World Cars
1973

ISBN 0-910714-05-3

Published in the United States of America in 1973

by

HERALD BOOKS

Pelham, New York

WORLD CARS

Published annually by
THE AUTOMOBILE CLUB OF ITALY

Edited by
L'EDITRICE DELL'AUTOMOBILE LEA

HERALD BOOKS, PELHAM, NEW YORK

Cover pictures

Ferrari B.B. Berlinetta Boxer (front)
Alfa Romeo Alfetta Spider (back)
bodies by Pininfarina

Contributors and correspondents

Gianfilippo Elti di Rodeano
Antonio di Fazio
Antonio Cataldo (Argentina)
Gianni Costa (China, India)
Paul Frère
Felix Lagmann
Alan Langley (Great Britain)
Giovanni Lurani
Jan P. Norbye (USA)
Gianni Rogliatti (Italy)
Pier Luigi Sagona
Hilmar Schmitt (Germany)
L.J.K. Setright
Luis M. Varela (Brazil)
Jack K. Yamaguchi (Japan)

Language consultant

Jean Gribble

Editorial offices

L'Editrice dell'Automobile
Viale Regina Margherita 279
00198 Rome, Italy

Composition, printing and binding

Arnoldo Mondadori Editore
Verona, Italy

Colour illustrations

Riproduzioni-Lith
Rome, Italy

Black-and-white illustrations

Fotolito Bernardino Gamba
Rome, Italy

SUMMARY

Editor's note

As publishers of *World Cars*, our aim is to give our readers as much accurate information as possible and to present it as concisely as possible. It is not always easy to reconcile the search for accuracy and completeness, for clarity and uniformity, and so one or two preliminary remarks may be of assistance to the reader consulting this reference book.

The technical data published is based on questionnaires completed by motor manufacturers throughout the world, and only when this information was incomplete or not made available, has it been supplemented from other reliable sources.

Performance figures are expressed in DIN, CUNA and SAE values according to country. DIN and CUNA standards for measuring horsepower vary from SAE standards (for instance, a maximum power expressed as 100 hp (SAE) would be slightly lower if expressed as a DIN or CUNA figure). The difference varies considerably but is rarely more than 20%. The horsepower for cars manufactured by English-speaking countries represents a slightly higher power (1.0139:1) than the horsepower of cars made by other countries.

Finally, fuel consumption, indicated by figures that are inevitably approximative, is calculated for a medium load and at a cruising speed of about 60% of the car's maximum speed on a varied run.

Since two valves per cylinder are now the norm and dual braking circuits are prevalent, only exceptions to these two cases have been indicated. Wherever not otherwise indicated, a car will have two valves per cylinder. Since all American V8 engines have the cylinders slanted at 90°, this indication has been omitted for United States production.

The technical information is grouped in basic descriptions relative to the fundamental models, and similar models differing only in price and in some characteristics refer back to these basic descriptions.

It often happens that one car is available with engines differing both in engine capacity and power. For American production and cars from other countries in which American influence is strongly felt in this field (Canada, South Africa and Australia), each of these engines is described separately. For other countries, the various engines have been listed under "Variations" at the foot of the basic description and—except when otherwise specifically indicated—should be taken as being available for all the models that refer back to the basic description.

The "Optional Accessories", which appear immediately after the "Variations" (if there are any) also apply to all the models that refer back to the basic description, except when otherwise specified. Some accessories may become "standard", or not be available, and others may be added, but this is always specified.

The prices expressed in sterling are before adding purchase tax or VAT. The prices for American cars refer to models equipped with a standard engine of the lowest power listed (generally a 4- or 6-cylinder engine). Any extra price for higher power standard engines is indicated at the foot of the list of models and prices. Unfortunately the present uncertain international monetary situation, the introduction of new taxes in many countries, and the continual rise in prices prevents any price list from remaining valid for long. Editorial problems have prevented us from making certain corrections to the prices in the main body of the volume after the end of 1972 and so the reader is advised to refer to the price index for more recent prices of models. When prices are shown in the currency of the country of origin, these should be taken as ex-factory and therefore subject to revision if the car is imported into another country.

Technical and photographic coverage is given to about 1,200 models at present in production. It has sometimes been necessary to exclude models produced in very small numbers or visually almost identical to others illustrated, and also models that, even if built or assembled under another name outside the country of origin, are practically a repetition of the model presented as part of the maker's standard range.

The major competitions

MOTOR RACING IN 1972

by Giovanni Lurani

The 1972 season saw the continuation of the exceptional development and amazing variety of motor racing. Racing formulas both international and national, categories, classes, groups and sub-groups, various kinds of competitions at every level also confirmed the utter impossibility of an analytical synthesis of activities that now involve enormous interests stretching far beyond purely technical and sporting ones.
A fair idea of the cream of the 1972 racing season can however be given by confining our comments almost entirely to the great races of the World Championship for Formula 1 cars and the Makers' Championship.

THE WORLD CHAMPIONSHIP FOR FORMULA 1 CARS

As always, this series of Grand Prix races, fought out at the highest level of technical perfection and driving skill, has been the focal point of interest.
The Formula has remained unaltered (except for one or two regulations aimed at safeguarding drivers in the event of an accident). That is to say, the engines were again three-litre jobs, using commercial fuel, and once more they were allowed to carry on board the enormous quantities of petrol needed to cover the full distance without refuelling. There is little doubt that, technically and competitively speaking, this is nonsense and means that the regulations have been eased under the pressure of varied interests in a manner that is often in contrast with any logic.
During 1972, as was to be expected, the Formula 1 monocoques underwent further development even though there was no outstanding progress on the engineering side. Here, indeed, stagnation would seem to be the applicable word, since the world title was carried off by a Lotus designed some years ago and powered by an eight-cylinder

Emerson Fittipaldi a few moments after his victory in the British Grand Prix. This is the moment of triumph.

Ford Cosworth engine that made its victorious debut as far back as 1967.

There were however many improvements in details and these allowed new and sensational records to be set up on all the circuits in the world.

The monocoque frames are now standard equipment. Even Ferrari has finally been converted. Prototype type nose cones are also used by everyone. Greater attention has been paid to the aerodynamic qualities of the cars, tapering them off and covering up certain unproductive bare extremities, shifting radiators and—in most cases—mounting airfoils further back.

Chassis specialists have taken care to work out the ideal point for the centre of gravity and to arrange weights in relation to the most suitable polar moment for obtaining greater stability. Since most of the world championship circuits are twisting, pure top speed has been sacrificed in favour of greater stability and the resulting higher speeds on the bends.

One of the factors contributing to this increased stability has been the constant and marked progress made in tyres, the chief protagonists of the great 1972 races. But the contribution was not entirely positive. The enormous tubeless tyres with their very low and wide sections, blown up to pressures that in some cases are little more than 14 psi, have often been the arbitrators of the result. From one race to another, Firestone and Goodyear, the two great makes of American tyres, in fierce competition, presented new designs, new blends, tyres suited to every track, to every type of road surface, to every kind of atmospheric conditions or temperatures, to every type of suspension and mechanical layout and even to individual driving styles. The choice of tyres was a matter of chance but always decisive, and on the superiority—in the conditions of the day—of one make or the other often depended the result.

One of the aces of Formula 1 racing told us that a noticeable difference in engine power could mean at most a second per lap on the average circuit, while the choice of the tyres could be worth from two to three seconds per lap. This goes to show how tyres were more than ever the real protagonists of Grand Prix racing, since the cars were fairly evenly matched in most other ways.

Dynamic air intakes, a solution that dates back to the early days of motor racing, are now practically standard equipment, like fuel injection, four valves per cylinder, extremely light titanium alloys and other precious metal alloys, plus every other trick of the trade that can bring the best F 1 engines up to specific powers in the region of 160 hp/1, with optimum utilization characteristics.

Now that four-wheel drive and turbine engines have finally been put on the shelf, on paper 1972 should have seen the decisive revenge of the 12-cylinder engines over the 'old' Ford-Cosworths. Yet, out of the 12 races qualifying for the title, no less than 10 were won by cars powered by the famous 8-cylinder engine (Tyrrells, McLarens and Lotuses) and only 2 by cars using a 12-cylinder engine (Ferrari and B.R.M.). This was a rather disappointing score-sheet for the 12-cylinders which seemed to stand a better chance than the results would indicate. The great rivals and most worthy adversaries of the many cars mounting Ford-Cosworth engines were undoubtedly the Ferraris. Their engines appeared to be the finest of the 12-cylinders and also the most flexible. But the chassis used were not up to the situation and tuning faults prevented them from putting up a better showing. Some of the Grand Prix were lost by the 12-cylinder cars when it seemed that they had already been worthily won, often due to external factors—blown tyres, collisions and so on. The best of the 12-cylinders were undoubtedly the Ferraris, for the French Matra, with only one car entered, did not have a strong enough team and was particularly unlucky.

B.R.M., which fielded a very large team, won one race—by mistake, if the remark may be forgiven. In fact, after the Monte-carlo victory, achieved in abnormal conditions, the B.R.Ms. were never again seen among the victors for the rest of the season. The Italian Tecno-Martini, another 12-cylinder like the Williams-Politoys, never completely got over its teething troubles.

Thus the Ford-Cosworth engine, mounted on three-quarters of the cars in the field, won 10 out of the 12 races in the world championship programme and so totalled the fantastic haul of 52 wins in championship Grand Prix races since its debut (victorious of course) in far-away 1967.

The vitality of this engine is unbelievable and, since in 1973 Ferrari will apparently be fielding only one top-ranking car, since Matra is not yet a certain starter and it is unlikely that Tecno will be in the top class, the 12-cylinder cars are not going to have an easy time of it. We do not feel that the moment is yet ripe for entering cars with Ford-Weslake 12-cylinder engines or with

On this page: Ronnie Peterson (top photo) in the March-Ford at grips with the famous Karussell bend on the Nürburgring circuit during the German Grand Prix. 1972 was a very good year for the McLaren. Hulme (in the bottom photo) and Revson finished well on numerous occasions. Opposite: Stewart (Tyrrell-Ford) leading Ickx (Ferrari) and Fittipaldi (Lotus-Ford) at one stage of the Austrian Grand Prix which was won by the Brazilian.

Alfa Romeo 12-cylinder engines, for both of these were originally destined for prototype sports rather than Formula 1 cars. The best of the Ford-Cosworth engined cars appeared to be Fittipaldi's extremely stable and well-prepared Lotus. The McLarens, beautifully tuned, sturdy and thrusting were also very impressive. The Tyrrels, famed for their road-holding, did not match up to their renown in 1972 and Stewart (like Gevert) suffered for some failings in the necessary preparation.

Of the other cars competing, the most impressive were the Surtees; the Marches improved, even if they broke down too often, while the Brabhams lagged behind. In any case, the winter truce allows valuable time for the preparation of new vehicles capable of doing even better than the exceptional results that last season provided.

1972 was also a very good year for drivers. Even so, there was a fall in the number classifying in the world championship tables. In 1970 there were 25 names, only 22 in 1971 and 21 in 1972. This is a sign that, even though the Formula 1 fields are larger than ever, the élite who appear in the first six places are even more than ever a high-level minority.

Seven of the names in the 1971 table have disappeared. Two of them, the much missed Rodriguez and Siffert, even though they figured in the 1971 list, were dead before that season closed.

The others missing are Wisell, Pescarolo, Donohue, Stommelen and Surtees. The Swede Reine Wisell was not able to find a competitive car and the same is true of Henri Pescarolo who had too many accidents to come anywhere near the top of the list. Donohue, a great champion and victorious at Indianapolis, had to withdraw from practically the whole series following a bad accident that kept him out of driving for a long period.

Rolf Stommelen too was without a top-ranking car, while the ex-world champion, John Surtees, opted for constructing rather than driving.

The new names in the world table are the Americans Revson and Redman, the Italians De Adamich and Merzario, the Brazilian Pace and the Argentinian Reutemann. In all six drivers with great talent who can certainly be relied on for the future.

Emerson Fittipaldi is the 1972 World Champion. The results in the 1972 table speak for themselves. In the races qualifying, only two drivers, Fittipaldi and Hulme, managed to obtain eight placings. In 1971, only Stewart—world champion for that year—obtained eight placings. Fittipaldi's record, considering it was made up of five wins and only two second places and a third, means wonderful consistency, surprising regularity, a capacity for avoiding errors and not pushing the car beyond its limits, and finally exceptional self-control. Fittipaldi is an authentic champion in the absolute sense of the word. In 1970 he was tenth in the world table, in 1971 he moved up to sixth and now last year his admirable steady improvement gained him the highest honours.

With a peremptory return to form, Jackie Stewart climbed back to second place in the 1972 world table with no less than four wins in Grand Prix races, plus a second and a fifth place. The outgoing champion's season was marked by alternating phases: after a dazzling start, the Scotsman had to drop out of racing for health reasons. When he did drive, he was always among the leaders and showed that he had lost nothing of his skill.

Third place went to another ex-world champion, Denny Hulme. The New Zealander is the only driver to share with Fittipaldi the honour of conquering eight placings. Hulme confirmed that he was in his best form.

Jackie Ickx took fourth place with a single win on the fearsome Nürburgring track with the authoritative flair and marked superio-

rity that confirm him as worthy to figure among the finest drivers in the world.
The likeable American millionaire Peter Revson was not a sufficiently regular entrant, but his exceptional performances were brilliant enough to confirm him one of the élite and to merit a significant fifth place. Gevert, inevitably overshadowed by the formidable first driver in his stable, Jackie Stewart, had to take the consequences of the unexpected failures of the Tyrrells.
Seventh in 1971, Clay Regazzoni moved up to share sixth place with Gevert in 1972, throwing away chances of better placing often because of his excessive impulsiveness. However, the Swiss ace remains one of the best drivers around.
From eighteenth in 1971, Mike Hailwood did well to come eighth in the 1972 table, while Ronnie Peterson, second in 1971, dropped back to eighth due to his car's mechanical failures and shares this placing with the most unlucky ace of the wheel there has ever been, Chris Amon. This fine driver has never yet won a Grand Prix in spite of being so often on the brink of a well-deserved victory.
The Frenchman Beltoise won the Montecarlo Grand Prix in 1972. In our opinion, this performance was an exceptional one for him and due, apart from a start that only just respected the regulations, to the ghastly atmospheric conditions. In fact, Beltoise did nothing much in the other Grand Prix races.
Next in the table, but with far fewer points, came Mario Andretti who made only rare appearances in Formula 1 racing, Ganley who did what he could within the B.R.M. fold, Graham Hill bereft of a competitive car and probably by now somewhat resigned to his fate, and Redman.
At the bottom of the table, some of the names are familiar, like de Adamich and Gethin, while Schenken, Pace, Reutemann and Merzario are faces we shall no doubt be seeing a great deal of in the future.

THE 1972 WORLD MAKERS' CHAMPIONSHIP

Justly promoted for the first time to 'world' status (previously it was merely 'international'), this championship—even if it was monotonously simple to predict the results, —was engrossing from the technical point of view.
For the first time, the championship was reserved for the so-called 3000 cc prototypes: the use of commercial fuel was made compulsory the minimum weight was fixed at 650 kg and fuel tank capacity at 120 litres. As was to be expected, the cars that dominated the field were no more than Formula 1 monocoques disguised in a pretence at a two-seater hull. Since aerodynamically speaking they are much more efficient than their Formula 1 sisters with unenclosed wheels, they outdid them in pure, outright speed. And to think that, in the big-sounding words of the racing legislators, these 'prototypes' were to be cars "designed as the forerunners of a future production sports car". Ingenuousness, a utopian dream or... window dressing.
The best of the cars were the Ferrari 312 Ps (derived from the famous 12-cylinder boxer-engined Formula 1), the Alfa Romeo 33.3s with a V8 engine, the 8-cylinder Ford-Cosworth-engined Lolas (Formula 1 type but tamed down to render them less fragile), the V12 Matra-Simcas and finally the new Gulf-Mirages with V12 Ford-Weslake engines.
In the bitterly fought out battles for this world title, disputed at extremely high speeds, the great outsider was the privately entered 1971 Porsche 8-cylinder, whose brilliant performances often assumed a semi-official character.
The only car of all these with a propellant remotely resembling a production engine was the Alfa Romeo 33.3 with an engine whose geometry was not very different from the 8-cylinder mounted on the Montreal grand touring. The 1972 season proved that to be close kin to an authentic production car meant to be defeated.
Alfa Romeo, after a fine 1971 season with a series of great performances culminating in three clamorous victories including the Targa Florio, had perhaps placed too great trust in the qualities of its 33.3 TT (with

Above the Matra MS670, victor of the Le Mans 24 Heures. At the wheel the Frenchman Cévert. Right, Marko's Alfa Romeo 33TT3 in the pits during the Sebring Grand Prix. Below, the Gulf Mirage M6 made its debut at the beginning of the 1972 season. Here the Dutchman Van Lennep is at the controls. On the opposite page, Matra, Lola and Alfa Romeo tracking one another on the Tertre Rouge bend of the Le Mans circuit.

extra-light tubular chassis). In fact 1972 marked its condemnation. After a series of defeats, the bitterest of which must have been the Targa Florio lost by a handful of seconds to the only Ferrari entered and the most crushing the Le Mans 24 Heures where the Matra, in the Ferraris' absence, demonstrated its clear superiority, Alfa Romeo decided to withdraw its 8-cylinders, now outclassed, while waiting for the new 12-cylinders destined for 1973. And thus the last fine thread linking the 'prototypes' and production cars disappeared.

It is a singular fact that, while in the Formula 1 field 10 out of 12 races were won by 8-cylinder engined cars, all 11 races qualifying for the World Makers' Championship were won with 12-cylinder engines.

The gesture made by Ferrari in this Championship is unique of its kind and possibly unrepeatable. Even though the world title was theirs when only about half the season was over, Enzo Ferrari decided to demonstrate the superb quality and unchallengeable superiority of his cars by running them in all the qualifying events except the Le Mans 24 Heures, and won every race in which his cars took part. The risk he ran was a calculated one and one which it was worth taking only because he knew the team he had available was outstanding both in men and machines.

Of the 11 races of the 1972 World Championship, nine were fairly similar in length and duration (1000 kilometres or 6 hours) while one (Sebring) was a 12-hour race and the eleventh, Le Mans, was of course 24 hours. It is obvious that cars designed for races lasting roughly six hours can hardly be suitable for races twice as long, let alone four times as long. Enzo Ferrari, whose policy was to enter for everything and try to sweep the board, endeavoured to win at Sebring (12 hours) and pulled it off. He then set his sights on Le Mans, entering cars with even more tapered off bodies in the spring events and making long tests at Turin and Monza to see if his cars were suitable for Le Mans. The conviction he came to was that his cars would not have had a fair chance in the gruelling 24 Heures and therefore, with unimpeachable logic, he decided not to enter them.

This withdrawal left everyone unsatisfied, for the Ferraris, which had wiped the floor with the Alfa Romeos, the Lolas and the Gulf Mirages (plus the privately entered Porsche) had not beaten the Matras which had been prepared solely for Le Mans where they won handsomely. So the 1972 season concluded with a question mark to be held over till the 1973 season. These two makes will have to meet and everyone is eagerly awaiting the occasion.

In every sense, this championship was dominated by the Ferraris. Not only did they win all ten races in which they took part but in seven of them they carried off the first two places and in one achieved the sensational feat of placing the four Ferraris competing in the first four places. And all this was clinched by an outstanding series of fastest laps both in practice and during the races. An unprecedented record.

The Lolas proved themselves to be the fastest machines competing. Unsustained by adequate preparation and fundamentally fragile, they made an excellent showing but never achieved a truly valid result. Nevertheless, they are extremely competitive.

Matra-Simca, as we said, concentrated on the minutely detailed preparation indispensable for the Le Mans 24 Heures and so their cars were not fit for competing on level terms with the Ferraris in the shorter races. The long-awaited Matra-Ferrari clash may take place in 1973 and this will certainly be one of the most interesting themes of the championship, together with the expected return of Alfa Romeo with 12-cylinder boxer engines. It is worth remembering that, way back before the war Alfa Romeo planned a 12-cylinder boxer engine (1500 cc supercharged) and again in 1951 a 2500 cc 12-cylinder boxer for Grand Prix racing. So, for the Milan makers it is not a case of copying other people's schemes but of picking up where they left off.

The 12-cylinder Ford-Weslake engined Gulf-Mirage was not really ready at the tail-end of the 1972 season but there is reason to believe that 1973 will be another story. This contender should add interest to a season that is full of question marks.

THE CAN-AM SERIES

This is the richest series of races existing today and for the last seven years has polarized the attention of the motor racing world in the United States. The Can-Am or Canada-America series is disputed over nine races that feature the most monstrous cars to be seen in track racing today. In fact the Can-Am cars are subjected to practically no regulation except that they must be two-seaters. With their aerodynamic, wrap-round hulls, they are the most powerful racing cars of all time.

Though up to 1972 American engines derived for the series and with engine capacities even higher than eight litres regularly dominated the field, in 1972 the victor was Porsche which, concentrating officially on the Can-Am series, prepared 12-cylinder 5000 cc engines with turbo chargers (that is to say turbo-compressors powered by exhaust gases) with a power nudging 1000 cc. What purpose monsters of this kind utterly lacking in any future in motor manufacturing can have, it is hard to say. But there is no doubt that the battles between these startlingly powerful machines are a gripping attraction.

In the seven years of its history, the Can-Am series was won the first year by a Lola with Surtees at the wheel and then five times running by McLarens (twice driven by the late constructor, twice by Hulme and once by Revson). This year instead it was the turn of the Porsches driven by Follmer and Donohue, managed by the wizard Roger Penske.

Such then was 1972 motor racing in synthesis, a season when Porsche switched to the Can-Am series, Ferraris dominated the Makers' Championship and the Ford-Cosworth engine remained unchallenged in the Formula 1 field.

PROTOTYPE SPORTS CARS

by Felix Lagmann

It is commonly said that the Formula 1 monocoque is the launching pad of the most advanced motor engineering: however, the characteristics and performance of prototype sports cars make it possible to affirm that it is not the only one. In fact, not only do three-litre engined sports cars have the same characteristics as the monocoques and use the same engines, brakes and so on but—thanks to their aerodynamic bodies—manage to reach even higher speeds in the region of 200 miles an hour.

There is an extra problem that sports cars have to face—the length of the races. These are generally run over 1,000 kilometres, but last as long as 24 hours like the gruelling Le Mans race. This means the meticulous preparation and study of the car from the point of view of reliability, easy maintenance and repair work to make good anything that might happen during the race—from a break-down to running off the track. In a long-distance race, vital parts such as a gearbox or suspension often have to be repaired or replaced and the car can still come out of the pits to finish well placed in spite of the hold-up, just as long as the work has been done at top speed.

Today constructors are concentrating their efforts above all on the three-litre class competing for the world title and the two-litre class competing for the European title. But from the sporting and spectacular point of view, the races of the Can-Am series—with some pale imitations in Europe—cannot be forgotten. In this field the results obtained by the Porsches are of particular interest: this car won nearly all the races of the 1972 series thanks to its formidable 12-cylinder engine with two turbo-compressors developing no less than 900 brake horse power. Both the engine and the rest of the car are derived from the famed 917, with modifications to make it suitable for the different racing conditions.

Coming back to the World Makers' Championship in which the protagonists are three-litre sports prototypes, it may be said that 1973 is a particularly intense year: besides the legendary Ford Cosworth V8s, there will be many 12-cylinder engined cars facing the chequered flag.

The Ferraris dominated the 1972 season with their 12-cylinder boxer engines identical to the ones mounted on the Formula 1 cars. In 1973 they take up the challenge again, revised to keep abreast of the rapid progress made in racing engineering. The Ferraris have many years' racing experience behind them and can count on meticulous tuning and preparation. One innovation is the adoption of Goodyear tyres, which was decided on after a period of uncertainty due to the curtailing of the Firestone racing programme.

The great novelty of the 1973 season is the new Alfa Romeo with a boxer type 12-cylinder engine and a totally redesigned chassis. The makers hope that this car will bring them back to a salient position after the disappointing 1972 season. Like most engines in this field, the Alfa Romeo has twin overhead camshafts, four valves

The Gulf Mirage M6, above, mounts a Ford Cosworth V8 engine similar to the one used in Formula 1 racing. The 3-fitre Cosworth-engined Lola T280 took part in almost all the races qualifying for the World Makers' Championship. In the photo on the opposite page the Swede Wisell is at the wheel.

The Abarth Osella driven by Arturo Merzario (in the photo above) won the European title for 2-litre sports cars. Below, the winner of the World Makers' Championship was the Ferrari 312P, here seen with the Belgian Jackie Ickx at the wheel. Top right, the Chevron B21 was one of the leading contenders in the European Championship for 2-litre sports. Bottom right, the Porsche 917/10 won the two championships reserved for Group 7 cars: the Can-Am series with George Follmer at the wheel and the Interseries with Leo Kinnunen.

per cylinder, Lucas injection in the inlet pipes and electronic ignition with discharge through the condenser (Marelli Dinoplex). The chassis is derived from the model 33 TT 3 tubular trellis frame with reinforcement panels.

Another Italian make, Abarth, is making a strong comeback, though this time in the class up to two litres, with the backing of the official Osella stable. In 1972, with its four-cylinder engine, the Abarth showed itself to be the most powerful in the field and, further developed, will be a strong contender in 1973.

The French Matra will try to repeat in 1973 its performance of winning on its home ground the longest race of the series—the Le Mans 24 Heures. Matra, too, is mounting a 12-cylinder engine but with the cylinders arranged in a 60° Vee; it is a sufficiently powerful engine and, as was seen at Le Mans, very reliable. Adverse circumstances and factors quite unconnect-

ed with the engine itself were the only reason why this engine failed to do much better in Formula 1 racing. There is no doubt that these French cars, produced by the finest engineers, are an extremely interesting example of motor engineering employing the most advanced techniques derived from missile construction, a field in which Matra specialises.

The English Lolas and Mirages place their trust in two types of engines, both commissioned from Ford by two different constructors: one is the famed Cosworth V8 which has a long series of successes in F 1 racing behind it including 51 wins by the end of the 1972 season, and the other is the new Weslake V12, constructed specially for the sports cars.

For that matter, the 'little' Cosworth, the four-cylinder, is a valid contender in the under two-litre class and it should not be forgotten that this engine inspired the eight-cylinder one that allowed the brilliant designer Keith Duckworth to work the miracle of producing a new engine for the Formula 1 car in record time and to win the first time out.

The German motor industry, on the other hand, seems somewhat loath to engage in the contest once more. With the Porsche victories with the three-litre 908s and the five-litre 917s still fresh in our minds, it does not appear that there will be a return. Porsche will be competing with grand touring cars which are of course lion-hearted and well-prepared but cannot compete from the spectator's point of view with the prototypes.

In this regard 1973 will mark a pause. Will the Mercedes be back in 1974 to take advantage of the thesis of the twenty-year cycle? It is hard to say: what is certain is that Mercedes built an exceptionally fine car for the Automobile Club de France Grand Prix in 1914, returned to racing in 1934 to begin the epic duel with Auto Union, made another comeback in 1954 with the fabulous 196 with its extremely complicated eight-cylinder engine with desmodromic distribution and direct injection (no one else has ever managed to make a similar engine successfully), and now for years has made only sporadic appearances in rallies and touring car racing. But the engineering and human potential is still there and word has spread of the studies being carried out on very high-powered Wankel engines, so the

Above, Howden Ganley with the 7-litre Chevrolet-engined P167 he drove for BRM in the Interseries Championship, the European version of the Can-Am Series. Below, Hulme at the wheel of the McLaren M20 which failed to repeat the string of victories obtained in the last four editions of the Can-Am series, going under to a Porsche. Above left, the Lola T310 Hobbs drove in several Can-Am races. This car, like the others on these two pages, belongs to Group 7. In the races disputed in the United States and Canada, the only entirely American Group 7 car was the AVS Shadow (bottom left) driven by Jackie Oliver and Carlos Pace.

idea of another return after twenty years is fascinating.
The most characteristic technicalities of the modern sports car often derive from experiments in space but on the other hand they foreshadow possible improvements in production cars.
For instance, incredible results have been obtained in the sphere of tyres and suspensions with adherence in the transverse sense equal to at least 'g'—that is to say the acceleration of gravity—and adherence while accelerating that has been calculated as equal to 1.3 g, greater that is than the acceleration of gravity.
Braking is equally fine, as stands to reason. After the well-known disc brakes came ventilated discs with radial slits and finally with transverse holes. Experiments have been carried out with beryllium or copper discs to obtain more efficient dissipation of the heat generated during braking.
The material most commonly used in racing cars today is titanium which is both as light as aluminium and has a greater resistance than steel. This material is used both for the moving parts such as the connecting rods and for the hull structure, bolts and so on.
The construction technique employing a bearing box-type frame with drop-rivet connecting links is no longer new and has been refined, while light alloy castings have benefited from space technology. This is confirmed by the fact that Campagnolo, the most noted manufacturer of light alloy wheels, also makes parts for missiles and helicopters out of similar alloys.
This technology, if duly applied, could make it possible to build special vehicles—for example town cars with very low weights and performance suited to traffic conditions, in particular with powerful acceleration and good braking.

Special bodies

Illustrations and technical information

ITALY

Fiat X 1/9

BERTONE 

Safe handling and advanced engineering solutions are the most marked features of this central-engined sports car. The wedge-shaped body has a removable roof.

ITALY

Lancia Stratos HF

BERTONE 

First presented at the 1971 Turin Motor Show, the Stratos HF today mounts a 150 bhp central engine. This car, which is destined for homologation in Group 4 of the Grand Touring category, has a top speed of over 130 mph.

COGGIOLA — Alpine A 310 Special — ITALY

This 'study in form' was presented at the Paris Motor Show and then again at Turin. The dimensions of the special body are different from the standard Alpine: length 172.44 in, width 69.29 in, height 45.67 in.

COGGIOLA — Volvo 1800 ESC Coupé — ITALY

This 2 + 2 coupé made a favourable impression when it was presented at the 1971 Paris Motor Show. Both technically and from the point of view of comfort, it is very convincing. Wheelbase 96.46 in, length 175.79 in, width 67.13 in, height 49.80 in.

GREAT BRITAIN

Grosvenor Mk V Limousine

COLEMAN-MILNE 

The lines of this seven-seater limousine, while respecting the finest English traditions, are modern and pleasing to the eye. It is based on the Ford Consul 3000 GT and has automatic transmission. Servo steering and heated rear window are standard.

ITALY

Fiat 127 Familiare

CORIASCO 

The fine handling qualities and agility for which the Fiat 127 is famed are enhanced in this 'familiare' version. A special attraction of the car, whose tailgate opens flush with the roof, is the ample space for luggage.

CRAYFORD AUTO DEVELOPMENT — Mercedes-Benz 250 Estate Car — GREAT BRITAIN

Crayford Auto Development specializes in converting Mercedes-Benz saloons. The results are very convincing in this model which offers all the advantages of an estate car without losing the original lines.

FISSORE — Fiat 128 Berlina — ITALY

This is a 'de luxe' interpretation of one of the pillars of Fiat production. Apart from modifications to the body particular attention has been paid to the interior finishing. Leather upholstery can be supplied on request.

ITALY **FL 1** **FRANCIS LOMBARDI**

Presented at the 1972 Turin Motor Show, the FL 1 is a two-seater coupé of a clearly sporting nature with a central rear engine. The power unit used is the Lancia 2000 injection engine which allows a top speed of 125 mph to be reached.

ITALY **De Tomaso Longchamp** **GHIA**

This 2+2 coupé is the most recent result of collaboration between Ghia and De Tomaso. It is inspired by the Deauville but though sophisticated is tougher. A front-mounted Ford engine allows a maximum speed of nearly 175 mph.

ITAL DESIGN — Lotus Esprit — ITALY

This was one of the most admired models at the Turin Motor Show for its extremely low profile and the beauty of its lines.
The body is reinforced glassfibre and the engine is mounted centrally at the rear.

MICHELOTTI — Fiat 128 « Pulsar » — ITALY

The "Pulsar" is an attractive streamlined four-seater coupé with a Fiat 128 Rally engine. It was presented at the 1972 Geneva Motor Show. The flexible bumpers are both interesting and functional.

ITALY **Fiat 132 « Flares »** **MICHELOTTI** 

The most striking feature of the 2+2 coupé with Fiat 132 mechanics is the sharply sawn-off tail and the recessed lights. The lines are pleasantly sporting and aerodynamic. The bumpers are similar to the ones mounted on the "Pulsar".

ITALY **Fiat 132 Coupé**  **MORETTI** 

Safety in the paramount factor in this Moretti coupé.
It is based on the Fiat 132 launched this year.
A protective flexible element is used as a 'wrap-round' throughout the body.

OGLE — Sotheby Special — GREAT BRITAIN

At the 1972 Montreal Motor Show the futuristic lines and performance of this coupé made a great impression (it is based on the mechanics of the Aston Martin DBS V8). At the rear there are no less than twenty-two signal lights.

PININFARINA — Alfa Romeo Alfetta Spider — ITALY

This was undoubtedly one of the most interesting cars launched at the Turin Motor Show with its clearly sporting wedge-shaped lines. There are numerous technical innovations including the original 'variable transparency' roof.

ITALY **Ferrari 365 GT4 2+2** **PININFARINA**

The Ferrari 365 GT4 2 + 2, an extremely high-class coupé on view for the first time at the Paris Motor Show, mounts a 4,390 cc V12 engine. Bumpers in a special flexible material are fitted on a body with a sawn-off tail.

ITALY **Ferrari B.B. Berlinetta Boxer** **PININFARINA**

The Ferrari B.B. Berlinetta Boxer, which made its successful debut at the 1971 Turin Motor Show, is now, after more than a year, going into production. The streamlining is aesthetically pleasing and the car mounts a 360 bhp (DIN) 12-cylinder engine.

PININFARINA **Fiat Abarth 124 Rally** **ITALY**

Held with good reason to be the finest sporting car produced by the Turin firm, this car is greatly admired for its compact, sleek lines. The high level of driving comfort is also a pleasant surprise.

PININFARINA **Fiat 132 Giardinetta** **ITALY**

This is a car that does full justice to the concept of an estate car. Besides the greater space available for carrying belongings, the refined elegance of the finishings of this most successful car are greatly admired.

ITALY NSU Ro 80 PININFARINA 

Besides the obvious differences in style that distinguish this Pininfarina Ro 80 from the standard model there are the bonuses of a custom-made car — the luxurious finishing and a rational instrument panel where nothing is missing.

ITALY Fiat 127 Albarella SAVIO 

This amusing little fine weather car is called a 'seaside car'. The open four-seater body has a 87.60 in wheelbase and the overall dimensions are: length 142.12 in, width 59.84 in, height 64.17 in.

SCIONERI — Fiat 127 S — ITALY

Even more worthwhile than the important modifications to the body and the different radiator mask is the careful attention paid to improving the internal finishings.
The result confirms that this is a de luxe version.

ZAGATO — Fiat 132 « Aster » — ITALY

This is a sporting little 2 + 2 saloon with the following overall dimensions: length 167.13 in, width 65.83 in, height 48.62 in. The car weighs 1,984 lb. The front and rear elements are aluminium while the central structure is steel.

World automobile production

France

A FAVOURABLE MARKET

by Paul Frère

In spite of the economic recession in certain Common Market countries, the rising curve of French motor production continued its upward trend uninterrupted. In fact, during the 12 months from 1 January 1971 to 30 June 1972, 3,245,770 motor vehicles were manufactured (2,902,938 of them passenger or estate cars), an increase of more than 14% over the corresponding period 1970-1971. And that period had already shown a 9% advance over the previous period.

During the period July 1971 to the end of June 1972, 1,706,663 vehicles were exported, that is to say 54% of total production, and exports of passenger cars were no less than 56% of the total number manufactured. Moreover, this rise in the number of cars manufactured by French makers has not stemmed imports, since over 455,000 vehicles were imported over the same period, or 24.2% more than in the corresponding period 1970-1971. In the same period (July 1971 to end of June 1972) 26% of the passenger cars registered in France were imported and 25% of the industrial vehicles. In the field of passenger cars, Régie Renault is still by far the most important manufacturer, with a production of 1,186,282 vehicles in the 12 months from 1 July 1971 to 30 June 1972. Citroën has however ousted Peugeot from second place, with 633,630 cars against Peugeot's 567,148. In the previous 12 months Peugeot produced 22,000 more cars than Citroën. Chrysler-France, which holds the fourth place in French production, has also made an important leap forward which allowed it for the first time to top the half-million mark and by a good margin, manufacturing 512,555 vehicles.

Shown as percentage increases over the

The Rallye 2, the most sophisticated version of the Simca 1000, with radiator and electric fan, two twin-barrel carburators and a power of 82 bhp (DIN). It can reach a top speed of over 106 mph.

previous results, the following progress has been made:

Renault	+13.2%
Citroën	+20.6%
Peugeot	+ 3.8%
Chrysler-France	+14.5%

EVOLUTION OF MODELS

It would be incorrect to interpret the continuing increase in car imports as a failure of the French motor manufacturing industry. This is a normal trend, springing from lowered trade barriers, particularly within the Common Market area, and the same phenomenon is to be noted in Italy and Germany as well: the quota of imported cars rises but the quota of vehicles exported increases in the same manner. The day will no doubt come when the concepts of imports and exports will appear outdated in discussing the countries of Western Europe. While it is true that today more than a quarter of the cars on the road in France are imported, it must also be remembered that she exports 56% of her own production, whose characteristics are well attuned not only to the French road network but also to the tastes and demands of a large number of European purchasers. Today, all French cars are designed with an eye to economical running at high speeds on the motorways that are being completed or constructed everywhere and, for this reason, they are particularly prized in Germany and in Italy. On the whole, too, French cars are exceptionally comfortable, due perhaps to the relatively poor state of French secondary roads which nevertheless, thanks to the long straight stretches, invite high speeds. This comfort is appreciated by purchasers in many countries, but soft suspension is not always welcomed by more sporting customers. Care for comfort is one of the most striking features of French cars in general.

In the course of 1972 two new models destined for a very wide market were presented, the Renault 5 and the Peugeot 104. They are part of the new generation of four-seaters less than 12 feet long, with an engine capacity of less than 1,000 cc, with front-wheel drive and independent suspension on all four wheels. Others are the Autobianchi A 112, Nissan Cherry 1000 and the Fiat 127. Of all these models, the Renault is the only one mounting a longitudinal engine, for its general layout is similar to the R 4. The Peugeot, on the other hand, like the others in the group, has a transverse engine; it has an aluminium cylinder block and overhead camshaft. The engine already conforms to the anti-pollution standards proposed by the European Community for 1976. The chief card the Peugeot holds as compared with its rivals is its coachwork (designed by Pininfarina), a four-door body like one of the versions of the Nissan. But this alone hardly explains its price on the French market, 2,000 francs dearer than the Fiat 127. And on the Belgian market, its price is still a good deal higher than the Nissan four-door model which has none of the Common Market advantages nor the relatively short transport distance enjoyed by the Peugeot.

The other makers presented no new models. The major evolutions are the replacement of the Citroën DS 21 by the DS 23, with the engine capacity raised by 200 cc, the adoption of electronic injection for the Citroën SM and the evolution of the Citroën GS, to which Citroën chiefly owes its recovery over the last two years and is from now on offered in a second 1220 cc version. Chrysler-France has created two sports versions of the Simca 1000 mounting a 1300 cc engine.

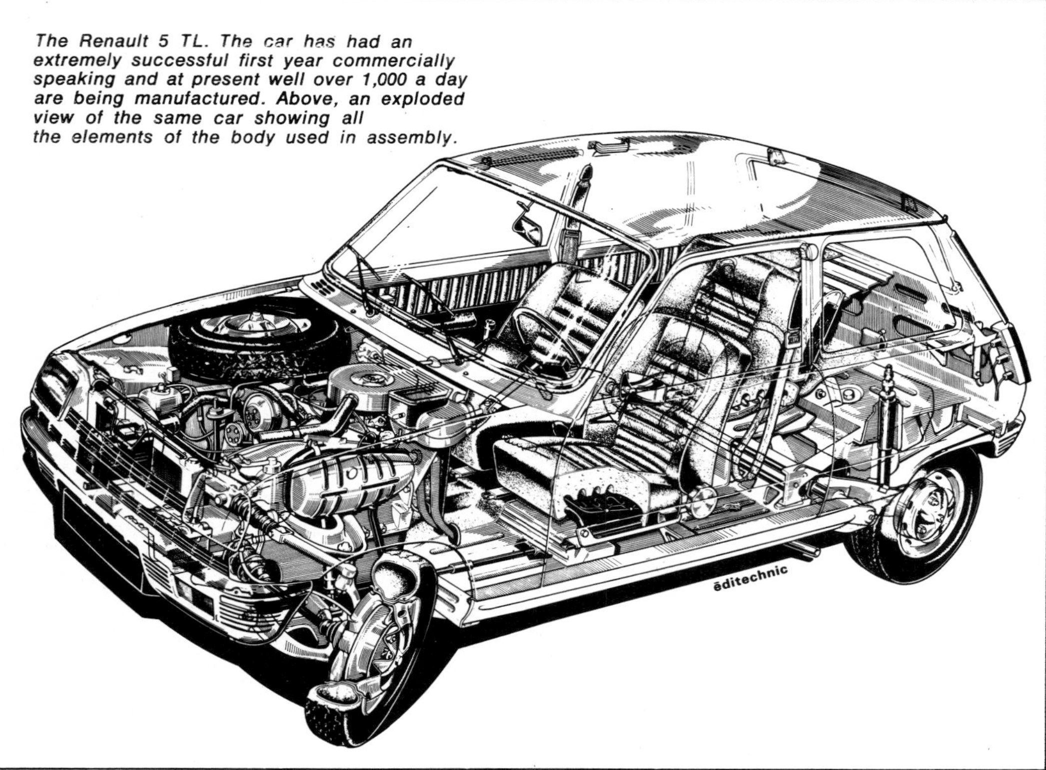

The Renault 5 TL. The car has had an extremely successful first year commercially speaking and at present well over 1,000 a day are being manufactured. Above, an exploded view of the same car showing all the elements of the body used in assembly.

POLLUTION AND SAFETY

Like the other European makers, the French firms dedicated large budgets and much of their research activities to the demands of safety and the construction of cars with a lower pollution factor. It is mainly in order to conform to the pollution regulations at present in force in European countries and generally based on regulation no. 15 of the special Working Group on Atmospheric Pollution set up by the United Nations Economic Commission for Europe, that Citroën has replaced the three carburettors previously mounted on the SM by an electronic injection system. This regulation will henceforth be respected by the whole of the European Economic Community. For 1976 it lays down a further 20% reduction in carbon monoxide emissions and 10% in hydro-carbons, so that research into this problem must be continued.

In order to reduce the share for each of the huge expenditure required by research in the fields of atmospheric pollution and safety, Renault and Peugeot have signed a

Citroën opted for the 1015 cc engine with horizontally opposed cylinders, already mounted on the GS, for the new Super version of the well-known Ami. The Super has a redesigned radiator grille and the internal finishings have been modified. With a 9 : 1 compression ratio, the engine develops 53.5 bhp (DIN) at 6,500 rpm and a torque of 50 lb/ft at 3,500 revs. The Super weighs 1,775 lb and has a top speed of 87 mph.

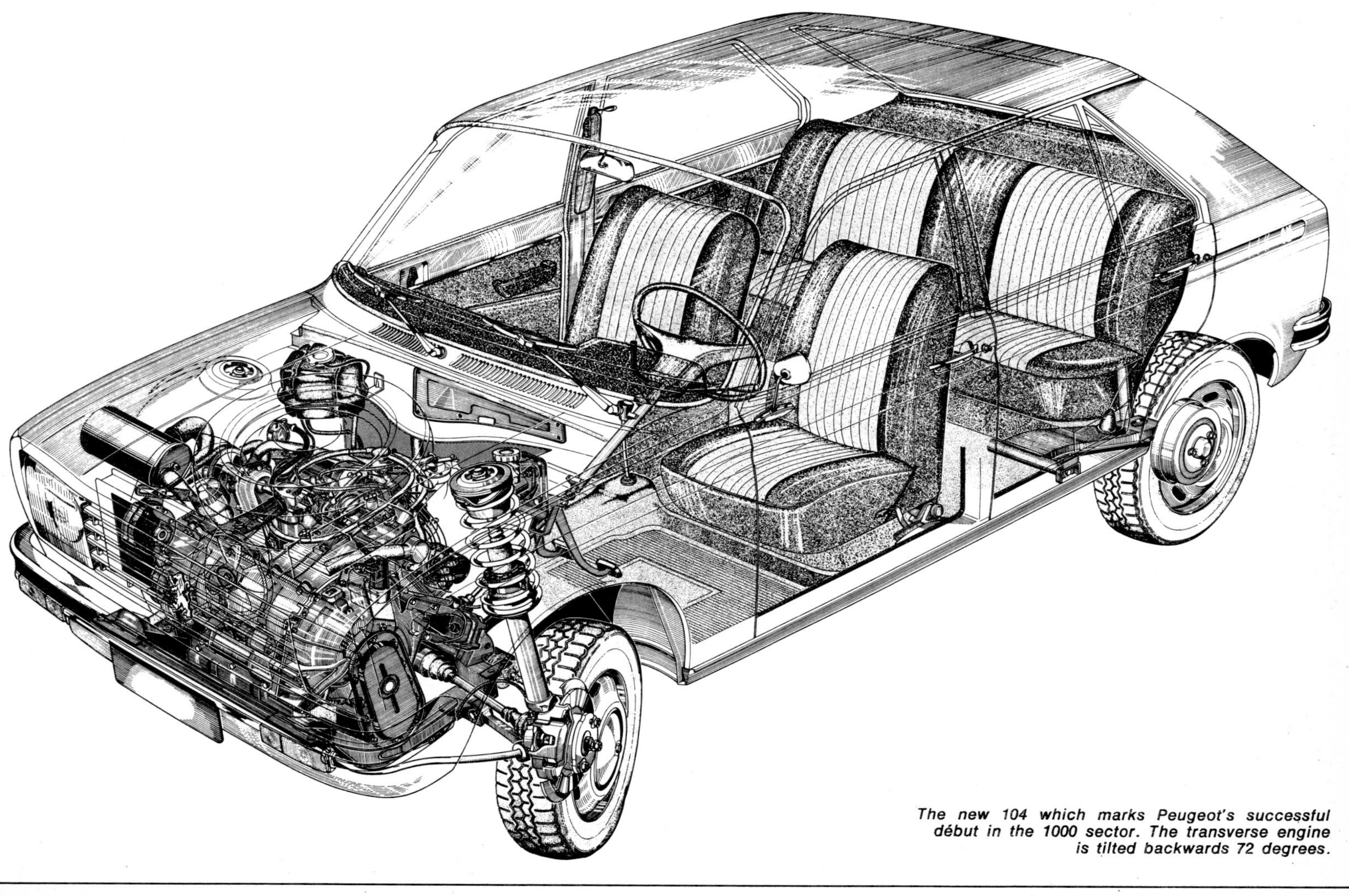

The new 104 which marks Peugeot's successful début in the 1000 sector. The transverse engine is tilted backwards 72 degrees.

collaboration agreement and set up a common Study and Research Centre financed by both firms. This agreement also turns on the study in common of certain mechanical groups destined for future models. From 1967 to 1971, the two companies have spent 67 million francs on investment and running expenses for the Research Centre in the field of pollution, and it is forecast that another 108 million francs will be spent from 1972 to 1975, bringing the total expenditure on the battle against atmospheric pollution to 175 million francs from 1967 to 1975. At the moment, Renault and Peugeot's joint investments in the struggle against pollution include 18 rolling test benches and 16 engine test beds. In 1975, these will be brought up to 27 rolling benches, 34 motor test beds and 9 automatic test beds with programmed cycles.

Another 175 million francs will be invested between 1967 and 1975 by these two makers on their joint research into the field of safety. 53 million had already been invested by the end of 1971 and a further investment of 122 million is forecast for the 1972-1975 period. In this case, the investment is relatively low compared with overheads which will exceed 159 million during the nine-year period in consideration.

Citroën never tends to hang back when faced by unorthodox solutions. It proposes, in order to give the occupants of a relatively small vehicle better protection and without prejudicing in any way the active safety, to create a car with no bumpers either in front or behind. The aim is to attain greater structural rigidity with a low weight. The occupants will be seated in a diamond shape, with the driver placed centrally in front and thus enjoying excellent visibility in all directions; slightly behind him there will be two seats side by side whose occupants will be well back from the windscreen and enjoy the greater clearance towards the centre of the car, while the fourth passenger will be accommodated on a single back seat. This layout will allow easy access even though the doors will be limited to two in order to ensure greater rigidity of the coachwork. However, in order for it to be acceptable, certain laws at present in force will have to be amended. Adopting in this respect an attitude very similar to Italian firms, the French manufacturers, though carrying out very serious research in the field of resistance to impact and with a view to the reduction of deceleration at passenger level, refuse to sacrifice primary safety (roadholding, handling qualities, braking and acceleration) to secondary safety. This is not simply a question of philosophy (better to avoid the accident than protect the passengers should it happen), but also an attitude springing from the very great diver-

Above, the Citroën Series D in a crash test against a concrete wall. Below and right, the new 2-litre Chrysler, the company's prestige car. Mechanically, it is based on the 180 but the engine capacity is brought up from 1,812 to 1,981 cc. The power has been raised to 110 bhp DIN at 5,600 rpm and the torque to 118 lb/ft DIN at 3,600 rpm. The standard version of the car has a 3-speed Chrysler automatic gearbox with torque converter. The width of the wheels has been increased from 13 to 14 inches and the tyres now have a 175 HR 14 section. The rims, which are pierced, mount a new type of hub cups. A vynil covered roof is standard equipment.

Left, the Diesel version of the Opel Rekord which can be recognised by the hump on the bonnet. The Diesel engine (above) develops 60 bhp DIN at 4,400 rpm. A top speed of approximately 87 mph can be reached. An automatic gearbox is available as an optional extra. Below, the BMW Turbo experimental prototype which repeats the gull-wing doors introduced in some Mercedes models in the 'fifties. Bottom picture, the new Volkswagen EA 400 which will be presented at Frankfurt in 1973. There is a choice of two- or four-door versions of this front-wheel drive car and three different water-cooled engines are available.

is roomier. In fact the length of the passenger cell is nearly 5 inches greater in the Opel, measuring from the accelerator to the upper edge of the rear seats. And finally consumption. The Opel does slightly more to the gallon than the Ford. The internal equipment of the two cars is very different: the Ford panel looks overcrowded while the Opel instruments are well-placed and clearly visible.

Are these the elements that influence customers in their choice of a car? It would seem that they are, even if it is true that the Opel also had almost two months' advantage over its rival.

In addition, Opel fully exploits the tendency of motorists to attach great importance to low running costs. The diesel Opel caters to many German drivers' preference for an economical car (this is confirmed by the fact that the number of foreign cars registered—particularly with low engine capacities—went up by 25% in 1972). But in this case the diesel engine is an expensive economy.

You have to pay over 2,000 marks more for the diesel version with a 2,100 cc engine and a 66 bhp without being able to run the car more economically because of the rise in the cost of diesel fuel. An acceleration of from 0 to 62 mph in 24 seconds and a top speed of 84 mph are clearly in contrast with present traffic tendencies.

1972 saw the introduction on German roads of the most important regulation yet introduced governing traffic: a maximum speed of 62 miles per hour on all roads except motorways and super highways with four lanes and a central barrier. This regution, which has been in force since the beginning of October 1972, has not been

mitigated by the possibility allowed by law of permitting speeds of 75 mph on two-lane roads which are particularly wide. The regulation, which it has been explicitly declared is a trial one, will be valid for three years. Then the German Minister for Traffic will be in a position to establish if a measure of this kind is able to halt the frightening rise or even reduce the number of fatal and serious accidents that occur daily on German roads.

Even though a sector of experts right up to the last moment went on expressing the opinion that the enforcement of a maximum speed might create new perils, motorists have adapted extremely well to the limit. It has also been made clear that, even if the limit did not exist, it would not be possible to do over 62 miles an hour by day on secondary roads, while the most serious accidents occur at night when clearly alcohol and the apparently deserted roads induce foolhardy drivers to travel at excessively high speeds. It is already being said that the 62 mph limit is too high. The analyses of accidents will presumably tell us this year if this is true.

Already there is no doubt that these regulations and traffic conditions have strictly curtailed the design of ever-faster cars. This is confirmed by the BMW 520 in which the BMW traditions of high maximum speeds have been abandoned. One would in fact be hard put to find the traditional BMW characteristics in the 520 engine. It is a car built to guarantee a high level of comfort and a restful drive, with excellent safety features including a roll bar, and is much heavier than the earlier models with a consequent loss of acceleration. It is a car with rather too much metal and lines which demand low seats but—unlike the ones in earlier models—extraordinarily comfortable ones. The engineering technique used in the construction is excellent even if it cannot be said to be in the vanguard of progress (the bodywork is a modified version of the six-cylinder models, and the engine is the one used on the 2-litre car with a few modifications). However, there is no doubt that this is a fine car. And even this BMW is no tortoise: 107 mph with the 115 bhp carburettor engine, 114 mph with the 130 bhp injection engine. The acceleration times are good—12 and 11 seconds respectively from 0 to 62 mph. The apparent contradiction between the comparatively low top speed and the brilliant acceleration is justified by the need for trouble-free overtaking on secondary roads.

One might complain that the standard fuel tank holds only about 12 gallons and the 15-gallon tank is an optional extra which of course must be paid for. A costly quartz clock is mounted on the facia but there are no seat belts or headrests. However, the many months required to obtain delivery of this model prove its success.

The Mercedes Series S cars pay little heed to the new speed limits and are in contrast to the compact shapes adopted by most makers. In fact, in 1972 Daimler Benz built for European roads cars that are over two inches longer and two inches wider than the earlier models. These models show more clearly than the BMW 520 that greater safety means greater weight and, in spite of the 160 and 180 bhp, these cars take a good deal more than ten seconds to accelerate from 0 to 62 mhp. Daimler-Benz should be successful with these models. It has however done nothing to meet the wishes of those of its customers who were hoping for a completely new rear axle to improve the handling of this high-class car. The old rear suspension has been used again with only slight modifications: swinging semi-trailing arms which are mounted even on the smaller models. For 1973 a more up-to-date model which is expected to mount the 4,500 cc engine is awaited. It will be possible to obtain the zero offset steering device and antiblocking mechanism announced some time ago that practically prevents the car from skidding on slippery road surfaces when the traction of one wheel is greater than the other, or if one of the tyres is suddenly damaged. The price has in the meantime risen by 100%, from 1,000 to 2,000 marks.

In this connexion the Audi 80 also comes to mind, for it mounts an anti-skid braking system with a negative offset device. Anyone who has seen the tests the Audi 80 has been put through, in which everything was tried from accidents artificially caused to tyres to trials over a stretch of soap-smeared road, cannot but be amazed at the extraordinary effect small technical modifications can have in situations of extreme hazard. The Audi does not alter direction when a knife slits the tyre cover. This development by Audi and Daimler-Benz is one of the most important made by the German motor manufacturing industry in 1972.

With regard to other developments in the motoring sphere the magazine of the German

Below, the Volkswagen ESV prototype, or the safety vehicle that adheres most closely aesthetically to the lines of contemporary average cars. It is over 186 in long, 70 in wide and weight 3.180 lb. On the opposite page, the latest Mercedes ESV. The V6 engine of this prototype, called ESF 13, develops 140 bhp DIN and the lines recall the new Series S. The ESF 13 has lateral protection along the door rabbets and the windows.

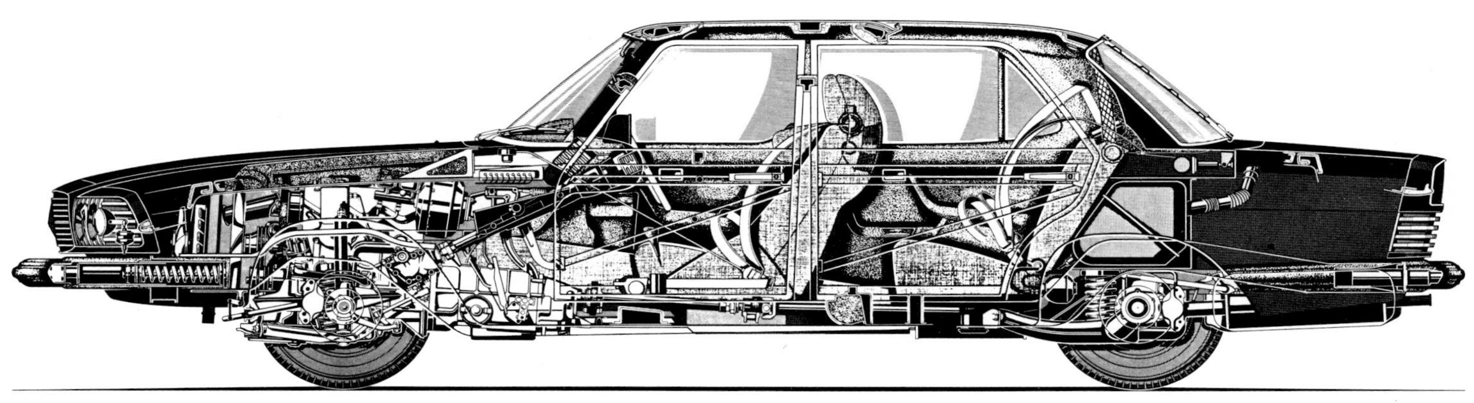

Automobile Club, which numbers two and a half million members, stated that: "In the opinion of the makers, the way to be followed in the future is indicated by the new BMW 520. If this were to prove true, the future would not be very different from the past. This is the case for all models. They are better (and dearer) than before, but they seek after perfection while remaining within the limits imposed by traditional criteria".

Will the future really be like the present? One might think so, since the most modern realizations being developed by German constructors at first sight look extraordinarily like present production cars: these are the 'safety cars' which are now in the experimental phase, after completing the design phase.

On rapid examination, the Daimler Benz ESF 13 looks like a standard car of the S class and the Volkswagen ESVM appears to be a slightly larger K 70. Great weight but rational dimensions are the bases of the safety cars which are destined to guarantee that passengers will survive in a crash at a speed of 50 miles per hour.

The Mercedes weighs no less than 4,630 pounds and, at over 19 feet long, is 10½ inches longer than a 350 SE. The experimental Volkswagen weighs 3,180 lb and is over 15 feet long, that is to say a foot longer than a K 70. The Mercedes has a 2.8-litre six-cylinder engine developing 140 bhp, while the Volkswagen's 100 bhp engine derived from the 1,600 cc model is air-cooled and can be mounted either at the front or rear of the car (at the front with front-wheel drive).

Opel, too, is working on a safety car and —like Fiat—has set itself a limit of 1,000 kilograms. At present it is carrying out experiments on the greater use of foam-rubber padding and reducing the areas subject to buckling.

BMW has made an original contribution to the safety theme by carrying out studies that also have a futuristic sense. The turbine-engined BMW in fact is not merely a dream car but, with its shock-absorbing bumpers, and safety 'cell' with its exemplary structure conforms to safety regulations. The power unit, a 2-litre 280 bhp injection engine with exhaust gas turbo-compressor allows the car, which weighs a mere 2,160 kg, to accelerate from 0 to 62 mph in a mere 6.6 seconds. The turbine car has not yet been tried out except on the BMW factory test circuit.

After this glance at the future, let us take a step back nearer the present. In the autumn of this year the Frankfurt Motor Show will be held once more. But this year new models will be thin on the ground for the German motor industry has expended much of its energies in the past. It is taken for granted that Ford will be presenting a new Escort and a new Capri but it is not certain which of the two models will be presented first. Opel should be presenting a modified Kadett while Audi will launch a new little NSU, since production of the old models has already been largely suspended. It is not known whether the new 'little Volkswagen' constructed according to the badge-engineering techniques the group has already used in the Audi 80 will be making its appearance, but in Volkswagen's interests it is certainly to be augured. BMW can rest on its laurels, though a 520 coupé might be forthcoming.

After a year of economic recession could come a year of reflection for the motor engineers before the German makers present a new generation of models for the 1974-1975 season.

There is however a slightly offbeat novelty: the first small series of electric cars will be placed on the market by Dornier of Münich. These cars are for sale to the public and are therefore the first electric cars of a new wave of automobiles better suited to the exigencies of modern traffic and the demands of motorists. Experiments are also being carried out by Messerschmitt, Bölkow, Blom, and BMW. In Germany the future of the motor car has hardly begun in spite of what the fathers of the new vehicles say...

Great Britain

UNREDEEMED PROMISES

by L.J.K. Setright

A year ago it hardly seemed possible that the great boom in British car-buying would continue unabated. While the potentates of the industry congratulated themselves on virtue being rewarded, other pundits argued that the record sales were attributable to the sudden relieving of numerous financial restrictions and labour problems, enabling the market to satiate itself after a period of what was either starvation or else self-denial. Even that distinguished commentator L.J.K. Setright observed that "In this particular case the success is unreal because it follows some very lean and hungry years, so that the record levels of production and sales attained in 1971 cannot be expected to be maintained in the immediate future".

It hardly seemed possible, but it happened. What drove the customers into the showrooms God alone knows, unless it was the old hedonistic cry "Buy, spend, and be merry, for tomorrow we join the Common Market". How in a year of vicious inflation they found the money, Mammon alone knows, but in the first nine months of 1972 they somehow found enough to buy 1,276, 874 cars, whereas the official SMMT figures for the corresponding months of 1971 totalled only 966,498. Enthusiasts for the products of the other European manufacturers raised the market share of imported cars from 19.51% in 1971 to 23.41% in 1972 (in the same nine-month periods) but even so the domestic producers sold more cars in Britain in the latter year than the nation bought from all sources in the earlier year.

Exports were up too, though in 1971 the value of motors and components sold abroad rose to a record £ 1,358,000,000. In 1972 for the first time the value of complete vehicles was exceeded by the value of the bits and pieces exported as original equipment for British vehicles manufactured outside the United Kingdom and for vehicles of non-British manufacture. Business seems to be gathering momentum all the time.

Momentum, however, is something that engineers understand in terms of inertia; and business of this kind promotes inertia of a kind that is inimical to engineering progress.

The British industry, finding that it can go on selling the things that it has been making for so long, is displaying a pronounced aversion to the introduction of new models. During 1971 the excuse was made that new safety legislation was demanding all the time of those engineers whose efforts might otherwise have been channelled into the creation of new and doubtless wonderful cars; and in view of the dreadful things that were being promulgated by politicians and bureaucrats the whole world over, the excuse was accepted as reasonable. In 1972, however, we had been led to expect a flood of new designs, no doubt delayed a bit but all the better for their prolonged gestation. We are still waiting.

The new four-in-line Ford Escort RS 1600, in light alloy throughout. Distribution is by two overhead camshafts and four valves per cylinder. The engine can develop up to 280 bhp.

There have been some new cars, it is true; but not one of the few could be called wholly new. That sort of cloistered bravery might be all very well for the likes of Citroën or Alfa Romeo, but in Britain the teachings of American experience held sway, and it was no longer considered safe to bring out a completely new car: engines and drivelines must be kept in production, and the quality of the old wine is subordinate to the appearance of the new bottle.

Only one of the major manufacturers reversed the order, putting a new engine into an existing bodyshell: British Leyland brought out a new 6-cylinder 2.2-litre version of the long-stroke Maxi transverse four, with which to enliven and refine that exceptionally sturdy and capacious car the Austin 1800. Those who still want the old four-cylinder 1800 can have it, somewhat improved but still essentially an eight-year-old car with a considerably older engine; those who can pay 11% more will prefer the Austin 2200, whose advantages in power and smoothness are accompanied by virtually no disadvantages, even in weight or fuel consumption.

Probably the year's most distinguished expression of the current theme of putting existing propellants in new packages is the Ford Granada, which also epitomises Ford's successful modern policy of giving its cars as international an appeal as possible, to justify making them in Germany as well as in Britain. The other well-established habit—of contriving luxury, economy, and high-performance versions of the basic design—is also indulged with a profusion and confusion of names and styles, from an under-engined under-privileged V4 Consul at the 2-litre end of the range to a lush Granada estate and a lusty Consul GT at the 3-litre end.

Collectively they replace the old Zephyr and Zodiac which started life on the wrong foot and never really justified the improvements that went into them over the years. The Granada presents a welcome contrast, being one of the most thoroughly developed Fords to come on to the market for years, as well as one of the most attractive.

The glaring faults of the old Z cars have all been eradicated, for the new car not only looks internationally acceptable (which to Ford means German styling) but also behaves well enough on the road to be acceptable to all kinds of drivers.

Thus, despite being much more compact than its predecessors, the Granada is more spacious; but although such aspects as comfort, quietness, visibility, luggage accommodation and ease of servicing have all been studied with obvious care, it is the roadworthiness that most clearly proclaims the care that has gone into the design. The respectable 109-inch wheelbase is long enough to give good pitch stability and steering response, the very wide track confers lateral stability, and Ford's bad old habits of offering different types of tyres all conflicting with the suspension have been overcome with generous radials on wheels of decent width. The rear suspension is still independent, but instead of the troublesome toggle links (which the old Z cars inherited from even older and more erratic American Fords) at the inboard ends of the semi-trailing single wishbones, the pivots are now more positively located in adjustable bushes; new constant velocity sliding joints are built into the half-axle driveshafts, precluding the need for sliding splines and the danger of the suspension binding when full tractive torque is transmitted. Mechanical refinement such as this in a bodyshell of such robustness justifies all the popularity the Granada is now enjoying.

There is an interesting contrast between the attitudes to the British market of Ford and of General Motors.

The latter seem content to leave to Opel the business of making cars of international appeal (even to the extent of selling these increasingly popular German cars in Britain) while Vauxhall cater for the domestic tastes with which they should by now be so familiar. There seems no better way to explain the new range of Victors (the FE series) which Vauxhall brought out early in the year, and which combined all the usual improvements expected of a new bodyshell with typically GM increments in engine size and in vulgarity of styling.

Virtually all the many claimed improvements are real ones and worthwhile: the body detailing is essentially practical but is internally also tasteful, and whereas the previous Victor range had good roadholding and stability the new one adds agility and responsiveness. The most memorable feature I recall is the outstanding braking behaviour; conversely, none of the variants (even the Ventora, with the old 3.3 litre pushrod six-cylinder engine) could be described as fast by current standards.

Vauxhall's improved Victors are heavier Victors, and enlargement of their engines has done no more than preserve a modest status quo. The overhead-camshaft four-cylinder engines now have longer strokes, the larger version also having a bigger bore: so the old 1600 cc job is now a 1759, the 2000 new musters 2279... and a new camshaft for the larger engine deprives it of so much top-end liveliness as to promote a keen driver's despair at the depredations of emission control.

On the whole, the British manufacturers have done well to keep most of their engines up to established marks of performance despite the detrimental effects of the emission control addenda that have become necessary. According to all the theories, their engines ought by now to be a lot more feeble, intractable, and thirsty, than in the dear dirty old days when a polluted state was considered preferable to a Police State. In fact most of them have managed to maintain their verve; sometimes their inlet and (especially) exhaust manifolding was so crude that the simple substitution of a fairly efficient set of pipework has sufficed to

Above, the Ford Consul/Granada available on the English market with either 2- or 3-litre engines. Left, the up-dated edition of the Triumph Stag with reinforced bumpers. On the opposite page, the Avenger Tiger II, the more sporting version of the Hillman, which is produced in limited numbers. With an engine capacity of 1,498 cc, it can reach 105 mph.

restore the power lost in new carburettors and distributors. Before long there will be a new and more onerous set of regulations to be obeyed, and then the engines that have been enlarged will come into their own. Maybe the Vauxhalls are merely the first and most far-sighted of these in Britain, anticipating the enlarged Rolls-Royce engine by a matter of weeks. Rolls-Royce have long been diligent pursuers in the wake of General Motors.

At least we have one really new engine to show for 1972, even if it does appear to owe a lot to Vauxhall inspiration. The 2-litre Lotus engine, an inclined four-cylinder engine with two overhead camshafts and 16 valves, is intended to power all sorts of new cars that have long been expected to issue from the Lotus factory but have been deferred until 1973 or later. It is fairly powerful considering the cleanliness of its exhaust, or very clean considering its power, having been detuned from the racing

standards of its prototype; and pending the arrival of the new Loti, it already finds a use in the new Jensen Healey. This two-seater, intended to occupy that place in the affections of America's sporting motorists once the preserve of the big brutal 3-litre Austin Healey, is essentially an old-fashioned car with new-fangled gimmicks, a sporty fresh-air funster with lively acceleration and reasonable roadworthiness. As an exercise in marketeering and keeping the factory busy (the old Austin Healey was put together in the Jensen factory) it is exemplary; and were it not for the fact that the Vauxhall Viva provides all its suspension and running gear while the Sunbeam Rapier provides a suitable gearbox, it would stand out as the only wholly new car to enter the British lists in the past twelve months.

Just as strong a claim may be maintained by the Clan Crusader. This is a tiny little two-seater, in which the engine and all running gear and suspension and so forth are out of the 50 bhp Sunbeam Sport version of the 875 cc Hillman Imp. The rest was conceived by a young project engineer at Lotus, who left to form his own company and has created one of the best-engineered GRP bodies ever to go into production. The styling may look peculiar (as is so often the case when a small firm is let loose with some glassfibre and plastics) but structurally the hull is uncommonly sturdy and has displayed exceptional merits in the statutory 30 mph crash test, on prolonged rough-road trials, and in rallying. The car is not particularly fast but handles with great agility and precision, despite deliberate efforts to ensure that it should be a practical runabout and not just a boy's racer. Carefully made and nicely finished, it is not—and does not look—cheap; and in all these things it is the antithesis of all that we have come to know and fear from Britain's motley rabble of small 'specialist' manufacturers.

The number of such firms may soon be reduced. Prompted by imminent integration with the EEC, Britain arranged to adopt the European idea of Value Added Tax in 1973; and in one fell swoop this has deprived many of the more sporting small-production cars of their principal attraction, which was that they could be bought as a kit of parts and sub-assemblies that the customer could finish putting together at home and thus avoid the purchase tax that is levied on complete cars. Firms such as Clan, TVR, Gilbern, Ginetta and even Lotus have all thrived on this trade; but the foreknowledge of the tax loophole's closure has prompted them all to concentrate on improving their own factory standards, in the hope that even when they have to compete with their more conventional opponents their cars will have sufficient quality and individuality to maintain their appeal. Some of these little firms have already introduced new models that are only available fully finished: Gilbern's latest Invader has a new chassis as well as emendations to the body, the same may be said of the latest TVR, and Ginetta now make a car with the Sunbeam Rapier 1750 cc engine.

Above, the driving seat of the Range Rover. Various improvements, including making extra instruments previously supplied on request standard, have been made. The standard version now also has windscreen wipers on the rear window. Below, the redesigned interior of the Triumph Spitfire Mk IV. Other modifications have also been incorporated, including a wide rear track, to improve its roadholding.

All these, with the exception of Lotus, are manufacturers on a very small scale, and most of them attract customers who are prepared to forego the enjoyment of high quality and refinement in return for lively performance and distinctive styling at modest cost. Yet the prize for real individuality and exclusiveness continues to go to a firm at the other end of the price spectrum: Bristol continue to restrict themselves to making three cars a week—but of such refinement, ability and quality as to make all other things subordinate. They introduced some styling and mechanical alterations to the 411 early in the year: by November they had taken orders (at nearly £ 8000 each) that would take the Bristol factory's full production up to next May!

While the Bristol skims the cream of what we used to call the carriage trade, the Rolls-Royce remains for most Britons the epitome of expensive living. At last the Silver Shadow will not be quite so expensive in its rate of tyre consumption, for Rolls-Royce announced late in the year that they had now done all that was necessary to reconcile the car to the radial-ply tyres that had so long seemed an essential element in its continuing development. The provision of appropriate compliance involved a complete redesign of the front suspension; so the RR is no longer the only car in Europe (or perhaps the world) whose front suspension sub-frame is so flexibly mounted that it has to be anchored laterally by its own Panhard rod! Its other claims to fame or notoriety appear to have survived unaltered.

Detailed revision, often very extensive, has been a feature of many models. Ford's Capri series is one, and their Cortina Mark 3 (which went through a very difficult early stage in production, so that during the first year it became the most altered car in the country, has not yet settled down completely—despite which it took from the BLMC 1100/1300 the honour of being the biggest-selling car in Britain. The Escort 1600 RS now has an aluminium alloy cylinder block to encourage the homologationers, while the uprated V6 of the Granada aforesaid now lends extra verve to that most competent grand tourer the Reliant Scimitar GTE, as well as to sundry glassfibre rollerskates from the 'specialists'. Reliant's own engine, the 700 cc lightweight for the little Rebel saloon, has gone up to 750 cc. British Leyland's list of alterations starts with an addition to the Maxi range, called the Maxi HL or Hi-Line. This expression, I am credibly informed, will be understood by Americans to imply a sort of *ne plus ultra;* but it is translated in England to mean a livelier camshaft, two carburettors and some nice interior trim. Another and potentially more interesting branch of the Maxi line adopts the AP automatic transmission, an ingenious combination of converter coupling and four-speed gear train that once seemed doomed to confinement among Minis and 1100s, only to be revived by the promise of employment by Alfa Romeo in the near future.

It has been an interesting year for automatic transmission enthusiasts. Not only AP have been active, but also Borg Warner, who have a new four-speed automatic gearbox of compact dimensions and impeccable manners, while Hobbs have a new kind of four-element converter coupling that is claimed to make the gearbox redundant.

I dare say all the motor manufacturers in Britain would happily lay all their gearboxes end to end if it would lead them to a satisfactory engine for the future. Jaguar wax proud with their V12, having put it into the XJ saloon (which was designed for it in the first place) which becomes as the XJ12 one of the most formidable saloons in the world, regardless of price. But what they all want to know is how they are going to manage in the years to come, they who have so glibly dismissed the Wankel engine that now promises to return in about 1975 to its rightful inheritance. They are working on it, of course; but they have lost a lot of leeway. If as a result they founder, Browning leaves an epitaph ready:

"This could but have happened once,
And we missed it, lost it for ever".

Above, the head-up display speedometer designed by Smiths Industries Ltd as it is seen from the driving seat. This eliminates any need for the driver to take his eyes of the road. Below, the 'safety arm', a new device with many advantages. In the drawing, the arm is in the 'rest' position. When the ignition key is inserted, in fact, it moves very close to the chest of the driver and the front-seat passenger.

Italy

THE ITALIAN WAY TO SAFETY

by Pier Luigi Sagona

A good starting point for a consideration of the new Italian cars launched in 1972 is the Fiat 126. This car—together with the 500 which remains in production in a single revised version—is aimed at a very large market. It is a very compact little car with low fuel consumption but able to keep up a very fair average speed over distances and can therefore be used for out of town travelling. The rear air-cooled engine is directly derived from the well-tried 500 engine but the engine capacity has been brought up to 594 cc developing 23 bhp (DIN). The top three gears of the four-speed gearbox are synchronized. The 126 is manufactured not only in Turin but also in the new Cassino plant.

Fiat also presented a new car in the large family car range—the 132. This car is available with a choice of engines (1600 and 1800 cc) and a choice of bodies—standard and special. The mechanical layout is traditional and the car is both fast and comfortable. Fiat has revised all the cars in the 124 range, both mechanically by mounting engines derived from the 132 and in the details of the coachwork. The bodies of 128 saloons have also been modified. Other new cars from Fiat are the XI-9 coupé-spider designed by Bertone with a central 1300 cc engine and the Fiat-Abarth 124 sport 1800 which is directly derived from the car that in 1972 took many first places in the most important international rallies.

The Beta is the first Lancia model realized in collaboration with Fiat by whom it was taken over in 1969. The front-wheel drive Beta is a fairly large car with the high standards of finishing that have always been associated with Lancia. Five different models are produced in standard or de luxe versions and with engines derived from the Fiat 132, with 1400, 1600 and 1800 cc engine capacities. The standard 1800 cc version has a maximum power of 110 hp (DIN) and a top speed nudging 110 mph. The engine is mounted transversely and inclined towards the rear; there is a five-speed gearbox and independent suspension on all four wheels.

Alfa Romeo, the second largest Italian motor manufacturing company, brought out two very interesting cars in 1972. The Alfasud, first presented at the 1971 Turin Motor Show but not placed on the market until June 1972, is a revolutionary model for Alfa Romeo. Besides being the first model to be manufactured by the new Pomigliano d'Arco factory, it is also the first car with front-wheel drive they have made. Designed by Giorgio Giugiaro of Ital Design, the car is compact and modern in appearance; its engine capacity (1186 cc) places it in a sector of the market in which the competition is particularly sharp. The engine is the work of Rodolfo Hrusca, the General Manager of the Pomigliano d'Arco factory.

The other new car is the Alfetta, a commodious grand touring saloon with striking performance figures. The name it has been given is a glorious one, for the famous 158-159 racing car, victorious in two world championships, was affectionately called 'Alfetta'. At the Turin Motor Show, Alfa

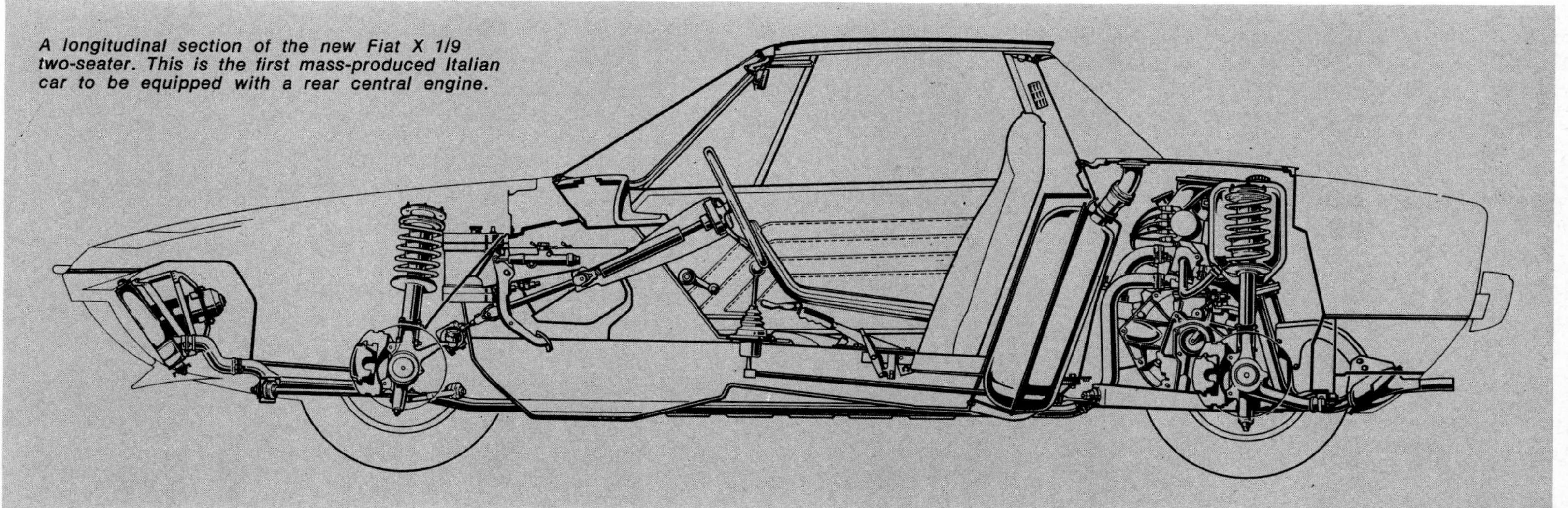

A longitudinal section of the new Fiat X 1/9 two-seater. This is the first mass-produced Italian car to be equipped with a rear central engine.

Romeo presented a 1600 cc version of the Junior-Zagato coupé.
In the sector of high performance de luxe cars, Ferrari launched the Pininfarina-bodied 365 GY4 2+2 and the central-engined B.B. Berlinetta Boxer which goes into production after its 1971 appearance as a prototype. Both mount a 12-cylinder engine with an engine capacity of over 4 litres and can reach extremely high speeds (the BB can do over 185 mph).
Maserati brought out the Merak with a centrally-mounted engine derived from the one used on the Citroën SM and body designed by Giugiaro.
The Bertone Countach with 5000 cc engine developing 440 bhp (DIN) is now being regularly produced by Lamborghini.
The Italian coachbuilders, as usual, did not fail to keep their appointments with the major international motor shows and presented a large number of novelties. The running gear most commonly used was from the Fiat 132 which appeared in Pininfarina, Michelotti, Zagato and Moretti versions. Pininfarina also showed a car with Alfetta mechanics, while Francis Lombardi chose the Lancia 2000 IE and Ital Design the Maserati Bora 4.7. There were also numerous bodies using the chassis and running gear of foreign cars.
A few words must also be dedicated to the prototype ESV (Experimental Safety Vehicle) presented by Fiat at the great Transpo '72 Exhibition in Washington and illustrated in the Third ESV Conference already mentioned. This is the first prototype ESV in the world with a weight in the region of 700 kilograms. The project was programmed in October 1971, the engineering work on the various units of the body was begun in the November and by the end of March 1972 the first two prototypes had been completed.
The Fiat ESV has the same wheelbase as the Fiat 500 (72.44 inches), is 133 inches long and 57 inches wide, and the height when fully loaded is 52.75 inches. The overhang at the front and rear is 27.5 inches and 33 inches respectively. The terminal elements of the body, which are identical front and rear, are composed of two crushable elements fixed to the metallic part of the coachwork and easy to dismantle. Their purpose is not merely to endow the car with a front and rear protective system in head-on or angled crashes at low speeds but also minimise its aggressiveness, especially with regard to pedestrians.
The study of the car's *structure* was the most exacting part of the development project, for it involved overcoming marked difficulties deriving not only from the limitation imposed by the decision to use already existing mechanical elements but also the need to make substantial modifications to the provisional structures previously tried out on the 500 saloon.
The elements of the body *skeleton* belong to three structural groups arranged at different heights.
A comparison between the ESV and the 500 saloon is particularly significant and affords a clear picture of the heavy consequences to be expected in this class of vehicle should manufacturers in future be obliged to conform to the safety requirements laid down in the 1972 formulation of the ESV specification: increases in weight in the region of 29% for survival space alone and 9% for low-speed protection, with a consequent further increase of at least 6% and 2% respectively for strengthening the mechanical elements. These percentages correspond to an overall price increase of roughly Lit. 240,000, or about 40% of the car's original selling price.
This comparison shows how important it is to tackle the question of road safety in a global manner, estimating the costs and benefits of each projected modification or innovation.
The growing collaboration between the major European motor manufacturers leads us to believe that before the end of 1973 there may be a more realistic attitude towards the problem of the ESV and road safety in general.

THE PROBLEM OF SAFETY

"We must aim towards greater safety on the roads and an improved relationship between the motor vehicle and its natural and urban surroundings. This must be achieved without bringing about—due to a swift spiral in the costs of production and the operating costs of motor vehicles—the exclusion from motorization of vast numbers of users and potential users. We must seek safety without stifling the role of 'accelerator' of economic and social develop-

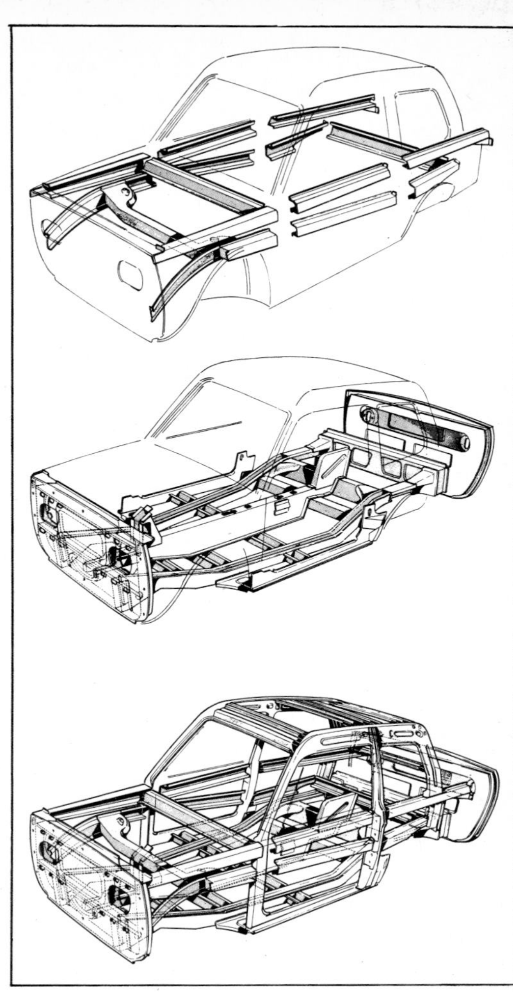

Fiat's first design for the development of a small experimental safety vehicle in the 700 kg class. In the photos on the opposite page, it can clearly be seen how far the flexible bumpers protrude at the front and rear. In the drawings above, starting from the top: a diagram of the lateral structures, of the floor and the complete box-type structure of the body. Due to the reinforced body, it is inevitably half as heavy again as a 500.

Comparative table for 700 ESV experimental safety vehicle and Fiat 500

	Fiat 500	ESV 700 Forecast*	ESV 700 Current**
Overall dimensions in mm:			
Length	2,970	3,250	3,380
Width	1,320	1,440	1,450
Height	1,292	1,340	1,340
Weight in kg:			
Kerb weight	520	670	760
Fully loaded	840	990	1,080
Selling price	600,000	780,000	840,000

* For survival space only.
** For survival space, low-speed protection, and aggressivity reduction.

Increases in overall dimensions, weight and cost of 700 ESV experimental safety vehicle as compared with Fiat 500

	Survival space	Low-speed protection and aggressivity reduction	Total
Overall dimensions:			
Length	+ 4%	+14%	+18%
Width	+ 4%	+ 6%	+10%
Height	+ 4%	+ 0%	+ 4%
Overall surface	+ 8%	+17%	+25%
Weight:	+35%	+11%	+46%
Cost:			+40%

ment played by the automobile and without stirring up new imbalances of unforeseeable range and effect. There is no doubt that the burning question of motoring is today, and in the coming years will be, the increase in individual and social costs that the use of a car will mean. The interests of the user therefore coincide with those of the entire industrial society in the search for every solution capable of slowing down this upward spiral. Naturally this does not mean closing one's eyes to the serious problems that lie before us, but rather searching for causes and solutions with an open mind, with intellectual courage and a lively sense of criticism and self-criticism."

This is how the Italian motorist's point of view was summed up by Filippo Carpi, President of the Automobile Club of Italy and vice-president of the Fédération Internationale de l'Automobile (FIA), during the 29th Conference on Traffic and Road Usage, held at Stresa in September 1972. The theme of the Conference ("the motor car in society" with particular reference to the "costs and benefits of safety") permitted a direct confrontation between the policies of political figures, car designers and motorists' representatives on the vital problems of motoring in the present situation.

The congestion of urban areas, the pollution of the atmosphere, and road accidents: these are the chief charges laid against motoring today. From the sporadic and generic criticism of the motor vehicle that has been gradually developing since the 'sixties in countries with the highest levels of motorization, we have moved on to a series of initiatives at all levels, beginning with the international level. All these undoubtedly today need vigorous coordinating action into a single policy, if we are not to get bogged down in contradictions, in squandering funds and energies that should be directed towards a real need: that of paring down the negative aspects of motorization and heightening its positive ones, of 'bending' the use of motor vehicles to the ends of modern society and of improving the quality of the life we lead today.

Did the Stresa meeting serve to define 'an Italian policy' with relation to the complex network of problems, initiatives and policies that are springing up?

At the Third Conference on the Experimental Safety Vehicle held in Washington in May 1972, Oscar Montabone—head of Fiat's Research and Development sector—stated that: "Motorization in Europe is in many aspects very different from motorization in the United States. In Europe for many years to come there will still be the problem of the first car, one destined for low income brackets. This is why we need to know at once what the additional cost will be in a small car that conforms to the safety standards that have been proposed up to now. It could in the future become extremely difficult to satisfy the demand for motorization in a large sector of the population." And he concluded: "We have been able to establish that the costs of research on the ESV and the additional costs that small cars would entail constitute a commitment to enormous expenditure by the community. Should we not ask ourselves if there is not a less onerous solution, one for instance linking the safe car to the safe road? For instance why not aim at a different road layout in order to avoid any possibility of lateral or head-on collisions? Safety is based on a triangle whose three points are: man, the road and the vehicle."

The Stresa Conference (the report on "The Technical and Economic Aspects of Safety" was contributed by Oscar Montabone) concluded with the unanimous affirmation that "an optimal programme of road safety can be attained only at the level of a study of the system 'man-road-vehicle'. The representatives of the government who spoke at the Conference—the Italian Minister of Public Works, Gulloti, of Education, Scalfaro and Transport, Bozzi—were in full agreement with the working proposal put forward by the President of the Italian Automobile Club to set up an organisation that would allow the problem of safety in all its aspects to tackled as a whole, thus overcoming the formal separations of jurisdiction between the various ministerial organs. This proposal was swiftly put into force with the constitution of a committee on safety composed of representatives of the ministries concerned in all three aspects of the question (man-road-vehicle). The Automobile Club of Italy—as Sig. Scalfaro said—will have to be the moving force in the various initiatives for the road education of young people and the preparation of motorists.

The formation of this committee is in itself a significant event in the panorama of Italian motoring in 1972. It is a sign of a trend that—tenaciously upheld in recent years by numerous designers and experts and in particular by exponents of the Italian Automobile Club—will succeed in establishing itself if, in the coming months, a way is found of equipping the new organism with the technical policy and that effective incisiveness demanded by the situation. One question it will have to deal with is Italy's position in relation to initiatives at the international level. It should not be forgotten that the Economic Commission for Europe in Geneva, the Common Market Commission in Brussels and OECD in Paris, as well as NATO with their special agencies, commissions and working groups, have for many years been working on the problems of the relationship between the motor vehicle and society, and questions of road safety in particular. It will be a question of, on the one hand, achieving concerted action in the questions already raised and on the other hand applying, more rapidly than has hitherto been done in Italy, the policies and formal agreements reached in the various international bodies. For instance, on 15 November 1972 the twice-yearly meeting of the NATO "Committee for the Challenges of the Modern World" was held in London and all the countries taking part, including Italy, undertook fresh commitments for research in the sector of pollution-free motor vehicles.

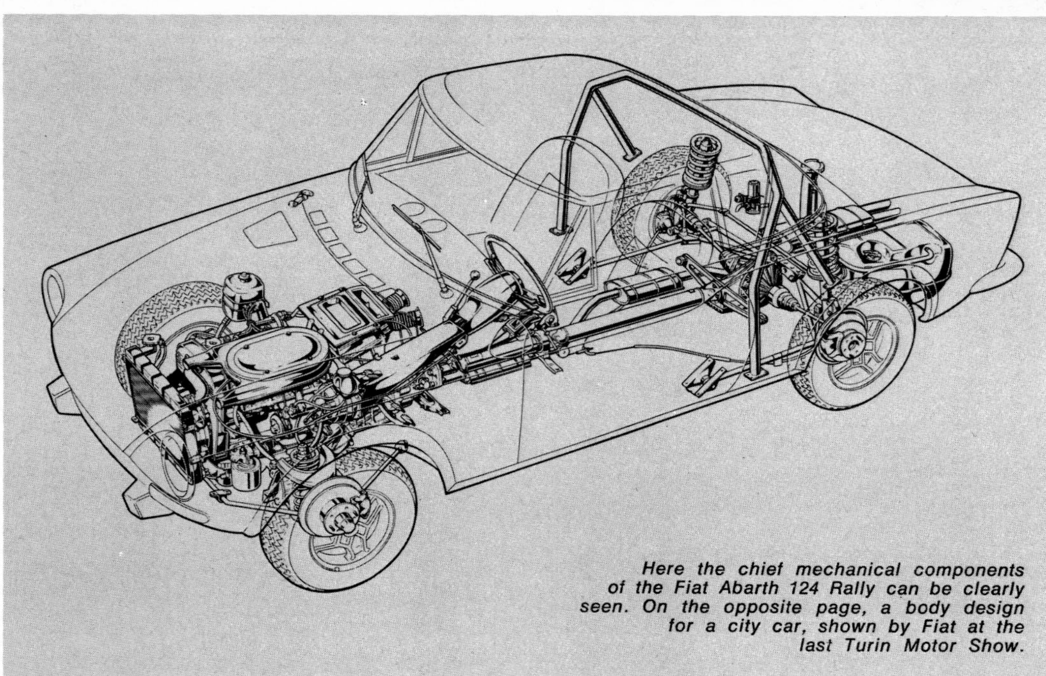

Here the chief mechanical components of the Fiat Abarth 124 Rally can be clearly seen. On the opposite page, a body design for a city car, shown by Fiat at the last Turin Motor Show.

For their part, the motor manufacturers of the Common Market, again in November, formed a special committee to evaluate the technical, political and economic problems deriving from the trends that are developing in the fields of safety, pollution and congestion. Giovanni Agnelli, president of Fiat, was appointed chairman of this committee. This initiative will certainly lead to a more united front in facing these problems and European manufacturers will probably demonstrate this during the Fourth ESV Conference in the spring of 1973 in Tokyo. For that matter, in Washington they showed signs (particularly on the themes of the aggressivity and compatibility of ESVs within the framework of motoring in Europe) of moving more closely together than at the Second ESV Conference at Stuttgart in the autumn of 1971.

THE GENERAL PANORAMA

In view of the more explicit terms on which certain problems have been faced both in Italy and internationally, it may be said that 1972 has shown itself to be the turning point for private motoring both in Italy and throughout the world. The future of the automobile in the industrialized world appears to be increasingly conditioned by the need to mediate between the development of motorization and the defence of the ambient, the survival of the town, and road safety. This has led to important consequences (but even more important ones must be expected) in design, manufacturing, sales and operation; and it is also imposing a new series of problems in the sphere of territorial programming, in the conception and construction of infrastructures, in the organization and design of transport systems and so on. All this has meant the inversion of previous tendencies in the field of costs and prices. The downward trend—due to technological progress, more efficient industrial organization and an expansion of production—that had marked the more prosperous years of the post-war period, has been fading out in recent years and an upward trend has begun, even if establishing itself slowly and in an irregular manner. 1972 and the early months of 1973 (in Italy partly due to the introduction of the Value Added Tax) have confirmed and generalized this new trend.

Confirmation of this tendency and reasons for its existence were given by the major figures of the Italian motor manufacturing industry during the 1972 International Motor Show in Turin (this was the last of the series of annual motor shows in Turin; the next one will be in 1974 and then every other year like the other European motor shows).

The President of Alfa Romeo, Giuseppe Luraghi, advanced three explanations for the continued increase in the price of cars.

1) prevalent causes connected with the fall in the value of money and the general rise in prices (including the prices of raw materials);

2) causes specifically concerning motor ma-

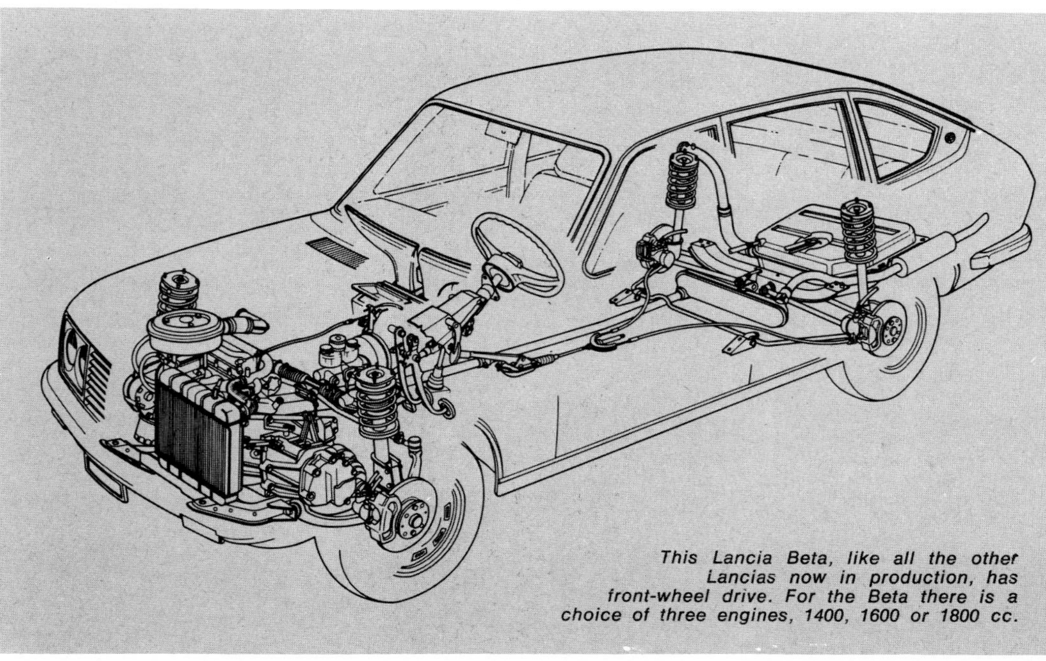

This Lancia Beta, like all the other Lancias now in production, has front-wheel drive. For the Beta there is a choice of three engines, 1400, 1600 or 1800 cc.

nufacturing which involve a rise in costs in real and not merely monetary terms. These include the costs of reducing pollution and improving safety factors in vehicles that are increasingly sophisticated from the technical point of view;

3) situations and phenomena which are to be met with only in Italy or which occur in Italy in a more aggravated form than elsewhere, and which have a direct influence on costs. Sig. Luraghi in this regard spoke of a marked fall in productivity which is attributed above all to absenteeism and frequent trades union unrest.

Gianni Agnelli, too, stressed the fall in productivity during a press conference held on the occasion of the Turin Motor Show. Defining the situation from the point of view of the Fiat management, Agnelli stated that: "Since 1968 we have spent 500 billion lire on investments, given jobs to another twenty thousand people, we have increased our labour force by one third, but production has only risen by about a seventh. In 1968 Fiat accounted for 5.2% of world production, today its share has fallen to 4.3%". The president of Fiat gave the following figures on absenteeism: "In 1960 absenteeism at Fiat stood at 4%, in 1970 it was 8% and today it is 15%". The phenomenon is not confined to Italy alone and is viewed with anxiety on all sides even if at the Renault press conference in Turin it was stated that absenteeism at Régie is today 5%, only a little higher than in the past). Another significant piece of information was supplied by Agnelli: in the south of Italy absenteeism is almost unknown; in the Fiat works in Lecce it stands at 2% and in Bari at 4%.

With regard to the Mezzogiorno, an event has taken place that could be defined of historic importance for Italian motoring: the launching of a mass-produced car entirely manufactured in a factory in the south of Italy, specially built for the purpose. We are of course speaking of the Alfasud; of "the eruption of a factory at the foot of Vesuvius", as a French newspaper wrote. The foundation stone of the Alfasud factory was laid on 29 April 1968. When the new car was launched commercially (in June 1972) the Pomigliano d'Arco factory was producing 70 cars a day. In 1973 it should reach a thousand units a day and 15,000 employees (90% of them coming from the south of Italy). The factory represents an investment of about 250 billion lire.

Fiat, too, has chosen the Mezzogiorno for its new production centres. The Cassino plant (an investment amounting to over 60 billion lire with 4,000 employees) was responsible for the first Fiat 126 which rolled off the production lines in the autumn of 1972; when the plant is working at full capacity, 250,000 cars a year will be manufactured. The new Fiat factories at Termini Imerese have also started operating. Italian production, in spite of the fall in productivity, absenteeism and strikes connected with the renewal of the engineering industries' labour contract, rose by about 7% in the passenger car sector and fell in the industrial vehicle sector. All the same, in 1972 it topped for the first time two million units (the million watershed was left behind by Italian industry in 1963). There was a marked increase in Italian exports which, with 750,000 vehicles, were 15% higher than in 1971. More than half a million vehicles were exported for the first time in 1968. The home market, on the other hand, remained practically stationary with 1,600,000 registrations, 400,000 of them foreign cars. (It was in 1963 that more than a million vehicles were registered for the first time). The share of the market held by cars imported into Italy (about 25%) averages out with the percentages registered in other Common Market countries.

As a whole the Fiat Group (including Autobianchi and Lancia) has maintained the quota of about 89% of all the cars produced in Italy. Vehicles registered in Italy in 1972 topped the thirteen and a half million mark (the 10 million mark was reached in Italy in 1969, in France and Germany in 1965 and in the United Kingdom in 1964).

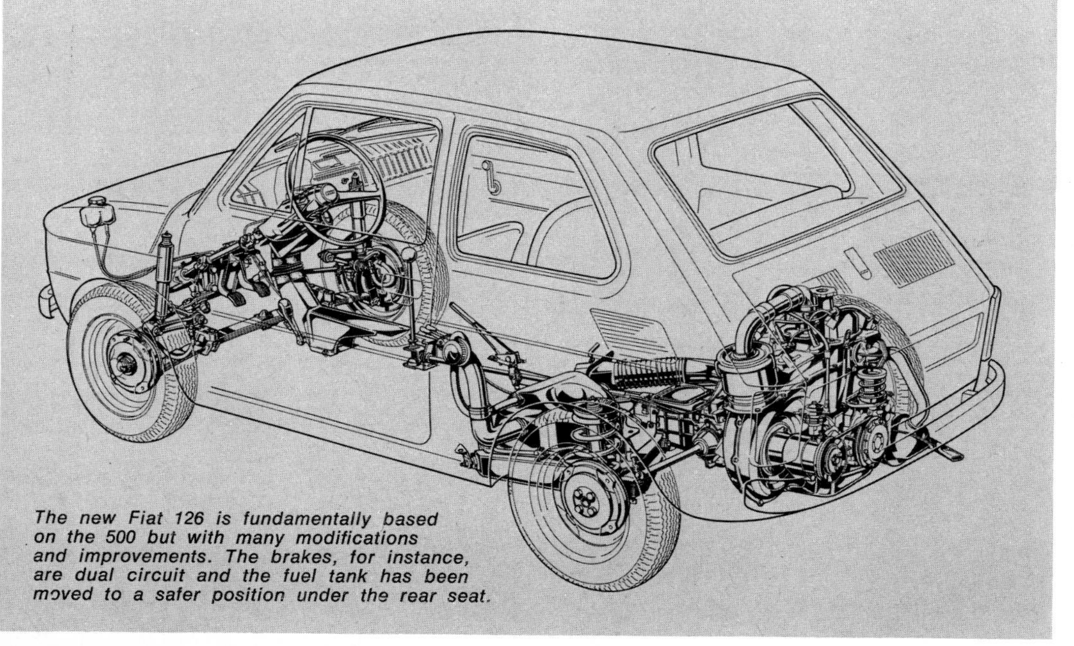

The new Fiat 126 is fundamentally based on the 500 but with many modifications and improvements. The brakes, for instance, are dual circuit and the fuel tank has been moved to a safer position under the rear seat.

only) automatic transmission, as well as an efficient air-conditioning system, are offered to the American buyer. Exports to Europe and other markets should follow soon. The Suzuka factory has a maximum capacity of 10,000 Civics a month, which now appears totally insufficient, and plans are underway to expand the facilities. Honda has also replaced the complex aircooled transverse 4-cylinder engine of the 1300 range with a Civic-inspired watercooled 1.45-litre four, the car being renamed the Honda 145. Production of this model is held deliberately low, at 1,000 per month, in order to make room for Civics at Suzuka.
The intermediate class, as represented by Toyota's Mark II and Nissan-Datsun's Laurel and Skyline twins, is gaining popularity, indicating the accumulated wealth of the upper middle class buyer.
Earlier in the year, Toyota followed Nissan's suit when it updated the Mark II. Nissan was extremely successful with its Skyline 6-cylinder (known as the 2400 GT or 240K GT in Europe) version, which was a stretched four-cylinder body into which a 2-litre six was dropped. The new Mark II has six-cylinder models, both in single and twin carburetter tune. Likewise, Nissan added six-cylinder models when the Laurel was due for a major model change in mid-year. There was, however, a curious design reversal in the case of the Laurel, which had adopted an independent rear suspension on all models. The new Laurel sedan has a rigid rear axle and semi-elliptic springs, while the pillarless hardtop retains the i.r.s. This was repeated in the new Skyline which appeared later in the season, in a different manner. The four-cylinder Skyline, both with 4-door sedan and 2-door hardtop bodies, gets a rigid axle, while the "GT" six has the i.r.s.
The first new car of the season is again a Nissan-Datsun: the type 710 which replaces the type 510 which is better known as the Datsun 1400/1600 or the Bluebird. The Bluebird name has been dropped from this model, which is now called the Nissan Violet. The 710 also has a rigid axle, this time for the basic 1400 and the luxury 1600, and a semi-trailing arm independent rear suspension for the sportier 1600SSS. Three bodies are offered; 2- and 4-door sedans and a fashionable 2-door pillarless hardtop. Nissan is quickly expanding models which are fed by a locally produced Bosch-type electronic fuel injection system. One of them is the new Violet 1600SSS-E whose power output is increased to 115 hp at 6200 rpm, a gain of 10 hp over the twin SU SSS version.
Toyota also offers its own EFI (electronic fuel injection) jointly developed with Denso, Toyota's subsidiary specialist in electrics, on the Mark II and Corona 4-cylinder models. By contrast, Honda has adopted a mechanical injection system with radially placed plungers in the camshaft-driven pump on the 145 FI coupé.
Toyo Kogyo's Luce is Mazda's challenge to the Mark II and the Laurel/Skyline brigades. It is a thoroughly conventional front-engined, rear wheel drive car with two body styles, a 4-door sedan and the inevitable 2-door pillarless hardtop. Mazda has been reluctant to revert to this very popular body style (it had produced a limited number of front wheel drive R130 coupés with this type of body), but obviously the marketing people won. Mazda's Chief Designer Watanabe is one of very few Japanese engineers believing in fat tyres on wide rims, and he has gone so far as to fit 195/70SR13 tyres on the GSII/GRII Luce, a refined, smooth and extremely roadworthy car which should soon find its way to the export markets.
Although the 360 cc market is steadily shrinking, several new models have appeared in this class. Toyo Kogyo had been absent from this sector for some time, but it came back with the brand new Chantez sedan, powered by a 2-stroke watercooled 2-cylinder engine. It is a conventional design with the engine at the front driving the rear wheels via normal 4-speed gearbox transmission.
Despite its orthodox layout, the Chantez is a surprisingly roomy runabout with good road manners. Its only vice is typical 2-stroke noise. Mazda would have loved to fit a mini Wankel, but tooling up for an entirely new engine conforming to the existing 360 cc rule was not a viable proposition.
Fuji Heavy Industries also reclothed its Subaru rear-engined 360 cc car, and renamed it the Rex.
Mitsubishi replaced the 2-stroke engine of the Minica 360, and the new sohc 2-cylinder engined model is called the F4. Following the trend in larger cars, Honda removed the center pillar from the home market Z coupé (powered by a watercooled engine), which is now a proper hardtop coupé with wind-down rear quarter windows. Another interesting Honda addition is the Stepvan, a tall 4-door plus tailgate wagon based on the power unit and running gear of the Life sedan.

United States of America

THE YEAR OF THE FORWARD LOOK

by Jan P. Norbye

As 1969 was a year of 'Polarization', 1970 was the year of the Subcompact, 1971 was the Year of the Question Mark, and last year was the *Year of the Forward Look*. Chrysler Corporation once used the same expression to characterize its styling theme, but in this new context its meaning is more literal. The 1972 model year was a period when the market was expanding, factories were running at full throttle, and the industry leaders were able to concentrate their efforts not on next year or the year after, but on the future beyond that. The reasons why 1972 became the year for looking forward are simple: decisions affecting the cars of 1975-76 must be made NOW, and a program for the period up to about 1985 must be formulated without further delay. There were several reasons why pressure reached its climax in 1972. First, legislation covering emission control systems and safety standards. Second, the coming energy crisis and the search for future fuels and compatible power systems. The challenges and the possible solutions will be discussed after we have looked at the accomplishments of the auto industry in the '72-model year and its current status.

Retail sales of passenger cars and trucks in the United States during the 1972 model year were the highest ever. A total of 13.2 million vehicles were retailed, exceeding the previous peak of 11.7 million in 1969 by 13%. Strong demand for passenger cars was sustained throughout the year. Passenger car deliveries of 10.7 million units, including imports, were 10% above the former 1969 record. Compared with the 1971 model year, car sales in 1972 were up 14%. Chairman of the Board of the Ford Motor Company, Henry Ford II, gave a few impressive facts in a speech in September 1972: ...the motor vehicle industry and the entire range of closely related industries in the United States are able to:

- provide employment, directly or indirectly, for one of every four American workers;
- generate nearly one of every ten dollars of total federal, state and local tax revenues;
- contribute more than 15% of the Gross National Product;
- serve more than 80% of the total transportation needs of the nation;
- and earn sufficient profits to support the massive capital investments required to build new facilities, improve productivity and stay competitive with foreign industry investments that totaled approximately $ 1.8 billion in 1972 for the U.S. motor vehicle industry alone.

The flow of imports has not been stemmed, but is stabilizing around the 15% penetration mark. Here is the list of the top ten for the 12-month period corresponding to Detroit's 1972 model year, showing gains or losses compared with the previous 12-month period:

1.	Volkswagen	449,030	— 20.75%
2.	Toyota	284,098	— 1.9 %
3.	Datsun	177,907	— 3.73%
4.	Ford Capri	81,077	+ 55.1 %
5.	Opel	70,495	— 22.69%
6.	Fiat	54,896	+ 24.52%
7.	Volvo	50,633	— 6.99%
8.	Mazda	44,438	+186.97%
9.	Dodge Colt (Mitsubishi)	41,054	+121.36%
10.	Mercedes-Benz	38,657	+ 8.09%

The American public is continuing to favor smaller cars. 39% of all cars now sold in the U.S. are compact size or smaller. Changing driving conditions go a long way to explain this trend. About 85% of all trips are under 25 miles, with one or two persons in the car. 13% of driving time is spent idling, and overall average speed is 26 mph. More and more people agree that they don't need a $ 5,000 2½ ton 250 hp 6-seater sedan to do that job. Growing multi-car ownership is another cause.

In the past five years, total motor vehicle registrations have gone up by 20%, and the annual number of vehicle miles driven has increased by 27%, while the population has increased only 5%. Almost a third of all families now own at least two cars, compared with one-fourth of all families five years ago. The trend can only be accentuated by increasing population density in the large cities, coupled with a general lack of appropriate public transport.

In October 1972, Roy D. Chapin, Jr., Board Chairman of American Motors Corporation, told a business audience in New York that "reappraisal of the role for the automobile in central cities is necessary", and that "the auto industry will be more farsighted than it has been in the past if it makes positive recommendations as to how and when changes should be made".

To stimulate both government and industry in this direction, a group known as SCORE (Student Competitions on Relevant Engineering) sponsored an Urban Vehicle Design Competition which attracted 65 entries from universities all over the U.S. and Canada. Overall winner was a superbly finished two-seater from Canada's University of British Columbia. This car was powered by a Fiat 128 4-cylinder engine converted to run on liquid natural gas.

Some of the cleanest emissions were recorded by cars from Brigham Young University, the University of California in Los Angeles, and the University of Detroit. The only entry to meet the '76 emission standards was a stock Volkswagen Super Beetle that ran on hydrogen fuel and water injection. "It only cost $ 100 to convert to the hydrogen system", said Kay Mortensen, faculty advisor to the Brigham Young University team. We just put in five hydrogen tanks and hooked them up to the carburetor. For

Two city car prototypes. The one developed by the University of Michigan (top photo) mounts a Wankel engine while the University of British Columbia prototype is based on the Fiat 128.

Above, a Ford Galaxie and the Ford ESV. The safety vehicle has a longer hood for better impact absorption while the rear part of the car is reduced to keep it down to a maximum length of 200 inches laid down by government regulations. On the opposite page, the AMF experimental safety vehicle prototype.

water injection we used the standard VW fuel system, including the regular fuel tank". General Motors has disclosed that the 1975 and 1976 emission standards can be met with modified production engines and lead-free gasoline. The limits imposed are (in grams per mile):

	1975	1976
hydrocarbons (HC)	0.41	0.41
carbon monoxide (CO)	3.4	3.4
oxides of nitrogen (NO)	3.0	0.4

In reporting on the "all-out efforts" being made by General Motors, President Edward N. Cole said, *We have been able to meet emission levels for 1975 and 1976, but only with prototype systems in experimental cars at low mileage.* Much more progress is required to get from these carefully-tuned experimental systems to mass-produced hardware that not only meets the federal requirements but also functions properly in the hands of our customers". In 1975 GM cars will use an oxidizing catalyst to control hydrocarbon and carbon monoxide emissions, and in 1976 GM will add a reducing catalyst to meet stricter standards for controlling oxides of nitrogen. A catalytic system acts to convert pollutants chemically into harmless vapor as the automobile's exhaust gases are passed through it.

Ford is in the process of linking up with Japan's Honda Motor Co. for rights to the Compound Vortex Controlled Combustion Engine. This is a normal piston engine with a modified carburetor-type induction system, plus special piston and cylinder head design, which has passed a 50,000-mile running test, conforming to '75 standards, without thermal reactors or catalytic converters.

Chrysler Corp. has a different approach, expressed in the argument that meeting the '75 and '76 standards won't bring about an improvement in air quality commensurate with the cost of conforming to those standards. Speaking to a meeting of the Society of Automotive Engineers in Detroit, Chrysler President, John J. Riccardo, said: I believe we have concentrated too much on the question of *how* these standards are to be met, instead of raising the far more relevant question: *why* should they be met?" He said most of the assumptions on which the 1975-76 standards were based have since been refuted by new scientific research. Will the standards be held to the strict limits now on the books? President Nixon's Committee Report on the Cumulative Regulatory Effects of the Cost of Automotive Transportation (RECAT) recommends easing the rules on NO_x emissions for '76 to 1 to 2 grams per mile in order to encourage development of power units such as the Wankel, and other alternative engines. The RECAT report went into detailed cost studies, and showed that emission controls alone for a proposed 1976 V8 engine would cost the customer $350!

As far as the Wankel engine is concerned, its imminent production in the U.S. is almost an accepted fact. General Motors President Cole has stated that it had been developed so far that the program has been handed over from the corporate research establishment to Chevrolet Motor Division.

The GMRE (General Motors Rotary Engine) will be built by Hydra-Matic Division for use in the Chevrolet Vega, and the target date for production start-up is March or April 1974. The GMRE will be a twinrotor Wankel engine, installed in the space normally occupied by the four-cylinder power unit. Next in the Wankel program, GM is preparing a front wheel drive prototype of compact dimensions. This is expected to result in a line of production cars to be sold by all GM car divisions including Cadillac, perhaps by 1977.

Why the switch to the Wankel? It's an internal combustion engine, which requires much the same emission control equipment as the reciprocating piston engine. Many factors combine in favor of the Wankel:

1. Emissions. It has far lower NO_x emission.

2. Packaging. The small size of the Wankel will make it easier to accommodate the emission control hardware.

3. Performance. The Wankel has a far superior power-to-weight ratio, and higher rpm capability.

4. Cost. The Wankel has fewer parts, weighs less, and can be manufactured and assembled on automated machinery, with consequently lower original and maintenance costs.

5. Comfort. The Wankel is essentially vibrationless.

6. Noise. The Wankel has lower noise levels.

7. Fuel. The Wankel has a very low octane requirement. It can use regular fuel, and does not need lead.

8. Lube oil. It has no need of costly oil additives to prevent foaming, sludge, corrosion or dilution.

9. Styling. The Wankel engine can be designed with a lower profile permitting lower hood lines and better visibility.

10. Conservation of resources. The Wankel uses less raw material for a given power output.

But General Motors is not alone in recognizing these facts. All the U.S. auto makers are eyeing the Wankel. American Motors expects to be able to buy engines from General Motors. Ford has a task force assigned to Wankel research, but does not yet have a license for North America (Ford of Germany holds a very restricted licence from NSU/Wankel). Chrysler is reportedly negotiating for a Wankel license, but the Wankel activity at Chrysler is restricted to tests, mostly with Mazda engines. Chrysler is, however, developing its seventh-generation automotive gas turbine, possibly in the hope of leapfrogging the Wankel. The turbine is extremely clean in terms of HC and CO emissions, but has a NO_x problem in its present state.

But the turbine field is no longer exclusively Chrysler's. A small 80 hp turbine of advanced design, built by Williams Research Corporation of Walled Lake, Michigan, has been installed in an AMC Hornet. The car was delivered to the City of New York under a federal grant for testing in the urban environment. It has been going from one test establishment to the other for a full year, and a conclusive report is expected soon. The only reliability problem so far has been failure to start once, which was due to filling the tank with the wrong fuel (heavy oil instead of low-octane gasoline). The Williams Research turbine car has successfully passed the '75 emission test, but has not met the '76 limits.

Ford is also investigating the Stirling engine (an external-combustion liquid-fuel power system) that is expected to meet the '76 standards. The basic engine has been developed by Philips Scientific Laboratories in Eindhoven, Holland, and Ford's program involves conversion of two Pinto cars by a fellow licensee, United Stirling AB in Sweden, plus evaluation in a Torino in the U.S.

In the area of safety, the goals of the National Highway Traffic Safety Administration (a branch of the Department of Transportation) are being re-evaluated, following tests of the Experimental Safety Vehicles built under federal contracts by AMF, Fairchild, Ford, and General Motors.

The winner was supposed to get a contract for the construction of 12 more ESVs. That did not happen. The AMF car was the winner, but the prize was a 'small' $2.15 million contract for more consumer oriented studies, analyses, and development tests to define the performance specifications for an improved ESV of family sedan size.

In December Federal Motor Vehicle Safety Standard 208 was suspended by a Federal Court in Cincinnati, Ohio, ruling on a suit against the air-bag rule by Ford

Motor Co., Chrysler Corporation, International Harvester Co., Volvo Inc. and the Association of Automobile Importers. As written, FMVSS 208 demanded a passive restraint system protecting all vehicle occupants in a 30 mph barrier crash in all new cars manufactured after 15 August 1975. The standard cannot be reactivated until passive restraint systems have been developed and proved their reliability. Behind the court's decision, lie some interesting facts.

The law does not specify 'air bags' but it is questionable whether any belt system can be devised to meet the requirements. Doubts have been raised as to the reliability of air bags, especially since they failed to inflate in the Fairchild ESV in the DoT crash test. To date there is only one instance of air bag inflation under actual accident conditions. Last spring Ford supplied All-State Insurance Co. with 200 Mercury cars equipped with Allied Chemical air bags for the right front passenger. The cars have been involved in over 40 accidents, but only one serious enough to activate the system. In this collision, the air bag did inflate. However, the driver was alone in the car, and he was wearing a seat belt. The experience is inconclusive.

The leading alternative to passive restraints is compulsory seat belt usage (following the sensible example from Victoria State, Australia). According to the RECAT report, the equipment needed for 1976 would cost the customer $523 per car. Legislation will cost nothing, and enforcement costs are optional.

Inseparable from any discussion of safety is the subject of callbacks. Quality is probably the worst problem Detroit has right now. Since the National Traffic and Motor Vehicle Safety Act was passed in 1966, almost 31 million vehicles—domestic and imported—have been called back for inspection by the factory.

The biggest campaign was Chevrolet's replacement of motor mounts on more than 6 million cars made between 1967 and 1972: Ford had a bad case with the '72 Torino and Montego, and 436,000 cars had to be called back for replacement of rear axle shafts. Ford's second-worst problem was a missing pin in the power steering gear on 900,000 '72-model intermediates, full-size cars and pickup trucks. Without the pin, a hard left turn could snap the steering shaft. The axle problem was a design flaw; the steering gear pin was a quality control matter.

Chevrolet also had a rear axle problem. About 4,400 Vega shafts were found too short and rejected. Somehow, they still found their way to the assembly line and were installed, but nobody had any record of which cars they had gone into. To find the shafts, Chevrolet had to call back 500,000 Vegas.

Callback campaigns have proved more costly than would effective inspection and quality control, and all auto companies are acting accordingly. Testing and checking are being given more importance in all assembly plants and the motivation is clear when GM admits that warranty repairs now cost the company almost $ 500 million a year.

Before leaving the subject of safety, it is on order to record that the Chevrolet Corvair has been cleared by the Academy of Science as not being "unsafe at any speed" (title of Ralph Nader's book, which was a direct attack on the rear-engined, air-cooled compact). Subsequent to the discontinuation of the Corvair in 1969, Mr. Nader has concentrated his attacks on the Volkswagen beetle, which he characterized as the "most dangerous car on the road". Mr. Nader has thoroughly discredited himself and his research organization by being unable to name the *second* most dangerous car; the attack has been invalidated.

What's new in the '73 models? Exhaust gas recirculation to meet the 0.34 gram/mile limit on oxides of nitrogen emissions set by the Environmental Protection Agency; front bumpers that can take a 5-mph barrier crash without permitting damage to any safety-oriented items such as headlights, parking lights, and so on (and rear bumpers meeting the same conditions in a 2½ mph barrier crash).

Most EGR (exhaust gas recirculation) systems are essentially similar. The exhaust manifold has a distribution passage that feeds into an EGR valve controlling the amount of gas sent around again. The exhaust gas is mixed with the fresh charge in the intake manifold. The EGR valve is controlled by intake manifold vacuum, and modified by a high-temperature compensator, a low-ambient compensator, and a coolant override valve. No exhaust gas is recirculated at idle or under wide-open-throttle operation, but 12-13% is recirculated on part-throttle load. The EGR systems have little effect on full performance but cause a significant rise in fuel consumption.

The automobile manufacturers have widely different approaches to the bumper standards. General Motors and American Motors have the most elaborate design. The bumper is backed up by hydraulic buffers. A front cylinder is filled with nitrogen gas, and a rear cylinder with mineral oil. On impact, the gas is compressed, and the oil is displaced through a flow-control orifice. Ford Motor Co. uses rubber blocks in shear, mounted between the bumper support rails and the chassis frame. Chrysler Corp. uses flexible rubber overriders, but no other elastic parts, on the theory that the shock loads are distributed throughout the body structure by energy management design. Body shells and front stub frames are reinforced and lengthened bumper support brackets add 4 to 9 inches to overall vehicle length.

The industry is drifting away from the two to three year restyling cycle towards a five to ten year cycle. The annual model change concerns only minor items such as grilles, taillight panels, trim and color. Styling trends are clear, and almost revolutionary in concept. The convertible is disappearing. Chrysler has none, Ford has two (Mustang and Cougar), and the GM divisions restrict them to B bodies and the Eldorado. Next to be eliminated is the hardtop. GM took this drastic step with all its '73 intermediates. Next year, the full size cars will follow. At the same time, glass area is radically increased. The Department of Transportation has proposed certain visibility standards, with a periscope-type rear view mirror, and the auto companies want to prove they can do just as well without giving up their full styling freedom. This is a long overdue but desirable development. Styling *per se* will be de-emphasized on future models. Many small cars are in the initial design stage now, at all companies, and reports

On the opposite page and above, the new Buick Apollo, the latest of the compacts. There is a choice of three versions, a four-door sedan, a coupé and a Hatchback coupé with top-hinged tailgate and a folding-down rear seat. The Apollo wheelbase is 111.42 in and the coupé version weighs 3,275 lb. The standard power group is a six-in-line four cylinder 250 cu in engine and a V8 five-litre engine is available as an optional. Below, the little Williams Research Corporation experimental turbine engine is mounted on a Hornet. This is the smallest turbine engine to date for automobiles. It develops 80 bhp and emission-wise is very clean.

indicate they will be boxy, practical designs with big windows.

Detroit's future is going to be increasingly dependent on a global approach to auto production. The domestic market does not promise much opportunity for expansion, but the 'third world' (collective name for the under-developed nations) most certainly does. Ford and General Motors have already taken action to start the process of motorization in Asia. General Motors started production of the Bedford Harimau at Tampoi in Malaysia in September 1972. The following month, Ford Asia-Pacific began building the Ford Fiera in its Philippines factory.

Both the Harimau and the Fiera are ultra-simple, basic vehicles, designed for low cost transportation in countries without a modern highway network. Both use a maximum of standard parts, however, from the British subsidiaries (Vauxhall engine in the Harimau, English Ford engine in the Fiera).

Following the invasion of the U.S. market by Japanese passenger cars, Detroit is reacting by buying into the Japanese industry and forming joint companies with Japanese firms for production in Japan. In July 1971 General Motors paid $ 56 million for a 34% share in Isuzu Motors. Ford tried to get a similar share of Toyo Kogyo, but failed to reach an angreement. However, Ford is a partner in the Japanese Automatic Transmission Company, together with Toyo Kogyo and Nissan Motors.

Chrysler have linked up with Mitsubishi Motor Co. and import the Colt into the U.S. They aimed originally for a 35% share in the Japanese company but, disappointed by Japan's business slowdown and worried about the revaluation of the yen, have decided to limit their share in Mitsubishi to 15%.

Only General Motors goes ahead, undaunted. In September 1972, a new company was formed, GM Allison Japan Ltd., with local participation by Isuzu (20%), Kawasaki (20%), and C. Itoh (10%). GM holds 50% of the joint venture, which will make transmissions and gas turbines.

All major U.S. auto manufacturers are, of course, multinational corporations. The profit picture at the end of 1972 was satisfactory for most divisions and subsidiaries, and the outlook for 1973 is full of promise. A number of decision-making functions, in the product and pricing ends, have been moved from Detroit to Washington D.C. in recent times, but American auto executives are learning to live with government although fighting vigorously to protect their interests. And in global terms, the men from Detroit are among the most enterprising in seeking and developing new markets, though with a new flexibility that allows much higher local participation.

On the whole, Detroit now seems more self-assured and more confident in its future than at any time in the past decade.

ELECTRIC VEHICLES

by Gianni Rogliatti

Added prominence has been given today to the question of the electric car by the strong opposition that has recently been springing up to the conventional internal combustion engine. The petrol engine is noisy and pollutes the air; the electric motor is quiet and causes no pollution. But laymen are rarely aware of a series of problems that arise when an attempt is made to introduce the electric car into practical use, the same problems that led to the abandon of this type of power unit in the early days of motoring, in spite of the fact that—as early as 1899—it was an electric car that first reached a speed of 100 km/h.

One of the problems to be overcome before the electric car can win the success that it will almost certainly obtain is the development of light-weight, economical and practical batteries. The choice would seem to lie now between the new, light accumulator type batteries and fuel cells. Then a choice must be made between alternate and direct current and, if the latter is chosen, between series, parallel and composite types. Finally speed control systems must be found that are more precise than the electro-mechanical commutation type but less expensive than electronic systems.

At present the production of autonomous electric vehicles, that is to say not linked to electric networks as are trolley buses and electric trains, is of two distinct types: the construction by industry of prototypes for the study of the problems mentioned above and the production of small series of vehicles for special usages. In the latter case, "vehicle" rather than "passenger cars" is the correct term inasmuch as electric traction with conventional lead-acid batteries has long been used for specific purposes, such as delivery rounds in towns, the transport of persons in airports and wherever noise and exhaust emissions are not tolerat-

Above, the little car manufactured in England by Enfield. It is a 2 + 2 with an autonomy of about 80 miles and a top speed of roughly 40 mph. The motor develops 5 bhp. Below, the commercial vehicle produced by the British Morrison Electricar. Here the top speed is about 30 mph with an autonomy of about 25 mph.

ed (hospitals, golf courses and so on), in fork lift trucks and for many other uses.
At the present stage of development, the only type of battery that can be used is the lead-acid battery, which is very heavy in relation to the energy it can store, but economical, easy to keep in an efficient state and with a life of at least two years' continuous use. On the other hand, the other types of batteries built industrially have drawbacks that make them unsuitable for traction; the nickel-cadmium and zinc-silver batteries are much more costly and are not capable of supplying the high voltage currents needed for starting up and acceleration. The same is true of fuel cells, while other batteries of a more advanced type still have to be fully adapted to practical use. The one which seems to be most promising is the zinc-air battery which can be rapidly recharged by introducing fresh zinc and removing the solution in which the zinc consumed has dissolved during discharging. The zinc is then salvaged electrolitically and thus a kind of indirect recharging is achieved.
Motors of the traditional type running on direct current are normally used but the possibility is being studied of using alternate current or direct current with electronic commutation to permit smaller and therefore lighter motors to be adopted. These rotate at very high speeds and are extremely efficient. Of great interest, too, are the studies being carried out on superconduction at very low temperatures, as these could lead to the development of motors of a power and efficiency hitherto unimagined.
The problem as far as control systems is concerned is the fact that fairly high currents must be regulated with a very compact unit, as fully automatic as possible and also adaptable to the countless driving conditions encountered in various traffic situations. Today this is possible thanks to an electronic system which utilizes controlled diodes or thyristors. In a very refined unit it is even possible to salvage part of the kinetic energy produced when the vehicle is braking, that is to say when the electric motor acts as a dynamo and recharges the batteries.
However the energy recovered in this manner should not be overestimated since it amounts to a maximum of 10% of the energy expended during acceleration. Then again it must not be overlooked that an electronic control system today costs almost as much as a small car due to the high cost of the special high-powered components. This is why electronic control systems are at present mounted only on experimental vehicles, either electric cars or larger vehicles where of course it would be easier to absorb the high costs. Even on mass-produced industrial vehicles, the comparatively simple electro-mechanical control system is still pre-

Above the MBB (Messerschmitt-Bölkow-Blohm) electric prototype which has a glassfibre bearing body. Below, the driver is faced with only two pedals in this electric version of the Renault 5 by the Société Electricité de France. Below, the Voiture Electronique, another French variation on the theme of the electric car. This one has a single central lever between the seats.

ferred, for it is strong and economical even if rougher in operation.
Experiments in electric vehicles are spread over a wide field. The ones being developed in the United States and Japan, in Great Britain, Holland and Italy come immediately to mind. Prototypes of various kinds are being presented every now and then, not only by most of the great motor manufacturers to show their interest in the problem, but also by chemical and electronics industries and by private enterprises that are anxious to play their part in the great race towards the electric car.
There is undoubtedly a serious purpose behind most of the models presented, both from the manufacturing and experimental points of view. However, in some cases misleading information has been divulged regarding performance—speed, autonomy, acceleration—due perhaps to scanty knowledge of the problem but conceivably to marketing interests. Nothing revolutionary has as yet come up in construction engineering, for lead batteries are still being used with direct current, generally with series excitation and electro-mechanical controls. The French 'Voiture Electronique' which was brought out a few years ago at the Paris Motor Show with electronic drive and variable reluctivity motors, took a step backwards in time since it returned to more orthodox motors and the 'cloche' driving system similar to the one used on the NASA lunar vehicle. Though very sensitive, it works well only at low speeds, and the average driver finds it difficult to get used to.
Various prototypes are being studied in the United States and form part of a vast research programme aimed at discovering new methods of urban transport. Given the problem posed by the heaviness of conventional lead batteries and the difficulty of finding a substitute for them, General Motors engineers are carrying out experiments both with conventional batteries and with a hybrid system: that is to say, batteries and an auxiliary motor for recharging them.
For its part Ford has built a small electric car called the Comuta in England and a new type of light sodium-sulphur battery has been elaborated in its laboratories. Small electric vehicles for special purposes are constructed by Westinghouse and Cushman (the latter specializing in golf buggies), while a very recent model has been realized by another specialized firm, Andersson. The most interesting feature of this model is the slide-out battery pack which is inserted into a central core formed by the welded structure of the frames and can easily be recharged or checked. The electronic control system, too, plugs in in order to reduce the loss of current in the cables.

Left and above: two prototypes developed by the American Andersson Electric, both with glassfibre body. The car shown above can carry four persons.

Japanese engineers, for their part, are at present engaged in research into various aspects of the motor-control system and batteries. Their efforts are favoured by the enormous development of the semi-conductor industry so that they have even faced the problem of the very high speed engines with direct current and electronic commutation —without, that is, the traditional carbon manifold and rotor arm.

Hideo Baba of Sony has developed a zinc-air battery in which the powdered zinc is continuously fed into the battery and thus acts as fuel, producing electric current while it combines in solution. In this manner, all that is needed to recharge the batteries is to put more zinc into them.

In Europe electric cars are already being manufactured in small series by a great variety of constructors, a few of whom we are mentioning as examples of the work that is being done.

The 'Vôiture Electronique' has a tubular chassis and glassfibre body. It is a three-wheeler driven by the two rear wheels, while the front wheel is free to turn in any direction inasmuch as steering is by the differentiated movement of the rear wheels. Each of these has its own electric motor and chain transmission; the electronic drive of the two motors provides for forward motion, reverse and also steering. The 24 volt batteries should ensure an autonomy of 25 to 37 miles at just over 15 miles an hour. The vehicle is nearly six feet long and four foot four inches wide with a dry weight of 440 pounds, and can carry a load of 353 lb, that is to say two persons sitting side by side. Both a closed version and a goods version of the same vehicle are at present being built.

The Enfield 8000 built in the United Kingdom has all the appearance of a small car with glassfibre body and 2 + 2 seating. It is about seven feet long and nearly four feet wide, weighing 1,786 pounds dry with the batteries accounting for about 675 lb of this. The direct current motor in series operates at 48 volts and develops about 5 bhp with electro-mechanical adjustment by means of relays. The mechanics of the vehicle are conventional with the front suspension independent and a rigid rear axle, 145 x 10 tyres and hydraulic brakes. Performance, according to the constructor, is good with a maximum speed of 40 mph and an autonomy of over 80 miles (which is however attainable at a top speed of under 20 miles an hour). In town traffic, the autonomy would drop to about 62 miles.

In Italy the Urbanina has been manufactured for some years and has now been adopted by Zagato for the elaboration of the Zele, an electric four-wheeler (independent front suspension with rigid rear axle incorporating the motor). Its main feature is the tiny area it covers which is made up for by its height (77 x 53 x 62 inches). It mounts 145 x 10 tyres and the kerb weight is 1,212 lb, about half of which is accounted for by the batteries which are mounted in a container that takes up the whole floor area of the vehicle between the suspension and the passenger cell.

The declared speed is 25 miles an hour and the autonomy between 37 and 43 miles. The engine has a nominal power of 1,000 watts, that is to say a little more than one horse power but an engine with double the power can be supplied, increasing the power but of course reducing the autonomy. The price indicated is about Lit. 800,000.

Zagato, the Italian coachbuilder, presented this 2-seater prototype called the Zele at the last Turin Motor Show.

Mention should also be made of one of the various prototypes built by Fiat to try out the possibilities of the electric car. This is a suitably modified 500, with a revised hull and of course without the petrol engine and its accessories. A lusty motor with independent series excitation has been installed, allowing electric braking, with a nominal power of 21 horse and a maximum power of 45 horse. The performance offered by this motor is clearly of a higher level than anything available in other cars of this kind, and even better than many cars running on petrol. In fact the top speed is 50 mph and it will accelerate from 0 to over 30 miles per hour in 4 seconds. The dry weight of the car is 1,609 kg and the batteries account for 353 lb of this. The autonomy is rather restricted and since it is only a prototype the cost is naturally not known.

We are encouraged to a fair degree of faith in the success of electric traction by the fact that a host of research workers are at present studying all these problems and their possible solutions, so that it would seem that mass production of electric cars must be only a question of time.

DIMENSIONS AND WEIGHT dry weight: 1,400 lb, 635 kg.

OPTIONAL ACCESSORIES larger engine sump and 5-speed mechanical gearbox not available.

A 310

PRICE EX WORKS: 46,800 francs.

ENGINE rear, 4 stroke; 4 cylinders, vertical, in line; 97.9 cu in, 1,605 cc (3.07 x 3.31 in, 78 x 84 mm); compression ratio: 10.25:1; max power (SAE): 140 hp at 6,250 rpm; max torque (SAE): 109 lb ft, 15 kg m at 5,000 rpm; max engine rpm: 6,800; 87.2 hp/l; light alloy cylinder block and head, wet liners; 5 crankshaft bearings; valves: overhead, Vee-slanted, push-rods and rockers; camshafts: 1, side; lubrication: rotary pump, full flow filter, oil cooler, 7.6 imp pt, 9.1 US pt, 4.3 l; 2 Weber 45 DCOE horizontal twin barrel carburettors; fuel feed: mechanical pump; sealed circuit cooling, water, 15.8 imp pt, 19 US pt, 9 l, front radiator, 2 electric thermostatically- or manually-controlled fans.

TRANSMISSION driving wheels: rear; clutch: single dry plate (diaphragm), hydraulically-controlled; gearbox: mechanical; gears: 5, fully synchronized; ratios: I 3.610, II 2.330, III 1.610, IV 1.210, V 1.030, rev 3.080; lever: central; final drive: hypoid bevel; axle ratio: 3.270; width of rims: 6.5"; tyres: 165 x 13 front, 185 x 13 rear.

PERFORMANCE max speeds: (I) 43 mph, 69 km/h; (II) 66 mph, 107 km/h; (III) 96 mph, 155 km/h; (IV) 129 mph, 207 km/h; (V) 130 mph, 210 km/h; power-weight ratio: 13 lb/hp, 5.9 kg/hp; speed in top at 1,000 rpm: 22.2 mph, 35.7 km/h; fuel consumption: 21.7 m/imp gal, 18.1 m/US gal, 13 l x 100 km.

CHASSIS integral, central steel backbone; front suspension: independent, wishbones, rubber elements, coil springs, anti-roll bar, telescopic dampers; rear suspension: independent, wishbones, coil springs, anti-roll bar, telescopic dampers.

STEERING rack-and-pinion; turns lock to lock: 2.50.

BRAKES disc (diameter 8.98 in, 228 mm front, 10 in, 254 mm rear), front internal radial fins, servo; swept area: front 78.8 sq in, 508 sq cm, rear 87.3 sq in, 563 sq cm, total 166.1 sq in, 1,071 sq cm.

ELECTRICAL EQUIPMENT 12 V; 45 Ah battery; 40 A alternator; Ducellier distributor; 6 headlamps.

DIMENSIONS AND WEIGHT wheel base: 89.37 in, 2,270 mm; tracks: 55.31 in, 1,405 mm front, 55.51 in, 1,410 mm rear; length: 164.57 in, 4,180 mm; width: 63.78 in, 1,620 mm; height: 42.28 in, 1,150 mm; ground clearance: 6.02 in, 153 mm; dry weight: 1,819 lb, 825 kg; turning circle (between walls): 33.5 ft, 10.2 m; fuel tank: 13.2 imp gal, 15.8 US gal, 60 l.

BODY coupé in plastic material; 2 doors; 2 + 2 seats.

PRACTICAL INSTRUCTIONS fuel 98-100 oct petrol; engine sump oil: 7.6 imp pt, 9.1 US pt, 4.3 l, change every 3,100 miles, 5,000 km; tappet clearances: inlet 0.010 in, 0.25 mm, exhaust 0.014 in, 0.35 mm; valve timing: 40° 72° 72° 40°; tyre pressure: front 22 psi, 1.5 atm, rear 30 psi, 2.1 atm.

OPTIONAL ACCESSORIES electrically-heated rear window; tinted glass; leather upholstery; metallic spray.

C.F.P.M. FRANCE

Monica

ENGINE front, 4 stroke; 8 cylinders, Vee-slanted at 90°; 208.9 cu in, 3,423 cc (3.43 x 2.84 in, 87 x 72.2 mm); compression ratio: 10.5:1; max power (DIN): 240 hp at 6,000 rpm; max torque (DIN): 236 lb ft, 32.5 kg m at 4,000-5,000 rpm; max engine rpm: 6,400; 70.1 hp/l; light alloy cylinder block and head, dry liners; 5 crankshaft bearings; valves: overhead, in line, push-rods and rockers; camshafts: 1, overhead, per cylinder block, cogged belt; lubrication: gear pump, full flow filter, dry sump, oil cooler, 24.6 imp pt, 29.6 US pt, 14 l; 4 Weber IDS 40 twin barrel carburettors; fuel feed: 2 electric pumps; water-cooled, 21.1 imp pt, 25.4 US pt, 12 l, 2 electric thermostatic fans.

TRANSMISSION driving wheels: rear; clutch: single dry plate, hydraulically controlled; gearbox: ZF mechanical; gears: 5, fully synchronized, with overdrive/top; ratios: I 3.100, II 1.800, III 1.300, IV 1, V 0.837, overdrive 0.820; lever: central; final drive: hypoid bevel; axle ratio: 4.375; tyres: 215/70 VR x 14.

PERFORMANCE max speed: 149 mph, 240 km/h; power-weight ratio: 13.4 lb/hp, 6.1 kg/hp; carrying capacity: 882 lb, 400 kg; speed in top at 1,000 rpm: 20.6 mph, 33.1 km/h; fuel consumption: not declared.

ALPINE Berlinette Tour de France 1600 S

ALPINE A 310

C.F.P.M. Monica

CHASSIS perimeter box-type; front suspension: independent, wishbones, coil springs, anti-roll bar, telescopic dampers; rear suspension: de Dion, rigid axle, torque arms, transverse linkage bar, coil springs, telescopic dampers.

STEERING rack-and-pinion.

BRAKES disc (diameter 138 in, 305 mm), internal radial fins, servo.

ELECTRICAL EQUIPMENT 12 V; 2 x 55 Ah battery; 890 W alternator; 4 headlamps, 2 retractable iodine long distance lights.

DIMENSIONS AND WEIGHT wheel base: 109.05 in, 2,770 mm; tracks: 59.84 in, 1,520 mm front, 59.84 in, 1,520 mm rear; length: 194.88 in, 4,950 mm; width: 71.65 in, 1,820 mm; height: 52.36 in, 1,330 mm; ground clearance: 5.90 in, 150 mm; dry weight: 3,197 lb, 1,450 kg; turning circle (between walls): 39.4 ft, 12 m; fuel tank: 24.2 imp gal, 29 US gal, 110 l (2 separate tanks).

BODY saloon/sedan; 4 doors; 4 seats, separate front seats; electrically-heated rear window; air-conditioning.

PRACTICAL INSTRUCTIONS engine sump oil: 24.6 imp pt, 29.6 US pt, 14 l, SAE 20W-40, change every 6,100 miles, 10,000 km.

CG FRANCE

1300 Coupé

PRICE EX WORKS: 25,970 francs.

ENGINE rear, 4 stroke; 4 cylinders, slanted at 15°, in line; 79 cu in, 1,294 cc (3.02 x 2.76 in, 76.7 x 70 mm); compression ratio: 9.8:1; max power (DIN): 82 hp at 6,000 rpm; max torque (DIN): 80 lb ft, 11 kg m at 4,400 rpm; max engine rpm: 6,500; 64.1 hp/l; cast iron cylinder block, light alloy head; 5 crankshaft bearings; valves: overhead, push-rods and rockers; camshafts: 1, side; lubrication: gear pump, full flow filter, 7 imp pt, 8.5 US pt, 4 l; 2 Solex 35 PHH 5 horizontal twin barrel carburettors; fuel feed: mechanical pump; water-cooled, 19.4 imp pt, 23.3 US pt, 11 l, electric thermostatic fan.

TRANSMISSION driving wheels: rear; clutch: single dry plate (diaphragm), hydraulically controlled; gearbox: mechanical; gears: 4, fully synchronized; ratios: I 3.546, II 2.119, III 1.408, IV 0.963, rev 3.436; lever: central; final drive: hypoid bevel; axle ratio: 4.111; width of rims: 4.5"; tyres: 145 x 13 front, 155 x 13 rear.

PERFORMANCE max speeds: (I) 34 mph, 54 km/h; (II) 53 mph, 85 km/h; (III) 76 mph, 122 km/h; (IV) 109 mph, 176 km/h; power-weight ratio: 19.4 lb/hp, 8.8 kg/hp; carrying capacity: 728 lb, 330 kg; acceleration: standing ¼ mile 17.2 sec; speed in top at 1,000 rpm: 17.8 mph, 28.6 km/h; fuel consumption: 31.4 m/imp gal, 26.1 m/US gal, 9 l x 100 km.

CHASSIS integral, tubular reinforced platform; front suspension: independent, wishbones, transverse leafspring lower arms, anti-roll bar, telescopic dampers; rear suspension: independent, semi-trailing arms, coil springs, anti-roll bar, telescopic dampers.

STEERING rack-and-pinion; turns lock to lock: 4.25.

BRAKES disc (diameter 8.70 in, 221 mm), servo; swept area: front 140.2 sq in, 904 sq cm, rear 140.2 sq in, 904 sq cm, total 280.4 sq in, 1,808 sq cm.

ELECTRICAL EQUIPMENT 12 V; 40/45 Ah battery; 35 A alternator; Ducellier distributor; 4 headlamps, iodine long distance lights.

DIMENSIONS AND WEIGHT wheel base: 87.87 in, 2,232 mm; tracks: 49.57 in, 1,259 mm front, 51.30 in, 1,303 mm rear; length: 155.91 in, 3,960 mm; width: 60.63 in, 1,540 mm; height: 47.44 in, 1,205 mm; ground clearance: 4.92 in, 125 mm; dry weight: 1,599 lb, 725 kg; turning circle (between walls): 34.1 ft, 10.4 m; fuel tank: 11.7 imp gal, 14 US gal, 53 l.

BODY coupé in plastic material; 2 doors; 2 seats.

PRACTICAL INSTRUCTIONS fuel: 98-100 oct petrol; engine sump oil: 7 imp pt, 8.5 US pt, 4 l, SAE 20W-40, change every 3,700 miles, 6,000 km; gearbox and final drive oil: 3.2 imp pt, 3.8 US pt, 1.8 l, SAE 90 EP, change every 6,200 miles, 10,000 km; greasing: none; tappet clearances (hot): inlet 0.014 in, 0.35 mm, exhaust 0.016 in, 0.40 mm; tyre pressure: front 23 psi, 1.6 atm, rear 30 psi, 2.1 atm.

VARIATIONS

ENGINE max power (DIN): 95 hp; 73.4 hp/l; 2 Weber 40 DCOE twin barrel carburettors.
PERFORMANCE max speed over 118 mph, 190 km/h.

1300 COUPÉ

ENGINE (supercharged) 79.3 cu in, 1,300 cc, 65.4 hp/l.
PERFORMANCE power-weight ratio 14.1 lb/h, 6.4 kg/hp.
DIMENSIONS AND WEIGHT dry weight 1,208 lb, 548 kg.

OPTIONAL ACCESSORIES 3.880 axle ratio; light alloy wheels; iodine fog lamps; headrests; metallic spray; roll bar.

1300 Spider

See 1300 Coupé, except for:

PRICE EX WORKS: 27,101 francs.

BODY convertible.

OPTIONAL ACCESSORIES hardtop.

CHRYSLER FRANCE FRANCE

Simca 1000 LS (5 CV)

PRICE IN GB: £ 670.
PRICE EX WORKS: 8,835 francs.

ENGINE rear, 4 stroke; 4 cylinders, slanted at 15°, in line; 57.6 cu in, 944 cc (2.68 x 2.56 in, 68 x 65 mm); compression ratio: 9.4:1; max power (DIN): 44 hp at 6,000 rpm; max torque (DIN): 46 lb ft, 6.4 kg m at 3,000 rpm; max engine rpm: 6,000; 46.6 hp/l; cast iron cylinder block, light alloy head; 5 crankshaft bearings; valves: overhead, in line, push-rods and rockers; camshafts: 1, side; lubrication: gear pump, centrifugal filter, 5.1 imp pt, 6.1 US pt, 2.9 l; 1 Weber 32 ICR-12 downdraught single barrel carburettor; fuel feed: mechanical pump; water-cooled, 11.3 imp pt, 13.5 US pt, 6.4 l.

TRANSMISSION driving wheels: rear; clutch: single dry plate (diaphragm), hydraulically controlled; gearbox: mechanical; gears: 4, fully synchronized; ratios: I 3.546, II 2.119, III 1.408, IV 0.963, rev 3.436; lever: central; final drive: hypoid bevel; axle ratio: 4.375; width of rims: 4.5"; tyres: 145 SR x 13.

PERFORMANCE max speeds: (I) 24 mph, 38 km/h; (II) 40 mph, 64 km/h; (III) 60 mph, 96 km/h; (IV) 87 mph, 140 km/h; power-weight ratio: 38.8 lb/hp, 17.6 kg/hp; carrying capacity: 882 lb, 400 kg; speed in top at 1,000 rpm: 15 mph, 24.1 km/h; fuel consumption: 44.1 m/imp gal, 36.8 m/US gal, 6.4 l x 100 km.

CHASSIS integral; front suspension: independent, wishbones, transverse leafspring lower arms, anti-roll bar, telescopic dampers; rear suspension: independent, semi-trailing arms, coil springs, telescopic dampers.

STEERING rack-and-pinion; turns lock to lock: 3.17.

BRAKES drum, single circuit; swept area: front 45 sq in, 290 sq cm, rear 39.4 sq in, 254 sq cm, total 84.4 sq in, 544 sq cm.

ELECTRICAL EQUIPMENT 12 V; 40 Ah battery; 240 W dynamo; Ducellier distributor; 2 headlamps.

DIMENSIONS AND WEIGHT wheel base: 87.40 in, 2,220 mm; tracks: 49.61 in, 1,260 mm front, 50.20 in, 1,275 mm rear; length: 149.41 in, 3,795 mm; width: 58.46 in, 1,485 mm; height: 54.96 in, 1,396 mm; ground clearance: 5.12 in, 130 mm; dry weight: 1,709 lb, 775 kg; turning circle (between walls): 30.2 ft, 9.2 m; fuel tank: 7.9 imp gal, 9.5 US gal, 36 l.

BODY saloon/sedan; 4 doors; 5 seats; separate front seats.

PRACTICAL INSTRUCTIONS fuel: 98 oct petrol; engine sump oil: 5.1 imp pt, 6.1 US pt, 2.9 l, SAE 20W-40, change every 3,100 miles, 5,000 km; gearbox and final drive oil: 3.2 imp pt, 3.8 US pt, 1.8 l, SAE 90 EP, change every 6,200 miles, 10,000 km; greasing: none; tappet clearances (hot): inlet 0.014 in, 0.35 mm, exhaust 0.016 in, 0.40 mm; valve timing: 16°30' 58° 60°30' 14°; tyre pressure: front 20 psi, 1.4 atm, rear 27 psi, 1.9 atm.

OPTIONAL ACCESSORIES Ferodo-Verto 3-speed semi-automatic transmission, hydraulic torque converter (I 2.532, II 1.524, III 0.765, rev 3.436), max ratio of converter at stall 2, possible manual selection; back seat folding down to luggage table.

Simca 1000 GLS Automatic (5 CV)

See Simca 1000 LS (5 CV), except for:

PRICE EX WORKS: 10,035 francs.

TRANSMISSION gearbox: Ferodo-Verto semi-automatic transmission (standard).

BODY reclining backrests.

CG 1300 Coupé

CHRYSLER FRANCE Simca 1000 Rallye 2

CHRYSLER FRANCE Simca 1100 GLS Berline

Simca 1000 GLS (6 CV)

See Simca 1000 LS (5 CV), except for:

PRICE IN GB: £ 710.
PRICE EX WORKS: 9,735 francs.

ENGINE 68.2 cu in, 1,118 cc (2.91 x 2.56 in, 74 x 65 mm); compression ratio: 9.6:1; max power (DIN): 55 hp at 5,800 rpm; max torque (DIN): 59 lb ft, 8.2 kg m at 3,400 rpm; 49.1 hp/l; 1 Weber 32 ICR-3 downdraught single barrel carburettor.

TRANSMISSION axle ratio: 4.111; tyres: 145 SR x 13.

PERFORMANCE max speeds: (I) 25 mph, 41 km/h; (II) 42 mph, 68 km/h; (III) 64 mph, 103 km/h; (IV) 91 mph, 147 km/h; power weight ratio: 31.5 lb/hp, 14.3 kg/hp; speed in top at 1,000 rpm: 16.1 mph, 25.9 km/h; fuel consumption: 37.7 m/imp gal, 31.4 m/US gal, 7.5 l x 100 km.

BRAKES front disc (diameter 9.21 in, 234 mm), rear drum, single circuit; swept area: front 161.9 sq in, 1,044 sq cm, rear 39.5 sq in, 255 sq cm, total 201.4 sq in, 1,299 sq cm.

DIMENSIONS AND WEIGHT dry weight: 1,731 lb, 785 kg.

OPTIONAL ACCESSORIES none.

Simca 1000 Special

See Simca 1000 LS (5 CV), except for:

PRICE IN GB: £ 782.
PRICE EX WORKS: 10,295 francs.

ENGINE 79 cu in, 1,294 cc (3.02 x 2.76 in, 76.7 x 70 mm); compression ratio: 9.8-10:1; max power (DIN): 60 hp at 5,400 rpm; max torque (DIN): 71 lb ft, 9.8 kg m at 2,600 rpm; 46.3 hp/l; 1 Solex 34 ICR downdraught single barrel carburettor.

TRANSMISSION axle ratio: 4.111.

PERFORMANCE max speed: 96 mph, 155 km/h; power-weight ratio: 29.1 lb/hp, 13.2 kg/hp; speed in top at 1,000 rpm: 16.1 mph, 25.9 km/h; fuel consumption: 35.3 m/imp gal, 29.4 m/US gal, 8 l x 100 km.

BRAKES front disc (diameter 9.21 in, 234 mm), rear drum; swept area: front 161.9 sq in, 1,044 sq cm, rear 39.5 sq in, 255 sq cm, total 201.4 sq in, 1,299 sq cm.

ELECTRICAL EQUIPMENT 25 A alternator; 2 headlamps; 2 iodine fog lamps.

DIMENSIONS AND WEIGHT dry weight: 1,742 lb, 790 kg.

BODY luxury interior.

OPTIONAL ACCESSORIES 4.375 axle ratio; 145 HR x 13 tyres; Ferodo-Verto semi-automatic transmission not available.

Simca 1000 Rallye 1

See Simca 1000 Special, except for:

PRICE IN GB: £ 780.
PRICE EX WORKS: 9,995 francs.

ENGINE 1 Solex 34 BICSA downdraught single barrel carburettor.

OPTIONAL ACCESSORIES electrically-heated rear window.

Simca 1000 Rallye 2

See Simca 1000 Rallye 1, except for:

PRICE EX WORKS: 12,995 francs.

ENGINE max power (DIN): 82 hp at 6,000 rpm; max torque (DIN): 80 lb ft, 11 kg m at 4,400 rpm; 53.3 hp/l; lubricating system capacity: 7 imp pt, 8.5 US pt, 4 l; 2 Solex 35 PHHE 4 horizontal twin barrel carburettors; water-cooled, radiator on front, electric thermostatic fan, 18.5 imp pt, 22.2 US pt, 10.5 l.

TRANSMISSION tyres: 145 HR x 13 (standard).

PERFORMANCE max speed: 99 mph, 160 km/h; power-weight ratio: 22.9 lb/hp, 10.4 kg/hp.

BRAKES disc, rear compensator; swept area: front 161.9 sq in, 1,044 sq cm, rear 143.9 sq in, 928 sq cm, total 205.8 sq in, 1,972 sq cm.

ELECTRICAL EQUIPMENT 36 A alternator.

CG 1300 Coupé

CHRYSLER FRANCE Simca 1000 Rallye 2

CHRYSLER FRANCE Simca 1100 GLS Break

DIMENSIONS AND WEIGHT dry weight: 1,896 lb, 860 kg; fuel tank: 11 imp gal, 13.2 US gal, 50 l.

BODY electrically-heated rear window (standard).

OPTIONAL ACCESSORIES light alloy wheels.

Simca 1100 LS Berline (5 CV)

PRICE IN GB: £ 815.
PRICE EX WORKS: 11,235 francs.

ENGINE front, transverse, 4 stroke; 4 cylinders, slanted at 41°, in line; 57.6 cu in, 944 cc (2.68 x 2.56 in, 68 x 65 mm); compression ratio: 9.5:1; max power (DIN): 45 hp at 6,000 rpm; max torque (DIN): 48 lb ft, 6.6 kg m at 4,000 rpm; max engine rpm: 6,000; 47.6 hp/l; cast iron cylinder block, light alloy head; 5 crankshaft bearings; valves: overhead, push-rods and rockers; camshafts: 1, side; lubrication: gear pump, full flow filter, 5.3 imp pt, 6.3 US pt, 3 l; 1 Solex 32 BISA downdraught carburettor; fuel feed: mechanical pump; water-cooled, 10.6 imp pt, 12.7 US pt, 6 l, electric thermostatic fan.

TRANSMISSION driving wheels: front; clutch: single dry plate (diaphragm), hydraulically controlled; gearbox: mechanical; gears: 4, fully synchronized; ratios: I 3.906, II 2.315, III 1.524, IV 1.080, rev 3.773; lever: central; final drive: cylindrical gears; axle ratio: 4.062; width of rims: 4.5"; tyres: 145 SR x 13.

PERFORMANCE max speeds: (I) 23 mph, 37 km/h; (II) 39 mph, 62 km/h; (III) 58 mph, 94 km/h; (IV) 84 mph, 135 km/h; power-weight ratio: 43 lb/hp, 19.5 kg/hp; carrying capacity: 882 lb, 400 kg; speed in top at 1,000 rpm: 13.7 mph, 22 km/h; fuel consumption: 44.1 m/imp gal, 36.8 m/US gal, 6.4 l x 100 km.

CHASSIS integral; front suspension: independent, wishbones, longitudinal torsion bars, anti-roll bar, telescopic dampers; rear suspension: independent, longitudinal trailing arms, transverse torsion bars, anti-roll bar, telescopic dampers.

STEERING rack-and-pinion; turns lock to lock: 3.25.

BRAKES front disc (diameter 9.21 in, 234 mm), rear drum, single circuit, rear compensator; swept area: front 161.9 sq in, 1,044 sq cm, rear 73.8 sq in, 476 sq cm, total 235.7 sq in, 1,520 sq cm.

ELECTRICAL EQUIPMENT 12 V; 40 Ah battery; 330 W alternator; Ducellier distributor; 2 headlamps.

DIMENSIONS AND WEIGHT wheel base: 99.21 in, 2,520 mm; tracks: 54.37 in, 1,381 mm front, 52.13 in, 1,324 mm rear; length: 155.28 in, 3,944 mm; width: 62.52 in, 1,588 mm; height: 57.40 in, 1,458 mm; ground clearance: 4.72 in, 120 mm; dry weight: 1,940 lb, 880 kg; turning circle (between walls): 35.4 ft, 10.8 m; fuel tank: 9.2 imp gal, 11.1 US gal, 42 l.

BODY saloon/sedan; 4 doors; 5 seats, separate front seats; back seat folding down to luggage table.

PRACTICAL INSTRUCTIONS fuel: 98 oct petrol; engine sump oil: 5.3 imp pt, 6.3 US pt, 3 l, SAE 20W-40, change every 3,100 miles, 5,000 km; gearbox and final drive oil: 3.2 imp pt, 3.8 US pt, 1.8 l, SAE 90 EP, change every 6,200 miles, 10,000 km; greasing: none; tyre pressure: front 24 psi, 1.7 atm, rear 26 psi, 1.8 atm.

Simca 1100 LS Berline (6 CV)

See Simca 1100 LS Berline (5 CV), except for:

PRICE IN GB: £ 784.
PRICE EX WORKS: 11,435 francs.

ENGINE 68.2 cu in, 1,118 cc (2.91 x 2.56 in, 74 x 65 mm); compression ratio: 9.6:1; max power (DIN): 60 hp at 6,000 rpm; max torque (DIN): 62 lb ft, 8.6 kg m at 3,200 rpm; 53.7 hp/l.

TRANSMISSION axle ratio: 3.937.

PERFORMANCE max speeds: (I) 25 mph, 40 km/h; (II) 42 mph, 68 km/h; (III) 64 mph, 103 km/h; (IV) 87 mph, 140 km/h; power-weight ratio: 33.5 lb/hp, 15.2 kg/hp; speed in top at 1,000 rpm: 15 mph, 24.1 km/h; fuel consumption: 38.7 m/imp gal, 32.2 m/US gal, 7.3 l x 100 km.

DIMENSIONS AND WEIGHT dry weight: 2,007 lb, 910 kg.

OPTIONAL ACCESSORIES Ferodo 3-speed semi-automatic transmission, hydraulic torque converter (I 2.469, II 1.650, III 1.080, rev 3.774), max ratio of converter at stall 2, possible manual selection, max speeds (I) 40 mph, 64 km/h, (II) 59 mph, 95 km/h, (III) 87 mph, 140 km/h; servo brake.

Simca 1100 GLS Berline

See Simca 1100 LS Berline (6 CV), except for:

PRICE IN GB: £ 867.
PRICE EX WORKS: 12,635 francs.

BRAKES servo.

OPTIONAL ACCESSORIES semi-automatic transmission and electrically-heated rear window.

Simca 1100 LS Break

See Simca 1100 LS Berline (6 CV), except for:

PRICE EX WORKS: 12,135 francs.

TRANSMISSION tyres: 155 SR x 13.

PERFORMANCE power-weight ratio: 34.6 lb/hp, 15.7 kg/hp; carrying capacity: 992 lb, 450 kg.

DIMENSIONS AND WEIGHT length: 154.33 in, 3,920 mm; height: 55.83 in, 1,418 mm; dry weight: 2,073 lb, 940 kg.

BODY estate car/station wagon; 4+1 doors.

Simca 1100 GLS Break

See Simca 1100 LS Break, except for:

PRICE IN GB: 935.
PRICE EX WORKS: 13,335 francs.

BRAKES servo.

OPTIONAL ACCESSORIES semi-automatic transmission and electrically-heated rear window.

Simca 1100 Special 2-door

See Simca 1100 LS Berline (5 CV), except for:

PRICE IN GB: £ 955.
PRICE EX WORKS: 13,335 francs.

ENGINE 79 cu in, 1,294 cc (3.02 x 2.76 in, 76.7 x 70 mm); compression ratio: 9.8:1; max power (DIN): 75 hp at 5,800 rpm; max torque (DIN): 72 lb ft, 10 kg m at 3,400 rpm; 57.9 hp/l; 1 downdraught twin barrel carburettor.

TRANSMISSION axle ratio: 3.706; width of rims: 4.5''; tyres: 145 HR x 13.

PERFORMANCE max speeds: (I) 27 mph, 43 km/h; (II) 45 mph, 72 km/h; (III) 68 mph, 109 km/h; (IV) 96 mph, 154 km/h; power-weight ratio: 27.1 lb/hp, 12.3 kg/hp; speed in top at 1,000 rpm: 15.9 mph, 25.6 km/h; fuel consumption: 35.3 m/imp gal, 29.4 m/US gal, 8 l x 100 km.

BRAKES servo.

ELECTRICAL EQUIPMENT 30 A alternator; 2 iodine fog lamps.

DIMENSIONS AND WEIGHT dry weight: 2,029 lb, 920 kg.

BODY 2 + 1 doors.

OPTIONAL ACCESSORIES semi-automatic transmission and electrically-heated rear window.

Simca 1100 Special 4-door

See Simca 1100 Special 2-door, except for:

PRICE IN GB: £ 985.
PRICE EX WORKS: 13,835 francs.

PERFORMANCE power-weight ratio: 27.6 lb/hp, 12.5 kg/hp.

DIMENSIONS AND WEIGHT dry weight: 2,073 lb, 940 kg.

BODY 4 + 1 doors.

Simca 1301 Special Berline

PRICE IN GB: £ 980.
PRICE EX WORKS: 13,535 francs.

ENGINE front, 4 stroke; 4 cylinders, vertical, in line; 87.7 cu in, 1,290 cc (2.91 x 2.95 in, 74 x 75 mm); compression ratio: 9.1:1; max power (DIN): 70 hp at 5,400 rpm; max

CHRYSLER FRANCE Simca 1100 Special 4-door

CHRYSLER FRANCE Simca 1301 Special Berline

CHRYSLER FRANCE Chrysler 180

torque (DIN): 68-72 lb ft, 9.4-10 kg m at 2,400-4,600 rpm; max engine rpm: 5,300; 54.2 hp/l; cast iron cylinder block, light alloy head; 5 crankshaft bearings; valves: overhead, push-rods and rockers; camshafts: 1, side; lubrication: gear pump, centrifugal filter, 7 imp pt, 8.5 US pt, 4 l; 1 Weber 32 ICB 3 downdraught carburettor; fuel feed: mechanical pump; water-cooled, 11.3 imp pt, 13.5 US pt, 6.4 l.

TRANSMISSION driving wheels: rear; clutch: single dry plate (diaphragm), hydraulically controlled; gearbox: mechanical; gears: 4, fully synchronized; ratios: I 3.546, II 2.391, III 1.418, IV 1, rev 3.222; lever: central; final drive: hypoid bevel; axle ratio: 4.222; width of rims: 4''; tyres: 165 SR x 13.

PERFORMANCE max speeds: (I) 27 mph, 43 km/h; (II) 45 mph, 72 km/h; (III) 70 mph, 112 km/h; (IV) 91 mph, 147 km/h; power-weight ratio: 31.7 lb/hp, 14.4 kg/hp; carrying capacity: 926 lb, 420 kg; speed in direct drive at 1,000 rpm: 15.5 mph, 25 km/h; fuel consumption: 39.2 m/imp gal, 32.7 US gal, 7.2 l x 100 km.

CHASSIS integral; front suspension: independent, wishbones, lower trailing links, coil springs/telescopic dampers, anti-roll bar; rear suspension: rigid axle, trailing lower radius arms, upper torque arms, transverse linkage bar, coil springs/telescopic dampers.

STEERING worm and roller; turns lock to lock: 4.

BRAKES front disc (diameter 10.04 in, 255 mm), rear drum, rear compensator, servo; swept area: front 189.8 sq in, 1,224 sq cm, rear 111.6 sq in, 720 sq cm, total 301.4 sq in, 1,944 sq cm.

ELECTRICAL EQUIPMENT 12 V; 40 Ah battery; 350 W dynamo; Ducellier distributor; 4 headlamps.

DIMENSIONS AND WEIGHT wheel base: 99.21 in, 2,520 mm; tracks: 52.05 in, 1,322 mm front, 51.18 in, 1,300 mm rear; length: 175.47 in, 4,457 mm; width: 62.20 in, 1,580 mm; height: 55.12 in, 1,400 mm; ground clearance: 4.72 in, 120 mm; dry weight: 2,227 lb, 1,010 kg; distribution of weight: 52% front, 48% rear; turning circle (between walls): 34.1 ft, 10.4 m; fuel tank: 12.1 imp gal, 14.5 US gal, 55 l.

BODY saloon/sedan; 4 doors; 5-6 seats, separate front seats.

PRACTICAL INSTRUCTIONS fuel: 98-100 oct petrol; engine sump oil: 7 imp pt, 8.5 US pt, 4 l, SAE 20W-40, change every 3,100 miles, 5,000 km; gearbox oil: 2.8 imp pt, 3.4 US pt, 1.6 l, SAE 90 EP, change every 12,400 miles, 20,000 km; final drive oil: 1.9 imp pt, 2.3 US pt, 1.1 l, SAE 90 EP, change every 12,400 miles, 20,000 km; greasing: every 6,200 miles, 10,000 km, 4 points; tappet clearances (hot): inlet 0.010 in, 0.25 mm, exhaust 0.010 in, 0.25 mm; valve timing: 12° 60° 52° 20°; tyre pressure: front 23 psi, 1.6 atm, rear 24 psi, 1.7 atm.

OPTIONAL ACCESSORIES Borg-Warner automatic transmission with 3 ratios; 4.444 axle ratio; electrically-heated rear window.

Simca 1301 Special Break

See Simca 1301 Special Berline, except for:

PRICE IN GB: £ 1,066.
PRICE EX WORKS: 14,035 francs.

TRANSMISSION lever: steering column; axle ratio: 4.444; tyres: 175 SR x 13.

PERFORMANCE power-weight ratio: 33.9 lb/hp, 15.4 kg/hp; carrying capacity: 1,103 lb, 500 kg.

DIMENSIONS AND WEIGHT rear track: 51.97 in, 1,320 mm; length: 169.88 in, 4,315 mm; ground clearance: 4.92 in, 125 mm; dry weight: 2,381 lb, 1,080 kg; distribution of weight: 49% front, 51% rear.

BODY estate car/station wagon; 4 + 1 doors; bench front seats.

OPTIONAL ACCESSORIES separate front seats with central lever; electrically-heated rear window not available.

Simca 1501 Special Berline

(only for export).

See Simca 1301 Special Berline, except for:

PRICE IN GB: £ 1,046.

ENGINE 90 cu in, 1,475 cc (2.96 x 3.27 in, 75.2 x 83 mm); compression ratio: 9.3:1; max power (DIN): 81 hp at 5,200 rpm; max torque (DIN): 88 lb ft, 12.2 kg m at 4,000 rpm; max engine rpm: 5,700; 54.9 hp/l; 1 Weber DCB 3 downdraught twin barrel carburettor; cooling system: electric thermostatic fan.

TRANSMISSION axle ratio: 3.818.

CHRYSLER FRANCE Simca 1100 Special

CHRYSLER FRANCE Simca 1301 Special Berline

CHRYSLER FRANCE Chrysler 180

PERFORMANCE max speeds: (I) 27 mph, 44 km/h; (II) 47 mph, 75 km/h; (III) 72 mph, 116 km/h; (IV) 100 mph, 161 km/h; power-weight ratio: 27.8 lb/hp, 12.6 kg/hp; speed in direct drive at 1,000 rpm: 17.6 mph, 28.3 km/h; fuel consumption: 31.4 m/imp gal, 26.1 m/US gal, 9 l x 100 km.

DIMENSIONS AND WEIGHT dry weight: 2,249 lb, 1,020 kg.

PRACTICAL INSTRUCTIONS tappet clearances (hot): inlet 0.012 in, 0.30 mm, exhaust 0.016 in, 0.40 mm; valve timing: 22° 60° 56° 24°.

OPTIONAL ACCESSORIES Borg-Warner automatic transmission, hydraulic torque converter and planetary gears with 3 ratios (I 2.390, II 1.450, III 1, rev 2.090), max ratio of converter at stall 2, possible manual selection, max speeds (I) 42 mph, 67 km/h, (II) 69 mph, 111 km/h, (III) 100 mph, 161 km/h; electrically-heated rear window.

Simca 1501 Special Break

(only for export).

See Simca 1501 Special Berline, except for:

PRICE IN GB: £ 1,204.

TRANSMISSION lever: steering column; tyres: 175 SR x 13.

PERFORMANCE power-weight ratio: 29.5 lb/hp, 13.4 kg/hp; carrying capacity: 1,080 lb, 490 kg.

DIMENSIONS AND WEIGHT rear track: 51.97 in, 1,320 mm; length: 169.88 in, 4,315 mm; ground clearance: 4.92 in, 125 mm; dry weight: 2,403 lb, 1,090 kg.

BODY estate car/station wagon; 4 + 1 doors; bench front seats.

OPTIONAL ACCESSORIES separate front seats with central lever; electrically-heated rear window not available.

Chrysler 160

PRICE EX WORKS: 15,070 francs.

ENGINE front, 4 stroke; 4 cylinders, slanted at 15°, in line; 100 cu in, 1,639 cc (3.28 x 2.95 in, 83.4 x 75 mm); compression ratio: 9.4-9.6:1; max power (DIN): 80 hp at 5,600 rpm; max torque (DIN): 91 lb ft, 12.5 kg m at 3,000 rpm; max engine rpm: 5,700; 48.8 hp/l; cast iron cylinder block, light alloy head; 5 crankshaft bearings; valves: overhead, rockers; camshafts: 1, overhead; lubrication: gear pump, full flow filter, 7 imp pt, 8.5 US pt, 4 l; 1 Weber 34 ICR 8 downdraught carburettor; fuel feed: mechanical pump; water-cooled, 16.7 imp pt, 20.1 US pt, 9.5 l.

TRANSMISSION driving wheels: rear; clutch: single dry plate (diaphragm), hydraulically controlled; gearbox: mechanical; gears: 4, fully synchronized; ratios: I 3.560, II 2.185, III 1.422, IV 1, rev 3.239; lever: central; final drive: hypoid bevel; axle ratio: 3.909; width of rims: 4.5''; tyres: 165 HR x 13.

PERFORMANCE max speeds: (I) 27 mph, 44 km/h; (II) 45 mph, 73 km/h; (III) 70 mph, 113 km/h; (IV) 98 mph, 157 km/h; power-weight ratio: 29.3 lb/hp, 13.3 kg/hp; carrying capacity: 937 lb, 425 kg; speed in direct drive at 1,000 rpm: 17.1 mph, 27.5 km/h; fuel consumption: 28.2 m/imp gal, 23.5 m/US gal, 10 l x 100 km.

CHASSIS integral; front suspension: independent, by McPherson, coil springs/telescopic damper struts, lower wishbones, anti-roll bar; rear suspension: rigid axle, lower longitudinal trailing arms, upper torque arms, transverse linkage bar, coil springs, anti-roll bar, telescopic dampers.

STEERING rack-and-pinion; turns lock to lock: 4.

BRAKES front disc, rear drum, servo; swept area: front 25.4 sq in, 164 sq cm, rear 62.9 sq in, 406 sq cm, total 88.3 sq in, 570 sq cm.

ELECTRICAL EQUIPMENT 12 V; 40 Ah battery; 300 W alternator; Ducellier distributor; 2 headlamps.

DIMENSIONS AND WEIGHT wheel base: 105 in, 2,667 mm; tracks: 55.12 in, 1,400 mm front, 55 in, 1,397 mm rear; length: 178.27 in, 4,527 mm; width: 67.83 in, 1,723 mm; height: 56.30 in, 1,430 mm; ground clearance: 4.72 in, 120 mm; dry weight: 2,348 lb, 1,065 kg; distribution of weight: 53.8% front, 46.2% rear; turning circle (between walls): 36.1 ft, 11 m; fuel tank: 14.3 imp gal, 17.2 US gal, 65 l.

BODY saloon/sedan; 4 doors; 5 seats, separate front seats.

PRACTICAL INSTRUCTIONS fuel: 98-100 oct petrol; engine sump oil: 7 imp pt, 8.5 US pt, 4 l, SAE 10W-50, change every 3,100 miles, 5,000 km; gearbox oil: 2.6 imp pt, 3.2 US pt, 1.5 l, SAE 90 EP, change every 12,400 miles, 20,000 km; final drive oil: 2.5 imp pt, 3 US pt, 1.4 l, SAE 90 EP, change every 12,400 miles, 20,000 km; greasing: none;

CHRYSLER 160

sparking plug type: 225°; tappet clearances: inlet 0.010 in, 0.25 mm, exhaust 0.014 in, 0.35 mm; tyre pressure: front 24 psi, 1.7 atm, rear 27 psi, 1.9 atm.

OPTIONAL ACCESSORIES automatic transmission, hydraulic torque converter and planetary gears with 3 ratios (I 2.450, II 1.450, III 1, rev 2.200); electrically-heated rear window; iodine long-distance lights.

Chrysler 180

See Chrysler 160, except for:

PRICE EX WORKS: 16,995 francs.

ENGINE 110.6 cu in, 1,812 cc (3.45 x 2.95 in, 87.7 x 75 mm); max power (DIN): 100 hp at 5,600 rpm; max torque (DIN): 111 lb ft, 55.1 kg m at 3,400 rpm; max engine rpm: 5,800; 55.1 hp/l; 1 Weber 38 ADS downdraught twin barrel carburettor; water-cooled, 17.6 imp pt, 21.1 US pt, 10 l, electric thermostatic fan.

TRANSMISSION axle ratio: 3.702.

PERFORMANCE max speed: 106 mph, 170 km/h; power-weight ratio: 24.1 lb/hp, 10.9 kg/hp; fuel consumption: 25.7 m/imp gal, 21.4 m/US gal, 11 l x 100 km.

BRAKES disc; swept area: front 23.6 sq in, 152 sq cm, rear 16.7 sq in, 108 sq cm, total 40.3 sq in, 260 sq cm.

ELECTRICAL EQUIPMENT 35 A alternator.

DIMENSIONS AND WEIGHT dry weight: 2,414 lb, 1,095 kg.

CITROËN FRANCE

2 CV 4

PRICE EX WORKS: 7,896 francs.

ENGINE front, 4 stroke; 2 cylinders, horizontally opposed; 26.5 cu in, 435 cc (2.70 x 2.32 in, 68.5 x 59 mm); compression ratio: 8.5:1; max power (SAE): 26 hp at 6,750 rpm; max torque (SAE): 22 lb ft, 3.1 kg m at 4,000 rpm; max engine rpm: 6,750; 59.8 hp/l; cast iron cylinder block, light alloy head, dry liners, light alloy sump, hemispherical combustion chambers; 2 crankshaft bearings; valves: overhead, Vee-slanted at 70°, push-rods and rockers; camshafts: 1, central, lower; lubrication: rotary pump, filter in sump, oil cooler, 3.5 imp pt, 4.2 US pt, 2 l; 1 Solex 34 PICS 4 downdraught carburettor; fuel feed: mechanical pump; air-cooled.

TRANSMISSION driving wheels: front (double homokinetic joints); clutch: single dry plate; gearbox: mechanical; gears: 4, fully synchronized; ratios: I 6.964, II 3.555, III 2.134, IV 1.474, rev 6.964; lever: on facia; final drive: spiral bevel; axle ratio: 4.125; tyres: 125 x 380.

PERFORMANCE max speeds: (I) 16 mph, 26 km/h; (II) 32 mph, 51 km/h; (III) 53 mph, 85 km/h; (IV) 63 mph, 102 km/h; power-weight ratio: 47.4 lb/hp, 21.5 kg/hp; carrying capacity: 706 lb, 320 kg; speed in top at 1,000 rpm: 11.3 mph, 18.2 km/h; fuel consumption: 51.4 m/imp gal, 42.8 m/US gal, 5.5 l x 100 km.

CHASSIS platform; front suspension: independent, swinging leading arms, 2 friction dampers, 2 inertia-type patter dampers; rear suspension: independent, swinging longitudinal trailing arms linked to front suspension by longitudinal coil springs, 2 inertia-type patter dampers, 2 telescopic dampers.

STEERING rack-and-pinion; turns lock to lock: 2.25.

BRAKES drum, single circuit; swept area: front 29.1 sq in, 188 sq cm, rear 30.7 sq in, 198 sq cm, total 59.8 sq in, 386 sq cm.

ELECTRICAL EQUIPMENT 12 V; 32 Ah battery; 390 W alternator; 2 headlamps, height adjustable from driving seat.

DIMENSIONS AND WEIGHT wheel base: 94.49 in, 2,400 mm; tracks: 49.61 in, 1,260 mm front, 49.61 in, 1,260 mm rear; length: 150.79 in, 3,830 mm; width: 58.27 in, 1,480 mm; height: 62.99 in, 1,600 mm; ground clearance: 5.91 in, 150 mm; dry weight: 1,235 lb, 560 kg; turning circle (between walls): 35.1 ft, 10.7 m; fuel tank: 4.4 imp gal, 5.3 US gal, 20 l.

BODY saloon/sedan; 4 doors; 4 seats, bench front seats; back seat folding down to luggage table, fully opening canvas sunshine roof.

CITROËN 2 CV 4

CITROËN Dyane

CITROËN Mehari 2+2

PRACTICAL INSTRUCTIONS fuel: 86 oct petrol; engine sump oil: 3.5 imp pt, 4.2 US pt, 2 l, SAE 10W-30, change every 3,100 miles, 5,000 km; gearbox and final drive oil: 1.8 imp pt, 2.1 US pt, 1 l, SAE 80, change every 12,400 miles, 20,000 km; greasing: every 1,900 miles, 3,000 km, 4 points; tyre pressure: front 18 psi, 1.3 atm, rear 26 psi, 1.8 atm.

OPTIONAL ACCESSORIES centrifugal clutch; separate front seats.

2 CV 6

See 2 CV 4, except for:

PRICE EX WORKS: 8,380 francs.

ENGINE 36.7 cu in, 602 cc (2.91 x 2.76 in, 74 x 70 mm); max power (SAE): 33 hp at 7,000 rpm; max torque (SAE): 31 lb ft, 4.3 kg m at 3,500-4,000 rpm; max engine rpm: 7,000; 54.8 hp/l; lubricating system capacity: 4.4 imp pt, 5.3 US pt, 2.5 l; 1 Solex 34 PICS 4 or 34 PCIS 4 downdraught carburettor.

TRANSMISSION gearbox ratios: I 5.203, II 2.657, III 1.786, IV 1.316, rev 5.203.

PERFORMANCE max speeds: (I) 19 mph, 30 km/h; (II) 40 mph, 65 km/h; (III) 59 mph, 95 km/h; (IV) 68 mph, 110 km/h; power-weight ratio: 37.5 lb/hp, 17 kg/hp; fuel consumption: 50.4 m/imp gal, 42 m/US gal, 5.6 l x 100 km.

Dyane

PRICE IN GB: £ 585.
PRICE EX WORKS: 8,580 francs.

ENGINE front, 4 stroke; 2 cylinders, horizontally opposed; 26.2 cu in, 435 cc (2.70 x 2.32 in, 68.5 x 59 mm); compression ratio: 8.5:1; max power (SAE): 26 hp at 6,750 rpm; max torque (SAE): 22 lb ft, 3.1 kg m at 4,000 rpm; max engine rpm: 6,750; 59.8 hp/l; cast iron cylinder block, light alloy head, dry liners, light alloy sump, hemispherical combustion chambers; 2 crankshaft bearings; valves: overhead, Vee-slanted at 70°, push-rods and rockers; camshafts: 1, central, lower; lubrication: rotary pump, filter in sump, oil cooler, 4.4 imp pt, 5.3 US pt, 2.5 l; 1 Solex 34 PICS 4 downdraught carburettor; fuel feed: mechanical pump; air-cooled.

TRANSMISSION driving wheels: front (double universal joints); clutch: single dry plate; gearbox: mechanical; gears: 4, fully synchronized; ratios: I 6.964, II 3.555, III 2.134, IV 1.474, rev 6.964; lever: on facia; final drive: spiral bevel; axle ratio: 4.125; tyres: 125 x 380.

PERFORMANCE max speeds: (I) 16 mph, 26 km/h; (II) 32 mph, 51 km/h; (III) 53 mph, 85 km/h; (IV) 65 mph, 104 km/h; power-weight ratio: 50.1 lb/hp, 22.9 kg/hp; carrying capacity: 706 lb, 320 kg; speed in top at 1,000 rpm: 11.3 mph, 18.2 km/h; fuel consumption: 51.4 m/imp gal, 42.8 m/US gal, 5.5 l x 100 km.

CHASSIS platform; front suspension: independent, swinging leading arms, 2 friction dampers, 2 inertia-type patter dampers; rear suspension: independent, swinging longitudinal trailing arms linked to front suspension by longitudinal coil springs, 2 inertia-type patter dampers, 2 telescopic dampers.

STEERING rack-and-pinion; turns lock to lock: 2.25.

BRAKES drum, single circuit; swept area: front 29.1 sq in, 188 sq cm, rear 30.7 sq in, 198 sq cm, total 59.8 sq in, 386 sq cm.

ELECTRICAL EQUIPMENT 12 V; 32 Ah battery; 390 W alternator; 2 headlamps.

DIMENSIONS AND WEIGHT wheel base: 94.49 in, 2,400 mm; tracks: 49.61 in, 1,260 mm front, 49.61 in, 1,260 mm rear; length: 148.82 in, 3,780 mm; width: 59.06 in, 1,500 mm; height: 60.63 in, 1,540 mm; ground clearance: 6.30 in, 160 mm; dry weight: 1,312 lb, 595 kg; turning circle (between walls): 35.1 ft, 10.7 m; fuel tank: 4.4 imp gal, 5.3 US gal, 20 l.

BODY saloon/sedan; 4 + 1 doors; 4 seats, bench front seats; fully opening canvas sunshine roof.

PRACTICAL INSTRUCTIONS fuel: 80-85 oct petrol; engine sump oil: 4.4 imp pt, 5.3 US pt, 2.5 l, SAE 10W-30, change every 3,100 miles, 5,000 km; gearbox and final drive oil: 1.8 imp pt, 2.1 US pt, 1 l, SAE 80, change every 12,400 miles, 20,000 km; greasing: every 1,900 miles, 3,000 km, 4 points; tyre pressure: front 18 psi, 1.3 atm, rear 26 psi, 1.8 atm.

OPTIONAL ACCESSORIES centrifugal clutch; back seat folding down to luggage table; Commerciale version.

CITROËN 2 CV 4

CITROËN Dyane

CITROËN Mehari 2+2

Dyane 6

See Dyane, except for:

PRICE IN GB: **£ 635.**
PRICE EX WORKS: **8,980 francs.**

ENGINE 36.7 cu in, 602 cc (2.91 x 2.76 in, 74 x 70 mm); compression ratio: 9:1; max power (SAE): 35 hp at 5,750 rpm; max torque (SAE): 34 lb ft, 4.7 kg m at 4,750 rpm; max engine rpm: 6,000; 58.1 hp/l; 1 Solex 26-35 CSIC or 26-35 SCIC downdraught twin barrel carburettor.

TRANSMISSION gearbox ratios: I 5.747, II 2.935, III 1.923, IV 1.350, rev 5.747; axle ratio: 3.875.

PERFORMANCE max speeds: (I) 19 mph, 30 km/h; (II) 36 mph, 58 km/h; (III) 55 mph, 89 km/h; (IV) 73 mph, 118 km/h; power-weight ratio: 37.7 lb/hp, 17.1 kg/hp; speed in top at 1,000 rpm: 13.1 mph, 21.1 km/h; fuel consumption: 47.1 m/imp gal, 39.2 m/US gal, 6 l x 100 km.

BRAKES swept area: total 84.8 sq in, 547 sq cm.

DIMENSIONS AND WEIGHT dry weight: 1,323 lb, 600 kg; fuel tank: 5.5 imp gal, 6.6 US gal, 25 l.

Mehari 2 + 2

See Dyane 6, except for:

PRICE EX WORKS: **9,680 francs.**

TRANSMISSION gearbox ratios: I 6.060, II 3.125, III 1.920, IV 1.420, rev 6.060; tyres: 135 x 380.

PERFORMANCE max speed: 62 mph, 100 km/h; power-weight ratio: 35.1 lb/hp, 15.9 kg/hp; carrying capacity: 882 lb, 400 kg; fuel consumption: 51.4 m/imp gal, 42.8 m/US gal, 5.5 l x 100 km.

DIMENSIONS AND WEIGHT length: 138.98 in, 3,530 mm; width: 60.24 in, 1,530 mm; dry weight: 1,158 lb, 525 kg.

BODY open, in plastic material; no doors; 2 + 2 seats, separate front seats.

OPTIONAL ACCESSORIES only centrifugal clutch.

Ami 8 Berline Confort

PRICE IN GB: **£ 701.**
PRICE EX WORKS: **9,980 francs.**

ENGINE front, 4 stroke; 2 cylinders, horizontally opposed; 36.7 cu in, 602 cc (2.91 x 2.76 in, 74 x 70 mm); compression ratio: 9:1; max power (SAE): 35 hp at 5,750 rpm; max torque (SAE): 34 lb ft, 4.7 kg m at 4,750 rpm; max engine rpm: 6,000; 58.1 hp/l; cast iron cylinder block, light alloy head, dry liners, light alloy sump, hemispherical combustion chambers; 2 crankshaft bearings; valves: overhead, Vee-slanted at 70°; camshafts: 1, central; lubrication: gear pump, filter in sump, oil cooler, 3.9 imp pt, 4.7 US pt, 2.2 l; 1 Solex 26-35 CSIC or 26-35 SCIC downdraught carburettor; fuel feed: mechanical pump; air-cooled.

TRANSMISSION driving wheels: front (double universal joints); clutch: single dry plate; gearbox: mechanical; gears: 4, fully synchronized; ratios: I 5.760, II 2.940, III 1.920, IV 1.350, rev 5.760; lever: on facia; final drive: spiral bevel; axle ratio: 3.875; tyres: 125 x 380.

PERFORMANCE max speeds: (I) 19 mph, 30 km/h; (II) 36 mph, 58 km/h; (III) 55 mph, 89 km/h; (IV) 76 mph, 123 km/h; power-weight ratio: 44.1 lb/hp, 20 kg/hp; carrying capacity: 706 lb, 320 kg; speed in top at 1,000 rpm: 13.1 mph, 21.1 km/h; fuel consumption: 44.1 m/imp gal, 36.8 m/US gal, 6.4 l x 100 km.

CHASSIS platform; front suspension: independent, swinging leading arms, 2 telescopic dampers, 2 inertia-type patter dampers, anti-roll bar; rear suspension: independent, swinging longitudinal trailing arms linked to front suspension by longitudinal coil springs, 2 telescopic dampers, 2 inertia-type patter dampers.

STEERING rack-and-pinion; turns lock to lock: 2.25.

BRAKES front disc, rear drum, single circuit.

ELECTRICAL EQUIPMENT 12 V; 30 Ah battery; 390 W alternator; 2 headlamps.

DIMENSIONS AND WEIGHT wheel base: 94.49 in, 2,400 mm; tracks: 49.61 in, 1,260 mm front, 48.03 in, 1,220 mm rear; length: 157.09 in, 3,990 mm; width: 59.84 in, 1,520 mm; height: 58.46 in, 1,485 mm; ground clearance: 6.30 in, 160 mm; dry weight: 1,544 lb, 700 kg; turning circle (between walls): 37.4 ft, 11.4 m; fuel tank: 7 imp gal, 8.4 US gal, 32 l.

BODY saloon/sedan; 4 doors; 4-5 seats, bench front seats.

AMI 8 BERLINE CONFORT

PRACTICAL INSTRUCTIONS fuel: 80-85 oct petrol; engine sump oil: 3.9 imp pt, 4.7 US pt, 2.2 l, SAE 10W-30, change every 3,100 miles, 5,000 km; gearbox and final drive oil: 1.8 imp pt, 2.1 US pt, 1 l, SAE 80, change every 12,400 miles, 20,000 km; greasing: every 1,900 miles, 3,000 km, 4 points; tyre pressure: front 18 psi, 1.3 atm, rear 21 psi, 1.5 atm.

OPTIONAL ACCESSORIES centrifugal clutch; separate front seats, reclining backrests.

Ami 8 Berline Club

See Ami 8 Berline Confort, except for:

PRICE IN GB: £ 738.
PRICE EX WORKS: 10,440 francs.

BODY separate front seats, reclining backrests (standard); luxury interior.

Ami 8 Break Confort

See Ami 8 Berline Confort, except for:

PRICE IN GB: £ 763.
PRICE EX WORKS: 10,440 francs.

TRANSMISSION tyres: 135 x 380.

PERFORMANCE carrying capacity: 882 lb, 400 kg.

CHASSIS reinforced suspension.

BODY estate car/station wagon; 4 + 1 doors.

Ami 8 Commerciale

See Ami 8 Break Confort, except for:

BODY Commerciale equipment.

GS Berline

PRICE IN GB: £ 958.
PRICE EX WORKS: 12,900 francs.

ENGINE front, 4 stroke; 4 cylinders, horizontally opposed; 61.9 cu in, 1,015 cc (2.91 x 2.32 in, 74 x 59 mm); compression ratio: 9:1; max power (SAE): 61 hp at 6,750 rpm; max torque (SAE): 54 lb ft, 7.5 kg m at 3,500 rpm; max engine rpm: 6,750; 60.1 hp/l; light alloy cylinder block, head with cast iron liners, light alloy fins, hemispherical combustion chambers; 3 crankshaft bearings; valves: overhead, Vee-slanted; camshafts: 1 per cylinder block, overhead, cogged belt; lubrication: gear pump, full flow filter, oil cooler, 7.4 imp pt, 8.9 US pt, 4.2 l; 1 Solex 28 CIC downdraught twin barrel carburettor; fuel feed: mechanical pump; air-cooled.

TRANSMISSION driving wheels: front; clutch: single dry plate (diaphragm); gearbox: mechanical; gears: 4, fully synchronized; ratios: I 3.818, II 2.312, III 1.524, IV 1.120, rev 4.182; lever: central; final drive: spiral bevel; axle ratio: 4.375; width of rims: 4.5"; tyres: 145 x 380.

PERFORMANCE max speeds: (I) 28 mph, 45 km/h; (II) 45 mph, 73 km/h; (III) 71 mph, 114 km/h; (IV) 91 mph, 147 km/h; power-weight ratio: 31.7 lb/hp, 14.4 kg/hp; carrying capacity: 915 lb, 415 kg; acceleration: standing ¼ mile 20.4 sec; speed in top at 1,000 rpm: 14.2 mph, 22.9 km/h; fuel consumption: 30.4 m/imp gal, 25.3 m/US gal, 9.3 l x 100 km.

CHASSIS integral; front suspension: independent, wishbones, hydropneumatic suspension, anti-roll bar, automatic levelling control; rear suspension: independent, swinging trailing arms, hydropneumatic suspension, anti-roll bar, automatic levelling control.

STEERING rack-and-pinion; turns lock to lock: 3.75.

BRAKES disc (front diameter 10.63 in, 270 mm, rear diameter 6.93 in, 176 mm), servo; swept area: front 22.5 sq in, 145 sq cm, rear 10.4 sq in, 67 sq cm, total 32.9 sq in, 212 sq cm.

ELECTRICAL EQUIPMENT 12 V; 30 Ah battery; 390 W alternator; Sev distributor; 2 headlamps.

DIMENSIONS AND WEIGHT wheel base: 100.39 in, 2,550 mm; tracks: 54.25 in, 1,378 mm front, 52.28 in, 1,328 mm rear; length: 162.20 in, 4,120 mm; width: 63.39 in, 1,610 mm; constant height: 53.15 in, 1,350 mm; ground clearance (variable): 6.06 in, 154 mm; dry weight: 1,940 lb, 880 kg; distribution of weight: 62.5% front, 37.5% rear; turning

CITROËN Ami 8 Berline Confort

CITROËN GS 1220 Berline

CITROËN DSpecial Berline

circle (between walls): 33.5 ft, 10.2 m; fuel tank: 9.5 imp gal, 11.4 US gal, 43 l.

BODY saloon/sedan; 4 doors; 4-5 seats, separate front seats.

PRACTICAL INSTRUCTIONS fuel: 98 oct petrol; engine sump oil: 7.4 imp pt, 8.9 US pt, 4.2 l, SAE 20W-50 change every 3,100 miles, 5,000 km; gearbox and final drive oil: 2.5 imp pt, 3 US pt, 1.4 l, SAE 90, change every 12,400 miles, 20,000 km; hydropneumatic suspension oil: 5.8 imp pt, 7 US pt, 3.3 l; greasing: none; tappet clearances: inlet 0.008 in, 0.20 mm, exhaust 0.008 in, 0.20 mm; valve timing: 2°20' 34° 34°20' 2°; tyre pressure: front 26 psi, 1.8 atm, rear 27 psi, 1.9 atm.

OPTIONAL ACCESSORIES boosted heating for temperatures below −20°C, −4°F; electrically-heated rear window, tinted glass.

GS Break

See GS Berline, except for:

PRICE IN GB: £ 1,021.
PRICE EX WORKS: 13,500 francs.

BODY estate car/station wagon; 4 + 1 doors.

GS Commerciale

See GS Break, except for:

BODY Commerciale equipment.

GS 1220 Berline

See GS Berline, except for:

PRICE IN GB: £ 1,026.
PRICE EX WORKS: 13,700 francs.

ENGINE 74.4 cu in, 1,220 cc (3.03 x 2.58 in, 77 x 65.6 mm); compression ratio: 8.2:1; max power (SAE): 65.5 hp at 6,000 rpm; max torque (SAE): 67 lb ft, 9.2 kg m at 3,250 rpm; max engine rpm: 6,500; 53.6 hp/l.

TRANSMISSION axle ratio: 4.125.

PERFORMANCE max speeds: (I) 29 mph, 46 km/h; (II) 48 mph, 77 km/h; (III) 72 mph, 116 km/h; (IV) 94 mph, 151 km/h; power-weight ratio: 30.2 lb/hp, 13.7 kg/hp; acceleration: standing ¼ mile 19.7 sec; speed in top at 1,000 rpm: 15.1 mph, 24.3 km/h.

ELECTRICAL EQUIPMENT 35 Ah battery; 490 W alternator.

DIMENSIONS AND WEIGHT dry weight: 1,985 lb, 900 kg.

BODY electrically-heated rear window (standard).

PRACTICAL INSTUCTIONS valve timing: 4°10' 31°50' 36°10' 0°10.

OPTIONAL ACCESSORIES semi-automatic transmission, hydraulic torque converter and planetary gears with 3 ratios (I 2.786, II 1.453, III 1,120, rev 2.500), max ratio of converter at stall 2.

GS 1220 Break

See GS 1220 Berline, except for:

PRICE IN GB: £ 1,097.
PRICE EX WORKS: 14,300 francs.

BODY estate car/station wagon: 4 + 1 doors.

GS 1220 Commerciale

See GS 1220 Break, except for:

BODY Commerciale equipment.

GS 1220 Berline Club

See GS 1220 Berline, except for:

PRICE IN GB: £ 1,087.
PRICE EX WORKS: 14,300 francs.

ELECTRICAL EQUIPMENT 490 W alternator; iodine headlamps.

BODY luxury equipment.

CITROËN Ami 8

CITROËN GS 1220

CITROËN DSpecial Berline

GS 1220 Break Club

See GS 1220 Berline Club, except for:

PRICE IN GB: £ 1,153.
PRICE EX WORKS: 14,900 francs.

BODY estate car/station wagon; 4 + 1 doors.

GS 1220 Commerciale Club

See GS 1220 Break Club, except for:

BODY Commerciale equipment.

DSpecial Berline

PRICE IN GB: £ 1,404.
PRICE IN USA: $ 3,750.

ENGINE front, 4 stroke; 4 cylinders, vertical, in line; 121.1 cu in, 1,985 cc (3.39 x 3.37 in, 86 x 85.5 mm); compression ratio: 8.7:1; max power (SAE): 108 hp at 5,750 rpm; max torque (SAE): 112 lb ft, 15.5 kg m at 4,000 rpm; max engine rpm: 6,000; 54.4 hp/l; cast iron cylinder block, light alloy head, wet liners, hemispherical combustion chambers; 5 crankshaft bearings; valves: overhead, Vee-slanted at 60°, push-rods and rockers; camshafts: 1, side; lubrication: gear pump, filter in sump and full flow, 8.8 imp pt, 10.6 US pt, 5 l; 1 Weber 28/36 DLEA 2 downdraught carburettor; fuel feed: mechanical pump; water-cooled, 18.7 imp pt, 22.4 US pt, 10.6 l.

TRANSMISSION driving wheels: front; clutch: single dry plate (diaphragm); gearbox: mechanical; gears: 4, fully synchronized; ratios: I 3.250, II 1.833, III 1.133, IV 0.786, rev 3.154; lever: steering column; final drive: spiral bevel; axle ratio: 4.857; width of rims: 5.5"; tyres: 180 x 380 front, 155 x 380 rear.

PERFORMANCE max speeds: (I) 29 mph, 47 km/h; (II) 52 mph, 83 km/h; (III) 84 mph, 135 km/h; (IV) 105 mph, 169 km/h; power-weight ratio: 28.4 lb/hp, 12.9 kg/hp; carrying capacity: 1,058 lb, 480 kg; acceleration: standing ¼ mile, 18.7 sec; speed in top at 1,000 rpm: 20.2 mph, 32.5 km/h; fuel consumption: 25.7 m/imp gal, 21.4 m/US gal, 11 l x 100 km.

CHASSIS platform, lateral box members; front suspension: independent, wishbones, hydropneumatic suspension, anti-roll bar, automatic levelling control; rear suspension: independent, trailing radius arms, hydropneumatic suspension, anti-roll bar, automatic levelling control.

STEERING rack-and-pinion; turns lock to lock: 3.20.

BRAKES front disc (diameter 11.81 in, 300 mm), rear drum, rear compensator, servo; swept area: total 447 sq in, 2,883 sq cm.

ELECTRICAL EQUIPMENT 12 V; 40 Ah battery; 520 W alternator; Sev or Ducellier distributor; 4 headlamps.

DIMENSIONS AND WEIGHT wheel base: 123.03 in, 3,125 mm; tracks: 59.68 in, 1,516 mm front, 51.81 in, 1,316 mm rear; length: 191.73 in, 4,870 mm; width: 70.87 in, 1,800 mm; height: 57.87 in, 1,470 mm; ground clearance: 2.56 5.31 9.84 in, 65 135 250 mm; dry weight: 2,822 lb, 1,280 kg; distribution of weight: 65.1% front, 34.9% rear; turning circle (between walls): 39.4 ft, 12 m; fuel tank: 14.3 imp gal, 17.2 US gal, 65 l.

BODY saloon/sedan; 4 doors; 5 seats, separate front seats; warning light on facia for worn brakes, plastic roof.

PRACTICAL INSTRUCTIONS fuel: 90-95 oct petrol; engine sump oil: 8.8 imp pt, 10.6 US pt, 5 l, SAE 20W-40, change every 3,100 miles, 5,000 km; gearbox and final drive oil: 3.5 imp pt, 4.2 US pt, 2 l, SAE 80, change every 12,400 miles, 20.000 km; hydraulic suspension oil: 9.2 imp pt, 11 US pt, 5.2 l; greasing: every 3,100 miles, 5,000 km, 8 points; tappet clearances: (hot) inlet 0.008 in, 0.20 mm, exhaust 0.010 in, 0.25 mm; valve timing: 0°30' 42°30' 38°30' 4°30'; tyre pressure: front 28 psi, 2 atm, rear 28 psi, 2 atm.

OPTIONAL ACCESSORIES power-assisted steering, 4 headlamps automatically adjustable in height while running with 2 iodine long-distance lights automatically directed on bends by steering; iodine long-distance lights; headlamps automatically adjustable in height while running; boosted heating for temperatures below −15°C, 5°F; electrically-heated rear window.

DSuper Berline

See DSpecial Berline, except for:

PRICE EX WORKS: 19,700 francs.

STEERING servo (standard).

BODY electrically-heated rear window (standard).

DS 20 Berline

See DSpecial Berline, except for:

PRICE IN GB: £ 1,707.
PRICE EX WORKS: 22,800 francs.

ENGINE 1 Weber 28/36 DLE2 downdraught carburettor.

TRANSMISSION clutch: automatically hydraulically-controlled; gearbox: servo-assisted; ratios: I 3.250, II 1.833, III 1.207, IV 0.852, rev 3.154; axle ratio: 4.375.

PERFORMANCE max speeds: (I) 32 mph, 52 km/h; (II) 58 mph, 93 km/h; (III) 88 mph, 141 km/h; (IV) 105 mph, 169 km/h; power-weight ratio: 26.5 lb/hp, 12 kg/hp; carrying capacity: 1,014 lb, 460 kg; acceleration: standing 1/4 mile 19.6 sec; speed in top at 1,000 rpm: 20.7 mph, 33.3 km/h; fuel consumption: 28.5 m/imp gal, 23.8 m/US gal, 9.9 l x 100 km.

STEERING servo (standard).

DIMENSIONS AND WEIGHT dry weight: 2,867 lb, 1,300 kg.

BODY electrically-heated rear window (standard).

DS 20 Pallas

See DS 20 Berline, except for:

PRICE EX WORKS: 24,800 francs.

PERFORMANCE power-weight ratio: 26.9 lb/hp, 12.2 kg/hp.

ELECTRICAL EQUIPMENT 4 iodine headlamps automatically adjustable in height while running with 2 long-distance lights automatically directed on bends by steering (standard).

DIMENSIONS AND WEIGHT dry weight: 2,911 lb, 1,320 kg.

Familiale Confort 20

See DSpecial Berline, except for:

PRICE EX WORKS: 24,300 francs.

TRANSMISSION gearbox ratios: I 3.250, II 1.833, III 1.207, IV 0.852, rev 3.154; axle ratio: 4.375; tyres: 180 x 380 (front and rear).

PERFORMANCE max speeds: (I) 32 mph, 52 km/h; (II) 58 mph, 93 km/h; (III) 88 mph, 141 km/h; (IV) 103 mph, 165 km/h; power-weight ratio: 26.7 lb/hp, 12.1 kg/hp; carrying capacity: 1,323 lb, 600 kg; acceleration: standing 1/4 mile 19.4 sec; speed in top at 1,000 rpm: 20.7 mph, 33.3 km/h; fuel consumption: 26.2 m/imp gal, 21.8 m/US gal, 10.8 l x 100 km.

STEERING servo (standard).

BRAKES swept area: total 78.9 sq in, 509 sq cm.

DIMENSIONS AND WEIGHT length: 197.87 in, 5,026 mm; width: 72.83 in, 1,850 mm; height: 59.84 in, 1,520 mm; dry weight: 3,087 lb, 1,400 kg.

BODY estate car/station wagon; 4 + 1 doors; 7 seats, bench front seats.

Break Confort 20

See Familiale Confort 20, except for:

PRICE EX WORKS: 24,300 francs.

Commerciale 20

See Familiale Confort 20, except for:

PRICE EX WORKS: 21,508 francs.

BODY Commerciale equipment.

DSuper 5 Berline

PRICE IN GB: £ 1,545.
PRICE EX WORKS: 20,900 francs.

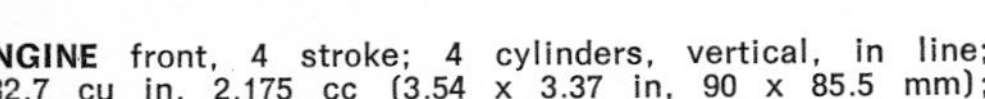

ENGINE front, 4 stroke; 4 cylinders, vertical, in line; 132.7 cu in, 2,175 cc (3.54 x 3.37 in, 90 x 85.5 mm); compression ratio: 8.7:1; max power (SAE): 115 hp at 5,750 rpm; max torque (SAE): 126 lb ft, 17.4 kg m at 4,000 rpm; max engine rpm: 6,000; 52.9 hp/l; cast iron cylinder block, light alloy head, hemispherical combustion chambers; 5 crankshaft bearings; valves: overhead, Vee-slanted at 60°, push-rods and rockers; camshafts: 1, side; lubrication: gear pump, filter in sump and full flow, 8.8 imp pt, 10.6 US pt, 5 l; 1 Weber 28/36 DLE downdraught twin barrel carburettor; fuel feed: mechanical pump; water-cooled, 24.3 imp pt, 29.2 US pt, 13.8 l.

CITROËN DSuper 5 Berline

CITROËN DS 23

CITROËN SM Injection

TRANSMISSION driving wheels: front; clutch: single dry plate (diaphragm); gearbox: mechanical; gears: 5, fully synchronized; ratios: I 3.250, II 1.941, III 1.321, IV 0.970, V 0.784, rev 3.154; lever: steering column; final drive: spiral bevel; axle ratio: 4.375; width of rims: 5.5"; tyres: 180 x 380 front, 165 x 380 rear.

PERFORMANCE max speeds: (I) 32 mph, 52 km/h; (II) 54 mph, 87 km/h; (III) 80 mph, 129 km/h; (IV) 96 mph, 155 km/h; (V) 109 mph, 175 km/h; power-weight ratio: 25.1 lb/hp, 11.4 kg/hp; carrying capacity: 1,080 lb, 490 kg; acceleration: standing ¼ mile 18.5 sec; speed in top at 1,000 rpm: 22.5 mph, 36.2 km/h; fuel consumption: 26.4 m/imp gal, 22 m/US gal, 10.7 l x 100 km.

CHASSIS platform, lateral box members; front suspension: independent, wishbones, hydropneumatic suspension, anti-roll bar, automatic levelling control; rear suspension: independent, trailing radius arms, hydropneumatic suspension, anti-roll bar, automatic levelling control.

STEERING rack-and-pinion, servo; turns lock to lock: 3.20.

BRAKES front disc (diameter 11.81 in, 300 mm), rear drum, rear compensator, servo; swept area: total 69.3 sq in, 447 sq cm.

ELECTRICAL EQUIPMENT 12 V; 40 Ah battery; 520 W alternator; Sev or Ducellier distributor; 4 headlamps.

DIMENSIONS AND WEIGHT wheel base: 123.03 in, 3,125 mm; tracks: 59.68 in, 1,516 mm front, 51.81 in, 1,316 mm rear; length: 191.73 in, 4,870 mm; width: 70.87 in, 1,800 mm; height: 57.87 in, 1,470 mm; ground clearance: 2.56 5.31 9.84 in, 65 135 250 mm; dry weight: 2,889 lb, 1.310 kg; turning circle (between walls): 39.4 ft, 12 m; fuel tank: 14.3 imp gal, 17.2 US gal, 65 l.

BODY saloon/sedan; 4 doors; 5 seats, separate front seats, warning light on facia for worn brakes; electrically-heated rear window.

PRACTICAL INSTRUCTIONS fuel: 90-95 oct petrol; engine sump oil: 8.8 imp pt, 10.6 US pt, 5 l, SAE 20W-40, change every 3,100 miles, 5,000 km; gearbox and final drive oil: 3.5 imp pt, 4.2 US pt, 2 l, SAE 80, change every 12,400 miles, 20,000 km; hydraulic suspension oil: 9.2 imp pt, 11 US pt, 5.2 l; greasing: every 3,100 miles, 5,000 km, 6 points; tappet clearances: inlet 0.008 in, 0.20 mm, exhaust 0.010 in, 0.25 mm; tyre pressure: front 28 psi, 2 atm, rear 28 psi, 2 atm.

DS 23 Berline

PRICE IN GB: £ 1,887.
PRICE EX WORKS: 25,000 francs.

ENGINE front, 4 stroke; 4 cylinders, vertical, in line, 143.2 cu in, 2,347 cc (3.68 x 3.37 in, 93.5 x 85.5 mm); compression ratio: 8.7:1; max power (SAE): 124 hp at 5,750 rpm; max torque (SAE): 138 lb ft, 19.1 kg m at 4,000 rpm; max engine rpm: 6,000; 52.8 hp/l; cast iron cylinder block, light alloy head, hemispherical combustion chambers; 5 crankshaft bearings; valves: overhead, Vee-slanted at 60°, push-rods and rockers; camshafts: 1, side; lubrication: gear pump, filter in sump and full flow, 8.8 imp pt, 10.6 US pt, 5 l; 1 Weber 28/36 DLE downdraught twin barrel carburettor; fuel feed: mechanical pump; water-cooled, 24.3 imp pt, 29.2 US pt, 13.8 l.

TRANSMISSION driving wheels: front; clutch: single dry plate (diaphragm); gearbox: mechanical; gears: 5, fully synchronized; ratios: I 3.250, II 1.941, III 1.321, IV 0.970, V 0.784, rev 3.154; lever: steering column; final drive: hypoid bevel; axle ratio: 4.375; width of rims: 5.5"; tyres: 180 x 380 front, 165 x 380 rear.

PERFORMANCE max speeds: (I) 32 mph, 52 km/h; (II) 54 mph, 87 km/h; (III) 80 mph, 129 km/h; (IV) 96 mph, 155 km/h; (V) 111 mph, 179 km/h; power-weight ratio: 23.3 lb/hp, 10.6 kg/hp; carrying capacity: 1,058 lb, 480 kg; acceleration: standing ¼ mile 18.2 sec; speed in top at 1,000 rpm: 22.5 mph, 36.2 km/h; fuel consumption: 26.4 m/imp gal, 22 m/US gal, 10.7 l x 100 km.

CHASSIS platform, lateral box members; front suspension: independent, wishbones, hydropneumatic suspension, anti-roll bar, automatic levelling control; rear suspension: independent, trailing radius arms, hydropneumatic suspension, anti-roll bar, automatic levelling control.

CITROËN DSuper 5 Berline

CITROËN DS 23 Pallas

CITROËN SM Injection

STEERING rack-and-pinion, servo; turns lock to lock: 3.20.

BRAKES rear drum, rear compensator, servo; swept area: total 69.3 sq in, 447 sq cm.

ELECTRICAL EQUIPMENT 12 V; 40 Ah battery; 520 W alternator; Sev or Ducellier distributor; 4 headlamps.

DIMENSIONS AND WEIGHT wheel base: 123.03 in, 3,125 mm; tracks: 59.68 in, 1,516 mm front, 51.81 in, 1,316 mm rear; length: 191.73 in, 4,870 mm; width: 70.87 in, 1,800 mm; height: 57.87 in, 1,470 mm; ground clearance: 2.48 5.31 9.84 in, 63 135 250 mm; dry weight: 2,911 lb, 1,320 kg; turning circle (between walls): 39.4 ft, 12 m; fuel tank: 14.3 imp gal, 17.2 US gal, 65 l.

BODY saloon/sedan; 4 doors; 5 seats; separate front seats; warning light on facia for worn brakes; electrically-heated rear window.

PRACTICAL INSTRUCTIONS fuel: 95-98 oct petrol; gearbox and final drive oil: 3.9 imp pt, 4.7 US pt, 2.2 l, SAE 80; hydraulic suspension oil: 9.2 imp pt, 11 US pt, 5.2 l; greasing; every 3,100 miles, 5,000 km, 8 points; tappet clearances (hot): inlet 0.008 in, 0.20 mm, exhaust 0.010 in, 0.25 mm; valve timing: 0°30' 42°30' 38°30' 4°30'; tyre pressure: front 28 psi, 2 atm, rear 28 psi, 2 atm.

VARIATIONS

ENGINE (injection) max power (SAE) 141 hp at 5,500 rpm, max torque (SAE) 149 lb ft, 20.5 kg m at 4,000 rpm, 60.1 hp/l, oil cooler, Bosch electronically-controlled injection system, cooling system capacity 22.9 imp pt, 27.5 US pt, 13 l.
TRANSMISSION 185 x 380 tyres.
PERFORMANCE max speed 117 mph, 188 km/h, power-weight ratio 20.1 lb/hp, 9.5 kg/hp, carrying capacity: 1,103 lb, 500 kg, acceleration standing 1/4 mile 17.3 sec, fuel consumption 24.4 m/imp gal, 20.3 m/US gal, 11.6 l x 100 km.
DIMENSIONS AND WEIGHT dry weight 2,955 lb, 1,340 kg.
PRACTICAL INSTRUCTIONS rear tyre pressure 26 psi, 1.8 atm.

OPTIONAL ACCESSORIES 4-speed servo-assisted mechanical gearbox with automatically hydraulically controlled clutch (I 3.250, II 1.833, III 1.207, IV 0.852, rev 3.154) max speed 111 mph, 178 km/h (117 mph, 188 km/h with injection engine), fuel consumption 25 m/imp gal, 20.8 m/US gal, 11.3 l x 100 km (23.5 m/imp gal, 19.6 m/US gal, 12 l x x 100 km with injection engine); Borg-Warner automatic transmission, hydraulic torque converter and planetary gears with 3 ratios (I 2.075, II 1.260, III 0.868, rev 1.850), max ratio of converter at stall 2, possible manual selection, max speed 107 mph, 173 km/h (112 mph, 180 km/h with injection engine), fuel consumption 22.2 m/imp gal, 18.5 m/US gal, 12.7 l x 100 km (21.1 m/imp gal, 17.6 m/US gal, 13.4 l x 100 km with injection engine); 4 headlamps automatically adjustable in height while running with 2 iodine long-distance lights automatically directed on bends by steering; iodine long distance lights; boosted heating for temperatures below −15°C, 5°F; air-conditioning.

DS 23 Pallas

See DS 23 Berline, except for:

PRICE IN GB: £ 2,107.
PRICE EX WORKS: 27,000 francs.

PERFORMANCE power-weight ratio: 22.6 lb/hp, 10.7 kg/hp.

ELECTRICAL EQUIPMENT 4 iodine headlamps, automatically adjustable in height while running with 2 long-distance lights automatically directed on bends by steering (standard).

DIMENSIONS AND WEIGHT dry weight: 2,933 lb, 1,330 kg.

Familiale Confort 23

See DS 23 Berline, except for:

PRICE EX WORKS: 26,500 francs.

TRANSMISSION tyres: 180 x 380 (front and rear).

PERFORMANCE max speed: 107 mph, 173; power-weight ratio: 25.6 lb/hp, 11.6 kg/hp; carrying capacity: 1,411 lb, 640 kg; acceleration: standing 1/4 mile 18.9 sec; fuel consumption: 23 m/imp gal, 19.1 m/US gal, 12.3 l x 100 km.

BRAKES swept area: total 78.9 sq in, 509 sq cm.

DIMENSIONS AND WEIGHT length: 197.87 in, 5,026 mm;

FAMILIALE CONFORT 23

width: 72.83 in, 1,850 mm; height: 59.84 in, 1,520 mm; dry weight: 3,164 lb, 1,435 kg.

BODY estate car/station wagon; 4+1 doors; 7 seats, bench front seats.

VARIATIONS

None.

OPTIONAL ACCESSORIES 4-speed servo-assisted mechanical gearbox and Borg-Warner automatic transmission not available.

Break Confort 23

See Familiale Confort 23, except for:

PRICE EX WORKS: 26,500 francs.

Commerciale 23

See Familiale Confort 23, except for:

BODY Commerciale equipment.

SM Injection

PRICE IN GB: £ 4,420.
PRICE IN USA: $ 11,700.

ENGINE Maserati front, 4 stroke; 6 cylinders, Vee-slanted at 90°; 162.9 cu in, 2,670 cc (3.43 x 2.95 in, 87 x 75 mm); compression ratio: 9:1; max power (SAE): 188 hp at 6,250 rpm; max torque (SAE): 175 lb ft, 24.1 kg m at 4,000 rpm; max engine rpm: 6.000; 70.4 hp/l; light alloy cylinder block and head, wet liners; 4 crankshaft bearings; valves: overhead, Vee-slanted; camshafts: 2, overhead, per cylinder block; lubrication: gear pump, full flow filter, oil cooler, 12.3 imp pt, 14.8 US pt, 7 l; Bosch electronically-controlled injection system; fuel feed: electric pump; water-cooled, 22.9 imp pt, 27.5 US pt, 13 l, 2 electric thermostatic fans.

TRANSMISSION driving wheels: front; clutch: single dry plate (diaphragm), hydraulically controlled; gearbox: mechanical; gears: 5, fully synchronized; ratios: I 2.923, II 1.941, III 1.321, IV 0.970, V 0.757, rev 3.154; lever: central; final drive: spiral bevel; axle ratio: 4.375; width of rims: 6"; tyres: 205 x 380.

PERFORMANCE max speeds: (I) 36 mph, 58 km/h; (II) 54 mph, 87 km/h; (III) 80 mph, 128 km/h; (IV) 108 mph, 174 km/h; (V) 142 mph, 228 km/h; power-weight ratio: 16.8 lb/hp, 7.6 kg/hp; carrying capacity: 772 lb, 350 kg; acceleration: standing ¼ mile 16.2 sec; speed in top at 1,000 rpm; 27.2 mph, 37.3 km/h; fuel consumption: 25.2 m/imp gal, 21.8 m/US gal, 25.2 l x 100 km.

CHASSIS platform, lateral box members; front suspension: independent, wishbones, hydropneumatic suspension, anti-roll bar, automatic levelling control; rear suspension: independent, swinging longitudinal trailing arms, hydropneumatic suspension, anti-roll bar, automatic levelling control.

STEERING rack-and-pinion, adjustable steering wheel, variable ratio servo; turns lock to lock: 2.

BRAKES disc (front diameter 11.81 in, 300 mm, rear 10.08 in, 256 mm), compensator, servo; swept area: total 47.8 sq in, 308 sq cm.

ELECTRICAL EQUIPMENT 12 V; 70 Ah battery; 940 W alternator; Sev or Ducellier distributor; 6 iodine headlamps, automatically adjustable in height while running, with long-distance lights automatically directed on bends by steering.

DIMENSIONS AND WEIGHT wheel base: 116.14 in, 2,950 mm; tracks: 60.08 in, 1,526 mm front, 52.20 in, 1,326 mm rear; length: 192.52 in, 4,890 mm; width: 72.44 in, 1,840 mm; height: 51.97 in, 1,320 mm; ground clearance: 6.10 in, 155 mm; dry weight: 3,197 lb, 1,450 kg; distribution of weight: 66% front, 34% rear; turning circle (between walls): 37.7 ft, 11.5 m; fuel tank: 19.8 imp gal, 23.8 US gal, 90 l.

BODY coupé; 2 doors; 2 + 2 seats, separate front seats, adjustable backrests; electrically-controlled windows, electrically-heated rear window.

PRACTICAL INSTRUCTIONS fuel: 98-100 oct petrol; engine sump oil: 12.3 imp pt, 14.8 US pt, 7 l, SAE 10W-30, change every 3,100 miles, 5,000 km; gearbox and final drive oil: 3.9 imp pt, 4.7 US pt, 2.2 l, SAE 80, change every 12,400

LIGIER JS 2

MATRA SPORTS 530 SX

PEUGEOT 104 Berline

miles, 20,000 km; hydraulic suspension oil: 9.5 imp pt, 11.4 US pt, 5.4 l; tappet clearances: inlet 0.012-0.014 in, 0.30-0.35 mm, exhaust 0.020-0.022 in, 0.50-0.55 mm; tyre pressure: front 33 psi, 2.3 atm, rear 30 psi, 2.1 atm.

OPTIONAL ACCESSORIES air-conditioning; wheels in reinforced plastic material; tinted glass; leather upholstery.

LIGIER FRANCE

JS 2

ENGINE Maserati, central, 4 stroke; 6 cylinders, Vee-slanted at 90°; 162.90 cu in, 2,670 cc (3.43 x 2.95 in, 87 x 75 mm); compression ratio: 9:1; max power (DIN): 170 hp at 5,500 rpm; max torque (DIN): 170 lb ft, 23.5 kg m at 4,000 rpm; max engine rpm: 6,000; 64.4 hp/l; light alloy cylinder block and head, wet liners; 4 crankshafts bearings; valves: overhead, Vee-slanted, thimble tappets, camshafts: 2, overhaed, per cylinder block; lubrication: gear pump, full flow filter, oil cooler, 12.3 imp pt, 14.8 US pt, 7 l; 3 Weber 42 DCNF downdraught twin barrel carburettors; fuel feed: electric pump; water-cooled, 24.6 imp pt, 29.6 US pt, 14 l; 2 electric thermostatic fans.

TRANSMISSION driving wheels: rear; clutch: single dry plate (diaphragm), hydraulically controlled; gearbox: mechanical; gears: 5, fully synchronized; ratios: I 2.923, II 1.941, III 1.321, IV 0.970, V 0.757, rev 3.154; lever: central; final drive: spiral bevel; axle ratio: 4.375; width of rims: 6.5"; tyres: 195/70 VR x 14.

PERFORMANCE max speed: 150 mph, 242 km/h; power-weight ratio: 11 lb/hp, 5 kg/hp; carrying capacity: 992 lb, 450 kg; speed in top at 1,000 rpm: 21.7 mph, 35 km/h; fuel consumption: 17.7 m/imp gal, 14.7 m/US gal, 16 l x 100 km.

CHASSIS backbone; front suspension: independent, wishbones, coil springs, anti-roll bar, telescopic dampers; rear suspension: independent, wishbones, torque arms, coil springs, anti-roll bar, telescopic dampers.

STEERING rack-and-pinion.

BRAKES disc (diameter 10.75 in, 273 mm), servo; swept area: front 22.9 sq in, 148 sq cm, rear 16.7 sq in, 108 sq cm, total 39.6 sq in, 256 sq cm.

ELECTRICAL EQUIPMENT 12 V; 70 Ah battery; 900 W alternator; 4 retractable iodine headlamps.

DIMENSIONS AND WEIGHT wheel base: 95.52 in, 2,350 mm; tracks: 55.51 in, 1,410 mm front, 55.51 in, 1,410 mm rear; length: 167.32 in, 4,250 mm; width: 67.72 in, 1,720 mm; height: 45.28 in, 1,150 mm; ground clearance: 5.51 in, 140 mm; dry weight: 1,874 lb, 850 kg; turning circle (between walls): 44.3 ft, 13.5 m; fuel tanks: 20.7 imp gal, 24.8 US gal, 94 l.

BODY coupé in plastic material; 2 doors; 2 seats.

PRACTICAL INSTRUCTIONS fuel: 98-100 oct petrol; engine sump oil: 12.3 imp pt, 14.8 US pt, 7 l, SAE lOW-30, change every 3,100 miles, 5,000 km; gearbox and final drive oil: 3.9 imp pt, 4.7 US pt, 2.2 l, SAE 80, change every 3,100 miles, 5,000 km; greasing: every 6,200 miles, 10,000 km, 3 points.

OPTIONAL ACCESSORIES limited slip differential.

MATRA SPORTS FRANCE

530 LX

PRICE EX WORKS: 22,695 francs.

ENGINE rear, 4 stroke; 4 cylinders, Vee-slanted at 60°; 103.7 cu in, 1,699 cc (3.54 x 2.63 in, 90 x 66.8 mm); compression ratio: 9:1; max power (DIN): 75 hp at 5,000 rpm; max torque (DIN): 104 lb ft, 14.4 kg m at 3,000 rpm; max engine rpm: 5,500; 44.1 hp/l; cast iron cylinder block and head; 3 crankshaft bearings; valves: overhead, in line, push-rods and rockers; camshafts: 1, central; lubrication: gear pump, full flow filter, 7.9 imp pt, 9.5 US pt, 4.5 l; 1 Solex 32 TDID downdraught twin barrel carburettor; fuel feed: mechanical pump; sealed circuit cooling, water, 17.6 imp pt, 21.1 US pt, 10 l, electric thermostatic fan.

TRANSMISSION driving wheels: rear; clutch: single dry plate; gearbox: mechanical; gears: 4, fully synchronized; ratios: I 3.400, II 1.990, III 1.370, IV 1, rev 3.960; lever: central; final drive: hypoid bevel; axle ratio: 3.500; width of rims: 4.5"; tyres: 145 x 14 front, 165 x 14 rear.

PERFORMANCE max speeds: (I) 32 mph, 51 km/h; (II) 55 mph, 88 km/h; (III) 80 mph, 129 km/h; (IV) 109 mph,

LIGIER JS 2

MATRA SPORTS 530 LX

PEUGEOT 104 Berline

175 km/h; power-weight ratio: 27.6 lb/hp, 12.5 kg/hp; carrying capacity: 838 lb, 380 kg; speed in direct drive at 1,000 rpm: 19.8 mph, 31.9 km/h; fuel consumption: 31.4 m/imp gal, 26.1 m/US gal, 9 l x 100 km.

CHASSIS platform; front suspension: independent, wishbones, lower trailing arms, coil springs, anti-roll bar, telescopic dampers; rear suspension: independent, longitudinal trailing arms, coil springs, anti-roll bar, telescopic dampers.

STEERING rack-and-pinion; turns lock to lock: 2.80.

BRAKES disc (diameter 8.31 in, 211 mm); swept area: front 18.6 sq in, 120 sq cm, rear 18.6 sq in, 120 sq cm, total 37.2 sq in, 240 sq cm.

ELECTRICAL EQUIPMENT 12 V; 40 Ah battery; 490 W alternator; Bosch distributor; 2 retractable iodine headlamps.

DIMENSIONS AND WEIGHT wheel base: 100.79 in, 2,560 mm; tracks: 52.76 in, 1,340 mm front, 53.15 in, 1,350 mm rear; length: 165.24 in, 4,197 mm; width: 63.78 in, 1,620 mm; height: 47.24 in, 1,200 mm; ground clearance: 5.51 in, 140 mm; dry weight: 2,062 lb, 935 kg; distribution of weight: 51.5% front, 48.5% rear; turning circle (between walls): 32.8 ft, 10 m; fuel tank: 9.5 imp gal, 11.4 US gal, 43 l.

BODY coupé in plastic material; 2 doors; 2 + 2 seats, separate front seats, reclining backrests; detachable roof.

PRACTICAL INSTRUCTIONS fuel: 98-100 oct petrol; engine sump oil: 7.9 imp pt, 9.5 US pt, 4.5 l, SAE 10W-30, change every 3,100 miles, 5,000 km; gearbox and final drive oil: 5.6 imp pt, 6.8 US pt, 3.2 l, SAE 90 EP, change every 12,400 miles, 20,000 km; greasing: every 12,400 miles, 20,000 km, 2 points; tappet clearances: inlet 0.014 in, 0.35 mm, exhaust 0.016 in, 0.40 mm; valve timing: 20° 55° 62° 14°; tyre pressure: front 24 psi, 1.7 atm, rear 27 psi, 1.9 atm.

OPTIONAL ACCESSORIES light alloy wheels; fixed top version.

530 SX

See 530 LX, except for:

PRICE EX WORKS: 19,900 francs.

ELECTRICAL EQUIPMENT 4 headlamps.

BODY fixed top.

OPTIONAL ACCESSORIES only light alloy wheels.

PEUGEOT FRANCE

104 Berline

PRICE EX WORKS: 12,200 francs.

ENGINE front, transverse, slanted 72° to rear, 4 stroke; 4 cylinders, in line; 58.2 cu in, 954 cc (2.76 x 2.44 in, 70 x 62 mm); compression ratio: 8.8:1; max power (SAE): 50 hp at 6,250 rpm; max torque (SAE): 54 lb ft, 7.4 kg m at 3,000 rpm; max engine rpm: 6,250; 52.5 hp/l; light alloy cylinder block and head, wet liners, bi-hemispherical combustion chambers; 5 crankshaft bearings; valves: overhead, Vee-slanted, rockers, cogged belt; camshafts: 1, overhead; lubrication: gear pump, full flow filter, 7.9 imp pt, 9.5 US pt, 4.5 l; 1 Solex 32 HNSA horizontal carburettor; fuel feed: mechanical pump; water-cooled, 9.9 imp pt, 11.8 US pt, 5.6 l, electric thermostatic fan.

TRANSMISSION driving wheels: front: clutch: single dry plate (diaphragm); gearbox: mechanical; in unit with engine and final drive; gears: 4, fully synchronized; ratios: I 3.883, II 2.296, III 1.502, IV 1.042, rev 3.568; lever: central; final drive: spiral bevel; axle ratio: 4.060; width of rims: 4"; tyres: 135 x 13.

PERFORMANCE max speed: 84 mph, 135 km/h; power-weight ratio: 17.4 lb/hp, 7.9 kg/hp; acceleration: standing 1/4 mile 20.5 sec; speed in top at 1,000 rpm: 14.7 mph, 23.6 km/h; fuel consumption: 35.3 m/imp gal, 29.4 m/US gal, 8 l x 100 km.

CHASSIS integral; front suspension: independent, by McPherson, coil springs/telescopic damper struts, lower wishbones, anti-roll bar; rear suspension: independent, wishbones, coil springs, telescopic dampers.

STEERING rack-and-pinion; turns lock to lock: 3.43.

BRAKES front disc (diameter 9.49 in, 241 mm), rear drum, single circuit, rear compensator; swept area: front 176.1 sq in, 1,136 sq cm, rear 68.4 sq in, 441 sq cm, total 244.5 sq in, 1,577 sq cm.

ELECTRICAL EQUIPMENT 12 V; 30 Ah battery; 350 W alternator; Ducellier or Paris-Rhone distributor; 2 headlamps.

104 BERLINE

DIMENSIONS AND WEIGHT wheel base: 95.28 in, 2,420 mm; tracks: 50.79 in, 1,290 mm front, 48.82 in, 1,240 mm rear; length: 140.94 in, 3,580 mm; width: 59.84 in, 1,520 mm; height: 54.72 in, 1,390 mm; ground clearance: 5.04 in, 128 mm; dry weight: 1,676 lb, 760 kg; turning circle (between walls): 32.1 ft, 9.8 m; fuel tank: 8.8 imp gal, 10.6 US gal, 40 l.

BODY saloon/sedan; 4 doors; 4 seats, separate front seats.

PRACTICAL INSTRUCTIONS fuel: 95 oct petrol; engine sump, gearbox and final drive oil: 7 imp pt, 8.5 US pt, 4 l, SAE 10W-40, change every 3,100 miles, 5,000 km; greasing: every 3,100 miles, 5,000 km, 1 point; tyre pressure: front 26 psi, 1.8 atm, rear 28 psi, 2 atm.

OPTIONAL ACCESSORIES electrically-heated rear window.

204 Berline Grand Luxe

PRICE IN GB: £ 990.
PRICE EX WORKS: 13,060 francs.

ENGINE front, transverse, 4 stroke; 4 cylinders, slanted 20° to front, in line; 69 cu in, 1,130 cc (2.95 x 2.52 in, 75 x 64 mm); compression ratio: 8.8:1; max power (SAE): 60 hp at 5,900 rpm; max torque (SAE): 66 lb ft, 9.1 kg m at 3,500 rpm; max engine rpm: 5,900; 53.1 hp/l; light alloy cylinder block head, wet liners, bi-hemispherical combustion chambers; 5 crankshaft bearings; valves: overhead, Vee-slanted, rockers; camshafts: 1, overhead; lubrication: gear pump, full flow filter, 7 imp pt, 8.5 US pt, 4 l; 1 Solex 34 PBISA-4 downdraught single barrel carburettor; fuel feed: mechanical pump; water-cooled, 10.2 imp pt, 12.3 US pt, 58 l, electromagnetically-operated fan.

TRANSMISSION driving wheels: front; clutch: single dry plate (diaphragm), hydraulically controlled; gearbox: mechanical; gears: 4, fully synchronized; ratios: I 3.731, II 2.268, III 1.486, IV 1.009, rev 4.032; lever: steering column; final drive: helical spur gears; axle ratio: 4.066; width of rims: 4''; tyres: 135 x 14.

PERFORMANCE max speeds: (I) 25 mph, 40 km/h; (II) 41 mph, 66 km/h; (III) 63 mph, 101 km/h; (IV) 87 mph, 140 km/h; power-weight ratio: 32.4 lb/hp, 14.7 kg/hp; carrying capacity: 937 lb, 425 kg; acceleration: standing ¼ mile 20.2 sec; speed in top at 1,000 rpm: 15.8 mph, 25.4 km/h; fuel consumption: 30.7 m/imp gal, 25.6 m/US gal, 9.2 l x 100 km.

CHASSIS integral; front suspension: independent, by McPherson, coil springs/telescopic dampers, lower wishbones, anti-roll bar; rear suspension: independent, swinging longitudinal trailing arms, coil springs/telescopic dampers, anti-roll bar.

STEERING rack-and-pinion; turns lock to lock: 3.75.

BRAKES front disc (diameter 10.08 in, 256 mm), rear drum, rear compensator, servo; swept area: front 192.2 sq in, 1,240 sq cm, rear 89.1 sq in, 575 sq cm, total 281.3 sq in, 1,815 sq cm.

ELECTRICAL EQUIPMENT 12 V; 40 Ah battery; 350 W alternator; Sev or Ducellier distributor; 2 headlamps.

DIMENSIONS AND WEIGHT wheel base: 102.7 in, 2,595 mm; tracks: 51.97 in, 1,320 mm front, 50.79 in, 1,290 mm rear; length: 157.09 in, 3,990 mm; width: 61.42 in, 1,560 mm; height: 55.12 in, 1,400 mm; ground clearance: 5.51 in, 140 mm; dry weight: 1,940 lb, 880 kg; distribution of weight: 58.5% front, 41.5% rear; turning circle (between walls): 32.8 ft, 10.6 m; fuel tank: 9.2 imp gal, 11.1 US gal, 42 l.

BODY saloon/sedan; 4 doors; 5 seats, separate front seats, reclining backrests.

PRACTICAL INSTRUCTIONS fuel: 95 oct petrol; engine sump, gearbox and final drive oil: 7 imp pt, 8.5 US pt, 4 l, SAE 20W-40, change every 3,100 miles, 5,000 km; greasing: every 3,100 miles, 5,000 km, 5 points; tappet clearances: inlet 0.004 in, 0.10 mm, exhaust 0.010 in, 0.25 mm; valve timing: 1°20' 32° 33° 2°30'; tyre pressure: front 24 psi, 1.7 atm, rear 28 psi, 2 atm.

OPTIONAL ACCESSORIES 145 x 14 tyres only for export; electrically-heated rear window; headrests; sunshine roof.

204 Break Grand Luxe

See 204 Berline Grand Luxe, except for:

PRICE IN GB: £ 1,048.
PRICE EX WORKS: 13,700 francs.

TRANSMISSION width of rims: 4.5''; tyres: 145 x 14.

PEUGEOT 204 Berline Grand Luxe

PEUGEOT 304 S Berline

PEUGEOT 304 S Cabriolet

PERFORMANCE power-weight ratio: 34.4 lb/hp, 15.6 kg/hp; acceleration: standing ¼ mile 21.1 sec; speed in top at 1,000 rpm: 16.3 mph, 26.2 km/h; fuel consumption: 30.4 m/imp gal, 25.3 m/US gal, 9.3 l x 100 km.

DIMENSIONS AND WEIGHT length: 156.30 in, 3,970 mm; dry weight: 2,062 lb, 935 kg.

BODY estate car/station wagon; 4 + 1 doors.

PRACTICAL INSTRUCTIONS tyre pressure: front 22 psi, 1.6 atm, rear 36 psi, 2.5 atm.

204 Break Grand Luxe Diesel

See 204 Break Grand Luxe, except for:

PRICE EX WORKS: 16,330 francs.

ENGINE Diesel; 76.6 cu in, 1,255 cc (2.95 x 2.80 in, 75 x 71 mm); compression ratio: 22.3:1; max power (SAE): 45 hp at 5,000 rpm; max torque (SAE): 53 lb ft, 7.3 kg m at 3,000 rpm; max engine rpm: 5,450; 35.9 hp/l; lubricating system capacity: 8.8 imp pt, 10.6 US pt, 5 l; heating plugs on cylinder head; Bosch injection pump; cooling system capacity: 8.8 imp pt, 10.6 US pt, 5 l.

PERFORMANCE max speeds: (I) 24 mph, 39 km/h; (II) 40 mph, 64 km/h; (III) 61 mph, 98 km/h; (IV) 78 mph, 125 km/h; power-weight ratio: 46.7 lb/hp, 21.2 kg/hp; fuel consumption: 42.2 m/imp gal, 35.1 m/US gal, 6.7 l x 10 km.

ELECTRICAL EQUIPMENT 65 Ah battery; 330 W dynamo.

DIMENSIONS AND WEIGHT dry weight: 2,106 lb, 955 kg; fuel tank: 9.2 imp gal, 11.1 US gal, 42 l.

PRACTICAL INSTRUCTIONS engine sump, gearbox and final drive oil: 8.8 imp pt, 10.6 US pt, 5 l, change every 1,600 miles, 2,500 km; tyre pressure: front 24 psi, 1.7 atm.

304 Berline

PRICE IN GB: £ 1,107.
PRICE IN USA: $ 2,560.

ENGINE front, transverse, 4 stroke; 4 cylinders, slanted 20° to front, in line; 78.6 cu in, 1,288 cc (2.99 x 2.80 in, 76 x 71 mm); compression ratio: 8.8:1; max power (SAE): 70 hp at 6,100 rpm; max torque (SAE): 74 lb ft, 10.2 kg m at 3,750 rpm; max engine rpm: 6,100; 54.3 hp/l; light alloy cylinder block and head, wet liners, bi-hemispherical combustion chambers; 5 crankshaft bearings; valves: overhead, Vee-slanted, rockers; camshafts: 1, overhead; lubrication: rotary pump, cartridge on by-pass, 7 imp pt, 8.5 US pt, 4 l; 1 Solex 34 PBISA-4 downdraught single barrel carburettor; fuel feed: mechanical pump; water-cooled, 10.2 imp pt, 12.3 US pt, 5.8 l, electromagnetically-operated fan.

TRANSMISSION driving wheels: front; clutch: single dry plate (diaphragm), hydraulically controlled; gearbox: mechanical; gears: 4, fully synchronized; ratios: I 3.650, II 2.217, III 1.451, IV 0.986, rev 3.953; lever: steering column; final drive: helical spur gears; axle ratio: 4.066; width of rims: 4.5''; tyres: 145 x 14.

PERFORMANCE max speeds: (I) 27 mph, 44 km/h; (II) 45 mph, 73 km/h; (III) 69 mph, 111 km/h; (IV) 93 mph, 150 km/h; power-weight ratio: 29.1 lb/hp, 13.2 kg/hp; carrying capacity: 816 lb, 370 kg; acceleration: standing ¼ mile 19.5 sec; speed in top at 1,000 rpm: 16.7 mph, 26.9 km/h; fuel consumption: 28 m/imp gal, 23.3 m/US gal, 10.1 l x 100 km.

CHASSIS integral; front suspension: independent, by McPherson, coil springs/telescopic dampers, lower wishbones, anti-roll bar; rear suspension: independent, swinging longitudinal trailing arms, anti-roll bar, coil springs/telescopic dampers.

STEERING rack-and-pinion; turns lock to lock: 3.75.

BRAKES front disc (diameter 10.08 in, 256 mm), rear drum, rear compensator, servo; swept area: front 192.2 sq in, 1,240 sq cm, rear 89.1 sq in, 575 sq cm, total 281.3 sq in, 1,815 sq cm.

ELECTRICAL EQUIPMENT 12 V; 40 Ah battery; 350 W alternator; Ducellier distributor; 2 headlamps.

DIMENSIONS AND WEIGHT wheel base: 101.97 in, 2,590 mm; tracks: 51.97 in, 1,320 mm front, 50.79 in, 1,290 mm rear; length: 162.99 in, 4,140 mm; width: 61.81 in, 1,570 mm; height: 56.30 in, 1,430 mm; ground clearance: 4.72 in, 120 mm; dry weight: 2.051 lb, 930 kg; turning circle (between walls): 34.8 ft, 10.6 m; fuel tank: 9.2 imp gal, 11.1 US gal, 42 l.

BODY saloon/sedan; 4 doors; 5 seats, separate front seats, reclining backrests.

PRACTICAL INSTRUCTIONS fuel: 95 oct petrol; engine

PEUGEOT 204 Berline Grand Luxe

PEUGEOT 304 S Berline

PEUGEOT 304 S Coupé

sump, gearbox and final drive oil: 7 imp pt, 8.5 US pt, 4 l, SAE 20W-40, change every 3,100 miles, 5,000 km; greasing: every 3,100 miles, 5,000 km, 5 points; tyre pressure: front 23 psi, 1.6 atm, rear 27 psi, 1.9 atm.

OPTIONAL ACCESSORIES sunshine roof; electrically-heated rear window.

304 Coupé

See 304 Berline, except for:

PRICE EX WORKS: 15,270 francs.

TRANSMISSION lever: central.

PERFORMANCE max speed: 94 mph, 152 km/h; power-weight ratio: 27.6 lb/hp, 12.5 kg/hp; carrying capacity: 706 lb, 320 kg; acceleration: standing ¼ mile 19.3 sec.

ELECTRICAL EQUIPMENT 500 W alternator.

DIMENSIONS AND WEIGHT wheel base: 90.75 in, 2,305 mm; length: 148.03 in, 3,760 mm; height: 51.97 in, 1,320 mm; dry weight: 1,929 lb, 875 kg; turning circle (between walls): 31.8 ft, 9.7 m.

BODY coupé; 2 doors; 4 seats; electrically-heated rear window (standard).

304 Break Super-Luxe

See 304 Berline, except for:

PRICE IN GB: £ 1,153.
PRICE IN USA: $ 2,830.

PERFORMANCE power-weight ratio: 30 lb/hp, 13.6 kg/hp; fuel consumption: 28 m/imp gal, 23.3 m/US gal, 10.1 l x 100 km.

DIMENSIONS AND WEIGHT length: 157.09 in, 3,990 mm; height: 56.30 in, 1,430 mm; dry weight: 2,095 lb, 950 kg.

BODY estate car/station wagon; 4 + 1 doors.

PRACTICAL INSTRUCTIONS tyre pressure: rear 35 psi, 2.5 atm.

OPTIONAL ACCESSORIES only sunshine roof.

304 S Berline

See 304 Berline, except for:

PRICE IN GB: £ 1,212.
PRICE EX WORKS: 15,390 francs.

ENGINE max power (SAE): 80 hp at 6,100 rpm; max torque (SAE): 80 lb ft, 11.1 kg m at 4,500 rpm; 62.1 hp/l; 1 Solex 35 EEISA twin barrel carburettor.

TRANSMISSION lever: central.

PERFORMANCE max speeds: (I) 27 mph, 44 km/h; (II) 45 mph, 73 km/h; (III) 69 mph, 111 km/h; (IV) 99 mph, 160 km/h; power-weight ratio: 25.6 lb/hp, 11.6 kg/hp; acceleration: standing ¼ mile 18.6 sec; fuel consumption: 28.2 m/imp gal, 23.5 m/US gal, 10 l x 100 km.

ELECTRICAL EQUIPMENT iodine long distance lights.

BODY built-in headrests; sunshine roof (standard).

304 S Coupé

See 304 S Berline, except for:

PRICE IN GB: £ 1,381.
PRICE EX WORKS: 15,270 francs.

PERFORMANCE carrying capacity: 706 lb, 320 kg.

ELECTRICAL EQUIPMENT 500 W alternator.

DIMENSIONS AND WEIGHT wheel base: 90.63 in, 2,302 mm; length: 147.64 in, 3,750 mm; turning circle (between walls): 31.5 ft, 9.6 m.

BODY coupé; 2 doors; 4 seats; electrically-heated rear window (standard).

PRACTICAL INSTRUCTIONS tyre pressure: front 24 psi, 1.7 atm, rear 31 psi, 2.2 atm.

304 S Cabriolet

See 304 S Coupé, except for:

PRICE IN GB: £ 1,345.
PRICE EX WORKS: 15,940 francs.

PERFORMANCE power-weight ratio: 24.7 lb/hp, 11.2 kg/hp; carrying capacity: 419 lb, 190 kg; acceleration: standing ¼ mile 18.5 sec.

DIMENSIONS AND WEIGHT ground clearance: 5.12 in, 130 mm; dry weight: 1,973 lb, 895 kg.

BODY convertible; 2 seats.

PRACTICAL INSTRUCTIONS tyre pressure: rear 28 psi, 2 atm.

OPTIONAL ACCESSORIES hardtop.

404 Berline Grand Tourisme

PRICE IN GB: £ 1,214.
PRICE EX WORKS: 14,820 francs.

ENGINE front, 4 stroke; 4 cylinders, slanted at 45°, in line; 98.7 cu in, 1,618 cc (3.31 x 2.87 in, 84 x 73 mm); compression ratio: 7.6:1; max power (SAE): 73 hp at 5,600 rpm; max torque (SAE): 94 lb ft, 13 kg m at 2,500 rpm; max engine rpm: 5,600; 45.1 hp/l; cast iron cylinder block, wet liners, light alloy head, hemispherical combustion chambers; 5 crankshaft bearings; valves: overhead, Vee-slanted, push-rods and rockers; camshafts: 1, side; lubrication: gear pump, metal gauze filter, 7 imp pt, 8.5 US pt, 4 l; 1 Solex 34 PBICA-9 downdraught carburettor; fuel feed: electric pump; water-cooled, 13.2 imp pt, 15.9 US pt, 7.5 l, electromagnetically-operated fan.

TRANSMISSION driving wheels: rear; clutch: single dry plate (diaphragm), hydraulically controlled; gearbox: mechanical; gears: 4, fully synchronized; ratios: I 3.663, II 2.169, III 1.408, IV 1, rev 3.745; lever: steering column; final drive: worm and wheel; axle ratio: 4.200; width of rims: 4.5"; tyres: 165 x 15.

PERFORMANCE max speeds: (I) 25 mph, 40 km/h; (II) 44 mph, 71 km/h; (III) 68 mph, 110 km/h; (IV) 92 mph, 148 km/h; power-weight ratio: 30.9 lb/hp, 14 kg/hp; carrying capacity: 1,125 lb, 510 kg; acceleration: standing ¼ mile 20.2 sec; speed in direct drive at 1,000 rpm: 17.7 mph, 28.5 km/h; fuel consumption: 26.2 m/imp gal, 21.8 m/US gal, 10.8 l x 100 km.

CHASSIS integral; front suspension: independent, by McPherson, coil springs/telescopic damper struts, lower wishbones, anti-roll bar; rear suspension: rigid axle, coil springs, transverse linkage bar, anti-roll bar, telescopic dampers.

STEERING rack-and-pinion; turns lock to lock: 3.75.

BRAKES front disc (diameter 11.30 in, 287 mm), rear drum, rear compensator, servo; swept area: front 207.1 sq in, 1,336 sq cm, rear 111.6 sq in, 720 sq cm, total 318.7 sq in, 2,056 sq cm.

ELECTRICAL EQUIPMENT 12 V; 40 Ah battery; 350 W alternator; Sev or Ducellier distributor; 2 headlamps.

DIMENSIONS AND WEIGHT wheel base: 104.33 in, 2,650 mm; tracks: 52.95 in, 1,345 mm front, 50.39 in, 1,280 mm rear; length: 175.20 in, 4,450 mm; width: 63.98 in, 1,625 mm; height: 57.09 in, 1,450 mm; ground clearance: 5.90 in, 150 mm; dry weight: 2,249 lb, 1,020 kg; distribution of weight: 53.9% front, 46.1% rear; turning circle (between walls): 35.4 ft, 10.8 m; fuel tank: 12.1 imp gal, 14.5 US gal, 55 l.

BODY saloon/sedan; 4 doors; 5 seats, separate front seats.

PRACTICAL INSTRUCTIONS fuel: 86 oct petrol; engine sump oil: 7 imp pt, 8.5 US pt, 4 l, SAE 20W-40, change every 3,100 miles, 5,000 km; gearbox oil: 2.1 imp pt, 2.5 US pt, 1.2 l, SAE 20W-40, change every 6,200 miles, 10,000 km; final drive oil: 3 imp pt, 3.6 US pt, 1.7 l, GP 90, change every 18,600 miles, 30,000 km; greasing: every 3,100 miles, 5,000 km, 10 points; sparking plug type: 200°; tappet clearances: inlet 0.004 in, 0.10 mm, exhaust 0.010 in, 0.25 mm; valve timing: 0° 30°30' 35° 4°30'; tyre pressure: front 20 psi, 1.4 atm, rear 23 psi, 1.6 atm.

OPTIONAL ACCESSORIES ZF automatic transmission, hydraulic torque converter and planetary gears with 3 ratios (I 2.564, II 1.520, III 1, rev 2), max ratio of converter at stall 2.3, with engine max power (SAE) 76 hp, max torque (SAE) 96 lb ft, 13.3 kg m, 47 hp/l, max speed 89 mph, 144 km/h; sunshine roof.

404 Berline Diesel

See 404 Berline Grand Tourisme, except for:

PRICE EX WORKS: 17,480 francs.

ENGINE Diesel; 118.9 cu in, 1,948 cc (3.46 x 3.15 in, 88 x 80 mm); compression ratio: 21.5:1; max power (SAE): 68 hp

PEUGEOT 404 Berline Grand Tourisme

PEUGEOT 504 G.L. Berline

PEUGEOT 504 Break Super-Luxe

at 4,500 rpm; max torque (SAE): 87 lb ft, 12.1 kg m at 2,250 rpm; max engine rpm: 4,800; 34.9 hp/l; Bosch injection pump.

PERFORMANCE max speeds: (I) 21 mph, 34 km/h; (II) 38 mph, 61 km/h; (III) 58 mph, 94 km/h; (IV) 81 mph, 130 km/h; power-weight ratio: 35.7 lb/hp, 16.2 kg/hp; fuel consumption: 34.4 m/imp gal, 28.7 m/US gal, 8.2 l x 100 km.

BRAKES drum, 2 front leading shoes; swept area: total 288.8 sq in, 1,863 sq cm.

ELECTRICAL EQUIPMENT 65 Ah battery; 500 W alternator.

DIMENSIONS AND WEIGHT dry weight: 2,426 lb, 1,100 kg.

OPTIONAL ACCESSORIES automatic transmission not available.

504 G.L. Berline

PRICE IN GB: £ 1,494.
PRICE IN USA: $ 3,630.

ENGINE front, 4 stroke; 4 cylinders, slanted at 45°, in line; 120.3 cu in, 1,971 cc (3.46 x 3.19 in, 88 x 81 mm); compression ratio: 8.35:1; max power (SAE): 98 hp at 5,600 rpm; max torque (SAE): 125 lb ft, 17.2 kg m at 3,000 rpm; max engine rpm: 5,500; 49.7 hp/l; cast iron cylinder block, wet liners, light alloy head, hemispherical combustion chambers; 5 crankshaft bearings; valves: overhead, Vee-slanted, push-rods and rockers; camshafts: 1, side; lubrication: gear pump, metal gauze filter, 7 imp pt, 8.5 US pt, 4 l; 1 Solex 32-35 SEIEA downdraught twin barrel carburettor; fuel feed: mechanical pump; water-cooled, 13.7 imp pt, 16.5 US pt, 7.8 l, electromagnetic thermostatic fan.

TRANSMISSION driving wheels: rear; clutch: single dry plate (diaphragm), hydraulically controlled; gearbox: mechanical; gears: 4, fully synchronized; ratios: I 3.558, II 2.105, III 1.366, IV 1, rev 3.636; lever: central; final drive: hypoid bevel; axle ratio: 3.888; width of rims: 5"; tyres: 175 x 14.

PERFORMANCE max speeds: (I) 27 mph, 44 km/h; (II) 47 mph, 75 km/h; (III) 71 mph, 115 km/h; (IV) 101 mph, 162 km/h; power-weight ratio: 27.6 lb/hp, 12.5 kg/hp; carrying capacity: 1,058 lb, 480 kg; acceleration: standing ¼ mile 18.3 sec; speed in direct drive at 1,000 rpm: 18.5 mph, 29.7 km/h; fuel consumption: 23.7 m/imp gal, 19.8 m/US gal, 11.9 l x 100 km.

CHASSIS integral; front suspension: independent, by McPherson, coil springs/telescopic dampers struts, lower wishbones, anti-roll bar; rear suspension: independent, oblique semi-trailing arms, coil springs/telescopic dampers, anti-roll bar.

STEERING rack-and-pinion; turns lock to lock: 4.50.

BRAKES disc (diameter 10.75 in, 273 mm), rear compensator, servo; swept area: front 236.9 sq in, 1,528 sq cm, rear 201.6 sq in, 1,300 sq cm, total 438.5 sq in, 2,828 sq cm.

ELECTRICAL EQUIPMENT 12 V; 45 Ah battery; 500 W alternator; Ducellier distributor; 2 iodine headlamps.

DIMENSIONS AND WEIGHT wheel base: 107.87 in, 2,740 mm; tracks: 55.91 in, 1,420 mm front, 53.54 in, 1,360 mm rear; length: 176.77 in, 4,490 mm; width: 66.54 in, 1,690 mm; height: 57.48 in, 1,460 mm; ground clearance: 6.30 in, 160 mm; dry weight: 2,712 lb, 1,230 kg; turning circle (between walls): 35.8 ft, 10.9 m; fuel tank: 12.3 imp gal, 14.8 US gal, 56 l.

BODY saloon/sedan; 4 doors; 5 seats, separate front seats, reclining backrests; built-in adjustable headrests.

PRACTICAL INSTRUCTIONS fuel: 95 oct petrol; engine sump oil: 7 imp pt, 8.5 US pt, 4 l, SAE 20W-40, change every 3,100 miles, 5,000 km; gearbox oil: 1.9 imp pt, 2.3 US pt, 1.1 l, SAE 20W-40, change every 6,200 miles, 10,000 km; final drive oil: 2.1 imp pt, 2.5 US pt, 1.2 l, GP 90, change every 6,200 miles, 10,000 km; greasing: every 3,100 miles, 5,000 km, 6 points; tappet clearances: inlet 0.004 in, 0.10 mm, exhaust 0.010 in, 0.25 mm; valve timing: 1°30' 36° 35°30' 9°; tyre pressure: front 21 psi, 1.5 atm, rear 26 psi, 1.8 atm.

VARIATIONS

ENGINE (injection) max power (SAE) 110 hp at 5,600 rpm, max torque (SAE) 131 lb ft, 18.1 kg m at 3,000 rpm, 55.8 hp/l, 4-cylinder injection pump in inlet pipes (Kugelfischer system).
PERFORMANCE max speeds (I) 29 mph, 46 km/h, (II) 48 mph, 78 km/h, (III) 75 mph, 121 km/h, (IV) 107 mph, 173 km/h, power-weight ratio 22.9 lb/hp, 10.4 kg/hp, acceleration standing ¼ mile 17.8 sec, speed in direct drive at 1,000 rpm 19 mph, 30.6 km/h, fuel consumption 28.2 m/imp gal, 23.5 m/US gal, 10 l x 100 km.

OPTIONAL ACCESSORIES ZF automatic transmission, hydraulic torque converter and planetary gears with 3 ratios (I 2.564, II 1.520, III 1, rev 2), max ratio of converter at stall 2.3, max speed 97 mph, 156 km/h (with injection engine max speed 104 mph, 167 km/h); leather upholstery; sushine roof (standard with injection engine); electrically-heated rear window (standard with injection engine).

PEUGEOT 404 Berline Grand Tourisme

PEUGEOT 504 G.L. Berline

PEUGEOT 504 Break Super-Luxe

504 G.L. Berline Diesel

See 504 G.L. Berline, except for:

PRICE EX WORKS: 20,800 francs.

ENGINE Diesel; 128.9 cu in, 2,112 cc (3.58 x 3.27 in, 90 x 83 mm); compression ratio: 22.2:1; max power (DIN): 65 hp at 4,500 rpm; max torque (DIN): 91 lb ft, 12.6 kg m at 2,000 rpm; 30.8 hp/l; heating plugs on cylinder block; Bosch injection pump.

PERFORMANCE max speeds: (I) 23 mph, 37 km/h; (II) 39 mph, 62 km/h; (III) 59 mph, 95 km/h; (IV) 84 mph, 135 km/h; power-weight ratio: 43.4 lb/hp, 19.7 kg/hp; fuel consumption: 30.4 m/imp gal, 25.3 m/US gal, 9.3 l x 100 km.

ELECTRICAL EQUIPMENT 65 Ah battery.

DIMENSIONS AND WEIGHT dry weight: 2,822 lb, 1,280 kg.

VARIATIONS

None.

OPTIONAL ACCESSORIES only sunshine roof and electrically-heated rear window.

504 Break

See 504 G.L. Berline, except for:

PRICE IN GB: £ 1,598.
PRICE EX WORKS: 18,720 francs.

TRANSMISSION lever: steering column; axle ratio: 4.111; tyres: 185 x 14.

PERFORMANCE max speed: 99 mph, 160 km/h; power-weight ratio: 28.7 lb/hp, 13 kg/hp; carrying capacity: 1,411 lb, 640 kg; speed in direct drive at 1,000 rpm: 17.8 mph, 28.7 km/h.

CHASSIS rear suspension: 4 coil springs.

BRAKES rear drum; swept area: total 400.5 sq in, 2,583 sq cm.

ELECTRICAL EQUIPMENT 45 Ah battery.

DIMENSIONS AND WEIGHT length: 189.09 in, 4,803 mm; width: 66.73 in, 1,695 mm; height: 61.02 in, 1,550 mm; ground clearance: 6.50 in, 165 mm; dry weight: 2,800 lb, 1,270 kg; turning circle (between walls): 37.4 ft, 11.4 m.

BODY estate car/station wagon; 4 + 1 doors.

VARIATIONS

None.

OPTIONAL ACCESSORIES automatic transmission, max speed 96 mph, 154 km/h.

504 Break Super-Luxe

See 504 Break, except for:

PRICE IN GB: £ 1,680.
PRICE EX WORKS: 19,790 francs.

504 Break Familiale

See 504 Break, except for:

PRICE IN GB: £ 1,652.
PRICE IN USA: $ 3,990.

BODY 7 seats.

VARIATIONS

(with 65 hp Diesel engine).

TRANSMISSION 4.222 axle ratio.
PERFORMANCE max speed 80 mph, 128 km/h, power-weight ratio 44.5 lb/hp, 20.2 kg/hp, acceleration standing ¼ mile

504 BREAK FAMILIALE

22.5 sec, speed in direct drive at 1,000 rpm 17.4 mph, 28 km/h, fuel consumption 29.4 m/imp gal, 24.5 m/US gal, 9.6 l x 100 km.
DIMENSIONS AND WEIGHT dry weight 2,900 lb, 1,315 kg.

504 Commerciale

See 504 G.L. Berline, except for:

PRICE EX WORKS: 15,830 francs.

ENGINE 109.6 cu in, 1,796 cc (3.31 x 3.19 in, 84 x 81 mm); compression ratio: 7.5:1; max power (SAE): 80 hp at 5,500 rpm; max torque (DIN): 103 lb ft, 14.2 kg m at 2,500 rpm; 44.5 hp/l.

TRANSMISSION axle ratio: 4.222.

PERFORMANCE max speed: 91 mph, 146 km/h; power-weight ratio: 32.8 lb/hp, 14.9 kg/hp; carrying capacity: 1,477 lb, 670 kg; acceleration: standing ¼ mile 20 sec.

CHASSIS rear suspension without anti-roll bar.

ELECTRICAL EQUIPMENT 40 Ah battery.

DIMENSIONS AND WEIGHT height: 57.48 in, 1,460 mm; dry weight: 2,635 lb, 1,195 kg.

BODY estate car/station wagon; 4 + 1 doors; Commerciale equipment.

VARIATIONS

ENGINE Diesel, 118.9 cu in, 1,948 cc (3.36 x 3.15 in, 88 x 80 mm), 21:1 compression ratio, max power (DIN) 50 hp at 4,500 rpm, max torque (DIN) 83 lb ft, 11.4 kg m at 2,000 rpm, max engine rpm 4,750, 25.6 hp/l.
TRANSMISSION 4.625 axle ratio.
PERFORMANCE max speed 73 mph, 118 km/h, power-weight ratio 52.7 lb/hp, 23.9 kg/hp, acceleration standing ¼ mile 24.1 sec, fuel consumption 26.9 m/imp gal, 22.4 m/US gal, 10.5 l x 100 km.

504 Coupé

See 504 G.L. Berline, except for:

PRICE IN GB: £ 2,512.
PRICE EX WORKS: 30,100 francs.

ENGINE max power (SAE): 110 hp at 5,600 rpm; max torque (SAE): 131 lb ft, 18.1 kg m at 3,000 rpm; max engine rpm: 5,600; 55.8 hp/l; lubricating system capacity: 8.8 imp pt, 10.6 US pt, 5 l; 4-cylinder injection pump in inlet pipes (Kugelfischer system).

TRANSMISSION axle ratio: 3.700.

PERFORMANCE max speeds: (I) 30 mph, 48 km/h; (II) 50 mph, 80 km/h; (III) 77 mph, 124 km/h; (IV) 111 mph, 179 km/h; power-weight ratio: 24.5 lb/hp, 11.1 kg/hp; carrying capacity: 706 lb, 320 kg; acceleration: standing ¼ mile 17.5 sec; speed in direct drive at 1,000 rpm: 19.3 mph, 31.1 km/h; fuel consumption: 27.7 m/imp gal, 23.1 m/US gal, 10.2 l x 100 km.

ELECTRICAL EQUIPMENT 4 iodine headlamps.

DIMENSIONS AND WEIGHT wheel base: 100.39 in, 2,550 mm; rear track: 55.51 in, 1,410 mm; length: 171.65 in, 4,360 mm; width: 66.93 in, 1,700 mm; height: 53.15 in, 1,350 mm; dry weight: 2,690 lb, 1,220 kg; distribution of weight: 52.5% front, 47.5% rear; turning circle (between walls): 33.8 ft, 10.4 m.

BODY coupé; 2 doors; 4 seats.

OPTIONAL ACCESSORIES with automatic transmission max speed 106 mph, 170 km/h; sunshine roof not available.

504 Cabriolet

See 504 Coupé, except for:

PRICE IN GB: £ 2,440.
PRICE EX WORKS: 29,090 francs.

DIMENSIONS AND WEIGHT height: 53.54 in, 1,360 mm.

BODY convertible.

PEUGEOT 504 Cabriolet

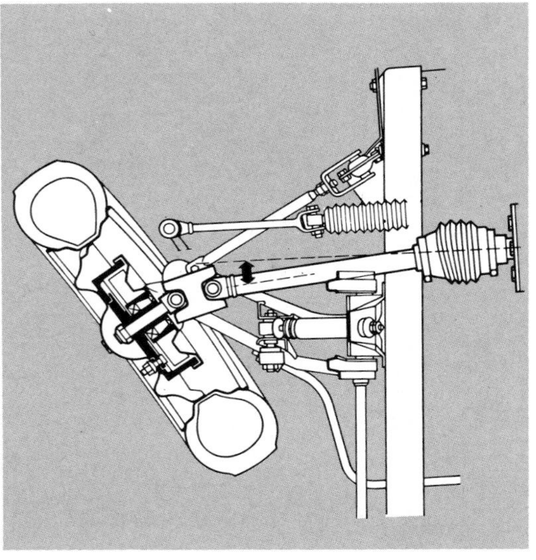

RENAULT 4 (front suspension)

RENAULT 5 TL

RENAULT FRANCE

4 Luxe

PRICE IN GB: £ 590.
PRICE EX WORKS: 8,500 francs.

ENGINE front, 4 stroke; 4 cylinders, vertical, in line; 47.7 cu in, 782 cc (2.20 x 3.15 in, 55.8 x 80 mm); compression ratio: 8.5:1; max power (DIN): 27 hp at 5,000 rpm; max torque (DIN): 38 lb ft, 5.3 kg m at 2,500 rpm; max engine rpm: 5,000; 34.5 hp/l; cast iron cylinder block, wet liners, light alloy head; 3 crankshaft bearings; valves: overhead, in line, push-rods and rockers; camshafts: 1, side; lubrication: gear pump, filter in sump, 4.4 imp pt, 5.3 US pt, 2.5 l; 1 Solex 26 DIS 5 or Zenith 28 IF downdraught single barrel carburettor; fuel feed: mechanical pump; sealed circuit cooling, liquid, 8.4 imp pt, 10.1 US pt, 4.8 l.

TRANSMISSION driving wheels: front; clutch: single dry plate (diaphragm); gearbox: mechanical; gears: 4, fully synchronized; ratios: I 3.800, II 2.059, III 1.364, IV 1.036, rev 3.800; lever: on facia; final drive: spiral bevel; axle ratio: 4.125; width of rims: 4"; tyres: 130 x 330.

PERFORMANCE max speeds: (I) 19 mph, 30 km/h; (II) 35 mph, 56 km/h; (III) 53 mph, 85 km/h; (IV) 68 mph, 110 km/h; power-weight ratio: 51.8 lb/hp, 23.5 kg/hp; carrying capacity: 783 lb, 355 kg; acceleration: standing ¼ mile 27.1 sec, 0-50 mph (0-80 km/h) 34.2 sec; speed in top at 1,000 rpm: 14.5 mph, 23.3 km/h; fuel consumption: 51.4 m/imp gal, 42.8 m/US gal, 5.5 l x 100 km.

CHASSIS platform; front suspension: independent, wishbones, longitudinal torsion bars, anti-roll bar, telescopic dampers; rear suspension: independent, swinging longitudinal trailing arms, transverse torsion bars, telescopic dampers.

STEERING rack-and-pinion; turns lock to lock: 3.75.

BRAKES drum (diameter 7.87 in, 200 mm front, 6.30 in, 160 mm rear), single circuit, rear compensator; swept area: front 68.2 sq in, 440 sq cm, rear 38.9 sq in, 251 sq cm, total 107.1 sq in, 691 sq cm.

ELECTRICAL EQUIPMENT 12 V; 30 Ah battery; 22 A dynamo; 2 headlamps.

DIMENSIONS AND WEIGHT wheel base: 96.42 in, 2,449 mm (right), 94.53 in, 2,401 mm (left); tracks: 50.35 in, 1,279 mm front, 48.98 in, 1,244 mm rear; length: 144.41 in, 3,668 mm; width: 58.46 in, 1,485 mm; height: 61.02 in, 1,550 mm; ground clearance: 7.87 in, 200 mm; dry weight: 1,400 lb, 635 kg; distribution of weight: 57.8% front, 42.2% rear; turning circle (between walls): 33.1 ft, 10.1 m; fuel tank: 5.7 imp gal, 6.9 US gal, 26 l.

BODY estate car/station wagon; 4 + 1 doors; 4 seats, bench front seats.

PRACTICAL INSTRUCTIONS fuel: 98-100 oct petrol; engine sump oil: 4.4 imp pt, 5.3 US pt, 2.5 l, SAE 10W-40, change every 3,100 miles, 5,000 km; gearbox and final drive oil: 1.9 imp pt, 2.3 US pt, 1.1 l, SAE 80 EP; greasing: none; tappet clearances: inlet 0.006-0.007 in, 0.15-0.18 mm, exhaust 0.007-0.009 in, 0.18-0.22 mm; valve timing: 10° 34° 49° 11° tyre pressure: front 20 psi, 1.4 atm, rear 23 psi, 1.6 atm.

OPTIONAL ACCESSORIES back seat folding down to luggage table.

4 Export

See 4 Luxe, except for:

PRICE IN GB: £ 660.
PRICE EX WORKS: 9,300 francs.

TRANSMISSION tyres: 135 x 330.

PERFORMANCE max speed: over 68 mph, 110 km/h; power-weight ratio: 53.8 lb/hp, 24.4 kg/hp; carrying capacity: 728 lb, 330 kg.

DIMENSIONS AND WEIGHT dry weight: 1,455 lb, 660 kg.

OPTIONAL ACCESSORIES sunshine roof; separate front seats; reclining backrests; metallic spray.

5 L

PRICE IN GB: £ 706.
PRICE EX WORKS: 10,100 francs.

ENGINE front, 4 stroke; 4 cylinders, vertical, in line; 47.7 cu in, 782 cc (2.20 x 3.15 in, 55.8 x 80 mm); compression ratio: 8.5:1; max power (DIN): 34 hp at 5,200 rpm; max torque (DIN): 38 lb ft, 5.3 kg m at 3,000 rpm; max engine rpm: 6,000; 43.4 hp/l; cast iron cylinder block, wet liners,

PEUGEOT 504 Coupé

RENAULT 4 Luxe

RENAULT 5 L

light alloy head; 3 crankshaft bearings; valves: overhead, in line, push-rod and rockers; camshafts: 1, side; lubrication: gear pump, filter in sump (cartridge), 4.4 imp pt, 5.3 US pt, 2.5 l; 1 Solex 32 SEI downdraught single barrel carburettor; fuel feed: mechanical pump; sealed circuit cooling, liquid, 10.2 imp pt, 12.3 US pt, 5.8 l.

TRANSMISSION driving wheels: front; clutch: single dry plate (diaphragm); gearbox: mechanical; gears: 4, fully synchronized; ratios: I 3.670, II 2.230, III 1.450, IV 1.030, rev 2.230; lever: on facia; final drive: spiral bevel; axle ratio: 4.125; width of rims: 4''; tyres: 135 x 330.

PERFORMANCE max speeds: (1) 21 mph, 34 km/h; (II) 35 mph, 57 km/h; (III) 53 mph, 86 km/h; (IV) 76 mph, 122 km/h; power-weight ratio: 47.2 lb/hp, 21.4 kg/hp; carrying capacity: 662 lb, 300 kg; speed in top at 1,000 rpm: 14.5 mph, 23.4 km/h; fuel consumption: 47.1 m/imp gal, 39.2 m/US gal, 6 l x 100 km.

CHASSIS integral; front suspension: independent, wishbones, longitudinal torsion bar, anti-roll bar, telescopic dampers; rear suspension: independent, swinging longitudinal trailing arms, transverse torsion bars, telescopic dampers.

STEERING rack-and-pinion; turns lock to lock: 3.75.

BRAKES drum (diameter 7.87 in, 200 mm front, 6.30 in, 160 mm rear), single circuit, rear compensator; swept area: front 68.2 sq in, 440 sq cm, rear 38.9 sq in, 251 sq cm, total 107.1 sq in, 691 sq cm.

ELECTRICAL EQUIPMENT 12 V; 30 Ah battery; 26 A dynamo; R 220 distributor; 2 headlamps.

DIMENSIONS AND WEIGHT wheel base: 95.28 in, 2,420 mm; tracks: 50.39 in, 1,280 mm front, 48.82 in, 1,240 mm rear; length: 137.80 in, 3,500 mm; width: 59.84 in, 1,520 mm; height: 55.12 in, 1,400 mm; ground clearance: 5.12 in, 130 mm; dry weight: 1,610 lb, 730 kg; turning circle (between walls): 33.1 ft, 10.1 m; fuel tank: 9 imp gal, 10.8 US gal, 41 l.

BODY saloon/sedan; 2+1 doors; 4 seats, separate front seats.

PRACTICAL INSTRUCTIONS fuel: 98-100 oct petrol; engine sump oil: 4.4 imp pt, 5.3 US pt, 2.5 l, SAE 20W-40, change every 3,100 miles, 5,000 km; gearbox and final drive oil: 3.2 imp pt, 3.8 US pt, 1.8 l, SAE 80 EP, change every 6,200 miles, 10,000 km; greasing: none; tappet clearances: inlet 0.006 in, 0.15 mm; exhaust 0.008 in, 0.20 mm; valve timing: 20° 56° 53° 23°; tyre pressure: front 24 psi, 1.7 atm, rear 28 psi, 1.9 atm.

OPTIONAL ACCESSORIES luxury interior; metallic spray; back seat folding down to luggage table.

5 TL

See 5 L, except for:

PRICE IN GB: £ 768.
PRICE EX WORKS: 11,300 francs.

ENGINE 58.3 cu in, 956 cc (2.56 x 2.83 in, 65 x 72 mm); compression ratio: 9.25:1; max power (DIN): 44 hp at 5,500 rpm; max torque (DIN): 48 lb ft, 6.6 kg m at 3,500 rpm; max engine rpm: 6,000; 46 hp/l; 5 crankshaft bearings; lubricating system capacity: 5.3 imp pt, 6.3 US pt, 3 l; sealed circuit cooling, liquid, electric thermostatic fan, 11.1 imp pt, 13.3 US pt, 6.3 l.

TRANSMISSION tyres: 135 x 13.

PERFORMANCE max speeds: (I) 24 mph, 39 km/h; (II) 40 mph, 64 km/h; (III) 61 mph, 98 km/h; (IV) 86 mph, 138 km/h; power-weight ratio: 37.9 lb/hp, 17.2 kg/hp; carrying capacity: 882 lb, 400 kg; fuel consumption: 41.5 m/imp gal, 34.6 m/US gal, 6.8 l x 100 km.

BRAKES front disc (diameter 8.98 in, 228 mm), rear drum, rear compensator; swept area: front 157.2 sq in, 1,014 sq cm, rear 52.6 sq in, 339 sq cm, total 209.8 sq in, 1,353 sq cm.

ELECTRICAL EQUIPMENT 40 A alternator; R 248 C 33 distributor.

DIMENSIONS AND WEIGHT dry weight: 1,676 lb, 760 kg.

BODY reclining backrests; back seat folding down to luggage table.

PRACTICAL INSTRUCTIONS engine sump oil: 5.3 imp pt, 6.3 US pt, 3 l; tappet clearances: inlet 0.005 in, 0.12 mm, exhaust 0.008 in, 0.20 mm; valve timing: 18° 54° 53° 23°.

OPTIONAL ACCESSORIES central lever; tinted glass; sunshine roof; electrically-heated rear window.

6 (850)

PRICE IN GB: £ 735.
PRICE EX WORKS: 10,500 francs.

ENGINE front, 4 stroke; 4 cylinders, vertical, in line; 51.6 cu in, 845 cc (2.28 x 3.15 in, 58 x 80 mm); compression ratio: 8:1; max power (DIN): 34 hp at 5,000 rpm; max torque (DIN): 42 lb ft, 5.8 kg m at 3,000 rpm; max engine rpm: 5,200; 40.2 hp/l: cast iron cylinder block, light alloy head, wet liners; 3 crankshaft bearings; valves: overhead, in line, push-rods and rockers; camshafts: 1, side; lubrication: gear pump, filter in sump, 4.4 imp pt, 5.3 US pt, 2.5 l; 1 Solex 32 EISA downdraught carburettor; fuel feed: mechanical pump; sealed circuit cooling, liquid, 8.8 imp pt, 10.6 US pt, 5 l.

TRANSMISSION driving wheels: front; clutch: single dry plate (diaphragm); gearbox: mechanical; gears: 4, fully synchronized; ratios: I 3.670, II 2.230, III 1.450, IV 1.030, rev 3.230; lever: on facia; final drive: spiral bevel; axle ratio: 4.125; width of rims: 4''; tyres: 135 x 330.

PERFORMANCE max speeds: (I) 21 mph, 33 km/h; (II) 38 mph, 61 km/h; (III) 57 mph, 92 km/h; (IV) over 75 mph, 120 km/h; power-weight ratio: 49.8 lb/hp, 22.6 kg/hp; carrying capacity: 816 lb, 370 kg; speed in top at 1,000 rpm; 14.6 mph, 23.4 km/h; fuel consumption: 70.6 m/imp gal, 58.8 m/US gal, 4 l x 100 km.

CHASSIS platform; front suspension: independent, wishbones, longitudinal torsion bars, anti-roll bar, telescopic dampers; rear suspension: independent, swinging longitudinal trailing arms, transverse torsion bars, telescopic dampers.

STEERING rack-and-pinion; turns lock to lock: 3.75.

BRAKES drum, rear compensator; swept area: front 89 sq in, 574 sq cm, rear 38.9 sq in, 251 sq cm, total 127.9 sq in, 825 sq cm.

ELECTRICAL EQUIPMENT 12 V; 30 Ah battery; 22 A dynamo; Lucas distributor; 2 headlamps.

DIMENSIONS AND WEIGHT wheel base: 94.53 in, 2,401 mm; tracks: 50.35 in, 1,279 mm front, 48.98 in, 1,244 mm rear; length: 151.61 in, 3,851 mm; width: 60.47 in, 1,536 mm; height: 59.06 in, 1,500 mm; ground clearance: 4.92 in, 125 mm; dry weight: 1,698 lb, 770 kg; distribution of weight: 56% front, 44% rear; turning circle (between walls): 34.4 ft, 10.5 m; fuel tank: 8.8 imp gal, 10.6 US gal, 40 l.

BODY saloon/sedan; 4 + 1 doors; 4-5 seats, separate front seats; back seat folding down to luggage table.

PRACTICAL INSTRUCTIONS fuel: 90 oct petrol; engine sump oil: 4.4 imp pt, 5.3 US pt, 2.5 l, change every 3,100 miles, 5,000 km; gearbox and final drive: 3.2 imp pt, 3.8 US pt, 1.8 l, SAE 80 EP; greasing: none; tappet clearances: inlet 0.006-0.007 in, 0.15-0.18 mm, ehaust 0.007-0.009 in, 0.18-0.22 mm; valve timing: 16° 52° 52° 22°; tyre pressure: front 21 psi, 1.5 atm, rear 24 psi, 1.7 atm.

OPTIONAL ACCESSORIES reclining backrests; headrests; sunshine roof.

6 TL (1100)

See 6 (850), except for:

PRICE IN GB: £ 818.
PRICE EX WORKS: 11,600 francs.

ENGINE 67.6 cu in, 1,108 cc (2.76 x 2.83 in, 70 x 72 mm); compression ratio: 9.5:1; max power (DIN): 47 hp at 5,500 rpm; max torque (DIN): 57 lb ft, 7.9 kg m at 3,000 rpm; max engine rpm: 5,700; 42.4 hp/l; 5 crankshaft bearings; lubrication: full flow filter, 5.3 imp pt, 6.3 US pt, 3 l; cooling system capacity: 11.1 imp pt, 13.3 US pt, 6.3 l, electric thermostatic fan.

TRANSMISSION tyres: 145 x 330.

PERFORMANCE max speeds: (I) 22 mph, 35 km/h; (II) 39 mph, 63 km/h; (III) 60 mph, 97 km/h; (IV) 84 mph, 135 km/h; power-weight ratio: 38.4 lb/hp, 17.4 kg/hp; carrying capacity: 882 lb, 400 kg; speed in top at 1,000 rpm: 15 mph, 24.1 km/h; fuel consumption: 37.7 m/imp gal, 31.4 m/US gal, 7.5 l x 100 km.

CHASSIS rear suspension: anti-roll bar.

BRAKES front disc (diameter 8.98 in, 228 mm), rear drum, rear compensator; swept area: front 157.2 sq in, 1,014 sq cm, rear 52.7 sq in, 340 sq cm, total 209.9 sq in, 1,354 sq cm.

ELECTRICAL EQUIPMENT 30/40 A alternator.

DIMENSIONS AND WEIGHT wheel base: 94.53 in, 2,401 mm (left), 96.42 in, 2,449 mm (right); tracks: 50.63 in, 1,286 mm front, 49.13 in, 1,248 mm rear; length: 151.93 in, 3,859

RENAULT 6 TL (1100)

RENAULT 12 Break

RENAULT 12 TS Berline

mm; dry weight: 1,808 lb, 820 kg; distribution of weight: 56.1% front, 43.9% rear.

BODY reclining backrests (standard).

PRACTICAL INSTRUCTIONS engine sump oil: 5.3 imp pt, 6.3 US pt, 3 l; valve timing: 18° 54° 53° 23°; tyre pressure: front 20 psi, 1.4 atm, rear 24 psi, 1.7 atm.

OPTIONAL ACCESSORIES electrically-heated rear window.

8

PRICE EX WORKS: 10,500 francs.

ENGINE rear, 4 stroke; 4 cylinders, vertical, in line; 67.6 cu in, 1,108 cc (2.76 x 2.83 in, 70 x 72 mm); compression ratio: 8.5:1; max power (DIN): 43 hp at 4,600 rpm; max torque (DIN): 57 lb ft, 7.9 kg m at 3,000 rpm: max engine rpm: 5,300; 38.8 hp/l; cast iron cylinder block, light alloy head, wet liners; 5 crankshaft bearings; valves: overhead, in line, slanted, push-rods and rockers; camshafts: 1, side; lubrication: gear pump, filter in sump, 4.4 imp pt, 5.3 US pt, 2.5 l; 1 Solex 32 DITA 3 downdraught carburettor; fuel feed: mechanical pump; sealed circuit cooling, liquid, 12.5 imp pt, 15 US pt, 7.1 l.

TRANSMISSION driving wheels: rear; clutch: single dry plate (diaphragm); gearbox: mechanical; gears: 4, fully synchronized; ratios: I 3.610, II 2.260, III 1.480, IV 1.030, rev 3.080; lever: central; final drive: hypoid bevel; axle ratio: 4.125; width of rims: 4"; tyres: 135 x 380.

PERFORMANCE max speeds: (I) 26 mph, 42 km/h; (II) 42 mph, 68 km/h; (III) 64 mph, 103 km/h; (IV) 84 mph, 135 km/h; power-weight ratio: 41 lb/hp, 18 kg/hp; carrying capacity: 706 lb, 320 kg; speed in top at 1,000 rpm: 16.3 mph, 26.3 km/h; fuel consumption: 41.5 m/imp gal, 34.6 m/US gal, 6.8 l x 100 km.

CHASSIS integral; front suspension: independent, wishbones, coil springs, anti-roll bar, telescopic dampers; rear suspension: independent, swinging semi-axles, swinging longitudinal trailing arms articulated at centre, coil springs, telescopic dampers.

STEERING rack-and-pinion; turns lock to lock: 3.60.

BRAKES front disc, (diameter 10.28 in, 261 mm), rear drum (diameter 8.98 in, 228 mm), rear compensator; swept area: front 171.2 sq in, 1,104 sq cm, rear 34.1 sq in, 220 sq cm, total 205.3 sq in, 1,324 sq cm.

ELECTRICAL EQUIPMENT 12 V; 40 Ah battery; 22 A dynamo; 2 headlamps.

DIMENSIONS AND WEIGHT wheel base: 89.37 in, 2,270 mm; tracks: 49.45 in, 1,256 mm front, 48.27 in, 1,226 mm rear; lenght: 157.28 in, 3,995 mm; width: 58.66 in, 1,490 mm; height: 55.31 in, 1,405 mm; ground clearance: 4.72 in, 120 mm; dry weight: 1,764 lb, 800 kg; distribution of weight: 36.4% front, 63.6% rear; turning circle (between walls): 33.5 ft, 10.2 m; fuel tank: 8.4 imp gal, 10 US gal, 38 l.

BODY saloon/sedan; 4 doors; 4-5 seats, separate front seats.

PRACTICAL INSTRUCTIONS fuel: 86 oct petrol; engine sump oil: 4.4 imp pt, 5.3 US pt, 2.5 l, SAE 10W-40, change every 3,100 miles, 5,000 km; gearbox and final drive oil: 3.3 imp pt, 4 US pt, 1.9 l, SAE 80 EP, change every 6,200 miles, 10,000 km; greasing: every 12,400 miles, 20,000 km, 1 point; tappet clearances: inlet 0.004-0.006 in, 0.10-0.14 mm, exhaust 0.007-0.009 in, 0.18-0.22 mm; valve timing: 10° 34° 46° 10°; tyre pressure: front 14 psi, 1 atm, rear 28 psi, 2 atm.

OPTIONAL ACCESSORIES reclining backrests.

12 L Berline

PRICE IN GB: £ 851.
PRICE EX WORKS: 12,800 francs.

ENGINE front, 4 stroke; 4 cylinders, vertical, in line; 78.7 cu in, 1,289 cc (2.87 x 3.03 in, 73 x 77 mm); compression ratio: 8.5:1; max power (DIN): 54 hp at 5,250 rpm; max torque (DIN): 70 lb ft, 9.7 kg m at 3,000 rpm; max engine rpm: 6,000; 41.8 hp/l; cast iron cylinder block, wet liners, light alloy head; 5 crankshaft bearings; valves: overhead, push-rods and rockers; camshafts: 1, side; lubrication: gear pump, filter in sump, 5.3 imp pt, 6.3 US pt, 3 l; 1 Solex 32 EISA downdraught carburettor; fuel feed: mechanical pump; sealed circuit cooling, liquid, 8.8 imp pt, 10.6 US pt, 5 l.

TRANSMISSION driving wheels: front; clutch: single dry plate (diaphragm); gearbox: mechanical; gears: 4, fully synchronized; ratios: I 3.615, II 2.263, III 1.480, IV 1.032, rev 3.076; lever: central; final drive: hypoid bevel; axle ratio: 3.770; width of rims: 4.5"; tyres: 145 x 330.

PERFORMANCE max speeds: (I) 27 mph, 43 km/h; (II) 43 mph, 70 km/h; (III) 67 mph, 108 km/h; (IV) 90 mph, 145 km/h; power-weight ratio: 36.8 lb/hp, 16.7 kg/hp; carrying capacity: 882 lb, 400 kg; speed in top at 1,000 rpm: 16.3 mph, 26.2 km/h; fuel consumption: 33.2 m/imp gal, 27.7 m/US gal, 8.5 l x 100 km.

RENAULT 6 TL (1100)

RENAULT 12

RENAULT 12 TS Berline

CHASSIS integral; front suspension: independent, wishbones, anti-roll bar, coil springs/telescopic dampers; rear suspension: rigid axle, trailing arms, A-bracket, anti-roll bar, coil springs/telescopic dampers.

STEERING rack-and-pinion; turns lock to lock: 3.50.

BRAKES front disc (diameter 8.98 in, 228 mm), rear drum, rear compensator; swept area: front 171.2 sq in, 1,014 sq cm, rear 70.1 sq in, 452 sq cm, total 241.3 sq in, 1,466 sq cm.

ELECTRICAL EQUIPMENT 12 V; 40 Ah battery; 40 A alternator; 2 headlamps.

DIMENSIONS AND WEIGHT wheel base: 96.10 in, 2,441 mm; tracks: 51.65 in, 1,312 mm front, 51.65 in, 1,312 mm rear; length: 170.87 in, 4,340 mm; width: 64.41 in, 1,636 mm; height: 56.46 in, 1,434 mm; ground clearance: 5.51 in, 140 mm; dry weight: 1,985 lb, 900 kg; distribution of weight: 58.5% front, 41.5% rear; turning circle (between walls): 35.1 ft, 10.7 m; fuel tank: 11 imp gal, 13.2 US gal, 50 l.

BODY saloon/sedan; 4 doors; 4-5 seats, separate front seats.

PRACTICAL INSTRUCTIONS fuel: 92 oct petrol; engine sump oil: 5.3 imp pt, 6.3 US pt, 3 l, SAE 10W-40, change every 3,100 miles, 5,000 km; gearbox and final drive oil: 3.5 imp pt, 4.2 US pt, 2 l, SAE 80 EP, change every 6,200 miles, 10,000 km; greasing: none; tappet clearances: inlet 0.004-0.006 in, 0.10-0.14 mm, exhaust 0.007-0.009 in, 0.18-0.22 mm; valve timing: 22° 62° 60° 20°; tyre pressure: front 26 psi, 1.6 atm, rear 26 psi, 1.8 atm.

OPTIONAL ACCESSORIES separate front seats; electrically-heated rear window; tinted glass.

12 TL Berline

See 12 L Berline, except for:

PRICE IN GB: £ 917.
PRICE EX WORKS: 13,600 francs.

BODY separate front seats, reclining backrests.

12 Break

See 12 L Berline, except for:

PRICE IN GB: £ 1,009.
PRICE EX WORKS: 13,980 francs.

TRANSMISSION tyres: 155 x 330.

PERFORMANCE max speed: over 90 mph, 145 km/h; power-weight ratio: 38.6 lb/hp, 17.5 kg/hp; carrying capacity: 937 lb, 425 kg; speed in top at 1,000 rpm: 16.8 mph, 27.1 km/h.

BRAKES servo; swept area: front 157.2 sq in, 1,014 sq cm, rear 89 sq in, 574 sq cm, total 246.2 sq in, 1,588 sq cm.

DIMENSIONS AND WEIGHT length: 173.39 in, 4,404 mm; height: 57.28 in, 1,455 mm; dry weight: 2,095 lb, 950 kg; distribution of weight: 54.7% front, 45.3% rear.

BODY estate car/station wagon; 4 + 1 doors.

OPTIONAL ACCESSORIES reclining backrests with head-rests.

12 TS Berline

See 12 L Berline, except for:

PRICE IN GB: £ 991.
PRICE EX WORKS: 14,900 francs.

ENGINE compression ratio: 9.5:1; max power (DIN): 65 hp at 5,500 rpm; max torque (DIN): 71 lb ft, 9.8 kg m at 3,500 rpm; 50.4 hp/l; 1 Weber 39 DIR downdraught carburettor.

PERFORMANCE max speed: (I) 27 mph, 43 km/h; (II) 43 mph, 69 km/h; (III) 72 mph, 116 km/h; (IV) 94 mph, 152 km/h; power-weight ratio: 30.8 lb/hp, 14 kg/hp; carrying capacity: 860 lb, 390 kg; speed in top at 1,000 rpm: 16.5 mph, 26.5 km/h.

BRAKES servo.

ELECTRICAL EQUIPMENT R 24C 34 distributor; 4 headlamps, iodine long distance lights.

DIMENSIONS AND WEIGHT tracks: 52.13 in, 1,324 mm

12 TS BERLINE

front, 52.13 in, 1,324 mm rear; width: 63.62 in, 1,616 mm; height: 53.35 in, 1,355 mm; ground clearance: 4.41 in, 112 mm; dry weight: 2,007 lb, 910 kg.

BODY separate front seats, reclining backrets, built-in headrests; electrically-heated rear window (standard).

PRACTICAL INSTRUCTIONS engine sump oil: 5.3 imp pt, 6.3 US pt, 3 l, SAE 20W-40; tappet clearances: inlet 0.006 in, 0.15 mm; exhaust 0.012 in, 0.20 mm; valve timing: 22° 62° 65° 25°; tyre pressure front 26 psi, 1.8 atm, rear 28 psi, 2 atm.

12 Gordini

See 12 L Berline, except for:

PRICE EX WORKS: 19,200 francs.

ENGINE 95.5 cu in, 1,565 cc (3.03 x 3.31 in, 77 x 84 mm); compression ratio: 10.2:1; max power (DIN): 113 hp at 6,250 rpm; max torque (DIN): 104 lb ft, 14.3 kg m at 5,500 rpm; max engine rpm: 6,500; 72.2 hp/l; light alloy cylinder block, wet liners; valves: Vee-slanted; lubrication: rotary pump, full flow filter, oil cooler, 8.4 imp pt, 10.1 US pt, 4.8 l; 2 Weber 45 DCOE 38/39 horizontal twin barrel carburettors; cooling system capacity: 9.9 imp pt, 11.8 US pt, 5.6 l, electric thermostatic fan.

TRANSMISSION gears: 5, fully synchronized; ratios: I 3.610, II 2.330, III 1.610, IV 1.210, V 0.970, rev 3.080; width of rims: 5.5"; tyres: 155 x 330.

PERFORMANCE max speeds: (I) 32 mph, 51 km/h; (II) 49 mph, 79 km/h; (III) 71 mph, 115 km/h; (IV) 94 mph, 152 km/h; (V) 115 mph, 185 km/h; power-weight ratio: 19 lb/hp, 8.6 kg/hp; speed in top at 1,000 rpm: 18.1 mph, 29.1 km/h; fuel consumption: 28.2 m/imp gal, 23.5 m/US gal, 10 l x 100 km.

STEERING turns lock to lock: 2.60.

BRAKES disc, front internal radial fins, dual circuit, servo; swept area: front 157.2 sq in, 1,014 sq cm, rear 157.2 sq in, 1,014 sq cm, total 314.4 sq in, 2,028 sq cm.

ELECTRICAL EQUIPMENT 45 Ah battery; 30/40 A alternator; 4 headlamps, iodine long distance lights.

DIMENSIONS AND WEIGHT tracks: 52.76 in, 1,340 mm front, 50.87 in, 1,292 mm rear; length: 169.29 in, 4,300 mm; width: 64.41 in, 1,536 mm; height: 54.92 in, 1,395 mm; dry weight: 2,161 lb, 980 kg; distribution of weight: 58.2% front, 41.8% rear; fuel tank: 19.6 imp gal, 23.5 US gal, 89 l.

PRACTICAL INSTRUCTIONS fuel: 98-100 oct petrol; engine sump oil: 7 imp pt, 8.5 US pt, 4 l; tappet clearances: inlet 0.010 in, 0.25 mm, exhaust 0.014 in, 0.35 mm; valve timing: 40° 72° 72° 40°; tyre pressure: front 27 psi, 1.9 atm, rear 27 psi, 1.9 atm.

OPTIONAL ACCESSORIES headrests.

15 TL

PRICE IN GB: £ 1,133.
PRICE EX WORKS: 16,500 francs.

ENGINE front, 4 stroke; 4 cylinders, vertical, in line; 78.7 cu in, 1,289 cc (2.87 x 3.03 in, 73 x 77 mm); compression ratio: 9.5:1; max power (DIN): 60 hp at 5,500 rpm; max torque (DIN): 71 lb ft, 9.8 kg m at 3,500 rpm; max engine rpm: 6,000; 46.5 hp/l; cast iron cylinder block, light alloy head, wet liners; 5 crankshaft bearings; valves: overhead, in line, slanted, push-rods and rockers; camshafts: 1, side; lubrication: gear pump, full flow filter, 5.3 imp pt, 6.3 US pt, 3 l; 1 Weber 32 DIR downdraught twin barrel carburettor; fuel feed: mechanical pump; sealed circuit cooling, liquid, 9.7 imp pt, 11.6 US pt, 5.5 l, electric thermostatic fan.

TRANSMISSION driving wheels: front; clutch: single dry plate (diaphragm); gearbox: mechanical; gears: 4, fully synchronized; ratios: I 3.610, II 2.260, III 1.480, IV 1.030, rev 3.080; lever: central; final drive: hypoid bevel; axle ratio: 3.770; width of rims: 4.5"; tyres: 145 x 13.

PERFORMANCE max speeds: (I) 29 mph, 46 km/h; (II) 46 mph, 74 km/h; (III) 70 mph, 113 km/h; (IV) over 93 mph, 150 km/h; power-weight ratio: 35.3 lb/hp, 16 kg/hp; carrying capacity: 706 lb, 320 kg; speed in top at 1,000 rpm: 16.8 mph, 27 km/h; fuel consumption: 28.5 m/imp gal, 23.8 m/US gal, 9 l x 100 km.

CHASSIS integral; front suspension: independent, wishbones, anti-roll bar, coil springs/telescopic dampers; rear suspension: rigid axle, trailing arms, A-bracket, anti-roll bar, coil springs/telescopic dampers.

RENAULT 15 TS

RENAULT 16 L

RENAULT 17 TS Convertible

STEERING rack-and-pinion; turns lock to lock: 3.50.

BRAKES front disc, rear drum, rear compensator, servo; swept area: front 157.2 sq in, 1,014 sq cm, rear 70.1 sq in, 452 sq cm, total 227.3 sq in, 1,466 sq cm.

ELECTRICAL EQUIPMENT 12 V; 40 Ah battery; 40 A alternator; 2 headlamps.

DIMENSIONS AND WEIGHT wheel base: 96.06 in, 2,440 mm; tracks: 51.57 in, 1,310 mm front, 51.57 in, 1,310 mm rear; length: 167.72 in, 4,260 mm; width: 64.17 in, 1,630 mm; height: 51.57 in, 1,310 mm; ground clearance: 5.31 in, 135 mm; dry weight: 2,128 lb, 965 kg; turning circle (between walls): 35.1 ft, 10.7 m; fuel tank: 12.1 imp gal, 14.5 US gal, 55 l.

BODY saloon/sedan; 2 doors; 4 seats, separate front seats, reclining backrests.

PRACTICAL INSTRUCTIONS fuel: 98-100 oct petrol; engine sump oil: 5.3 imp pt, 6.3 US pt, 3 l, change every 3,100 miles, 5,000 km; gearbox and final drive oil: 3.5 imp pt, 4.2 US pt, 2 l, change every 6,200 miles, 10,000 km; greasing: none; tappet clearances: inlet 0.006 in, 0.15 mm, exhaust 0.008 in, 0.20 mm; valve timing: 22° 62° 65° 25°; tyre pressure: front 26 psi, 1.8 atm, rear 27 psi, 1.9 atm.

OPTIONAL ACCESSORIES headrests; electrically-controlled windows; electrically-heated rear window; luxury interior; metallic spray.

15 TS

See 15 TL, except for:

PRICE IN GB: £ 1,240.
PRICE EX WORKS: 18,500 francs.

ENGINE 95.5 cu in, 1,565 cc (3.03 x 3.31 in, 77 x 84 mm); compression ratio: 9.2:1; max power (DIN): 90 hp at 5,500 rpm; max torque (DIN): 91 lb ft, 12.5 kg m at 3,000 rpm; 57.5 hp/l; light alloy cylinder block, hemispherical combustion chambers; valves: Vee-slanted; lubrication: eccentric pump, 7 imp pt, 8.5 US pt, 4 l.

TRANSMISSION axle ratio: 3.550; tyres: 155 x 13.

PERFORMANCE max speeds: (I) 30 mph, 49 km/h; (II) 48 mph, 78 km/h; (III) 75 mph, 120 km/h; (IV) 106 mph, 170 km/h; power-weight ratio: 24.7 lb/hp, 11.2 kg/hp; speed in top at 1,000 rpm: 17.8 mph, 28.7 km/h; fuel consumption: 26.9 m/imp gal, 22.4 m/US gal, 10.5 l x 100 km.

BRAKES front disc with internal radial fins; swept area: rear 89 sq in, 574 sq cm, total 246.2 sq in, 1,588 sq cm.

DIMENSIONS AND WEIGHT front track: 52.76 in, 1,340 mm; dry weight: 2,216 lb, 1,005 kg; turning circle (between walls): 35.4 ft, 10.8 m.

PRACTICAL INSTRUCTIONS engine sump oil: 7 imp pt, 8.5 US pt, 4 l; tappet clearances: inlet 0.008 in, 0.20 mm, exhaust 0.010 in, 0.25 mm; valve timing: 24° 68° 68° 24°.

OPTIONAL ACCESSORIES automatic transmission, hydraulic torque converter and planetary gears with 3 ratios (I 2.396, II 1.484, III 1.027, rev 2.054), max ratio of converter at stall 2.3, possible manual selection, max speed about 103 mph, 165 km/h.

16 L

PRICE IN GB: £ 1,009.
PRICE IN USA: $ 2,825.

ENGINE front, 4 stroke; 4 cylinders, vertical, in line; 95.5 cu in, 1,565 cc (3.03 x 3.31 in, 77 x 84 mm); compression ratio: 8.6:1; max power (DIN): 64.5 hp at 5,200 rpm; max torque (DIN): 78 lb ft, 10.7 kg m at 3,000 rpm; max engine rpm: 5,500; 41.2 hp/l; light alloy cylinder block and head, wet liners; 5 crankshaft bearings; valves: overhead, in line, slanted at 20°, push-rods and rockers; camshafts: 1, side; lubrication: eccentric pump, filter in sump, 7 imp pt, 8.5 US pt, 4 l; 1 Weber 32 DIR downdraught carburettor; fuel feed: mechanical pump; sealed circuit cooling, liquid, 11.6 imp pt, 14 US pt, 6.6 l, electric thermostatic fan.

TRANSMISSION driving wheels: front; clutch: single dry plate (diaphragm); gearbox: mechanical; gears: 4, fully synchronized; ratios: I 3.610, II 2.260, III 1.480, IV 1.030, rev 3.080; lever: steering column; final drive: hypoid bevel; axle ratio: 3.770; width of rims: 4.5"; tyres: 145 x 355.

PERFORMANCE max speeds: (I) 27 mph, 43 km/h; (II) 43 mph, 70 km/h; (III) 67 mph, 108 km/h; (IV) over 93 mph, 150 km/h; power-weight ratio: 34.5 lb/hp, 15.7 kg/hp; carrying capacity: 882 lb, 400 kg; acceleration: 0-50 mph (0-80 km/h) 10.7 sec; speed in top at 1,000 rpm: 17.2 mph, 27.7 km/h; fuel consumption: 28.2 m/imp gal, 23.5 m/US gal, 10 l x 100 km.

RENAULT 15 TS

RENAULT 16 TS

RENAULT 17 TS Coupé

CHASSIS integral; front suspension: independent, wishbones, longitudinal torsion bars, anti-roll bar, telescopic dampers; rear suspension: independent, swinging longitudinal trailing arms, transverse torsion bars, anti-roll bar, telescopic dampers.

STEERING rack-and-pinion; turns lock to lock: 4.

BRAKES front disc (diameter 10 in, 254 mm), rear drum, rear compensator, servo; swept area: front 180.2 sq in, 1,162 sq cm, rear 41.9 sq in, 270 sq cm, total 222 sq in, 1,432 sq cm.

ELECTRICAL EQUIPMENT 12 V; 40 Ah battery; 30/40 A alternator; 2 headlamps.

DIMENSIONS AND WEIGHT wheel base: 104.33 in, 2,650 mm (right), 106.97 in, 2,717 mm (left); tracks: 52.83 in, 1,342 mm front, 50.87 in, 1,292 mm rear; length: 166.81 in, 4,237 mm; width: 64.88 in, 1,648 mm; height: 57.09 in, 1,450 mm; ground clearance: 4.53 in, 115 mm; dry weight: 2,227 lb, 1,010 kg; distribution of weight: 56.2% front, 43.8% rear; turning circle (between walls): 34.8 ft, 10.6 m; fuel tank: 11 imp gal, 13.2 US gal, 50 l.

BODY saloon/sedan; 4 + 1 doors; 5-6 seats, separate front seats; back seat folding down to luggage table.

PRACTICAL INSTRUCTIONS engine sump oil: 7 imp pt, 8.5 US pt, 4 l, SAE 10W-40, change every 3,100 miles, 5,000 km; gearbox and final drive oil: 2.8 imp pt, 3.4 US pt, 1.6 l, SAE 80 EP, change every 6,200 miles, 10,000 km; greasing: none; tappet clearances: inlet 0.008 in, 0.20 mm, exhaust 0.010 in, 0.25 mm; valve timing: 10° 42° 46° 10°; tyre pressure: front 23 psi, 1.6 atm, rear 28 psi, 2 atm.

OPTIONAL ACCESSORIES automatic transmission, hydraulic torque converter and planetary gears with 3 ratios (I 2.396, II 1.484, III 1.027, rev 2.054), max ratio of converter at stall 2.3, possible manual selection; headrests; electrically-heated rear window; luxury interior; metallic spray.

16 Commerciale

See 16 L, except for:

PRICE EX WORKS: 14,840 francs.

TRANSMISSION tyres: 155 x 355.

OPTIONAL ACCESSORIES automatic transmission not available; reclining backrests.

16 TL

See 16 L, except for:

PRICE IN GB: £ 1,083.
PRICE EX WORKS: 15,700 francs.

BODY reclining backrests; electrically-heated rear window (standard).

OPTIONAL ACCESSORIES tinted glass; electrically-controlled sunshine roof.

16 TS

See 16 L, except for:

PRICE IN GB: £ 1,216.
PRICE EX WORKS: 17,700.

ENGINE max power (DIN): 83 hp at 5,750 rpm; max torque (DIN): 88 lb ft, 12.2 kg m at 3,500 rpm; max engine rpm: 6,000; 53 hp/l; hemispherical combustion chambers; valves: Vee-slanted; 1 Weber 32 DIR downdraught twin barrel carburettor; cooling system capacity: 12 imp pt, 14.4 US pt, 6.8 l.

TRANSMISSION tyres: 155 x 355.

PERFORMANCE max speeds: (I) 30 mph, 49 km/h; (II) 49 mph, 79 km/h; (III) 75 mph, 120 km/h; (IV) 103 mph, 165 km/h; power-weight ratio: 28 lb/hp, 12.7 kg/hp; speed in top at 1,000 rpm: 17.8 mph, 28.6 km/h.

ELECTRICAL EQUIPMENT iodine long distance lights.

DIMENSIONS AND WEIGHT dry weight: 2,337 lb, 1,060 kg.

BODY separate front seats, reclining backrests; electrically-controlled windows; electrically-heated rear window (standard).

PRACTICAL INSTRUCTIONS valve timing: 21° 59° 59° 21°.

OPTIONAL ACCESSORIES leather upholstery; tinted glass; electrically-controlled sunshine roof.

16 TS Commerciale

See 16 TS, except for:

PRICE EX WORKS: 17,260 francs.

17 TL Coupé

See 15 TS, except for:

PRICE IN GB: £ 1,360.
PRICE EX WORKS: 19,600 francs.

PERFORMANCE power-weight ratio: 24.9 lb/hp, 11.3 kg/hp.

ELECTRICAL EQUIPMENT 4 headlamps, iodine long distance lights.

DIMENSIONS AND WEIGHT rear track: 52.76 in, 1,340 mm; dry weight: 2,238 lb, 1,015 kg.

BODY coupé; electrically-heated rear window (standard); electrically-controlled windows (standard).

OPTIONAL ACCESSORIES leather upholstery.

17 TL Convertible

See 17 TL Coupé, except for:

PRICE EX WORKS: 21,100 francs.

PERFORMANCE power-weight ratio: 25.4 lb/hp, 11.5 kg/hp.

DIMENSIONS AND WEIGHT dry weight: 2,282 lb, 1,035 kg.

BODY convertible.

OPTIONAL ACCESSORIES hardtop; electrically-controlled soft-top.

17 TS Coupé

See 15 TS, except for:

PRICE IN GB: £ 1,704.
PRICE EX WORKS: 24,600 francs.

ENGINE compression ratio: 10.25:1; max power (DIN): 90 hp at 5,500 rpm; max torque (DIN): 91 lb ft, 12.5 kg m at 3,000 rpm; max engine rpm: 6,500; 56.8 hp/l; lubrication: eccentric pump, oil cooler, 8.4 imp pt, 10.1 US pt, 4.8 l; electronically-controlled injection system; cooling system capacity: 9.9 imp pt, 11.8 US pt, 5.6 l.

TRANSMISSION gears: 5, fully synchronized; ratios: I 3.620, II 2.340, III 1.610, IV 1.220, V 0.940, rev 3.080; axle ratio: 3.770; width of rims: 5.5''; tyres: 165 x 13.

PERFORMANCE max speeds: (I) 32 mph, 52 km/h; (II) 50 mph, 80 km/h; (III) 73 mph, 117 km/h; (IV) 96 mph, 154 km/h; (V) over 112 mph, 180 km/h; power-weight ratio: 25.8 lb/hp, 11.7 kg/hp; speed in top at 1,000 rpm: 19.1 mph, 30.7 km/h; fuel consumption: 27.7 m/imp gal, 23.1 m/US gal, 10.2 l x 100 km.

BRAKES disc, front internal radial fins, rear compensator, servo; swept area: front 157.2 sq in, 1,014 sq cm, rear 157.2 sq in, 1,014 sq cm, total 314.4 sq in, 2,028 sq cm.

ELECTRICAL EQUIPMENT 4 headlamps, iodine long distance lights.

DIMENSIONS AND WEIGHT rear track: 52.76 in, 1,340 mm; dry weight: 2,326 lb, 1,055 kg.

BODY coupé; electrically-heated rear window (standard); electrically-controlled windows (standard).

PRACTICAL INSTRUCTIONS tappet clearances: inlet 0.010 in, 0.25 mm, exhaust 0.012 in, 0.30 mm; valve timing: 40° 72° 72° 40°; tyre pressure: front 24 psi, 1.7 atm, rear 27 psi, 1.9 atm.

OPTIONAL ACCESSORIES automatic transmission not available; leather upholstery; tinted glass.

17 TS Convertible

See 17 TS Coupé, except for:

PRICE EX WORKS: 26,100 francs.

PERFORMANCE power-weight ratio: 26.2 lb/hp, 11.9 kg/hp.

DIMENSIONS AND WEIGHT dry weight: 2,370 lb, 1,075 kg.

BODY convertible.

OPTIONAL ACCESSORIES **hardtop;** electrically-controlled soft-top.

TRABANT 601

WARTBURG 353 De Luxe

NSU Prinz 4L

TRABANT GERMANY (D.D.R.)

601 Limousine

ENGINE front, transverse, 2 stroke; 2 cylinders, in line; 36.2 cu in, 594 cc (2.83 x 2.87 in, 72 x 73 mm); compression ratio: 7.6:1; max power (SAE): 30 hp at 4,200 rpm; max torque (SAE): 46 lb ft, 6.3 kg m at 3,000 rpm; max engine rpm: 4,500; 50.5 hp/l; light alloy cylinder block and head; 3 crankshaft bearings; valves: 1 per cylinder, rotary; lubrication: mixture; 1 BVF type 28 HB 2-7 horizontal single barrel carburettor; fuel feed: gravity; air-cooled.

TRANSMISSION driving wheels: front; clutch: single dry plate; gearbox: mechanical; gears: 4, fully synchronized; ratios: I 4.080, II 2.320, III 1.520, IV 1.030, rev 3.830; lever: on facia; final drive: conic bevel; axle ratio: 4.330; width of rims: 4''; tyres: 5.20 x 13.

PERFORMANCE max speeds: (I) 16 mph, 25 km/h; (II) 28 mph, 45 km/h; (III) 43 mph, 70 km/h; (IV) 62 mph, 100 km/h; power-weight ratio: 45.2 lb/hp, 20.5 kg/hp; carrying capacity: 849 lb, 385 kg; acceleration: 0-50 mph (0-80 km/h) 18 sec; speed in top at 1,000 rpm: 14.6 mph, 23.5 km/h; fuel consumption: 40.4 m/imp gal, 33.6 m/US gal, 7 l x 100 km.

CHASSIS integral; front suspension: independent, wishbones, transverse leafspring upper arms, telescopic dampers; rear suspension: independent, swinging semi-axles, transverse semi-elliptic leafspring, telescopic dampers.

STEERING rack-and-pinion; turns lock to lock: 2.60.

BRAKES drum, single circuit; swept area: front 38.9 sq in, 251 sq cm, rear 34.1 sq in, 220 sq cm, total 73 sq in, 471 sq cm.

ELECTRICAL EQUIPMENT 6 V; 56 Ah battery; 220 W dynamo; AKA distributor; 2 headlamps.

DIMENSIONS AND WEIGHT wheel base: 79.53 in, 2,020 mm; tracks: 47.48 in, 1,206 mm front, 49.41 in, 1,255 mm rear. length: 139.96 in, 3,555 mm; width: 59.25 in, 1,505 mm; height: 56.69 in, 1,440 mm; ground clearance: 6.10 in, 155 mm; dry weight: 1,356 lb, 615 kg; distribution of weight: 45% front, 55% rear; turning circle (between walls): 32.8 ft, 10 m; fuel tank: 5.3 imp gal, 6.3 US gal, 24 l.

BODY saloon/sedan; 2 doors; 4 seats, separate front seats, reclining backrests.

PRACTICAL INSTRUCTIONS fuel: mixture 1:33.3, 88 oct petrol, SAE 10W-30, oil in separate tank; gearbox and final drive oil: 2.6 imp pt, 3.2 US pt, 1.5 l, SAE 20W-30, change every 9,300 miles, 15,000 km; greasing: every 3,100 miles, 5,000 km, 9 points; sparking plug type: 260°; valve timing: 45° 45° 72°5' 72°5'; tyre pressure: front 20 psi, 1.4 atm, rear 20 psi, 1.4 atm.

OPTIONAL ACCESSORIES Hycomat automatic clutch.

601 Universal

See 601 Limousine, except for:

PERFORMANCE power-weight ratio: 47.6 lb/hp, 21.6 kg/hp; carrying capacity: 860 lb, 390 kg.

DIMENSIONS AND WEIGHT length: 140.16 in, 3,560 mm; width: 59.45 in, 1,510 mm; height: 57.87 in, 1,470 mm; dry weight: 1,433 lb, 650 kg; distribution of weight: 44% front, 56% rear.

BODY estate car/station wagon; 2 + 1 doors.

WARTBURG GERMANY (D.D.R.)

353

PRICE IN GB: £ 746.

ENGINE front, 2 stroke; 3 cylinders, vertical, in line; 60.5 cu in, 992 cc (2.89 x 3.07 in, 73.5 x 78 mm); compression ratio: 7.5:1; max power (SAE): 55 hp at 4,250 rpm; max torque (DIN): 72 lb ft, 10 kg m at 3,000 rpm; max engine rpm: 5,000; 55.4 hp/l; cast iron cylinder block, light alloy head; 4 crankshaft bearings; lubrication: mixture 1:33; 1 BVF 40 F 1-11 single barrel carburettor; fuel feed: mechanical pump; sealed circuit cooling, liquid, 13.2 imp pt, 15.9 US pt, 7.5 l.

TRANSMISSION driving wheels: front; clutch: single dry plate; gearbox: mechanical; gears: 4, fully synchronized; ratios: I 3.769, II 2.160, III 1.347, IV 0.906, rev 3.385; lever: steering column; final drive: spiral bevel; axle ratio: 4.222; width of rims: 4.5''; tyres: 6.00 x 13.

TRABANT 601 Limousine

WARTBURG 353 De Luxe

NSU Prinz 4L

PERFORMANCE max speeds: (I) 20 mph, 32 km/h; (II) 35 mph, 57 km/h; (III) 56 mph, 90 km/h; (IV) 81 mph, 130 km/h; power-weight ratio: 35.9 lb/hp, 16.3 kg/hp; carrying capacity: 882 lb, 400 kg; acceleration: standing ¼ mile 22.6 sec, 0-50 mph (0-80 km/h) 14 sec; speed in top at 1,000 rpm: 18 mph, 29 km/h; fuel consumption: 30.4 m/imp gal, 25.3 m/US gal, 9.3 l x 100 km.

CHASSIS box-type ladder frame; front suspension: independent, wishbones, coil springs, rubber elements, telescopic dampers; rear suspension: independent, semi-trailing arms, coil springs, rubber elements, anti-roll bar, telescopic dampers.

STEERING rack-and-pinion; turns lock to lock: 3.50.

BRAKES drum, single circuit, rear compensator; swept area: front 65.9 sq in, 425 sq cm, rear 61.2 sq in, 395 sq cm, total 127.1 sq in, 820 sq cm.

ELECTRICAL EQUIPMENT 12 V; 42 Ah battery; 220 W dynamo; FEK distributor; 2 headlamps.

DIMENSIONS AND WEIGHT wheel base: 96.46 in, 2,450 mm; tracks: 49.61 in, 1,260 mm front, 51.18 in, 1,300 mm rear; length: 166.14 in, 4,220 mm; width: 64.65 in, 1,642 mm; height: 58.86 in, 1,495 mm; ground clearance: 6.10 in, 155 mm; dry weight: 1,985 lb, 900 kg; distribution of weight: 57% front, 43% rear; turning circle (between walls): 33.5 ft, 10.2 m; fuel tank: 9.7 imp gal, 11.6 US gal, 44 l.

BODY saloon/sedan; 4 doors; 5 seats, separate front seats, reclining backrests.

PRACTICAL INSTRUCTIONS fuel: mixture 1:33, SAE 20-40, oil in separate tank; gearbox and final drive oil: 3.2 imp pt, 3.8 US pt, 1.8 l, SAE 90 EP, change every 15,500 miles, 25,000 km; greasing: every 31,100 miles, 50,000 km, 2 points; sparking plug type: 240°; opening timing: 62°17' 62°17' 78°2' 78°2'; tyre pressure: front 23 psi, 1.6 atm, rear 24 psi, 1.7 atm.

OPTIONAL ACCESSORIES 165 SR x 13 tyres; sunshine roof; luxury version.

353 Tourist

See 353, except for:

PRICE IN GB: £ 832.

PERFORMANCE max speed: 78 mph, 125 km/h; power-weight ratio: 38.4 lb/hp, 17.4 kg/hp; carrying capacity: 992 lb, 450 kg; fuel consumption 29.7 m/imp gal, 24.8 m/US gal, 9.5 l x 100 km.

DIMENSIONS AND WEIGHT length: 172.44 in, 4,380 mm; dry weight: 2,117 lb, 960 kg.

BODY estate car/station wagon; 4 + 1 doors.

PRACTICAL INSTRUCTIONS tyre pressure: front 24 psi, 1.7 atm, rear 36 psi, 2.5 atm.

AUDI NSU GERMANY (F.R.)

NSU Prinz 4L

PRICE EX WORKS: 5,190 marks.

ENGINE rear, transverse, 4 stroke; 2 cylinders, in line; 36.5 cu in, 598 cc (2.99 x 2.60 in, 76 x 66 mm); compression ratio: 7.5:1; max power (DIN): 30 hp at 5,600 rpm; max torque (DIN): 33 lb ft, 4.5 kg m at 3,000 rpm; max engine rpm: 6,500; 50.2 hp/l; cast iron cylinder block, light alloy head; 2 crankshaft bearings; valves: overhead, Vee-slanted, rockers; camshafts: 1, overhead, driven by connecting rods; lubrication: gear pump, full flow filter, 4.8 imp pt, 5.7 US pt, 2.7 l; 1 Solex 34 PCI downdraught carburettor; fuel feed: mechanical pump; air-cooled.

TRANSMISSION driving wheels: rear; clutch: single dry plate; gearbox: mechanical; engine-gearbox ratio: 2.08; gears: 4, fully synchronized; ratios: I 4.140, II 2.210, III 1.410, IV 1, rev 5.380; lever: central; final drive: hypoid bevel; axle ratio: 2.310; width of rims: 4"; tyres: 5.65/135 x 12

PERFORMANCE max speeds: (I) 21 mph, 33 km/h; (II) 38 mph, 61 km/h; (III) 60 mph, 96 km/h; (IV) 75 mph, 120 km/h; power-weight ratio: 40.8 lb/hp, 18.5 kg/hp; carrying capacity: 981 lb, 445 kg; acceleration: standing ¼ mile 23.6 sec, 0-50 mph (0-80 km/h) 15.8 sec; speed in direct drive at 1,000 rpm: 13 mph, 20.9 km/h; fuel consumption: 49.6 m/imp gal, 41.3 m/US gal, 5.7 l x 100 km.

CHASSIS integral; front suspension: independent, wishbones, coil springs, anti-roll bar, telescopic dampers; rear suspension: independent, swinging semi-axles, wide-based wishbones, coil springs, Prinzair auxiliary air rubber springs, telescopic dampers.

NSU PRINZ 4L

STEERING rack-and-pinion; turns lock to lock: 3.

BRAKES drum, 2 front leading shoes; swept area: total 58.5 sq in, 377 sq cm.

ELECTRICAL EQUIPMENT 12 V; 32 Ah battery; 130 W dynamo; Bosch distributor; 2 headlamps.

DIMENSIONS AND WEIGHT wheel base: 80.31 in, 2,040 mm; tracks: 48.43 in, 1,230 mm front, 47.24 in, 1,200 mm rear; length: 135.43 in, 3,440 mm; width: 58.66 in, 1,490 mm; height: 53.54 in, 1,360 mm; ground clearance: 7.09 in, 180 mm; dry weight: 1,224 lb, 555 kg; distribution of weight: 44% front, 56% rear; turning circle (between walls): 28.9 ft, 8.8 m; fuel tank: 8.1 imp gal, 9.8 US gal, 37 l.

BODY saloon/sedan; 2 doors; 4 seats, separate front seats.

PRACTICAL INSTRUCTIONS fuel: 85-90 oct petrol; engine sump, gearbox and final drive oil: 4.2 imp pt, 5.1 US pt, 2.4 l, SAE 20 (winter) 30 (summer), change every 4,700 miles, 7,500 km; greasing: every 4,700 miles, 7,500 km, 2 points; sparking plug type: 225°; tappet clearances: inlet 0.008 in, 0.20 mm, exhaust 0.008 in, 0.20 mm; valve timing: 48° 72° 78° 42°; tyre pressure: front 20 psi, 1.4 atm, rear 24 psi, 1.7 atm.

OPTIONAL ACCESSORIES front disc brakes, diameter 8.94 in, 227 mm; sunshine roof.

NSU 1000 C

PRICE EX WORKS: 5,990 marks.

ENGINE rear, transverse, 4 stroke; 4 cylinders, in line; 60.8 cu in, 996 cc (2.72 x 2.62 in, 69 x 66.6 mm); compression ratio: 7.5:1; max power (DIN): 40 hp at 5,500 rpm; max torque (DIN): 51 lb ft, 7 kg m at 3,500 rpm; max engine rpm: 5,800; 40.2 hp/l; light alloy cylinder block and head; 5 crankshaft bearings; valves: overhead, Vee-slanted, rockers; camshafts: 1, overhead; lubrication: gear pump, full flow filter, 6.2 imp pt, 7.4 US pt, 3.5 l; 1 Solex 34 PCI downdraught single barrel carburettor; fuel feed: mechanical pump; air-cooled.

TRANSMISSION driving wheels: rear; clutch: single dry plate; gearbox: mechanical; engine-gearbox ratio: 2.05; gears: 4, fully synchronized; ratios: I 4.356, II 2.403, III 1.538, IV 1.100, rev 4.869; lever: central; final drive: cylindrical gears; axle ratio: 3.786; width of rims: 4.5"; tyres: 5.50 x 12.

PERFORMANCE max speeds: (I) 22 mph, 36 km/h; (II) 40 mph, 65 km/h; (III) 63 mph, 102 km/h; (IV) 81 mph, 130 km/h; power-weight ratio: 36.4 lb/hp, 16.5 kg/hp; carrying capacity: 882 lb, 400 kg; speed in top at 1,000 rpm: 15.5 mph, 25 km/h; fuel consumption: 33.6 m/imp gal, 28 m/US gal, 8.4 l x 100 km.

CHASSIS integral; front suspension: independent, wishbones, coil springs, anti-roll bar, telescopic dampers; rear suspension: independent, semi-trailing arms, coil springs, telescopic dampers.

STEERING rack-and-pinion; turns lock to lock: 3.50.

BRAKES drum; swept area: front 45.3 sq in, 292 sq cm, rear 28.5 sq in, 184 sq cm, total 73.8 sq in, 476 sq cm.

ELECTRICAL EQUIPMENT 12 V; 32 Ah battery; 350 W dynamo; Bosch distributor; 2 headlamps.

DIMENSIONS AND WEIGHT wheel base: 88.58 in, 2,250 mm; tracks: 49.61 in, 1,260 mm front, 49.13 in, 1,248 mm rear; length: 149.33 in, 3,793 mm; width: 58.66 in, 1,490 mm; height: 53.70 in, 1,364 mm; ground clearance: 5.31 in, 135 mm; dry weight: 1,455 lb, 660 kg; distribution of weight: 41.6% front, 58.4% rear; turning circle (between walls): 30.8 ft, 9.4 m; fuel tank: 8.1 imp gal, 9.8 US gal, 37 l.

BODY saloon/sedan; 2 doors; 5 seats, separate front seats.

PRACTICAL INSTRUCTIONS fuel: 85-90 oct petrol; engine sump oil: 6.2 imp pt, 7.4 US pt, 3.5 l, SAE 10W-30, change every 4,700 miles, 7,500 km; gearbox and final drive oil: 3.5 imp pt, 4.2 US pt, 2 l, SAE 80, change every 4,700 miles, 7,500 km; greasing: none; sparking plug type: 225°; tappet clearances: inlet 0.008 in, 0.20 mm, exhaust 0.008 in, 0.20 mm; tyre pressure: front 18 psi, 1.3 atm, rear 27 psi, 1.9 atm.

OPTIONAL ACCESSORIES 145 x 12 tyres; front disc brakes (diameter 9.02 in, 229 mm); sunshine roof.

NSU 1200 C

PRICE EX WORKS: 6,690 marks.

ENGINE rear, transverse, 4 stroke; 4 cylinders, in line; 71.8 cu in, 1,177 cc (2.95 x 2.62 in, 75 x 66.6 mm); compression ratio: 7.8:1; max power (DIN): 55 hp at 5,600 rpm; max torque (DIN): 62 lb ft, 8.5 kg m at 2,500-4,500 rpm; max engine rpm: 5,800; 46.7 hp/l; light alloy cylinder block and head; 5 crankshaft bearings; valves: overhead, Vee-slanted, rockers; camshafts: 1, overhead; lubrication: gear pump, full flow filter, 6.2 imp pt, 7.4 US pt, 3.5 l; 1 Solex 34 PCI downdraught single barrel carburettor; fuel feed: mechanical pump; air-cooled.

TRANSMISSION driving wheels: rear; clutch: single dry plate, hydraulically controlled; gearbox: mechanical; gears: 4, fully synchronized; ratios: I 4.356, II 2.403, III 1.538, IV 1.100, rev 4.869; lever: central; final drive: cylindrical gears; axle ratio: 3.786, width of rims: 4.5"; tyres: 6.15/155 x 13.

PERFORMANCE max speeds: (I) 23 mph, 37 km/h; (II) 41 mph, 66 km/h; (III) 65 mph, 104 km/h; (IV) 90 mph, 145 km/h; power-weight ratio: 28.9 lb/hp, 13.1 kg/hp; carrying capacity: 904 lb, 410 kg; acceleration: 0-50 mph (0-80 km/h) 9.4 sec; speed in top at 1,000 rpm: 15.5 mph, 25 km/h; fuel consumption: 32.1 m/imp gal, 26.7 m/US gal, 8.8 l x 100 km.

CHASSIS integral; front suspension: independent, wishbones, lower trailing links, coil springs, anti-roll bar, telescopic dampers; rear suspension: independent, semi-trailing arms, coil springs, telescopic dampers.

STEERING rack-and-pinion; turns lock to lock: 3.20.

BRAKES drum; swept area: total 90.5 sq in, 584 sq cm.

ELECTRICAL EQUIPMENT 12 V; 32 Ah battery; 350 W dynamo; Bosch distributor; 2 headlamps.

DIMENSIONS AND WEIGHT wheel base: 96.06 in, 2,440 mm; tracks: 50.39 in, 1,280 mm front, 49.13 in, 1,248 mm rear; length: 157.48 in, 4,000 mm; width: 59.06 in, 1,500 mm; height: 54.72 in, 1,390 mm; ground clearance: 7.48 in, 190 mm; dry weight: 1,588 lb, 720 kg; distribution of weight: 45% front, 55% rear; turning circle (between walls): 32.5 ft, 9.9 m; fuel tank: 9.7 imp gal, 11.6 US gal, 44 l.

BODY saloon/sedan; 2 doors; 4-5 seats, separate front seats.

PRACTICAL INSTRUCTIONS fuel: 85-90 oct petrol; engine sump oil: 6.2 imp pt, 7.4 US pt, 3.5 l, SAE 10W-30, change every 4,700 miles, 7,500 km; gearbox and final drive oil: 3.5 imp pt, 4.2 US pt, 2 l, SAE 80; greasing: none; sparking plug type: 225°; tappet clearances: inlet 0.008 in, 0.20 mm, exhaust 0.008 in, 0.20 mm; valve timing: 20° 50° 55° 25°; tyre pressure: front 17 psi, 1.2 atm, rear 21 psi, 1.5 atm.

OPTIONAL ACCESSORIES front disc brakes, diameter 9.02 in, 229 mm; sunshine roof.

NSU 1200 C Automatic

See NSU 1200 C, except for:

PRICE EX WORKS: 7,190 marks.

TRANSMISSION gearbox: 3-speed semi-automatic transmission; ratios: I 2.995, II 1.679, III 1.095, rev 3.845.

NSU Ro 80

PRICE IN GB: £ 2,439.
PRICE EX WORKS: 17,590 marks.

ENGINE front, 4 stroke, Wankel type; 2 co-axial 3-lobe rotors; 30.3 x 2 cu in, 495.5 x 2 cc; compression ratio: 9:1; max power (DIN): 115 hp at 5,500 rpm; max torque (DIN): 121 lb ft, 16.7 kg m at 4,500 rpm; max engine rpm: 6,500; engine block: light alloy; rotors: light alloy; 2 crankshaft bearings; lubrication: gear pump, full flow filter, oil-water heat exchanger, 13.4 imp pt, 16.1 US pt, 7.6 l; 2 Solex 18/32 HHD horizontal carburettors, cleaner air system; fuel feed: mechanical pump; water-cooled engine block, oil-cooled rotors, 16.7 imp pt, 20.1 US pt, 9.5 l.

TRANSMISSION driving wheels: front; clutch: single dry plate automatically operated by gear lever; gearbox: 3-speed semi-automatic transmission, hydraulic torque converter, max ratio of converter at stall 2, possible manual selection; ratios: I 2.056, II 1.208, III 0.788, rev 2.105; lever: central; final drive: cylindrical gears; axle ratio: 4.857; width of rims: 5"; tyres: 175 HR x 14.

PERFORMANCE max speeds: (I) 47 mph, 75 km/h; (II) 80 mph, 129 km/h; (III) 112 mph, 180 km/h; power-weight ratio: 24.5 lb/hp, 11.1 kg/hp; carrying capacity: 992 lb, 450 kg; speed in top at 1,000 rpm: 18.8 mph, 30.3 km/h; fuel consumption: 25.2 m/imp gal, 21 m/US gal, 11.2 l x 100 km.

CHASSIS integral; front suspension: independent, by McPherson, coil springs/telescopic damper struts, lower articulated wishbones, anti-roll bar; rear suspension: independent, semi-trailing arms, coil springs, telescopic dampers.

STEERING rack-and-pinion, ZF servo; turns lock to lock: 3.80.

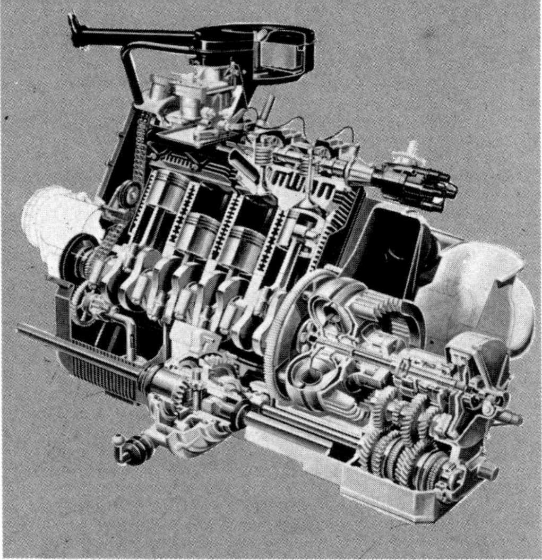

NSU 1200 C Automatic

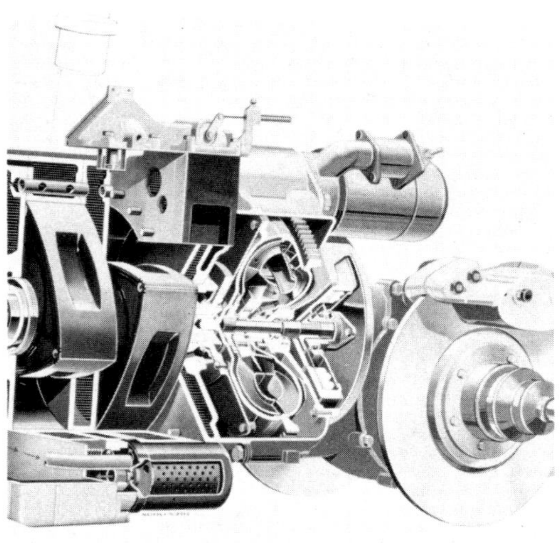

NSU Ro 80

AUDI 80 LS 2-door Limousine

NSU 1200 C

NSU Ro 80

AUDI 80 LS 2-door Limousine

BRAKES disc (front diameter 11.18 in, 284 mm, rear 10.71 in, 272 mm), servo; swept area: front 30.4 sq in, 196 sq cm, rear 12.9 sq in, 83 sq cm, total 43.3 sq in, 279 sq cm.

ELECTRICAL EQUIPMENT 12 V; 66 Ah battery; 770 W alternator; Bosch distributor; 4 headlamps.

DIMENSIONS AND WEIGHT wheel base: 112.60 in, 2,860 mm; tracks: 58.27 in, 1,480 mm front, 56.46 in, 1,434 mm rear; length: 188.19 in, 4,780 mm; width: 69.29 in, 1,760 mm; height: 55.51 in, 1,410 mm; ground clearance: 4.49 in, 114 mm; dry weight: 2,822 lb, 1,280 kg; distribution of weight: 62% front, 38% rear; turning circle (between walls): 38.7 ft, 11.8 m; fuel tank: 18 imp gal, 21.6 US gal, 82 l.

BODY saloon/sedan; 4 doors; 5 seats, separate front seats.

PRACTICAL INSTRUCTIONS fuel: 92 oct petrol; engine sump oil: 13.4 imp pt, 16.1 US pt, 7.6 l, SAE 10W-30; gearbox and final drive oil: 3.5 imp pt, 4.2 US pt, 2 l, SAE 90 change every 12,400 miles, 20,000 km; tyre pressure: front 28 psi, 2 atm, rear 24 psi, 1.7 atm.

OPTIONAL ACCESSORIES light alloy wheels; sunshine roof.

Audi 80 2-door Limousine

PRICE EX WORKS: 7,990 marks.

ENGINE front, 4 stroke; 4 cylinders, in line; 79.1 cu in, 1,297 cc (2.95 x 2.89 in, 75 x 73.4 mm); compression ratio: 8.5:1; max power (DIN): 60 hp at 5,500 rpm; max torque (DIN): 68 lb ft, 9.4 kg m at 2,500 rpm; max engine rpm: 6,500; 46.3 hp/l; cast iron cylinder block, light alloy head; 5 crankshaft bearings; valves: overhead, in line, thimble tappets; camshafts: 1, overhead, cogged belt; lubrication: gear pump, full flow filter, 6.2 imp pt, 7.4 US pt, 3.5 l; 1 Solex 30-35 PDSIT downdraught single barrel carburettor; fuel feed: mechanical pump; water-cooled, 10.9 imp pt, 13.1 US pt, 6.2 l.

TRANSMISSION driving wheels: front; clutch: single dry plate (diaphragm); gearbox: mechanical; gears: 4, fully synchronized; ratios: I 3.454, II 2.055, III 1.370, IV 0.969, rev 3.166; lever: central; final drive: hypoid bevel; axle ratio: 4.556; width of rims: 4.5''; tyres: 6.15 or 155 x 13.

PERFORMANCE max speeds: (I) 25 mph, 41 km/h; (II) 42 mph, 68 km/h; (III) 68 mph, 110 km/h; (IV) 90 mph, 145 km/h; power-weight ratio: 30.7 lb/hp, 13.9 kg/hp; acceleration: 0-50 mph (0-80 km/h) 10.8 sec; speed in top at 1,000 rpm: 14.9 mph, 24 km/h; fuel consumption: 32.1 m/imp gal, 26.7 m/US gal, 8.8 l x 100 km.

CHASSIS integral, front auxiliary subframe; front suspension: independent, by McPherson, lower wishbones, anti-roll bar, coil springs/telescopic damper struts; rear suspension: rigid axle trailing radius arms, transverse linkage bar, telescopic damper struts.

STEERING rack-and-pinion; turns lock to lock: 3.94.

BRAKES front disc (diameter 9.43 in, 239 mm), rear drum.

ELECTRICAL EQUIPMENT 12 V; 36 Ah battery; 490 W alternator; Bosch distributor; 2 headlamps.

DIMENSIONS AND WEIGHT wheel base: 97.24 in, 2,470 mm; tracks: 52.76 in, 1,340 mm front, 52.56 in, 1,335 mm rear; length: 164.37 in, 4,175 mm; width: 62.99 in, 1,600 mm; height: 53.94 in, 1,370 mm; ground clearance: 7.40 in, 188 mm; dry weight: 1,841 lb, 835 kg; turning circle (between walls): 33.8 ft, 10.3 m; fuel tank: 9.9 imp gal, 11.9 US gal, 45 l.

BODY saloon/sedan; 2 doors; 5 seats, separate front seats.

PRACTICAL INSTRUCTIONS fuel: 90 oct petrol; engine sump oil: 5.6 imp pt, 6.8 US pt, 3.2 l, SAE 10W-30, change every 9,300 miles, 15,000 km; gearbox and final drive oil: 2.8 imp pt, 3.4 US pt, 1.6 l, SAE 80 or 90, change every 27,900 miles, 45,000 km; greasing: none; sparking plug type: 175°; tappet clearances: inlet 0.008-0.010 in, 0.20-0.25 mm, exhaust 0.016-0.018 in, 0.40-0.45 mm; valve timing: 9° 29° 45° 3°; tyre pressure: front 24 psi, 1.7 atm, rear 24 psi, 1.7 atm.

OPTIONAL ACCESSORIES 5'' wide rims; servo brake; halogen headlamps; electrically-heated rear window; air-conditioning; sunshine roof.

Audi 80 4-door Limousine

See Audi 80 2-door Limousine, except for:

PRICE EX WORKS: 8,365 marks.

Audi 80 L 2-door Limousine

See Audi 80 2-door Limousine, except for:

PRICE IN GB: £ 1,070.
PRICE EX WORKS: 8,440 marks.

Audi 80 L 4-door Limousine

See Audi 80 2-door Limousine, except for:

PRICE IN GB: £ 1,095.
PRICE EX WORKS: 8,815 marks.

Audi 80 S 2-door Limousine

See Audi 80 2-door Limousine, except for:

PRICE EX WORKS: 8,340 marks.

ENGINE 89.8 cu in, 1,471 cc (3.01 x 3.15 in, 76.5 x 80 mm); compression ratio: 9.7:1; max power (DIN): 75 hp at 5,800 rpm; max torque (DIN): 84 lb ft, 11.6 kg m at 3,500 rpm; max engine rpm: 6,500; 51 hp/l.

TRANSMISSION gearbox ratios: I 3.455, II 2.055, III 1.037, IV 0.969, rev 3.167; axle ratio: 4.111; tyres: 155 SR x 13.

PERFORMANCE max speeds: (I) 27 mph, 44 km/h; (II) 47 mph, 75 km/h; (III) 70 mph, 112 km/h; (IV) 99 mph, 160 km/h; power-weight ratio: 25 lb/hp, 11.3 kg/hp; acceleration: 0-50 mph (0-80 km/h) 8.6 sec; speed in top at 1,000 rpm: 16.2 mph, 26 km/h; fuel consumption: 32.8 m/imp gal, 27.3 m/US gal, 8.6 l x 100 km.

DIMENSIONS AND WEIGHT dry weight: 1,874 lb, 850 kg.

PRACTICAL INSTRUCTIONS fuel: 98 oct petrol; sparking plug type: 200°; valve timing: 9° 41° 49° 1°.

Audi 80 S 4-door Limousine

See Audi 80 S 2-door Limousine, except for:

PRICE EX WORKS: 8,715 marks.

Audi 80 LS 2-door Limousine

See Audi 80 S 2-door Limousine, except for:

PRICE EX WORKS: 8,790 marks.

Audi 80 LS 4-door Limousine

See Audi 80 S 2-door Limousine, except for:

PRICE IN GB: £ 1,175.
PRICE EX WORKS: 9,165 marks.

Audi 80 GL 2-door Limousine

See Audi 80 2-door Limousine, except for:

PRICE IN GB: £ 1,239.
PRICE EX WORKS: 9,250 marks.

ENGINE 89.8 cu in, 1,471 cc (3.01 x 3.15 in, 76.5 x 80 mm); compression ratio: 9.7:1; max power (DIN): 85 hp at 5,800 rpm; max torque (DIN): 89 lb ft, 12.3 kg m at 4,000 rpm; max engine rpm: 6,500; 57.8 hp/l; 1 Solex 32-35 TDID carburettor.

TRANSMISSION gearbox ratios: I 3.455, II 2.055, III 1.037, IV 0.939, rev 3.167; axle ratio: 4.111; tyres: 155 SR x 13.

PERFORMANCE max speeds: (I) 29 mph, 46 km/h; (II) 48 mph, 78 km/h; (III) 73 mph, 117 km/h; (IV) 106 mph, 170 km/h; power-weight ratio: 22.2 lb/hp, 10 kg/hp; acceleration: 0-50 mph (0-80 km/h) 8 sec; speed in top at 1,000 rpm: 17.4 mph, 28 km/h; fuel consumption: 32.8 m/imp gal, 27.3 m/US gal, 8.6 l x 100 km.

ELECTRICAL EQUIPMENT 4 headlamps.

DIMENSIONS AND WEIGHT dry weight: 1,885 lb, 855 kg.

PRACTICAL INSTRUCTIONS fuel: 98 oct petrol; sparking plug type: 225°; valve timing: 9° 41° 49° 1°.

Audi 80 GL 4-door Limousine

See Audi 80 GL 2-door Limousine, except for:

PRICE IN GB: £ 1,305.
PRICE EX WORKS: 9,625 marks.

AUDI 100 LS 2-door Limousine

AUDI 100 GL 2-door Limousine

AUDI 100 Coupé S

Audi 100 2-door Limousine

PRICE EX WORKS: 10,600 marks.

ENGINE front, 4 stroke; 4 cylinders, in line; 107.4 cu in, 1,760 cc (3.21 x 3.32 in, 81.5 x 84.4 mm); compression ratio: 8.5:1; max power (DIN): 85 hp at 5,100 rpm; max torque (DIN): 100 lb ft, 13.8 kg m at 3,000 rpm; max engine rpm: 5,800; 48.3 hp/l; cast iron cylinder block, light alloy head; 5 crankshaft bearings; valves: overhead, push-rods and rockers; camshafts: 1, side; lubrication: gear pump, full flow filter, 7 imp pt, 8.5 US pt, 4 l; 1 Solex 35 PDSIT downdraught carburettor; fuel feed: mechanical pump; water-cooled, 13.2 imp pt, 15.9 US pt, 7.5 l.

TRANSMISSION driving wheels: front; clutch: single dry plate; gearbox: mechanical; gears: 4, fully synchronized; ratios: I 3.400, II 1.944, III 1.360, IV 0.966, rev 3.100; lever: steering column; final drive: spiral bevel; axle ratio: 3.888; width of rims: 4.5"; tyres: 165 x 14.

PERFORMANCE max speeds: (I) 27 mph, 44 km/h; (II) 52 mph, 83 km/h; (III) 75 mph, 121 km/h; (IV) 100 mph, 161 km/h; power weight ratio: 28 lb/hp, 12.6 kg/hp; carrying capacity: 1,058 lb, 480 kg; speed in top at 1,000 rpm: 16.8 mph, 27 km/h; fuel consumption: 31.7 m/imp gal, 26.4 m/US gal, 8.9 l x 100 km.

CHASSIS integral; front suspension: independent, wishbones, anti-roll bar, coil springs/telescopic dampers; rear suspension: rigid axle, swinging longitudinal trailing arms, transverse linkage bar, transverse torsion bars, anti-roll bar in axle tube, telescopic dampers.

STEERING rack-and-pinion; turns lock to lock: 3.88.

BRAKES front disc (diameter 11.02 in, 280 mm), rear drum; swept area: front 16.3 sq in, 105 sq cm, rear 45.3 sq in, 292 sq cm, total 61.6 sq in, 397 sq cm.

ELECTRICAL EQUIPMENT 12 V; 45 Ah battery; 770 W alternator; Bosch distributor; 2 headlamps.

DIMENSIONS AND WEIGHT wheel base: 105.31 in, 2,675 mm; tracks: 55.91 in, 1,420 mm front, 56.10 in, 1,425 mm rear; length: 180.71 in, 4,590 mm; width: 68.07 in, 1,729 mm; height: 55.79 in, 1,417 mm; ground clearance: 6.18 in, 157 mm; dry weight: 2,370 lb, 1,075 kg; distribution of weight: 50% front, 50% rear; turning circle (between walls): 36.7 ft, 11.2 m; fuel tank: 12.8 imp gal, 15.3 US gal, 58 l.

BODY saloon/sedan; 2 doors; 5-6 seats, separate front seats.

PRACTICAL INSTRUCTIONS fuel: 88 oct petrol; engine sump oil: 7 imp pt, 8.5 US pt, 4 l, SAE 10W-30, change every 3,100 miles, 5,000 km; gearbox and final drive oil: 3.5 imp pt, 4.2 US pt, 2 l, SAE 80, change every 18,600 miles, 30,000 km; greasing: none; tappet clearances: inlet 0.006 in, 0.15 mm, exhaust 0.016 in, 0.40 mm; valve timing: 5° 37° 39° 3°; tyre pressure: front 26 psi, 1.8 atm, rear 26 psi, 1.8 atm.

OPTIONAL ACCESSORIES central gear lever; servo brake; sunshine roof; reclining backrests; electrically-heated rear window.

Audi 100 4-door Limousine

See Audi 100 2-door Limousine, except for:

PRICE EX WORKS: 10,950 marks.

Audi 100 LS 2-door Limousine

See Audi 100 2-door Limousine, except for:

PRICE IN GB: £ 1,487.
PRICE EX WORKS: 11,200 marks.

ENGINE compression ratio: 9.8:1; max power (DIN): 100 hp at 5,500 rpm; max torque (DIN): 111 lb ft, 15.3 kg m at 3,200 rpm; max engine rpm: 5,800; 56.8 hp/l; 1 Solex 32/35 TDID downdraught twin barrel carburettor.

PERFORMANCE max speeds: (I) 31 mph, 50 km/h; (II) 54 mph, 87 km/h; (III) 81 mph, 130 km/h; (IV) 106 mph, 170 km/h; power-weight ratio: 24 lb/hp, 10.9 kg/hp; acceleration: 0-50 mph (0-80 km/h) 8.8 sec; speed in top at 1,000 rpm: 17.7 mph, 28.5 km/h.

BRAKES servo (standard).

DIMENSIONS AND WEIGHT dry weight: 2,403 lb, 1,090 kg.

BODY reclining backrests (standard).

PRACTICAL INSTRUCTIONS fuel: 98 oct petrol.

AUDI 100, 100 LS Limousine (rear suspension)

AUDI 100 GL

AUDI 100 Coupé S

OPTIONAL ACCESSORIES automatic transmission, hydraulic torque converter and planetary gears with 3 ratios (I 2.650, II 1.590, III 1, rev 1.800), max ratio of converter at stall 2.5, possible manual selection, 3.727 axle ratio, max speeds (I) 40 mph, 65 km/h, (II) 71 mph, 115 km/h, (III) 104 mph, 167 km/h, fuel consumption 28 m/imp gal, 23.3 m/US gal, 10.1 l x 100 km, front disc brakes (diameter 11.46 in, 291 mm), 54 Ah battery; central gear lever; sunshine roof; electrically-heated rear window.

Audi 100 LS 4-door Limousine

See Audi 100 LS 2-door Limousine, except for:

PRICE IN GB: £ 1,545.
PRICE EX WORKS: 11,550 marks.

Audi 100 GL 2-door Limousine

See Audi 100 LS 2-door Limousine, except for:

PRICE IN GB: £ 1,650.
PRICE EX WORKS: 12,000 marks.

ENGINE 114,2 cu in, 1,871 cc (3.31 x 3.32 in, 84 x 84.4 mm); max power (DIN): 112 hp at 5,600 rpm; max torque (DIN): 118 lb ft, 16.3 kg m at 3,500 rpm; 59.9 hp/l.

TRANSMISSION lever: central (standard).

PERFORMANCE max speed: 111 mph, 179 km/h; power-weight ratio: 21.7 lb/hp, 9.8 kg/hp; acceleration: 0-50 mph (0-80 km/h) 7.5 sec.

ELECTRICAL EQUIPMENT 4 headlamps.

DIMENSIONS AND WEIGHT dry weight: 2,426 lb, 1,100 kg.

Audi 100 GL 4-door Limousine

See Audi 100 GL 2-door Limousine, except for:

PRICE IN GB: £ 1,650.
PRICE EX WORKS: 12,350 marks.

Audi 100 Coupé S

See Audi 100 2-door Limousine, except for:

PRICE IN GB: £ 2,130.
PRICE EX WORKS: 14,700 marks.

ENGINE 114.2 cu in, 1,871 cc (3.31 x 3.32 in, 84 x 84.4 mm); compression ratio: 9.8:1; max power (DIN): 112 hp at 5,600 rpm; max torque (DIN): 118 lb ft, 16.3 kg m at 3,500 rpm; max engine rpm: 6,200; 59.9 hp/l; 1 Solex 32/35 TDID downdraught twin barrel carburettor.

TRANSMISSION lever: central; axle ratio: 3.700; width of rims: 5"; tyres: 185/70 HR x 14.

PERFORMANCE max speeds: (I) 34 mph, 55 km/h; (II) 60 mph, 96 km/h; (III) 85 mph, 137 km/h; (IV) 115 mph, 185 km/h; power-weight ratio: 19.8 lb/hp, 9 kg/hp; carrying capacity: 772 lb, 350 kg; speed in top at 1,000 rpm: 19.3 mph, 31 km/h.

BRAKES servo (standard).

ELECTRICAL EQUIPMENT 4 headlamps.

DIMENSIONS AND WEIGHT wheel base: 100.79 in, 2,560 mm; tracks: 56.81 in, 1,443 mm front, 56.69 in, 1,440 mm rear; length: 173.15 in, 4,398 mm; width: 68.07 in, 1.729 mm; height: 51.54 in, 1.309 mm (max load); turning circle (between walls): 36.1 ft, 11 m.

BODY coupé; 4 seats, separate front seats, reclining backrests.

OPTIONAL ACCESSORIES automatic transmission, hydraulic torque converter and planetary gears with 3 ratios (I 2.650, II 1.590, III 1, rev 1.800), max ratio of converter at stall 2.5, possible manual selection, 3.727 axle ratio, max speeds (I) 40 mph, 65 km/h, (II) 71 mph, 115 km/h, (III) 104 mph, 167 km/h, fuel consumption 28 m/imp gal, 23.3 m/US gal, 10.1 l x 100 km, front disc brakes (diameter 11.46 in, 291 mm), 54 Ah battery; sunshine roof.

BMW GERMANY (F.R.)

1602 Limousine

PRICE IN GB: £ 1,570.
PRICE EX WORKS: 10,645 marks.

ENGINE front, 4 stroke; 4 cylinders, slanted at 30°; 96 cu in, 1,573 cc (3.31 x 2.80 in, 84 x 71 mm); compression ratio: 8.6:1; max power (DIN): 85 hp at 5,700 rpm; max torque (DIN): 96 lb ft, 13.2 kg m at 3,500 rpm; max engine rpm: 6,200; 54 hp/l; cast iron cylinder block, light alloy head, hemispherical combustion chambers; 5 crankshaft bearings; valves: overhead, Vee-slanted at 52°, rockers; camshafts: 1, overhead; lubrication: gear pump, full flow filter, 7.4 imp pt, 8.9 US pt, 4.2 l; 1 Solex 38 PDSI downdraught carburettor; fuel feed: mechanical pump; water-cooled, 12.3 imp pt, 14.8 US pt, 7 l.

TRANSMISSION driving wheels: rear; clutch: single dry plate, hydraulically controlled; gearbox: mechanical; gears: 4, fully synchronized; ratios: I 3.764, II 2.020, III 1.320, IV 1, rev 4.096; lever: central; final drive: hypoid bevel; axle ratio: 4.110; width of rims: 4.5"; tyres: 165 SR x 13.

PERFORMANCE max speeds: (I) 25 mph, 41 km/h; (II) 48 mph, 77 km/h; (III) 73 mph, 118 km/h; (IV) 99 mph, 160 km/h; power-weight ratio: 25.1 lb/hp, 11.4 kg/hp; carrying capacity: 882 lb, 400 kg; acceleration: standing ¼ mile 18.4 sec, 0-50 mph (0-80 km/h) 9 sec; speed in direct drive at 1,000 rpm: 16.5 mph, 26.5 km/h; fuel consumption: 28.5 m/imp gal, 23.8 m/US gal, 9.9 l x 100 km.

CHASSIS integral; front suspension: independent, by McPherson, coil springs/telescopic damper struts, lower wishbones, lower trailing links; rear suspension: independent, oblique semi-trailing arms, auxiliary rubber springs, coil springs, telescopic dampers.

STEERING ZF, worm and roller; turns lock to lock: 3.50.

BRAKES front disc (diameter 9.45 in, 240 mm), rear drum, rear compensator, servo; swept area: front 16.3 sq in, 105 sq cm, rear 45.6 sq in, 294 sq cm, total 61.9 sq in, 399 sq cm.

ELECTRICAL EQUIPMENT 12 V; 36 Ah battery; 630 W alternator; Bosch distributor; 2 headlamps.

DIMENSIONS AND WEIGHT wheel base: 98.43 in, 2,500 mm; tracks: 52.36 in, 1,330 mm front, 52.36 in, 1,330 mm rear; length: 166.54 in, 4,230 mm; width: 62.60 in, 1,590 mm; height: 55.51 in, 1,410 mm; ground clearance: 6.30 in, 160 mm; dry weight: 2,139 lb, 970 kg; distribution of weight: 54.5% front, 45.5% rear; turning circle (between walls): 34.1 ft, 10.4 m; fuel tank: 10.1 imp gal, 12.1 US gal, 46 l.

BODY saloon/sedan; 2 doors; 5 seats, separate front seats.

PRACTICAL INSTRUCTIONS fuel: 98-100 oct petrol; engine sump oil: 7.4 imp pt, 8.9 US pt, 4.2 l, SAE 20W-50, change every 3,700 miles, 6,000 km; gearbox oil: 1.8 imp pt, 2.1 US pt, 1 l, SAE 80, change every 14,800 miles, 24,000 km; final drive oil: 1.6 imp pt, 1.9 US pt, 0.9 l, SAE 90, no change recommended; greasing: every 3,700 miles, 6,000 km, 4 points; sparking plug type: 200°; tappet clearances: inlet 0.006 in, 0.15 mm, exhaust 0.008 in, 0.20 mm; valve timing: 4° 52° 52° 4°; tyre pressure: front 26 psi, 1.8 atm, rear 26 psi, 1.8 atm.

OPTIONAL ACCESSORIES 4.100 axle ratio; 5-speed fully synchronized mechanical gearbox (I 3.368, II 2.160, III 1.579, IV 1.241, V 1, rev 4); limited slip differential; anti-roll bar on front and rear suspensions; iodine headlamps; reclining backrests; sunshine roof; electrically-heated rear window; rev counter.

1600 Touring

See 1602 Limousine, except for:

PRICE EX WORKS: 11,320 marks.

PERFORMANCE power-weight ratio: 26.7 lb/hp, 12.1 kg/hp; carrying capacity: 926 lb, 420 kg.

DIMENSIONS AND WEIGHT length: 161.81 in, 4,110 mm; height: 54.33 in, 1,380 mm; dry weight: 2,271 lb, 1,030 kg; turning circle (between walls): 31.5 ft, 9.6 m; fuel tank: 11.4 imp gal, 13.7 US gal, 52 l.

BODY 2 + 1 doors; 4 seats.

1802 Limousine

See 1602 Limousine, except for:

PRICE EX WORKS: 11,195 marks.

ENGINE 107.8 cu in, 1,766 cc (3.50 x 2.80 in, 89 x 71 mm); max power (DIN): 90 hp at 5,250 rpm; max torque (DIN): 106 lb ft, 14.6 kg m at 3,000 rpm; 51 hp/l.

PERFORMANCE max speed: 103 mph, 165 km/h; power-weight ratio: 22.9 lb/hp, 10.4 kg/hp; acceleration: standing ¼ mile 18.1 sec; fuel consumption: 28.2 m/imp gal, 23.5 m/US gal, 10 l x 100 km.

ELECTRICAL EQUIPMENT 44 Ah battery.

BODY 4 doors.

BMW 2002 Cabriolet

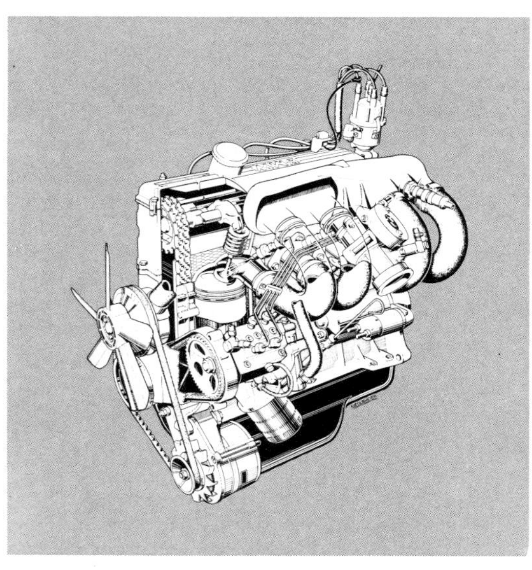

BMW 2002 Tii Limousine

BMW 2000 Tii Touring

1800 Touring

See 1802 Limousine, except for:

PRICE EX WORKS: 11,870 marks.

PERFORMANCE power-weight ratio: 25.1 lb/hp, 11.4 kg/hp; carrying capacity: 926 lb, 420 kg.

DIMENSIONS AND WEIGHT length: 161.81 in, 4,110 mm; height: 54.33 in, 1,380 mm; dry weight: 2,271 lb, 1,030 kg; turning circle (between walls): 31.5 ft, 9.6 m; fuel tank: 11.4 imp gal, 13.7 US gal, 52 l.

BODY 2 + 1 doors; 4 seats.

2002 Limousine

See 1602 Limousine, except for:

PRICE IN GB: £ 1,774.
PRICE IN USA: $ 3,571.

ENGINE 121.4 cu in, 1,990 cc (3.50 x 3.15 in, 89 x 80 mm); compression ratio: 8.5:1; max power (DIN): 100 hp at 5,500 rpm; max torque (DIN): 116 lb ft, 16 kg m at 3,500 rpm; 52.9 hp/l; 1 Solex 40 PDSIT downdraught carburettor.

TRANSMISSION axle ratio: 3.640.

PERFORMANCE max speeds: (I) 27 mph, 44 km/h; (II) 51 mph, 82 km/h; (III) 78 mph, 125 km/h; (IV) 106 mph, 170 km/h; power-weight ratio: 20.7 lb/hp, 9.4 kg/hp; acceleration: standing ¼ mile 17.6 sec, 0-50 mph (0-80 km/h) 7.3 sec; speed in direct drive at 1,000 rpm: 18.5 mph, 29.7 km/h; fuel consumption: 28.2 m/imp gal, 23.5 m/US gal, 10 l x 100 km.

CHASSIS front and rear suspensions: anti-roll bar (standard).

BRAKES swept area: front 19.5 sq in, 126 sq cm, rear 50.2 sq in, 324 sq cm, total 69.7 sq in, 450 sq cm.

ELECTRICAL EQUIPMENT 44 Ah battery.

DIMENSIONS AND WEIGHT dry weight: 2,183 lb, 990 kg.

BODY reclining backrests (standard).

2002 Automatic Limousine

See 2002 Limousine, except for:

PRICE IN GB: £ 1,955.
PRICE EX WORKS: 12,995 marks.

TRANSMISSION gearbox: ZF automatic transmission, hydraulic torque converter and planetary gears with 3 ratios, max ratio of converter at stall 2.1, possible manual selection; ratios: I 2.560, II 1.520, III 1, rev 2.

PERFORMANCE max speeds: (I) 40 mph, 65 km/h; (II) 68 mph, 110 km/h; (III) 103 mph, 165 km/h.

2000 Touring

See 2002 Limousine, except for:

PRICE IN GB: £ 1,943.
PRICE EX WORKS: 12,370 marks.

TRANSMISSION width of rims: 4.5"; tyres: 165 x 13.

PERFORMANCE max speed: 106 mph, 170 km/h; power-weight ratio: 22.7 lb/hp, 10.3 kg/hp; carrying capacity: 926 lb, 420 kg; speed in direct drive at 1,000 rpm: 16.5 mph, 26.5 km/h.

DIMENSIONS AND WEIGHT length: 161.81 in, 4,110 mm; height: 54.33 in, 1,380 mm; dry weight: 2,271 lb, 1,030 kg; turning circle (between walls): 31.5 ft, 9.6 m; fuel tank: 11.4 imp gal, 13.7 US gal, 52 l.

BODY 2 + 1 doors; 4 seats.

BMW 2002 Cabriolet

BMW 2002 Tii Limousine

BMW 2000 Tii Touring

2000 Automatic Touring

See 2002 Limousine, except for:

PRICE IN GB: £ 2,124.
PRICE EX WORKS: 13,670 marks.

TRANSMISSION gearbox: ZF automatic transmission, hydraulic torque converter and planetary gears with 3 ratios + reverse, max ratio of converter at stall 2.1, possible manual selection; ratios: I 2.560, II 1.520, III 1, rev 2; width of rims: 4.5''; tyres: 165 x 13.

PERFORMANCE max speeds: (I) 41 mph, 66 km/h; (II) 70 mph, 112 km/h; (III) 103 mph, 165 km/h; power-weight ratio: 22.7 lb/hp, 10.3 kg/hp; carrying capacity: 926 lb, 420 kg; speed in direct drive at 1,000 rpm: 16.5 mph, 26.5 km/h.

DIMENSIONS AND WEIGHT length: 161.81 in 4,110 mm; height: 54.33 in, 1,380 mm; dry weight: 2,271 lb, 1,030 kg; turning circle (between walls): 31.5 ft, 9.6 m; fuel tank: 11.4 imp gal, 13.7 US gal, 52 l.

BODY 2 + 1 doors; 4 seats.

2002 Cabriolet

See 2002 Limousine, except for:

PRICE EX WORKS: 15,490 marks.

PERFORMANCE power-weight ratio: 21.8 lb/hp, 9.9 kg/hp; carrying capacity: 772 lb, 350 kg.

DIMENSIONS AND WEIGHT height: 53.54 in, 1,360 mm; dry weight: 2,183 lb, 990 kg.

BODY convertible; 2 + 2 seats.

2002 Tii Limousine

See 2002 Limousine, except for:

PRICE IN GB: £ 2,067.
PRICE IN USA: $ 4,286.

ENGINE compression ratio: 9.5; max power (DIN): 130 hp at 5,800 rpm; max torque (DIN): 131 lb ft, 18.1 kg m at 4,500 rpm; 65.3 hp/l; 4-cylinder injection pump, injectors in inlet pipes (Kugelfischer system).

TRANSMISSION axle ratio: 3.450; width of rims: 5''; tyres: 165 HR x 13.

PERFORMANCE max speed: 118 mph, 190 km/h; power-weight ratio: 15.9 lb/hp, 7.2 kg/hp; acceleration: standing ¼ mile 16.7 sec; speed in direct drive at 1,000 rpm: 18.3 mph, 29.5 km/h.

BRAKES front disc (diameter 10.08 in, 256 mm).

DIMENSIONS AND WEIGHT front and rear track: 53.07 in, 1,348 mm.

OPTIONAL ACCESSORIES 3.450 axle ratio with 5-speed mechanical gearbox.

2000 Tii Touring

See 2002 Limousine, except for:

PRICE EX WORKS: 14,415 marks.

PERFORMANCE max speed: 118 mph, 190 km/h; power-weight ratio: 22.7 lb/hp, 10.3 kg/hp; speed in direct drive at 1,000 rpm: 19.6 mph, 31.5 km/h; carrying capacity: 926 lb, 420 kg.

DIMENSIONS AND WEIGHT length: 161.81 in, 4,110 mm; height: 54.33 in, 1.380 mm; dry weight: 2,271 lb, 1,030 kg; turning circle (between walls): 31.5 ft, 9.6 m; fuel tank: 11.4 imp gal, 13.7 US gal, 52 l.

BODY 2 + 1 doors; 4 seats.

520

PRICE EX WORKS: 14,490 marks.

ENGINE front, 4 stroke; 4 cylinders, in line; 121.4 cu in, 1,990 cc (3.50 x 3.15 in, 89 x 80 mm); compression ratio: 9:1; max power (DIN): 115 hp at 5,800 rpm; max torque (DIN): 120 lb ft, 16.5 kg m at 3,700 rpm; max engine rpm: 6,400; 57.8 hp/l; cast iron cylinder block, light alloy head, hemispherical combustion chambers; 5 crankshaft bearings; valves: overhead, Vee-slanted at 52°, rockers; camshafts: 1, overhead; lubrication: rotary pump, full flow filter, 7.4 imp pt, 8.9 US pt, 4.2 l; 2 Stromberg 175 CDET

520

horizontal carburettors; fuel feed: mechanical pump; water-cooled, 12.3 imp pt, 14.8 US pt, 7 l.

TRANSMISSION driving wheels: rear; clutch: single dry plate; gearbox: mechanical; gears: 4, fully synchronized; ratios: I 3.764, II 2.020, III 1.320, IV 1, rev 4.090; lever: central; final drive: hypoid bevel; axle ratio: 4.100; width of rims: 5.5"; tyres: 175 SR x 14.

PERFORMANCE max speed: 107 mph, 173 km/h; power-weight ratio: 23.6 lb/hp, 10.7 kg/hp; carrying capacity: 1,036 lb, 470 kg; acceleration: standing ¼ mile 18.2 sec, 0-50 mph (0-80 km/h) 8.5 sec; speed in direct drive at 1,000 rpm: 17.1 mph, 27.5 km/h; fuel consumption: 26.4 m/imp gal, 22 m/US gal, 10.7 l x 100 km.

CHASSIS integral; front suspension: independent, by McPherson, coil springs/telescopic damper struts, lower wishbones, lower trailing links; rear suspension: independent, oblique semi-trailing arms, auxiliary rubber springs, coil springs, telescopic dampers.

STEERING ZF, worm and roller.

BRAKES front disc (diameter 10.71 in, 272 mm), rear drum, rear compensator, servo; swept area: front 29.8 sq in, 192 sq cm, rear 53.3 sq in, 344 sq cm, total 83.1 sq in, 536 sq cm.

ELECTRICAL EQUIPMENT 12 V; 44 Ah battery; 630 W alternator; Bosch distributor; 4 iodine headlamps.

DIMENSIONS AND WEIGHT wheel base: 103.78 in, 2,636 mm; tracks: 55.35 in, 1,406 mm front, 56.77 in, 1,442 mm rear; length: 181.89 in, 4,620 mm; width: 66.54 in, 1,690 mm; height: 56.10 in, 1,425 mm; ground clearance: 5.51 in, 140 mm; dry weight: 2,712 lb, 1,230 kg; turning circle (between walls): 34.4 ft, 10.5 m; fuel tank: 12.3 imp gal, 14.8 US gal, 56 l.

BODY saloon/sedan; 4 doors; 5 seats, separate front seats, reclining backrests; electrically-heated rear window.

PRACTICAL INSTRUCTIONS fuel: 98-100 oct petrol; engine sump oil: 7.4 imp pt, 8.9 US pt, 4.2 l, SAE 20W-50, change every 3,700 miles, 6,000 km; gearbox oil: 1.8 imp pt, 2.1 US pt, 1 l, SAE 80, change every 14,800 miles, 24,000 km; final drive oil: 1.6 imp pt, 1.9 US pt, 0.9 l, SAE 90, no change recommended.

OPTIONAL ACCESSORIES 5-speed fully synchronized mechanical gearbox (I 3.360, II 2.160, III 1.580, IV 1.240, V 1, rev 4); adjustable steering wheel; larger fuel tank.

520 Automatic

See 520, except for:

PRICE EX WORKS: 15,790 marks.

TRANSMISSION gearbox: ZF automatic transmission, hydraulic torque converter and planetary gears with 3 ratios + reverse, max ratio of converter at stall 2, possible manual selection; ratios: I 2.560, II 1.520, III 1, rev 2.

PERFORMANCE max speed: 104 mph, 168 km/h.

520 i

See 520, except for:

PRICE EX WORKS: 15,670 marks.

ENGINE compression ratio: 9.5:1; max power (DIN): 130 hp at 5,800 rpm; max torque (DIN): 131 lb ft, 18.1 kg m at 4,500 rpm; 65.3 hp/l; 4-cylinder injection pump, injectors in inlet pipes (Kugelfischer system).

TRANSMISSION axle ratio: 3.900.

PERFORMANCE max speed: 114 mph, 183 km/h; power-weight ratio: 21.4 lb/hp, 9.7 kg/hp; carrying capacity: 992 lb, 450 kg; acceleration: standing ¼ mile 11.1 sec, 0-50 mph (0-80 km/h) 7.4 sec; speed in direct drive at 1,000 rpm: 18.3 mph, 29.5 km/h; fuel consumption: 28.5 m/imp gal, 23.8 m/US gal, 9.9 l x 100 km.

DIMENSIONS AND WEIGHT dry weight: 2,756 lb, 1,250 kg.

520 i Automatic

See 520 i, except for:

PRICE EX WORKS: 16,970 marks.

TRANSMISSION gearbox: ZF automatic transmission, hydraulic torque converter and planetary gears with 3 ratios +

BMW 520 - 520 i

BMW 2500 Limousine

BMW 3.0 Si Limousine

reverse, max ratio of converter at stall, 2 possible manual selection; ratios: I 2.560, II 1.520, III 1, rev 2.

PERFORMANCE max speed: 111 mph, 178 km/h.

2500 Limousine

PRICE IN GB: £ 2,729.
PRICE EX WORKS: 18,280 marks.

ENGINE front, 4 stroke; 6 cylinders, in line; 152.2 cu in, 2,494 cc (3.39 x 2.82 in, 86 x 71.6 mm); compression ratio: 9:1; max power (DIN): 150 hp at 6,000 rpm; max torque (DIN): 156 lb ft, 21.5 kg m at 3,700 rpm; max engine rpm: 6,200; 60.1 hp/l; cast iron cylinder block, light alloy head, polispherical combustion chambers; 7 crankshaft bearings; valves: overhead, Vee-slanted, rockers; camshafts: 1, overhead; lubrication: rotary pump, full flow filter, 10 imp pt, 12 US pt, 5.7 l; 2 Solex 35/40 INAT downdraught twin barrel carburettors; fuel feed: mechanical pump; water-cooled, 21.1 imp pt, 25.4 US pt, 12 l.

TRANSMISSION driving wheels: rear; clutch: single dry plate, hydraulically controlled; gearbox: mechanical; gears: 4, fully synchronized; ratios: I 3.850, II 2.080, III 1.375, IV 1, rev 4.130; lever: central; final drive: hypoid bevel; axle ratio: 3.640; width of rims: 6''; tyres: 175 HR x 14.

PERFORMANCE max speeds: (I) 31 mph, 50 km/h; (II) 56 mph, 90 km/h; (III) 86 mph, 138 km/h; (IV) 118 mph, 190 km/h; power-weight ratio: 19.6 lb/hp, 8.9 kg/hp; carrying capacity: 1,036 lb, 470 kg; acceleration: standing ¼ mile 17.1 sec, 0-50 mph (0-80 km/h) 7.2 sec; speed in direct drive at 1,000 rpm: 19.8 mph, 31.8 km/h; fuel consumption: 25.9 m/imp gal, 21.6 m/US gal, 10.9 l x 100 km.

CHASSIS integral; front suspension: independent, by McPherson, coil springs/telescopic damper struts, auxiliary rubber springs, anti-roll bar, lower wishbones; rear suspension: independent, semi-trailing arms, auxiliary rubber springs, coil springs, telescopic dampers.

STEERING worm and roller; turns lock to lock: 4.40.

BRAKES disc (diameter 10.71 in, 272 mm), rear compensator, servo; swept area: front 29.5 sq in, 190 sq cm, rear 11.9 sq in, 77 sq cm, total 41.4 sq in, 267 sq cm.

ELECTRICAL EQUIPMENT 12 V; 55 Ah battery; 630 W alternator; Bosch distributor; 4 iodine headlamps.

DIMENSIONS AND WEIGHT wheel base: 105.98 in, 2,692 mm; tracks: 56.93 in, 1,446 mm front, 57.64 in, 1,464 mm rear; length: 185.04 in, 4,700 mm; width: 68.90 in, 1,750 mm; height: 57.09 in, 1,450 mm; ground clearance: 5.51 in, 140 mm; dry weight: 2,955 lb, 1,340 kg; distribution of weight: 54% front, 46% rear; turning circle (between walls): 34.4 ft, 10.5 m; fuel tank: 16.5 imp gal, 19.8 US gal, 75 l.

BODY saloon/sedan; 4 doors; 5 seats, separate front seats, reclining backrests.

PRACTICAL INSTRUCTIONS fuel: 98 oct petrol; engine sump oil: 10 imp pt, 12 US pt, 5.7 l, SAE 20W-50; gearbox oil: 2.1 imp pt, 2.5 US pt, 1.2 l, SAE 80, change every 14,800 miles, 24,000 km; final drive oil: 2.6 imp pt, 3.2 US pt, 1.5 l, SAE 90, no change recommended; greasing: none; sparking plug type: 175°; tappet clearances: inlet 0.010 in, 0.25 mm, exhaust 0.012 in, 0.30 mm; valve timing: 6° 50° 50° 6°; tyre pressure: front 28 psi, 2 atm, rear 27 psi, 1.9 atm.

OPTIONAL ACCESSORIES limited slip differential; DR 70 x 14 tyres; Nivomat (Boge system) units and anti-roll bar on rear suspension; sunshine roof; power-assisted steering; air-conditioning; electrically-controlled windows; electrically-heated rear window.

2500 Automatic Limousine

See 2500 Limousine, except for:

PRICE IN GB: £ 2,952.
PRICE EX WORKS: 19,780 marks.

TRANSMISSION gearbox: ZF automatic transmission, hydraulic torque converter and planetary gears with 3 ratios + reverse, max ratio of converter at stall 2, possible manual selection; ratios: I 2.500, II 1.500, III 1, rev 2.

PERFORMANCE max speeds: (I) 50 mph, 80 km/h; (II) 81 mph, 130 km/h; (III) 114 mph, 184 km/h.

2800 Limousine

See 2500 Limousine, except for:

PRICE IN USA: $ 5,555.
PRICE EX WORKS: 19,250 marks.

ENGINE 170.1 cu in, 2,788 cc (3.39 x 3.15 in, 86 x 80 mm); max power (DIN): 170 hp at 6,000 rpm; max torque (DIN): 174 lb ft, 24 kg m at 3,700 rpm; 61 hp/l.

TRANSMISSION final drive: limited slip differential (standard); axle ratio: 3.450; tyres: DR 70 x 14.

PERFORMANCE max speeds: (I) 33 mph, 53 km/h; (II) 59 mph, 95 km/h; (III) 91 mph, 146 km/h; (IV) 124 mph, 200 km/h; power-weight ratio: 17.4 lb/hp, 7.9 kg/hp; acceleration: standing ¼ mile 16.6 sec; speed in direct drive at 1,000 rpm: 20.8 mph, 33.4 km/h.

CHASSIS rear suspension: Nivomat (Boge system) units, anti-roll bar (standard).

BODY electrically-heated rear window (standard).

BMW 520 - 520 i

BMW 2500

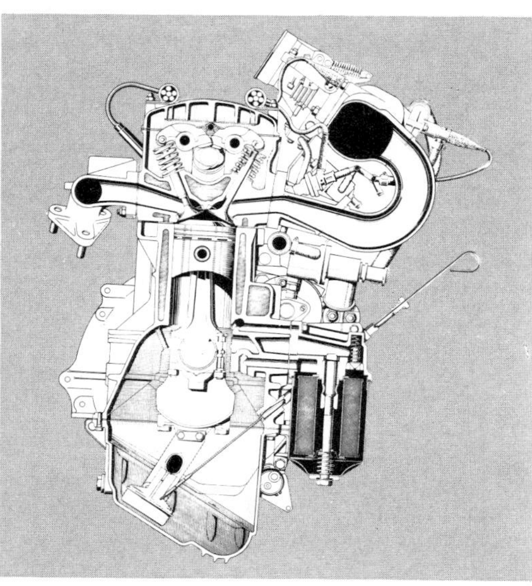

BMW 3.0 Si Limousine

2800 Automatic Limousine

See 2800 Limousine, except for:

PRICE EX WORKS: 20,750 marks.

TRANSMISSION gearbox: ZF automatic transmission, hydraulic torque converter and planetary gears with 3 ratios + reverse, max ratio of converter at stall 2, possible manual selection; ratios: I 2.500, II 1.500, III 1, rev 2.

PERFORMANCE max speeds: (I) 52 mph, 83 km/h; (II) 86 mph, 138 km/h; (III) 120 mph, 193 km/h.

3.0 S Limousine

See 2500 Limousine, except for:

PRICE IN GB: £ 3,334.
PRICE EX WORKS: 21,490 marks.

ENGINE 182.1 cu in, 2,985 cc (3.50 x 3.15 in, 89 x 80 mm); max power (DIN): 180 hp at 6,000 rpm; max torque (DIN): 188 lb ft, 26 kg m at 4,300 rpm; 60.3 hp/l.

TRANSMISSION final drive: limited slip differential (standard); axle ratio: 3.450; tyres: DR 70 or 195/70 x 14.

PERFORMANCE max speeds: (I) 33 mph, 53 km/h; (II) 59 mph, 95 km/h; (III) 91 mph, 146 km/h; (IV) 127 mph, 205 km/h; power-weight ratio: 17 lb/hp, 7.7. kg/hp; acceleration: standing ¼ mile 16.2 sec; speed in direct drive at 1,000 rpm: 20.8 mph, 33.4 km/h; fuel consumption: 24.8 m/imp gal, 20.6 m/US gal, 11.4 l x 100 km.

STEERING servo (standard).

DIMENSIONS AND WEIGHT dry weight: 3,043 lb, 1,380 kg.

BODY electrically-heated rear window (standard).

PRACTICAL INSTRUCTIONS sparking plug type: 248°; valve timing: 14° 54° 54° 14°; tyre pressure: front 28 psi, 2 atm, rear 28 psi, 2 atm.

3.0 S Automatic Limousine

See 3.0 S Limousine, except for:

PRICE IN GB: £ 3,556.
PRICE EX WORKS: 22,990 marks.

TRANSMISSION gearbox: ZF automatic transmission, hydraulic torque converter and planetary gears with 3 ratios + reverse, max ratio of converter at stall 2, possible manual election; ratios: I 2.500, II 1.500, III 1, rev 2.

PERFORMANCE max speeds: (I) 49 mph, 79 km/h; (II) 82 mph, 132 km/h; (III) 123 mph, 198 km/h.

3.0 CS Coupé

See 3.0 S Limousine, except for:

PRICE IN GB: £ 4,093.
PRICE IN USA: $ 8,712.

PERFORMANCE max speeds: (I) 35 mph, 56 km/h; (II) 60 mph, 97 km/h; (III) 95 mph, 153 km/h; (IV) 137 mph, 220 km/h; carrying capacity: 816 lb, 370 kg; acceleration: standing ¼ mile 15.7 sec.
CHASSIS anti-roll bar on rear suspension.

DIMENSIONS AND WEIGHT wheel base: 103.35 in, 2,625 mm; tracks: 56.93 in, 1,446 mm front, 55.20 in, 1,402 mm rear; length: 183.46 in, 4,660 mm; width: 65.75 in, 1,670 mm; height: 53.94 in, 1,370 mm; ground clearance: 5.51 in, 140 mm; fuel tank: 15.4 imp gal, 18.5 US gal, 70 l.

BODY coupé; 2 doors; 4 seats.

3.0 CS Automatic Coupé

See 3.0 CS Coupé, except for:

PRICE IN GB: £ 5,129.
PRICE EX WORKS: 30,450 marks.

TRANSMISSION gearbox: ZF automatic transmission, hydraulic torque converter and planetary gears with 3 ratios + reverse, max ratio of converter at stall 2, possible manual selection; ratios: I 2.500, II 1.500, III 1, rev 2.

PERFORMANCE max speeds: (I) 69 mph, 111 km/h; (II) 115 mph, 185 km/h; (III) 173 mph, 218 km/h.

3.0 Si Limousine

See 3.0 S Limousine, except for:

PRICE IN GB: £ 3,556.
PRICE EX WORKS: 23,590 marks.

ENGINE compression ratio: 9.5:1; max power (DIN): 200 hp at 5,500 rpm; max torque (DIN): 201 lb ft, 27.7 kg m at 4,300 rpm; 67 hp/l; Bosch electrically-controlled injection system.

TRANSMISSION gearbox ratios: I 3.855, II 2.203, III 1.402, IV 1, rev 4.300; tyres: 70 VR or 195/70 VR x 14.

PERFORMANCE max speed: 131 mph, 211 km/h; power-weight ratio: 15.2 lb/hp, 6.9 kg/hp; acceleration: standing ¼ mile 15.8 sec. 0-50 mph (0-80 km/h) 7.8 sec; fuel consumption: 27.7 m/imp gal, 23.1 m/US gal, 10.2 l x 100 km.

ELECTRICAL EQUIPMENT 770 W alternator.

3.0 Si Automatic Limousine

See 3.0 Si Limousine, except for:

PRICE EX WORKS: 25,090 marks.

TRANSMISSION gearbox: Borg-Warner 35 automatic transmission, hydraulic torque converter and planetary gears with 3 ratios + reverse, possible manual selection; ratios: I 2.400, II 1.460, III 1, rev 2.400.

PERFORMANCE max speed: 127 mph, 204 km/h.

3.0 CSi Coupé

See 3.0 CS Coupé, except for:

PRICE IN GB: £ 5,129.
PRICE EX WORKS: 30,650 marks.

ENGINE compression ratio: 9.5:1; max power (DIN): 200 hp at 5,500 rpm; max torque (DIN): 201 lb ft, 27.7 kg m at 4,300 rpm; 67 hp/l; Bosch electrically-controlled injection system.

TRANSMISSION axle ratio: 3.250; tyres: 195/70 VR x 14.

PERFORMANCE max speeds: (I) 35 mph, 56 km/h; (II) 60 mph, 97 km/h; (III) 95 mph, 153 km/h; (IV) 137 mph, 220 km/h; acceleration: standing ¼ mile 15.7 sec, 0-50 mph (0-80 km/h) 7.7 sec; fuel consumption: 28.5 m/imp gal, 23.8 m/US gal, 9.9 l x 100 km.

STEERING servo (standard).

3.0 CSi Automatic Coupé

See 3.0 CSi Coupé, except for:

PRICE EX WORKS: 32,150 marks.

TRANSMISSION gearbox: Borg-Warner 35 automatic transmission, hydraulic torque converter and planetary gears with 3 ratios + reverse, possible manual selection; ratios: I 2.400, II 1.460, III 1, rev 2.400.

PERFORMANCE max speed: 133 mph, 214 km/h.

3.0 CSL Coupé

See 3.0 CSi Coupé, except for:

PRICE IN GB: £ 5,294.
PRICE EX WORKS: 31,950 marks.

PERFORMANCE max speed: 138 mph, 222 km/h; power-weight ratio: 12.8 lb/hp, 5.8 kg/hp.

DIMENSIONS AND WEIGHT length: 182.28 in, 4,630 mm; width: 71.26 in, 1,810 mm; dry weight: 2,569 lb, 1,165 kg.

BMW 3.0 CSi Coupé

FIBERFAB Bonito

FORD Escort GT

FIBERFAB — GERMANY (F.R.)

Bonito

ENGINE Volkswagen, rear, 4 stroke; 4 cylinders, horizontally opposed; 72.7 cu in, 1,192 cc (3.03 x 2.52 in, 77 x 64 mm); compression ratio: 7:1; max power (DIN): 34 hp at 3,600 rpm; max torque (DIN): 61 lb ft, 8.4 kg m at 2,000 rpm; max engine rpm: 4,500; 28.5 hp/l.

TRANSMISSION width of rims: 4" or 6"; tyres: 165 x 15 or 175 x 14.

DIMENSIONS AND WEIGHT wheel base: 94.49 in, 2,400 mm; tracks: 51.38 in, 1,305 mm front, 53.46 in, 1,358 mm rear; length: 171.26 in, 4,350 mm; width: 66.14 in, 1,680 mm; height: 45.28 in, 1,150 mm; ground clearance: 5.91 in, 150 mm; dry weight: 1,499 lb, 680 kg; fuel tank: 9.2 imp gal, 11.1 US gal, 42 l.

BODY coupé in plastic material; 2 doors; 2 + 2 seats, separate front seats.

VARIATIONS

ENGINE Volkswagen, 78.4 cu in, 1,285 cc (3.03 x 2.72 in, 77 x 69 mm).

ENGINE Volkswagen, 91.1 cu in, 1,493 cc (3.27 x 2.72 in, 83 x 69 mm).

ENGINE Volkswagen, 96.7 cu in, 1,584 cc (3.37 x 2.72 in, 85.5 x 69 mm).

For further technical information see Volkswagen.

FORD — GERMANY (F.R.)

Escort Series, see FORD GREAT BRITAIN (only for data not mentioned)

Escort 2-door Limousine

PRICE EX WORKS: 6,485 marks.

ENGINE compression ratio: 8:1; max power (DIN): 44 hp at 5,500 rpm; max torque (DIN): 52 lb ft, 7.2 kg m at 3,000 rpm; 41 hp/l; lubrication: gear pump; water-cooled, 8.8 imp pt, 10.6 US pt, 5 l.

TRANSMISSION axle ratio: 4.110; tyres: 6.00 x 12.

PERFORMANCE max speed: 78 mph, 126 km/h; power-weight ratio: 41.2 lb/hp, 18.7 kg/hp.

CHASSIS rear suspension: torque trailing links.

ELECTRICAL EQUIPMENT 12 V; 44 Ah battery; 25 A alternator.

DIMENSIONS AND WEIGHT tracks: 49.49 in, 1,257 mm front, 50.28 in, 1,277 mm rear; length: 159.53 in, 4,052 mm; height: 55.35 in, 1,406 mm; dry weight: 1,819 lb, 825 kg.

VARIATIONS

ENGINE 9:1 compression ratio, max power (DIN) 48 hp at 5,500 rpm, max torque (DIN) 54 lb ft, 7.5 kg m. at 3,000 rpm, 44.7 hp/l.
PERFORMANCE max speed: 82 mph, 132 km/h.

ENGINE 77.1 cu in, 1,263 cc (3.19 x 2.48 in, 81 x 63 mm), 9:1 compression ratio, max power (DIN) 57 hp at 5,500 rpm, max torque (DIN) 67 lb ft, 9.3 km m, at 3,000 rpm, 45 hp/l.
TRANSMISSION 3.890 axle ratio.
PERFORMANCE max speed 90 mph, 145 km/h, fuel consumption 32.5 m/imp gal, 27 m/US gal, 8.7 l x 100 km.
BRAKES front disc brakes with servo.

OPTIONAL ACCESSORIES automatic transmission, hydraulic torque converter and planetary gears with 3 ratios (I 2.393, II 1.450, III 1, rev 2.094), max ratio of converter at stall 2, possible manual selection, central gear lever, 3.890 axle ratio (only for 77.1 cu in, 1,263 cc engine); 155 SR x 12 tyres (only for 77.1 cu in, 1,263 cc engine); front disc brakes with servo.

Escort 4-door Limousine

See Escort 2-door Limousine, except for:

PRICE EX WORKS: 6,775 marks.

PERFORMANCE power-weight ratio: 41.9 lb/hp, 19 kg/hp.

DIMENSIONS AND WEIGHT height: 55.20 in, 1,402 mm; dry weight: 1,163 lb, 845 kg.

BMW 3.0 CSL Coupé

FIBERFAB Bonito

FORD Escort XL 4-door Limousine

Escort Turnier

See Escort 2-door Limousine, except for:

PRICE EX WORKS: 7,035 marks.

PERFORMANCE power-weight ratio: 44.1 lb/hp, 20 kg/hp.

DIMENSIONS AND WEIGHT rear track: 50.51 in, 1,283 mm; length: 163.15 in, 4,144 mm; height: 56.18 in, 1,427 mm; dry weight: 1,940 lb, 880 kg.

BODY estate car/station wagon; 2 + 1 doors.

OPTIONAL ACCESSORIES 4.110 axle ratio (only for automatic transmission and 77.1 cu in, 1,263 cc engine).

Escort L 2-door Limousine

See Escort 2-door Limousine, except for:

PRICE EX WORKS: 6,715 marks.

Escort L 4-door Limousine

See Escort 4-door Limousine, except for:

PRICE EX WORKS: 7,005 marks.

Escort L Turnier

See Escort Turnier, except for:

PRICE EX WORKS: 7,265 marks.

Escort XL 2-door Limousine

See Escort 2-door Limousine, except for:

PRICE EX WORKS: 7,130 marks.

Escort XL 4-door Limousine

See Escort 4-door Limousine, except for:

PRICE EX WORKS: 7,420 marks.

Escort XL Turnier

See Escort Turnier, except for:

PRICE EX WORKS: 7,680 marks.

Escort GT 2-door Limousine

See Escort 2-door Limousine, except for:

PRICE EX WORKS: 7,920 marks.

TRANSMISSION axle ratio: 3.890; tyres: 155 SR x 15.

VARIATIONS

None.

Escort GT 4-door Limousine

See Escort GT 2-door Limousine, except for:

PRICE EX WORKS: 8,210 marks.

Escort 2-door Sport Limousine

See Escort GT 2-door Limousine, except for:

PRICE EX WORKS: 7,375 marks.

PERFORMANCE fuel consumption: 31 m/imp gal, 25.8 m/US gal, 9.1 l x 100 km.

Taunus 2-door Limousine

PRICE EX WORKS: 7,625 marks.

ENGINE front, 4 stroke; 4 cylinders, in line; 78.9 cu in, 1,293 cc (3.11 x 2.60 in, 79 x 66 mm); compression ratio: 8.2:1; max power (DIN): 55 hp at 5,500 rpm; max torque (DIN): 67 lb ft, 9.2 kg m at 3,000 rpm; max engine rpm:

TAUNUS 2-DOOR LIMOUSINE

6,000; 42.5 hp/l; cast iron cylinder block and head; 5 crankshaft bearings; valves: overhead, Vee-slanted, rockers; camshafts: 1, overhead; lubrication: gear pump, full flow filter, 6.5 imp pt, 7.8 US pt, 3.7 l; 1 Ford 71 HW 9510/AA downdraught carburettor; fuel feed: mechanical pump; water-cooled, 11.4 imp pt, 13.7 US pt, 6.5 l.

TRANSMISSION driving wheels: rear; clutch: single dry plate; gearbox: mechanical; gears: 4, fully synchronized; ratios: I 3.660, II 2.180, III 1.430, IV 1, rev 4.240; lever: central; final drive: hypoid bevel; axle ratio: 4.110; width of rims: 4.5"; tyres: 5.60 x 13.

PERFORMANCE max speeds: (I) 23 mph, 37 km/h; (II) 39 mph, 62 km/h; (III) 58 mph, 94 km/h; (IV) 84 mph, 135 km/h; power-weight ratio: 33.3 lb/hp, 15.1 kg/hp; carrying capacity: 882 lb, 400 kg; speed in direct drive at 1,000 rpm: 14 mph, 22.5 km/h; fuel consumption: 31 m/imp gal, 25.8 m/US gal, 9.1 l x 100 km.

CHASSIS integral, front subframe; front suspension: independent, wishbones, lower trailing links, coil springs/telescopic dampers; rear suspension: rigid axle, lower trailing arms, upper oblique trailing arms, coil springs, telescopic dampers.

STEERING rack-and-pinion.

BRAKES front disc (diameter 9.76 in, 248 mm), rear drum; swept area: front 46.8 sq in, 302 sq cm, rear 92.1 sq in, 594 sq cm, total 138.9 sq in, 896 sq cm.

ELECTRICAL EQUIPMENT 12 V; 44 Ah battery; 28 A alternator; Bosch distributor; 2 headlamps.

DIMENSIONS AND WEIGHT wheel base: 101.50 in, 2,578 mm; tracks: 55.98 in, 1,422 mm front, 55.98 in, 1,422 mm rear; length: 167.99 in, 4,267 mm: width: 66.97 in, 1,701 mm height: 53.50 in, 1,359 mm; ground clearance: 3.94 in, 100 mm; dry weight: 2,095 lb, 950 kg; turning circle (between walls): 31.5 ft, 9.6 m; fuel tank: 11.9 imp gal, 14.3 US gal, 54 l.

BODY saloon/sedan; 2 doors; 5 seats, separate front seats, reclining backrests.

PRACTICAL INSTRUCTIONS fuel: 97 oct petrol; engine sump oil: 5.6 imp pt, 6.8 US pt, 3.2 l, SAE 10W-40, change every 6,200 miles, 10,000 km; gearbox oil: 1.4 imp pt, 1.7 US pt, 0.8 l, SAE 80 EP, change every 12,400 miles, 20,000 km; final drive oil: 1.8 imp pt, 2.1 US pt, 1 l, SAE 90, change every 12,400 miles, 20,000 km; greasing: every 34,100 miles, 55,000 km, 2 points; tyre pressure: front 24 psi, 1.7 atm, rear 24 psi, 1.7 atm.

VARIATIONS

ENGINE (export) 9.2:1 compression ratio, max power (DIN) 67 hp at 5,700 rpm, max torque (DIN) 79 lb ft, 10.9 kg m at 3,000 rpm, 51.8 hp/l, lubrication system capacity 7 imp pt, 8.5 US pt, 4 l, 1 Ford 71 HHW/9510/BA carburettor.
PERFORMANCE max speed 86 mph, 138 km/h, power-weight ratio 31.3 lb/hp, 14.2 kg/hp, fuel consumption 31.4 m/imp gal, 26.1 m/US gal, 9 l x 100 km.

ENGINE 97.1 cu in, 1,592 cc (3.45 x 2.60 in, 87.6 x 66 mm), 9.2:1 compression ratio, max power (DIN) 72 hp at 5,500 rpm, max torque (DIN) 87 lb ft, 12 kg m at 2,700 rpm, 45.2 hp/l, 1 Ford 71 HW/9510/YA carburettor.
TRANSMISSION gearbox ratios I 3.650, II 1.970, III 1.370, IV 1, rev 3.660, 3.890 axle ratio (4.110 for Turnier, see below), 6.45 x 13 tyres (165 x 13 on request for L Coupé and L Turnier, see below).
PERFORMANCE max speed 94 mph, 152 km/h, power-weight ratio 29.5 lb/hp, 13.4 kg/hp, fuel consumption 27.2 m/imp gal, 22.6 m/US gal, 10.4 l x 100 km.
BRAKES servo.
DIMENSIONS AND WEIGHT dry weight 2,161 lb, 980 kg.

OPTIONAL ACCESSORIES Borg-Warner 35 automatic transmission with 55 Ah battery (only with 97.1 cu in, 1,592 cc engine), hydraulic torque converter and planetary gears with 3 ratios (I 2.393, II 1.450, III 1, rev 2.094), max ratio of converter at stall 1.91, possible manual selection; 4.440 axle ratio; 165 x 13 tyres; 5.5" wide rims; heavy-duty suspension; servo brake; sunshine roof; electrically-heated rear window.

Taunus 4-door Limousine

See Taunus 2-door Limousine, except for:

PRICE EX WORKS: 8,000 marks.

PERFORMANCE power-weight ratio: 34.2 lb/hp, 15.5 kg/hp.

DIMENSIONS AND WEIGHT dry weight: 2,150 lb, 975 kg.

FORD Taunus 2-door Limousine

FORD Taunus GXL 4-door Limousine

FORD Taunus GXL Coupé

Taunus 5-door Turnier

See Taunus 2-door Limousine, except for:

PRICE EX WORKS: 8,435 marks.

TRANSMISSION axle ratio: 4.440; tyres: 6.45 x 13.

PERFORMANCE power-weight ratio: 36.4 lb/hp, 16.5 kg/hp.

DIMENSIONS AND WEIGHT length: 172.01 in, 4,369 mm; height: 53.94 in, 1,370 mm; dry weight: 2,293 lb, 1,040 kg.

BODY estate car/station wagon; 4 + 1 doors.

Taunus L 2-door Limousine

See Taunus 2-door Limousine, except for:

PRICE EX WORKS: 7,935 marks.

Taunus L 4-door Limousine

See Taunus 4-door Limousine, except for:

PRICE EX WORKS: 8,310 marks.

Taunus L Coupé

See Taunus 2-door Limousine, except for:

PRICE EX WORKS: 8,480 marks.

PERFORMANCE power-weight ratio: 33.7 lb/hp, 15.3 kg/hp.

DIMENSIONS AND WEIGHT width: 67.24 in, 1,708 mm; height: 52.40 in, 1,331 mm; dry weight: 2,128 lb, 965 kg.

BODY coupé.

Taunus L 5-door Turnier

See Taunus 5-door Turnier, except for:

PRICE EX WORKS: 8,745 marks.

Taunus XL 2-door Limousine

See Taunus 2-door Limousine, except for:

PRICE EX WORKS: 8,815 marks.

ELECTRICAL EQUIPMENT 35 A alternator.

Taunus XL 4-door Limousine

See Taunus 4-door Limousine, except for:

PRICE EX WORKS: 9,190 marks.

ELECTRICAL EQUIPMENT 35 A alternator.

Taunus XL Coupé

See Taunus L Coupé, except for:

PRICE EX WORKS: 9,325 marks.

ELECTRICAL EQUIPMENT 35 A alternator.

Taunus XL 5-door Turnier

See Taunus 5-door Turnier, except for:

PRICE EX WORKS: 9,625 marks.

ELECTRICAL EQUIPMENT 35 A alternator.

Taunus GT 2-door Limousine

See Taunus 2-door Limousine, except for:

PRICE EX WORKS: 9,520 marks.

ENGINE 97.1 cu in, 1,592 cc (3.45 x 2.60 in, 87.6 x 66 mm); compression ratio: 9.2:1; max power (DIN): 88 hp at 5,700 rpm; max torque (DIN): 92 lb ft, 12.7 kg m at 4,000 rpm; max engine rpm: 6,200; 55.2 hp/l; lubricating system capacity: 7 imp pt, 8.5 US pt, 4 l; 1 Weber carburettor.

TRANSMISSION gearbox ratios: I 3.650, II 1.970, III 1.370, IV 1, rev 3.660; axle ratio: 3.890; width of rims: 5.5"; tyres: 155 x 13.

PERFORMANCE max speeds: (I) 27 mph, 44 km/h; (II) 51 mph, 82 km/h; (III) 73 mph, 118 km/h; (IV) 101 mph, 162 km/h; power-weight ratio: 24.9 lb/hp, 11.3 kg/hp; speed in direct drive at 1,000 rpm: 16.8 mph, 27 km/h; fuel consumption: 27.4 m/imp gal, 22.8 m/US gal, 10.3 l x 100 km.

CHASSIS front suspension: anti-roll bar.

BRAKES servo (standard); swept area: front 76.8 sq in, 486 sq cm, rear 121 sq in, 780 sq cm, total 197.8 sq in, 1,266 sq cm.

ELECTRICAL EQUIPMENT 35 A alternator.

DIMENSIONS AND WEIGHT dry weight: 2,194 lb, 995 kg.

VARIATIONS

ENGINE 6 cylinders, Vee-slanted 60°, 120.9 cu in, 1,981 cc (3.31 x 2.37 in, 84 x 60.1 mm), 9:1 compression ratio, max power (DIN) 90 hp at 5,000 rpm, max torque (DIN) 110 lb ft, 15.2 kg m at 3,000 rpm, 45.4 hp/l, 4 crankshaft bearings, lubricating system capacity 7.9 imp pt, 9.5 US pt, 4.5 l, 1 Solex twin barrel carburettor, cooling system capacity 13.7 imp pt, 16.5 US pt, 7.8 l.
TRANSMISSION 3.440 axle ratio.
PERFORMANCE max speed 102 mph, 163 km/h, power-weight ratio 27.3 lb/hp, 12.4 kg/hp, fuel consumption 26.2 m/imp gal, 21.8 m/US gal, 10.8 l x 100 km.
ELECTRICAL EQUIPMENT 55 Ah battery.
DIMENSIONS AND WEIGHT dry weight 2,459 lb, 1,115 kg.

ENGINE 6 cylinders, Vee-slanted at 60°, 138.8 cu in, 2,274 cc (3.54 x 2.37 in, 90 x 60.1 mm), max power (DIN) 108 hp at 5,000 rpm, max torque (DIN) 130 lb ft, 18 kg m at 3,000 rpm, 54.1 hp/l, 4 crankshaft bearings, lubricating system capacity 7.9 imp pt, 9.5 US pt, 4.5 l, 1 Solex twin barrel carburettor.
TRANSMISSION 3.440 axle ratio.
PERFORMANCE max speed 107 mph, 173 km/h, power-weight ratio 22.7 lb/hp, 10.3 kg/hp, fuel consumption 28 m/imp gal, 23.3 m/US gal, 10.1 l x 100 km.
ELECTRICAL EQUIPMENT 55 Ah battery, 35 A alternator.
DIMENSIONS AND WEIGHT dry weight 2,459 lb, 1,115 kg.

OPTIONAL ACCESSORIES only Borg-Warner 35 automatic transmission with 4.110 axle ratio; 185/70 HR x 13 tyres with 5.5" wide rims.

Taunus GT 4-door Limousine

See Taunus GT 2-door Limousine, except for:

PRICE EX WORKS: 9,895 marks.

PERFORMANCE power-weight ratio: 22.5 lb/hp, 10.2 kg/hp.

DIMENSIONS AND WEIGHT dry weight: 2,249 lb, 1,020 kg.

Taunus GT Coupé

See Taunus GT 2-door Limousine, except for:

PRICE EX WORKS: 10,030 marks.

PERFORMANCE power-weight ratio: 25.4 lb/hp, 11.5 kg/hp.

DIMENSIONS AND WEIGHT width: 67.24 in, 1,708 mm; height: 52.40 in, 1,331 mm; dry weight: 2,227 lb, 1,010 kg.

BODY coupé.

Taunus GXL 2-door Limousine

See Taunus GT 2-door Limousine, except for:

PRICE EX WORKS: 10,195 marks.

BODY electrically-heated rear window.

Taunus GXL 4-door Limousine

See Taunus GT 4-door Limousine, except for:

PRICE EX WORKS: 10,570 marks.

BODY electrically-heated rear window.

FORD Taunus Series

FORD Taunus XL Series

FORD Taunus GXL Series

Taunus GXL Coupé

See Taunus GT Coupé, except for:

PRICE EX WORKS: 10,705 marks.

BODY electrically-heated rear window.

Capri 1300

PRICE EX WORKS: 8,365 marks.

ENGINE front, 4 stroke; 4 cylinders, Vee-slanted at 60°; 78.6 cu in, 1,288 cc (3.31 x 2.32 in, 84 x 58.9 mm); compression ratio: 8.2:1; max power (DIN): 50 hp at 5,000 rpm; max torque (DIN): 69 lb ft, 9.5 kg m at 2,500 rpm; max engine rpm: 5,000; 39 hp/l; cast iron cylinder block and head; 3 crankshaft bearings; valves: overhead, push-rods and rockers; camshafts: 1, at centre of Vee; lubrication: rotary pump, full flow filter, 6.2 imp pt, 7.4 US pt, 3.5 l; 1 Ford C8GH-A downdraught carburettor; fuel feed: mechanical pump; water-cooled, 11.3 imp pt, 13.5 US pt, 6.4 l, thermostatic fan.

TRANSMISSION driving wheels: rear; clutch: single dry plate; gearbox: mechanical; gears: 4, fully synchronized; ratios: I 3.650, II 1.970, III 1.370, IV 1, rev 3.660; lever: central; final drive: hypoid bevel; axle ratio: 4.110; width of rims: 4.5''; tyres: 6.00 x 13.

PERFORMANCE max speeds: (I) 24 mph, 38 km/h; (II) 42 mph, 67 km/h; (III) 60 mph, 96 km/h; (IV) 83 mph, 133 km/h; power-weight ratio: 43 lb/hp, 19.5 kg/hp; carrying capacity: 706 lb, 320 kg; speed in direct drive at 1,000 rpm: 16.5 mph, 26.5 km/h; fuel consumption: 31.4 m/imp gal, 26.1 m/US gal, 9 l x 100 km.

CHASSIS integral; front suspension: independent, by McPherson, coil springs/telescopic damper struts, lower transverse arms, anti-roll bar; rear suspension: rigid axle, semi-elliptic leafsprings, rubber springs, telescopic dampers.

STEERING rack-and-pinion.

BRAKES front disc (diameter 9.49 in, 241 mm), rear drum; swept area: front 34.8 sq in, 224 sq cm, rear 75.6 sq in 488 sq cm, total 110.4 sq in, 712 sq cm.

ELECTRICAL EQUIPMENT 12 V; 44 Ah battery; 25 A dynamo; Bosch distributor; 2 headlamps.

DIMENSIONS AND WEIGHT wheel base: 100.75 in, 2,559 mm; tracks: 52.99 in, 1,346 mm front, 51.97 in, 1,320 mm rear; length: 167.79 in, 4,262 mm; width: 64.76 in, 1,645 mm; height: 52.36 in, 1,330 mm; ground clearance: 5 in, 127 mm; dry weight: 2,150 lb, 975 kg; turning circle (between walls): 33.5 ft, 10.2 m; fuel tank: 12.8 imp gal, 15.3 US gal, 58 l.

BODY coupé; 2 doors; 4 seats, separate front seats.

PRACTICAL INSTRUCTIONS fuel: 90 oct petrol; engine sump oil: 5.3 imp pt, 6.3 US pt, 3 l, SAE 20W-40, change every 6,200 miles, 10,000 km; gearbox oil: 2.3 imp pt, 2.7 US pt, 1.3 l, SAE 80, change every 12,400 miles, 20,000 km; final drive oil: 1.9 imp pt, 2.3 US pt, 1.1 l, SAE 90, change every 12,400 miles, 20,000 km; greasing: none; tappet clearances: inlet 0.014 in, 0.35 mm, exhaust 0.016 in, 0.40 mm; valve timing: 23° 84° 65° 42°; tyre pressure: front 24 psi, 1.7 atm, rear 27 psi, 1.9 atm.

OPTIONAL ACCESSORIES 5'' wheels; 165 x 13 tyres; servo brake; alternator; sunshine roof; L equipment; XL equipment.

Capri 1500

See Capri 1300, except for:

PRICE EX WORKS: 8,330 marks.

ENGINE 90.8 cu in, 1,488 cc (3.54 x 2.32 in, 90 x 58.9 mm); compression ratio: 9:1; max power (DIN): 65 hp at 5,000 rpm; max torque (DIN) 85 lb ft, 11.7 kg m at 2,500 rpm; 34.2 hp/l.

TRANSMISSION axle ratio: 3.890.

PERFORMANCE max speeds: (I) 25 mph, 41 km/h; (II) 44 mph, 71 km/h; (III) 63 mph, 102 km/h; (IV) 90 mph, 145 km/h; power-weight ratio: 33 lb/hp, 15 kg/hp; speed in direct drive at 1,000 rpm: 17.4 mph, 28 km/h; fuel consumption: 28.8 m/imp gal, 24 m/US gal, 9.8 l x 100 km.

ELECTRICAL EQUIPMENT 44 Ah battery.

OPTIONAL ACCESSORIES automatic transmission with 55 Ah battery, hydraulic torque converter and planetary gears with 3 ratios (I 2.393, II 1.450, III 1, rev 2.094), max ratio of converter at stall 2.28, possible manual selection.

FORD Capri XL Series

FORD Capri GXL Series

FORD Consul Series

Capri GT 1700

See Capri 1300, except for:

PRICE EX WORKS: 9,125 marks.

ENGINE 103 cu in, 1,688 cc (3.54 x 2.63 in, 90 x 66.8 mm) compression ratio: 9:1; max power (DIN): 75 hp at 5,000 rpm; max torque (DIN): 94 lb ft, 13 kg m at 2,500 rpm; max engine rpm: 5,200; 43.2 hp/l; 1 Solex 32 TDID carburettor.

TRANSMISSION clutch: diaphragm; axle ratio: 3.700; tyres 165 x 13 (standard).

PERFORMANCE max speeds: (I) 28 mph, 45 km/h; (II) 48 mph, 78 km/h; (III) 70 mph, 113 km/h; (IV) 96 mph, 155 km/h; power-weight ratio: 31 lb/hp, 13 kg/hp; speed in direct at 1,000 rpm: 18.5 mph, 29.8 km/h; fuel consumption 28.5 m/imp gal, 23.8 m/US gal, 9.9 l x 100 km.

BRAKES front disc (diameter 9.61 in, 244 mm), servo (standard); swept area: front 46.8 sq in, 302 sq cm, rear 99 sq in, 638 sq cm, total 145.8 sq in, 940 sq cm.

ELECTRICAL EQUIPMENT 44 Ah battery.

DIMENSIONS AND WEIGHT dry weight: 2,161 lb, 980 kg.

OPTIONAL ACCESSORIES automatic transmission (for other elements see optional accessories of Capri 1500 mentioned above); L equipment; XL equipment; XLR equipment.

Capri GT 2000

See Capri 1300, except for:

PRICE EX WORKS: 9,670 marks.

ENGINE 6 cylinders, Vee-slanted at 60°; 121.1 cu in, 1,985 cc (3.31 x 2.37 in, 84 x 60.1 mm); compression ratio: 9:1; max power (DIN): 90 hp at 5,000 rpm; max torque (DIN) 112 lb ft, 15.5 kg m at 3,000 rpm; max engine rpm: 5,300; 45.3 hp/l; 4 crankshaft bearings; lubricating system capacity: 7.9 imp pt, 9.5 US pt, 4.5 l; 1 Solex 32 DDIST downdraught twin barrel carburettor; cooling system capacity: 13.7 imp pt, 16.5 US pt, 7.8 l.

TRANSMISSION clutch: diaphragm; axle ratio: 3.440; tyres: 165 x 13 (standard).

PERFORMANCE max speeds: (I) 30 mph, 48 km/h; (II) 52 mph, 83 km/h (III) 75 mph, 120 km/h; (IV) 104 mph, 168 km/h; power-weight ratio: 25.2 lb/hp, 11.4 kg/hp; speed in direct drive at 1,000 rpm: 19.4 mph, 31.2 km/h; fuel consumption: 26.6 m/imp gal, 22.2 m/US gal, 10.6 l x 100 km.

BRAKES front disc (diameter 9.61 in, 244 mm), servo (standard); swept area: front 46.8 sq in, 302 sq cm, rear 99 sq in, 638 sq cm, total 145.8 sq in, 940 sq cm.

ELECTRICAL EQUIPMENT 44 Ah battery; 28 A alternator; 2 halogen headlamps.

DIMENSIONS AND WEIGHT dry weight: 2,271 lb, 1,030 kg

OPTIONAL ACCESSORIES see Capri GT 1700.

Capri GT 2300

See Capri 1300, except for:

PRICE EX WORKS: 10,230 marks.

ENGINE 6 cylinders, Vee-slanted at 60°; 138.8 cu in, 2,274 cc (3.54 x 2.37 in, 90 x 60.1 mm); compression ratio: 9:1; max power (DIN): 108 hp at 5,100 rpm; max torque (DIN): 134 lb ft, 18.5 kg m at 3,500 rpm; max engine rpm: 5,600; 47.5 hp/l; 4 crankshaft bearings; lubricating system capacity: 7.9 imp pt, 9.5 US pt, 4.5 l; 1 Solex 35 DDIST downdraught twin barrel carburettor; cooling system capacity: 13.7 imp pt, 16.5 US pt, 7.8 l.

TRANSMISSION clutch: diaphragm; axle ratio: 3.220; tyres: 165 x 13 (standard).

PERFORMANCE max speeds: (I) 32 mph, 51 km/h; (II) 56 mph, 90 km/h; (III) 81 mph, 130 km/h; (IV) 111 mph, 178 km/h; power-weight ratio: 20.9 lb/hp, 9.6 kg/hp; speed in direct drive at 1,000 rpm: 19.9 mph, 32 km/h; fuel consumption: 27.4 m/imp gal, 22.8 m/US gal, 10.3 l x 100 km.

BRAKES front disc (diameter 9.61 in, 244 mm), servo (standard); swept area: front 46.8 sq in, 302 sq cm, rear 99 sq in, 638 sq cm, total 145.8 sq in, 940 sq cm.

ELECTRICAL EQUIPMENT 55 Ah battery; 28 A alternator.

DIMENSIONS AND WEIGHT dry weight: 2,293 lb, 1,040 kg.

OPTIONAL ACCESSORIES see Capri GT 1700 (with automatic transmission, 66 Ah battery).

FORD Capri XL

FORD Capri GXL

FORD Consul L 2-door Limousine

Capri GT 2600

See Capri GT 2300, except for:

PRICE EX WORKS: 10,760 marks.

ENGINE 155.5 cu in, 2,520 cc (3.54 x 2.63 in, 90 x 66.8 mm); compression ratio: 9:1; max power (DIN): 125 hp at 5,300 rpm; max torque (DIN): 149 lb ft, 20.5 kg m at 3,100 rpm; 36.4 hp/l.

TRANSMISSION width of rims: 5''; tyres: 185/70 x 13.

PERFORMANCE max speed: 118 mph, 190 km/h; power-weight ratio: 17.1 lb/hp, 8.3 kg/hp; fuel consumption: 27.2 m/imp gal, 22.6 m/US gal, 10.4 l x 100 km.

BRAKES swept area: rear 127.2 sq in, 820 sq cm.

Capri RS 2600

See Capri 2300 GT, except for:

PRICE EX WORKS: 16,195 marks.

ENGINE 159.6 cu in, 2,615 cc (3.54 x 2.72 in, 90 x 69 mm); compression ratio: 10.5:1; max power (DIN): 150 hp at 5,800 rpm; max torque (DIN): 159 lb ft, 21.9 kg m at 4,000 rpm; max engine rpm: 6,000; 57.6 hp/l; injection pump in inlet pipes (Kugelfischer system); fuel feed: mechanical pump.

TRANSMISSION ratios I 3.160, II 1.940, III 1.410, IV 1, rev 3.346; axle ratio: 3.090; width of rims: 6''; tyres: 185/70 x 13.

PERFORMANCE max speed: 127 mph, 205 km/h; power-weight ratio: 15.8 lb/hp, 7.2 kg/hp; fuel consumption: 32.1 m/imp gal, 26.7 m/US gal, 8.8 l x 100 km.

BRAKES swept area: front 41 sq in, 264 sq cm, rear 119 sq in, 768 sq cm, total 160 sq in, 1,032 sq cm.

DIMENSIONS AND WEIGHT tracks: 54.80 in, 1,392 mm front, 54.80 in, 1,392 mm rear; length: 166.93 in, 4,240 mm; width: 65.83 in, 1,672 mm; height: 50.51 in, 1,283 mm; dry weight: 2,381 lb, 1,080 kg; fuel tank: 12.8 imp gal, 16.3 US gal, 58 l.

Consul 2-door Limousine

PRICE EX WORKS: 9,830 marks.

ENGINE front, 4 stroke; 4 cylinders, Vee-slanted at 60°; 102.5 cu in, 1,680 cc (3.54 x 2.63 in, 90 x 66.8 mm); compression ratio: 9:1; max power (DIN): 75 hp at 5,000 rpm; max torque (DIN): 94 lb ft, 13 kg m at 2,500 rpm; max engine rpm: 5,500; 44.5 hp/l; cast iron cylinder block and head; 3 crankshaft bearings; valves: overhead, in line; camshafts: 1, at centre of Vee; lubrication: gear pump, full flow filter, 6.5 imp pt, 7.8 US pt, 3.7 l; 1 Solex 32 TDID downdraught carburettor; fuel feed: mechanical pump; water-cooled, 10.6 imp pt, 12.7 US pt, 6 l.

TRANSMISSION driving wheels: rear; clutch: single dry plate (diaphragm); gearbox: mechanical; gears: 4, fully synchronized; ratios: I 3.650, II 1.970, III 1.370, IV 1, rev 3.660; final drive: hypoid bevel; axle ratio: 4.110; width of rims: 5.5''; tyres: 6.45 x 14.

PERFORMANCE max speed: 90 mph, 145 km/h; power-weight ratio: 35.1 lb/hp, 15.9 kg/hp; speed in direct drive at 1,000 rpm: 16.8 mph, 27.1 km/h; fuel consumption: 26.9 m/imp gal, 22.4 m/US gal, 10.5 l x 100 km.

CHASSIS integral, front and rear auxiliary frames; front suspension: independent, wishbones (lower trailing links), coil springs, anti-roll bar, telescopic dampers; rear suspension: independent, oblique semi-trailing arms, coil springs, telescopic dampers.

STEERING rack-and-pinion.

BRAKES front disc (diameter 10.31 in, 262 mm), rear drum, servo.

ELECTRICAL EQUIPMENT 12 V; 44 A battery; 28 A alternator; Ford distributor; 2 headlamps.

DIMENSIONS AND WEIGHT wheel base: 109.02 in, 2,769 mm; tracks: 59.49 in, 1,511 mm front, 60.51 in, 1,537 mm rear; length: 180 in, 4,572 mm; width: 70.51 in, 1,791 mm; height: 54.68 in, 1,389 mm; ground clearance: 5.04 in, 128 mm; dry weight: 2,635 lb, 1,195 kg; turning circle (between walls): 36.7 ft, 11.2 m; fuel tank: 14.5 imp gal, 17.4 US gal, 66 l.

BODY saloon/sedan; 2 doors; 5 seats, reclining backrests.

PRACTICAL INSTRUCTIONS fuel: 90 oct petrol; engine sump oil: 5.6 imp pt, 6.8 US pt, 3.2 l, SAE 10W-40, change every 6,200 miles, 10,000 km; gearbox oil: 3 imp pt, 3.6 US pt, 1.7 l, SAE 80, no change recommended; final drive

CONSUL 2-DOOR LIMOUSINE

oil: 3.2 imp pt, 3.8 US pt, 1.8 l, SAE 90, no change recommended; greasing: none; tappet clearances: inlet 0.014 in, 0.35 mm, exhaust 0.016 in, 0.40 mm; valve timing: 24° 84° 65° 42°; tyre pressure: front 20 psi, 1.4 atm, rear 22 psi, 1.6 atm.

VARIATIONS

ENGINE 119.3 cu in, 1,955 cc (3.57 x 3.13 in, 90.8 x 79.6 mm), 9.2:1 compression ratio, max power (DIN) 99 hp at 5,500 rpm, max torque (DIN) 112 lb ft, 15.4 kg m at 4,000 rpm; max engine rpm 5,500, 51.1 hp/l; 5 crankshaft bearings, Vee-slanted valves, rockers, camshafts 1, overhead, 1 Weber downdraught carburettor, water-cooled, 12.3 imp pt, 14.8 US pt, 7 l.
TRANSMISSION 6.95 S x 14 tyres.
PERFORMANCE max speed 100 mph, 161 km/h, power-weight ratio 27.1 lb/hp, 12.3 kg/hp, speed in top at 1,000 rpm 17.3 mph, 27.9 km/h, fuel consumption 27.4 m/imp gal, 22.8 m/US gal, 10.3 l x 100 km.
ELECTRICAL EQUIPMENT 55 Ah battery.
DIMENSIONS AND WEIGHT dry weight 2,712 lb, 1,230 kg.

ENGINE 6 cylinders, Vee-slanted at 60°, 138.8 cu in, 2,274 cc (3.54 x 2.37 in, 90 x 60.1 mm), 9:1 compression ratio, max power (DIN) 108 hp at 5,000 rpm, max torque (DIN) 130 lb ft, 18 kg m at 3,000 rpm, max engine rpm 5,000, 47.5 hp/l, 4 crankshaft bearings, lubricating system capacity 7.4 imp pt, 8.9 US pt, 4.2 l, 1 Solex downdraught twin barrel carburettor, cooling system capacity 18 imp pt, 21.6 US pt, 10.2 l.
TRANSMISSION 6.95 S x 14 tyres, 3.890 axle ratio.
PERFORMANCE max speed 102 mph, 164 km/h, power-weight ratio 26 lb/hp, 11.8 kg/hp, speed in top at 1,000 rpm 18.3 mph, 29.5 km/h, consumption 26.4 m/imp gal, 22 m/US gal, 10.7 l x 100 km.
ELECTRICAL EQUIPMENT 55 Ah battery.
DIMENSIONS AND WEIGHT dry weight 2,822 lb, 1,280 kg.

OPTIONAL ACCESSORIES Automatic transmission, hydraulic torque converter and planetary gears with 3 ratios (I 2.460, II 1.460, III 1, rev 2.200), max ratio of converter at stall 2.1, 66 Ah battery; 175 x 14 tyres with 5.5" wide rims; 185 SR x 14 with 6" wide rims; 4.400 axle ratio; sunshine roof; electrically-heated rear window.

Consul 4-door Limousine

See Consul 2-door Limousine, except for:

PRICE EX WORKS: 10,200 marks.

ELECTRICAL EQUIPMENT 35 A alternator.

DIMENSIONS AND WEIGHT height: 55.63 in, 1,413 mm.

Consul Turnier

See Consul 2-door Limousine, except for:

PRICE EX WORKS: 10,750 marks.

TRANSMISSION tyres: 7.35 x 14; axle ratio: 4.440 (only for 102.5 cu in, 1,680 cc engine).

BRAKES front disc (diameter 10 in, 254 mm).

DIMENSIONS AND WEIGHT length: 184.02 in, 4,674 mm; height: 56.57 in, 1,437 mm; ground clearance: 5.39 in, 137 mm; fuel tank: 13.6 imp gal, 16.4 US gal, 62 l.

OPTIONAL ACCESSORIES 7.35 S x 14 tyres (only with 119.3 cu in, 1,955 cc and 138.8 cu in, 2,274 cc engine).

Consul L 2-door Limousine

See Consul 2-door Limousine, except for:

PRICE EX WORKS: 10,420 marks.

ELECTRICAL EQUIPMENT 35 A alternator.

DIMENSIONS AND WEIGHT height: 55.63 in, 1,413 mm.

Consul L 4-door Limousine

See Consul 4-door Limousine, except for:

PRICE EX WORKS: 10,790 marks.

FORD Consul GT 2-door Limousine

FORD Granada Turnier

FORD Granada GXL 4-door Limousine

Consul L Turnier

See Consul Turnier, except for:

PRICE EX WORKS: 11,340 marks.

ELECTRICAL EQUIPMENT 35 A alternator.

Consul GT 2-door Limousine

See Consul 2-door Limousine, except for:

PRICE EX WORKS: 11,595 marks.

ENGINE 6 cylinders; Vee-slanted at 60°; 138.8 cu in, 2,274 cc (3.54 x 2.37 in, 90 x 60.1 mm); compression ratio: 9:1; max power (DIN): 108 hp at 5,000 rpm; max torque (DIN): 130 lb ft, 18 kg m at 3,000 rpm; max engine rpm: 5,000; 47.5 hp/l; 4 crankshaft bearings; lubricating system capacity: 7.4 imp pt, 8.9 US pt, 4.2 l; 1 Solex downdraught twin barrel carburettor; cooling system capacity: 18 imp pt, 21.6 US pt, 10.2 l.

TRANSMISSION tyres: 6.95 S x 14; axle ratio: 3.890.

PERFORMANCE max speed: 102 mph, 164 km/h; power-weight ratio: 26 lb/hp, 11.8 kg/hp; speed in top at 1,000 rpm: 18.3 mph, 29.5 km/h; fuel consumption: 26.4 m/imp gal, 22 m/US gal, 10.7 l x 100 km.

ELECTRICAL EQUIPMENT 35 Ah battery.

DIMENSIONS AND WEIGHT dry weight: 2,822 lb, 1,280 kg.

VARIATIONS

ENGINE 179.7 cu in, 2,945 cc (3.69 x 2.85 in, 93.7 x 72.4), 8.9:1 compression ratio, max power (DIN) 138 hp at 5,000 rpm, max torque (DIN) 174 lb ft, 24 kg m at 3,000 rpm, max engine rpm 5,000, 46.8 hp/l, lubricating system capacity 8.8 imp pt, 10.6 US pt, 5 l, 1 Weber downdraught twin barrel carburettor, cooling system capacity 20.1 imp pt, 24.1 US pt, 114 l.
TRANSMISSION ratios I 3.160, II 1.950, III 1.410, IV 1, rev 3.350, axle ratio 3.450, 6" wide rims, 185 SR x 14 tyres.
PERFORMANCE max speed 113 mph, 182 km/h; power-weight ratio 22.1 lb/hp, 10 kg/hp, speed in top at 1,000 rpm 20.8 mph, 33.4 km/h, fuel consumption 24.8 m/imp gal, 20.6 m/US gal, 11.4 l x 100 km.
ELECTRICAL EQUIPMENT 55 Ah battery, 35 A alternator.
DIMENSIONS AND WEIGHT dry weight 3,043 lb, 1,380 kg.

Consul GT 4-door Limousine

See Consul GT 2-door Limousine, except for:

PRICE EX WORKS: 11,965 marks.

DIMENSIONS AND WEIGHT height: 55.63 in, 1,413 mm.

Granada 2-door Limousine

See Consul 2-door Limousine, except for:

PRICE EX WORKS: 12,475 marks.

ENGINE 6 cylinders, Vee-slanted at 60°; 138.8 cu in, 2,274 cc (3.54 x 2.37 in, 90 x 60.1 mm); compression ratio: 9:1; max power (DIN): 108 hp at 5,000 rpm; max torque (DIN): 130 lb ft, 18 kg m at 3,000 rpm; max engine rpm: 5,000; 47.5 hp/l; 4 crankshaft bearings; lubricating system capacity: 7.4 imp pt, 8.9 US pt, 4.2 l; 1 Solex downdraught twin barrel carburettor; cooling system capacity: 18 imp pt, 21.6 US pt, 10.2 l.

TRANSMISSION axle ratio: 3.890; tyres: 6.95 S x 14.

PERFORMANCE max speed: 102 mph, 164 km/h; power-weight ratio: 26.9 lb/hp, 12.2 kg/hp; speed in direct drive at 1,000 rpm: 18.3 mph, 29.5 km/h; fuel consumption: 26.4 m/imp gal, 22 m/US gal, 10.7 l x 100 km.

ELECTRICAL EQUIPMENT 35 A alternator.

DIMENSIONS AND WEIGHT dry weight: 2,922 lb, 1,325 kg.

VARIATIONS

ENGINE 153.8 cu in, 2,520 cc (3.54 x 2.63 in, 90 x 66.8 mm), max power (DIN) 125 hp at 5,000 rpm, max torque (DIN) 149 lb ft, 20.5 kg m at 3,500 rpm, 49.5 hp/l.
TRANSMISSION ratios I 3.160, II 1.950, III 1.410, IV 1, rev 3.350, axle ratio 3.640, 175 SR x 14 tyres.
PERFORMANCE max speed 109 mph, 175 km/h, power-weight ratio 23.8 lb/hp, 10.8 kg/hp, speed in top at 1,000 rpm 19.6 mph, 31.6 km/h; fuel consumption 26.9 m/imp gal, 22.4 m/US gal, 10.5 l x 100 km.
DIMENSION AND WEIGHT dry weight 2,977 lb, 1,350 kg.

FORD Consul GT Series

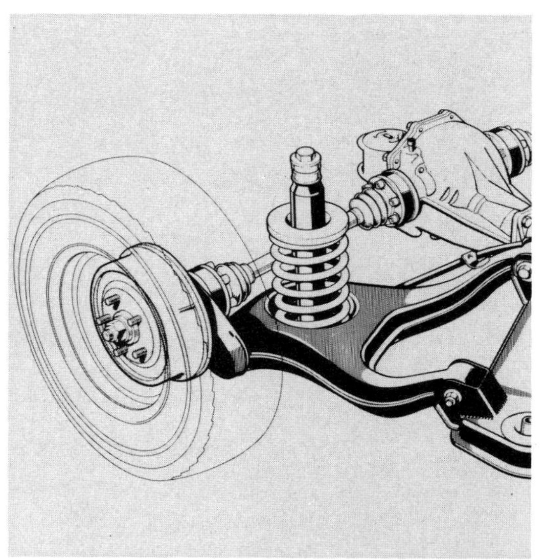

FORD Consul/Granada Series

FORD Granada Series

ENGINE 179.7 cu in, 2,945 cc (3.69 x 2.85 in, 93.7 x 72.4 mm); compression ratio 8.9:1, max power (DIN) 138 hp at 5,000 rpm, max torque (DIN) 174 lb ft, 24 kg m at 3,000 rpm, 46.8 hp/l, lubricating system capacity 8.8 imp pt, 10.6 US pt, 5 l, cooling system capacity 20.1 imp pt, 24.1 US pt, 11.4 l.
TRANSMISSION ratios I 3.160, II 1.950, III 1.410, IV 1, rev 3.350, axle ratio 3.450, tyres 175 HR x 14.
PERFORMANCE max speed 113 mph, 182 km/h, power-weight ratio 22.1 lb/hp, 10 kg/hp, speed in top at 1,000 rpm 20.8 mph, 33.4 km/h, fuel consumption 24.8 m/imp gal, 20.6 m/ US gal, 11.4 l x 100 km.
DIMENSIONS AND WEIGHT dry weight 3,043 lb, 1,380 kg.

OPTIONAL ACCESSORIES power-assisted steering.

Granada 4-door Limousine

See Granada 2-door Limousine, except for:

PRICE EX WORKS: 12,845 marks.

DIMENSIONS AND WEIGHT height: 55.63 in, 1,413 mm.

Granada Turnier

See Granada 2-door Limousine, except for:

PRICE EX WORKS: 13,395 marks.

TRANSMISSION tyres: 7.35 S x 14.

DIMENSIONS AND WEIGHT length: 184.02 in, 4,674 mm; height: 56.57 in, 1,437 mm; ground clearance: 5.39 in, 137 mm; fuel tank: 13.6 imp gal, 16.4 US gal, 62 l.

VARIATIONS

ENGINE 153.8 cu in, 2,520 cc not available.

Granada GXL 2-door Limousine

See Granada 2-door Limousine, except for:

PRICE EX WORKS: 15,185 marks.

Granada GXL 4-door Limousine

See Granada 2-door Limousine, except for:

PRICE EX WORKS: 15,555 marks.

DIMENSIONS AND WEIGHT height: 55.63 in, 1,413 mm.

MERCEDES-BENZ GERMANY (F.R.)

200

PRICE EX WORKS: 13,930 marks.

ENGINE front, 4 stroke; 4 cylinders, vertical, in line; 121.3 cu in, 1,988 cc (3.43 x 3.29 in, 87 x 83.6 mm); compression ratio: 9:1; max power (DIN): 95 hp at 4,800 rpm; max torque (DIN): 115 lb ft, 15.9 kg m at 2,800 rpm; max engine rpm: 6,000; 47.6 hp/l; cast iron cylinder block, light alloy head; 5 crankshaft bearings; valves: overhead, in line, finger levers; camshafts: 1, overhead; lubrication: gear pump, oil-water heat exchanger, full flow filter, 7.9 imp pt, 9.5 US pt, 4.5 l; 1 Stromberg 175 CD horizontal carburettor; fuel feed: mechanical pump; water-cooled, 18.8 imp pt, 22.6 US pt, 10.7 l.

TRANSMISSION driving wheels: rear; clutch: single dry plate, hydraulically controlled; gearbox: mechanical; gears: 4, fully synchronized; ratios: I 3.900, II 2.300, III 1.410, IV 1, rev 3.660; lever: steering column; final drive: hypoid bevel; axle ratio: 3.920; tyres: 6.95 S x 14 or 175 S x 14.

PERFORMANCE max speeds: (I) 28 mph, 45 km/h; (II) 47 mph, 75 km/h; (III) 78 mph, 125 km/h; (IV) 99 mph, 160 km/h; power-weight ratio: 30.9 lb/hp, 14 kg/hp; carrying capacity: 1,147 lb, 520 kg; fuel consumption: 25.9 m/imp gal, 21.6 m/US gal, 10.9 l x 100 km.

CHASSIS integral, front auxiliary frame; front suspension: independent, wishbones, coil springs, auxiliary rubber springs, anti-roll bar, telescopic dampers; rear suspension: independent, oblique semi-trailing arms, coil springs, auxiliary rubber springs, anti-roll bar, telescopic dampers.

200

STEERING recirculating ball, damper; turns lock to lock: 4.60.

BRAKES disc (front diameter 10.75 in, 273 mm, rear 10.98 in, 279 mm), servo; swept area: front 23.6 sq in, 152 sq cm, rear 15.5 sq in, 100 sq cm, total 39.1 sq in, 252 sq cm.

ELECTRICAL EQUIPMENT 12 V; 55 Ah battery; 490 W alternator; Bosch distributor; 2 headlamps.

DIMENSIONS AND WEIGHT wheel base: 108.27 in, 2,750 mm; tracks: 57 in, 1,448 mm front, 56.69 in, 1,440 mm rear; length: 184.45 in, 4,685 mm; width: 69.68 in, 1,770 mm; height: 56.69 in, 1,440 mm; ground clearance: 6.85 in, 174 mm; dry weight: 2,933 lb, 1,330 kg; turning circle (between walls): 35.4 ft, 10.8 m; fuel tank: 14.3 imp gal, 17.2 US gal, 65 l.

BODY saloon/sedan; 4 doors; 5-6 seats, separate front seats, reclining backrests.

PRACTICAL INSTRUCTIONS fuel: 98 oct petrol; engine sump oil: 7.9 imp pt, 9.5 US pt, 4.5 l, SAE 20W-30, change every 6,200 miles, 10,000 km; gearbox oil: 2.8 imp pt, 3.4 US pt, 1.6 l, ATF, change every 12,400 miles, 20,000 km; final drive oil: 1.9 imp pt, 2.3 US pt, 1.1 l, SAE 90, change every 12,400 miles, 20,000 km; greasing: none; tyre pressure: front 21 psi, 1.5 atm, rear 26 psi, 1.8 atm.

OPTIONAL ACCESSORIES central gear lever; MB automatic transmission, hydraulic coupling and planetary gears with 4 ratios (I 3.980, II 2.390, III 1.460, IV 1, rev 5.470), possible manual selection; automatic levelling control on rear suspension; power-assisted steering; air-conditioning system; sunshine roof; electrically-heated rear window.

200 D

See 200, except for:

PRICE EX WORKS: 14,430 marks.

ENGINE Diesel; compression ratio: 21:1; max power (DIN): 55 hp at 4,200 rpm; max torque (DIN): 83 lb ft, 11.5 kg m at 2,400 rpm; max engine rpm: 4,350; 27,6 hp/l; cast iron cylinder head; 4-cylinder Bosch injection pump.

PERFORMANCE max speeds: (I) 21 mph, 33 km/h; (II) 35 mph, 56 km/h; (III) 57 mph, 92 km/h; (IV) 81 mph, 130 km/h; power-weight ratio: 54,7 lb/hp, 24.8 kg/hp; fuel consumption: 34.9 m/imp gal, 29 m/US gal, 8.1 l x 100 km.

ELECTRICAL EQUIPMENT 66 Ah battery.

DIMENSIONS AND WEIGHT dry weight: 3,010 lb, 1,365 kg.

PRACTICAL INSTRUCTIONS fuel: Diesel oil.

220

See 200, except for:

PRICE IN GB: £ 2,397.
PRICE IN USA: $ 6,267.

ENGINE 134.1 cu in, 2,197 cc (3.43 x 3.64 in, 87 x 92.4 mm); max power (DIN): 105 hp at 4,800 rpm; max torque (DIN): 132 lb ft, 18.2 kg m at 2,800 rpm; 47 hp/l.

PERFORMANCE max speed: 104 mph, 168 km/h; power-weight ratio: 28 lb/hp, 12.7 kg/hp; fuel consumption: 25.4 m/imp gal, 21.2 m/US gal, 11.1 l x 100 km.

DIMENSIONS AND WEIGHT dry weight: 2,944 lb, 1,335 kg.

220 D

See 200 D, except for:

PRICE IN GB: £ 2,680.
PRICE IN USA: $ 6,020.

ENGINE 134.1 cu in, 2,197 cc (3.43 x 3.64 in, 87 x 92.4 mm); max power (DIN): 60 hp at 4,200 rpm; max torque (DIN): 93 lb ft, 12.8 kg m at 2,400 rpm; 27.3 hp/l.

PERFORMANCE max speeds: (I) 21 mph, 33 km/h; (II) 35 mph, 56 km/h; (III) 57 mph, 92 km/h; (IV) 84 mph, 135 km/h; power-weight ratio: 50.5 lb/hp, 22.9 kg/hp; fuel consumption: 33.2 m/imp gal, 27.7 m/US gal, 8.5 l x 100 km.

ELECTRICAL EQUIPMENT 88 Ah battery.

DIMENSIONS AND WEIGHT dry weight: 3,032 lb, 1,375 kg.

MERCEDES-BENZ 200 D

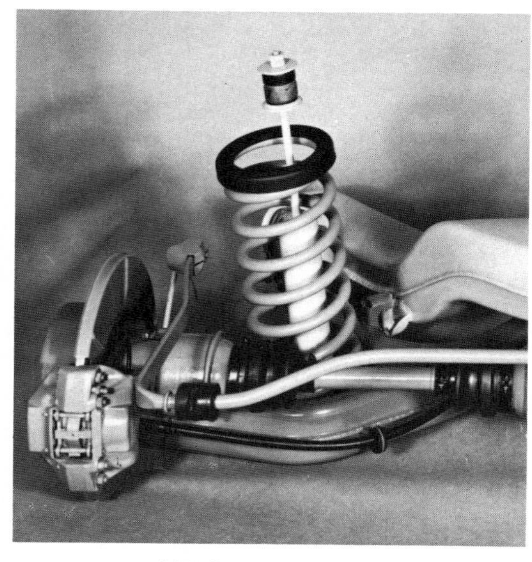

MERCEDES-BENZ 250

MERCEDES-BENZ 280

220 D Lang

See 220 D, except for:

PRICE IN GB: £ 3,881.
PRICE EX WORKS: 21,534 marks.

TRANSMISSION axle ratio: 4.080; tyres: 185 HR x 15.

PERFORMANCE power-weight ratio: 56.7 lb/hp, 25.7 kg/hp; carrying capacity: 1,422 lb, 645 kg.

CHASSIS rear suspension: automatic levelling control (standard).

DIMENSIONS AND WEIGHT wheel base: 133.86 in, 3,400 mm; length: 210.04 in, 5,335 mm; height: 58.46 in, 1,485 mm; dry weight: 3,407 lb, 1,545 kg; turning circle (between walls): 42.3 ft, 12.9 m.

BODY 7-8 seats.

230

See 200, except for:

PRICE EX WORKS: 16,095 marks.

ENGINE 6 cylinders; 139.9 cu in, 2,292 cc (3.22 x 2.87 in, 81.7 x 72.8 mm); max power (DIN): 120 hp at 5,400 rpm; max torque (DIN): 132 lb ft, 18.2 kg m at 3,500 rpm; max engine rpm: 6,300; 52 hp/l; 4 crankshaft bearings; lubrication: oil cooler, 9.7 imp pt, 11.6 US pt, 5.5 l; 2 Zenith 35-40 INAT downdraught twin barrel carburettors.

TRANSMISSION axle ratio: 3.690.

PERFORMANCE max speeds: (I) 31 mph, 50 km/h; (II) 52 mph, 84 km/h; (III) 88 mph, 142 km/h; (IV) 109 mph, 175 km/h; power-weight ratio: 24.7 lb/hp, 11.2 kg/hp; fuel consumption: 25.2 m/imp gal, 21 m/US gal, 11.2 l x 100 km.

DIMENSIONS AND WEIGHT dry weight: 2,988 lb, 1,355 kg.

OPTIONAL ACCESSORIES 5-speed mechanical gearbox (I 3.960, II 2.340, III 1.435, IV 1, V 0.880, rev 3.720), 3.920 axle ratio.

230 Lang

See 230, except for:

PRICE IN GB: £ 3,932.
PRICE EX WORKS: 22,477 marks.

TRANSMISSION axle ratio: 3.920; tyres: 185 x 15.

PERFORMANCE power-weight ratio: 28 lb/hp, 12.7 kg/hp; carrying capacity: 1,422 lb, 645 kg.

CHASSIS rear suspension: automatic levelling control (standard).

DIMENSIONS AND WEIGHT wheel base: 133.86 in, 3,400 mm; length: 210.04 in, 5,335 mm; dry weight: 3,363 lb, 1,525 kg; turning circle (between walls): 42.3 ft, 12.9 m.

BODY 7-8 seats.

250 Limousine

See 200, except for:

PRICE IN GB: £ 2,891.
PRICE IN USA: $ 7,218.

ENGINE 6 cylinders; 169.5 cu in, 2,778 cc (3.41 x 3.10 in, 86.5 x 78.8 mm); max power (DIN): 130 hp at 5,000 rpm; max torque (DIN): 159 lb ft, 22.4 kg m at 3,000 rpm; max engine rpm: 6,500; 46.7 hp/l; 7 crankshaft bearings; lubrication: oil cooler, 7.9 imp pt, 9.5 US pt, 4.5 l; 2 Zenith INAT downdraught twin barrel carburettors; cooling system capacity: 18.5 imp pt, 22.2 US pt, 10.5 l.

TRANSMISSION axle ratio: 3.690.

PERFORMANCE max speeds: (I) 31 mph, 50 km/h; (II) 52 mph, 84 km/h; (III) 88 mph, 142 km/h; (IV) 112 mph, 180 km/h; power-weight ratio: 13.9 lb/hp, 10.6 kg/hp; fuel consumption: 22.6 m/imp gal, 18.8 m/US gal, 12.5 l x 100 km.

DIMENSIONS AND WEIGHT dry weight: 3,065 lb, 1,390 kg.

OPTIONAL ACCESSORIES 5-speed mechanical gearbox (I 3.960, II 2.340, III 1.435, IV 1, V 0.880, rev 3.720), 3.920 axle ratio.

MERCEDES-BENZ 200

MERCEDES-BENZ 250 Limousine

MERCEDES-BENZ 280 CE Coupé

250 C Coupé

See 250 Limousine, except for:

PRICE IN USA: $ 8,069.
PRICE EX WORKS: 19,369 marks.

DIMENSIONS AND WEIGHT width: 70.47 in, 1,790 mm; height: 54.92 in, 1,395 mm.

BODY coupé; 2 doors.

280 Limousine

PRICE EX WORKS: 18,981 marks.

ENGINE front, 4 stroke: 6 cylinders, vertical, in line; 167.6 cu in, 2,746 cc (3.39 x 3.10 in, 86 x 78.8); compression ratio: 9:1; max power (DIN): 160 hp at 5,500 rpm; max torque (DIN): 167 lb ft, 23 kg m at 4,000 rpm; max engine rpm: 6,500; 50.8 hp/l; cast iron cylinder block, light alloy head; 7 crankshaft bearings; valves: overhead, Vee-slanted, finger levers; camshafts: 2, overhead, cogged belt; lubrication: gear pump, oil-water heat exchanger, filter on by-pass, oil cooler, 10.6 imp pt, 12.7 US pt, 6 l; 1 Solex 4AI downdraught twin barrel carburettor; fuel feed: mechanical pump, water-cooled, 17.1 imp pt, 20.5 US pt, 9.7 l, thermostatic fan.

TRANSMISSION driving wheels: rear; clutch: single dry plate, hydraulically controlled; gearbox: mechanical; gears: 4, fully synchronized; ratios: I 3.900, II 2.380, III 1.410, IV, 1, rev 3.660; lever: steering column; final drive: hypoid bevel; axle ratio: 3.690; width of rims: 6"; tyres: 185 HR x 14.

PERFORMANCE max speed: 118 mph, 190 km/h; 19.8 lb/hp, 9 kg/hp; carrying capacity: 1,103 lb, 500 kg; fuel consumption: 22.6 m/imp gal, 18.8 m/US gal, 12.5 l x 100 km.

CHASSIS integral, front auxiliary frame; front suspension: independent, wishbones, coil springs, anti-roll bar, telescopic dampers; rear suspension: independent, oblique semi-trailing arms, coil springs, automatic levelling control, auxiliary rubber springs, telescopic dampers.

STEERING recirculating ball, dampers; turns lock to lock: 4.

BRAKES disc, rear compensator, servo; swept area: front 23.6 sq in, 152 sq cm, 16.3 sq in, 105 sq cm, total 39.9 sq in, 257 sq cm.

ELECTRICAL EQUIPMENT 12 V; 55 Ah battery; 770 W alternator; Bosch distributor; 2 headlamps.

DIMENSIONS AND WEIGHT wheel base: 108.27 in, 2,750 mm; tracks: 58.35 in, 1,482 mm front, 56.69 in, 1,440 mm rear; length: 184.25 in, 4,680 mm; width: 67.72 in, 1,720 mm; height: 56.69 in, 1,440 mm; ground clearance: 5.71 in, 145 mm; dry weight: 3,175 lb, 1,440 kg; turning circle (between walls): 36.1 ft, 11 m; fuel tank: 17.2 imp gal, 20.6 US gal, 78 l.

BODY saloon/sedan; 5-6 seats, separate front seats, reclining backrests.

PRACTICAL INSTRUCTIONS fuel: 96 oct petrol; engine sump oil: 10.6 imp pt, 12.7 US pt, 6 l, SAE 20W-30, change every 3,600 miles, 6,000 km; gearbox oil: 3.2 imp pt, 3.8 US pt, 1.8 l, ATF, change every 12,400 miles, 20,000 km; final drive oil: 4.4 imp pt, 5.3 US pt, 2.5 l, SAE 90, change every 12,400 miles, 20,000 km; greasing: every 3,100 miles, 5,000 km; 20 points; tyre pressure: front 22 psi, 1.6 atm, rear 28 psi, 1.9 atm.

OPTIONAL ACCESSORIES central lever; 5-speed mechanical gearbox (I 3.960, II 2.340, III 1.430, IV 1, V 0.870, rev 3.720), 3.920 axle ratio; MB automatic transmission, hydraulic coupling and planetary gears with 4 ratios (I 3.980, II 2.390, III 1.460, IV 1, rev 5.470), possible manual selection; power-assisted steering; sunshine roof.

280 C Coupé

See 280 Limousine, except for:

PRICE EX WORKS: 21,423 marks.

BODY coupé; 2 doors.

280 E Limousine

See 280 Limousine, except for:

PRICE IN GB: £ 3,305.
PRICE EX WORKS: 20,535 marks.

ENGINE max power (DIN): 185 hp at 6,000 rpm; max torque (DIN): 176 lb ft, 24.3 kg m at 4,500 rpm; 60.7 hp/l;

280 E LIMOUSINE

6-cylinder Bosch intermittent injection pump in inlet pipes; fuel feed: electric pump.

PERFORMANCE max speed: 124 mph, 200 km/h; power-weight ratio: 17.2 lb/hp, 7.8 kg/hp.

280 CE Coupé

See 280 E Limousine, except for:

PRICE IN GB: £ 3,719.
PRICE EX WORKS: 22,977 marks.

BODY coupé; 2 doors.

280 S Limousine

PRICE IN GB: £ 2,958.
PRICE EX WORKS: 23,809 marks.

ENGINE front, 4 stroke; 6 cylinders, vertical, in line; 167.6 cu in, 2,746 cc (3.46 x 3.10 in, 88 x 78.8 mm) compression ratio: 9:1; max power (DIN): 160 hp at 5,500 rpm; max torque (DIN): 167 lb ft, 23 kg m at 4,000 rpm; max engine rpm: 6,500; 58.2 hp/l; cast iron cylinder block, light alloy head; 7 crankshaft bearings; valves: overhead, Vee-slated, finger levers; camshafts: 2, overhead, cogged belt; lubrication: gear pump, full flow filter, oil cooler, 10.6 imp pt, 12.7 US pt, 6 l; 1 Solex 4AI downdraught twin barrel carburettor; fuel feed: mechanical pump; water-cooled, 17.1 imp pt, 20.5 US pt, 9.7 l, thermostatic fan.

TRANSMISSION driving wheels: rear; clutch: single dry plate, hydraulically controlled; gearbox: mechanical; gears: 4, fully synchronized; ratios: I 3.900, II 2.380, III 1.410, IV 1, rev 3.660; lever: central; final drive: hypoid bevel; axle ratio: 3.690; width of rims: 6''; tyres: 185 HR x 14.

PERFORMANCE max speed: 118 mph, 190 km/h; power-weight ratio: 22 lb/hp, 10 kg/hp; carrying capacity: 1,147 lb, 520 kg; speed in direct drive at 1,000 rpm: 19,8 mph, 31.8 km/h; fuel consumption: 22.6 m/imp gal, 18.9 m/US gal, 12.5 l x 100 km.

CHASSIS integral; front suspension: independent, upper wishbones with single transverse rod, longitudinal leading arm in one with anti-roll bar, coil springs, telescopic dampers; rear suspension: independent, oblique semi-trailing arms, coil springs, anti-roll bar, auxiliary rubber springs, telescopic dampers.

STEERING recirculating ball, dampers, servo.

BRAKES disc, servo.

ELECTRICAL EQUIPMENT 12 V; 55 Ah battery; 770 W alternator; Bosch distributor; 4 headlamps.

DIMENSIONS AND WEIGHT wheel base: 112.80 in, 2,865 mm; tracks: 60.04 in, 1,525 mm front, 59.25 in, 1,505 mm rear; length: 195.28 in, 4,960 mm; width: 73.43 in, 1,865 mm; height: 56.10 in, 1,425 mm; ground clearance: 5.71 in, 145 mm; dry weight: 3,550 lb, 1,610 kg; turning circle (between walls): 37.4 ft, 11.4 m; fuel tank: 21.1 imp gal, 25.3 US gal, 96 l.

BODY saloon/sedan; 4 doors; 5 seats, separate front seats; reclining backrests.

PRACTICAL INSTRUCTIONS fuel: 98 oct petrol; engine sump oil: 10.6 imp pt, 12.7 US pt, 6 l, SAE 20W-30, change every 3,600 miles, 6,000 km; gearbox oil 3.2 imp pt, 3.8 US pt, 1.8 l, ATF, change every 12,400 miles, 20,000 km; final drive oil: 4.4 imp pt, 5.3 US pt, 2.5 l, SAE 90, change every 12,400 miles, 20,000 km; pressure: front 22 psi, 1.6 atm, 28 psi, 1.9 atm.

OPTIONAL ACCESSORIES 5-speed fully synchronized mechanical gearbox (I 3.690, II 2.340, III 1.435, IV 1, V 0.880, rev 3.720), 3.920 axle ratio; MB automatic transmission, hydraulic torque converter and planetary gears with 4 ratios (I 3.980, II 2.390, III 1.460, IV 1, rev 5.480), max ratio of converter at stall 2.3, possible manual selection, steering column or central lever; 205/70 VR x 14 tyres with 6'' wide rims; automatic levelling control; electrically-controlled sunshine roof.

280 SE Limousine

See 280 S Limousine, except for:

PRICE IN GB: £ 3,305.
PRICE IN USA: $ 9,503.

ENGINE max power (DIN): 185 hp at 6,000 rpm; max torque (DIN): 176 lb ft, 24.3 kg m at 4,500 rpm; 67.4 hp/l;

MERCEDES-BENZ 350 SE Limousine

MERCEDES-BENZ 350 SL Roadster

MERCEDES-BENZ 350 SLC Coupé

6-cylinder Bosch electronically-controlled injection system, injectors in inlet pipes; fuel feed: electric pump.

PERFORMANCE max speed: 124 mph, 200 km/h; power-weight ratio: 19.2 lb/hp, 8.7 kg/hp.

ELECTRICAL EQUIPMENT transistorized ignition.

DIMENSIONS AND WEIGHT dry weight: 3,561 lb, 1,615 kg.

350 SE Limousine

See 280 S Limousine, except for:

PRICE IN GB: £ 4,447.
PRICE EX WORKS: 28,860 marks.

ENGINE 8 cylinders, Vee-slanted at 90°; 213.5 cu in, 3,499 cc (3.62 x 2.59 in, 92 x 65.8 mm); compression ratio: 9.5:1; max power (DIN): 200 hp at 5,800 rpm; max torque (DIN): 212 lb ft, 29.2 kg m at 4,000 rpm; 57.1 hp/l; 5 crankshaft bearings; valves: overhead, finger levers; camshafts: 1, overhead, per cylinder block; lubricating system capacity: 13.2 imp pt, 15.9 US pt, 7.5 l; Bosch electronically-controlled injection system, injectors in inlet pipes; fuel feed: electric pump; cooling system capacity: 23.8 imp pt, 28.5 US pt, 13.5 l.

TRANSMISSION gearbox ratios: I 3.960, II 2.340, III 1.430, IV 1, rev 3.720; axle ratio: 3.460; width of rims: 6.5"; tyres: 205/70 VR x 14 (standard).

PERFORMANCE max speed: 127 mph, 205 km/h; power-weight ratio: 18.5 lb/hp, 8.4 kg/hp; fuel consumption: 21.7 m/imp gal, 18.1 m/US gal, 13 l x 100 km.

ELECTRICAL EQUIPMENT 66 Ah battery; transistorized ignition.

DIMENSIONS AND WEIGHT dry weight: 3,693 lb, 1,675 kg.

OPTIONAL ACCESSORIES MB automatic transmission, hydraulic torque converter and planetary gears with 3 ratios (I 2.310, II 1.460, III 1, rev 1.840), max ratio of converter at stall 2.3, possible manual selection, steering column or central lever; 5-speed fully synchronized mechanical gearbox not available.

350 SL Roadster

PRICE IN GB: £ 5,121.
PRICE IN USA: $ 10,540.

ENGINE front, 4 stroke; 8 cylinders, Vee-slanted at 90°; 213 cu in, 3,499 cc (3.62 x 2.59 in, 92 x 65.8 mm); compression ratio: 9.5:1; max power (DIN): 200 hp at 5,800 rpm; max torque (DIN): 212 lb ft, 29.2 kg m at 4,000 rpm; max engine rpm: 6,300; 57.1 hp/l; cast iron cylinder block, light alloy head; 5 crankshaft bearings; valves: overhead, finger levers; camshafts: 1 per cylinder block, overhead; lubrication: gear pump, full flow filter, oil cooler, 12.3 imp pt, 14.8 US pt, 7 l; Bosch electronically-controlled injection system; fuel feed: electric pump; water-cooled, fan with revolutions limiting device (1,900 rpm), 25.2 imp pt, 30.2 US pt, 14.3 l.

TRANSMISSION driving wheels: rear; clutch: single dry plate, hydraulically controlled; gearbox: mechanical; gears: 4, fully synchronized; ratios: I 3.960, II 2.340, III 1.430, IV 1, rev 3.720; lever: central; final drive: hypoid bevel; axle ratio: 3.460; width of rims: 6.5"; tyres: 205/70 VR x 14.

PERFORMANCE max speeds: (I) 34 mph, 54 km/h; (II) 56 mph, 90 km/h; (III) 93 mph, 150 km/h; (IV) 130 mph, 210 km/h; power-weight ratio: 17.8 lb/hp, 7.7 kg/hp; carrying capacity: 937 lb, 425 kg; fuel consumption: 21.7 m/imp gal, 18.1 m/US gal, 13 l x 100 km.

CHASSIS backbone platform with box-type ladder frame; front suspension: independent, wishbones, coil springs, auxiliary rubber springs, anti-roll bar, telescopic dampers; rear suspension: independent, oblique semi-trailing arms, coil springs, auxiliary rubber springs, anti-roll bar, telescopic dampers.

STEERING recirculating ball, damper, servo.

BRAKES disc (front diameter 10.75 in, 273 mm, rear 10.98 in, 279 mm), front internal radial fins, rear compensator, servo.

ELECTRICAL EQUIPMENT 12 V; 66 Ah battery; 770 W alternator; Bosch (transistorized) distributor; 2 iodine headlamps.

DIMENSIONS AND WEIGHT wheel base: 96.85 in, 2,460 mm; tracks: 57.17 in, 1,452 mm front, 56.69 in, 1,440 mm rear; length: 172.44 in, 4,380 mm; width: 70.47 in, 1,790 mm; heigth: 51.18 in, 1,300 mm; ground clearance: 5.32 in, 135 mm; dry weight: 3,407 lb, 1,545 kg; turning circle (between walls): 33.8 ft, 10.3 m; fuel tank: 19.8 imp gal, 23.8 US gal, 90 l.

MERCEDES-BENZ 350 SE Limousine

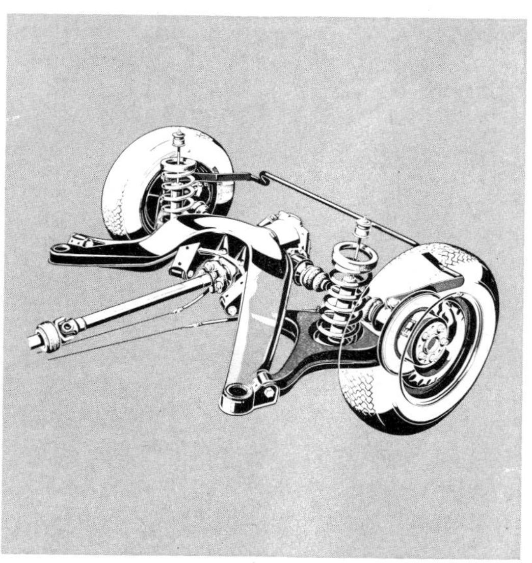

MERCEDES-BENZ 350 SL, 350 SLC (rear suspension)

MERCEDES-BENZ 350 SLC Coupé

BODY convertible; 2 doors; 2 seats, reclining backrests.

PRACTICAL INSTRUCTIONS fuel: 96 oct petrol; engine sump oil: 11.4 imp pt, 13.7 US pt, 6.5 l, SAE 20W-40, change every 3,700 miles, 6,000 km; gearbox oil: 9.5 imp pt, 11.4 US pt, 5.4 l; sparking plug type: 215°; tyre pressure: front 30 psi, 2.1 atm, rear 34 psi, 2.4 atm.

OPTIONAL ACCESSORIES 5-speed fully synchronized mechanical gearbox (I 3.570, II 2.110, III 1.290, IV 1, V 0.866, rev 3.360), central lever; MB automatic transmission, hydraulic coupling and planetary gears with 4 ratios (I 3.980, II 2.390, III 1.460, IV 1, rev 5.480), central or steering column lever, max speed 127 mph, 205 km/h; limited slip differential; hardtop; air-conditioning; electrically-controlled windows.

350 SLC Coupé

See 350 SL Roadster, except for:

PRICE IN GB: £ 6,785.
PRICE EX WORKS: 35,631 marks.

PERFORMANCE power-weight ratio: 17.6 lb/hp, 7.9 kg/hp; carrying capacity: 838 lb, 380 kg.

DIMENSIONS AND WEIGHT wheel base: 111.02 in, 2,820 mm; length: 186.61 in, 4,740 mm; height: 52.36 in, 1,330 mm; dry weight: 3,517 lb, 1,595 kg; turning circle (between walls): 37.7 ft, 11.5 m.

BODY coupé; 4-5 seats.

600 Limousine

PRICE IN GB: £ 11,818.
PRICE IN USA: $ 32,695.

ENGINE front, 4 stroke; 8 cylinders, Vee-slanted at 90°; 386.4 cu in, 6,332 cc (4.06 x 3.74 in, 103 x 95 mm); compression ratio: 9:1; max power (DIN): 250 hp at 4,000 rpm; max torque (DIN): 370 lb ft, 51 kg m at 2,800 rpm; max engine rpm: 4,800; 39.5 hp/l; cast iron cylinder block, light alloy head; 5 crankshaft bearings; valves: overhead, finger levers; camshafts: 1 per cylinder block, overhead; lubrication: gear pump, full flow and by-pass filters, 10.6 imp pt, 12.7 US pt, 6 l; 8-cylinder Bosch intermittent injection pump in inlet pipes; fuel feed: electric pump; water-cooled, 40.5 imp pt, 48.6 US pt, 23 l, thermostatic fan.

TRANSMISSION driving wheels: rear; gearbox: MB automatic transmission, hydraulic coupling and twin planetary gears with 4 ratios; ratios: I 3.980, II 2.460, III 1.580, IV 1, rev 4.150; lever: steering column; final drive: hypoid bevel, limited slip differential; axle ratio: 3.230; width of rims: 6.5"; tyres: 9.00 H x 15.

PERFORMANCE max speeds: (I) 31 mph, 50 km/h; (II) 50 mph, 80 km/h; (III) 81 mph, 130 km/h; (IV) 127 mph, 205 km/h; power-weight ratio: 21.8 lb/hp, 9.9 kg/hp; carrying capacity: 1,297 lb, 580 kg; acceleration: 0-50 mph (0-80 km/h) 6.9 sec; speed in direct drive at 1,000 rpm: 26.4 mph, 42.5 km/h; fuel consumption: 15.9 m/imp gal, 13.2 m/US gal, 17.8 l x 100 km.

CHASSIS integral, front auxiliary frame; front suspension: independent, wishbones, air rubber springs, auxiliary rubber springs, automatically and manually controlled levelling system, anti-roll bar, telescopic dampers adjustable while running; rear suspension: independent, single joint low pivot, swinging semi-axles, trailing lower radius arms, air rubber springs, auxiliary rubber springs, automatically and manually controlled levelling system, anti-roll bar, telescopic dampers adjustable while running.

STEERING recirculating ball, damper, servo, adjustable height of steering wheel; turns lock to lock: 3.30.

BRAKES disc [front diameter (twin calipers) 11.46 in, 291 mm, rear 11.57 in, 294 mm], rear compensator, servo; swept area: front 31.6 sq in, 204 sq cm, rear 24.7 sq in, 159 sq cm, total 56.3 sq in, 363 sq cm.

ELECTRICAL EQUIPMENT 12 V; 88 Ah battery; 2 490 W alternators; Bosch distributor; 2 headlamps.

DIMENSIONS AND WEIGHT wheel base: 125.98 in, 3,200 mm; tracks: 62.48 in, 1,587 mm front, 62.24 in, 1,581 mm rear; length: 218.11 in, 5,540 mm; width: 76.77 in, 1,950 mm; height: 58.46 in, 1,485 mm; ground clearance: 6.50 in, 165 mm; dry weight: 5,457 lb, 2,475 kg; distribution of weight: 50.6% front, 49.4% rear; turning circle (between walls): 41.7 ft, 12.7 m; fuel tank: 24.6 imp gal, 29.6 US gal, 112 l.

BODY limousine; 4 doors; 6 seats, bench front seats; windows, locks, glass partition and front and rear seats (shifting horizontally and vertically) hydraulically controlled.

PRACTICAL INSTRUCTIONS fuel: 96 oct petrol; engine sump oil: 10.6 imp pt, 12.7 US pt, 6 l, SAE 20W-20, change every 3,700 miles, 6,000 km; gearbox oil: 13.6 imp pt, 16.3 US

600 LIMOUSINE

pt, 7.7 l, ATF, change every 12,400 miles, 20,000 km; final drive oil: 5.6 imp pt, 6.8 US pt, 3.2 l, SAE 90, change every 12,400 miles, 20,000 km; greasing: none; sparking plug type: 215°; tappet clearances: inlet 0.004 in, 0.10 mm, exhaust 0.010 in, 0.25 mm; valve timing: 2°30' 52°30' 37°30' 18°; tyre pressure: front 28 psi, 2 atm, rear 33 psi, 2.3 atm.

OPTIONAL ACCESSORIES air-conditioning; sunshine roof.

600 Pullman-Limousine

See 600 Limousine, except for:

PRICE IN GB: £ 12,902.
PRICE IN USA: $ 37,928.

PERFORMANCE power-weight ratio: 23.4 lb/hp, 10.6 kg/hp; carrying capacity: 1,544 lb, 700 kg.

DIMENSIONS AND WEIGHT wheel base: 153.54 in, 3,900 mm; length: 245.67 in, 6,240 mm; height: 59.06 in, 1,500 mm; dry weight: 5,843 lb, 2,650 kg; distribution of weight: 51.5% front, 48.5% rear; turning circle (between walls): 49.2 ft, 15 m.

BODY 4 or 6 doors; 7-8 seats.

OPEL GERMANY (F.R.)

Kadett 2-door Limousine

PRICE IN GB: £ 751.
PRICE EX WORKS: 6,540 marks.

ENGINE front, 4 stroke; 4 cylinders, in line; 65.8 cu in, 1,078 cc (2.95 x 2.40 in, 75 x 61 mm); compression ratio: 7.8:1; max power (DIN): 50 hp at 5,600 rpm; max torque (DIN): 54 lb ft, 7.4 kg m at 2,400-3,000 rpm; max engine rpm: 5,800; 46.4 hp/l; cast iron cylinder block and head; 3 crankshaft bearings; valves: overhead, push-rods and rockers; camshafts: 1, side; lubrication: gear pump, full flow filter, 4.8 imp pt, 5.7 US pt, 2.7 l; 1 Solex 35 PDSI downdraught carburettor; fuel feed: mechanical pump; sealed circuit cooling, liquid, 8.6 imp pt, 10.4 US pt, 4.9 l.

TRANSMISSION driving wheels: rear; clutch: single dry plate (diaphragm); gearbox: mechanical; gears: 4, fully synchronized; ratios: I 3.733, II 2.243, III 1.432, IV 1, rev 3.900; lever: central; final drive: hypoid bevel; axle ratio: 4.110; width of rims: 4''; tyres: 6.00 x 12.

PERFORMANCE max speeds: (I) 24 mph, 38 km/h; (II) 42 mph, 67 km/h; (III) 63 mph, 102 km/h; (IV) 81 mph, 130 km/h; power-weight ratio: 33.1 lb/hp, 15 kg/hp; carrying capacity: 882 lb, 400 kg; acceleration: 0-50 mph (0-80 km/h) 13.5 sec; speed in direct drive at 1,000 rpm: 15.5 mph, 24.9 km/h; fuel consumption: 35.8 m/imp gal, 29.8 m/US gal, 7.9 l x 100 km.

CHASSIS integral; front suspension: independent, wishbones, lower transverse semi-elliptic leafspring, telescopic dampers; rear suspension: rigid axle (torque tube), trailing radius arms, transverse linkage bar, coil springs, telescopic dampers.

STEERING rack-and-pinion; turns lock to lock: 3.

BRAKES drum.

ELECTRICAL EQUIPMENT 12 V; 38 Ah battery; 28 A dynamo; Bosch distributor; 2 headlamps.

DIMENSIONS AND WEIGHT wheel base: 95.12 in, 2,416 mm; tracks: 49.29 in, 1,252 mm front, 50.47 in, 1,282 mm rear; length: 161.61 in, 4,105 mm; width: 61.93 in, 1,573 mm; height: 55.12 in, 1,400 mm; ground clearance: 4.72 in, 120 mm; dry weight: 1,654 lb, 750 kg; turning circle (between walls): 34.8 ft, 10.6 m; fuel tank: 8.8 imp gal, 10.6 US gal, 40 l.

BODY saloon/sedan; 2 doors; 5 seats, separate front seats.

PRACTICAL INSTRUCTIONS fuel: 90 oct petrol; engine sump oil: 4.8 imp pt, 5.7 US pt, 2.7 l, SAE 20W-30, change every 6,200 miles, 10,000 km; gearbox oil: 1.2 imp pt, 1.5 US pt, 0.7 l, SAE 80, no change recommended; final drive oil: 1.1 imp pt, 1.3 US pt, 0.6 l, SAE 90, no change recommended; greasing: none; sparking plug type: 200°; tappet clearances: inlet 0.006 in, 0.15 mm, exhaust 0.010 in, 0.25 mm; valve timing: 40° 60° 70° 30°; tyre pressure: front 18 psi, 1.3 atm, rear 20 psi, 1.4 atm.

VARIATIONS

ENGINE 1.2-litre S, 73 cu in, 1,196 cc (3.11 x 2.40 in, 79 x 61 mm), max power (DIN) 60 hp at 5,400 rpm, max torque (DIN) 65 lb ft, 9 kg m at 3,000-3,800 rpm, 9:1 compression ratio, 50.2 hp/l, cooling system capacity 8.3 imp pt, 9.9 US pt, 4.7 l.

MERCEDES-BENZ 600 Limousine

OPEL Kadett Limousine (1.2-litre S engine)

OPEL Kadett Rallye Coupé

TRANSMISSION 5'' wide rims, 155 x 13 tyres (standard).
PERFORMANCE max speed 87 mph, 140 km/h, power-weight ratio 28.2 lb/hp, 12.8 kg/hp, fuel consumption 34 m/imp gal, 28.3 m/US gal, 8.3 l x 100 km.
CHASSIS anti-roll bar on front and rear suspensions.
BRAKES front disc (diameter 9.37 in, 238 mm).
DIMENSIONS AND WEIGHT tracks 49.37 in, 1,254 mm front, 50.31 in, 1,278 mm rear; dry weight 1,720 lb, 780 kg.
PRACTICAL INSTRUCTIONS valve timing 46° 90° 70° 30°.

OPTIONAL ACCESSORIES Opel automatic transmission with 3 ratios (I 2.400, II 1.480, III 1, rev 1.920) and 4.375 axle ratio only with 1.2-litre S engine; 155 x 13 tyres; 5'' wide rims; limited slip differential; anti-roll bar on rear suspension; front disc brakes only with 155 x 13 tyres and servo brake; 44 Ah battery; 35 A alternator; sunshine roof; electrically-heated rear window (only with alternator).

Kadett 4-door Limousine

See Kadett 2-door Limousine, except for:

PRICE IN GB: £ 852.
PRICE EX WORKS: 6,890 marks.

PERFORMANCE power-weight ratio: 33.9 lb/hp, 15.4 kg/hp.

DIMENSIONS AND WEIGHT width: 63.54 in, 1,614 mm; dry weight: 1,698 lb, 770 kg.

Kadett L 2-door Limousine

See Kadett 2-door Limousine, except for:

PRICE IN GB: £ 909.
PRICE EX WORKS: 7,125 marks.

PERFORMANCE power-weight ratio: 33.3 lb/hp, 15.1 kg/hp.

DIMENSIONS AND WEIGHT length: 164.65 in, 4,182 mm; dry weight: 1,665 lb, 755 kg.

Kadett L 4-door Limousine

See Kadett 2-door Limousine, except for:

PRICE IN GB: £ 951.
PRICE EX WORKS: 7,475 marks.

PERFORMANCE power-weight ratio: 34.2 lb/hp, 15.5 kg/hp.

DIMENSIONS AND WEIGHT length: 164.65 in, 4,182 mm; width: 63.54 in, 1,614 mm; dry weight: 1,709 lb, 775 kg.

Kadett Coupé

See Kadett 2-door Limousine, except for:

PRICE IN GB: £ 961.
PRICE EX WORKS: 7,580 marks.

PERFORMANCE power-weight ratio: 33.5 lb/hp, 15.2 kg/hp.

DIMENSIONS AND WEIGHT length: 164.65 in, 4,182 mm; height: 55.31 in, 1,405 mm; dry weight: 1,676 lb, 760 kg.

BODY coupé; 4 seats.

VARIATIONS

(with 1.2-litre S engine)

PERFORMANCE power-weight ratio 29.1 lb/hp, 13.2 kg/hp.
DIMENSIONS AND WEIGHT dry weight 1,742 lb, 790 kg.

Kadett 3-door Caravan

See Kadett 2-door Limousine, except for:

PRICE IN GB: £ 901.
PRICE EX WORKS: 7,090 marks.

PERFORMANCE power-weight ratio: 34.4 lb/hp, 15.6 kg/hp.

CHASSIS anti-roll bar on rear suspension (standard).

DIMENSIONS AND WEIGHT length: 161.42 in, 4,100 mm; height: 54.92 in, 1,395 mm; dry weight: 1,720 lb, 780 kg.

BODY estate car/station wagon; 2 + 1 doors.

VARIATIONS

(with 1.2-litre S engine)

PERFORMANCE power-weight ratio 30 lb/hp, 13.6 kg/hp.
DIMENSIONS AND WEIGHT dry weight 1,797 lb, 815 kg.

MERCEDES-BENZ 600 Limousine

OPEL Kadett L 4-door Limousine

OPEL Kadett Rallye Coupé

Kadett L 3-door Caravan

See Kadett 2-door Limousine, except for:

PRICE IN GB: 973.
PRICE EX WORKS: 7,620 marks.

PERFORMANCE power-weight ratio: 34.6 lb/hp, 15.7 kg/hp.

CHASSIS anti-roll bar on rear suspension (standard).

DIMENSIONS AND WEIGHT length: 164.45 in, 4,177 mm; height: 54.92 in, 1,395 mm; dry weight: 1,731 lb, 785 kg.

BODY estate car/station wagon; 2 + 1 doors.

Kadett Rallye Coupé

PRICE IN GB: £ 1,134.
PRICE EX WORKS: 3,904 marks.

ENGINE front, 4 stroke; 4 cylinders, in line; 73 cu in, 1,196 cc (3.11 x 2.40 in, 79 x 61 mm); compression ratio: 9.2:1; max power (DIN): 60 hp at 5,400 rpm; max torque (DIN): 65 lb ft, 9 kg m at 3,000-3,800 rpm; max engine rpm: 5,400; 50.2 hp/l: cast iron cylinder block and head; 3 crankshaft bearings; valves: overhead, push-rods and rockers; camshafts: 1, side; lubrication: gear pump, full flow filter, 4.8 imp pt, 5.7 US pt, 2.7 l; 1 Solex 35 PDSI downdraught carburettors; fuel feed: mechanical pump; sealed circuit cooling, liquid, 8.3 imp pt, 9.9 US pt, 4.7 l.

TRANSMISSION driving wheels: rear; clutch: single dry plate (diaphragm); gearbox: mechanical; gears: 4, fully synchronized; ratios: I 3.733, II 2.243, III 1.432, IV 1, rev 3.900; lever: central; final drive: hypoid bevel; axle ratio: 4.110; width of rims: 5''; tyres: 155 SR x 13.

PERFORMANCE max speeds: (I) 27 mph, 43 km/h; (II) 47 mph, 75 km/h; (III) 72 mph, 116 km/h; (IV) 89 mph, 143 km/h; power-weight ratio: 29.4 lb/hp, 13.3 kg/hp; carrying capacity: 684 lb, 310 kg; acceleration: 0-50 mph (0-80 km/h) 10.5 sec; speed in direct drive at 1,000 rpm: 16.5 mph, 26.5 km/h; fuel consumption: 33.6 m/imp gal, 28 m/US gal, 8.4 l x 100 km.

CHASSIS integral; front suspension: independent, wishbones, lower transverse semi-elliptic leafspring, anti-roll bar, telescopic dampers; rear suspension: rigid axle (torque tube), trailing radius arms, coil springs, anti-roll bar, telescopic dampers.

STEERING recirculating ball; turns lock to lock: 3.

BRAKES front disc (diameter 9.37 in, 238 mm), rear drum, servo.

ELECTRICAL EQUIPMENT 12 V; 36 Ah battery; 35 A alternator; Bosch distributor; 4 headlamps.

DIMENSIONS AND WEIGHT wheel base: 95.12 in, 2,416 mm; tracks: 49.37 in, 1,254 mm front, 50.31 in, 1,278 mm rear; length: 164.65 in, 4,182 mm; width: 61.93 in, 1,573 mm; height: 55.31 in, 1,405 mm; ground clearance: 4.45 in, 113 mm; dry weight: 1,764 lb, 800 kg; turning circle (between walls): 34.8 ft, 10.6 m; fuel tank: 8.8 imp gal, 10.6 US gal, 40 l.

BODY coupé; 2 doors; 4 seats, separate front seats.

PRACTICAL INSTRUCTIONS fuel: 98 oct petrol; engine sump oil: 4.4 imp pt, 5.3 US pt, 2.5 l, SAE 20W-30, change every 6,200 miles, 10,000 km; gearbox oil: 1.2 imp pt, 1.5 US pt, 0.7 l, SAE 80, no change recommended; final drive oil: 1.1 imp pt, 1.3 US pt, 0.6 l, SAE 90, no change recommended; greasing: none; sparking plug type: 200°; tappet clearances: inlet 0.006 in, 0.15 mm, exhaust 0.010 in, 0.25 mm; valve timing: 46° 90° 70° 30°; tyre pressure: front 18 psi, 1.3 atm, rear 24 psi, 1.7 atm.

VARIATIONS

ENGINE 1.9-litre S, 115.8 cu in, 1,897 cc (3.66 x 2.75 in, 93 x 69.8 mm), max power (DIN) 90 hp at 5,100 rpm, max torque (DIN) 108 lb ft, 14.9 kg m at 2,500-3,100 rpm, 47.4 hp/l, 5 crankshaft bearings, 1 overhead camshaft, lubricating system capacity 5.3 imp pt, 6.3 US pt, 3 l, 1 Solex 32 DIDTA downdraught carburettor, cooling system capacity 10.7 imp pt, 12.9 US pt, 6.1 l.
TRANSMISSION 4-speed mechanical gearbox (I 3.428, II 2.156, III 1.366, IV 1, rev 3.317), 3.670 axle ratio.
PERFORMANCE max speeds (I) 30 mph, 49 km/h, (II) 48 mph, 78 km/h, (III) 76 mph, 123 km/h, (IV) 102 mph, 164 km/h, power-weight ratio 21.8 lb/hp, 9.9 kg/hp, fuel consumption 30.7 m/imp gal, 25.6 m/US gal, 9.2 l x 100 km.
ELECTRICAL EQUIPMENT 44 Ah battery.
DIMENSIONS AND WEIGHT rear track 50.47 in, 1,282 mm, dry weight 1,962 lb, 890 kg.
PRACTICAL INSTRUCTIONS valve timing 44° 86° 84° 46°.

OPTIONAL ACCESSORIES limited slip differential; electrically-heated rear window.

Ascona 2-door Limousine

PRICE IN GB: £ 1,182.
PRICE EX WORKS: 7,895 marks.

ENGINE front, 4 stroke; 4 cylinders, in line; 96.6 cu in, 1,583 cc (3.35 x 2.75 in, 85 x 69.8 mm); compression ratio: 8.2:1; max power (DIN): 68 hp at 5,200 rpm; max torque (DIN): 80 lb ft, 11 kg m at 3,400 rpm; max engine rpm: 6,000; 42.9 hp/l; cast iron cylinder block and head; 5 crankshaft bearings; valves: overhead, in line, rockers; camshafts: 1, overhead; lubrication: gear pump, full flow filter, 6.2 imp pt, 7.4 US pt, 3.5 l; 1 Solex 35 PDSI downdraught carburettor; fuel feed: mechanical pump; sealed circuit cooling, liquid, 11.4 imp pt, 13.7 US pt, 6.5 l.

TRANSMISSION driving wheels: rear; clutch: single dry plate (diaphragm); gearbox: mechanical; gears: 4, fully synchronized; ratios: I 3.428, II 2.156, III 1.366, IV 1, rev 3.317; lever: central; final drive: hypoid bevel; axle ratio: 3.700; width of rims: 5"; tyres: 155 x 13.

PERFORMANCE max speeds: (I) 26 mph, 42 km/h; (II) 42 mph, 67 km/h; (III) 66 mph, 106 km/h; (IV) 90 mph, 145 km/h; power-weight ratio: 29.5 lb/hp, 13.4 kg/hp; carrying capacity: 882 lb, 400 kg; speed in direct drive at 1,000 rpm: 16.2 mph, 26 km/h; fuel consumption: 28.2 m/imp gal, 23.5 m/US gal, 10 l x 100 km.

CHASSIS integral; front suspension: independent, wishbones, coil springs, anti-roll bar, telescopic dampers; rear suspension: rigid axle (torque tube), trailing radius arms, transverse linkage bar, coil springs, anti-roll bar, telescopic dampers.

STEERING rack-and-pinion; turns lock to lock: 3.

BRAKES front disc (diameter 9.37 in, 238 mm), rear drum, servo.

ELECTRICAL EQUIPMENT 12 V; 44 Ah battery; 28 A alternator; Bosch distributor; 2 headlamps.

DIMENSIONS AND WEIGHT wheel base: 95.67 in, 2,430 mm; tracks: 52.40 in, 1,331 mm front, 51.97 in, 1,320 mm rear; length: 162.36 in, 4,124 mm; width: 64.02 in, 1,626 mm; height: 54.53 in, 1,385 mm; ground clearance: 4.72 in, 120 mm; dry weight: 2,007 lb, 910 kg; turning circle (between walls): 33.4 ft, 10.2 m; fuel tank: 9.9 imp gal, 11.9 US gal, 45 l.

BODY saloon/sedan; 2 doors; 5 seats, separate front seats, adjustable backrests.

PRACTICAL INSTRUCTIONS fuel: 90 oct petrol; engine sump oil: 5.3 imp pt, 6.3 US pt, 3 l, SAE 20W-30, change every 6,200 miles, 10,000 km; gearbox oil: 1.9 imp pt, 2.3 US pt, 1.1 l, SAE 80, no change recommended; final drive oil: 1.9 imp pt, 2.3 US pt, 1.1 l, SAE 90, no change recommended; greasing: none; sparking plug type: 200°; tappet clearances (hot): inlet 0.012 in, 0.30 mm, exhaust 0.012 in, 0.30 mm; valve timing: 44° 86° 84° 46°; tyre pressure: front 23 psi, 1.6 atm, rear 26 psi, 1.8 atm.

VARIATIONS

ENGINE 1.2-litre S, max power (DIN) 60 hp at 5,400 rpm, max torque (DIN) 65 lb ft, 9 kg m at 3,000-3,800 rpm, 9:1 compression ratio, 50.2 hp/l, cooling system capacity 8.3 imp pt, 9.9 US pt, 4.7 l.
TRANSMISSION 5" wide rims, 155 x 13 tyres (standard).
PERFORMANCE max speed 87 mph, 140 km/h, power-weight ratio 30.9 lb/hp, 14 kg/hp, fuel consumption 34 m/imp gal, 28.3 m/US gal, 8.3 l x 100 km/h.
CHASSIS anti-roll bar on front and rear suspensions.
BRAKES front disc (diameter 9.73 in, 238 mm).
DIMENSIONS AND WEIGHT dry weight 1,863 lb, 845 kg.
PRACTICAL INSTRUCTIONS valve timing 46° 90° 70° 30°.

ENGINE 1.6-litre S, max power (DIN) 80 hp at 5,200 rpm, max torque (DIN) 87 lb ft, 12 kg m at 3,800 rpm, 9.5:1 compression ratio, 50.5 hp/l, 1 Solex 32 DIDTA-4 carburettor.
TRANSMISSION 3.670 axle ratio, 165 S x 13 tyres (standard).
PERFORMANCE max speed 96 mph, 155 km/h, power-weight ratio 25.8 lb/hp, 11.7 kg/hp, fuel consumption 30.7 m/imp gal, 25.6 m/US gal, 9.2 l x 100 km.
BRAKES swept area: total 79.1 sq in, 510 sq cm.
DIMENSIONS AND WEIGHT dry weight 2,073 lb, 940 kg.
PRACTICAL INSTRUCTIONS 98 oct petrol.

ENGINE 1.9-litre S, 115.8 cu in, 1,897 cc (3.66 x 2.75 in, 93 x 69.8 mm), max power (DIN) 90 hp at 5,100 rpm, max torque (DIN) 108 lb ft, 14.9 kg m at 2,500-3,100 rpm, 9:1 compression ratio, 47.4 hp/l, 1 Solex 32 DIDTA-4 carburettor, cooling system capacity 10.7 imp pt, 12.9 US pt, 6.1 l.
TRANSMISSION 3.440 axle ratio, 165 S x 13 tyres (standard).
PERFORMANCE max speed 99 mph, 160 km/h, power-weight ratio 22.9 lb/hp, 10.4 kg/hp, fuel consumption 29.1 m/imp gal, 24.2 m/US gal, 9.7 l x 100 km.
BRAKES swept area: total 79.1 sq in, 510 sq cm.
DIMENSIONS AND WEIGHT dry weight 2,073 lb, 940 kg.
PRACTICAL INSTRUCTIONS 98 oct petrol.

OPTIONAL ACCESSORIES Opel automatic transmission (only with 1.6-litre S and 1.9-litre S engines) with 3 ratios (I

OPEL Ascona 2-door Limousine

OPEL Ascona Voyage

OPEL Manta SR

2.400, II 1.480, III 1, rev 1.920), max ratio of converter at stall 2.5; 165 x 13 or 185/70 SR x 13 tyres, 5.5" wide rims; 35 A alternator; sunshine roof; electrically-heated rear window; limited slip differential.

Ascona 4-door Limousine

See Ascona 2-door Limousine, except for:

PRICE IN GB: £ 1,184.
PRICE EX WORKS: 7,988 marks.

PERFORMANCE power-weight ratio: 30.2 lb/hp, 13.7 kg/hp.

DIMENSIONS AND WEIGHT dry weight: 2,051 lb, 930 kg.

Ascona L 2-door Limousine

See Ascona 2-door Limousine, except for:

PRICE EX WORKS: 8,545 marks.

DIMENSIONS AND WEIGHT length: 164.57 in, 4,180 mm; width: 64.25 in, 1,632 mm; dry weight: 2,018 lb, 915 kg.

Ascona L 4-door Limousine

See Ascona 4-door Limousine, except for:

PRICE EX WORKS: 8,985 marks.

DIMENSIONS AND WEIGHT length: 164.57 in, 4,180 mm; width: 64.25 in, 1,632 mm; dry weight: 2,062 lb, 935 kg.

Ascona Voyage

See Ascona 2-door Limousine, except for:

PRICE IN GB: £ 1,221.
PRICE EX WORKS: 9,195 marks.

TRANSMISSION tyres: 165 x 13 (standard).

PERFORMANCE power-weight ratio: 32.2 lb/hp, 14.6 kg/hp; carrying capacity: 1,125 lb, 510 kg; fuel consumption: 27.7 m/imp gal, 23.1 m/US gal, 10.2 l x 100 km.

DIMENSIONS AND WEIGHT length: 164.57 in, 4,180 mm; width: 64.25 in, 1,632 mm; height: 55.12 in, 1,400 mm; dry weight: 2,194 lb, 995 kg.

BODY estate car/station wagon; 2 + 1 doors.

VARIATIONS

(with 1.6-litre S engine)

PERFORMANCE fuel consumption 29.1 m/imp gal, 24.2 m/US gal, 9.7 l x 100 km.

(with 1.9-litre S engine)

PERFORMANCE fuel consumption 28.5 m/imp gal, 23.8 m/US gal, 9.9 l x 100 km.

Manta

See Ascona 2-door Limousine, except for:

PRICE IN GB: £ 1,272.
PRICE EX WORKS: 8,875 marks.

TRANSMISSION tyres: 165 S x 13.

PERFORMANCE max speed: 96 mph, 155 km/h; power-weight ratio: 30.2 lb/hp, 13.7 kg/hp; fuel consumption: 31.4 m/imp gal, 26.1 m/US gal, 9 l x 100 km.

DIMENSIONS AND WEIGHT length: 168.98 in, 4,292 mm; height: 53.35 in, 1,355 mm; dry weight: 2,051 lb, 930 kg.

BODY coupé.

VARIATIONS

(with 1.2-litre S engine)

PERFORMANCE power-weight ratio 31.8 lb/hp, 14.4 kg/hp, fuel consumption 33.6 m/imp gal, 28 m/US gal, 8.4 l x 100 km.
DIMENSIONS AND WEIGHT dry weight 1,907 lb, 865 kg.

(with 1.6-litre S engine)

PERFORMANCE max speed 102 mph, 164 km/h, power-weight ratio 26.2 lb/hp, 11.9 kg/hp, fuel consumption 32.8 m/imp gal, 27.3 m/US gal, 8.6 l x 100 km.
DIMENSIONS AND WEIGHT dry weight 2,095 lb, 950 kg.

(with 1.9-litre S engine)

PERFORMANCE max speed 106 mph, 170 km/h, power-weight ratio 23.1 lb/hp, 10.5 kg/hp, fuel consumption 33.2 m/imp gal, 27.7 m/US gal, 8.5 l x 100 km.
DIMENSIONS AND WEIGHT dry weight 2,095 lb, 950 kg.

OPEL Ascona

OPEL Ascona Voyage

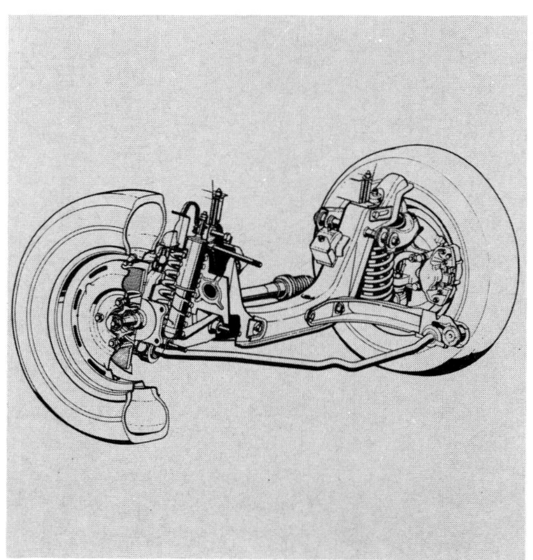

OPEL Manta (front suspension)

Manta L

See Manta, except for:

PRICE EX WORKS: 9,360 marks.

PERFORMANCE power-weight ratio: 30.4 lb/hp, 13.2 kg/hp.

DIMENSIONS AND WEIGHT length: 170.98 in, 4,343 mm; width: 64.25 in, 1,632 mm; dry weight: 2,084 lb, 945 kg.

Manta SR

See Manta L, except for:

PRICE IN GB: £ 1,405.
PRICE EX WORKS: 10,431 marks.

ENGINE 1.6-litre S (standard); compression ratio: 9.5:1; max power (DIN): 80 hp at 5,200 rpm; max torque (DIN): 87 lb ft, 12 kg m at 3,800 rpm; 50.5 hp/l; 1 Solex 32 DIDTA-4 carburettor.

TRANSMISSION axle ratio: 3.890; width of rims: 5.5"; tyres: 185/70 SR x 13 (standard).

PERFORMANCE max speed: 102 mph, 164 km/h; power-weight ratio: 26.7 lb/hp, 12.1 kg/hp; fuel consumption: 31.7 m/imp gal, 26.4 m/US gal, 8.9 l x 100 km.

ELECTRICAL EQUIPMENT 35 A alternator (standard).

DIMENSIONS AND WEIGHT height: 52.95 in, 1,345 mm; dry weight: 2,139 lb, 970 kg.

PRACTICAL INSTRUCTIONS fuel: 98 oct petrol.

VARIATIONS

ENGINE 1.2-litre and 1.6-litre not available.

(with 1.9-litre S engine)

TRANSMISSION 3.670 axle ratio (3.440 with automatic transmission).
PERFORMANCE fuel consumption 32.5 m/imp gal, 27 m/US gal, 8.7 l x 100 km.

OPTIONAL ACCESSORIES automatic transmission with 3.890 axle ratio.

Rekord 2-door Limousine

PRICE EX WORKS: 9,285 marks.

ENGINE front, 4 stroke; 4 cylinders, in line; 103.6 cu in, 1,698 cc (3.46 x 2.75 in, 88 x 69.8 mm); compression ratio: 8.2:1; max power (DIN): 66 hp at 5,300 rpm; max torque (DIN): 87 lb ft, 12 kg m at 2,000-3,100 rpm; max engine rpm: 6,000; 38.9 hp/l; cast iron cylinder block and head; 5 crankshaft bearings; valves: overhead, in line, rockers; camshafts: 1, overhead; lubrication: gear pump, full flow filter, 7.2 imp pt, 8.7 US pt, 4.1 l; 1 Solex 35 PDSI downdraught carburettor; fuel feed: mechanical pump; anti-freeze liquid-cooled, 8.8 imp pt, 10.6 US pt, 6.5 l.

TRANSMISSION driving wheels: rear; clutch: single dry plate (diaphragm); gearbox: mechanical; gears: 4, fully synchronized; ratios: I 3.428, II 2.156, III 1.366, IV 1, rev 3.317; lever: steering column; final drive: hypoid bevel; axle ratio: 3.890; width of rims: 5"; tyres: 6.40 x 13.

PERFORMANCE max speeds: (I) 25 mph, 40 km/h; (II) 40 mph, 65 km/h; (III) 62 mph, 100 km/h; (IV) 89 mph, 143 km/h; power-weight ratio: 35.5 lb/hp, 16.1 kg/hp; carrying capacity: 882 lb, 400 kg; speed in direct drive at 1,000 rpm: 15.8 mph, 25.5 km/h; fuel consumption: 28.8 m/imp gal, 24 m/US gal, 9.8 l x 100 km.

CHASSIS integral; front suspension: independent, wishbones, lower trailing links, coil springs, anti-roll bar, telescopic dampers; rear suspension: rigid axle, trailing lower radius arms, upper torque arms, transverse linkage bar, anti-roll bar, coil springs, telescopic dampers.

STEERING recirculating ball; turns lock to lock: 4.

BRAKES front disc (diameter 9.37 in, 238 mm), rear drum, servo.

REKORD 2-DOOR LIMOUSINE

ELECTRICAL EQUIPMENT 12 V; 44 Ah battery; 28 A alternator; Bosch distributor; 2 headlamps.

DIMENSIONS AND WEIGHT wheel base: 105.04 in, 2,668 mm; tracks: 56.18 in, 1,427 mm front, 55.59 in, 1,412 mm rear; length: 179.80 in, 4,567 mm; width: 67.64 in, 1718 mm; height: 55.31 in, 1,405 mm; ground clearance: 5.08 in, 129 mm; dry weight: 2,348 lb, 1,065 kg; turning circle (between walls): 37.4 ft, 11.4 m; fuel tank: 15.4 imp gal, 18.5 US gal, 70 l.

BODY saloon/sedan; 2 doors; 5 seats, separate front seats, reclining backrests.

PRACTICAL INSTRUCTIONS fuel: 90 oct petrol; engine sump oil: 6.7 imp pt, 8 US pt, 3.8 l, SAE 20W-30, change every 3,100 miles, 5,000 km; gearbox oil: 1.9 imp pt, 2.3 US pt, 1.1 l, SAE 80, no change recommended; final drive oil: 2.1 imp pt, 2.5 US pt, 1.2 l, SAE 90, no change recommended; greasing: none; sparking plug type: 200°; tappet clearances: inlet 0.012 in, 0.30 mm exhaust 0.012 in, 0.30 mm; valve timing: 34° 76° 70° 28°; tyre pressure: front 24 psi, 1.7 atm, rear 26 psi, 1.8 atm.

VARIATIONS

ENGINE 1.7-litre S, max power (DIN) 83 hp at 5,400 rpm, max torque (DIN) 94 lb ft, 13 kg m at 2,500-2,900 rpm, 9.8:1 compression ratio, 48.8 hp/l, 1 Solex 32 DIDTA downdraught carburettor, cooling system capacity 10 imp pt, 12 US pt, 5.7 l.
TRANSMISSION 6.40 S x 13 tyres.
PERFORMANCE max speeds (I) 28 mph, 45 km/h, (II) 44 mph, 71 km/h, (III) 70 mph, 112 km/h, (IV) 96 mph, 155 km/h, power-weight ratio 30.8 lb/hp, 14 kg/hp, fuel consumption 28.5 m/imp gal, 23.8 m/US gal, 9.9 l x 100 km.
PRACTICAL INSTRUCTIONS fuel: 98 oct petrol, valve timing 44° 86° 84° 46°.

ENGINE 1.9-litre S, 115.8 cu in, 1,897 cc (3.66 x 2.75 in, 93 x 69.8 mm), max power (DIN) 97 hp at 5,200 rpm, max torque (DIN) 109 lb ft, 15 kg m at 3,800 rpm, 9.8:1 compression ratio, hydraulic tappets, 41.1 hp/l, 1 Zenith 35/4 INAT carburettor.
TRANSMISSION 6.40 S x 13 tyres.
PERFORMANCE max speeds (I) 29 mph, 47 km/h, (II) 46 mph, 74 km/h, (III) 73 mph, 117 km/h, (IV) 100 mph, 161 km/h, power-weight ratio 24 lb/hp, 10.9 kg/hp, fuel consumption 28.8 m/imp gal, 24 m/US gal, 9.8 l x 100 km.
PRACTICAL INSTRUCTIONS fuel: 98 oct petrol, valve timing 40° 88° 80° 48°.

OPTIONAL ACCESSORIES central gear lever; Opel automatic transmission with 3 ratios (I 2.400, II 1.480, III 1, rev 1.920), max ratio of converter at stall 2.5; 175 SR x 14 tyres with 5.5" x 14 wide rims; 185/70 SR x 14 tyres with 5.5" x 14 wide rims; limited slip differential; sunshine roof; electrically-heated rear window; halogen headlamps.

Rekord 2100 D 2-door Limousine

See Rekord 2-door Limousine, except for:

PRICE EX WORKS: 11,520 marks.

ENGINE Diesel; 126.1 cu in, 2,067 cc (3.46 x 3.35 in, 88 x 85 mm); compression ratio: 22:1; max power (DIN): 60 hp at 4,400 rpm; max torque (DIN): 87 lb ft, 12 kg m at 2,500 rpm; max engine rpm: 4,600; 29 hp/l; lubricating system capacity: 10.2 imp pt, 12.3 US pt, 5.8 l; Bosch injection system; cooling system capacity: 18.8 imp pt, 22.6 US pt, 10.7 l.

TRANSMISSION tyres: 165 x 14.

PERFORMANCE max speed: 84 mph, 135 km/h; power-weight ratio: 44.4 lb/hp, 20.1 kg/hp; fuel consumption: 32.5 m/imp gal, 27 m/US gal, 8.7 l x 100 km.

ELECTRICAL EQUIPMENT 88 Ah battery; 35 A alternator.

DIMENSIONS AND WEIGHT tracks: 55.71 in, 1,415 mm front, 55.12 in, 1,400 mm rear; dry weight: 2,688 lb, 1,210 kg.

PRACTICAL INSTRUCTIONS tappet clearances: inlet 0.008 in, 0.20 mm, exhaust 0.012 in, 0.30 mm; valve timing: 24° 36° 48° 27°; tyre pressure: front 28 psi, 2 atm, rear 28 psi, 2 atm.

OPTIONAL ACCESSORIES 185/70 SR x 14 tyres not available.

Rekord 4-door Limousine

See Rekord 2-door Limousine, except for:

PRICE EX WORKS: 9,675 marks.

PERFORMANCE power-weight ratio: 36.1 lb/hp, 16.4 kg/hp.

DIMENSIONS AND WEIGHT dry weight: 2,392 lb, 1,085 kg.

OPEL Rekord 2100 D

OPEL Rekord L Caravan

OPEL GT

Rekord 2100 D 4-door Limousine

See Rekord 2100 D 2-door Limousine, except for:

PRICE EX WORKS: 11,910 marks.

PERFORMANCE power-weight ratio: 45.1 lb/hp, 20.5 kg/hp.

DIMENSIONS AND WEIGHT dry weight: 2,712 lb, 1,230 kg.

Rekord 3-door Caravan

See Rekord 2-door Limousine, except for:

PRICE EX WORKS: 9,765 marks.

TRANSMISSION axle ratio: 4.220.

PERFORMANCE max speed: 87 mph, 140 km/h; power-weight ratio: 36.9 lb/hp, 16.8 kg/hp; fuel consumption: 27.4 m/imp gal, 22.8 m/US gal, 10.3 l x 100 km.

DIMENSIONS AND WEIGHT length: 180.87 in, 4,594 mm; width: 67.64 in, 1,718 mm; height: 56,50 in, 1,435 mm; dry weight: 2,448 lb, 1,110 kg.

BODY estate car/station wagon; 2 + 1 doors.

VARIATIONS

(with 1.7-litre S engine)

PERFORMANCE max speed 94 mph, 152 km/h, fuel consumption 28 m/imp gal, 23.3 m/US gal, 10.1 l x 100 km.

(with 1.9-litre S engine)

PERFORMANCE max speed 98 mph, 158 km/h, fuel consumption 28.2 m/imp gal, 23.5 m/US gal, 10 l x 100 km.

Rekord 5-door Caravan

See Rekord 2-door Limousine, except for:

PRICE EX WORKS: 10,225 marks.

VARIATIONS

(with 1.7-litre S engine)

TRANSMISSION 4.220 axle ratio.
PERFORMANCE power-weight ratio 37.7 lb/hp, 17.1 kg/hp, fuel consumption 27.4 m/imp gal, 22.8 m/US gal, 10.3 l x 100 km.
DIMENSIONS AND WEIGHT length 180.87 in, 4,594 mm, width 67.64 in, 1,718 mm, height 56.50 in, 1,435 mm, dry weight 2,503 lb, 1,135 kg.
BODY estate car/station wagon 4 + 1 doors.

(with 1.9-litre S engine)

TRANSMISSION 4.220 axle ratio (only with automatic transmission).
PERFORMANCE max speed 98 mph, 158 km/h, fuel consumption 28.2 m/imp gal, 23.5 m/US gal, 10 l x 100 km.

Rekord L 2-door Limousine

See Rekord 2-door Limousine, except for:

PRICE EX WORKS: 9,795 marks.

PERFORMANCE power-weight ratio: 38.1 lb/hp, 16.1 kg/hp.

DIMENSIONS AND WEIGHT length: 181.31 in, 4,607 mm; width: 67.64 in, 1,728 mm; dry weight: 2,359 lb, 1,070 kg.

Rekord L 2100 D 2-door Limousine

See Rekord 2100 D 2-door Limousine, except for:

PRICE EX WORKS: 12,030 marks.

PERFORMANCE power-weight ratio: 44.5 lb/hp, 20.2 kg/hp.

DIMENSIONS AND WEIGHT length: 181.38 in, 4,607 mm; width: 68.03 in, 1,728 mm; dry weight: 2,679 lb, 1,215 kg.

Rekord L 4-door Limousine

See Rekord L 2-door Limousine, except for:

PRICE IN GB: £ 1,399.
PRICE EX WORKS: 10,185 marks.

PERFORMANCE power-weight ratio: 36.4 lb/hp, 16.5 kg/hp.

DIMENSIONS AND WEIGHT length: 181.38 in, 4,607 mm; width: 67.64 in, 1,728 mm; dry weight: 2,403 lb, 1,090 kg.

AC 428 Fastback

ASTON MARTIN V8

AUSTIN 1300 Mk III 4-door Super De Luxe Saloon

rpm; max torque (DIN): 60 lb ft, 8.3 kg m at 2,500 rpm; max engine rpm: 6,000; 43.7 hp/l; cast iron cylinder block and head; 3 crankshaft bearings; valves: overhead, in line, push-rods and rockers; camshafts: 1, side; lubrication: eccentric pump, full flow filter, 9 imp pt, 10.8 US pt, 5.1 l; 1 SU type HS 2 semi-downdraught carburettor; fuel feed: electric pump; water-cooled, 6.7 imp pt, 8 US pt, 3.8 l.

TRANSMISSION driving wheels: front; clutch: single dry plate (diaphragm), hydraulically controlled; gearbox: mechanical, in unit with engine; gears: 4, fully synchronized; ratios: I 3.530, II 2.220, III 1.430, IV 1, rev 3.540; lever: central; final drive: helical spur gears, in unit with engine; axle ratio: 4.133; width of rims: 4"; tyres: 5.50 x 12.

PERFORMANCE max speeds: (I) 22 mph, 36 km/h; (II) 36 mph, 58 km/h; (III) 56 mph, 90 km/h; (IV) 79 mph, 127 km/h; power-weight ratio: 36.4 lb/hp, 16.5 kg/hp; carrying capacity: 882 lb, 400 kg; acceleration: standing ¼ mile 22 sec, 0-50 mph (0-80 km/h) 14.7 sec; speed in direct drive at 1,000 rpm: 14.8 mph, 23.8 km/h; fuel consumption: 34.4 m/imp gal, 28.7 m/US gal, 8.2 l x 100 km.

CHASSIS integral, front and rear auxiliary frames; front suspension: independent, wishbones, hydrolastic (liquid) rubber cone springs, hydraulic connecting pipes to rear wheels; rear suspension: independent, swinging longitudinal trailing arms, hydrolastic (liquid) rubber cone springs, hydraulic connecting pipes to front wheels, combined with transverse torsion bars, anti-roll bar.

STEERING rack-and-pinion; turns lock to lock: 3.12.

BRAKES front disc (diameter 8.40 in, 213 mm), rear drum, rear compensator; swept area: front 148 sq in, 955 sq cm, rear 63 sq in, 407 sq cm, total 211 sq in, 1,362 sq cm.

ELECTRICAL EQUIPMENT 12 V; 40 Ah battery; 264 W dynamo; Lucas distributor; 2 headlamps.

DIMENSIONS AND WEIGHT wheel base: 93.50 in, 2,375 mm; tracks: 51.50 in, 1,308 mm front, 50.87 in, 1,292 mm rear; length: 146.73 in, 3,727 mm; width: 60.35 in, 1,533 mm; height: 52.99 in, 1,346 mm; ground clearance: 6.10 in, 155 mm; dry weight: 1,749 lb, 793 kg; distribution of weight: 62% front, 38% rear; turning circle (between walls): 36.1 ft, 11 m; fuel tank: 7.9 imp gal, 9.5 US gal, 36 l.

BODY saloon/sedan; 2 doors; 4-5 seats, separate front seats.

PRACTICAL INSTRUCTIONS fuel: 96 oct petrol; engine sump, gearbox and final drive oil: 7.9 imp pt, 9.5 US pt, 4.5 l, SAE 10W-30 (winter) 20W-50 (summer), change every 6,000 miles, 9,700 km; greasing: every 3,000 miles, 4,800 km, 4 points; sparking plug type: 225°; tappet clearances: inlet 0.012 in, 0.30 mm, exhaust 0.012 in, 0.30 mm; valve timing: 5° 45° 51° 21°; tyre pressure: front 28 psi, 2 atm, rear 24 psi, 1.7 atm.

VARIATIONS

ENGINE 7.5:1 compression ratio.

OPTIONAL ACCESSORIES AP automatic transmission, hydraulic torque converter with 2 conic bevel gears (twin concentric differential-like gear clusters) with 4 ratios (I 2.689, II 1.846, III 1.460, IV 1, rev 2.689), operated by 3 brake bands and 2 multi-disc clutches, max ratio of converter at stall 2, possible manual selection, 3.760 axle ratio, with 8.9:1 compression ratio, 1 SU type HS 4 semi-downdraught carburettor, speed in direct drive at 1,000 rpm 18.8 mph, 30.2 km/h, swept area front 148 sq in, 955 sq cm, rear 63 sq in, 407 sq cm, total 211 sq in, 1,362 sq cm; reclining backrests; electrically-heated rear window.

1100 Mk III 4-door Super De Luxe Saloon

See 1100 Mk III 2-door De Luxe Saloon, except for:

PRICE IN GB: £ 779.

PERFORMANCE power-weight ratio: 37.6 lb/hp, 17.1 kg/hp.

DIMENSIONS AND WEIGHT dry weight: 1,804 lb, 818 kg.

1300 Mk III 2-door Super De Luxe Saloon

See 1100 Mk III 2-door De Luxe Saloon, except for:

PRICE IN GB: £ 775.

ENGINE 77.8 cu in, 1,275 cc (2.78 x 3.20 in, 70.6 x 81.3 mm); compression ratio: 8.8:1; max power (DIN): 60 hp at 5,250 rpm; max torque (DIN): 69 lb ft, 9.5 kg m at 2,500 rpm; 47.1 hp/l; 1 SU type HS 4 semi-downdraught carburettor.

TRANSMISSION axle ratio: 3.647.

PERFORMANCE max speeds: (I) 28 mph, 45 km/h; (II) 45 mph, 72 km/h; (III) 69 mph, 111 km/h; (IV) 87 mph,

1300 MK III 2-DOOR SUPER DE LUXE SALOON

140 km/h; power-weight ratio: 28.5 lb/hp, 12.9 kg/hp; acceleration: standing ¼ mile 20 sec, 0-50 mph (0-80 km/h) 11.4 sec; speed in direct drive at 1,000 rpm: 16.8 mph, 27 km/h; fuel consumption: 34 m/imp gal, 28.3 m/US gal, 8.3 l x 100 km.

DIMENSIONS AND WEIGHT dry weight: 1,711 lb, 776 kg.

PRACTICAL INSTRUCTIONS fuel: 98-100 oct petrol.

VARIATIONS

ENGINE 7.5:1 compression ratio not available.

1300 Mk III 4-door Super De Luxe Saloon

See 1300 Mk III 2-door Super De Luxe Saloon, except for:

PRICE IN GB: £ 803.

PERFORMANCE power-weight ratio: 29.4 lb/hp, 13.3 kg/hp.

DIMENSIONS AND WEIGHT dry weight: 1,766 lb, 801 kg.

1300 Mk III Countryman

See 1300 Mk III 2-door Super De Luxe Saloon, except for:

PRICE IN GB: £ 884.

TRANSMISSION tyres: 145 x 12 (5.50 x 12 only for export).

PERFORMANCE max speed: 85 mph, 136 km/h; power-weight ratio: 30.2 lb/hp, 13.7 kg/hp; acceleration: 0-50 mph (0-80 km/h) 11.6 sec.

DIMENSIONS AND WEIGHT dry weight: 1,815 lb, 823 kg.

BODY estate car/station wagon; 2 + 1 doors.

OPTIONAL ACCESSORIES electrically-heated rear window not available.

1300 G.T. Saloon

See 1300 Mk III 2-door Super De Luxe Saloon, except for:

PRICE IN GB: £ 932.

ENGINE compression ratio: 9.7:1; max power (DIN): 70 hp at 6,000 rpm; max torque (DIN): 74 lb ft, 10.2 kg m at 3,250 rpm; 54.9 hp/l; 2 SU type HS 2 semi-downdraught carburettors.

TRANSMISSION gearbox ratios: I 3.330, II 2.090, III 1.350, IV 1, rev 3.350; width of rims: 4''; tyres: 145 x 12.

PERFORMANCE max speeds: (I) 32 mph, 51 km/h; (II) 50 mph, 80 km/h; (III) 77 mph, 124 km/h; (IV) 92 mph, 148 km/h; power-weight ratio: 24.4 lb/hp, 11.1 kg/hp; acceleration: standing ¼ mile 19.7 sec, 0-50 mph (0-80 km/h) 9.8 sec; speed in direct drive at 1,000 rpm: 16.7 mph, 26.8 km/h.

BRAKES servo.

DIMENSIONS AND WEIGHT length: 145.81 in, 3,703 mm; width: 60.38 in, 1,534 mm; height: 53.50 in, 1,359 mm; ground clearance: 5.50 in, 140 mm.

BODY reclining backrests (standard).

OPTIONAL ACCESSORIES only electrically-heated rear window.

Maxi 1500

PRICE IN GB: £ 992.

ENGINE front, transverse, 4 stroke; 4 cylinders, in line; 90.6 cu in, 1,485 cc (3 x 3.20 in, 76.2 x 81.3 mm); compression ratio: 9:1; max power (DIN): 74 hp at 5,500 rpm; max torque (DIN): 84 lb ft, 11.6 kg m at 3,500 rpm; max engine rpm: 6,000; 49.8 hp/l; cast iron cylinder block and head; 5 crankshaft bearings; valves: overhead; camshafts: 1, overhead; lubrication: rotary pump, full flow filter, 9.5 imp pt, 11.4 US pt, 5.4 l; 1 SU type HS 6 horizontal carburettor; fuel feed: mechanical pump; water-cooled, 9.1 imp pt, 10.8 US pt, 5.1 l.

TRANSMISSION driving wheels: front; clutch: single dry plate (diaphragm), hydraulically controlled; gearbox: mechanical; gears: 5, fully synchronized; ratios: I 3.202, II 2.004, III 1.372, IV 1, V 0.795, rev 3.467; lever: central; final drive: helical spur gears; axle ratio: 3.938; width of rims: 4.5''; tyres: 155 x 13.

AUSTIN Maxi 1750 HL

AUSTIN 1800 De Luxe Saloon

AUSTIN 2200 De Luxe Saloon

PERFORMANCE max speeds: (I) 30 mph, 48 km/h; (II) 50 mph, 80 km/h; (III) 70 mph, 112 km/h; (IV) 90 mph, 145 km/h; (V) 87 mph, 140 km/h; power-weight ratio: 28.8 lb/hp, 13.1 kg/hp; carrying capacity: 882 lb, 400 kg; acceleration: standing ¼ mile 21 sec, 0-50 mph (0-80 km/h) 11 sec; speed in 4th gear at 1,000 rpm: 15.6 mph, 25.2 km/h; fuel consumption: 31.5 m/imp gal, 26.1 m/US gal, 9 l x 100 km.

CHASSIS integral; front suspension: independent, wishbones, hydrolastic (liquid) rubber cone springs, hydraulic connecting pipes to rear wheels; rear suspension: independent, swinging longitudinal trailing arms, hydrolastic (liquid) rubber cone springs, hydraulic connecting pipes to front wheels.

STEERING rack-and-pinion; turns lock to lock: 3.90.

BRAKES front disc (diameter 9.68 in, 246 mm), rear drum, servo; swept area: front 184 sq in, 1,187 sq cm, rear 76 sq in, 490 sq cm, total 260 sq in, 1,677 sq cm.

ELECTRICAL EQUIPMENT 12 V; 40 Ah battery; dynamo; Lucas distributor; 2 headlamps.

DIMENSIONS AND WEIGHT wheel base: 104 in, 2,641 mm; tracks: 53.80 in, 1,366 mm front, 53.20 in, 1,351 mm rear; length: 158.33 in, 4,021 mm; width: 64.12 in, 1,629 mm; height: 55.28 in, 1,404 mm; ground clearance: 5.50 in, 140 mm; dry weight: 2,128 lb, 965 kg; distribution of weight: 62.3% front, 37.7% rear; turning circle (between walls): 33.9 ft, 10.3 m; fuel tank: 9 imp gal, 10.8 US gal, 41 l.

BODY saloon/sedan; 4 + 1 doors; 4-5 seats, separate front seats.

PRACTICAL INSTRUCTIONS fuel: 98-100 oct petrol; engine sump, gearbox and final drive oil: 9.5 imp pt, 11.4 US pt, 5.4 l, SAE 10W-30 (winter) 20W-50 (summer), change every 6,000 miles, 9,700 km; greasing: none; tappet clearances: inlet 0.016-0.018 in, 0.40-0.45 mm, exhaust 0.020-0.022 in, 0.50-0.55 mm; valve timing: 9°4' 50°56' 48°56' 11°4'; tyre pressure: front 26 psi, 1.8 atm, rear 24 psi, 1.7 atm.

OPTIONAL ACCESSORIES electrically-heated rear window.

Maxi 1750

See Maxi 1500, except for:

PRICE IN GB: £ 1,032.

ENGINE 106.7 cu in, 1,748 cc (3 x 3.77 in, 76.2 x 95.7 mm); compression ratio: 8.7:1; max power (DIN): 84 hp at 5,000 rpm; max torque (DIN): 105 lb ft, 14.5 kg m at 3,000 rpm; 48.1 hp/l.

TRANSMISSION gearbox ratios: V 0.869; axle ratio: 3.647.

PERFORMANCE max speeds: (I) 34 mph, 54 km/h; (II) 56 mph, 90 km/h; (III) 78 mph, 125 km/h; (IV) 92 mph, 148 km/h; (V) 88 mph, 141 km/h; power-weight ratio: 25.4 lb/hp, 11.5 kg/hp; acceleration: standing ¼ mile 19.5 sec, 0-50 mph (0-80 km/h) 10 sec; speed in 4th gear at 1,000 rpm: 16.8 mph, 27 km/h; fuel consumption: 24.1 m/imp gal, 20.1 m/US gal, 11.7 l x 100 km.

DIMENSIONS AND WEIGHT dry weight: 2,128 lb, 965 kg; distribution of weight: 63% front, 37% rear.

PRACTICAL INSTRUCTIONS tappet clearances: inlet 0.012 in, 0.30 mm, exhaust 0.012 in, 0.30 mm; valve timing: 9° 51° 49° 11°.

OPTIONAL ACCESSORIES AP automatic transmission, hydraulic torque converter with 2 conic bevel gears (twin concentric differential-like gear clusters) with 4 ratios (I 2.612, II 1.807, III 1.446, IV 1, rev 2.612), operated by 3 brake bands and 2 multi-disc clutches, max ratio of converter at stall 2, possible manual selection, max speeds (I) 41 mph, 66 km/h, (II) 59 mph, 95 km/h, (III) 73 mph, 118 km/h, (IV) 88 mph, 141 km/h; alternator.

Maxi 1750 HL

See Maxi 1750, except for:

PRICE IN GB: £ 1,137.

ENGINE compression ratio: 9.5:1; max power (DIN): 95 hp at 5,350 rpm; max torque (DIN): 107 lb ft, 14.7 kg m at 3,500 rpm; 54.3 hp/l; 2 SU type HS 6 carburettors.

TRANSMISSION tyres: 165 x 13.

PERFORMANCE max speeds: (I) 35 mph, 56 km/h; (II) 56 mph, 90 km/h; (III) 82 mph, 132 km/h; (IV) 98 mph, 158 km/h; (V) 97.5 mph, 157 km/h; power-weight ratio: 22.4 lb/hp, 10.1 kg/hp; acceleration: 0-50 mph (0-80 km/h) 11 sec; speed in top at 1,000 rpm: 19.9 mph, 32 km/h.

STEERING turns lock to lock: 4.20.

ELECTRICAL EQUIPMENT 16 A alternator (standard).

AUSTIN Maxi 1750 HL

AUSTIN 1800 De Luxe Saloon

AUSTIN 2200 De Luxe Saloon

1800 De Luxe Saloon

PRICE IN GB: £ 1,073.

ENGINE front, transverse, 4 stroke; 4 cylinders, in line; 109.7 cu in, 1,798 cc (3.16 x 3.50 in, 80.3 x 88.9 mm); compression ratio: 9:1; max power (DIN): 86 hp at 5,400 rpm; max torque (DIN): 101 lb ft, 13.9 kg m at 3,000 rpm; max engine rpm: 5,600; 48.1 hp/l; cast iron cylinder block and head; 5 crankshaft bearings: valves: overhead, push-rods and rockers; camshafts: 1, side; lubrication: rotary pump, magnetic metal gauze filter in sump and full flow, 11.2 imp pt, 13.5 US pt, 6.4 l; 1 SU type HS 6 semi-downdraught carburettor; fuel feed: mechanical pump; water-cooled, 9.5 imp pt, 11.4 US pt, 5.4 l.

TRANSMISSION driving wheels: front; clutch: single dry plate (diaphragm), hydraulically controlled; gearbox: mechanical, in unit with engine; gears: 4, fully synchronized; ratios: I 3.292, II 2.059, III 1.384, IV 1, rev 3.075; lever: central; final drive: spiral bevel; axle ratio: 3.882; width of rims: 4.5''; tyres: 165 x 14.

PERFORMANCE max speeds: (I) 32 mph, 51 km/h; (II) 51 mph, 82 km/h; (III) 76 mph, 122 km/h; (IV) 92 mph, 148 km/h; power-weight ratio: 28.5 lb/hp, 13 kg/hp; carrying capacity: 882 lb, 400 kg; acceleration: 0-50 mph (0-80 km/h) 11.7 sec; speed in direct drive at 1,000 rpm: 13.2 mph, 21.3 km/h; fuel consumption: 23.4 m/imp gal, 19.6 m/US gal, 12 l x 100 km.

CHASSIS integral; front suspension: independent, wishbones, lower trailing links, hydrolastic (liquid) rubber cone springs, hydraulic connecting pipes to rear wheels; rear suspension: independent, swinging longitudinal trailing arms, hydrolastic (liquid) rubber cone springs, hydraulic connecting pipes to front wheels, anti-roll bar.

STEERING rack-and-pinion; turns lock to lock: 3.56.

BRAKES front disc (diameter 9.28 in, 236 mm), rear drum, servo; swept area: front 183 sq in, 1,181 sq cm, rear 99 sq in, 639 sq cm, total 282 sq in, 1,820 sq cm.

ELECTRICAL EQUIPMENT 12 V; 55 Ah battery; 40 A dynamo; Lucas distributor; 4 headlamps.

DIMENSIONS AND WEIGHT wheel base: 105.87 in, 2,689 mm; tracks: 55.91 in, 1,420 mm front, 55.47 in, 1,409 mm rear; length: 166.18 in, 4,221 mm; width: 66.93 in, 1,700 mm; height: 56,14 in, 1,426 mm; ground clearance: 6.50 in, 165 mm; dry weight: 2,464 lb, 1,117 kg; distribution of weight: 63% front, 37% rear; turning circle (between walls): 40.3 ft, 12.3 m; fuel tank: 10.5 imp gal, 12.7 US gal, 48 l.

BODY saloon/sedan; 4 doors; 4-5 seats, separate front seats.

PRACTICAL INSTRUCTIONS fuel: 96-98 oct petrol; engine sump, gearbox and final drive oil: 11 imp pt, 13.1 US pt, 6.2 l, SAE 10W-30 (winter) 20W-50 (summer), change every 6,000 miles, 9,700 km; tappet clearances: inlet 0.015 in, 0.38 mm, exhaust 0.015 in, 0.38 mm; valve timing: 5° 45° 40° 10°; tyre pressure: front 30 psi, 2.1 atm, rear 24 psi, 1.7 atm.

OPTIONAL ACCESSORIES Borg-Warner automatic transmission, hydraulic torque converter and planetary gears with 3 ratios (I 2.388, II 1.449, III 1, rev 2.388), max ratio of converter at stall 2, 3.940 axle ratio, speed in direct drive at 1,000 rpm 17.8 mph, 28.7 km/h, max speeds (I) 42 mph, 68 km/h, (II) 69 mph, 111 km/h, (III) 100 mph, 161 km/h; power-assisted steering; alternator; reclining backrests; electrically-heated rear window.

2200 De Luxe Saloon

See 1800 De Luxe Saloon, except for:

PRICE IN GB: £ 1,197.

ENGINE 6 cylinders; 135.9 cu in, 2,227 cc (3 x 3.30 in, 76.1 x 83.7 mm); max power (DIN): 110 hp at 5,250 rpm; max torque (DIN): 126 lb ft, 17.4 kg m at 3,500 rpm; 49.4 hp/l; 4 crankshaft bearings; lubricating system capacity: 13 imp pt, 15.6 US pt, 7.4 l; 2 SU type HS 6 carburettors; fuel feed: electric pump; water-cooled, 17 imp pt, 20.3 US pt, 9.6 l, electric thermostatic fan.

TRANSMISSION tyres: 165 SR x 14.

PERFORMANCE max speed: 103 mph, 165 km/h; power-weight ratio: 22.8 lb/hp, 10.3 kg/hp; fuel consumption: 20.5 m/imp gal, 17 m/US gal, 13.8 l x 100 km.

BRAKES disc (diameter 9.70 in, 246 mm); swept area: front 195 sq in, 1,258 sq cm, rear 99 sq in, 638 sq cm, total 294 sq in, 1,896 sq cm.

ELECTRICAL EQUIPMENT 16 A alternator (standard).

DIMENSIONS AND WEIGHT dry weight: 2,511 lb, 1,139 kg; fuel tank: 12.5 imp gal, 15 US gal, 57 l.

PRACTICAL INSTRUCTIONS engine sump, gearbox and final drive oil: 12 imp pt, 14.4 US pt, 6.8 l.

BENTLEY GREAT BRITAIN

T Series 4-door Saloon

PRICE IN GB: £ 8,730.
PRICE IN USA: $ 25,000.

ENGINE front, 4 stroke; 8 cylinders, Vee-slanted at 90°; 411.9 cu in, 6,750 cc (4.10 x 3.90 in, 104.1 x 99 mm); compression ratio: 9:1; light alloy cylinder block and head, wet liners; 5 crankshaft bearings; valves: overhead, in line, slanted, push-rods and rockers, hydraulic tappets; camshafts: 1, at centre of Vee; lubrication: gear pump, full flow filter, 14.4 imp pt, 17.3 US pt, 8.2 l; 2 SU type HD 8 horizontal carburettors; fuel feed: 2 electric pumps; water-cooled, 28 imp pt, 33.6 US pt, 15.9 l.

TRANSMISSION driving wheels: rear; gearbox: automatic transmission, hydraulic torque converter and planetary gears with 3 ratios, max ratio of converter at stall 2.04, possible manual selection; ratios: I 2.480, II 1.480, III 1, rev 2.080; lever: steering column; final drive: hypoid bevel; axle ratio: 3.080; tyres: 8.45 x 15.

PERFORMANCE max speeds: (I) 40 mph, 64 km/h; (II) 74 mph, 119 km/h; (III) 119 mph, 191 km/h; carrying capacity: 1,058 lb, 480 kg; speed in direct drive at 1,000 rpm: 26.2 mph, 42.2 km/h; fuel consumption: 15 m/imp gal, 12.5 m/US gal, 18.8 l x 100 km.

CHASSIS integral, front and rear auxiliary frames; front suspension: independent, wishbones, coil springs, automatic levelling control, telescopic dampers; rear suspension: independent, semi-trailing arms, coil springs, automatic levelling control, telescopic dampers.

STEERING recirculating ball, progressive servo, right-hand drive; turns lock to lock: 3.25.

BRAKES disc [diameter (twin caliper) 11 in, 279 mm], 3 independent circuits, servo; swept area: front 227 sq in, 1,464 sq cm, rear 287 sq in, 1,851 sq cm, total 514 sq in, 3,315 sq cm.

ELECTRICAL EQUIPMENT 12 V; 64 Ah battery; 35 A alternator; Lucas distributor; 4 headlamps.

DIMENSIONS AND WEIGHT wheel base: 119.50 in, 3,035 mm; tracks: 57.50 in, 1,460 mm front, 57.50 in, 1,460 mm rear; length: 203.50 in, 5,169 mm; width: 71 in, 1,803 mm; height: 59.75 in, 1,518 mm; ground clearance: 6.50 in, 165 mm; dry weight: 4,556 lb, 2,067 kg; turning circle (between walls): 38 ft, 11.6 m; fuel tank: 24 imp gal, 28.8 US gal, 109 l.

BODY saloon/sedan; 4 doors; 5-6 seats, separate front seats, adjustable and reclining backrests; headrests, air-conditioning system, electrically-controlled windows.

PRACTICAL INSTRUCTIONS fuel: 98-100 oct petrol; engine sump oil: 14.1 imp pt, 16.9 US pt, 8 l, SAE 10W-30, change every 6,000 miles, 9,700 km; gearbox oil: 23.9 imp pt, 28.8 US pt, 13.6 l, change every 24,000 miles, 38,600 km; final drive oil: 4 imp pt, 4.9 US pt, 2.3 l, change every 24,000 miles, 38,600 km; power-assisted steering and automatic levelling control oil: change every 12,000 miles, 19,300 km; greasing: every 12,000 miles, 19,300 km; valve timing: 26° 52° 68° 10°; tyre pressure: front 26 psi, 1.8 atm, rear 26 psi, 1.8 atm.

VARIATIONS

ENGINE 8:1 compression ratio.

OPTIONAL ACCESSORIES iodine headlamps.

2-door Corniche

See T Series 4-door Saloon, except for:

PRICE IN GB: £ 11,400.
PRICE IN USA: $ 32,800.

TRANSMISSION tyres: 205 x 15.

PERFORMANCE max speed: 120 mph, 193 km/h; fuel consumption: 14.5 m/imp gal, 12.1 m/US gal, 19.5 l x 100 km.

DIMENSIONS AND WEIGHT height: 58.66 in, 1,490 mm.

BODY coupé; 2 doors.

Corniche Convertible

See 2-door Corniche, except for:

PRICE IN GB: £ 11,915.

BODY convertible.

BENTLEY T Series 4-door Saloon (rear suspension)

BRISTOL 411

CLAN Crusader

BIOTA GREAT BRITAIN

Mini Sports Car

PRICE IN GB: £ 675.

ENGINE Mini (British Leyland), front, transverse, 4 stroke; 4 cylinders, vertical, in line; 51.7 cu in, 848 cc (2.48 x 2.69 in, 63 x 68.4 mm); max power (DIN): 34 hp at 5,500 rpm; max torque (DIN): 44 lb ft, 6.1 kg m at 2,900 rpm.

PERFORMANCE power-weight ratio: 23.6 lb/hp, 10.7 kg/hp.

CHASSIS tubular.

DIMENSIONS AND WEIGHT wheel base: 74 in, 1,880 mm; tracks: 51 in, 1,296 mm front, 51 in, 1,296 mm rear; length: 117 in, 2,972 mm; width: 59 in, 1,499 mm; height: 40 in, 1,016 mm; ground clearance: 4.50 in, 114 mm; dry weight: 800 lb, 363 kg; distribution of weight: 75% front, 25% rear; turning circle (between walls): 28 ft, 8.5 m.

BODY open in plastic material; 2 seats.

VARIATIONS

ENGINE Mini (British Leyland), 60.9 cu in, 998 cc.

ENGINE Mini (British Leyland), 77.8 cu in, 1,275 cc.

For further technical information see Mini (British Leyland).

BRISTOL GREAT BRITAIN

411

PRICE IN GB: £ 6,450.

ENGINE front, 4 stroke; 8 cylinders, Vee-slanted at 90°; 383 cu in, 6,277 cc (4.25 x 3.37 in, 108 x 85.7 mm); compression ratio: 9.5:1; max power (SAE): 335 hp at 5,200 rpm; max torque (SAE): 425 lb ft, 58.6 kg m at 3,400 rpm; max engine rpm: 5,500; 53 hp/l; cast iron cylinder block and head; 5 crankshaft bearings; valves: overhead, push-rods and rockers, hydraulic tappets; camshafts: 1, at centre of Vee; lubrication: rotary pump, full flow filter, 10.5 imp pt, 12.5 US pt, 5.9 l; 1 Holley downdraught 4-barrel carburettor; fuel feed: mechanical pump; water-cooled, 29 imp pt, 34.9 US pt, 16.5 l, thermostatically-controlled twin electric fan.

TRANSMISSION driving wheels: rear; gearbox: Torqueflite automatic transmission, hydraulic torque converter and planetary gears with 3 ratios, max ratio of converter at stall 2, possible manual selection; ratios: I 2.450, II 1.450, III 1, rev 2.200; lever: central; final drive: hypoid bevel; axle ratio: 3.070; width of rims: 6"; tyres: 205 x 15.

PERFORMANCE max speeds: (I) 50 mph, 80 km/h; (II) 90 mph, 145 km/h; (III) 140 mph, 225 km/h; power-weight ratio: 11 lb/hp, 5 kg/hp; carrying capacity: 904 lb, 410 kg; acceleration: 0-50 mph (0-80 km/h) 6 sec; speed in direct drive at 1,000 rpm: 26 mph, 41.8 km/h; fuel consumption: 16 m/imp gal, 13.3 m/US gal, 17.7 l x 100 km.

CHASSIS box-type ladder frame; front suspension: independent, wishbones, coil springs, anti-roll bar, adjustable telescopic dampers; rear suspension: rigid axle, longitudinal torsion bars, trailing lower radius arms, upper torque arms, transverse Watt linkage, automatic levelling control, adjustable telescopic dampers.

STEERING recirculating ball, servo; turns lock to lock: 3.

BRAKES disc (front diameter 10.91 in, 277 mm, rear 10.60 in, 269 mm), servo; swept area: front 224 sq in, 1,445 sq cm, rear 196 sq in, 1,264 sq cm, total 420 sq in, 2,709 sq cm.

ELECTRICAL EQUIPMENT 12 V; 71 Ah battery; 720 W alternator; Chrysler distributor; 4 headlamps.

DIMENSIONS AND WEIGHT wheel base: 114 in, 2,896 mm; tracks: 54.50 in, 1,384 mm front, 55.25 in, 1,403 mm rear; length: 194 in, 4,990 mm; width: 68 in, 1,727 mm; height: 57.50 in, 1,460 mm; ground clearance: 5 in, 127 mm; dry weight: 3,700 lb, 1,678 kg; distribution of weight: 53% front, 47% rear; turning circle (between walls): 40 ft, 12.2 m; fuel tank: 18 imp gal, 21.6 US gal, 82 l.

BODY saloon/sedan; 2 doors; 4 seats, separate front seats, reclining backrests; electrically-controlled windows, electrically-heated rear window.

PRACTICAL INSTRUCTIONS fuel: 100 oct petrol; engine sump oil: 10.5 imp pt, 12.7 US pt, 6 l, 20W-50, change every 4,000 miles, 6,400 km; gearbox oil: 13 imp pt, 15.6 US pt, 7.4 l, Dexron, change every 32,000 miles, 51,500 km; final drive oil: 3.5 imp pt, 4.2 US pt, 2 l, SAE 90 EP, change every 20,000 miles, 32,200 km; greasing: every 20,000 miles, 32,200 km, 4 points; valve timing: 21° 67° 79° 25°; tyre pressure: front 28 psi, 2 atm, rear 28 psi, 2 atm.

OPTIONAL ACCESSORIES air-conditioning; automatic speed control.

BENTLEY 2-door Corniche

BIOTA Mini Sports Car

CLAN Crusader

CLAN GREAT BRITAIN

Crusader

PRICE IN GB: £ 1,125.

ENGINE rear, 4 stroke; 4 cylinders, in line, slanted at 45°; 53.4 cu in, 875 cc (2.68 x 2.38 in, 68 x 60.4 mm); compression ratio: 10; max power (DIN): 51 hp at 6,100 rpm; max torque (DIN): 52 lb ft, 377 kg m at 4,300 rpm; max engine rpm: 6,500-7,000; 58.2 hp/l; light alloy cylinder block and head, dry liners; 3 crankshaft bearings; camshafts: 1, overhead; lubrication: eccentric pump, full flow filter, oil cooler, 7 imp pt, 8.5 US pt, 4 l; 2 Stromberg 125 CDS semi-downdraught carburettors; fuel feed: mechanical pump; water-cooled, 11 imp pt, 13.1 US pt, 6.2 l.

TRANSMISSION driving wheels: rear; clutch: single dry plate, (diaphragm), hydraulically controlled; gearbox: mechanical; gears: 4, fully synchronized; ratios: I 3.417, II 1.833, III 1.174, IV 1, rev 2.846; lever: central; final drive: hypoid bevel; axle ratio: 4.875; width of rims: 4.5''; tyres: 155 x 12.

PERFORMANCE max speeds: (I) 28 mph, 45 km/h; (II) 50 mph, 80 km/h; (III) 77 mph, 124 km/h; (IV): 101 mph, 162 km/h; power-weight ratio: 25.4 lb/hp, 10.8 kg/hp; acceleration: standing ¼ mile 18.9 sec, 0-50 mph (0-80 km/h) 9.7 sec; speed in direct drive at 1,000 rpm: 15.1 mph, 24.3 km/h; fuel consumption: 35.6 m/imp gal, 29.8 m/US gal, 7.9 l x 100 km.

CHASSIS integral in plastic material with steel longitudinal reinforcements; front suspension: independent, U-shaped swinging semi-axles, coil springs, telescopic dampers; rear suspension: independent, semi-trailing arms, coil springs, telescopic dampers.

STEERING rack-and-pinion.

BRAKES drum, servo; swept area: total 75 sq in, 484 sq cm.

ELECTRICAL EQUIPMENT 12 V; 32 Ah battery; 27 A alternator.

DIMENSIONS AND WEIGHT wheel base: 82.01 in, 2,083 mm; tracks: 50.98 in, 1,295 mm front, 50.98 in, 1,295 mm rear; length: 152.52 in, 3,874 mm; width: 59.02 in, 1,499 mm; height: 74.88 in, 1,902 mm; dry weight: 1,290 lb, 552 kg; turning circle (between walls): 32.5 ft, 9.9 m; fuel tank: 6 imp gal, 7.1 US gal, 27 l.

BODY coupé, in plastic material; 2 doors; 2 seats, separate front seats.

PRACTICAL INSTRUCTIONS fuel: 100 oct petrol; engine sump oil: 6 imp pt, 7.2 US pt, 3.4 l, SAE 20W-50, change every 5,000 miles, 8,000 km; gearbox and final drive oil: 4.6 imp pt, 5.5 US pt, 2.6 l, SAE 80 EP; greasing: every 5,000 miles, 8,000 km, 4 points; tappet clearances: inlet 0.007 in, 0.18 mm, exhaust 0.014 in, 0.36 mm; tyre pressure: front 18 psi, 1.3 atm, rear 30 psi, 2.1 atm.

OPTIONAL ACCESSORIES 5'' wide rims; halogen headlamps; sunshine roof.

DAIMLER GREAT BRITAIN

Sovereign 2.8-litre

PRICE IN GB: £ 2,443.

ENGINE front, 4 stroke; 6 cylinders, vertical, in line; 170 cu in, 2,791 cc (3.27 x 3.39 in, 83 x 86 mm); compression ratio: 8.5:1; max power (DIN): 140 hp at 5,150 rpm; max torque (DIN): 150 lb ft, 20.7 kg m at 4,250 rpm; max engine rpm: 6,500; 50.2 hp/l; cast iron cylinder block with dry liners, light alloy head with hemispherical combustion chambers; 7 crankshaft bearings; valves: overhead, Vee-slanted at 70°, thimble tappets; camshafts: 2, overhead; lubrication: mechanical pump, full flow filter, 14.4 imp pt, 17.3 US pt, 8.2 l; 2 SU type HD 8 horizontal carburettors; fuel feed: 2 electric pumps; water-cooled, 30 imp pt, 35.9 US pt, 17 l, viscous coupling thermostatic fan.

TRANSMISSION driving wheels: rear; clutch: single dry plate (diaphragm), hydraulically controlled; gearbox: mechanical; gears: 4, fully synchronized, and overdrive/top; ratios: I 3.040, II 1.970, III 1.330, IV 1, overdrive 0.780, rev 3.374; lever: central; final drive: hypoid bevel; axle ratio: 4.550; width of rims: 6''; tyres: E 70 VR x 15.

PERFORMANCE max speeds: (I) 34 mph, 55 km/h; (II) 53 mph, 85 km/h; (III) 72 mph, 116 km/h; (IV) 100 mph, 161 km/h; (overdrive) 117 mph, 189 km/h; power-weight ratio: 24.2 lb/hp, 11 kg/hp; carrying capacity: 926 lb, 420 kg; acceleration: standing ¼ mile 17.9 sec, 0-50 mph (0-80 km/h) 8.5 sec; speed in overdrive/top at 1,000 rpm: 21.4 mph, 34.4 km/h; fuel consumption: 20.5 m/imp gal, 17 m/US gal, 13.8 l x 100 km.

SOVEREIGN 2.8-LITRE

CHASSIS integral, front and rear auxiliary frames; front suspension: independent, wishbones, coil springs, anti-roll bar, telescopic dampers; rear suspension: independent, wishbones, semi-axle as upper arm, trailing lower radius arms, 4 coil springs, 4 telescopic dampers.

STEERING rack-and-pinion, adjustable steering wheel, variable ratio gearing servo; turns lock to lock: 3.50.

BRAKES disc (front diameter 11.18 in, 284 mm, rear 10.40 in, 264 mm), servo; swept area: front 243.7 sq in, 1,572 sq cm, rear 197.8 sq in, 1,276 sq cm, total 441.5 sq in, 2,848 sq cm.

ELECTRICAL EQUIPMENT 12 V; 50 Ah battery; 45 A alternator: Lucas distributor; 4 headlamps.

DIMENSIONS AND WEIGHT wheel base: 108.87 in, 2,765 mm; tracks: 58 in, 1,473 mm front, 58.33 in, 1,481 mm rear; length: 189.60 in, 4,816 mm; width: 69.75 in, 1,772 mm; height: 52.87 in, 1,343 mm; ground clearance: 6 in, 152 mm; dry weight: 3,389 lb, 1,537 kg; distribution of weight: 52% front, 48% rear; turning circle (between walls): 36 ft, 11 m; fuel tank: 20 imp gal, 24 US gal, 91 l.

BODY saloon/sedan; 4 doors; 5 seats, separate front seats, reclining backrests; electrically-heated rear window.

PRACTICAL INSTRUCTIONS fuel: 98 oct petrol; engine sump oil: 14.4 imp pt, 17.3 US pt, 8.2 l, SAE 10W-40 (winter) 20W-50 (summer), change every 6,000 miles, 9,700 km; gearbox oil: 3 imp pt, 3.6 US pt, 1.7 l, SAE 30, change every 12,000 miles, 19,000 km; final drive oil: 2.7 imp pt, 3.4 US pt, 1.6 l, SAE 90, change every 12,000 miles, 19,000 km; greasing: none; tappet clearances: inlet 0.012-0.014 in, 0.31-0.36 mm, exhaust 0.012-0.014 in, 0.31-0.36 mm; valve timing: 17° 59° 59° 17°; tyre pressure: front 25 psi, 1.7 atm, rear 26 psi, 1.8 atm.

OPTIONAL ACCESSORIES Borg-Warner 35 automatic transmission, hydraulic torque converter and planetary gears with 3 ratios (I 2.401, II 1.450, III 1, rev 2.078), max ratio of converter at stall 2, possible manual selection, 4.090 axle ratio, max speeds (I) 53 mph, 85 km/h, (II) 86 mph, 139 km/h, (III) 116 mph, 186 km/h; air-conditioning; electrically-controlled windows.

Sovereign 4.2-litre

See Sovereign 2.8-litre, except for:

PRICE IN GB: £ 2,696.

ENGINE 258 cu in, 4,235 cc (3.63 x 4.17 in, 92.1 x 106 mm); compression ratio: 8:1; max power (DIN): 173 hp at 4,750 rpm; max torque (DIN): 227 lb ft, 31.3 kg m at 3,000 rpm; max engine rpm: 5,500; 40.8 hp/l.

TRANSMISSION axle ratio: 3.540.

PERFORMANCE max speeds: (I) 37 mph, 60 km/h; (II) 56 mph, 90 km/h; (III) 77 mph, 124 km/h; (IV) 107 mph, 172 km/h; (overdrive) 124 mph, 200 km/h; power-weight ratio: 19.8 lb/hp, 9 kg/hp; acceleration: standing ¼ mile 16.5 sec, 0-50 mph (0-80 km/h) 6.6 sec; speed in overdrive/top at 1,000 rpm: 27.5 mph, 44.2 km/h.

DIMENSIONS AND WEIGHT dry weight: 3,440 lb, 1,560 kg.

VARIATIONS

Long Wheelbase model.

OPTIONAL ACCESSORIES Borg-Warner model 12 automatic transmission, hydraulic torque converter and planetary gears with 3 ratios (I 2.401, II 1.450, III 1, rev 2.078), max ratio of converter at stall 2, possible manual selection, 3.310 axle ratio, max speed 120 mph, 193 km/h.

Double-Six

See Sovereign 2.8-litre, except for:

PRICE IN GB: £ 3,184.

ENGINE 12 cylinders, Vee-slanted at 60°; 326 cu in, 5,343 cc (3.54 x 2.76 in, 90 x 70 mm); compression ratio: 9.1:1; max power (DIN): 265 hp at 6,000 rpm; max torque (DIN): 301 lb ft, 41.5 kg m at 3,500 rpm; max engine rpm: 6,500; 20.1 hp/l; light alloy cylinder block with wet liners, aluminium alloy head with hemispherical combustion chambers; valves: in line, thimble tappets; camshafts: 1, per cylinder block, overhead; lubrication: gear pump, full flow filter, 17.6 imp pt, 21.1 US pt, 10 l; 4 Zenith 175 CDSE semi-downdraught carburettors; fuel feed: electric pump; water-cooled, 36 imp pt, 43.3 US pt, 20.5 l.

TRANSMISSION gearbox: Borg-Warner automatic transmission, hydraulic torque converter and planetary gears with 3

DAIMLER Double-Six - Vanden Plas Saloon

DAIMLER Limousine

FAIRTHORPE TX-S

ratios, max ratio of converter at stall 2, possible manual selection; ratios: I 2.400, II 1.450, III 1, rev 2; lever: central; final drive: hypoid bevel; axle ratio: 3.310; tyres: 205/70 VR x 15.

PERFORMANCE max speeds: (I) 65 mph, 104 km/h; (II) 102 mph, 164 km/h; (III) 140 mph, 225 km/h; power-weight ratio: 12.1 lb/hp, 5.5 kg/hp; carrying capacity: 408 lb, 185 kg; acceleration: standing ¼ mile 15.7 sec, 0-50 mph (0-80 km/h) 6.2 sec; speed in direct drive at 1,000 rpm: 21.5 mph, 34.6 km/h; fuel consumption: 18.8 m/imp gal, 15.7 m/US gal, 20 l x 100 km.

CHASSIS integral, front and rear auxiliary frames; front suspension: independent, wishbones, coil springs, anti-roll bar, telescopic dampers; rear suspension: independent, wishbones, semi-axles as upper arm, trailing lower radius arms, 4 coil springs, 4 telescopic dampers.

BRAKES swept area: front 234.5 sq in, 1,513 sq cm, rear 213.7 sq in, 1,379 sq cm, total 448.2 sq in, 2,892 sq cm.

ELECTRICAL EQUIPMENT 68 Ah battery; 60 A alternator; Lucas electronic distributor; 4 headlamps.

DIMENSIONS AND WEIGHT wheel base: 108.87 in, 2,765 mm; tracks: 58 in, 1,473 mm front, 58.33 in, 1,481 mm rear; length: 189.60 in, 4,816 mm; width: 69.75 in, 1,772 mm; height: 52.87 in, 1,343 mm; ground clearance: 6 in, 152 mm; dry weight: 3,232 lb, 1,466 kg.

BODY convertible; 2 doors; 2 seats; reclining backrests.

PRACTICAL INSTRUCTIONS fuel: 97 oct petrol; engine sump oil: 16 imp pt, 19.2 US pt, 9 l, change every 3,100 miles, 5,000 km; final drive oil: 2.6 imp pt, 3.2 US pt, 1.5 l, change every 12,400 miles, 20,000 km; greasing: every 6,000 miles, 9,700 km, 17 points; tyre pressure: front 26 psi, 1.8 atm, rear 26 psi, 1.8 atm.

OPTIONAL ACCESSORIES electrically-controlled windows; air-conditioning.

Double-Six - Vanden Plas Saloon

PRICE IN GB: £ 4,500.

ENGINE front, 4 stroke; 12 cylinders, Vee-slanted at 60°; 326 cu in, 5,343 cc (3.54 x 2.76 in, 90 x 70 mm); compression ratio: 9.1:1; max power (DIN): 265 hp at 6,000 rpm; max torque (DIN): 301 lb ft, 41.5 kg m at 3,500 rpm; max engine rpm: 6,500; 20.1 hp/l; cylinder block with light alloy wet liners head with aluminium alloy hemispherical combustion chambers; 7 crankshaft bearings; valves: in line, thimble tappets; camshafts: 1 per cylinder block, overhead; lubrication: gear pump, full flow filter, 17.6 imp pt, 21.1 US pt; 10 l; 4 Zenith 175 CDSE semi-downdraught carburettors; fuel feed: electric pump; water-cooled: 36 imp pt, 43.3 US pt, 20.5 l.

TRANSMISSION driving wheels: rear; gearbox: Borg Warner automatic transmission, hydraulic torque converter and planetary gears with 3 ratios, max ratio of converter at stall 2, possible manual selection; ratios: I 2.400, II 1.450, III 1, rev 2; lever: central; final drive: hypoid bevel; axle ratio: 3.310; width of rims: 6''; tyres: 205/70 VR x 15.

PERFORMANCE max speeds: (I) 65 mph, 104 km/h; (II) 102 mph, 164 km/h; (III) 140 mph, 225 km/h; power-weight ratio: 15 lb/hp, 6.8 kg/hp; carrying capacity: 408 lb, 185 kg; acceleration: standing ¼ mile 15.7 sec, 0-50 mph (0-80 km/h) 6.2 sec; speed in direct drive at 1,000 rpm: 21.5 mph, 34.6 km/h; fuel consumption: 18.8 m/imp gal, 15.7 m/US gal, 20 l x 100 km.

CHASSIS integral, front and rear auxiliary frames; front suspension: independent, wishbones, coil springs, anti-roll bar, telescopic dampers; rear suspension: independent, wishbones, semi-axles as upper arm, trailing lower radius arms, 4 coil springs, 4 telescopic dampers.

STEERING rack-and-pinion, adjustable steering wheel, variable ratio gearing servo; turns lock to lock: 3.50.

BRAKES disc (front diameter 11.18 in, 284 mm, rear 10.40 in, 264 mm), servo; swept area: front, 243.7 sq in, 1,572 sq cm, rear 197.8 sq in, 1,276 sq cm, total 441.5 sq in, 2,848 sq cm.

ELECTRICAL EQUIPMENT 12 V; 50 Ah battery: 45 A alternator; Lucas distributor; 4 halogen headlamps.

DIMENSIONS AND WEIGHT wheel base: 112.80 in, 2,865 mm; tracks: 58 in 1,473 mm front, 58.30 in, 1,481 mm rear; length: 193.60 in, 4,917 mm; width: 69.70 in, 1,771 mm; height: 52.80 in, 1,341 mm; ground clearance: 6 in, 152 mm; dry weight: 4,116 lb, 1,821 kg; turning circle (between walls): 36 ft, 11 m; fuel tank: 20 imp gal, 24 US gal, 91 l.

BODY convertible; 2 doors; 2 seats, reclining backrests; electrically-controlled windows; air-conditioning.

PRACTICAL INSTRUCTIONS fuel: 97 oct petrol; engine sump oil: 16 imp pt, 19.2 US pt, 9 l, SAE 10W-40 (winter) 20W-50 (summer), change every 3,100 miles, 5,000 km; final drive oil: 2.6 imp pt, 3.2 US pt, 1.5 l, SAE 30, change every 12,400 miles, 20,000 km; gearbox oil: 3 imp pt, 3.6

DAIMLER Double-Six

DAIMLER Limousine

FAIRTHORPE TX-GT

US pt, 1.7 l, SAE 30, change every 12,000 miles, 19,000 km; greasing: every 6,000 miles, 9,700 km, 17 points; tappet clearances: inlet 0.012-0.014 in, 0.31-0.36 mm, exhaust 0.012-0.014 in, 0.31-0.036 mm; valve timing: 17° 59° 59° 17°; tyre pressure: front 26 psi, 1.8 atm, rear 26 psi, 1.8 atm.

Limousine

PRICE IN GB: £ 4,900.

ENGINE front, 4 stroke; 6 cylinders, vertical, in line; 258 cu in, 4,235 cc (3.63 x 4.17 in, 92.1 x 106 mm); compression ratio: 8:1; max power (DIN): 173 hp at 4,750 rpm; max torque (DIN): 227 lb ft, 31.3 kg m at 3,000 rpm; max engine rpm: 5,500; 40.8 hp/l; cast iron cylinder block with dry liners, light alloy head with hemispherical combustion chambers; 7 crankshaft bearings; valves: overhead, Vee-slanted at 70°, thimble tappets; camshafts: 2, overhead; lubrication: mechanical pump, full flow filter, 12 imp pt, 14.4 US pt, 6.8 l; 2 SU type HD 8 horizontal carburettors; fuel feed: 2 electric pumps; water-cooled, 25.5 imp pt, 30.7 US pt, 14.5 l, thermostatic fan.

TRANSMISSION driving wheels: rear; gearbox: Borg-Warner automatic transmission, hydraulic torque converter and planetary gears with 3 ratios, max ratio of converter at stall 2, possible manual selection; ratios: I 2.401, II 1.458, III 1, rev 2; lever: steering column; final drive: hypoid bevel; axle ratio: 3.540; tyres: 205 x 15 HR SP41.

PERFORMANCE max speeds: (I) 48 mph, 78 km/h; (II) 79 mph, 127 km/h; (III) 115 mph, 185 km/h; power-weight ratio: 27.6 lb/hp, 12.5 kg/hp; carrying capacity: 1,235 lb, 560 kg; fuel consumption: 17.6 m/imp gal, 14.7 m/US gal, 16 l x 100 km.

CHASSIS integral, front and rear auxiliary frames; front suspension: independent, wishbones, coil springs, anti-roll bar, telescopic dampers; rear suspension: independent, wishbones, semi-axle as upper arm, trailing lower radius arms, 4 coil springs, 4 telescopic dampers.

STEERING recirculating ball, adjustable steering wheel, variable ratio gearing servo; turns lock to lock: 2.75.

BRAKES disc, servo.

ELECTRICAL EQUIPMENT 12 V; 60 Ah battery; 45 A alternator; Lucas distributor; 4 headlamps.

DIMENSIONS AND WEIGHT wheel base: 141 in, 3,582 mm; tracks: 58 in, 1,473 mm front, 58 in, 1,473 mm rear; length: 226 in, 5,741 mm; width: 77.50 in, 1,968 mm; height: 63.75 in, 1,619 mm; ground clearance: 7 in, 177 mm; dry weight: 4,787 lb, 2,172 kg; turning circle (between walls): 46 ft, 14 m; fuel tank: 20 imp gal, 24 US gal, 91 l (2 separate tanks).

BODY limousine; 4 doors; 7 seats, separate front seats; glass partition.

PRACTICAL INSTRUCTIONS fuel: 97 oct petrol; engine sump oil: 12 imp pt, 14.4 US pt, 6.8 l, multigrade, change every 3,000 miles, 5,000 km; tappet clearances: inlet 0.012-0.014 in, 0.31-0.36 mm, exhaust 0.012-0.014 in, 0.31-0.36 mm.

OPTIONAL ACCESSORIES electrically-controlled windows; electrically-controlled glass partition; electrically-heated rear window.

FAIRTHORPE GREAT BRITAIN

Mark VI EM

PRICE IN GB: £ 1,061.

ENGINE front, 4 stroke; 4 cylinders, in line; 79.1 cu in, 1,296 cc (2.90 x 2.99 in, 73.7 x 76 mm); compression ratio: 9.5:1; max power (DIN): 75 hp at 6,000 rpm; max torque (DIN): 75 lb ft, 10.3 kg m at 4,000 rpm; max engine rpm: 6,500; 57.9 hp/l; cast iron cylinder block and head; 3 crankshaft bearings; valves: overhead, in line, push-rods and rockers; camshafts: 1, side; lubrication: gear pump, full flow filter, 7 imp pt, 8.5 US pt, 4 l; 2 SU type HS 2 semi-downdraught carburettors; fuel feed: mechanical pump; water-cooled, 9 imp pt, 10.8 US pt, 5.1 l.

TRANSMISSION driving wheels: rear; clutch: single dry plate (diaphragm), hydraulically controlled; gearbox: mechanical; gears: 4, fully synchronized; ratios: I 3.753, II 2.159, III 1.306, IV 1, rev 3.753; lever: central; final drive: hypoid bevel; axle ratio: 3.890; width of rims: 4.5''; tyres: 155 x 13.

PERFORMANCE max speed: 104 mph, 168 km/h; power-weight ratio: 13.7 lb/hp, 6.2 kg/hp; carrying capacity: 397 lb, 180 kg; speed in direct drive at 1,000 rpm: 16 mph, 25.7 km/h; fuel consumption: 40 m/imp gal, 33.1 m/US gal, 7.1 l x 100 km.

CHASSIS double backbone, box section with outriggers; front suspension: independent, wishbones, coil springs, anti-

MARK VI EM

roll bar, telescopic dampers; rear suspension: independent, wishbones, transverse leafspring as upper arms, lower trailing links, telescopic dampers.

STEERING rack-and-pinion; turns lock to lock: 3.50.

BRAKES front disc (diameter 9 in, 229 mm), rear drum, single circuit; swept area: front 197 sq in, 1,270 sq cm, rear 63 sq in, 406 sq cm, total 260 sq in, 1,676 sq cm.

ELECTRICAL EQUIPMENT 12 V; 45 Ah battery; 16 A alternator; Lucas distributor; 2 headlamps.

DIMENSIONS AND WEIGHT wheel base: 83 in, 2,108 mm; tracks: 49.50 in, 1,257 mm front, 49.50 in, 1,257 mm rear; length: 143 in, 3,632 mm; width: 58 in, 1,473 mm; height: 46 in, 1,168 mm; ground clearance: 5 in, 127 mm; dry weight: 1,030 lb, 467 kg; distribution of weight: 52% front, 48% rear; fuel tank: 10.5 imp gal, 12.7 US gal, 48 l.

BODY sports in plastic material; 2 doors; 2 seats.

PRACTICAL INSTRUCTIONS fuel: 100 oct petrol; engine sump oil: 6 imp pt, 7.2 US pt, 3.4 l, SAE 20-30; gearbox oil: 1.5 imp pt, 1.7 US pt, 0.8 l, SAE 20-30; final drive oil: 1.2 imp pt, 1.5 US pt, 0.7 l, SAE 90 EP; greasing: every 6,000 miles, 9,700 km, 3 points; tyre pressure: front 18 psi, 1.3 atm, rear 18 psi, 1:3 atm.

OPTIONAL ACCESSORIES servo brake; electrically-heated rear window; supercharger.

TX-S

PRICE IN GB: £ 1,520.

ENGINE front, 4 stroke; 6 cylinders, in line; 121.9 cu in, 1,998 cc (2.94 x 2.99 in, 74.7 x 76 mm); compression ratio: 9.2:1; max power (DIN): 114 hp at 5,300 rpm; max torque (DIN): 120 lb ft, 16.6 kg m at 3,000 rpm; max engine rpm: 6,000; 57.1 hp/l; cast iron cylinder block and head; 4 crankshaft bearings; valves: overhead, push-rods and rockers; camshafts: 1, side; lubrication: gear pump, full flow filter, 9 imp pt, 10.8 US pt, 5.1 l; 2 Stromberg 150 CD horizontal carburettors; fuel feed: mechanical pump; water-cooled, 10.9 imp pt, 13.1 US pt, 6.2 l.

TRANSMISSION driving wheels: rear; clutch: single dry plate (diaphragm), hydraulically controlled; gearbox: mechanical; gears: 4, fully synchronized; ratios: I 2.648, II 1.780, III 1.257, IV 1, rev 3.104; lever: central; final drive: hypoid bevel; axle ratio: 3.270; width of rims: 5.5"; tyres: 165 x 13.

PERFORMANCE max speeds: (I) 42 mph, 67 km/h; (II) 65 mph, 104 km/h; (III) 90 mph, 145 km/h; (IV) 115 mph, 185 km/h; power-weight ratio: 15.2 lb/hp, 6.9 kg/hp; carrying capacity: 353 lb, 160 kg; speed in direct drive at 1,000 rpm: 20.1 mph, 32.3 km/h; fuel consumption: 28 m/imp gal, 23.3 m/US gal, 10.1 l x 100 km.

CHASSIS double backbone, box section with outriggers; front suspension: independent, wishbones, coil springs, anti-roll bar, telescopic dampers; rear suspension: independent, longitudinal trailing arms, transverse arms from top of articulated uprights to ends of longitudinal trailing arms (Torix-Bennett system), coil springs, telescopic dampers.

STEERING rack-and-pinion; turns lock to lock: 3.50.

BRAKES front disc (diameter 9 in, 229 mm), rear drum; swept area: total 260.5 sq in, 1,680 sq cm.

ELECTRICAL EQUIPMENT 12 V; 52 Ah battery; 17 A alternator; Lucas distributor; 2 headlamps.

DIMENSIONS AND WEIGHT wheel base: 83 in, 2,108 mm; tracks: 49.50 in, 1,257 mm front, 49.50 in, 1,257 mm rear; length: 146.46 in, 3,720 mm; width: 60 in, 1,524 mm; height: 44.49 in, 1,130 mm; ground clearance: 5 in, 127 mm; dry weight: 1,742 lb, 790 kg; distribution of weight: 52% front, 48% rear; turning circle (between walls): 25.3 ft, 7.7 m; fuel tank: 9.7 imp gal, 11.6 US gal, 44 l.

BODY coupé in plastic material; 2 doors; 2 seats; electrically-heated rear window, rear window wiper.

PRACTICAL INSTRUCTIONS fuel: 98-100 oct petrol; engine sump oil: 6 imp pt, 7.2 US pt, 3.4 l, SAE 20W-30, change every 6,000 miles, 9,700 km; gearbox oil: 1.5 imp pt, 1.7 US pt, 0.8 l, SAE 20W-30, change every 3,700 miles, 6,000 km; final drive oil: 1.2 imp pt, 1.5 US pt, 0.7 l, SAE 90 EP, no change recommended; greasing: every 5,000 miles, 8,000 km, 3 points; tappet clearances: inlet 0.010 in, 0.25 mm; exhaust 0.010 in, 0.25 mm; valve timing: 18° 58° 58° 18°; tyre pressure: front 23 psi, 1.6 atm, rear 23 psi, 1.6 atm.

VARIATIONS

ENGINE light alloy cylinder head, 1 overhead camshaft.

OPTIONAL ACCESSORIES 3.900 or 4.110 axle ratio; servo brake; 4 halogen headlamps.

FORD Escort L

FORD Escort 1300 XL Estate Car

FORD Escort GT

TX-SS

See TX-S, except for:

PRICE IN GB: £ 1,720.

ENGINE 152.5 cu in, 2,499 cc (2.94 x 3.74 in, 74.7 x 95 mm); compression ratio: 9.5:1; max power (DIN): 134 hp at 5,450 rpm; max torque (DIN): 146 lb ft, 20.2 kg m at 2,000 rpm; max engine rpm: 6,500; 53.6 hp/l; Lucas injection pump, injectors in inlet pipes.

PERFORMANCE max speed: 130 mph, 209 km/h; power-weight ratio: 13 lb ft, 5.9 kg/hp; speed in top at 1,000 rpm: 20.7 mph, 33.3 km/h; fuel consumption: 25 m/imp gal, 20.8 m/US gal, 11.3 l x 100 km.

BRAKES front disc (diameter 9.80 in, 250 mm).

PRACTICAL INSTRUCTIONS tyre pressure: front 25 psi, 1.7 atm, rear 25 psi, 1.7 atm.

TX-GT

See TX-S, except for:

ENGINE max power (DIN): 105 hp at 5,300 rpm; max torque (DIN): 117 lb ft, 16.1 kg m at 3,000 rpm; 52.6 hp/l.

TRANSMISSION gears: 4 and overdrive (1.220 ratio).

PERFORMANCE max speed: 112 mph, 180 km/h; power-weight ratio: 17 lb/hp, 7.7 kg/hp.

DIMENSIONS AND WEIGHT length: 132.28 in, 3,360 mm; height: 46.53 in, 1,182 mm; dry weight: 1,793 lb, 813 kg.

FORD GREAT BRITAIN

Escort 1100 Standard 2-door Saloon

PRICE IN GB: £ 679.

ENGINE front, 4 stroke; 4 cylinders, vertical, in line; 67 cu in, 1,098 cc (3.19 x 2.10 in, 81 x 53.3 mm); compression ratio: 9:1; max power (SAE): 55 hp at 6,000 rpm; max torque (SAE): 60 lb ft, 8.3 kg m at 3,000 rpm; max engine rpm: 6,000; 50.1 hp/l; cast iron cylinder block and head; 5 crankshaft bearings; valves: overhead, in line, push-rods and rockers; camshafts: 1, side; lubrication: rotary or vane-type pump, full flow filter, 6.3 imp pt, 7.6 US pt, 3.6 l; 1 Autolite downdraught single barrel carburettor; fuel feed: mechanical pump; water-cooled, 9 imp pt, 10.8 US pt, 5.1 l.

TRANSMISSION driving wheels: rear; clutch: single dry plate (diaphragm); gearbox: mechanical; gears: 4, fully synchronized; ratios: I 3.656, II 2.185, III 1.425, IV 1, rev 4.235; lever: central; final drive: hypoid bevel; axle ratio: 3.900; width of rims: 4.5"; tyres: 5.50 x 12.

PERFORMANCE max speeds: (I) 24 mph, 38 km/h; (II) 41 mph, 66 km/h; (III) 62 mph, 100 km/h; (IV) 82 mph, 132 km/h; power-weight ratio: 32.2 lb/hp, 14.6 kg/hp; carrying capacity: 882 lb, 400 kg; acceleration: standing ¼ mile 21.3 sec, 0-50 mph (0-80 km/h) 13.1 sec; speed in direct drive at 1,000 rpm: 15.8 mph, 25.4 km/h; fuel consumption: 33 m/imp gal, 27.7 m/US gal, 8.5 l x 100 km.

CHASSIS integral; front suspension: independent, by McPherson, coil springs/telescopic damper struts; rear suspension: rigid axle, semi-elliptic leafsprings, telescopic dampers.

STEERING rack-and-pinion; turns lock to lock: 3.50.

BRAKES drum; swept area: front 75.4 sq in, 486 sq cm, rear 75.4 sq in, 486 sq cm, total 150.8 sq in, 972 sq cm.

ELECTRICAL EQUIPMENT 12 V; 38 Ah battery; 264 W dynamo; Motorcraft distributor; 2 headlamps.

DIMENSIONS AND WEIGHT wheel base: 94.50 in, 2,400 mm; tracks: 49 in, 1,245 mm front, 50 in, 1,270 mm rear; length: 156.60 in, 3,978 mm; width: 61.80 in, 1,570 mm; height: 53 in, 1,346 mm; ground clearance: 5 in, 127 mm; dry weight: 1,775 lb, 805 kg; distribution of weight: 54.3% front, 45.7% rear; turning circle (between walls): 29.5 ft, 9 m; fuel tank: 9 imp gal, 10.8 US gal, 41 l.

BODY saloon/sedan; 2 doors; 4-5 seats, separate front seats.

PRACTICAL INSTRUCTIONS fuel: 94 oct petrol; engine sump oil: 5.5 imp pt, 6.6 US pt, 3.1 l, SAE 10W-30, change every 5,000 miles, 8,000 km; gearbox oil: 1.6 imp pt, 1.9 US pt, 0.9 l, SAE 80, no change recommended; final drive oil: 2.6 imp pt, 3.2 US pt, 1.5 l, SAE 90, no change recommended; greasing: none; tappet clearances: inlet 0.010 in, 0.25 mm,

TRANSMISSION gearbox ratios: I 3.337, II 1.995, III 1.418, IV 1, rev 3.868; axle ratio: 4.110; width of rims: 5''; tyres: 165 x 13.

PERFORMANCE max speeds: (I) 29 mph, 47 km/h; (II) 48 mph, 79 km/h; (III) 68 mph, 109 km/h; (IV) 98 mph, 158 km/h; power-weight ratio: 21.6 lb/hp, 9.8 kg/hp; acceleration: standing ¼ mile 19 sec, 0-50 mph (0-80 km/h) 8.5 sec; speed in direct drive at 1,000 rpm: 16.2 mph, 26 km/h; fuel consumption: 30 m/imp gal, 25 m/US gal, 9.4 l x 100 km.

CHASSIS front suspension: anti-roll bar.

BRAKES front disc (diameter 8.60 in, 218 mm), rear drum, servo; swept area: front 143.5 sq in, 925 sq cm, rear 75.4 sq in, 486 sq cm, total 218.9 sq in, 1,411 sq cm.

DIMENSIONS AND WEIGHT dry weight: 1,775 lb, 805 kg.

PRACTICAL INSTRUCTIONS final drive oil: 1.9 imp pt, 2.3 US pt, 1.1 l; tappet clearances: inlet 0.012 in, 0.31 mm, exhaust 0.022 in, 0.55 mm; tyre pressure: rear 28 psi, 2 atm.

Escort GT 2-door Saloon

See Escort Sport, except for:

PRICE IN GB: £ 861.

TRANSMISSION width of rims: 4.5''; tyres: 155 x 12.

PERFORMANCE power-weight ratio: 21.8 lb/hp, 9.9 kg/hp.

CHASSIS front suspension: no anti-roll bar.

DIMENSIONS AND WEIGHT wheel base: 94.80 in, 2,408 mm; dry weight: 1,795 lb, 814 kg.

OPTIONAL ACCESSORIES only centre console.

Escort GT 4-door Saloon

See Escort GT 2-door Saloon, except for:

PRICE IN GB: £ 890.

PERFORMANCE power-weight ratio: 22.5 lb/hp, 10.2 kg/hp.

DIMENSIONS AND WEIGHT dry weight: 1,839 lb, 834 kg.

Escort Mexico

PRICE IN GB: £ 1,072.

ENGINE front, 4 stroke; 97.5 cu in, 1,598 cc (3.19 x 3.06 in, 81 x 77.6 mm); compression ratio: 9:1; max power (SAE): 98 hp at 6,000 rpm; max torque (SAE): 102 lb ft, 14.1 kg m at 4,000 rpm; max engine rpm: 6,600; 61.3 hp/l; cast iron cylinder block and head; 5 crankshaft bearings; valves: overhead, in line, push-rods and rockers; camshafts: 1, side; lubrication: rotary or vane-type pump, full flow filter, 7.7 imp pt, 9.3 US pt, 4.4 l; 1 Weber 32 DFM downdraught twin barrel carburettor; fuel feed: mechanical pump; water-cooled, 11.6 imp pt, 14 US pt, 6.6 l.

TRANSMISSION driving wheels: rear; clutch: single dry plate (diaphragm); gearbox: mechanical; gears: 4, fully synchronized; ratios: I 2.972, II 2.210, III 1.397, IV 1, rev 3.324; lever: central; final drive: hypoid bevel; axle ratio: 3.777; width of rims: 5.5''; tyres: 165 x 13.

PERFORMANCE max speeds: (I) 34 mph, 54 km/h; (II) 45 mph, 73 km/h; (III) 71 mph, 115 km/h; (IV) 100 mph, 161 km/h; power-weight ratio: 17.6 lb/hp, 8 kg/hp; speed in direct drive at 1,000 rpm: 15.2 mph, 24.4 km/h; fuel consumption: 23.5 m/imp gal, 19.6 m/US gal, 12 l x 100 km.

CHASSIS integral; front suspension: independent, by McPherson, coil springs/telescopic damper struts, anti-roll bar; rear suspension: rigid axle, semi-elliptic leafsprings, trailing radius arms, telescopic dampers.

STEERING rack-and-pinion; turns lock to lock: 3.60.

BRAKES front disc (diameter 9.25 in, 235 mm), rear drum, servo; swept area: front 189.9 sq in, 1,225 sq cm, rear 96 sq in, 619 sq cm, total 285.9 sq in, 1,844 sq cm.

ELECTRICAL EQUIPMENT 12 V; 38 Ah battery; 28 A alternator; Motorcraft distributor; 2 headlamps.

DIMENSIONS AND WEIGHT wheel base: 94.49 in, 2,400 mm; tracks: 49.02 in, 1,245 mm front, 50 in, 1,270 mm rear; length: 160.79 in, 4,084 mm; width: 61.81 in, 1,570 mm; height: 52.99 in, 1,346 mm; ground clearance: 5.79 in, 147 mm; dry weight: 1,731 lb, 785 kg; distribution of weight: 51.6% front, 48.4% rear; turning circle (between walls): 29.8 ft, 9.1 m; fuel tank: 9 imp gal, 10.8 US gal, 41 l.

BODY saloon/sedan; 2 doors; 2 bucket seats.

PRACTICAL INSTRUCTIONS fuel: 100 oct petrol; engine sump oil: 7.2 imp pt, 8.7 US pt, 4.1 l, change every 2,500 miles, 4,000 km; gearbox oil: 1.8 imp pt, 2.1 US pt, 1 l, SAE 80, no change recommended; final drive oil: 2.6 imp pt, 3.2 US pt, 1.5 l, SAE 90, no change recommended; greasing: none; tappet clearances: inlet 0.012 in, 0.30 mm, exhaust 0.022 in, 0.55 mm; valve timing: 27° 65° 65° 27°; tyre pressure: front 24 psi, 1.7 atm, rear 24 psi, 1.7 atm.

OPTIONAL ACCESSORIES limited slip differential; 4.700 5.100 5.000 axle ratios; light alloy wheels with 6'' wide rims; heavy-duty front suspension; adjustable rear telescopic dampers; off-road equipment (comprising magnesium sump shield and oil cooler).

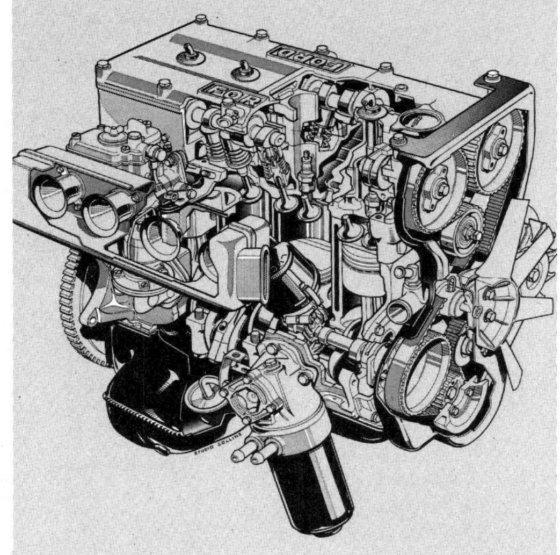

FORD Escort RS 1600

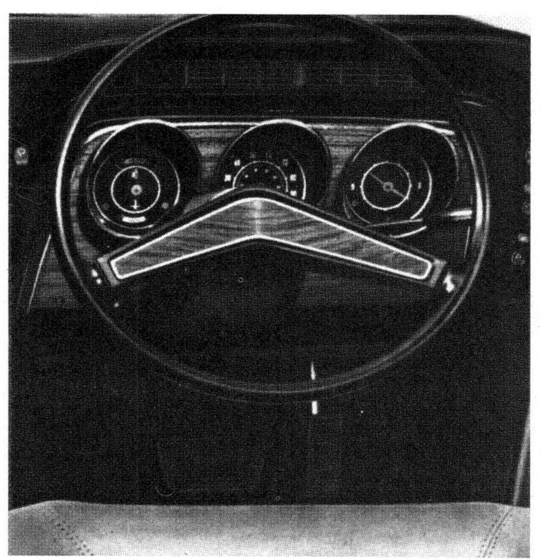

FORD Cortina XL

FORD Cortina GT

Escort RS 1600

See Escort Mexico, except for:

PRICE IN GB: £ 1,480.

ENGINE 97.7 cu in, 1,601 cc (3.19 x 3.06 in, 81 x 77.6 mm); compression ratio: 10:1; max power (DIN): 120 hp at 6,500 rpm; max torque (DIN): 112 lb ft, 15.4 kg m at 4,000 rpm; 74.9 hp/l; light alloy cylinder head; valves: 4 per cylinder, overhead, Vee-slanted; camshafts: 2, overhead, cogged belt.

PERFORMANCE max speeds: (I) 40 mph, 64 km/h; (II) 60 mph, 96 km/h; (III) 85 mph, 136 km/h; (IV) 113 mph, 182 km/h; power-weight ratio: 14.3 lb/hp, 6.5 kg/hp; acceleration: standing ¼ mile 16.7 sec, 0-50 mph (0-80 km/h) 6.8 sec; speed in direct drive at 1,000 rpm: 17.1 mph, 27.6 km/h; fuel consumption: 22 m/imp gal, 18.4 m/US gal, 12.8 l x 100 km.

ELECTRICAL EQUIPMENT Lucas distributor.

PRACTICAL INSTRUCTIONS tappet clearances: inlet 0.005-0.007 in, 0.12-0.17 mm, exhaust 0.006-0.008 in, 0.15-0.20 mm; valve timing: — 107° 112° —; tyre pressure: front 28 psi, 2 atm, rear 28 psi, 2 atm.

Cortina 1300 2-door Saloon

PRICE IN GB: £ 803.

ENGINE front, 4 stroke; 4 cylinders, vertical, in line; 79.2 cu in, 1,298 cc (3.19 x 2.48 in, 81.1 x 63.1 mm); compression ratio: 9:1; max power (DIN): 57 hp at 5,500 rpm; max torque (DIN): 67 lb ft, 9.2 kg m at 3,000 rpm; max engine rpm: 6,000; 44.1 hp/l; cast iron cylinder block and head; 5 crankshaft bearings; valves: overhead, push-rods and rockers; camshafts: 1, side; lubrication: rotary pump, full flow filter, 6 imp pt, 7.2 US pt, 3.4 l; 1 Ford GPD downdraught single barrel carburettor; fuel feed: mechanical pump; water-cooled, 10 imp pt, 12 US pt, 5.7 l.

TRANSMISSION driving wheels: rear; clutch: single dry plate (diaphragm); gearbox: mechanical; gears: 4, fully synchronized; ratios: I 3.540, II 2.400, III 1.410, IV 1, rev 3.960; lever: central; final drive: hypoid bevel; axle ratio: 4.444; width of rims: 4.5''; tyres: 6.00 x 13.

PERFORMANCE max speeds: (I) 24 mph, 39 km/h; (II) 37 mph, 60 km/h; (III) 63 mph, 102 km/h; (IV) 85 mph, 136 km/h; power-weight ratio: 36.4 lb/hp, 16.5 kg/hp; carrying capacity: 959 lb, 435 kg; speed in direct drive at 1,000 rpm: 14.9 mph, 24 km/h; fuel consumption: 35.9 m/imp gal, 29.8 m/US gal, 7.9 l x 100 km.

CHASSIS integral, front auxiliary frame; front suspension: independent, wishbones, coil spring/telescopic dampers; rear suspension: rigid axle, lower trailing arms, upper oblique torque arms, coil springs, telescopic dampers.

STEERING rack-and-pinion; turns lock to lock: 3.70.

BRAKES front disc (diameter 9.70 in, 247 mm), rear drum; swept area: front 194.6 sq in, 1,255 sq cm, rear 75.3 sq in, 486 sq cm, total 269.9 sq in, 1,741 sq cm.

ELECTRICAL EQUIPMENT 12 V; 38 Ah battery; 38 A alternator; Ford distributor; 2 headlamps.

DIMENSIONS AND WEIGHT wheel base: 101.50 in, 2,578 mm; tracks: 56 in, 1,422 mm front, 56 in, 1,422 mm rear; length: 168 in, 4,267 mm; width: 67.05 in, 1,703 mm; height: 52 in, 1,321 mm; ground clearance: 5 in, 127 mm; dry weight: 2,084 lb, 945 kg; distribution of weight: 53% front, 47% rear; turning circle (between walls): 33.5 ft, 10.2 m; fuel tank: 12 imp gal, 14.3 US gal, 54 l.

BODY saloon/sedan; 2 doors; 5 seats, separate front seats.

PRACTICAL INSTRUCTIONS fuel: 97 oct petrol; engine sump oil: 6 imp pt, 7.2 US pt, 3.4 l, SAE 10W-30, change every 6,000 miles, 9,700 km; gearbox oil: 1.6 imp pt, 1.9 US pt, 0.9 l, SAE 80 EP, no change recommended; final drive oil: 1.7 imp pt, 2.1 US pt, 1 l, SAE 90 EP, no change recommended; greasing: none; tappet clearances: inlet 0.004 in, 0.10 mm, exhaust 0.007 in, 0.17 mm; valve timing: 17° 51° 51° 17°; tyre pressure: front 27 psi, 1.9 atm, rear 34 psi, 2.4 atm.

OPTIONAL ACCESSORIES 5.5'' sport road wheels with 175 x 15 tyres; servo brake; alternator; reclining backrests.

Cortina 1300 L 2-door Saloon

See Cortina 1300 2-door Saloon, except for:

PRICE IN GB: £ 824.

Cortina 1300 4-door Saloon

See Cortina 1300 2-door Saloon, except for:

PRICE IN GB: £ 832.

PERFORMANCE power-weight ratio: 37.2 lb/hp, 16.9 kg/hp.

DIMENSIONS AND WEIGHT dry weight: 2,139 lb, 970 kg.

Cortina 1300 L 4-door Saloon

See Cortina 1300 4-door Saloon, except for:

PRICE IN GB: £ 853.

Cortina 1300 Estate Car

See Cortina 1300 2-door Saloon, except for:

PRICE IN GB: £ 929.

PERFORMANCE power-weight ratio: 39.7 lb/hp, 18.5 kg/hp.

DIMENSIONS AND WEIGHT dry weight: 2,293 lb, 1,040 kg.

BODY estate car/station wagon; 4 + 1 doors.

Cortina 1300 L Estate Car

See Cortina 1300 Estate Car, except for:

PRICE IN GB: £ 950.

Cortina 1600 2-door Saloon

See Cortina 1300 2-door Saloon, except for:

PRICE IN GB: £ 843.

ENGINE 97.5 cu in, 1,598 cc (3.19 x 3.06 in, 81 x 77.6 mm); max power (DIN): 68 hp at 5,700 rpm; max torque (DIN): 85 lb ft, 11.6 kg m at 2,600 rpm; 42.5 hp/l.

TRANSMISSION axle ratio: 3.890.

PERFORMANCE max speeds: (I) 29 mph, 47 km/h; (II) 43 mph, 69 km/h; (III) 73 mph, 117 km/h; (IV) 91 mph, 146 km/h; power-weight ratio: 31.1 lb/hp, 14.1 kg/hp; carrying capacity: 992 lb, 450 kg; speed in direct drive at 1,000 rpm: 17.1 mph, 27.5 km/h; fuel consumption: 32.1 m/imp gal, 26.7 m/US gal, 8.8 l x 100 km.

ELECTRICAL EQUIPMENT alternator (standard).

DIMENSIONS AND WEIGHT dry weight: 2,117 lb, 960 kg; distribution of weight: 54% front, 46% rear.

OPTIONAL ACCESSORIES Borg-Warner 35/3 automatic transmission, hydraulic torque converter and planetary gears with 3 ratios (I 2.390, II 1.450, III 1, rev 2.094), max ratio of converter at stall 2, possible manual selection.

Cortina 1600 L 2-door Saloon

See Cortina 1600 2-door Saloon, except for:

PRICE IN GB: £ 864.

Cortina 1600 XL 2-door Saloon

See Cortina 1600 2-door Saloon, except for:

PRICE IN GB: £ 936.

Cortina 1600 4-door Saloon

See Cortina 1600 2-door Saloon, except for:

PRICE IN GB: £ 872.

PERFORMANCE power-weight ratio: 31.8 lb/hp, 14.4 kg/hp.

DIMENSIONS AND WEIGHT dry weight: 2,172 lb, 985 kg.

FORD Cortina (rear suspension)

FORD Capri 1600 XL

FORD Capri 1600 XL

Cortina 1600 L 4-door Saloon

See Cortina 1600 4-door Saloon, except for:

PRICE IN GB: £ 893.

Cortina 1600 XL 4-door Saloon

See Cortina 1600 4-door Saloon, except for:

PRICE IN GB: £ 965.

Cortina 1600 Estate Car

See Cortina 1600 2-door Saloon, except for:

PRICE IN GB: £ 969.

PERFORMANCE power-weight ratio: 33.8 lb/hp, 15.3 kg/hp.

DIMENSIONS AND WEIGHT dry weight: 2,326 lb, 1,055 kg.

BODY estate car/station wagon; 4 + 1 doors.

Cortina 1600 L Estate Car

See Cortina 1600 Estate Car, except for:

PRICE IN GB: £ 990.

Cortina 1600 XL Estate Car

See Cortina 1600 Estate Car, except for:

PRICE IN GB: £ 1,062.

Cortina 1600 GT 2-door Saloon

See Cortina 1300 2-door Saloon, except for:

PRICE IN GB: £ 987.

ENGINE 97.2 cu in, 1,593 cc (3.57 x 2.60 in, 87.6 x 66 mm); compression ratio: 9.2:1; max power (DIN): 88 hp at 5,700 rpm; max torque (DIN): 92 lb ft, 12.7 kg m at 4,000 rpm; max engine rpm: 6,500; 55.2 hp/l; valves: overhead, rockers; camshafts: 1, overhead; 1 Weber downdraught carburettor; cooling system capacity: 7.1 imp pt, 8.5 US pt, 4 l.

TRANSMISSION gearbox ratios: I 2.970, II 2.010, III 1.400, IV 1, rev 3.320; axle ratio: 3.890; width of rims: 5.5"; tyres: 175 x 13.

PERFORMANCE max speeds: (I) 35 mph, 57 km/h; (II) 52 mph, 84 km/h; (III) 75 mph, 121 km/h; (IV) 101 mph, 162 km/h; power-weight ratio: 24.9 lb/hp, 11.3 kg/hp; speed in direct drive at 1,000 rpm: 17.6 mph, 28.3 km/h; fuel consumption: 30.3 m/imp gal, 25.3 m/US gal, 9.3 l x 100 km.

CHASSIS front suspension: anti-roll bar.

BRAKES servo; swept area: rear 98.9 sq in, 638 sq cm.

ELECTRICAL EQUIPMENT alternator; 4 iodine headlamps.

DIMENSIONS AND WEIGHT dry weight: 2,194 lb, 995 kg; distribution of weight: 54% front, 46% rear.

PRACTICAL INSTRUCTIONS tappet clearances: inlet 0.008 in, 0.20 mm, exhaust 0.010 in, 0.25 mm; valve timing: 18° 70° 64° 24°.

OPTIONAL ACCESSORIES only Borg-Warner 35/3 automatic transmission, hydraulic torque converter and planetary gears with 3 ratios (I 2.390, II 1.450, III 1, rev 2.094), max ratio of converter at stall 2, possible manual selection and 185 x 13 tyres.

Cortina 1600 GT 4-door Saloon

See Cortina 1600 GT 2-door Saloon, except for:

PRICE IN GB: £ 1,016.

PERFORMANCE power-weight ratio: 25.6 lb/hp, 11.6 kg/hp.

DIMENSIONS AND WEIGHT dry weight: 2,249 lb, 1,020 kg.

Cortina 1600 GXL 4-door Saloon

See Cortina 1600 GT 4-door Saloon, except for:

PRICE IN GB: £ 1,123.

BODY special interior and trimmed body.

FORD Cortina 2000 XL Estate Car

FORD Capri 1600 XL

FORD Capri 1600 GT

Cortina 2000 L 4-door Saloon

See Cortina 1300 2-door Saloon, except for:

PRICE IN GB: £ 948.

ENGINE 121.6 cu in, 1,993 cc (3.89 x 3.03 in, 90.8 x 76.9 mm); compression ratio: 9.2:1; max power (DIN): 98 hp at 5,500 rpm; max torque (DIN): 111 lb ft, 15.3 kg m at 3,500 rpm; max engine rpm: 6,500; 49.2 hp/l; valves: rockers; camshafts: 1, overhead; 1 Weber downdraught carburettor; cooling system capacity: 7.1 imp pt, 8.5 US pt, 4 l.

TRANSMISSION gearbox ratios: I 3.650, II 1.970, III 1.370, IV 1; axle ratio: 3.440; width of rims: 5.5"; tyres: 175 x 13.

PERFORMANCE max speeds: (I) 30 mph, 49 km/h; (II) 57 mph, 91 km/h; (III) 81 mph, 131 km/h; (IV) 103 mph, 165 km/h; power-weight ratio: 22.7 lb/hp, 10.3 kg/hp; carrying capacity: 992 lb, 450 kg; speed in direct drive at 1,000 rpm: 17.7 mph, 28.5 km/h; fuel consumption: 33 m/imp gal, 27.3 m/US gal, 8.6 l x 100 km.

CHASSIS front suspension: anti-roll bar.

ELECTRICAL EQUIPMENT 44 A alternator; 4 iodine headlamps.

DIMENSIONS AND WEIGHT dry weight: 2,238 lb, 1,015 kg; distribution of weight: 54.5% front, 45.5% rear.

PRACTICAL INSTRUCTIONS tappet clearances: inlet 0.008 in, 0.20 mm, exhaust 0.010 in, 0.25 mm; valve timing: 18° 70° 64° 24°.

OPTIONAL ACCESSORIES only Borg-Warner 35/3 automatic transmission, hydraulic torque converter and planetary gears with 3 ratios (I 2.390, II 1.450, III 1, rev 2.094), max ratio of converter at stall 2, possible manual selection; 185 x 13 tyres.

Cortina 2000 XL 2-door Saloon

See Cortina 2000 L 4-door Saloon, except for:

PRICE IN GB: £ 991.

Cortina 2000 XL 4-door Saloon

See Cortina 2000 L 4-door Saloon, except for:

PRICE IN GB: £ 1,020.

Cortina 2000 L Estate Car

See Cortina 2000 L 4-door Saloon, except for:

PRICE IN GB: £ 1,045.

PERFORMANCE power-weight ratio: 24.5 lb/hp, 11.1 kg/hp.

DIMENSIONS AND WEIGHT dry weight: 2,392 lb, 1,085 kg.

BODY estate car/station wagon; 4 + 1 doors.

Cortina 2000 XL Estate Car

See Cortina 2000 L Estate Car, except for:

PRICE IN GB: £ 1,117.

Cortina 2000 GT 2-door Saloon

See Cortina 2000 L 4-door Saloon, except for:

PRICE IN GB: £ 1,028.

BODY special interior and trimmed body.

OPTIONAL ACCESSORIES only Borg-Warner 35/3 automatic transmission and 185 x 13 tyres.

Cortina 2000 GT 4-door Saloon

See Cortina 2000 GT 2-door Saloon, except for:

PRICE IN GB: £ 1,057.

PERFORMANCE power-weight ratio: 23.2 lb/hp, 10.5 kg/hp.

DIMENSIONS AND WEIGHT dry weight: 2,238 lb, 1,015 kg.

Cortina 2000 GXL 4-door Saloon

See Cortina 2000 L 4-door Saloon, except for:

PRICE IN GB: £ 1,164.

PERFORMANCE power-weight ratio: 23.2 lb/hp, 10.5 kg/hp.

DIMENSIONS AND WEIGHT dry weight: 2,238 lb, 1,015 kg.

Capri 1300 L

PRICE IN GB: £ 902.

ENGINE front, 4 stroke; 4 cylinders, vertical, in line; 79.2 cu in, 1,298 cc (3.19 x 2.48 in, 81.1 x 63.1 mm); compression ratio: 9,2:1; max power (DIN): 57 hp at 5,500 rpm; max torque (DIN): 67 lb ft, 9.3 kg m at 3,000 rpm; max engine rpm: 6,000; 50.1 hp/l; cast iron cylinder block and head; 5 crankshaft bearings; valves: overhead, in line, push-rods and rockers; camshafts: 1, side; lubrication: rotary or vane-type pump, full flow filter, 5.7 imp pt, 6.8 US pt, 3.2 l; 1 Ford GPD downdraught single barrel carburettor; fuel feed: mechanical pump; water-cooled, 8.2 imp pt, 9.7 US pt, 4.6 l.

TRANSMISSION driving wheels: rear; clutch: single dry plate (diaphragm), hydraulically controlled; gearbox: mechanical; gears: 4, fully synchronized; ratios: I 3.543, II 2.936, III 1.412, IV 1, rev 3.963; lever: central; final drive: hypoid bevel; axle ratio: 4.125; width of rims: 5''; tyres: 6.00 x 13.

PERFORMANCE max speeds: (I) 27 mph, 44 km/h; (II) 33 mph, 53 km/h; (III) 69 mph, 111 km/h; (IV) 86 mph, 138 km/h; power-weight ratio: 30.2 lb/hp, 13.7 kg/hp; speed in direct drive at 1,000 rpm: 16.3 mph, 26.2 km/h; fuel consumption: 31 m/imp gal, 25.8 m/US gal, 9.1 l x 100 km.

CHASSIS integral; front suspension: independent, by McPherson, coil springs/telescopic damper struts, lower wishbones (trailing arms), anti-roll bar; rear suspension: rigid axle, semi-elliptic leafsprings, anti-roll bar (acting as torque radius arms), twin upper radius arms, telescopic dampers.

STEERING rack-and-pinion.

BRAKES front disc (diameter 9.50 in, 241 mm), rear drum; swept area: front 95.5 sq in, 616 sq cm, rear 75.6 sq in, 487 sq cm, total 171.1 sq in, 1,103 sq cm.

ELECTRICAL EQUIPMENT 12 V; 38 Ah battery; 22 A dynamo; Motorcraft distributor; 2 headlamps.

DIMENSIONS AND WEIGHT wheel base: 100.80 in, 2,560 mm; tracks: 53 in, 1,346 mm front, 52 in, 1,321 mm rear; length: 167.80 in, 4,262 mm; width: 64.80 in, 1,646 mm; height: 48.35 in, 1,228 mm; ground clearance: 4.50 in, 114 mm; dry weight: 1,960 lb, 889 kg; distribution of weight: 52.5% front, 47.5% rear; turning circle (between walls): 32 ft, 9.8 m; fuel tank: 10.5 imp gal, 12.7 US gal, 48 l.

BODY coupé; 2 doors; 4 seats, separate front seats.

PRACTICAL INSTRUCTIONS fuel: 97 oct petrol; engine sump oil: 5.4 imp pt, 6.3 US pt, 3 l, SAE 10W-30, change every 5,000 miles, 8,000 km; gearbox oil: 2 imp pt, 2.3 US pt, 1.1 l, SAE 80, no change recommended; final drive oil: 2 imp pt, 2.3 US pt, 1.1 l, SAE 90, no change recommended; greasing: none; tappet clearances: inlet 0.010 in, 0.25 mm, exhaust 0.017 in, 0.44 mm; valve timing: 17° 51° 51° 17°.

VARIATIONS

ENGINE 8:1 compression ratio, max power (SAE) 62 hp at 5,000 rpm, max torque (SAE) 72 lb ft, 9.9 kg m at 2,500 rpm, 47.8 hp/l.

OPTIONAL ACCESSORIES 165 x 13 tyres; servo brake; 28 A alternator; reclining backrests; sunshine roof; vinyl roof; sport road wheels; electrically-heated rear window and alternator.

Capri 1600 L

See Capri 1300 L, except for:

PRICE IN GB: £ 973.

ENGINE 97.2 cu in, 1,593 cc (3.57 x 2.60 in, 87.6 x 66 mm); max power (DIN): 72 hp at 5,500 rpm; max torque (DIN): 87 lb ft, 12 kg m at 2,700 rpm; 45.1 hp/l; valves: rockers; camshaft: 1, overhead; lubricating system capacity: 6.5 imp pt, 7.8 US pt, 3.7 l; 1 Ford GPD downdraught carburettor; cooling system capacity: 10.1 imp pt, 12 US pt, 5.7 l.

TRANSMISSION axle ratio: 3.900; tyres: 165 x 13.

PERFORMANCE max speed: 92 mph, 148 km/h; power-weight ratio: 27.8 lb/hp, 12.6 kg/hp; speed in direct drive at 1,000 rpm: 17.3 mph, 27.8 km/h; fuel consumption: 31.4 m/imp gal, 26.1 m/US gal, 9 l x 100 km.

FORD Capri 3000 GXL

FORD Consul Saloon

FORD Consul L Saloon

BRAKES front disc (diameter 9.62 in, 244 mm); swept area: front 108 sq in, 696 sq cm, rear 98.8 sq in, 637 sq cm, total 206.8 sq in, 1,333 sq cm.

ELECTRICAL EQUIPMENT 28 A alternator.

DIMENSIONS AND WEIGHT dry weight: 2,005 lb, 909 kg; distribution of weight: 52.6% front, 47.4% rear.

OPTIONAL ACCESSORIES 4.125 axle ratio; Borg-Warner 35/3 automatic transmission, hydraulic torque converter and planetary gears with 3 ratios (I 2.393, II 1.450, III 1, rev 2.094), max ratio of converter at stall 2, possible manual selection, max speeds (I) 38 mph, 61 km/h, (II) 63 mph, 102 km/h, (III) 92 mph, 148 km/h.

Capri 1600 XL

See Capri 1600 L, except for:

PRICE IN GB: £ 999.

Capri 1600 GT

See Capri 1300 L, except for:

PRICE IN GB: £ 1,101.

ENGINE 97.2 cu in, 1,593 (3.57 x 2.60 in, 90.6 x 66 mm); max power (DIN): 88 hp at 5,700 rpm; max torque (DIN): 92 lb ft, 12.7 kg m at 4,000 rpm; max engine rpm: 6,500; 55.2 hp/l; valves: rockers; camshaft: 1, overhead; lubricating system capacity: 6.5 imp pt, 7.8 US pt, 3.7 l; 1 Weber downdraught twin barrel carburettor; cooling system capacity: 10.1 imp pt, 12 US pt, 5.7 l.

TRANSMISSION gearbox ratios: I 2.972, II 2.010, III 1.397, IV 1, rev 3.324; axle ratio: 3.770; tyres: 165 x 13.

PERFORMANCE max speeds: (I) 34 mph, 54 km/h; (II) 50 mph, 80 km/h; (III) 71 mph, 114 km/h; (IV) 99 mph, 160 km/h; power-weight ratio: 22.7 lb/hp, 10.3 kg/hp; speed in direct drive at 1,000 rpm: 17.9 mph, 28.8 km/h; fuel consumption: 28.8 m/imp gal, 24 m/US gal, 9.8 l x 100 km.

BRAKES front disc (diameter 9.62 in, 244 mm), servo; swept area: front 108 sq in, 696 sq cm, rear 98.8 sq in, 637 sq cm, total 206.8 sq in, 1,333 sq cm.

ELECTRICAL EQUIPMENT 28 A alternator.

DIMENSIONS AND WEIGHT height: 50.20 in, 1,275 mm; dry weight: 2,010 lb, 911 kg; distribution of weight: 52.6% front, 47.4% rear.

PRACTICAL INSTRUCTIONS tappet clearances: inlet 0.008 in, 0.20 mm, exhaust 0.010 in, 0.25 mm; valve timing: 18° 0° 69° 24°.

VARIATIONS

None.

OPTIONAL ACCESSORIES Borg-Warner 35/3 automatic transmission, hydraulic torque converter and planetary gears with 3 ratios (I 2.393, II 1.450, III 1, rev 2.094), max ratio of converter at stall 2, possible manual selection, max speeds (I) 42 mph, 67 km/h, (II) 68 mph, 110 km/h, (III) 99 mph, 160 km/h; 55 57 66 Ah battery; 28 A alternator; reclining backrests; heavy-duty equipment; sunshine roof; sport road wheels.

Capri 2000 GT

See Capri 1300 L, except for:

PRICE IN GB: £ 1,125.

ENGINE 4 cylinders, Vee-slanted at 60°; 121.8 cu in, 1,996 cc (3.69 x 2.85 in, 93.7 x 72.4 mm); compression ratio: 8.9:1; max power (DIN): 92 hp at 5,250 rpm; max torque (DIN): 104 lb ft, 14.4 kg m at 4,000 rpm; 46.1 hp/l; 3 crankshaft bearings; camshafts: 1, at centre of Vee; lubricating system capacity: 7.5 imp pt, 8.9 US pt, 4.2 l; 1 Weber downdraught twin barrel carburettor; cooling system capacity: 10.5 imp pt, 12.5 US pt, 5.9 l.

TRANSMISSION gearbox ratios: I 2.972, II 2.010, III 1.397, IV 1, rev 3.324; axle ratio: 3.545; tyres: 165 x 13.

PERFORMANCE max speeds: (I) 39 mph, 62 km/h; (II) 57 mph, 91 km/h; (III) 81 mph, 131 km/h; (IV) 106 mph, 171 km/h; power-weight ratio: 23.2 lb/hp, 10.5 kg/hp; speed in direct drive at 1,000 rpm: 19 mph, 30.6 km/h; fuel consumption: 23 m/imp gal, 19.1 m/US gal, 12.3 l x 100 km.

BRAKES front disc (diameter 9.62 in, 244 mm), servo; swept area: front 108 sq in, 696 sq cm, rear 98.8 sq in, 637 sq cm, total 206.8 sq in, 1,333 sq cm.

FORD Capri XL

FORD Consul Series

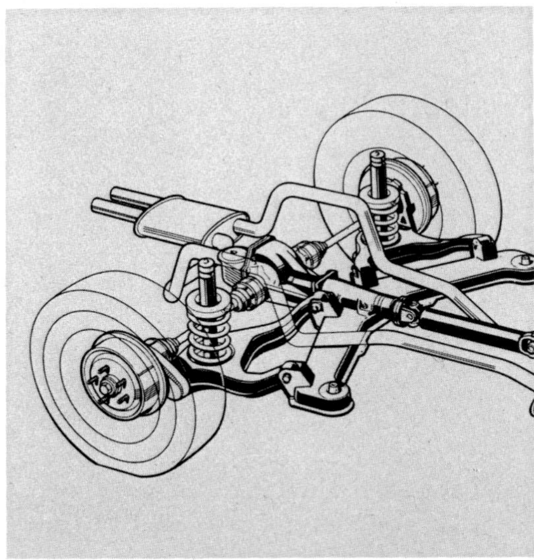

FORD Consul Series

DIMENSIONS AND WEIGHT height: 50.20 in, 1,275 mm; dry weight: 2,130 lb, 966 kg; distribution of weight: 55.1% front, 44,9% rear.

PRACTICAL INSTRUCTIONS engine sump oil: 6.6 imp pt, 7.8 US pt, 3.7 l.

VARIATIONS

None.

OPTIONAL ACCESSORIES Borg-Warner 35/3 automatic transmission, hydraulic torque converter and planetary gears with 3 ratios (I 2.393, II 1.450, III 1, rev 2.094), max ratio of converter at stall 2, possible manual selection, max speeds (I) 44 mph, 71 km/h, (II) 73 mph, 118 km/h, (III) 106 mph, 171 km/h; 5" wide rims; 55 57 66 Ah battery; 28 A alternator; reclining backrests; sunshine roof; sport road wheels.

Capri 3000 GT

See Capri 1300 L, except for:

PRICE IN GB: £ 1,329.

ENGINE 6 cylinders, Vee-slanted at 60°; 182.7 cu in, 2,994 cc (3.69 x 2.85 in, 93.7 x 72.4 mm); compression ratio: 8.9:1; max power (DIN): 140 hp at 5,300 rpm; max torque (DIN): 174 lb ft, 24 kg m at 3,000 rpm; max engine rpm: 5,500; 46.7 hp/l; 4 crankshaft bearings; camshafts: 1, at centre of Vee; lubricating system capacity: 8.8 imp pt, 10.6 US pt, 5 l; 1 Weber downdraught twin barrel carburettor; cooling system capacity: 16.4 imp pt, 19.7 US pt, 9.3 l.

TRANSMISSION gearbox ratios: I 3.160, II 1.950, III 1.912, IV 1, rev 3.346; axle ratio: 3.090; width of rims: 5"; tyres: 185 x 13.

PERFORMANCE max speeds: (I) 39 mph, 62 km/h; (II) 55 mph, 88 km/h; (III) 86 mph, 139 km/h; (IV) 122 mph, 196 km/h; power-weight ratio: 17 lb/hp, 7.7 kg/hp; speed in direct drive at 1,000 rpm: 21.8 mph, 35.1 km/h; fuel consumption: 23.4 m/imp gal, 19.4 m/US gal, 12.1 l x 100 km.

BRAKES front disc (diameter 9.62 in, 244 mm), servo; swept area: front 108 sq in, 696 sq cm, rear 127.2 sq in, 820 sq cm, total 235.2 sq in, 1,516 sq cm.

ELECTRICAL EQUIPMENT 55 Ah battery; 44 A alternator.

DIMENSIONS AND WEIGHT height: 50.20 in, 1,275 mm; dry weight: 2,380 lb, 1,079 kg; distribution of weight: 56% front, 44% rear; turning circle (between walls): 34 ft, 10.4 m; fuel tank: 13.5 imp gal, 16.1 US gal, 61 l.

PRACTICAL INSTRUCTIONS fuel: 94 oct petrol; engine sump oil: 6.7 imp pt, 8 US pt, 3.8 l; gearbox oil: 3.2 imp pt, 3.8 US pt, 1.8 l; final drive oil: 1.9 imp pt, 2.3 US pt, 1.1 l; tappet clearances: inlet 0.012 in, 0.30 mm, exhaust 0.012 in, 0.30 mm; valve timing: 20° 56° 62° 14°.

VARIATIONS

None.

OPTIONAL ACCESSORIES only Borg-Warner 35/3 automatic transmission, hydraulic torque converter and planetary gears with 3 ratios (I 2.393, II 1.450, III 1, rev 2.094), max ratio of converter at stall 2, possible manual selection, max speeds (I) 48 mph, 77 km/h, (II) 79 mph, 127 km/h, (III) 118 mph, 190 km/h; 60 Ah battery; reclining backrests; sunshine roof; sport road wheels; electrically-heated rear window.

Capri 3000 GXL

See Capri 3000 GT, except for:

PRICE IN GB: £ 1,471.

PERFORMANCE power-weight ratio: 17.2 lb/hp, 7.8 kg/hp.

ELECTRICAL EQUIPMENT 4 halogen headlamps.

DIMENSIONS AND WEIGHT dry weight: 2,435 lb, 1,104 kg; distribution of weight: 55.7% front, 44.3% rear.

BODY reclining backrests (standard); special interior and body trim.

Consul 2000 Saloon

PRICE IN GB: £ 1,070.

ENGINE front, 4 stroke; 4 cylinders, Vee-slanted at 60°; 121.8 cu in, 1,996 cc (3.69 x 2.85 in, 93.7 x 72.4 mm); compression ratio: 8.9:1; max power (DIN): 82 hp at 5,000 rpm; max torque (DIN): 106 lb ft, 14.6 kg m at 3,000 rpm; max engine rpm: 5,400; 41 hp/l; cast iron cylinder block and head; 3 crankshaft bearings; valves: overhead, push-rods and rockers; camshafts: 1, at centre of Vee; lubrication: rotary pump, full flow filter, 7.8 imp pt, 9.3 US pt, 4.4 l; 1 Weber downdraught carburettor; fuel feed: mechanical pump; water-cooled, 13.9 imp pt, 16.7 US pt, 7.9 l.

CONSUL 2000 SALOON

TRANSMISSION driving wheels: rear; clutch: single dry plate (diaphragm); gearbox: mechanical; gears: 4, fully synchronized; ratios: I 3.650, II 1.970, III 1.370, IV 1, rev 3.660; lever: central; final drive: hypoid bevel; axle ratio: 3.890; width of rims: 5.5"; tyres: 6.45 x 14.

PERFORMANCE max speeds: (I) 29 mph, 47 km/h; (II) 54 mph, 87 km/h; (III) 78 mph, 125 km/h; (IV) 90 mph, 145 km/h; power-weight ratio: 30.2 lb/hp, 13.7 kg/hp; acceleration: standing ¼ mile 19.2 sec; speed in direct drive at 1,000 rpm: 17.8 mph, 28.6 km/h; fuel consumption: 27.6 m/imp gal, 23.1 m/US gal, 10.2 l x 100 km.

CHASSIS integral; front suspension: independent, wishbones, coil springs, anti-roll bar, telescopic dampers; rear suspension: independent, semi-trailing arms, coil springs, telescopic dampers.

STEERING rack-and-pinion; turns lock to lock: 4.20.

BRAKES front disc (diameter 10.30 in, 262 mm), rear drum, servo; swept area: front 209.9 sq in, 1,354 sq cm, rear 94.7 sq in, 611 cm, total 304.6 sq in, 1,965 sq cm.

ELECTRICAL EQUIPMENT 12 V; 44 Ah battery; 28 A alternator; Motorcraft distributor; 2 headlamps.

DIMENSIONS AND WEIGHT wheel base: 109.02 in, 2,769 mm; tracks: 59.49 in, 1,511 mm front, 60.51 in, 1,537 mm rear; length: 180 in, 4,572 mm; width: 70.50 in, 1,791 mm; height: 53.90 in, 1,369 mm; ground clearance: 5.04 in, 128 mm; dry weight: 2,481 lb, 1,125 kg; turning circle (between walls): 34 ft, 10.4 m; fuel tank: 14.3 imp gal, 17.2 US gal, 65 l.

BODY saloon/sedan: 4 doors; 5 seats, separate front seats.

PRACTICAL INSTRUCTIONS fuel: 97 oct petrol; engine sump oil: 7.5 imp pt, 8.9 US pt, 4.2 l, 20W-50, change every 6,000 miles, 9,700 km; gearbox oil: 2.9 imp pt, 3.4 US pt, 1.6 l, SAE 90 EP, no change recommended; final drive oil: 3.5 imp pt, 4.2 US pt, 2 l, SAE 90 EP, no change recommended; greasing: none; tappet clearances: inlet 0.012 in, 0.30 mm, exhaust 0.018 in, 0.45 mm; tyre pressure: front 24 psi, 1.7 atm, rear 26 psi, 1.8 atm.

OPTIONAL ACCESSORIES automatic transmission, hydraulic torque converter and planetary gears with 3 ratios (I 2.460, II 1.460, III 1, rev 2.200), max ratio of converter at stall 2, possible manual selection; reclining backrests on front seats; sunshine roof; electrically-heated rear window.

Consul 2000 L Saloon

See Consul 2000 Saloon, except for:

PRICE IN GB: £ 1,126.

ELECTRICAL EQUIPMENT 35 A alternator.

Consul 2500 Saloon

See Consul 2000 Saloon, except for:

PRICE IN GB: £ 1,157.

ENGINE 6 cylinders, Vee-slanted at 60°; 152.2 cu in, 2,495 cc (3.69 x 2.38 in, 93.7 x 60.4 mm); compression ratio: 9.1:1; max power (DIN): 120 hp at 5,300 rpm; max torque (DIN): 132 lb ft, 18.2 kg m at 3,800 rpm; max engine rpm: 5,500; 48.1 hp/l; 4 crankshaft bearings; lubricating system capacity: 9.8 imp pt, 11.6 US pt, 5.5 l; cooling system capacity: 20.1 imp pt, 24.1 US pt, 11.4 l.

TRANSMISSION axle ratio: 3.640; tyres: 175 x 14.

PERFORMANCE max speeds: (I) 29 mph, 46 km/h; (II) 53 mph, 86 km/h; (III) 77 mph, 124 km/h; (IV) 106 mph, 170 km/h; power-weight ratio: 22.9 lb/hp, 10.4 kg/hp; speed in direct drive at 1,000 rpm: 19.6 mph, 31.6 km/h; fuel consumption: 24.3 m/imp gal, 20.3 m/US gal, 11.6 l x 100 km.

ELECTRICAL EQUIPMENT 55 Ah battery.

DIMENSIONS AND WEIGHT dry weight: 2,734 lb, 1,240 kg.

OPTIONAL ACCESSORIES 185 x 14 tyres with 6" wide rims; power-assisted steering.

Consul 2500 L Saloon

See Consul 2500 Saloon, except for:

PRICE IN GB: £ 1,213.

ELECTRICAL EQUIPMENT 35 A alternator.

FORD Granada GXL Series

FORD Granada 3000 Estate Car

GILBERN Invader Mk III Saloon

Consul 2500 L Estate Car

See Consul 2500 Saloon, except for:

PRICE IN GB: £ 1,473.

TRANSMISSION width of rims: 5.5"; tyres: 185 x 14.

PERFORMANCE max speed: 105 mph, 169 km/h; power-weight ratio: 24.8 lb/hp, 10.8 kg/hp; fuel consumption: 23 m/imp gal, 19.1 m/US gal, 12.3 l x 100 km.

DIMENSIONS AND WEIGHT length: 184 in, 4,673 mm; height: 53.50 in, 1,359 mm; dry weight: 2,844 lb, 1,290 kg.

BODY estate car/station wagon; 4 + 1 doors.

Consul 3000 GT Saloon

See Consul 2000 Saloon, except for:

PRICE IN GB: £ 1,414.

ENGINE 6 cylinders, Vee-slanted at 60°; 182.7 cu in, 2,994 cc (3.69 x 2.85 in, 93.7 x 72.4 mm); max power (DIN): 138 hp at 5,000 rpm; max torque (DIN): 174 lb ft, 24 kg m at 3,000 rpm; max engine rpm: 5,400; 46 hp/l; 4 crankshaft bearings.

TRANSMISSION ratios: I 3.160, II 1.941, III 1.410, IV 1, rev 3.350; axle ratio: 3.450; width of rims: 6"; tyres: 185 x 14.

PERFORMANCE max speed: 113 mph, 182 km/h; fuel consumption: 24 m/imp gal, 19.9 m/ US gal, 11.8 l x 100 km.

BRAKES swept area: total 310.2 sq in, 2,001 sq cm.

ELECTRICAL EQUIPMENT 55 Ah battery; 35 A alternator.

Granada 2500 Saloon

PRICE IN GB: £ 1,400.

ENGINE front, 4 stroke; 6 cylinders, Vee-slanted at 60°; 152.2 cu in, 2,495 cc (3.69 x 2.73 in, 93.7 x 60.4 mm); compression ratio: 9.1:1; max power (DIN): 120 hp at 5,300 rpm; max torque (DIN): 132 lb ft, 18.2 kg m at 3,800 rpm; max engine rpm: 5,400; 48.1 hp/l; cast iron cylinder block and head; 4 crankshaft bearings; valves: overhead, push-rods and rockers; camshafts: 1, at centre of Vee; lubrication: rotary pump, full flow filter, 9.8 imp pt, 11.6 US pt, 5.5 l; 1 Weber downdraught carburettor; fuel feed: mechanical pump; water-cooled, 20.1 imp pt, 24.1 US pt, 11.4 l.

TRANSMISSION driving wheels: rear; clutch: single dry plate (diaphragm); gearbox: mechanical; gears: 4, fully synchronized; ratios: I 3,650, II 1.980, III 1.370, IV 1, rev 3.660; lever: central; final drive: hypoid bevel; axle ratio: 3.640; width of rims: 5.5"; tyres: 6.95 x 14.

PERFORMANCE max speed: 106 mph, 170 km/h; power-weight ratio: 33.5 lb/hp, 10.5 kg/hp; speed in direct drive at 1,000 rpm: 19.7 mph, 31.7 km/h; fuel consumption: 24.3 m/imp gal, 20.3 m/US gal, 11.6 l x 100 km.

CHASSIS integral; front suspension: independent, wishbones, coil springs, anti-roll bar, telescopic dampers; rear suspension: independent, semi-trailing arms, coil springs, telescopic dampers.

STEERING rack-and-pinion.

BRAKES front disc (diameter 10.60 in, 269 mm), rear drum, servo; swept area: total 310.2 sq in, 2,001 sq cm.

ELECTRICAL EQUIPMENT 12 V; 55 Ah battery; alternator; 2 headlamps.

DIMENSIONS AND WEIGHT wheel base: 109.02 in, 2,769 mm; tracks: 59.49 in, 1,511 mm front, 60.51 in, 1,537 mm rear; length: 180 in, 4,572 mm; width: 70.51 in, 1,791 mm; height: 53.90 in, 1,369 mm; ground clearance: 5.04 in, 128 mm; dry weight: 2,778 lb, 1,260 kg; turning circle (between walls): 34 ft, 10.4 m; fuel tank: 14.3 imp gal, 17.2 US gal, 65 l.

BODY saloon/sedan; 4 doors; 5 seats, separate front seats, reclining backrests.

PRACTICAL INSTRUCTIONS engine sump oil: 8 imp pt, 9.5 US pt, 4.5 l, SAE 20W-50, change every 6,000 miles, 9,700 km; gearbox oil: SAE 90 EP; final drive oil: 3.1 imp pt, 3.6 US pt, 1.7 l, SAE 90 EP, change every 6,000 miles, 9,700 km; greasing: none; tappet clearances: inlet 0.012 in, 0.30 mm, exhaust 0.018 in, 0.45 mm; tyre pressure: front 24 psi, 1.7 atm, rear 26 psi, 1.8 atm.

OPTIONAL ACCESSORIES automatic transmission, hydraulic torque converter and planetary gears with 3 ratios; power-assisted steering; sunshine roof; electrically-heated rear window.

FORD Granada 3000 GXL Saloon

FORD Granada 3000 Estate Car

GILBERN Invader Mk III Saloon

Granada 2500 GXL Saloon

See Granada 2500 Saloon, except for:

PRICE IN GB: £ 1,680.

TRANSMISSION tyres: 175 x 14.

Granada 3000 Saloon

See Granada 2500 Saloon, except for:

PRICE IN GB: £ 1,451.

ENGINE 182.7 cu in, 2,994 cc (3.69 x 2.85 in, 93.7 x 72.4 mm); compression ratio: 8.9:1; max power (DIN): 138 hp at 5,000 rpm; max torque (DIN): 174 lb ft, 24 kg m at 3,000 rpm; max engine rpm: 5,400; 46 hp/l.

TRANSMISSION gearbox ratios: I 3.160, II 1.950, III 1.420, IV 1, rev 3.350; axle ratio: 3.450; tyres: 175 x 14.

PERFORMANCE max speeds: (I) 35 mph, 57 km/h; (II) 58 mph, 93 km/h; (III) 80 mph, 128 km/h; (IV) 113 mph, 182 km/h; fuel consumption: 24 m/imp gal, 19.9 m/US gal, 11.8 l x 100 km.

Granada 3000 GXL Saloon

See Granada 3000 Saloon, except for:

PRICE IN GB: £ 1,731.

BRAKES front disc, ventilated.

Granada 3000 Estate Car

See Granada 3000 Saloon, except for:

PRICE IN GB: £ 1,728.

TRANSMISSION width of rims: 5.5''; tyres: 185 x 14.

DIMENSIONS AND WEIGHT length: 184 in, 4,673 mm; height: 53.50 in, 1,359 mm.

BODY estate car/station wagon; 4 + 1 doors.

GILBERN GREAT BRITAIN

Invader Mk III Saloon

PRICE IN GB: £ 2,063.

ENGINE front, 4 stroke; 6 cylinders, Vee-slanted at 60°; 182.7 cu in, 2,994 cc (3.69 x 2.85 in, 93.7 x 72.4 mm); compression ratio: 8.9:1; max power (DIN): 140 hp at 5,000 rpm; max torque (DIN): 179 lb ft, 24.7 kg m at 3,500 rpm; max engine rpm: 6,100; 46.8 hp/l; cast iron cylinder block and head; 4 crankshaft bearings; valves: overhead, in line, push-rods and rockers; camshafts: 1, at centre of Vee; lubrication: rotary pump, full flow filter, 9 imp pt, 10.8 US pt, 5.1 l; 1 Weber 40 DFA downdraught twin barrel carburettor; fuel feed: mechanical pump; water-cooled, 19.8 imp pt, 23.7 US pt, 11.2 l, electric thermostatic fan.

TRANSMISSION driving wheels: rear; clutch: single dry plate (diaphragm); gearbox: mechanical; gears: 4 + overdrive on III and IV, fully synchronized; ratios: I 3.160, II 2.210, III 1.410, IV 1, overdrive 0.820, rev 3.350; lever: central; final drive: hypoid bevel; axle ratio: 3.090; width of rims: 5.5'; tyres: 185/70 x 13.

PERFORMANCE max speeds: (I) 41 mph, 66 km/h; (II) 58 mph, 93 km/h; (III) 92 mph, 148 km/h; (IV) 129 mph, 207 km/h; power-weight ratio: 17.6 lb/hp, 8 kg/hp; carrying capacity: 706 lb, 320 kg; speed in direct drive at 1,000 rpm: 22 mph, 35.4 km/h; fuel consumption: 25 m/imp gal, 20.8 m/US gal, 11.3 l x 100 km.

CHASSIS tubular; front suspension: independent, wishbones, coil springs, anti-roll bar, telescopic dampers; rear suspension: rigid axle, twin trailing radius arms, transverse linkage bar, coil springs/telescopic dampers unit.

STERING rack-and-pinion; turns lock to lock: 3.07.

BRAKES front disc (diameter 9.60 in, 244 mm), rear drum, servo; swept area: total 334 sq in, 2,154 sq cm.

ELECTRICAL EQUIPMENT 12 V; 53 Ah battery; 36 A alternator; 2 halogen headlamps; 2 fog lamps.

INVADER MK III SALOON

DIMENSIONS AND WEIGHT wheel base: 92.75 in, 2,432 mm; tracks: 56 in, 1,423 mm front, 56 in, 1,423 mm rear; length: 160.50 in, 4,077 mm; width: 67 in, 1,702 mm; height: 53 in, 1,346 mm; ground clearance: 5.50 in, 139 mm; dry weight: 2,464 lb, 1,117 kg turning circle (between walls): 32.6 ft, 9.9 m; fuel tank: 12 imp gal, 14.3 US gal, 54 l.

BODY coupé in plastic material; 2 doors; 2 seats; electrically-controlled windows.

PRACTICAL INSTRUCTIONS fuel: 97 oct petrol; engine sump oil: 8 imp pt, 9.5 US pt, 4.5 l, SAE 20W-50, change every 6,000 miles, 9,600 km; gearbox oil: 3.2 imp pt, 3.8 US pt, 1.8 l, SAE 80; final drive oil: 1.9 imp pt, 2.3 US pt, 1.1 l, SAE 90 EP; greasing: every 35,000 miles, 56.000 km, 5 points; tappet clearances: inlet 0.010 in, 0.25 mm, exhaust 0.018 in, 0.46 mm; valve timing: 20° 56° 62° 14°; tyre pressure: front 25 psi, 1.8 atm, rear 27 psi, 1.9 atm.

OPTIONAL ACCESSORIES automatic transmission; sunshine roof.

GINETTA — GREAT BRITAIN

G15

PRICE IN GB: £ 958.

ENGINE Sunbeam Sport, rear, 4 stroke; 4 cylinders, in line; 53.4 cu in, 875 cc (2.68 x 2.37 in, 68 x 60.3 mm); compression ratio: 10:1; max power (DIN): 55 hp at 6,100 rpm; max torque (DIN): 52 lb ft, 7.2 kg m at 4,300 rpm; max engine rpm: 7,000; 62.9 hp/l; light alloy cylinder block and head; 3 crankshaft bearings; valves: overhead, in line, thimble tappets; camshafts: 1, overhead; lubrication: eccentric pump, full flow filter, oil cooler, 6.5 imp pt, 7.8 US pt, 3.7 l; 2 Stromberg 125 CDS horizontal carburettors; fuel feed: mechanical pump; water-cooled, 14.1 imp pt, 16.9 US pt, 8 l.

TRANSMISSION driving wheels: rear; clutch: single dry plate (diaphragm), hydraulically controlled; gearbox: mechanical; gears: 4, fully synchronized; ratios: I 4.317, II 1.833, III 1.174, IV 0.852, rev 2.846; lever: central; final drive: hypoid bevel; axle ratio: 4.875; width of rims: 4"; tyres: 5.20 x 13.

PERFORMANCE max speeds: (I) 21 mph, 33 km/h; (II) 56 mph, 90 km/h; (III) 88 mph, 141 km/h; (IV) 101 mph, 162 km/h; power-weight ratio: 21.4 lb/hp, 9.7 kg/hp; carrying capacity: 380 lb, 172 kg; acceleration: standing ¼ mile 18.4 sec, 0-50 mph (0-80 km/h) 8.6 sec; speed in top at 1,000 rpm: 14.9 mph, 23.9 km/h; fuel consumption: 40 m/imp gal, 33.1 m/US gal, 7.1 l x 100 km.

CHASSIS tubular; front suspension: independent, wishbones, coil springs, telescopic dampers; rear suspension: independent, semi-trailing arms, coil springs, telescopic dampers.

STEERING rack-and-pinion; turns lock to lock: 2.75.

BRAKES front disc (diameter 9 in, 229 mm), rear drum, single circuit.

ELECTRICAL EQUIPMENT 12 V; 32 Ah battery; 264 W dynamo; Lucas distributor; 2 headlamps.

DIMENSIONS AND WEIGHT wheel base: 82 in, 2,083 mm; tracks: 49 in, 1,245 mm front, 48.75 in, 1,238 mm rear; length: 144.50 in, 3,670 mm; width: 57 in, 1,448 mm; height: 44.50 in, 1,130 mm; ground clearance: 6 in, 152 mm; dry weight: 1,176 lb, 533 kg; distribution of weight: 45% front, 55% rear; turning circle (between walls): 33 ft, 10.1 m; fuel tank: 7 imp gal, 8.4 US gal, 32 l.

BODY coupé in plastic material; 2 doors; 2 seats.

PRACTICAL INSTRUCTIONS fuel: 97 oct petrol; engine sump oil: 6.5 imp pt, 7.8 US pt, 3.7 l, SAE 20W-50, change every 5,000 miles, 8,000 km; gearbox and final drive oil: 3 imp pt, 3.6 US pt, 1.7 l, SAE 90 EP, change every 10,000 miles, 16,100 km; greasing: every 5,000 miles, 8,000 km, 2 points, tappet clearances: inlet 0.008 in, 0.20 mm, exhaust 0.008 in, 0.20 mm; tyre pressure: front 16 psi, 1.1 atm, rear 26 psi 1.8 atm.

OPTIONAL ACCESSORIES light alloy wheels; sunshine roof

G21

PRICE IN GB: £ 2,065.

ENGINE Ford, front, 4 stroke; 6 cylinders, Vee-slanted at 60°; 182.7 cu in, 2,994 cc (3.69 x 2.85 in, 93.7 x 72.4 mm); compression ratio: 8.9:1; max power (DIN): 128 hp at 4,750 rpm; max torque (DIN): 174 lb ft, 24 kg m at 3,000 rpm;

GINETTA G21

G.T.M. 1-3 Super 90

HILLMAN Imp

max engine rpm: 5,500; 42.7 hp/l; cast iron cylinder block and head; 4 crankshaft bearings; valves: overhead, in line, push-rods and rockers; camshafts: 1, at centre of Vee; lubrication: eccentric or vane-type pump, full flow filter, 10 imp pt, 12 US pt, 5.7 l; 1 Weber DFA 2 downdraught twin barrel carburettor; fuel feed: mechanical pump; water-cooled, 12.5 imp pt, 15 US pt, 7.1 l.

TRANSMISSION driving wheels: rear; clutch: single dry plate, gearbox: mechanical; gears: 4, fully synchronized; ratios: I 3.163, II 2.214, III 1.412, IV 1, rev 3.346; lever: central; final drive: hypoid bevel, limited slip differential; axle ratio: 2.880; width of rims: 5.5"; tyres: 165 x 13.

PERFORMANCE max speeds: (I) 45 mph, 72 km/h; (II) 61 mph, 98 km/h; (III) 98 mph, 157 km/h; (IV) 128 mph, 206 km/h; power-weight ratio: 15.4 lb/hp, 7 kg/hp; acceleration: standing ¼ mile 14.9 sec, 0-50 mph (0-80 km/h) 5.5 sec; speed in direct drive at 1,000 rpm: 23.4 mph, 37.6 km/h; fuel consumption: 26 m/imp gal, 21.6 m/US gal, 10.9 l x 100 km.

CHASSIS tubular; front suspension: independent, wishbones, coil springs, anti-roll bar, telescopic dampers; rear suspension: independent, wishbones, semi-axles as upper arms, twin trailing longitudinal radius arms, coil springs, telescopic dampers.

STEERING rack-and-pinion; turns lock to lock: 2.75.

BRAKES disc; swept area: front 196.9 sq in, 1,270 sq cm, rear 193.2 sq in, 1,246 sq cm, total 390.1 sq in, 2,516 sq cm.

ELECTRICAL EQUIPMENT 12 V; 36 Ah battery; 516 W alternator; Autolite distributor; 4 headlamps.

DIMENSIONS AND WEIGHT wheel base: 91 in, 2,311 mm; tracks: 50.75 in, 1,289 mm front, 51 in, 1,295 mm rear; length: 156.50 in, 3,975 mm; width: 63 in, 1,600 mm; height: 46 in, 1,168 mm; ground clearance: 4.75 in, 121 mm; dry weight: 1,920 lb, 871 kg; distribution of weight: 49% front, 51% rear; turning circle (between walls): 35 ft, 10.7 m; fuel tank: 10 imp gal, 11.9 US gal, 45 l.

BODY coupé in plastic material; 2 doors; 4 seats, separate front seats, reclining backrests.

PRACTICAL INSTRUCTIONS fuel: 96 oct petrol; engine sump oil: 9.5 imp pt, 11.4 US pt, 5.4 l, SAE 20W-50, change every 10,000 miles, 16,100 km; gearbox oil: 3.2 imp pt, 3.8 US pt, 1.8 l, SAE 80 EP, change every 10,000 miles, 16,100 km; final drive oil: 2.8 imp pt, 3.4 US pt, 1.6 l, SAE 90 EP, change every 10,000 miles, 16,100 km; tappet clearances: inlet 0.012 in, 0.30 mm, exhaust 0.018 in, 0.45 mm; valve timing: 20° 56° 62° 14°; tyre pressure: front 22 psi, 1.6 atm, rear 24 psi, 1.7 atm.

VARIATIONS

ENGINE Sunbeam Rapier, 4 cylinders, slanted at 10°, in line, 105.3 cu in, 1,725 cc (3.21 x 3.25 in, 81.5 x 82.5 mm), max power (DIN) 79 hp at 5,200 rpm, max torque (DIN) 91 lb ft, 12.5 kg m at 3,800 rpm, 9.2:1 compression ratio, max engine rpm 6,200, 45.8 hp/l, light alloy cylinder head, 5 crankshaft bearings, 1 side camshaft, lubricating system capacity 7.5 imp pt, 8.9 US pt, 4.2 l, 2 Zenith-Stromberg semi-downdraught carburettors, cooling system capacity 13.7 imp pt, 16.5 US pt, 7.8 l.
TRANSMISSION 3.700 axle ratio.
PERFORMANCE max speed 112 mph, 180 km/h, power-weight ratio 24.3 lb/hp, 11 kg/hp, speed in direct drive at 1,000 rpm 19.3 mph, 31 km/h, fuel consumption 25.7 m/imp gal, 21.4 m/US gal, 11 l x 100 km.
CHASSIS rear suspension: rigid axle, longitudinal trailing arms, transverse linkage bar.
DIMENSIONS AND WEIGHT rear track 50.50 in, 1,283 mm.

OPTIONAL ACCESSORIES Laycock-de Normanville overdrive/top (0.820 ratio); automatic transmission, hydraulic torque converter and planetary gears with 3 ratios (I 2.460, II 1.460, III 1, rev 2.200), max ratio of converter at stall 2; head-rests; electrically-heated rear window; sunshine roof.

G.T.M. GREAT BRITAIN

1-3 Super 90

PRICE IN GB: £ 1,175.

ENGINE Mini (British Leyland), central, transverse, 4 stroke; 4 cylinders, vertical, in line; 77.8 cu in, 1,275 cc (2.78 x 3.20 in, 70.7 x 81.4 mm); compression ratio: 9.9:1; max power (SAE): 90 hp at 5,800 rpm; max torque (SAE): 83 lb ft, 11.4 kg m at 3,200 rpm; max engine rpm: 7,600; 70.6 hp/l; cast iron cylinder block and head; 3 crankshaft bearings; valves: overhead, in line, push-rods and rockers; camshafts: 1, side; lubrication: rotary pump, full flow filter, oil cooler, 8 imp pt, 9.5 US pt, 4.5 l; 2 SU carburettors; fuel feed: electric pump; water-cooled, 8 imp pt, 9.5 US pt, 4.5 l, rear mounted radiator.

TRANSMISSION driving wheels: rear; clutch: single dry

GINETTA G21 (79 hp engine)

G.T.M. 1-3 Super 90

HILLMAN Super Imp

plate (diaphragm); gearbox: mechanical; gears: 4, fully synchronized; ratios: I 3.203, II 1.919, III 1.358, IV 1, rev 3.350; lever: central; final drive: helical spur gears; axle ratio: 3.440; width of rims: 5"; tyres: 145 x 10 or 165 x 10.

PERFORMANCE max speeds: (I) 39 mph, 62 km/h; (II) 61 mph, 98 km/h; (III) 90 mph, 145 km/h; (IV) 120 mph, 193 km/h; power-weight ratio: 13.2 lb/hp, 6 kg/hp; carrying capacity: 500 lb, 225 kg; acceleration: standing ¼ mile 17.5 sec, 0-50 mph (0-80 km/h) 7 sec; speed in direct drive at 1,000 rpm: 16 mph, 25.7 km/h; fuel consumption: 34 m/imp gal, 28.3 m/US gal, 8.3 l x 100 km.

CHASSIS integral with front and rear tubular frame sections; front suspension: independent, wishbones, coil springs, telescopic dampers; rear suspension: independent, wishbones, rubber elements, telescopic dampers.

STEERING rack-and-pinion; turns lock to lock: 2.25.

BRAKES front disc, rear drum.

ELECTRICAL EQUIPMENT 12 V; 75 Ah battery; dynamo; Lucas distributor; 2 headlamps.

DIMENSIONS AND WEIGHT wheel base: 84 in, 2,133 mm; tracks: 48 in, 1,219 mm front, 48 in, 1,219 mm rear; length: 129 in, 3,276 mm; width: 56 in, 1,422 mm; height: 43 in, 1,092 mm; ground clearance: 5.50 in, 140 mm; dry weight: 1,200 lb, 544 kg; distribution of weight: 43% front, 57% rear; fuel tank: 5 imp gal, 6.1 US gal, 23 l.

BODY coupé in plastic material; 2 doors; 2 seats.

PRACTICAL INSTRUCTIONS engine sump, gearbox and final drive oil: 8 imp pt, 9.5 US pt, 4.5 l, SAE 20W-50, change every 6,000 miles, 9,600 km; greasing: every 6,000 miles, 9,600 km, 9 points; tappet clearances: inlet 0.015 in, 0.37 mm, exhaust 0.015 in, 0.37 mm; valve timing: 5° 45° 51° 21°; tyre pressure: front 20 psi, 1.3 atm, rear 30 psi, 2.1 atm.

OPTIONAL ACCESSORIES larger fuel tank.

HILLMAN GREAT BRITAIN

Imp

PRICE IN GB: £ 546.

ENGINE rear, 4 stroke; 4 cylinders, slanted at 45°, in line; 53.4 cu in, 875 cc (2.68 x 2.38 in, 68 x 60.4 mm); compression ratio: 10:1; max power (DIN): 37 hp at 4,800 rpm; max torque (DIN): 49 lb ft, 6.7 kg m at 2,600 rpm; max engine rpm: 5,600; 42.3 hp/l; light alloy cylinder block and head, dry liners; 3 crankshaft bearings; valves: overhead, in line, thimble tappets; camshafts: 1, overhead; lubrication: eccentric pump, full flow filter, 5.5 imp pt, 6.6 US pt, 3.1 l; 1 Solex 30 PIH-5 semi-downdraught single barrel carburettor; fuel feed: mechanical pump; water-cooled, 11.2 imp pt, 13.3 US pt, 6.3 l.

TRANSMISSION driving wheels: rear; clutch: single dry plate (diaphragm), hydraulically controlled; gearbox: mechanical; gears: 4, fully synchronized; ratios: I 3.417, II 1.833, III 1.174, IV 0.852, rev 2.846; lever: central; final drive: hypoid bevel; axle ratio: 4.857; width of rims: 4.5"; tyres: 5.50 x 12.

PERFORMANCE max speeds: (I) 23 mph, 37 km/h; (II) 43 mph, 69 km/h; (III) 68 mph, 109 km/h; (IV) 80 mph, 129 km/h; power-weight ratio: 40 lb/hp, 18.1 kg/hp; carrying capacity: 706 lb, 320 kg; acceleration: 0-50 mph (0-80 km/h) 14.6 sec; speed in top at 1,000 rpm: 15.1 mph, 24.3 km/h; fuel consumption: 43.7 m/imp gal, 36.2 m/US gal, 6.5 l x 100 km.

CHASSIS integral; front suspension: independent, U-shaped swinging semi-axles, coil springs, telescopic dampers; rear suspension: independent, semi-trailing arms, coil springs, telescopic dampers.

STEERING rack-and-pinion; turns lock to lock: 2.63.

BRAKES drum, 2 front leading shoes; swept area: total 150.8 sq in, 972 sq cm.

ELECTRICAL EQUIPMENT 12 V; 32 Ah battery; 297 W dynamo; Lucas distributor; 2 headlamps.

DIMENSIONS AND WEIGHT wheel base: 82 in, 2,083 mm; tracks: 50.50 in, 1,283 mm front, 48 in, 1,219 mm rear; length: 139 in, 3,531 mm; width: 60.25 in, 1,530 mm; height: 54.50 in, 1,384 mm; ground clearance: 6.50 in, 165 mm; dry weight: 1,480 lb, 671 kg; distribution of weight: 38% front, 62% rear; turning circle (between walls): 31.5 ft, 9.6 m; fuel tank: 6 imp gal, 7.1 US gal, 27 l.

BODY saloon/sedan; 2 doors; 4 seats, separate front seats.

PRACTICAL INSTRUCTIONS fuel: 97 oct petrol; engine sump oil: 5.5 imp pt, 6.6 US pt, 3.1 l, SAE 20W-50, change every 5,000 miles, 8,000 km; gearbox and final drive oil: 4.5 imp pt, 5.3 US pt, 2.5 l, SAE 80 EP, no change recommended;

IMP

tappet clearances: inlet 0.005 in, 0.13 mm, exhaust 0.011 in, 0.28 mm; valve timing: 36° 76° 43° 3°; tyre pressure: front 18 psi, 1.3 atm, rear 30 psi, 2.1 atm.

Imp De Luxe

See Imp, except for:

PRICE IN GB: £ **600.**

PERFORMANCE power-weight ratio: 40.2 lb/hp, 18.2 kg/hp.

DIMENSIONS AND WEIGHT dry weight: 1,486 lb, 674 kg.

Super Imp

See Imp, except for:

PRICE IN GB: £ **634.**

PERFORMANCE power-weight ratio: 41 lb/hp, 18.6 kg/hp.

DIMENSIONS AND WEIGHT dry weight: 1,518 lb, 688 kg.

Avenger

PRICE IN GB: £ **729.**

ENGINE front, 4 stroke; 4 cylinders, in line; 76.2 cu in, 1,248 cc (3.09 x 2.53 in, 78.6 x 64.3 mm); compression ratio: 9.2:1; max power (DIN): 53 hp at 5,000 rpm; max torque (DIN): 66 lb ft, 9.1 kg m at 3,000 rpm; max engine rpm: 6,700; 42.5 hp/l; cast iron cylinder block and head; 5 crankshaft bearings; valves: overhead, in line, push-rods and rockers; camshafts: 1, side; lubrication: rotary pump, full flow filter, 7 imp pt, 8.5 US pt, 4 l; 1 Zenith-Stromberg 150 CD3 carburettor; fuel feed: mechanical pump; water-cooled, 12.9 imp pt, 15.6 US pt, 7.4 l.

TRANSMISSION driving wheels: rear; clutch: single dry plate (diaphragm); gearbox: mechanical; gears: 4, fully synchronized; ratios: I 3.538, II 2.165, III 1.387, IV 1, rev 3.680; lever: central; final drive: hypoid bevel; axle ratio: 4.375; width of rims: 4.5"; tyres: 5.60 x 13.

PERFORMANCE max speeds: (I) 25 mph, 40 km/h; (II) 45 mph, 72 km/h; (III) 65 mph, 104 km/h; (IV) 84 mph, 135 km/h; power-weight ratio: 33.1 lb/hp, 15 kg/hp; carrying capacity: 948 lb, 430 kg; acceleration: 0-50 mph (0-80 km/h) 11.1 sec; speed in direct drive at 1,000 rpm: 15.5 mph, 24.9 km/h; fuel consumption: 34 m/imp gal, 28.3 m/US gal, 8.3 l x 100 km.

CHASSIS integral; front suspension: independent, by McPherson, coil springs/telescopic damper struts, wishbones; rear suspension: rigid axle, swinging longitudinal trailing arms, upper oblique torque arms, coil springs, telescopic dampers.

STEERING rack-and-pinion; turns lock to lock: 3.66.

BRAKES front disc (diameter 9.50 in, 241 mm), rear drum; swept area: front 164 sq in, 1,058 sq cm, rear 74 sq in, 477 sq cm, total 238 sq in, 1,535 sq cm.

ELECTRICAL EQUIPMENT 12 V; 33 Ah battery; 264 W dynamo; Lucas distributor; 2 headlamps.

DIMENSIONS AND WEIGHT wheel base: 98 in, 2,489 mm; tracks: 51 in, 1,295 mm front, 51.30 in, 1,303 mm rear; length: 161.40 in, 4,100 mm; width: 62.50 in, 1,587 mm; height: 56 in, 1,422 mm; ground clearance: 5.50 in, 140 mm; dry weight: 1,763 lb, 800 kg; distribution of weight: 55% front, 45% rear; turning circle (between walls): 34 ft, 10.4 m; fuel tank: 9 imp gal, 10.8 US gal, 41 l.

BODY saloon/sedan; 4 doors; 4-5 seats, separate front seats.

PRACTICAL INSTRUCTIONS fuel: 97 oct petrol; engine sump oil: 7 imp pt, 8.5 US pt, 4 l, SAE 20W-50, change every 5,000 miles, 8,000 km; gearbox oil: 3 imp pt, 3.6 US pt, 1.7 l, SAE 20W-50, no change recommended; final drive oil: 1.5 imp pt, 1.9 US pt, 0.9 l, SAE 90 EP, no change recommended; greasing: none; tappet clearances: inlet 0.008 in, 0.20 mm, exhaust 0.016 in, 0.40 mm; valve timing: 38° 66° 72° 20°; tyre pressure: front 24 psi, 1.7 atm, rear 24 psi, 1.7 atm.

VARIATIONS

ENGINE 91.4 cu in, 1,498 cc (3.39 x 2.53 in, 86 x 64.2 mm), max power (DIN) 63 hp at 5,000 rpm, max torque (DIN) 80 lb ft, 11 kg m at 3,000 rpm, 42.1 hp/l.
TRANSMISSION ratios: III 1.361; 3.889 axle ratio.
PERFORMANCE max speeds (I) 30 mph, 48 km/h, (II) 50 mph, 80 km/h, (III) 75 mph, 120 km/h, (IV) 90 mph, 145 km/h, power-weight ratio 28.7 lb/hp, 13 kg/hp, acceleration 0-50 mph (0-80 km/h) 9.1 sec, fuel consumption 32 m/imp gal, 26.7 m/US gal, 8.8 l x 100 km.
CHASSIS anti-roll bar on front suspension.
ELECTRICAL EQUIPMENT 34 A alternator.
PRACTICAL INSTRUCTIONS valve timing 35° 69° 69° 23°.

OPTIONAL ACCESSORIES Borg-Warner 35/3 automatic transmission, hydraulic torque converter and planetary gears with 3 ratios (I 2.390, II 1.450, III 1, rev 2.090), max ratio of converter at stall 2, possible manual selection (only with 1.5 - litre engine), servo brake.

HILLMAN Avenger Super

HILLMAN Avenger Super Estate Car

HILLMAN Avenger GLS

Avenger De Luxe

See Avenger, except for:

PRICE IN GB: £ **754.**

Avenger De Luxe Estate Car

See Avenger, except for:

PRICE IN GB: £ **840.**

PERFORMANCE power-weight ratio: 36.6 lb/hp, 16.6 kg/hp; acceleration: 0-50 mph (0-80 km/h) 12.7 sec; fuel consumption: 31 m/imp gal, 25.8 m/US gal, 9.1 l x 100 km.

CHASSIS front suspension: anti-roll bar; rear suspension: transverse linkage bar.

DIMENSIONS AND WEIGHT length: 165.50 in, 4,204 mm; dry weight: 1,949 lb, 884 kg; distribution of weight: 51% front, 49% rear; fuel tank: 10 imp gal, 11.9 US gal, 45 l.

BODY estate car; 4 + 1 doors.

PRACTICAL INSTRUCTIONS tyre pressure: front 24 psi, 1.7 atm, rear 24 psi, 1.7 atm.

OPTIONAL ACCESSORIES 155 x 13 tyres (only for 91.4 cu in, 1,498 cc engine).

Avenger Super

See Avenger, except for:

PRICE IN GB: £ **782.**

PERFORMANCE power-weight ratio: 33.5 lb/hp, 15.2 kg/hp.

DIMENSIONS AND WEIGHT dry weight: 1,781 lb, 808 kg.

Avenger Super Estate Car

See Avenger De Luxe Estate Car, except for:

PRICE IN GB: £ **889.**

PERFORMANCE power-weight ratio: 36.8 lb/hp, 16.7 kg/hp.

DIMENSIONS AND WEIGHT dry weight: 1,964 lb, 891 kg.

Avenger GL

See Avenger, except for:

PRICE IN GB: £ **882.**

ENGINE 91.4 cu in, 1,498 cc (3.39 x 2.53 in, 86 x 64.2 mm); max power (DIN): 63 hp at 5,000 rpm; max torque (DIN): 80 lb ft, 11 kg m at 3,000 rpm; 42.1 hp/l.

TRANSMISSION axle ratio: 3.889.

PERFORMANCE max speeds: (I) 30 mph, 48 km/h; (II) 50 mph, 80 km/h; (III) 75 mph, 120 km/h; (IV) 90 mph, 145 km/h; power-weight ratio: 28.2 lb/hp, 12.8 kg/hp; acceleration: 0-50 mph (0-80 km/h) 9.1 sec.

CHASSIS front suspension: anti-roll bar.

ELECTRICAL EQUIPMENT 408 W alternator; 4 headlamps.

DIMENSIONS AND WEIGHT dry weight: 1,810 lb, 821 kg.

BODY reclining backrests.

PRACTICAL INSTRUCTIONS valve timing: 35° 69° 69° 23°.

VARIATIONS

None.

HILLMAN Avenger

HILLMAN Avenger Super Estate Car

HILLMAN Avenger GLS

Avenger GLS

See Avenger, except for:

PRICE IN GB: £ 991.

ENGINE 91.4 cu in, 1,498 cc (3.39 x 2.53 in, 86 x 64.2 mm); max power (DIN): 78 hp at 5,600 rpm; max torque (DIN): 81 lb ft, 11.2 kg m at 3,750 rpm; 52 hp/l; 2 Zenith-Stromberg 150 CD3 carburettors; viscous coupling fan.

TRANSMISSION ratios: III 1.361; axle ratio: 3.890; width of rims: 5''; tyres: 155 x 13.

PERFORMANCE max speeds: (I) 30 mph, 48 km/h; (II) 50 mph, 80 km/h; (III) 75 mph, 120 km/h; (IV) 99 mph, 159 km/h; power-weight ratio: 29.5 lb/hp, 13.4 kg/hp; acceleration: 0-50 mph (0-80 km/h) 8.9 sec; speed in direct drive at 1,000 rpm: 16.9 mph, 27.2 km/h; fuel consumption: 31 m/imp gal, 25.8 m/US gal, 9.1 l x 100 km.

CHASSIS front suspension: anti-roll bar.

BRAKES servo (standard).

ELECTRICAL EQUIPMENT 34 A alternator; 4 headlamps.

DIMENSIONS AND WEIGHT tracks: 51.50 in, 1,308 mm front, 51.50 in, 1,308 mm rear; dry weight: 1,873 lb, 849 kg.

PRACTICAL INSTRUCTIONS tappet clearances: inlet 0.010 in, 0.25 mm, exhaust 0.016 in, 0.40 mm; valve timing: 44° 78° 69° 23°; tyre pressure: front 24 psi, 1.7 atm, rear 24 psi, 1.7 atm.

VARIATIONS

None.

Hunter De Luxe Saloon

PRICE IN GB: £ 825.

ENGINE front, 4 stroke; 4 cylinders, in line; 91.3 cu in, 1,496 cc (3.21 x 2.82 in, 81.5 x 71.6 mm); compression ratio: 8.4:1; max power (DIN): 54 hp at 4,600 rpm; max torque (DIN): 73 lb ft, 10.1 kg m at 2,500 rpm; max engine rpm: 5,500; 36.1 hp/l; cast iron cylinder block and head; 5 crankshaft bearings; valves: overhead, in line, push-rods and rockers; camshafts: 1, side; lubrication: rotary pump, full flow filter, 7.5 imp pt, 8.9 US pt, 4.2 l; 1 Zenith-Stromberg 150 CD3 semi-downdraught carburettor; fuel feed: mechanical pump; water-cooled: 12.6 imp pt, 15 US pt, 7.1 l.

TRANSMISSION driving wheels: rear; clutch: single dry plate (diaphragm), hydraulically controlled; gearbox: mechanical; gears: 4, fully synchronized; ratios: I 3.352, II 2.139, III 1.391, IV 1, rev 3.568; lever: central; final drive: hypoid bevel; axle ratio: 3.890; width of rims: 4.5''; tyres: 5.60 x 13.

PERFORMANCE max speeds: (I) 29 mph, 46 km/h; (II) 45 mph, 72 km/h; (III) 69 mph, 111 km/h; (IV) 83 mph, 133 km/h; power-weight ratio: 36.1 lb/hp, 16.4 kg/hp; carrying capacity: 882 lb, 400 kg; acceleration: 0-50 mph (0-80 km/h) 12.5 sec; speed in direct drive at 1,000 rpm: 17.4 mph, 28 km/h; fuel consumption: 32 m/imp gal, 26.7 m/US gal, 8.8 l x 100 km.

CHASSIS integral; front suspension: independent, coil springs/telescopic damper struts, lower wishbones (trailing links), anti-roll bar; rear suspension: rigid axle, semi-elliptic leafsprings, telescopic dampers.

STEERING recirculating ball; turns lock to lock: 3.75.

BRAKES front disc (diameter 9.61 in, 244 mm), rear drum; swept area: front 179 sq in, 1,155 sq cm, rear 99 sq in, 639 sq cm, total 278 sq in, 1,794 sq cm.

ELECTRICAL EQUIPMENT 12 V; 40 Ah battery; 34 A alternator; Lucas distributor; 2 headlamps.

DIMENSIONS AND WEIGHT wheel base: 98.50 in, 2,502 mm; tracks: 52 in, 1,321 mm front, 52 in, 1,321 mm rear; length: 168 in, 4,267 mm; width: 63.50 in, 1,613 mm; height: 56 in, 1,422 mm; ground clearance: 6.73 in, 171 mm; dry weight: 1,952 lb, 885 kg; distribution of weight: 55% front, 45% rear; turning circle (between walls): 36 ft, 11 m; fuel tank: 10 imp gal, 11.9 US gal, 45 l.

BODY saloon/sedan; 4 doors; 4-5 seats, separate front seats.

PRACTICAL INSTRUCTIONS fuel: 97 oct petrol; engine sump oil: 7 imp pt, 8.5 US pt, 4 l, SAE 20W-50, change every 5,000 miles, 8,000 km; gearbox oil: 3.5 imp pt, 4.2 US pt, 2 l, SAE 20W-50, no change recommended; final drive oil: 1.8 imp pt, 2.1 US pt, 1 l, SAE 90 EP, no change recommended; greasing: none; tappet clearances: inlet 0.012 in, 0.30 mm, exhaust 0.014 in, 0.36 mm; valve timing: 37° 64° 67° 22°; tyre pressure: front 24 psi, 1.7 atm, rear 24 psi, 1.7 atm.

OPTIONAL ACCESSORIES Borg-Warner 35/3 automatic transmission, hydraulic torque converter and planetary gears with 3 ratios (I 2.393, II 1,450, III 1, rev 2.094), max ratio

HUNTER DE LUXE SALOON

of converter at stall 1.9, max speeds (I) 42 mph, 67 km/h, (II) 70 mph, 112 km/h, (III) 86 mph, 138 km/h, with engine capacity 105.3 cu in, 1,725 cc (3.21 x 3.25 in, 81.5 x 82.6 mm), max power (DIN) 61 hp at 4,700 rpm, max torque (DIN) 85 lb ft, 11.7 kg m at 2,600 rpm, max engine rpm 5,800; servo brake.

Hunter De Luxe Estate Car

See Hunter De Luxe Saloon, except for:

PRICE IN GB: £ 936.

TRANSMISSION axle ratio: 4.222; tyres: 6.00 x 13.

PERFORMANCE max speeds: (I) 26 mph, 42 km/h; (II) 41 mph, 66 km/h; (III) 64 mph, 103 km/h; (IV) 81 mph, 130 km/h; power-weight ratio: 38.8 lb/hp, 17.6 kg/hp; acceleration: 0-50 mph (0-80 km/h) 12.6 sec; speed in direct drive at 1,000 rpm: 16.4 mph, 26.4 km/h.

BRAKES servo.

DIMENSIONS AND WEIGHT length: 171 in, 4,343 mm; dry weight: 2,096 lb, 951 kg; distribution of weight: 51% front, 49% rear.

BODY estate car/station wagon; 4 + 1 doors.

VARIATIONS

ENGINE 1.7-litre, max power (DIN) 61 hp at 4,700 rpm (for other elements see Hunter Super).

Hunter Super

PRICE IN GB: £ 884.

ENGINE front, 4 stroke; 4 cylinders, slanted at 10°, in line; 105.3 cu in, 1,725 cc (3.21 x 3.25 in, 81.5 x 82.5 mm); compression ratio: 8.4:1; max power (DIN): 61 hp at 4,700 rpm; max torque (DIN): 85 lb ft, 11.7 kg m at 2,600 rpm; max engine rpm: 6,100; 35.4 hp/l; cast iron cylinder block and head; 5 crankshaft bearings; valves: overhead, in line, push-rods and rockers; camshafts: 1, side; lubrication: rotary pump, full flow filter, 7.5 imp pt, 8.9 US pt, 4.2 l; 1 Zenith-Stromberg 150 CD3 single barrel carburettor; fuel feed: mechanical pump; water-cooled, 12.6 imp pt, 15 US pt, 7.1 l.

TRANSMISSION driving wheels: rear; clutch: single dry plate (diaphragm), hydraulically controlled; gearbox: mechanical; gears: 4, fully synchronized; ratios: I 3.354, II 2.140, III 1.392, IV 1, rev 3.568; lever: central; final drive: hypoid bevel; axle ratio: 3.890; width of rims: 4.5"; tyres: 5.60 x 13.

PERFORMANCE max speeds: (I) 31 mph, 50 km/h; (II) 48 mph, 77 km/h; (III) 75 mph, 120 km/h; (IV) 89 mph, 143 km/h; power-weight ratio: 32.1 lb/hp, 14.6 kg/hp; carrying capacity: 882 lb, 400 kg; acceleration: 0-50 mph (0-80 km/h) 11 sec; speed in direct drive at 1,000 rpm: 17.4 mph, 28 km/h; fuel consumption: 34 m/imp gal, 28.3 m/US gal, 8.3 l x 100 km.

CHASSIS integral; front suspension: independent, coil springs/telescopic damper struts, lower wishbones (trailing links), anti-roll bar; rear suspension: rigid axle, semi-elliptic leafsprings, telescopic dampers.

STEERING recirculating ball; turns lock to lock: 3.75.

BRAKES front disc (diameter 9.61 in, 244 mm), rear drum; swept area: front 179 sq in, 1,155 sq cm, rear 99 sq in, 639 sq cm, total 278 sq in, 1,794 sq cm.

ELECTRICAL EQUIPMENT 12 V; 40 Ah battery; 34 A alternator; Lucas distributor; 2 headlamps.

DIMENSIONS AND WEIGHT wheel base: 98.50 in, 2,502 mm; tracks: 52 in, 1,321 mm front, 52 in, 1,321 mm rear; length: 168 in, 4,267 mm; width: 63.50 in, 1,613 mm; height: 56 in, 1,422 mm; ground clearance: 6.73 in, 171 mm; dry weight: 1,961 lb, 889 kg; distribution of weight: 54% front, 46% rear; turning circle (between walls): 36 ft, 11 m; fuel tank: 10 imp gal, 11.9 US gal, 45 l.

BODY saloon/sedan; 4 doors; 4-5 seats, separate front seats.

PRACTICAL INSTRUCTIONS fuel: 97 oct petrol; engine sump oil: 7 imp pt, 8.5 US pt, 4 l, SAE 20W-50, change every 5,000 miles, 8,000 km; gearbox oil: 3.5 imp pt, 4.2 US pt, 2 l, SAE 20W-50, no change recommended; final drive oil: 1.8 imp pt, 2.1 US pt, 1 l, SAE 90 EP, no change recommended; greasing: none; tappet clearances: inlet 0.012 in, 0.30 mm, exhaust 0.014 in, 0.36 mm; valve timing: 47° 86° 82° 36°.

OPTIONAL ACCESSORIES overdrive; Borg-Warner 35/3 automatic transmission, hydraulic torque converter and planetary gears with 3 ratios (I 2.393, II 1.450, III 1, rev 2.049), max ratio of converter at stall 1.94; servo brake; electrically-heated rear window; reclining backrests.

HILLMAN Hunter Super

HILLMAN Hunter GLS

HUMBER Sceptre

Hunter GL Saloon

PRICE IN GB: £ 963.

ENGINE front, 4 stroke; 4 cylinders, slanted at 10°, in line; 105.3 cu in, 1,725 cc (3.21 x 3.25 in, 81.5 x 82.5 mm); compression ratio: 9.2:1; max power (DIN): 72 hp at 5,000 rpm; max torque (DIN): 90 lb ft, 12.5 kg m at 3,000 rpm; max engine rpm: 6,100; 41.7 hp/l; cast iron cylinder block, light alloy head; 5 crankshaft bearings; valves: overhead, in line, push-rods and rockers; camshafts: 1, side; lubrication: rotary pump, full flow filter, 7.5 imp pt, 8.9 US pt, 4.2 l; 1 Zenith-Stromberg 150 CD3 semi-downdraught single barrel carburettor; fuel feed: mechanical pump; water-cooled, 12.6 imp pt, 15 US pt, 7.1 l.

TRANSMISSION driving wheels: rear; clutch: single dry plate (diaphragm), hydraulically controlled; gearbox: mechanical; gears: 4, fully synchronized; ratios: I 3.354, II 2.140, III 1.392, IV 1, rev 3.568; lever: central; final drive: hypoid bevel; axle ratio: 3.700; width of rims: 4.5"; tyres: 5.60 x 13.

PERFORMANCE max speeds: (I) 33 mph, 53 km/h; (II) 52 mph, 84 km/h; (III) 80 mph, 129 km/h; (IV) 90 mph, 145 km/h; power-weight ratio: 26.9 lb/hp, 12.2 kg/hp; carrying capacity: 882 lb, 400 kg; acceleration: 0-50 mph (0-80 km/h) 9.9 sec; speed in direct drive at 1,000 rpm: 18.3 mph, 29.5 km/h; fuel consumption: 34 m/imp gal, 28.3 m/US gal, 8.3 l x 100 km.

CHASSIS integral; front suspension: independent, coil springs/telescopic damper struts, lower wishbones (trailing links), anti-roll bar; rear suspension: rigid axle, semi-elliptic leafsprings, telescopic dampers.

STEERING recirculating ball; turns lock to lock: 3.75.

BRAKES front disc (diameter 9.61 in, 244 mm), rear drum, servo; swept area: front 179 sq in, 1,154 sq cm, rear 99 sq in, 638 sq cm, total 278 sq in, 1,792 sq cm.

ELECTRICAL EQUIPMENT 12 V; 40 Ah battery; 408 W alternator; Lucas distributor; 2 headlamps.

DIMENSIONS AND WEIGHT wheel base: 98.50 in, 2,502 mm; tracks: 52.01 in, 1,321 mm front, 52.01 in, 1,321 mm rear; length: 168 in, 4,267 mm; width: 63.50 in, 1,613 mm; height: 56 in, 1,422 mm; ground clearance: 6.73 in, 171 mm; dry weight: 1,948 lb, 884 kg; distribution of weight: 54% front, 46% rear; turning circle (between walls): 36.8 ft, 11.2 m; fuel tank: 10 imp gal, 11.9 US gal, 45 l.

BODY saloon/sedan; 4 doors; 4-5 seats, separate front seats, reclining backrests.

PRACTICAL INSTRUCTIONS fuel: 97 oct petrol; engine sump oil: 7.5 imp pt, 8.9 US pt, 4.2 l, SAE 20W-50, change every 5,000 miles, 8,000 km; gearbox oil: 3.5 imp pt, 4.2 US pt, 2 l, multigrade, no change recommended; final drive oil: 1.7 imp pt, 2.1 US pt, 1 l, SAE 90 EP, no change recommended; greasing: none; tappet clearances: inlet 0.013 in, 0.32 mm, exhaust 0.013 in, 0.32 mm; valve timing: 38° 72° 72° 38°; tyre pressure: front 24 psi, 1.7 atm, rear 24 psi, 1.7 atm.

OPTIONAL ACCESSORIES Laycock overdrive on III and IV (0.803 ratio), 3.890 axle ratio; Borg-Warner 35/3 automatic transmission, hydraulic torque converter and planetary gears with 3 ratios (I 2.393, II 1.450, III 1, rev 2.094), max ratio of converter at stall 1.9, steering column selector lever.

Hunter GL Estate Car

See Hunter GL Saloon, except for:

PRICE IN GB: £ 1,078.

TRANSMISSION axle ratio: 3.890; tyres: 6.00 x 13.

PERFORMANCE max speeds: (I) 32 mph, 51 km/h; (II) 50 mph, 80 km/h; (III) 76 mph, 122 km/h; (IV) 90 mph, 145 km/h; power-weight ratio: 31.4 lb/hp, 14.2 kg/hp; acceleration: 0-50 mph (0-80 km/h) 11.2 sec; speed in direct drive at 1,000 rpm: 17.8 mph, 28.6 km/h.

DIMENSIONS AND WEIGHT length: 171 in, 4,343 mm; dry weight: 2,107 lb, 956 kg; distribution of weight: 50% front, 50% rear.

BODY estate car/station wagon; 4 + 1 doors.

Hunter GT

PRICE IN GB: £ 973.

ENGINE front, 4 stroke; 4 cylinders, slanted at 10°, in line; 105.3 cu in, 1,725 cc (3.21 x 3.25 in, 81.5 x 82.5 mm); compression ratio: 9.2:1; max power (DIN): 79 hp at 5,100 rpm; max torque (DIN): 93 lb ft, 12.9 kg m at 3,800 rpm; max engine rpm: 6,400; 45.8 hp/l; cast iron cylinder block, light alloy head; 5 crankshaft bearings; valves: overhead, in line, push-rods and rockers; camshafts: 1, side; lubrication: rotary pump, full flow filter, 7.5 imp pt, 8.9 US pt, 4.2 l; 2 Zenith-Stromberg 150 CD3 semi-downdraught carburettors;

HILLMAN Hunter GL Estate Car

HILLMAN Hunter GLS

HUMBER Sceptre

fuel feed: mechanical pump; water-cooled, 12.6 imp pt, 15 US pt, 7.1 l.

TRANSMISSION driving wheels: rear; clutch: single dry plate (diaphragm), hydraulically controlled; gearbox: mechanical; gears: 4, fully synchronized; ratios: I 3.122, II 1.993, III 1.296, IV 1, rev 3.323; lever: central; final drive: hypoid bevel; axle ratio: 3.700; width of rims: 5"; tyres: 165 x 13.

PERFORMANCE max speeds: (I) 33 mph, 53 km/h; (II) 51 mph, 82 km/h; (III) 79 mph, 127 km/h; (IV) 100 mph, 161 km/h; power-weight ratio: 25.4 lb/hp, 11.5 kg/hp; carrying capacity: 871 lb, 395 kg; acceleration: 0-50 mph (0-80 km/h) 8.5 sec; speed in direct drive at 1,000 rpm: 18.3 mph, 29.3 km/h; fuel consumption: 34 m/imp gal, 28.3 m/US gal, 8.3 l x 100 km.

CHASSIS integral; front suspension: independent, coil springs/telescopic damper struts, lower wishbones (trailing links), anti-roll bar; rear suspension: rigid axle, semi-elliptic leafsprings, telescopic dampers.

STEERING recirculating ball; turns lock to lock: 3.75.

BRAKES front disc (diameter 9.60 in, 244 mm), rear drum, servo; swept area: front 175 sq in, 1,129 sq cm, rear 97 sq in, 626 sq cm, total 272 sq in, 1,755 sq cm.

ELECTRICAL EQUIPMENT 12 V; 40 Ah battery; 408 W alternator; Lucas distributor; 2 headlamps.

DIMENSIONS AND WEIGHT wheel base: 98.50 in, 2,502 mm; tracks: 51.80 in, 1,316 mm front, 51.80 in, 1,316 rear; length: 168 in, 4,267 mm; width: 63.50 in, 1,613 mm; height: 56 in, 1,422 mm; ground clearance: 6.50 in, 165 mm; dry weight: 2,011 lb, 912 kg; turning circle (between walls): 36.7 ft, 11.2 m; fuel tank: 10 imp gal, 11.9 US gal, 45 l.

BODY saloon/sedan; 4 doors; 4-5 seats, separate front seats.

PRACTICAL INSTRUCTIONS fuel: 97 oct petrol; engine sump oil: 7.5 imp pt, 8.9 US pt, 4.2 l, SAE 20W-50, change every 5,000 miles, 8,000 km; gearbox oil: 3.5 imp pt, 4.2 US pt, 2 l, SAE 20W-50, no change recommended; final drive oil: 7.5 imp pt, 8.9 US pt, 4.2 l, SAE 20W-50, no change recommended; greasing: none; tappet clearances: inlet 0.013 in, 0.32 mm, exhaust 0.013 in, 0.32 mm; valve timing: 38° 72° 72° 38°; tyre pressure: front 24 psi, 1.7 atm, rear 24 psi, 1.7 atm.

OPTIONAL ACCESSORIES Laycock overdrive on III and IV (0.803 ratio) with 3.890 axle ratio; reclining backrests; electrically-heated rear window.

Hunter GLS

See Hunter GT, except for:

PRICE IN GB: £ 1,091.

ENGINE compression ratio 9.6:1; max power (DIN): 93 hp at 5,200 rpm; max torque (DIN): 106 lb ft, 14.6 kg m at 4,000 rpm; max engine rpm: 6,500; 53.9 hp/l; 2 Weber 40DCOE twin barrel carburettors; water-cooled, 12.5 imp pt, 15 US pt, 7.1 l.

TRANSMISSION tyres: 165 x 13.

PERFORMANCE max speeds: (I) 36 mph, 58 km/h; (II) 55 mph, 88 km/h; (III) 84 mph, 135 km/h; (IV) 103 mph, 165 km/h; power-weight ratio: 21.4 lb/hp, 9.7 kg/hp; acceleration: 0-50 mph (0-80 km/h) 7 sec; speed in direct drive at 1,000 rpm: 18.2 mph, 29.3 km/h.

ELECTRICAL EQUIPMENT 4 headlamps.

DIMENSIONS AND WEIGHT tracks: 52.50 in, 1,333 mm front, 52.50 in, 1,333 mm rear; ground clearance: 6.30 in, 160 mm; dry weight: 2,000 lb, 907 kg; distribution of weight: 55% front, 45% rear.

PRACTICAL INSTRUCTIONS valve timing: 58° 66° 84° 40°; tyre pressure: front 26 psi, 1.8 atm, rear 24 psi, 1.7 atm.

OPTIONAL ACCESSORIES overdrive on III and IV (0.803 ratio); Borg Warner 35/3 automatic transmission, hydraulic torque converter and planetary gears with 3 ratios (I 2.393, II 1.450, III 1, rev 2.094), max ratio of converter at stall 1.9, steering column selector lever; electrically-heated rear window.

HUMBER GREAT BRITAIN

Sceptre

PRICE IN GB: £ 1,175.

ENGINE front, 4 stroke; 4 cylinders, vertical, in line; 105.3 cu in, 1,725 cc (3.21 x 3.25 in, 81.5 x 82.5 mm); compression ratio: 9.2:1; max power (DIN): 79 hp at 5,100 rpm; max torque (DIN): 93 lb ft, 12.9 kg m at 3,300 rpm; max engine rpm: 6,400; 45.8 hp/l; cast iron cylinder block, light alloy head; 5 crankshaft bearings; valves: overhead, in line,

SCEPTRE

push-rods and rockers; camshafts: 1, side; lubrication: rotary pump, full flow filter, 7.5 imp pt, 8.9 US pt, 4.2 l; 2 Zenith-Stromberg 150 CD3 semi-downdraught carburettors; fuel feed: mechanical pump; water-cooled, 12.5 imp pt, 15 US pt, 7.1 l.

TRANSMISSION driving wheels: rear; clutch: single dry plate (diaphragm), hydraulically controlled; gearbox: mechanical; gears: 4, fully synchronized, and overdrive on III and IV; ratios: I 3.352, II 1.993, III 1.296, IV 1, overdrive/top 0.802, rev 3.323; lever: central; final drive: hypoid bevel; axle ratio: 3.890; width of rims: 5"; tyres: 155 x 13.

PERFORMANCE max speeds: (I) 33 mph, 53 km/h; (II) 51 mph, 82 km/h; (III) 79 mph, 127 km/h; (IV) 97 mph, 156 km/h; power-weight ratio: 26.2 lb/hp, 11.9 kg/hp; carrying capacity: 882 lb, 400 kg; acceleration: 0-50 mph (0-80 km/h) 9 sec; speed in top at 1,000 rpm: 17.8 mph, 28.7 km/h; fuel consumption: 29.7 m/imp gal, 24.8 m/US gal, 9.5 l x 100 km.

CHASSIS integral; front suspension: independent, coil springs/telescopic damper struts, lower wishbones (trailing links), anti-roll bar; rear suspension: rigid axle, semi-elliptic leafsprings, telescopic dampers.

STEERING recirculating ball, adjustable steering wheel; turns lock to lock: 3.75.

BRAKES front disc (diameter 9.60 in, 244 mm), rear drum, servo; swept area: total 278 sq in, 1,793 sq cm.

ELECTRICAL EQUIPMENT 12 V; 40 Ah battery; 34 A alternator; Lucas distributor; 4 headlamps.

DIMENSIONS AND WEIGHT wheel base: 98.50 in, 2,502 mm; tracks: 51.80 in, 1,316 mm front, 51.80 in, 1,316 mm rear; length: 169.50 in, 4,305 mm; width: 64.75 in, 1,645 mm; height: 56 in, 1,422 mm; ground clearance: 6.75 in, 171 mm; dry weight: 2,082 lb, 944 kg; distribution of weight: 55% front, 45% rear; turning circle (between walls): 36 ft, 11 m; fuel tank: 10 imp gal, 11.9 US gal, 45 l.

BODY saloon/sedan; 4 doors; 5 seats, separate front seats, reclining backrests.

PRACTICAL INSTRUCTIONS fuel: 97 oct petrol; engine sump oil: 7.5 imp pt, 8.9 US pt, 4.2 l, SAE 20W-50, change every 5,000 miles, 8,000 km; gearbox oil: 4.5 imp pt, 5.3 US pt, 2.5 l, SAE 20W-50, no change recommended; final drive oil: 1.8 imp pt, 2.1 US pt, 1 l, SAE 80-90 EP, no change recommended; greasing: none; tappet clearances: inlet 0.013 in, 0.32 mm, exhaust 0.014 in, 0.36 mm; valve timing: 38° 72° 72° 38°; tyre pressure: front 26 psi, 1.8 atm, rear 26 psi, 1.8 atm.

OPTIONAL ACCESSORIES Borg-Warner 35/3 automatic transmission, hydraulic torque converter and planetary gears with 3 ratios (I 2.390, II 1.450, III 1, rev 2.090), max ratio of converter at stall 1.9, 3.700 axle ratio, 57 Ah battery.

JAGUAR — GREAT BRITAIN

XJ6 2.8-litre Saloon

PRICE IN GB: £ 2,285.
PRICE IN USA: $ 7,683 (with automatic transmission).

ENGINE front, 4 stroke; 6 cylinders, vertical, in line; 170.2 cu in, 2,790 cc (3.27 x 3.39 in, 63 x 86 mm); compression ratio: 8.5:1; max power (DIN): 140 hp a 5,150 rpm; max torque (DIN): 150 lb ft, 20.7 kg m at 4,250 rpm; max engine rpm: 6,500; 50.2 hp/l; cast iron cylinder block, dry liners, light alloy head, hemispherical combustion chambers; 7 crankshaft bearings; valves: overhead, Vee-slanted at 70°, thimble tappets; camshafts: 2, overhead; lubrication: mechanical pump, full flow filter, 14.4 imp pt, 17.3 US pt, 8.2 l; 2 SU type HD 8 horizontal carburettors; fuel feed: electric pump; water-cooled, 29.9 imp pt, 35.9 US pt, 17 l, viscous coupling thermostatic fan.

TRANSMISSION driving wheels: rear; clutch: single dry plate (diaphragm), hydraulically controlled; gearbox: mechanical; gears: 4, fully synchronized; ratios: I 2.933, II 1.905, III 1.389, IV 1, rev 3.378; lever: central; final drive: hypoid bevel; axle ratio: 4.270; width of rims: 6"; tyres: E70 VR x 15.

PERFORMANCE max speeds: (I) 38 mph, 61 km/h; (II) 58 mph, 93 km/h; (III) 81 mph, 130 km/h; (IV) 118 mph, 190 km/h; power-weight ratio: 24.2 lb/hp, 11 kg/hp; carrying capacity: 926 lb, 420 kg; acceleration: standing ¼ mile 17.7 sec, 0-50 mph (0-80 km/h) 8.5 sec; speed in direct drive at 1,000 rpm: 16.8 mph, 27 km/h; fuel consumption: 21.5 m/imp gal, 17.8 m/US gal, 13.2 l x 100 km.

CHASSIS integral, front and rear auxiliary frames; front suspension: independent, wishbones, coil springs, anti-roll bar, telescopic dampers; rear suspension: independent,

JAGUAR XJ6 2.8-litre Saloon

JAGUAR XJ12

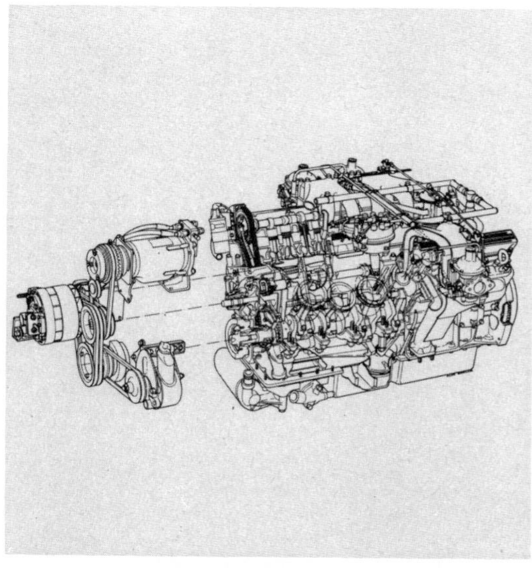

JAGUAR 12V

wishbones, semi-axles as upper arm, trailing lower radius arms, 4 coil springs, 4 telescopic dampers.

STEERING rack-and-pinion, adjustable steering wheel, variable ratio, servo; turns lock to lock: 3.50.

BRAKES disc (front diameter 11.18 in, 284 mm, rear 10.40 in, 264 mm), servo; swept area: front 242.4 sq in, 1,563 sq cm, rear 189.6 sq in, 1,223 sq cm, total 432 sq in, 2,786 sq cm.

ELECTRICAL EQUIPMENT 12 V; 51 Ah battery; 45 A alternator; Lucas distributor; 4 headlamps.

DIMENSIONS AND WEIGHT wheel base: 108.87 in, 2,765 mm; tracks: 58 in, 1,473 mm front, 58.33 in, 1,481 mm rear; length: 189.60 in, 4,816 mm; width: 69.75 in, 1,772 mm; height: 52.87 in, 1,343 mm; ground clearance: 6 in, 152 mm; dry weight: 3,389 lb, 1,537 kg; distribution of weight: 52% front, 48% rear; turning circle (between walls): 36 ft, 11 m; fuel tank: 20 imp gal, 24 US gal, 91 l.

BODY saloon/sedan; 4 doors; 5 seats, separate front seats, reclining backrests; luxury interior.

PRACTICAL INSTRUCTIONS fuel: 98-100 oct petrol; engine sump oil: 14.4 imp pt, 17.3 US pt, 8.2 l, SAE 10W-40 (winter) 20W-50 (summer), change every 6,000 miles, 9,700 km; gearbox oil: 2.5 imp pt, 3 US pt, 1.4 l, SAE 30, change every 12,000 miles, 19,300 km; final drive oil: 2.7 imp pt, 3.2 US pt, 1.5 l, SAE 90, change every 12,000 miles, 19,300 km; greasing: every 6,000-12,000 miles, 9,700-19,300 km; tappet clearances: inlet and exhaust 0.012-0.014 in, 0.30-0.35 mm; valve timing: 17° 59° 59° 17°; tyre pressure: front 25 psi, 1.8 atm, rear 27 psi, 1.9 atm.

OPTIONAL ACCESSORIES Laycock-de Normanville overdrive/top (0.779 ratio), 4.550 axle ratio; Borg-Warner automatic transmission, hydraulic torque converter and planetary gears with 3 ratios (I 2.389, II 1.450, III 1, rev 2.089), max ratio of converter at stall 2, possible manual selection, max speeds (I) 51 mph, 82 km/h, (II) 83 mph, 133 km/h, (III) 118 mph, 190 km/h; electrically-controlled windows; air-conditioning; electrically-heated rear window.

XJ6 4.2-litre Saloon

See XJ6 2.8-litre Saloon, except for:

PRICE IN GB: £ 2,540.

ENGINE 258.4 cu in, 4,235 cc (3.63 x 4.17 in, 92.1 x 105.9 mm); compression ratio: 8:1; max power (DIN): 173 hp at 4,750 rpm; max torque (DIN): 227 lb ft, 31.3 kg m at 3,000 rpm; max engine rpm: 5,500; 40.9 hp/l; cooling system capacity: 32 imp pt, 36.4 US pt, 18.2 l.

TRANSMISSION axle ratio: 3.310.

PERFORMANCE max speeds: (I) 44 mph, 71 km/h; (II) 67 mph, 108 km/h; (III) 92 mph, 148 km/h; (IV) 124 mph, 200 km/h; power-weight ratio: 19.8 lb/hp, 9 kg/hp; speed in direct drive at 1,000 rpm: 21.4 mph, 34.4 km/h; fuel consumption: 17.9 m/imp gal, 14.9 m/US gal, 15.8 l x 100 km.

ELECTRICAL EQUIPMENT 60 Ah battery.

DIMENSIONS AND WEIGHT dry weight: 3,444 lb, 1,562 kg.

VARIATIONS

ENGINE 7:1 or 9:1 compression ratio.

Long wheelbase model.

OPTIONAL ACCESSORIES Borg-Warner automatic transmission, hydraulic torque converter and planetary gears with 3 ratios (I 2.401, II 1.458, III 1, rev 2), max ratio of converter at stall 2, possible manual selection, 3.310 axle ratio, max speeds (I) 53 mph, 85 km/h, (II) 88 mph, 141 km/h, (III) 121 mph, 194 km/h.

XJ12 Saloon

See XJ6 2.8-litre Saloon, except for:

PRICE IN GB: £ 3,082.

ENGINE 12 cylinders, Vee-slanted at 60°; 326 cu in, 5,343 cc (3.54 x 2.76 in, 90 x 70 mm); compression ratio: 9:1; max power (DIN): 272 hp at 5,850 rpm; max torque (DIN): 304 lb ft, 41.9 kg m at 3,600 rpm; max engine rpm: 6,500; 50.9 hp/l; cylinder block with light alloy wet liners, head with aluminium alloy hemispherical combustion chambers; 7 crankshaft bearings; valves: in line, thimble tappets; camshafts: 1, per cylinder block, overhead; lubrication: gear pump, full flow filter, 17.6 imp pt, 21.1 US pt, 10 l; 4 Zenith 175 CDSE variable choke side-draught carburettors; fuel feed: electric pump; water-cooled, 36 imp pt, 43.3 US pt, 20.5 l.

TRANSMISSION gearbox: Borg Warner automatic transmission, hydraulic torque converter and planetary gears with 3 ratios, max ratio of converter at stall 2, possible manual selection; ratios: I 2.400, II 1.450, III 1, rev 2; final drive: hypoid bevel; axle ratio: 3.310; width of rims: 6"; tyres: 205/70 VR x 15.

JAGUAR XJ6 4.2-litre Saloon

JAGUAR XJ12 Saloon

JAGUAR E Type 12V Series III 2+2 Coupé

PERFORMANCE max speeds: (I) 65 mph, 104 km/h; (II) 102 mph, 164 km/h; (III) 140 mph, 225 km/h; power-weight ratio: 6.4 lb/hp, 2.9 kg/hp; acceleration: standing ¼ mile 15.7 sec, 0-50 mph (0-80 km/h) 6.1 sec; speed in direct drive at 1,000 rpm: 22.9 mph, 36.9 km/h; fuel consumption: 14.1 m/imp gal, 16.7 m/US gal, 20 l x 100 km.

BRAKES swept area: front 234.5 sq in, 1,513 sq cm, rear 213.7 sq in, 1,379 sq cm, total 448.2 sq in, 2,892 sq cm.

ELECTRICAL EQUIPMENT 68 Ah battery; 60 A alternator; Lucas electronic distributor.

DIMENSIONS AND WEIGHT dry weight: 1,760 lb, 798 kg; distribution of weight 48.7% front, 51.3% rear.

PRACTICAL INSTRUCTIONS engine sump oil: 16 imp pt, 19.2 US pt, 9.1 l; gearbox oil: 2.8 imp pt, 3.4 US pt, 1.6 l, 90 SAE, no change recommended; final drive oil: 2.6 imp pt, 3.2 US pt, 1.5 l, SAE 90; greasing: every 6,000 miles, 9,700 km, 17 points; sparking plug type: Campion; tyre pressure: front 26 psi, 1.8 atm, rear 26 psi, 1.8 atm.

VARIATIONS

Long wheelbase model.

OPTIONAL ACCESSORIES electrically-controlled windows; air-conditioning.

E Type 12V Series III Convertible

PRICE IN GB: £ 2,785.
PRICE IN USA: $ 7,338.

ENGINE front, 4 stroke; 12 cylinders, Vee-slanted at 60°; 326 cu in, 5,343 cc (3.54 x 2.76 in, 90 x 70 mm); compression ratio: 9:1; max power (DIN): 272 hp at 5,850 rpm; max torque (DIN): 304 lb ft, 41.9 kg m at 3,600 rpm; max engine rpm: 6,500 ; 50.9 hp/l; cylinder block with light alloy wet liners; 7 crankshaft hearings; valves in line, thimble tappets; camshafts: 1, per cylinder block, overhead; lubrication: gear pump, full flow filter, 17.6 imp pt, 21.1 US pt, 10 l; 4 Zenith 175 CDSE variable choke side-draught carburettors; fuel feed: electric pump; water-cooled, 36 imp pt, 43.3 US pt, 20.5 l, automatic thermostatic fan.

TRANSMISSION driving wheels: rear; clutch: single dry plate (diaphragm), hydraulically controlled; gearbox: mechanical; gear: 4, fully synchronized; ratios: I 2.933, II 1.905, III 1.389, IV 1, rev 3.378; lever: central; final drive: hypoid bevel, limited slip differential; axle ratio: 3.310; width of rims: 6"; tyres: E70 VR x 15.

PERFORMANCE max speeds: (I) 50 mph, 81 km/h; (II) 78 mph, 125 km/h; (III) 101 mph, 162 km/h; (IV) 150 mph, 241 km/h; power-weight ratio: 11.9 lb/hp, 5.4 kg/hp; carrying capacity: 408 lb, 185 kg; acceleration: standing ¼ mile 14.5 sec, 0-50 mph (0-80 km/h) 4.8 sec; speed in direct drive at 1,000 rpm: 22.9 mph, 36.8 km/h; fuel consumption: 15.5 m/imp gal, 12.9 m/US gal, 18.2 l x 100 km.

CHASSIS integral, front and rear tubular auxiliary frames; front suspension: independent, wishbones, longitudinal torsion bars, anti-roll bar, telescopic dampers; rear suspension: independent, wishbones, semi-axles as upper arm, trailing lower radius arms, 4 coil springs, 4 telescopic dampers.

STEERING rack-and-pinion, servo; turns lock to lock: 3.50.

BRAKES disc (front diameter 11.18 in, 284 mm, rear 10.38 in, 264 mm), servo; swept area: front 234.5 sq in, 1,512 sq cm, rear 213.7 sq in, 1,378 sq cm, total 448.2 sq in, 2,890 sq cm.

ELECTRICAL EQUIPMENT 12 V; 68 Ah battery; 60 A alternator; Lucas electronic distributor; 2 headlamps.

DIMENSIONS AND WEIGHT wheel base: 105 in, 2,667 mm; tracks: 54.25 in, 1,378 mm front, 53.25 in, 1,352 mm rear; length: 184.38 in, 4,683 mm; width: 66 in, 1,676 mm; height: 48.40 in, 1,229 mm; ground clearance: 5.92 in, 150 mm; dry weight: 3,232 lb, 1,466 kg; distribution of weight: 53.4% front, 46.6% rear; turning circle (between walls): 36 ft, 11 m; fuel tank: 18 imp gal, 21.6 US gal, 82 l.

BODY convertible; 2 doors; 2 seats, reclining backrests.

PRACTICAL INSTRUCTIONS fuel: 97 oct petrol; engine sump oil: 17.6 imp pt, 21.1 US pt, 10 l, change every 3,100 miles 5,000 km; gearbox oil: 3 imp pt, 3.6 US pt, 1.7 l, change every 12,000 miles, 19,300 km; final drive oil: 2.6 imp pt, 3.2 US pt, 1.5 l, change every 12,000 miles, 19,300 km; greasing: every 6,000-12,000 miles, 9,700-19,300 km; tappet clearances: inlet and exhaust 0.012-0.014 in, 0.30-0.35 mm; valve timing: 17° 59° 59° 15°; tyre pressure: front 25 psi, 1.7 atm, rear 28 psi, 2 atm.

OPTIONAL ACCESSORIES Borg-Warner automatic transmission, hydraulic torque converter and planetary gears with 3 ratios (I 2.400, II 1.450, III 1, rev 2), max ratio of converter at stall 2, 3.070 axle ratio; air-conditioning.

E Type 12V Series III 2 + 2 Coupé

See E Type 12V Series III Convertible, except for:

PRICE IN GB: £ 3,004.
PRICE IN USA: $ 7,732.

PERFORMANCE carrying capacity: 717 lb, 325 kg.

DIMENSIONS AND WEIGHT dry weight: 3,226 lb, 1,463 kg.

BODY coupé; 2 + 2 seats

OPTIONAL ACCESSORIES electrically-heated rear window.

JENSEN GREAT BRITAIN

Jensen - Healey

PRICE IN GB: £ 1,620.
PRICE IN USA: $ 4,595.

ENGINE front, 4 stroke; 4 cylinders, in line, slanted at 45°; compression ratio: 8.4:1; max power (DIN): 140 hp at 6,500 rpm; max torque (DIN): 130 lb ft, 17.9 kg m at 5,000 rpm; max engine rpm: 7,000; light alloy cylinder block and head; 5 crankshaft bearings; valves: Vee-slanted; camshafts: 2, overhead, cogged belt; lubrication: electric pump, full flow filter, 11 imp pt, 13.1 US pt, 6.2 l; 2 Dell'Orto or Stromberg twin barrel carburettors; fuel feed: electric pump; water-cooled, 12 imp pt, 14.4 US pt, 6.8 l.

TRANSMISSION driving wheels: rear; clutch: single dry plate (diaphragm); gearbox: mechanical; gears: 4, fully synchronized; ratios: I 3.122, II 1.993, III 1.296, IV 1, overdrive 0.797, rev 3.320; final drive: hypoid bevel; axle ratio: 3.730; width of rims: 5.5''; tyres: 185/70HR x 13.

PERFORMANCE max speeds: (I) 40 mph, 64 km/h; (II) 63 mph, 101 km/h; (III) 97 mph, 156 km/h; (IV) 123 mph, 198 km/h; power-weight ratio: 19 lb/hp, 8.6 kg/hp; acceleration: standing ¼ mile 16 sec, 0-50 mph (0-80 km/h) 5.7 sec; speed in direct drive at 1,000 rpm: 18 mph, 28.9 km/h; fuel consumption: 22 m/imp gal, 18.2 m/US gal, 12.9 l x 100 km.

CHASSIS integral; front suspension: independent, wishbones, coil springs, telescopic dampers; rear suspension: rigid axle, lower longitudinal trailing arms, upper oblique torque arms, coil springs, telescopic dampers.

STEERING rack-and-pinion; turns lock to lock: 3.16.

BRAKES disc front, rear drum; swept area: front 193.8 sq in, 1,250 sq cm, rear 99.2 sq in, 640 sq cm, total 293 sq in, 1,890 sq cm.

ELECTRICAL EQUIPMENT 12 V; 50 Ah battery; 35 A alternator; Lucas 23 D4 distributor; 2 headlamps.

DIMENSIONS AND WEIGHT wheel base: 92.01 in, 2,337 mm; tracks: 53.31 in, 1,354 mm front, 52.44 in, 1,332 mm rear; length: 161.93 in, 4,113 mm; width: 63.23 in, 1,606 mm; height: 47.64 in, 1,210 mm; ground clearance: 5 in, 127 mm; dry weight: 2,650 lb, 1,202 kg; turning circle (between walls): 32 ft, 9.8 m; fuel tank: 11 imp gal, 13.2 US gal, 50 l.

BODY open roadster; 2 doors, 2 seats, separate front seats.

PRACTICAL INSTRUCTIONS fuel: 91 oct petrol; engine sump oil: 10 imp pt, 12 US pt, 5.7 l, SAE 20W-50, change every 6,000 miles, 9,700 km; gearbox oil: 3.5 imp pt, 4.2 US pt, 2 l, SAE 20W-50, change every 6,000 miles, 9,700 km; final drive oil: 2.5 imp pt, 3 US pt, 1.4 l, SAE 90, change every 6,000 miles, 9,700 km; greasing: 4 points, every 6,000 miles, 9,700 km; valve timing: 21° 71° 71° 21°; tyre pressure: front 24 psi, 1.7 atm, rear 24 psi, 1.7 atm.

OPTIONAL ACCESSORIES tonneau cover.

Interceptor III

PRICE IN GB: £ 5,580.
PRICE IN USA: $ 13,970.

ENGINE front, 4 stroke; 8 cylinders, Vee-slanted at 90°; 440 cu in, 7,212 cc (4.32 x 3.75 in, 109.7 x 952 mm); compression ratio: 8.2:1; max power (SAE): 300 hp at 4,800 rpm; max torque (SAE): 410 lb ft, 56.6 kg m at 3,400 rpm; max engine rpm: 5,200; 41.5 hp/l; cast iron cylinder block and head; 5 crankshaft bearings; valves: overhead, in line, push-rods and rockers, hydraulic tappets; camshafts: 1, at centre of Vee; lubrication: rotary pump, full flow filter, 6.5 imp pt, 7.8 US pt, 3.7 l; 1 Holley downdraught 4-barrel carburettor; fuel feed: mechanical pump; water-cooled, 28.2 imp pt, 33.8 US pt, 16 l, 2 electric thermostatic fans.

TRANSMISSION driving wheels: rear; gearbox: Torqueflite

JENSEN Jensen-Healey

JENSEN Interceptor III

LOTUS Europa Twin Cam

automatic transmission, hydraulic torque converter and planetary gears with 3 ratios, max ratio of converter at stall 2, possible manual selection; ratios: I 2.448, II 1.444, III 1, rev 2.194; lever: central; final drive: hypoid bevel, limited slip differential; axle ratio: 2.880; tyres: ER70 x VR15.

PERFORMANCE max speeds: (I) 56 mph, 90 km/h; (II) 95 mph, 153 km/h; (III) 135 mph, 217 km/h; power-weight ratio: 11.7 lb/hp, 5.3 kg/hp; carrying capacity: 706 lb, 320 kg; acceleration: 0-50 mph (0-80 km/h) 5 sec; speed in direct drive at 1,000 rpm: 26.5 mph, 42.6 km/h; fuel consumption: 17 m/imp gal, 14.2 m/US gal, 16.6 l x 100 km.

CHASSIS tubular; front suspension: independent, wishbones, coil springs, anti-roll bar, telescopic dampers; rear suspension: de Dion rigid axle, semi-elliptic leafsprings, transverse linkage bar, telescopic dampers.

STEERING rack-and-pinion, adjustable steering wheel, servo; turns lock to lock: 3.40.

BRAKES disc (diameter 10.75 in, 273 mm), internal radial fins, servo; swept area: front 219 sq in, 1,412 sq cm, rear 198 sq in, 1,277 sq cm, total 417 sq in, 2,689 sq cm.

ELECTRICAL EQUIPMENT 12 V; 67 Ah battery; 60 A alternator; Chrysler distributor; 4 halogen headlamps.

DIMENSIONS AND WEIGHT wheel base: 105.12 in, 2,670 mm; tracks: 55.91 in, 1,420 mm front, 56.69 in, 1,440 mm rear; length: 188 in, 4,775 mm; width: 69.05 in, 1,754 mm; height: 53 in, 1,346 mm; ground clearance: 5.50 in, 140 mm; dry weight: 3,506 lb, 1,590 kg; turning circle (between walls): 38 ft, 11.6 m; fuel tank: 20 imp gal, 24 US gal, 91 l.

BODY coupé; 2 doors; 4 seats, separate front seats, reclining backrests; electrically-controlled windows, electrically-heated rear window; air-conditioning.

PRACTICAL INSTRUCTIONS fuel: 91 oct petrol; engine sump oil: 6.5 imp pt, 7.8 US pt, 3.7 l, SAE 10W-30, change every 4,000 miles, 6,400 km; gearbox oil: 15.2 imp pt, 18.2 US pt, 8.6 l, Dexron automatic transmission fluid, change every 36,000 miles, 58,000 km; final drive oil: 3 imp pt, 3.6 US pt, 1.7 l, change every 12,000 miles, 19,300 km; greasing: every 4,000 miles, 6,400 km, 4 points.

SP

See Interceptor III, except for:

PRICE IN GB: £ 5,950.

ENGINE 440.1 cu in, 7,212 cc (4.33 x 3.75 in, 110 x 95.3 mm); compression ratio: 10.3:1; max power (SAE): 385 hp at 4,700 rpm; max torque (SAE): 490 lb ft, 67.6 kg m at 3,200 rpm; 53.4 hp/l; 3 Holley downdraught twin barrel carburettors; cooling system capacity: 28 imp pt, 33.6 US pt, 15.9 l.

TRANSMISSION width of rims: 6.5"; tyres: GR 70 VR x 15.

PERFORMANCE max speed: 150 mph, 241 km/h; power-weight ratio: 10.4 lb/hp, 4.7 kg/hp; fuel consumption: 14 m/imp gal, 11.6 m/US gal, 20.2 l x 100 km.

PRACTICAL INSTRUCTIONS fuel: 97 oct petrol; valve timing: 21° 67° 79° 25°; tyre pressure: front 28 psi, 2 atm, rear 32 psi, 2.2 atm.

LOTUS GREAT BRITAIN

Europa Twin Cam

PRICE IN GB: £ 1,595.

ENGINE central, 4 stroke; 4 cylinders, vertical, in line; 95.1 cu in, 1,558 cc (3.25 x 2.86 in, 82.5 x 72.7 mm); compression ratio: 9.5:1; max power (SAE): 105 hp at 6,000 rpm; max torque (SAE): 103 lb ft, 14.2 kg m at 4,500 rpm; max engine rpm: 6,500; 67.3 hp/l; cast iron cylinder block, light alloy head; 5 crankshaft bearings; valves: overhead, Vee-slanted, thimble tappets; camshafts: 2, overhead; lubrication: rotary pump, full flow filter by cartridge, 7.5 imp pt, 8.9 US pt, 4.2 l; 2 Dell'Orto 40 DHLA twin barrel carburettors; fuel feed: mechanical pump; water-cooled, 19 imp pt, 22.8 US pt, 10.8 l.

TRANSMISSION driving wheels: rear; clutch: single dry plate (diaphragm); gearbox: mechanical; gears: 4, fully synchronized; ratios: I 3.600, II 2.260, III 1.480, IV 1.030, rev 3.080; lever: central; final drive: hypoid bevel; axle ratio: 3.550; width of rims: 4.5"; tyres: 155 HR x 13.

PERFORMANCE max speed: 117 mph, 188 km/h; power-weight ratio: 14.7 lb/hp, 6.7 kg/hp; carrying capacity: 485 lb, 220 kg; acceleration: 0-50 mph (0-80 km/h) 5.3 sec; speed in top at 1,000 rpm: 17.9 mph, 28.8 km/h; fuel consumption: 32 m/imp gal, 26.7 m/US gal, 8.8 l x 100 km.

CHASSIS box-type backbone; front suspension: independent,

JENSEN Jensen-Healey

JENSEN Interceptor III

LOTUS Europa Twin Cam

wishbones, coil springs, anti-roll bar, telescopic dampers; rear suspension: independent, wishbones, semi-axles as upper arm, oblique lower trailing radius arms, coil springs/telescopic dampers units.

STEERING rack-and-pinion.

BRAKES front disc, rear drum, servo; swept area: front 8.6 sq in, 55 sq cm, rear 19.2 sq in, 124 sq cm, total 27.8 sq in, 179 sq cm.

ELECTRICAL EQUIPMENT 12 V; 39 Ah battery; alternator; Lucas distributor; 2 headlamps.

DIMENSIONS AND WEIGHT wheel base: 92 in, 2,337 mm; tracks: 53.50 in, 1,359 mm front, 53 in, 1,346 mm rear; length: 157.50 in, 4,000 mm; width: 64.50 in, 1,638 mm; height: 42.50 in, 1,080 mm; ground clearance: 6 in, 152 mm; dry weight: 1,513 lb, 686 kg; turning circle (between walls): 41 ft, 12.5 m; fuel tank: 12.5 imp gal, 15 US gal, 57 l.

BODY coupé in reinforced plastic material; 2 doors; 2 seats.

PRACTICAL INSTRUCTIONS fuel: 100 oct petrol; engine sump oil: 7 imp pt, 8.5 US pt, 4 l, SAE 20W-50; greasing: every 5,000 miles, 8,000 km, 4 points; tappet clearances: inlet 0.005-0.007 in, 0.12-0.17 mm, exhaust 0.009-0.011 in, 0.22-0.27 mm; valve timing: 26° 66° 66° 26°; tyre pressure: front 18 psi, 1.3 atm, rear 28 psi, 2 atm.

OPTIONAL ACCESSORIES 5.5" light alloy wheels with 175/70 front and 185/70 rear tyres.

Europa Special

See Europa Twin Cam, except for:

PRICE IN GB: £ 1,960.

ENGINE compression ratio: 10.3:1; max power (DIN): 126 hp at 6,500 rpm; max torque (DIN): 113 lb/ft, 15.6 kg m at 5,500 rpm; 80.8 hp/l.

TRANSMISSION width of rims: 5.5"; tyres: 175/70 x 13 front, 185/70 x 13 rear.

PERFORMANCE max speed: 125 mph, 201 km/h.

OPTIONAL ACCESSORIES 5-speed mechanical gearbox (I 3.620, II 2.330, III 1.600, IV 1.250, V 0.870).

Elan Sprint Drophead Coupé

PRICE IN GB: £ 1,940.

ENGINE front, 4 stroke; 4 cylinders, vertical, in line; 95.1 cu in, 1,558 cc (3.25 x 2.86 in, 82.5 x 72.7 mm); compression ratio: 10.3:1; max power (SAE): 126 hp at 6,500 rpm; max torque (SAE): 113 lb ft, 15.6 kg m at 5,500 rpm; max engine rpm: 6,800; 80.1 hp/l; cast iron cylinder block, light alloy head; 5 crankshaft bearings; valves: overhead, Vee-slanted, thimble tappets; camshafts: 2, overhead; lubrication: rotary pump, full flow filter, 7.5 imp pt, 8.9 US pt, 4.2 l; Dell'Orto 40 DMLA twin barrel carburettors; fuel feed: mechanical pump; water-cooled, 16.8 imp pt, 20.1 US pt, 9.5 l.

TRANSMISSION driving wheels: rear; clutch: single dry plate; gearbox: mechanical; gears: 4, fully synchronized; ratios: I 2.972, II 2.009, III 1.397, IV 1, rev 3.325; lever: central; final drive: hypoid bevel; axle ratio: 3.770; width of rims: 4.5"; tyres 155 HR x 13.

PERFORMANCE max speeds: (I) 41 mph, 66 km/h; (II) 61 mph, 98 km/h; (III) 88 mph, 141 km/h; (IV) 121 mph, 194 km/h; power-weight ratio: 12.1 lb/hp, 5 kg/hp; carrying capacity: 353 lb, 160 kg; speed in direct drive at 1,000 rpm: 17.4 mph, 28 km/h; fuel consumption: 30.5 m/imp gal, 25.3 m/US gal, 9.3 l x 100 km.

CHASSIS box-type backbone; front suspension: independent, wishbones, coil springs, anti-roll bar, telescopic dampers; rear suspension: independent, lower wishbones, coil springs/telescopic dampers struts.

STEERING rack-and-pinion, adjustable steering wheel; turns lock to lock: 2.67.

BRAKES disc (front diameter 9.50 in, 241 mm, rear 10 in, 254 mm), servo; swept area: front 144 sq in, 929 sq cm, rear 160 sq in, 1,032 sq cm, total 304 sq in, 1,961 sq cm.

ELECTRICAL EQUIPMENT 12 V; 39 Ah battery; 22 A dynamo; Lucas distributor; 2 retractable headlamps.

DIMENSIONS AND WEIGHT wheel base: 84 in, 2,134 mm; tracks: 47.09 in, 1,196 mm front, 47,06 in, 1,195 mm rear; length: 145 in, 3,683 mm; width: 56 in, 1,422 mm; height: 45.25 in, 1,149 mm; ground clearance: 6 in, 152 mm; dry weight: 1,540 lb, 698 kg; distribution of weight: 48% front, 52% rear; turning circle (between walls): 33.5 ft, 10.2 m; fuel tank: 9.2 imp gal, 11.1 US gal, 42 l.

ELAN SPRINT DROPHEAD COUPÉ

BODY convertible in plastic material; 2 doors; 2 seats.

PRACTICAL INSTRUCTIONS fuel: 98-100 oct petrol; engine sump oil: 7.5 imp pt, 8.7 US pt, 4.1 l, SAE 10W-30, change every 3,000 miles, 4,800 km; gearbox oil: 1.8 imp pt, 2.1 US pt, 1 l, SAE 80 EP, change every 6,000 miles, 9,700 km; final drive oil: 1.9 imp pt, 2.3 US pt, 1.1 l, SAE 90 EP, no change recommended; greasing: every 3,100 miles, 5,000 km, 2 points; tappet clearances: inlet 0.005-0.007 in, 0.13-0.17 mm, exhaust 0.009-0.011 in, 0.22-0.27 mm; valve timing: 26° 66° 66° 26°; tyre pressure: front 18 psi, 1.3 atm, rear 23 psi, 1.6 atm.

OPTIONAL ACCESSORIES 5-speed mechanical gearbox (I 3.200, II 2.000, III 1.370, IV 1, V 0.800); 3.550 axle ratio.

Elan Sprint Coupé

See Elan Sprint Drophead Coupé, except for:

PRICE IN GB: £ 1,940.

DIMENSIONS AND WEIGHT dry weight: 1,550 lb, 703 kg.

BODY coupé.

+ 2 'S' 130

See Elan Sprint Drophead Coupé, except for:

PRICE IN GB: £ 2,250.

TRANSMISSION width of rims: 5.5"; tyres: 165 HR x 13.

PERFORMANCE power-weight ratio: 16.5 lb/hp, 7.5 kg/hp; speed in direct drive at 1,000 rpm: 17.8 mph, 28.7 km/h; acceleration: standing ¼ mile 16.4 sec.

BRAKES disc (diameter 10 in, 254 mm); swept area: front 159 sq in, 1,025 sq cm, rear 159 sq in, 1,025 sq cm, total 318 sq in, 2,050 sq cm.

ELECTRICAL EQUIPMENT alternator.

DIMENSIONS AND WEIGHT wheel base: 96 in, 2,438 mm; tracks: 54 in, 1,372 mm front, 55 in, 1,397 mm rear; length: 169 in, 4,293 mm; width: 66 in, 1,676 mm; height: 47 in, 1,194 mm; dry weight: 2,086 lb, 946 kg; distribution of weight: 51% front, 49% rear; turning circle (between walls): 28 ft, 8.6 m.

BODY coupé; 2 + 2 seats, separate front seats, reclining backrests.

PRACTICAL INSTRUCTIONS tyre pressure: front 20 psi, 1.3 atm, rear 24 psi, 1.7 atm.

OPTIONAL ACCESSORIES only 5-speed mechanical gearbox.

MG GREAT BRITAIN

Midget Mk III

PRICE IN GB: £ 829.
PRICE IN USA: £ 2,520.

ENGINE front, 4 stroke; 4 cylinders, vertical, in line; 77.8 cu in, 1,275 cc (2.78 x 3.20 in, 70.6 x 81.3 mm); compression ratio: 8.8:1; max power (DIN): 64 hp at 5,800 rpm; max torque (DIN): 72 lb ft, 9.9 kg m at 3,000 rpm; max engine rpm: 6,200; 50.2 hp/l; cast iron cylinder block and head; 3 crankshaft bearings; valves: overhead, push-rods and rockers; camshafts: 1, side; lubrication: eccentric pump, full flow filter, 7 imp pt, 8.5 US pt, 4 l; 2 SU type HS 2 semi-downdraught carburettors; fuel feed: electric pump; water-cooled, 10.6 imp pt, 12.7 US pt, 6 l.

TRANSMISSION driving wheels: rear; clutch: single dry plate (diaphragm), hydraulically controlled; gearbox: mechanical; gears: 4, II, III and IV synchronized; ratios: I 3.205, II 1.949, III 1.359, IV 1, rev 4.123; lever: central; final drive: hypoid bevel; axle ratio: 3.900; tyres: 145 x 13.

PERFORMANCE max speeds: (I) 30 mph, 48 km/h; (II) 50 mph, 80 km/h; (III) 71 mph, 114 km/h; (IV) 95 mph, 153 km/h; power-weight ratio: 23.6 lb/hp, 10.7 kg/hp; carrying capacity: 353 lb, 160 kg; acceleration: standing ¼ mile 19.1 sec, 0-50 mph (0-80 km/h) 9.2 sec; speed in direct drive at 1,000 rpm: 15.5 mph, 24.9 km/h; fuel consumption: 35.3 m/imp gal, 29.4 m/US gal, 8 l x 100 km.

CHASSIS integral; front suspension: independent, wishbones, coil springs, lever dampers as upper arms; rear suspension: rigid axle, semi-elliptic leafsprings, lever dampers.

LOTUS + 2 'S' 130

MG Midget Mk III

MG MGB GT

STEERING rack-and-pinion; turns lock to lock: 2.30.

BRAKES front disc (diameter 8.23 in, 209 mm), rear drum.

ELECTRICAL EQUIPMENT 12 V; 43 Ah battery; 22 A dynamo; Lucas distributor; 2 headlamps.

DIMENSIONS AND WEIGHT wheel base: 80 in, 2,032 mm; tracks: 46.30 in, 1,176 mm front, 44.75 in, 1,137 mm rear; length: 137.60 in, 3,495 mm; width: 54.90 in, 1,394 mm; height: 48.62 in, 1,235 mm; ground clearance: 5 in, 127 mm; dry weight: 1,510 lb, 685 kg; distribution of weight: 52.4% front, 47.6% rear; turning circle (between walls): 32 ft, 9.8 m; fuel tank: 6 imp gal, 7.1 US gal, 27 l.

BODY convertible; 2 doors; 2 seats.

PRACTICAL INSTRUCTIONS fuel: 98 oct petrol; engine sump oil: 6.5 imp pt, 7.8 US pt, 3.7 l, SAE 10W-30 (winter) 20W-50 (summer), change every 6,000 miles, 9,700 km; gearbox oil: 2.3 imp pt, 2.7 US pt, 1.3 l, SAE 10W-30 (winter) 20W-50 (summer); final drive oil: 1.4 imp pt, 1.7 US pt, 0.8 l, SAE 90; greasing: every 3,000 miles, 4,800 km, 8 points; tappet clearances: inlet 0.012 in, 0.30 mm, exhaust 0.012 in, 0.30 mm; valve timing: 5° 45° 51° 21°; tyre pressure: front 18 psi, 1.3 atm, rear 20 psi, 1.4 atm.

VARIATIONS

ENGINE 8:1 compression ratio.
TRANSMISSION (only for export) 5.20 x 13 tyres.

OPTIONAL ACCESSORIES oil cooler; wire wheels; anti-roll bar on front suspension; hardtop; tonneau cover.

MGB GT

PRICE IN GB: £ 1,298.
PRICE IN USA: $ 3,615.

ENGINE front, 4 stroke; 4 cylinders, in line; 109.7 cu in, 1,798 cc (3.16 x 3.50 in, 80.3 x 88.9 mm); compression ratio: 8.8:1; max power (DIN): 95 hp at 5,400 rpm; max torque (DIN): 110 lb ft, 15.2 kg m at 3,000 rpm; max engine rpm: 6,200; 52.8 hp/l; cast iron cylinder block and head; 5 crankshaft bearings; valves: overhead, push-rods and rockers; camshafts: 1, side; lubrication: eccentric pump, full flow filter, oil cooler, 6.5 imp pt, 7.8 US pt, 3.7 l; 2 SU type HS 4 (HIF4 only for export) semi-downdraught carburettors; fuel feed: electric pump; water-cooled, 10 imp pt, 12 US pt, 5.7 l.

TRANSMISSION driving wheels: rear; clutch: single dry plate (diaphragm), hydraulically controlled; gearbox: mechanical; gears: 4, II, III and IV synchronized; ratios: I 3.439, II 2.166, III 1.381, IV 1, rev 3.094; lever: central; final drive: hypoid bevel; axle ratio: 3.909; width of rims 5"; tyres: 165 SR x 14.

PERFORMANCE max speeds: (I) 32 mph, 51 km/h; (II) 51 mph, 82 km/h; (III) 81 mph, 130 km/h; (IV) 107 mph, 173 km/h; power-weight ratio: 20.1 lb/hp, 9.1 kg/hp; carrying capacity: 529 lb, 240 kg; acceleration: 0-50 mph (0-80 km/h) 9 sec; speed in direct drive at 1,000 rpm: 18 mph, 28.9 km/h; fuel consumption: 25.4 m/imp gal, 21.2 m/US gal 11.1 l x 100 km.

CHASSIS integral; front suspension: independent, wishbones, coil springs, anti-roll bar, lever dampers as upper arms; rear suspension: rigid axle, semi-elliptic leafsprings lever dampers.

STEERING rack-and-pinion; turns lock to lock: 2.93.

BRAKES front disc (diameter 10.75 in, 273 mm), rear drum; swept area: front 209.2 sq in, 1,350 sq cm, rear 106 sq in 684 sq cm, total 315.2 sq in, 2,034 sq cm.

ELECTRICAL EQUIPMENT 12 V; 2 60 Ah batteries; 16 A alternator; Lucas distributor; 2 headlamps.

DIMENSIONS AND WEIGHT wheel base: 91 in, 2,311 mm tracks: 49 in, 1,245 mm front, 49.25 in, 1,251 mm rear length: 153.18 in, 3,891 mm; width: 59.94 in, 1,522 mm height: 49.50 in, 1,257 mm; ground clearance: 5 in, 127 mm dry weight: 2,220 lb, 1,007 kg; turning circle (between walls): 32.6 ft, 9.9 m; fuel tank: 12 imp gal, 14.5 US gal 55 l.

BODY coupé; 2 doors; 2 + 2 seats, separate front seats

PRACTICAL INSTRUCTIONS fuel: 98-100 oct petrol; engine sump oil: 6 imp pt, 7.2 US pt, 3.4 l, SAE 10W-30 (winter) 20W-50 (summer), change every 3,000 miles, 4,800 km gearbox oil: 4.6 imp pt, 5.5 US pt, 2.6 l, SAE 20W-50 final drive oil: 1.5 imp pt, 1.9 US pt, 0.9 l, SAE 90 greasing: every 3,000 miles, 4,800 km, 8 points; tappet clearances: inlet 0.015 in. 0.38 mm, exhaust 0.015 in 0.38 mm; valve timing: 16° 56° 51° 21°; tyre pressure front 21 psi, 1.5 atm, rear 24 psi, 1.7 atm.

LOTUS Elan Sprint Coupé

MG Midget Mk III

MG MGB GT

OPTIONAL ACCESSORIES Borg-Warner 35 automatic transmission, hydraulic torque converter and planetary gears with 3 ratios (I 2.389, II 1.450, III 1, rev 2.090), max ratio of converter at stall 2, possible manual selection, with 8:1 compression ratio engine, max power (DIN) 91 hp at 5,400 rpm, max torque (DIN) 105 lb ft, 14.5 kg m at 3,000 rpm, 50.6 hp/l, max speeds (I) 47 mph, 75 km/h, (II) 77 mph, 124 km/h, (III) 100 mph, 161 km/h, power-weight ratio 24.5 lb/hp, 11 kg/hp; Laycock-de Normanville overdrive on III and IV, 0.820 ratio; servo brake; wire wheels with 4.5'' wide rims; electrically-heated rear window.

MGB Sports

See MGB GT, except for:

PRICE IN GB: £ 1,169.
PRICE IN USA: $ 3,320.

TRANSMISSION tyres: 165 SR x 14.

PERFORMANCE power-weight ratio: 19.1 lb/hp, 8.7 kg/hp; acceleration: standing ¼ mile 18.7 sec, 0-50 mph (0-80 km/h) 8.5 sec.

DIMENSIONS AND WEIGHT dry weight: 2,100 lb, 953 kg.

BODY sports; 2 seats.

OPTIONAL ACCESSORIES hardtop; tonneau cover; electrically-heated rear window not available.

MINI (BRITISH LEYLAND)
GREAT BRITAIN

---

850 Saloon

PRICE IN GB: £ 574.

ENGINE front, transverse, 4 stroke; 4 cylinders, vertical, in line; 51.7 cu in, 848 cc (2.48 x 2.69 in, 63 x 68.4 mm); compression ratio: 8.3:1; max power (DIN): 34 hp at 5,500 rpm; max torque (DIN): 44 lb ft, 6.1 kg m at 2,900 rpm; max engine rpm: 5,500; 40.1 hp/l; cast iron cylinder block and head; 3 crankshaft bearings; valves: overhead, in line, push-rods and rockers; camshafts: 1, side; lubrication: eccentric pump, full flow filter, 8.4 imp pt, 10.1 US pt, 4.8 l; 1 SU type HS 2 semi-downdraught carburettor; fuel feed: mechanical pump; water-cooled, 6.2 imp pt, 7.4 US pt, 3.5 l.

TRANSMISSION driving wheels: front; clutch: single dry plate (diaphragm), hydraulically controlled; gearbox: mechanical, in unit with engine; gears: 4, fully synchronized; ratios: I 3.525, II 2.218, III 1.433, IV 1, rev 3.544; lever: central; final drive: helical spur gears, in unit with engine and gearbox; axle ratio: 3.765; tyres: 5.20 x 10.

PERFORMANCE max speeds: (I) 22 mph, 35 km/h; (II) 35 mph, 56 km/h; (III) 54 mph, 87 km/h; (IV) 73 mph, 117 km/h; power-weight ratio: 39.2 lb/hp, 17.8 kg/hp; carrying capacity: 706 lb, 320 kg; acceleration: standing ¼ mile 23.6 sec, 0-50 mph (0-80 km/h) 18.3 sec; speed in direct drive at 1,000 rpm: 14.8 mph, 23.8 km/h; fuel consumption: 42.8 m/imp gal, 35.6 m/US gal, 6.6 l x 100 km.

CHASSIS integral, front and rear auxiliary frames; front suspension: independent, wishbones, hydrolastic (liquid) rubber cone springs, hydraulic connecting pipes to rear wheels; rear suspension: independent, swinging longitudinal trailing arms, hydrolastic (liquid) rubber cone springs, hydraulic connecting pipes to front wheels, pitch control tension springs.

STEERING rack-and-pinion; turns lock to lock: 2.33.

BRAKES drum, single circuit, 2 front leading shoes; swept area: front 60.9 sq in, 393 sq cm, rear 54.9 sq in, 354 sq cm, total 115.8 sq in, 747 sq cm.

ELECTRICAL EQUIPMENT 12 V; 30 Ah battery; 22 A dynamo; Lucas distributor; 2 headlamps.

DIMENSIONS AND WEIGHT wheel base: 80.16 in, 2,036 mm; tracks: 47.44 in, 1,205 mm front, 45.87 in, 1,165 mm rear; length: 120.24 in, 3,054 mm; width: 55.51 in, 1,410 mm; height: 52.99 in, 1,346 mm; ground clearance: 6.14 in, 156 mm; dry weight: 1,398 lb, 634 kg; distribution of weight: 61% front, 39% rear; turning circle (between walls): 29.5 ft, 9 m; fuel tank: 5.5 imp gal, 6.6 US gal, 25 l.

BODY saloon/sedan; 2 doors; 4 seats, separate front seats.

PRACTICAL INSTRUCTIONS fuel: 94 oct petrol; engine sump, gearbox and final drive oil: 7.6 imp pt, 9.1 US pt, 4.3 l, SAE 20W-50, change every 6,000 miles, 9,700 km; greasing: every 3,000 miles, 4,800 km, 8 points; tappet clearances: inlet 0.012 in, 0.30 mm, exhaust 0.012 in, 0.30

850 SALOON

mm; valve timing: 5° 45° 40° 10°; tyre pressure: front 24 psi, 1.7 atm, rear 21 psi, 1.5 atm.

VARIATIONS

ENGINE 8.8:1 compression ratio.

OPTIONAL ACCESSORIES AP automatic transmission, hydraulic torque converter with 2 conic bevel gears (twin concentric differential-like gear clusters) with 4 ratios (I 2.690, II 1.845, III 1.460, IV 1.269, rev 2.690), operated by 3 brake bands and 2 multi-disc clutches, max ratio of converter at stall 2, possible manual selection, with 8.8:1 compression ratio; reclining backrests; electrically-heated rear window.

1000 Saloon

See 850 Saloon, except for:

PRICE IN GB: £ 658.

ENGINE 60.9 cu in, 998 cc (2.54 x 3 in, 64.6 x 76.2 mm); max power (DIN): 38 hp at 5,250 rpm; max torque (DIN): 52 lb ft, 7.2 kg m at 2,700 rpm; 38.1 hp/l.

TRANSMISSION axle ratio: 3.444.

PERFORMANCE max speeds: (I) 26 mph, 42 km/h; (II) 49 mph, 79 km/h; (III) 62 mph, 100 km/h; (IV) 75 mph, 120 km/h; power-weight ratio: 36.8 lb/hp, 16.7 kg/hp; carrying capacity: 706 lb, 320 kg; acceleration: standing ¼ mile 22.5 sec, 0-50 mph (0-80 km/h) 13.7 sec; speed in direct drive at 1,000 rpm: 16.5 mph, 26.5 km/h.

OPTIONAL ACCESSORIES AP automatic transmission with 8.9:1 compression ratio, max power (SAE) 41 hp at 4,850 rpm, max torque (SAE) 52 lb ft, 7.2 kg m at 2,750 rpm, 1 SU type HS 4 semi-downdraught carburettor, power-weight ratio 34 lb/hp, 15.4 kg/hp, fuel consumption 39.8 m/imp gal, 33.1 m/US gal, 7.1 l x 100 km.

Clubman Saloon

See 1000 Saloon, except for:

PRICE IN GB: £ 702.

TRANSMISSION tyres: 145 x 10 (5.20 x 10 only for export).

PERFORMANCE max speeds: (I) 25 mph, 40 km/h; (II) 41 mph, 66 km/h; (III) 64 mph, 103 km/h; (IV) 73 mph, 117 km/h; power-weight ratio: 37 lb/hp, 16.8 kg/hp; acceleration: 0-50 mph (0-80 km/h) 14.9 sec.

STEERING turns lock to lock: 2.72.

DIMENSIONS AND WEIGHT wheel base: 80.16 in, 2,036 mm; tracks: 47.44 in, 1,205 mm front, 45.88 in, 1,165 mm rear; length: 124.64 in, 3,166 mm; dry weight: 1,406 lb, 637 kg; turning circle (between walls): 30 ft, 9.2 m.

OPTIONAL ACCESSORIES AP automatic transmission, hydraulic torque converter with 2 conic bevel gears (twin concentric differential-like gears clusters) with 4 ratios (I 2.690, II 1.845, III 1.460, IV 1.269, rev 2.690), operated by 3 brake bands and 2 multi-disc clutches, max ratio of converter at stall 2, possible manual selection, with 8.9:1 compression ratio, max power (SAE) 41 hp at 4,850 rpm, max torque (SAE) 52 lb ft, 7.2 kg m at 2,750 rpm, 1 SU type HS 4 semi-downdraught carburettor, power-weight ratio 34.3 lb/hp, 15.6 kg/hp, fuel consumption 39.8 m/imp gal, 33.1 m/US gal, 7.1 l x 100 km; alternator (with 45 Ah battery).

Clubman Estate Car

See Clubman Saloon, except for:

PRICE IN GB: £ 755.

PERFORMANCE power-weight ratio: 38 lb/hp, 17.2 kg/hp; acceleration: 0-50 mph (0-80 km/h) 15.1 sec.

CHASSIS integral, front and rear auxiliary frames; front suspension: independent, wishbones, rubber cone springs, telescopic dampers; rear suspension: independent, swinging longitudinal trailing arms, rubber cone springs, telescopic dampers.

DIMENSIONS AND WEIGHT wheel base: 84.15 in, 2,138 mm; length: 133.92 in, 3,401 mm; height: 53.50 in, 1,359 mm; dry weight: 1,444 lb, 655 kg; fuel tank: 6.7 imp gal, 7.9 US gal, 30 l.

BODY estate car/station wagon; 2 + 1 doors.

OPTIONAL ACCESSORIES electrically-heated rear window not available.

MINI (BRITISH LEYLAND) 850 Saloon

MINI (BRITISH LEYLAND) Clubman Saloon

MORGAN Plus 8

RELIANT Regal 3/30 Saloon

RELIANT Scimitar GTE

ROLLS-ROYCE Silver Shadow 4-door Saloon

26.2 mph, 42.2 km/h; fuel consumption: 15 m/imp gal, 12.5 m/US gal, 18.8 l x 100 km.

CHASSIS integral, front and rear auxiliary frames; front suspension: independent, wishbones, coil springs, automatic levelling control, telescopic dampers; rear suspension: independent, semi-trailing arms, coil springs, automatic levelling control, telescopic dampers.

STEERING recirculating ball, progressive servo, right-hand drive; turns lock to lock: 3.25.

BRAKES disc [diameter (twin calipers) 11 in, 279 mm], 3 independent circuits, servo; swept area: front 227 sq in, 1,464 sq cm, rear 287 sq in, 1,851 sq cm, total 514 sq in, 3,315 sq cm.

ELECTRICAL EQUIPMENT 12 V; 64 Ah battery; 35 A alternator; Lucas distributor; 4 headlamps.

DIMENSIONS AND WEIGHT wheel base: 119.50 in, 3,035 mm; tracks: 57.50 in, 1,460 mm front, 57.50 in, 1,460 mm rear; length: 203.50 in, 5,169 mm; width: 72 in, 1,829 mm; height: 59.75 in, 1,518 mm; ground clearance: 6.50 in, 165 mm; dry weight: 4,556 lb, 2,067 kg; turning circle (between walls): 38 ft, 11.6 m; fuel tank: 24 imp gal, 28.8 US gal, 109 l.

BODY saloon/sedan; 4 doors; 5-6 seats, separate front seats, adjustable reclining backrests; headrests, air-conditioning, electrically-controlled windows.

PRACTICAL INSTRUCTIONS fuel: 98-100 oct petrol; engine sump oil: 14.1 imp pt, 16.9 US pt, 8 l, SAE 10W-30, change every 6,000 miles, 9,700 km; gearbox oil: 23.9 imp pt, 28.8 US pt, 13.6 l, change every 24,000 miles, 38,600 km; final drive oil: 4 imp pt, 4.9 US pt, 2.3 l, change every 24,000 miles, 38,600 km; power-assisted steering and automatic levelling control oil: change every 20,000 miles, 32,000 km; greasing: every 12,000 miles, 19,300 km; valve timing: 26° 52° 68° 10°; tyre pressure: front 26 psi, 1.8 atm, rear 26 psi, 1.8 atm.

VARIATIONS

ENGINE 8:1 compression ratio.

OPTIONAL ACCESSORIES iodine headlamps.

Silver Shadow Long Wheelbase 4-door Saloon

See Silver Shadow 4-door Saloon, except for:

PRICE IN GB: £ 10,020.
PRICE IN USA: $ 28,700.

TRANSMISSION gearbox ratios: I 2.050, II 1.050, III 1, rev 2.

PERFORMANCE max speeds: (I) 59 mph, 95 km/h; (II) 114 mph, 183 km/h; (III) 120 mph, 193 km/h.

DIMENSIONS AND WEIGHT wheel base: 123.50 in, 3,137 mm; length: 207.50 in, 5,270 mm; turning circle (between walls): 39 ft, 11.9 m.

Silver Shadow Long Wheelbase 4-door Saloon with division

See Silver Shadow Long Wheelbase 4-door Saloon, except for:

PRICE IN GB: £ 10,685.

BODY glass partition.

2-door Corniche

See Silver Shadow 4-door Saloon, except for:

PRICE IN GB: £ 11,400.
PRICE IN USA: $ 33,000.

TRANSMISSION tyres: 205 x 15.

PERFORMANCE max speed: 120 mph, 193 km/h; fuel consumption: 14.5 m/imp gal, 12.1 m/US gal, 19.5 l x 100 km.

DIMENSIONS AND WEIGHT height: 58.66 in, 1,490 mm.

BODY coupé; 2 doors.

Corniche Convertible

See 2-door Corniche, except for:

PRICE IN GB: £ 11,915.
PRICE IN USA $ 35,600.

BODY convertible.

Phantom VI 7-passenger Limousine

PRICE IN GB: £ 12,875.

ENGINE front, 4 stroke; 8 cylinders, Vee-slanted at 90°; 380 cu in, 6,230 cc; compression ratio: 9:1; light alloy cylinder block and head, wet liners; 5 crankshaft bearings; valves: overhead, in line, slanted, push-rods and rockers, hydraulic tappets; camshafts: 1, at centre of Vee; lubrication: gear pump, full flow filter, 14.1 imp pt, 16.9 US pt, 8 l; 2 SU type HD 8 horizontal carburettors; fuel feed: 2 electric pumps; water-cooled, 23.1 imp pt, 27.7 US pt, 13.1 l.

TRANSMISSION driving wheels: rear; gearbox: Rolls-Royce automatic transmission, hydraulic coupling and planetary gears with 4 ratios, possible manual selection; ratios: I 3.310, II 2.620, III 1.440, IV 1, rev 4.290; lever: steering column; final drive: hypoid bevel; axle ratio: 3.890; tyres: 8.90 x 15.

PERFORMANCE max speeds: (I) 18 mph, 29 km/h; (II) 32 mph, 51 km/h; (III) 62 mph, 100 km/h; (IV) 100 mph, 161 km/h; carrying capacity: 1,235 lb, 560 kg; acceleration: standing ¼ mile 19.4 sec, 0-50 mph (0-80 km/h) 9.7 sec; speed in direct drive at 1,000 rpm: 22.5 mph, 36.2 km/h; fuel consumption: 14 m/imp gal, 11.6 m/US gal, 20.2 l x 100 km.

CHASSIS box-type ladder frame; front suspension: independent, wishbones, coil springs, anti-roll bar, lever dampers; rear suspension: rigid axle, asymmetrical semi-elliptic leafsprings, Z-type transverse linkage bar, electrically-adjustable lever dampers.

STEERING worm and roller, progressive servo (50%-80%); turns lock to lock: 4.25.

BRAKES drum, 2 independent hydraulic circuits, mechanical servo; swept area: total 424 sq in, 2,735 sq cm.

ELECTRICAL EQUIPMENT 12 V; 68 Ah battery; 472 W dynamo; AC Delco distributor; 4 headlamps.

DIMENSIONS AND WEIGHT wheel base: 144 in, 3,658 mm; tracks: 60.87 in, 1,546 mm front, 64 in, 1,626 mm rear; length: 238 in, 6,045 mm; width: 79 in, 2,007 mm; height: 69 in, 1,753 mm; ground clearance: 7.25 in, 184 mm; dry weight: 5,713 lb, 2,591 kg; distribution of weight: 48% front, 52% rear; turning circle (between walls): 49.2 ft, 15 m; fuel tank: 24 imp gal, 28.8 US gal, 109 l.

BODY limousine; 4 doors; 7 seats, separate front seats; glass partition, air-conditioning electrically-controlled windows.

PRACTICAL INSTRUCTIONS fuel: 100 oct petrol; engine sump oil: 12 imp pt, 14.4 US pt, 6.8 l, SAE 10W-30, change every 6,000 miles, 9,700 km; gearbox oil: 20.1 imp pt, 24.1 US pt, 11.4 l, change every 24,000 miles, 38,600 km; final drive oil: 1.6 imp pt, 1.9 US pt, 0.9 l, SAE 90, change every 24,000 miles, 38,600 km; greasing: every 12,000 miles, 19,300 km, 21 points; valve timing: 20° 61° 62° 19°; tyre pressure: front 22 psi, 1.5 atm, rear 27 psi, 1.9 atm.

VARIATIONS

ENGINE 8:1 compression ratio.

ROLLS-ROYCE Phantom VI 7-passenger Limousine

ROVER 2000 SC

ROVER 3500

ROVER GREAT BRITAIN

2000 SC

PRICE IN GB: £ 1,545.

ENGINE front, 4 stroke; 4 cylinders, vertical, in line; 120.7 cu in, 1,978 cc (3.37 x 3.37 in, 85.5 x 85.5 mm); compression ratio: 9:1; max power (DIN): 89 hp at 5,000 rpm; max torque (DIN): 108 lb ft, 15 kg m at 2,500 rpm; max engine rpm: 6,000; 45 hp/l; cast iron cylinder block, light alloy head; 5 crankshaft bearings; valves: overhead, thimble tappets; camshafts: 1, overhead; lubrication: rotary pump, full flow filter, 8.5 imp pt, 10.2 US pt, 4.8 l; 1 SU type HS 6 horizontal carburettor; fuel feed: mechanical pump; water-cooled, 14 imp pt, 16.9 US pt, 8 l.

TRANSMISSION driving wheels: rear; clutch: single dry plate (diaphragm), hydraulically controlled; gearbox: mechanical; gears: 4, fully synchronized; ratios: I 3.625, II 2.133, III 1.391, IV 1, rev 3.430; lever: central; final drive: hypoid bevel; axle ratio: 3.540; width of rims: 5"; tyres: 165 SR x 14.

PERFORMANCE max speeds: (I) 32 mph, 51 km/h; (II) 55 mph, 88 km/h; (III) 84 mph, 135 km/h; (IV) 100 mph, 161 km/h; power-weight ratio: 30.2 lb/hp, 13.7 kg/hp; carrying capacity: 882 lb, 400 kg; acceleration: standing ¼ mile 19.6 sec, 0-50 mph (0-80 km/h) 10.1 sec; speed in direct drive at 1,000 rpm: 19.1 mph, 30.7 km/h; fuel consumption: 26.2 m/imp gal, 21.8 m/US gal, 10.8 l x 100 km.

CHASSIS integral; front suspension: independent, upper leading arm, lower transverse arm, horizontal coil springs, anti-roll bar, telescopic dampers; rear suspension: de Dion rigid axle with variable track, fixed length semi-axle, transverse linkage bar from final drive, longitudinal Watt linkage, coil springs, telescopic dampers.

STEERING worm and roller, adjustable steering wheel; turns lock to lock: 3.75.

BRAKES disc (front diameter 10.37 in, 263 mm, rear 10.70 in, 272 mm), servo; swept area: front 204 sq in, 1,316 sq cm, rear 152 sq in, 980 sq cm, total 354 sq in, 2,296 sq cm.

ELECTRICAL EQUIPMENT 12 V; 60 Ah battery; 45 A alternator; Lucas distributor; 4 headlamps.

DIMENSIONS AND WEIGHT wheel base: 103.37 in, 2,625 mm; tracks: 53.37 in, 1,355 mm front, 52.50 in, 1,333 mm rear; length: 179.31 in, 4,554 mm; width: 66 in, 1,676 mm; height: 55.25 in, 1,403 mm; ground clearance: 6 in, 152 mm; dry weight: 2,692 lb, 1221 kg; distribution of weight: 53.7% front, 46.3% rear; turning circle (between walls): 35.4 ft, 10.8 m; fuel tank: 11.9 imp gal, 14.3 US gal, 54 l.

BODY saloon/sedan; 4 doors; 4-5 seats, separate front seats, reclining backrests.

PRACTICAL INSTRUCTIONS fuel: 95 oct petrol; engine sump oil: 8.5 imp pt, 10.2 US pt, 4.8 l, change every 6,000 miles, 9,000 km; gearbox oil: 1.7 imp pt, 2.1 US pt, 1 l, 90 EP, change every 20,000 miles, 32,000 km; final drive oil: 2.2 imp pt, 2.5 US pt, 1.2 l, 90 EP, change every 20,000 miles, 32,000 km; greasing: every 5,000 miles, 8,000 km, 1 point; tappet clearances: inlet 0.008-0.010 in, 0.20-0.25 mm, exhaust 0.013-0.015 in, 0.33-0.38 mm; valve timing: 14° 46° 44° 16°; tyre pressure: front 26 psi, 1.8 atm, rear 28 psi, 2 atm.

OPTIONAL ACCESSORIES electric immersion heater for cylinder block; headrests on front and rear seats; air-conditioning; sunshine roof; electrically-heated rear window.

2000 Automatic

See 2000 SC, except for:

PRICE IN GB: £ 1,645.

TRANSMISSION gearbox: Borg-Warner 35 automatic transmission, hydraulic torque converter and planetary gears with 3 ratios, max ratio of converter at stall 2.1, possible manual selection; ratios: I 2.390, II 1.450, III 1, rev 2.090.

PERFORMANCE max speeds: (I) 39 mph, 62 km/h; (II) 68 mph, 109 km/h; (III) 100 mph, 161 km/h; power-weight ratio: 31.4 lb/ hp, 14.3 kg/hp; acceleration: standing ¼ mile 21.3 sec, 0-50 mph (0-80 km/h) 12.7 sec; fuel consumption: 24 m/imp gal, 20.1 m/US gal, 11.7 l x 100 km.

DIMENSIONS AND WEIGHT dry weight: 2,797 lb, 1,269 kg.

PRACTICAL INSTRUCTIONS valve timing: 18° 42° 48° 12°.

2000 TC

See 2000 SC, except for:

PRICE IN GB: £ 1,640.

ENGINE compression ratio: 10:1; max power (DIN): 109 hp at 5,500 rpm; max torque (DIN): 124 lb ft, 17.2 kg m at 2,750 rpm; max engine rpm: 6,500; 57.4 hp/l; 2 SU type HIF6 horizontal carburettors.

PERFORMANCE max speeds: (I) 36 mph, 58 km/h; (II) 59 mph, 95 km/h; (III) 91 mph, 146 km/h; (IV) 112 mph, 180 km/h; power-weight ratio: 25 lb/hp, 11.3 kg/hp; acceleration: standing ¼ mile 18.5 sec, 0-50 mph (0-80 km/h) 8.2 sec; speed in direct drive at 1,000 rpm: 19.1 mph, 30.7 km/h; fuel consumption: 25.6 m/imp gal, 21.4 m/US gal, 11 l x 100 km.

DIMENSIONS AND WEIGHT dry weight: 2,739 lb, 1,242 kg.

PRACTICAL INSTRUCTIONS fuel: 100 oct petrol; valve timing: 14° 46° 44° 16°.

VARIATIONS

ENGINE (only for export), 9:1 compression ratio, max power (DIN) 104 hp at 5,500 rpm, max torque (DIN) 118 lb ft, 16.3 kg m at 3,750 rpm, 52.8 hp/l.
PERFORMANCE max speed 110 mph, 177 km/h, power-weight ratio 26.2 lb/hp, 11.9 kg/hp.
PRACTICAL INSTRUCTIONS 95 oct petrol.

OPTIONAL ACCESSORIES oil cooler; wire wheels.

ROLLS-ROYCE Phantom VI 7-passenger Limousine

ROVER 2000 SC

ROVER 3500

3500

PRICE IN GB: £ 1,890.

ENGINE front, 4 stroke; 8 cylinders, Vee-slanted at 90°; 215 cu in, 3,528 cc (3.50 x 2.80 in, 88.9 x 71.1 mm); compression ratio: 10.5:1; max power (DIN): 144 hp at 5,000 rpm; max torque (DIN): 197 lb ft, 27.2 kg m at 2,700 rpm; max engine rpm: 5,200; 40.8 hp/l; light alloy cylinder block and head, dry liners; 5 crankshaft bearings; valves: overhead, in line, push-rods and rockers, hydraulic tappets; camshafts: 1, at centre of Vee; lubrication: gear pump, full flow filter, 9 imp pt, 10.8 US pt, 5.1 l; 2 SU type HIF 6 semi-downdraught carburettors; fuel feed: mechanical pump; water-cooled, 15.3 imp pt, 18.4 US pt, 8.7 l.

TRANSMISSION driving wheels: rear; gearbox: Borg-Warner 35 automatic transmission, hydraulic torque converter and planetary gears with 3 ratios, max ratio of converter at stall 2.1, possible manual selection; ratios: I 2.390, II 1.450, III 1, rev 2.090; lever: central; final drive: hypoid bevel; axle ratio: 3.080; width of rims: 5.5"; tyres: 185 HR x 14.

PERFORMANCE max speeds: (I) 50 mph, 80 km/h; (II) 80 mph, 128 km/h; (III) 118 mph, 190 km/h; power-weight ratio: 19.9 lb/hp, 9 kg/hp; carrying capacity: 975 lb, 442 kg; acceleration: standing ¼ mile 18 sec, 0-50 mph (0-80 km/h) 7.7 sec; speed in direct drive at 1,000 rpm: 23.5 mph, 37.8 km/h; fuel consumption: 22.7 m/imp gal, 19 m/US gal, 12.4 l x 100 km.

CHASSIS integral; front suspension: independent, upper leading arm, lower transverse arm, horizontal coil springs, anti-roll bar, telescopic dampers; rear suspension: de Dion rigid axle with variable track, fixed length semi-axles, transverse linkage bar from final drive, longitudinal Watt linkage, coil springs, telescopic dampers.

STEERING recirculating ball, adjustable steering wheel, variable ratio servo; turns lock to lock: 4.50.

BRAKES disc (front diameter 10.82 in, 275 mm, rear 10.69 in, 271 mm), servo; swept area: front 220 sq in, 1,419 sq cm, rear 152 sq in, 980 sq cm, total 372 sq in, 2,399 sq cm.

ELECTRICAL EQUIPMENT 12 V; 60 Ah battery; 45 A alternator; Lucas distributor; 4 headlamps.

DIMENSIONS AND WEIGHT wheel base: 103.37 in, 2,625 mm; tracks: 53.37 in, 1,355 mm front, 51.75 in, 1,314 mm rear; length: 179.75 in, 4,566 mm; width: 66 in, 1,676 mm; height: 55.75 in, 1,416 mm; ground clearance: 6.13 in, 155 mm; dry weight: 2,861 lb, 1,298 kg; turning circle (between walls): 35.7 ft, 10.9 m; fuel tank: 15 imp gal, 18 US gal, 68 l.

BODY saloon/sedan; 4 doors; 4-5 seats, separate front seats, reclining backrests.

PRACTICAL INSTRUCTIONS fuel: 100 oct petrol; engine sump oil: 9 imp pt, 10.8 US pt, 5.1 l, SAE 20-30, change every 6,000 miles, 9,000 km; gearbox oil: 14 imp pt, 16.7 US pt, 7.9 l, ATF, no change recommended; final drive oil: 2.3 imp pt, 2.7 US pt, 1.3 l, SAE 90 EP, change every 20,000 miles, 32,000 km; greasing: every 6,000 miles, 9,000 km, 1 point; valve timing: 30° 75° 68° 37°; tyre pressure: front 28 psi, 2 atm, rear 30 psi, 2.1 atm.

OPTIONAL ACCESSORIES headrests on front and rear seats; sushine roof; air-conditioning.

3500 S

See 3500, except for:

PRICE IN GB: £ 1,825.

ENGINE max power (DIN): 150 hp at 5,000 rpm; max torque (DIN): 204 lb ft, 28.2 kg m at 2,700 rpm; 42.5 hp/l.

TRANSMISSION gearbox: mechanical; gears: 4, fully synchronized; ratios: I 3.625, II 2.133, III 1.391, IV 1, rev 3.430.

PERFORMANCE max speeds: (I) 34 mph, 55 km/h; (II) 58 mph, 94 km/h; (III) 89 mph, 144 km/h; (IV) 125 mph, 201 km/h; power-weight ratio: 19.2 lb/hp, 8.7 kg/hp; carrying capacity: 975 lb, 442 kg; acceleration: standing ¼ mile 17 sec, 0-50 mph (0-80 km/h) 6.7 sec.

DIMENSIONS AND WEIGHT dry weight: 2,868 lb, 1,301 kg.

3.5-litre Saloon

PRICE IN GB: £ 2,265.

ENGINE front, 4 stroke; 8 cylinders, Vee-slanted at 90°; 215 cu in, 3,523 cc (3.50 x 2.80 in, 88.9 x 71.1 mm); compression ratio: 10.5:1; max power (DIN): 150 hp at 5,000 rpm; max torque (DIN): 202.5 lb ft, 27.9 kg m at 2,625 rpm; max engine rpm: 5,200; 42.5 hp/l; light alloy cylinder block and head, dry liners; 5 crankshaft bearings; valves: overhead, in line, push-rods and rockers, hydraulic tappets;

3.5-LITRE SALOON

camshafts: 1, at centre of Vee; lubrication: gear pump, full flow filter, 9 imp pt, 10.8 US pt, 5.1 l; 2 SU type HS 6 semi-downdraught carburettors; fuel feed: mechanical pump; water-cooled, 16 imp pt, 19.2 US pt, 9.1 l.

TRANSMISSION driving wheels: rear; gearbox: Borg-Warner 35 automatic transmission, hydraulic torque converter and planetary gears with 3 ratios, max ratio of converter at stall 2.1, possible manual selection; ratios: I 2.390, II 1.450, III 1, rev 2.090; lever: central; final drive: hypoid bevel; axle ratio: 3.540; width of rims: 5''; tyres: 6.70 x 15.

PERFORMANCE max speeds: (I) 46 mph, 74 km/h; (II) 77 mph, 124 km/h; (III) 115 mph, 185 km/h; power-weight ratio: 23.3 lb/hp, 10.6 kg/hp; carrying capacity: 960 lb, 435 kg; acceleration: standing ¼ mile 18.6 sec, 0-50 mph (0-80 km/h) 9 sec; speed in direct drive at 1,000 rpm: 21.5 mph, 34.6 km/h; fuel consumption: 18.2 m/imp gal, 15.2 m/US gal, 15.5 l x 100 km.

CHASSIS integral, front auxiliary frame; front suspension: independent, wishbones, lower trailing links, longitudinal laminated torsion bars, anti-roll bar, telescopic dampers; rear suspension: rigid axle, semi-elliptic leafsprings, telescopic dampers.

STEERING worm and peg, variable ratio servo; turns lock to lock: 2.50.

BRAKES front disc (diameter 10.75 in, 273 mm), rear drum, servo; swept area: front 260 sq in, 1.677 sq cm, rear 154.8 sq in, 998 sq cm, total 414.8 sq in, 2,675 sq cm.

ELECTRICAL EQUIPMENT 12 V; 58 Ah battery; 45 A alternator; Lucas distributor; 2 headlamps.

DIMENSIONS AND WEIGHT wheel base: 110.50 in, 2,807 mm; tracks: 56.20 in, 1,427 mm front, 56.90 in, 1,445 mm rear; length: 187 in, 4,750 mm; width: 70.50 in, 1,791 mm; height: 61 in, 1,549 mm; ground clearance: 6.60 in, 167 mm; dry weight: 3,498 lb, 1,587 kg; distribution of weight: 51% front, 49% rear; turning circle (between walls): 40 ft, 12.2 m; fuel tank: 14.1 imp gal, 16.9 US gal, 64 l.

BODY saloon/sedan; 4 doors; 4-5 seats, separate front seats, reclining backrests.

PRACTICAL INSTRUCTIONS fuel: 100 oct petrol; engine sump oil: 9 imp pt, 10.8 US pt, 5.1 l, SAE 20-30, change every 6,000 miles, 9,000 km; gearbox oil: 14.1 imp pt, 16.9 US pt, 8 l, automatic transmission fluid; final drive oil: 3 imp pt, 3.6 US pt, 1.7 l, SAE 90 EP, change every 20,000 miles, 32.000 km; greasing: every 6,000 miles, 9.000 km, 1 point; valve timing: 30° 75° 68° 37°; tyre pressure: front 26 psi, 1.8 atm, rear 26 psi, 1.8 atm.

OPTIONAL ACCESSORIES headrests on front and rear seats; sunshine roof; air-conditioning.

3.5-litre Coupé

See 3.5-litre Saloon, except for:

PRICE IN GB: £ 2,360.

PERFORMANCE power-weight ratio: 23.2 lb/hp, 10.5 kg/hp.

DIMENSIONS AND WEIGHT height: 58 in, 1,473 mm; dry weight: 3,479 lb, 1,578 kg.

BODY coupé.

Land Rover 88" Regular

PRICE IN GB: £ 1,115.
PRICE IN USA: $ 3,998.

ENGINE front, 4 stroke; 4 cylinders, vertical, in line; 139.5 cu in, 2,286 cc (3.56 x 3.50 in, 90.5 x 88.9 mm); compression ratio: 8:1; max power (DIN): 70 hp at 4,000 rpm; max torque (DIN): 120 lb ft, 16.5 kg m at 1,500 rpm; max engine rpm: 5,000; 30.6 hp/l; cast iron cylinder block and head; 3 crankshaft bearings; valves: overhead, in line, roller tappets, push-rods and rockers; camshafts: 1, side; lubrication: gear pump, full flow filter, 12.5 imp pt, 14.8 US pt, 7 l; 1 Zenith 36 IV downdraught single barrel carburettor; fuel feed: mechanical pump; water-cooled, 15.2 imp pt, 18.3 US pt, 8.7 l.

TRANSMISSION driving wheels: front (automatically engaged with transfer box low ratio) and rear; clutch: single dry plate, hydraulically controlled; gearbox: mechanical; gears: 4, fully synchronized and 2-ratio transfer box (high 1.150, low 2.350); ratios: I 3.680, II 2.220, III 1.500, IV 1, rev 4.020; gear and transfer lever: central; final drive: spiral bevel; axle ratio: 4.700; width of rims: 5''; tyres: 6.00 x 16.

PERFORMANCE max speeds: (I) 21 mph, 33 km/h; (II) 34 mph, 54 km/h; (III) 50 mph, 80 km/h; (IV) 66 mph, 106

ROVER 3.5-litre Saloon

ROVER Land Rover 88" Regular

ROVER Range Rover

km/h; power-weight ratio: 42.2 lb/hp, 19.1 kg/hp; carrying capacity: 1,499 lb, 680 kg; acceleration: 0-50 mph (0-80 km/h) 16.3 sec; speed in direct drive at 1,000 rpm: 15 mph, 24.1 km/h; fuel consumption: 19.1 m/imp gal, 15.9 m/US gal, 14.8 l x 100 km.

CHASSIS box-type ladder frame; front suspension: rigid axle, semi-elliptic leafsprings, telescopic dampers; rear suspension: rigid axle, semi-elliptic leafsprings, telescopic dampers.

STEERING recirculating ball; turns lock to lock: 3.35.

BRAKES drum; swept area: total 189 sq in, 1,219 sq cm.

ELECTRICAL EQUIPMENT 12 V; 58 Ah battery; 408 W alternator; Lucas distributor; 2 headlamps.

DIMENSIONS AND WEIGHT wheel base: 88 in, 2,235 mm; tracks: 51.50 in, 1,308 mm front, 51.50 in, 1,308 mm rear; length: 142.35 in, 3,616 mm; width: 66 in, 1,676 mm; height: 77.85 in, 1,977 mm; ground clearance: 7 in, 178 mm; dry weight: 2,953 lb, 1,339 kg; distribution of weight: 52.5% front, 47.5% rear; turning circle (between walls): 38 ft, 11.6 m; fuel tank: 10 imp gal, 12 US gal, 45 l.

BODY estate car/station wagon; 2 + 1 doors; 7-8 seats, separate front seats.

PRACTICAL INSTRUCTIONS fuel: 91 oct petrol; engine sump oil: 12.5 imp pt, 14.8 US pt, 7 l, SAE 20W, change every 3,000 miles, 4,800 km; gearbox oil: 2.5 imp pt, 3 US pt, 1.4 l; transfer box oil: 4.4 imp pt, 5.3 US pt, 2.5 l, SAE 90 EP, change every 12,000 miles, 19,300 km; final drive oil: 3 imp pt, 3.6 US pt, 1.7 l, SAE 90 EP, change every 12,000 miles, 19,300 km; greasing: every 4,000 miles, 6,400 km, 1 point; tappet clearances: inlet 0.010 in, 0.25 mm, exhaust 0.010 in, 0.25 mm; valve timing: 6° 52° 34° 24°; tyre pressure: front 25 psi, 1.7 atm, rear 25 psi, 1.7 atm.

VARIATIONS

ENGINE Diesel, compression ratio 23:1; max power (DIN) 62 hp at 4,000 rpm, max torque (DIN) 103 lb ft, 14.2 kg m at 1,800 rpm, max engine rpm 4,000, 27.1 hp/l, cast iron cylinder head with precombustion chambers.
PERFORMANCE power-weight ratio 47.6 lb/hp, 21.6 kg/hp.

OPTIONAL ACCESSORIES oil cooler; front and rear power take-off; 7/7.50 x 16 tyres; servo brake; 45 Ah alternator.

Land Rover 109" Estate Car

See Land Rover 88" Regular, except for:

PRICE IN GB: £ 1,615.

TRANSMISSION width of rims: 5.5"; tyres: 7.50 x 16.

PERFORMANCE power-weight ratio: 53,6 lb/hp, 24.3 kg/hp.

DIMENSIONS AND WEIGHT wheel base: 109 in, 2,769 mm; length: 175 in, 4,445 mm; height: 81.35 in, 2,066 mm; ground clearance: 8.25 in, 210 mm; dry weight: 3,752 lb, 1,702 kg; distribution of weight: 46.5% front, 53.5% rear; turning circle (between walls): 48 ft, 14.6 m; fuel tank: 16 imp gal, 19.3 US gal, 73 l.

BODY 10-12 seats.

VARIATIONS

ENGINE Diesel (62 hp).

ENGINE 6 cylinders, 160.2 cu in, 2,625 cc (3.06 x 3.63 in, 77.8 x 92.1 mm), compression ratio 7.8:1, max power (DIN) 86 hp at 4,500 rpm, max torque (DIN) 132 lb ft, 18.2 kg m at 1,500 rpm, 32.8 hp/l, 1 Zenith 175-CD2S carburettor.
PERFORMANCE max speed 72 mph, 116 km/h, power-weight ratio 45.5 lb/hp, 20.6 kg/hp.
DIMENSIONS AND WEIGHT dry weight 3,910 lb, 1,774 kg.

Range Rover

PRICE IN GB: £ 2,025.

ENGINE front, 4 stroke; 8 cylinders, Vee-slanted at 90°; 215 cu in, 3,523 cc (3.50 x 2.80 in, 88.9 x 71.1 mm); compression ratio: 8.5:1; max power (DIN): 130 hp at 5,000 rpm; max torque (DIN): 185 lb ft, 25.5 kg m at 2,500 rpm; max engine rpm: 5,200; 36.8 hp/l; light alloy cylinder block and head, dry liners; 5 crankshaft bearings; valves: overhead, in line, push-rods and rockers, hydraulic tappets; camshafts: 1, at centre of Vee; lubrication: gear pump, full flow filter, 10 imp pt, 12 US pt, 5.7 l; 2 Zenith-Stromberg CD2 semi-downdraught carburettors; fuel feed: mechanical pump; water-cooled, 20 imp pt, 23.9 US pt, 11.3 l.

TRANSMISSION driving wheels: front (automatically engaged with transfer box low ratio) and rear; clutch: single dry plate (diaphragm), hydraulically controlled; gearbox: mechanical; gears: 4, fully synchronized, and 2-ratio transfer box (high 1.174, low 3.321); ratios: I 4.069, II 2.448, III 1.505, IV 1, rev 3.664; gear and transfer lever: central; final

ROVER 3.5-litre Saloon

ROVER Land Rover 88" Regular

ROVER Range Rover

drive: spiral bevel; axle ratio: 3.540; width of rims: 6"; tyres: 205 x 16.

PERFORMANCE max speeds: (I) 24 mph, 39 km/h; (II) 41 mph, 66 km/h; (III) 68 mph, 109 km/h; (IV) 96 mph, 154 km/h; power-weight ratio: 29.2 lb/hp, 13.3 kg/hp; carrying capacity: 1,720 lb, 780 kg; acceleration: standing ¼ mile 19.3 sec, 0-50 mph (0-80 km/h) 11.1 sec; speed in direct drive at 1,000 rpm: 18.9 mph, 30.4 km/h; fuel consumption: 18.2 m/imp gal, 15.1 m/US gal, 15.5 l x 100 km.

CHASSIS box-type ladder frame; front suspension: rigid axle, longitudinal radius arms, transverse linkage bar, coil springs/telescopic dampers units; rear suspension: rigid axle, longitudinal radius arms, upper A bracket, Boge Hydromat self-energizing levelling device, coil springs, telescopic dampers.

STEERING Burman, recirculating ball, worm and nut; turns lock to lock: 5.55.

BRAKES disc (front diameter 11.75 in, 298 mm, rear 11.42 in, 290 mm); swept area: front 261 sq in, 1,683 sq cm, rear 235 sq in, 1,516 sq cm, total 496 sq in, 3,199 sq cm.

ELECTRICAL EQUIPMENT 12 V; 57 Ah battery; 408 W alternator; Lucas distributor; 2 headlamps.

DIMENSIONS AND WEIGHT wheel base: 100 in, 2,540 mm; tracks: 58.50 in, 1,486 mm front, 58.50 in, 1,486 mm rear; length: 175.98 in, 4,470 mm; width: 70 in, 1,778 mm; height: 70 in, 1,778 mm; ground clearance: 7.50 in, 190 mm; dry weight: 3,800 lb, 1,724 kg; distribution of weight: 50% front, 50% rear; turning circle (between walls): 37 ft, 11.3 m; fuel tank: 19 imp gal, 22.7 US gal, 86 l.

BODY estate car/station wagon; 2 + 1 doors; 5 seats, separate front seats, reclining backrests.

PRACTICAL INSTRUCTIONS fuel: 91-93 oct petrol; engine sump oil: 10 imp pt, 12 US pt, 5.7 l, SAE 20W, change every 6,000 miles, 9,000 km; gearbox oil: 4.5 imp pt, 5.5 US pt, 2.6 l, SAE 80 EP, change every 24,000 miles, 40,000 km; transfer box oil: 5.5 imp pt, 6.6 US pt, 3.1 l, SAE 80 EP, change every 6,000 miles, 9,000 km; final drive oil: rear 2.7 imp pt, 3.2 US pt, 1.5 l, SAE 80 EP, change every 24,000 miles, 40,000 km, front 3 imp pt, 3.6 US pt, 1.7 l, SAE 80 EP, change every 24,000 miles, 40.000 km; greasing every 6,000 miles, 9,000 km, 6 points; valve timing: 30° 75° 68° 37°; tyre pressure: front 25 psi, 1.7 atm, rear 25 psi, 1.7 atm.

OPTIONAL ACCESSORIES power-assisted steering; electrically-heated rear window.

SUNBEAM GREAT BRITAIN

Sport

PRICE IN GB: £ 712.

ENGINE rear, 4 stroke; 4 cylinders, slanted at 45°, in line; 53.4 cu in, 875 cc (2.68 x 2.38 in, 68 x 60.4 mm); compression ratio: 10:1; max power (DIN): 50 hp at 5,800 rpm; max torque (DIN): 49 lb ft, 6.7 kg m at 4,500 rpm; max engine rpm: 7,000; 57.1 hp/l; light alloy cylinder block and head, dry liners; 3 crankshaft bearings; valves: overhead, in line, thimble tappets; camshafts: 1, overhead; lubrication: eccentric pump, full flow filter, oil cooler, 6 imp pt, 7.2 US pt, 3.4 l; 2 Zenith-Stromberg 125 CD horizontal carburettors; fuel feed: mechanical pump; water-cooled, 11.2 imp pt, 13.3 US pt, 6.3 l.

TRANSMISSION driving wheels: rear; clutch: single dry plate (diaphragm), hydraulically controlled; gearbox: mechanical; gears: 4, fully synchronized; ratios: I 3.417, II 1.833, III 1.174, IV 0.852, rev 2.846; lever: central; final drive: hypoid bevel; axle ratio: 4.857; width of rims: 4.5"; tyres: 155 x 12.

PERFORMANCE max speeds: (I) 26 mph, 42 km/h; (II) 49 mph, 79 km/h; (III) 77 mph, 124 km/h; (IV) 90 mph, 145 km/h; power-weight ratio: 31.9 lb/hp, 14.5 kg/hp; carrying capacity: 706 lb, 320 kg; acceleration: 0-50 mph (0-80 km/h) 12.4 sec; speed in top at 1,000 rpm: 15.1 mph, 24.3 km/h; fuel consumption: 40 m/imp gal, 33.1 m/US gal, 7.1 l x 100 km.

CHASSIS integral; front suspension: independent, U-shaped swinging semi-axles, coil springs, telescopic dampers; rear suspension: independent, semi-trailing arms, coil springs, telescopic dampers.

STEERING rack-and-pinion; turns lock to lock: 2.63.

BRAKES drum, 2 front leading shoes, servo; swept area: total 151 sq in, 974 sq cm.

ELECTRICAL EQUIPMENT 12 V; 32 Ah battery; 297 W dynamo; Lucas distributor; 4 headlamps.

DIMENSIONS AND WEIGHT wheel base: 82 in, 2,083 mm; tracks: 49.70 in, 1,262 mm front, 48 in, 1,219 rear; length: 139 in, 3,531 mm; width: 60.25 in, 1,530 mm; height: 54.50

SPORT

in, 1,384 mm; ground clearance: 6.50 in, 165 mm; dry weight: 1,596 lb, 724 kg; distribution of weight: 38% front, 62% rear; turning circle (between walls): 31.5 ft, 9.6 m; fuel tank: 6 imp gal, 7.1 US gal, 27 l.

BODY saloon/sedan; 2 doors; 4 seats, separate front seats, reclining backrests.

PRACTICAL INSTRUCTIONS fuel: 95-97 oct petrol; engine sump oil: 5.5 imp pt, 6.6 US pt, 3.1 l, SAE 20W-50, change every 5,000 miles, 8,000 km; gearbox and final drive oil: 4.6 imp pt, 5.5 US pt, 2.6 l, SAE 80 EP; greasing: every 5,000 miles, 8,000 km, 4 points; tappet clearances: inlet 0.007 in, 0.18 mm, exhaust 0.014 in, 0.36 mm; valve timing: 67° 93° 63° 13°; tyre pressure: front 18 psi, 1.3 atm, rear 30 psi, 2.1 atm.

Rapier

PRICE IN GB: £ 1,209.

ENGINE front, 4 stroke; 4 cylinders, slanted at 10°, in line; 105.3 cu in, 1,725 cc (3.21 x 3.25 in, 81.5 x 82.5 mm); compression ratio: 9.2:1; max power (DIN): 79 hp at 5,700 rpm; max torque (DIN): 93 lb ft, 12.9 kg m at 3,300 rpm; max engine rpm: 6,200; 45.8 hp/l; cast iron cylinder block, light alloy head: 5 crankshaft bearings; valves: overhead, in line, push-rods and rockers; camshafts: 1, side; lubrication: rotary pump, full flow filter, 7.5 imp pt, 8.9 US pt, 4.2 l; 2 Zenith-Stromberg semi-downdraught carburettors; fuel feed: mechanical pump; water-cooled, 12.6 imp pt, 15 US pt, 7.1 l.

TRANSMISSION driving wheels: rear; clutch: single dry plate (diaphragm), hydraulically controlled; gearbox: mechanical; gears: 4, fully synchronized and overdrive on III and IV; ratios: I 3.123, II 1.993, III 1.296, IV 1, overdrive/top 0.803, rev 3.325; lever: central; final drive: hypoid bevel; axle ratio: 4.220; width of rims: 5"; tyres: 155 x 13.

PERFORMANCE max speeds: (I) 31 mph, 50 km/h; (II) 48 mph, 77 km/h; (III) 75 mph, 120 km/h; (IV) 100 mph, 161 km/h; power-weight ratio: 27.1 lb/hp, 12.3 kg/hp; acceleration: 0-50 mph (0-80 km/h) 9 sec; speed in direct drive at 1,000 rpm: 15.6 mph, 25.1 km/h, fuel consumption: 30 m/imp gal, 25 m/US gal, 9.4 l x 100 km.

CHASSIS integral; front suspension: independent, coil springs/telescopic damper struts, lower wishbones (trailing links), anti-roll bar; rear suspension: rigid axle, semi-elliptic leafsprings, telescopic dampers.

STEERING recirculating ball; turns lock to lock: 3.75.

BRAKES front disc (diameter 9.60 in, 244 mm), rear drum, servo; swept area: front 179 sq in, 1,154 sq cm, rear 99 sq in, 638 sq cm, total 278 sq in, 1,792 sq cm.

ELECTRICAL EQUIPMENT 12 V; 40 Ah battery; 34 A alternator; Lucas distributor; 4 headlamps.

DIMENSIONS AND WEIGHT wheel base: 98.50 in, 2,502 mm; tracks: 51.80 in, 1,316 mm front, 51.80 in, 1,316 mm rear; length: 174.50 in, 4,432 mm; width: 64.75 in, 1,645 mm; height: 55 in, 1,397 mm; ground clearance: 5 in, 127 mm; dry weight: 2,145 lb, 973 kg; distribution of weight: 53% front, 47% rear; turning circle (between walls): 36.8 ft, 11.2 m; fuel tank: 15 imp gal, 17.9 US gal, 68 l.

BODY saloon/sedan (fastback); 2 doors; 4-5 seats, separate front seats, reclining backrests.

PRACTICAL INSTRUCTIONS fuel: 97 oct petrol; engine sump oil: 7.5 imp pt, 8.9 US pt, 4.2 l, SAE 20W-50 change every 5,000 miles, 8,000 km; gearbox oil: 4.5 imp pt, 5.4 US pt, 2.6 l, multigrade; final drive oil: 1.7 imp pt, 1.9 US pt, 0.9 l, SAE 90 EP; greasing: none; tappet clearances: inlet 0.013 in, 0.32 mm, exhaust 0.014 in, 0.35 mm; valve timing: 38° 72° 72° 38°; tyre pressure: front 26 psi, 1.8 atm, rear 26 psi, 1.8 atm.

OPTIONAL ACCESSORIES Borg-Warner 35/3 automatic transmission, hydraulic torque converter and planetary gears with 3 ratios (I 2.393, II 1.450, III 1, rev 2.094), max ratio of converter at stall 1.9, 3.700 axle ratio; electrically-heated rear window.

Rapier H120

See Rapier, except for:

PRICE IN GB: £ 1,385.

ENGINE compression ratio: 9.6:1; max power (DIN): 93 hp at 5,200 rpm; max torque (DIN): 106 lb ft, 14.6 kg m at 4,000 rpm; 53.9 hp/l; 2 Weber 40 DCOE horizontal twin barrel carburettors.

SUNBEAM Rapier

SUNBEAM Alpine

TECHNICAL EXPONENTS TX Tripper Series

TRANSMISSION axle ratio: 3.890; width of rims: 5"; tyres: 165 x 13.

PERFORMANCE max speeds: (I) 34 mph, 54 km/h; (II) 54 mph, 87 km/h; (III) 83 mph, 133 km/h; (IV) 107 mph, 172 km/h; (overdrive/top) 110 mph, 177 km/h; power-weight ratio: 34 lb/hp, 15.4 kg/hp; acceleration: 0-50 mph (0-80 km/h) 8 sec; speed in direct drive at 1,000 rpm; 17.3 mph, 27.9 km/h; fuel consumption: 25.7 m/imp gal, 21.4 m/US gal, 11 l x 100 km.

DIMENSIONS AND WEIGHT dry weight: 2,170 lb, 984 kg.

Alpine

PRICE IN GB: £ 1,069.

ENGINE front, 4 stroke; 4 cylinders, in line; 105.3 cu in, 1,725 cc (3.21 x 3.25 in, 81.5 x 82.5 mm); compression ratio: 9.2:1; max power (DIN): 72 hp at 5,000 rpm; max torque (DIN): 90 lb ft, 12.5 kg m at 3,000 rpm; max engine rpm: 6,300; 38.8 hp/l; cast iron cylinder block, light alloy head; 5 crankshaft bearings; valves: overhead, in line, push-rods and rockers; camshafts: 1, side; lubrication: eccentric pump, full flow filter, 7.5 imp pt, 8.9 US pt, 4.2 l; 1 Zenith Stromberg 150 CD3 semi-downdraught carburettor; fuel feed: mechanical pump; water-cooled, 12.6 imp pt, 15 US pt, 7.1 l.

TRANSMISSION driving wheels: rear; clutch: single dry plate (diaphragm), hydraulically controlled; gearbox: mechanical; gears: 4, fully synchronized; ratios: I 3.353, II 2.141, III 1.392, IV 1, rev 3.569; lever: central; final drive: hypoid bevel; axle ratio: 3.889; width of rims: 4.5"; tyres: 155 x 13.

PERFORMANCE max speeds: (I) 27 mph, 43 km/h; (II) 45 mph, 72 km/h; (III) 70 mph, 112 km/h; (IV) 96 mph, 154 km/h; power-weight ratio: 28.9 lb/hp, 13.1 kg/hp; carrying capacity: 882 lb, 400 kg; acceleration: 0-50 mph (0-80 km/h) 10 sec; speed in direct drive at 1,000 rpm: 16.8 mph, 28.6 km/h; fuel consumption: 34 m/imp gal, 28.3 m/US gal, 8.3 l x 100 km.

CHASSIS integral; front suspension: independent, coil springs/telescopic damper struts, lower wishbones (trailing links), anti-roll bar; rear suspension rigid axle, semi-elliptic leafsprings, telescopic dampers.

STEERING recirculating ball; turns lock to lock: 3.75.

BRAKES front disc (diameter 9.60 in, 244 mm), rear drum, servo; swept area: front 175 sq in, 1,129 sq cm, rear 97 sq in, 625 sq cm, total 272 sq in, 1,754 sq cm.

ELECTRICAL EQUIPMENT 12 V; 40 Ah battery; 408 W alternator; Lucas distributor; 4 headlamps.

DIMENSIONS AND WEIGHT wheel base: 98.50 in, 2,502 mm; tracks: 52 in, 1,321 mm front, 52 in, 1,321 mm rear; length: 174.10 in, 4,422 mm; width: 64.75 in, 1,645 mm; height: 55 in, 1,397 mm; ground clearance: 5 in, 127 mm; dry weight: 2,091 lb, 948 kg; turning circle (between walls): 36 ft, 11 m; fuel tank: 15 imp gal, 17.9 US gal, 68 l.

BODY coupé (fastback); 2 doors; 4 seats, separate front seats.

PRACTICAL INSTRUCTIONS fuel: 97 oct petrol; engine sump oil: 7.5 imp pt, 8.9 US pt, 4.2 l, SAE 20W-50, change every 5,000 miles, 8,000 km; gearbox oil: 3.5 imp pt, 4.2 US pt, 2 l, multigrade, no change recommended; final drive oil: 1.7 imp pt, 1.9 US pt, 0.9 l, SAE 90 EP, no change recommended; greasing: none; tappet clearances: inlet 0.013 in, 0.32 mm, exhaust 0.013 in, 0.32 mm; valve timing: 38° 72° 72° 38°; tyre pressure: front 26 psi, 1.8 atm, rear 26 psi, 1.8 atm.

OPTIONAL ACCESSORIES Laycock overdrive on III and IV, 0.803 ratio; Borg-Warner 35/3 automatic transmission, hydraulic torque converter and planetary gears with 3 ratios (I 2.393, II 1.450, III 1, rev 2.094), max ratio of converter at stall 1.9, 3.890 axle ratio; reclining backrests; electrically-heated rear window.

TECHNICAL EXPONENTS

GREAT BRITAIN

TX Tripper 1300

PRICE IN GB: £ 1,100.

ENGINE front, 4 stroke; 4 cylinders, in line; 79.1 cu in, 1,296 cc (2.90 x 2.99 in, 73.7 x 76 mm); compression ratio: 9.5:1; max power (DIN): 75 hp at 6,000 rpm; max torque (DIN): 75 lb ft, 10.3 kg m at 4,000 rpm; max engine rpm: 6,500; 57.9 hp/l; cast iron cylinder block and head; 5 crank-

BRAKES front disc (diameter 10.60 in, 269 mm), rear drum, servo; swept area: front 220.2 sq in, 1,420 sq cm, rear 127 sq in, 819 sq cm, total 347.2 sq in, 2,239 sq cm.

ELECTRICAL EQUIPMENT 12 V; 56 Ah battery; alternator; Lucas distributor; 4 halogen headlamps.

DIMENSIONS AND WEIGHT wheel base: 100 in, 2,540 mm; tracks: 52.60 in, 1,336 mm front, 53 in, 1,346 mm rear; length: 174.01 in, 4,420 mm; width: 63.46 in, 1,612 mm; height: 49.53 in, 1,258 mm; ground clearance: 4.02 in, 102 mm; dry weight: 2,640 lb, 1,197 kg; distribution of weight: 47.4% front, 52.6% rear; turning circle (between walls): 34.1 ft, 10.4 m; fuel tank: 13.9 imp gal, 16.6 US gal, 63 l.

BODY convertible; 2 doors; 2 + 2 seats, separate front seats.

PRACTICAL INSTRUCTIONS fuel: 97 oct petrol; engine sump oil: 8 imp pt, 9.5 US pt, 4.5 l, SAE 20W-40, change every 6,000 miles, 9,700 km; gearbox oil: 2.6 imp pt, 3.2 US pt, 1.5 l, SAE 90, no change recommended; final drive oil: 1.9 imp pt, 2.3 US pt, 1.1 l, SAE 90, no change recommended; greasing: 3 points, every 6,000 miles, 9,700 km; tappet clearances: inlet 0.008 in, 0.20 mm, exhaust 0.018 in, 0.46 mm; valve timing: 16° 56° 56° 16°; tyre pressure: front 26 psi, 1.8 atm, rear 30 psi, 2.1 atm.

OPTIONAL ACCESSORIES (standard for Great Britain) Laycock-de Normanville overdrive on III and IV (0.797 ratio); Borg-Warner 35 automatic transmission, hydraulic torque converter and planetary gears with 3 ratios (I 2.390, II 1.450, III 1, rev 2.090); max ratio of converter at stall 2.275, possible manual selection; air-conditioning; tonneau cover; hardtop.

TVR — GREAT BRITAIN

1600 M

PRICE IN GB: £ 1,638.

ENGINE front, 4 stroke; 4 cylinders, in line; 97.6 cu in, 1,599 cc (3.19 x 3.06 in, 80.98 x 77.62 mm); compression ratio: 9:1; max power (DIN): 86 hp at 5,500 rpm; max torque (DIN): 92 lb ft, 12.7 kg m at 4,000 rpm; max engine rpm: 6,000; 62.8 hp/l; cast iron cylinder block and head; 5 crankshaft bearings; valves: overhead, in line, push-rods and rockers; camshafts: 1, side; lubrication: eccentric pump, full flow filter, 7.4 imp pt, 8.9 US pt, 4.2 l; 1 Weber downdraught twin barrel carburettor; fuel feed: mechanical pump; water-cooled, 14.3 imp pt, 17.1 US pt, 8.1 l.

TRANSMISSION driving wheels: rear; clutch: single dry plate (diaphragm); gearbox: mechanical; gears: 4, fully synchronized; ratios: I 2.972, II 2.010, III 1.397, IV 1, rev 3.324; lever: central; final drive: hypoid bevel; axle ratio: 4.100; width of rims: 5.5"; tyres: 165 SR x 15.

PERFORMANCE max speeds: (I) 42 mph, 67 km/h; (II) 62 mph, 99 km/h; (III) 89 mph, 143 km/h; (IV) 110 mph, 177 km/h; power-weight ratio: 20.1 lb/hp, 9.1 kg/hp; carrying capacity: 360 lb, 160 kg; acceleration: standing ¼ mile 17 sec, 0-50 mph (0-80 km/h) 6.9 sec; speed in direct drive at 1,000 rpm: 17.8 mph, 28.6 km/h; fuel consumption: 30 m/imp gal, 25 m/US gal, 9.4 l x 100 km.

CHASSIS multi-tubular backbone; front suspension: independent, wishbones, coil springs, anti-roll bar, telescopic dampers; rear suspension: independent, wishbones, coil springs, telescopic dampers.

STEERING rack-and-pinion; turns lock to lock: 3.50.

BRAKES front disc (diameter 10.85 in, 276 mm), rear drum, servo; swept area: front 233 sq in, 1,503 sq cm, rear 99 sq in, 639 sq cm, total 332 sq in, 2,142 sq cm.

ELECTRICAL EQUIPMENT 12 V; 40 Ah battery; dynamo; Lucas distributor; 2 headlamps.

DIMENSIONS AND WEIGHT wheel base: 90 in, 2,286 mm; tracks: 53.74 in, 1,365 mm front, 53.74 in, 1,365 mm rear; length: 163.98 in, 4,165 mm; width: 64 in, 1,626 mm; height: 47.01 in, 1,194 mm; ground clearance: 5 in, 127 mm; dry weight: 1,736 lb, 787 kg; distribution of weight: 50% front, 50% rear; turning circle (between walls): 35.9 ft, 11.9 m; fuel tank: 12 imp gal, 14.3 US gal, 54 l.

BODY coupé in fibre glass; 2 doors; 2 seats.

PRACTICAL INSTRUCTIONS fuel: 95-100 oct petrol; engine sump oil: 7.4 imp pt, 8.9 US pt, 4.2 l, SAE 20W-50, change every 6,000 miles, 9,700 km; gearbox oil: 1.8 imp pt, 2.1 US pt, 1 l, SAE 90, change every 6,000 miles, 9,700 km; final drive oil: 1.1 imp pt, 1.3 US pt, 0.6 l, SAE 90 EP, no change recommended; greasing: every 3,000 miles, 4,800 km, 11 points; tappet clearances: inlet 0.012 in, 0.30 mm, exhaust 0.022 in, 0.56 mm; valve timing: 18° 70° 64° 24°; tyre pressure: front 20 psi, 1.3 atm, rear 22 psi, 1.5 atm.

OPTIONAL ACCESSORIES oil cooler; light alloy wheels; reclining backrests; sunshine roof.

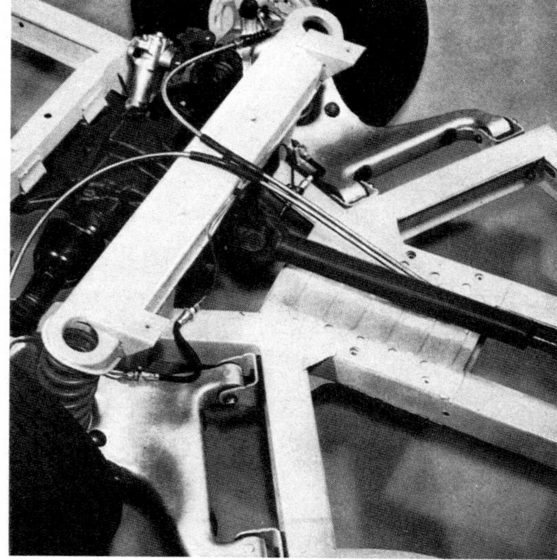

TRIUMPH TR6 P.I.

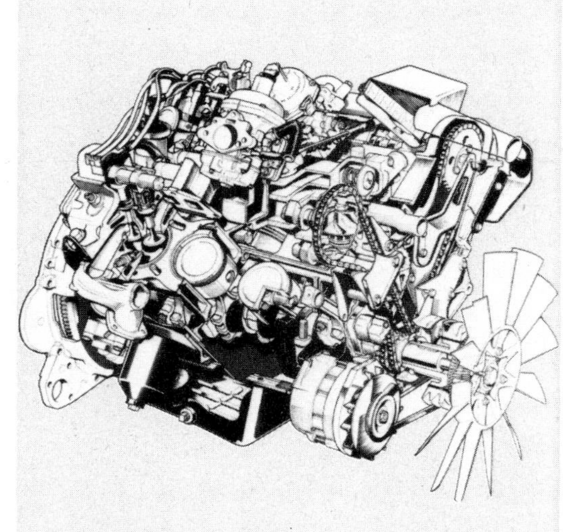

TRIUMPH Stag

TVR 1600 M

2500 M

See 1600 M, except for:

PRICE IN GB: £ 1,779.

ENGINE 6 cylinders, in line; 152 cu in, 2,498 cc (2.94 x 3.74 in, 74.7 x 95 mm); compression ratio: 8.5:1; max power (DIN): 106 hp at 4,600 rpm; max torque (DIN): 117 lb ft, 16.2 kg m at 3,000 rpm; 42.4 hp/l; 4 crankshaft bearings; lubricating system capacity: 9 imp pt, 10.8 US pt, 5.1 l; 2 Solex carburettors; cooling system capacity: 11 imp pt, 13.3 US pt, 6.3 l.

TRANSMISSION gearbox ratios: I 3.140, II 2.010, III 1.330, IV 1, rev 3.220; axle ratio: 3.450.

PERFORMANCE max speeds: (I) 38 mph, 61 km/h; (II) 59 mph, 95 km/h; (III) 89 mph, 143 kg/h; (IV) 116 mph, 186 km/h; power-weight ratio: 18.5 lb/hp, 8.4 kg/hp; carrying capacity: 380 lb, 170 kg; acceleration: standing ¼ mile 17 sec, 0-50 mph (0-80 km/h) 6 sec; speed in direct drive at 1,000 rpm: 21.6 mph, 34.7 km/h; fuel consumption: 29 m/imp gal, 24.2 m/US gal, 9.7 l x 100 km.

ELECTRICAL EQUIPMENT 264 W alternator.

DIMENSIONS AND WEIGHT dry weight: 1,960 lb, 889 kg.

PRACTICAL INSTRUCTIONS engine sump oil: 8 imp pt, 9.5 US pt, 4.5 l; gearbox oil: 2 imp pt, 2.4 US pt, 1.1 l; final drive oil: 2.5 imp pt, 3 US pt, 1.4 l; tappet clearances: (cold) inlet 0.010 in, 0.25 mm, exhaust 0.012 in, 0.30 mm; tyre pressure: front 22 psi, 1.5 atm, rear 24 psi, 1.7 atm.

OPTIONAL ACCESSORIES overdrive.

3000 M

See 1600 M, except for:

PRICE IN GB: £ 1,884.

ENGINE 6 cylinders, in line; 182.7 cu in, 2,994 cc (3.70 x 2.85 in, 93.97 x 72.41 mm); compression ratio: 8.9:1; max power (DIN): 138 hp at 5,000 rpm; max torque (DIN): 172 lb ft, 23.8 kg m at 3,000 rpm; 46.1 hp/l; 4 crankshaft bearings; lubricating system capacity: 9 imp pt, 10.8 US pt, 5.1 l; 2 Weber carburettors; cooling system capacity: 12 imp pt, 14.4 US pt, 6.8 l.

TRANSMISSION gearbox ratios: I 3.160, II 1.950, III 1.410, IV 1, rev 3.350; axle ratio: 3.450; tyres: 165 HR x 15.

PERFORMANCE max speeds: (I) 40 mph, 65 km/h; (II) 65 mph, 104 km/h; (III) 90 mph, 145 km/h; (IV) 125 mph, 201 km/h; power-weight ratio: 14.2 lb/hp, 6.4 kg/hp; acceleration: standing ¼ mile 17 sec, 0-50 mph (0-80 km/h) 6 sec; speed in direct drive at 1,000 rpm: 21.6 mph, 34.7 km/h; fuel consumption: 22 m/imp gal, 18.4 m/US gal, 12.8 l x 100 km.

ELECTRICAL EQUIPMENT 264 W alternator.

DIMENSIONS AND WEIGHT dry weight: 1,960 lb, 889 kg.

PRACTICAL INSTRUCTIONS engine sump oil: 8 imp pt, 9.5 US pt, 4.5 l; gearbox oil: 2 imp pt, 2.4 US pt, 1.1 l; final drive oil: 2.5 imp pt, 3 US pt, 1.4 l; tappet clearances: (cold) inlet 0.010 in, 0.25 mm, exhaust 0.012 in, 0.30 mm; tyre pressure: front 22 psi, 1.5 atm, rear 24 psi, 1.7 atm.

OPTIONAL ACCESSORIES overdrive.

VANDEN PLAS — GREAT BRITAIN

Princess 1300

PRICE IN GB: £ 1,129.

ENGINE front, transverse, 4 stroke; 4 cylinders, vertical, in line; 77.8 cu in, 1,275 cc (2.78 x 3.20 in, 70.6 x 81.3 mm); compression ratio: 8.8:1; max power (DIN): 65 hp at 5,750 rpm; max torque (DIN): 70.5 lb ft, 9.7 kg m at 3,000 rpm; max engine rpm: 5,900; 51 hp/l; cast iron cylinder block and head; 3 crankshaft bearings; valves: overhead, in line, push-rods and rockers; camshafts: 1, side; lubrication: gear or vane-type pump, full flow filter, 9 imp pt, 10.8 US pt, 5.1 l; 2 SU type HS 2 semi-downdraught carburettors; fuel feed: electric pump; water-cooled, 6.9 imp pt, 8.2 US pt, 3.9 l.

TRANSMISSION driving wheels: front; clutch: single dry plate (diaphragm), hydraulically controlled; gearbox: mechanical; gears: 4, fully synchronized; ratios: I 3.530, II 2.220, III 1.430, IV 1, rev 3.540; lever: central; final drive: helical spur gears; axle ratio: 3.650; width of rims: 4"; tyres: 145 x 12.

PRINCESS 1300

PERFORMANCE max speeds: (I) 27 mph, 43 km/h; (II) 46 mph, 74 km/h; (III) 70 mph, 113 km/h; (IV) 90 mph, 145 km/h; power-weight ratio: 30.2 lb/hp, 13.7 kg/hp; carrying capacity: 882 lb, 400 kg; acceleration: 0-50 mph (0-80 km/h) 11.4 sec; speed in direct drive at 1,000 rpm: 16.8 mph, 27 km/h; fuel consumption: 32.4 m/imp gal, 27 m/US gal, 8.7 l x 100 km.

CHASSIS integral, front and rear auxiliary frames; front suspension: independent, wishbones, hydrolastic (liquid) rubber cone springs, hydraulic connecting pipes to rear wheels; rear suspension: independent, swinging longitudinal trailing arms, hydrolastic (liquid) rubber cone springs, hydraulic connecting pipes to front wheels, combined with transverse torsion bars, anti-roll bar.

STEERING rack-and-pinion; turns lock to lock: 3.12.

BRAKES front disc (diameter 8.40 in, 213 mm), rear drum, rear compensator.

ELECTRICAL EQUIPMENT 12 V; 40 Ah battery; 264 W dynamo; Lucas distributor; 4 headlamps.

DIMENSIONS AND WEIGHT wheel base: 93.50 in, 2,375 mm; tracks: 51.50 in, 1,308 mm front, 50.85 in, 1,292 mm rear; length: 146.75 in, 3,727 mm; width: 60.35 in, 1,533 mm; height: 53 in, 1,346 mm; ground clearance: 5.30 in, 135 mm; dry weight: 1,962 lb, 890 kg; distribution of weight: 62% front, 38% rear; turning circle (between walls): 36 ft, 11 m; fuel tank: 8 imp gal, 9.5 US gal, 36 l.

BODY saloon/sedan; 4 doors; 4-5 seats, separate front seats.

PRACTICAL INSTRUCTIONS fuel: 98-100 oct petrol; engine sump, gearbox and final drive oil: 7.6 imp pt, 9.1 US pt, 4.3 l, SAE 10W-30, change every 6,000 miles, 9,700 km; greasing: every 3,000 miles, 4,800 km, 4 points; sparking plug type: 225°; tappet clearances: inlet 0.012 in, 0.30 mm, exhaust 0.012 in, 0.30 mm; valve timing: 5° 45° 51° 21°; tyre pressure: front 28 psi, 2 atm, rear 24 psi, 1.7 atm.

OPTIONAL ACCESSORIES AP automatic transmission, hydraulic torque converter with 2 conic bevel gears (twin concentric differential-like gear clusters) with 4 ratios (I 2.690, II 1.850, III 1.460, IV 1, rev 2.690) operated by 3 brake bands and 2 multi-disc clutches, max ratio of converter at stall 2, possible manual selection, with engine max power (DIN) 60 hp at 5,250 rpm, max torque (DIN) 69.5 lb ft, 9.6 kg m at 2,500 rpm, 47.1 hp/l, 1 SU type HS 4 carburettor, 3.270 axle ratio, max speeds (I) 37 mph, 59 km/h, (II) 53 mph, 85 km/h, (III) 66 mph, 106 km/h, (IV) 87 mph, 140 km/h, power-weight ratio 32.7 lb/hp, 14.8 kg/hp, speed in direct drive at 1,000 rpm 16.3 mph, 26.2 km/h, fuel consumption 34 m/imp gal, 28.3 m/US gal, 8.3 l x 100 km; sunshine roof; electrically-heated rear window.

VANDEN PLAS Princess 1300

VAUXHALL Viva De Luxe Series

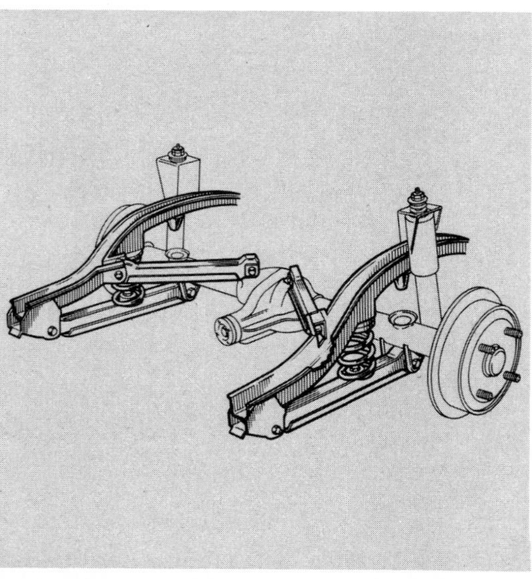

VAUXHALL Viva (rear suspension)

VAUXHALL — GREAT BRITAIN

Viva 1256 2-door Saloon

PRICE IN GB: £ 741.

ENGINE front, 4 stroke; 4 cylinders, vertical, in line; 76.6 cu in, 1,256 cc (3.19 x 2.40 in, 81 x 61 mm); compression ratio: 8.5:1; max power (DIN): 53 hp at 5,200 rpm; max torque (DIN): 65 lb ft, 9.8 kg m at 2,600 rpm; max engine rpm: 6,000; 42.1 hp/l; cast iron cylinder block and head; 3 crankshaft bearings; valves: overhead, in line, push-rods and rockers; camshafts: 1, side; lubrication: gear pump, full flow filter, 5.5 imp pt, 6.6 US pt, 3.1 l; 1 Zenith 30 IZE downdraught single barrel carburettor; fuel feed: mechanical pump; water-cooled, 10.2 imp pt, 12.3 US pt, 5.8 l.

TRANSMISSION driving wheels: rear; clutch: single dry plate (diaphragm); gearbox: mechanical; gears: 4, fully synchronized; ratios: I 3.460, II 2.213, III 1.404, IV 1, rev 3.707; lever: central; final drive: hypoid bevel; axle ratio: 4.125; width of rims: 4"; tyres: 5.60 x 13.

PERFORMANCE max speeds: (I) 27 mph, 43 km/h; (II) 43 mph, 70 km/h; (III) 74 mph, 119 km/h; (IV) 82 mph, 132 km/h; power-weight ratio: 31.5 lb/hp, 14.3 kg/hp; carrying capacity: 1,056 lb, 480 kg; speed in direct drive at 1,000 rpm: 15.8 mph, 25.3 km/h; fuel consumption: 33 m/imp gal, 27.7 m/US gal, 8.5 l x 100 km.

CHASSIS integral; front suspension: independent, wishbones, coil springs, telescopic dampers; rear suspension: rigid axle, trailing lower radius arms, upper oblique radius ams, coil springs, telescopic dampers.

STEERING rack-and-pinion; turns lock to lock: 3.16.

BRAKES drum; swept area: front 62.9 sq in, 405 sq cm, rear 62.9 sq in, 405 sq cm, total 125.8 sq in, 810 sq cm.

ELECTRICAL EQUIPMENT 12 V; 32 Ah battery; 336 W alternator; AC Delco distributor; 2 headlamps.

DIMENSIONS AND WEIGHT wheel base: 97 in, 2,464 mm; tracks: 51.40 in, 1,306 mm front, 51.50 in, 1,308 mm rear; length: 162 in, 4,115 mm; width: 64.70 in, 1,643 mm; height: 53.10 in, 1,349 mm; ground clearance: 5.30 in, 135 mm; dry weight: 1,684 lb, 763 kg; distribution of weight: 53% front, 47% rear; turning circle (between walls): 34.1 ft, 10.4 m; fuel tank: 8 imp gal, 9.5 US gal, 36 l.

BODY saloon/sedan; 2 doors; 4-5 seats, separate front seats.

PRACTICAL INSTRUCTIONS fuel: 98 oct petrol; engine sump oil: 4.9 imp pt, 5.9 US pt, 2.8 l, SAE 20W-20, change every 6,000 miles, 9,700 km; gearbox oil: 0.9 imp pt, 1.1 US pt, 0.5 l, SAE 90, change every 6 months; final drive oil: 1.2 imp pt, 1.5 US pt, 0.7 l, SAE 90, no change recommended; greasing every 6 months, 4 points; tappet clearances: inlet 0.008 in, 0.20 mm, exhaust 0.008 in, 0.20 mm; valve timing: 39° 73° 71° 41°; tyre pressure: front 22 psi, 1.5 atm, rear 22 psi, 1.5 atm.

VARIATIONS

ENGINE 7.3:1 compression ratio (only for export).

OPTIONAL ACCESSORIES 155 x 13 tyres; front disc brakes with servo.

Viva 1256 De Luxe 2-door Saloon

See Viva 1256 2-door Saloon, except for:

PRICE IN GB: £ 819.

PERFORMANCE power-weight ratio: 34 lb/hp, 15.4 kg/hp.

BRAKES front disc (diameter 8.46 in, 215 mm), rear drum, servo; swept area: front 133.2 sq in, 861 sq cm, rear 62.9 sq in, 405 sq cm, total 196.1 sq in, 1,266 sq cm.

DIMENSIONS AND WEIGHT dry weight: 1,800 lb, 817 kg.

OPTIONAL ACCESSORIES G.M. automatic transmission, hydraulic torque converter and planetary gears with 3 ratios (I 2.390, II 1.480, III 1, rev 1.920), max ratio of converter at stall 2, possible manual selection; 6.20 x 13 tyres; 115 SR x 13 tyres; 6.50 x 13 tyres; electrically-heated rear window with heavy-duty alternator.

Viva 1256 De Luxe 4-door Saloon

See Viva 1256 De Luxe 2-door Saloon, except for:

PRICE IN GB: £ 853.

PERFORMANCE power-weight ratio: 34.6 lb/hp, 15.7 kg/hp.

DIMENSIONS AND WEIGHT dry weight: 1,840 lb, 835 kg.

Viva 1256 De Luxe Estate Car

See Viva 1256 De Luxe 2-door Saloon, except for:

PRICE IN GB: £ 920.

TRANSMISSION width of rims: 4.5"; tyres: 6.20 x 13 (standard).

PERFORMANCE power-weight ratio: 35.5 lb/hp, 16.1 kg/hp.

DIMENSIONS AND WEIGHT dry weight: 1,890 lb, 857 kg.

BODY estate car/station wagon; 2 + 1 doors.

OPTIONAL ACCESSORIES heavy-duty suspension.

Viva 1256 SL 2-door Saloon

See Viva 1256 2-door Saloon, except for:

PRICE IN GB: £ 905.

ENGINE 97.5 cu in, 1,599 cc (3.37 x 2.73 in, 85.7 x 69.2 mm); max power (SAE): 81 hp at 5,400 rpm; max torque (SAE): 96 lb ft, 13.3 kg m at 3,200 rpm; 50.7 hp/l; 5 crankshaft bearings; valves: thimble tappets; camshafts: 1, overhead; lubrication: rotary or vane-type pump, full flow filter, 8.5 imp pt, 10.1 US pt, 4.8 l; 1 Zenith 36 IV downdraught single barrel carburettor; cooling system capacity: 14 imp pt, 16.9 US pt, 7.9 l.

TRANSMISSION gearbox ratios: I 2.786, II 1.981, III 1.413, IV 1, rev 3.064; width of rims: 4.5"; tyres: 155 x 13.

PERFORMANCE max speeds: (I) 33 mph, 53 km/h; (II) 47 mph, 75 km/h; (III) 66 mph, 106 km/h; (IV) 91 mph, 146 km/h; power-weight ratio: 22.1 lb/hp, 10 kg/hp; speed in direct drive at 1,000 rpm: 15.6 mph, 25.1 km/h; fuel consumption: 28 m/imp gal, 23.3 m/US gal, 10.1 l x 100 km.

BRAKES front disc (diameter 8.54 in, 217 mm), rear drum, servo (standard); swept area: front 133.2 sq in, 861 sq cm, rear 62.9 sq in, 405 sq cm, total 196.1 sq in, 1,266 sq cm.

ELECTRICAL EQUIPMENT 38 Ah battery.

VANDEN PLAS Princess 1300

VAUXHALL Viva 1800 SL 2-door Saloon

VAUXHALL Viva 2300 SL Estate Car

DIMENSIONS AND WEIGHT height: 54.50 in, 1,356 mm; ground clearance: 5 in, 127 mm; dry weight: 1,790 lb, 812 kg; distribution of weight: 55.5% front, 44.5% rear; fuel tank: 12 imp gal, 14.3 US gal, 54 l.

PRACTICAL INSTRUCTIONS fuel: 97 oct petrol; engine sump oil: 8.5 imp pt, 10.1 US pt, 4.8 l; tappet clearances: inlet 0.007 in, 0.18 mm, exhaust 0.015 in, 0.38 mm; valve timing: 10° 42° 42° 10°; tyre pressure: front 24 psi, 1.7 atm, rear 24 psi, 1.7 atm.

OPTIONAL ACCESSORIES 175/70 HR x 13 tyres; reclining backrests.

Viva 1256 SL 4-door Saloon

See Viva 1256 SL 2-door Saloon, except for:

PRICE IN GB: £ 939.

PERFORMANCE power-weight ratio: 23.8 lb/hp, 10.8 kg/hp.

DIMENSIONS AND WEIGHT dry weight: 1,936 lb, 878 kg.

Viva 1256 SL Estate Car

See Viva 1256 SL 2-door Saloon, except for:

PRICE IN GB: £ 1,001.

PERFORMANCE power-weight ratio: 24.5 lb/hp, 11.1 kg/hp.

DIMENSIONS AND WEIGHT dry weight: 1,990 lb, 903 kg.

BODY estate car/station wagon; 2 + 1 doors.

Viva 1800 De Luxe 2-door Saloon

See Viva 1256 2-door Saloon, except for:

PRICE IN GB: £ 878.

ENGINE 4 cylinders, in line, slanted at 45°; 107.3 cu in, 1,759 cc (3.37 x 3 in, 85.7 x 76.2 mm); compression ratio: 8.5:1; max power (DIN): 77 hp at 5,200 rpm; max torque (DIN): 97 lb ft, 13.4 kg m at 3,000 rpm; max engine rpm: 6,250; 43.7 hp/l; 5 crankshaft bearings; camshafts: 1, overhead, push-rods, cogged belt; lubricating system capacity: 8.5 imp pt, 10.1 US pt, 4.8 l; 1 Zenith 36 VE downdraught single barrel carburettor; water-cooled, 8 imp pt, 14.1 US pt, 16.9 l.

TRANSMISSION ratios: I 3.300, II 2.141, III 1.362, IV 1, rev 3.064; axle ratio: 3.727; width of rims: 4.5"; tyres 155 x 13.

PERFORMANCE max speeds: (I) 35 mph, 56 km/h; (II) 54 mph, 87 km/h; (III) 84 mph, 135 km/h; (IV) 100 mph, 161 km/h; power-weight ratio: 24.5 lb/hp, 11.1 kg/hp; acceleration: standing ¼ mile 18.7 sec, 0-50 mph (0-80 km/h) 9.3 sec; speed in top et 1,000 rpm: 17.6 mph, 28.4 km/h; fuel consumption: 27 m/imp gal, 22.4 m/US gal, 10.5 l.

CHASSIS front suspension: anti-roll bar; rear suspension: anti-roll bar.

BRAKES front disc (diameter 10.03 in, 255 mm), rear drum, servo, swept area: front 188 sq in, 1,212 sq cm, rear 99 sq in, 638 sq cm, total 287 sq in, 1,850 sq cm.

ELECTRICAL EQUIPMENT 38 Ah battery; 44 W alternator.

DIMENSIONS AND WEIGHT dry weight: 1,958 lb, 859 kg; fuel tank: 12 imp gal, 14.3 US gal, 54 l.

PRACTICAL INSTRUCTIONS engine sump oil: 8 imp pt, 9.5 US pt, 4.5 l, 10W-40, change every 6,000 miles, 9,700 km; gearbox and final drive oil: 2.5 imp pt, 3 US pt, 1.4 l, 90 EP; tappet clearances: inlet 0.007-0.010 in, 0.17-0.25 mm, exhaust 0.015-0.018 in, 0.37-0.45 mm; valve timing: 33°26' 65°26' 65°26' 33°26'; tyres pressure: front 24 psi, 1.7 atm, rear 24 psi, 1.7 atm.

OPTIONAL ACCESSORIES 175/70 HR x 13 tyres; reclining front seats.

Viva 1800 De Luxe 4-door Saloon

See Viva 1800 De Luxe 2-door Saloon, except for:

PRICE IN GB: £ 912.

PERFORMANCE power-weight ratio: 26.2 lb/hp, 11.9 kg/hp.

DIMENSIONS AND WEIGHT: dry weight: 2,025 lb, 918 kg.

Viva 1800 De Luxe Estate Car

See Viva 1800 De Luxe 2-door Saloon, except for:

PRICE IN GB: £ **979.**

PERFORMANCE power-weight ratio: 27.3 lb/hp, 12.4 kg/hp.

DIMENSIONS AND WEIGHT dry weight: 2,110 lb, 957 kg.

BODY estate car/station wagon; 2 + 1 doors.

OPTIONAL ACCESSORIES heavy-duty suspension.

Viva 1800 SL 2-door Saloon

See Viva 1800 De Luxe 2-door Saloon, except for:

PRICE IN GB: £ **954.**

PERFORMANCE power-weight ratio: 25.8 lb/hp, 11.7 kg/hp.

DIMENSIONS AND WEIGHT dry weight: 1,995 lb, 905 kg.

Viva 1800 SL 4-door Saloon

See Viva 1800 De Luxe 2-door Saloon, except for:

PRICE IN GB: £ **988.**

PERFORMANCE power-weight ratio: 26.4 lb/hp, 12 kg/hp.

DIMENSIONS AND WEIGHT dry weight: 2,035 lb, 923 kg.

Viva 1800 SL Estate Car

See Viva 1800 De Luxe 2-door Saloon, except for:

PRICE IN GB: £ **1,050.**

PERFORMANCE power-weight ratio: 27.5 lb/hp, 12.5 kg/hp.

DIMENSIONS AND WEIGHT dry weight: 2,120 lb, 961 kg.

BODY estate car/station wagon; 2 + 1 doors.

OPTIONAL ACCESSORIES heavy-duty suspension.

Viva 2300 SL 2-door Saloon

See Viva 1800 De Luxe 2-door Saloon, except for:

PRICE IN GB: £ **1,072.**

ENGINE 139.1 cu in, 2,279 cc (3.84 x 3 in, 97.5 x 76.2 mm); max power (DIN): 110 hp at 5,200 rpm; max torque (DIN): 140 lb ft, 19.3 kg m at 3,000 rpm; max engine rpm: 5,500; 47 hp/l; 2 Zenith-Stromberg 175 CD-2 semi-downdraught carburettors.

TRANSMISSION axle ratio: 3.455; width of rims: 5"; tyres: 175/70 HR x 13.

PERFORMANCE max speeds: (I) 36 mph, 58 km/h; (II) 56 mph, 90 km/h; (III) 89 mph, 143 km/h; (IV) 104 mph, 167 km/h; power-weight ratio: 18.5 lb/hp, 8.3 kg/hp; acceleration: standing ¼ mile 18 sec, 0-50 mph (0-80 km/h) 8.3 sec; speed in top at 1,000 rpm: 19.2 mph, 30.9 km/h; fuel consumption: 25 m/imp gal, 20.8 m/US gal, 11.3 l x 100 km.

DIMENSIONS AND WEIGHT dry weight: 2,015 lb, 914 kg.

BODY reclining backrests.

PRACTICAL INSTRUCTIONS valve timing: 31°36' 63°36' 63°36' 31°36'.

Viva 2300 SL 4-door Saloon

See Viva 2300 SL 2-door Saloon, except for:

PRICE IN GB: £ **1,106.**

PERFORMANCE power-weight ratio: 18.9 lb/hp, 8.5 kg/hp.

DIMENSIONS AND WEIGHT dry weight: 2,055 lb, 932 kg.

Viva 2300 SL Estate Car

See Viva 2300 SL 2-door Saloon, except for:

PRICE IN GB: £ **1,168.**

PERFORMANCE power-weight ratio: 18.7 lb/hp, 8.4 kg/hp.

DIMENSIONS AND WEIGHT dry weight: 2,050 lb, 930 kg.

BODY estate car/station wagon; 2 + 1 doors.

OPTIONAL ACCESSORIES heavy-duty suspension.

VAUXHALL Firenza Sport SL

VAUXHALL Victor 1800 De Luxe Saloon

VAUXHALL VX 4/90

Firenza 1256 De Luxe

PRICE IN GB: £ 883.

ENGINE front, 4 stroke; 4 cylinders, vertical, in line; 76.6 cu in, 1,256 cc (3.19 x 2.40 in, 81 x 61 mm); compression ratio: 8.5:1; max power (SAE): 63 hp at 5,400 rpm; max torque (SAE): 71 lb ft, 9.8 kg m at 3,600 rpm; max engine rpm: 6,000; 50.3 hp/l; cast iron cylinder block and head; 3 crankshaft bearings; valves: overhead, in line, push-rods and rockers; camshafts: 1, side; lubrication: gear pump, full flow filter, 5.5 imp pt, 6.6 US pt, 3.1 l; 1 Zenith IZE downdraught single barrel carburettor; fuel feed: mechanical pump; water-cooled, 10.2 imp pt, 12.3 US pt, 5.8 l.

TRANSMISSION driving wheels: rear; clutch: single dry plate (diaphragm); gearbox: mechanical; gears: 4, fully synchronized; ratios: I 3.460, II 2.213, III 1.404, IV 1, rev 3.707; lever: central; final drive: hypoid bevel; axle ratio: 4.125; width of rims: 4"; tyres: 5.60 x 13.

PERFORMANCE max speeds: (I) 27 mph, 43 km/h; (II) 43 mph, 70 km/h; (III) 74 mph, 119 km/h; (IV) 82 mph, 132 km/h; power-weight ratio: 29.5 lb/hp, 13.4 kg/hp; carrying capacity: 917 lb, 415 kg; speed in direct drive at 1,000 rpm: 15.5 mph, 25 km/h; fuel consumption: 33 m/imp gal, 27.7 m/US gal, 8.5 l x 100 km.

CHASSIS integral; front suspension: independent, wishbones, coil springs, telescopic dampers; rear suspension: rigid axle, trailing lower radius arms, upper oblique radius arms, coil springs, telescopic dampers.

STEERING rack-and-pinion; turns lock to lock: 3.16.

BRAKES front disc (diameter 8.54 in, 217 mm), rear drum, servo; swept area: front 133.2 sq in, 861 sq cm, rear 62.9 sq in, 405 sq cm, total 196.1 sq in, 1,266 sq cm.

ELECTRICAL EQUIPMENT 12 V; 32 Ah battery; 444 W alternator; AC Delco distributor; 4 headlamps.

DIMENSIONS AND WEIGHT wheel base: 97 in, 2,464 mm; tracks: 51.40 in, 1,306 mm front, 51.50 in, 1,308 mm rear; length: 162.80 in, 4,135 mm; width: 64.70 in, 1,644 mm; height: 52.80 in, 1,341 mm; ground clearance: 5 in, 127 mm; dry weight: 1,865 lb, 846 kg; turning circle (between walls): 34.1 ft, 10.4 m; fuel tank: 8 imp gal, 9.5 US gal, 36 l.

BODY coupé; 2 doors; 4-5 seats, separate front seats; electrically-heated rear window.

PRACTICAL INSTRUCTIONS fuel: 98 oct petrol; engine sump oil: 4.9 imp pt, 5.9 US pt, 2.8 l, SAE 20W-20, change every 6,000 miles, 9,700 km; gearbox oil: 0.9 imp pt, 1.1 US pt, 0.5 l, SAE 90, change every 6 months; final drive oil: 1.2 imp pt, 1.5 US pt, 0.7 l, SAE 90, no change recommended; greasing: every 6 months, 4 points; tappet clearances: inlet 0.008 in, 0.20 mm, exhaust 0.008 in, 0.20 mm; valve timing: 39° 73° 71° 41°; tyre pressure: front 22 psi, 1.5 atm, rear 22 psi, 1.5 atm.

OPTIONAL ACCESSORIES G.M. automatic transmission, hydraulic torque converter and planetary gears with 3 ratios (I 2.390, II 1.480, III 1, rev 1.920), max ratio of converter at stall 2, possible manual selection.

Firenza 1800 SL

See Firenza 1256 De Luxe, except for:

PRICE IN GB: £ 1,051.

ENGINE 4 cylinders, in line; 107.3 cu in, 1,759 cc (3.38 x 3 in, 85.7 x 76.2 mm); compression ratio: 8.5:1; max power (DIN): 77 hp at 5,200 rpm; max torque (DIN): 97 lb ft, 13.4 kg m at 3,000 rpm; max engine rpm: 6,250; 43.7 hp/l; 5 crankshaft bearings; camshafts: 1, overhead, push-rods, cogged belt; lubricating system capacity: 8.5 imp pt, 10.1 US pt, 4.8 l; 1 Zenith 36 NE downdraught single barrel carburettor; cooling system capacity: 14.1 imp pt, 16.9 US pt, 8 l.

TRANSMISSION ratios: I 3.300, II 2.141, III 1.362, IV 1, rev 3.064; axle ratio: 3.700; width of rims: 5"; tyres: 175/70 HR x 13.

PERFORMANCE max speeds: (I) 35 mph, 56 km/h, (II) 54 mph, 87 km/h (III) 84 mph, 135 km/h, (IV) 100 mph, 161 km/h; power-weight ratio: 25.8 lb/hp, 11.7 kg/hp; speed in direct drive at 1,000 rpm: 19.2 mph, 30.9 km/h; fuel consumption: 27 m/imp gal, 22.4 m/US gal, 10.5 l.

CHASSIS front suspension: anti-roll bar; rear suspension: anti-roll bar.

BRAKES front disc (diameter 10.03 in, 255 mm), rear drum; swept area: front 188 sq in, 1,212 sq cm, rear 99 sq in, 638 sq cm, total 287 in, 1,850 sq cm.

ELECTRICAL EQUIPMENT 38 Ah battery; 4 headlamps.

DIMENSIONS AND WEIGHT dry weight: 1,990 lb, 902 kg; fuel tank: 12 imp gal, 14.3 US gal, 54 l.

VAUXHALL Firenza Sport SL

VAUXHALL Victor De Luxe Series

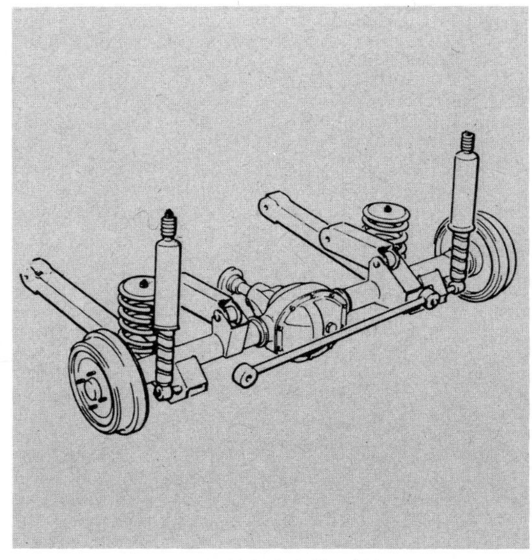

VAUXHALL VX 4/90

PRACTICAL INSTRUCTIONS engine sump oil: 8 imp pt, 9.5 US pt, 4.5 l, 10W-40, change every 6,000 miles, 9,700 km; gearbox and final drive oil: 2.5 imp pt, 3 US pt, 1.4 l, SAE 90 EP; tappets clearances: inlet 0.007-0.010 in, 0.17-0.25 mm, exhaust 0.015-0.018 in, 0.37-0.45 in; valve timing 33°26' 65°26' 65°26' 33°26'.

OPTIONAL ACCESSORIES automatic transmission.

Firenza Sport SL

See Firenza 1800 SL, except for:

PRICE IN GB: £ 1,140.

ENGINE 139.1 cu in, 2,279 cc (3.86 x 3 in, 97.5 x 76.2 mm); max power (DIN): 110 hp at 5,200 rpm; max torque (DIN): 140 lb ft, 19.3 kg m at 3,000 rpm; max engine rpm: 5,500; 47 hp/l; 2 Zenith Stromberg 175 CD-2 sidedraught single barrel carburettors.

TRANSMISSION axle ratio: 3.455; width of rims: 5"; tyres: 175/70HR x 13.

PERFORMANCE max speeds: (I) 36 mph, 58 km/h; (II) 56 mph, 90 km/h; (III) 89 mph, 143 km/h; (IV) 104 mph, 167 km/h; power-weight ratio: 18.7 lb/hp, 8.4 kg/hp; speed in direct drive at 1,000 rpm: 17.6 mph, 28.3 km/h; acceleration: standing ¼ mile 18 sec, 0-50 mph (0-80 km/h) 8.3 sec; fuel consumption: 25 m/imp gal, 20.8 m/US gal, 11.3 l x 100 km.

DIMENSIONS AND WEIGHT dry weight: 2,040 lb, 925 kg.

PRACTICAL INSTRUCTIONS engine sump oil: 8.5 imp pt, 10.1 US pt, 4.8 l; valve timing: 31°36' 63°35' 31°36' 63°36'.

Victor 1800 De Luxe Saloon

PRICE IN GB: £ 1,089.

ENGINE front, 4 stroke; 4 cylinders, in line; 107.3 cu in, 1,759 cc (3.37 x 3 in, 85.7 x 76.2 mm); compression ratio: 8.5:1; max power (DIN): 77 hp at 5,200 rpm; max torque (DIN): 97 lb ft, 13.4 kg m at 3,000 rpm; max engine rpm: 6,250; 43.7 hp/l; cast iron cylinder block and head; 5 crankshaft bearings; valves: overhead, in line, push-rods; camshafts: 1, overhead, cogged belt; lubrication: gear pump, full flow filter; 1 Zenith 36 NE downdraught single barrel carburettor; fuel feed: mechanical pump; water-cooled, 13.5 imp pt, 16.1 US pt, 7.6 l.

TRANSMISSION driving wheels: rear; clutch: single dry plate (diaphragm); gearbox: mechanical; gears: 4, fully synchronized; ratios: I 3.300, II 2.141, III 1.362, IV 1, rev 3.064; lever: central; final drive: hypoid bevel; axle ratio: 3.900; width of rims: 5"; tyres: 6.40 x 13.

PERFORMANCE max speeds: (I) 33 mph, 53 km/h; (II) 50 mph, 80 km/h; (III) 78 mph, 125 km/h; (IV) 96 mph, 154 km/h; power-weight ratio: 30.9 lb/hp, 14 kg/hp; acceleration: standing ¼ mile 20 sec, 0-50 mph (0-80 km/h) 9.7 sec; speed in direct drive at 1,000 rpm: 18.1 mph, 29.1 km/h; fuel consumption: 26.5 m/imp gal, 22 m/US gal, 10.7 l x 100 km.

CHASSIS integral: front suspension: independent, wishbones, coil springs, anti-roll bar, telescopic dampers; rear suspension: rigid axle, twin trailing radius arms, transverse linkage bar, coil springs, telescopic dampers.

STEERING rack-and-pinion; turns lock to lock: 4.

BRAKES front disc (diameter 10.03 in, 255 mm), rear drums, servo; swept area: front 188 sq in, 1,212 sq cm, rear 99 sq in, 638 sq cm, total 287 sq in, 1,850 sq cm.

ELECTRICAL EQUIPMENT 12 V; 38 Ah battery; 44 A alternator; Lucas distributor; 2 headlamps.

DIMENSIONS AND WEIGHT wheel base: 105 in, 2,667 mm; tracks: 56.20 in, 1,427 mm front, 55.40 in, 1,407 mm rear; length: 179.30 in, 4,554 mm; width: 66.90 in, 169 mm; height: 53.90 in, 1,370 mm; ground clearance: 5 in, 128 mm; dry weight: 2,385 lb, 1,081 kg; distribution of weight: 48% front, 52% rear; turning circle (between walls): 3.4 ft, 10.8 m; fuel tank: 14.2 imp pt, 16.9 US pt, 64 l.

BODY saloon/sedan; 4 doors; 4-5 seats, separate front seats; electrically-heated rear window.

PRACTICAL INSTRUCTIONS fuel: 98 oct petrol; engine sump oil: 8 imp pt, 9.5 US pt, 4.5 l, 20W-50, change every 6,000 miles, 9,700 km; gearbox and final drive oil: 2.5 imp pt, 3 US pt, 1.4 l, 90 EP; greasing: none; tappet clearances: inlet 0.007-0.010 in, 0.17-0.25 mm, exhaust 0.015 in, 0.019 in, 0.37-0.45 mm; valve timing 33°26' 65°26' 65°26' 33°26; tyre pressure: front 24 psi, 1.7 atm, rear 24 psi, 1.7 atm.

OPTIONAL ACCESSORIES G.M. automatic transmission, hydraulic torque converter and planetary gears with 3 ratios

VICTOR 1800 DE LUXE SALOON

(I 2.390, II 1.480, III 1, rev 2.920), max ratio of converter at stall 2, possible manual selection; 175 x 13 tyres; reclining backrests.

Victor 1800 De Luxe Estate Car

See Victor 1800 De Luxe Saloon, except for:

PRICE IN GB: £ 1,190.

PERFORMANCE power-weight ratio: 32 lb/hp, 14.5 kg/hp.

DIMENSIONS AND WEIGHT dry weight: 2,475 lb, 1,122 kg.

BODY estate car/station wagon; 4 + 1 doors.

Victor 2300 SL Saloon

See Victor 1800 De Luxe Saloon, except for:

PRICE IN GB: £ 1,185.

ENGINE 139.1 cu in, 2,279 cc (3.84 x 3 in, 97.5 x 76.2 mm); compression ratio: 8.5:1; max power (DIN): 100 hp at 5,200 rpm; max torque (DIN): 138 lb ft, 19 kg m at 3,000 rpm; max engine rpm: 5,500; 43.8 hp/l; 1 Zenith Stromberg 175 CD2 sidedraught single barrel carburettor.

TRANSMISSION axle ratio: 3.700; tyres 175 x 13.

PERFORMANCE max speeds: (I) 34 mph, 55 km/h; (II) 53 mph, 85 km/h; (III) 83 mph, 133 km/h; (IV) 100 mph, 161 km/h; power-weight ratio: 24.1 lb/hp, 10.9 kg/hp; acceleration: standing ¼ mile 18.2 sec, 0-50 (0-80 km/h) 8.3 sec; speed in direct drive at 1,000 rpm: 18.9 mph, 11.3 km/h; fuel consumption: 25 m/imp gal, 20.8 m/US gal, 11.3 l x 100 km.

CHASSIS rear suspension: anti-roll bar.

DIMENSIONS AND WEIGHT dry weight: 2,410 lb, 1,093 kg.

PRACTICAL INSTRUCTIONS valve timing: 31°36' 63°36' 31°36' 63°36'.

OPTIONAL ACCESSORIES overdrive/top (0.778 ratio).

Victor 2300 SL Estate Car

See Victor 2300 SL Saloon, except for:

PRICE IN GB: £ 1,278.

PERFORMANCE power-weight ratio: 24.7 lb/hp, 11.2 kg/hp; carrying capacity: 1,055 lb, 478 kg.

DIMENSIONS AND WEIGHT dry weight: 2,475 lb, 1,123 kg.

BODY estate car/station wagon; 4 + 1 doors.

Victor 3300 SL Estate Car

See Victor 1800 De Luxe Saloon, except for:

PRICE IN GB: £ 1,497.

ENGINE 6 cylinders, in line; 201 cu in, 3,294 cc (3.62 x 3.25 in, 92 x 82.5 mm); compression ratio: 8.5:1; max power (DIN): 123 hp at 4,600 rpm; max torque (DIN): 176 lb ft, 24.3 kg m at 2,400 rpm; max engine rpm: 5,300; 37 hp/l; 4 crankshaft bearings; valves: overhead, push-rods and rockers; camshafts: 1, side; lubricating system capacity: 9.5 imp pt, 11.4 US pt, 5.4 l; 1 Zenith WIAT 42 downdraught carburettor; cooling system capacity: 16.6 imp pt, 19.9 US pt, 9.4 l.

TRANSMISSION axle ratio: 3.090; width of rims: 6''; tyres: 185/70 HR x 14.

CHASSIS front and rear suspension: anti-roll bar.

STEERING servo; turns lock to lock: 2.80.

BRAKES disc (diameter 10.74 in, 273 mm); swept area: total 316.6 sq in, 2,042 sq cm.

ELECTRICAL EQUIPMENT 55 Ah battery.

DIMENSIONS AND WEIGHT turning circle (between walls): 37.1 ft, 11.3 m.

BODY estate car/station wagon; 4 + 1 doors.

VAUXHALL Ventora

WOLSELEY 1300

WOLSELEY Six

PRACTICAL INSTRUCTIONS engine sump oil: 9 imp pt, 10.8 US pt, 5.1 l; tappet clearances: inlet 0.013 in, 0.32 mm exhaust 0.018 in, 0.45 mm; valve timing: 39° 84° 81° 42°.

OPTIONAL ACCESSORIES reclining backrests.

VX 4/90

See Victor 2300 SL Saloon, except for:

PRICE IN GB: £ 1,336.

ENGINE slanted at 45°; max power (DIN): 110 hp at 5,200 rpm; max torque (DIN): 140 lb ft, 19.3 kg m at 3,000 rpm; 47 hp/l.

TRANSMISSION ratios: overdrive 0.778 on III and IV; width of rims: 6''; tyres: 185/70 HR x 14.

PERFORMANCE max speeds: (I) 35 mph, 56 km/h; (II) 54 mph, 87 km/h; (III) 85 mph, 136 km/h; (IV) 98 mph, 157 km/h, overdrive 102 mph, 164 km/h; power-weight ratio: 22.7 lb/hp, 10.3 kg/hp; acceleration: standing ¼ mile 18.4 sec, 0-50 mph, (0-80 km/h) 8.9 sec; speed in top at 1,000 rpm: 18.6 mph, 29.9 km/h.

BRAKES disc (diameter 10.74 in, 273 mm); swept area: total 316.6 sq in, 2,042 sq cm.

ELECTRICAL EQUIPMENT 4 headlamps.

DIMENSIONS AND WEIGHT dry weight: 2,520 lb, 1,143 kg.

PRACTICAL INSTRUCTIONS gearbox oil: 3 imp pt, 3.6 US pt, 1.7 l; valve timing: 31°36' 63°36' 31°36' 63°36'.

Ventora

See Victor 2300 SL Saloon, except for:

PRICE IN GB: £ 1,535.

PERFORMANCE power-weight ratio: 22.3 lb/hp, 10.3 kg/hp.

ELECTRICAL EQUIPMENT 4 headlamps.

DIMENSIONS AND WEIGHT dry weight: 2,750 lb, 1,247 kg.

BODY reclining backrests.

OPTIONAL ACCESSORIES overdrive on III and IV (ratio 0.778); automatic transmission.

WOLSELEY GREAT BRITAIN

1300

PRICE IN GB: £ 904.

ENGINE front, transverse, 4 stroke; 4 cylinders, vertical, in line; 77.8 cu in, 1,275 cc (2.78 x 3.20 in, 70.6 x 81.3 mm); compression ratio: 8.8:1; max power (DIN): 65 hp at 5,750 rpm; max torque (DIN): 70.5 lb ft, 9.7 kg m at 3,000 rpm; max engine rpm: 5,900; 51 hp/l; cast iron cylinder block and head; 3 crankshaft bearings; valves: overhead, in line, push-rods and rockers; camshafts: 1, side; lubrication: gear or vane-type pump, full flow filter, 9 imp pt, 10.8 US pt, 5.1 l; 2 SU type HS 2 semi-downdraught carburettors; fuel feed: electric pump; water-cooled, 6.9 imp pt, 8.2 US pt, 3.9 l.

TRANSMISSION driving wheels: front; clutch: single dry plate (diaphragm), hydraulically controlled; gearbox: mechanical; gears: 4, fully synchronized; ratios: I 3.530, II 2.220, III 1.430, IV 1, rev 3.540; lever: central; final drive: helical spur gears; axle ratio: 3.650; tyres: 5.50 x 12.

PERFORMANCE max speeds: (I) 28 mph, 45 km/h; (II) 44 mph, 71 km/h; (III) 69 mph, 111 km/h; (IV) 90 mph, 145 km/h; power-weight ratio: 28.5 lb/hp, 13 kg/hp; carrying capacity: 882 lb, 400 kg; acceleration: 0-50 mph (0-80 km/h) 11.4 sec; speed in direct drive at 1,000 rpm: 16.8 mph, 27 km/h; fuel consumption: 33.6 m/imp gal, 28 m/US gal, 8.4 l x 100 km.

CHASSIS integral, front and rear auxiliary frames; front suspension: independent, wishbones, hydrolastic (liquid) rubber cone springs, hydraulic connecting pipes to rear wheels; rear suspension: independent, swinging longitudinal trailing arms, hydrolastic (liquid) rubber cone springs, hydraulic connecting pipes to front wheels, combined with transverse torsion bars, anti-roll bar.

STEERING rack-and-pinion; turns lock to lock: 3.12.

VAUXHALL Ventora

WOLSELEY 1300

WOLSELEY Six

BRAKES front disc (diameter 8.40 in, 213 mm), rear drum.

ELECTRICAL EQUIPMENT 12 V; 40 Ah battery; 264 W dynamo; Lucas distributor; 2 headlamps.

DIMENSIONS AND WEIGHT wheel base: 93.50 in, 2,375 mm; tracks: 51.50 in, 1,308 mm front, 50.85 in, 1,292 mm rear; length: 146.75 in, 3,727 mm; width: 60.35 in, 1,533 mm; height: 53 in, 1,346 mm; ground clearance: 5.30 in, 135 mm; dry weight: 1,852 lb, 840 kg; distribution of weight: 62% front, 38% rear; turning circle (between walls): 36 ft, 11 m; fuel tank: 8 imp gal, 9.5 US gal, 36 l.

BODY saloon/sedan; 4 doors; 4-5 seats, separate front seats.

PRACTICAL INSTRUCTIONS fuel: 98-100 oct petrol; engine sump, gearbox and final drive oil: 7.6 imp pt, 9.1 US pt, 4.3 l, SAE 10W-30, change every 6,000 miles, 9,700 km; greasing: every 3,000 miles, 4,800 km, 4 points; sparking plug type: 225°; tappet clearances: inlet 0.012 in, 0.30 mm, exhaust 0.012 in, 0.30 mm; valve timing: 5° 45° 51° 21°; tyre pressure: front 28 psi, 2 atm, rear 24 psi, 1.7 atm.

OPTIONAL ACCESSORIES AP automatic transmission, hydraulic torque converter with 2 conic bevel gears (twin concentric differential-like gear clusters) with 4 ratios (I 2.690, II 1.850, III 1.460, IV 1, rev 2.690) operated by 3 brake bands and 2 multi-disc clutches, max ratio of converter at stall 2, possible manual selection, with engine max power (DIN) 60 hp at 5,250 rpm, max torque (DIN) 69.5 lb ft, 9.6 kg m at 2,500 rpm, 47.1 hp/l, 1 SU type HS 4 carburettor, 3.270 axle ratio, max speeds (I) 38 mph, 59 km/h, (II) 53 mph, 85 km/h, (III) 66 mph, 106 km/h, (IV) 87 mph, 140 km/h, power-weight ratio 30.9 lb/hp, 14 kg/hp, speed in direct drive at 1,000 rpm 16.3 mph, 26.2 km/h, fuel consumption 34 m/imp gal, 28.3 m/US gal, 8.3 l x 100 km; reclining backrests; electrically-heated rear window.

Six

PRICE IN GB: £ 1,328.

ENGINE front, transverse, 4 stroke; 6 cylinders, in line; 135.8 cu in, 2,227 cc (3 x 3.20 in, 76.2 x 81.28 mm); compression ratio: 9:1; max power (DIN): 110 hp at 5,250 rpm; max torque (DIN): 125.6 lb ft, 17.4 kg m at 3,500 rpm; max engine rpm: 5,400; 49.4 hp/l; cast iron cylinder block and head; 4 crankshaft bearings; valves: overhead, in line, thimble tappets; camshafts: 1, overhead; lubrication: rotary pump, full flow filter, 17 imp pt, 20.3 US pt, 9.6 l; 2 SU type HS6 semi-downdraught carburettors; fuel feed: 2 electric pumps; water-cooled, 17 imp pt, 20.3 US pt, 9.6 l, electric thermostatic fan.

TRANSMISSION driving wheels: front; clutch: single dry plate (diaphragm), hydraulically controlled; gearbox: mechanical; gears: 4, fully synchronized; ratios: I 3.290, II 2.060, III 1.380, IV 1, rev 3.070; lever: central; final drive: spiral bevel; axle ratio: 3.880; width of rims: 4.5"; tyres: 165 SR x 14.

PERFORMANCE max speed: 103 mph, 165 km/h; power-weight ratio: 22.8 lb/hp, 10.3 kg/hp; acceleration: 0-50 mph (0-80 km/h) 9 sec; speed in direct drive at 1,000 rpm: 13.3 mph, 21.4 km/h; fuel consumption: 20.5 m/imp gal, 17 m/US gal, 13.8 l x 100 km.

CHASSIS integral; front suspension: independent, wishbones, lower trailing links, hydrolastic (liquid) rubber cone springs, hydraulic connecting pipes to rear wheels; rear suspension: independent, swinging longitudinal trailing arms, hydrolastic (liquid) rubber cone springs, hydraulic connecting pipes to front wheels, anti-roll bar.

STEERING rack-and-pinion; turns lock to lock: 3.56.

BRAKES front disc (diameter 9.70 in, 246 mm), rear drum, servo; swept area: front 195 sq in, 1,258 sq cm, rear 99 sq in, 638 sq cm, total 294 sq in, 1,896 sq cm.

ELECTRICAL EQUIPMENT 12 V; 50 Ah battery; 16 A alternator; Lucas distributor; 2 headlamps.

DIMENSIONS AND WEIGHT wheel base: 105.87 in, 2,689 mm; tracks: 55.91 in, 1,420 mm front, 55.47 in, 1,409 mm rear; length: 166.18 in, 4,221 mm; width: 66.93 in, 1,700 mm; height: 56.14 in, 1,426 mm; ground clearance: 6.50 in, 165 mm; dry weight: 2,511 lb, 1,139 kg; turning circle (between walls): 38.5 ft, 11.7 m; fuel tank: 12.5 imp gal, 15 US gal, 57 l.

BODY saloon/sedan; 4 doors; 5 seats, separate front seats, reclining backrests.

PRACTICAL INSTRUCTIONS fuel: 99 oct petrol; engine sump, gearbox and final drive oil: 16 imp pt, 19.2 US pt, 9.1 l.

OPTIONAL ACCESSORIES Borg-Warner 35 automatic transmission; power-assisted steering; electrically-heated rear window.

DAF HOLLAND

33 Saloon

PRICE IN GB: £ 677.

ENGINE front, 4 stroke; 2 cylinders, horizontally opposed; 45.5 cu in, 746 cc (3.37 x 2.56 in, 85.5 x 65 mm); compression ratio: 7.5:1; max power (DIN): 28 hp at 4,200 rpm; max torque (DIN): 38 lb ft, 5.4 kg m at 2,700 rpm; max engine rpm: 4,500; 37.5 hp/l; light alloy cylinder block and head; 2 crankshaft bearings; valves: overhead, in line, push-rods and rockers; camshafts: 1, central, lower; lubrication: gear pump, full flow filter, 3.5 imp pt, 4.2 US pt, 2 l; 1 Solex 34 PICS-3 downdraught carburettor; fuel feed: mechanical pump; air-cooled.

TRANSMISSION driving wheels: rear; clutch: automatic, 2-stage centrifugal; transmission: Daf-Variomatic automatic acting as limited slip differential; gears: progressive, infinite number of ratios between 16.4 and 3.9; lever: central; axle ratio: 4.750; tyres: 135 x 13.

PERFORMANCE max speed: 70 mph, 112 km/h; power-weight ratio: 52.5 lb/hp, 23.8 kg/hp; carrying capacity: 706 lb, 320 kg; acceleration: 0-50 mph (0-80 km/h) 17 sec; fuel consumption: 42.1 m/imp gal, 35.1 m/US gal, 6.7 l x 100 km.

CHASSIS integral; front suspension: independent, transverse lower leafspring, vertical sliding pillars, co-axial telescopic dampers; rear suspension: independent, oblique semi-trailing arms, coil springs, telescopic dampers.

STEERING rack-and-pinion; turns lock to lock: 2.90.

BRAKES drum, single circuit; swept area: front 34 sq in, 219 sq cm, rear 34 sq in, 219 sq cm, total 68 sq in, 438 sq cm.

ELECTRICAL EQUIPMENT 12 V; 36 Ah battery; 420 W dynamo; Bosch distributor; 2 headlamps.

DIMENSIONS AND WEIGHT wheel base: 80.71 in, 2,050 mm; tracks: 47.01 in, 1,194 mm front, 47.01 in, 1,194 mm rear; length: 142.52 in, 3,620 mm; width: 56.69 in, 1,440 mm; height: 54.33 in, 1,380 mm; ground clearance: 7.48 in, 190 mm; dry weight: 1,477 lb, 670 kg; distribution of weight: 50% front, 50% rear; turning circle (between walls): 31.2 ft, 9.5 m; fuel tank: 7 imp gal, 8.4 US gal, 32 l.

BODY saloon/sedan; 2 doors; 4-5 seats, separate front seats.

PRACTICAL INSTRUCTIONS fuel: 88 oct petrol; engine sump oil: 3.5 imp pt, 4.2 US pt, 2 l, SAE 10W-30 (summer), 20W-40 (winter), change every 3,100 miles, 5,000 km; transmission oil: central conic bevels 0.9 imp pt, 11 US pt, 0.5 l, SAE 80-90, axle reduction gears and pulleys (one per wheel) 0.5 imp pt, 0.6 US pt, 0.3 l, SAE 80-90, Variomatic belt, pulley drums sealed for life; greasing: none; tappet clearances: inlet 0.004 in, 0.10 mm, exhaust 0.006 in, 0.15 mm; valve timing: 13° 27° 27° 13°; tyre pressure: front 20 psi, 1.4 atm, rear 24 psi, 1.7 atm.

OPTIONAL ACCESSORIES sunshine roof.

33 De Luxe Saloon

See 33 Saloon, except for:

PRICE IN GB: £ 715.

BODY luxury equipment.

44 Saloon

See 33 Saloon, except for:

PRICE IN GB: £ 772.

ENGINE 51.5 cu in, 844 cc (3.37 x 2.89 in, 85.5 x 73.5 mm); compression ratio: 7.6:1; max power (DIN): 34 hp at 4,500 rpm; max torque (DIN): 47 lb ft, 6.6 kg m at 2,200 rpm; max engine rpm: 5,200; 40.2 hp/l; 1 Solex 40 PICS-6 downdraught carburettor.

TRANSMISSION gears: progressive, infinite number of ratios between 15.44 and 3.87; axle ratio: 3.640; tyres: 135 x 14.

PERFORMANCE max speed: 76 mph, 123 km/h; power-weight ratio: 48.9 lb/hp, 21.8 kg/hp; carrying capacity: 728 lb, 330 kg; acceleration: 0-50 mph (0-80 km/h) 15 sec; fuel consumption: 37.6 m/imp gal, 31.4 m/US gal, 7.5 l x 100 km.

CHASSIS rear suspension: independent, swinging semi-axles (wide based transverse arm).

STEERING turns lock to lock: 3.25.

BRAKES swept area: front 48.7 sq in, 314 sq cm, rear 48.7 sq in, 314 sq cm, total 97.4 sq in, 628 sq cm.

DIMENSIONS AND WEIGHT wheel base: 88.58 in, 2,250 mm; tracks: 48.46 in, 1,310 mm front, 49.61 in, 1,260 mm rear; length: 151.57 in, 3,850 mm; ground clearance: 6.69 in, 170 mm; dry weight: 1,632 lb, 740 kg; distribution of weight 54% front, 46% rear; fuel tank: 8.4 imp gal, 10 US gal, 38 l

PRACTICAL INSTRUCTIONS tyre pressure: front 22 psi, 1.5 atm, rear 28 psi, 2 atm.

DAF 33 De Luxe Saloon

DAF 66 Marathon Series

DAF 66 Series

44 De Luxe Saloon

See 44 Saloon, except for:

PRICE IN GB: £ 800.

BODY luxury equipment.

44 C Estate Car

See 44 Saloon, except for:

PRICE IN GB: £ 907.

PERFORMANCE power-weight ratio: 50 lb/hp, 22.7 kg/hp carrying capacity: 772 lb, 350 kg.

DIMENSIONS AND WEIGHT dry weight: 1,698 lb, 770 kg; distribution of weight: 51% front, 49% rear.

BODY estate car/station wagon; 2 + 1 doors.

66 De Luxe Saloon

PRICE IN GB: £ 876.

ENGINE front, 4 stroke; 4 cylinders, vertical, in line, 67.6 cu in, 1,108 cc (2.76 x 2.83 in, 70 x 72 mm); compression ratio: 8.5:1; max power (DIN): 47 hp at 5,000 rpm; max torque (DIN): 54 lb ft, 7.6 kg m at 2,700 rpm; max engine rpm: 6,200; 42.4 hp/l; cast iron cylinder block, light alloy head; 5 crankshafts bearings; valves: overhead, in line push-rods and rockers; camshafts: 1, side; lubrication: gear pump, full flow filter, 5.3 imp pt, 6.3 US pt, 3 l; 1 Solex 32 EHSA-3 carburettor; fuel feed: mechanical pump; water-cooled, 8.4 imp pt, 10.1 US pt, 4.8 l.

TRANSMISSION driving wheels: rear; clutch: automatic, centrifugal; transmission: Daf-Variomatic automatic, acting as limited slip differential; gears: progressive, infinite number of ratios between 14.22 and 3.60; lever: central; axle ratio: 4.510; tyres: 135 SR x 14.

PERFORMANCE max speed: 85 mph, 136 km/h; power-weight ratio: 38.4 lb/hp, 17.4 kg/hp; carrying capacity: 838 lb, 380 kg; acceleration: 0-50 mph (0-80 km/h) 12 sec; fuel consumption: 34.4 m/imp gal, 28.7 m/US gal, 8.2 l x 100 km.

CHASSIS integral; front suspension: independent, longitudinal torsion bars, telescopic dampers struts, lower wishbones (trailing links), anti-roll bar; rear suspension: de Dion rigid axle, semi-elliptic leafsprings, upper torque arms, telescopic dampers.

STEERING rack-and-pinion; turns lock to lock: 3.34.

BRAKES drum; swept area: front 48.8 sq in, 315 sq cm, rear 27.9 sq in, 180 sq cm, total 76.7 sq in, 495 sq cm.

ELECTRICAL EQUIPMENT 12 V; 36 Ah battery; 420 W alternator; Ducellier distributor; 2 headlamps.

DIMENSIONS AND WEIGHT wheel base: 88.58 in, 2,250 mm; tracks: 51.57 in, 1,310 mm front, 48.82 in, 1,240 mm rear; lenght: 152.56 in, 3,875 mm; width: 60.63 in, 1,540 mm; height: 54.33 in, 1,380 mm; ground clearance: 4.92 in, 125 mm; dry weight: 1,808 lb, 820 kg; distribution of weight: 54% front, 46% rear; turning circle (between walls): 31.2 ft, 9.5 m; fuel tank: 9.2 imp gal, 11.1 US gal, 42 l.

BODY saloon/sedan; 2 doors; 4-5 seats, separate front seats.

PRACTICAL INSTRUCTIONS fuel: 88 oct petrol; engine sump oil: 5.3 imp pt, 6.3 US pt, 3 l, SAE 10W-30 (summer) 20W-40 (winter), change every 3,100 miles, 5,000 km; transmission oil: central conic bevel 0.9 imp pt, 1.1 US pt, 0.5 l, SAE 80; axle reduction gears and pulleys (one per wheel) 0.5 imp pt, 0.6 US pt, 0.3 l, SAE 80-90, Variomatic belt-pulley drums sealed for life; greasing: none; tappet clearances: 0.006 in, 0.15 mm, exhaust 0.008 in, 0.20 mm; valve timing: 2° 35°30' 39° 4°; tyre pressure: front 22 psi, 1.6 atm, rear 26 psi, 1.8 atm.

OPTIONAL ACCESSORIES 155 SR x 13 tyres; reclining backrests; electrically-heated rear window; sunshine roof.

66 De Luxe Estate Car

See 66 De Luxe Saloon, except for:

PRICE IN GB: £ 1,012.

PERFORMANCE power-weight ratio: 39 lb/hp, 17.7 kg/hp.

FIAT 127 2-door Berlina

FIAT 128 4-door Berlina

FIAT 128 Rally

km/h; fuel consumption: 32.8 m/imp gal, 27.3 m/US gal, 8.6 l x 100 km.

BRAKES servo.

ELECTRICAL EQUIPMENT 45 Ah battery; 580 W alternator; Marelli S 146 A distributor; 4 headlamps.

DIMENSIONS AND WEIGHT length: 152.60 in, 3,876 mm; height: 54.72 in, 1,390 mm; turning circle (between walls): 34.8 ft, 10.6 m.

BODY reclining backrests (standard); headrests (standard).

PRACTICAL INSTRUCTIONS tappet clearances: inlet 0.016 in, 0.40 mm, exhaust 0.018 in, 0.45 mm; valve timing: 24° 68° 64° 28°.

OPTIONAL ACCESSORIES light alloy wheels.

128 S 1100 Sport Coupé

PRICE EX WORKS: 1,257,000 liras.

ENGINE front, transverse, 4 stroke; 4 cylinders, vertical, in line; 68.1 cu in, 1,116 cc (3.15 x 2.19 in, 80 x 55.5 mm); compression ratio: 8.8:1; max power (DIN): 64 hp at 6,000 rpm; max torque (DIN): 61 lb ft, 8.4 kg m at 4,400 rpm; max engine rpm: 6,800; 57.3 hp/l; cast iron cylinder block, light alloy head; 5 crankshaft bearings; valves: overhead, thimble tappets; camshafts: 1, overhead; lubrication: gear pump, full flow filter (cartridge), 8.8 imp pt, 10.6 US pt, 5 l; 1 Weber DMTR 20 twin barrel carburettor; fuel feed: mechanical pump; water-cooled, 11.4 imp pt, 13.7 US pt, 6.5 l.

TRANSMISSION driving wheels: front; clutch: single dry plate; gearbox: mechanical; gears: 4, fully synchronized; ratios: I 3.583, II 2.235, III 1.454, IV 1.042, rev 3.714; lever: central; final drive: cylindrical gears; axle ratio: 4.077; width of rims: 4.5"; tyres: 145 x 13.

PERFORMANCE max speeds: (I) 31 mph, 50 km/h; (II) 50 mph, 80 km/h; (III) 75 mph, 120 km/h; (IV) 93 mph, 150 km/h; power-weight ratio: 28 lb/hp, 12.7 kg/hp; carrying capacity: 706 lb, 320 kg; acceleration: standing ¼ mile 19.8 sec, 0-50 mph (0-80 km/h) 10.1 sec; speed in top at 1,000 rpm: 15.2 mph, 24.4 km/h; fuel consumption: 32.8 m/imp gal, 27.3 m/US gal, 8.6 l x 100 km.

CHASSIS integral; front suspension: independent, by McPherson, coil springs, telescopic damper struts, lower wishbones, anti-roll bar; rear suspension: independent, single wide-based wishbone, transverse anti-roll bar leafspring, telescopic dampers.

STEERING rack-and-pinion; turns lock to lock: 3.50.

BRAKES front disc, rear drum, rear compensator; swept area: front 19.2 sq in, 124 sq cm, rear 33.5 sq in, 216 sq cm, total 52.7 sq in, 340 sq cm.

ELECTRICAL EQUIPMENT 12 V; 45 Ah battery; 400 W alternator; Marelli distributor; 2 headlamps.

DIMENSIONS AND WEIGHT wheel base: 87.52 in, 2,223 mm; tracks: 52.17 in, 1,325 mm front, 52.48 in, 1,333 mm rear; length: 149.92 in, 3,808 mm; width: 61.42 in, 1,560 mm; height: 51.57 in, 1,310 mm; ground clearance: 5.12 in, 130 mm; dry weight: 1,797 lb, 815 kg; turning circle (between walls): 34.1 ft, 10.4 m; fuel tank: 11 imp gal, 13.2 US gal, 50 l.

BODY coupé; 2 doors; 4 seats, separate front seats.

PRACTICAL INSTRUCTIONS fuel: 98 oct petrol; engine sump oil: 7.4 imp pt, 8.9 US pt, 4.2 l, SAE 20W (winter), 30W (summer), change every 6,200 miles, 10,000 km; gearbox and final drive oil: 5.5 imp pt, 6.6 US pt, 3.1 l, SAE 90, change every 18,600 miles, 30,000 km; greasing: homocinetic joints, every 18,600 miles, 30,000 km; sparking plug type: 240°; tappet clearances: inlet 0.016 in, 0.40 mm, exhaust 0.018 in, 0.45 mm; valve timing: 24° 68° 64° 28°; tyre pressure: front 26 psi, 1.8 atm, rear 24 psi, 1.7 atm.

OPTIONAL ACCESSORIES reclining backrests and headrests; light alloy wheels; tinted glass with electrically-heated rear window.

128 SL 1100 Sport Coupé

See 128 S 1100 Sport Coupé, except for:

PRICE IN GB: £ 1,168.
PRICE EX WORKS: 1,342,000 liras.

PERFORMANCE power-weight ratio: 28.2 lb/hp, 12.8 kg/hp.

ELECTRICAL EQUIPMENT 4 headlamps.

DIMENSIONS AND WEIGHT dry weight: 1,808 lb, 820 kg.

BODY reclining backrests (standard).

128 S 1300 Sport Coupé

See 128 S 1100 Sport Coupé, except for:

PRICE EX WORKS: 1,314,000 liras.

ENGINE 78.7 cu in, 1,290 cc (3.39 x 2.19 in, 86 x 55.5 mm): compression ratio: 8.9:1; max power (DIN): 75 hp at 6,600 rpm; max torque (DIN): 68 lb ft, 9.4 kg m at 3,600 rpm; 58.1 hp/l.

PERFORMANCE max speed: 99 mph, 160 km/h; power-weight ratio: 29.8 lb/hp, 10.8 kg/hp; acceleration: standing ¼ mile 19 sec, 0-50 mph (0-80 km/h) 9.2 sec; fuel consumption: 33.2 m/imp gal, 27.7 m/US gal, 8.5 l x 100 km.

128 SL 1300 Sport Coupé

See 128 S 1300 Sport Coupé, except for:

PRICE IN GB: £ 1,202.
PRICE IN USA: $ 2,650.

PERFORMANCE power-weight ratio: 24 lb/hp, 10.9 kg/hp.

ELECTRICAL EQUIPMENT 4 headlamps.

DIMENSIONS AND WEIGHT dry weight: 1,808 lb, 820 kg.

BODY reclining bachrests (standard).

X 1/9

PRICE EX WORKS: 1,701,000 liras.

ENGINE central, rear, transverse, 4 stroke; 4 cylinders, vertical, in line; 78.7 cu in, 1,290 cc (3.39 x 2.19 in, 86 x 55.5 mm); compression ratio: 8.9:1; max power (DIN): 75 hp at 6,000 rpm; max torque (DIN): 72 lb ft, 9.9 kg m at 3,400 rpm; max engine rpm: 6,900; 58.1 hp/l; cast iron cylinder block, light alloy head: 5 crankshafts bearings; valves: overhead, Vee-slanted, thimble tappets; camshafts: 1, overhead, cogged belt; lubrication: gear pump, full flow filter by cartridge, 8.6 imp pt, 10.4 US pt, 4.9 l; 1 Weber 32 DMTR 22 downdraught twin barrel carburettor; fuel feed: mechanical pump; water-cooled, 19.4 imp pt, 23.3 US pt, 11 l, electric thermostatic fan.

TRANSMISSION driving wheels: rear; clutch: single dry plate (diaphragm), hydraulically controlled; gearbox: mechanical; gears: 4, fully synchronized; ratios: I 3.583, II 2.235, III 1.454, IV 0.959, rev 3.714; lever: central; final drive: cylindrical gears; axle ratio: 4.077; width of rims: 4.5"; tyres: 145 HR x 13.

PERFORMANCE max speeds: (I) 31 mph, 50 km/h; (II) 50 mph, 80 km/h; (III) 75 mph, 120 km/h; (IV) over 106 mph, 170 km/h; power-weight ratio: 25.8 lb/hp, 11.7 kg/hp; carrying capacity: 441 lb, 200 kg; acceleration: standing ¼ mile 18.5 sec; speed in direct drive at 1,000 rpm: 16.4 mph, 26.4 km/h.

CHASSIS integral; front suspension: independent, by McPherson (lower trailing links), coil springs, telescopic damper struts, lower wishbones; rear suspension: independent, lower wishbones, each with articulated transverse control bar, coil springs/telescopic damper struts.

STEERING rack-and-pinion; turns lock to lock: 3.

BRAKES disc (diameter 8.94 in, 227 mm); swept area: front 136.4 sq in, 880 sq cm, rear 136.4 sq in, 880 sq cm, total 272.8 sq in, 1,760 sq cm.

ELECTRICAL EQUIPMENT 12 V; 45 Ah battery; 33 A alternator; Marelli distributor; 2 retractable headlamps.

DIMENSIONS AND WEIGHT wheel base: 86.69 in, 2,202 mm; tracks: 52.56 in, 1,335 mm front, 52.87 in, 1,343 mm rear; length: 150.79 in, 3,830 mm; width: 61.81 in, 1,570 mm; height: 46.06 in, 1,170 mm; ground clearance: 4.92 in, 125 mm; dry weight: 1,940 lb, 880 kg; distribution of weight: 41% front, 59% rear; turning circle (between walls): 35.4 ft, 10.8 m; fuel tank: 10.6 imp gal, 12.7 US gal, 48 l.

BODY sports; 2 doors; 2 seats, reclining backrests, built-in headrests, roll bar, detachable roof.

PRACTICAL INSTRUCTIONS fuel 98-100 oct petrol; engine sump oil: 7.4 imp pt, 8.9 US pt, 4.2 l, SAE 30W (summer), 20W (winter), change every 6,200 miles, 10,000 km; gearbox and final drive oil: 5.5 imp pt, 6.6 US pt, 3.1 l, FIAT ZC 90, change every 18,600 miles, 30,000 km; tappet clearances: inlet 0.018 in, 0.45 mm, exhaust 0.020 in, 0.50 mm; valve timing: 24° 68° 64° 28°; tyre pressure: front 26 psi, 1.8 atm, rear 28 psi, 2 atm.

124 Berlina

PRICE IN GB: £ 867.
PRICE EX WORKS: 1,266,000 liras.

ENGINE front, 4 stroke; 4 cylinders, in line; 73 cu in, 1,197 cc (2.87 x 2.81 in, 73 x 71.5 mm); compression ratio: 8.8:1;

FIAT 128 SL 1100 - 1300 Sport Coupé

FIAT X 1/9

FIAT 124 Berlina

ISO Varedo

LAMBORGHINI Urraco 250

LAMBORGHINI Espada 400 GT

plate (diaphragm), hydraulically controlled; gearbox: mechanical; gears: 5, fully synchronized; ratios: I 2.520, II 1.735, III 1.225, IV 1, IV 0.815, rev 2.765; lever: central; final drive: hypoid bevel; axle ratio: 4.500; width of rims: 7''; tyres: HS 205 VR x 15.

PERFORMANCE max speeds: (I) 47 mph, 75 km/h; (II) 68 mph, 110 km/h; (III) 93 mph, 150 km/h; (IV) 124 mph, 200 km/h; (V) 155 mph, 250 km/h; power-weight ratio: 10.3 lb/hp, 4.7 kg/hp; carrying capacity: 937 lb, 425 kg; acceleration: standing ¼ mile 15.5 sec; speed in top at 1,000 rpm: 21.6 mph, 34.8 km/h; fuel consumption: 16.6 m/imp gal, 13.8 m/US gal, 17 l x 100 km.

CHASSIS integral; front suspension: independent, wishbones, coil springs, anti-roll bar, telescopic dampers; rear suspension: independent, wishbones, coil springs, anti-roll bar, telescopic dampers.

STEERING ZF screw and sector; turns lock to lock: 3.80.

BRAKES disc (front diameter 11.81 in, 300 mm, rear 11.02 in, 280 mm), internal radial fins, dual circuit, each with servo; swept area: front 285.3 sq in, 1,840 sq cm, rear 206.2 sq in, 1,330 sq cm, total 491.5 sq in, 3,170 sq cm.

ELECTRICAL EQUIPMENT 12 V; 72 Ah battery; 2 x 770 W alternators; Marelli distributor; 2 iodine headlamps; 2 iodine fog lamps.

DIMENSIONS AND WEIGHT wheel base: 104.33 in, 2,650 mm; tracks: 58.66 in, 1,490 mm front, 58.66 in, 1,490 mm rear; length: 186.54 in, 4,738 mm; width: 73.23 in, 1,860 mm; height: 46.65 in, 1,185 mm; ground clearance: 4.92 in, 125 mm; dry weight: 3,605 lb, 1,635 kg; distribution of weight: 49.5% front, 50.5% rear; turning circle (between walls): 39.4 ft, 12 m; fuel tank: 20.5 imp gal, 24.6 US gal, 93 l (2 separate tanks).

BODY coupé; 2 doors; 4 seats, separate front seats, reclining backrests; air-conditioning, tinted glass, electrically-controlled windows, electrically-heated rear window.

PRACTICAL INSTRUCTIONS fuel: 98-100 oct petrol; engine sump oil: 25.2 imp pt, 30.2 US pt, 14.3 l, SAE 20W-50, change every 2,500 miles, 4,000 km; gearbox oil: 7 imp pt, 8.5 US pt, 4 l, SAE 90, change every 6,200 miles, 10,000 km; final drive oil: 2.6 imp pt, 3.2 US pt, 1.5 l, SAE 90, change every 6,200 miles, 10,000 km; greasing: every 6,200 miles, 10,000 km, 2 points, every 12,400 miles, 20,000 km, 2 points; sparking plug type: 235°; tappet clearances: inlet 0.010 in, 0.25 mm, exhaust 0.010 in, 0.25 mm; valve timing: 32° 76° 64° 32°; tyre pressure: front 34 psi, 2.4 atm, rear 37 psi, 2.6 atm.

OPTIONAL ACCESSORIES limited slip differential; 4.090 axle ratio; power-assisted steering; right-hand drive; VIP interior; metallic spray; special spray.

Jarama 400 GT S

PRICE IN GB: £ 7,580.
PRICE EX WORKS: 9,000,000 liras.

ENGINE front, 4 stroke; 12 cylinders, Vee-slanted at 60°; 239.7 cu in, 3,929 cc (2.23 x 2.44 in, 82 x 62 mm); compression ratio: 10.7:1; max power (DIN): 365 hp at 7,500 rpm; max torque (DIN): 301 lb ft, 41.5 kg m at 5,500 rpm; max engine rpm: 7,900; 92.8 hp/l; light alloy cylinder block and head, wet liners; 7 crankshaft bearings; valves: overhead, Vee-slanted at 70°, thimble tappets; camshafts: 2, per cylinder block, overhead, cogged belts; lubrication: gear pump, full flow filter, 22 imp pt, 26.4 US pt, 12.5 l; 6 Weber 40 DCOE 20-21 horizontal twin barrel carburettors; fuel feed: electric pump; water-cooled, 24.6 imp pt, 29.6 US pt, 14 l, 2 electric thermostatic fans.

TRANSMISSION driving wheels: rear; clutch: single dry plate; gearbox: mechanical; gears: 5, fully synchronized; ratios: I 2.520, II 1.735, III 1.225, IV 1, V 0.815, rev 2.765; lever: central; final drive: hypoid bevel, limited slip differential; axle ratio: 4.500; width of rims: 7''; tyres: 215/70 VR x 15.

PERFORMANCE max speeds: (I) 52 mph, 83 km/h; (II) 75 mph, 121 km/h; (III) 96 mph, 154 km/h; (IV) 130 mph, 210 km/h; (V) 162 mph, 260 km/h; power-weight ratio: 8.8 lb/hp, 4.1 kg/hp; carrying capacity: 948 lb, 430 kg; acceleration: standing ¼ mile 15 sec; speed in top at 1,000 rpm: 17.4 mph, 28 km/h; fuel consumption: 12 m/imp gal, 10 m/US gal, 23.5 l x 100 km.

CHASSIS integral; front suspension: independent, wishbones, coil springs, anti-roll bar, telescopic dampers; rear suspension: independent, wishbones, coil springs, anti-roll bar, telescopic dampers.

STEERING ZF screw and sector; turns lock to lock: 4.50.

BRAKES disc, internal radial fins, servo; swept area: front 35.3 sq in, 228 sq cm, rear 20.8 sq in, 134 sq cm, total 56.1 sq in, 362 sq cm.

ELECTRICAL EQUIPMENT 12 V; 72 Ah battery; 2 Bosch 770

JARAMA 400 GT S

W alternators; Marelli distributor; 4 iodine retractable headlamps.

DIMENSIONS AND WEIGHT wheel base: 93.70 in, 2,380 mm; tracks: 58.66 in, 1,490 mm front, 58.66 in, 1,490 mm rear; length: 176.57 in, 4,485 mm; width: 71.65 in, 1,820 mm; height: 46.85 in, 1,190 mm; ground clearance: 4.92 in, 125 mm; dry weight: 3,219 lb, 1,460 kg; distribution of weight: 49.5% front, 50.5% rear; turning circle (between walls): 39.4 ft, 12 m; fuel tank: 22 imp gal, 26.4 US gal, 100 l.

BODY coupé; 2 doors; 2 + 2 seats, separate front seats, reclining backrests, leather upholstery, tinted glass, electrically-heated rear window, back seat folding down to luggage table, air-conditioning.

PRACTICAL INSTRUCTIONS fuel: 98-100 oct petrol; engine sump oil: 20.8 imp pt, 24.9 US pt, 11.8 l, SAE 20W-50, change every 3,100 miles, 5,000 km; gearbox oil: 5.8 imp pt, 7 US pt, 3.3 l, SAE 90, change every 6,200 miles, 10,000 km; final drive oil: 2.1 imp pt, 2.5 US pt, 1.2 l, SAE 90; greasing: every 3,100 miles, 5,000 km, 5 points; sparking plug type: 235°; tappet clearances: inlet 0.010 in, 0.25 mm, exhaust 0.010 in, 0.25 mm; valve timing: 32° 76° 64° 32°; tyre pressure: front 34 psi, 2.4 atm, rear 37 psi, 2.6 atm.

OPTIONAL ACCESSORIES right-hand drive; power-assisted steering; special spray; metallic spray.

Countach LP 500

ENGINE rear, central, longitudinal, 4 stroke; 12 cylinders, Vee-slanted at 60°; 303.3 cu in, 4,971 cc (3.35 x 2.87 in, 85 x 73 mm); compression ratio: 10.5:1; max power (DIN): 440 hp at 7,400 rpm; max torque (DIN): 366 lb ft, 50.5 kg m at 5,000 rpm; max engine rpm: 7,900; 88.5 hp/l; light alloy cylinder block and head, wet liners; 7 crankshaft bearings; valves: overhead, Vee-slanted, thimble tappets; camshafts: 2, per cylinder block, overhead, cogged belts; 6 Weber 42 DCOE horizontal twin barrel carburettors; water-cooled, 2 radiators, 4 electric fans.

TRANSMISSION driving wheels: rear; clutch: single dry plate; gearbox: mechanical; gears: 5, fully synchronized; ratios: I 2.520, II 1.735, III 1.225, IV 1, V 0.815, rev 2.765; lever: central; width of rims: front 7", rear 9".

PERFORMANCE max speed: about 186 mph, 300 km/h; power-weight ratio: 5.7 lb/hp, 2.6 kg/hp; fuel consumption: not declared.

CHASSIS integral, box-type platform; front suspension: independent, wishbones, coil springs, anti-roll bar, telescopic dampers; rear suspension: independent, wishbones, coil springs, anti-roll bar, telescopic dampers.

STEERING ZF screw and sector.

BRAKES disc, internal radial fins, dual circuit, each with servo.

ELECTRICAL EQUIPMENT 12 V; 56 Ah battery; 770 W alternator; Marelli distributor; 4 iodine retractable headlamps.

DIMENSIONS AND WEIGHT wheel base: 96.46 in, 2,450 mm; tracks: 59.06 in, 1,500 mm front, 59.84 in, 1,520 mm rear; length: 157.87 in, 4,010 mm; width: 73.62 in, 1,870 mm; height: 40.55 in, 1,030 mm; dry weight: 2,492 lb, 1,130 kg.

BODY coupé; 2 doors; 2 seats, tinted glass, electrically-controlled windows, light alloy wheels.

PRACTICAL INSTRUCTIONS fuel: 98-100 oct petrol.

LANCIA ITALY

Fulvia Berlina 2ª Serie

PRICE IN GB: £ 1,156 (with electrically-heated rear window).
PRICE EX WORKS: 1,835,000 liras.

ENGINE front, 4 stroke; 4 cylinders, Vee-slanted at 12°53'28"; 79.2 cu in, 1,298 cc (3.03 x 2.74 in, 77 x 69.7 mm); compression ratio: 9:1; max power (DIN): 85 hp at 6,000 rpm; max torque (DIN): 83 lb ft, 11.5 kg m at 4,500 rpm; max engine rpm: 6,200; 65.4 hp/l; cast iron cylinder block, light alloy head, hemispherical combustion chambers; 3 crankshaft bearings; valves: Vee-slanted at 60°, rockers; camshafts: 2, overhead; lubrication: rotary pump, full flow filter (cartridge), 7.6 imp pt, 9.1 US pt, 4.3 l; 2 Solex C 35 PHH 18 horizontal twin barrel carburettors; fuel feed: mechanical pump; liquid-cooled, 11.1 imp pt, 13.3 US pt, 6.3 l, electric thermostatic fan.

TRANSMISSION driving wheels: front; clutch: single dry plate (diaphragm); gearbox: mechanical; gears: 5, fully

LAMBORGHINI Countach LP 500

LANCIA Fulvia Coupé 1.3 S 2ª Serie Monte-Carlo

LANCIA Fulvia Sport 1600

synchronized; ratios: I 4.159, II 2.698, III 1.793, IV 1.284, V 1, rev 4.239; lever: central; final drive: hypoid bevel; axle ratio: 4.100; width of rims: 4.5"; tyres: 155 x 14.

PERFORMANCE max speeds: (I) 25 mph, 40 km/h; (II) 39 mph, 62 km/h; (III) 58 mph, 93 km/h; (IV) 81 mph, 131 km/h; (V) over 99 mph, 160 km/h; power-weight ratio: 27.6 lb/hp, 12.5 kg/hp; carrying capacity: 882 lb, 400 kg; speed in direct drive at 1,000 rpm: 16.8 mph, 27 km/h; fuel consumption: 32.1 m/imp gal, 26.7 m/US gal, 8.8 l x 100 km.

CHASSIS integral, front auxiliary frame; front suspension: independent, wishbones, transverse upper leafspring, anti-roll bar, telescopic dampers; rear suspension: rigid axle, semi-elliptic leafsprings, transverse linkage bar, telescopic dampers.

STEERING worm and roller; turns lock to lock: 4.17.

BRAKES disc (front diameter 10.24 in, 260 mm, rear 10.91 in, 277 mm), rear compensator, servo; swept area: front 29.8 sq in, 192 sq cm, rear 16.1 sq in, 104 sq cm, total 45.9 sq in, 296 sq cm.

ELECTRICAL EQUIPMENT 12 V; 45 Ah battery; 400 W alternator; Marelli distributor; 4 iodine headlamps.

DIMENSIONS AND WEIGHT wheel base: 98.43 in, 2,500 mm; tracks: 51.18 in, 1,300 mm front, 50.39 in, 1,280 mm rear; length: 163.58 in, 4,155 mm; width: 61.22 in, 1,555 mm; height: 55.12 in, 1,400 mm; ground clearance: 4.72 in, 120 mm; dry weight: 2,337 lb, 1,060 kg; distribution of weight: 62.9% front, 37.1% rear; turning circle (between walls): 36.4 ft, 11.1 m; fuel tank: 9.2 imp gal, 11.1 US gal, 42 l.

BODY saloon/sedan; 4 doors; 5 seats, separate front seats, reclining backrests.

PRACTICAL INSTRUCTIONS fuel: 96 oct petrol; engine sump oil: 7.6 imp pt, 9.1 US pt, 4.3 l, SAE 10W-40, change every 4,300 miles, 7,000 km; gearbox and final drive oil: 4.8 imp pt, 5.7 US pt, 2.7 l, SAE 90, change every 8,700 miles, 14,000 km; greasing: every 4,300 miles, 7,000 km, 5 points; tappet clearances: inlet 0.006 in, 0.15 mm, exhaust 0.010 in, 0.25 mm; valve timing: 17° 65° 65° 17°; tyre pressure: front 24 psi, 1.7 atm, rear 24 psi, 1.7 atm.

OPTIONAL ACCESSORIES luxury interior; leather upholstery; electrically-heated rear window; metallic spray.

Fulvia Coupé 1.3 S 2ª Serie

See Fulvia Berlina 2ª Serie, except for:

PRICE IN GB: £ 1,542 (with electrically-heated rear window).
PRICE EX WORKS: 1,975,000 liras.

ENGINE compression ratio: 9.5:1; max power (DIN): 90 hp at 6,000 rpm; max torque (DIN): 84 lb ft, 11.6 kg m at 5,000 rpm; 69.3 hp/l; oil cooler, 9.3 imp pt, 11.2 US pt, 5.3 l; 2 Solex C 35 PHH 19 - C 35 PHH 16 horizontal twin barrel carburettors.

TRANSMISSION axle ratio: 3.909; tyres: 165 x 14.

PERFORMANCE max speeds: (I) 27 mph, 43 km/h; (II) 41 mph, 66 km/h; (III) 62 mph, 100 km/h; (IV) 87 mph, 140 km/h; (V) over 106 mph, 170 km/h; power-weight ratio: 23.6 lb/hp, 10.7 kg/hp; carrying capacity: 706 lb, 320 kg; speed in direct drive at 1,000 rpm: 18 mph, 28.9 km/h; fuel consumption: 31.7 m/imp gal, 26.4 m/US gal, 8.9 l x 100 km.

CHASSIS rear suspension: anti-roll bar.

DIMENSIONS AND WEIGHT wheel base: 91.73 in, 2,330 mm; length: 156.50 in, 3,975 mm; height: 51.97 in, 1,320 mm; dry weight: 2,139 lb, 970 kg; distribution of weight: 63.3% front, 36.7% rear; turning circle (between walls): 34.4 ft, 10.5 m; fuel tank: 8.4 imp gal, 10 US gal, 38 l.

BODY coupé; 2 doors; 2 + 2 seats.

PRACTICAL INSTRUCTIONS engine sump oil: 9.3 imp pt, 11.2 US pt, 5.3 l; valve timing: 28° 66° 66° 28°; tyre pressure: front 26 psi, 1.8 atm, rear 26 psi, 1.8 atm.

Fulvia Coupé 1.3 S 2ª Serie Monte-Carlo

See Fulvia Coupé 1.3 S 2ª Serie, except for:

PRICE EX WORKS: 2,050,000 liras.

ELECTRICAL EQUIPMENT 2 fog lamps.

BODY special equipment.

Fulvia Sport 1.3 S 2ª Serie

See Fulvia Coupé 1.3 S 2ª Serie, except for:

PRICE IN GB: £ 1,880 (with electrically-heated rear window).
PRICE EX WORKS: 2,350,000 liras.

TRANSMISSION axle ratio: 3.700.

PERFORMANCE max speeds: (I) 29 mph, 46 km/h; (II) 43 mph, 70 km/h; (III) 66 mph, 106 km/h; (IV) 92 mph, 148

LAMBORGHINI Jarama 400 GT S

LANCIA Fulvia Coupé 1.3 S 2ª Serie Monte-Carlo

LANCIA Fulvia Sport 1600

km/h; (V) over 112 mph, 180 km/h; power-weight ratio: 23.4 lb/hp, 10.6 kg/hp; speed in direct drive at 1,000 rpm: 19 mph, 30.5 km/h; fuel consumption: 32.8 m/imp gal, 27.3 m/US gal, 8.6 l x 100 km.

ELECTRICAL EQUIPMENT 2 iodine headlamps.

DIMENSIONS AND WEIGHT length: 161.02 in, 4,090 mm; width: 61.81 in, 1,570 mm; height: 50.39 in, 1,280 mm; dry weight: 2,117 lb, 960 kg; distribution of weight: 67.8% front, 32.2% rear.

OPTIONAL ACCESSORIES headrests.

Fulvia Coupé 1600 HF 2ª Serie

PRICE IN GB: £ 1,981 (luxury version).
PRICE EX WORKS: 2,575,000 liras.

ENGINE front, 4 stroke; 4 cylinders, Vee-slanted at 12°35'; 96.7 cu in, 1,584 cc (3.23 x 2.95 in, 82 x 75 mm); compression ratio: 10.5:1; max power (DIN): 114 hp at 6,000 rpm; max torque (DIN): 113 lb ft, 15.6 kg m at 4,500 rpm; max engine rpm: 6,500; 72 hp/l; cast iron cylinder block, light alloy head, hemispherical combustion chambers; 3 crankshaft bearings; valves: overhead, Vee-slanted at 60°, rockers; camshafts: 2, overhead; lubrication: rotary pump, full flow filter (cartridge), 7.6 imp pt, 9.1 US pt, 4.3 l; 2 Solex C 42 DDHF front, C 42 DDHF/1 rear, horizontal twin barrel carburettors; fuel feed: mechanical pump; liquid-cooled, 12.3 imp pt, 14.8 US pt, 7 l, electric thermostatic fan.

TRANSMISSION driving wheels: front; clutch: single dry plate; gearbox: mechanical; gears: 5, fully synchronized; ratios: I 3.646, II 2.473, III 1.719, IV 1.317, V 1, rev 4.063; lever: central; final drive: hypoid bevel; axle ratio: 3.909; width of rims: 6"; tyres: 175 x 14.

PERFORMANCE max speeds: (I) 33 mph, 53 km/h; (II) 48 mph, 78 km/h; (III) 70 mph, 112 km/h; (IV) 91 mph, 146 km/h; (V) over 112 mph, 180 km/h; power-weight ratio: 17.4 lb/hp, 7.9 kg/hp; carrying capacity: 706 lb, 320 kg; acceleration: standing ¼ mile 16.5 sec, 0-50 mph (0-80 km/h) 6.5 sec; speed in direct drive at 1,000 rpm: 18.4 mph, 29.6 km/h; fuel consumption: 26.2 m/imp gal, 21.8 m/US gal, 10.8 l x 100 km.

CHASSIS integral, front auxiliary frame; front suspension: independent, wishbones, lower transverse leafspring, anti-roll bar, telescopic dampers; rear suspension: rigid axle, semi-elliptic leafsprings, transverse linkage bar, anti-roll bar, telescopic dampers.

STEERING worm and roller; turns lock to lock: 4.17.

BRAKES disc (front diameter 10.24 in, 260 mm, rear 10.91 in, 277 mm), rear compensator, servo; swept area: front 29.8 sq in, 192 sq cm, rear 16.1 sq in, 104 sq cm, total 45.9 sq in, 296 sq cm.

ELECTRICAL EQUIPMENT 12 V; 45 Ah battery; 400 W alternator; Marelli distributor; 4 iodine headlamps.

DIMENSIONS AND WEIGHT wheel base: 91.73 in, 2,330 mm; tracks: 54.72 in, 1,390 mm front, 52.56 in, 1,335 mm rear; length: 154.92 in, 3,935 mm; width: 61.81 in, 1,570 mm; height: 52.36 in, 1,330 mm; ground clearance: 4.88 in, 124 mm; dry weight: 1,958 lb, 900 kg; distribution of weight: 64.5% front, 35.5% rear; turning circle (between walls): 35.4 ft, 10.8 m; fuel tank: 8.4 imp gal, 10 US gal, 38 l.

BODY coupé; 2 doors; 2 + 2 seats, separate front seats, reclining backrests.

PRACTICAL INSTRUCTIONS fuel: 96 oct petrol; engine sump oil: 7.6 imp pt, 9.1 US pt, 4.3 l, SAE 20W-50, change every 4,300 miles, 7,000 km; gearbox and final drive oil: 4.8 imp pt, 5.7 US pt, 2.7 l, SAE 90, change every 8,700 miles, 14,000 km; greasing: every 4,300 miles, 7,000 km, 5 points; tappet clearances: inlet 0.008 in, 0.20 mm, exhaust 0.012 in, 0.30 mm; valve timing: 28° 66° 66° 28°; tyre pressure: front 21 psi, 1.5 atm, rear 21 psi, 1.5 atm.

OPTIONAL ACCESSORIES electrically-heated rear window; headrests; metallic spray; luxury version with special bumpers, deflectors and headrests.

Fulvia Sport 1600

See Fulvia Coupé 1600 HF 2ª Serie, except for:

PRICE IN GB: £ 2,229 (with electrically-heated rear window).
PRICE EX WORKS: 2,700,000 liras.

TRANSMISSION axle ratio: 3.545; width of rims: 4.5"; tyres: 165 x 14.

PERFORMANCE max speeds: (I) 35 mph, 57 km/h; (II) 52 mph, 84 km/h; (III) 76 mph, 122 km/h; (IV) 99 mph, 159 km/h; (V) 118 mph, 190 km/h; power-weight ratio: 18.5 lb/hp, 8.4 kg/hp; speed in direct drive at 1,000 rpm: 19.9 mph, 32.1 km/h; fuel consumption: 27.4 m/imp gal, 22.8 m/US gal, 10.3 l x 100 km.

ELECTRICAL EQUIPMENT 2 iodine headlamps.

DIMENSIONS AND WEIGHT tracks: 51.18 in, 1,300 mm front,

FULVIA SPORT 1600

50.39 in, 1,280 mm rear; length: 162.99 in, 4,140 mm; height: 50.39 in, 1,280 mm; ground clearance: 5.12 in, 130 mm; dry weight: 2,117 lb, 960 kg.

OPTIONAL ACCESSORIES electrically-heated rear window; luxury interiors; metallic spray.

Beta 1400

PRICE EX WORKS: 2,050,000 liras.

ENGINE front, transverse, slanted at 20° to rear, 4 stroke; 4 cylinders, in line; 87.7 cu in, 1,438 cc (3.15 x 2.81 in, 80 x 71.5 mm); compression ratio: 8.9:1; max power (DIN): 90 hp at 6,000 rpm; max torque (DIN): 86 lb ft, 11.8 kg m at 3,800 rpm; max engine rpm: 6,400; 62,5 hp/l; cast iron cylinder block, light alloy head, hemispherical combustion chambers; 5 crankshaft bearings; valves: overhead, Vee-slanted, thimble tappets; camshafts: 2, overhead, cogged belt; lubrication: gear pump, full flow filter, 7.9 imp pt, 9.5 US pt, 4.5 l; 1 Weber 32 DMTR24 or Solex C 32 CIC-I downdraught twin barrel carburettor; fuel feed: mechanical pump; liquid-cooled, 14.4 imp pt, 17.3 US pt, 8.2 l, electric thermostatic fan.

TRANSMISSION driving wheels: front; clutch: single dry plate; gearbox mechanical, in unit with engine; gears: 5, fully synchronized; ratios: I 3.500, II 2.235, III 1.522, IV 1.152, V 0.925, rev 3.071; lever: central; final drive: cylindrical gears, in unit with engine and gearbox; axle ratio: 4.461; width of rims: 5"; tyres: 155 SR x 14.

PERFORMANCE max speeds: (I) 28 mph, 45 km/h; (II) 44 mph, 71 km/h; (III) 65 mph, 104 km/h; (IV) 85 mph, 137 km/h; (V) 103 mph, 165 km/h; power-weight ratio: 26.7 lb/hp, 11.9 kg/hp; carrying capacity: 937 lb, 425 kg; acceleration: standing ¼ mile 18.2 sec; speed in top at 1,000 rpm: 16.6 mph, 26.7 km/h; fuel consumption: 28.5 m/imp gal, 23.8 m/US gal, 9.9 l x 100 km.

CHASSIS integral; front suspension: independent, lower wide-based wishbones, coil springs, telescopic damper struts, anti-roll bar; rear suspension: independent, wishbones, coil springs, telescopic dampers struts, anti-roll bar acting as longitudinal torque arm.

STEERING rack-and-pinion; turns lock to lock: 4.

BRAKES disc (diameter 9.88 in, 251 mm), rear compensator, servo.

ELECTRICAL EQUIPMENT 12 V; 45 Ah battery; 750 W alternator; Marelli distributor; 4 iodine headlamps.

DIMENSIONS AND WEIGHT wheel base: 100 in, 2,540 mm; tracks: 55.35 in, 1,406 mm front, 54.80 in, 1,392 mm rear; length: 168.90 in, 4,290 mm; width: 66.54 in, 1,690 mm; height: 55.12 in, 1,400 mm; ground clearance: 4.72 in, 120 mm; dry weight: 2,591 lb, 1,075 kg; turning circle (between walls): 34.8 ft, 10.6; fuel tank: 11.2 imp gal, 13.5 US gal, 51 l.

BODY saloon/sedan; 4 doors; 5 seats, separate front seats, reclining backrests.

PRACTICAL INSTRUCTIONS fuel: 96 oct petrol; engine sump, gearbox and final drive oil: 7.9 imp pt, 9.5 US pt, 4.5 l; valve timing: 12° 42° 46° 8°; tyre pressure: front 24 psi, 1.7 atm, rear 24 psi, 1.7 atm.

OPTIONAL ACCESSORIES light alloy wheels; fog lamps; manually-controlled sunshine roof; tinted glass; electrically-controlled windows; luxury interior; leather upholstery; air-conditioning with tinted glass; metallic spray; headrests; electrically-heated rear window.

Beta 1600

See Beta 1400, except for:

PRICE EX WORKS: 2,300,000 liras.

ENGINE 97.1 cu in, 1,592 cc (3.15 x 3.12 in, 80 x 79.2 mm); max power (DIN): 100 hp at 6,000 rpm; max torque (DIN): 95 lb ft, 13.1 kg m at 3,000 rpm; 62.8 hp/l; 1 Weber 34 DMTR21 or Solex C34 CIC-I downdraught twin barrel carburettor; cooling system capacity: 14.6 imp pt, 17.5 US pt, 8.3 l.

TRANSMISSION axle ratio: 4.214; width of rims: 5.5"; tyres: 175/70 SR x 14.

PERFORMANCE max speeds: (I) 31 mph, 50 km/h; (II) 47 mph, 75 km/h; (III) 68 mph, 110 km/h; (IV) 90 mph, 145 km/h; (V) 106 mph, 170 km/h; power-weight ratio: 23.9 lb/hp, 10.8 kg/hp; acceleration: standing ¼ mile per 17.7 sec; speed in top at 1,000 rpm: 17.6 mph, 28.3 km/h; fuel consumption: not declared.

DIMENSIONS AND WEIGHT dry weight: 2,392 lb, 1,085 kg.

PRACTICAL INSTRUCTIONS valve timing: 13° 45° 49° 9°.

LANCIA Beta 1800 LX

LANCIA 2000 Berlina

LANCIA 2000 Coupé HF

Beta 1600 LX

See Beta 1600, except for:

BODY luxury interior; built-in headrests (standard).

OPTIONAL ACCESSORIES special electrically-heated rear window.

Beta 1800

See Beta 1400, except for:

PRICE EX WORKS: 2,400,000 liras.

ENGINE 107.2 cu in, 1,756 cc (3.31 x 3.12 in, 84 x 79.2 mm); max power (DIN): 110 hp at 6,000 rpm; max torque (DIN): 107 lb ft, 14.7 kg m at 3,000 rpm; 62.6 hp/l; 1 Weber 34 DMTR 21 or Solex C 34 CIC-I downdraught twin barrel carburettor; cooling system capacity: 14.6 imp pt, 17.5 US pt, 8.3 l.

TRANSMISSION axle ratio: 4.071; width of rims: 5.5"; tyres: 175/70 SR x 14.

PERFORMANCE max speeds: (I) 31 mph, 50 km/h; (II) 48 mph, 78 km/h; (III) 71 mph, 114 km/h; (IV) 94 mph, 151 km/h; (V) 109 mph, 175 km/h; power-weight ratio: 21.8 lb/hp, 9.9 kg/hp; acceleration: standing ¼ mile 17.2 sec; speed in top at 1,000 rpm: 18.2 mph, 29.3 km/h; fuel consumption: not declared.

DIMENSIONS AND WEIGHT dry weight: 2,414 lb, 1,095 kg.

PRACTICAL INSTRUCTIONS valve timing: 13° 45° 49° 9°.

Beta 1800 LX

See Beta 1800, except for:

BODY luxury interior; built-in headrests (standard).

OPTIONAL ACCESSORIES special electrically-heated rear window.

2000 Berlina

PRICE IN GB: £ 1,860 (with electrically-controlled windows and tinted glass).
PRICE EX WORKS: 2,700,000 liras.

ENGINE front, 4 stroke; 4 cylinders, horizontally opposed; 121.5 cu in, 1,991 cc (3.50 x 3.15 in, 89 x 80 mm); compression ratio: 9.2:1; max power (DIN): 115 hp at 5,500 rpm; max torque (DIN): 123 lb ft, 17 kg m at 3,500 rpm; max engine rpm: 6,000; 57.7 hp/l; light alloy cylinder block and head; 3 crankshaft bearings; valves: overhead, Vee-slanted, push-rods and rockers; camshafts: 2, side, lower; lubrication: rotary pump, full flow filter (cartridge), 12.7 imp pt, 15.2 US pt, 7.2 l; 1 Solex C 36 EIES downdraught twin barrel carburettor; fuel feed: mechanical pump; sealed circuit cooling, water, 14.1 imp pt, 16.9 US pt, 8 l, electric thermostatic fan.

TRANSMISSION driving wheels: front; clutch: single dry plate; gearbox: mechanical; gears: 5, fully synchronized; ratios: I 3.922, II 2.543, III 1.691, IV 1.211, V 1, rev 3.997; lever central; final drive: hypoid bevel; axle ratio: 3.818; width of rims: 5"; tyres: 175 x 14.

PERFORMANCE max speeds: (I) 29 mph, 47 km/h; (II) 45 mph, 72 km/h; (III) 68 mph, 109 km/h; (IV) 94 mph, 152 km/h; (V) over 109 mph, 175 km/h; power-weight ratio: 23.6 lb/hp, 10.7 kg/hp; carrying capacity: 882 lb, 400 kg; speed in direct drive at 1,000 rpm: 19.1 mph, 30.7 km/h; fuel consumption: 26.4 m/imp gal, 22 m/US gal, 10.7 l x 100 km.

CHASSIS integral, front auxiliary frame; front suspension: independent, wishbones, transverse upper leafspring, anti-roll bar, telescopic dampers; rear suspension: rigid axle, semi-elliptic leafsprings, transverse linkage bar, anti-roll bar, telescopic dampers.

STEERING recirculating ball, ZF servo; turns lock to lock: 3.50.

BRAKES disc (front diameter 10.24 in, 260 mm, rear 10.91 in, 277 mm), rear compensator, servo; swept area: front 29.8 sq in, 192 sq cm, rear 16.1 sq in, 104 sq cm, total 45.9 sq in, 296 sq cm.

ELECTRICAL EQUIPMENT 12 V; 45 Ah battery; 750 W alternator; Marelli distributor; 4 iodine headlamps.

DIMENSIONS AND WEIGHT wheel base: 104.33 in, 2,650 mm; tracks: 52.44 in, 1,332 mm front, 50.71 in, 1,288 mm rear; length: 181.89 in, 4,620 mm; width: 63.39 in, 1,610 mm; height: 57.48 in, 1,460 mm; ground clearance: 4.80 in, 122 mm; dry weight: 2,723 lb, 1,235 kg; turning circle (between walls): 36.1 ft, 11 m; fuel tank: 12.1 imp gal, 14.5 US gal, 55 l.

BODY saloon/sedan; 4 doors; 5 seats, separate front seats, reclining backrests; electrically-heated rear window.

SEAT 600 E

SEAT 850 Especial Berlina 4 Puertas Lujo

SEAT 850 Sport Coupé

mm; tracks: 46.06 in, 1,170 mm front, 48.11 in, 1,222 mm rear; length: 143.78 in, 3,652 mm; width: 59.06 in, 1,500 mm; height: 51.18 in, 1,300 mm; ground clearance: 4.92 in, 125 mm; dry weight: 1,521 lb, 690 kg; turning circle (between walls): 33.5 ft, 10.2 m; fuel tank: 6.6 imp gal, 7.9 US gal, 30 l.

BODY coupé; 2 doors; 2 + 2 seats, separate front seats.

PRACTICAL INSTRUCTIONS fuel: 98 oct petrol; engine sump oil: 6.5 imp pt; 7.8 US pt, 3.7 l, SAE 20W (winter) 30 (summer), change every 5,200 miles, 10,000 km; gearbox and final drive oil: 3.7 imp pt, 4.4 US pt, 2.1 l, SAE 90 EP, change every 18,600 miles, 30,000 km; greasing: every 1,600 miles, 2,500 km, 2 points; sparking plug type: 260°; tappet clearances: inlet 0.006 in, 0.15 mm, exhaust 0.008 in, 0.20 mm; valve timing: 25° 51° 64° 12°; tyre pressure: front 16 psi, 1.1 atm, rear 26 psi, 1.8 atm.

850 Sport Spider

See 850 Sport Coupé, except for:

ENGINE lubricating system capacity: 7.9 imp pt, 9.5 US pt, 4.5 l.

PERFORMANCE max speed: 95 mph, 153 km/h; power-weight ratio: 30.9 lb/hp, 14 kg/hp; carrying capacity: 463 lb, 210 kg; acceleration: standing ¼ mile 19.8 sec, 0-50 mph (0-80 km/h) 11.8 sec; fuel consumption: 39.8 m/imp gal, 33.1 m/US gal, 7.1 l x 100 km.

ELECTRICAL EQUIPMENT 2 headlamps.

DIMENSIONS AND WEIGHT length: 150.55 in, 3,824 mm; width: 58.98 in, 1,498 mm; height: 48.03 in, 1,220 mm; ground clearance: 5.12 in, 130 mm; dry weight: 1,610 lb, 730 kg.

BODY sports; 2 seats.

OPTIONAL ACCESSORIES hardtop.

1430 Berlina

PRICE EX WORKS: 147,700 pesetas.

ENGINE front, 4 stroke; 4 cylinders, in line; 87.7 cu in, 1,438 cc (3.15 x 2.81 in, 80 x 71.5 mm); compression ratio: 9:1; max power (DIN): 70 hp at 5,400 rpm; max torque (DIN): 80 lb ft, 11 kg m at 3,400 rpm; max engine rpm: 6,000; 48.7 hp/l; cast iron cylinder block, light alloy head; 5 crankshaft bearings; valves: overhead, push-rods and rockers; camshafts: 1, side; lubrication: gear pump, full flow filter, 6.9 imp pt, 8.2 US pt, 3.9 l; 1 Weber 32 DHS 21 or Solex 32 EIES-31 downdraught twin barrel carburettor; fuel feed: mechanical pump; water-cooled, 13.2 imp pt, 15.9 US pt, 7.5 l.

TRANSMISSION driving wheels: rear; clutch: single dry plate; gearbox: mechanical; gears: 4, fully synchronized; ratios: I 3.797, II 2.175, III 1.410, IV 1, rev 3.655; lever: central; final drive: hypoid bevel; axle ratio: 4.100; width of rims: 4.5"; tyres: 150 SR x 13.

PERFORMANCE max speeds: (I) 25 mph, 40 km/h; (II) 43 mph, 70 km/h; (III) 65 mph, 105 km/h; (IV) 96 mph, 155 km/h; power-weight ratio: 28.7 lb/hp, 13 kg/hp; carrying capacity: 937 lb, 425 kg; acceleration: standing ¼ mile 19.5 sec; speed in direct drive at 1,000 rpm: 15.7 mph, 25.3 km/h; fuel consumption: 33.2 m/imp gal, 27.7 m/US gal, 8.5 l x 100 km.

CHASSIS integral; front suspension: independent, wishbones, coil springs, anti-roll bar, telescopic dampers; rear suspension: rigid axle, twin trailing radius arms, transverse linkage bar, coil springs, telescopic dampers.

STEERING worm and roller; turns lock to lock: 2.75.

BRAKES disc, rear compensator; swept area: front 19.2 sq in, 124 sq cm, rear 19.2 sq in, 124 sq cm, total 38.4 sq in, 248 sq cm.

ELECTRICAL EQUIPMENT 12 V; 45 Ah battery; 540 W alternator; Femsa distributor; 4 headlamps.

DIMENSIONS AND WEIGHT wheel base: 95.28 in, 2,420 mm; tracks: 52.36 in, 1,330 mm front, 51.18 in, 1,300 mm rear; length: 159.57 in, 4,053 mm; width: 63.43 in, 1,611 mm; height: 55.91 in, 1,420 mm; ground clearance: 5.12 in, 130 mm; dry weight: 2,007 lb, 910 kg; distribution of weight: 53% front, 47% rear; turning circle (between walls): 37.4 ft, 11.4 m; fuel tank: 8.6 imp gal, 10.3 US gal, 39 l.

BODY saloon/sedan; 4 doors; 5 seats, separate front seats, reclining backrests.

PRACTICAL INSTRUCTIONS fuel: 98 oct petrol; engine sump oil: 6.7 imp pt, 8 US pt, 3.8 l, SAE 30W-40, change every 6,200 miles, 10,000 km; gearbox oil: 2.3 imp pt, 2.7 US pt, 1.3 l, SAE 90 EP, change every 18,600 miles, 30,000 km; final drive oil: 1.2 imp pt, 1.5 US pt, 0.7 l, SAE 90 EP, change every 18,600 miles, 30,000 km; greasing: none; sparking plug type: 240°; tappet clearances: inlet 0.008 in, 0.20 mm, exhaust 0.008 in, 0.20 mm; valve timing: 19° 48° 59° 8°; tyre pressure: front 24 psi, 1.7 atm, rear 26 psi, 1.8 atm.

1430 Familiar

See 1430 Berlina, except for:

PRICE EX WORKS: 154,800 pesetas.

PERFORMANCE power-weight ratio: 29.1 lb/hp, 15.2 kg/hp; carrying capacity: 1,014 lb, 460 kg.

DIMENSIONS AND WEIGHT height: 56.69 in, 1,440 mm; dry weight: 2,051 lb, 930 kg; fuel tank: 10.5 imp gal, 12.4 US gal, 47 l.

BODY estate car/station wagon; 4 + 1 doors.

1500 Berlina

ENGINE front, 4 stroke; 4 cylinders, vertical, in line; 90.4 cu in, 1,481 cc (3.03 x 3.13 in, 77 x 79.5 mm); compression ratio: 9:1; max power (DIN): 75 hp at 5,000 rpm; max torque (DIN): 85 lb ft, 11.7 kg m at 3,200 rpm; max engine rpm: 5,500; 50.6 hp/l; cast iron cylinder block, light alloy head; 3 crankshaft bearings; valves: overhead, push-rods and rockers; camshafts: 1, side; lubrication: gear pump, centrifugal filter, 7.6 imp pt, 9.1 US pt, 4.3 l; 1 Brussel-Weber 28/36 DCDI 1 downdraught carburettor; fuel feed: mechanical pump; water-cooled, 15 imp pt, 18 US pt, 8.5 l.

TRANSMISSION driving wheels: rear; clutch: single dry plate, hydraulically controlled; gearbox: mechanical; gears: 4, fully synchronized; ratios: I 3.750, II 2.300, III 1.490, IV 1, rev 3.870; lever: steering column; final drive: hypoid bevel; axle ratio: 4.444; width of rims: 4.5"; tyres: 5.90 S x 14.

PERFORMANCE max speeds: (I) 25 mph, 40 km/h; (II) 40 mph, 65 km/h; (III) 62 mph, 100 km/h; (IV) 87 mph, 140 km/h; power-weight ratio: 33.3 lb/hp, 15.1 kg/hp; carrying capacity: 1,058 lb, 480 kg; acceleration: standing ¼ mile 23 sec, 0-50 mph (0-80 km/h) 15.7 sec; speed in direct drive at 1,000 rpm: 16.2 mph, 26 km/h; fuel consumption: 29.7 m/imp gal, 24.8 m/US gal, 9.5 l x 100 km.

CHASSIS integral; front suspension: independent, wishbones, lower trailing links, longitudinal torsion bars, coil springs, anti-roll bar, telescopic dampers; rear suspension: rigid axle, coil springs, ¼-elliptic leafsprings as leading arms, anti-roll bar, telescopic dampers.

STEERING worm and roller; turns lock to lock: 3.25.

BRAKES disc (diameter 9.21 in, 234 mm), servo; swept area: front 19.2 sq in, 124 sq cm, rear 19.2 sq in, 124 sq cm, total 38.4 sq in, 248 sq cm.

ELECTRICAL EQUIPMENT 12 V; 48 Ah battery; 540 W alternator; Femsa distributor; 4 headlamps.

DIMENSIONS AND WEIGHT wheel base: 104.33 in, 2,650 mm; tracks: 52.36 in, 1,330 mm front, 51.57 in, 1,310 mm rear; length: 175.79 in, 4,465 mm; width: 63.78 in, 1,620 mm; height: 56.30 in, 1,430 mm; ground clearance: 8.27 in, 210 mm; dry weight: 2,503 lb, 1,135 kg; turning circle (between walls): 35.1 ft, 10.7 m; fuel tank: 13.2 imp gal, 15.8 US gal, 60 l.

BODY saloon/sedan; 4 doors; 6 seats, bench front seats.

PRACTICAL INSTRUCTIONS fuel: 96 oct petrol; engine sump oil: 6.2 imp pt, 7.4 US pt, 3.5 l, SAE 20W (winter) 30 (summer), change every 6,200 miles, 10,000 km; gearbox oil: 2.3 imp pt, 2.7 US pt, 1.3 l, SAE 90 EP; final drive oil: 2.6 imp pt, 3.2 US pt, 1.5 l, SAE 90 EP, change every 18,600 miles, 30,000 km; greasing: every 3,100 miles, 5,000 km, 11 points; sparking plug type: 240°; tappet clearances: inlet 0.008 in, 0.20 mm; exhaust 0.010 in, 0.25 mm; valve timing: 25° 51° 64° 12°; tyre pressure: front 22 psi, 1.6 atm, rear 26 psi, 1.8 atm.

1500 Familiar

See 1500 Berlina, except for:

PERFORMANCE power-weight ratio: 36.8 lb/hp, 16.7 kg/hp.

DIMENSIONS AND WEIGHT dry weight: 2,778 lb, 1,260 kg.

BODY estate car/station wagon; 4 + 1 doors.

Diesel 2000

See 1500 Berlina, except for:

ENGINE Mercedes-Benz Diesel; 4 cylinders, vertical, in line; 121.3 cu in, 1,988 cc (3.43 x 2.29 in, 87 x 83.6 mm); compression ratio: 21:1; max power (DIN): 55 hp at 4,200 rpm; max torque (DIN): 83 lb ft, 11.5 kg m at 2,400 rpm; max engine rpm: 4,350; 27.6 hp/l; cast iron cylinder head; 5 crankshaft bearings; valves: overhead, in line, finger levers; camshafts: 1, overhead; dry sump, full flow and by-pass filter; 4-cylinder Bosch injection pump.

TRANSMISSION axle ratio: 3.900.

PERFORMANCE max speed: 81 mph, 130 km/h; power-weight ratio: 46 lb/hp, 21.1 kg/hp; speed in direct drive

SEAT 1430 Berlina

SAAB 95 V4

SAAB 99 2.0 L 4-door Saloon

AZLK Moskvich 427

VAZ Lada

ZAZ 966

VAZ USSR

Lada

ENGINE front, 4 stroke; 4 cylinders, in line; 73.1 cu in, 1,198 cc (2.99 x 2.60 in, 76 x 66 mm); compression ratio: 8.8:1; max power (DIN): 60 hp at 5,600 rpm; max torque (DIN): 64 lb ft, 8.9 kg m at 3,400 rpm; max engine rpm: 6,500; 50.1 hp/l; cast iron cylinder block, light alloy head; 5 crankshaft bearings; valves: overhead, in line, rockers; camshafts: 1, overhead; lubrication: gear pump, full flow filter, 7.7 imp pt, 9.3 US pt, 4.4 l; 1 Weber downdraught twin barrel carburettor; fuel feed: mechanical pump; water-cooled, 15 imp pt, 18 US pt, 8.5 l.

TRANSMISSION driving wheels: rear; clutch: single dry plate (diaphragm), hydraulically controlled; gearbox: mechanical; gears: 4, fully synchronized; ratios: I 3.753, II 2.303, III 1.493, IV 1, rev 3.867; lever: central; final drive: hypoid bevel; axle ratio: 4.300; width of rims: 4.5''; tyres: 6.15 x 13 or 155 SR x 13.

PERFORMANCE max speeds: (I) 19 mph, 30 km/h; (II) 31 mph, 50 km/h; (III) 43 mph, 70 km/h; (IV) 88 mph, 142 km/h; power-weight ratio: 34.7 lb/hp, 15.7 kg/hp; carrying capacity: 882 lb, 400 kg; speed in direct drive at 1,000 rpm: 15.2 mph, 24.5 km/h; fuel consumption: 33.2 m/imp gal, 27.7 m/US gal, 8.5 l x 100 km.

CHASSIS integral; front suspension: independent, wishbones, coil springs, anti-roll bar, telescopic dampers; rear suspension: rigid axle, twin trailing radius arms, transverse linkage bar, coil springs, telescopic dampers.

STEERING worm and roller; turns lock to lock: 2.75.

BRAKES front disc, rear drum, rear compensator; swept area: front 20.9 sq in, 135 sq cm, rear 76.9 sq in, 496 sq cm, total 97.8 sq in, 631 sq cm.

ELECTRICAL EQUIPMENT 12 V; 55 Ah battery; 40 A alternator; R 125 distributor; 2 headlamps.

DIMENSIONS AND WEIGHT wheel base: 95.47 in, 2,425 mm; tracks: 52.95 in, 1,345 mm front, 51.38 in, 1,305 mm rear; length: 160.43 in, 4,075 mm; width: 63.43 in, 1,611 mm; height: 56.69 in, 1,440 mm; ground clearance: 6.69 in, 170 mm; dry weight: 2,084 lb, 945 kg; turning circle (between walls): 37.4 ft, 11.4 m; fuel tank: 8.6 imp gal, 10.3 US gal, 39 l.

BODY saloon/sedan; 4 doors; 5 seats, separate front seats.

PRACTICAL INSTRUCTIONS fuel: 92 oct petrol; engine sump oil: 6.5 imp pt, 7.8 US pt, 3.7 l; gearbox oil: 2.3 imp pt, 2.7 US pt, 1.3 l; final drive oil: 2.6 imp pt, 3.2 US pt, 1.5 l; greasing: none; tappet clearances: inlet 0.006 in, 0.15 mm, exhaust 0.006 in, 0.15 mm; tyre pressure: front 24 psi, 1.7 atm, rear 26 psi, 1.8 atm.

Lada Kombi

See Lada, except for:

TRANSMISSION axle ratio: 4.440.

PERFORMANCE power-weight ratio: 36 lb/hp, 16.3 kg/hp; carrying capacity: 948 lb, 430 kg.

DIMENSIONS AND WEIGHT dry weight: 2,161 lb, 980 kg; fuel tank: 10.3 imp gal, 12.4 US gal, 47 l.

BODY estate car/station wagon; 4 + 1 doors.

ZAZ USSR

966

ENGINE rear, 4 stroke; 4 cylinders, Vee-slanted at 90°; 73 cu in, 1,196 cc (2.99 x 2.60 in, 76 x 66 mm); compression ratio: 8.4:1 max power (DIN): 40 hp at 4,400 rpm; max torque (DIN): 55 lb ft, 7.6 kg m at 2,900 rpm; 33.4 hp/l; cast iron cylinder block, light alloy head; 3 crankshaft bearings; valves: overhead, push-rods and rockers; camshafts: 1, at centre of Vee; lubrication: gear pump, full flow filter, 5.8 imp pt, 7 US pt, 3.3 l; 1 K 125 downdraught carburettor; fuel feed: mechanical pump; air-cooled.

TRANSMISSION driving wheels: rear; clutch: single dry plate, hydraulically controlled; gearbox: mechanical; gears: II, III and IV synchronized; ratios: I 3.800, II 2.120, III 1.410, IV 0.964, rev 4.165; lever: central; final drive: hypoid bevel; axle ratio: 4.125; tyres: 145 x 13.

PERFORMANCE max speed: 84 mph, 135 km/h; power-weight ratio: 43 lb/hp, 19.5 kg/hp; carrying capacity: 882 lb, 400 kg; speed in top at 1,000 rpm: 16.5 mph, 26.5 km/h; fuel consumption: 40.4 m/imp gal, 33.6 m/US gal, 7 l x 100 km.

CHASSIS integral; front suspension: independent, swinging longitudinal trailing arms, transverse torsion bars, telescopic dampers; rear suspension: independent, semi-trailing arms, coil springs, telescopic dampers.

STEERING worm and double roller.

966

BRAKES drum, single circuit; swept area: front 44.2 sq in, 285 sq cm, rear 44.2 sq in, 285 sq cm, total 88.4 sq in, 570 sq cm.

ELECTRICAL EQUIPMENT 12 V; 48 Ah battery; 250 W alternator; 2 headlamps.

DIMENSIONS AND WEIGHT wheel base: 85.04 in, 2,160 mm; tracks: 48.03 in, 1,220 mm front, 47.24 in, 1,200 mm rear; length: 146.85 in, 3,730 mm; width: 60.43 in, 1,535 mm; height: 53.94 in, 1,370 mm; ground clearance: 7.48 in, 190 mm; dry weight: 1,720 lb, 780 kg; turning circle (between walls): 36.1 ft, 11 m; fuel tank: 6.6 imp gal, 7.9 US gal, 30 l.

BODY saloon/sedan; 2 doors; 5 seats, separate front seats, reclining backrests, independent heating.

PRACTICAL INSTRUCTIONS fuel: 93 oct petrol; engine sump oil: 4.6 imp pt, 5.5 US pt, 2.6 l, SAE 20W-30, change every 2,400 miles, 4,000 km; gearbox and final drive oil: 2.5 imp pt, 3 US pt, 1.4 l, SAE 80-90, change every 14,900 miles, 24,000 km; greasing: 10 points, every 3,700 miles, 6,000 km; tappet clearances: inlet 0.003 in, 0.08 mm, exhaust 0.004 in, 0.10 mm; tyre pressure: front 21 psi, 1.5 atm, rear 24 psi, 1.7 atm.

ZIL USSR

114 Limousine

ENGINE front, 4 stroke; 8 cylinders, Vee-slanted at 90°; 427.1 cu in, 7,000 cc; compression ratio: 9.5:1; max power (SAE): 300 hp at 4,400 rpm; max torque (SAE): 420 lb ft, 58 kg m at 2,900 rpm; max engine rpm: 4,500; 43 hp/l; cast iron cylinder block, light alloy head; 7 crankshaft bearings; valves: overhead, push-rods and rockers; camshafts: 1, at centre of vee; lubrication: gear pump, full flow filter, 13.2 imp pt, 15.9 US pt, 7.5 l; 1 K 85 downdraught 4-barrel carburettor; fuel feed: electric pump; water-cooled, 39.9 imp pt, 48 US pt, 22.7 l.

TRANSMISSION driving wheels: rear; gearbox: automatic transmission, hydraulic torque converter and planetary gears with 2 ratios, max ratio of converter at stall 2.5; ratios: I 1.720, II 1, rev 2.930; lever: push button control; final drive: hypoid bevel; axle ratio: 3.540; width of rims: 6.5"; tyres: 8.90 x 15.

PERFORMANCE max speed: 118 mph, 190 km/h; power-weight ratio: 23.4 lb/hp, 10.6 kg/hp; carrying capacity: 1,411 lb, 640 kg; fuel consumption: not declared.

CHASSIS box-type ladder frame and X cross members; front suspension: independent, wishbones, coil springs, anti-roll bar, lever dampers; rear suspension: rigid axle, semi-elliptic leafsprings, telescopic dampers.

STEERING recirculating ball, servo; turns lock to lock: 4.30.

BRAKES front disc, rear drum, servo.

ELECTRICAL EQUIPMENT 12 V; 2 x 54 Ah batteries; 500 W dynamo; R-4 distributor; 4 headlamps; 2 fog lamps.

DIMENSIONS AND WEIGHT wheel base: 148.03 in, 3,760 mm; tracks: 61.81 in, 1,570 mm front, 63.78 in, 1,620 mm rear; length: 247.44 in, 6,285 mm; width: 81.50 in, 2,070 mm; height: 59.45 in, 1,510 mm; ground clearance: 7.09 in, 180 mm; dry weight: 7,001 lb, 3,175 kg; turning circle (between walls): 52.4 ft, 16 m; fuel tank: 26.4 imp gal, 31.7 US gal, 120 l.

BODY limousine; 4 doors; 7 seats, separate front seats; air-conditioning.

PRACTICAL INSTRUCTIONS fuel: 95 oct petrol; engine sump oil: 12.3 imp pt, 14.8 US pt, 7 l, SAE 10W-30, change every 2,400 miles, 4,000 km; gearbox oil: 22 imp pt, 26.4 US pt, 12.5 l, A type automatic transmission fluid, change every 12 months; final drive oil: 6 imp pt, 7.2 US pt, 3.4 l, SAE 80-90, change every 7,500 miles, 12,000 km; tyre pressure: front 31 psi, 2.2 atm, rear 31 psi, 2.2 atm.

ZCZ YUGOSLAVIA

Zastava 750 M

ENGINE rear, 4 stroke; 4 cylinders, vertical, in line; 46.8 cu in, 767 cc (2.44 x 2.50 in, 62 x 63.5 mm); compression ratio: 7.5:1; max power (DIN) 25 hp at 4,600 rpm; max torque (DIN): 37 lb ft, 5.1 kg m at 2,500 rpm; max engine rpm: 4,800; 32.6 hp/l; cast iron cylinder block, light alloy head; 3 crankshafts bearings; valves: overhead, in line, push-rods and rockers; camshafts: 1, side; lubrication: gear pump, centrifugal filter, 6.5 imp pt, 7.8 US pt, 3.7 l; 1 Weber 28 ICP 6 or Solex C28PIB 3 or Holley 28 ICP 6 downdraught single barrel carburettor; fuel feed: mechanical pump; water-cooled, 7.9 imp pt, 9.5 US pt, 4.5 l.

ZCZ Zastava 750 Luxe

ZCZ Zastava 101

ZCZ Zastava 1300

ANSMISSION driving wheels: rear; clutch: single dry ate; gearbox: mechanical; gears: 4, II, III and IV synch-nized; ratios: I 3.385, II 2.055, III 1.333, IV 0.896, rev 275; lever: central; final drive: spiral bevel; axle ratio: 375; width of rims: 3.5''; tyres: 5.20 x 12.

RFORMANCE max speeds: (I) 19 mph, 30 km/h; (II) 28 oh, 45 km/h; (III) 43 mph, 70 km/h; (IV) about 68 mph, 0 km/h; power-weight ratio: 54.2 lb/hp, 24.6 kg/hp; carry-g capacity: 706 lb, 320 kg; acceleration: standing ¼ mile .7 sec, 0-50 mph (0-80 km/h) 24 sec; speed in top at 000 rpm: 14.1 mph, 22.7 km/h; fuel consumption: 48.7 /imp gal, 40.6 m/US gal, 5.8 l x 100 km.

HASSIS integral; front suspension: independent, wish-ones, transverse leafspring lower arms, telescopic dam-ers; rear suspension: independent, oblique semi-trailing ms, coil springs, telescopic dampers.

TEERING screw and sector; turns lock to lock: 2.12.

RAKES drum, single circuit; swept area: front 33.5 sq in, 6 sq cm, rear 33.5 sq in, 216 sq cm, total 67 sq in, 2 sq cm.

LECTRICAL EQUIPMENT 12 V; 32 Ah battery; 230 W ynamo; Marelli distributor; 2 headlamps.

IMENSIONS AND WEIGHT wheel base: 78.74 in, 2,000 mm; acks: 45.28 in, 1,150 mm front, 45.67 in, 1,160 mm rear; ngth: 129.72 in, 3,295 mm; width: 54.25 in, 1,378 mm; eight: 55.12 in, 1,400 mm; ground clearance: 5.71 in, 145 m; dry weight: 1,356 lb, 615 kg; distribution of weight: % front, 54% rear; turning circle (between walls): 30.5 , 9.3 m; fuel tank: 6.6 imp gal, 7.9 US gal, 30 l.

ODY saloon/sedan; 2 doors; 4 seats, separate front seats; ack seats folding down to luggage table.

RACTICAL INSTRUCTIONS fuel: 80-85 oct petrol; engine ump oil: 5.6 imp pt, 6.8 US pt, 3.2 l, SAE 30W (summer) W (winter), change every 6,200 miles, 10,000 km; gearbox d final drive oil: 2.6 imp pt, 3.2 US pt, 1.5 l, SAE 90 EP, ange every 18,60 miles, 30,000 km; greasing: every 1,600 iles, 2,500 km, 2 points; sparking plug type: 225°; tappet earances: inlet 0.006 in, 0.15 mm, exhaust 0.006 in, 0.15 m; valve timing: 4° 34° 29° 1°; tyre pressure: front 14 psi, atm, rear 28 psi, 1.6 atm.

Zastava 750 Luxe

ee Zastava 750 M, except for:

ODY reclining backrests; luxury interior.

Zastava 101

NGINE front, transverse, 4 stroke; 4 cylinders, in line; 3.1 cu in, 1,116 cc (3.15 x 2.19 in, 80 x 55.5 mm); com-ression ratio: 8.8:1; max power (DIN): 55 hp at 6,000 rpm; ax torque (DIN): 57 lb ft, 7.9 kg m at 3,000 rpm; max ngine rpm: 6,000; 49.3 hp/l; cast iron cylinder block, light lloy head; 5 crankshaft bearings; valves: overhead, thimble appets; camshafts: 1, overhead; lubrication: gear pump, artridge filter, 8.8 imp. pt, 10.6 US pt, 5 l; 1 Weber 32 CEV or Solex C 32 DISA downdraught carburettor; fuel eed: mechanical pump; water-cooled, 11.4 imp pt, 13.7 S pt, 6.5 l, electric thermostatic fan.

RANSMISSION driving wheels: front; clutch: single dry late; gearbox: mechanical; gears: 4, fully synchronized; atios: I 3.583, II 2.235, III 1.454, IV 1.042, rev 3.714; lever: entral; final drive: cylindrical gears; axle ratio: 4.077; vidth of rims: 4.5''; tyres: 145 SR x 13.

ERFORMANCE max speeds: (I) 28 mph, 45 km/h; (II) 47 mph, 75 km/h; (III) 71 mph, 115 km/h; (IV) over 84 mph, 35 km/h; power-weight ratio: 32.6 lb/hp, 14.8 kg/hp; carry-ng capacity: 882 lb, 400 kg; acceleration: standing ¼ mile 1 sec, 0-50 mph (0-80 km/h) 12.7 sec; speed in top at 1,000 pm: 15.5 mph, 25 km/h; fuel consumption: 35.3 m/imp gal, 9.4 m/US gal, 8 l x 100 km.

CHASSIS integral; front suspension: independent, by McPherson, coil springs, telescopic dampers struts, lower vishbones, anti-roll bar; rear suspension: independent, single wide-based wishbone, transverse leafspring, teles-copic dampers.

STEERING rack-and-pinion; turns lock to lock: 3.50.

BRAKES front disc (diameter 8.94 in, 227 mm), rear drum, ear compensator; swept area: front 19.2 sq in, 124 sq cm, ear 33.5 sq in, 216 sq cm, total 52.7 sq in, 340 sq cm.

ELECTRICAL EQUIPMENT 12 V; 34 Ah battery; 400 W alternator; Marelli distributor; 2 headlamps.

DIMENSIONS AND WEIGHT wheel base: 96.42 in, 2,449 mm; tracks: 51.34 in, 1,304 mm front, 51.18 in, 1,300 mm rear; ength: 151.02 in, 3,836 mm; width: 62.60 in, 1,590 mm; height: 54.02 in, 1,372 mm; ground clearance: 5.71 in, 145 mm; dry weight: 1,797 lb, 815 kg; distribution of weight: 61.5% front, 38.5% rear; turning circle (between walls): 35.8 ft, 10.9 m; fuel tank: 8.4 imp gal, 10 US gal, 38 l.

BODY saloon/sedan; 4 + 1 doors; 5 seats, separate front seats.

PRACTICAL INSTRUCTIONS fuel: 98 oct petrol; engine sump oil: 7.4 imp pt, 8.9 US pt, 4.2 l, SAE 20W (winter) 30 (sum-mer), change every 6,200 miles, 10,000 km; gearbox and

ZCZ Zastava 750 Luxe

ZCZ Zastava 101

ZCZ Zastava 1500 De Luxe

final drive oil: 5.5 imp pt, 6.6 US pt, 3.1, SAE 90, change every 18,600 miles, 30,000 km; greasing: none; sparking plug type: 240°; tappet clearances: inlet 0.012 in, 0,30 mm, ex-haust 0.016 in, 0.40 mm; valve timing: 12° 52° 52° 12°; tyre pressure: front 26 psi, 1.8 atm, rear 24 psi, 1.7 atm.

OPTIONAL ACCESSORIES reclining backrests; luxury in-terior; electrically-heated rear window.

Zastava 1300

ENGINE front, 4 stroke; 4 cylinders, vertical, in line, 79 cu in, 1,295 cc (2.83 x 3.13 in, 72 x 79.5 mm); compression ratio: 9:1; max power (DIN): 60 hp at 5,000 rpm; max torque (DIN): 69 lb ft, 9.5 kg m at 3,200 rpm; max engine rpm: 5,500; 43.6 hp/l; cast iron cylinder block, light alloy head; 3 crankshaft bearings; valves: overhead, Vee-slanted, push-rods and rockers; camshafts: 1, side; lubrication: gear pump, centrifugal filter, cartridge on by-pass, 7.6 imp pt, 9.1 US pt, 4.3 l; 1 Weber 34 DCHD or Solex C 34 PAIA 2 downdraught twin barrel carburettor; fuel feed: mechanical pump; water-cooled, 11.8 imp pt, 14.2 US pt, 6.7 l.

TRANSMISSION driving wheels: rear; clutch: single dry plate, hydraulically controlled; gearbox: mechanical; gears: 4, fully synchronized; ratios: I 3.750, II 2.300, III 1.490, IV 1, rev 3.870; lever: steering column; final drive: hypoid bevel; axle ratio: 4.100; width of rims: 4.5''; tyres: 5.60 S x 13.

PERFORMANCE max speeds: (I) 25 mph, 40 km/h; (II) 40 mph, 65 km/h; (III) 62 mph, 100 km/h; (IV) over 87 mph, 140 km/h; power-weight ratio: 35.3 lb/hp, 16 kg/hp; carrying capacity: 882 lb, 400 kg; acceleration: standing ¼ mile 23.1 sec, 0-50 mph (0-80 km/h) 13.9 sec; speed in direct drive at 1,000 rpm: 16.1 mph, 25.9 km/h; fuel consumption: 32.8 m/imp gal, 27.3 m/US gal, 8.6 l x 100 km.

CHASSIS integral; front suspension: independent, wish-bones, lower trailing links, coil springs, anti-roll bar, telescopic dampers; rear suspension: rigid axle, semi-elliptic leafsprings, telescopic dampers.

STEERING worm and roller; turns lock to lock: 3.

BRAKES disc, servo.

ELECTRICAL EQUIPMENT 12 V; 48 Ah battery; 400 W dynamo; Marelli distributor; 4 headlamps.

DIMENSIONS AND WEIGHT wheel base: 95.47 in, 2,425 mm; tracks: 50.98 in, 1,295 mm front, 50.08 in, 1,272 mm rear; length: 158.66 in, 4,030 mm; width: 60.83 in, 1,545 mm; height: 56.69 in, 1,440 mm; ground clearance: 5.12 in, 130 mm; dry weight: 2,117 lb, 960 kg; distribution of weight: 56% front, 44% rear; turning circle (between walls): 33.5 ft, 10.2 m; fuel tank: 9.9 imp gal, 11.9 US gal, 45 l.

BODY saloon/sedan; 4 doors; 5 seats, separate front seats, reclining backrests.

PRACTICAL INSTRUCTIONS fuel: 92 oct petrol; engine sump oil: 6.2 imp pt, 7.4 US pt, 3.5 l, SAE 10W (winter 40 summer), change every 6,200 miles, 10,000 km; gearbox oil: 2.3 imp pt, 2.7 US pt, 1.3 l, SAE 90, change every 18,600 miles, 30,000 km; final drive oil: 1.6 imp pt, 1.9 US pt, 0.9 l, SAE 90, change every 18,600 miles, 30,000 km; greasing: every 1,600 miles, 2,500 km, 3 points; sparking plug type: 240°; tappet clearances: inlet 0.008 in, 0.20 mm, exhaust 0.008 in, 0.20 mm; valve timing: 9° 61° 49° 21°; tyre pressure: front 20 psi, 1.4 atm, rear 24 psi, 1.7 atm.

Zastava 1300 Luxe

See Zastava 1300, except for:

PERFORMANCE power-weight ratio: 35.5 lb/hp, 16.1 kg/hp.

DIMENSIONS AND WEIGHT dry weight: 2,139 lb, 970 kg.

BODY luxury interior.

Zastava 1500

See Zastava 1300, except for:

ENGINE 90.4 cu in, 1,481 cc (3.03 x 3.13 in, 77 x 79.5 mm); max power (DIN): 75 hp at 5,000 rpm; max torque (DIN): 86 lb ft, 11.8 kg m at 3,200 rpm; 50.6 hp/l.

PERFORMANCE max speeds: (I) 25 mph, 41 km/h; (II) 42 mph, 68 km/h; (III) 65 mph, 104 km/h; (IV) 96 mph, 155 km/h; power-weight ratio: 28.7 lb/hp, 13 kg/hp; accele-ration: standing ¼ mile 20.6 sec, 0-50 mph (0-80 km/h) 11.5 sec; fuel consumption: 30.1 m/imp gal, 25 m/US gal, 9.4 l x 100 km.

DIMENSIONS AND WEIGHT wheel base: 98.62 in, 2,505 mm; length: 162.60 in, 4,130 mm; ground clearance: 4.84 in, 123 mm; dry weight: 2,161 lb, 980 kg; distribution of weight: 55% front, 45% rear; turning circle (between walls): 37.1 ft, 11.3 m.

Zastava 1500 De Luxe

See Zastava 1500, except for:

BODY luxury interior.

The Americas

Models now in production

Illustrations and technical information

ANDINO ARGENTINA

GT 1100

ENGINE rear, 4 stroke; 4 cylinders, vertical, in line; 68.2 cu in, 1,118 cc (2.68 x 3.03 in, 68 x 77 mm); compression ratio: 8.5:1; max power (SAE): 56 hp at 5,500 rpm; max torque (SAE): 62 lb ft, 8.5 kg m at 3,500 rpm; max engine rpm: 6,200; 50.1 hp/l; cast iron cylinder block, light alloy head, wet liners; 5 crankshaft bearings; valves: overhead, push-rods and rockers; camshafts: 1, side; lubrication: gear pump, full flow filter, 5.3 imp pt, 6.3 US pt, 3 l; 1 Solex F 32 PDIS-3 carburettor; fuel feed: mechanical pump; water-cooled, 9.7 imp pt, 11.6 US pt, 5.5 l.

TRANSMISSION driving wheels: rear; clutch: single dry plate; gearbox: mechanical; gears: 4, fully synchronized; ratios: I 3.615, II 2.263, III 1.480, IV 1.032, rev 3.080; gear lever: central; final drive: hypoid bevel; axle ratio: 3.875; width of rims: 5.5"; tyres: 690 x 14.

PERFORMANCE max speeds: (I) 29 mph, 47 km/h; (II) 47 mph, 75 km/h; (III) 71 mph, 115 km/h; (IV) 106 mph, 170 km/h; power-weight ratio: 24 lb/hp, 10.9 kg/hp; carrying capacity: 397 lb, 180 kg; speed in top at 1,000 rpm: 16.8 mph, 27 km/h; fuel consumption: 40.4 m/imp gal, 33.6 m/US gal, 7 l x 100 km.

CHASSIS tubular backbone; front suspension: independent, wishbones, lower links, coil springs, anti-roll bar, telescopic dampers; rear suspension: independent, swinging semi-axles, swinging longitudinal trailing arms articulated at centre, coil springs, anti-roll bar, telescopic dampers.

STEERING rack-and-pinion; turns lock to lock: 3.

BRAKES disc (diameter 10.28 in, 261 mm); swept area: total 342.9 sq in, 2,212 sq cm.

ELECTRICAL EQUIPMENT 12 V; 55 Ah battery; 500 W alternator; 2 headlamps.

DIMENSIONS AND WEIGHT wheel base: 89.37 in, 2,270 mm; tracks: 50.39 in, 1,280 mm front, 51.18 in, 1,300 mm rear; length: 155.51 in, 3,950 mm; width: 62.99 in, 1,600 mm; height: 42.52 in, 1,080 mm; ground clearance: 5.91 in, 150 mm; dry weight: 1,345 lb, 610 kg; distribution of weight: 45% front, 55% rear; turning circle (between walls): 32.8 ft, 10 m; fuel tank: 9.9 imp gal, 11.9 US gal, 45 l.

BODY coupé in plastic material; 2 doors; 2 seats.

PRACTICAL INSTRUCTIONS fuel: 90-95 oct petrol; engine sump oil: 4.4 imp pt, 5.3 US pt, 2.5 l, SAE 10W-40, change every 1,600 miles, 2,500 km; gearbox and final drive oil: 3.3 imp pt, 4 US pt, 1.9 l, SAE 80, change every 6,200 miles, 10,000 km; greasing: every 12,400 miles, 20,000 km, 1 point; tappet clearances: inlet 0.006-0.007 in, 0.15-0.18 mm, exhaust 0.007-0.009 in, 0.18-0.22 mm; tyre pressure: front 21 psi, 1.5 atm, rear 23 psi, 1.6 atm.

VARIATIONS

ENGINE 79.3 cu in, 1,300 cc, max power (SAE) 80 hp at 7,000 rpm.
PERFORMANCE max speed 121 mph, 195 km/h, power-weight ratio 16.8 lb/hp, 7.6 kg/hp.

CHEVROLET ARGENTINA

Special

ENGINE front, 4 stroke; 6 cylinders, vertical, in line; 194 cu in, 3,185 cc (3.56 x 3.25 in, 90.5 x 82.5 mm); compression ratio: 7.5:1; max power (SAE): 110 hp at 4,400 rpm; max torque (SAE): 169 lb ft, 23.3 kg m at 2,200 rpm; max engine rpm: 4,600; 34.5 hp/l; cast iron cylinder block and head; 7 crankshaft bearings; valves: overhead, in line, push-rods and rockers; hydraulic tappets; camshafts: 1, side; lubrication: gear pump, full flow filter, 7 imp pt, 8.5 US pt, 4 l; 1 Zenith downdraught carburettor; fuel feed: mechanical pump; water-cooled, 21.6 imp pt, 26 US pt, 12.3 l.

TRANSMISSION driving wheels: rear; clutch: single dry plate; gearbox: mechanical; gears: 3, fully synchronized; ratios: I 2.800, II 1.690, III 1, rev 3.800; lever: steering column; final drive: hypoid bevel; axle ratio: 3.310; width of rims: 5.5"; tyres: 7.35 x 14.

PERFORMANCE max speed: 93 mph, 150 km/h; power-weight ratio: 26.2 lb/hp, 11.9 kg/hp; carrying capacity: 882 lb, 400 kg; speed in direct drive at 1,000 rpm: 23.3 mph, 37.5 km/h; fuel consumption: 22.6 m/imp gal, 18.8 m/US gal, 12.5 l x 100 km.

CHASSIS integral; front suspension: independent, wishbones, coil springs, telescopic dampers; rear suspension: rigid axle, semi-elliptic leafsprings, telescopic dampers.

STEERING recirculating ball.

BRAKES front disc, rear drum.

ANDINO GT 1100

CHEVROLET Rally Sport 250

CHEVROLET Chevy Super Sport Coupé

ELECTRICAL EQUIPMENT 12 V; 55 Ah battery; 33 A alte nator; Delco-Remy distributor; 2 headlamps.

DIMENSIONS AND WEIGHT wheel base: 110 in, 2,794 mm tracks: 56.50 in, 1,435 mm front, 55.98 in, 1,422 mm rea length: 182.79 in, 4,643 mm; width: 70.47 in, 1,790 mr height: 57.28 in, 1,455 mm; ground clearance: 6.30 in, 16 mm; dry weight: 2,889 lb, 1,310 kg; turning circle (betwee walls): 40.7 ft, 12.4 m; fuel tank: 13.2 imp gal, 15.8 U gal, 60 l.

BODY saloon/sedan; 4 doors; 5 seats, separate front seat

OPTIONAL ACCESSORIES 3.360 axle ratio; anti-roll bar c front and rear suspension.

Rally Sport

See Special, except for:

TRANSMISSION gears: 4, fully synchronized; ratios: I 2.85 II 2.020, III 1.350, IV 1, rev 2.850; lever; central.

PERFORMANCE power-weight ratio: 26.6 lb/hp, 12.1 kg/h

DIMENSIONS AND WEIGHT dry weight: 2,955 lb, 1,340 k

Rally Sport 250

See Rally Sport, except for:

ENGINE 250 cu in, 4,097 cc (3.87 x 3.53 in, 98.4 x 89.7 mm) compression ratio: 8.1:1; max power (SAE): 150 hp 4,400 rpm; max torque (SAE): 225 lb ft, 31.1 kg m at 1,80 rpm; 36.6 hp/l; lubricating system capacity: 7.4 imp pt, 8 US pt, 4.2 l; 1 Holley downdraught carburettor.

PERFORMANCE max speed: 99 mph, 160 km/h; power-weig ratio: 19.6 lb/hp, 8.9 kg/hp; speed in direct drive at 1,00 rpm: 23.6 mph, 38 km/h; fuel consumption: 18.8 m/imp ga 15.7 m/US gal, 15 l x 100 km.

CHASSIS front suspension: anti-roll bar (standard).

Chevy Standard

ENGINE front, 4 stroke; 6 cylinders, vertical, in line; 23 cu in, 3,769 cc (3.87 x 3.25 in, 98.4 x 82.6 mm); compres sion ratio: 8.1:1; max power (SAE): 137 hp at 4,400 rpm max torque (SAE): 204 lb ft, 28.2 kg m at 2,000 rpm; ma engine rpm: 4,600; 36.4 hp/l; cast iron cylinder block an head; 7 crankshaft bearings; valves: overhead, in line push-rods and rockers, hydraulic tappets; camshafts: 1 side; lubrication: gear pump, full flow filter, 7.4 imp pt 8.9 US pt, 4.2 l; 1 Holley downdraught carburettor; fue feed: mechanical pump; water-cooled, 21.6 imp pt, 26 U pt, 12.3 l.

TRANSMISSION driving wheels: rear; clutch: single dr plate; gearbox: mechanical; gears: 3, fully synchronized ratios: I 2.800, II 1.690, III 1, rev 3.800; lever: steerin column; final drive: hypoid bevel; axle ratio: 3.080; widt of rims: 5.5"; tyres: 7.35 x 14.

PERFORMANCE max speed: 99 mph, 160 km/h; power-weig ratio: 23.1 lb/hp, 10.5 kg/hp; carrying capacity: 882 lb 400 kg; speed in direct drive at 1,000 rpm: 23.6 mph, 3 km/h; fuel consumption: 20.9 m/imp gal, 17.4 m/US ga 13.5 l x 100 km.

CHASSIS integral; front auxiliary frame; front suspensior independent, wishbones, coil springs, telescopic dampers rear suspension: rigid axle, semi-elliptic leafsprings, tele scopic dampers.

STEERING recirculating ball.

BRAKES front disc, rear drum.

ELECTRICAL EQUIPMENT 12 V; 55 Ah battery; 32 A alterna tor; Delco-Remy distributor; 2 headlamps.

DIMENSIONS AND WEIGHT wheel base: 110.98 in, 2,81 mm; tracks: 59.53 in, 1,512 mm front, 59.41 in, 1,509 mr rear; length: 191.26 in, 4,858 mm; width: 72.56 in, 1,84 mm; height: 56.06 in, 1,424 mm; ground clearance: 5.12 ir 130 mm; dry weight: 3,197 lb, 1,450 kg; turning circl (between walls): 41 ft, 12.5 m; fuel tank: 15 imp gal, 1 US gal, 68 l.

BODY saloon/sedan; 4 doors; 5 seats, separate front seats

OPTIONAL ACCESSORIES servo brake.

Chevy Super

See Chevy Standard, except for:

BODY luxury interior.

VARIATIONS

ENGINE 250 cu in, 4,097 cc (3.87 x 3.53 in, 98.4 x 89.7 mm)

ANDINO GT 1100

CHEVROLET Rally Sport 250

CHEVROLET Chevy Super Sport Coupé

max power (SAE) 150 hp at 4,400 rpm, max torque (SAE) 225 lb ft, 31.1 kg m at 1,800 rpm, 36.6 hp/l.

PERFORMANCE max speed 99 mph, 160 km/h, power-weight ratio 21.4 lb/hp, 9.7 kg/hp, speed in direct drive at 1,000 rpm 23.6 mph, 38 km/h, fuel consumption 18.8 m/imp gal, 15.7 m/US gal, 15 l x 100 km.

Chevy De Luxe

See Chevy Standard, except for:

ENGINE 250 cu in, 4,097 cc (3.87 x 3.53 in, 98.4 x 89.7 mm); max power (SAE): 150 hp at 4,400 rpm; max torque (SAE): 225 lb ft, 31.1 kg m at 1,800 rpm; 36.6 hp/l.

TRANSMISSION gearbox: Chevromatic automatic transmission, hydraulic torque converter and planetary gears with 3 ratios + reverse; ratios: I 2,400, II 1.480, III 1, rev 1.920.

PERFORMANCE max speed: 99 mph, 160 km/h; power-weight ratio: 21.4 lb/hp, 9.7 kg/hp; fuel consumption: 18.8 m/imp gal, 15.7 m/US gal, 15 l x 100 km.

DIMENSIONS AND WEIGHT dry weight: 3,222 lb, 1,461 kg.

Chevy Super Sport

See Chevy Standard, except for:

ENGINE 250 cu in, 4,097 cc (3.87 x 3.53 in, 98.4 x 89.7 mm); max power (SAE): 150 hp at 4,400 rpm; max torque (SAE): 225 lb ft, 31.1 kg m at 1,800 rpm; 36.3 hp/l.

TRANSMISSION gears: 4, fully synchronized; ratios: I 2.850, II 2.020, III 1.350, IV 1, rev 2.850; lever: central.

PERFORMANCE max speed: (I) 36 mph, 58 km/h; (II) 52 mph, 83 km/h; (III) 78 mph, 125 km/h; (IV) 104 mph, 168 km/h; power-weight ratio: 22.3 lb/hp, 10.1 kg/hp; speed in direct drive at 1,000 rpm: 24.9 mph, 40 km/h; fuel consumption: 18.2 m/imp gal, 15.2 m/US gal, 15.5 l x 100 km.

CHASSIS front suspension: anti-roll bar.

DIMENSIONS AND WEIGHT dry weight: 3,345 lb, 1,517 kg.

Chevy Super Sport Coupé

See Chevy Super Sport, except for:

PERFORMANCE power-weight ratio: 21.8 lb/hp, 9.9 kg/hp.

DIMENSIONS AND WEIGHT height: 55.04 in, 1,398 mm; dry weight: 3,296 lb, 1,495 kg.

BODY coupé; 2 doors; separate front seats, reclining backrests.

DODGE ARGENTINA

Dodge 1500

PRICE EX WORKS: 23,510 new pesos.

ENGINE front, 4 stroke; 4 cylinders, vertical, in line; 91.4 cu in, 1,498 cc (3.39 x 2.53 in, 86.1 x 64.3 mm); compression ratio: 8:1; max power (SAE): 72 hp at 5,400 rpm; max torque (SAE): 88 lb ft, 12.2 kg m at 3,200 rpm; max engine rpm: 5,400; 48 hp/l; cast iron cylinder block and head; 5 crankshaft bearings; valves: overhead, in line, push-rods and rockers; camshafts: 1, side; lubrication: rotary pump, full flow filter, 7 imp pt, 8.5 US pt, 4 l, 1 Stromberg 150 CDS single barrel carburettor; fuel feed: mechanical pump; water-cooled, 10.6 imp pt, 12.7 US pt, 6 l.

TRANSMISSION driving wheels: rear; clutch: single dry plate (diaphragm); gearbox: mechanical; gears: 4, fully synchronized; ratios: I 3.317, II 2.029, III 1.366, IV 1, rev 3.450; lever: central; final drive: hypoid bevel; axle ratio: 3.890; width of rims: 5"; tyres: 5.60 x 13.

PERFORMANCE max speeds: (I) 29 mph, 46 km/h; (II) 48 mph, 77 km/h; (III) 71 mph, 114 km/h; (IV) 90 mph, 145 km/h; power-weight ratio: 27.6 lb/hp, 12.5 kg/hp; carrying capacity: 882 lb, 400 kg; acceleration: 0-50 mph (0-80 km/h) 9.5 sec; speed in direct drive at 1,000 rpm: 18.6 mph, 30 km/h; fuel consumption: 25.7 m/imp gal, 21.4 m/US gal, 11 l x 100 km.

CHASSIS integral; front suspension: independent, by McPherson, lower trailing links, coil springs, anti-roll bar, telescopic dampers; rear suspension: rigid axle, lower trailing radius arms, upper oblique torque arms, coil springs, telescopic dampers.

STEERING rack-and-pinion; turns lock to lock: 3.66.

BRAKES front disc, rear drum; swept area: front 42.5 sq in, 274 sq cm, 26.7 sq in, 172 sq cm, total 69,2 sq in, 446 sq cm.

DODGE 1500

ELECTRICAL EQUIPMENT 12 V; 48 Ah battery; 32 A alternator; TRIA distributor; 2 headlamps.

DIMENSIONS AND WEIGHT wheel base: 97.99 in, 2,489 mm; tracks: 50.98 in, 1,295 mm front, 51.26 in, 1,302 mm rear; length: 162.99 in, 4,140 mm; width 62.52 in, 1,588 mm; height: 53.15 in, 1,350 mm; ground clearance: 5.59 in, 142 mm; dry weight: 1,958 lb, 900 kg; distribution of weight: 54.2% in, 45.8% rear; turning circle (between walls): 30.8 ft, 9.4 m; fuel tank: 9.9 imp gal, 11.9 US gal, 45 l.

BODY saloon/sedan; 4 doors; 5 seats, separate front seats, reclining backrests.

PRACTICAL INSTRUCTIONS fuel: 98-100 oct petrol; engine sump oil: 7 imp pt, 8.5 US pt, 4 l; gearbox oil: 3 imp pt, 3.6 US pt, 1.7 l; final drive oil: 2.3 imp pt, 2.7 US pt, 1.3 l; greasing: 1 point; tappet clearances (hot): inlet 0.008 in, 0.20 mm, exhaust 0.016 in, 0.40 mm; valve timing: 17° 51° 55° 9°; tyre pressure: front 22 psi, 1.6 atm, rear 24 psi, 1.7 atm.

OPTIONAL ACCESSORIES luxury interior.

Polara

PRICE EX WORKS: 31,269 new pesos.

ENGINE front, 4 stroke; 6 cylinders, vertical, in line; 225 cu in, 3,688 cc (3.40 x 4.13 in, 86.4 x 104.8 mm); compression ratio: 8.4:1; max power (SAE): 145 hp at 4,400 rpm; max torque (SAE): 158 lb ft, 21.8 kg m at 2,400 rpm; max engine rpm: 4,600; 39.3 hp/l; cast iron cylinder block and head; 4 crankshaft bearings; valves: overhead, in line, push-rods and rockers; camshafts: 1, side; lubrication: rotary pump, full flow filter, 8.8 imp pt, 10.6 US pt, 5 l; 1 Holley R 2535A downdraught single barrel carburettor; fuel feed: mechanical pump: water-cooled, 21.6 imp pt, 26 US pt, 12.3 l.

TRANSMISSION driving wheels: rear; clutch: single dry plate; gearbox: mechanical; gears: 3, fully synchronized; ratios: I 2.830, II 1.560, III 1, rev 2.660; lever: steering column; final drive: hypoid bevel; axle ratio: 3.070; width of rims: 5.5"; tyres: 6.95 x 14.

PERFORMANCE max speeds: (I) 34 mph, 55 km/h; (II) 71 mph, 115 km/h; (III) 99 mph, 160 km/h; power-weight ratio: 21.4 lb/hp, 9.6 kg/hp; carrying capacity: 1,213 lb, 550 kg; acceleration: 0-50 mph (0-80 km/h) 9 sec; speed in direct drive at 1,000 rpm: 24.9 mph, 40 km/h; fuel consumption: 21.7 m/imp gal, 18.1 m/US gal, 13 l x 100 km.

CHASSIS integral; front suspension: independent, wishbones, lower trailing links, longitudinal torsion bars, telescopic dampers; rear suspension: rigid axle, semi-elliptic leafsprings, telescopic dampers.

STEERING recirculating ball; turns lock to lock: 5.30.

BRAKES front disc, rear drum; swept area: front 60.5 sq in, 390 sq cm, rear 32.4 sq in, 209 sq cm, total 92.9 sq in, 599 sq cm.

ELECTRICAL EQUIPMENT 12 V; 56 Ah battery; 40 A alternator; Chrysler distributor; 2 headlamps.

DIMENSIONS AND WEIGHT wheel base: 110/98 in, 2,819 mm; tracks: 56.30 in, 1,430 mm front, 57,72 in, 1,466 mm rear; length: 197.24 in, 5,010 mm; width: 73.23 in, 1,860 mm; height: 55.51 in, 1,410 mm; ground clearance: 6.38 in, 162 mm; dry weight: 3,109 lb, 1,410 kg; distribution of weight: 55% front, 45% rear; turning circle (between walls): 38.7 ft, 11.8 m; fuel tank: 15 imp gal, 18 US gal, 68 l.

BODY saloon/sedan; 4 doors; 6 seats, bench front seats.

PRACTICAL INSTRUCTIONS fuel: 98-100 oct petrol; engine sump oil: 7.9 imp pt 9.5 US pt, 4.5 l, change every 3,700 miles, 6,000 km; gearbox oil: 3.5 imp pt, 4.2 US pt, 2 l, change every 24,000 miles, 36,000 km; final drive oil: 1.8 imp pt, 2.1 US pt, 1 l, change every 24,000 miles, 36,000 km; greasing: every 24,000 miles, 36,000 km, 2 points; tappet clearances: inlet 0.010 in, 0.25 mm, exhaust 0.020 in, 0.50 mm; valve timing: 10° 50° 50° 6°; tyre pressure: front 26 psi, 1.8 atm, 26 psi, 1.8 atm.

OPTIONAL ACCESSORIES luxury interior.

Polara Coupé

See Polara, except for:

PRICE EX WORKS: 33,355 new pesos.

PERFORMANCE power-weight ratio: 21.4 lb/hp, 9.7 kg/hp.

DIMENSIONS AND WEIGHT length: 197.64 in, 5,020 mm; width: 74.92 in, 1,903 mm; height: 53.54 in, 1,360 mm;

DODGE Dodge 1500

DOGE GTX

FIAT 125 Sport

ground clearance: 5.98 in, 152 mm; dry weight: 3,131 lb, 1,420 kg.

BODY coupé; 2 doors; separate front seats, reclining backrests.

Coronado Automatic

See Polara, except for:

PRICE EX WORKS: 41,491 new pesos.

TRANSMISSION gearbox: Torqueflite automatic transmission, hydraulic torque converter and planetary gears with 3 ratios + reverse, max ratio of converter at stall 2.1, possible manual selection; ratios: I 2.450, II 1.450, III 1, rev 2.200; tyres: 7.35 x 14.

PERFORMANCE max speeds: (I) 32 mph, 52 km/h; (II) 68 mph, 110 km/h; (III) 96 mph, 155 km/h; acceleration: 0-50 mph (0-80 km/h) 10 sec; fuel consumption: 20.2 m/imp gal, 16.8 m/US gal, 14 l x 100 km.

STEERING servo; turns lock to lock: 3.50.

BRAKES servo.

GTX

See Polara, except for:

PRICE EX WORKS: 43,705 new pesos.

ENGINE 8 cylinders, Vee-slanted at 90°; 318 cu in, 5,210 cc (3.91 x 3.31 in, 99.3 x 84 mm); compression ratio: 8.8:1; max power (SAE): 230 hp at 4,400 rpm; max torque (SAE): 345 lb ft, 47.6 kg m at 2,000 rpm; 44.2 hp/l; 5 crankshaft bearings; valves: hydraulic tappets; camshafts: 1, at centre of Vee; lubricating system capacity: 10.6 imp pt, 12.7 US pt, 6 l; 1 Carter BBD 7495 downdraught twin barrel carburettor; cooling system capacity: 26.9 imp pt, 32.3 US pt, 15.3 l.

TRANSMISSION gears: 4, fully synchronized; ratios: I 3.090, II 2.100, III 1.450, IV 1, rev 2.680; lever: central; axle ratio: 2.870; width of rims: 6''; tyres: E70H x 14.

PERFORMANCE max speeds: (I) 43 mph, 70 km/h; (II) 56 mph, 90 km/h; (III) 87 mph, 140 km/h; (IV) 121 mph, 195 km/h; power-weight ratio: 14.1 lb/hp, 6.4 kg/hp; acceleration: 0-50 mph, (0-80 km/h) 7 sec; speed in direct drive at 1,000 rpm: 28 mph, 45 km/h; fuel consumption: 20.2 m/imp gal, 16.8 m/US gal, 14 l x 100 km.

BRAKES servo.

ELECTRICAL EQUIPMENT iodine headlamps.

DIMENSIONS AND WEIGHT length: 197.64 in, 5,020 mm; width: 74.92 in, 1,903 mm; height: 53.54 in, 1,360 mm; ground clearance: 5.98 in, 152 mm; dry weight: 3,303 lb, 1,480 kg; distribution of weight: 56% front, 44% rear.

BODY coupé; 2 doors; 5 seats, separate front seats, reclining backrests.

PRACTICAL INSTRUCTIONS engine sump oil: 8.3 imp pt, 9.9 US pt, 4.7 l; gearbox oil: 4.2 imp pt, 5.1 US pt, 2.4 l; valve timing: 10° 50° 58° 10°.

FIAT — ARGENTINA

125 Familiar

ENGINE front, 4 stroke; 4 cylinders, vertical, in line; 98.1 cu in, 1,608 cc (3.15 x 3.15 in, 80 x 80 mm); compression ratio: 8.8:1; max power (DIN): 100 hp at 6,200 rpm; max torque (DIN): 96 lb ft, 13.3 kg m at 4,000 rpm; max engine rpm: 6,200; 62 hp/l; cast iron cylinder block, light alloy head; 5 crankshaft bearings; valves: overhead; camshafts: 2, overhead, cogged belt; lubrication: gear pump, full flow filter, 8.6 imp pt, 10.4 US pt, 4.9 l; 1 Weber 34 DCHE 2 or Solex C34 PAIA/3 downdraught twin barrel carburettor; fuel feed: mechanical pump; water-cooled, 13.2 imp pt, 15.9 US pt, 7.5 l, electric thermostatic fan.

TRANSMISSION driving wheels: rear; clutch: single dry plate; gearbox: mechanical; gears: 4, fully synchronized; ratios: I 3.750, II 2.300, III 1.490, IV 1, rev 3.870; lever: central; final drive: hypoid bevel; axle ratio: 3.900; width of rims: 5''; tyres: 175 x 13.

PERFORMANCE max speeds: (I) 28 mph, 45 km/h; (II) 50 mph, 80 km/h; (III) 78 mph, 125 km/h; (IV) 103 mph, 165 km/h; power-weight ratio: 24 lb/hp, 10.9 kg/hp; carrying capacity: 882 lb, 400 kg; acceleration: standing ¼ mile 19 sec, 0-50 mph (0-80 km/h) 9.5 sec; speed in direct drive at 1,000 rpm: 17.5 mph, 28.2 km/h; fuel consumption: 28.5 m/imp gal, 23.8 m/US gal, 9.9 l x 100 km.

CHASSIS integral; front suspension: independent, wishbones, coil springs, anti-roll bar, telescopic dampers; rear

DODGE Polara Coupé

DODGE GTX

FIAT 125 Familiar

suspension: rigid axle: upper torque arms, semi-elliptic leafsprings, telescopic dampers.

STEERING worm and roller; turns lock to lock: 3.

BRAKES front disc, rear drum, servo; swept area: front 22 sq in, 142 sq cm, rear 70.7 sq in, 456 sq cm, total 92.7 sq in, 598 sq cm.

ELECTRICAL EQUIPMENT 12 V; 48 Ah battery; 550 W alternator; Garef-Marelli distributor; 4 headlamps.

DIMENSIONS AND WEIGHT wheel base: 98.62 in, 2,505 mm; tracks: 50.98 in, 1,295 mm front, 50.08 in, 1,272 mm rear; length: 167.05 in, 4,263 mm; width: 64.17 in, 1,630 mm; height: 55.35 in, 1,406 mm; ground clearance: 7.28 in, 185 mm; dry weight: 2,403 lb, 1,090 kg; distribution of weight: 50% front, 50% rear; turning circle (between wall) 35.4 ft, 10.8 m; fuel tank: 9.9 imp gal, 11.9 US gal, 45 l.

BODY estate car/station wagon; 4 + 1 doors; 5 seats, separate front seats, reclining backrests.

PRACTICAL INSTRUCTIONS fuel 95 oct petrol; engine sump oil: 6.5 imp pt, 7.8 US pt, 3.7 l, SAE 20W-40, change every 3,100 miles, 5,000 km; gearbox oil: 2.3 imp pt, 2.7 US pt, 1.3 l, SAE 90 EP, change every 18,600 miles, 30,000 km; final drive oil: 2.5 imp pt, 3 US pt, 1.4 l, SAE 90 EP, change every 18,600 miles, 30,000 km; greasing: every 3,100 miles, 5,000 km, 8 points; tappet clearances: inlet 0.018 in, 0.45 mm, exhaust 0.020 in, 0.50 mm; valve timing: 26° 66° 66° 26°; tyre pressure: front 20 psi, 1.5 atm, rear 24 psi, 1.7 atm.

125 Sport

See 125 Familiar, except for:

TRANSMISSION width of rims: 5.5''; tyres: 175 SR x 13.

PERFORMANCE max speed: 106 mph, 170 km/h; power-weight ratio: 32 lb/hp, 10.5 kg/hp; carrying capacity: 728 lb, 330 kg; acceleration: standing ¼ mile 18.6 sec, 0-50 mph (0-80 km/h) 9 sec.

ELECTRICAL EQUIPMENT 2 headlamps.

DIMENSIONS AND WEIGHT tracks: 52.48 in, 1,333 mm front, 51.10 in, 1,298 mm rear; length: 166.34 in, 4,225 mm; width: 60.24 in, 1,530 mm; height: 54.33 in, 1,380 mm; ground clearance: 5.91 in, 150 mm; dry weight: 2,315 lb, 1,050 kg; distribution of wieght: 55% front, 45% rear.

BODY coupé; 2 doors; 4 seats, separate front seats, reclining backrests.

IKA-RENAULT — ARGENTINA

Torino L

PRICE EX WORKS: 22,300 new pesos.

ENGINE front, 4 stroke; 6 cylinders, in line; 230 cu in, 3,770 cc (3.34 x 4.37 in, 84.9 x 111.1 mm); compression ratio: 7.5:1; max power (SAE): 140 hp at 4,200 rpm; max torque (SAE): 196 lb ft, 27 kg m at 2,200 rpm; max engine rpm: 4,600; 37.1 hp/l; cast iron cylinder block and head; 4 crankshaft bearings; valves: overhead, Vee-slanted at 64°; rockers; camshafts: 1, overhead; lubrication: gear pump, full flow filter, 7.9 imp pt, 9.5 US pt, 4.5 l; 1 Carter RBS downdraught carburettor; fuel feed: mechanical pump; water-cooled, 20.4 imp pt, 24.5 US pt, 11.6 l.

TRANSMISSION driving wheels: rear; clutch: single dry plate, hydraulically-controlled; gearbox: ZF mechanical; gears: 4, fully synchronized; ratios: I 2.830, II 1.850, III 1.320, IV 1, rev 3.150; lever: central; final drive: hypoid bevel; axle ratio: 3.310; width of rims: 5.5''; tyres: 6.85 x 15.

PERFORMANCE max speeds: (I) 36 mph, 58 km/h; (II) 55 mph, 89 km/h; (III) 78 mph, 125 km/h; (IV) 99 mph, 160 km/h; power-weight ratio: 21.6 lb/hp, 9.8 kg/hp; carrying capacity: 882 lb, 400 kg; acceleration: 0-50 mph (0-80 km/h) 8.2 sec; speed in direct drive at 1,000 rpm: 22.3 mph, 35.9 km/h; fuel consumption: 26.6 m/imp gal, 22.2 m/US gal, 10.6 l x 100 km.

CHASSIS integral; front suspension: independent, wishbones, coil springs, anti-roll bar, telescopic dampers; rear suspension: rigid axle, trailing lower radius arms, oblique upper torque arms, coil springs, telescopic dampers.

STEERING recirculating ball; turns lock to lock: 5.50.

BRAKES drum; swept area: front 78.9 sq in, 509 sq cm, rear 62.6 sq in, 404 sq cm, total 141.5 sq in, 913 sq cm.

ELECTRICAL EQUIPMENT 12 V; 55 Ah battery; 40 A alternator; Prestolite distributor; 2 headlamps.

DIMENSIONS AND WEIGHT wheel base: 107.20 in, 2,723 mm; tracks: 56.69 in, 1,440 mm front, 56.38 in, 1,432 mm rear; length: 186.46 in, 4,736 mm; width: 70.87 in, 1,800 mm; height: 56.69 in, 1,440 mm; ground clearance: 5.98 in, 152

TORINO L

mm; dry weight: 3,014 lb, 1,367 kg; distribution of weight: 56.5% front, 43.5% rear; turning circle (between walls): 39 ft, 11.9 m; fuel tank: 14.1 imp gal, 16.9 US gal, 64 l.

BODY saloon/sedan; 4 doors; 5 seats, bench front seats.

PRACTICAL INSTRUCTIONS fuel: 83-85 oct petrol; engine sump oil: 6.9 imp pt, 8.2 US pt, 3.9 l, SAE 30, change every 3,100 miles, 5,000 km; gearbox oil: 2.1 imp pt, 2.5 US pt, 1.2 l, SAE 90 EP, change every 12,400 miles, 20,000 km; final drive oil: 2.1 imp pt, 2.5 US pt, 1.2 l, SAE 90 EP, change every 12,400 miles, 20,000 km; greasing: every 3,100 miles, 5,000 km, 16 points; tappet clearances: inlet 0.007 in, 0.18 mm, exhaust 0.008 in, 0.20 mm; valve timing: 20° 52° 50° 10°; tyre pressure: front 24 psi, 1.7 atm, rear 28 psi, 2 atm.

OPTIONAL ACCESSORIES power-assisted steering; defroster on rear window.

Torino S

See Torino L, except for:

PRICE EX WORKS: 27,700 new pesos.

ENGINE compression ratio: 8:1; max power (SAE): 143 hp at 4,200 rpm; 37.9 hp/l.

PERFORMANCE max speed: 106 mph, 170 km/h; power-weight ratio: 21.8 lb/hp, 9.9 kg/hp.

BRAKES front disc, rear drum, servo; swept area: front 27.9 sq in, 180 sq cm, rear 76.6 sq in, 494 sq cm, total 104.5 sq in, 674 sq cm.

ELECTRICAL EQUIPMENT 4 headlamps.

DIMENSIONS AND WEIGHT dry weight: 3,122 lb, 1,416 kg; distribution of weight: 56.4% front, 43.6% rear.

BODY separate front seats, reclining backrests.

Torino TS Berlina

See Torino S, except for:

PRICE EX WORKS: 29,500 new pesos.

ENGINE max power (SAE): 160 hp at 4,300 rpm; max torque (SAE): 225 lb ft, 31 kg m at 2,200 rpm; 42.4 hp/l; 1 Holley 2300 C downdraught twin barrel carburettor.

PERFORMANCE max speed: 109 mph, 175 km/h; power-weight ratio: 19.8 lb/hp, 9 kg/hp; fuel consumption: 25.4 m/imp gal, 21.2 m/US gal, 11.1 l x 100 km.

DIMENSIONS AND WEIGHT dry weight: 3,171 lb, 1,438 kg.

OPTIONAL ACCESSORIES air-conditioning.

Torino TS Coupé

See Torino TS Berlina, except for:

PRICE EX WORKS: 30,900 new pesos.

TRANSMISSION tyres: 7.35 x 15.

PERFORMANCE max speed: 112 mph, 180 km/h; power-weight ratio: 20.3 lb/hp, 9.2 kg/hp; acceleration: 0-50 mph (0-80 km/h) 8 sec; speed in direct drive at 1,000 rpm: 22.9 mph, 36.9 km/h.

DIMENSIONS AND WEIGHT height: 55.91 in, 1,420 mm; dry weight: 3,244 lb, 1,471 kg.

BODY coupé; 2 doors.

Torino GS Coupé

See Torino TS Coupé, except for:

PRICE EX WORKS: 33,500 new pesos.

ENGINE max power (SAE): 185 hp at 4,500 rpm; max torque (SAE): 239 lb ft, 33 kg m at 3,500 rpm; max engine rpm: 4,800; 49.1 hp/l; 3 Weber 45 DCOE 17 horizontal twin barrel carburettors.

TRANSMISSION axle ratio: 3.070; tyres: 7.75 x 15.

PERFORMANCE max speed: 124 mph, 199 km/h; power-weight ratio: 17.9 lb/hp, 8.1 kg/hp; acceleration: 0-50 mph (0-80 km/h) 7.4 sec; speed in direct drive at 1,000 rpm: 25.5 mph, 41 km/h.

DIMENSIONS AND WEIGHT dry weight: 3,301 lb, 1,497 kg; distribution of weight: 53.2% front, 46.8% rear.

IKA-RENAULT Torino TS and GS Coupé

IKA-RENAULT Rambler Cross Country

CHEVROLET Opala Coupé SS

Rambler Ambassador

ENGINE front, 4 stroke; 6 cylinders, vertical, in line; 230 cu in, 3,770 cc (3.34 x 4.37 in, 84.9 x 111.1 mm); compression ratio: 7.5:1; max power (SAE): 155 hp at 4,300 rpm; max torque (SAE): 225 lb ft, 31 kg m at 2,200 rpm; max engine rpm: 4,600; 42.4 hp/l; cast iron cylinder block and head; 4 crankshaft bearings; valves: overhead, Vee-slanted at 64°, rockers; camshafts: 1, overhead, cogged belt; lubrication: gear pump, full flow filter, 20.4 imp pt, 24.5 US pt, 5.5 l; 1 Holley 2.300 C or Argelite downdraught twin barrel carburettor; fuel feed: mechanical pump; water-cooled, 20.4 imp pt, 24.5 US pt, 11.6 l.

TRANSMISSION driving wheels: rear; clutch: single dry plate, hydraulically controlled; gearbox: ZF mechanical; gears: 4, fully synchronized; ratios: I 2.830, II 1.850, III 1.380, IV 1, rev 3.150; lever: steering column; final drive: hypoid bevel; axle ratio: 3.540; tyres: 8.15 x 15.

PERFORMANCE max speed: 101 mph, 162 km/h; power-weight ratio: 21.6 lb/hp, 9.8 kg/hp; carrying capacity: 882 lb, 400 kg; speed in direct drive at 1,000 rpm: 22.3 mph, 35.9 km/h; fuel consumption: 25.4 m/imp gal, 21.2 m/US gal, 11.1 l x 100 km.

CHASSIS integral; front suspension: independent, wishbones, coil springs, anti-roll bar, telescopic dampers; rear suspension: rigid axle; semi-elliptic leafsprings, telescopic dampers.

STEERING recirculating ball, servo.

BRAKES front disc, rear drum, rear compensator, servo.

ELECTRICAL EQUIPMENT 12 V; 55 Ah battery; 40 A alternator; Prestolite distributor; 4 iodine headlamps.

DIMENSIONS AND WEIGHT wheel base: 115.98 in, 2,946 mm; tracks: 58.58 in, 1,488 mm front, 57.91 in, 1,471 mm rear; length: 198.88 in, 5,077 mm; width. 74.49 in, 1,892 mm; height: 55.71 in, 1,415 mm; ground clearance: 7.16 in, 182 mm; dry weight: 3,376 lb, 1,531 kg; turning circle (between walls): 42 ft, 12.8 m; fuel tank: 15.8 imp gal, 19 US gal, 72 l.

BODY saloon/sedan; 4 doors; 5 seats, separate front seats, reclining backrests.

Rambler Classic

See Rambler Ambassador, except for:

TRANSMISSION axle ratio: 3.310; tyres: 7.75 x 15.

PERFORMANCE power-weight ratio: 20.7 lb/hp, 9.4 kg/hp.

DIMENSIONS AND WEIGHT wheel base: 112.01 in, 2,845 mm; length: 195.91 in, 4,976 mm; height: 55.91 in, 1,420 mm; ground clearance: 6.97 in, 177 mm; dry weight: 3,230 lb, 1,465 kg.

Rambler Cross Country

See Rambler Ambassador, except for:

TRANSMISSION tyres: 7.75 x 15.

PERFORMANCE power-weight ratio: 21.2 lb/hp, 9.6 kg/hp; carrying capacity: 1,103 lb, 500 kg.

DIMENSIONS AND WEIGHT wheel base: 112.01 in, 2,845 mm; length: 192.89 in, 4,902 mm; height: 57.28 in, 1,455 mm; ground clearance: 6.97 in, 177 mm; dry weight: 3,303 lb, 1,498 kg.

BODY estate car/station wagon; 4 + 1 doors; 5-6 seats, separate front seats, reclining backrests.

CHEVROLET BRAZIL

Opala Especial

ENGINE front, 4 stroke; 4 cylinders, in line; 152.6 cu in, 2,500 cc (3.87 x 3.25 in, 98.4 x 82.5 mm); compression ratio: 7:1; max power (SAE): 80 hp at 4,000 rpm; max torque (SAE): 130 lb ft, 18 kg m at 2,600 rpm; max engine rpm: 4,400; 31.9 hp/l; cast iron cylinder block and head; 5 crankshaft bearings; valves: overhead, push-rods and rockers, hydraulic tappets; camshafts: 1, side; lubrication: gear pump, full flow filter, 6.2 imp pt, 7.4 US pt, 3.5 l; 1 Brosol-Solex H 40/44 DIS downdraught carburettor; fuel feed: mechanical pump; water-cooled, 15.1 imp pt, 18.2 US pt, 8.6 l.

TRANSMISSION driving wheels: rear; clutch: single dry plate; gearbox: mechanical; gears: 3, fully synchronized; ratios: I 2.790, II 1.680, III 1, rev 3.570; lever: steering column; final drive: hypoid bevel; axle ratio: 3.540; width of rims: 4.5''; tyres: 5.90 x 14.

PERFORMANCE max speed: 90 mph, 145 km/h; power-weight ratio: 28.2 lb/hp, 12.8 kg/hp; carrying capacity: 882 lb

IKA-RENAULT Torino GS Coupé

IKA-RENAULT Rambler Ambassador

CHEVROLET Opala Coupé SS

400 kg; fuel consumption: 26.9 m/imp gal, 22.4 m/US gal, 10.5 l x 100 km.

CHASSIS integral; front suspension: independent, wishbones, coil springs, anti-roll bar, telescopic dampers; rear suspension: rigid axle, twin trailing radius arms, transverse linkage bar, telescopic dampers.

STEERING screw and sector; turns lock to lock: 3.20.

BRAKES drum, single circuit; swept area: total 123.6 sq in, 797 sq cm.

ELECTRICAL EQUIPMENT 12 V; 44 Ah battery; 32 A alternator; Arno distributor; 2 headlamps.

DIMENSIONS AND WEIGHT wheel base: 105 in, 2,667 mm; tracks: 55.51 in, 1,410 mm front, 55.51 in, 1,410 mm rear; length: 180.24 in, 4,578 mm; width: 69.21 in, 1,758 mm; height: 54.49 in, 1,384 mm; ground clearance: 5.79 in, 147 mm; dry weight: 2,254 lb, 1,022 kg; turning circle (between walls): 38.7 ft, 11.8 m; fuel tank: 11.9 imp gal, 14.3 US gal, 54 l.

BODY saloon/sedan; 4 doors; 6 seats, bench front seats.

PRACTICAL INSTRUCTIONS fuel: 73 oct petrol; engine sump oil: 6.2 imp pt, 7.4 US pt, 3.5 l, SAE 20W-30, change every 3,100 miles, 5,000 km; gearbox oil: 1.4 imp pt, 1.7 US pt, 0.8 l; final drive oil: 1.2 imp pt, 1.5 US pt, 0.7 l; greasing: none; valve timing: 16° 48° 46°30' 17°30'; tyre pressure: front 20 psi, 1.4 atm, rear 21 psi, 1.5 atm.

VARIATIONS

ENGINE 6 cylinders, in line, 250.2 cu in, 4,100 cc (3.87 x 3.52 in, 98.4 x 89.7 mm), max power (SAE) 138 hp at 4,000 rpm, max torque (SAE) 210 lb ft, 29 kg m at 2,400 rpm, 34.1 hp/l, 7 crankshaft bearings, lubricating system capacity 7 imp pt, 8.5 US pt, 4 l, 1 Brosol-Solex H 40/41 downdraught carburettor, cooling system capacity 18 imp pt, 21.6 US pt, 10.2 l.
TRANSMISSION 3.080 axle ratio; tyres 7.35 S x 14.
CHASSIS anti-roll bar on rear suspension (standard).
BRAKES front disc, rear drum, servo (standard).

OPTIONAL ACCESSORIES 4-speed fully synchronized mechanical gearbox (I 2.790, II 2.020, III 1.390, IV 1, rev 3.570), central gear lever; anti-roll bar on rear suspension; front disc brakes with servo; separate front seats with reclining backrests; air-conditioning (only with 6-cylinder engine); vynil roof; metallic spray.

Opala Coupé Especial

See Opala Especial, except for:

DIMENSIONS AND WEIGHT height: 53.50 in, 1,359 mm.

BODY coupé; 2 doors.

OPTIONAL ACCESSORIES limited slip differential.

Opala De Luxo

See Opala Especial, except for:

TRANSMISSION tyres: 6.45 x 14.

BODY L equipment.

Opala Coupé De Luxo

See Opala Especial, except for:

TRANSMISSION tyres: 6.45 x 14.

DIMENSIONS AND WEIGHT height: 53.50 in, 1,359 mm.

BODY coupé; 2 doors; 5 seats, separate front seats (standard); L equipment.

OPTIONAL ACCESSORIES limited slip differential.

Opala Gran Luxo

See Opala Especial, except for:

ENGINE 6 cylinders, in line; 250.2 cu in, 4,100 cc (3.87 x 3.52 in, 98.4 x 89.7 mm); max power (SAE): 138 hp at 4,000 rpm; max torque (SAE): 210 lb ft, 29 kg m at 2,400 rpm; 33.6 hp/l; 7 crankshaft bearings; lubricating system capacity: 7 imp pt, 8.5 US pt, 4 l; 1 Brosol-Solex H 40/41 downdraught carburettor; cooling system capacity: 18 imp pt, 21.6 US pt, 10.2 l.

TRANSMISSION axle ratio: 3.080; width of rims: 5"; tyres: 7.35S x 14.

PERFORMANCE max speed: about 106 mph, 170 km/h; power-weight ratio: 17.4 lb/hp, 8 kg/hp; speed in direct drive at 1,000 rpm: 23.9 mph, 38.4 km/h; fuel consumption: 18.8 m/imp gal, 15.7 m/US gal, 15 l x 100 km.

CHASSIS rear suspension: anti-roll bar (standard).

OPALA GRAN LUXO

BRAKES front disc, rear drum, servo (standard).

DIMENSIONS AND WEIGHT dry weight: 2,426 lb, 1,100 kg.

BODY L equipment.

VARIATIONS

None.

OPTIONAL ACCESSORIES tinted glass; rev counter.

Opala Coupé Gran Luxo

See Opala Gran Luxo, except for:

DIMENSIONS AND WEIGHT height: 53.50 in, 1,359 mm.

BODY coupé; 2 doors; 5 seats; separate front seats (standard).

Opala Coupé SS

See Opala Gran Luxo, except for:

TRANSMISSION gears: 4, fully synchronized; ratios: I 2.790, II 2.020, III 1.390, IV 1, rev 3.570; lever: central.

DIMENSIONS AND WEIGHT height: 53.50 in, 1,359 mm.

BODY coupé; 2 doors; 5 seats, separate front seats, reclining backrests (standard); rev counter.

OPTIONAL ACCESSORIES limited slip differential.

Veraneio

ENGINE front, 4 stroke; 6 cylinders, vertical, in line, 261 cu in, 4,277 cc (3.75 x 3.94 in, 95.2 x 100.1 mm); compression ratio: 7.8:1; max power (SAE): 151 hp at 3,800 rpm; max torque (SAE): 233 lb ft, 32.1 kg m at 2,400 rpm; max engine rpm: 4,200; 35.3 hp/l; cast iron cylinder block and head; 4 crankshafts bearings; valves: overhead, in line, push-rods and rockers; camshafts: 1, side; lubrication: gear pump, full flow filter, 8.3 imp pt, 9.9 US pt, 4.7 l; 1 DF Vasconcelos downdraught carburettor; fuel feed: mechanical pump; water-cooled, 29.9 imp pt, 35.9 US pt, 17 l.

TRANSMISSION driving wheels: rear; clutch: single dry plate (diaphragm); gearbox: mechanical; gears: 3, fully synchronized; ratios: I 2.918, II 1.753, III 1, rev 3.761; lever: steering column; final drive: hypoid bevel, limited slip differential; axle ratio: 3.900; tyres: 7.10 x 15.

PERFORMANCE max speed: 90 mph, 145 km/h; carrying capacity: 1,058 lb, 480 kg; speed in direct drive at 1,000 rpm: 20.9 mph, 33.6 km/h; fuel consumption: 17.7 m/imp gal, 14.7 m/US gal, 16 l x 100 km.

CHASSIS box-type ladder frame; front suspension: independent, wishbones, coil springs, telescopic dampers; rear suspension: rigid axle, longitudinal leading arms, coil springs, telescopic dampers.

STEERING worm and roller.

BRAKES drum; swept area: total 174.4 sq in, 1,125 sq cm.

ELECTRICAL EQUIPMENT 12 V; 65 Ah battery; 37 A alternator; Arno distributor; 2 headlamps.

DIMENSIONS AND WEIGHT wheel base: 114.96 in, 2,920 mm; tracks: 63.39 in, 1,610 mm front, 64.96 in, 1,550 mm rear; length: 203.15 in, 5,160 mm; width: 77.95 in, 1,980 mm; height: 68.11 in, 1,730 mm; ground clearance: 9.06 in, 230 mm; dry weight: 4,271 lb, 1,937 kg; turning circle (between walls): 42.6 ft, 13 m; fuel tank: 15 imp gal, 18 US gal, 68 l.

BODY estate car/station wagon; 4 + 1 doors; 6 seats, bench front seats.

OPTIONAL ACCESSORIES power-assisted steering.

DODGE — BRAZIL

Dart 4-door Sedan

ENGINE front, 4 stroke; 8 cylinders, Vee-slanted at 90°; 318 cu in, 5,212 cc (3.91 x 3.31 in, 99.3 x 84.1 mm); compression ratio: 7.5:1; max power (SAE): 198 hp at 4,400 rpm; max torque (SAE): 301 lb ft, 41.5 kg m at 2,400 rpm; max engine rpm: 4,800; 38.6 hp/l; cast iron cylinder block and head; 5 crankshafts bearings; valves: overhead, push-rods and rockers, hydraulic tappets; camshafts: 1, at centre of Vee; lubrication: rotary pump, full flow filter, 8.4 imp pt, 10.1 US pt, 4.8 l; 1 Bendix WW 3-272 A or DF

CHEVROLET Veraneio

DODGE Dart 2-door Coupé De Luxo

DODGE Charger R/T 2-door Coupé

Vasconcelos downdraught twin barrel carburettor: fuel feed: mechanical pump; water-cooled, 31.7 imp pt, 38.1 US pt, 18 l.

TRANSMISSION driving wheels: rear; clutch: single dry plate; gearbox: mechanical; gears: 3, fully synchronized; ratios: I 2.670, II 1.600, III 1, rev 3.440; lever: steering column; final drive: hypoid bevel; axle ratio: 3.150; width of rims: 4.5"; tyres: 6.95 x 14.

PERFORMANCE max speed: 109 mph, 175 km/h; power-weight ratio: 16.3 lb/hp, 7.4 kg/hp; carrying capacity: 1,059 lb, 480 kg; speed in direct drive at 1,000 rpm: 23 mph, 37 km/h; fuel consumption: 17.1 m/imp gal, 14.3 m/US gal, 16.5 l x 100 km.

CHASSIS integral; front suspension: independent, wishbones, lower trailing links, longitudinal torsion bars, telescopic dampers; rear suspension: rigid axle, semi-elliptic leafsprings, telescopic dampers.

STEERING recirculating ball.

BRAKES drum; swept area: total 194.7 sq in, 1,256 sq cm.

ELECTRICAL EQUIPMENT 12 V; 45 Ah battery; 40 A alternator; Chrysler distributor; 2 headlamps.

DIMENSIONS AND WEIGHT wheel base: 111.02 in, 2,820 mm; tracks: 58.66 in, 1,490 mm front, 56.30 in, 1,430 mm rear; length: 195.28 in, 4,960 mm; width: 71.26 in, 1,810 mm; height: 54.72 in, 1,390 mm; ground clearance: 6.30 in, 160 mm; dry weight: 3,268 lb, 1,482 kg; turning circle (between walls): 41.3 ft, 12.6 m; fuel tank: 13.6 imp gal, 16.4 US gal, 62 l.

BODY saloon/sedan; 4 doors; 6 seats, bench front seats.

PRACTICAL INSTRUCTIONS fuel: 80 oct petrol; engine sump oil: 8.4 imp pt, 10.1 US pt, 4.8 l, change every 3,100 miles, 5,000 km; gearbox oil: 4.4 imp pt, 5.3 US pt, 2.5 l, change every 3,100 miles, 5,000 km; final drive oil: 2.6 imp pt, 3.2 US pt, 1.5 l, change every 3,100 miles, 5,000 km; greasing: every 3,100 miles, 5,000 km, 12 points.

OPTIONAL ACCESSORIES Torqueflite automatic transmission, hydraulic torque converter and planetary gears with 3 ratios (I 2.450, II 1.450, III 1, rev 2.200), max ratio of converter at stall 2.1, possible manual selection, 3.150 axle ratio; 7.35 x 14 tyres with 5" wide rims; anti-roll bar on front suspension; front disc brakes with servo; air-conditioning.

Dart 2-door Coupé De Luxo

See Dart 4-door Sedan, except for:

PERFORMANCE power-weight ratio: 16.1 lb/hp, 7.3 kg/hp.

DIMENSIONS AND WEIGHT dry weight: 3,226 lb, 1,463 kg.

BODY coupé; 2 doors.

Charger 2-door Coupé

ENGINE front, 4 stroke; 8 cylinders, Vee-slanted at 90°; 318 cu in, 5,212 cc (3.91 x 3.31 in, 99.3 x 84.1 mm); compression ratio: 7.5:1; max power (SAE): 205 hp at 4,400 rpm; max torque (SAE): 301 lb ft, 41.5 kg m at 2,400 rpm; max engine rpm: 4,800; 39.9 hp/l; cast iron cylinder block and head; 5 crankshaft bearings; valves: overhead, in line, push-rods and rockers, hydraulic tappets; camshafts: 1, at centre of Vee; lubrication: rotary pump, full flow filter, 8.3 imp pt, 9.9 US pt, 4.7 l; 1 Bendix WW 3-272 A or DF Vasconcelos downdraught twin barrel carburettor; fuel feed: mechanical pump; water-cooled, 31.7 imp pt, 38.1 US pt, 18 l.

TRANSMISSION driving wheels: rear; clutch: single dry plate; gearbox: mechanical; gears: 3, fully synchronized; ratios: I 2.670, II 1.600, III 1, rev 3.440; lever: steering column; final drive: hypoid bevel; axle ratio: 3.150; width of rims: 5"; tyres: 7.35 x 14.

PERFORMANCE max speed: about 118 mph, 190 km/h; power-weight ratio: 16.1 lb/hp, 7.3 kg/hp; carrying capacity: 1,058 lb, 480 kg; speed in direct drive at 1,000 rpm: 23 mph, 37 km/h; fuel consumption: 14.9 m/imp gal 12.4 m/US gal, 19 l x 100 km.

CHASSIS integral; front suspension: independent, wishbones, lower trailing links, longitudinal torsion bars, telescopic dampers; rear suspension: rigid axle, semi-elliptic leafsprings, telescopic dampers.

STEERING recirculating ball.

BRAKES front disc (diameter 10.90 in, 277 mm), rear drum, servo; swept area: total 354.3 sq in, 2,285 sq cm.

ELECTRICAL EQUIPMENT 12 V; 45 Ah battery; 40 A alternator; Chrysler distributor; 4 headlamps.

DIMENSIONS AND WEIGHT wheel base: 111.02 in, 2,820 mm; tracks: 59.06 in, 1,500 mm front, 56.30 in, 1,430 mm rear; length: 195.28 in, 4,960 mm; width: 71.26 in, 1,810 mm; height: 54.72 in, 1,390 mm; ground clearance: 6.30 in, 160 mm; dry weight: 3,296 lb, 1,495 kg; turning circle (between walls): 41.3 ft, 12.6 m; fuel tank: 13.6 imp gal, 16.4 US gal, 62 l.

CHEVROLET Veraneio

DODGE Dart 4-door Sedan

DODGE Charger 2-door Coupé

BODY coupé; 2 doors; 6 seats, bench front seats.

PRACTICAL INSTRUCTIONS fuel: 80 oct petrol; engine sump oil: 8.3 imp pt, 9.9 US pt, 4.7 l, change every 3,100 miles, 5,000 km; gearbox oil: 4.4 imp pt, 5.3 US pt, 2.5 l, change every 3,100 miles, 5,000 km; final drive oil: 2.6 imp pt, 3.2 US pt, 1.5 l, change every 3,100 miles, 5,000 km; greasing: every 3,100 miles, 5,000 km, 12 points.

OPTIONAL ACCESSORIES 4-speed fully synchronized mechanical gearbox (I 2.670, II 1.860, III 1.300, IV 1, rev 3.140), central lever, 3.150 axle ratio; Torqueflite automatic transmission, hydraulic torque converter and planetary gears with 3 ratios (I 2.450, II 1.450, III 1, rev 2.200), max ratio of converter at stall 2.1, possible manual selection, steering column lever, 3.150 axle ratio; anti-roll bar on front suspension; power-assisted steering; disc brakes with servo; separate front seats with reclining backrests; air-conditioning.

Charger R/T 2-door Coupé

See Charger 2-door Coupé, except for:

ENGINE compression ratio: 8.4:1; max power (SAE): 215 hp at 4,400 rpm; max torque (SAE): 311 lb ft, 42.9 kg m at 2,400 rpm; 41.9 hp/l; dual exhaust system.

PERFORMANCE power-weight ratio: 15.4 lb/hp, 7 kg/hp; carrying capacity: 882 lb, 400 kg.

STEERING servo (standard).

DIMENSIONS AND WEIGHT dry weight: 3,358 lb, 1,523 kg.

BODY 5 seats, separate front seats with reclining backrests (standard).

FNM BRAZIL

2150

PRICE EX WORKS: 20,000 cruzeiros.

ENGINE front, 4 stroke; 4 cylinders, in line; 130.1 cu in, 2,132 cc (3.33 x 3.74 in, 84.5 x 95 mm); compression ratio: 8.2:1; max power (SAE): 125 hp at 5,700 rpm; max torque (SAE): 133 lb ft, 18.3 kg m at 3,900 rpm; max engine rpm: 5,700; 58.6 hp/l; cast iron cylinder block, light alloy head; 5 crankshaft bearings; valves: overhead, Vee-slanted at 90°; camshafts: 2, overhead; lubrication: mechanical pump, filter on by pass, 12.3 imp pt, 14.8 US pt, 7 l; 1 Solex APAI-G downdraught twin barrel carburettor; fuel feed: mechanical pump; water-cooled, 19.4 imp pt, 23.3 US pt, 11 l.

TRANSMISSION driving wheels: rear; clutch: single dry plate; gearbox: mechanical; gears: 5, fully synchronized; ratios: I 3.258, II 1.985, III 1.357, IV 1, V 0.854, rev 3.252; lever: steering column; final drive: hypoid bevel; axle ratio: 5.123; tyres: 175 x 400.

PERFORMANCE max speeds: (I) 25 mph, 40 km/h; (II) 42 mph, 67 km/h; (III) 60 mph, 97 km/h; (IV) 82 mph, 132 km/h; (V) 103 mph, 165 km/h; power-weight ratio: 24 lb/hp, 10.9 kg/hp; carrying capacity: 1,014 lb, 460 kg; acceleration: 0-50 mph (0-80 km/h) 9 sec; speed in top at 1,000 rpm: 17.4 mph, 28 km/h; fuel consumption: 23.5 m/imp gal, 19.6 m/US gal, 12 l x 100 km.

CHASSIS integral; front suspension: independent, wishbones, coil springs, anti-roll bar, telescopic dampers; rear suspension: rigid axle, trailing lower radius arms, upper A-bracket, coil springs, telescopic dampers.

STEERING worm and roller; turns lock to lock: 4.50.

BRAKES drum, servo; swept area: front 120.2 sq in, 775.50 sq cm, rear 120.2 sq in, 775.50 sq cm, total 240.4 sq in, 1,551 sq cm.

ELECTRICAL EQUIPMENT 12 V; 50 Ah battery; 360 W alternator; Bosch distributor; 2 headlamps.

DIMENSIONS AND WEIGHT wheel base: 107.09 in, 2,720 tracks: 55.12 in, 1,400 mm front, 53.94 in, 1,370 mm rear; length: 185.63 in, 4,715 mm; width: 66.93 in, 1,700 mm; height: 57.17 in, 1,452 mm; ground clearance: 5.91 in, 150 mm; dry weight: 2,999 lb, 1,360 kg; distribution of weight: 53% front, 47% rear; turning circle (between walls): 34.1 ft, 10.4 m; fuel tank: 13.2 imp gal, 15.8 US gal, 60 l.

BODY saloon/sedan; 4 doors; 6 seats, bench front seats.

PRACTICAL INSTRUCTIONS fuel: 98-100 oct petrol; engine sump oil: 11.4 imp pt, 13.7 US pt, 6.5 l, SAE 40, change every 2,500 miles, 4,000 km; gearbox oil: 3 imp pt, 3.6 US pt, 1.7 l, SAE 90, change every 5,000 miles, 8,000 km; final drive oil: 5.1 imp pt, 6.1 US pt, 2.9 l, SAE 90, change every 5,000 miles, 8,000 km; greasing: every 2,500 miles, 4,000 km, 25 points; tappet clearances: inlet 0.018 in, 0.45 mm, exhaust 0.020 in, 0.50 mm; valve timing: 5°25' 52°33' 52°33' 5°25'; tyre pressure: front 24 psi, 1.7 atm, rear 26 psi, 1.8 atm.

OPTIONAL ACCESSORIES front disc brakes.

2150 Luxo

See 2150, except for:

PRICE EX WORKS: 22,000 cruzeiros.

TRANSMISSION lever: central.

BODY 5 seats, separate front seats.

FORD BRAZIL

4-door Corcel Sedan

ENGINE front, 4 stroke; 4 cylinders, vertical, in line; 78.7 cu in, 1,289 cc (2.87 x 3.03 in, 73 x 77 mm); compression ratio: 8:1; max power (SAE): 68 hp at 5,200 rpm; max torque (SAE): 75 lb ft, 10.4 kg m at 3,200 rpm; max engine rpm: 5,200; 52.7 hp/l; cast iron cylinder block, wet liners, light alloy head; 5 crankshaft bearings; valves: overhead, push-rods and rockers; camshafts: 1, side; lubrication: gear pump, full flow filter, 5.3 imp pt, 6.3 US pt, 3 l; 1 Bosch Solex 32 PDIS downdraught single barrel carburettor; fuel feed: mechanical pump; sealed circuit cooling, water, 7.9 imp pt, 9.5 US pt, 4.5 l.

TRANSMISSION driving wheels: front; clutch: single dry plate; gearbox: mechanical; gears: 4, fully synchronized; ratios: I 3.615, II 2,263, III 1.480, IV 1.032, rev 3.077; lever: central; final drive: hypoid bevel; axle ratio: 4.125; width of rims: 4.5''; tyres: 165 SR x 13.

PERFORMANCE max speeds: (I) 23 mph, 37 km/h; (II) 37 mph, 59 km/h; (III) 57 mph, 91 km/h; (IV) 84 mph, 135 km/h; power-weight ratio: 30.6 lb/hp, 13.9 kg/hp; carrying capacity: 827 lb, 375 kg; acceleration: standing ¼ mile 22 sec; speed in top at 1,000 rpm: 16.8 mph, 27 km/h; fuel consumption: 34 m/imp gal, 28.3 m/US gal, 8.3 l x 100 km.

CHASSIS integral; front suspension: independent, wishbones, upper trailing arms, coil springs, anti-roll bar, telescopic dampers; rear suspension: rigid axle, trailing lower radius arms, upper Vee bracket, coil springs, telescopic dampers.

STEERING rack-and-pinion; turns lock to lock: 3.50.

BRAKES front disc (diameter 8.98 in, 228 mm), rear drum; swept area: front 64.7 sq in, 417 sq cm, rear 36.7 sq in, 237 sq cm, total 101.4 sq in, 654 sq cm.

ELECTRICAL EQUIPMENT 12 V; 40 Ah battery; 40 A alternator; Bosch distributor; 2 headlamps.

DIMENSIONS AND WEIGHT wheel base: 96.06 in, 2,440 mm; tracks: 51.57 in, 1,310 mm front, 50.39 in, 1,280 mm rear; length: 173.23 in, 4,400 mm; width: 63.39 in, 1,610 mm; height: 57.09 in, 1,450 mm; ground clearance: 5.12 in, 130 mm; dry weight: 2,082 lb, 944 kg; distribution of weight: 56.3% front, 43.7% rear; turning circle (between walls): 34.4 ft, 10.5 m; fuel tank: 11.2 imp gal, 13.5 US gal, 51 l.

BODY saloon/sedan; 4 doors; 5 seats, separate front seats.

PRACTICAL INSTRUCTIONS fuel: 70 oct petrol; engine sump oil: 4.4 imp pt, 5.3 US pt, 2.5 l, SAE 30, change every 3,100 miles, 5,000 km; gearbox and final drive oil: 2.8 imp pt, 3.4 US pt, 1.6 l, SAE 90, change every 6,200 miles, 10,000 km; greasing: none; tappet clearances: inlet 0.006 in, 0.15 mm, exhaust 0.008 in, 0.20 mm; valve timing: 20° 60° 60° 20°; tyre pressure: front 17 psi, 1.2 atm, rear 17 psi, 1.2 atm.

OPTIONAL ACCESSORIES reclining backrests.

4-door Corcel Sedan Luxo

See 4-door Corcel Sedan, except for:

BODY L equipment.

Corcel Coupé

See 4-door Corcel Sedan, except for:

DIMENSIONS AND WEIGHT height: 53.94 in, 1,370 mm; dry weight: 2,080 lb, 943 kg.

BODY coupé; 2 doors.

Corcel Coupé Luxo

See 4-door Corcel Sedan, except for:

DIMENSIONS AND WEIGHT height: 53.94 in, 1,370 mm; dry weight: 2,080 lb, 943 kg.

BODY coupé; 2 doors; L equipment.

Corcel Belina Station Wagon

See 4-door Corcel Sedan, except for:

PERFORMANCE max speed: 82 mph, 132 km/h; power-weight ratio: 32.4 lb/hp, 14.7 kg/hp; carrying capacity: 926 lb, 420 kg; fuel consumption: 31.4 m/imp gal, 26.1 m/US gal, 9 l x 100 km.

DIMENSIONS AND WEIGHT length: 173.62 in, 4,410 mm; dry weight: 2,201 lb, 998 kg; fuel tank: 13.9 imp gal, 16.6 US gal, 63 l.

BODY estate car/station wagon; 2 + 1 doors.

FNM 2150 Luxo

FORD Corcel Coupé Luxo

FORD Galaxie 500

Corcel Belina Luxo Station Wagon

See Corcel Belina Station Wagon, except for:

BODY L equipment.

Corcel Belina Luxo Especial Station Wagon

See Corcel Belina Station Wagon, except for:

PERFORMANCE power-weight ratio: 32.6 lb/hp, 14.8 kg/hp.

DIMENSIONS AND WEIGHT dry weight: 2,214 lb, 1,004 kg.

BODY L equipment.

Corcel GT Coupé

See 4-door Corcel Sedan, except for:

ENGINE 83.7 cu in, 1,372 mm (2.96 x 3.03 in, 75.3 x 77 mm); max power (SAE): 85 hp at 5,400 rpm; max torque (SAE): 84 lb ft, 11.6 kg m at 3,600 rpm; max engine rpm: 6,000; 62 hp/l; 1 DFV downdraught twin barrel carburettor.

PERFORMANCE max speeds: (I) 30 mph, 48 km/h; (II) 43 mph, 69 km/h; (III) 70 mph, 113 km/h; (IV) 88 mph, 141 km/h; power-weight ratio: 24.9 lb/hp, 11.3 kg/hp; acceleration: standing ¼ mile 21.5 sec; fuel consumption: 29.7 m/imp gal, 24.8 m/US gal, 9.5 l x 100 km.

DIMENSIONS AND WEIGHT dry weight: 2,121 lb, 962 kg.

BODY coupé; 2 doors.

Aero-Willys

ENGINE front, 4 stroke; 6 cylinders, vertical, in line; 161 cu in, 2,638 cc (3.13 x 3.50 in, 79.4 x 88.9 mm); compression ratio: 7.6:1; max power (SAE): 130 hp at 4,800 rpm; max torque (SAE): 143 lb ft, 19.7 kg m at 2,000 rpm; max engine rpm: 4,800; 49.3 hp/l; cast iron cylinder block and head; 4 crankshaft bearings; valves: overhead, push-rods and rockers, side exhaust, roller rockers; camshafts: 1, side; lubrication: gear pump, filter on by-pass, 12.3 imp pt, 14.8 US pt, 7 l; 2 DF Vasconcelos-Zenith downdraught single barrel carburettors; fuel feed: mechanical pump; water-cooled, 18.3 imp pt, 22 US pt, 10.4 l.

TRANSMISSION driving wheels: rear; clutch: single dry plate; gearbox: mechanical; gears: 4, fully synchronized; ratios: I 2.991, II 1.992, III 1.390, IV 1, rev 3.544; lever: steering column; final drive: hypoid bevel; axle ratio: 4.090; width of rims: 5''; tyres: 6.45 x 13.

PERFORMANCE max speeds: (I) 28 mph, 45 km/h; (II) 42 mph, 67 km/h; (III) 60 mph, 96 km/h; (IV) 86 mph, 138 km/h; power-weight ratio: 25.1 lb/hp, 11.4 kg/hp; carrying capacity: 1,058 lb, 480 kg; acceleration: standing ¼ mile 22.5 sec; speed in direct drive at 1,000 rpm: 16.5 mph, 26.5 km/h; fuel consumption: 20.9 m/imp gal, 17.4 m/US gal, 13.5 l x 100 km.

CHASSIS integral; front suspension: independent, wishbones, coil springs, telescopic dampers; rear suspension: rigid axle, semi-elliptic leafsprings, telescopic dampers.

STEERING worm and roller; turns lock to lock: 4.30.

BRAKES drum; swept area: total 159.7 sq in, 1,030 sq cm.

ELECTRICAL EQUIPMENT 12 V; 54 Ah battery; 380 W alternator; Bosch or Autolite distributor; 2 headlamps.

DIMENSIONS AND WEIGHT wheel base: 107.87 in, 2,740 mm; tracks: 58.19 in, 1,478 mm front, 57.87 in, 1,470 mm rear; length: 189.41 in, 4,811 mm; width: 72.40 in, 1,839 mm; height: 59.96 in, 1,523 mm; ground clearance: 7.32 in, 186 mm; dry weight: 3,263 lb, 1,480 kg; turning circle (between walls): 41 ft, 12.5 m; fuel tank capacity: 14.5 imp gal, 17.4 US gal, 66 l.

BODY saloon/sedan; 4 doors; 6 seats, bench front seats.

PRACTICAL INSTRUCTIONS fuel: 70 oct petrol; engine sump oil: 10.6 imp pt, 12.7 US pt, 6 l, SAE 30, change every 1,900 miles, 3,000 km; gearbox oil: 3 imp pt, 3.6 US pt, 1.7 l, SAE 90, change every 12,100 miles, 19,500 km; final drive oil: 2.6 imp pt, 3.2 US pt, 1.5 l, SAE 90, change every 12,100

150 hp power team

See 100 hp power team, except for:

ENGINE 8 cylinders; 304 cu in, 4,982 cc (3.75 x 3.44 in, 95.2 x 87.3 mm); compression ratio: 8.4:1; max power (DIN): 150 hp at 4,200 rpm; max torque (DIN): 245 lb ft, 33.8 kg m at 2,500 rpm; max engine rpm: 4,600; 30.5 hp/l; 5 crankshaft bearings; camshafts: 1, at centre of Vee; 1 Motorcraft 3DM2 downdraught twin barrel carburettor; cleaner air system; cooling system capacity: 23.2 imp pt, 27.9 US pt, 13.2 l.

TRANSMISSION axle ratio: 3.540; width of rims: Javelin AMX 6"; tyres: Javelin AMX E70 x 14.

PERFORMANCE max speed: about 104 mph, 167 km/h; power-weight ratio: Javelin 19.8 lb/hp, 9 kg/hp - Javelin AMX 20.1 lb/hp, 9.1 kg/hp; speed in direct drive at 1,000 rpm: 24.3 mph, 39.1 km/h; fuel consumption: 18.1 m/imp gal, 15.1 m/US gal, 15.6 l x 100 km.

CHASSIS front suspension: anti-roll bar (standard).

BRAKES swept area: total 267.04 sq in, 1,722 sq cm.

DIMENSIONS AND WEIGHT front track: Javelin AMX 59.08 in, 1,501 mm; height: Javelin AMX 51.49 in, 1,308 mm; ground clearance: Javelin AMX 4.97 in, 126 mm; dry weight Javelin plus 236 lb, 107 kg - Javelin AMX 3,200 lb, 1,451 kg.

OPTIONAL ACCESSORIES Torque-Command automatic transmission with max ratio of converter at stall 2, central or steering column lever, 2.870 3.150 axle ratios; 3.910 axle ratio; E60 x 15 tyres with 7" wide rims; FR70 x 14 tyres with 6" wide rims.

175 hp power team

See 100 hp power team, except for:

ENGINE 8 cylinders; 360 cu in, 5,899 cc (4.08 x 3.44 in, 103.6 x 87.3 mm); compression ratio: 8.5:1; max power (DIN): 175 hp at 4,000 rpm; max torque (DIN): 285 lb ft, 39.3 kg m at 2,400 rpm; max engine rpm: 4,400; 29.7 hp/l; 5 crankshaft bearings; camshafts: 1, at centre of Vee; 1 Motorcraft 3RA2 downdraught twin barrel carburettor; cleaner air system; cooling system capacity: 21.6 imp pt, 26 US pt, 12.3 l.

TRANSMISSION gearbox: Torque-Command automatic transmission (standard), hydraulic torque converter and planetary gears with 3 ratios, max ratio of converter at stall 2, possibile manual selection; ratios: I 2.450, II 1.450, III 1, rev 2.200; lever: steering column or central; axle ratio: 2.870; width of rims: Javelin AMX 6"; tyres: Javelin AMX E70 x 14.

PERFORMANCE max speed: about 110 mph, 177 km/h; power-weight ratio: Javelin 18.3 lb/hp, 8.3 kg/hp - Javelin AMX 18.5 lb/hp, 8.4 kg/hp; speed in direct drive at 1,000 rpm: 25.2 mph, 40.5 km/h; fuel consumption: 17.5 m/imp gal, 14.6 m/US gal, 16.1 l x 100 km.

CHASSIS front suspension: anti-roll bar (standard).

BRAKES swept area: total 267 sq in, 1,722 sq cm.

ELECTRICAL EQUIPMENT 60 Ah battery; 55 A alternator.

DIMENSIONS AND WEIGHT (see 150 hp power team) dry weight: Javelin plus 299 lb, 136 kg - Javelin AMX plus 63 lb, 28 kg.

OPTIONAL ACCESSORIES 3.150 axle ratio; E60 x 15 tyres with 7" wide rims; FR70 x 14 tyres with 6" wide rims.

220 hp power team

See 100 hp power team, except for:

ENGINE 8 cylinders; 360 cu in, 5,899 cc (4.08 x 3.44 in, 103.6 x 87.3 mm); compression ratio: 8.5:1; max power (DIN): 220 hp at 4,400 rpm; max torque (DIN): 315 lb ft, 43.5 kg m at 3,100 rpm; max engine rpm: 4,800; 37.3 hp/l; 5 crankshaft bearings; camshafts: 1, at centre of Vee; 1 Motorcraft 3TM4 downdraught 4-barrel carburettor; cleaner air system; dual exhaust system; cooling system capacity: 21.6 imp pt, 26 US pt, 12.3 l.

TRANSMISSION gears: 4, fully synchronized; ratios: I 2.230, II 1.770, III 1.350, IV 1, rev 2.160; lever: central; axle ratio: 3.540; width of rims: Javelin AMX 6"; tyres: Javelin AMX E70 x 14.

PERFORMANCE max speed: about 120 mph, 193 km/h; power-weight ratio: Javelin 14.6 lb/hp, 6.6 kg/hp - Javelin AMX 14.8 lb/hp, 6.7 kg/hp; speed in direct drive at 1,000 rpm: 24.7 mph, 39.7 km/h; fuel consumption: 15.3 m/imp gal, 12.7 m/US gal, 18.5 l x 100 km.

CHASSIS front suspension: anti-roll bar (standard).

AMERICAN MOTORS Hornet Series

AMERICAN MOTORS Javelin AMX 2-door Hardtop

AMERICAN MOTORS Matador 2-door Hardtop

BRAKES swept area: total 267 sq in, 1,722 sq cm.

ELECTRICAL EQUIPMENT 60 Ah battery; 55 A alternator.

DIMENSIONS AND WEIGHT (see 150 hp power team) dry weight Javelin plus 309 lb, 140 kg - Javelin AMX plus 73 lb, 33 kg.

OPTIONAL ACCESSORIES 3.910 axle ratio; Torque-Command automatic transmission with max ratio of converter at stall 2, 2.870 3.150 axle ratios, steering column or central lever; E60 x 15 tyres with 7" wide rims; FR70 x 14 tyres with 6" wide rims.

255 hp power team

See 100 hp power team, except for:

ENGINE 8 cylinders; 401 cu in, 6,571 cc (4.16 x 3.68 in, 105.6 x 93.4 mm); compression ratio: 8.5:1; max power (DIN): 255 hp at 4,600 rpm; max torque (DIN): 345 lb ft, 47.6 kg m at 3,300 rpm; max engine rpm: 5,000; 38.8 hp/l; 5 crankshaft bearings; camshafts: 1, at centre of Vee; 1 Motorcraft 3TM4 downdraught 4-barrel carburettor; cleaner air system; dual exhaust system; cooling system capacity: 21.6 imp pt, 26 US pt, 12.3 l.

TRANSMISSION gears: 4, fully synchronized; ratios: I 2.320, II 1.770, III 1.350, IV 1, rev 2.160; lever: central; axle ratio: 3.540; width of rims: Javelin AMX 6"; tyres: Javelin AMX E70 x 14.

PERFORMANCE max speed: about 124 mph, 199 km/h; power-weight ratio: Javelin 17.8 lb/hp, 5.9 kg/hp - Javelin AMX 17.6 lb/hp, 5.8 kg/hp; speed in direct drive at 1,000 rpm: 24.7 mph, 39.7 km/h; fuel consumption: 14.1 m/imp gal, 11.7 m/US gal, 20.1 l x 100 km.

CHASSIS front suspension: anti-roll bar (standard).

BRAKES swept area: total 267 sq in, 1,722 sq cm.

ELECTRICAL EQUIPMENT 60 Ah battery; 55 A alternator.

DIMENSIONS AND WEIGHT (see 150 hp power team) dry weight Javelin plus 449 lb, 204 kg - Javelin AMX plus 113 lb, 51 kg.

OPTIONAL ACCESSORIES 3.910 axle ratio; Torque-Command automatic transmission with max ratio of converter at stall 2, 2.870 3.150 3.540 axle ratios, central lever; E60 x 15 tyres with 7" wide rims; FR70 x 14 tyres with 6" wide rims.

Matador Series

PRICES IN USA:

1 Matador	2-door Hardtop	**$ 2,848**
2 Matador	4-door Sedan	**$ 2,814**
3 Matador	Station Wagon	**$ 3,140**

For V8 engines add $ 99.

Power team:	Standard for:	Optional for:
100 hp	1,2	—
110 hp	3	1,2
150 hp	—	all
175 hp	—	all
195 hp	—	all
220 hp	—	all
255 hp	—	all

100 hp power team

ENGINE front, 4 stroke; 6 cylinders, in line; 232 cu in, 3,802 cc (3.75 x 3.50 in, 95.2 x 88.8 mm); compression ratio: 8:1; max power (DIN): 100 hp at 3,600 rpm; max torque (DIN): 185 lb ft, 25.5 kg m at 1,800 rpm; max engine rpm: 4,000; 26.3 hp/l; cast iron cylinder block and head; 7 crankshafts bearings; valves: overhead, in line, push-rods and rockers, hydraulic tappets; camshafts: 1, side; lubrication: gear pump, full flow filter, 8.3 imp pt, 9.9 US pt, 4.7 l; 1 Carter YF 6299 downdraught single barrel carburettor; cleaner air system; fuel feed: mechanical pump; water-cooled, 17.4 imp pt, 20.9 US pt, 9.9 l.

TRANSMISSION driving wheels: rear; clutch: single dry plate; gearbox: mechanical; gears: 3, fully synchronized; ratios: I 2.636, II 1.605, III 1, rev 2.636; lever: steering column; final drive: hypoid bevel; axle ratios: 3.150; width of rims: 5"; tyres: E78 x 14.

PERFORMANCE max speed: about 90 mph, 145 km/h; power-weight ratio: Matador 4-dr. sedan 33.4 lb/hp, 15.2 kg/hp; speed in direct drive at 1,000 rpm: 24.9 mph, 40 km/h; fuel consumption: 19.3 m/imp gal, 16.1 m/US gal, 14.6 l x 100 km.

CHASSIS integral; front suspension: independent, wishbones, coil springs, anti-roll bar, telescopic dampers; rear suspension: rigid axle, lower trailing radius arms, upper oblique torque arms, coil springs, telescopic dampers.

100 HP POWER TEAM

STEERING recirculating ball; turns lock to lock: 6.

BRAKES drum; swept area: total 267 sq in, 1,722 sq cm.

ELECTRICAL EQUIPMENT 12 V; 50 Ah battery; 37 A alternator; Delco-Remy or Prestolite distributor; 4 headlamps.

DIMENSIONS AND WEIGHT wheel base: 118 in, 2,997 mm; tracks: 59.94 in, 1,522 mm front, 60 in, 1,524 mm rear; length: 208.48 in, 5,296 mm; width: hardtop 77.22 in, 1,961 mm - sedan 77.28 in, 1,963 mm; height: hardtop 54.33 in, 1,380 mm - sedan 55.55 in, 1,411 mm; ground clearance: hardtop 5.98 in, 152 mm - sedan 6.48 in, 165 mm; dry weight: hardtop 3,368 lb, 1,527 kg - sedan 3,340 lb, 1,515 kg; turning circle (between walls): 41 ft, 12.5 m; fuel tank: 14.3 imp gal, 19.5 US gal, 74 l.

OPTIONAL ACCESSORIES Torque-Command automatic transmission with 3 ratios (I 2.450, II 1.450, III 1, rev 2.200), max ratio of converter at stall 2.10, possible manual selection, steering column lever, 3.150 3.540 axle ratios; limited slip differential; 3.540 axle ratio; F78 x 14 tyres; FR70 x 14 tyres with 6'' wide rims; E60 x 15 tyres with 7'' wide rims; anti-roll bar on rear suspension; adjustable telescopic dampers on rear suspension; power-assisted steering, variable ratio; tilt of steering wheel; servo brake; front disc brakes; front disc brakes with servo, total swept area 375.3 sq in, 2,420 sq cm; tinted glass; electrically-heated rear window; air-conditioning.

110 hp power team

See 100 hp power team, except for:

ENGINE 258 cu in, 4,228 cc (3.75 x 3.90 in, 95.2 x 99 mm); max power (DIN): 110 hp at 3,500 rpm; max torque (DIN): 195 lb ft, 26.9 kg m at 2,000 rpm; max engine rpm: 3,900; 26 hp/l; 1 Carter YF 6299 (6300 for station wagon) downdraught single barrel carburettor; cleaner air system.

TRANSMISSION gearbox: Torque-Command automatic transmission (standard only for hardtop and sedan models); axle ratio: station wagon 3.540; width of rims: station wagon 6''; tyres: station wagon H78 x 14.

PERFORMANCE max speed: about 99 mph, 160 km/h; power-weight ratio: 30.6 lb/hp, 13.9 kg/hp; speed in direct drive at 1,000 rpm: 25.9 mph, 41.7 km/h; fuel consumption: 18.1 m/imp gal, 15.1 m/US gal, 15.6 l x km 100.

BRAKES swept area: station wagon total 314.2 sq in, 2,026 sq cm.

DIMENSIONS AND WEIGHT length: station wagon 207.66 in, 5,274 mm; width: station wagon 77.18 in, 1,960 mm; height: station wagon 57.42 in, 1,458 mm; ground clearance: station wagon 7.45 in, 189 mm; dry weight: hardtop and sedan plus 39 lb, 18 kg - station wagon 3,681 lb, 1,669 kg; fuel tank: station wagon 16.7 imp gal, 20 US gal, 76 l.

OPTIONAL ACCESSORIES only for station wagon 3.150 axle ratio and HR78 x 14 tyres.

150 hp power team

See 100 hp power team, except for:

ENGINE 8 cylinders; 304 cu in, 4,982 cc (3.75 x 3.44 in, 95.2 x 87.3 mm); compression ratio: 8.4:1; max power (DIN): 150 hp at 4,200 rpm; max torque (DIN): 245 lb ft, 33.8 kg m at 2,500 rpm; max engine rpm: 4.600; 30.5 hp/l; 5 crankshaft bearings; camshafts: 1, at centre of Vee; 1 Motorcraft 3DA2 downdraught twin barrel carburettor; cleaner air system; cooling system capacity: 23.2 imp pt, 27.9 US pt, 13.2 l.

TRANSMISSION gearbox: Torque-Command automatic transmission (standard), hydraulic torque converter and planetary gears with 3 ratios, max ratio of converter at stall 2, possible manual selection; ratios: I 2.450, II 1.450, III 1, rev 2.200; axle ratio: 3.150; width of rims: station wagon 6''; tyres: station wagon H78 x 14.

PERFORMANCE max speed: about 101 mph, 162 km/h; power-weight ratio: Matador 4-dr. sedan 22.5 lb/hp, 10.2 kg/hp; speed in direct drive at 1,000 rpm: 26 mph, 41.8 km/h; fuel consumption: 17.9 m/imp gal, 14.9 m/US gal, 15.8 l x 100 km.

BRAKES swept area: station wagon total 314.2 sq in, 2,026 sq cm.

DIMENSIONS AND WEIGHT (see 110 hp power team) dry weight: plus 213 lb, 96 kg - station wagon plus 188 lb, 85 kg.

OPTIONAL ACCESSORIES only for station wagon HR78 x 14 tyres.

AMERICAN MOTORS Matador 4-door Sedan

AMERICAN MOTORS Matador Station Wagon

AMERICAN MOTORS Ambassador Brougham 2-door Hardtop

175 hp power team

See 100 hp power team, except for:

ENGINE 8 cylinders; 360 cu in, 5,899 cc (4.08 x 3.44 in, 103.6 x 87.3 mm); compression ratio: 8.5:1; max power (DIN): 175 hp at 4,000 rpm; max torque (DIN): 285 lb ft, 39.3 kg m at 2,400 rpm; max engine rpm: 4,400; 29.7 hp/l; 5 crankshaft bearings; camshafts: 1, at centre of Vee; 1 Motorcraft 2RA2 downdraught twin barrel carburettor; cleaner air system; cooling system capacity: 21.6 imp pt, 26 US pt, 12.3 l.

TRANSMISSION gearbox: Torque-Command automatic transmission (standard), hydraulic torque converter and planetary gears with 3 ratios, max ratio of converter at stall 2, possible manual selection; ratios: I 2.450, II 1.450, III 1, rev 2.200; axle ratio: 3.150; width of rims: station wagon 6''; tyres: station wagon H78 x 14.

PERFORMANCE max speed: about 105 mph, 169 km/h; power-weight ratio: Matador 4-dr. sedan 20.7 lb/hp, 9.4 kg/hp; speed in direct drive at 1,000 rpm: 26 mph, 41.8 km/h; fuel consumption: 17.3 m/imp gal, 14.4 m/US gal, 16.3 l x 100 km.

BRAKES swept area: station wagon total 314.2 sq in, 2,026 sq cm.

ELECTRICAL EQUIPMENT 60 Ah battery; 55 A alternator.

DIMENSIONS AND WEIGHT (see 110 hp power team) dry weight: plus 281 lb, 127 kg - station wagon plus 227 lb, 103 kg.

OPTIONAL ACCESSORIES only for station wagon HR78 x 14 tyres.

195 hp power team

See 100 hp power team, except for:

ENGINE 8 cylinders; 360 cu in, 5,899 cc (4.08 x 3.44 in, 103.6 x 87.3 mm); compression ratio: 8.5:1; max power (DIN): 195 hp at 4,400 rpm; max torque (DIN): 295 lb ft, 40.7 kg m at 2,900 rpm; max engine rpm: 4,800; 33 hp/l; 5 crankshaft bearings; camshafts: 1, at centre of Vee; 1 Motorcraft 3TA4 downdraught 4-barrel carburettor; cleaner air system; cooling system capacity: 21.6 imp pt, 26 US pt, 12.3 l.

TRANSMISSION gearbox: Torque-Command automatic transmission (standard), hydraulic torque converter and planetary gears with 3 ratios, max ratio of converter at stall 2, possible manual selection; ratios: I 2.450, II 1.450, III 1, rev 2.200; axle ratio: 3.150; width of rims: station wagon 6''; tyres: station wagon H78 x 14.

PERFORMANCE max speed: about 108 mph, 174 km/h; power-weight ratio: Matador 4-dr. sedan 18.5 lb/hp, 8.4 kg/hp; speed in direct drive at 1,000 rpm: 26 mph, 41.8 km/h; fuel consumption: 16.6 m/imp gal, 13.8 m/US gal, 17 l x 100 km.

BRAKES swept area: station wagon total 314.2 sq in, 2,026 sq cm.

ELECTRICAL EQUIPMENT 60 Ah battery; 55 A alternator.

DIMENSIONS AND WEIGHT (see 110 hp power team) dry weight: plus 291 lb, 132 kg - station wagon plus 237 lb, 108 kg.

OPTIONAL ACCESSORIES only for station wagon HR78 x 14 tyres.

220 hp power team

See 100 hp power team, except for:

ENGINE 8 cylinders; 360 cu in, 5,899 cc (4.08 x 3.44 in, 103.6 x 87.3 mm); compression ratio: 8.5:1; max power (DIN): 220 hp at 4,400 rpm; max torque (DIN): 315 lb ft, 43.5 kg m at 3,100 rpm; max engine rpm: 4,800; 37.3 hp/l; 5 crankshaft bearings; camshafts: 1, at centre of Vee; 1 Motorcraft 3TA4 downdraught 4-barrel carburettor; cleaner air system; dual exhaust system; cooling system capacity: 21.6 imp pt, 26 US pt, 12.3 l.

TRANSMISSION gearbox: Torque-Command automatic transmission (standard), hydraulic torque converter and planetary gears with 3 ratios, max ratio of converter at stall 2, possible manual selection; ratios: I 2.450, II 1.450, III 1, rev 2.200; axle ratio: 3.150; width of rims: station wagon 6''; tyres: station wagon H78 x 14.

PERFORMANCE max speed: about 113 mph, 182 km/h; power-weight ratio: Matador 4-dr. sedan 15.4 lb/hp, 7 kg/hp; speed in direct drive at 1,000 rpm: 26 mph, 41.8 km/h; fuel consumption: 15 m/imp gal, 12.5 m/US gal, 18.8 l x 100 km.

BRAKES swept area: station wagon total 314.2 sq in, 2,026 sq cm.

BUICK Century Luxus Colonnade Hardtop Sedan

BUICK Century Regal Colonnade Hardtop Coupé

BUICK Le Sabre Hardtop Sedan

BRAKES front disc (diameter 11.86 in, 301 mm), internal radial fins, rear drum, servo; swept area: total 373.08 sq in, 2,406 sq cm.

ELECTRICAL EQUIPMENT 12 V; 2,900 W battery; 42 A alternator; Delco-Remy distributor; 4 headlamps.

DIMENSIONS AND WEIGHT wheel base: 124 in, 3,150 mm; tracks: 63.60 in, 1,615 mm front, 64 in, 1,626 mm rear; length: 224.20 in, 5,695 mm; width: 79.60 in, 2,022 mm; height: hardtop coupés 53.60 in, 1,361 mm - hardtop sedans 53.80 in, 1,367 mm - 4-dr. sedans 54.40 in, 1,382 mm; dry weight: Le Sabre hardtop coupé 4,865 lb, 2,207 kg - hardtop sedan 4,899 lb, 2,222 kg - 4-dr. sedan 4,869 lb, 2,209 kg - Le Sabre Custom hardtop coupé 4,934 lb, 2,238 kg - hardtop sedan 4,988 lb, 2,263 kg - 4-dr sedan 4,878 lb, 2,213 kg; turning circle (between walls): 44.1 ft, 13.5 m; fuel tank: 20.9 imp gal, 25 US gal, 95 l.

OPTIONAL ACCESSORIES limited slip differential; 2.730 3.420 axle ratios; J78 x 15, H78 x 15, 8.55 x 15 tyres; tilt of steering wheel; automatic levelling control; air-conditioning.

175 hp power team

See 150 hp power team, except for:

ENGINE max power (DIN): 175 hp at 3,800 rpm; max torque (DIN): 270 lb ft, 37.3 kg m at 2,400 rpm; max engine rpm: 4,200; 30.5 hp/l; 1 Rochester 4MV downdraught 4-barrel carburettor.

PERFORMANCE max speed: about 106 mph, 170 km/h; power-weight ratio: Centurion hardtop sedan 28.7 lb/hp, 13 kg/hp; fuel consumption: 15.1 m/imp gal, 12.6 m/US gal, 18.7 l x 100 km.

DIMENSIONS AND WEIGHT height: Centurion convertible 54.20 in, 1,377 mm; dry weight: Le Sabre and Le Sabre Custom Series plus 45 lb, 20 kg - Centurion hardtop coupé 4,954 lb, 2,247 kg - convertible 4,983 lb, 2,260 kg - hardtop sedan 5,028 lb, 2,281 kg.

225 hp power team

See 150 hp power team, except for:

ENGINE 455 cu in, 7,456 cc (4.31 x 3.90 in, 109.4 x 99 mm); max power (DIN): 225 hp at 4,000 rpm; max torque (DIN): 360 lb ft, 49.7 kg m at 2,600 rpm; max engine rpm: 4,400; 30.2 hp/l; 1 Rochester 4MV downdraught 4-barrel carburettor.

TRANSMISSION axle ratio: 2.730.

PERFORMANCE max speed: about 108 mph, 174 km/h; power-weight ratio: Le Sabre 4-dr. sedan 22.2 lb/hp, 10 kg/hp - Le Sabre Custom 4-dr. sedan 22.3 lb/hp, 10.1 kg/hp; speed in direct drive at 1,000 rpm: 25.8 mph, 41.5 km/h; fuel consumption: 14.4 m/imp gal, 12 m/US gal, 19.6 l x 100 km.

STEERING turns lock to lock: 2.94.

ELECTRICAL EQUIPMENT 3,000 W battery.

DIMENSIONS AND WEIGHT dry weight: plus 134 lb, 61 kg.

250 hp power team

See 150 hp power team, except for:

ENGINE 455 cu in, 7,456 cc (4.31 x 3.90 in, 109.4 x 99 mm); max power (DIN); 250 hp at 4,000 rpm; max torque (DIN): 375 lb ft, 51.7 kg m at 2,800 rpm; max engine rpm: 4,400; 33.5 hp/l; 1 Rochester 4MV downdraught 4-barrel carburettor; dual exhaust system.

TRANSMISSION axle ratio: 2.730.

PERFORMANCE max speed: about 110 mph, 177 km/h; power-weight ratio: Le Sabre 4-dr. coupé 19.6 lb/hp, 8.8 kg/hp - Le Sabre Custom 4-dr. coupé 19.7 lb/hp, 8.9 kg/hp - Centurion hardtop sedan 20.1 lb/hp, 9.1 kg/hp; speed in direct drive at 1,000 rpm: 25.8 mph, 41.5 km/h; fuel consumption: 14 m/imp gal, 11.6 m/US gal, 20.2 l x 100 km.

STEERING turns lock to lock: 2.94.

ELECTRICAL EQUIPMENT 3,000 W battery.

DIMENSIONS AND WEIGHT (see 175 hp power team); dry weight: plus 134 lb, 61 kg.

OPTIONAL ACCESSORIES 3.230 axle ratio.

260 hp power team

See 150 hp power team, except for:

ENGINE 455 cu in, 7,456 cc (4.31 x 3.90 in, 109.4 x 99 mm); max power (DIN): 260 hp at 4,400 rpm; max torque (DIN):

260 HP POWER TEAM

380 lb ft, 52.4 kg m at 2,800 rpm; max engine rpm: 4,800; 34.9 hp/l; 1 Rochester 4MV downdraught 4-barrel carburettor; dual exhaust system.

TRANSMISSION axle ratio: 2.730.

PERFORMANCE max speed: about 111 mph, 178 km/h; power-weight ratio: Centurion hardtop sedan 20 lb/hp, 9.1 kg/hp; speed in direct drive at 1,000 rpm: 25.8 mph, 41.5 km/h, fuel consumption: 13.7 m/imp gal, 11.4 m/US gal, 20.6 l x 100 km.

STEERING turns lock to lock: 2.94.

ELECTRICAL EQUIPMENT 3,000 W battery.

DIMENSIONS AND WEIGHT (see 175 hp power team); dry weight: plus 134 lb, 61 kg.

OPTIONAL ACCESSORIES 3.230 axle ratio.

Estate Wagon - Electra 225 - Electra 225 Custom - Riviera Series

PRICES IN USA:

1 Estate Wagon	6-passenger	**$ 4,589**
2 Estate Wagon	9-passenger	**$ 4,728**
3 Electra 225	Hardtop Coupé	**$ 4,781**
4 Electra 225	Hardtop Sedan	**$ 4,889**
5 Electra 225 Custom	Hardtop Coupé	**$ 4,951**
6 Electra 225 Custom	Hardtop Sedan	**$ 5,059**
7 Riviera	Hardtop Coupé	**$ 5,149**

Power team:	Standard for:	Optional for:
225 hp	all except 7	—
250 hp	7	3,4,5,6
260 hp	—	7

225 hp power team

ENGINE front, 4 stroke; 8 cylinders; 455 cu in, 7,456 cc (4.31 x 3.90 in, 109.4 x 99 mm); compression ratio: 8.5 : 1; max power (DIN): 225 hp at 4,000 rpm; max torque (DIN): 360 lb ft, 49.7 kg m at 2,600 rpm; max engine rpm: 4,400; 30.2 hp/l; cast iron cylinder block and head; 5 crankshaft bearings; valves: overhead, in line, push-rods and rockers, hydraulic tappets; camshafts: 1, at centre of Vee; lubrication: gear pump, full flow filter, 8.3 imp pt, 9.9 US pt, 4.7 l; 1 Rochester 4MV downdraught 4-barrel carburettor; cleaner air system; fuel feed: mechanical pump; water-cooled; 31.2 imp pt, 37.4 US pt, 17.7 l.

TRANSMISSION driving wheels: rear; gearbox: Turbo-Hydramatic 400 automatic transmission, hydraulic torque converter and planetary gears with 3 ratios, max ratio of converter at stall 2.20, possible manual selection; ratios: 2.480, II 1.480, III 1, rev 2.080; lever: steering column; final drive: hypoid bevel; axle ratio: 2.730 - Estate Wagon 2.930; width of rims: 6"; tyres: Estate Wagon L78 x 15 - Electra 225 and Electra 225 Custom J78 x 15.

PERFORMANCE max speed: about 105 mph, 169 km/h; power-weight ratio: Electra 225 hardtop sedan 22.6 lb/hp, 10.3 kg/hp - Electra 225 Custom hardtop sedan 23 lb/hp, 10.4 kg/hp; speed in direct drive at 1,000 rpm: 25.7 mph, 41.3 km/h; fuel consumption: 14.2 m/imp gal, 11.8 m/US gal, 19.9 l x 100 km.

CHASSIS perimeter box-type; front suspension: independent, wishbones, lower trailing links, coil springs, anti-roll bar, telescopic dampers; rear suspension: rigid axle, lower trailing arms, upper oblique torque arms, coil springs, telescopic dampers (only for Estate Wagon rigid axle, semi-elliptic leafsprings, telescopic dampers).

STEERING recirculating ball, servo; turns lock to lock: 2.94 - Estate Wagon 3.17.

BRAKES front disc (diameter 11.86 in, 301 mm), internal radial fins, rear drum, servo; swept area: total 373.08 sq in, 2,406 sq cm, - Estate Wagon total 385.64 sq in, 2,487 sq cm.

ELECTRICAL EQUIPMENT 12 V; 3,000 W battery; 42 A alternator; Delco-Remy distributor; 4 headlamps.

DIMENSIONS AND WEIGHT wheel base: 127 in, 3,226 mm; tracks: 63.60 in, 1,615 mm front, 64 in, 1,626 mm rear; length: 229.80 in, 5,837 mm - Estate Wagon 229.50 in, 5,829 mm; width: 79.30 in, 2,014 mm - Estate Wagon 79.60 in, 2,022 mm; height: 54.40 in, 1,382 mm - hardtop sedans 54.90 in, 1,394 mm - Estate Wagon 57.30 in, 1,455 mm; dry weight: Estate Wagon 6-pass. 5,549 lb, 2,517 kg - 9-pass. 5,629 lb, 2,553 kg - Electra 225 hardtop coupé 5,018 lb, 2,276 kg - hardtop sedan 5,074 lb, 2,302 kg - Electra 225 Custom hardtop coupé 5,099 lb, 2,313 kg - hardtop sedan 5,180 lb, 2,350 kg; turning circle (between walls): 46.8 ft, 14.3 m; fuel tank: 20.9 imp gal, 25 US gal, 95 l (Estate Wagon 18 imp gal, 22 US gal, 83 l).

BUICK Centurion Hardtop Sedan

BUICK Riviera Hardtop Coupé

CADILLAC Fleetwood Seventy-Five Sedan

OPTIONAL ACCESSORIES limited slip differential; 2.930 axle ratio (Estate Wagon 3.230); LR78 x 15 tyres only for Electra 225 and Electra 225 Custom Series; automatic levelling control; heavy-duty cooling system; limited equipment only for Electra 225 Custom hardtop sedan; tilt of steering wheel; air-conditioning.

250 hp power team

See 225 hp power team, except for:

ENGINE max power (DIN): 250 hp at 4,000 rpm; max torque (DIN): 375 lb ft, 51.8 kg m at 2,800 rpm; max engine rpm: 4,400; 33.5 hp/l; dual exhaust system.

TRANSMISSION axle ratio: Riviera 2.930 - Electra 225 and Electra 225 Custom 2.730; tyres: Riviera H78 x 15 - Electra 225 and Electra 225 Custom J78 x 15.

PERFORMANCE max speed: about 112 mph, 180 km/h; power-weight ratio: 20.2 lb/hp, 9.2 kg/hp; speed in direct drive at 1,000 rpm: 25.5 mph, 41 km/h; fuel consumption: 13.8 m/imp gal, 11.5 m/US gal, 20.4 l x 100 km.

STEERING tilt (standard).

DIMENSIONS AND WEIGHT wheel base: 122 in, 3,099 mm; length: 223.40 in, 5,674 mm; width: 79.90 in, 2,029 mm; height: 54 in, 1,372 mm; dry weight: Electra 225 and Electra 225 Custom plus 35 lb, 16 kg - Riviera hardtop coupé 5,047 lb, 2,289 kg; turning circle (between walls): 46.5 ft, 14.2 m.

OPTIONAL ACCESSORIES central lever and HR70 x 15 tyres (only for Riviera); 3.230 axle ratio; GS equipment with H70 x 15 tyres only for Riviera.

260 hp power team

See 225 hp power team, except for:

ENGINE max power (DIN): 260 hp at 4,400 rpm; max torque (DIN): 380 lb ft, 52.4 kg m at 2,800 rpm; max engine rpm: 4,800; 34.9 hp/l.

TRANSMISSION axle ratio: 2.930.

PERFORMANCE max speed: about 113 mph, 182 km/h; power-weight ratio: 19.4 lb/hp, 8.8 kg/hp; speed in direct drive at 1,000 rpm: 25.5 mph, 41 km/h; fuel consumption: 13.5 m/imp gal, 11.3 m/US gal, 20.9 l x 100 km.

STEERING tilt (standard).

DIMENSIONS AND WEIGHT (see 250 hp power team).

OPTIONAL ACCESSORIES central lever; 3.230 axle ratio; HR70 x 15 tyres; GS equipment with H70 x 15 tyres.

CADILLAC USA

Calais - De Ville - Fleetwood Series

PRICES IN USA:

Calais	Sedan	$ 5,938
Calais	Coupé	$ 5,771
De Ville	Sedan	$ 6,390
De Ville	Coupé	$ 6,168
Fleetwood Sixty	Special Brougham	$ 7,637
Fleetwood Seventy-Five	Sedan	$ 11,748
Fleetwood Seventy-Five	Limousine	$ 11,880

220 hp power team

(standard).

ENGINE front, 4 stroke; 8 cylinders; 472 cu in, 7,735 cc (4.30 x 4.06 in, 109.2 x 103.1 mm); compression ratio: 8.5:1; max power (DIN): 220 hp at 4,000 rpm; max torque (DIN): 365 lb ft, 50.5 kg m at 2,400 rpm; max engine rpm: 4,800; 28.4 hp/l; cast iron cylinder block and head; 5 crankshaft bearings; valves: overhead, in line, push-rods and rockers, hydraulic tappets; camshafts: l, at centre of Vee; lubrication: gear pump, full flow filter, 8.3 imp pt, 9.9 US pt, 4.7 l; 1 Rochester downdraught 4-barrel carburettor; cleaner air system; fuel feed: mechanical pump; water-cooled, 42.7 imp pt, 53.3 US pt, 20.2 l - Fleetwood Seventy-Five 44 imp pt, 52.9 US pt, 25 l.

TRANSMISSION driving wheels: rear; gearbox: Turbo-Hydramatic automatic transmission, hydraulic torque converter and planetary gears with 3 ratios, max ratio of converter at stall 2.03, possible manual selection; ratios: I 2.480, II 1.480, III 1, rev 2.090; lever: steering column; final drive: hypoid bevel; axle ratio: 2.930 - limousine 3.150; width of rims: 6"; tyres: L78 x 15.

BUICK Centurion Hardtop Sedan

BUICK Electra 225 Series

CADILLAC De Ville Series

PERFORMANCE max speed: about 119 mph, 191 km/h; power-weight ratio: Calais sedan 22.7 lb/hp, 10.3 kg/hp - De Ville sedan 22.9 lb/hp, 10.4 kg/hp - Fleetwood Seventy-Five sedan 12.7 lb/hp, 5.8 kg/hp; speed in direct drive at 1,000 rpm: 29 mph, 46.6 km/h; fuel consumption: 11.8 m/imp gal, 9.8 m/US gal, 24 l x 100 km.

CHASSIS perimeter box-type; front suspension: independent, wishbones, coil springs, anti-roll bar, telescopic dampers; rear suspension: rigid axle, lower-trailing arms, upper oblique torque arms, coil springs, telescopic dampers (for Fleetwood Sixty special Brougham and Fleetwood Seventy-Five Limousine automatic levelling control).

STEERING recirculating ball, variable ratio, servo; turns lock to lock: 3.25 - Fleetwood Seventy-Five 3.75.

BRAKES front disc (diameter 11.90 in, 302 mm), internal radial fins, rear drum (diameter 12 in, 305 mm), servo; swept area: front 240 sq in, 1,548 sq cm, rear 188.5 sq in, 1,216 sq cm, total 428.5 sq in, 2,764 sq cm.

ELECTRICAL EQUIPMENT 12 V; 3,600 W battery; 42 A alternator (limousine 80 A); Delco-Remy distributor; 4 headlamps.

DIMENSIONS AND WEIGHT wheel base: 130 in, 3,302 mm - Fleetwood Sixty 133 in, 3,378 mm - Fleetwood Seventy-Five 151.50 in, 3,848 mm; tracks: 63.30 in, 1,608 mm front, 63.30 in, 1,608 mm rear; length: 228.50 in, 5,004 mm - Fleetwood Sixty 231.50 in, 5,880 mm - Fleetwood Seventy-Five 250 in, 6,350 mm; width: 79.80 in, 2,027 mm; height: Calais and De Ville coupés 54.10 in, 1,374 mm - Calais and De Ville sedans 54.60 in, 1,387 mm - Fleetwood Sixty 55.50 in, 1,410 mm - Fleetwood Seventy-Five sedan 57.80 in, 1,468 mm - limousine 57.70 in, 1,466 mm; ground clearance: 5.90 in, 150 mm - Fleetwood Sixty 6.30 in, 160 mm - Fleetwood Seventy-Five 7 in, 178 mm; dry weight: Calais sedan 4,996 lb, 2,316 kg - coupé 4,943 lb, 2,292 kg - De Ville sedan 5,028 lb, 2,331 kg - coupé 4,968 lb, 2,303 kg - Fleetwood Sixty special brougham 5,145 lb, 2,385 kg - Fleetwood Seventy-Five sedan 5,783 lb, 2,681 kg - limousine 5,905 lb, 2,738 kg; turning circle (between walls): 48.2 ft, 14.7 m - Fleetwood Sixty 49.1 ft, 15 m - Fleetwood Seventy-Five 54.7 ft, 16.7 m; fuel tank: 22 imp gal, 27 US gal, 102 l.

BODY 4 doors (coupé 2); 6 seats (Fleetwood Seventy-Five 9), bench front seats, separate reclining backrests; built-in headrests; electrically-controlled windows (Fleetwood Seventy-Five with air-conditioning).

OPTIONAL ACCESSORIES limited slip differential; automatic levelling control only for Calais De Ville and Fleetwood Seventy-Five sedan; computerized rear wheel skid-control braking system; tilt and telescopic steering wheel; electrically-heated rear window except for Fleetwood Seventy-Five; electrically-controlled sunshine roof only for Fleetwood Sixty and De Ville Series; air-conditioning.

Fleetwood Eldorado Series

PRICES IN USA:

Fleetwood Eldorado	Coupé	$ 7,230
Fleetwood Eldorado	Convertible	$ 7,546

235 hp power team

(standard).

ENGINE front, 4 stroke; 8 cylinders; 500 cu in, 8,193 cc (4.30 x 4.30 in, 109.2 x 109.2 mm); compression ratio: 8.5:1; max power (DIN): 235 hp at 3,800 rpm; max torque (DIN): 385 lb ft, 53.1 kg m at 2,400 rpm; max engine rpm: 4,600; 28.7 hp/l; cast iron cylinder block and head; 5 crankshaft bearings; valves: overhead, in line, push-rods and rockers, hydraulic tappets; camshafts: 1, at centre of Vee; lubrication: gear pump, full flow filter, 10 imp pt, 12 US pt, 5.7 l; 1 Rochester downdraught 4-barrel carburettor; cleaner air system; fuel feed: mechanical pump; water-cooled, 35.5 imp pt, 42.7 US pt, 20.2 l.

TRANSMISSION driving wheels: front; gearbox: Turbo-Hydramatic automatic transmission, hydraulic torque converter and planetary gears (chain torque by engine-mounted converter) with 3 ratios, max ratio of converter at stall 2.03, possible manual selection; ratios: I 2.480, II 1.480, III 1, rev 2.090; lever: steering column; axle ratio: 3.070; width of rims: 6"; tyres: L78 x 15.

PERFORMANCE max speed: about 121 mph, 194 km/h; power-weight ratio: coupé 20.3 lb/hp, 9.2 kg/hp - convertible 20.7 lb/hp, 9.4 kg/hp; speed in direct drive at 1,000 rpm: 28.8 mph, 46.3 km/h; fuel consumption: 12.3 m/imp gal, 10.3 m/US gal, 22.9 l x 100 km.

CHASSIS perimeter box-type; front suspension: independent, wishbones, longitudinal torsion bars, anti-roll bar, telescopic dampers, rear suspension: rigid axle, lower trailing arms, upper oblique torque arms, automatic levelling control, coil springs, telescopic dampers.

235 HP POWER TEAM

STEERING recirculating ball, variable ratio, servo; turns lock to lock: 2.75.

BRAKES front disc (diameter 11 in, 279 mm), internal radial fins, rear drum, servo; swept area: front 224 sq in, 1,445 sq cm, rear 138 sq in, 890 sq cm, total 362 sq in, 2,335 sq cm.

ELECTRICAL EQUIPMENT 12 V; 3,600 W battery; 42 A alternator; Delco-Remy distributor; 4 headlamps.

DIMENSIONS AND WEIGHT wheel base: 126.30 in, 3,208 mm; tracks: 63.70 in, 1,618 mm front, 63.60 in, 1,615 mm rear; length: 222 in, 5,639 mm; width: 79.80 in, 2,027 mm; height: 53.90 in, 1,369 mm - convertible 54.30 in, 1,379 mm; ground clearance: 5.80 in, 147 mm; dry weight: coupé 4,777 lb, 2,167 kg - convertible 4,863 lb, 2,206 kg; turning circle (between walls): 46.8 ft, 14.3 m; fuel tank: 22 imp gal, 27 US gal, 102 l.

BODY 2 doors; 6 seats.

OPTIONAL ACCESSORIES computerized rear wheel skid-control braking system; tilt and telescopic steering wheel; electrically-heated rear window; electrically-controlled sunshine roof only for coupé; air-conditioning.

CHECKER USA

Marathon Series

PRICES IN USA:

1 Marathon	4-door Sedan	**$ 3,954**
2 Marathon	Station Wagon	**$ 4,211**
3 Marathon De Luxe	Limousine	**$ 4,612**

For V8 engine add $ 109.

Power team:	Standard for:	Optional for:
100 hp	all	—
145 hp	—	all

100 hp power team

ENGINE front, 4 stroke; 6 cylinders, in line; 250 cu in, 4,097 cc (3.88 x 3.53 in, 98.5 x 89.6 mm); compression ratio: 8.25:1; max power (DIN): 100 hp at 3,600 rpm; max torque (DIN): 175 lb ft, 24.1 kg m at 1,600 rpm; max engine rpm: 4,000; 24.4 hp/l; cast iron cylinder block and head; 7 crankshaft bearings; valves: overhead, in line, push-rods and rockers, hydraulic tappets; camshafts: 1, side; lubrication: gear pump, full flow filter, 8.3 imp pt, 9.9 US pt, 4.7 l; 1 Rochester 7043014 downdraught single barrel carburettor; cleaner air system; fuel feed: mechanical pump; water-cooled, 20.1 imp pt, 24.1 US pt, 11.4 l.

TRANSMISSION driving wheels: rear; gearbox: Warner Gear 11 D.R. automatic transmission, hydraulic torque converter and planetary gears with 3 ratios, max ratio of converter at stall 2.1, possible manual selection; ratios: I 2.400, II 1.470, III 1, rev 2; lever: steering column; final drive: hypoid bevel; axle ratio: 3.310; width of rims: 6"; tyres: G78 x 15.

PERFORMANCE max speed: about: 88 mph, 141 km/h; power-weight ratio: 4-dr. sedan 37.7 lb/hp, 17 kg/hp; speed in direct drive at 1,000 rpm: 23.8 mph, 38.3 km/h; fuel consumption: 21.4 m/imp gal, 17.8 m/US gal, 13.2 l x 100 km.

CHASSIS box-type ladder frame, X reinforcements; front suspension: independent, wishbones, coil springs, anti-roll bar, telescopic dampers; rear suspension: rigid axle, semi-elliptic leafsprings, telescopic dampers.

STEERING recirculating ball; turns lock to lock: 6.14.

BRAKES front disc (diameter 11.68 in, 296 mm), internal radial fins, rear drum, servo; swept area: total 380 sq in, 2,451 sq cm.

ELECTRICAL EQUIPMENT 12 V; 80 Ah battery; 55 A alternator: Delco-Remy distributor; 4 headlamps.

DIMENSIONS AND WEIGHT wheel base: 120 in, 3,048 mm - limousine 129 in, 3,277 mm; tracks: 64.45 in, 1,637 mm front, 63.31 in, 1,608 mm rear; length: 206.94 in, 5,256 mm - limousine 215.94 in, 5,485 mm; width: 76 in, 1,930 mm; height: 62.75 in, 1,594 mm; ground clearance: 7.50 in, 190 mm; dry weight: Marathon 4-dr. sedan 3,772 lb, 1,710 kg - station wagon 3,975 lb, 1,802 kg - Marathon De Luxe limousine 3,972 lb, 1,801 kg; turning circle (between walls): 42.3 ft, 12.9 m - limousine 43.3 ft, 13.2 m; fuel tank: 17.8 imp gal, 21.5 US gal, 81 l.

OPTIONAL ACCESSORIES oil cooler; limited slip differential; power-assisted steering; auxiliary rear seats; tinted glass; air-conditioning; vinyl roof except for station wagon.

CADILLAC Fleetwood Eldorado Coupé

CHECKER V8 engine

CHEVROLET Vega Hatchback Coupé

145 hp power team

See 100 hp power team, except for:

ENGINE 8 cylinders; 350 cu in, 5,736 cc (4 x 3.48 in, 101.6 x 88.3 mm); compression ratio: 8.5:1; max power (DIN): 145 hp at 4,000 rpm; max torque (DIN): 255 lb ft, 35.2 kg m at 2,400 rpm; max engine rpm: 4,400; 25.3 hp/l; 5 crankshaft bearings; camshafts: 1, at centre of Vee; 1 Rochester 7043114 downdraught twin barrel carburettor; cleaner air system; cooling system capacity: 28.3 imp pt, 34 US pt, 16.1 l.

TRANSMISSION gearbox: Warner Gear 12 D.R. automatic transmission.

PERFORMANCE max speed: about 94 mph, 152 km/h; power-weight ratio: 4-dr. sedan 26.8 lb/hp, 12.1 kg/hp; fuel consumption: 19.8 m/imp gal, 16.4 m/US gal, 14.3 l x 100 km.

STEERING servo (standard); turns lock to lock: 3.46.

DIMENSIONS AND WEIGHT dry weight: plus 110 lb, 50 kg - station wagon plus 100 lb, 45 kg.

CHEVROLET USA

Vega Series

PRICES IN USA:

1 Vega	Notchback Sedan	**$ 2,059**
2 Vega	Hatchback Coupé	**$ 2,159**
3 Vega	Kammback Station Wagon	**$ 2,284**

Power team:	Standard for:	Optional for:
72 hp	all	—
85 hp	—	all

72 hp power team

ENGINE front, 4 stroke; 4 cylinders, in line, 140 cu in, 2,294 cc (3.50 x 3.62 in, 88.8 x 91.9 mm); compression ratio: 8:1; max power (DIN): 72 hp at 4,400 rpm; max torque (DIN): 110 hp ft, 15.2 kg m at 2,000-2,400 rpm; max engine rpm: 4,800; 31.4 hp/l; light alloy cylinder block, cast iron head; 5 crankshaft bearings; valves: overhead, in line, thimble tappets; camshafts: 1, overhead, cogged belt; lubrication: eccentric pump, full flow filter, 6.7 imp pt, 8 US pt, 3.8 l; 1 Rochester 7043023 (7043323 for California only) downdraught single baller carburettor; fuel feed: electric pump; water-cooled, 10.7 imp pt, 12.9 US pt, 6.1 l.

TRANSMISSION driving wheels: rear; clutch: single dry plate (diaphragm); gearbox: mechanical; gears: 3, fully synchronized; ratios: I 3.110, II 1.840, III 1, rev 3.220; lever: central; final drive: hypoid bevel; axle ratio: 2.530; width of rims: 5"; tyres: A78 x 13.

PERFORMANCE max speed: about 90 mph, 141 km/h; power-weight ratio: sedan 31.5 lb/hp, 14.3 kg/hp - coupé 32.8 lb/hp, 14.9 kg/hp - station wagon 33 lb/hp, 15 kg/hp speed in direct drive at 1,000 rpm: 21 mph, 33.8 km/h; fuel consumption: 21.4 m/imp gal, 17.8 m/US gal, 13.2 l x 100 km.

CHASSIS integral; front suspension: independent, wishbones, coil springs, anti-roll bar, telescopic dampers; rear suspension: rigid axle, lower trailing radius arms, upper oblique torque arms, coil springs, telescopic damper.

STEERING recirculating ball; turns lock to lock: 4.40.

BRAKES front disc (diameter 9.88 in, 251 mm), rear drum; swept area: total 225.8 sq in, 1,457 sq cm.

ELECTRICAL EQUIPMENT 12 V; 2,300 W battery; 32 A alternator; Delco-Remy distributor; 2 headlamps.

DIMENSIONS AND WEIGHT wheel base: 97 in, 2,464 mm; tracks: 55.20 in, 1,402 mm front, 54.10 in, 1,374 mm rear; length: 172.20 in, 4,374 mm; width: 65.40 in, 1,661 mm; height: sedan 51.90 in, 1,318 mm - coupé 49.80 in, 1,265 mm - station wagon 51.70 in, 1,313 mm; ground clearance: 5 in, 127 mm - sedan 5.20 in, 132 mm; dry weight: sedan 2,268 lb, 1,028 kg - coupé 2,362 lb, 1,071 kg - station wagon 2,376 lb, 1,087 kg; turning circle (between walls): 34.7 ft, 10.7 m; fuel tank: 9.2 imp gal, 11 US gal, 42 l.

BODY 2 doors; 4 seats, separate front seats.

OPTIONAL ACCESSORIES 2.920 axle ratio; 4-speed fully synchronized mechanical gearbox (I 3.110, II 2.200, III 1.470, IV 1, rev. 3.110), 2.920 3.360 axle ratios; Powerglide automatic transmission with 2 ratios (I 1.820, II 1, rev 1.820), max ratio of converter at stall 2.10, possible manual selection, 2.920 3.360 axle ratios; Turbo-Hydramatic automatic transmission with 3 ratios (1 2.520, II 1.520, III 1, rev 1.930), max ratio of converter at stall 2.10,

CADILLAC Fleetwood Eldorado Convertible

CHECKER Marathon 4-door Sedan

CHEVROLET Vega Notchback Sedan

possible manual selection, 2.920, 3.360 axle ratios; limited slip differential; BR70 x 13 tyres with 6" wide rims; A70 x 13 tyres only for GT equipment; power-assisted steering; anti-roll bar on rear suspension; air-conditioning; electrically-heated rear window; GT equipment.

85 hp power team

See 72 hp power team, except for:

ENGINE max power (DIN): 85 hp at 4,800 rpm; max torque (DIN): 115 lb ft, 15.9 kg m at 2,400-2,800 rpm; max engine rpm: 5,000; 37.1 hp/l; 1 Holley 331157 (331159 for California only) downdraught twin barrel carburettor.

TRANSMISSION axle ratio: 2.920.

PERFORMANCE max speed: about 95 mph, 153 km/h; power-weight ratio: sedan 26.7 lb/hp, 12.1 kg/hp coupé and station wagon 27.8 lb/hp, 12.6 kg/hp; speed in direct drive at 1,000 rpm: 19 mph, 30.5 km/h; fuel consumption: 20.2 m/imp gal, 16.8 m/US gal, 14 l x 100 km.

OPTIONAL ACCESSORIES Powerglide automatic transmission with 3.360 axle ratio.

Nova - Nova Custom Series

PRICES IN USA:

1 Nova	Hatchback Coupé	**$ 2,503**
2 Nova	Coupé	**$ 2,354**
3 Nova	4-door Sedan	**$ 2,382**
4 Nova Custom	Hatchback Coupé	**$ 2,660**
5 Nova Custom	Coupé	**$ 2,511**
6 Nova Custom	4-door Sedan	**$ 2,539**

For V8 engines add $ 86.

Power team:	Standard for:	Optional for:
100 hp	all	—
115 hp	—	all
145 hp	—	all
175 hp	—	all

100 hp power team

ENGINE front, 4 stroke; 6 cylinders, in line; 250 cu in, 4,097 cc (3.87 x 3.53 in, 98.2 x 89.6 mm); compression ratio: 8.5:1; max power (DIN): 100 hp at 3,600 rpm; max torque (DIN): 175 lb ft, 24.1 kg m at 1,600 rpm; max engine rpm: 4,200; 24.4 hp/l; cast iron cylinder block and head; 7 crankshaft bearings; valves: overhead, in line, push-rods and rockers, hydraulic tappets; camshafts: 1, side; lubrication: gear pump, full flow filter, 8.3 imp pt, 9.9 US pt, 4.7 l; 1 Rochester 7043017 (7043317 for California only) downdraught single barrel carburettor; cleaner air system; fuel feed: mechanical pump; water-cooled, 20.1 imp pt, 24.1 US pt, 11.4 l.

TRANSMISSION driving wheels: rear; clutch: single dry plate (diaphragm); gearbox: mechanical; gears: 3, fully synchronized; ratios: I 2.850, II 1.680, III 1, rev 2.950; lever: steering column; final drive: hypoid bevel; axle ratio: 3.080; width of rims: 5"; tyres: E78 x 14.

PERFORMANCE max speed: about 96 mph, 154 km/h; power-weight ratio: Nova 4-dr. sedan 31.7 lb/hp, 14.4 kg/hp - Nova Custom 4-dr. sedan 32.1 lb/hp, 14.5 kg/hp; speed in direct drive at 1,000 rpm: 25 mph, 40.2 km/h; fuel consumption: 19.8 m/imp gal, 16.4 m/US gal, 14.3 l x 100 km.

CHASSIS integral, separate partial front box-type frame; front suspension: independent, wishbones, coil springs, anti-roll bar, telescopic dampers; rear suspension: rigid axle, semi-elliptic leafsprings, anti-roll bar, telescopic dampers.

STEERING recirculating ball; turns lock to lock: 5.65.

BRAKES: drum; swept area: total 268.6 sq in, 1,732 sq cm.

ELECTRICAL EQUIPMENT 12 V; 2,300 W battery; 37 A alternator; Delco-Remy distributor; 2 headlamps.

DIMENSIONS AND WEIGHT wheel base: 111 in, 2,820 mm; tracks: 59.80 in, 1,519 mm front, 59.60 in, 1.514 mm rear; length: 194.30 in, 4,935 mm; width: 72.40 in, 1,839 mm; height: 52.50 in, 1,333 mm - sedans 53.90 in, 1,369 mm; ground clearance: 4.90 in, 124 mm; dry weight: Nova hatchback coupé 3,249 lb, 1,474 kg - Nova coupé 3,177 lb, 1,441 kg - Nova 4-dr. sedan 3,169 lb, 1,437 kg - Nova Custom hatchback coupé 3,256 lb, 1,476 kg - Nova Custom coupé 3,177 lb, 1,441 kg - Nova Custom 4-dr. sedan 3,209 lb, 1,455 kg; turning circle (between walls): 43.8 ft, 13.4 m; fuel tank: 17.6 imp gal, 21 US gal, 80 l.

OPTIONAL ACCESSORIES Powerglide automatic transmission

100 HP POWER TEAM

with 2 ratios (I 1.820, II 1, rev 1.820), max ratio of converter at stall 2, possible manual selection; limited slip differential; E70 x 14 tyres with 7" wide rims; power-assisted steering; tilt of steering wheel; servo brake; ventilated front disc brakes with servo; air-conditioning; SS package (only for coupé models).

115 hp power team

See 100 hp power team, except for:

ENGINE 8 cylinders; 307 cu in, 5,031 cc (3.87 x 3.25 in, 98.2 x 82.5 mm); max power (DIN): 115 hp at 3,600 rpm; max torque (DIN): 205 lb ft, 28.3 kg m at 2,000 rpm; max engine rpm: 4,400; 22.8 hp/l; 5 crankshaft bearings; camshafts: 1, at centre of Vee; 1 Rochester 7043101 (7043401 for California only) downdraught twin barrel carburettor; cooling system capacity: 25 imp pt, 30 US pt, 14.2 l.

PERFORMANCE max speed: about 99 mph, 159 km/h; power-weight ratio: Nova 4-dr. sedan 27.5 lb/hp, 12.5 kg/hp - Nova Custom 4-dr. sedan 27.9 lb/hp, 12.6 kg/hp; fuel consumption: 18.5 m/imp gal, 15.4 m/US gal, 15.3 l x 100 km.

ELECTRICAL EQUIPMENT 2,900 W battery.

OPTIONAL ACCESSORIES Powerglide automatic transmission not available; Turbo-Hydramatic automatic transmission with 3 ratios (I 2.520, II 1.520, III 1, rev 1.930), max ratio of converter at stall 2, possible manual selection, 2.730, 3.420 axle ratios.

145 hp power team

See 100 hp power team, except for:

ENGINE 8 cylinders; 350 cu in, 5,736 cc (4 x 3.48 in, 101.6 x 88.3 mm); max power (DIN) 145 hp at 4,000 rpm; max torque (DIN): 255 lb ft, 35.2 kg m at 2,400 rpm; max engine rpm: 4,400; 25.1 hp/l; 5 crankshaft bearings; camshafts: 1, at centre of Vee; 1 Rochester 7043113 (7043413 for California only) downdraught twin barrel carburettor; cooling system capacity: 26.6 imp pt, 31.9 US pt, 15.1 l.

TRANSMISSION clutch; centrifugal; gearbox ratios: I 2.540, II 1.500, III 1, rev 2.630.

PERFORMANCE max speed: about 104 mph, 167 km/h; power-weight ratio: Nova 4-dr. sedan 22.8 lb/hp, 10.3 kg/hp - Nova Custom 4-dr. sedan 23.1 lb/hp, 10.5 kg/hp; fuel consumption: 17.1 m/imp gal, 14.3 m/US gal, 16.5 l x 100 km.

ELECTRICAL EQUIPMENT 2,900 W battery.

DIMENSIONS AND WEIGHT dry weight: plus 143 lb, 64 kg.

OPTIONAL ACCESSORIES Powerglide automatic transmission not available; Turbo-Hydramatic automatic transmission with 3 ratios (I 2.520, II 1.520, III 1, rev 1.930), max ratio of converter at stall 2, possible manual selection, 2.730, 3.420 axle ratios.

175 hp power team

See 100 hp power team, except for:

ENGINE 8 cylinders; 350 cu in, 5,736 cc (4 x 3.48 in, 101.6 x 88.3 mm); max power (DIN): 175 hp at 4,000 rpm; max torque (DIN): 260 lb ft, 35.9 kg m at 2,800 rpm; max engine rpm: 4,800; 30.5 hp/l; 5 crankshaft bearings; camshafts: 1, at centre of Vee; 1 Rochester 7043203 (7043503 for California only) downdraught 4-barrel carburettor; dual exhaust system; cooling system capacity: 26.6 imp pt, 31.9 US pt, 15.1 l.

TRANSMISSION clutch: centrifugal; gears: 4, fully synchronized; ratios: I 2.540, II 1.800, III 1.440, IV 1, rev 2.540; lever: central; axle ratio: 3.420; width of rims: 7"; tyres: E70 x 14.

PERFORMANCE max speed: about 109 mph, 175 km/h; power-weight ratio: Nova 4-dr sedan 19.2 lb/hp, 8.7 kg/hp - Nova Custom 4-dr sedan 19.5 lb/hp, 8.8 kg/hp; speed in direct drive at 1,000 rpm: 22.9 mph, 36.8 km/h; fuel consumption: 15.7 m/imp gal, 13.1 m/US gal, 18 l x 100 km.

BRAKES front disc (diameter 11 in, 279 mm), internal radial fins, rear drum, servo; swept area: total 337.3 sq in, 2,176 sq cm.

DIMENSIONS AND WEIGHT dry weight: plus 198 lb, 90 kg.

CHEVROLET Vega Kammback GT Station Wagon

CHEVROLET Nova Hatchback Coupé

CHEVROLET Nova SS Coupé

100 hp power team

ENGINE front, 4 stroke; 6 cylinders, in line; 250 cu in, 4,097 cc (3.87 x 3.53 in, 98.2 x 89.6 mm); compression ratio: 8.25:1; max power (DIN): 100 hp at 3,600 rpm; max torque (DIN): 175 lb ft, 24.1 kg m at 1,600 rpm; max engine rpm: 4,200; 24.4 hp/l; cast iron cylinder block and head; 7 crankshaft bearings; valves: overhead, in line, push-rods and rockers, hydraulic tappets; camshafts: 1, side; lubrication: gear pump, full flow filter, 8.3 imp pt, 9.9 US pt, 4.7 l; 1 Rochester 7043017 (7043317 for California only) downdraught single barrel carburettor; cleaner air system; fuel feed: mechanical pump; water-cooled, 20.1 imp pt, 24.1 US pt, 11.4 l.

TRANSMISSION driving wheels: rear: clutch: single dry plate (diaphragm); gearbox: mechanical; gears: 3, fully synchronized; ratios: I 2,850, II 1.680, III 1, rev 2.950; lever: steering column; final drive: hypoid bevel; axle ratio: 3.420; width of rims: 6''; tyres: G78 x 15.

PERFORMANCE max speed: about 91 mph, 146 km/h; power-weight ratio: 40.4 lb/hp, 18.3 kg/hp; speed in direct drive at 1,000 rpm: 23.9 mph, 38.4 km/h; fuel consumption: 19 m/imp gal, 15.8 m/US gal, 14.9 l x 100 km.

CHASSIS perimeter box-type with cross members; front suspension: independent, wishbones, coil springs, telescopic dampers; rear suspension: rigid axle, lower trailing radius arms, upper oblique torque arms, coil springs, telescopic dampers.

STEERING recirculating ball, servo; turns lock to lock: 3.06.

BRAKES front disc (diameter 11 in, 279 mm), internal radial fins, rear drum, servo; swept area: total 380 sq in, 2,451 sq cm.

ELECTRICAL EQUIPMENT 12 V; 2,300 W battery; 37 A alternator; Delco-Remy distributor; 4 headlamps.

DIMENSIONS AND WEIGHT wheel base: 121.50 in, 3,086 mm; tracks: 64.10 in, 1,628 mm front, 64 in, 1,625 mm rear; length: 221.90 in, 5,636 mm; width: 79.50 in, 2,019 mm; height: 54.50 in, 1,384 mm; ground clearance: 5.60 in, 142 mm; dry weight: 4,041 lb, 1,832 kg; turning circle (between walls): 45.2 ft, 13.8 m; fuel tank: 21.6 imp gal, 26 US gal, 98 l.

BODY saloon/sedan; 4 doors; 6 seats.

OPTIONAL ACCESSORIES limited slip differential; H78 x 15 tyres; tilt of steering wheel.

145 hp power team

ENGINE front, 4 stroke; 8 cylinders; 350 cu in, 5,736 cc (4 x 3.48 in, 101.6 x 88.3 mm); compression ratio: 8.5:1; max power (DIN): 145 hp at 4,000 rpm; max torque (DIN): 255 lb ft, 35.2 kg m at 2,400 rpm; max engine rpm: 4,400; 25.1 hp/l; cast iron cylinder block and head; 5 crankshaft bearings; valves: overhead, in line, push-rods and rockers, hydraulic tappets; camshafts: 1, at centre of Vee; lubrication: gear pump, full flow filter, 8.3 imp pt, 9.9 US pt, 4.7 l; 1 Rochester 7043114 (7043414 for California only) downdraught twin barrel carburettor; cleaner air system; fuel feed: mechanical pump; water-cooled, 26.6 imp pt, 31.9 US pt, 15.1 l.

TRANSMISSION driving wheels: rear; gearbox: Turbo-Hydramatic automatic transmission, hydraulic torque converter and planetary gears with 3 ratios: max ratio of converter at stall 2.10, possible manual selection; ratios: I 2.520, II 1.520, III 1, rev 1.930; lever: steering column; final drive: hypoid bevel; axle ratio: 2.730 - station wagons: 3.080; width of rims: 6''; tyres: G78 x 15 - station wagons L78 x 15.

PERFORMANCE max speed: about 104 mph, 167 km/h; power-weight ratio: Bel Air 4-dr. sedan 29 lb/hp, 13.1 kg/hp - Impala 4-dr. sedan 29.5 lb/hp, 13.4 kg/hp; speed in direct drive at 1,000 rpm: 28.8 mph, 46.3 km/h; fuel consumption: 16.1 m/imp gal, 13.4 m/US gal, 17.5 l x 100 km.

CHASSIS perimeter box-type with cross members; front suspension: independent wishbones, coil springs, anti-roll bar, telescopic dampers; rear suspension: rigid axle, lower trailing radius arms, upper oblique torque arms, coil springs, telescopic dampers (for station wagons only rigid axle, semi-elliptic leafsprings, telescopic dampers).

STEERING recirculating ball, servo; turns lock to lock: 3.06.

BRAKES front disc (diameter 11 in, 279 mm - station wagons 12 in, 304 mm), internal radial fins, rear drum, servo; swept area: total 380 sq in, 2,451 sq cm - station wagons total 392.6 sq in, 2,532 sq cm.

ELECTRICAL EQUIPMENT 12 V; 2,900 W battery; 37 A alternator; Delco-Remy distributor; 4 headlamps.

DIMENSIONS AND WEIGHT wheel base: 121.50 in, 3,086 mm - station wagons 125 in, 3,175 mm; tracks: 64.10 in, 1,628 mm front, 64 in, 1,625 mm rear; length: 221.90 in, 5,636 mm - station wagons 226.80 in, 5,761 mm; width: 79.50 in,

CHEVROLET Chevelle Laguna Estate Station Wagon

CHEVROLET Monte Carlo 2-door Sport Coupé

CHEVROLET Impala 2-door Custom Coupé

2,019 mm; height 53.70 in, 1,364 mm - sedans and sports sedans 54.50 in, 1,384 mm - 6-pass. station wagons 58.30 in, 1,481 mm - 9-pass. station wagons 57.50 in, 1,460 mm; ground clearance: 5.60 in, 142 mm - station wagons 6.50 in, 165 mm; dry weight: Bel Air 4-dr. sedan 4,201 lb, 1,905 kg - 6-pass. station wagon 4,856 lb, 2,202 kg - 9-pass. station wagon 4,909 lb, 2,226 kg - Impala 4-dr. sport sedan 4,308 lb, 1,953 kg - 2-dr. custom coupé 4,256 lb, 1,930 kg - 2-dr. sport coupé 4,242 lb, 1,924 kg - 4-dr. sedan 4,284 lb, 1,943 kg - 6-pass. station wagon 4,881 lb, 2,213 kg - 9-pass. station wagon 4,946 lb, 2,243 kg; turning circle (between walls): 45.2 ft, 13.8 m - station wagons 46.2 ft, 14.1 m; fuel tank: 21.6 imp gal, 26 US gal, 98 l - station wagons 18.3 imp gal, 22 US gal, 83 l.

OPTIONAL ACCESSORIES limited slip differential; 3.080 3.420 axle ratios; H78 x 15 tyres (station wagons L78 x 15); tilt of steering wheel; air-conditioning.

150 hp power team

See 145 hp power team, except for:

ENGINE max power (DIN): 150 hp at 3,200 rpm; max torque (DIN) 295 lb ft, 40.7 kg m at 2,000 rpm; max engine rpm: 3,600; 26.1 hp/l; 1 Rochester 7043202 (7043502 for California only) downdraught 4-barrel carburettor; cleaner air system; dual exhaust system.

TRANSMISSION axle ratio: 2.730.

PERFORMANCE max speed: about 108 mph, 174 km/h; power-weight ratio: Bel Air 4-dr. sedan 29 lb/hp, 13.2 kg/hp - Impala 4-dr. sedan 28.8 lb/hp, 13.1 kg/hp; speed in direct drive at 1,000 rpm: 28.8 mph, 46.3 km/h; fuel consumption: 15.6 m/imp gal, 13 m/US gal, 18.1 l x 100 km.

DIMENSIONS AND WEIGHT dry weight: Bel Air 4-dr. sedan plus 160 lb, 72 kg - Impala plus 42 lb, 19 kg.

175 hp power team

See 145 hp power team, except for:

ENGINE 400 cu in, 6,555 cc (4.13 x 3.75 in, 104.8 x 95.2 mm); max power (DIN): 175 hp at 4,400 rpm; max torque (DIN): 260 lb ft, 35.9 kg m at 2,800 rpm; max engine rpm: 4,800; 26.7 hp/l; 1 Rochester 7043118 (7043418 for California only) downdraught twin barrel carburettor; cleaner air system.

TRANSMISSION axle ratio: 2.730.

PERFORMANCE max speed: about 107 mph, 172 km/h; power-weight ratio: Caprice Classic 4-dr. sedan 24.7 lb/hp, 11.2 kg/hp; speed in direct drive at 1,000 rpm: 28.8 mph, 46.3 km/h; fuel consumption: 15.4 m/imp gal, 12.8 m/US gal, 18.4 l x 100 km.

DIMENSIONS AND WEIGHT dry weight: Bel Air and Impala plus 14 lb, 6 kg - Caprice Classic 4-dr. sport sedan 4,354 lb, 1,974 kg - 2-dr. sport coupé 4,289 lb, 1,945 kg - 2-dr. convertible 4,337 lb, 1,967 kg - 4-dr. sedan 4,322 lb, 1,960 kg - Caprice Estate 6-pass. station wagon 4,937 lb, 2,239 kg - 9-pass. station wagon 4,997 lb, 2,266 kg.

215 hp power team

See 145 hp power team, except for:

ENGINE 454 cu in, 7,440 cc (4.25 x 4 in, 107.9 x 101.6 mm); compression ratio: 8.25:1; max power (DIN): 215 hp at 4,000 rpm; max torque (DIN): 345 lb ft, 47.6 kg m at 2,400 rpm; max engine rpm: 4,400; 28.9 hp/l; 1 Rochester 7043200 (7043500 for California only) downdraught 4-barrel carburettor; cleaner air system; dual exhaust system; cooling system capacity: 36.6 imp pt, 44 US pt, 20.8 l.

TRANSMISSION gearbox: Turbo-Hydramatic automatic transmission, hydraulic torque converter and planetary gears with 3 ratios, max ratio of converter at stall 2.10, possible manual selection; ratios: I 2.480, II 1.480, III 1, rev 2.080; axle ratio: 2.730; tyres: L78 x 15.

PERFORMANCE max speed: about 110 mph, 177 km/h; power-weight ratio: Bel Air 6-pass. 23.6 lb/hp, 10.6 kg/hp - Impala 6-pass. 23.7 lb/hp, 10.7 kg/hp - Caprice Estate 6-pass. 24 lb/hp, 10.9 kg/hp; speed in direct drive at 1,000 rpm: 29.3 mph, 47.1 km/h; fuel consumption: 14.1 m/imp gal, 11.7 m/US gal, 20.1 l x 100 km.

DIMENSIONS AND WEIGHT (see 175 hp power team) dry weight: plus 215 lb, 97 kg.

OPTIONAL ACCESSORIES 3.420 axle ratio.

245 hp power team

See 145 hp power team, except for:

ENGINE 454 cu in, 7,440 cc (4.25 x 4 in, 107.9 x 101.6 mm);

245 HP POWER TEAM

compression ratio: 8.25:1; max power (DIN): 245 hp at 4,000 rpm; max torque (DIN): 375 lb ft, 51.9 kg m at 2,800 rpm; max engine rpm: 4,400; 32.9 hp/l; 1 Rochester 7043200 (7043500 for California only) downdraught 4-barrel carburettor; cleaner air system; dual exhaust system; cooling system capacity: 36.6 imp pt, 44 US pt, 20.8 l.

TRANSMISSION gearbox: Turbo-Hydramatic automatic transmission, hydraulic torque converter and planetary gears with 3 ratios, max ratio of converter at stall 2.10, possible manual selection; ratios: I 2.480, II 1.480, III 1, rev 2.080; axle ratio: 2.730; tyres: H78 x 15 (standard).

PERFORMANCE max speed: about 113 mph, 182 km/h; power-weight ratio: Bel Air 4-dr. sedan 18.4 lb/hp, 8.3 kg/hp - Impala and Caprice Classic 4-dr. sedan 18.8 lb/hp, 8.6 kg/hp; speed in direct drive at 1,000 rpm: 29 mph, 46.6 km/h; fuel consumption: 13.8 m/imp gal, 11.5 m/US gal, 20.4 l x 100 km.

DIMENSIONS AND WEIGHT (see 175 hp power team) dry weight: plus 305 lb, 138 kg.

OPTIONAL ACCESSORIES 3.420 axle ratio.

Corvette Series

PRICES IN USA:

1 Corvette	2-door Sport Coupé	**$ 5,561**
2 Corvette	2-door Convertible	**$ 5,335**

Power team:	Standard for:	Optional for:
190 hp	both	—
250 hp	—	both
275 hp	—	both

190 hp power team

ENGINE front, 4 stroke; 8 cylinders; 350 cu in, 5,736 cc (4 x 3.48 in, 101.6 x 88.3 mm); compression ratio: 8.5:1; max power (DIN): 190 hp at 4,400 rpm; max torque (DIN): 270 lb ft, 37.3 kg m at 2,800 rpm; max engine rpm: 4,800; 33.1 hp/l; cast iron cylinder block and head; 5 crankshaft bearings; valves: overhead, in line, push-rods and rockers, hydraulic tappets; camshafts: 1, at centre of Vee, lubrication: gear pump, full flow filter, 8.3 imp pt, 9.9 US pt, 4.7 l; 1 Rochester 7043203 (7043202 for California only) downdraught 4-barrel carburettor; cleaner air system, dual exhaust system; fuel feed: mechanical pump; water-cooled, 28.3 imp pt, 34 US pt, 16.1 l.

TRANSMISSION driving wheels: rear; clutch: single dry plate, semi-centrifugal; gearbox: mechanical; gears: 4, fully synchronized; ratios: I 2.520, II 1.880, III 1.460, IV 1, rev 2.590; lever: central; final drive: hypoid bevel, limited slip differential; axle ratio: 3.360; width of rims: 8"; tyres: GR70 x 15.

PERFORMANCE max speed: about 118 mph, 190 km/h; power-weight ratio: coupé 17.9 lb/hp, 8.1 kg/hp - convertible 18 lb/hp, 8.2 kg/hp; speed in direct drive at 1,000 rpm: 25.4 mph, 40.8 km/h; fuel consumption: 14.9 m/imp gal, 12.4 m/US gal, 19 l x 100 km.

CHASSIS box-type ladder frame; front suspension: independent, wishbones, coil springs, anti-roll bar, telescopic dampers; rear suspension: independent, wishbones, semi-axle as upper arms, transverse semi-elliptic leafsprings, trailing radius arms, anti-roll bar, telescopic dampers.

STEERING recirculating ball; turns lock to lock: 3.40.

BRAKES disc (diameter 11.75 in, 298 mm); swept area: total 639.4 sq in, 4,124 sq cm.

ELECTRICAL EQUIPMENT 12 V; 3,250 W battery; 42 A alternator; Delco-Remy distributor; 4 retractable headlamps.

DIMENSIONS AND WEIGHT wheel base: 98 in, 2,489 mm; tracks: 58.70 in, 1,491 mm front, 59.59 in, 1,511 mm rear; length: 184.70 in, 4,691 mm; width: 69 in, 1,752 mm; height: coupé 47.70 in, 1,211 mm - convertible 47.80 in, 1,214 mm; ground clearance: 4.30 in, 109 mm; dry weight: coupé 3,407 lb, 1,545 kg - convertible 3,414 lb, 1,548 kg; turning circle (between walls): 38.6 ft, 11.8 m; fuel tank: 15 imp gal, 18 US gal, 68 l.

BODY in plastic material; 2 doors; 2 seats, built-in headrests.

OPTIONAL ACCESSORIES 3.080 axle ratio; Turbo-Hydramatic automatic transmission with 3 ratios (I 2.480, II 1.480, III 1, rev 2.080), max ratio of converter at stall 2.10, possible manual selection, 3.080 and 3.360 axle ratios; tilt of steering wheel; power-assisted steering; servo brake; electrically-controlled windows; air-conditioning; hardtop only for convertible.

CHEVROLET Caprice Classic Series

CHEVROLET Corvette Series

CHRYSLER Newport Series

250 hp power team

See 190 hp power team, except for:

ENGINE compression ratio: 9:1; max power (DIN) 250 hp at 5,200 rpm; max torque (DIN): 285 lb ft, 39.3 kg m at 4,000 rpm; max engine rpm: 5,600 43.6 hp/l; 1 Rochester 7043213 (7043513 for California only) downdraught 4-barrel carburettor; cleaner air system.

TRANSMISSION axle ratio: 3.550.

PERFORMANCE max speed: about 123 mph, 198 km/h; power-weight ratio: 13.8 lb/hp, 6.2 kg/hp; speed in direct drive at 1,000 rpm: 24 mph, 38.6 km/h; fuel consumption: 14.2 m/imp gal, 11.8 m/US gal, 19.9 l x 100 km.

DIMENSIONS AND WEIGHT dry weight: plus 42 lb, 19 kg.

OPTIONAL ACCESSORIES 3.700 axle ratio; 4-speed fully synchronized mechanical gearbox (I 2.200, II 1.640, III 1.270, IV 1, rev 2.260), 3.700 or 3.550 axle ratio; Turbo-Hydramatic automatic transmission with 3.550 or 3.700 axle ratios.

275 hp power team

See 190 hp power team, except for:

ENGINE 454 cu in, 7,440 cc (4.25 x 4 in, 107.9 x 101.6 mm); compression ratio: 8.25:1; max power (DIN): 275 hp at 4,400 rpm; max torque (DIN): 395 lb ft, 54.6 kg m at 2,800 rpm; max engine rpm: 4,800; 37 hp/l; lubricating system capacity: 10 imp pt, 12 US pt, 5.7 l; 1 Rochester 7043201 (7043501 for California only) downdraught 4-barrel carburettor; cleaner air system; cooling system capacity: 36.6 imp pt, 44 US pt, 20.8 l.

TRANSMISSION axle ratio: 3.080.

PERFORMANCE max speed: about 126 mph, 202 km/h; power-weight ratio: sport coupé 13.1 lb/hp, 5.9 kg/hp - convertible 13.2 lb/hp, 6 kg/hp; speed in direct drive at 1,000 rpm: 25.9 mph, 41.7 km/h; fuel consumption: 13.9 m/imp gal, 11.6 m/US gal, 20.3 l x 100 km.

ELECTRICAL EQUIPMENT 3,750 W battery.

DIMENSIONS AND WEIGHT dry weight: plus 211 lb, 96 kg.

OPTIONAL ACCESSORIES 4-speed fully synchronized mechanical gearbox (I 2.200, II 1.640, III 1.270, IV 1, rev 2.260), 3.360 3.080 3.550 axle ratios; 3.360 axle ratio; Turbo-Hydramatic automatic transmission with 3.080 or 3.360 axle ratios.

CHRYSLER USA

Newport - Newport Custom - New Yorker - New Yorker Brougham - Town and Country Series

PRICES IN USA:

1	Newport	2-door Hardtop	**$ 4,153**
2	Newport	4-door Sedan	**$ 4,080**
3	Newport	4-door Hardtop	**$ 4,215**
4	Newport Custom	2-door Hardtop	**$ 4,383**
5	Newport Custom	4-door Sedan	**$ 4,313**
6	Newport Custom	4-door Hardtop	**$ 4,461**
7	New Yorker	4-door Sedan	**$ 4,891**
8	New Yorker	4-door Hardtop	**$ 5,019**
9	New Yorker Brougham	2-door Hardtop	**$ 5,297**
10	New Yorker Brougham	4-door Sedan	**$ 5,248**
11	New Yorker Brougham	4-door Hardtop	**$ 5,376**
12	Town and Country	6-passenger Station Wagon	**$ 5,181**
13	Town and Country	9-passenger Station Wagon	**$ 5,265**

Power team:	Standard for:	Optional for:
185 hp	1,2,3,4,5,6	—
208 hp	7,8,9,10,11,12,13	1,2,3,4,5,6
215 hp	7,8,9,10,11,12,13	1,2,3,4,5,6

185 hp power team

ENGINE front, 4 stroke; 8 cylinders; 400 cu in, 6,555 cc (4.34 x 3.38 in, 110.2 x 85.8 mm); compression ratio: 8.2:1; max power (DIN): 185 hp at 3,600 rpm; max torque (DIN): 310 lb ft, 42.8 kg m at 2,400 rpm; max engine rpm: 4,000; 28.2 hp/l; cast iron cylinder block and head; 5 crankshaft bearings; valves: overhead, in line, push-rods and rockers, hydraulic tappets; camshafts: 1, at centre of Vee; lubrication: rotary pump, full flow filter, 8.3 imp pt, 9.9 US pt, 4.7 l; 1 Holley R-6454A (R-6472 A for California only) downdraught twin barrel carburettor; cleaner air system; fuel feed: mechanical pump; water-cooled, 26.6 imp pt, 31.9 US pt, 15.1 l.

TRANSMISSION driving wheels: rear; gearbox: Torqueflite

CHEVROLET Caprice Classic 4-door Sport Sedan

CHEVROLET Corvette 2-door Sport Coupé

CHRYSLER Newport 4-door Hardtop

automatic transmission, hydraulic torque converter and planetary gears with 3 ratios, max ratio of converter at stall 2.02, possible manual selection; ratios: I 2.450, II 1.450; III 1, rev 2.200; lever: steering column; final drive: hypoid bevel; axle ratio: 2.710; width of rims: 5.5''; tyres: H78 x 15.

PERFORMANCE max speed: about 105 mph, 169 km/h; power-weight ratio: Newport 4-dr. sedan and Newport Custom 4-dr. sedan 23.3 lb/hp, 10.6 kg/hp; speed in direct drive at 1,000 rpm: 27.6 mph, 44.4 km/h; fuel consumption: 15.1 m/imp gal, 12.6 m/US gal, 18.7 l x 100 km.

CHASSIS integral, front auxiliary frame; front suspension: independent, wishbones, lower trailing links, longitudinal torsion bars, anti-roll bar, telescopic dampers; rear suspension: rigid axle, semi-elliptic leafsprings, telescopic dampers.

STEERING recirculating ball, servo; turns lock to lock: 3.50.

BRAKES front disc (diameter 11.56 in, 294 mm), internal radial fins, rear drum (diameter 11 in, 279 mm), servo; swept area: total 393.6 sq in, 2,539 sq cm.

ELECTRICAL EQUIPMENT 12 V; 375 A battery; 41 A alternator; Chrysler Essex or Chrysler Prestolite electronic ignition; 4 headlamps.

DIMENSIONS AND WEIGHT wheel base: 124 in, 3,150 mm; tracks: 62.10 in, 1,577 mm front, 63.40 in, 1,610 mm rear; length: 230.10 in, 5,844 mm; width: 79.40 in, 2,017 mm; height: 2-dr. hardtops 55 in, 1,397 mm - 4-dr. sedans 56.20 in, 1,427 mm - 4-dr. hardtops 55.70 in, 1,415 mm; ground clearance: 5.90 in, 150 mm; dry weight: Newport 2-dr. hardtop 4,270 lb, 1,937 kg - 4-dr. sedan 4,315 lb, 1,957 kg - 4-dr. hardtop 4,330 lb, 1,964 kg - Newport Custom 2-dr. hardtop 4.260 lb, 1,932 kg - 4-dr sedan 4,315 lb, 1,957 kg - 4-dr. hardtop 4,345 lb, 1,971 kg; turning circle (between walls): 46.7 ft, 14.2 m; fuel tank: 19.1 imp gal, 23 US gal, 87 l.

OPTIONAL ACCESSORIES limited slip differential; 3.230 axle ratio; HR78 x 15 or J78 x 15 tyres with 6'' wide rims; tilt and telescopic steering wheel; security alarm system; electronic digital clock; air-conditioning; sunshine roof.

208 hp power team

(only for California).

See 185 hp power team, except for:

ENGINE 440 cu in, 7,210 cc (4.32 x 3.75 in, 109.7 x 95.2 mm); max power (DIN): 208 hp at 3,600 rpm; max torque (DIN): 340 lb ft, 46.9 kg m at 2,000 rpm; max engine rpm: 4,000; 28.8 hp/l; 1 Carter TQ-6410'S' downdraught 4-barrel carburettor; cleaner air system with air pump; cooling system capacity: 25.9 imp pt, 31.2 US pt, 14.7 l.

TRANSMISSION axle ratio: 2.760; width of rims: 6'' - station wagons 6.5''; tyres: J78 x 15 (standard) - station wagons L84 x 15.

PERFORMANCE max speed: about 110 mph, 177 km/h; power-weight ratio: New Yorker 4-dr. sedan 21.5 lb/hp, 9.8 kg/hp - New Yorker Brougham 4-dr. sedan 21.8 lb/hp, 9.9 kg/hp - Town and Country 6-pass. 23 lb/hp, 10.4 kg/hp; speed in direct drive at 1,000 rpm: 27.9 mph, 44.9 km/h; fuel consumption: 14.9 m/imp gal, 12.4 m/US gal, 19 l x 100 km.

ELECTRICAL EQUIPMENT 440 A battery.

DIMENSIONS AND WEIGHT wheel base: station wagons 122 in, 3,099 mm; length: New Yorker and New Yorker Brougham 230.80 in, 5,862 mm - station wagons 229.60 in, 5,832 mm; height: New Yorker Brougham 2-dr. hardtop 55.30 in, 1,405 mm - New Yorker and New Yorker Brougham 4-dr. sedans 56.40 in, 1,432 mm - New Yorker and New Yorker Brougham 4-dr. hardtops 55.90 in, 1,420 mm - station wagons 58 in, 1,473 mm; ground clearance: New Yorker and New Yorker Brougham 6.20 in, 157 mm - station wagons 6.70 in, 170 mm; dry weight: Newport and Newport Custom plus 65 lb, 29 kg - New Yorker 4-dr. sedan 4,470 lb, 2,028 kg - 4-dr. hardtop 4,495 lb, 2,039 kg - New Yorker Brougham 2-dr hardtop 4,450 lb, 2,019 kg - 4-dr. sedan 4,540 lb, 2,059 kg - 4-dr. hardtop 4,555 lb, 2,066 kg - Town and Country 6-pass. station wagon 4,790 lb, 2,173 kg - 9-pass. station wagon 4,845 lb, 2,198 kg; turning circle (between walls): station wagons 45.9 ft, 14 m.

OPTIONAL ACCESSORIES LR78 x 15 or L84 x 15 tyres (station wagons LR78 x 15 tyres with 6.5'' wide rims).

215 hp power team

See 185 hp power team, except for:

ENGINE 440 cu in, 7,210 cc (4.32 x 3.75 in, 109.7 x 95.2 mm); max power (DIN): 215 hp at 3,600 rpm; max torque (DIN): 345 lb ft, 47,6 kg m at 2,000 rpm; max engine rpm: 4,000; 29.8 hp/l; 1 Carter TQ-6322'S' (TQ-64104S' for Cali-

215 HP POWER TEAM

fornia only) downdraught 4-barrel carburettor; cooling system capacity: 25.9 imp pt, 31.2 US pt, 14.7 l.

TRANSMISSION axle ratio: 2.760; width of rims: 6" - station wagons 6.5"; tyres: J78 x 15 (standard) - station wagons L84 x 15.

PERFORMANCE max speed: about 112 mph, 180 km/h; power-weight ratio: New Yorker 4-dr. sedan 20.8 lb/hp, 9.4 kg/hp; speed in direct drive at 1,000 rpm: 27.9 mph, 44.9 km/h; fuel consumption: 14.6 m/imp gal, 12.2 m/US gal, 19.31 x 100 km.

ELECTRICAL EQUIPMENT 440 A battery.

DIMENSIONS AND WEIGHT (see 208 hp power team).

OPTIONAL ACCESSORIES LR78 x 15 or L84 x 15 tyres (station wagons LR78 x 15 tyres with 6.5" wide rims).

DODGE USA

Dart - Dart Custom - Dart Sport - Dart 340 Sport - Dart Swinger - Dart Swinger Special Series

PRICES IN USA:

1 Dart	4-door Sedan	**$ 2,454**
2 Dart Custom	4-door Sedan	**$ 2,608**
3 Dart Sport	2-door Coupé	**$ 2,369**
4 Dart 340 Sport	2-door Coupé	**$ 2,793**
5 Dart Swinger	2-door Hardtop	**$ 2,562**
6 Dart Swinger Special	2-door Hardtop	**$ 2,407**

For V8 engines add $ 142.

Power team:	Standard for:	Optional for:
95 hp	all except 4	—
98 hp	—	all except 4
105 hp	—	all except 4
150 hp	all except 4	—
240 hp	4	—

95 hp power team

ENGINE front, 4 stroke; 6 cylinders, in line; 198 cu in, 3,245 cc (3.40 x 3.64 in, 86.3 x 92.4 mm); compression ratio: 8.4:1; max power (DIN): 95 hp at 4,000 rpm; max torque (DIN): 150 lb ft, 20.7 kg m at 1,600 rpm; max engine rpm: 4,600; 29.3 hp/l; cast iron cylinder block and head; 4 crankshaft bearings; valves: overhead, in line, push-rods and rockers; camshafts: 1, side; lubrication: rotary pump, full flow filter, 8.3 imp pt, 9.9 US pt, 4.7 l; 1 Holley R-6447A downdraught single barrel carburettor; cleaner air system; fuel feed: mechanical pump; water-cooled, 21.6 imp pt, 26 US pt, 12.3 l.

TRANSMISSION driving wheels: rear; clutch: single dry plate; gearbox: mechanical; gears: 3, II and III synchronized; ratios: I 3.180, II 1.830, III 1, rev 3.970; lever: stearing column or central; final drive: hypoid bevel; axle ratio: 3.230; width of rims: 4.5"; tyres: 6.95 x 14.

PERFORMANCE max speed: about 93 mph, 149 km/h; power-weight ratio: Dart and Dart Custom 4-dr. sedan 31.4 lb/hp, 14.2 kg/hp; speed in direct drive at 1,000 rpm: 25 mph, 40.2 km/h; fuel consumption: 21.6 m/imp gal, 18 m/US gal, 13.1 l x 100 km.

CHASSIS integral; front suspension: independent, wishbones, lower trailing links, longitudinal torsion bars, telescopic dampers; rear suspension: rigid axle, semi-elliptic leafsprings, telescopic dampers.

STEERING recirculating ball; turns lock to lock: 5.30.

BRAKES drum; swept area: total 254.5 sq in, 1,641 sq cm.

ELECTRICAL EQUIPMENT 12 V; 280 A battery; 34 A alternator; Chrysler Essex or Chrysler Prestolite electronic ignition; 2 headlamps.

DIMENSIONS AND WEIGHT wheel base: 111 in, 2,819 mm - coupé 108 in, 2,743 mm; tracks: 59.10 in, 1,501 mm front, 55.60 in, 1,412 mm rear; length: 203.80 in, 5,177 mm - coupé 200 in, 5,080 mm; width: 69.60 in, 1,768 mm - coupé 71.80 in, 1,824 mm; height: 52.80 in, 1,341 mm - sedans 54.10 in, 1,374 mm - coupé 53.10 in, 1,349 mm; ground clearance: hardtops 4.80 in, 122 mm - coupés 5.20 in 132 mm - sedans 5.80 in, 147 mm; dry weight: Dart and Dart Custom 4-dr. sedans 2,985 lb, 1,354 kg - Dart Sport 2,930 lb, 1,329 kg - Dart Swinger 2,970 lb, 1,347 kg - Dart Swinger Special 2,975 lb, 1,349 kg; turning circle (between

CHRYSLER New Yorker Brougham 4-door Sedan

DODGE Dart Swinger 2-door Hardtop

DODGE Challenger Rallye 2-door Hardtop

walls): 40.9 ft, 12.5 m - coupé 39.9 ft, 12.2 m; fuel tank: 19.3 imp gal, 16 US gal, 73 l.

OPTIONAL ACCESSORIES Torqueflite automatic transmission with 3 ratios (I 2.450, II 1.450, III 1, rev 2.200), max ratio of converter at stall 2.16, 2.760 3.210 3.230 3.550 axle ratios; limited slip differential; 3.210 3.550 axle ratios; D78 x 14 tyres; E70 x 14 tyres with 5.5" wide rims; anti-roll bar on front suspension; power-assisted steering; servo brake; disc brakes (diameter 10.82 in, 275 mm) with servo, total swept area 361.6 sq in, 2,332 sq cm; electrically-heated rear window; sunshine roof.

98 hp power team

(for California only).

See 95 hp power team, except for:

ENGINE 225 cu in, 3,687 cc (3.40 x 4.12 in, 86.4 x 104.6 mm); max power (DIN): 98 hp at 4,000 rpm; max torque (DIN): 178 lb ft, 24.5 kg m at 1,600 rpm; max engine rpm: 4,400; 26.6 hp/l; 1 Holley R-6595A downdraught single barrel carburettor.

PERFORMANCE max speed: about 96 mph, 154 km/h; power-weight ratio: Dart and Dart Custom 4-dr. sedan 30.5 lb/hp, 13.8 kg/hp; fuel consumption: 19.8 m/imp gal, 16.4 m/US gal, 14.3 l x 100 km.

DIMENSIONS AND WEIGHT dry weight: plus 7 lb, 3 kg.

OPTIONAL ACCESSORIES air-conditioning.

105 hp power team

See 95 hp power team, except for:

ENGINE 225 cu in, 3,687 cc (3.40 x 4.12 in, 86.4 x 104.6 mm); max power (DIN): 105 hp at 4,000 rpm; max torque (DIN): 185 lb ft, 25.5 kg m at 1,600 rpm; max engine rpm: 4,600; 28.5 hp/l; 1 Holley R-6593A (R-6595A for California only) downdraught single barrel carburettor.

PERFORMANCE max speed: about 98 mph, 158 km/h; power-weight ratio: Dart and Dart Custom 4-dr. sedan 28.5 lb/hp, 12.9 kg/hp; fuel consumption: 17.9 m/imp gal, 14.9 m/US gal, 15.8 l x 100 km.

DIMENSIONS AND WEIGHT dry weight: plus 7 lb, 3 kg.

OPTIONAL ACCESSORIES air-conditioning.

150 hp power team

See 95 hp power team, except for:

ENGINE 8 cylinders; 318 cu in, 5,211 cc (3.91 x 3.31 in, 99.2 x 84 mm); compression ratio: 8.6:1; max power (DIN): 150 hp at 3,600 rpm; max torque (DIN): 265 lb ft, 36.6 kg m at 2,000 rpm; max engine rpm: 4,000; 28.8 hp/l; 5 crankshaft bearings; valves: hydraulic tappets; camshafts: 1, at centre of Vee; 1 Carter BBD-6316S (BBD-6343S for California only) downdraught twin barrel carburettor; cooling system capacity: 26.6 imp pt, 31.9 US pt, 15.1 l.

TRANSMISSION gears: 3, fully synchronized; ratios: I 3.080, II 1,700, III 1, rev 2.900; axle ratio: 3.210.

PERFORMANCE max speed: about 106 mph, 170 km/h; power-weight ratio: Dart and Dart Custom 4-dr. sedan 20.7 lb/hp, 9.4 kg/hp; speed in direct drive at 1,000 rpm: 25.8 mph, 41.5 km/h; fuel consumption: 16.6 m/imp gal, 13.8 m/US gal, 17 l x 100 km.

ELECTRICAL EQUIPMENT 41 A alternator.

DIMENSIONS AND WEIGHT dry weight: Dart and Dart Custom 4-dr. sedan 3,105 lb, 1,408 kg - Dart Sport 3,045 lb, 1,381 kg - Dart Swinger 3,090 lb, 1,402 kg - Dart Swinger Special 3,095 lb, 1,404 kg.

OPTIONAL ACCESSORIES 3.550 axle ratio; 2.760 3.250 3.550 axle ratios; air-conditioning.

240 hp power team

See 95 hp power team, except for:

ENGINE 8 cylinders; 340 cu in, 5,572 cc (4.04 x 3.31 in, 102.5 x 84 mm); compression ratio: 8.5:1; max power (DIN): 240 hp at 4.800 rpm; max torque (DIN): 295 lb ft, 40.7 kg m at 3,600 rpm; max engine rpm: 5,000; 43.1 hp/l; 5 crankshaft bearings; valves: hydraulic tappets; camshafts: 1, at centre of Vee; 1 Carter TQ-6318S (TQ-6339S for California only) downdraught 4-barrel carburettor; dual exhaust system; cooling system capacity: 25.9 imp pt, 31.2 US pt, 14.7 l.

TRANSMISSION gears: 3, fully synchronized; gears: I 2.550,

CHRYSLER New Yorker Brougham 4-door Sedan

DODGE Dart Swinger 2-door Hardtop

DODGE Challenger Rallye 2-door Hardtop

II 1.490, III 1, rev 3.340; axle ratio: 3.210; width of rims: 5.5"; tyres: E70 x 14 (standard).

PERFORMANCE max speed: about 118 mph, 190 km/h; power-weight ratio: 13.7 lb/hp, 6.2 kg/hp; speed in direct drive at 1,000 rpm: 23.9 mph, 38.4 km/h; fuel consumption: 15.1 m/imp gal, 12.6 m/US gal, 18.7 l x 100 km.

CHASSIS front suspension: anti-roll bar (standard).

BRAKES swept area: total 361.6 sq in, 2,332 sq cm.

ELECTRICAL EQUIPMENT 41 A alternator.

DIMENSIONS AND WEIGHT height: 53.20 in, 1,351 mm; ground clearance: 5.30 in, 134 mm; dry weight: 3,280 lb, 1,488 kg.

OPTIONAL ACCESSORIES Torqueflite transmission, 3.210 3.555 axle ratios; 4-speed fully synchronized mechanical gearbox (I 2.470, II 1.770, III 1.340, IV 1, rev 2.400), central lever; 3.550 axle ratio; air-conditioning.

Challenger Series

PRICE IN USA:

Challenger	2-door Hardtop	**$ 2,924**

150 hp power team

(standard).

ENGINE front, 4 stroke; 8 cylinders; 318 cu in, 5,211 cc (3.91 x 3.31 in, 99.2 x 84 mm); compression ratio: 8.6:1; max power (DIN): 150 hp at 3,600 rpm; max torque (DIN): 265 lb ft, 36.6 kg m at 2,000 rpm; max engine rpm: 4,000; 28.8 hp/l; cast iron cylinder block and head; 5 crankshaft bearings; valves: overhead, in line, push-rods and rockers; hydraulic tappets; camshafts: 1, at centre of Vee; lubrication: rotary pump, full flow filter, 8.3 imp pt, 9.9 US pt, 4.7 l; 1 Carter 6316S (BBD-6343S for California only) downdraught twin barrel carburettor; cleaner air system; fuel feed: mechanical pump; water-cooled, 26.6 imp pt, 31.9 US pt, 15.1 l.

TRANSMISSION driving wheels: rear; clutch: single dry plate; gearbox: mechanical; gears: 3, fully synchronized; ratios: I 3.080, II 1.700, III 1, rev 2.900; lever: steering column or central; final drive: hypoid bevel; axle ratio: 3.230; width of rims: 5"; tyres: 7.35 x 14.

PERFORMANCE max speed: about 105 mph, 169 km/h; power-weight ratio: 21.6 lb/hp, 9.8 kg/hp; speed in direct drive at 1,000 rpm: 26.7 mph, 42.9 km/h; fuel consumption: 17.4 m/imp gal, 14.5 m/US gal, 16.2 l x 100 km.

CHASSIS integral; front suspension: independent, wishbones, lower trailing links, longitudinal torsion bars, telescopic dampers; rear suspension: rigid axle, semi-elliptic leafsprings, telescopic dampers.

STEERING recirculating ball; turns lock to lock: 5.30.

BRAKES front disc (diameter 10.84 in, 275 mm), rear drum; swept area: total 365.2 sq in, 2,356 sq cm.

ELECTRICAL EQUIPMENT 12 V; 280 A battery; 41 A alternator; Chrysler Essex or Chrysler Prestolite electronic ignition; 4 headlamps.

DIMENSIONS AND WEIGHT wheel base: 110 in, 2,794 mm; tracks: 60.20 in, 1,529 mm front, 60.70 in, 1,542 mm rear; length: 198.20 in, 5,034 mm; width: 76.40 in, 1,940 mm; height: 50.90 in, 1,293 mm; ground clearance: 4.90 in 124 mm; dry weight: 3,245 lb, 1,472 kg; turning circle (between walls): 42.3 ft, 12.9 m; fuel tank: 15 imp gal, 18 US gal, 68 l.

BODY hardtop; 2 doors; 4 seats, separate front seats.

OPTIONAL ACCESSORIES Torqueflite automatic transmission with 3 ratios (I 2.450, II 1.450, III 1, rev 2.450), max ratio of converter at stall 2.16, possible manual selection, 2.760 3.230 axle ratios; limited slip differential; F78 x 14 tyres; F70 x 14 tyres with 5.5" wide rims; anti-roll bar on front suspension; power-assisted steering; servo brake; air-conditioning; electrically-heated rear window; Rallye equipment.

240 hp power team

(optional).

See 150 hp power team, except for:

ENGINE 340 cu in, 5,572 cc (4.04 x 3.31 in, 102.5 x 84 mm); compression ratio: 8.5:1; max power (DIN): 240 hp at 4,800 rpm; max torque (DIN): 295 lb ft, 40.7 kg m at 3,600 rpm; max engine rpm: 5,000; 43.1 hp/l; 1 Carter TQ-6318S (TQ-6339S for California only) downdraught 4-barrel carburettor; dual exhaust system; cooling system capacity· 25 imp pt, 30 US pt, 14.2 l.

240 HP POWER TEAM

TRANSMISSION gearbox ratios: I 2.550, II 1.480, III 1, rev 3.340; width of rims: 5.5"; tyres: F70 x 14 (standard).

PERFORMANCE max speed: about 115 mph, 185 km/h; power-weight ratio: 14.4 lb/hp, 6.5 kg/hp; speed in direct drive at 1,000 rpm: 26.5 mph, 42.6 km/h; fuel consumption: 16 m/imp gal, 13.4 m/US gal, 17.6 l x 100 km.

CHASSIS front and rear suspension: anti-roll bar (standard).

DIMENSIONS AND WEIGHT dry weight: plus 210 lb, 95 kg.

OPTIONAL ACCESSORIES Torqueflite automatic transmission with 3.230 axle ratio; 4-speed fully synchronized mechanical gearbox (I 2.470, II 1.770, III 1.340, IV 1, rev 2.400); 3.550 axle ratio.

Coronet - Coronet Custom - Coronet Crestwood - Charger - Charger SE Series

PRICES IN USA:

1	Coronet	4-door Sedan	$ **2,782**
2	Coronet	6-passenger Station Wagon	$ **3,209**
3	Coronet Custom	4-door Sedan	$ **2,952**
4	Coronet Custom	6-passenger Station Wagon	$ **3,382**
5	Coronet Custom	9-passenger Station Wagon	$ **3,460**
6	Coronet Crestwood	6-passenger Station Wagon	$ **3,632**
7	Coronet Crestwood	9-passenger Station Wagon	$ **3,711**
8	Charger	2-door Coupé	$ **2,725**
9	Charger	2-door Hardtop	$ **2,995**
10	Charger SE	2-door Coupé	$ **3,290**

For V8 engines add $ 92.

Power team:	Standard for:	Optional for:
98 hp	1,3,8,9	—
105 hp	1,3,8,9	—
150 hp	all	—
175 hp	—	all
240 hp	—	1,3,8,9
260 hp	—	all
280 hp	—	1,3,8,9,10

98 hp power team

(for California only).

ENGINE front, 4 stroke; 6 cylinders, in line; 225 cu in, 3,687 cc (3.40 x 4.12 in, 86.4 x 104.6 mm); compression ratio: 8.4:1; max power (DIN): 98 hp at 4,000 rpm; max torque (DIN): 178 lb ft, 24.5 kg m at 1,600 rpm; max engine rpm: 4,400; 26.6 hp/l; cast iron cylinder block and head; 4 crankshaft bearings; valves: overhead, in line, push-rods and rockers; camshafts: 1, side; lubrication: rotary pump, full flow filter, 8.3 imp pt, 9.9 US pt, 4.7 l; 1 Holley R-6595A downdraught single barrel carburettor; cleaner air system; fuel feed: mechanical pump; water-cooled, 21.6 imp pt, 26 US pt, 12.3 l.

TRANSMISSION driving wheels: rear; clutch: single dry plate; gearbox: mechanical; gears: 3, fully synchronized; ratios: I 3.080, II 1.700, III 1, rev 2.900; lever: steering column; final drive: hypoid bevel; axle ratio: 3.210; width of rims: 5"; tyres: E78 x 14.

PERFORMANCE max speed: about 94 mph, 151 km/h; power-weight ratio: Coronet 4-dr. sedan 36.2 lb/hp, 16.4 kg/hp - Coronet Custom 4-dr. sedan 36.1 lb/hp, 16.3 kg/hp - Charger 2-dr. coupé 35.8 lb/hp, 16.2 kg/hp - 2-dr. hardtop 36.3 lb/hp, 16.5 kg/hp; speed in direct drive at 1,000 rpm: 25.3 mph, 40.7 kh/h; fuel consumption: 19.3 m/imp gal, 16.1 m/US gal, 14.6 l x 100 km.

CHASSIS integral; front suspension: independent, wishbones, lower trailing links, longitudinal torsion bars, telescopic dampers; rear suspension: rigid axle, semi-elliptic leafsprings, telescopic dampers.

STEERING recirculating ball; turns lock to lock: 5.30.

BRAKES front disc (diameter 10.84 in, 275 mm), rear drum; swept area: total 365.2 sq in, 2,356 sq cm.

ELECTRICAL EQUIPMENT 12 V; 280 A battery; 41 A alternator; Chrysler Essex or Chrysler Prestolite electronic ignition; 4 headlamps.

DIMENSIONS AND WEIGHT wheel base: 115 in, 2,921 mm - sedans 118 in, 2,997 mm; tracks: 61.90 in, 1,572 mm front, 62 in, 1,573 mm rear; length: 212.70 in, 5,402 mm - sedans 212.90 in, 5,407 mm; width: 77 in, 1,956 mm - sedans 77.80 in, 1,976 mm; height: coupé 52.20 in 1,326 mm - hardtop 52.50 in, 1,333 mm - sedans 53.60 in, 1,361 mm; ground clearance: coupé 5 in, 127 mm - hardtop 5.40 in, 137 mm - sedans 5.20 in, 132 mm; dry weight. Coronet 4-dr. sedan 3,550 lb, 1,610 kg - Coronet Custom 4-dr. sedan 3,540 lb, 1,605 kg - Charger 2-dr. coupé 3,505 lb, 1,589 kg - 2-dr. hardtop 3,555 lb, 1,612 kg; turning circle (between walls): 44.7 ft, 13.6 m - sedans 45 ft, 13.8 m; fuel tank: 16.3 imp gal, 19.5 US gal, 74 l.

OPTIONAL ACCESSORIES Torqueflite automatic transmission with 3 ratios (I 2.450, II 1.450, III 1, rev 2.200), max ratio of converter at stall 2.16, possible manual selection, steering column or central lever, 2.940, 3.210, 3.230, 3.550 axle ratios; limited slip differential; 3.230 3.550 axle ratios; F78 x 14 tyres; H78 x 14 tyres with 5.5" wide rims; anti-roll bar on front suspension; power-assisted steering; servo brake; air-conditioning.

DODGE Coronet Custom Series

DODGE Coronet Crestwood Series (V8 150 hp engine)

DODGE Charger SE 2-door Coupé

105 hp power team

See 98 hp power team, except for:

ENGINE max power (DIN): 105 hp at 4,000 rpm; max torque (DIN): 185 lb ft, 25.5 kg m at 1,600 rpm; max engine rpm: 4,600; 28.5 hp/l; 1 Holley R-6593A (R-6595A for California only) downdraught single barrel carburettor.

PERFORMANCE max speed: about 98 mph, 157 km/h; power-weight ratio: Coronet 4-dr. sedan and Charger 2-dr. hardtop 33.8 lb/hp, 15.3 kg/hp - Coronet Custom 4-dr. sedan 33.7 lb/hp, 15.2 kg/hp - Charger 2-dr. coupé 33.4 lb/hp, 15.1 kg/hp; fuel consumption: 17.8 m/imp gal, 14.8 m/US gal, 15.9 l x 100 km.

150 hp power team

ENGINE front, 4 stroke; 8 cylinders; 318 cu in, 5,211 cc (3.91 x 3.31 in, 99.2 x 84 mm); compression ratio: 8.6:1; max power (DIN): 150 hp at 3,600 rpm; max torque (DIN): 265 lb ft, 36.6 kg m at 2,000 rpm; max engine rpm: 4,000; 28.8 hp/l; cast iron cylinder block and head; 5 crankshaft bearings; valves: overhead, in line, push-rods and rockers, hydraulic tappets; camshafts: 1, at centre of Vee; lubrication: rotary pump, full flow filter, 8.3 imp pt, 9.9 US pt, 4.7 l; 1 Carter BBD-6316S (BBD-6343S for California only) downdraught twin barrel carburettor; cleaner air system; fuel feed: mechanical pump; water-cooled, 26.6 imp pt, 31.9 US pt, 15.1 l.

TRANSMISSION driving wheels: rear; clutch: single dry plate; gearbox: mechanical; gears: 3, fully synchronized; ratios: I 3.080, II 1.700, III 1, rev 2.900; lever: steering column; final drive: hypoid bevel; axle ratio: 2.940 - station wagons 3.230; width of rims: 5" - station wagons 5.5"; tyres: F78 x 14 - station wagons H78 x 14.

PERFORMANCE max speed: about 108 mph, 174 km/h; power-weight ratio: Coronet and Coronet Custom 4-dr. sedan 24 lb/hp, 10.9 kg/hp - Charger Series 23.9 lb/hp, 10.8 kg/hp - Charger SE 24.3 lb/hp, 11 kg/hp; speed in direct drive at 1,000 rpm: 25.9 mph, 41.7 km/h; fuel consumption: 16.3 m/imp gal, 13.6 m/US gal, 17.3 l x 100 km.

CHASSIS integral; front suspension: independent, wishbones, lower trailing links, longitudinal torsion bars (anti-roll bar standard only for station wagon and Charger SE), telescopic dampers; rear suspension: rigid axle, semi-elliptic leafsprings, telescopic dampers.

STEERING recirculating ball; turns lock to lock: 5.30.

BRAKES front disc (diameter 10.84 in, 275 mm); swept area: total 365.2 sq in, 2,356 sq cm (station wagons 380.9 sq in, 2,457 sq cm).

ELECTRICAL EQUIPMENT 12 V; 280 A battery; 41 A alternator; Chrysler Essex or Chrysler Prestolite electronic ignition; 4 headlamps.

DIMENSIONS AND WEIGHT wheel base: 115 in, 2,921 mm - sedans and station wagons 118 in, 2,997 mm; tracks: 61.90 in, 1,572 mm front, 62 in, 1,573 mm (station wagons 63.40 in, 1,610 mm) rear; length: 212.70 in, 5,402 mm - sedans 212.90 in, 5,408 mm - station wagons 217.60 in, 5,527 mm; width: 77 in, 1,956 mm - sedans 77.80 in, 1,976 mm - station wagons 78.80 in 2,001 mm; height: 52.50 in, 1,326 mm - sedans 54 in, 1,371 mm - station wagons 56.40 in, 1,432 mm; ground clearance: 5.40 in, 137 mm - sedans 5.60 in, 142 mm - station wagons 6.50 in, 165 mm; dry weight: Coronet 4-dr. sedan 3,615 lb, 1,639 kg - 6-pass. station wagon 4,065 lb, 1,843 kg - Coronet Custom 4-dr. sedan 3,605 lb, 1,635 kg - 6-pass. station wagon 4,065 lb, 1,843 kg - 9-pass. station wagon 4,110 lb, 1,864 kg - Coronet Crestwood 6-pass. station wagon 4,075 lb, 1,848 kg - 9-pass. station wagon 4,115 lb, 1,866 kg - Charger 2-dr. coupé 3,570 lb, 1,619 kg - 2-dr. hardtop 3,950 lb, 1,628 kg - Charger SE 2-dr. coupé 3,650 lb, 1,655 kg; turning circle (between walls): 44.7 ft, 13.6 m - sedans and station wagons 45 ft, 13.8 m; fuel tank: 16.3 imp gal, 19.5 US gal, 74 l - station wagons 17.6 imp gal, 21 US gal, 80 l.

OPTIONAL ACCESSORIES Torqueflite automatic transmission with 3 ratios (I 2.450, II 1.450, III 1, rev 2.200), max ratio of converter at stall 2.16, possible manual selection, steering column or central lever, 2.710 3.210 3.230 3.550

DUESENBERG SSJ Roadster

EXCALIBUR SS Roadster

FORD Pinto 3-door Runabout

BODY 4 seats, separate front seats; back seat folding down to luggage table standard for runabout.

OPTIONAL ACCESSORIES 4-speed fully synchronized mechanical gearbox (I 3.540, II 2.400, III 1.410, IV 1, rev 3.960); A78 x 13 tyres; A70 x 13 and 175R x 13 tyres with 5" wide rims; sunshine roof; vinyl roof; tinted glass; tinted rear window; light alloy wheels; Accent Group equipment; Sports Accent Group equipment; Convenience Group equipment; Luxury Decor Group equipment; back seat folding down to luggage table only for 2-dr. sedan.

83 hp power team

See 54 hp power team, except for:

ENGINE 122 cu in, 2,000 cc (3.58 x 3.03 in, 90.6 x 76.9 mm); compression ratio: 8.2:1; max power (DIN): 83 hp at 5,200 rpm; max torque (DIN): 98 lb ft, 13.5 kg m at 3,800 rpm; max engine rpm: 5,600; 41.5 hp/l; camshafts: 1, overhead; lubricating system capacity: 8.3 imp pt, 9.9 US pt, 4.7 l; 1 Holley-Weber 9510 D3ZF-AB downdraught twin barrel carburettor; cleaner air system; cooling system capacity: 14.1 imp pt, 16.9 US pt, 8 l.

TRANSMISSION axle ratio: 3.400; width of rims: 5''; tyres: A78 x 13.

PERFORMANCE max speed: about 92 mph, 148 km/h; power-weight ratio: 30 lb/hp, 13.6 kg/hp; speed in direct drive at 1,000 rpm: 15.2 mph, 24.4 km/h; fuel consumption: 23 m/imp gal, 19.1 m/US gal, 12.3 l x 100 km.

BRAKES front disc (diameter 9.30 in, 236 mm), rear drum; swept area: front 156.7 sq in, 1,011 sq cm, rear 98.5 sq in, 635 sq cm, total 255.2 sq in, 1,646 sq cm.

DIMENSIONS AND WEIGHT length: 173.80 in, 4,414 mm; width: 69.70 in, 1,770 mm; height: 51.30 in, 1,303 mm; dry weight: 2,490 lb, 1,129 kg; fuel tank: 9.9 imp gal 12 US gal, 45 l.

BODY estate car/station wagon; 2+1 doors; separate front seats; back seat folding down to luggage table.

OPTIONAL ACCESSORIES Select-Shift Cruise-O-Matic automatic transmission with 3 ratios (I 2.460, II 1.460, III 1, rev 2.200), max ratio of converter at stall 2.60, central lever, 3.400 axle ratio; 54 Ah battery; electrically-heated rear window; air-conditioning; Squire equipment; 4-speed fully synchronized mechanical gearbox; vinyl roof and sunshine roof not available.

85 hp power team

See 54 hp power team, except for:

ENGINE 122 cu in, 2,000 cc (3.58 x 3.03 in, 90.9 x 76.9 mm); compression ratio: 8.2:1; max power (DIN): 85 hp at 5,600 rpm; max torque (DIN): 98 lb ft, 13.5 kg m at 3,800 rpm; max engine rpm: 6,000; 42.5 hp/l; camshafts: 1, overhead; lubricating system capacity: 8.3 imp pt, 9.9 US pt, 4.7 l; 1 Holley-Weber 9510 D3Z-AB downdraught twin barrel carburettor; cleaner air system; cooling system capacity: 14.1 imp pt, 16.9 US pt, 8 l.

TRANSMISSION axle ratio: 3.400.

PERFORMANCE max speed: about 95 mph, 153 km/h; power-weight ratio: Pinto 2-dr. sedan 26.8 lb/hp, 12.2 kg/hp; speed in direct drive at 1,000 rpm; 15.2 mph, 24.4 km/h; fuel consumption: 22.2 m/imp gal, 18.5 m/US gal, 12.7 l x 100 km.

DIMENSIONS AND WEIGHT dry weight: plus 68 lb, 31 kg.

OPTIONAL ACCESSORIES Select-Shift Cruise-O-Matic automatic transmission with 3 ratios (I 2.460, II 1.460, III 1, rev 2.200), max ratio of converter at stall 2.60, central lever, 3.400 axle ratio; front disc brakes (diameter 9.30 in, 236 mm), total swept area 241.5 sq in, 1,558 sq cm; 54 Ah battery; electrically-heated rear window; air-conditioning; 4-speed fully synchronized mechanical gearbox not available.

Maverick - Maverick Grabber Series

PRICES IN USA:

1 Maverick	2-door Sedan	**$ 2,208**
2 Maverick	4-door Sedan	**$ 2,263**
3 Maverick Grabber	2-door Sport Sedan	**$ 2,389**

Power team:	Standard for:	Optional for:
84 hp	all	—
88 hp	—	all
138 hp	—	all

84 hp power team

ENGINE front, 4 stroke; 6 cylinders, in line; 200 cu in, 3,277 cc (3.67 x 3.13 in, 93.5 x 79.5 mm); compression ratio: 8.3:1; max power (DIN): 84 hp at 3,800 rpm; max torque (DIN): 151 lb ft, 20.8 kg m at 1,800 rpm; max engine rpm: 4,200; 25.6 hp/l; cast iron cylinder block and head; 7 crankshafts bearings; valves: overhead, in line, push-rods and rockers; hydraulic tappets; camshafts: 1, side; lubrication: rotary pump, full flow filter, 8.3 imp pt, 9.9 US pt, 4.7 l; 1 Carter 9510 D3DF-AA downdraught single barrel carburettor; cleaner air system; fuel feed: mechanical pump; water-cooled, 15 imp pt, 18 US pt, 8.5 l.

TRANSMISSION driving wheels: rear; clutch: single dry plate, semi-centrifugal; gearbox: mechanical; gears: 3; ratios: I 2.990, II 1.750, III 1, rev 3.170; lever: steering column; final drive: hypoid bevel; axle ratio: 3.000; width of rims: 4.5" - Maverick Grabber 6"; tyres: 6.45 x 14 - Maverick Grabber D70 x 14.

PERFORMANCE max speed: about 89 mph, 143 km/h; power-weight ratio: Maverick 4-dr. sedan 33 lb/hp, 15 kg/hp; speed in direct drive at 1,000 rpm: 26 mph, 41.8 km/h; fuel consumption: 21.6 m/imp gal, 18 m/US gal, 13.1 l x 100 km.

CHASSIS integral; front suspension: independent, wishbones, lower trailing links, coil springs, anti-roll bar, telescopic dampers; rear suspension: rigid axle, semi-elliptic leafsprings, telescopic dampers.

STEERING recirculating ball; turns lock to lock: 5.40.

BRAKES drum; swept area: total 267.2 sq in, 1,723 sq cm.

ELECTRICAL EQUIPMENT 12 V; 45 Ah battery; 38 A alternator; Motorcraft distributor; 2 headlamps.

DIMENSIONS AND WEIGHT wheel base: 103 in, 2,616 mm - 4-dr. sedan 109.90 in, 2,791 mm; tracks: 56.50 in, 1,435 mm front, 56.50 in, 1,435 mm rear; length: 183.30 in, 4,656 mm - 4-dr. sedan 190.20 in, 4,831 mm; width: 70.50 in, 1,791 mm; height: 53 in, 1,346 mm - 4-dr. sedan 53.10 in, 1,349 mm; ground clearance: 5.20 in, 132 mm - 4-dr. sedan 5 in, 127 mm; dry weight: Maverick 2-dr. sedan 2,681 lb, 1,216 kg - 4-dr. sedan 2,776 lb, 1,259 kg - Maverick Grabber 2-dr. sport sedan 2,736 lb, 1,241 kg; turning circle (between walls): 39.5 ft, 12 m; fuel tank: 12.5 imp gal, 15 US gal, 57 l.

BODY saloon/sedan; 4-5 seats.

OPTIONAL ACCESSORIES Select Shift Cruise-O-Matic automatic transmission with 3 ratios (I 2.460, II 1.460, III 1, rev 2.200), max ratio of converter at stall 2.14, possible manual selection, steering column lever, 2.790 3.000 axle ratios; C78 x 14 or DR78 x 14 tyres with 6" wide rims; power-assisted steering; 55 Ah battery; electrically-heated rear window; sunshine roof; vinyl roof; Base Accent Group equipment; Luxury Decor Group equipment; air-conditioning.

88 hp power team

See 84 hp power team, except for:

ENGINE 250 cu in, 4,097 cc (3.68 x 3.91 in, 93.5 x 99.3 mm); compression ratio: 8:1; max power (DIN): 88 hp at 3,200 rpm; max torque (DIN): 196 lb ft, 27 kg m at 1,600 rpm; max engine rpm: 3,600; 21.5 hp/l; 1 Carter 9510 D3DF-CA downdraught single barrel carburettor; cleaner air system; cooling system capacity: 16.2 imp pt, 19.4 US pt, 9.2 l.

TRANSMISSION gearbox: Select Shift Cruise-O-Matic automatic transmission (standard), hydraulic torque converter and planetary gears with 3 ratios, max ratio of converter at stall 2.01, possible manual selection; ratios: I 2.460, II 1.460, III 1, rev 2.200; lever: steering column; axle ratio: 2.790.

PERFORMANCE max speed: about 93 mph, 149 km/h; power-weight ratio: Maverick 4-dr. sedan 32.6 lb/hp, 14.8 kg/hp; speed in direct drive at 1,000 rpm: 26.9 mph, 43.3 km/hp; fuel consumption: 20.2 m/imp gal, 16.8 m/US gal, 14 l x 100 km.

DIMENSIONS AND WEIGHT dry weight: plus 90 lb, 41 kg.

OPTIONAL ACCESSORIES central lever; 3.000 axle ratio.

138 hp power team

See 84 hp power team, except for:

ENGINE 8 cylinders; 302 cu in, 4,950 cc (4 x 3 in, 101.6 x 76.2 mm); compression ratio: 8:1; max power (DIN): 138 hp at 4,200 rpm; max torque (DIN): 234 lb ft, 32.3 kg m at 2,200 rpm; max engine rpm: 4,600; 27.9 hp/l; 5 crankshaft bearings; camshafts: 1, at centre of Vee; 1 Rawsonville 9510 D3ZF-EA (9510 D3ZF-AD for California only) downdraught twin barrel carburettor; cleaner air

FORD Pinto Station Wagon

FORD Maverick 4-door Sedan

FORD Maverick Grabber 2-door Sport Sedan

FORD Country Squire Station Wagon

FORD Thunderbird 2-door Hardtop

GLASSIC Roadster

BRAKES front disc (diameter 11.72 in, 298 mm), internal radial fins, rear drum, servo; swept area: front 232 sq in, 1,497 sq cm, rear 173.2 sq in, 2,407 sq cm, total 405.2 sq in, 3,904 sq cm.

ELECTRICAL EQUIPMENT 12 V; 77 Ah battery; 65 A alternator; Autolite distributor; 4 headlamps.

DIMENSIONS AND WEIGHT wheel base: 120.40 in, 3,058 mm; tracks: 63.01 in, 1,600 mm front, 63.09 in, 1,602 mm rear; length: 218.90 in, 5,560 mm; width: 79.70 in, 2,024 mm; height: 53.07 in, 1,348 mm; ground clearance: 5.40 in, 137 mm; dry weight: 4,742 lb, 2,150 kg; turning circle (between walls): 46.7 ft, 14.2 m; fuel tank: 18.7 imp gal, 22.5 US gal, 85 l.

BODY hardtop; 2 doors; 6 seats, bench front seats.

OPTIONAL ACCESSORIES limited slip differential; 3.250 axle ratio; tyres: LR78 x 15; automatic levelling control; adjustable tilt of steering wheel; heavy duty suspension; Sure Track Brake Control system; 70 A alternator; electrically controlled sunshine roof; vinyl roof; electrically heated rear window; separate front seats; tinted glass; air-conditioning.

208 hp power team

(optional).

See 208 hp power team, except for:

ENGINE 460 cu in, 7,539 cc (4.36 x 3.85 in, 110.7 x 97.8 mm); max torque (DIN): 338 lb ft, 46.6 kg m at 2,800 rpm; max engine rpm: 4,800; 26.9 hp/l; 1 Rawsonville 9510 D3VF-AC downdraught 4-barrel carburettor; cleaner air system; cooling system capacity: 32.4 imp pt, 38.9 US pt, 18.4 l.

TRANSMISSION gearbox: max ratio of converter at stall 2.06.

GLASSIC USA

Glassic Series

PRICES IN USA:

Glassic	Phaeton	**$ 6,995**
Glassic	Roadster	**$ 6,995**

210 hp power team

(standard).

ENGINE Ford, front, 4 stroke; 8 cylinders; 302 cu in, 4,950 cc (4 x 3 in, 101.6 x 76.2 mm); compression ratio: 9:1; max power (SAE): 210 hp; 42.4 hp/l; cast iron cylinder block and head; 5 crankshaft bearings; valves: overhead, in line, push-rods and rockers, hydraulic tappets; camshafts: 1, at centre of Vee; lubrication: gear pump, full flow filter, 8.3 imp pt, 9.9 US pt, 4.7 l; 1 Autolite downdraught twin barrel carburettor; fuel feed: mechanical pump; water-cooled, 22.4 imp pt, 26.8 US pt, 12.7 l.

TRANSMISSION gearbox: mechanical; gears: 3, fully synchronized; ratios: I 3.340, II 1.850, III 1, rev 4.530; lever: central; final drive: hypoid bevel; axle ratio: 3.000; width of rims: 5"; tyres: 7.35 x 15.

PERFORMANCE max speed: not declared; power-weight ratio: 11 lb/hp, 5 kg/hp; speed in direct drive at 1,000 rpm: not declared; fuel consumption: not declared.

CHASSIS box-type ladder frame with cross members; front suspension: rigid axle, semi-elliptic leafsprings, telescopic dampers; rear suspension: rigid axle, semi-elliptic leafsprings, telescopic dampers.

STEERING worm and roller; turns lock to lock: 3.75.

BRAKES drum; swept area: total 175.7 sq in, 1,134 sq cm.

ELECTRICAL EQUIPMENT 12 V; 40 Ah battery; 32 A alternator; Autolite distributor; 2 headlamps.

DIMENSIONS AND WEIGHT wheel base: 102 in, 2,591 mm; tracks: 54 in, 1,372 mm front, 56.50 in, 1,435 mm rear; length: 156 in, 3,962 mm; width: 61 in, 1,549 mm; height: 60 in, 1,524 mm; ground clearance: 9 in, 229 mm; dry weight: 2,300 lb, 1,043 kg; turning circle (between walls): 40 ft, 12.2 m; fuel tank: 11 imp gal, 13 US gal, 50 l.

BODY in plastic material.

OPTIONAL ACCESSORIES Select-Shift automatic transmission.

IMPERIAL USA

Le Baron Series

PRICES IN USA:

1 Le Baron	2-door Hardtop	**$ 6,669**
2 Le Baron	4-door Hardtop	**$ 6,897**

Power team:	Standard for:	Optional for:
208 hp	both	—
215 hp	both	—

208 hp power team

(only for California).

ENGINE front, 4 stroke: 8 cylinders; 440 cu in, 7,210 cc (4.32 x 3.75 in, 109.7 x 95.2 mm); compression ratio: 8.2:1; max power (DIN): 208 hp at 3,600 rpm; max torque (DIN): 340 lb ft, 46.9 kg m at 2,000 rpm; max engine rpm: 4,000; 28.8 hp/l; cast iron cylinder block and head; 5 crankshaft bearings; valves: overhead, in line, push-rods and rockers, hydraulic tappets; camshafts: 1, at centre of Vee; lubrication: rotary pump, full flow filter, 8.3 imp pt, 9.9 US pt, 4.7 l; 1 Carter TQ-6411S downdraught 4-barrel carburettor; cleaner air system with air pump; fuel feed: mechanical pump; water-cooled, 29.9 imp pt, 35.9 US pt, 17 l.

TRANSMISSION driving wheels: rear; gearbox: Torqueflite automatic transmission, hydraulic torque converter and planetary gears with 3 ratio, max ratio of converter at stall 2.02, possible manual selection; ratios: I 2.450, II 1.450, III 1, rev 2.200; lever: steering column; final drive: hypoid bevel; axle ratio: 3.230; width of rims: 6''; tyres: L84 x 15.

PERFORMANCE max speed: about 111 mph, 178 km/h; power-weight ratio: 2-dr. hardtop 24.1 lb/hp, 10.9 kg/hp - 4-dr. hardtop 24.8 lb/hp, 11.2 kg:hp; speed in direct drive at 1,000 rpm: 28.6 mph, 46 km/h; fuel consumption: 13.9 m/imp gal, 11.6 m/US gal, 20,3 l x 100 km.

CHASSIS integral, front auxiliary frame with cross members; front suspension: independent, wishbones, longitudinal torsion bars, anti-roll bar, telescopic dampers; rear suspension: rigid axle, semi-elliptic leafsprings, telescopic dampers.

STEERING recirculating ball, servo; turns lock to lock: 3.50.

BRAKES front disc (diameter 11.56 in, 294 mm), internal radial fins; rear drum (diameter 11 in, 279 mm), servo; swept area: total 428.1 sq in, 2,761 sq cm.

ELECTRICAL EQUIPMENT 12 V; 380 A battery; 60 A alternator; Chrysler Essex or Chrysler Prestolite electronic ignition; 4 headlamps.

DIMENSIONS AND WEIGHT wheel base: 127 in, 3,226 mm; tracks: 62.40 in, 1,585 mm front, 63.40 in, 1,610 mm rear; length: 235.30 in, 5,982 mm; width: 79.60 in, 2,022 mm; height: 55.60 in, 1,412 mm - 4-dr. hardtop 56.20 in, 1,427 mm; ground clearance: 6.60 in, 168 mm; dry weight: 2-dr. hardtop 5,020 lb, 2,277 kg - 4-dr. hardtop 5,150 lb, 2,336 kg; turning circle (between walls): 47.9 ft, 14.6 m; fuel tank: 19.1 imp gal, 23 US gal, 87 l.

BODY hardtop; 6 seats; electrically-controlled windows; electronic digital clock; air-conditioning.

OPTIONAL ACCESSORIES tilt and telescopic steering wheel; security alarm system; electrically-controlled sunshine roof.

215 hp power team

See 208 hp power team, except for:

ENGINE max power (DIN): 215 hp at 3,600 rpm; max torque (DIN): 345 lb ft, 47.6 kg m at 2,000 rpm; max engine rpm: 4,000; 29.8 hp/l; 1 Carter TQ-6324S (TQ-6411S for California only) downdraught 4-barrel carburettor.

PERFORMANCE max speed: about 114 mph, 183 km/h; power-weight ratio: 2-dr. hardtop 23.3 lb/hp, 10.6 kg/hp - 4-dr. hardtop 24 lb/hp, 10.9 kg/hp; fuel consumption: 13.8 m/imp gal, 11.5 m/US gal, 20.5 l x 100 km.

INTERNATIONAL USA

Scout Series

PRICE IN USA:

Scout	Station Wagon	**$ 3,422**

IMPERIAL Le Baron 2-door Hardtop

INTERNATIONAL Scout Station Wagon

INTERNATIONAL Travelall 1110 Station Wagon

113.1 hp power team

(standard).

ENGINE front, 4 stroke; 6 cylinders, in line; 258 cu in, 4,228 cc (3.75 x 3.89 in, 95.2 x 98.8 mm); compression ratio: 8:1; max power (DIN): 113.1 hp at 4,000 rpm; max torque (DIN): 191 lb ft, 26.4 kg m at 2,000 rpm; max engine rpm: 4,000 26.7 hp/l; cast iron cylinder block and head; 5 crankshaft bearings; valves: overhead, in line, push-rods and rockers, hydraulic tappets; camshafts: 1, side; lubrication: gear pump, full flow filter, 11.6 imp pt, 14 US pt,, 6.6 l; 1 Holley downdraught single barrel carburettor; fuel feed: mechanical pump; water-cooled, 19.9 imp pt, 24 US pt, 11.3 l.

TRANSMISSION driving wheels: rear; clutch: single dry plate; gearbox: mechanical; gears: 3, II and III synchronized; ratios: I 3.339, II 1.851, III 1, rev 4.351; lever: central; final drive: hypoid bevel; axle ratio: 3.310; width of rims: 5.5"; tyres: E78 x 15.

PERFORMANCE max speed: about 81 mph, 136 km/h; power-weight ratio: 30 lb/hp, 13.6 kg/hp; carrying capacity: 950 lb, 430 kg; speed in direct drive at 1,000 rpm: 20.5 mph, 33 km/h; fuel consumption: 12.1 m/imp gal, 10 m/US gal, 23.3 l x 100 km.

CHASSIS box-type ladder frame; front suspension: rigid axle, semi-elliptic leafsprings, telescopic dampers; rear suspension: rigid axle, semi-elliptic leafsprings, telescopic dampers.

STEERING worm and roller.

BRAKES drum; swept area: front 93.7 sq in, 604 sq cm, rear 82 sq in, 529 sq cm, total 175.7 sq in, 1,133 sq cm.

ELECTRICAL EQUIPMENT 12 V; 50 Ah battery; 37 A alternator; 2 iodine headlamps.

DIMENSIONS AND WEIGHT wheel base: 100 in, 2,540 mm; tracks: 57.20 in, 1,453 mm front, 57.20 in, 1,453 mm rear; length: 165.20 in, 4,196 mm; width: 70 in, 1,778 mm; height: 67.20 in, 1,707 mm; dry weight: 3,390 lb, 1,538 kg; distribution of weight: 53.1% front, 46.9% rear; turning circle (between walls): 36.7 ft, 11.2 m; fuel tank: 15.8 imp gal, 19 US gal, 72 l.

BODY estate car/station wagon; 2+1 doors; 5 seats, bench front seats.

OPTIONAL ACCESSORIES 3.730 or 4.270 axle ratio; 3-speed automatic transmission; 4-wheel drive; gearbox with transfer box; limited slip differential; servo brake; air-conditioning; front bucket seats with console; heavy-duty off-road equipment, recirculating ball steering system with servo.

137 hp power team

(optional).

See 113.1 hp power team, except for:

ENGINE 8 cylinders; 304 cu in, 4,982 cc (3.88 x 3.22 in, 98.5 x 81.7 mm); compression ratio: 8.19:1 max power (DIN): 137 hp at 4,000 rpm; max torque (DIN): 233 lb ft, 32.1 kg m at 2,400 rpm; max engine rpm: 4.000; 27.4 hp/l; camshafts: 1, at centre of Vee; lubricating system capacity: 16.7 imp pt, 20 US pt, 9.5 l; 1 Holley downdraught twin barrel carburettor; cooling system capacity: 31.7 imp pt, 38 US pt, 18 l.

TRANSMISSION gearbox ratios: I 2.800, II 1.851, III 1, rev 4.351.

PERFORMANCE max speed: about 90 mph, 145 km/h; power-weight ratio: 26.1 lb/hp, 11.1 kg/hp; fuel consumption: 12.4 m/imp gal, 10.2 m/US gal, 22.7 l x 100 km.

DIMENSIONS AND WEIGHT dry weight: 3,584 lb, 1,625 kg.

OPTIONAL ACCESSORIES dual exhaust system.

143.5 hp power team

(optional).

See 113.1 hp power team, except for:

ENGINE 8 cylinders; 345 cu in, 5,654 cc (3.88 x 3.66 in, 98.5 x 92.9 mm); compression ratio: 8.05:1; max power (DIN): 143.5 hp at 3,600 rpm; max torque (DIN): 263 lb ft, 36.3 kg m at 2,000 rpm; max engine rpm: 3,800; 25.3 hp/l; camshafts: 1, at centre of Vee; lubricating system capacity: 11.6 imp pt, 14 US pt, 6.6 l; 1 Holley downdraught twin barrel carburettor; cooling system capacity: 33.3 imp pt, 40 US pt, 18.9 l.

TRANSMISSION gearbox ratios: I 2.800, II 1.851, III 1, rev 4.351.

PERFORMANCE max speed: about 93 mph, 149 km/h; power-weight ratio: 25.1 lb/hp, 11.4 kg/hp; fuel consumption: 12.3 m/imp gal, 10.5 m/US gal, 22.3 l x 100 km.

IMPERIAL Le Baron Series

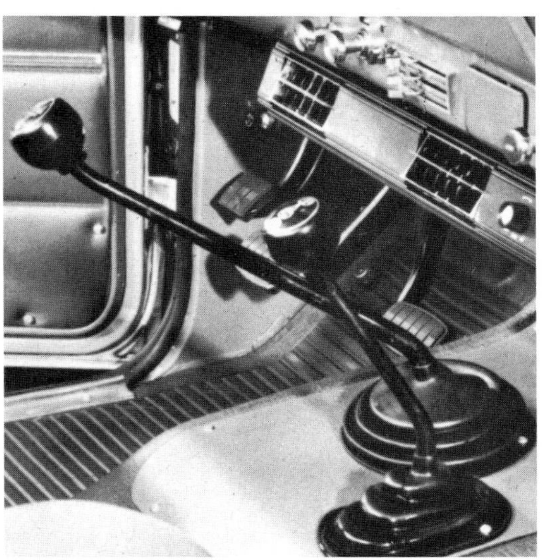

INTERNATIONAL Scout Station Wagon

INTERNATIONAL 143.5 hp engine

DIMENSIONS AND WEIGHT dry weight: 3,609 lb, 1,637 kg.

OPTIONAL ACCESSORIES dual exhaust system.

Travelall Series

PRICES IN USA:

Travelall 1010	Station Wagon	**$ 3,652**
Travelall 1110	Station Wagon	**$ 3,579**
Travelall 1210	Station Wagon	**$ 3,706**

Power team:	Standard for:	Optional for:
113.1 hp	all	—
137 hp	—	all
143.5 hp	—	all
178.8 hp	—	all

113.1 hp power team

ENGINE front, 4 stroke; 6 cylinders, in line; 258 cu in, 4,228 cc (3.75 x 3.89 in, 95.2 x 98.8 mm); compression ratio: 8:1; max power (DIN): 113.1 hp at 4,000 rpm; max torque (DIN): 191 lb ft, 26.3 kg m at 2,000 rpm; max engine rpm: 4,000; 26.8 hp/l; cast iron cylinder block and head; 7 crankshaft bearings; valves: overhead, in line, push-rods and rockers, hydraulic tappets; camshafts: 1, side; lubrication: gear pump, full flow filter, 10 imp pt, 12 US pt, 5.7 l; 1 Holley downdraught single barrel carburettor; fuel feed: mechanical pump; water-cooled, 23.2 imp pt, 27.9 US pt, 13.2 l.

TRANSMISSION driving wheels: rear; clutch: single dry plate; gearbox: mechanical; gears: 3, fully synchronized; ratios: I 3.060, II 1.500, III 1, rev 3.390; lever: steering column; final drive: hypoid bevel; axle ratio: 3.070; width of rims: 5.5" - Travelall 1210 6"; tyres: G78 x 15 - Travelall 1210 8.00 x 16.5.

PERFORMANCE max speed: about 82 mph, 132 km/h; power-weight ratio: Travelall 1010 37.6 lb/hp, 17.1 kg/hp - Travelall 1110 37.4 lb/hp, 17 kg/hp - Travelall 1210 40.1 lb/hp, 18.2 kg/hp; carrying capacity: 1,554 lb, 705 kg - Travelall 1210 1,995 lb, 905 kg; speed in direct drive at 1,000 rpm: 23 mph, 37 km/h; fuel consumption: 12.5 m/imp gal, 10.4 m/US gal, 22.6 l x 100 km.

CHASSIS ladder frame (for Travelall 1010 box-type ladder frame); front suspension: rigid axle, semi elliptic leafsprings, telescopic dampers (for Travelall 1010 independent, wishbones, longitudinal torsion bars, telescopic dampers); rear suspension: rigid axle, semi-elliptic leafsprings, telescopic dampers.

STEERING recirculating ball.

BRAKES drum (for Travelall 1010 only: front disc, rear drum, servo); swept area: Travelall 1010 front 135.6 sq in, 874 sq cm, rear 101.8 sq in, 656 sq cm, total 237.4 sq in, 1,530 sq cm - Travelall 1110 front 143 sq in, 923 sq cm, rear 101.8 sq in, 656 sq cm, total 244.8 sq in, 1,579 sq cm - Travelall 1210 front 122.8 sq in, 792 sq cm, rear 122.7 sq in, 791 sq cm, total 245.5 sq in, 1,583 sq cm.

ELECTRICAL EQUIPMENT 12 V; 50 Ah battery; 37 A alternator; 2 headlamps.

DIMENSIONS AND WEIGHT wheel base: 119 in, 3,023 mm; tracks: Travelall 1010 63 in, 1,600 mm (Travelall 1110 61.40 in, 1,560 mm - Travelall 1210 63.60 in, 1,615 mm) front, 61.40 in, 1,560 mm (Travelall 1210 63 in, 1,600 mm) rear; length: 203.90 in, 5.179 mm; width: 77.60 in, 1,971 mm; height: Travelall 1010 66.50 in, 1,689 mm - Travelall 1110 68.90 in, 1,750 mm - Travelall 1210 69 in, 1,753 mm; ground clearance: Travelall 1010 7.50 in, 191 mm - Travelall 1110 7.10 in, 180 mm - Travelall 1210 8.40 in, 213 mm; dry weight: Travelall 1010 4,250 lb, 1,928 kg - Travelall 1110 4,230 lb, 1,919 kg - Travelall 1210 4,535 lb, 2,057 kg; distribution of weight: 51% front, 49% rear - Travelall 1210 45% front, 55% rear; turning circle (between walls): Travelall 1010 47.8 ft, 14.6 m - Travelall 1110 43.8 ft, 13.4 m - Travelall 1210 43.4 ft, 13.2 m; fuel tank: 16.7 imp gal, 20 US gal, 76 l.

BODY estate car/station wagon; 4 + 1 doors; 6 or 9 seats, bench front seats.

OPTIONAL ACCESSORIES 3.310 3.540 3.730 4.090 4.560 axle ratios; automatic transmission; 4-speed mechanical gearbox; 5-speed mechanical gearbox; 5-speed mechanical gearbox with overdrive; 4-wheel drive, gearbox with transfer box (for Travelall 1110 and 1210 only); limited slip differential; power-assisted steering; servo brake (for Travelall 1110 and 1210 only); Anti-Skid device brake system (for Travelall 1010 and 1110 only); separate front seats; air-conditioning; automatic cruise control system.

137 hp power team

See 113.1 hp power team, except for:

ENGINE 8 cylinders; 304 cu in, 4,982 cc (3.88 x 3.22 in, 98.5 x 81.7 mm); compression ratio: 8.19:1; max power

137 HP POWER TEAM

(DIN): 137 hp at 4,000 rpm; max torque (DIN): 233 lb ft, 32.1 kg m at 2,400 rpm; 27.4 hp/l; 5 crankshaft bearings; camshafts: 1, at centre of Vee; lubricating system capacity: 11.6 imp pt, 14 US pt, 6.6 l; cooling system capacity: 31.7 imp pt, 38.1 US pt, 18 l.

PERFORMANCE max speed: about 90 mph, 145 km/h; power-weight ratio: Travelall 1010 31 lb/hp, 14 kg/hp - Travelall 1110 30.9 lb/hp, 13.9 kg/hp - Travelall 1210 33.1 lb/hp, 15 kg/hp; fuel consumption: 12.4 m/imp gal, 10.2 m/US gal, 22.7 l x km 100.

143.5 hp power team

See 113.1 hp power team, except for:

ENGINE 8 cylinders; 345 cu in, 5,654 cc (3.88 x 3.66 in, 98.5 x 92.9 mm); compression ratio: 8.05:1; max power (DIN): 143.5 hp at 3,600 rpm; max torque (DIN): 262 lb ft, 36.1 kg m at 2,000 rpm; max engine rpm: 3,800; 25.4 hp/l; lubricating system capacity: 11.6 imp pt, 14 US pt, 6.6 l; cooling system capacity: 33.3 imp pt, 40 US pt, 18.9 l.

PERFORMANCE max speed: about 92 mph, 148 km/h; power-weight ratio: Travelall 1010 29.6 lb/hp, 13.4 kg/hp - Travelall 1110 29.5 lb/hp, 13.3 kg/hp - Travelall 1210 31.6 lb/hp, 14.3 kg/hp; fuel consumption: 13.2 m/imp gal, 11 m/US gal, 21.4 l x 100 km.

178.8 hp power team

See 113.1 hp power team, except for:

ENGINE 8 cylinders; 392 cu in, 6,424 cc (4.12 x 3.66 in, 104.6 x 92.9 mm); compression ratio: 8.02:1; max power (DIN): 178.8 hp at 3,600 rpm; max torque (DIN): 297 lb ft, 41 kg m at 2,400 rpm; max engine rpm: 3,600; 27.8 hp/l; 5 crankshaft bearings; camshafts: 1, at centre of Vee; lubricating system capacity: 16.7 imp pt, 20.1 US pt, 9.5 l; cooling system capacity: 35 imp pt, 42.1 US pt, 19.9 l.

PERFORMANCE max speed: about 98 mph, 157 km/h; power-weight ratio: Travelall 1010 23.8 lb/hp, 10.8 kg/hp - Travelall 1110 23.7 lb/hp, 10.7 kg/hp - Travelall 1210 25.4 lb/hp, 11.5 kg/hp; fuel consumption: 13.5 m/imp gal, 11.2 m/US gal, 21 l x 100 km.

JEEP CORPORATION USA

Jeep CJ5 - Jeep CJ6 - Jeep Renegade Series

PRICES IN USA:

1 Jeep CJ5	Roadster	**$ 3,021**
2 Jeep CJ6	Roadster	**$ 3,111**
3 Jeep Renegade	Roadster	**$ —**

Power team:	Standard for:	Optional for:
100 hp	1,2	—
110 hp	—	1,2
150 hp	3	1,2

100 hp power team

ENGINE front, 4 stroke; 6 cylinders, in line; 232 cu in, 3,802 mm (3.75 x 3.50 in, 95.2 x 88.8 mm); compression ratio: 8:1; max power (DIN): 100 hp at 3,600 rpm; max torque (DIN): 185 lb ft, 25.5 kg m at 1,800 rpm; max engine rpm: 4,000; 26.3 hp/l; cast iron cylinder block and head; 7 crankshaft bearings; valves: overhead, in line, push-rods and rockers, hydraulic tappets; camshafts: 1, side; lubrication: gear pump, full flow filter, 10 imp pt, 12 US pt, 5.7 l; 1 downdraught single barrel carburettor; fuel feed: mechanical pump; water-cooled, 17.4 imp pt, 21 US pt, 9.9 l.

TRANSMISSION driving wheels: front (automatically engaged with transfer box low ratio) and rear; clutch: single dry plate; gearbox: mechanical; gears: 3, with high and low ratios, fully synchronized; ratios: I 3,100, II 1,612, III 1, rev 3,100; low ratios: I 2,030, II 1; levers: central; axle ratio: 3,730; width of rims: 6''; tyres: F78 x 15.

PERFORMANCE max speed: about 91 mph, 147 km/h; power-weight ratio: Jeep CJ5 23.4 lb/hp, 10.6 kg/hp - Jeep CJ6 24 lb/hp, 10.9 kg/hp; speed in direct drive at 1,000 rpm: 25 mph, 40.2 km/h; fuel consumption: 12.8 m/imp gal, 10.6 m/US gal, 22.1 l x 100 km.

CHASSIS box-type ladder frame; front suspension: rigid axle, semi-elliptic leafsprings, telescopic dampers; rear suspension: rigid axle, semi-elliptic leafsprings, telescopic dampers.

JEEP CORPORATION Jeep CJ5 Roadster

JEEP CORPORATION Jeep Commando Station Wagon

JEEP CORPORATION Jeep Wagoneer Custom Station Wagon

STEERING recirculating ball.

BRAKES drum; swept area: front 90.4 sq in, 583 sq cm, rear 90.4 sq in, 583 sq cm, total 180.8 sq in, 1,166 sq cm.

ELECTRICAL EQUIPMENT 12 V; 50 Ah battery; 37 A alternator; Delco-Remy distributor; 2 headlamps.

DIMENSIONS AND WEIGHT wheel base: 84 in, 2,134 mm - Jeep CJ6 104 in, 2,642 mm; tracks: 51.50 in, 1,308 mm front, 50 in, 1,270 mm rear; length: 138.90 in, 3,528 mm - Jeep CJ6 158.90 in, 4,036 mm; width: 71.70 in, 1,821 mm; height: 69.50 in, 1,765 mm - Jeep CJ6 68.30 in, 1,735 mm; ground clearance: 8.60 in, 218 mm front, 8 in, 203 mm rear; dry weight: Jeep CJ5 2,337 lb, 1,060 kg - Jeep CJ6 2,399 lb, 1,088 kg; turning circle (between walls): 32.9 ft, 10 m - Jeep CJ6 37.8 ft, 11.5 m; fuel tank: 13 imp gal, 15.5 US gal, 59 l.

OPTIONAL ACCESSORIES 4-speed mechanical gearbox only for Jeep CJ5; rear limited slip differential; power-assisted steering; servo brake; all or half metal top; all or half fabric top; rear bench seats; racing style roll bar; heavy-duty cooling system.

110 hp power team

See 100 hp power team, except for:

ENGINE 258 cu in, 4,228 cc (3.75 x 3.90 in, 95.2 x 99 mm); max power (DIN): 110 hp at 3,500 rpm; max torque (DIN): 195 lb ft, 26.9 kg m at 2,000 rpm; max engine rpm: 3,900; 26 hp/l.

PERFORMANCE max speed: about 95 mph, 153 km/h; power-weight ratio: Jeep CJ5 21.2 lb/hp, 9.6 kg/hp - Jeep CJ6 21.8 lb/hp, 9.9 kg/hp; fuel consumption: 12.5 m/imp gal, 10.4 m/US gal, 22.6 l x 100 km.

150 hp power team

See 100 hp power team, except for:

ENGINE 8 cylinders; 304 cu in, 4,982 cc (3.75 x 3.44 in, 95.2 x 87.3 mm); compression ratio: 8.4:1; max power (DIN): 150 hp at 4,200 rpm; max torque (DIN): 245 lb ft, 33.8 kg m at 2,500 rpm; max engine rpm: 4,600; 30.1 hp/l; 5 cranksnaft bearings; camshafts: 1, at centre of Vee; lubricating system capacity: 8.3 imp pt, 9.9 US pt, 4.7 l; 1 downdraught twin barrel carburettor; cooling system capacity: 23.2 imp pt, 28 US pt, 13.2 l.

TRANSMISSION gearbox ratios: I 2.997, II 1.832, III 1, rev 2.997; tyres: Jeep Renegade H78 x 15.

PERFORMANCE max speed: about 102 mph, 164 km/h; power-weight ratio: Jeep CJ5 16.6 lb/hp, 7.5 kg/hp - Jeep CJ6 17 lb/hp, 7.7 kg/hp; fuel consumption: 12.1 m/imp gal, 10.1 m/US gal, 23.4 l x 100 km.

DIMENSIONS AND WEIGHT dry weight: plus 154 lb, 70 kg.

BODY (only for Jeep Renegade) racing style roll bar (standard); luxury equipment.

OPTIONAL ACCESSORIES 4-speed mechanical gearbox not available.

Jeep Commando Series

PRICES IN USA:

1 Jeep Commando	Roadster	**$ 3,305**
2 Jeep Commando	Station Wagon	**$ 3,456**

Power team:	Standard for:	Optional for:
100 hp	both	—
110 hp	—	both
150 hp	—	both

100 hp power team

ENGINE front, 4 stroke; 6 cylinders, in line; 232 cu in, 3,802 cc (3.75 x 3.50 in, 95.2 x 88.8 mm); compression ratio: 8:1; max power (DIN): 100 hp at 3,600 rpm; max torque (DIN): 185 lb ft, 25.5 kg m at 1,800 rpm; max engine rpm: 4,000; 26.3 hp/l; cast iron cylinder block and head; 7 crankshafts bearings; valves: overhead, in line, push-rods and rockers, hydraulic tappets; camshafts: 1, side; lubrication: gear pump, full flow filter, 10 imp pt, 12 US pt, 5.7 l; 1 single barrel carburettor fuel feed: mechanical pump; water-cooled, 17.4 imp pt, 21 US pt, 9.9 l.

JEEP CORPORATION Jeep CJ5 Roadster

JEEP CORPORATION Jeep Commando Station Wagon

JEEP CORPORATION Jeep Wagoneer Custom Station Wagon

TRANSMISSION driving wheels: front (automatically engaged with transfer box low ratio) and rear; clutch: single dry plate; gearbox: mechanical; gears: 3, with high and low ratios, fully synchronized; ratios: I 3,100, II 1,612, III 1, rev 3,100; low ratios: I 2,030, II 1; levers: central; final drive: hypoid bevel; axle ratio: 3.730; width of rims: 6"; tyres: F78 x 15.

PERFORMANCE max speed: about 81 mph, 131 km/h; power-weight ratio: roadster 26.9 lb/hp, 12.2 kg/hp - station wagon 30.1 lb/hp, 13.7 kg/hp; speed in direct drive at 1,000 rpm: 25 mph, 40.2 km/h; fuel consumption 12.7 m/imp gal, 10.6 m/US gal, 22.2 l x 100 km.

CHASSIS box-type ladder frame; front suspension: rigid axle, semi-elliptic leafsprings, anti-roll bar, telescopic dampers; rear suspension: rigid axle semielliptic leafsprings, telescopic dampers.

STEERING recirculating ball.

BRAKES drum; swept area: front 90.4 sq in, 583 sq cm, rear 90.4 sq in, 583 sq cm, total 180.8 sq in, 1,166 sq cm.

ELECTRICAL EQUIPMENT 12 V; 50 Ah battery; 37 A alternator; Delco-Remy distributor; 2 headlamps.

DIMENSIONS AND WEIGHT wheel base: 104 in, 2,642 mm; tracks: 51.50 in 1,308 mm front, 50 in, 1,270 mm rear; length: 174.50 in, 4,432 mm; width: 65.20 in, 1,656 mm; height: 62.40 in, 1,585 mm; ground clearance: 7.50 in, 191 mm; dry weight: roadster 2,690 lb, 1,220 kg - station wagon 3,010 lb, 1,375 kg; turning circle (between walls): 37.8 ft, 11.5 m; fuel tank: 13 imp gal, 15.5 US gal, 59 l.

OPTIONAL ACCESSORIES 4-speed mechanical gearbox; rear limited slip differential; power-assisted steering; servo brake; heavy-duty cooling system; front bench seats; tinted glass; air-conditioning; all fabric top only for roadster.

110 hp power team

See 100 hp power team, except for:

ENGINE 258 cu in, 4,228 cc (3.75 x 3.90 in, 95.2 x 99 mm); max power (DIN): 110 hp at 3,500 rpm; max torque (DIN): 195 lb ft, 26.9 kg m at 2,000 rpm; max engine rpm: 3,900; 26 hp/l

PERFORMANCE max speed: about 85 mph, 136 km/h; power-weight ratio: roadster 24.5 lb/hp, 11.1 kg/hp - station wagon 27.3 lb/hp, 12.5 kg/hp; fuel consumption: 12.4 m/imp gal, 10.4 m/US gal, 22.7 l x 100 km.

OPTIONAL ACCESSORIES Turbo-Hydramatic automatic transmission.

150 hp power team

See 100 hp power team, except for:

ENGINE 8 cylinders; 304 cu in, 4,982 cc (3.75 x 3.44 in, 95.2 x 87.3 mm); compression ratio: 8.4:1; max power (DIN): 150 hp at 4,200 rpm; max torque (DIN): 245 lb ft, 33.8 kg m at 2,500 rpm; max engine rpm: 4,600; 30.1 hp/l; 5 crankshaft bearings; camshafts: 1, at centre of Vee; lubricating system capacity: 8.3 imp pt, 9.9 US pt, 4.7 l; 1 downdraught twin barrel carburettor; cooling system capacity: 23.2 imp pt, 28 US pt, 13.2 l.

TRANSMISSION gearbox ratios: I 2.997, II 1.832, III 1, rev 2.997.

PERFORMANCE max speed: about 93 mph, 150 km/h; power-weight ratio: roadster 17.9 lb/hp, 8.1 kg/hp - station wagon 20.1 lb/hp, 9.2 kg/hp; fuel consumption: 12 m/imp gal, 10 m/US gal, 23.5 l x 100 km.

OPTIONAL ACCESSORIES Turbo-Hydramatic automatic transmission; 4-speed mechanical gearbox not available.

Jeep Wagoneer Series

PRICES IN USA:

1 Jeep Wagoneer Standard	Station Wagon	**$ 4,451**
2 Jeep Wagoneer Custom	Station Wagon	**$ 4,689**

Power team:	Standard for:	Optional for:
110 hp	both	—
175 hp	—	both
195 hp	—	both

110 hp power team

ENGINE front, 4 stroke; 6 cylinders, in line; 258 cu in, 4,228 cc (3.75 x 3.90 in, 95.2 x 99 mm); compression ratio: 8:1; max power (DIN): 110 hp at 3,500 rpm; max torque

110 HP POWER TEAM

(DIN): 195 lb ft, 26.9 kg m at 2,000 rpm; max engine rpm: 3,900; 26 hp/l; cast iron cylinder block and head; 7 crankshaft bearings; valves: overhead, in line, push-rods and rockers, hydraulic tappets; camshafts: 1, side; lubrication: gear pump, full flow filter, 10 imp pt, 12 US pt, 5.7 l; 1 downdraught single barrel carburettor; fuel feed: mechanical pump; water cooled, 17.4 imp pt, 21 US pt, 9.9 l.

TRANSMISSION driving wheels: front (automatically engaged with transfer box low ratio) and rear; clutch: single dry plate; gearbox: mechanical; gears: 3, with high and low ratios, fully synchronized; ratios: I 3.100, II 1.612, III 1, rev 3.100; low ratios: I 2.030, II 1; levers: central; final drive: hypoid bevel; axle ratio: 3.730; width of rims: 6"; tyres: F78 x 15.

PERFORMANCE max speed: about 90 mph, 145 km/h; power-weight ratio: 34.6 lb/hp, 15.7 kg/hp; speed in direct drive at 1,000 rpm: 25 mph, 40.2 km/h; fuel consumption: 12.4 m/imp gal, 10.3 m/US gal, 22.8 l x 100 km.

CHASSIS box-type ladder frame; front suspension: rigid axle, semi-elliptic leafsprings, telescopic dampers; rear suspension: rigid axle, semi-elliptic leafsprings, telescopic dampers.

STEERING recirculating ball; turns lock to lock: 5.25.

BRAKES drum; swept area: front 90.4 sq in, 583 sq cm, rear 90.4 sq in, 583 sq cm, total 180.8 sq in, 1,166 sq cm.

ELECTRICAL EQUIPMENT 12 V; 50 Ah battery; 37 A alternator: Delco-Remy distributor; 2 headlamps.

DIMENSIONS AND WEIGHT wheel base: 110 in, 2,794 mm; tracks: 57.30 in, 1,455 mm front, 57.50 in, 1,460 mm rear; length: 183.70 in, 4,666 mm; width: 75.60 in, 1,920 mm; height: 65.30 in, 1,659 mm; ground clearance: 7.80 in, 198 mm; dry weight: 3,810 lb, 1,728 kg; turning circle (between walls): 44.4 ft, 13.5 m; fuel tank: 18.3 imp gal, 22 US gal, 83 l.

BODY 4+1 doors; 5 seats, separate front seats.

OPTIONAL ACCESSORIES 4-speed mechanical gearbox; Turbo-Hydramatic automatic transmission with steering column lever; rear limited slip differential; power-assisted steering; servo brake; heavy-duty cooling system; tinted glass; air-conditioning.

175 hp power team

See 110 hp power team, except for:

ENGINE 8 cylinders; 360 cu in, 5,899 cc (4.08 x 3.44 in, 103.6 x 87.3 mm); compression ratio: 8.5:1; max power (DIN): 175 hp at 4,000 rpm; max torque (DIN): 285 lb ft, 39.3 kg m at 2,400 rpm; max engine rpm: 4,400; 29.7 hp/l; 5 crankshaft bearings; camshafts: 1, at centre of Vee; lubricating system capacity: 8.3 imp pt, 9.9 US pt, 4.7 l; 1 downdraught twin barrel carburettor; cooling system capacity: 21.6 imp pt, 26 US pt, 12.3 l.

TRANSMISSION gearbox ratios: I 2.997, II 1.832, III 1, rev 2.997; axle ratio: 3.310.

PERFORMANCE max speed: about 99 mph, 160 km/h; power-weight ratio: 25.7 lb/hp, 11.6 kg/hp; speed in direct drive at 1,000 rpm: 25.9 mph, 41.7 km/h; fuel consumption: 11.9 m/imp gal, 9.9 m/US gal, 23.7 l x 100 km.

ELECTRICAL EQUIPMENT 60 Ah battery; 55 A alternator.

DIMENSIONS AND WEIGHT dry weight: plus 200 lb, 91 kg.

OPTIONAL ACCESSORIES 4-wheel drive Quadra-Trac system only with Turbo-Hydramatic automatic transmission.

195 hp power team

See 110 hp power team, except for:

ENGINE 360 cu in, 5,899 cc (4.08 x 3.44 in, 103.6 x 87.3 mm); compression ratio: 8.5:1; max power (DIN): 195 hp at 4,400 rpm; max torque (DIN): 295 lb ft, 40.7 kg m at 2,900 rpm; max engine rpm: 4,800; 33 hp/l; 5 crankshaft bearings; camshafts: 1, at centre of Vee; lubricating system capacity: 8.3 imp pt, 9.9 US pt, 4.7 l; 1 downdraught 4-barrel carburettor; cooling system capacity: 21.6 imp pt, 26 US pt, 12.3 l.

TRANSMISSION gearbox ratios: I 2.997, II 1.832, III 1, rev 2.997; axle ratio: 3.310.

PERFORMANCE max speed: about 104 mph, 167 km/h; power-weight ratio: 20.5 lb/hp, 9.3 kg/hp; speed in direct drive at 1,000 rpm: 25.9 mph, 41.7 km/h; fuel consumption: 11.8 m/imp gal, 9.8 m/US gal, 24 l x 100 km.

LINCOLN Continental 4-door Sedan

LINCOLN Continental Mk IV 2-door Hardtop

MERCURY Comet 2-door Sedan

MERCURY Marquis 2-door Hardtop

MERCURY Colony Park Station Wagon

MOHS Ostentatienne Opera Sedan

202 hp power team

See 161 hp power team, except for:

ENGINE 460 cu in, 7,539 cc (4.36 x 3.85 in, 110.7 x 97.8 mm); max power (DIN): 202 hp at 4,400 rpm; max torque (DIN): 330 lb ft, 45.5 kg m at 2,800 rpm; max engine rpm: 4,800; 26.8 hp/l; lubricating system capacity: 11.6 imp pt, 14 US pt, 6.6 l; 1 Carter 9510 D3VF-AC downdraught 4-barrel carburettor; cleaner air system; cooling system capacity: 32.4 imp pt, 38.9 US pt, 18.4 l.

TRANSMISSION gearbox ratios: I 2.460, II 1.460, III 1, rev 2.180.

PERFORMANCE max speed: about 110 mph, 177 km/h; power-weight ratio: Marquis 4-dr. hardtop 23.4 lb/hp, 10.5 kg/hp - Marquis Brougham 4-dr. hardtop 24.3 lb/hp, 11 kg/hp; fuel consumption: 15.8 m/imp gal, 13.1 m/US gal, 17.9 l x 100 km.

ELECTRICAL EQUIPMENT 85 Ah battery.

DIMENSIONS AND WEIGHT (see 171 hp power team) height: Marquis and Marquis Brougham 2-dr. hardtops 55 in, 1,397 mm; dry weight: Monterey plus 202 lb, 91 kg - Monterey Custom plus 113 lb, 51 kg - Marquis 2-dr. hardtop 4,676 lb, 2,120 kg - 4-dr. pillared hardtop 4,731 lb, 2,145 kg - 4-dr. hardtop 4,736 lb, 2,148 kg - Marquis Brougham 2-dr. hardtop 4,746 lb, 2,152 kg - 4-dr. pillared hardtop 4,801 lb, 2,177 kg - 4-dr. hardtop 4,806 lb, 2,179 kg.

267 hp power team

See 161 hp power team, except for:

ENGINE 460 cu in, 7,539 cc (4.36 x 3.85 in, 110.7 x 97.8 mm); compression ratio: 8.8:1; max power (DIN): 267 hp at 4,600 rpm; max torque (DIN): 383 lb ft, 52.8 kg m at 2,800 rpm; max engine rpm: 5,000; 35.1 hp/l; lubricating system capacity: 11.6 imp pt, 14 US pt, 6.6 l; 1 Carter 9510 D3AF-EB downdraught 4-barrel carburettor; cleaner air system; dual exhaust system; cooling system capacity: 33.1 imp pt, 39.7 US pt, 18.8 l.

TRANSMISSION gearbox ratios: I 2.460, II 1.460, III 1, rev 2.180; axle ratio 3.250; width of rims: station wagons 6.5''; tyres: station wagon JR78 x 15 (standard).

PERFORMANCE max speed: about 119 mph, 191 km/h; power-weight ratio: Marquis 4-dr. hardtop 17.7 lb/hp, 8 kg/hp - Marquis Brougham 4-dr. hardtop 18.6 lb/hp, 8.5 kg/hp; speed in direct drive at 1,000 rpm: 27.4 mph, 44.1 km/h; fuel consumption: 12.7 m/imp gal, 10.5 m/US gal, 22.3 l x 100 km.

BRAKES swept area: station wagons total 405.2 sq in, 2,613 sq cm.

ELECTRICAL EQUIPMENT 85 Ah battery; 61 A alternator.

DIMENSIONS AND WEIGHT (see 167 and 171 power teams) height: Marquis and Marquis Brougham 2-dr. hardtops 55 in, 1,397 mm; dry weight: Monterey plus 202 lb, 91 kg - Monterey Custom and station wagons plus 113 lb, 51 kg - Marquis 2-dr. hardtop 4,676 lb, 2,120 kg - 4-dr. pillared hardtop 4,731 lb, 2,145 kg - 4-dr. hardtop 4,736 lb, 2,148 kg - Marquis Brougham 2-dr. hardtop 4,746 lb, 2,152 kg - 4-dr. pillared hardtop 4,801 lb, 2,177 kg - 4-dr. hardtop 4,806 lb, 2,179 kg.

OPTIONAL ACCESSORIES with petrol injection 3.250 axle ratio.

MOHS — USA

Ostentatienne Opera

PRICE IN USA:

Ostentatienne Opera	Sedan	**$ 19,600**

193 hp power team

(standard).

ENGINE front, 4 stroke; 8 cylinders; 304 cu in, 4,982 cc (3.87 x 3.22 in, 98.2 x 81.7 mm); compression ratio: 8.2:1; max power (SAE): 193 hp at 4,400 rpm; max torque (SAE): 272 lb ft, 37.5 kg m at 2,800 rpm; max engine rpm: 4,400; 38.7 hp/l; cast iron cylinder block and head; 5 crankshaft bearings; valves: overhead, in line, push-rods and rockers, hydraulic tappets; camshafts: 1, at centre of Vee; lubrication: gear pump, full flow filter, 8.3 imp pt, 9.9 US pt, 4.7 l; 1 Holley downdraught twin barrel carburettor; fuel feed: mechanical pump; water-cooled, 28.3 imp pt, 34 US pt, 16.1 l.

TRANSMISSION driving wheels: rear; gearbox: Borg-Warner automatic transmission, hydraulic torque converter and pla-

193 HP POWER TEAM

netary gears with 3 ratios; final drive: hypoid bevel, limited slip differential; axle ratio: 3.110; width of rims: 7''; tyres: 7.50 x 20.

PERFORMANCE max speed: about 100 mph, 161 km/h; power-weight ratio: 29.7 lb/hp, 13.5 kg/hp; fuel consumption: 16.3 m/imp gal, 13.6 m/US gal, 17.3 l x 100 km.

CHASSIS box-type ladder frame; front suspension: independent, wishbones, longitudinal torsion bars, telescopic dampers; rear suspension: rigid axle, semi-elliptic leafsprings, telescopic dampers.

STEERING recirculating ball, servo; turns lock to lock: 3.50.

BRAKES drum, servo; swept area: total 237.4 sq in, 1,531 sq cm.

ELECTRICAL EQUIPMENT 12 V; 72 Ah battery; 60 A alternator; Prestolite distributor; 4 headlamps.

DIMENSIONS AND WEIGHT wheel base: 119 in, 3,023 mm; tracks: 74 in, 1,880 mm front, 74 in, 1,880 mm rear; length: 246 in, 6,250 mm; width: 90 in, 2,286 mm; height: 69 in, 1,753 mm; ground clearance: 8-9 in, 203-229 mm; dry weight: 5,740 lb, 2,604 kg; distribution of weight: 60% front, 40% rear; turning circle (between walls): 44,5 ft, 13.6 m; fuel tank: 14.1 imp gal, 17 US gal, 64 l.

BODY saloon/sedan; 1 rear door; 4 seats, separate front and rear seats; special pivoting safety bucket seats; independent heating, air-conditioning.

250 hp power team

(optional).

See 193 hp power team, except for:

ENGINE 549 cu in, 8,990 cc; max power (SAE): 250 hp at 4,400 rpm; 27.8 hp/l; lubricating system capacity: 10 imp pt, 12 US pt, 5.7 l.

PERFORMANCE max speed: about 115 mph, 185 km/h; power-weight ratio: 24.5 lb/hp, 11.1 kg/hp.

DIMENSIONS AND WEIGHT dry weight: 6,100 lb, 2,767 kg.

OLDSMOBILE USA

Omega Series

PRICES IN USA:

1 Omega	2-door Hatchback Coupé	**$ 2,733**
2 Omega	2-door Pillar Coupé	**$ 2,584**
3 Omega	4-door Pillar Sedan	**$ 2,612**

Power team:	Standard for:	Optional for:
100 hp	all	—
180 hp	—	all

100 hp power team

ENGINE front, 4 stroke; 6 cylinders, in line; 250 cu in, 4,097 cc (3.87 x 3.53 in, 98.2 x 89.6 mm); compression ratio: 8.25:1; max power (DIN): 100 hp at 3,600 rpm; max torque (DIN): 175 lb ft, 24.1 kg m at 1,600 rpm; max engine rpm: 4,000; 24.4 hp/l; cast iron cylinder block and head; 7 crankshaft bearings; valves: overhead, in line, push-rods and rockers, hydraulic tappets; camshafts: 1, side; lubrication: gear pump, full flow filter, 8.3 imp pt, 9.9 US pt, 4.7 l; 1 Rochester 7043017 (7043317 for California only) downdraught single barrel carburettor; fuel feed: mechanical pump; water-cooled, 20.1 imp pt, 24.1 US pt, 11.4 l.

TRANSMISSION driving wheels: rear; clutch: single dry plate; gearbox: mechanical; gears: 3, fully synchronized; ratios: I 2.540, II 1.500, III 1, rev 2.630; lever: steering column; final drive: hypoid bevel; axle ratio: 3.080; width of rims: 5''; tyres: E78 x 14.

PERFORMANCE max speed: about 107 mph, 172 km/h; power-weight ratio: 4-dr. pillar sedan 32.9 lb/hp, 14.9 kg/hp; speed in direct drive at 1,000 rpm: 26.7 mph, 42.9 km/h; fuel consumption: 20.6 m/imp gal, 17.2 m/US gal, 13.7 l x 100 km.

CHASSIS integral, front sub frame; front suspension: independent, wishbones, coil springs, anti-roll bar, telescopic dampers; rear suspension: rigid axle, semi-elliptic leafsprings, telescopic dampers.

STEERING recirculating ball; turns lock to lock: 5.65.

BRAKES drum; swept area: total 268.8 sq in, 1,734 sq cm.

OLDSMOBILE Omega 2-door Hatchback Coupé

OLDSMOBILE Cutlass Colonnade Hardtop Sedan

OLDSMOBILE Cutlass Supreme Colonnade Hardtop Coupé

ELECTRICAL EQUIPMENT 12 V; 2,300 W battery; 37A alternator; Delco-Remy distributor; 2 headlamps.

DIMENSIONS AND WEIGHT wheel base: 111 in, 2,819 mm; tracks: 59.10 in, 1,501 mm front, 58.80 in, 1,493 mm rear; length: 197.50 in, 5,016 mm; width: 72.40 in, 1,839 mm; height: 52.40 in, 1,331 mm - 4-door pillar sedan 53.80 in, 1,367 mm; ground clearance: 4.90 in, 124 mm; dry weight: 2-dr. hatchback coupé 3,339 lb, 1,514 kg - 2-dr. pillar coupé 3,227 lb, 1,463 kg - 4-dr. pillar sedan 3,290 lb, 1,492 kg; turning circle (between walls): 41.2 ft, 12.6 m; fuel tank: 13.4 imp gal, 16 US gal, 61 l.

BODY 5 seats, separate front seats.

OPTIONAL ACCESSORIES Turbo-Hydramatic 350 automatic transmission with 3 ratios (I 2.520, II 1.520, III 1, rev 1.930), max ratio of converter at stall 2.25, steering column lever, 2.730 or 3.080 axle ratio; central lever; limited slip differential; power-assisted steering, variable ratio; servo brake; front disc brakes with servo; air-conditioning.

180 hp power team

See 100 hp power team, except for:

ENGINE 8 cylinders; 350 cu in, 5,736 cc (4.06 x 3.38 in, 103.1 x 85.8 mm); compression ratio: 8.5:1; max power (DIN): 180 hp at 3,800 rpm; max torque (DIN): 275 lb ft, 37.9 kg m at 2,800 rpm; max engine rpm: 4,200; 31.4 hp/l; 5 crankshaft bearings; camshafts: 1, at centre of Vee; 1 Rochester 4MC downdraught 4-barrel carburettor; cooling system capacity: 8.3 imp pt, 9.9 US pt, 4.7 l.

PERFORMANCE max speed: about 115 mph, 185 km/h; power-weight ratio: 4-dr. pillar sedan 19.4 lb/hp, 8.8 kg/hp; fuel consumption: 15.8 m/imp gal, 13.1 m/US gal, 17.9 l x 100 km.

DIMENSIONS AND WEIGHT dry weight: plus 200 lb, 91 kg.

OPTIONAL ACCESSORIES 2.730 axle ratio; Turbo-Hydramatic 350 automatic transmission with max ratio of converter at stall 2.50.

Cutlass - Cutlass "S" - Cutlass Supreme Series

PRICES IN USA:

1 Cutlass	Colonnade Hardtop Coupé	**$ 3,002**
2 Cutlass	Colonnade Hardtop Sedan	**$ 3,086**
3 Cutlass 'S'	Colonnade Hardtop Coupé	**$ 3,107**
4 Cutlass Supreme	Colonnade Hardtop Coupé	**$ 3,265**
5 Cutlass Supreme	Colonnade Hardtop Sedan	**$ 3,336**

Power team:	Standard for:	Optional for:
160 hp	1,2,3	—
180 hp	all	—
250 hp	—	all
270 hp	—	all

160 hp power team

ENGINE front, 4 stroke; 8 cylinders; 350 cu in, 5,736 cc (4.06 x 3.38 in, 103.1 x 85.8 mm); compression ratio: 8.5:1; max power (DIN): 160 hp 3,800 rpm; max torque (DIN): 275 lb ft, 37.9 kg m at 2,400 rpm; max engine rpm: 4,200; 27.9 hp/l; cast iron cylinder block and head; 5 crankshaft bearings; valves: overhead, in line, push-rods and rockers, hydraulic tappets; camshafts: 1, at centre of Vee; lubrication: gear pump, full flow filter, 8.3 imp pt, 9.9 US pt, 4.7 l; 1 Rochester 2GC downdraught twin barrel carburettor; fuel feed: mechanical pump; water-cooled, 25.3 imp pt, 30.4 US pt, 14.4 l.

TRANSMISSION driving wheels: rear; gearbox: Turbo-Hydramatic 350 automatic transmission, hydraulic torque converter and planetary gears with 3 ratios, max ratio of converter at stall 2.50, possible manual selection; ratios: I 2.520, II 1.520, III 1, rev 1.930; lever: steering column or central; final drive: hypoid bevel, axle ratio: 2.730; width of rims: 6"; tyres: F78 x 14.

PERFORMANCE max speed: 98 mph, 157 km/h; power-weight ratio: Cutlass Colonnade hardtop sedan 24.4 lb/hp, 11.1 kg/hp; speed in direct drive at 1,000 rpm: 28 mph, 45 km/h; fuel consumption: 17.4 m/imp gal, 14.5 m/US gal, 16.2 l x 100 km.

CHASSIS channel section perimeter type frame; front suspension: independent, wishbones, coil springs, anti-roll bar, telescopic dampers; rear suspension rigid axle, lower trailing radius arms, upper oblique torque arms, coil springs, telescopic dampers.

STEERING recirculating ball; turns lock to lock: 6.20.

BRAKES front disc (diameter 10.90 in, 256 mm), internal radial fins, rear drum; swept area: total 345.6 sq in, 2,229 sq cm.

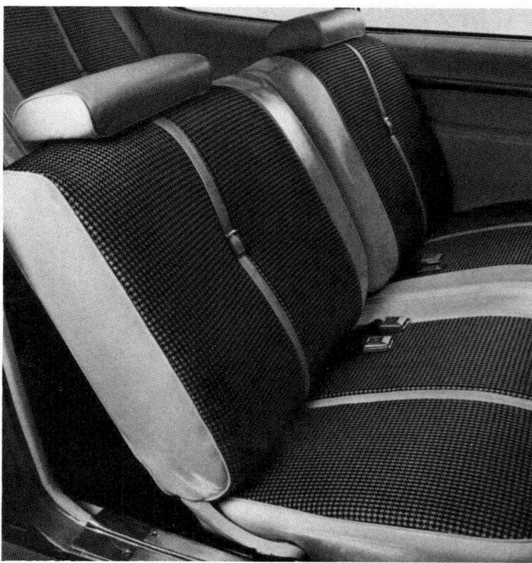

OLDSMOBILE Omega 2-door Hatchback Coupé

OLDSMOBILE Cutlass Colonnade Hardtop Sedan

OLDSMOBILE Cutlass Supreme Colonnade Hardtop Coupé

ELECTRICAL EQUIPMENT 12 V; 61 Ah battery; 37 A alternator; Delco-Remy distributor; 2 headlamps.

DIMENSIONS AND WEIGHT wheel base: 112 in, 2,845 mm - hardtop sedan 116 in, 2,946 mm; tracks: 61.40 in, 1,560 mm front, 60.70 in, 1,542 mm rear; length: 207 in, 5,258 mm - hardtop sedan 211 in, 5,359 mm; width: 76.50 in, 1,943 mm; height: 53.30 in, 1,359 mm - hardtop sedan 54 in, 1,371 mm; ground clearance: 5.40 in, 137 mm; dry weight: Cutlass Colonnade hardtop coupé 3,829 lb, 1,736 kg - hardtop sedan 3,902 lb, 1,769 kg - Cutlass 'S' 3,837 lb, 1,740 kg; turning circle (between walls): 46.6 ft, 14.2 m; fuel tank: 18.3 imp gal, 22 US gal, 83 l.

OPTIONAL ACCESSORIES limited slip differential; G78 x 14 tyres; G70 x 14 tyres with 7" wide rims; power-assisted steering; tilt of steering wheel; servo brake; air-conditioning.

180 hp power team

See 160 hp power team, except for:

ENGINE max power (DIN): 180 hp at 3,800 rpm; max torque (DIN): 275 lb ft, 37.9 kg m at 2,800 rpm; 31.4 hp/l; 1 Rochester 4MC downdraught 4-barrel carburettor; dual exhaust system.

TRANSMISSION clutch: single dry plate; gearbox: mechanical; gears: 3, fully synchronized; ratios: I 2.540, II 1.500, III 1, rev 2.630; lever; steering column; axle ratio: 3.230.

PERFORMANCE: max speed: about 105 mph, 169 km/h; power-weight ratio: Cutlass Supreme hardtop sedan 21.2 lb/hp, 9.6 kg/hp; speed in direct drive at 1,000 rpm: 27.3 mph, 43.9 km/h; fuel consumption: 15.4 m/imp gal, 12.9 m/US gal, 18.3 l x 100 km.

DIMENSIONS AND WEIGHT length: Cutlass Supreme hardtop coupé 208.90 in, 5,306 mm - hardtop sedan 212.90 in, 5,408 mm; height: Cutlass Supreme hardtop coupé 53.10 in, 1,349 mm - hardtop sedan 54 in, 1,371 mm; dry weight: Cutlass Supreme hardtop coupé 3,810 lb, 1,728 kg - hardtop sedan 3,824 lb, 1,734 kg.

OPTIONAL ACCESSORIES Turbo-Hydramatic 350 automatic transmission with 3 ratios (I 2.520, II 1.520, III 1, rev 1.930), max ratio of converter at stall 2.50, possible manual selection, 2.730 or 3.080 axle ratio; only for hardtop coupés 4-speed fully synchronized mechanical gearbox (I 2.520, II 1.880, III 1.460, IV 1, rev 2.600), central lever, 3.230 axle ratio.

250 hp power team

See 160 hp power team, except for:

ENGINE 455 cu in, 7,456 cc (4.13 x 4.25 in, 104.8 x 107.9 mm); max power (DIN): 250 hp at 4,000 rpm; max torque (DIN): 370 lb ft, 51 kg m at 2,800 rpm; max engine rpm: 4,400; 33.5 hp/l; 1 Rochester 4MC downdraught 4-barrel carburettor.

TRANSMISSION gearbox: Turbo-Hydramatic 400 automatic transmission, hydraulic torque converter and planetary gears with 3 ratios, max ratio of converter at stall 2.50, possible manual selection; ratios: I 2.520, II 1.520, III 1, rev 1.930 (only for hardtop coupés 4-speed fully synchronized mechanical gearbox I 2.520, II 1.880, III 1.460, IV 1, rev 2.600); axle ratio: 2.730 - hardtop coupés 3.230.

PERFORMANCE max speed: about 110 mph, 177 km/h; power-weight ratio: Cutlass hardtop sedan 16.2 lb/hp, 7.3 kg/hp - Cutlass Supreme hardtop sedan 15.9 lb/hp, 7.2 kg/hp; fuel consumption: 14.9 m/imp gal, 12.4 m/US gal, 18.9 l x 100 km.

DIMENSIONS AND WEIGHT (see 180 hp power team) dry weight: plus 157 lb, 71 kg.

OPTIONAL ACCESSORIES 3.080 3.230 3.420 axle ratios; only for hardtop coupés 3.420 axle ratio.

270 hp power team

See 160 hp power team, except for:

ENGINE 455 cu in, 7,456 cc (4.13 x 4.25 in, 104.8 x 107.9 mm); max power (DIN): 270 hp at 4,200 rpm; max torque (DIN): 370 lb ft, 51 kg m at 3,200 rpm; max engine rpm: 4,600; 36.2 hp/l; 1 Rochester 4MC downdraught 4-barrel carburettor; dual exhaust system.

TRANSMISSION gearbox: Turbo-Hydramatic 400 automatic transmission, hydraulic torque converter and planetary gears with 3 ratios, max ratio of converter at stall 2.50, possible manual selection; ratios: I 2.520, II 1.520, III 1, rev 1.930 (only for hardtop coupés 4-speed fully synchronized mechanical gearbox I 2.520, II 1.880, III 1.460, IV 1, rev 2.600); axle ratio: 2.730 - hardtop coupés 3.230.

270 HP POWER TEAM

PERFORMANCE max speed: about 116 mph, 186 km/h; power-weight ratio: Cutlass hardtop sedan 15 lb/hp, 6.8 kg/hp - Cutlass Supreme hardtop sedan 14.7 lb/hp, 6.7 kg/hp; fuel consumption: 14.7 m/imp gal, 12.3 m/US gal, 19.2 l x 100 km.

DIMENSIONS AND WEIGHT (see 180 hp power team) dry weight: plus 157 lb, 71 kg.

OPTIONAL ACCESSORIES 3.080 3.230 3.420 axle ratios; only for hardtop coupés 3.420 axle ratio with 4-speed mechanical gearbox.

Vista Cruiser - Custom Cruiser Series

PRICES IN USA:

1 Vista Cruiser	6-passenger Station Wagon	$ **3,723**
2 Vista Cruiser	9-passenger Station Wagon	$ **3,836**
3 Custom Cruiser	6-passenger Station Wagon	$ **4,556**
4 Custom Cruiser	9-passenger Station Wagon	$ **4,690**

Power team:	Standard for:	Optional for:
180 hp	1,2	—
225 hp	3,4	—
250 hp	—	1,2

180 hp power team

ENGINE front, 4 stroke; 8 cylinders; 350 cu in, 5,736 cc (4.06 x 3.38 in, 103.1 x 85.8 mm); compression ratio: 8.5:1; max power (DIN): 180 hp at 3,800 rpm; max torque (DIN): 275 lb ft, 37.9 kg m at 2,800 rpm; max engine rpm: 4,200; 31.4 hp/l; cast iron cylinder block and head; 5 crankshaft bearings; valves: overhead, in line, push-rods and rockers, hydraulic tappets; camshafts: 1, at centre of Vee; lubrication: gear pump, full flow filter, 8.3 imp pt, 9.9 US pt, 4.7 l; 1 Rochester 4MC downdraught 4-barrel carburettor; fuel feed: mechanical pump; water-cooled, 25.3 imp pt, 30.4 US pt, 14.4 l.

TRANSMISSION driving wheels: rear; clutch: single dry plate; gearbox: mechanical; gears: 3, fully synchronized; ratios: I 2.540, II 1.500, III 1, rev 2.630; lever: steering column; final drive: hypoid bevel; axle ratio: 3.230; width of rims: 6"; tyres: H78 x 14.

PERFORMANCE max speed: about 105 mph, 169 km/h; power-weight ratio: 6-pass. 24.2 lb/hp, 11 kg/hp; speed in direct drive at 1,000 rpm: 26.4 mph, 42.5 km/h; fuel consumption: 15.2 m/imp gal, 12.6 m/US gal, 18.6 l x x 100 km.

CHASSIS channel section (perimeter type) frame; front suspension: independent, wishbones, coil springs, anti-roll bar, telescopic dampers; rear suspension: rigid axle, lower trailing radius arms, upper oblique torque arms, coil springs, telescopic dampers.

STEERING recirculating ball; turns lock to lock: 6.20.

BRAKES front disc (diameter 10.90 in, 256 mm), internal radial fins, rear drum (diameter 11 in, 279 mm), servo; swept area: front 226.2 sq in, 1,459 sq cm, rear 137 sq in, 883 sq cm, total 363.2 sq in, 2,342 sq cm.

ELECTRICAL EQUIPMENT 12 V; 61 Ah battery; 37 A alternator; Delco-Remy distributor; 2 headlamps.

DIMENSIONS AND WEIGHT wheel base: 116 in, 2,946 mm; tracks: 61.40 in, 1,559 mm front, 60.70 in, 1,542 mm rear; length: 219.30 in, 5,570 mm; width: 76.80 in, 1,951 mm; height: 55.30 in, 1,405 mm; ground clearance: 5.60 in, 142 mm; dry weight: 6-pass. 4,357 lb, 1,976 kg - 9-pass. 4,392 lb, 1,992 kg; turning circle (between walls): 46.6 ft, 14.2 m; fuel tank: 18.3 imp gal, 22 US gal, 83 l.

OPTIONAL ACCESSORIES limited slip differential; Turbo-Hydramatic 375 automatic transmission with 3 ratios (I 2.520, II 1.520, III 1, rev 1.930), max ratio of converter at stall 2.40, possible manual selection; power-assisted steering; tilt of steering wheel; air-conditioning.

225 hp power team

See 180 hp power team, except for:

ENGINE 455 cu in, 7,456 cc (4.13 x 4.25 in, 104.8 x 107.9 mm); max power (DIN): 225 hp at 3,600 rpm; max torque (DIN): 360 lb ft, 49.8 kg m at 2,600 rpm; max engine rpm: 4,000; 30.2 hp/l; 1 Rochester 4MC downdraught 4-barrel carburettor: cooling system capacity: 28.3 imp pt, 34 US pt, 16.1 l.

TRANSMISSION gearbox: Turbo-Hydramatic 400 automatic transmission, hydraulic torque converter and planetary gears with 3 ratios, max ratio of converter at stall 2.20, possible manual selection; ratios: 1 2.480, II 1.480, III 1, rev 2.080; lever: steering column; axle ratio: 2.930; tyres: L78 x 15.

PERFORMANCE max speed: about 108 mph, 174 km/h; power-weight ratio: 6-pass. 22.5 lb/hp, 10.2 kg/hp; speed in direct drive at 1,000 rpm: 26.9 mph, 43.3 km/h; fuel consumption: 15 m/imp gal, 12.5 m/US gal, 18.8 l x 100 km.

CHASSIS rear suspension: rigid axle, semi-elliptic leafsprings, telescopic dampers.

BRAKES front disc (diameter 11.70 in, 281 mm), internal radial fins, rear drum (diameter 12 in, 305 mm), servo; swept area: front 249.2 sq in, 1,608 sq cm, rear 150.4 sq in, 970 sq cm, total 399.6 sq in, 2,578 sq cm.

ELECTRICAL EQUIPMENT 73 Ah battery; 42 A alternator.

DIMENSIONS AND WEIGHT wheel base: 127 in, 3,226 mm; tracks: 63.30 in, 1,608 mm front, 63.70 in, 1,618 mm rear; length: 228.30 mm 5,799 mm; width: 79.50 in, 2,019 mm; height: 57.20 in, 1,453 mm; ground clearance: 5.30 in, 134 mm; dry weight: 6-pass. 5,058 lb, 2,294 kg - 9-pass. 5,151 lb, 2,336 kg; turning circle (between walls): 48.7 ft, 14.8 m.

OPTIONAL ACCESSORIES 3.230 axle ratio; electronic ignition; Turbo-Hydramatic 375 automatic transmission not available.

OLDSMOBILE Vista Cruiser Station Wagon

OLDSMOBILE Delta 88 Royale Hardtop Coupé

OLDSMOBILE Ninety-Eight Hardtop Luxury Coupé

250 hp power team

See 180 hp power team, except for:

ENGINE 455 cu in, 7,456 cc (4.13 x 4.25 in, 104.8 x 107.9 mm); max power (DIN): 250 hp at 4,000 rpm; max torque (DIN): 370 lb ft, 51 kg m at 2,800 rpm; max engine rpm: 4,400; 33.5 hp/l; 1 Rochester 4MC downdraught 4-barrel carburettor; cooling system capacity: 28.3 imp pt, 34 US pt, 16.1 l.

TRANSMISSION Turbo-Hydramatic 400 automatic transmission, hydraulic torque converter and planetary gears with 3 ratios (I 2.480, II 1.480, III 1, rev 2.080); lever: steering column; axle ratio: 2.730.

PERFORMANCE max speed: about 111 mph, 178 km/h; power-weight ratio: 6-pass. 18 lb/hp, 8.2 kg/hp; speed in direct drive at 1,000 rpm: 26.4 mph, 42.5 km/h; fuel consumption: 14.7 m/imp gal, 12.3 m/US gal, 19.2 l x 100 km.

DIMENSIONS AND WEIGHT dry weight: plus 154 lb, 70 kg.

OPTIONAL ACCESSORIES Turbo-Hydramatic 375 automatic transmission not available; 3.080 3.230 3.420 axle ratios.

Delta 88 - Delta 88 Royale - Ninety-Eight Series

PRICES IN USA:

1 Delta 88	Hardtop Sedan	**$ 4,060**
2 Delta 88	Hardtop Coupé	**$ 4,001**
3 Delta 88	Town Sedan	**$ 3,948**
4 Delta 88 Royale	Hardtop Sedan	**$ 4,238**
5 Delta 88 Royale	Hardtop Coupé	**$ 4,179**
6 Delta 88 Royale	Convertible	**$ 4,387**
7 Delta 88 Royale	Town Sedan	**$ 4,101**
8 Ninety-Eight	Hardtop Coupé	**$ 4,747**
9 Ninety-Eight	Hardtop Sports Sedan	**$ 4,806**
10 Ninety-Eight	Hardtop Luxury Coupé	**$ 5,008**
11 Ninety-Eight	Hardtop Luxury Sedan	**$ 5,097**
12 Ninety-Eight Regency	Hardtop Sedan	**$ 5,348**

Power team:	Standard for:	Optional for:
160 hp	1,2,3,4,5,6,7	—
225 hp	8,9,10,11,12	1,2,3,4,5,6,7
250 hp	8,9,10,11,12	1,2,3,4,5,6,7

160 hp power team

ENGINE front, 4 stroke; 8 cylinders; 350 cu in, 5,736 cc (4.06 x 3.38 in, 103.1 x 85.8 mm); compression ratio: 8.5:1; max power (DIN): 160 hp at 3.800 rpm; max torque (DIN): 275 lb ft, 37.9 kg m at 2,400 rpm; max engine rpm: 4,200; 27.9 hp/l; cast iron cylinder block and head; 5 crankshaft bearings; valves: overhead, in line, push-rods and rockers, hydraulic tappets; camshafts: 1, at centre of Vee; lubrication: gear pump, full flow filter, 8.3 imp pt, 9.9 US pt, 4.7 l; 1 Rochester 2GC downdraught twin barrel carburettor; fuel feed: mechanical pump; water-cooled, 26.9 imp pt, 32.3 US pt, 15.3 l.

TRANSMISSION driving wheels: rear; gearbox: Turbo-Hydramatic 375 automatic transmission, hydraulic torque converter and planetary gears with 3 ratios, max ratio of converter at stall 2.20, possible manual selection; ratios: I 2.480, II 1.480, III 1, rev 2.080; lever: steering column; final drive: hypoid bevel; axle ratio: 3.080; width of rims: 6"; tyres: H78 x 15.

OLDSMOBILE Custom Cruiser Station Wagon

OLDSMOBILE Delta 88 Royale Hardtop Coupé

OLDSMOBILE Ninety-Eight Hardtop Luxury Coupé

PERFORMANCE max speed: about 105 mph, 169 km/h; power-weight ratio: Delta 88 hardtop sedan 27.5 lb/hp, 12.5 kg/hp - Delta 88 Royale hardtop sedan 27.7 lb/hp, 12.6 kg/hp; speed in direct drive at 1,000 rpm: 26.6 mph, 42.8 km/h; fuel consumption: 16.4 m/imp gal, 13.7 m/US gal, 17.2 l x 100 km.

CHASSIS channel section (perimeter type) frame; front suspension: independent, wishbones, coil springs, anti-roll bar, telescopic dampers; rear suspension: rigid axle, lower trailing radius arms, upper oblique torque arms, coil springs, telescopic dampers.

STEERING recirculating ball, servo; turns lock to lock: 2.97.

BRAKES front disc (diameter 11.74 in, 298 mm), rear drum (diameter 11 in, 279 mm), servo; swept area: total 386.2 sq in, 2,491 sq cm.

ELECTRICAL EQUIPMENT 12 V; 61 Ah battery; 42 A alternator; Delco-Remy distributor; 4 headlamps.

DIMENSIONS AND WEIGHT wheel base: 124 in, 3,150 mm; tracks: 63.70 in, 1,618 mm front, 64 in, 1,625 mm rear; length: 226.30 in, 5,748 mm - Delta 88 Royale town sedan 226.20 in, 5,745 mm - Delta 88 Series 225 in, 5,715 mm; width: 79.50 in, 2,019 mm - Delta 88 Royale Series 79.60 in, 2,022 mm; height: 53.40 in, 1,356 mm - hardtop sedans 53.60 in, 1,361 mm - town sedans 54.30 in, 1,379 mm; ground clearance: 5.30 in, 134 mm; dry weight: Delta 88 hardtop sedan 4,410 lb, 2,000 kg - hardtop coupé 4,332 lb, 1,964 kg - town sedan 4,383 lb, 1,987 kg - Delta 88 Royale hardtop sedan 4,436 lb, 2,012 kg - hardtop coupé 4,346 lb, 1,971 kg - convertible 4,436 lb, 2,012 kg - town sedan 4,395 lb, 1,993 kg; turning circle (between walls): 47.7 ft, 14.5 m; fuel tank: 21.6 imp gal, 26 US gal, 98 l.

OPTIONAL ACCESSORIES limited slip differential; tilt and telescopic steering wheel; air-conditioning.

225 hp power team

See 160 hp power team, except for:

ENGINE 455 cu in, 7,456 cc (4.13 x 4.25 in, 104.8 x 107.9 mm); max power (DIN): 225 hp at 3,600 rpm; max torque (DIN): 360 lb ft, 49.8 kg m at 2,600 rpm; max engine rpm: 4,000; 30.2 hp/l; 1 Rochester 4MC downdraught 4-barrel carburettor; cooling system capacity: 28.3 imp pt, 34 US pt, 16.1 l.

TRANSMISSION gearbox: Turbo-Hydramatic 400 automatic transmission, hydraulic torque converter and planetary gears with 3 ratios, possible manual selection; ratios: I 2.480, II 1.480, III 1, rev 2.080; axle ratio: 2.730; tyres: J78 x 15.

PERFORMANCE max speed: about 111 mph, 178 km/h; power-weight ratio: Ninety-Eight hardtop sports sedan 20.7 lb/hp, 9.4 kg/hp; speed in direct drive at 1,000 rpm: 27.7 mph, 44.5 km/h; fuel consumption: 14.9 m/imp gal, 12.4 m/US gal, 19 l x 100 km.

CHASSIS (for Ninety-Eight only) box-type perimeter frame.

STEERING turns lock to lock: 3.05 - Ninety-Eight 2.83.

ELECTRICAL EQUIPMENT 73 Ah battery.

DIMENSIONS AND WEIGHT (for Ninety-Eight only) wheel base: 127 mm, 3,226 mm; length: 230.30 in, 5,850 mm; width: 79.60 in, 2,022 mm; height: 54.20 in, 1,377 mm - hardtop sports sedan and hardtop luxury sedan 54.70 in, 1,389 mm; dry weight: Delta 88 and Delta 88 Royale plus 157 lb, 71 kg - Ninety-Eight hardtop coupé 4,575 lb, 2,075 kg - hardtop sports sedan 4,662 lb, 2,114 kg - hardtop luxury coupé 4,611 lb, 2,091 kg - hardtop luxury sedan 4,700 lb, 2,131 kg; turning circle (between walls): 48.7 ft, 14.8 m.

OPTIONAL ACCESSORIES 2.930 3.080 3.230 axle ratios; electronic ignition.

250 hp power team

See 160 hp power team, except for:

ENGINE 455 cu in, 7,456 cc (4.13 x 4.25 in, 104.8 x 107.9 mm); max power (DIN): 250 hp at 4,000 rpm; max torque (DIN): 370 lb ft, 51 kg m at 2,800 rpm; max engine rpm: 4,400; 33.5 hp/l; 1 Rochester 4MC downdraught 4-barrel carburettor; dual exhaust system; cooling system capacity: 28.3 imp pt, 34 US pt, 16.1 l.

TRANSMISSION gearbox: Turbo-Hydramatic 400 automatic transmission, hydraulic torque converter and planetary gears with 3 ratios, possible manual selection; ratios: I 2.480, II 1.480, III 1, rev 2.080; axle ratio: 2.730; tyres J78 x 15.

PERFORMANCE max speed: about 113 mph, 182 km/h; power-weight ratio: Ninety-Eight hardtop sports sedan 18.6 lb/hp, 8.5 kg/hp; speed in direct drive at 1,000 rpm: 27.7 mph, 44.5 km/h; fuel consumption: 13.4 m/imp gal, 11.1 m/US gal, 21.1 l x 100 km.

CHASSIS (for Ninety-Eight only) box-type perimeter frame.

250 HP POWER TEAM

STEERING turns lock to lock: 3.05 - Ninety-Eight 2.83.

ELECTRICAL EQUIPMENT 73 Ah battery.

DIMENSIONS AND WEIGHT (see 225 hp power team).

OPTIONAL ACCESSORIES 2.930 3.080 3.230 axle ratios; electronic ignition.

Toronado

PRICE IN USA:

Toronado	Custom Coupé	$ 5,340

250 hp power team

(standard).

ENGINE front, 4 stroke; 8 cylinders; 455 cu in, 7,456 cc (4.13 x 4.25 in, 104.8 x 107.9 mm); compression ratio: 8.5:1; max power (DIN): 250 hp at 4,000 rpm; max torque (DIN): 375 lb ft, 51.7 kg m at 2,800 rpm; max engine rpm: 4,400; 33.5 hp/l; cast iron cylinder block and head; 5 crankshaft bearings; valves: overhead, in line, push-rods and rockers, hydraulic tappets; camshafts: 1, at centre of Vee; lubrication: gear pump, full flow filter, 10 imp pt, 12 US pt, 5.7 l; 1 Rochester 4MC downdraught 4-barrel carburettor; dual exhaust system: fuel feed: mechanical pump; water-cooled, 32.4 imp pt, 38.9 US pt, 18.4 l.

TRANSMISSION driving wheels: front; gearbox: Turbo-Hydramatic 425 automatic transmission, hydraulic torque converter and planetary gears (chain torque by engine-mounted converter) with 3 ratios, possible manual selection; ratios: I 2.480, II 1.480, III 1, rev 2.080; lever: steering column; final drive: spiral bevel; axle ratio: 2.730; width of rims: 6"; tyres: J78 x 15.

PERFORMANCE max speed: about 106 mph, 170 km/h; power-weight ratio: 19.2 lb/hp, 8.7 kg/hp; speed in direct drive at 1,000 rpm: 26 mph, 41.8 km/h; fuel consumption: 12.7 m/imp gal, 10.6 m/US gal, 22.2 l x 100 km.

CHASSIS channel section (perimeter type) frame; front suspension: independent, wishbones, longitudinal torsion bars, anti-roll bar, telescopic dampers; rear suspension: rigid axle, lower trailing radius arms, upper oblique torque arms, coil springs, telescopic dampers.

STEERING recirculating ball, servo; turns lock to lock: 3.24.

BRAKES front disc (diameter 10.90 in, 256 mm), internal radial fins, rear drum (diameter 11 in, 279 mm), servo; swept area: total 364.4 sq in, 2,350 sq cm.

ELECTRICAL EQUIPMENT 12 V; 73 Ah battery; 42 A alternator; Delco-Remy distributor; 4 headlamps.

DIMENSIONS AND WEIGHT wheel base: 122 in, 3,099 mm; tracks: 63.50 in, 1,613 mm front, 63.60 in, 1,615 mm rear; length: 226.80 in, 5,761 mm; width: 79.80 in, 2,027 mm; height: 53.20 in, 1,351 mm; ground clearance: 4.80 in, 122 mm; dry weight: 4,794 lb, 2,174 kg; turning circle (between walls): 48.9 ft, 14.9 m; fuel tank: 21.6 imp gal, 26 US gal, 98 l

BODY 2 doors; 5 seats, separate front seats.

OPTIONAL ACCESSORIES 3.070 axle ratio; tilt and telescopic steering wheel; electronic ignition; air-conditioning; Brougham equipment.

PLYMOUTH USA

Valiant - Duster - Valiant Scamp - Duster 340 Series

PRICES IN USA:

1 Valiant	4-door Sedan	$ 2,397
2 Duster	2-door Coupé	$ 2,321
3 Valiant Scamp	2-door Hardtop	$ 2,562
4 Duster 340	2-door Coupé	$ 2,762

For V8 engines add $ 142.

Power team:	Standard for:	Optional for:
95 hp	1,2,3	—
98 hp	—	1,2,3
105 hp	—	1,2,3
150 hp	1,2,3	—
240 hp	4	—

OLDSMOBILE Toronado Custom Coupé

PLYMOUTH Valiant 4-door Sedan

PLYMOUTH Valiant Scamp 2-door Hardtop

at 4,800 rpm; max torque (DIN): 380 lb ft, 52.4 kg m at 3,200 rpm; max engine rpm: 5,200; 38.8 hp/l; 1 Carter TQ-6324S (TQ-6411S for California only) downdraught 4-barrel carburettor; cleaner air system; dual exhaust system; cooling system capacity: 27.5 imp pt, 33 US pt, 15.6 l.

TRANSMISSION gearbox: Torqueflite automatic transmission (standard); axle ratio: 3.230; width of rims: 6"; tyres: F70 x 14.

PERFORMANCE max speed: about 111 mph, 178 km/h; power-weight ratio: 13.6 lb/hp, 6.2 kg/hp; speed in direct drive at 1,000 rpm: 25.5 mph, 41 km/h; fuel consumption: 12.4 m/imp gal, 10.4 m/US gal, 22.7 l x 100 km.

CHASSIS front and rear suspension: anti-roll bar (standard).

BRAKES servo (standard).

ELECTRICAL EQUIPMENT 440 A battery.

DIMENSIONS AND WEIGHT (see 170 hp power team) dry weight: plus 194 lb, 88 kg.

OPTIONAL ACCESSORIES 3.550 axle ratio; G70 x 14 tyres; G60 x 15 tyres with 7" wide rims; air-conditioning; 4-speed fully synchronized mechanical gearbox not available.

Fury I - Fury II - Suburban - Fury III - Custom Suburban - Gran Coupé - Gran Sedan - Sport Suburban Series

PRICES IN USA:

1 Fury I	4-door Sedan	$ **3,486**
2 Fury II	4-door Sedan	$ **3,605**
3 Suburban	6-passenger Station Wagon	$ **4,046**
4 Fury III	2-door Hardtop	$ **3,804**
5 Fury III	4-door Sedan	$ **3,782**
6 Fury III	4-door Hardtop	$ **3,848**
7 Custom Suburban	6-passenger Station Wagon	$ **4,142**
8 Custom Suburban	9-passenger Station Wagon	$ **4,220**
9 Gran Coupé	2-door Hardtop	$ **3,960**
10 Gran Sedan	4-door Hardtop	$ **4,006**
11 Sport Suburban	6-passenger Station Wagon	$ **4,408**
12 Sport Suburban	9-passenger Station Wagon	$ **4,485**

Power team:	Standard for:	Optional for:
150 hp	1,2,4,5,6,9,10	—
163 hp	3,7,8,11,12	1,2,4,5,6,9,10
170 hp	3,7,8,11,12	1,2,4,5,6,9,10
185 hp	—	all
213 hp	—	all
220 hp	—	all

150 hp power team

ENGINE front, 4 stroke; 8 cylinders; 318 cu in, 5,211 cc (3.91 x 3.38 in, 99.2 x 85.8 mm); compression ratio: 8.6:1; max power (DIN): 150 hp at 3,600 rpm; max torque (DIN): 265 lb ft, 36.6 kg m at 2,000 rpm; max engine rpm: 4,000; 28.8 hp/l; cast iron cylinder block and head; 5 crankshaft bearings; valves: overhead, in line, push-rods and rockers, hydraulic tappets; camshafts: 1, at centre of Vee; lubrication: rotary pump, full flow filter, 8.3 imp pt, 9.9 US pt, 4.7 l; 1 Carter BBD-6317S (BBD-6344S for California only) downdraught twin barrel carburettor; cleaner air system; fuel feed: mechanical pump; water-cooled, 26.6 imp pt, 31.9 US pt, 15.1 l.

TRANSMISSION driving wheels: rear; gearbox: Torqueflite automatic transmission, hydraulic torque converter and planetary gears with 3 ratios, max ratio of converter at stall 2.16, possible manual selection; ratios: I 2.450, II 1.450, III 1, rev 2.200; lever: steering column; final drive: hypoid bevel; axle ratio: 2.710; width of rims: 5"; tyres: F78 x 15.

PERFORMANCE max speed: about 98 mph, 157 km/h; power-weight ratio: Fury I and Fury III 4-dr. sedans 26.5 lb/hp, 12 kg/hp - Fury II 4-dr. sedan and Gran Coupé 2-dr. hardtop 26.4 lb/hp, 11.9 kg/hp - Gran Sedan 4-dr. hardtop 26.7 lb/hp, 12.1 kg/hp; speed in direct drive at 1,000 rpm: 29 mph, 46.6 km/h; fuel consumption: 16.4 m/imp gal, 13.7 m/US gal, 17.2 l x 100 km.

CHASSIS integral, auxiliary front frame; front suspension: independent, wishbones, longitudinal torsion bars, anti-roll bar, telescopic dampers; rear suspension: rigid axle, semi-elliptic leafsprings, telescopic dampers.

STEERING recirculating ball, servo; turns lock to lock: 3.50.

BRAKES front disc (diameter 11.56 in, 294 mm), rear drum, servo; swept area: total 359 sq in, 2,316 sq cm.

ELECTRICAL EQUIPMENT 12 V; 280 A battery; 41 A alternator; Chrysler Essex or Chrysler Prestolite electronic ignition; 4 headlamps.

DIMENSIONS AND WEIGHT wheel base: 120 in, 3,048 mm;

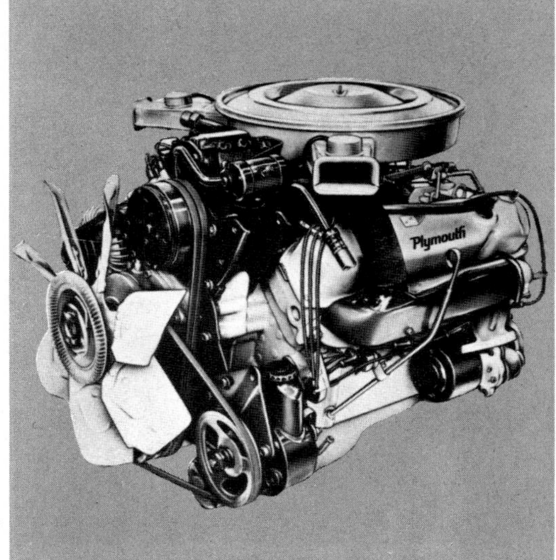

PLYMOUTH Satellite Sebring Plus 2-door Hardtop (260 hp V8 engine)

PLYMOUTH Satellite Regent Station Wagon

PLYMOUTH Gran Coupé 2-door Hardtop

tracks: 62.10 in, 1,577 mm front, 63.40 in, 1,610 mm rear; length: 223.40 in, 5,674 mm; width: 79.80 in, 2,027 mm; height: 2-dr. hardtops 54.90 in, 1,395 mm - sedans 56.10 in, 1,425 mm - 4-dr. hardtops 55.40 in, 1,407 mm; ground clearance: 5.60 in, 142 mm; dry weight: Fury I 4-dr. sedan 3,980 lb, 1,805 kg - Fury II 4-dr. sedan 3,960 lb, 1,796 kg - Fury III 2-dr. hardtop 3,930 lb, 1,782 kg - 4-dr. sedan 3,975 lb, 1,802 kg - 4-dr. hardtop 3,995 lb, 1,812 kg - Gran Coupé 2-dr. hardtop 3,960 lb, 1,796 kg - Gran Sedan 4-dr. hardtop 4,005 lb, 1,816 kg; turning circle (between walls): 45.5 ft, 13.9 m; fuel tank: 19.1 imp gal, 23 US gal, 87 l.

OPTIONAL ACCESSORIES limited slip differential; 3.210 3.230 3.550 axle ratios; GR78 x 15 or H78 x 15 tyres with 5.5" wide rims; tilt of steering wheel; security alarm system; air-conditioning.

163 hp power team

(for California only).

See 150 hp power team, except for:

ENGINE 360 cu in, 5,900 cc (4 x 3,58 in, 101.6 x 89.6 mm); compression ratio: 8.4:1; max power (DIN): 163 hp at 4,000 rpm; max torque (DIN): 280 lb ft, 38.6 kg m at 2,400 rpm; max engine rpm: 4,400; 27.6 hp/l; 1 Holley R-6575A downdraught twin barrel carburettor; cleaner air system; cooling system capacity: 25.9 imp pt, 31.2 US pt, 14.7 l.

TRANSMISSION axle ratio: station wagons 2.760; width of rims: 5.5" - station wagons 6.5"; tyres: G78 x 15 - 6-pass. J78 x 15 - 9-pass. L84 x 15.

PERFORMANCE max speed: about 100 mph, 161 km/h; power-weight ratio: Fury I and Fury III 4-dr. sedans 24.4 lb/hp, 11.1 kg/hp - Fury II 4-dr. sedan and Gran Coupé 2-dr. hardtop 24.3 lb/hp, 11 kg/hp - Gran Sedan 4-dr. hardtop 24.6 lb/hp, 11.2 kg/hp; speed in direct drive at 1,000 rpm: 28.7 mph, 46.2 km/h; fuel consumption: 15.7 m/imp gal, 13.1 m/US gal, 18 l x 100 km.

BRAKES swept area: station wagons total 393.6 sq in, 2,539 sq cm.

ELECTRICAL EQUIPMENT 315 A battery.

DIMENSIONS AND WEIGHT wheel base: station wagons 122 in, 3,099 mm; length: station wagons 227.50 in, 5,779 mm; height: 6-pass. 57.80 in, 1,468 mm - 9-pass. 58.30 in, 1,481 mm; ground clearance: 6-pass. station wagon 6.20 in, 157 mm - 9-pass. station wagon 6.70 in, 170 mm; dry weight: plus 93 lb, 43 kg - Suburban 6-pass. station wagon 4,535 lb, 2,056 kg - Custom Suburban 6-pass. station wagon 4,545 lb, 2,061 kg - 9-pass. station wagon 4,590 lb, 2,081 kg - Sport Suburban 6-pass. station wagon 4,560 lb, 2,068 kg - 9-pass. station wagon 4,620 lb, 2,095 kg.

OPTIONAL ACCESSORIES 3.230 axle ratio.

170 hp power team

See 150 hp power team, except for:

ENGINE 360 cu in, 5,900 cc (4 x 3.58 in, 101.6 x 89.6 mm); compression ratio: 8.4:1; max power (DIN): 170 hp at 4,000 rpm; max torque (DIN): 285 lb ft, 39.3 kg m at 2,400 rpm; max engine rpm: 4,400; 28.8 hp/l; 1 Holley R-6452A (R-6575A for California only) downdraught twin barrel carburettor; cleaner air system; cooling system capacity: 25.9 imp pt, 31.2 US pt, 14.7 l.

TRANSMISSION axle ratio: station wagons 2.760; width of rims: 5.5" - station wagons 6.5"; tyres: G78 x 15 - 6-pass. J78 x 15 - 9-pass. L84 x 15.

PERFORMANCE max speed: about 101 mph, 162 km/h; power-weight ratio: Fury I and Fury III 4-dr. sedans 23.4 lb/hp, 10.6 kg/hp - Fury II 4-dr. sedan and Gran Coupé 2-dr. hardtop 23.3 lb/hp, 10.5 kg/hp - Gran Sedan 4-dr. hardtop 23.5 lb/hp, 10.7 kg/hp; speed in direct drive at 1,000 rpm: 28.7 mph, 46.2 km/h; fuel consumption 15.3 m/imp gal, 12.7 m/US gal, 18.5 l x 100 km.

BRAKES swept area: station wagons total 393.6 sq in, 2,539 sq cm.

ELECTRICAL EQUIPMENT 315 A battery.

DIMENSIONS AND WEIGHT (see 163 hp power team).

OPTIONAL ACCESSORIES 3.230 axle ratio.

185 hp power team

See 150 hp power team, except for:

ENGINE 400 cu in, 6,555 cc (4.34 x 3.38 in, 110.2 x 85.8 mm); compression ratio: 8.2:1; max power (DIN): 185 hp at

185 HP POWER TEAM

3,600 rpm; max torque (DIN): 310 lb ft, 42.8 kg m at 2,400 rpm; max engine rpm: 4,000; 28.2 hp/l; 1 Holley R-6454A (R-6472A for California only) downdraught twin barrel carburettor; cleaner air system.

TRANSMISSION gearbox: max ratio of converter at stall 2.02; axle ratio: station wagons 2.760; width of rims: 5.5" - station wagons 6.5"; tyres: G78 x 15 - 6-pass. J78 x 15 - 9-pass. L84 x 15.

PERFORMANCE max speed: about 103 mph, 165 km/h; power-weight ratio: Fury I and Fury III 4-dr. sedans 22.4 lb/hp, 10.2 kg/hp - Fury II 4-dr. sedan and Gran Coupé 2-dr. hardtop 22.3 lb/hp, 10.1 kg/hp - Gran Sedan 4-dr. hardtop 22.6 lb/hp, 10.3 kg/hp; speed in direct drive at 1,000 rpm: 28.7 mph, 46.2 km/h; fuel consumption: 14.9 m/imp gal, 12.4 m/US gal, 18.9 l x 100 km.

BRAKES swept area: station wagons total 393.6 sq in, 2,539 sq cm.

ELECTRICAL EQUIPMENT 375 A battery.

DIMENSIONS AND WEIGHT (see 163 hp power team) dry weight: plus 170 lb, 77 kg - station wagons plus 81 lb, 37 kg.

OPTIONAL ACCESSORIES 3.230 axle ratio.

213 hp power team

(for California only).

See 150 hp power team, except for:

ENGINE 440 cu in, 7,210 cc (4.32 x 3.75 in, 109.7 x 95.2 mm); compression ratio: 8.2:1; max power (DIN): 213 hp at 3,600 rpm; max torque (DIN): 345 lb ft, 47.6 kg m at 2,400 rpm; max engine rpm: 4,000; 29.5 hp/l; 1 Carter TQ-6411S downdraught 4-barrel carburettor; cleaner air system; cooling system capacity: 25.9 imp pt, 31.2 US pt, 14.7 l.

TRANSMISSION gearbox: max ratio of converter at stall: 2.02; axle ratio: 2.760; width of rims: 5.5" - station wagons 6.5"; tyres: G78 x 15 - 6-pass. J78 x 15 - 9-pass. L84 x 15.

PERFORMANCE max speed: about 105 mph, 169 km/h; power-weight ratio: Fury I and Fury III 4-dr. sedans 19.8 lb/hp, 9 kg/hp - Fury II 4-dr. sedan and Gran Coupé 2-dr. hardtop 19.3 lb/hp, 8.9 kg/hp - Gran Sedan 4-dr. hardtop 20 lb/hp, 9.1 kg/hp; speed in direct drive at 1,000 rpm: 28.7 mph, 46.2 km/h; fuel consumption 14.6 m/imp gal, 12.1 m/US gal, 19.4 l x 100 km.

BRAKES swept area: total 393.6 sq in, 2,539 sq cm.

ELECTRICAL EQUIPMENT 440 A battery.

DIMENSIONS AND WEIGHT (see 163 hp power team) dry weight: plus 245 lb, 112 kg - station wagons plus 135 lb, 61 kg.

OPTIONAL ACCESSORIES 3.230 axle ratio.

220 hp power team

See 150 hp power team, except for:

ENGINE 440 cu in, 7,210 cc (4.32 x 3.75 in, 109.7 x 95.2 mm); compression ratio: 8.2:1; max power (DIN): 220 hp at 3,600 rpm; max torque (DIN): 350 lb ft, 48.3 kg m at 2,400 rpm; max engine rpm: 4,000; 30.5 hp/l; 1 Carter TQ-6324S (TQ-6411S for California only) downdraught 4-barrel carburettor; cleaner air system; cooling system capacity: 25.9 imp pt, 31.2 US pt, 14.7 l.

TRANSMISSION gearbox: max ratio of converter at stall 2.02; axle ratio: 2.760; width of rims: 5.5" - station wagons 6.5"; tyres: G78 x 15 - 6-pass. J78 x 15 - 9-pass. L84 x 15.

PERFORMANCE max speed: about 106 mph, 170 km/h; power-weight ratio: Fury I and Fury III 4-dr. sedans 19.2 lb/hp, 8.7 kg/hp - Fury II 4-dr. Sedan and Gran Coupé 2-dr. hardtop 19.1 lb/hp, 8.6 kg/hp - Gran Sedan 4-dr. hardtop 19.3 lb/hp, 8.8 kg/hp; speed in direct drive at 1,000 rpm: 28.7 mph, 46.2 km/h; fuel consumption: 14.3 m/imp gal, 11.9 m/US gal, 19.7 l x 100 km.

BRAKES swept area: total 393.6 sq in, 2,539 sq cm.

ELECTRICAL EQUIPMENT 440 A battery.

DIMENSIONS AND WEIGHT (see 163 hp power team) dry weight: plus 245 lb, 112 kg - station wagon plus 135 lb, 61 kg.

OPTIONAL ACCESSORIES 3.230 axle ratio.

PLYMOUTH Gran Sedan 4-door Hardtop

PLYMOUTH Sport Suburban Station Wagon (220 hp V8 engine)

PONTIAC Ventura 2-door Hatchback Coupé

PONTIAC USA

Ventura - Ventura Custom Series

PRICES IN USA:

1 Ventura	2-door Hatchback Coupé	**$ 2,574**
2 Ventura	2-door Coupé	**$ 2,425**
3 Ventura	4-door Sedan	**$ 2,453**
4 Ventura Custom	2-door Hatchback Coupé	**$ 2,729**
5 Ventura Custom	2-door Coupé	**$ 2,580**
6 Ventura Custom	4-door Sedan	**$ 2,608**

Power team:	Standard for:	Optional for:
100 hp	all	—
150 hp	—	all
175 hp	—	all

100 hp power team

ENGINE front, 4 stroke; 6 cylinders, in line; 250 cu in, 4,097 cc (3.87 x 3.53 in, 98.2 x 89.6); compression ratio: 8.2:1; max power (DIN): 100 hp at 3,600 rpm; max torque (DIN): 175 lb ft, 24.1 kg m at 1,600 rpm; max engine rpm: 4,000; 24.4 hp/l; cast iron cylinder block and head; 7 crankshaft bearings; valves: overhead, in line, push-rods and rockers, hydraulic tappets; camshafts: 1, side; lubrication: gear pump, full flow filter, 8.3 imp pt, 9.9 US pt, 4.7 l; 1 Rochester 7043017 (7043317 for California only) downdraught single barrel carburettor; cleaner air system; fuel feed: mechanical pump; water-cooled, 20.1 imp pt, 24.1 US pt, 11.4 l.

TRANSMISSION driving wheels: rear; clutch: single dry plate; gearbox: mechanical; gears: 3, fully synchronized; ratios: I 2.850, II 1.680, III 1, rev 2.950; lever: steering column; final drive: hypoid bevel; axle ratio: 3.080; width of rims: 5"; tyres: E78 x 14.

PERFORMANCE max speed: about 95 mph, 153 km/h; power-weight ratio: Ventura 4-dr. sedan 32.3 lb/hp, 14.7 kg/hp - Ventura Custom 4-dr. sedan 32.7 lb/hp, 14.8 kg/hp; speed in direct drive at 1,000 rpm: 25.9 mph, 41.7 km/h; fuel consumption: 20.8 m/imp gal, 17.3 m/US gal, 13.6 l x 100 km.

CHASSIS integral with front ladder type frame section; front suspension: independent, wishbones, coil springs, anti-roll bar, telescopic dampers; rear suspension: rigid axle, semi-elliptic leafsprings, anti-roll bar, telescopic dampers.

STEERING recirculating ball; turns lock to lock: 5.65.

BRAKES drum (diameter 9.50 in, 241 mm); swept area: total 268.6 sq in, 1,732 sq cm.

ELECTRICAL EQUIPMENT 12 V; 45 Ah battery; 37 A alternator; Delco-Remy distributor; 2 headlamps.

DIMENSIONS AND WEIGHT wheel base: 111 in, 2,814 mm; tracks: 59.90 in, 1,521 mm front, 59.60 in, 1,514 mm rear; length: 197.50 in, 5,016 mm; width: 72.40 in, 1,839 mm; height: 52.60 in, 1,336 mm - sedans 53.90 in, 1,369 mm; dry weight: Ventura 2-dr. hatchback coupé 3,280 lb, 1,487 kg - 2-dr. coupé 3,174 lb, 1,439 kg - 4-dr. sedan 3,234 lb, 1,466 kg - Ventura Custom 2-dr. hatchback coupé 3,313 lb, 1,502 kg - 2-dr. coupé 3,207 lb, 1,454 kg - 4-dr. sedan 3,267 lb, 1,481 kg; turning circle (between walls): 42.6 ft, 13 m; fuel tank: 18 imp gal, 21.5 US gal, 82 l.

OPTIONAL ACCESSORIES « Automatic » transmission with 2 ratios (I 1.820, II 1, rev 1.820), max ratio of converter at stall 2.15, 3.080 axle ratio; central lever; limited slip differential; E70 x 14 tyres with 6" wide rims; power-assisted steering; adjustable tilt of steering wheel; servo brake; front disc brakes (diameter 11 in, 279 mm) with servo, total swept area 337.3 sq in, 2,175 sq cm; sunshine roof and Sprint equipment except for sedans.

150 hp power team

See 100 hp power team, except for:

ENGINE 8 cylinders; 350 cu in, 5,736 cc (3.87 x 3.75 in, 98.2 x 89.3 mm); compression ratio: 7.6:1; max power (DIN): 150 hp at 4,000 rpm; max torque (DIN): 270 lb ft, 37.2 kg m at 2,000 rpm; max engine rpm: 4,400; 26.1 hp/l; 5 crankshaft bearings; camshafts: 1, at centre of Vee; lubricating system capacity: 10 imp pt, 12 US pt, 5.7 l; 1 Rochester 7043071 downdraught twin barrel carburettor; cleaner air-system; cooling system capacity: 32 imp pt, 38.5 US pt, 18.2 l.

TRANSMISSION gearbox ratios: I 2.540, II 1.500, III 1, rev 2.630; lever: central (standard).

PERFORMANCE max speed: about 108 mph, 174 km/h; power-weight ratio: Ventura 4-dr. sedan 23 lb/hp, 10.4 kg/hp

PLYMOUTH Gran Sedan 4-door Hardtop

PLYMOUTH Sport Suburban Station Wagon

PONTIAC Ventura 2-door Hatchback Coupé

- Ventura Custom 4-dr. sedan 23.2 lb/hp, 10.5 kg/hp; fuel consumption: 17.7 m/imp gal, 14.7 m/US gal, 16 l x 100 km.

ELECTRICAL EQUIPMENT 53 Ah battery.

DIMENSIONS AND WEIGHT dry weight: plus 212 lb, 96 kg.

OPTIONAL ACCESSORIES 4-speed fully synchronized mechanical gearbox (I 2.540, II 1.800, III 1.440, IV 1, rev 2.540), central lever, 3.080 axle ratio; Turbo-Hydramatic automatic transmission with 3 ratios (I 2.520, II 1.520, III 1, rev 1.920), max ratio of converter at stall 2.50, 2.730 or 3.080 axle ratio; air-conditioning; « Automatic » transmission not available.

175 hp power team

See 100 hp power team, except for:

ENGINE 8 cylinders; 350 cu in, 5,736 cc (3.87 x 3.75 in, 98.2 x 89.3 mm); compression ratio: 7.6:1; max power (DIN): 175 hp at 4,400 rpm; max torque (DIN): 280 lb ft, 38.6 kg m at 2,400 rpm; max engine rpm: 4,800; 30.5 hp/l; 5 crankshaft bearings; camshafts: 1, at centre of Vee; lubricating system capacity: 10 imp pt, 12 US pt, 5.7 l; 1 Rochester 7043071 downdraught twin barrel carburettor; cleaner air system; dual exhaust system; cooling system capacity: 32 imp pt, 38.5 US pt, 18.2 l.

TRANSMISSION gearbox ratios: I 2.450, II 1.500, III 1, rev 2.630; lever: central (standard).

PERFORMANCE max speed: about 114 mph, 183 km/h; power-weight ratio: Ventura 4-dr. sedan 19.8 lb/hp, 9 kg/hp - Ventura Custom 4-dr. sedan 20 lb/hp, 9.1 kg/hp; fuel consumption: 16 m/imp gal, 13.4 m/US gal, 17.6 l x 100 km.

ELECTRICAL EQUIPMENT 53 Ah battery.

DIMENSIONS AND WEIGHT dry weight: plus 239 lb, 108 kg.

OPTIONAL ACCESSORIES 4-speed fully synchronized mechanical gearbox (I 2.540, II 1.800, III 1.440, IV 1, rev 2.540), central lever, 3.080 axle ratio; Turbo-Hydramatic automatic transmission with 3 ratios (I 2.520, II 1.520, III 1, rev 1.920), max ratio of converter at stall 2.50, 2.730 or 3.080 axle ratios; air-conditioning; « Automatic » transmission not available.

Firebird Series

PRICES IN USA:

1 Firebird	2-door Hardtop Coupé	**$ 2,838**
2 Firebird Esprit	2-door Hardtop Coupé	**$ 3,194**
3 Firebird Formula	2-door Hardtop Coupé	**$ 3,221**
4 Firebird Trans Am	2-door Hardtop Coupé	**$ 4,103**

For V8 engines add $ 118.

Power team:	Standard for:	Optional for:
100 hp	1	—
150 hp	2	1
170 hp	—	2
175 hp	3	—
230 hp	—	3
250 hp	4	3
310 hp	—	3,4

100 hp power team

ENGINE front, 4 stroke; 6 cylinders, in line; 250 cu in, 4,097 cc (3.87 x 3.53 in, 98.2 x 89.6 mm); compression ratio: 8.2:1; max power (DIN): 100 hp at 3,600 rpm; max torque (DIN): 175 lb ft, 24.1 kg m at 1,600 rpm; max engine rpm: 4,000; 24.4 hp/l; cast iron cylinder block and head; 7 crankshaft bearings; valves: overhead, in line, push-rods and rockers, hydraulic tappets; camshafts: 1, side; lubrication: gear pump, full flow filter, 8.3 imp pt, 9.9 US pt, 4.7 l; 1 Rochester 7043017 (7043317 for California only) downdraught single barrel carburettor; cleaner air system; fuel feed: mechanical pump; water-cooled, 20.8 imp pt, 24.9 US pt, 11.8 l.

TRANSMISSION driving wheels: rear; clutch: single dry plate; gearbox: mechanical; gears: 3, fully synchronized; ratios: I 2.850, II 1.680, III 1, rev 2.950; lever: central; final drive: hypoid bevel; axle ratio: 3.080; width of rims: 6"; tyres: E78 x 14.

PERFORMANCE max speed: about 100 mph, 161 km/h; power-weight ratio: 32.5 lb/hp, 14.7 kg/hp; speed in direct drive at 1,000 rpm: 26.3 mph, 42.3 km/h; fuel consumption: 20 m/imp gal, 16.7 m/US gal, 14.1 l x 100 km.

CHASSIS integral with separate partial frame; front suspension: independent, wishbones, lower trailing links, coil springs, anti-roll bar, telescopic dampers; rear suspension: rigid axle, semi-elliptic leafsprings, anti-roll bar, telescopic dampers.

STEERING recirculating ball; turns lock to lock: 6.30.

100 HP POWER TEAM

BRAKES front disc (diameter 11 in, 279 mm), rear drum; swept area: total 337.3 sq in, 2,175 sq cm.

ELECTRICAL EQUIPMENT 12 V; 45 Ah battery; 37 A alternator; Delco-Remy distributor; 2 headlamps.

DIMENSIONS AND WEIGHT wheel base: 108 in, 2,743 mm; tracks: 61.30 in, 1,557 mm front, 60 in, 1,524 mm rear; length: 192.10 in, 4,879 mm; width: 73.40 in, 1,864; height: 50.40 in, 1,280 mm; dry weight: 3,248 lb, 1,473 kg; turning circle (between walls): 39.8 ft, 12.1 m; fuel tank: 15 imp gal, 18 US gal, 68 l.

BODY 2 doors; 4 seats, separate front seats, built-in headrests.

OPTIONAL ACCESSORIES Turbo-Hydramatic automatic transmission with 3 ratios (I 2.520, II 1.520, III 1, rev 1.920), max ratio of converter at stall 2.30, steering column or central lever, 3.080 axle ratio; limited slip differential; F78 x 14 or F70 x 14 tyres with 7" wide rims; power-assisted steering; tilt and vertically adjustable steering wheel; servo brake; air-conditioning.

150 hp power team

See 100 hp power team, except for:

ENGINE 8 cylinders; 350 cu in, 5,736 cc (3.87 x 3.75 in, 98.2 x 89.3 mm); compression ratio: 7.6:1; max power (DIN): 150 hp at 4,000 rpm; max torque (DIN): 270 lb ft, 37.2 kg m at 2,000 rpm; max engine rpm: 4,400; 26.1 hp/l; 5 crankshaft bearings; camshafts: 1, at centre of Vee; lubricating system capacity: 10 imp pt, 12 US pt, 5.7 l; 1 Rochester 7043071 downdraught twin barrel carburettor; cleaner air system; cooling system capacity: 37 imp pt, 44.4 US pt, 21 l.

TRANSMISSION gearbox ratios: I 2.540, II 1.500, III 1, rev 2.630.

PERFORMANCE max speed: about 108 mph, 174 km/h; power-weight ratio: Firebird Esprit 23.4 lb/hp, 10.6 kg/hp; fuel consumption: 17.7 m/imp gal, 14.7 m/US gal, 16 l x 100 km.

ELECTRICAL EQUIPMENT 53 Ah battery.

DIMENSIONS AND WEIGHT dry weight: plus 221 lb, 100 kg - Firebird Esprit 3,511 lb, 1,592 kg.

OPTIONAL ACCESSORIES 3.420 axle ratio; Turbo-Hydramatic automatic transmission with max ratio of converter at stall 2.50 and 2.730 3.080 axle ratios; 4-speed fully synchronized mechanical gearbox (I 2.540, II 1.800, III 1.440, IV 1, rev 2.540) 3.080 or 3.420 axle ratio.

170 hp power team

See 100 hp power team, except for:

ENGINE 8 cylinders; 400 cu in, 6,555 cc (4.12 x 3.75 in, 104.6 x 95.2 mm); compression ratio: 8:1; max power (DIN): 170 hp at 3,600 rpm; max torque (DIN): 320 lb ft, 44.1 kg m at 2,000 rpm; max engine rpm: 4,000; 25.9 hp/l; 5 crankshaft bearings; camshafts: 1, at centre of Vee; lubricating system capacity: 10 imp pt, 12 US pt, 5.7 l; 1 Rochester 7043060 (1043061 for California only) downdraught twin barrel carburettor; cleaner air system; cooling system capacity: 37 imp pt, 44.4 US pt, 21 l.

TRANSMISSION gearbox: Turbo-Hydramatic automatic transmission (standard), max ratio of converter at stall 2.20; ratios: I 2.480, II 1.480, III 1, rev 2.080; axle ratio: 2.730.

PERFORMANCE max speed: about 112 mph, 180 km/h; power-weight ratio: 22 lb/hp, 10 kg/hp; speed in direct drive at 1,000 rpm: 26.5 mph, 42.6 km/h; fuel consumption: 17.1 m/imp gal, 14.3 m/US gal, 16.5 l x 100 km.

ELECTRICAL EQUIPMENT 61 Ah battery.

DIMENSIONS AND WEIGHT dry weight: Firebird Esprit 3,736 lb, 1,694 kg.

OPTIONAL ACCESSORIES 3.080 axle ratio.

175 hp power team

See 100 hp power team, except for:

ENGINE 8 cylinders; 350 cu in, 5,736 cc (3.87 x 3.75 in, 98.2 x 89.3 mm); compression ratio: 7.6:1; max power (DIN): 175 hp at 4,400 rpm; max torque (DIN): 280 lb ft, 38.6 kg m at 2,400 rpm; max engine rpm: 4,800; 30.5 hp/l; 5 crankshaft bearings; camshafts: 1, at centre of Vee; lubricating system capacity: 10 imp pt, 12 US pt, 5.7 l; 1 Rochester 7043071 downdraught twin barrel carburettor; cleaner air system; dual exhaust system; cooling system capacity: 37 imp pt, 44.4 US pt, 21 l.

PONTIAC Firebird 2-door Hardtop Coupé

PONTIAC Firebird Trans Am 2-door Hardtop Coupé

PONTIAC Le Mans Sport Coupé 2-door Colonnade Hardtop

TRANSMISSION gearbox ratios: I 2.540, II 1.500, III 1, rev 2.630; width of rims: 7"; tyres: F70 x 14 (standard).

PERFORMANCE max speed: about 113 mph, 182 km/h; power-weight ratio: 20.1 lb/hp, 9.1 kg/hp; speed in direct drive at 1,000 rpm: 26.4 mph, 42.5 km/h; fuel consumption: 15.7 m/imp gal, 13.1 m/US gal, 18 l x 100 km.

ELECTRICAL EQUIPMENT 53 Ah battery.

DIMENSIONS AND WEIGHT tracks: 61.60 in, 1,565 mm front, 60.30 in, 1,532 mm rear; dry weight: 3,528 lb, 1,600 kg.

OPTIONAL ACCESSORIES Turbo-Hydramatic automatic transmission with max ratio of converter at stall 2.50 and 2.730 3.080 axle ratios; 4-speed fully synchronized mechanical gearbox (I 2.540, II 1.800, III 1.440, IV 1, rev 2.540) 3.080 or 3.420 axle ratio; GR70 x 15 tyres with 7" wide rims.

230 hp power team

See 100 hp power team, except for:

ENGINE 8 cylinders; 400 cu in, 6,555 cc (4.12 x 3.75 in, 104.6 x 95.2 mm); compression ratio: 8:1; max power (DIN): 230 hp at 4,400 rpm; max torque (DIN): 325 lb ft, 44.8 kg m at 3,200 rpm; max engine rpm: 4,800; 35.1 hp/l; 5 crankshaft bearings; camshafts: 1, at centre of Vee; lubricating system capacity: 10 imp pt, 12 US pt, 5.7 l; 1 Rochester 7043263 downdraught 4-barrel carburettor; cleaner air system; dual exhaust system; cooling system capacity: 37 imp pt, 44.4 US pt, 21 l.

TRANSMISSION gears: 4, fully synchronized; ratios: I 2.520, II 1.880, III 1.460, IV 1, rev 2.590; axle ratio: 3.420; width of rims: 7"; tyres: F70 x 14 (standard).

PERFORMANCE max speed: about 117 mph, 188 km/h; power-weight ratio: 16.3 lb/hp, 7.4 kg/hp; speed in direct drive at 1,000 rpm: 26.6 mph, 42.8 km/h; fuel consumption: 15.3 m/imp gal, 12.7 m/US gal, 18.5 l x 100 km.

ELECTRICAL EQUIPMENT 61 Ah battery.

DIMENSIONS AND WEIGHT tracks: 61.60 in, 1,565 mm front, 60.30 in, 1,532 mm rear; dry weight: 3,766 lb, 1,708 kg.

OPTIONAL ACCESSORIES Turbo-Hydramatic automatic transmission with 3 ratios (I 2.480, II 1.480, III 1, rev 2.080), max ratio of converter at stall 2.20, 3.080 3.420 axle ratios; 4-speed fully synchronized mechanical gearbox (I 2.200, II 1.640, III 1.280, IV 1, rev 2.270), 3.420 axle ratio; GR70 x 15 tyres with 7" wide rims; electronic ignition.

250 hp power team

See 100 hp power team, except for:

ENGINE 8 cylinders; 455 cu in, 7,456 cc (4.15 x 4.21 in, 105.3 x 106.9 mm); compression ratio: 8:1; max power (DIN): 250 hp at 4,000 rpm; max torque (DIN): 370 lb ft, 51 kg m at 2,800 rpm; max engine rpm: 4,400; 33.5 hp/l; 5 crankshaft bearings; camshafts: 1, at centre of Vee; lubricating system capacity: 10 imp pt, 12 US pt, 5.7 l; 1 Rochester 7043265 downdraught 4-barrel carburettor; cleaner air system; dual exhaust system; cooling system capacity: 34.8 imp pt, 41.9 US pt, 19.8 l.

TRANSMISSION gears: 4, fully synchronized; gearbox ratios: I 2.200, II 1.640, III 1.280, IV 1, rev 2.270; axle ratio: 3.420; final drive: limited slip differential (standard); width of rims: 7"; tyres: F60 x 15.

PERFORMANCE max speed: about 119 mph, 191 km/h; power-weight ratio: Firebird Trans Am 14.8 lb/hp, 6.7 kg/hp; speed in direct drive at 1,000 rpm: 27.1 mph, 43.6 km/h; fuel consumption: 15.1 m/imp gal, 12.6 m/US gal, 18.7 l x 100 km.

STEERING servo (standard).

BRAKES servo (standard).

ELECTRICAL EQUIPMENT 62 Ah battery.

DIMENSIONS AND WEIGHT tracks: 61.60 in, 1,565 mm front, 60.30 in, 1,532 mm rear; dry weight: 3,711 lb, 1,683 kg.

OPTIONAL ACCESSORIES Turbo-Hydramatic automatic transmission with 3 ratios (I 2.480, II 1.480, III 1, rev 2.080), max ratio of converter at stall 2.20, 3.080 3.420 axle ratios; GR70 x 15 tyres with 7" wide rims; electronic ignition.

310 hp power team

See 100 hp power team, except for:

ENGINE 8 cylinders; 455 cu in, 7,456 cc (4.15 x 4.21 in, 105.3 x 106.9 mm); compression ratio: 8.4:1; max power (DIN): 310 hp at 4,000 rpm; max torque (DIN): 390 lb ft, 53.8 kg m at 3,600 rpm; max engine rpm: 4,400; 41.6 hp/l; 5 crankshaft bearings; camshafts: 1, at centre of Vee; lubricating system capacity: 10 imp pt, 12 US pt, 5.7 l; 1 Rochester 7043273 downdraught 4-barrel carburettor; cleaner air system; dual exhaust system; cooling system capacity: 34.8 imp pt, 41.9 US pt, 19.8 l.

PONTIAC Firebird Formula 2-door Hardtop Coupé

PONTIAC Firebird Trans Am 2-door Hardtop Coupé

PONTIAC Le Mans Sport Coupé 2-door Colonnade Hardtop

TRANSMISSION gears: 4, fully synchronized; ratios: I 2.520, II 1.880, III 1.460, IV 1, rev 2.590; final drive: limited slip differential (standara); axle ratio: 3.420; width of rims: 7"; tyres: F60 x 15.

PERFORMANCE max speed: about 125 mph, 201 km/h; power-weight ratio: Firebird Formula 12.2 lb/hp, 5.5 kg/hp - Firebird Trans Am 12.8 lb/hp, 5.8 kg/hp; speed in direct drive at 1,000 rpm: 29 mph, 46.6 km/h; fuel consumption: 14.2 m/imp gal, 11.8 m/US gal, 19.9 l x 100 km.

STEERING servo (standard).

BRAKES servo (standard).

ELECTRICAL EQUIPMENT 62 Ah battery.

DIMENSIONS AND WEIGHT tracks: 61.60 in, 1,565 mm front, 60.30 in, 1.532 mm rear; dry weight: Firebird Formula 3,780 lb, 1,714 kg - Firebird Trans Am 3,963 lb, 1,797 kg.

OPTIONAL ACCESSORIES Turbo-Hydramatic automatic transmission with 3 ratios (I 2.480, II 1.480, III 1, rev 2.080), max ratio of converter at stall 2.20, 3.080 3.420 axle ratios; GR70 x 15 tyres with 7" wide rims; electronic ignition.

Le Mans - Le Mans Safari - Le Mans Sport Coupé - GTO - Luxury Le Mans - Grand Am Series

PRICES IN USA:

1	Le Mans	2-door Colonnade Hardtop	$ **2,870**
2	Le Mans	4-door Colonnade Hardtop	$ **2,846**
3	Le Mans Safari	6-passenger Station Wagon	$ **3.230**
4	Le Mans Safari	9-passenger Station Wagon	$ **3,357**
5	Le Mans Sport Coupé	2-door Colonnade Hardtop	$ —
6	GTO	2-door Colonnade Hardtop	$ —
7	Luxury Le Mans	2-door Colonnade Hardtop	$ **3,215**
8	Luxury Le Mans	4-door Colonnade Hardtop	$ **3,338**
9	Grand Am	2-door Colonnade Hardtop	$ **4,178**
10	Grand Am	4-door Colonnade Hardtop	$ **4,267**

Power team:	Standard for:	Optional for:
100 hp	1,2,3,4,5	—
150 hp	7,8	1,2,3,4,5
170 hp	9,10	1,2,3,4,5,7,8
175 hp	7,8	1,2,3,4,5
185 hp	9,10	1,2,3,4,5,7,8
230 hp	6	1,2,3,4,5,7,8,9,10
250 hp	—	all
310 hp	—	1,5,6,9

100 hp power team

ENGINE front, 4 stroke; 6 cylinders, in line, 250 cu in, 4,097 cc (3.87 x 3.53 in, 98.2 x 89.6); compression ratio: 8.2:1; max power (DIN): 100 hp at 3,600 rpm; max torque (DIN): 175 lb ft, 24.1 kg m at 1,600 rpm; max engine rpm: 4,000; 24.4 hp/l; cast iron cylinder block and head; 7 crankshaft bearings; valves: overhead, in line, push-rods and rockers, hydraulic tappets; camshafts: 1, side; lubrication: gear pump, full flow filter, 8.3 imp pt, 9.9 US pt, 4.7 l; 1 Rochester 7043017 (7043317 for California only) downdraught single barrel carburettor; cleaner air system; fuel feed: mechanical pump; water-cooled, 22.2 imp pt, 26.6 US pt, 12.6 l.

TRANSMISSION driving wheels: rear; clutch: single dry plate; gearbox: mechanical; gears: 3, fully synchronized; ratios: I 2.850, II 1.680, III 1, rev 2.950; lever: steering column; final drive: hypoid bevel; axle ratio: 3.230 - station wagons 3.420; width of rims: 6"; tyres: F78 x 14 - station wagons H78 x 14.

PERFORMANCE max speed: about 99 mph, 160 km/h; power-weight ratio: Le Mans 4-dr. Colonnade hardtop 37.1 lb/hp, 16.9 kg/hp; speed in direct drive: 27.1 mph, 43.6 km/h; fuel consumption: 20.1 m/imp gal, 16.7 m/US gal, 14.1 l x 100 km.

CHASSIS perimeter; front suspension: independent, wishbones, lower trailing links, coil springs, anti-roll bar, telescopic dampers; rear suspension: rigid axle, lower trailing radius arms, upper oblique torque arms, coil springs, anti-roll bar, telescopic dampers.

STEERING recirculating ball; turns lock to lock: 5.60.

BRAKES front disc (diameter 11 in, 279 mm), rear drum (station wagons servo); swept area: total 337.3 sq in, 2,175 sq cm - station wagons 356.1 sq in, 2,297 sq cm.

100 HP POWER TEAM

ELECTRICAL EQUIPMENT 12 V; 45 Ah battery; 37 A alternator; Delco-Remy distributor; 2 headlamps.

DIMENSIONS AND WEIGHT wheel base: 112 in, 2,845 mm - 4-dr. Colonnade hardtop and station wagons 116 in, 2,946 mm; tracks: 61.50 in, 1,562 mm front, 60.70 in, 1,542 mm rear; length: 207.40 in, 5,293 mm - 4-dr. Colonnade hardtop 211.40 in, 5,369 mm - station wagons 213.30 in, 5,418 mm; width: 77.70 in, 1,973 mm; height: 52.90 in, 1,344 mm - 4-dr. Colonnade hardtop 54.30 in, 1,379 mm - station wagons 55 in, 1,397 mm; dry weight: Le Mans 2-dr. Colonnade hardtop 3,609 lb, 1,637 kg - 4-dr. Colonnade hardtop 3,715 lb, 1,685 kg - Le Mans Safari 6-pass. station wagon 4,069 lb, 1,845 kg - 9-pass. station wagon 4,106 lb, 1,862 kg - Le Mans Sport Coupé 2-dr. Colonnade hardtop 3,633 lb, 1,647 kg; turning circle (between walls): 39.5 ft, 12 m - 4-dr. Colonnade hardtop 44 ft, 13.4 m - station wagons 45 ft, 13.7 m; fuel tank: 18.3 imp gal, 21.8 US gal, 83 l - station wagons 18.5 imp gal, 22 US gal, 84 l.

OPTIONAL ACCESSORIES Turbo-Hydramatic automatic transmission with 3 ratios (I 2.520, II 1.520, III 1, rev 1.920), max ratio of converter at stall 2.30, 3.080 3.230 3.420 axle ratios; limited slip differential; G78 x 14 or G70 x 14 tyres with 7" wide rims (except station wagons); anti-roll bar on rear suspension; tilt and vertically adjustable steering wheel; power-assisted steering; servo brake; manually or electrically controlled sunshine roof only for 2-door Colonnade hardtop models; air-conditioning; Custom equipment only for station wagons.

150 hp power team

See 100 hp power team, except for:

ENGINE 8 cylinders; 350 cu in, 5,736 cc (3.87 x 3.75 in, 98.2 x 89.3 mm); compression ratio: 7.6:1; max power (DIN): 150 hp at 4,000 rpm; max torque (DIN): 260 lb ft, 37.2 kg m at 2,000 rpm; max engine rpm: 4,400; 26.1 hp/l; 5 crankshaft bearings; camshaft: 1, at centre of Vee; lubricating system capacity: 10 imp pt, 12 US pt, 5.7 l; 1 Rochester 7043071 downdraught twin barrel carburettor; cleaner air system; cooling system capacity: 36.6 imp pt, 44 US pt, 20.8 l.

TRANSMISSION gearbox ratios: I 2.540, II 1.500, III 1, rev 2.630.

PERFORMANCE max speed: about 106 mph, 170 km/h; power-weight ratio: Luxury Le Mans 4-dr. Colonnade hardtop 26.5 lb/hp, 12 kg/hp; fuel consumption: 17.8 m/imp gal, 14.8 m/US gal, 15.9 l x 100 km.

ELECTRICAL EQUIPMENT 53 Ah battery.

DIMENSIONS AND WEIGHT dry weight: Le Mans, Le Mans Safari and Le Mans Sport Coupé plus 216 lb, 98 kg - Luxury Le Mans 2-dr. Colonnade hardtop 3,839 lb, 1,741 kg - 4-dr. Colonnade hardtop 3,977 lb, 1,804 kg.

OPTIONAL ACCESSORIES 3.080 axle ratio; Turbo-Hydramatic automatic transmission with max ratio of converter at stall 2.50 and 2.730 3.080 axle ratios; 4-speed fully synchronized mechanical gearbox (I 2.540, II 1.800, III 1.440, IV 1, rev 2,540), central lever, 3.230 3.080 axle ratios.

170 hp power team

See 100 hp power team, except for:

ENGINE 8 cylinders; 400 cu in, 6,555 cc (4.12 x 3.75 in, 104.6 x 95.2 mm); compression ratio: 8:1; max power DIN): 170 hp at 3,600 rpm; max torque (DIN): 320 lb ft, 44.1 kg m at 2,000 rpm; max engine rpm: 4,000; 25.9 hp/l; 5 crankshaft bearings; camshafts: 1, at centre of Vee; lubricating system capacity: 10 imp pt, 12 US pt, 5.7 l; 1 Rochester 7043060 (7043061 for California only) downdraught twin barrel carburettor; cleaner air system; cooling system capacity: 36.6 imp pt, 44 US pt, 20.8 l.

TRANSMISSION gearbox: Turbo-Hydramatic automatic transmission (standard), max ratio of converter at stall 2.20; ratios: I 2.480, II 1.480, III 1, rev 2.080; axle ratio: 3.080 - station wagons 2.730; width of rims: 7"; tyres: GR70 x 15.

PERFORMANCE max speed: about 110 mph, 177 km/h; power-weight ratio: Grand Am 4-dr. Colonnade hardtop 24.4 lb/hp, 11 kg/hp; speed in direct drive at 1,000 rpm: 27.6 mph, 44.4 km/h; fuel consumption: 17 m/imp gal, 14.2 m/US gal, 16.6 l x 100 km.

STEERING servo (standard).

BRAKES servo (standard).

ELECTRICAL EQUIPMENT 61 Ah battery.

PONTIAC Luxury Le Mans Series

PONTIAC Grand Am Series

PONTIAC Grand Ville Series

DIMENSIONS AND WEIGHT tracks: 61.90 in, 1,572 mm front, 61.10 in, 1,552 mm rear; length: 2-dr. Colonnade hardtop 208.60 in, 5,298 mm - 4-dr. Colonnade hardtop 212.60 in, 5,400 mm; dry weight: plus 221 lb, 100 kg - Grand Am 2-dr. Colonnade hardtop 4,054 lb, 1,838 kg - 4-dr. Colonnade hardtop 4,150 lb, 1,882 kg; turning circle (between walls): 2-dr. Colonnade hardtop 42.2 ft, 12.9 m - 4-dr. Colonnade hardtop 43.2 ft, 13.2 m; fuel tank: 20.9 imp gal, 25 US gal, 95 l.

OPTIONAL ACCESSORIES 2.930 axle ratio: G60 x 15 tyres with 7" wide rims.

175 hp power team

See 100 hp power team, except for:

ENGINE 8 cylinders; 350 cu in, 5,736 cc (3.87 x 3.75 in, 98.2 x 89.3 mm); compression ratio: 7.6:1; max power (DIN): 175 hp at 4,400 rpm; max torque (DIN): 280 lb ft, 38.6 kg m at 2,400 rpm; max engine rpm: 4,800; 30.5 hp/l; 5 crankshaft bearings; camshaft: 1, at centre of Vee; lubricating system capacity: 10 imp pt, 12 US pt, 5.7 l; 1 Rochester 7043071 downdraught twin barrel carburettor; cleaner air system; dual exhaust system; cooling system capacity: 36.6 imp pt, 44 US pt, 20.8 l.

TRANSMISSION (only for Le Mans and Le Mans Sport Coupé Series) gearbox ratios: I 2.420, II 1.580, III 1, rev 2.410; lever; central; axle ratio: 3.230.

PERFORMANCE max speed: about 112 mph, 180 km/h; power-weight ratio: Luxury Le Mans 4-dr. Colonnade hardtop 22.9 lb/hp, 10.4 kg/hp; fuel consumption: 15.4 m/imp gal, 12.9 m/US gal, 18.3 l x 100 km.

ELECTRICAL EQUIPMENT 53 Ah battery.

DIMENSIONS AND WEIGHT (see 150 hp power team) dry weight: plus 27 lb, 12 kg.

OPTIONAL ACCESSORIES Turbo-Hydramatic automatic transmission not available; 3.080 axle ratio.

185 hp power team

See 100 hp power team, except for:

ENGINE 8 cylinders; 400 cu in, 6,555 cc (4.12 x 3.75 in, 104.6 x 95.2 mm); compression ratio: 8:1; max power (DIN): 185 hp at 4,000 rpm; max torque (DIN): 320 lb ft, 44.1 kg m at 2,400 rpm; max engine rpm: 4,400; 28.2 hp/l; 5 crankshaft bearings; camshafts: 1, at centre of Vee; lubricating system capacity: 10 imp pt, 12 US pt, 5.7 l; 1 Rochester 7043060 (7043061 for California only) downdraught twin barrel carburettor; cleaner air system; dual exhaust system; cooling system capacity: 36.6 imp pt, 44 US pt, 20.8 l.

TRANSMISSION gearbox: Turbo-Hydramatic automatic transmission (standard), max ratio of converter at stall 2.20; ratios: I 2.480, II 1.480, III 1, rev 2.080; axle ratio: 3.080 - station wagons 2.730; width of rims: 7"; tyres: GR70 x 15.

PERFORMANCE max speed: about 114 mph, 183 km/h; power-weight ratio: Grand Am 4-dr. Colonnade hardtop 22.6 lb/hp, 10.2 kg/ hp; speed in direct drive at 1,000 rpm: 27.6 mph, 44.4 km/h; fuel consumption: 15.4 m/imp gal, 12.8 m/US gal, 18.4 l x 100 km.

STEERING servo (standard).

BRAKES servo (standard).

ELECTRICAL EQUIPMENT 61 Ah battery.

DIMENSIONS AND WEIGHT (see 170 hp power team) dry weight: plus 27 lb, 12 kg.

OPTIONAL ACCESSORIES 2.930 axle ratio; G60 x 15 tyres with 7" wide rims.

230 hp power team

See 100 hp power team, except for:

ENGINE 8 cylinders; 400 cu in, 6,555 cc (4.12 x 3.75 in, 104.6 x 95.2 mm); compression ratio: 8:1; max power (DIN): 230 hp at 4,400 rpm; max torque (DIN): 325 lb ft, 44.8 kg m at 3,200 rpm; max engine rpm: 4,800; 35.1 hp/l; 5 crankshaft bearings; camshafts: 1, at centre of Vee; lubricating system capacity: 10 imp pt, 12 US pt, 5.7 l; 1 Rochester 7043263 downdraught 4-barrel carburettor; cleaner air system; dual exhaust system; cooling system capacity: 38.4 imp pt, 46 US pt, 21.8 l.

TRANSMISSION gears: 4, fully synchronized; ratios: I 2.520, II 1,880, III 1.460, IV 1, rev 2.590; lever: central; axle ratio: 3.420 - station wagons 3.230; width of rims: 7"; tyres: G60 x 15.

PONTIAC Luxury Le Mans 2-door Colonnade Hardtop

PONTIAC Grand Am 4-door Colonnade Hardtop

PONTIAC Catalina 2-door Hardtop Coupé

PERFORMANCE max speed: about 116 mph, 186 km/h; power-weight ratio: Le Mans 4-dr. Colonnade hardtop 17.3 lb/hp, 7.8 kg/hp - Luxury Le Mans 4-dr. Colonnade hardtop 17.5 lb/hp, 7.9 kg/hp - Grand Am 4-dr. Colonnade hardtop 18.2 lb/hp, 8.3 kg/hp; speed in direct drive at 1,000 rpm: 26.9 mph, 43.3 km/h; fuel consumption: 15.2 m/imp gal, 12.6 m/US gal, 18.6 l x 100 km.

STEERING servo (standard).

BRAKES servo (standard).

ELECTRICAL EQUIPMENT 61 Ah battery.

DIMENSIONS AND WEIGHT (see 170 hp power team) tracks: 61.90 in, 1,572 mm front, 61.10 in, 1,552 mm rear; dry weight: Le Mans, Le Mans Sport Coupé and Le Mans Safari plus 261 lb, 118 kg - Luxury Le Mans and Grand Am plus 45 lb, 21 kg.

OPTIONAL ACCESSORIES Turbo-Hydramatic automatic transmission with 3 ratios (I 2.480, II 1.480, III 1, rev 2.080), max ratio of converter at stall 2.20, 3.420 3.230 3.080 axle ratios (station wagons 3.230 3.080); only for GTO and Le Mans Series 3-speed fully synchronized mechanical gearbox (I 2.420, II 1.580, III 1, rev 2.410), central lever, 3.420 3.230 axle ratios; electronic ignition.

250 hp power team

See 100 hp power team, except for:

ENGINE 8 cylinders; 455 cu in, 7,456 cc (4.15 x 4.21 in, 105.3 x 106.9 mm); compression ratio: 8:1; max power (DIN): 250 hp at 4,000 rpm; max torque (DIN): 370 lb ft, 51 kg m at 2,800 rpm; max engine rpm: 4,400; 33.5 hp/l; 5 crankshaft bearings; camshafts: 1, at centre of Vee; lubricating system capacity: 10 imp pt, 12 US pt, 5.7 l; 1 Rochester 7043262 downdraught 4-barrel carburettor; cleaner air system; dual exhaust system; cooling system capacity: 37 imp pt, 44.4 US pt, 21 l.

TRANSMISSION gearbox: Turbo-Hydramatic automatic transmission (standard) max ratio of converter at stall 2.20; ratios: I 2.480, II 1.480, III 1, rev 2.080; axle ratio: 3.230; width of rims: 7''; tyres: G60 x 15.

PERFORMANCE max speed: about 118 mph, 190 km/h; power-weight ratio: Le Mans 4-dr. Colonnade hardtop 15.9 lb/hp, 7.2 kg/hp - Luxury Le Mans 4-dr. Colonnade hardtop 16.1 lb/hp, 7.3 kg/hp - Grand Am 4-dr. Colonnade hardtop 16.8 lb/hp, 7.6 kg/hp; speed in direct drive at 1,000 rpm: 27 mph, 43.4 km/h; fuel consumption: 14.9 m/imp gal, 12.4 m/US gal, 18.9 l x 100 km.

STEERING servo (standard).

BRAKES servo (standard).

ELECTRICAL EQUIPMENT 62 Ah battery.

DIMENSIONS AND WEIGHT (see 230 hp power team) dry weight: Le Mans, Le Mans Sport Coupé and Le Mans Safari plus 265 lb, 121 kg - Luxury Le Mans and Grand Am plus 49 lb, 23 kg.

OPTIONAL ACCESSORIES 3.080 axle ratio; electronic ignition.

310 hp power team

See 100 hp power team, except for:

ENGINE 8 cylinders; 455 cu in, 7,456 cc (4.15 x 4.21 in, 105.3 x 106.9 mm); compression ratio: 8.4:1; max power (DIN): 310 hp at 4,000 rpm; max torque (DIN): 390 lb ft, 53.8 kg m at 3,600 rpm; max engine rpm: 4,400; 41.6 hp/l; 5 crankshaft bearings; camshafts: 1, at centre of Vee; lubricating system capacity: 10 imp pt, 12 US pt, 5.7 l; 1 Rochester 7043273 downdraught 4-barrel carburettor; cleaner air system; dual exhaust system; cooling system capacity: 37 imp pt, 44.4 US pt, 21 l.

TRANSMISSION gears: 4, fully synchronized; ratios: I 2.520, II 1.880, III 1.460, IV 1, rev 2.590; lever: central; axle ratio: 3.420; width of rims: 7''; tyres: G60 x 15.

PERFORMANCE max speed: about 120 mph, 193 km/h; power-weight ratio: Le Mans 2-dr. Colonnade hardtop 12.8 lb/hp, 6 kg/hp - Le Mans Sport Coupé 2-dr. Colonnade hardtop 11.9 lb/hp, 5 kg/hp; speed in direct drive at 1,000 rpm: 26.9 mph, 43.3 km/h; fuel consumption: 14.1 m/imp gal, 11.8 m/US gal, 20 l x 100 km.

STEERING servo (standard).

BRAKES servo (standard).

ELECTRICAL EQUIPMENT 62 Ah battery.

310 HP POWER TEAM

DIMENSIONS AND WEIGHT (see 230 hp power team) dry weight: Le Mans plus 275 lb, 125 kg - Le Mans Sport Coupé plus 54 lb, 25 kg.

OPTIONAL ACCESSORIES Turbo-Hydramatic automatic transmission with 3 ratios (I 2.480, II 1.480, III 1, rev 2.080), max ratio of converter at stall 2.20, 3.420 axle ratio; electronic ignition.

Catalina - Safari - Bonneville - Grand Ville - Grand Safari Series

PRICES IN USA:

1	Catalina	2-door Hardtop Coupé	**$ 3,807**
2	Catalina	4-door Hardtop	**$ 3,873**
3	Catalina	4-door Sedan	**$ 3,712**
4	Safari	6-passenger Station Wagon	**$ 4,232**
5	Safari	9-passenger Station Wagon	**$ 4,372**
6	Bonneville	2-door Hardtop Coupé	**$ 4,155**
7	Bonneville	4-door Hardtop	**$ 4,220**
8	Bonneville	4-door Sedan	**$ 4,096**
9	Grand Ville	2-door Hardtop Coupé	**$ 4,442**
10	Grand Ville	2-door Convertible	**$ 4,640**
11	Grand Ville	4-door Hardtop Sedan	**$ 4,507**
12	Grand Safari	6-passenger Station Wagon	**$ 4,564**
13	Grand Safari	9-passenger Station Wagon	**$ 4,704**

Power team:	Standard for:	Optional for:
150 hp	1,2,3	—
170 hp	4,5,6,7,8	1,2,3
175 hp	1,2,3	—
185 hp	6,7,8	1,2,3
200 hp	12,13	1,2,3,4,5,6,7,8
215 hp	9,10,11	all except 9,10,11
230 hp	12,13	1,2,3,6,7,8
250 hp	9,10,11	1,2,3,6,7,8

150 hp power team

ENGINE front, 4 stroke; 8 cylinders; 350 cu in, 5,736 cc (3.87 x 3.75 in, 98.2 x 89.3 mm); compression ratio: 7.6:1; max power (DIN): 150 hp at 4,000 rpm; max torque (DIN): 270 lb ft, 37.2 kg m at 2,000 rpm; max engine rpm: 4,400; 26.1 hp/l; cast iron cylinder block and head; 5 crankshaft bearings; valves: overhead, in line, push-rods and rockers, hydraulic tappets; camshafts: 1, at centre of Vee; lubrication: gear pump, full flow filter, 10 imp pt, 12 US pt, 5.7 l; 1 Rochester 7043073 (7043063 for California only) downdraught twin barrel carburettor; cleaner air system; fuel feed: mechanical pump; water-cooled, 36.6 imp pt, 44 US pt, 20.8 l.

TRANSMISSION driving wheels: rear; gearbox: Turbo-Hydramatic automatic transmission, hydraulic torque converter and planetary gears with 3 ratios, max ratio of converter at stall 2.40, possible manual selection; ratios: I 2.480, II 1.480, III 1, rev 2.080; lever: steering column; final drive: hypoid bevel; axle ratio: 3.080; width of rims: 6"; tyres G78 x 15.

PERFORMANCE max speed: about 97 mph, 156 km/h; power-weight ratio: Catalina 4-dr. sedan 29.1 lb/hp, 13.2 kg/hp; speed in direct drive at 1,000 rpm: 26.4 mph, 42.5 km/h; fuel consumption: 17.2 m/imp gal, 14.3 m/US gal, 16.4 l x 100 km.

CHASSIS perimeter; front suspension: independent, wishbones, coil springs, anti-roll bar, telescopic dampers; rear suspension: rigid axle (semi-elliptic leafsprings on station wagons), lower trailing radius arms, upper torque arms, coil springs, telescopic dampers.

STEERING recirculating ball, variable ratio, servo; turns lock to lock: 3.50.

BRAKES front disc (diameter 11.86 in, 301 mm), rear drum, servo; swept area: total 380 sq in, 2,451 sq cm.

ELECTRICAL EQUIPMENT 12 V; 53 Ah battery; 37 A alternator; Delco-Remy distributor; 4 headlamps.

DIMENSIONS AND WEIGHT wheel base: 124 in, 3,149 mm; tracks: 64.10 in, 1,628 mm front, 64 in, 1,625 mm rear; length: 224.80 in, 5,710 mm; width 79.60 in, 2,022 mm; height: 2-dr. hardtop coupé 53.50 in, 1,359 mm - 4-dr. hardtop 53.60 in, 1,361 mm - 4-dr. sedan 54.20 in, 1,377 mm; dry weight: Catalina 2-dr. hardtop coupé 4,326 lb, 1,962 kg - 4-dr. hardtop 4,407 lb, 1,998 kg - 4-dr. sedan 4,370 lb, 1,982 kg; turning circle (between walls): 46.5 ft, 14.2 m; fuel tank: 21.6 imp gal, 25.8 US gal, 98 l.

OPTIONAL ACCESSORIES limited slip differential; 3.230 axle ratio; J78 x 15 tyres; automatic or manual levelling control or rear suspension; air-conditioning.

PONTIAC Safari Station Wagon

PONTIAC Bonneville 4-door Hardtop

PONTIAC Grand Ville 4-door Hardtop Sedan

170 hp power team

See 150 hp power team, except for:

ENGINE 400 cu in, 6,555 cc (4.12 x 3.75 in, 104.6 x 95.2 mm); compression ratio: 8:1; max power (DIN): 170 hp at 3,600 rpm; max torque (DIN): 320 lb ft, 44.1 kg m at 2,000 rpm; max engine rpm: 4,000; 25.9 hp/l; 1 Rochester 7043060 (7043067 for California only) downdraught twin barrel carburettor; cleaner air system.

TRANSMISSION max ratio of converter at stall 2.20; axle ratio: 2.730 - station wagons 2.930; tyres: Bonneville H78 x 15 - station wagons L78 x 15.

PERFORMANCE max speed: about 100 mph, 161 km/h; power-weight ratio: Bonneville 4-dr. sedan 26.2 lb/hp, 11.9 kg/hp; speed in direct drive at 1,000 rpm: 26.6 mph, 42.8 km/h; fuel consumption: 16.4 m/imp gal, 13.7 m/US gal, 17.2 l x 100 km.

BRAKES (only for station wagons) swept area: total 392.6 sq in, 2,532 sq cm.

ELECTRICAL EQUIPMENT 61 Ah battery.

DIMENSIONS AND WEIGHT wheel base: station wagons 127 in, 3,226 mm; length: station wagons 230.20 in, 5,847 mm; height: Bonneville 4-dr. hardtop 53.70 in, 1,364 mm - 4-dr. sedan 54.40 in, 1,382 mm - station wagons 57.50 in, 1,460 mm; dry weight: Safari 6-pass. station wagon 4,904 lb, 2,224 kg - 9-pass. station wagon 4,986 lb, 2,261 kg - Bonneville 2-dr. hardtop coupé 4,428 lb, 2,008 kg - 4-dr. hardtop 4,505 lb, 2,043 kg - 4-dr. sedan 4,469 lb, 2,027 kg; turning circle (between walls): station wagons 47.1 ft, 14.4 m; fuel tank: station wagons 20.9 imp gal, 22 US gal, 95 l.

OPTIONAL ACCESSORIES 2.930 3.080 axle ratios (station wagons 2.730 3.080 axle ratios).

175 hp power team

See 150 hp power team, except for:

ENGINE max power (DIN): 175 hp at 4,400 rpm; max torque (DIN): 280 lb ft, 38.6 kg m at 2,400 rpm; max engine rpm: 4,800; 30.5 hp/l; dual exhaust system.

PERFORMANCE max speed: about 102 mph, 164 km/h; power-weight ratio: Catalina 4-dr sedan 25.2 lb/hp, 11.4 kg/hp; speed in direct drive at 1,000 rpm: 26.6 mph, 42.8 km/h; fuel consumption: 15.4 m/imp gal, 12.8 m/US gal, 18.4 l x 100 km.

DIMENSIONS AND WEIGHT dry weight: plus 42 lb, 19 kg.

185 hp power team

See 150 hp power team, except for:

ENGINE 400 cu in, 6,555 cc (4.12 x 3.75 in, 104.6 x 95.2 mm); compression ratio: 8:1; max power (DIN): 185 hp at 4,000 rpm; max torque (DIN): 320 lb ft, 44.1 kg m at 2,400 rpm; max engine rpm: 4,400; 28.2 hp/l; 1 Rochester 7043066 (7043067 for California only) downdraught twin barrel carburettor; cleaner air system; dual exhaust system.

TRANSMISSION max ratio of converter at stall 2.20; axle ratio: 2.930; tyres: Bonneville H78 x 15.

PERFORMANCE max speed: about 103 mph, 165 km/h; power-weight ratio: Bonneville 4-dr. sedan 24.4 lb/hp, 11.1 kg/hp; speed in direct drive at 1,000 rpm: 26.7 mph, 42.9 km/h; fuel consumption: 15.3 m/imp gal, 12.7 m/US gal, 18.5 l x 100 km.

ELECTRICAL EQUIPMENT 61 Ah battery.

DIMENSIONS AND WEIGHT (see 170 hp power team) dry weight: plus 55 lb, 25 kg.

OPTIONAL ACCESSORIES 2.730 3.080 axle ratios.

200 hp power team

See 150 hp power team, except for:

ENGINE 400 cu in, 6,555 cc (4.12 x 3.75 in, 104.6 x 95.2 mm); compression ratio: 8:1; max power (DIN): 200 hp at 4,000 rpm; max torque (DIN): 310 lb ft, 42.8 kg m at 2,400 rpm; max engine rpm: 4,400; 30.5 hp/l; 1 Rochester 7043264 downdraught 4-barrel carburettor; cleaner air system.

TRANSMISSION gearbox: max ratio of converter at stall 2.20; axle ratio: 3.080; tyres: Bonneville H78 x 15 - station wagons L78 x 15.

PONTIAC Safari Station Wagon

PONTIAC Grand Safari Series

PONTIAC Grand Ville Series

PERFORMANCE max speed: about 106 mph, 170 km/h; power-weight ratio: Grand Safari 6-pass. 24.7 lb/hp, 11.2 kg/hp; speed in direct drive at 1,000 rpm: 26.7 mph, 42.9 km/h; fuel consumption: 15.1 m/imp gal, 12.6 m/US gal, 18.7 l x 100 km.

BRAKES (only for station wagons) swept area: total 392.6 sq in, 2,532 sq cm.

ELECTRICAL EQUIPMENT 61 Ah battery.

DIMENSIONS AND WEIGHT (see 170 hp power team) dry weight: Safari and Bonneville plus 10 lb, 4,5 kg - Catalina plus 34 lb, 15 kg - Grand Safari 6-pass. station wagon 4,936 lb, 2,238 kg - 9-pass. station wagon 2,285 kg.

OPTIONAL ACCESSORIES 2.730 or 3,230 axle ratio; electronic ignition.

215 hp power team

See 150 hp power team, except for:

ENGINE 455 cu in, 7,456 cc (4.15 x 4.21 in, 105.3 x 106.7 mm); compression ratio: 8:1; max power (DIN): 215 hp at 3,600 rpm; max torque (DIN): 350 lb ft, 43.5 kg m at 2,400 rpm; max engine rpm: 4,000; 27.2 hp/l; 1 Rochester 7043262 downdraught 4-barrel carburettor; cleaner air system; cooling system capacity: 35.2 imp pt, 42.3 US pt, 20 l.

TRANSMISSION gearbox: max ratio of converter at stall 2.20; axle ratio: 2.930 - station wagons 3.080; tyres: H78 x 15 - station wagons L78 x 15.

PERFORMANCE max speed: about 107 mph, 172 km/h; power-weight ratio: Grand Ville 4-dr. hardtop sedan 20.9 lb/hp, 9.5 kg/hp; speed in direct drive at 1,000 rpm: 26.7 mph, 42.9 km/h; fuel consumption: 15 m/imp gal, 12.5 m/US gal, 18.8 l x 100 km.

BRAKES (only for station wagons) swept area: total 392.6 sq in, 2,532 sq cm.

ELECTRICAL EQUIPMENT 62 Ah battery.

DIMENSIONS AND WEIGHT (see 200 hp power team) height: Grand Ville 2-dr. hardtop coupé and 2-dr. convertible 54.20 in, 1,377 mm - 4-dr. hardtop sedan 53.80 in, 1,366 mm; dry weight: Grand Safari plus 9 lb, 4 kg - Safari and Bonneville plus 19 lb, 8.6 kg - Catalina plus 42 lb, 19 kg - Grand Ville 2-dr. hardtop coupé 4,455 lb, 2,020 kg - 2-dr. convertible 4,475 lb, 2,029 kg - 4-dr. hardtop sedan 4,512 lb, 2,046 kg.

OPTIONAL ACCESSORIES 2.730 3.080 axle ratios (station wagons 3.230); electronic ignition.

230 hp power team

See 150 hp power team, except for:

ENGINE 400 cu in, 6,555 cc (4.12 x 3.75 in, 104.6 x 95.2 mm); compression ratio: 8:1; max power (DIN): 230 hp at 4,400 rpm; max torque (DIN): 325 lb ft, 44.8 kg m at 3,200 rpm; max engine rpm: 4,800; 35.1 hp/l; 1 Rochester 7043264 downdraught 4-barrel carburettor; cleaner air system; dual exhaust system.

TRANSMISSION gearbox: max ratio of converter at stall 2.20; axle ratio: 3.080; tyres: H78 x 15 - station wagons L78 x 15.

PERFORMANCE max speed: about 109 mph, 175 km/h; power-weight ratio: Grand Safari 6-pass. station wagon 21.5 lb/hp, 9.7 kg/hp; speed in direct drive at 1,000 rpm: 26.7 mph, 42.9 km/h; fuel consumption: 14.9 m/imp gal, 12.4 m/US gal, 18.9 l x 100 km.

BRAKES (only for station wagons) swept area: total 392.6 sq in, 2,532 sq cm.

ELECTRICAL EQUIPMENT 61 Ah battery.

DIMENSIONS AND WEIGHT (see 200 hp power team).

OPTIONAL ACCESSORIES 2.730 or 3.230 axle ratio; electronic ignition.

250 hp power team

See 150 hp power team, except for:

ENGINE 455 cu in, 7,456 cc (4.15 x 4.21 in, 105.3 x 106.9 mm); compression ratio: 8:1; max power (DIN): 250 hp at 4,000 rpm; max torque (DIN): 370 lb ft, 51 kg m at 2,800

250 HP POWER TEAM

rpm; max engine rpm: 4,400; 33.5 hp/l; 1 Rochester 7043262 downdraught 4-barrel carburettor; cleaner air system; dual exhaust system; cooling system capacity: 37 imp pt, 44.4 US pt, 21 l.

TRANSMISSION gearbox: max ratio of converter at stall 2.20; axle ratio: 2.930; tyres: H78 x 15.

PERFORMANCE max speed: about 110 mph, 177 km/h; power-weight ratio: Grand Ville 4-dr hardtop sedan 18.1 lb/hp, 8.2 kg/hp; speed in direct drive at 1,000 rpm: 26.7 mph, 42.9 km/h; fuel consumption: 14.5 m/imp gal, 12.1 m/US gal, 19.5 l x 100 km.

ELECTRICAL EQUIPMENT 62 Ah battery.

DIMENSIONS AND WEIGHT (see 215 hp power team) dry weight: plus 27 lb, 13 kg.

OPTIONAL ACCESSORIES 2.730 or 3.080 axle ratio; electronic ignition.

Grand Prix

PRICE IN USA:

Grand Prix	2-door Hardtop Coupé	**$ 4,478**

230 hp power team

(standard).

ENGINE front, 4 stroke; 8 cylinders; 400 cu in, 6,555 cc (4.12 x 3.75 in, 104.6 x 95.2 mm); compression ratio: 8:1; max power (DIN): 230 hp at 4,400 rpm; max torque (DIN): 325 lb ft, 44.8 kg m at 3,200 rpm; max engine rpm: 4,800; 35.1 hp/l; cast iron cylinder block and head; 5 crankshaft bearings; valves: overhead, in line, push-rods and rockers, hydraulic tappets; camshafts: 1, at centre of Vee; lubrication: gear pump, full flow filter, 10 imp pt, 12 US pt, 5.7 l; 1 Rochester 7043264 downdraught 4-barrel carburettor; cleaner air system; dual exhaust system; fuel feed: mechanical pump; water-cooled, 38.7 imp pt, 46.5 US pt, 22 l.

TRANSMISSION driving wheels: rear; gearbox: Turbo-Hydramatic automatic transmission, hydraulic torque converter and planetary gears with 3 ratios, max ratio of converter at stall 2.20, possible manual selection; ratios: I 2.480, II 1.480, III 1, rev 2.080; lever: central; final drive: hypoid bevel; axle ratio: 2.930; width of rims: 7"; tyres: G78 x 14.

PERFORMANCE max speed: about 110 mph, 177 km/h; power-weight ratio: 17.9 lb/hp, 8.1 kg/hp; speed in direct drive at 1,000 rpm: 26.5 mph, 42.6 km/h; fuel consumption: 15 m/imp gal, 12.5 m/US gal, 18.8 l x 100 km.

CHASSIS perimeter; front suspension: independent, wishbones, coil springs, anti-roll bar, telescopic dampers; rear suspension: rigid axle, lower trailing radius arms, upper oblique torque arms, coil springs, telescopic dampers.

STEERING recirculating ball, variable ratio, servo; turns lock to lock: 3.50.

BRAKES front disc (diameter 11 in, 279 mm), rear drum, servo; swept area: total 337.3 sq in, 2,175 sq cm.

ELECTRICAL EQUIPMENT 12 V; 61 Ah battery; 37 A alternator; Delco-Remy distributor; 2 headlamps.

DIMENSIONS AND WEIGHT wheel base: 116 in, 2,946 mm; tracks: 61.90 in, 1,572 mm front, 61.10 in, 1,552 mm rear; length: 216.60 in, 5,502 mm; width: 78.70 in, 1,999 mm; height: 52.90 in, 1,344 mm; dry weight: 4,117 lb, 1,867 kg; turning circle (between walls): 43.9 ft, 13.4 m; fuel tank: 20.9 imp gal, 25 US gal, 95 l.

BODY hardtop coupé; 2 doors; 5 seats, separate front seats; built-in headrests.

OPTIONAL ACCESSORIES limited slip differential; 3.080 axle ratio: GR70 x 15 tyres; anti-roll bar on rear suspension; electronic ignition; SJ equipment; manually or electrically controlled sunshine roof; air-conditioning; bench front seats.

250 hp power team

See 230 hp power team, except for:

ENGINE 455 cu in, 7,456 cc (4.15 x 4.21 in, 105.3 x 106.9 mm); max power (DIN): 250 hp at 4,000 rpm; max torque

PONTIAC Grand Prix 2-door Hardtop Coupé

SQUIRE S.S. 100 Roadster

STUTZ Blackhawk 2-door Hardtop

(DIN): 370 lb ft, 51 kg m at 2,800 rpm; max engine rpm: 4,400; 33.5 hp/l; 1 Rochester 7043262 downdraught 4-barrel carburettor; cleaner air system; dual exhaust system; cooling system capacity: 37 imp pt, 44.4 US pt, 21 l.

TRANSMISSION axle ratio: 3.080.

PERFORMANCE max speed: about 111 mph, 178 km/h; power-weight ratio: 16.5 lb/hp, 7.5 kg/hp; speed in direct drive at 1,000 rpm: 27.3 mph, 43.9 km/h; fuel consumption: 14.6 m/imp gal, 12.1 m/US gal, 19.4 l x 100 km.

ELECTRICAL EQUIPMENT 62 Ah battery.

DIMENSIONS AND WEIGHT dry weight: plus 8 lb, 3.6 kg.

OPTIONAL ACCESSORIES 3.230 axle ratio.

310 hp power team

See 230 hp power team, except for:

ENGINE 455 cu in, 7,456 cc (4.15 x 4.21 in, 105.3 x 106.9 mm); compression ratio: 8.4:1; max power (DIN): 310 hp at 4,000 rpm; max torque (DIN): 390 lb ft, 53.8 kg m at 3,600 rpm; max engine rpm: 4,400; 41.5 hp/l; 1 Rochester 7043270 downdraught 4-barrel carburettor; cleaner air system; dual exhaust system; cooling system capacity: 37 imp pt, 44.4 US pt, 21 l.

TRANSMISSION axle ratio: 3.420.

PERFORMANCE max speed: about 119 mph, 191 km/h; power-weight ratio: 13.3 lb/hp, 6 kg/hp; speed in direct drive at 1,000 rpm: 28 mph, 45 km/h; fuel consumption: 14.1 m/imp gal, 11.7 m/US gal, 20.1 l x 100 km.

ELECTRICAL EQUIPMENT 73 Ah battery.

DIMENSIONS AND WEIGHT dry weight: plus 14 lb, 6 kg.

OPTIONAL ACCESSORIES electronic ignition not available.

SQUIRE USA

S.S. 100

170 hp power team

(standard).

ENGINE Ford, front, 4 stroke; 6 cylinders, in line; 250 cu in, 4,097 cc (3.68 x 3.91 in, 93.4 x 99.2 mm); max power (SAE): 170 hp at 4,500 rpm; max engine rpm: 5,000; 41.5 hp/l; cast iron cylinder block and head; 7 crankshaft bearings; valves: overhead, in line, push-rods and rockers, hydraulic tappets; camshafts: 1, side; lubrication: rotary pump, full flow filter, 7.4 imp pt, 9 US pt, 4 l; 1 Autolite downdraught twin barrel carburettor; fuel feed: mechanical pump; water-cooled, 22.5 imp pt, 27.2 US pt, 12.8 l.

TRANSMISSION driving wheels: rear; clutch: single dry plate; gearbox: mechanical; gears: 4, fully synchronized; ratios: I 2.201, II 1.661, III 1.311, IV 1, rev 2.200; lever: central; final drive: hypoid bevel; axle ratio: 3.250; width of rims: 5"; tyres: 6.00 x 16.

PERFORMANCE max speed: about 116 mph, 186 km/h; power-weight ratio: 12.9 lb/hp, 5.9 kg/hp; speed in direct drive at 1,000 rpm: 23.2 mph, 37.3 km/h; fuel consumption: 23.9 m/imp gal, 20 m/US gal, 11.8 l x 100 km.

CHASSIS box-type ladder frame; front suspension; independent, wishbones, coil springs, anti-roll bar, telescopic dampers; rear suspension: rigid axle, semi-elliptic leafsprings, telescopic dampers.

STEERING ZF recirculating ball; turns lock to lock: 3.50.

BRAKES drum; swept area: total 251.30 sq in, 2,221 sq cm.

ELECTRICAL EQUIPMENT 12 V; 55 A battery; alternator; Autolite distributor; 4 headlamps.

DIMENSIONS AND WEIGHT wheel base: 104.50 in, 2,654 mm; tracks: 59 in, 1,499 mm front, 58.95 in, 1,497 mm rear; length: 150 in, 3,810 mm; width: 61 in, 1,549 mm; height: 44 in, 1,118 mm; ground clearance: 8 in, 203 mm; dry weight: 2,200 lb, 998 kg; turning circle (between walls): 39 ft, 11.9 m; fuel tank: 18 imp gal, 22 US gal, 83 l.

BODY roadster in plastic material; 2 doors; 2 seats.

OPTIONAL ACCESSORIES Cruise-O-Matic automatic transmission with 3 ratios.

AUTOCARS Carmel 13/60

OTOSAN Anadol A2

EL NASR Nasr 128

ELECTRICAL EQUIPMENT 12 V; 34 Ah battery; 230 W dynamo; Marelli distributor; 2 headlamps.

DIMENSIONS AND WEIGHT wheel base: 96.38 in, 2,448 mm; tracks: 51.50 in, 1,308 mm front, 51.69 in, 1,313 mm rear; length: 151.81 in, 3,856 mm; width: 62.60 in, 1,590 mm; height: 55.91 in, 1,420 mm; ground clearance: 5.71 in, 145 mm; dry weight: 1,775 lb, 805 kg; distribution of weight: 61.5% front, 38.5% rear; turning circle (between walls): 35.8 ft, 10.9 m; fuel tank: 8.4 imp gal, 10 US gal, 38 l.

BODY saloon/sedan; 4 doors; 5 seats, separate front seats.

PRACTICAL INSTRUCTIONS fuel: 86 oct petrol; engine sump oil: 7.4 imp pt, 8.9 US pt, 4.2 l, SAE 30W (winter) 40 (summer), change every 6,200 miles, 10,000 km; gearbox and final drive oil: 5.5 imp pt, 6.6 US pt, 3.1 l, SAE 90 EP, change every 18,600 miles, 30,000 km; greasing: every 18,600 miles, 30,000 km, 1 point; sparking plug type: 240°; tappet clearances: inlet 0.012 in, 0.30 mm, exhaust 0.016 in, 0.40 mm; valve timing: 12° 52° 52° 12°; tyre pressure: front 26 psi, 1.8 atm, rear 24 psi, 1.7 atm.

Nasr 125

ENGINE front, 4 stroke; 4 cylinders, vertical, in line; 79 cu in, 1,295 cc (2.83 x 3.13 in, 72 x 79.5 mm); compression ratio: 9:1; max power (SAE): 70 hp at 5,400 rpm; max torque (SAE): 76 lb ft, 10.5 kg m at 3,200 rpm; max engine rpm: 5,500; 54.1 hp/l; cast iron cylinder block, light alloy head; 3 crankshaft bearings; valves: overhead, in line, push-rods and rockers; camshafts: 1, side; lubrication: gear pump, centrifugal filter, cartridge on by-pass, 7.5 imp pt, 9 US pt, 4.3 l; 1 Weber 34 DCHD 1 downdraught twin barrel carburettor; fuel feed: mechanical pump; water-cooled, 11.8 imp pt, 14.2 US pt, 6.7 l.

TRANSMISSION driving wheels: rear; clutch: single dry plate, hydraulically controlled; gearbox: mechanical; gears: 4, fully synchronized; ratios: I 3.750, II 2.300, III 1.490, IV 1, rev 3.870; lever: central; final drive: hypoid bevel; axle ratio: 4.100; width of rims: 4.5"; tyres: 5.60 S x 13.

PERFORMANCE max speeds: (I) 25 mph, 40 km/h; (II) 40 mph, 65 km/h; (III) 62 mph, 100 km/h; (IV) 87 mph, 140 km/h; power-weight ratio: 29 lb/hp, 13.1 kg/hp; carrying capacity: 882 lb, 400 kg; acceleration: 0-50 mph (0-80 km/h) 13 sec; speed in direct drive at 1,000 rpm: 16.1 mph, 25.9 km/h; fuel consumption: 29.7 m/imp gal, 24.8 m/US gal, 9.5 l x 100 km.

CHASSIS integral; front suspension: independent, wishbones, lower trailing links, coil springs, anti-roll bar, telescopic dampers; rear suspension: rigid axle, semi-elliptic leafsprings, telescopic dampers.

STEERING worm and roller; turns lock to lock: 3.

BRAKES disc, servo.

ELECTRICAL EQUIPMENT 12 V; 48 Ah battery; 770 W alternator; 4 headlamps.

DIMENSIONS AND WEIGHT wheel base: 95.28 in, 2,420 mm; tracks: 52.36 in, 1,330 mm front, 51.18 in, 1,300 mm rear; length: 166.65 in, 4,233 mm; width: 63.98 in, 1,625 mm; height: 56.69 in, 1,440 mm; ground clearance: 5.51 in, 140 mm; dry weight: 2,029 lb, 920 kg; turning circle (between walls): 36.1 ft, 11 m; fuel tank: 9.9 imp gal, 11.9 US gal, 45 l.

BODY saloon/sedan; 4 doors; 5 seats, separate front seats, reclining backrests.

PRACTICAL INSTRUCTIONS fuel: 92 oct petrol; engine sump oil: 6.2 imp pt, 7.4 US pt, 3.5 l, SAE 20W-30, change every 6,200 miles, 10,000 km; gearbox oil: 2.3 imp pt, 2,7 US pt, 1.3 l, SAE 90, change every 18,600 miles, 30,000 km; final drive oil: 1.6 imp pt, 1.9 US pt, 0.9 l, SAE 90, change every 18,600 miles, 30,000 km; greasing: every 1,600 miles, 2,500 km, 3 points; sparking plus type: 240°; tappet clearances: inlet 0.008 in, 0.20 mm, exhaust 0.008 in, 0.20 mm; valve timing: 9° 61° 49° 21°; tyre pressure: front 21 psi, 1.5 atm, rear 24 psi, 1.7 atm.

CHEVROLET SOUTH AFRICA

Firenza SL Series

1 Firenza SL	2-door Sedan
2 Firenza SL	4-door Sedan
3 Firenza SL	2-door Coupé
4 Firenza SL	Station Wagon

Power team:	Standard for:	Optional for:
75 hp	1,2,4	—
101 hp	3	2

75 hp power team

ENGINE front, 4 stroke; 4 cylinders, vertical, in line; 70.7 cu in, 1,159 cc (3.06 x 2.40 in, 77.8 x 61 mm); compression ratio: 8.5:1; max power (SAE): 75 hp at 5,800 rpm; max torque (SAE): 70 lb ft, 9.7 kg m at 4,200 rpm; max engine rpm: 6,000; 64.7 hp/l; cast iron cylinder block and head; 3 crankshaft bearings; valves: overhead, in line, push-rods and rockers; camshafts: 1, side; lubrication: gear pump, full flow filter, 5.8 imp pt, 7 US pt, 3.3 l; 1 Weber downdraught twin barrel carburettor; fuel feed: mechanical pump; water-cooled, 10.2 imp pt, 12.3 US pt, 5.8 l.

TRANSMISSION driving wheels: rear; clutch: single dry plate (diaphragm); gearbox: mechanical; gears: 4, fully synchronized; ratios: I 3.765, II 2.213, III 1.404, IV 1, rev 3.707; lever: central; final drive: hypoid bevel; axle ratio: 4.125; tyres: 5.20 x 13.

PERFORMANCE max speed: about 85 mph, 137 km/h; power-weight ratio: 4-dr. sedan 25 lb/hp, 11.3 kg/hp; carrying capacity: 882 lb, 400 kg; speed in direct drive at 1,000 rpm: 15.7 mph, 25.3 km/h; fuel consumption: 29.7 m/imp gal, 24.8 m/US gal, 9.5 l x 100 km.

CHASSIS integral; front suspension: independent, wishbones, coil springs, telescopic dampers; rear suspension: rigid axle, trailing lower radius arms, upper oblique radius arms, coil springs, telescopic dampers.

STEERING rack-and-pinion; turns lock to lock: 3.16.

BRAKES front disc (diameter 8.54 in, 217 mm), rear drum, servo; swept area: total 193.6 sq in, 1,266 sq cm.

ELECTRICAL EQUIPMENT 12 V; 32 Ah battery; 336 W alternator; 2 headlamps.

DIMENSIONS AND WEIGHT wheel base: 97.05 in, 2,465 mm; tracks: 51.77 in, 1,315 mm front, 51.57 in, 1,310 mm rear; length: 162.01 in, 4,115 mm; width: 64.76 in, 1,645 mm; height: 53.35 in, 1,355 mm; ground clearance: 5.31 in, 135 mm; dry weight: Firenza SL 2-dr. sedan 1,830 lb, 830 kg - 4-dr. sedan 1,874 lb, 850 kg - station wagon 1,918 lb, 870 kg; turning circle (between walls): 31.5 ft, 9.6 m; fuel tank: 7.9 imp gal, 9.5 US gal, 36 l.

OPTIONAL ACCESSORIES 155 SR x 13 tyres.

101 hp power team

See 75 hp power team, except for:

ENGINE 153 cu in, 2,507 cc (3.87 x 3.25 in, 98.4 x 82.5 mm); max power (SAE): 101 hp at 4,400 rpm; max torque (SAE): 159 lb ft, 22 kg m at 2,600 rpm; max engine rpm: 4,600; 40.3 hp/l; 5 crankshaft bearings; valves: hydraulic tappets; 1 Rochester downdraught single barrel carburettor; cooling system capacity: 14.8 imp pt, 17.8 US pt, 8.4 l.

TRANSMISSION clutch: single dry plate (diaphragm), hydraulically controlled; gearbox ratios: I 2.786, II 1.981, III 1.413, IV 1, rev 3.064; axle ratio: 3.450.

PERFORMANCE max speed: about 93 mph, 150 kmqh; power-weight ratio: 4-dr. sedan 20.7 lb/hp, 9.4 kg/hp; speed in direct drive at 1,000 rpm: 20.2 mph, 32.5 km/h; fuel consumption: 22.6 m/imp gal, 18.8 m/US gal, 12.5 l x 100 km.

DIMENSIONS AND WEIGHT dry weight: Firenza SL 4-dr. sedan 2,095 lb, 950 kg - 2-dr. coupé 2,117 lb, 960 kg.

OPTIONAL ACCESSORIES Tri-Matic automatic transmission with 3 ratios (I 2.400, II 1.480, III 1, rev 1.920), max ratio of converter at stall 2, possible manual selection, 3.450 axle ratio.

Kommando Series

1 Kommando	4-door Sedan
2 Kommando	Station Wagon

Power team:	Standard for:	Optional for:
142 hp	both	—
157 hp	—	both
182 hp	—	both

142 hp power team

ENGINE front, 4 stroke; 6 cylinders, vertical, in line; 229.9 cu in, 3,768 cc (3.87 x 3.25 in, 98.4 x 82.5 mm); compression ratio: 8.5:1; max power (SAE): 142 hp at 4,400 rpm; max torque (SAE): 220 lb ft, 30.4 kg m at 1,600 rpm; max engine rpm: 4,600; 37.7 hp/l; cast iron cylinder block and head; 7 crankshaft bearings; valves: overhead, in line, push-rods and rockers, hydraulic tappets; camshafts: 1, side; lubrication: gear pump, full flow filter, 6.7 imp pt, 8 US pt, 3.8 l; 1 Rochester downdraught carburettor; fuel feed: mechanical pump; water-cooled, 21.6 imp pt, 26 US pt, 12.3 l.

TRANSMISSION driving wheels: rear; clutch: single dry plate (diaphragm); gearbox: mechanical; gears: 3, fully

CHEVROLET Firenza SL 4-door Sedan

CHEVROLET Kommando 4-door Sedan

RANGER Ranger SS Coupé

Consorte Standard Sedan

PRICE EX WORKS: 407,000 yen.

ENGINE front, 4 stroke; 4 cylinders, vertical, in line; 58.5 cu in, 958 cc (2.68 x 2.60 in, 68 x 66 mm); compression ratio: 9:1; max power (DIN): 58 hp at 5,500 rpm; max torque (DIN): 58 lb ft, 8 kg m at 4,000 rpm; max engine rpm: 6,000; 60.5 hp/l; cast iron cylinder block, light alloy head; 3 crankshaft bearings; valves: overhead, push-rods and rockers; camshafts: 1, side; lubrication: rotary pump, full flow filter, 4.9 imp pt, 5.9 US pt, 2.8 l; 1 Aisan downdraught twin barrel carburettor; fuel feed: mechanical pump; water-cooled, 7.2 imp pt, 8.7 US pt, 4.1 l.

TRANSMISSION driving wheels: rear; clutch: single dry plate (diaphragm); gearbox: mechanical; gears: 4, fully synchronized; ratios: I 3.588, II 2.125, III 1.406, IV 1, rev 4.965; lever: central; final drive: hypoid bevel; axle ratio: 4.222; width of rims: 4"; tyres: 6.00 x 12.

PERFORMANCE max speeds: (I) 25 mph, 40 km/h; (II) 42 mph, 67 km/h; (III) 63 mph, 102 km/h; (IV) 87 mph, 140 km/h; power-weight ratio: 24.9 lb/hp, 11.3 kg/hp; carrying capacity: 882 lb, 400 kg; acceleration: standing ¼ mile 19.5 sec; speed in direct drive at 1,000 rpm: 14.5 mph, 23.3 km/h; fuel consumption: 38.7 m/imp gal, 32.2 m/US gal, 7.3 l x 100 km.

CHASSIS integral; front suspension: independent, by McPherson, coil springs/telescopic dampers struts, lower wishbones (trailing links), anti-roll bar; rear suspension: rigid axle, semi-elliptic leafsprings, telescopic dampers.

STEERING recirculating ball; turns lock to lock: 3.10.

BRAKES front disc, rear drum; swept area: front 19.7 sq in, 127 sq cm, rear 35.7 sq in, 230 sq cm, total 55.4 sq in, 357 sq cm.

ELECTRICAL EQUIPMENT 12 V; 32 Ah battery; 30 A alternator; Nihon-Denso distributor; 2 headlamps.

DIMENSIONS AND WEIGHT wheel base: 85.04 in, 2,160 mm; tracks: 48.62 in, 1,235 mm front, 47.24 in, 1,200 mm rear; length: 145.47 in, 3,695 mm; width: 57.09 in, 1,450 mm; height: 54.33 in, 1,380 mm; ground clearance: 6.69 in, 170 mm; dry weight: 1,444 lb, 655 kg; distribution of weight: 51% front, 49% rear; turning circle (between walls): 28.9 ft, 8.8 m; fuel tank: 8.8 imp gal, 10.6 US gal, 40 l.

BODY saloon/sedan; 2 doors; 4 seats, separate front seats.

PRACTICAL INSTRUCTIONS fuel: 85-90 oct petrol; engine sump oil: 4.9 imp pt, 5.9 US pt, 2.8 l, SAE 20W-30, change every 3,100 miles, 5,000 km; gearbox oil: 2.5 imp pt, 3 US pt, 1.4 l, SAE 90, change every 18,600 miles, 30,000 km; final drive oil: 3.7 imp pt, 4.4 US pt, 2.1 l, SAE 90, change every 18,600 miles, 30,000 km; tappet clearances: inlet 0.010 in, 0.25 mm, exhaust 0.010 in, 0.25 mm; valve timing: 15° 55° 55° 15°; tyre pressure: front 21 psi, 1.5 atm, rear 21 psi, 1.5 atm.

Consorte Super De Luxe Sedan

See Consorte Standard Sedan, except for:

PRICE EX WORKS: 487,000 yen.

Consorte PS Sedan

See Consorte Standard Sedan, except for:

PRICE EX WORKS: 484,000 yen.

Consorte GS

See Consorte Standard Sedan, except for:

PRICE EX WORKS: 514,000 yen.

ENGINE 71.1 cu in, 1,166 cc (2.95 x 2.60 in, 75 x 66 mm); max power (DIN): 68 hp at 6,000 rpm; max torque (DIN): 69 lb ft, 9.5 kg m at 3,800 rpm; max engine rpm: 6,500; 58.3 hp/l; 5 crankshaft bearings; lubricating system capacity: 6.2 imp pt, 7.4 US pt, 3.5 l; cooling system capacity: 8.3 imp pt, 9.9 US pt, 4.7 l.

TRANSMISSION gearbox ratios: I 3.684, II 2.050, III 1.383, IV 1, rev 4.316; tyres: 155 SR x 12.

PERFORMANCE max speeds: (I) 25 mph, 40 km/h; (II) 43 mph, 69 km/h; (III) 65 mph, 105 km/h; (IV) 93 mph, 150 km/h; power-weight ratio: 22.4 lb/hp, 10.2 kg/hp; acceleration: standing ¼ mile 18.5 sec; fuel consumption: not declared.

DIMENSIONS AND WEIGHT height: 54.53 in, 1,385 mm; dry weight: 1,521 lb, 690 kg; distribution of weight: 57% front, 43% rear.

BODY 5 seats.

DAIHATSU Fellow Max 4-door Hi Custom Sedan

DAIHATSU Fellow Max Hardtop GHL

DAIHATSU Consorte GS

PRACTICAL INSTRUCTIONS engine sump oil: 6.2 imp pt, 7.4 US pt, 3.5 l; gearbox oil: 3 imp pt, 3.6 US pt, 1.7 l, SAE 90; tappet clearances: inlet 0.008 in, 0.20 mm, exhaust 0.012 in, 0.30 mm; valve timing: 16° 50° 50° 16°.

HONDA JAPAN

Life De Luxe 2-door Sedan

PRICE EX WORKS: 346,000 yen.

ENGINE front, transverse, 4 stroke; 2 cylinders, in line; 21.7 cu in, 356 cc (2.64 x 1.99 in, 67 x 50.6 mm); compression ratio: 8.8:1; max power (DIN): 30 hp at 8,000 rpm; max torque (DIN): 21 lb ft, 2.9 kg m at 6,000 rpm; max engine rpm: 8,500; 84.3 hp/l; light alloy cylinder block with cast iron liners, light alloy head; 3 crankshaft bearings; valves: overhead, rockers; camshafts: 1, overhead; lubrication: eccentric pump, full flow filter, 5.3 imp pt, 6.3 US pt, 3 l; 1 Keihin downdraught twin barrel carburettor; fuel feed: electric pump; water-cooled, 5.3 imp pt, 6.3 US pt, 3 l.

TRANSMISSION driving wheels: front; clutch: single dry plate (diaphragm); gearbox: mechanical; gears: 4, fully synchronized; ratios: I 4.700, II 2.846, III 1.833, IV 1.272, rev 4.847; lever: central; final drive: helical spur gears; axle ratio: 5.429; width of rims: 3.5"; tyres: 5.20 x 10.

PERFORMANCE max speeds: (I) 19 mph, 30 km/h; (II) 30 mph, 48 km/h; (III) 47 mph, 76 km/h; (IV) 71 mph, 115 km/h; power-weight ratio: 35.6 lb/hp, 16.1 kg/hp; fuel consumption: not declared.

CHASSIS integral, front subframe; front suspension: independent, by McPherson, coil springs/telescopic damper struts, lower wishbones (trailing links), anti-roll bar; rear suspension: rigid axle, semi-elliptic leafsprings, telescopic dampers.

STEERING rack-and-pinion; turns lock to lock: 3.20.

BRAKES drum, single circuit; swept area: front 39.1 sq in, 252 sq cm, rear 39.1 sq in, 252 sq cm, total 78.2 sq in, 504 sq cm.

ELECTRICAL EQUIPMENT 12 V; 26 Ah battery; 30 A alternator; Nihon Denso distributor; 2 headlamps.

DIMENSIONS AND WEIGHT wheel base: 81.89 in, 2,080 mm; tracks: 44.49 in, 1,130 mm front, 43.70 in, 1,110 mm rear; length: 117.91 in, 2,995 mm; width: 50.98 in, 1,295 mm; height: 52.76 in, 1,340 mm; ground clearance: 6.50 in, 165 mm; dry weight: 1,069 lb, 485 kg; distribution of weight: 62.9% front, 37.1% rear; turning circle (between walls): 28.9 ft, 8.8 m; fuel tank: 5.7 imp gal, 6.9 US gal, 26 l.

BODY saloon/sedan; 2 doors; 4 seats, separate front seats.

PRACTICAL INSTRUCTIONS fuel: 85-90 oct petrol; engine sump oil: 5.3 imp pt, 6.3 US pt, 3 l, SAE 10W-30, change every 3,100 miles, 5,000 km; gearbox and final drive oil: 3.5 imp pt, 4.2 US pt, 2 l, SAE 10W-30, change every 25,000 miles, 40,000 km; tappet clearances: inlet 0.003 in, 0.08 mm, exhaust 0.003 in, 0.08 mm; valve timing: 0° 30° 40° 0°; tyre pressure: front 21 psi, 1.5 atm, rear 21 psi, 1.5 atm.

Life De Luxe 2-door Automatic Sedan

See Life De Luxe 2-door Sedan, except for:

PRICE EX WORKS: 397,000 yen.

TRANSMISSION gearbox: Honda automatic transmission, hydraulic torque converter with 3 ratios; ratios: I 3.444, II 1.791, III 1.161, rev 3.719; lever: steering column.

Life De Luxe 4-door Sedan

See Life De Luxe 2-door Sedan, except for:

PRICE EX WORKS: 366,000 yen.

PERFORMANCE power-weight ratio: 37.5 lb/hp, 17 kg/hp.

DIMENSIONS AND WEIGHT dry weight: 1,125 lb, 510 kg.

BODY 4 doors.

Life De Luxe 4-door Automatic Sedan

See Life De Luxe 2-door Automatic Sedan, except for:

PRICE EX WORKS: 417,000 yen.

PERFORMANCE power-weight ratio: 37.5 lb/hp, 17 kg/hp.

DIMENSIONS AND WEIGHT dry weight: 1,125 lb, 510 kg.

BODY 4 doors.

Life De Luxe Station Wagon

See Life De Luxe 2-door Sedan, except for:

PRICE EX WORKS: 394,000 yen.

PERFORMANCE power-weight ratio: 37.8 lb/hp, 17.1 kg/hp.

DIMENSIONS AND WEIGHT dry weight: 1,136 lb, 515 kg.

BODY estate car/station wagon; 2 + 1 doors.

Life De Luxe Automatic Station Wagon

See Life De Luxe 2-door Automatic Sedan, except for:

PRICE EX WORKS: 417,000 yen.

PERFORMANCE power-weight ratio: 39 lb/hp, 17.6 kg/hp.

DIMENSIONS AND WEIGHT dry weight: 1,169 lb, 530 kg.

BODY estate car/station wagon; 2 + 1 doors.

Life Custom 2-door Sedan

See Life De Luxe 2-door Sedan, except for:

PRICE EX WORKS: 428,000 yen.

Life Custom 2-door Automatic Sedan

See Life De Luxe 2-door Automatic Sedan, except for:

PRICE EX WORKS: 451,000 yen.

Life Custom 4-door Sedan

See Life De Luxe 4-door Sedan, except for:

PRICE EX WORKS: 448,000 yen.

Life Custom 4-door Automatic Sedan

See Life De Luxe 4-door Automatic Sedan, except for:

PRICE EX WORKS: 471,000 yen.

Life Custom Station Wagon

See Life De Luxe Station Wagon, except for:

PRICE EX WORKS: 448,000 yen.

Life Custom Automatic Station Wagon

See Life De Luxe Automatic Station Wagon, except for:

PRICE EX WORKS: 471,000 yen.

Life Touring SS 2-door Sedan

See Life De Luxe 2-door Sedan, except for:

PRICE EX WORKS: 389,000 yen.

ENGINE compression ratio: 9:1; max power (DIN): 36 hp at 9,000 rpm; max torque (DIN): 23 lb ft, 3.2 kg m at 7,000 rpm; max engine rpm: 10,000; 101.1 hp/l; 2 Keihin CV horizontal carburettors.

PERFORMANCE max speeds: (I) 21 mph, 33 km/h; (II) 33 mph, 53 km/h; (III) 51 mph, 82 km/h; (IV) 75 mph, 120 km/h; power-weight ratio: 29.7 lb/hp, 13.7 kg/hp.

PRACTICAL INSTRUCTIONS valve timing: 10° 30° 40° 0°.

OPTIONAL ACCESSORIES air-conditioning.

Life Touring SL 2-door Sedan

See Life Touring SS 2-door Sedan, except for:

PRICE EX WORKS: 419,000 yen.

PERFORMANCE power-weight ratio: 30.3 lb/hp, 13.8 kg/hp.

DIMENSIONS AND WEIGHT dry weight: 1,091 lb, 495 kg.

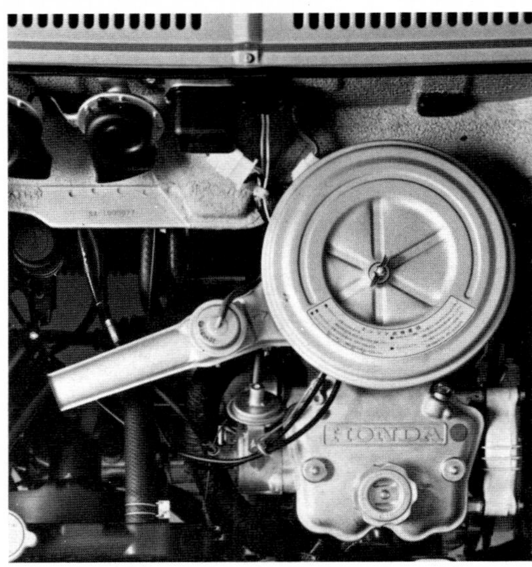

HONDA Life Custom Series

HONDA Life Touring GS 2-door Sedan

HONDA Vamos 4

Life Touring GS 2-door Sedan

See Life Touring SS 2-door Sedan, except for:

PRICE EX WORKS: 449,000 yen.

TRANSMISSION gears: 5, II, III, IV and V synchronized; ratios: I 4.700, II 3.166, III 2.187, IV 1.550, V 1.173, rev 4.758; tyres: 145 SR x 10.

PERFORMANCE max speeds: (I) 21 mph, 33 km/h; (II) 29 mph, 47 km/h; (III) 42 mph, 68 km/h; (IV) 60 mph, 96 km/h; (V) 75 mph, 120 km/h.

PRACTICAL INSTRUCTIONS tyre pressure: front 24 psi, 1.7 atm, rear 24 psi, 1.7 atm.

Life Twin De Luxe 4-door Sedan

See Life Touring SS 2-door Sedan, except for:

PRICE EX WORKS: 404,000 yen.

BODY 4 doors.

Life Twin Custom 4-door Sedan

See Life Touring SS 2-door Sedan, except for:

PRICE EX WORKS: 458,000 yen.

BODY 4 doors.

Vamos 4

PRICE EX WORKS: 345,000 yen.

ENGINE rear, 4 stroke; 2 cylinders, in line; 21.6 cu in, 354 cc (2.46 x 2.28 in, 62.5 x 57.8 mm); compression ratio: 8:1; max power (DIN): 30 hp at 8,000 rpm; max torque (DIN): 22 lb ft, 3 kg m at 5,500 rpm; max engine rpm: 8,600; 84.7 hp/l; light alloy cylinder block and head; 4 crankshaft bearings, on roller bearings; valves: overhead, rockers; camshafts: 1, overhead; lubrication: plunger pump, full flow filter, 5.3 imp pt, 6.3 US pt, 3 l; 1 Keihin CV horizontal carburettor; fuel feed: electric pump; air-cooled.

TRANSMISSION driving wheels: rear; clutch: single dry plate (diaphragm); gearbox: mechanical, in unit with engine; gears: 4, fully synchronized; ratios: I 2.529, II 1.565, III 1, IV 0.615, rev 2.438; lever: central; final drive: hypoid bevel, in unit with engine and gearbox; axle ratio: 4.273; width of rims: 3.5''; tyres: 5.00 x 10.

PERFORMANCE max speeds: (I) 16 mph, 25 km/h; (II) 26 mph, 42 km/h; (III) 40 mph, 64 km/h; (IV) 56 mph, 90 km/h; power-weight ratio: 38.1 lb/hp, 17.3 kg/hp; fuel consumption: 56.5 m/imp gal, 47 m/US gal, 5 l x 100 km.

CHASSIS platform; front suspension: independent, by McPherson, coil springs/telescopic damper struts, lower wishbones; rear suspension: de Dion rigid axle, semi-elliptic leafsprings, telescopic dampers.

STEERING rack-and-pinion.

BRAKES drum, single circuit; swept area: front 37.7 sq in, 243 sq cm, rear 37.7 sq in, 243 sq cm, total 75.4 sq in, 486 sq cm.

ELECTRICAL EQUIPMENT 12 V; 26 Ah battery; 250 W dynamo; Denso distributor; 2 headlamps.

DIMENSIONS AND WEIGHT wheel base: 70.08 in, 1,780 mm; tracks: 43.70 in, 1,110 mm front, 44.09 in, 1,120 mm rear; length: 117.91 in, 2,995 mm; width: 50.98 in, 1,295 mm; height: 65.16 in, 1,655 mm; ground clearance: 8.27 in, 210 mm; dry weight: 1,147 lb, 520 kg; distribution of weight: 49% front, 51% rear; turning circle (between walls): 24.9 ft, 7.6 m; fuel tank: 5.7 imp gal, 6.9 US gal, 26 l.

BODY open; no doors; 2-4 seats, separate front seats.

PRACTICAL INSTRUCTIONS fuel: 88 oct petrol; engine sump, gearbox and final drive oil: 5.3 imp pt, 6.3 US pt, 3 l, SAE 20W-30, change every 3,100 miles, 5,000 km; tappet clearances: inlet 0.004 in, 0.10 mm, exhaust 0.004 in, 0.10 mm; valve timing: 5° 25° 40° 5°; tyre pressure: front 24 psi, 1.7 atm, rear 24 psi, 1.7 atm.

Life Stepvan Super De Luxe

PRICE EX WORKS: 403,000 yen.

ENGINE front, transverse, 4 stroke; 2 cylinders, in line; 21.7 cu in, 356 cc (2.64 x 1.99 in, 67 x 50.6 mm); compression ratio: 8.8:1; max power (DIN): 30 hp at 8,000 rpm; max torque (DIN): 21 lb ft, 2.9 kg m at 6,000 rpm; max engine rpm: 9,000; 84.3 hp/l; light alloy cylinder block with cast iron liners, light alloy head; 3 crankshaft bearings; valves:

HONDA Life Custom 4-door Sedan

HONDA Life Touring GS 2-door Sedan

HONDA Vamos 4

overhead, rockers; camshafts: 1, overhead; lubrication: eccentric pump, full flow filter, 5.3 imp pt, 6.3 US pt, 3 l; 1 Keihin downdraught twin barrel carburettor; fuel feed: eccentric pump; water-cooled, 5.3 imp pt, 6.3 US pt, 3 l.

TRANSMISSION driving wheels: front; clutch: single dry plate (diaphragm); gearbox: mechanical; gears: 4, fully synchronized; ratios: I 4.700, II 2.846, III 1.833, IV 1.272, rev 4.847; lever: central; final drive: helical spur gears; axle ratio: 5.923; width of rims: 3.5"; tyres: 5.00 x 10.

PERFORMANCE max speeds: (I) 17 mph, 27 km/h; (II) 27 mph, 44 km/h; (III) 42 mph, 68 km/h; (IV) 62 mph, 100 km/h; power-weight ratio: 44.5 lb/hp, 20 kg/hp; carrying capacity: 882 lb, 400 kg; fuel consumption: not declared.

CHASSIS integral; front suspension: independent, by McPherson, coil springs/telescopic damper struts, lower wishbones (trailing links), anti-roll bar.

STEERING rack-and-pinion; turns lock to lock: 3.20.

BRAKES drum, single circuit; swept area: front 39.1 sq in, 252 sq cm, rear 39.1 sq in, 252 sq cm, total 78.2 sq in, 504 sq cm.

ELECTRICAL EQUIPMENT 12 V; 26 Ah battery; 35 A alternator; Hitachi distributor; 2 headlamps.

DIMENSIONS AND WEIGHT wheel base: 81.89 in, 2,080 mm; tracks: 44.49 in, 1,130 mm front, 43.70 in, 1,110 mm rear; length: 117.91 in, 2,995 mm; width: 50.98 in, 1,295 mm; height: 63.78 in, 1,620 mm; ground clearance: 6.50 in, 165 mm; dry weight: 1,334 lb, 605 kg; distribution of weight: 58.7% front, 41.3% rear; turning circle (between walls): 28.9 ft, 8.8 m; fuel tank: 5.7 imp gal, 6.9 US gal, 26 l.

BODY estate car/station wagon; 4 + 1 doors; 4 seats, separate front seats, back seat folding down to luggage table.

PRACTICAL INSTRUCTIONS fuel: 85-90 oct petrol; engine sump oil: 5.3 imp pt, 6.3 US pt, 3 l, SAE 10W-30, change every 3,100 miles, 5,000 km; gearbox and final drive oil: 3.5 imp pt, 4.2 US pt, 2 l, SAE 10W-30, change every 24,800 miles, 40,000 km; tappet clearances: inlet 0.003 in, 0.08 mm, exhaust 0.003 in, 0.08 mm; valve timing: 0° 30° 40° 0°; tyre pressure: front 23 psi, 1.6 atm, rear 23 psi, 1.6 atm.

Z Hardtop SS

PRICE EX WORKS: 368,000 yen.

ENGINE front, transverse, 4 stroke; 2 cylinders, in line; 21.7 cu in, 356 cc (2.64 x 1.99 in, 67 x 50.6 mm); compression ratio: 9:1; max power (DIN): 36 hp at 9,000 rpm; max torque (DIN): 23 lb ft, 3.2 kg m at 7,000 rpm; max engine rpm: 10,000; 101.1 hp/l; light alloy cylinder block with cast iron liners, light alloy head; 3 crankshaft bearings; valves: overhead, rockers; camshafts: 1, overhead; lubrication: eccentric pump, full flow filter, 5.3 imp pt, 6.3 US pt, 3 l; 2 Keihin CV horizontal carburettors; fuel feed: electric pump; water-cooled, 5.3 imp pt, 6.3 US pt, 3 l.

TRANSMISSION driving wheels: front; clutch: single dry plate (diaphragm); gearbox: mechanical; gears: 4, fully synchronized; ratios: I 4.700, II 2.846, III 1.833, IV 1.272, rev 4.847; lever: central; final drive: helical spur gears; axle ratio: 5.429; width of rims: 3.5" tyres: 5.20 x 10.

PERFORMANCE max speed: 75 mph, 120 km/h; power-weight ratio: 32.5 lb/hp, 14.7 kg/hp; fuel consumption: not declared.

CHASSIS integral; front suspension: independent, by McPherson, coil springs/telescopic damper struts, lower wishbones (trailing links), anti-roll bar; rear suspension: rigid axle, semi-elliptic leafsprings, telescopic dampers.

STEERING rack and-pinion; turns lock to lock: 3.20.

BRAKES drum, single circuit; swept area: front 39.1 sq in, 252 sq cm, rear 39.1 sq in, 252 sq cm, total 78.2 sq in, 504 sq cm.

ELECTRICAL EQUIPMENT 12 V; 35 Ah battery; 30 A alternator; Nihon Denso distributor; 2 headlamps.

DIMENSIONS AND WEIGHT wheel base: 81.89 in, 2,080 mm; tracks: 44.49 in, 1,130 mm front, 43.90 in, 1,115 mm rear; length: 117.91 in, 2,995 mm; width: 50.98 in, 1,295 mm; height: 50.20 in, 1,275 mm; ground clearance: 6.30 in, 160 mm; dry weight: 1,169 lb, 530 kg; distribution of weight: 60.8% front, 39.2% rear; turning circle (between walls): 28.9 ft, 8.8 m; fuel tank: 5.7 imp gal, 6.9 US gal, 26 l.

BODY hardtop; 2 doors; 4 seats, separate front seats.

PRACTICAL INSTRUCTIONS fuel: 85-90 oct petrol; engine sump oil: 5.3 imp pt, 6.3 US pt, 3 l, SAE 10W-30, change every 3,100 miles, 5,000 km; gearbox and final drive oil: 3.5 imp pt, 4.2 US pt, 2 l, SAE 10W-30, change every 24,800 miles, 40,000 km; tappet clearances: inlet 0.003 in, 0.08 mm, exhaust 0.003 in, 0.08 mm; valve timing: 0° 30° 40° 0°; tyre pressure: front 21 psi, 1.5 atm, rear 21 psi, 1.5 atm.

Z Hardtop GT

See Z Hardtop SS, except for:

PRICE EX WORKS: 429,000 yen.

Z Hardtop GL

See Z Hardtop SS, except for:

PRICE EX WORKS: 449,000 yen.

Z Hardtop GSS

See Z Hardtop SS, except for:

PRICE EX WORKS: 461,000 yen.

TRANSMISSION gears: 5, II, III, IV and V synchronized; ratios: I 4.700, II 3.166, III 2.187, IV 1.550, V 1.173, rev 4.758; tyres: 145 SR x 10.

N 600 Sedan

(only for export).

PRICE IN GB: £ 569.
PRICE IN USA: $ 1,473.

ENGINE front, 4 stroke; 2 cylinders, in line; 36.6 cu In, 599 cc (2.91 x 2.74 in, 74 x 69.6 mm); compression ratio: 8.5:1; max power (SAE): 36 hp at 6,000 rpm; max torque (SAE): 32 lb ft, 4.4 kg m at 2,500 rpm; max engine rpm: 8,000; 60.1 hp/l; light alloy cylinder block and head; 3 crankshaft bearings, on roller bearings; valves: overhead, rockers; camshafts: 1, overhead; lubrication: gear pump, full flow filter, 5.3 imp pt, 6.3 US pt, 3 l; 1 Keihin CV horizontal carburettor; fuel feed: electric pump; air-cooled.

TRANSMISSION driving wheels: front; clutch: single dry plate (diaphragm); gearbox: mechanical, in unit with engine; gears: 4, fully synchronized; ratios: I 2.529, II 1.565, III 1, IV 0.714, rev 2.437; lever: central; final drive: helical spur gears; axle ratio: 3.037; width of rims: 3.5"; tyres: 5.20 x 10.

PERFORMANCE max speeds: (I) 22 mph, 35 km/h; (II) 35 mph, 56 km/h; (III) 54 mph, 87 km/h; (IV) 75 mph, 120 km/h; power-weight ratio: 37.7 lb/hp, 17.1 kg/hp; carrying capacity: 706 lb, 320 kg; acceleration: standing ¼ mile 22.4 sec; speed in top at 1,000 rpm: 12.7 mph, 20.5 km/h; fuel consumption: 47.1 m/imp gal, 39.2 m/US gal, 6 l x 100 km.

CHASSIS integral; front suspension: independent, by McPherson, coil springs/telescopic damper struts, lower wishbones; rear suspension: rigid axle, semi-elliptic leaf-springs, telescopic dampers.

STEERING rack-and-pinion; turns lock to lock: 3.10.

BRAKES front disc, rear drum.

ELECTRICAL EQUIPMENT 12 V; 40 Ah battery; 300 W alternator; Denso distributor; 2 headlamps.

DIMENSIONS AND WEIGHT wheel base: 78.74 in, 2,000 mm; tracks: 45.28 in, 1,150 mm front, 43.50 in, 1,105 mm rear; length: 122.05 in, 3,100 mm; width: 50.98 in, 1,295 mm; height: 52.36 in, 1,330 mm; ground clearance: 6.30 in, 160 mm; dry weight: 1,356 lb, 615 kg; distribution of weight: 64% front, 36% rear; turning circle (between walls): 31.2 ft, 9.5 m; fuel tank: 5.7 imp gal, 6.9 US gal, 26 l.

BODY saloon/sedan; 2 doors; 4 seats, separate front seats.

PRACTICAL INSTRUCTIONS fuel: 88 oct petrol; engine sump, gearbox and final drive oil: 5.3 imp pt, 6.3 US pt, 3 l, SAE 20W-30, change every 3,100 miles, 5,000 km; tappet clearances: inlet 0.003 in, 0.08 mm, exhaust 0.005 in, 0.12 mm; tyre pressure: front 24 psi, 1.7 atm, rear 21 psi, 1.5 atm.

Z 600 Sedan

(only for export).

See N 600 Sedan, except for:

PRICE IN GB: £ 644.
PRICE IN USA: $ 1,610.

TRANSMISSION tyres: 144 SR x 10.

PERFORMANCE power-weight ratio: 36.4 lb/hp, 16.5 kg/hp.

DIMENSIONS AND WEIGHT tracks: 45.87 in, 1,165 mm front, 44.29 in, 1,125 mm rear; length: 123.42 in, 3,135 mm; height: 50.39 in, 1,280 mm; ground clearance: 6.10 in, 155 mm; dry weight: 1,312 lb, 595 kg.

HONDA Life Stepvan Super De Luxe

HONDA Z 600 Sedan

HONDA Civic GL 3-door Sedan

Civic Standard 2-door Sedan

PRICE EX WORKS: 425,000 yen.

ENGINE front, transverse, 4 stroke; 4 cylinders, in line; 71.3 cu in, 1,169 cc (2.76 x 2.99 in, 70 x 76 mm); compression ratio: 8.1:1; max power (DIN): 60 hp at 5,500 rpm; max torque (DIN): 69 lb ft, 9.5 kg m at 3,000 rpm; max engine rpm: 6,000; 51.3 hp/l; light alloy cylinder head with cast iron liners, light alloy head; 5 crankshaft bearings; valves: overhead, rockers; camshafts: 1, overhead; lubrication: rotary pump, full flow filter, 5.3 imp pt, 6.3 US pt, 3 l; 1 Hitachi DCG306 downdraught twin barrel carburettor; fuel feed: mechanical pump; water-cooled, 7 imp pt, 8.5 US pt, 4 l.

TRANSMISSION driving wheels: front; clutch: single dry plate (diaphragm); gearbox: mechanical; gears: 4, fully synchronized; ratios: I 3.000, II 1.798, III 1.182, IV 0.846, rev 2.916; lever: central; final drive: helical spur gears; axle ratio: 4.933; width of rims: 4"; tyres: 6.00 x 12.

PERFORMANCE max speeds: (I) 26 mph, 42 km/h; (II) 43 mph, 70 km/h; (III) 65 mph, 105 km/h; (IV) 90 mph, 145 km/h; power-weight ratio: 22 lb/hp, 10 kg/hp; fuel consumption: not declared.

CHASSIS integral, front auxiliary frame; front suspension: independent, by McPherson, coil springs/telescopic damper struts, lower wishbones (trailing links), anti-roll bar; rear suspension: independent, by McPherson, coil springs/telescopic damper struts, lower wishbones (torque arms).

STEERING rack-and-pinion; turns lock to lock: 3.10.

BRAKES drum; swept area: front 42.2 sq in, 272 sq cm, rear 34.7 sq in, 224 sq cm, total 76.9 sq in, 496 sq cm.

ELECTRICAL EQUIPMENT 12 V; 32 Ah battery; 35 A alternator; Mitsubishi distributor; 2 headlamps.

DIMENSIONS AND WEIGHT wheel base: 86.61 in, 2,200 mm; tracks: 51.18 in, 1,300 mm front, 50.39 in, 1,280 mm rear; length: 134.05 in, 3,405 mm; width: 59.25 in, 1,505 mm; height: 52.17 in, 1,305 mm; ground clearance: 6.89 in, 175 mm; dry weight: 1,323 lb, 600 kg; distribution of weight: 62.4% front, 37.6% rear; turning circle (between walls): 30.8 ft, 9.4 m; fuel tank: 8.4 imp gal, 10 US gal, 38 l.

BODY saloon/sedan; 2 doors; 5 seats, separate front seats.

PRACTICAL INSTRUCTIONS fuel: 85-90 oct petrol; engine sump oil: 5.3 imp pt, 6.3 US pt, 3 l, SAE 10W-30, change every 3,100 miles, 5,000 km; gearbox and final drive oil: 4.4 imp pt, 5.3 US pt, 2.5 l, SAE 10W-40; tappet clearances: inlet 0.005 in, 0.12 mm, exhaust 0.005 in, 0.12 mm; valve timing: 10° 20° 30° 10°; tyre pressure: front 21 psi, 1.5 atm, rear 21 psi, 1.5 atm.

OPTIONAL ACCESSORIES semi-automatic transmission with 2 ratios; air-conditioning.

Civic De Luxe 2-door-Sedan

See Civic Standard 2-door Sedan, except for:

PRICE EX WORKS: 475,000 yen.

PERFORMANCE power-weight ratio: 22.6 lb/hp, 10.2 kg/hp.

DIMENSIONS AND WEIGHT dry weight: 1,356 lb, 615 kg.

Civic De Luxe 3-door Sedan

See Civic Standard 2-door Sedan, except for:

PRICE EX WORKS: 490,000 yen.

PERFORMANCE power-weight ratio: 23 lb/hp, 10.4 kg/hp.

DIMENSIONS AND WEIGHT dry weight: 1,378 lb, 625 kg.

BODY 2 + 1 doors.

Civic Hi De Luxe 2-door Sedan

See Civic Standard 2-door Sedan, except for:

PRICE EX WORKS: 495,000 yen.

PERFORMANCE power-weight ratio: 23 lb/hp, 10.4 kg/hp.

DIMENSIONS AND WEIGHT dry weight: 1,378 lb, 625 kg.

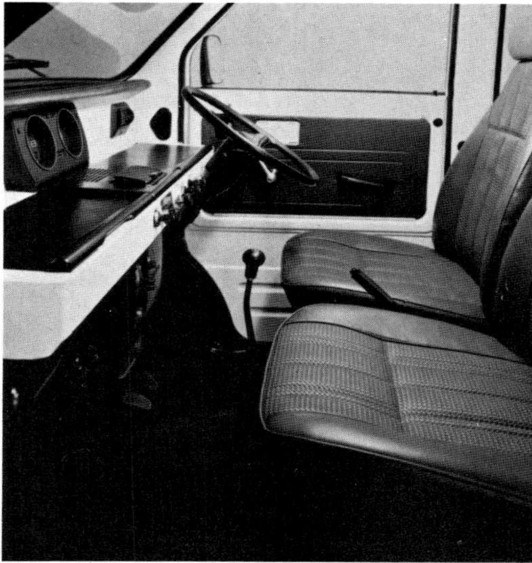

HONDA Life Stepvan Super De Luxe

HONDA Z 600 Sedan

HONDA Civic Hi De Luxe Series

Civic Hi De Luxe 3-door Sedan

See Civic Standard 2-door Sedan, except for:

PRICE EX WORKS: 510,000 yen.

PERFORMANCE power-weight ratio: 23.3 lb/hp, 10.6 kg/hp.

DIMENSIONS AND WEIGHT dry weight: 1,400 lb, 635 kg.

BODY 2 + 1 doors.

Civic GL 2-door Sedan

See Civic Standard 2-door Sedan, except for:

PRICE EX WORKS: 530,000 yen.

ENGINE compression ratio: 8.6:1; max power (DIN): 69 hp at 5,500 rpm; max torque (DIN): 74 lb ft, 10.2 kg m at 4,000 rpm; max engine rpm: 6,500; 59 hp/l; 1 Hitachi DCM328 downdraught twin barrel carburettor.

TRANSMISSION tyres: 6.00 S x 12.

PERFORMANCE max speeds: (I) 28 mph, 45 km/h; (II) 47 mph, 75 km/h; (III) 71 mph, 115 km/h; (IV) 99 mph, 160 km/h; power-weight ratio: 20.4 lb/hp, 9.3 kg/hp.

DIMENSIONS AND WEIGHT dry weight: 1,411 lb, 640 kg; distribution of weight: 61.7% front, 38.3% rear.

PRACTICAL INSTRUCTIONS valve timing: 10° 30° 40° 10°.

Civic GL 3-door Sedan

See Civic GL 2-door Sedan, except for:

PRICE EX WORKS: 545,000 yen.

PERFORMANCE power-weight ratio: 20.8 lb/hp, 9.4 kg/hp.

DIMENSIONS AND WEIGHT dry weight: 1,433 lb, 650 kg.

BODY 2 + 1 doors.

Civic

(only for export).

See Civic GL 2-door Sedan, except for:

TRANSMISSION tyres: 155 SR x 12.

BRAKES servo.

145 Standard Sedan

PRICE EX WORKS: 511,000 yen.

ENGINE front, transverse, 4 stroke; 4 cylinders, in line; 87.4 cu in, 1,433 cc (2.83 x 3.46 in, 72 x 88 mm); compression ratio: 8.6:1; max power (DIN): 80 hp at 5,500 rpm; max torque (DIN): 87 lb ft, 12 kg m at 3,500 rpm; max engine rpm: 6,500; 55.8 hp/l; cast iron cylinder block, light alloy head; 5 crankshaft bearings; valves: overhead, rochers; camshafts: 1, overhead; lubrication: rotary pump, full flow filter, 5.3 imp pt, 6.3 US pt, 3 l; 1 Hitachi downdraught twin barrel carburettor; fuel feed: mechanical pump; water-cooled, 7 imp pt, 8.5 US pt, 4 l.

TRANSMISSION driving wheels: front; clutch: single dry plate (diaphragm); gearbox: mechanical; gears: 4, fully synchronized; ratios: I 3.000, II 1.789, III 1.182, IV 0.846, rev 2.916; lever: central; final drive: helical spur gears; axle ratio: 4.733; width of rims: 4"; tyres: 6.20 S x 13.

PERFORMANCE max speeds: (I) 29 mph, 47 km/h; (II) 48 mph, 78 km/h; (III) 73 mph, 118 km/h; (IV) 99 mph, 160 km/h; power-weight ratio: 23.3 lb/hp, 10.6 kg/hp; fuel consumption: not declared.

CHASSIS integral, front auxiliary frame; front suspension: independent, by McPherson, coil springs/telescopic damper struts, lower wishbones (trailing links), anti-roll bar; rear suspension: independent, swinging semi-axles (cross beam system), semi-elliptic leafsprings, telescopic dampers.

STEERING rack-and-pinion; turns lock to lock: 3.30.

BRAKES front disc, rear drum, rear compensator, servo; swept area: front 16.1 sq in, 104 sq cm, rear 40 sq in, 258 sq cm, total 56.1 sq in, 362 sq cm.

ELECTRICAL EQUIPMENT 12 V; 35 Ah battery; 700 W alternator; Hitachi distributor; 2 headlamps.

DIMENSIONS AND WEIGHT wheel base: 88.58 in, 2,250 mm; tracks: 49.41 in, 1,255 mm front, 48.23 in, 1,225 mm

145 STANDARD SEDAN

rear; length: 157.28 in, 3,995 mm; width: 57.68 in, 1,465 mm; height: 53.54 in, 1,360 mm; ground clearance: 6.30 in, 160 mm; dry weight: 1,863 lb, 845 kg; turning circle (between walls): 31.5 ft, 9.6 m; fuel tank: 9.9 imp gal, 11.9 US gal, 45 l.

BODY saloon/sedan; 4 doors; 5 seats, separate front seats.

PRACTICAL INSTRUCTIONS fuel: 85-90 oct petrol; engine sump oil: 5.3 imp pt, 6.3 US pt, 3 l, SAE 10W-30, change every 3,100 miles, 5,000 km; gearbox and final drive oil: 4.4 imp pt, 5.3 US pt, 2.5 l, SAE 10W-30; tappet clearances: inlet 0.005 in, 0.12 mm, exhaust 0.005 in, 0.12 mm; valve timing: 10° 30° 40° 10°; tyre pressure: front 23 psi, 1.6 atm, rear 23 psi, 1.6 atm.

OPTIONAL ACCESSORIES air-conditioning.

145 De Luxe Sedan

See 145 Standard Sedan, except for:

PRICE EX WORKS: 591,000 yen.

PERFORMANCE power-weight ratio: 24 lb/hp, 10.9 kg/hp.

DIMENSIONS AND WEIGHT dry weight: 1,918 lb, 870 kg.

145 Custom Sedan

See 145 Standard Sedan, except for:

PRICE EX WORKS: 658,000 yen.

PERFORMANCE power-weight ratio: 28.2 lb/hp, 11 kg/hp.

DIMENSIONS AND WEIGHT length: 158.27 in, 4,020 mm; dry weight: 1,940 lb, 880 kg.

145 SL Coupé

See 145 Standard Sedan, except for:

PRICE EX WORKS: 623,000 yen.

PERFORMANCE power-weight ratio: 23.4 lb/hp, 10.6 kg/hp.

DIMENSIONS AND WEIGHT length: 162.99 in, 4,140 mm; height: 52.36 in, 1,330 mm; dry weight: 1,874 lb, 850 kg.

BODY coupé; 2 doors.

145 GL Coupé

See 145 SL Coupé, except for:

PRICE EX WORKS: 711,000 yen.

145 FI Coupé

See 145 SL Coupé, except for:

PRICE EX WORKS: 811,000 yen.

ENGINE max power (DIN): 90 hp at 6,000 rpm; max torque (DIN): 91 lb ft, 12.5 kg m at 4,000 rpm; max engine rpm: 6,800; 62.8 hp/l; Honda fuel injection system.

PERFORMANCE max speeds: (I) 30 mph, 48 km/h; (II) 52 mph, 84 km/h; (III) 78 mph, 125 km/h; (IV) 106 mph, 170 km/h; power-weight ratio: 20.8 lb/hp, 9.4 kg/hp.

PRACTICAL INSTRUCTIONS valve timing: 5° 30° 40° 5°.

ISUZU JAPAN

Bellett 1600 Special 2-door Sedan

PRICE EX WORKS: 561,000 yen.

ENGINE front, 4 stroke; 4 cylinders, in line; 96.7 cu in, 1,584 cc (3.23 x 2.95 in, 82 x 75 mm); compression ratio: 8.7:1; max power (DIN): 84 hp at 5,200 rpm; max torque (DIN): 91 lb ft, 12.5 kg m at 2,600 rpm; max engine rpm: 5,800; 53 hp/l; cast iron cylinder block, light alloy head; 5 crankshaft bearings; valves: overhead, push-rods and rockers; camshafts: 1, side; lubrication, rotary pump, full flow filter, 5.6 imp pt, 6.8 US pt, 3.2 l; 1 Nikki-Stromberg downdraught twin barrel carburettor; fuel feed: mechanical pump; water-cooled, 13.2 imp pt, 15.9 US pt, 7.5 l.

HONDA 145 FI Coupé

ISUZU Bellett 1600 Special

ISUZU Bellett 1800 Sports Sedan

TRANSMISSION driving wheels: rear; clutch: single dry plate; gearbox: mechanical; gears: 4, fully synchronized; ratios: I 3.507, II 2.175, III 1.418, IV 1, rev 3.927; lever: central; final drive: hypoid bevel; axle ratio: 4.100; width of rims: 4"; tyres: 5.60 x 13.

PERFORMANCE max speed: 93 mph, 150 km/h; power-weight ratio: 24.3 lb/hp, 11 kg/hp; carrying capacity: 882 lb, 400 kg; speed in direct drive at 1,000 rpm: 16.9 mph, 27.2 km/h; fuel consumption: 31.4 m/imp gal, 26.1 m/US gal, 9 l x 100 km.

CHASSIS integral; front suspension: independent, wishbones, coil springs, anti-roll bar, telescopic dampers; rear suspension: independent, oblique swinging trailing arms, transverse compensating leafspring (single), coil springs, anti-roll bar, telescopic dampers.

STEERING rack-and-pinion; turns lock to lock: 3.

BRAKES drum; swept area: front 44.8 sq in, 289 sq cm, rear 44.8 sq in, 289 sq cm, total 89.6 sq in, 578 sq cm.

ELECTRICAL EQUIPMENT 12 V; 35 Ah battery; 30 A alternator; Hitachi distributor; 4 headlamps.

DIMENSIONS AND WEIGHT wheel base: 92.52 in, 2,350 mm; tracks: 48.62 in, 1,235 mm front, 47.83 in, 1,215 mm rear; length: 157.09 in, 3,990 mm; width: 58.86 in, 1,495 mm; height: 54.72 in, 1,390 mm; ground clearance: 6.89 in, 175 mm; dry weight: 2,029 lb, 920 kg; distribution of weight: 55% front, 45% rear; turning circle (between walls): 32.8 ft, 10 m; fuel tank: 8.8 imp gal, 10.6 US gal, 40 l.

BODY saloon/sedan; 2 doors; 5 seats, separate front seats.

PRACTICAL INSTRUCTIONS fuel: 90 oct petrol; engine sump oil: 5.6 imp pt, 6.8 US pt, 3.2 l, SAE 20W-30, change every 3,100 miles, 5,000 km; gearbox oil: 3.5 imp pt, 4.2 US pt, 2 l, SAE 30, change every 24,900 miles, 40,000 km; final drive oil: 1.2 imp pt, 1.5 US pt, 0.7 l, SAE 90/140, change every 24,900 miles, 40,000 km.

Bellett 1600 Special 4-door Sedan

See Bellett 1600 Special 2-door Sedan, except for:

PRICE EX WORKS: 591,000 yen.

PERFORMANCE power-weight ratio: 24.5 lb/hp, 11.1 kg/hp.

DIMENSIONS AND WEIGHT dry weight: 2,051 lb, 930 kg.

Bellett 1600 GTR Coupé

See Bellett 1600 Special 2-door Sedan, except for:

PRICE EX WORKS: 1,110,000 yen.

ENGINE compression ratio: 10.3:1; max power (DIN): 120 hp at 6,400 rpm; max torque (DIN): 105 lb ft, 14.5 kg m at 5,000 rpm; max engine rpm: 7,000; 76 hp/l; valves: overhead, thimble tappets; camshafts: 2, overhead; lubricating system capacity: 7.9 imp pt, 9.5 US pt, 4.5 l; 2 Mikuni-Solex 40 PHH downdraught twin barrel carburettors; fuel feed: electric pump.

TRANSMISSION clutch: single dry plate (diaphragm); gearbox ratios: I 3.467, II 1.989, III 1.356, IV 1, rev 3.592; final drive: hypoid bevel, limited slip differential; tyres: 165 x 13.

PERFORMANCE max speeds: (I) 35 mph, 57 km/h; (II) 64 mph, 103 km/h; (III) 91 mph, 147 km/h; (IV) 118 mph, 190 km/h; power-weight ratio: 17.9 lb/hp, 8.1 kg/hp; acceleration: standing ¼ mile 16.6 sec; speed in direct drive at 1,000 rpm: 17.4 mph, 28 km/h; fuel consumption: 28.2 m/imp gal, 23.5 m/US gal, 10 l x 100 km.

CHASSIS rear suspension: no anti-roll bar.

BRAKES front disc, rear drum; swept area: front 16.7 sq in, 108 sq cm, rear 44.8 sq in, 289 sq cm, total 61.5 sq in, 397 sq cm.

ELECTRICAL EQUIPMENT 40 Ah battery; 40 A alternator.

DIMENSIONS AND WEIGHT tracks: 49.61 in, 1,260 mm front, 48.82 in, 1,240 mm rear; length: 157.68 in, 4,005 mm; height: 52.17 in, 1,325 mm; ground clearance: 7.68 in, 195 mm; dry weight: 2,139 lb, 970 kg.

BODY coupé; 2 + 2 seats.

PRACTICAL INSTRUCTIONS valve timing: 40° 44° 57° 15°; tyre pressure: front 26 psi, 1.8 atm, rear 31 psi, 2.2 atm.

Bellett 1800 Sports Sedan

See Bellett 1600 Special 2-door Sedan, except for:

PRICE EX WORKS: 717,000 yen.

ENGINE 110.9 cu in, 1,817 cc (3.31 x 3.23 in, 84 x 82 mm); compression ratio: 9.7:1; max power (DIN): 115 hp at 5,800 rpm; max torque (DIN): 112 lb ft, 15.5 kg m at 4,200 rpm;

Capella 1600 De Luxe Sedan

See Capella 1500 De Luxe Sedan, except for:

PRICE EX WORKS: 658,000 yen.

ENGINE 96.8 cu in, 1,586 cc (3.07 x 3.27 in, 78 x 83 mm); max power (DIN): 100 hp at 6,000 rpm; max torque (DIN): 101 lb ft, 14 kg m at 3,500 rpm; 63 hp/l.

PERFORMANCE max speeds: (I) 31 mph, 50 km/h; (II) 52 mph, 83 km/h; (III) 76 mph, 123 km/h; (IV) 103 mph, 165 km/h; power-weight ratio: 20.1 lb/hp, 9.1 kg/hp.

Capella 1600 Super De Luxe Sedan

See Capella 1600 De Luxe Sedan, except for:

PRICE EX WORKS: 698,000 yen.

BRAKES front disc, rear drum, servo.

Capella 1600 Super De Luxe Coupé

See Capella 1600 Super De Luxe Sedan, except for:

PRICE EX WORKS: 738,000 yen.

DIMENSIONS AND WEIGHT height: 54.92 in, 1,395 mm.

BODY coupé; 2 doors; 4 seats.

Capella 1600 GL Sedan

See Capella 1600 Super De Luxe Sedan, except for:

PRICE EX WORKS: 720,000 yen.

TRANSMISSION axle ratio: 3.900; width of rims: 4.5"; tyres: 6.45 x 13.

PERFORMANCE power-weight ratio: 20.7 lb/hp, 9.4 kg/hp.

DIMENSIONS AND WEIGHT tracks: 50.79 in, 1,290 mm front, 50.79 in, 1,290 mm rear; length: 165.75 in, 4,210 mm; height: 56.50 in, 1,435 mm; ground clearance: 6.69 in, 170 mm; dry weight: 2,073 lb, 940 kg.

Capella 1600 GF Coupé

See Capella 1600 GL Sedan, except for:

PRICE EX WORKS: 760,000 yen.

PERFORMANCE power-weight ratio: 20.5 lb/hp, 9.3 kg/hp.

DIMENSIONS AND WEIGHT height: 54.92 in, 1,395 mm; dry weight: 2,040 lb, 925 kg.

BODY coupé; 2 doors.

Capella RE De Luxe Sedan

PRICE EX WORKS: 748,000 yen.

ENGINE front, 4 stroke, Wankel type; 2 co-axial 3-lobe rotors; 35 x 2 cu in, 573 x 2 cc; compression ratio: 9.4:1; max power (DIN): 120 hp at 6,500 rpm; max torque (DIN): 116 lb ft, 16 kg m at 3,500 rpm; max engine rpm: 7,000; light alloy engine block, dual ignition, cast iron rotors; 2 crankshaft bearings; lubrication: rotary pump, full flow filter, oil-cooler, 9.7 imp pt, 11.6 US pt, 5.5 l; 1 Nikki-Stromberg downdraught 4-barrel carburettor; fuel feed: electric pump; water-cooled, 14.1 imp pt, 16.9 US pt, 8 l.

TRANSMISSION driving wheels: rear; clutch: single dry plate (diaphragm); gearbox: mechanical; gears: 4, fully synchronized; ratios: I 3.683, II 2.263, III 1.397, IV 1, rev 3.692; lever: central; final drive: hypoid bevel; axle ratio: 3.700; width of rims: 4"; tyres: 155 x 13.

PERFORMANCE max speeds: (I) 31 mph, 50 km/h; (II) 54 mph, 87 km/h; (III) 87 mph, 140 km/h; (IV) 115 mph, 185 km/h; power-weight ratio: 17.6 lb/hp, 8 kg/hp; carrying capacity: 882 lb, 400 kg; speed in direct drive at 1,000 rpm: 16.5 mph, 26.5 km/h; fuel consumption: 25.7 m/imp gal, 21.4 m/US gal, 11 l x 100 km.

CHASSIS integral; front suspension: independent, by McPherson, coil springs/telescopic damper struts, lower wishbones (trailing links), anti-roll bar; rear suspension: rigid axle, lower trailing arms, upper torque arms, transverse linkage bar, coil springs, telescopic dampers.

STEERING recirculating ball, variable ratio; turns lock to lock: 3.30.

BRAKES front disc, rear drum, servo; swept area: front 24.8 sq in, 160 sq cm, rear 39.7 sq in, 256 sq cm, total 64.5 sq in, 416 sq cm.

MAZDA Rotary Coupé GS

MAZDA Capella 1600 GL Sedan

MAZDA Capella GS II Coupé

ELECTRICAL EQUIPMENT 12 V; 45 Ah battery; 40 A alternator; Mitsubishi distributor; 2 headlamps.

DIMENSIONS AND WEIGHT wheel base: 97.24 in, 2,470 mm; tracks: 50.59 in, 1,285 mm front, 50.39 in, 1,280 mm rear; length: 163.39 in, 4,150 mm; width: 62.20 in, 1,580 mm; height: 55.91 in, 1,420 mm; ground clearance: 6.30 in, 160 mm; dry weight: 2,106 lb, 955 kg; distribution of weight: 53.6% front, 46.4% rear; turning circle (between walls): 33.5 ft, 10.2 m; fuel tank: 14.3 imp gal, 17.2 US gal, 65 l.

BODY saloon/sedan; 4 doors; 5 seats, separate front seats.

PRACTICAL INSTRUCTIONS fuel: 85-90 oct petrol; engine sump oil: 9.7 imp pt, 11.6 US pt, 5.5 l, SAE 10W-30, change every 3,700 miles, 6,000 km; gearbox oil: 4.4 imp pt, 5.3 US pt, 2.5 l, SAE 90, change every 31,000 miles, 50,000 km; final drive oil: 2.1 imp pt, 2.5 US pt, 1.2 l, SAE 90, change every 31,000 miles, 50,000 km; tyre pressure: front 24 psi, 1.7 atm, rear 24 psi, 1.7 atm.

Capella RE GS Coupé

See Capella RE De Luxe Sedan, except for:

PRICE EX WORKS: 845,000 yen.

PERFORMANCE max speed: 118 mph, 190 km/h.

DIMENSIONS AND WEIGHT height: 54.92 in, 1,395 mm; dry weight: 2,117 lb, 960 kg.

BODY coupé; 2 doors; 4 seats.

Capella GS II Coupé

See Capella RE GS Coupé, except for:

PRICE EX WORKS: 920,000 yen.

ENGINE max power (DIN): 125 hp at 7,000 rpm; max torque (DIN): 118 lb ft, 16.3 kg m at 4,000 rpm.

TRANSMISSION gears: 5, fully synchronized; ratios: I 3.683, II 2.263, III 1.397, IV 1, V 0.862, rev 3.692; axle ratio: 4.111.

PERFORMANCE power-weight ratio: 17.3 lb/hp, 7.9 kg/hp.

DIMENSIONS AND WEIGHT dry weight: 2,161 lb, 980 kg.

Capella GR Sedan

See Capella RE De Luxe Sedan, except for:

PRICE EX WORKS: 820,000 yen.

TRANSMISSION axle ratio: 3.900; width of rims: 4.5"; tyres: 6.45 x 13.

PERFORMANCE power-weight ratio: 18.1 lb/hp, 8.2 kg/hp; acceleration: standing ¼ mile 16.3 sec.

ELECTRICAL EQUIPMENT 4 headlamps.

DIMENSIONS AND WEIGHT tracks: 50.79 in, 1,290 mm front, 50.79 in, 1,290 mm rear; length: 165.75 in, 4,210 mm; height: 56.50 in, 1,435 mm; ground clearance: 6.69 in, 170 mm; dry weight: 2,161 lb, 980 kg; distribution of weight: 54% front, 46% rear.

Cappella GR Sedan RE-matic

See Capella GR Sedan, except for:

PRICE EX WORKS: 875,000 yen.

TRANSMISSION gearbox: Jatco 3N71B automatic transmission, hydraulic torque converter and planetary gears with 3 ratios, max ratio of converter at stall 1.95, possible manual selection; ratios: I 2.458, II 1.458, III 1, rev 2.181.

PERFORMANCE max speed: 109 mph, 175 km/h; acceleration: standing ¼ mile 18.4 sec.

Capella GS Coupé

See Capella GR Sedan, except for:

PRICE EX WORKS: 870,000 yen.

PERFORMANCE max speed: 118 mph, 190 km/h; power-weight ratio: 17.9 lb/hp, 8.1 kg/hp; acceleration: standing ¼ mile 16.2 sec.

DIMENSIONS AND WEIGHT length: 163.39 in, 4,150 mm; height: 54.92 in, 1,395 mm; dry weight: 2,150 lb, 975 kg.

BODY coupé; 2 doors.

Capella GS Coupé RE-matic

See Capella GS Coupé, except for:

PRICE EX WORKS: 925,000 yen.

TRANSMISSION gearbox: Jatco automatic transmission, hydraulic torque converter and planetary gears with 3 ratios, max ratio of converter at stall 1.95, possible manual selection; ratios: I 2.458, II 1.458, III 1, rev 2.181.

PERFORMANCE max speed: 112 mph, 180 km/h; acceleration: standing ¼ mile 18.3 sec.

Savanna RX Sedan

PRICE EX WORKS: 670,000 yen.

ENGINE front, 4 stroke, Wankel type; 2 co-axial 3-lobe rotors; 30 x 2 cu in, 491 x 2 cc; compression ratio: 9.4:1; max power (DIN): 105 hp at 7,000 rpm; max torque (DIN): 99 lb ft, 13.7 kg m at 3,500 rpm; max engine rpm: 7,000; light alloy engine block, dual ignition, cast iron rotors; 2 crankshaft bearings; lubrication: gear pump, full flow filter, oil-water heat exchanger, 8.6 imp pt, 10.4 US pt, 4.9 l; 1 Hitachi-Stromberg KCB306 4-barrel carburettor; fuel feed: electric pump; water-cooled engine block, oil-cooled rotors, 12.7 imp pt, 15.2 US pt, 7.2 l.

TRANSMISSION driving wheels: rear; clutch: single dry plate (diaphragm); gearbox: mechanical; gears: 4, fully synchronized; ratios: I 3.737, II 2.202, III 1.435, IV 1, rev 4.024; lever: central; final drive: hypoid bevel; axle ratio: 3.700; width of rims: 4.5"; tyres: 6.15 x 13.

PERFORMANCE max speeds: (I) 32 mph, 52 km/h; (II) 55 mph, 88 km/h; (III) 86 mph, 138 km/h; (IV) 109 mph, 175 km/h; power-weight ratio: 18.1 lb/hp, 8.2 kg/hp; acceleration: standing ¼ mile 16.8 sec.

CHASSIS integral; front suspension: independent, by McPherson, coil springs/telescopic damper struts, lower wishbones (trailing links), anti-roll bar; rear suspension: rigid axle, semi-elliptic leafsprings, telescopic dampers.

STEERING recirculating ball, variable ratio; turns lock to lock: 3.50.

BRAKES front disc, rear drum; swept area: front 19.8 sq in, 128 sq cm, rear 39.7 sq in, 256 sq cm, total 59.5 sq in, 384 sq cm.

ELECTRICAL EQUIPMENT 12 V; 45 Ah battery; 40 A alternator; 4 headlamps.

DIMENSIONS AND WEIGHT wheel base: 90.94 in, 2,310 mm; tracks: 51.18 in, 1,300 mm front, 50.79 in, 1,290 mm rear; length: 160.04 in, 4,065 mm; width: 62.80 in, 1,595 mm; height: 54.13 in, 1,375 mm; ground clearance: 6.50 in, 165 mm; dry weight: 1,896 lb, 860 kg; distribution of weight: 57% front, 43% rear; turning circle (between walls): 30.8 ft, 9.4 m; fuel tank: 13.2 imp gal, 15.8 US gal, 60 l.

BODY saloon/sedan; 4 doors; 5 seats, separate front seats.

PRACTICAL INSTRUCTIONS fuel: 85-90 oct petrol; engine sump oil: 8.6 imp pt, 10.4 US pt, 4.9 l, SAE 10W-30, change every 3,700 miles, 6,000 km; gearbox oil: 2.5 imp pt, 3 US pt, 1.4 l, SAE 90, change every 29,800 miles, 48,000 km; final drive oil: 2.5 imp pt, 3 US pt, 1.4 l, SAE 90, change every 29,800 miles, 48,000 km; tyre pressure: front 26 psi, 1.8 atm, rear 26 psi, 1.8 atm.

Savanna GR Sedan

See Savanna RX Sedan, except for:

PRICE EX WORKS: 700,000 yen.

PERFORMANCE power-weight ratio: 18.3 lb/hp, 8.3 kg/hp.

DIMENSIONS AND WEIGHT dry weight: 1,918 lb, 870 kg.

Savanna SX Coupé

See Savanna RX Sedan, except for:

PRICE EX WORKS: 670,000 yen.

PERFORMANCE max speed: 112 mph, 180 km/h; power-weight ratio: 17.9 lb/hp, 8.1 kg/hp; acceleration: standing ¼ mile 16.4 sec.

DIMENSIONS AND WEIGHT height: 53.15 in, 1,350 mm; dry weight: 1,885 lb, 855 kg.

BODY coupé; 2 doors.

Savanna GS II Coupé

See Savanna SX Coupé, except for:

PRICE EX WORKS: 750,000 yen.

TRANSMISSION tyres: Z78 x 13.

MAZDA Savanna GS II Coupé

MAZDA Savanna GT Coupé

MAZDA Luce Sedan GR AP

PERFORMANCE power-weight ratio: 18.3 lb/hp, 8.3 kg/hp.

BRAKES servo.

DIMENSIONS AND WEIGHT dry weight: 1,929 lb, 875 kg.

OPTIONAL ACCESSORIES 155 SR x 13 tyres.

Savanna GT Coupé

See Savanna GS II Coupé, except for:

PRICE EX WORKS: 795,000 yen.

ENGINE 35 x 2 cu in, 573 x 2 cc max power (DIN): 120 hp at 6,500 rpm; max torque (DIN): 116 lb ft, 16 kg m at 3,500 rpm.

TRANSMISSION gears: 5, fully synchronized; ratios: I 3.682, II 2.263, III 1.397, IV 1, V 0.862, rev 3.692.

PERFORMANCE max speeds: (I) 31 mph, 50 km/h; (II) 51 mph, 82 km/h; (III) 82 mph, 132 km/h; (IV) 113 mph, 182 km/h; (V) 118 mph, 190 km/h; power-weight ratio: 16.3 lb/hp, 7.4 kg/hp.

STEERING recirculating ball, variable ratio; turns lock to lock: 3.30.

DIMENSIONS AND WEIGHT dry weight: 1,951 lb, 885 kg.

R130 De Luxe Coupé

PRICE EX WORKS: 1,450,000 yen.

ENGINE front, 4 stroke, Wankel type; 2 co-axial 3-lobe rotors; 40 x 2 cu in, 655 x 2 cc; compression ratio: 9:1; max power (SAE): 126 hp at 6,000 rpm; max torque (SAE): 127 lb ft, 17.5 kg m at 3,500 rpm; max engine rpm: 6,500; light alloy engine block, dual ignition, cast iron rotors; 3 crankshaft bearings; lubrication: gear pump, full flow filter, oil-water heat exchanger, 8.8 imp pt, 10.6 US pt, 5 l; 1 Stromberg 4-barrel carburettor; fuel feed: electric pump; water-cooled engine block, oil-cooled rotors, 15.5 imp pt, 18.6 US pt, 8.8 l.

TRANSMISSION driving wheels: front; clutch: single dry plate (diaphragm); gearbox: mechanical; gears: 4, fully synchronized; ratios: I 3.727, II 2.176, III 1.391, IV 1.037, rev 3.727; lever: central; final drive: hypoid bevel; axle ratio: 3.900; width of rims: 4.5"; tyres: 165 x 15.

PERFORMANCE max speeds: (I) 30 mph, 48 km/h; (II) 55 mph, 88 km/h; (III) 87 mph, 140 km/h; (IV) 118 mph, 190 km/h; power-weight ratio: 20.7 lb/hp, 9.4 kg/hp; carrying capacity: 882 lb, 400 kg; acceleration: standing ¼ mile 16.9 sec, 0-50 mph (0-80 km/h) 6.2 sec; fuel consumption: 23.5 m/imp gal, 19.6 m/US gal, 12 l x 100 km.

CHASSIS integral; front suspension: independent, wishbones, rubber springs (torsion), anti-roll bar, telescopic dampers; rear suspension: independent, semi-trailing arms, coil springs, telescopic dampers.

STEERING rack-and-pinion; turns lock to lock: 3.80.

BRAKES front disc, rear drum, servo.

ELECTRICAL EQUIPMENT 12 V; 45 Ah battery; 560 W alternator; Mitsubishi distributor; 4 headlamps.

DIMENSIONS AND WEIGHT wheel base: 101.57 in, 2,580 mm; tracks: 52.36 in, 1,330 mm front, 52.17 in, 1,325 mm rear; length: 180.51 in, 4,585 mm; width: 64.37 in, 1,635 mm; height: 54.53 in, 1,385 mm; ground clearance: 7.28 in, 185 mm; dry weight: 2,613 lb, 1,185 kg; distribution of weight: 62% front, 38% rear; turning circle (between walls): 34.8 ft, 10.6 m; fuel tank: 14.3 imp gal, 17.2 US gal, 65 l.

BODY coupé; 2 doors; 5 seats, separate front seats.

PRACTICAL INSTRUCTIONS fuel: 85-90 oct petrol; engine sump oil: 8.8 imp pt, 10.6 US pt, 5 l, SAE 10W-40, change every 3,700 miles, 6,000 km; gearbox and final drive oil: 6.2 imp pt, 7.4 US pt, 3.5 l, SAE 90, change every 31,100 miles, 50,000 km; greasing: every 31,100 miles, 50,000 km, 6 points; tyre pressure: front 28 psi, 2 atm, rear 23 psi, 1.6 atm.

R130 Super De Luxe Coupé

See R130 De Luxe Coupé, except for:

PRICE EX WORKS: 1,750,000 yen.

PERFORMANCE power-weight ratio: 22 lb/hp, 10 kg/hp.

STEERING servo; turns lock to lock: 3.50.

DIMENSIONS AND WEIGHT dry weight: 2,767 lb, 1,255 kg.

BODY electrically-controlled windows, air-conditioning.

MAZDA Savanna GS II Coupé

MAZDA Savanna GT Coupé

MAZDA Luce Sedan GR AP

Luce Sedan RX

PRICE EX WORKS: 810,000 yen.

ENGINE front, 4 stroke, Wankel type; 2 coaxial 3-lobe rotors; 35 x 2 cu in, 573 x 2 cc; compression ratio: 9.4:1; max power (DIN): 120 hp at 6,500 rpm; max torque (DIN): 116 lb ft, 16 kg m at 3,500 rpm; max engine rpm: 7,000; cast iron and light alloy engine block; 2 crankshaft bearings; lubrication: rotary pump, full flow filter, oil cooler, 9.2 imp pt, 11 US pt, 5.2 l; 1 Nikki downdraught 4-barrel carburettor; fuel feed: electric pump; water-cooled, 15.8 imp pt, 19 US pt, 9 l.

TRANSMISSION driving wheels: rear; clutch: single dry plate (diaphragm); gearbox: mechanical; gears: 4, fully synchronized; ratios: I 3.683, II 2.263, III 1.397, IV 1, rev 3.692; lever: central; final drive: hypoid bevel; axle ratio: 3.900; width of rims: 5"; tyres: 6.45 x 13.

PERFORMANCE max speeds: (I) 33 mph, 53 km/h; (II) 53 mph, 86 km/h; (III) 87 mph, 140 km/h; (IV) 112 mph, 180 km/h; power-weight ratio: 18.5 lb/hp, 8.4 kg/hp; fuel consumption: not declared.

CHASSIS integral; front suspension: independent, by McPherson, coil springs/telescopic damper struts, lower wishbones, anti-roll bar; rear suspension: rigid axle, semi-elliptic leafsprings, telescopic dampers.

STEERING recirculating ball, variable ratio; turns lock to lock: 3.40.

BRAKES front disc, rear drum, servo.

ELECTRICAL EQUIPMENT 12 V; 45 Ah battery; 50 A alternator; Mitsubishi distributor; 4 headlamps.

DIMENSIONS AND WEIGHT wheel base: 98.82 in, 2,510 mm; tracks: 54.33 in, 1,380 mm front, 53.94 in, 1,370 mm rear; length: 166.93 in, 4,240 mm; width: 65.35 in, 1,660 mm; height: 55.51 in, 1,410 mm; ground clearance: 6.89 in, 175 mm; dry weight: 2,216 lb, 1,005 kg; turning circle (between walls): 35.4 ft, 10.8 m; fuel tank: 14.3 imp gal, 17.2 US gal, 65 l.

BODY saloon/sedan; 4 doors; 5 seats, separate front seats.

PRACTICAL INSTRUCTIONS fuel: 85-90 oct petrol; engine sump oil: 8.8 imp pt, 10.6 US pt, 5 l, SAE 10W-30, change every 3,700 miles, 6,000 km; gearbox oil: 3 imp pt, 3.6 US pt, 1.7 l, SAE 90, change every 31,100 miles, 50,000 km; final drive oil: 2.1 imp pt, 2.5 US pt, 1.2 l, SAE 90, change every 31,100 miles, 50,000 km; tyre pressure: front 24 psi, 1.7 atm, rear 24 psi, 1.7 atm.

Luce Sedan GR

See Luce Sedan RX, except for:

PRICE EX WORKS: 860,000 yen.

TRANSMISSION tyres: B 70 x 13.

PERFORMANCE power-weight ratio: 18.6 lb/hp, 8.4 kg/hp.

DIMENSIONS AND WEIGHT dry weight: 2,227 lb, 1,010 kg.

Luce Sedan GR Automatic

See Luce Sedan RX, except for:

PRICE EX WORKS: 910,000 yen.

TRANSMISSION gearbox: Jatco automatic transmission, hydraulic torque converter and planetary gears with 3 ratios, max ratio of converter at stall 1.95, possible manual selection; ratios: I 2.458, II 1.458, III 1, rev 2.181; tyres: B 70 x 13.

PERFORMANCE max speed: 109 mph, 175 km/h; power-weight ratio: 18.7 lb/hp, 8.5 kg/hp.

DIMENSIONS AND WEIGHT dry weight: 2,249 lb, 1,020 kg.

Luce Sedan GR AP

See Luce Sedan GR Automatic, except for:

ENGINE anti-pollution system with air injection, thermal reactor and computer controlled ignition system; max power (DIN): 115 hp at 6,500 rpm; max torque (DIN): 114 lb ft, 15.7 kg m at 3,500 rpm.

TRANSMISSION axle ratio: 4.111.

PERFORMANCE max speed: 106 mph, 170 km/h; power-weight ratio: 20 lb/hp, 9 kg/hp.

DIMENSIONS AND WEIGHT dry weight: 2,293 lb, 1,040 kg.

Luce Custom GR

See Luce Sedan RX, except for:

PRICE EX WORKS: 885,000 yen.

TRANSMISSION tyres: B 78 x 13.

PERFORMANCE power-weight ratio: 18.6 lb/hp, 8.5 kg/hp.

DIMENSIONS AND WEIGHT length: 170.28 in, 4,325 mm; width: 65.75 in, 1,670 mm; dry weight: 2,238 lb, 1,015 kg.

Luce Custom GR Automatic

See Luce Sedan RX, except for:

PRICE EX WORKS: 940,000 yen.

TRANSMISSION gearbox: Jatco automatic transmission, hydraulic torque converter and planetary gears with 3 ratios, max ratio of converter at stall 1.95, possible manual selection; ratios: I 2.458, II 1.458, III 1, rev 2.185.

PERFORMANCE max speed: 109 mph, 175 km/h; power-weight ratio: 18.8 lb/hp, 8.5 kg/hp.

DIMENSIONS AND WEIGHT length: 170.28 in, 4,325 mm; width: 65.75 in, 1,670 mm; dry weight: 2,260 lb, 1,025 kg.

Luce Custom GR II

See Luce Sedan RX, except for:

PRICE EX WORKS: 975,000 yen.

ENGINE max power (DIN): 130 hp at 7,000 rpm; max torque (DIN): 120 lb ft, 16.3 kg m at 4,000 rpm.

TRANSMISSION gears: 5, fully synchronized; ratios: I 3.683, II 2.263, III 1.397, IV 1, V 0.862, rev 3.692; axle ratio: 4.111; width of rims: 5.5"; tyres: B 70 x 13.

PERFORMANCE max speed: 115 mph, 185 km/h; power-weight ratio: 17.5 lb/hp, 8 kg/hp.

DIMENSIONS AND WEIGHT length: 170.28 in, 4,325 mm; width: 65.75 in, 1,670 mm; dry weight: 2,282 lb, 1,035 kg.

Luce Custom GR II AP

See Luce Custom GR II, except for:

PRICE EX WORKS: 1,085,000 yen.

ENGINE anti-pollution system with air injection, thermal reactor and computer controlled ignition system; max power (DIN): 125 hp at 7,000 rpm; max torque (DIN): 117 lb ft, 16.2 kg m at 4,000 rpm.

TRANSMISSION gearbox: Jatco automatic transmission, hydraulic torque converter and planetary gears with 3 ratios, max ratio of converter at stall 1.95, possible manual selection; ratios: I 2.458, II 1.458, III 1, rev 2.185; axle ratio: 4.111.

PERFORMANCE max speed: 109 mph, 175 km/h; power-weight ratio: 18.7 lb/hp, 8.5 kg/hp.

DIMENSIONS AND WEIGHT dry weight: 2,337 lb, 1,060 kg.

Luce Hardtop SX

See Luce Sedan RX, except for:

PRICE EX WORKS: 350,000 yen.

PERFORMANCE max speed: 115 mph, 185 km/h; power-weight ratio: 18.6 lb/hp, 8.4 kg/hp.

DIMENSIONS AND WEIGHT length: 170.08 in, 4,320 mm; width: 54.33 in, 1,380 mm; dry weight: 2,227 lb, 1,010 kg.

BODY hardtop; 2 doors.

Luce Hardtop GS

See Luce Hardtop SX, except for:

PRICE EX WORKS: 905,000 yen.

TRANSMISSION tyres: B 78 x 13.

PERFORMANCE power-weight ratio: 18.7 lb/hp, 8.5 kg/hp.

DIMENSIONS AND WEIGHT dry weight: 2,238 lb, 1,015 kg.

OPTIONAL ACCESSORIES 175 SR x 13 tyres.

MAZDA Luce Hardtop GS II

MITSUBISHI Minica F4 Custom Sedan

MITSUBISHI Minica Skipper LL

Luce Hardtop GS II

See Luce Hardtop SX, except for:

PRICE EX WORKS: 1,010,000 yen.

ENGINE max power (DIN): 130 hp at 7,000 rpm; max torque (DIN): 120 lb ft, 16.5 kg m at 4,000 rpm.

TRANSMISSION gears: 5, fully synchronized; ratios: I 3.683, II 2.263, III 1.387, IV 1, V 0.862, rev 3.692; axle ratio: 4.111; width of rims: 5.5"; tyres: B 70 x 13.

PERFORMANCE max speeds: (I) 31 mph, 50 km/h; (II) 52 mph, 83 km/h; (III) 81 mph, 130 km/h; (IV) 112 mph, 180 km/h; (V) 118 mph, 190 km/h; power-weight ratio: 17.5 lb/hp, 7.9 kg/hp.

CHASSIS rear suspension: torque arms.

DIMENSIONS AND WEIGHT width: 65.94 in, 1,675 mm; dry weight: 2,271 lb, 1,030 kg.

OPTIONAL ACCESSORIES 195/70 SR x 13 tyres.

Luce Hardtop GS II Automatic

See Luce Hardtop SX, except for:

PRICE EX WORKS: 1,045,000 yen.

TRANSMISSION gearbox: Jatco automatic transmission, hydraulic torque converter and planetary gears with 3 ratios, max ratio of converter at stall 1.95, possible manual selection; ratios: I 2.458, II 1.458, III 1, rev 2.181; axle ratio: 3.900.

PERFORMANCE max speed: 115 mph, 185 km/h; power-weight ratio: 19.1 lb/hp, 8.7 kg/hp.

DIMENSIONS AND WEIGHT dry weight: 2,293 lb, 1,040 kg.

OPTIONAL ACCESSORIES 195/70 SR x 13 tyres.

Luce Hardtop GS II AP

See Luce Hardtop GS II Automatic, except for:

ENGINE anti-pollution system with air injection, thermal reactor and computer controlled ignition system; max power (DIN): 125 hp at 7,000 rpm; max torque (DIN): 117 lb ft, 16.2 kg m at 4,000 rpm.

TRANSMISSION axle ratio: 4.111.

PERFORMANCE max speed: 112 mph, 180 km/h; power-weight ratio: 18.7 lb/hp, 8.5 kg/hp.

DIMENSIONS AND WEIGHT dry weight: 2,337 lb, 1,060 kg.

MITSUBISHI JAPAN

Minica F4 Standard Sedan

PRICE EX WORKS: 331,000 yen.

ENGINE front, 4 stroke; 2 cylinders, in line; 21.9 cu in, 359 cc (2.44 x 2.35 in, 62 x 59.6 mm); compression ratio: 9:1; max power (DIN): 32 hp at 8,000 rpm; max torque (DIN): 22 lb ft, 3 kg m at 5,500 rpm; max engine rpm: 8,700; 88.9 hp/l; cast iron cylinder block, light alloy head; 3 crankshaft bearings; valves: overhead, rockers; camshafts: 1, overhead; lubrication: rotary pump, full flow filter, 4 imp pt, 4.9 US pt, 2.3 l; 1 Mikuni-Solex downdraught twin barrel carburettor; fuel feed: mechanical pump; water-cooled, 5.1 imp pt, 6.1 US pt, 2.9 l.

TRANSMISSION driving wheels: rear; clutch: single dry plate (diaphragm); gearbox: mechanical; gears: 4, fully synchronized; ratios: I 3.576, II 2.265, III 1.473, IV 1, rev 4.271; lever: central; final drive: hypoid bevel; axle ratio: 6.667; width of rims: 3.5"; tyres: 5.20 x 10.

PERFORMANCE max speeds: (I) 20 mph, 32 km/h; (II) 32 mph, 51 km/h; (III) 48 mph, 78 km/h; (IV) 71 mph, 115 km/h; power-weight ratio: 34.8 lb/hp, 15.8 kg/hp; carrying capacity: 706 lb, 320 kg; fuel consumption: not declared.

CHASSIS integral; front suspension: independent, by McPherson, coil springs/telescopic damper struts, anti-roll bar, lower wishbones (trailing links); rear suspension: rigid axle, twin longitudinal trailing radius arms, transverse linkage bar, coil springs, telescopic dampers.

STEERING recirculating ball.

BRAKES drum, single circuit; swept area: total 67 sq in, 432 sq cm.

MAZDA Luce Hardtop GS II

MITSUBISHI Minica F4 Custom Sedan

MITSUBISHI Minica Skipper

ELECTRICAL EQUIPMENT 12 V; 24 Ah battery; 35 A alternator; Mitsubishi distributor; 2 headlamps.

DIMENSIONS AND WEIGHT wheel base: 78.84 in, 2,000 mm; tracks: 44.09 in, 1,120 mm front, 42.52 in, 1,080 mm rear; length: 117.91 in, 2,995 mm; width: 50.98 in, 1,295 mm; height: 51.77 in, 1,315 mm; ground clearance: 5.71 in, 145 mm; dry weight: 1,114 lb, 505 kg; turning circle (between walls): 24.9 ft, 7.6 m; fuel tank: 6.6 imp gal, 7.9 US gal, 30 l.

BODY saloon/sedan; 2 doors; 4 seats, separate front seats.

PRACTICAL INSTRUCTIONS fuel: 85-90 oct petrol; engine sump oil: 4.8 imp pt, 5.7 US pt, 2.7 l, SAE 30, change every 3,100 miles, 5,000 km; gearbox oil: 1.1 imp pt, 1.3 US pt, 0.6 l, SAE 80, change every 24,900 miles, 40,000 km; final drive oil: 1.1 imp pt, 1.3 US pt, 0,6 l, SAE 80, change every 24,900 miles, 40,000 km; tappet clearances (hot): inlet 0.006 in, 0.15 mm, exhaust 0.010 in, 0.25 mm; valve timing: 40° 60° 70° 30°; tyre pressure: front 21 psi, 1.5 atm, rear 21 psi, 1.5 atm.

Minica F4 De Luxe Sedan

See Minica F4 Standard Sedan, except for:

PRICE EX WORKS: 374,000 yen.

Minica F4 Custom Sedan

See Minica F4 Standard Sedan, except for:

PRICE EX WORKS: 430,000 yen.

PERFORMANCE power-weight ratio: 35.5 lb/hp, 16 kg/hp.

DIMENSIONS AND WEIGHT dry weight: 1,136 lb, 515 kg.

Minica F4 GS

See Minica F4 Standard Sedan, except for:

PRICE EX WORKS: 442,000 yen.

ENGINE compression ratio: 9.5:1; max power (DIN): 36 hp at 8,500 rpm; max torque (DIN): 23 lb ft, 3.2 kg m at 6,500 rpm; max engine rpm: 9,000; 100.3 hp/l.

TRANSMISSION tyres: 145 SR x 10.

PERFORMANCE max speeds: (I) 21 mph, 33 km/h; (II) 33 mph, 53 km/h; (III) 50 mph, 80 km/h; (IV) 75 mph, 120 km/h; power-weight ratio: 31.9 lb/hp, 14.4 kg/hp.

DIMENSIONS AND WEIGHT dry weight: 1,147 lb, 520 kg.

Minica F4 GSL

See Minica F4 GS, except for:

PRICE EX WORKS: 470,000 yen.

Minica Skipper FL Coupé

See Minica F4 Standard Sedan, except for:

PRICE EX WORKS: 377,000 yen.

ELECTRICAL EQUIPMENT 4 headlamps.

DIMENSIONS AND WEIGHT height: 51.38 in, 1,305 mm.

BODY coupé

Minica Skipper LL

See Minica Skipper FL Coupé, except for:

PRICE EX WORKS: 419,000 yen.

Minica Skipper GT

See Minica Skipper FL Coupé, except for:

PRICE EX WORKS: 452,000 yen.

ENGINE compression ratio: 9.5:1; max power (DIN): 36 hp at 8,500 rpm; max torque (DIN): 23 lb ft, 3.2 kg m at 6,500 rpm; max engine rpm: 9.000; 100.3 hp/l.

TRANSMISSION tyres: 145 SR x 10.

PERFORMANCE max speeds: (I) 21 mph, 33 km/h; (II) 33 mph, 53 km/h; (III) 50 mph, 80 km/h; (IV) 75 mph, 120 km/h; power-weight ratio: 31.9 lb/hp, 14.4 kg/hp.

DIMENSIONS AND WEIGHT dry weight: 1,147 lb, 520 kg.

Galant FTO GI Coupé

PRICE EX WORKS: 558,000 yen.

ENGINE front, 4 stroke; 4 cylinders, in line; 84.1 cu in, 1,378 cc (3.01 x 2.95 in, 76.5 x 75 mm); compression ratio: 9:1; max power (DIN): 86 hp at 6,000 rpm; max torque (DIN): 85 lb ft, 11.7 kg m at 4,000 rpm; max engine rpm: 6,600; 62.4 hp/l; cast iron cylinder block, light alloy head; 3 crankshaft bearings; valves: overhead, push-rods and rockers; camshafts: 1, side; lubrication: rotary pump, full flow filter, 6.2 imp pt, 7.4 US pt, 3.5 l; 1 Stromberg CA 28AA twin barrel carburettor; fuel feed: mechanical pump; water-cooled, 10.6 imp pt, 12.7 US pt, 6 l.

TRANSMISSION driving wheels: rear; clutch: single dry plate (diaphragm); gearbox: mechanical; gears: 4, fully synchronized; ratios: I 3.525, II 2.193, III 1.442, IV 1, rev 3.867; lever: central; final drive: hypoid bevel; axle ratio: 4.222; width of rims: 4"; tyres: 6.15 x 13.

PERFORMANCE max speeds: (I) 29 mph, 46 km/h; (II) 45 mph, 73 km/h; (III) 70 mph, 112 km/h; (IV) 99 mph, 160 km/h; power-weight ratio: 20.9 lb/hp, 9.5 kg/hp; fuel consumption: not declared.

CHASSIS integral; front suspension: independent, by McPherson, coil springs/telescopic damper struts, anti-roll bar, lower wishbones; rear suspension: rigid axle, semi-elliptic leafsprings, telescopic dampers.

STEERING recirculating ball; turns lock to lock: 3.50.

BRAKES drum; swept area: front 47.8 sq in, 308 sq cm, rear 47.8 sq in, 308 sq cm, total 95.6 sq in, 616 sq cm.

ELECTRICAL EQUIPMENT 12 V; 35 Ah battery; 35 A alternator; Mitsubishi distributor; 2 headlamps.

DIMENSIONS AND WEIGHT wheel base: 90.55 in, 2,300 mm; tracks: 50.47 in, 1,282 mm front, 50.71 in, 1,288 mm rear; length: 148.23 in, 3,765 mm; width: 62.20 in, 1,580 mm; height: 52.36 in, 1,330 mm; ground clearance: 6.50 in, 165 mm; dry weight: 1,808 lb, 820 kg; turning circle (between walls): 30.8 ft, 9.4 m; fuel tank: 9.9 imp gal, 11.9 US gal, 45 l.

BODY coupé; 2 doors; 5 seats, separate front seats.

PRACTICAL INSTRUCTIONS fuel: 85-90 oct petrol; engine sump oil: 6.2 imp pt, 7.4 US pt, 3.5 l, SAE 10W-30, change every 3,100 miles, 5,000 km; gearbox oil: 3 imp pt, 3.6 US pt, 1.7 l, SAE 90, change every 24,900 miles, 40,000 km; final drive oil: 1.9 imp pt, 2.3 US pt, 1.1 l, SAE 90, change every 24,900 miles, 40,000 km; tappet clearances: inlet 0.006 in, 0.15 mm, exhaust 0.010 in, 0.25 mm; valve timing: 24° 64° 64° 24°; tyre pressure: front 26 psi, 1.8 atm, rear 26 psi, 1.8 atm.

Galant FTO GII

See Galant FTO GI Coupé, except for:

PRICE EX WORKS: 608,000 yen.

PERFORMANCE power-weight ratio: 21.2 lb/hp, 9.6 kg/hp.

BRAKES front disc.

DIMENSIONS AND WEIGHT dry weight: 1,819 lb, 825 kg.

Galant FTO GIII

See Galant FTO GI Coupé, except for:

PRICE EX WORKS: 660,000 yen.

ENGINE compression ratio: 9.5:1; max power (DIN): 95 hp at 6,300 rpm; max torque (DIN): 89 lb ft, 12.3 kg m at 4,500 rpm; 68.9 hp/l; 2 Stromberg CA28AC downdraught carburettors.

TRANSMISSION width of rims: 4.5"; tyres: 155 SR x 13.

PERFORMANCE max speeds: (I) 30 mph, 48 km/h; (II) 47 mph, 76 km/h; (III) 73 mph, 117 km/h; (IV) 103 mph, 165 km/h; power-weight ratio: 19.4 lb/hp, 8.8 kg/hp; acceleration: standing ¼ mile 17.2 sec.

DIMENSIONS AND WEIGHT dry weight: 1,841 lb, 835 kg.

PRACTICAL INSTRUCTIONS valve timing: 32° 72° 72° 32°.

Galant 14 L Sedan

PRICE EX WORKS: 528,000 yen.

ENGINE front, 4 stroke; 4 cylinders, in line; 87.8 cu in, 1,439 cc (2.87 x 3.39 in, 73 x 86 mm); compression ratio: 9:1; max power (DIN): 92 hp at 6,300 rpm; max torque (DIN): 91 lb ft, 12.5 kg m at 4,000 rpm; max engine rpm: 6,500; 63.9 hp/l; cast iron cylinder block, light alloy head; 5 crankshaft bearings; valves: overhead, rockers; camshafts: 1, overhead; lubrication: rotary pump, full flow filter, 7 imp pt, 8.5 US pt, 4 l; 1 Stromberg downdraught twin barrel carburettor; fuel feed: mechanical pump; water-cooled, 10.6 imp pt, 12.7 US pt, 6 l.

MITSUBISHI Galant FTO GII

MITSUBISHI Galant Hardtop Grand Sports

MITSUBISHI Galant GTO XII

TRANSMISSION driving wheels: rear; clutch: single dry plate (diaphragm); gearbox: mechanical; gears: 3, fully synchronized; ratios: I 3.198, II 1.635, III 1, rev 4.021; lever: central; final drive: hypoid bevel; axle ratio: 3.889; width of rims: 4.5"; tyres: 6.15 x 13.

PERFORMANCE max speeds: (I) 34 mph, 54 km/h; (II) 65 mph, 105 km/h; (III) 99 mph, 160 km/h; power-weight ratio: 20.3 lb/hp, 9.2 kg/hp; fuel consumption: not declared.

CHASSIS integral; front suspension: independent, by McPherson, coil springs/telescopic damper struts, lower wishbones; rear suspension: rigid axle, semi-elliptic leaf-springs, telescopic dampers.

STEERING recirculating ball; turns lock to lock: 3.50.

BRAKES drum.

ELECTRICAL EQUIPMENT 12 V; 35 Ah battery; 40 A alternator; Mtisubishi distributor; 4 headlamps.

DIMENSIONS AND WEIGHT wheel base: 95.28 in, 2,420 mm; tracks: 50.59 in, 1,285 mm front, 50.59 in, 1,285 mm rear; length: 159.84 in, 4,060 mm; width: 61.42 in, 1,560 mm; height: 54.53 in, 1,385 mm; ground clearance: 6.89 in, 175 mm; dry weight: 1,874 lb, 850 kg; turning circle (between walls): 30.2 ft, 9.2 m; fuel tank: 9.9 imp gal, 11.9 US gal, 45 l.

BODY saloon/sedan; 4 doors; 5 seats, separate front seats.

PRACTICAL INSTRUCTIONS fuel: 85-90 oct petrol; engine sump oil: 6.2 imp pt, 7.4 US pt, 3.5 l, SAE 20W-30, change every 3,100 miles, 5,000 km; gearbox oil: 2.6 imp pt, 3.2 US pt, 1.5 l, SAE 90, change every 24,900 miles, 40,000 km; final drive oil: 1.9 imp pt, 2.3 US pt, 1.1 l, SAE 90, change every 24,900 miles, 40,000 km; tappet clearances: inlet 0.006 in, 0.15 mm, exhaust 0.010 in, 0.25 mm; valve timing: 20° 48° 51° 17°; tyre pressure: front 24 psi, 1.7 atm, rear 27 psi, 1.9 atm.

Galant 14 L Custom

See Galant 14 L Sedan, except for:

PRICE EX WORKS: 625,000 yen.

TRANSMISSION gears: 4, fully synchronized; ratios: I 3.525, II 2.193, III 1.442, IV 1; axle ratio: 3.889.

PERFORMANCE power-weight ratio: 20.7 lb/hp, 9.4 kg/hp.

DIMENSIONS AND WEIGHT dry weight: 1,907 lb, 865 kg.

Galant 14 L SL 5

See Galant 14 L Sedan, except for:

PRICE EX WORKS: 695,000 yen.

TRANSMISSION gears: 4, fully synchronized; ratios: I 3.238, II 1.955, III 1.341, IV 1, rev 3.054; axle ratio: 4.222.

PERFORMANCE max speed: 103 mph, 165 km/h; power-weight ratio: 21.6 lb/hp, 9.8 kg/hp.

BRAKES front disc.

DIMENSIONS AND WEIGHT dry weight: 1,985 lb, 900 kg.

Galant 16 L Custom

See Galant 14 L Sedan, except for:

PRICE EX WORKS: 648,000 yen.

ENGINE 97.4 cu in, 1,597 cc (3.03 x 3.39 in, 76.9 x 86 mm); compression ratio: 8.5:1; max power (DIN): 100 hp at 6,300 rpm; max torque (DIN): 101 lb ft, 14 kg m at 4,000 rpm; 62.6 hp/l.

TRANSMISSION gears: 4, fully synchronized; ratios: I 3.525, II 2.193, III 1.442, IV 1; axle ratio: 3.889.

PERFORMANCE max speed: 103 mph, 165 km/h; power-weight ratio: 19.6 lb/hp, 8.9 kg/hp.

DIMENSIONS AND WEIGHT dry weight: 1,951 lb, 885 kg.

Galant 16 L GL

See Galant 16 L Custom, except for:

PRICE EX WORKS: 700,000 yen.

BRAKES front disc.

OPTIONAL ACCESSORIES Borg Warner 35 automatic trans-

MITSUBISHI Galant FTO GII

MITSUBISHI Galant Hardtop Grand Sports

MITSUBISHI Galant GTO XII

mission, hydraulic torque converter and planetary gears with 3 ratios (I 2.393, II 1.450, III 1, rev 2.094), max ratio of converter at stall 2.

Galant Hardtop 16 L GL

See Galant 16 L GL, except for:

PRICE EX WORKS: 742,000 yen.

PERFORMANCE power-weight ratio: 21.7 lb/hp, 9.9 kg/hp.

DIMENSIONS AND WEIGHT height: 53.35 in, 1,355 mm; width: 61.81 in, 1,570 mm; dry weight: 1,996 lb, 905 kg.

BODY hardtop coupé; 2 doors.

OPTIONAL ACCESSORIES 5-speed fully synchronized mechanical gearbox (I 3.238, II 1.955, III 1.341, IV 1, V 0.854, rev 3.054), 4.222 axle ratio.

Galant 16 L Grand Sports

See Galant 16 L Custom, except for:

PRICE EX WORKS: 738,000 yen.

ENGINE compression ratio: 9.5:1; max power (DIN): 110 hp at 6,700 rpm; max torque (DIN): 103 lb ft, 14.2 kg m at 4,800 rpm; max engine rpm: 7,000; 76.4 hp/l; 2 Stromberg downdraught twin barrel carburettors.

PERFORMANCE max speed: 109 mph, 175 km/h; power-weight ratio: 17.8 lb/hp, 8.1 kg/hp.

BRAKES disc.

DIMENSIONS AND WEIGHT front track: 50.98 in, 1,295 mm; dry weight: 1,962 lb, 890 kg.

OPTIONAL ACCESSORIES 5-speed fully synchronized mechanical gearbox (I 3.238, II 1.955, III 1.341, IV 1, V 0.854, rev 3.054), 4.222 axle ratio.

Galant Hardtop Grand Sports

See Galant 16 L Grand Sports, except for:

PRICE EX WORKS: 780,000 yen.

PERFORMANCE power-weight ratio: 18 lb/hp, 8.2 kg/hp.

DIMENSIONS AND WEIGHT height: 52.76 in, 1,340 mm; dry weight: 1,985 lb, 900 kg.

BODY hardtop; 2 doors.

Galant GTO XI Coupé

ENGINE front, 4 stroke; 4 cylinders, vertical, in line; 102.9 cu in, 1,686 cc (3.11 x 3.39 in, 79 x 86 mm); compression ratio: 8.5:1; max power (DIN): 105 hp at 6,300 rpm; max torque (DIN): 109 lb ft, 15 kg m at 4,000 rpm; max engine rpm: 6,700; 62.2 hp/l; cast iron cylinder block, light alloy head; 5 crankshaft bearings; valves: overhead, rockers; camshafts: 2, overhead; lubrication: rotary pump, full flow filter, 7 imp pt, 8.5 US pt, 4 l; 1 Stromberg DIDSA-6 downdraught twin barrel carburettor; fuel feed: mechanical pump; water-cooled, 10.6 imp pt, 12.7 US pt, 6 l.

TRANSMISSION driving wheels: rear; clutch: single dry plate; gearbox: mechanical; gears: 4, fully synchronized; ratios: I 3.525, II 2.193, III 1.442, IV 1, rev 3.867; lever: central; final drive: hypoid bevel; axle ratio: 3.889 width of rims: 4.5"; tyres: 6.15 x 13.

PERFORMANCE max speeds: (I) 31 mph, 50 km/h; (II) 50 mph, 80 km/h; (III) 76 mph, 122 km/h; (IV) 109 mph, 175 km/h; power-weight ratio: 19.4 lb/hp, 8.8 kg/hp; carrying capacity: 882 lb, 400 kg; speed in direct drive at 1,000 rpm: 17.8 mph, 28.6 km/h; fuel consumption: not declared.

CHASSIS integral; front suspension: independent, by McPherson, coil springs/telescopic damper struts, anti-roll bar, lower wishbones; rear suspension: rigid axle, semi-elliptic leafsprings, telescopic dampers.

STEERING recirculating ball; turns lock to lock: 3.50.

BRAKES front disc, rear drum, servo.

ELECTRICAL EQUIPMENT 12 V; 35 Ah battery; 45 A alternator; Mitsubishi distributor; 4 headlamps.

DIMENSIONS AND WEIGHT wheel base: 95.28 in, 2,420 mm; tracks: 50.98 in, 1,295 mm front, 50.59 in, 1,285 mm rear; length: 162.40 in, 4,125 mm; width: 62.20 in, 1,580 mm; height: 52.17 in, 1,325 mm; ground clearance: 6.50 in, 165

GALANT GTO XI COUPÉ

mm; dry weight: 2,040 lb, 925 kg; turning circle (between walls): 30.2 ft, 9.2 m; fuel tank: 12.1 imp gal, 14.5 US gal, 55 l.

BODY coupé; 2 doors; 5 seats, separate front seats.

PRACTICAL INSTRUCTIONS fuel: 85-90 oct petrol; engine sump oil: 6.2 imp pt, 7.4 US pt, 3.5 l, SAE 30 W, change every 3,100 miles, 5,000 km; gearbox oil: 3 imp pt, 3.6 US pt, 1.7 l, SAE 80, change every 24,800 miles, 40,000 km; final drive oil: 1.9 imp pt, 2.3 US pt, 1.1 l, SAE 90, change every 24,800 miles, 40,000 km; tappet clearances: inlet 0.006 in, 0.15 mm, exhaust 0.010 in, 0.25 mm; valve timing: 32° 60° 63° 29°; tyre pressure: front 24 psi, 1.7 atm, rear 27 psi, 1.9 atm.

Galant GTO XII

See Galant GTO XI Coupé, except for:

PRICE EX WORKS: 853,000 yen.

ENGINE compression ratio: 9.5:1; max power (DIN): 115 hp at 6,500 rpm; max torque (DIN): 110 lb ft, 15.2 kg m at 4,500 rpm; 68.1 hp/l; 2 Stromberg downdraught twin barrel carburettors.

TRANSMISSION tyres: 165 SR x 13.

PERFORMANCE max speeds: (I) 33 mph, 53 km/h; (II) 54 mph, 87 km/h; (III) 82 mph, 132 km/h; (IV) 112 mph, 180 km/h; power-weight ratio: 18.1 lb/hp, 8.2 kg/hp.

DIMENSIONS AND WEIGHT front track: 50.98 in, 1,295 mm; height: 51.77 in, 1,315 mm; dry weight: 2,084 lb, 945 kg.

PRACTICAL INSTRUCTIONS fuel: 98-100 oct petrol.

VARIATIONS

ENGINE 8.5:1 compression ratio, max power (DIN) 100 hp at 6,500 rpm, max torque (DIN) 109 lb ft, 15 kg m at 4,000 rpm, 60 hp/l.
PERFORMANCE power-weight ratio 20.8 lb/hp, 9.4 kg/hp.
PRACTICAL INSTRUCTIONS 85-90 oct petrol.

OPTIONAL ACCESSORIES Borg Warner automatic transmission, hydraulic torque converter and planetary gears with 3 ratios, max ratio of converter at stall 2. (I 2.393, II 1.450, III 1, rev 2.094).

Debonair Executive

PRICE EX WORKS: 1,197,000 yen.

ENGINE front, 4 stroke; 6 cylinders, in line; 121.7 cu in, 1,994 cc (2.87 x 3.13 in, 73 x 79.4 mm); compression ratio: 10:1; max power (DIN): 130 hp at 6,000 rpm; max torque (DIN): 123 lb ft, 17 kg m at 4,000 rpm; max engine rpm: 5,500; 65.2 hp/l; cast iron cylinder block, light alloy head; 7 crankshaft bearings; valves: overhead, rockers; camshafts: 1, overhead; lubrication: rotary pump, full flow filter, 9.5 imp pt, 11.4 US pt, 5.4 l; 1 Nikki-Stromberg downdraught twin barrel carburettor; fuel feed: mechanical pump; water-cooled, 15.8 imp pt, 19 US pt, 9 l.

TRANSMISSION driving wheels: rear; clutch: single dry plate (diaphragm); gearbox: mechanical; gears: 4, fully synchronized; ratios: I 3.039, II 1.645, III 1, IV 0.797, rev 3.989; lever: steering column; final drive: hypoid bevel; axle ratio: 4.625; tyres: 6.95 x 14.

PERFORMANCE max speeds: (I) 32 mph, 52 km/h; (II) 59 mph, 95 km/h; (III) 98 mph, 157 km/h; (IV) 106 mph, 170 km/h; power-weight ratio: 22.5 lb/hp, 10.2 kg/hp; acceleration: standing ¼ mile 17.8 sec; speed in top at 1,000 rpm: 17.6 mph, 28.3 km/h; fuel consumption: 22.6 m/imp gal, 18.8 m/US gal, 12.5 l x 100 km.

CHASSIS integral; front suspension: independent, wishbones, coil springs, anti-roll bar, telescopic dampers; rear suspension: rigid axle, semi-elliptic leafsprings, telescopic dampers.

STEERING recirculating ball.

BRAKES front disc, rear drum, servo; swept area: total 75.3 sq in, 486 sq cm.

ELECTRICAL EQUIPMENT 12 V; 35 Ah battery; 48 A alternator; Mitsubishi distributor; 4 headlamps.

DIMENSIONS AND WEIGHT wheel base: 105.91 in, 2,690 mm; tracks: 54.72 in, 1,390 mm front, 54.72 in, 1,390 mm rear; length: 183.86 in, 4,670 mm; width: 66.54 in, 1,690 mm; height: 57.87 in, 1,470 mm; ground clearance: 7.09 in, 180 mm; dry weight: 2,923 lb, 1,330 kg; distribution of weight: 56% front, 44% rear; turning circle (between walls): 34.8 ft, 10.6 m; fuel tank: 12.1 imp gal, 14.5 US gal, 55 l.

MITSUBISHI Debonair Executive

NISSAN Cherry 1200 GL 4-door Sedan

NISSAN Cherry 1200 X-1 Coupé

Datsun Bluebird-U 1600 De Luxe Hardtop

See Datsun Bluebird-U 1600 De Luxe Sedan, except for:

PRICE EX WORKS: 709,000 yen.

PERFORMANCE power-weight ratio: 22 lb/hp, 10 kg/hp.

DIMENSIONS AND WEIGHT height: 54.92 in, 1,395 mm; dry weight: 2,205 lb, 1,000 kg.

BODY hardtop; 2 doors.

OPTIONAL ACCESSORIES 3-speed automatic transmission.

Datsun Bluebird-U 1600 GL Sedan

See Datsun Bluebird-U 1600 De Luxe Sedan, except for:

PRICE EX WORKS: 764,000 yen.

Datsun Bluebird-U 1600 GL Hardtop

See Datsun Bluebird-U 1600 De Luxe Hardtop, except for:

PRICE EX WORKS: 764,000 yen.

PERFORMANCE power-weight ratio: 22.2 lb/hp, 10.1 kg/hp.

DIMENSIONS AND WEIGHT dry weight: 2,216 lb, 1,005 kg.

Datsun Bluebird-U 1600 SSS Sedan

See Datsun Bluebird-U 1600 De Luxe Sedan, except for:

PRICE EX WORKS: 774,000 yen.

ENGINE compression ratio: 9.5:1; max power (DIN): 105 hp at 6,200 rpm; max torque (DIN): 100 lb ft, 13.8 kg m at 4,200 rpm; 65.8 hp/l; 2 Hitachi SU type HJL38W horizontal carburettors.

PERFORMANCE max speed: 103 mph, 165 km/h; power-weight ratio: 20.8 lb/hp, 9.4 kg/hp.

OPTIONAL ACCESSORIES 5-speed fully synchronized mechanical gearbox (I 3.321, II 2.077, III 1.308, IV 1, V 0.864, rev 3.382), 4.375 axle ratio.

Datsun Bluebird-U 1600 SSS Hardtop

See Datsun Bluebird-U 1600 SSS Sedan, except for:

PRICE EX WORKS: 794,000 yen.

PERFORMANCE power-weight ratio: 21.2 lb/hp, 9.6 kg/hp.

DIMENSIONS AND WEIGHT height: 54.92 in, 1,395 mm; dry weight: 2,227 lb, 1,010 kg.

BODY hardtop; 2 doors.

OPTIONAL ACCESSORIES 3-speed automatic transmission; 5-speed fully synchronized mechanical gearbox.

Datsun Bluebird-U 1600 SSS-E Sedan

See Datsun Bluebird-U 1600 De Luxe Sedan, except for:

PRICE IN GB: £ 1,040.
PRICE EX WORKS: 849,000 yen.

ENGINE max power (DIN): 115 hp at 6,200 rpm; max torque (DIN): 106 lb ft, 14.6 kg m at 4,400 rpm; max engine rpm: 6,200; 72.1 hp/l; Bosch electronically-controlled injection system; fuel feed: electric pump.

TRANSMISSION gears: 5, fully synchronized; ratios: I 3.321, II 2.077, III 1.308, IV 1, V 0.864, rev 3.382; axle ratio: 4.375.

PERFORMANCE max speed: 106 mph, 170 km/h; power-weight ratio: 19 lb/hp, 8.6 kg/hp.

Datsun Bluebird-U 1600 SSS-E Hardtop

See Datsun Bluebird-U 1600 SSS-E Sedan, except for:

PERFOMANCE power-weight ratio: 19.4 lb/hp, 8.8 kg/hp.

DIMENSIONS AND WEIGHT height: 54.92 in, 1,395 mm; dry weight: 2,227 lb, 1,010 kg.

BODY hardtop; 2 doors.

OPTIONAL ACCESSORIES 3-speed automatic transmission not available.

NISSAN Datsun Bluebird-U 1600 SSS-E

NISSAN Datsun Bluebird-U 1800 SSS-E

NISSAN Laurel 1800 De Luxe Sedan

Datsun Bluebird-U 1800 GL Sedan

See Datsun Bluebird-U 1600 GL Sedan, except for:

PRICE EX WORKS: 784,000 yen.

ENGINE 108 cu in, 1,770 cc (3.35 x 3.07 in, 85 x 78 mm); max power (DIN): 105 hp at 6,000 rpm; max torque (DIN): 109 lb ft, 15 kg m at 6,000 rpm; 59.3 hp/l.

TRANSMISSION gearbox ratios: I 3.382, II 2.013, III 1.312, IV 1, rev 3.365; axle ratio: 3.900.

PERFORMANCE max speed: 103 mph, 165 km/h; power-weight ratio: 21.3 lb/hp, 9.6 kg/hp.

DIMENSIONS AND WEIGHT dry weight: 2,238 lb, 1,015 kg.

OPTIONAL ACCESSORIES 3-speed automatic transmission.

Datsun Bluebird-U 1800 GL Hardtop

See Datsun Bluebird-U 1800 GL Sedan, except for:

PRICE EX WORKS: 804,000 yen.

PERFORMANCE power-weight ratio: 21.4 lb/hp, 9.7 kg/hp.

DIMENSIONS AND WEIGHT height: 54.92 in, 1,395 mm; dry weight: 2,249 lb, 1,020 kg.

BODY hardtop; 2 doors.

Datsun Bluebird-U 1800 GL Station Wagon

See Datsun Bluebird-U 1800 GL Sedan, except for:

PRICE EX WORKS: 789,000 yen.

TRANSMISSION axle ratio: 4.111.

PERFORMANCE power-weight ratio: 22.6 lb/hp, 10.3 kg/hp.

CHASSIS rear suspension: rigid axle, semi-elliptic leafsprings, telescopic dampers.

DIMENSIONS AND WEIGHT rear track: 52.36 in, 1,330 mm; length: 168.50 in, 4,280 mm; height: 56.10 in, 1,425 mm; dry weight: 2,381 lb, 1,080 kg.

BODY estate car/station wagon; 4 + 1 doors.

Datsun Bluebird-U 1800 SSS Sedan

See Datsun Bluebird-U 1800 GL Sedan, except for:

PRICE IN GB: £ 1,148.
PRICE EX WORKS: 814,000 yen.

ENGINE compression ratio: 9.5:1; max power (DIN): 115 hp at 6,000 rpm; max torque (DIN): 112 lb ft, 15.5 kg m at 4,000 rpm; 65 hp/l; 2 Hitachi SU type HJL38W-6 horizontal carburettors.

PERFORMANCE max speed: 109 mph, 175 km/h; power-weight ratio: 19.6 lb/hp, 8.8 kg/hp.

DIMENSIONS AND WEIGHT dry weight: 2,249 lb, 1,020 kg.

OPTIONAL ACCESSORIES 3-speed automatic transmission; 5-speed fully synchronized mechanical gearbox (I 3.321, II 2.077, III 1.308, IV 1, V 0.864, rev 3.382), 4.111 axle ratio.

Datsun Bluebird-U 1800 SSS Hardtop

See Datsun Bluebird-U 1800 SSS Sedan, except for:

PRICE IN GB: £ 1,239.
PRICE EX WORKS: 834,000 yen.

PERFORMANCE power-weight ratio: 19.7 lb/hp, 8.9 kg/hp.

DIMENSIONS AND WEIGHT height: 54.92 in, 1,395 mm; dry weight: 2,260 lb, 1,025 kg.

BODY hardtop; 2 doors.

Datsun Bleuebird-U 1800 SSS-E Hardtop

See Datsun Bluebird-U 1800 SSS Sedan, except for:

PRICE EX WORKS: 944,000 yen.

ENGINE max power (DIN): 125 hp at 6,200 rpm; max torque

DATSUN BLUEBIRD-U 1800 SSS-E HARDTOP

(DIN): 116 lb ft, 16 kg m at 3,600 rpm; 70.6 hp/l; Bosch electronically-controlled injection system; fuel feed: electric pump.

PERFORMANCE power-weight ratio: 18.3 lb/hp, 8.3 kg/hp.

DIMENSIONS AND WEIGHT height: 54.92 in, 1,395 mm; dry weight: 2,293 lb, 1,040 kg.

BODY hardtop; 2 doors.

Laurel 1800 De Luxe Sedan

PRICE EX WORKS: 720,000 yen.

ENGINE front, 4 stroke; 4 cylinders, in line; 110.8 cu in, 1,815 cc (3.35 x 3.15 in, 85 x 80 mm); compression ratio: 8.3:1; max power (DIN): 105 hp at 5,600 rpm; max torque (DIN): 111 lb ft, 15.3 kg m at 3,600 rpm; max engine rpm: 6,400; 57.9 hp/l; cast iron cylinder block, light alloy head; 5 crankshaft bearings; valves: overhead, Vee-slanted, rockers; camshafts: 1, overhead; lubrication: gear pump, full flow filter, 6.5 imp pt, 7.8 US pt, 3.7 l; 1 Hitachi DCK340 downdraught twin barrel carburettor; fuel feed: electric pump; water-cooled, 15.1 imp pt, 18.2 US pt, 8.6 l.

TRANSMISSION driving wheels: rear; clutch: single dry plate (diaphragm); gearbox: mechanical; gears: 3, fully synchronized; ratios: I 3.263, II 1.645, III 1, rev 3.355; lever: steering column; final drive: hypoid bevel; axle ratio: 4.111; width of rims: 4.5"; tyres: 6.45 x 14.

PERFORMANCE max speed: 103 mph, 165 km/h; power-weight ratio: 22.7 lb/hp, 10.2 kg/hp; carrying capacity: 992 lb, 450 kg; fuel consumption: not declared.

CHASSIS integral; front suspension: independent, by McPherson, coil springs/telescopic damper struts, lower wishbones (trailing links), anti-roll bar; rear suspension: rigid axle, semi-elliptic leafsprings, telescopic dampers.

STEERING recirculating ball; turns lock to lock: 4.

BRAKES drum; swept area: front 54 sq in, 348 sq cm, rear 54 sq in, 348 sq cm, total 108 sq in, 696 sq cm.

ELECTRICAL EQUIPMENT 12 V; 35 Ah battery; 50 A alternator; Hitachi distributor; 4 headlamps.

DIMENSIONS AND WEIGHT wheel base: 105.12 in, 2,670 mm; tracks: 53.15 in, 1,350 mm front, 52.36 in, 1,330 mm rear; length: 177.17 in, 4,500 mm; width: 65.75 in, 1,670 mm; height: 55.71 in, 1,415 mm; ground clearance: 6.89 in, 175 mm; dry weight: 2,381 lb, 1,080 kg; distribution of weight: 52.4% front, 47.6% rear; turning circle (between walls): 38 ft, 11.6 m; fuel tank: 13.2 imp gal, 15.8 US gal, 60 l.

BODY saloon/sedan; 4 doors; 6 seats, bench front seats.

PRACTICAL INSTRUCTIONS fuel: 85-90 oct petrol; engine sump oil: 6.5 imp pt, 7.8 US pt, 3.7 l, SAE 20W-30, change every 3,100 miles, 5,000 km; gearbox oil: 3 imp pt, 3.6 US pt, 1.7 l, SAE 90, change every 31,100 miles, 50,000 km; final drive oil: 1.8 imp pt, 2.1 US pt, 1 l, SAE 90, change every 31,100 miles, 50,000 km; greasing: none; tappet clearances (hot): inlet 0.010 in, 0.25 mm; exhaust 0.010 in, 0.25 mm; valve timing: 13° 53° 53° 13°; tyre pressure: front 21 psi, 1.5 atm, rear 21 psi, 1.5 atm.

OPTIONAL ACCESSORIES 4-speed fully synchronized mechanical gearbox (I 3.382, II 2.013, III 1.312, IV 1, rev 3.365); automatic transmission with 3 ratios (I 2.458, II 1.458, III 1, rev 2.182) with central lever.

Laurel 1800 De Luxe Hardtop

See Laurel 1800 De Luxe Sedan, except for:

PRICE EX WORKS: 775,000 yen.

TRANSMISSION gears: 4, fully synchronized; ratios: I 3.382, II 2.013, III 1.312, IV 1, rev 3.365; lever: central; axle ratio: 3.900.

PERFORMANCE power-weight ratio: 23.4 lb/hp, 10.6 kg/hp.

CHASSIS rear suspension: independent, semi-trailing arms, coil springs, telescopic dampers.

DIMENSIONS AND WEIGHT height: 55.31 in, 1,405 mm; dry weight: 2,459 lb, 1,115 kg.

BODY hardtop; 2 doors; 5 seats, separate front seats.

OPTIONAL ACCESSORIES only 3-ratio automatic transmission.

NISSAN Laurel 1800 De Luxe Hardtop

NISSAN Laurel 2000 SGL Sedan

NISSAN Laurel 2000 SGX Hardtop

Laurel 1800 Custom Sedan

See Laurel 1800 De Luxe Sedan, except for:

PRICE EX WORKS: 780,000 yen.

TRANSMISSION gears: 4, fully synchronized; ratios: I 3.382, II 2.013, III 1.312, IV 1, rev 3.365; lever: central.

PERFORMANCE power-weight ratio: 22.9 lb/hp, 10.4 kg/hp.

BRAKES front disc, rear drum, servo; swept area: front 15.5 sq in, 100 sq cm.

DIMENSIONS AND WEIGHT dry weight: 2,403 lb, 1,090 kg.

BODY separate front seats.

OPTIONAL ACCESSORIES only 3-ratio automatic transmission.

Laurel 1800 Custom Hardtop

See Laurel 1800 De Luxe Hardtop, except for:

PRICE EX WORKS: 820,000 yen.

PERFORMANCE power-weight ratio: 23.5 lb/hp, 10.7 kg/hp.

BRAKES front disc, rear drum, servo; swept area: front 15.5 sq in, 100 sq cm.

DIMENSIONS AND WEIGHT dry weight: 2,470 lb, 1,120 kg.

Laurel 2000 Custom Sedan

See Laurel 1800 Custom Sedan, except for:

PRICE IN GB: £ 1,446.
PRICE EX WORKS: 800,000 yen.

ENGINE 121.4 cu in, 1,990 cc (3.50 x 3.15 in, 89 x 80 mm); max power (DIN): 110 hp at 5,600 rpm; max torque (DIN): 120 lb ft, 16.5 kg m at 3,200 rpm; 55.3 hp/l; 1 Hitachi DCJ340-3 downdraught twin barrel carburettor.

TRANSMISSION gearbox ratios: I 3.592, II 2.246, III 1.415, IV 1, rev 3.657; lever: central; axle ratio: 3.889.

PERFORMANCE max speed: 106 mph, 170 km/h; power-weight ratio: 22 lb/hp, 10 kg/hp.

DIMENSIONS AND WEIGHT dry weight: 2,414 lb, 1,095 kg.

OPTIONAL ACCESSORIES only 3-ratio automatic transmission.

Laurel 2000 Custom Hardtop

See Laurel 2000 Custom Sedan, except for:

PRICE IN GB: £ 1,568.
PRICE EX WORKS: 845,000 yen.

PERFORMANCE power-weight ratio: 22.6 lb/hp, 10.2 kg/hp.

DIMENSIONS AND WEIGHT height: 55.31 in, 1,405 mm; dry weight: 2,481 lb, 1,125 kg.

BODY hardtop; 2 doors.

Laurel 2000 GX Hardtop

See Laurel 2000 Custom Hardtop, except for:

PRICE EX WORKS: 895,000 yen.

ENGINE max power (DIN): 120 hp at 5,800 rpm; max torque (DIN): 123 lb ft, 17 kg m at 3,600 rpm; max engine rpm: 6,300; 60.3 hp/l; 2 Hitachi SU type HMA42W-1 horizontal carburettors.

TRANSMISSION tyres: 6.45 S x 14.

PERFORMANCE max speed: 109 mph, 175 km/h; power-weight ratio: 20.9 lb/hp, 9.5 kg/hp.

DIMENSIONS AND WEIGHT dry weight: 2,514 lb, 1,140 kg.

OPTIONAL ACCESSORIES 5-speed fully synchronized mechanical gearbox (I 3.321, II 2.077, III 1.308, IV 1, V 0.864, rev 3.382), 4.111 axle ratio; 3-ratio automatic transmission.

Laurel 2000 Custom 6 Sedan

See Laurel 1800 De Luxe Sedan, except for:

PRICE EX WORKS: 860,000 yen.

ENGINE 6 cylinders, in line; 121.9 cu in, 1,998 cc (3.07 x 2.74 in, 78 x 69.7 mm); compression ratio: 8.6:1; max power

NISSAN Laurel 1800 De Luxe Hardtop

NISSAN Laurel 2000 SGL Sedan

NISSAN Laurel 2000 SGX Hardtop

(DIN): 115 hp at 5,600 rpm; max torque (DIN): 120 lb ft, 16.5 kg m at 3,600 rpm; max engine rpm: 6,000; 60 hp/l; 7 crankshaft bearings; lubrication: rotary pump, full flow filter, 10 imp pt, 12 US pt, 5.7 l; 1 Hitachi DAH342-5 downdraught twin barrel carburettor; cooling system capacity: 16.7 imp pt, 20.1 US pt, 9.5 l.

TRANSMISSION gears: 4, fully synchronized; ratios: I 3.592, II 2.246, III 1.415, IV 1, rev 3.657; lever: central; axle ratio: 3.889.

PERFORMANCE max speed: 106 mph, 170 km/h; power-weight ratio: 21.8 lb/hp, 9.9 kg/hp.

BRAKES front disc, rear drum, servo; swept area: front 20.5 sq in, 132 sq cm, rear 54 sq in, 348 sq cm, total 64.5 sq in, 480 sq cm.

DIMENSIONS AND WEIGHT dry weight: 2,514 lb, 1,140 kg; distribution of weight: 55.7% front, 44.3% rear.

BODY 5 seats, separate front seats.

PRACTICAL INSTRUCTIONS engine sump oil: 10 imp pt, 12 US pt, 5.7 l; gearbox oil: 2.8 imp pt, 3.4 US pt, 1.6 l; tappet clearances: exhaust 0.012 in, 0.30 mm; valve timing: 8° 44° 50° 10°; tyre pressure: front 23 psi, 1.6 atm, rear 23 psi, 1.6 atm.

OPTIONAL ACCESSORIES only 3-ratio automatic transmission.

Laurel 2000 Custom 6 Hardtop

See Laurel 2000 Custom 6 Sedan, except for:

PRICE EX WORKS: 905,000 yen.

PERFORMANCE power-weight ratio: 22.4 lb/hp, 10.1 kg/hp.

DIMENSIONS AND WEIGHT height: 55.31 in, 1,405 mm; dry weight: 2,580 lb, 1,170 kg.

BODY hardtop; 2 doors.

Laurel 2000 SGL Sedan

See Laurel 2000 Custom 6 Sedan, except for:

PRICE EX WORKS: 945,000 yen.

PERFORMANCE power-weight ratio: 22.4 lb/hp, 10.1 kg/hp.

DIMENSIONS AND WEIGHT dry weight: 2,580 lb, 1,170 kg.

Laurel 2000 GX-6 Sedan

See Laurel 2000 Custom 6 Sedan, except for:

PRICE EX WORKS: 920,000 yen.

ENGINE max power (DIN): 125 hp at 6,000 rpm; max torque (DIN): 123 lb ft, 17 kg m at 4,400 rpm; 62.6 hp/l; 2 Hitachi SU type HJG38W-3 horizontal carburettors.

TRANSMISSION tyres: 6.45 S x 14.

PERFORMANCE max speed: 109 mph, 175 km/h; power-weight ratio: 21.2 lb/hp, 9.6 kg/hp.

BRAKES rear compensator.

DIMENSIONS AND WEIGHT width: 66.14 in, 1,680 mm; dry weight: 2,657 lb, 1,205 kg.

PRACTICAL INSTRUCTIONS valve timing: 12° 48° 54° 14°.

VARIATIONS

ENGINE 9.5:1 compression ratio, max power (DIN) 130 hp at 6,000 rpm, max torque (DIN) 127 lb ft, 17.5 kg m at 4,400 rpm, 65.1 hp/l.
PERFORMANCE max speed 112 mph, 180 km/h, power-weight ratio 20.4 lb/hp, 9.3 kg/hp.
PRACTICAL INSTRUCTIONS 98-100 oct petrol.

OPTIONAL ACCESSORIES 5-speed fully synchronized mechanical gearbox (I 3.321, II 2.077, III 1.308, IV 1, V 0.864, rev 3.382), 4.111 axle ratio; automatic transmission with 3 ratios.

Laurel 2000 SGX Hardtop

See Laurel 2000 GX-6 Sedan, except for:

PRICE EX WORKS: 1,030,000 yen.

DIMENSIONS AND WEIGHT width: 66.14 in, 1,680 mm; height: 55.31 in, 1,405 mm.

BODY hardtop; 2 doors.

Skyline 1600 Standard Sedan

PRICE EX WORKS: 597,000 yen.

ENGINE front, 4 stroke; 4 cylinders, in line; 97.2 cu in, 1,593 cc (3.35 x 2.76 in, 85 x 70.2 mm); compression ratio: 8.5:1; max power (DIN): 100 hp at 6,000 rpm; max torque (DIN): 100 lb ft, 13.8 kg m at 4,000 rpm; max engine rpm: 6,300; 60.3 hp/l; cast iron cylinder block, light alloy head; 5 crankshaft bearings; valves: overhead, Vee-slanted, rockers; camshafts: 1, overhead; lubrication: gear pump, full flow filter, 6.7 imp pt, 8 US pt, 3.8 l; 1 Nikki downdraught twin barrel carburettor; fuel feed: electric pump; water-cooled, 14.8 imp pt, 17.8 US pt, 8.4 l.

TRANSMISSION driving wheels: rear; clutch: single dry plate (diaphragm); gearbox: mechanical; gears: 3, fully synchronized; ratios: I 3.263, II 1.645, III 1, rev 3.355; lever: steering column; final drive: hypoid bevel; axle ratio: 4.111; width of rims: 4"; tyres: 5.60 x 13.

PERFORMANCE max speeds: (I) 31 mph, 50 km/h; (II) 59 mph, 95 km/h; (III) 99 mph, 160 km/h; power-weight ratio: 21.3 lb/hp, 9.6 kg/hp; fuel consumption: not declared.

CHASSIS integral; front suspension: independent, by McPherson, coil springs/telescopic damper struts, lower wishbones (trailing links), anti-roll bar; rear suspension: rigid axle, semi-elliptic leafsprings, telescopic dampers.

STEERING recirculating ball; turns lock to lock: 3.60.

BRAKES drum; swept area: front 54 sq in, 348 sq cm, rear 54 sq in, 348 sq cm, total 108 sq in, 696 sq cm.

ELECTRICAL EQUIPMENT 12 V; 35 Ah battery; 50 A alternator; Hitachi distributor; 4 headlamps.

DIMENSIONS AND WEIGHT wheel base: 99.02 in, 2,515 mm; tracks: 53.15 in, 1,350 mm front, 52.76 in, 1,340 mm rear; length: 167.32 in, 4,250 mm; width: 63.98 in, 1,625 mm; height: 55.31 in, 1,405 mm; ground clearance: 6.50 in, 165 mm; dry weight: 2,128 lb, 965 kg; turning circle (between walls): 36.1 ft, 11 m; fuel tank: 12.1 imp gal, 14.5 US gal, 55 l.

BODY saloon/sedan; 4 doors; 5 seats, bench front seats.

PRACTICAL INSTRUCTIONS fuel: 85-90 oct petrol; engine sump oil: 6.7 imp pt, 8 US pt, 3.8 l, SAE 20W-30, change every 3,100 miles, 5,000 km; gearbox oil: 3 imp pt, 3.6 US pt, 1.7 l, SAE 90, change every 31,100 miles, 50,000 km; final drive oil: 1.8 imp pt, 2.1 US pt, 1 l, SAE 90, change every 31,100 miles, 50,000 km; tappet clearances: inlet 0.010 in, 0.25 mm, exhaust 0.010 in, 0.25 mm; valve timing: 13° 53° 53° 13°; tyre pressure: front 23 psi, 1.6 atm, rear 23 psi, 1.6 atm.

OPTIONAL ACCESSORIES 4-speed fully synchronized mechanical gearbox (I 3.657, II 2.177, III 1.419; IV 1, rev 3.638) with central lever.

Skyline 1600 De Luxe Sedan

See Skyline 1600 Standard Sedan, except for:

PRICE EX WORKS: 697,000 yen.

PERFORMANCE power-weight ratio: 21.6 lb/hp, 9.8 kg/hp.

BRAKES front disc, rear drum, servo; swept area: front 15.5 sq in, 100 sq cm.

DIMENSIONS AND WEIGHT dry weight: 2,161 lb, 980 kg.

OPTIONAL ACCESSORIES automatic transmission with 3 ratios (I 2.458, II 1.458, III 1, rev 2.182) and steering column lever.

Skyline 1600 De Luxe Hardtop

See Skyline 1600 De Luxe Sedan, except for:

PRICE EX WORKS: 717,000 yen.

TRANSMISSION gears: 4, fully synchronized (standard); ratios: I 3.657, II 2.177, III 1.419, IV 1, rev 3.638; lever: central; axle ratio: 4.111.

PERFORMANCE power-weight ratio: 21.8 lb/hp, 9.9 kg/hp.

DIMENSIONS AND WEIGHT height: 54.92 in, 1,395 mm; dry weight: 2,183 lb, 990 kg.

BODY hardtop; 2 doors; separate front seats.

Skyline 1600 GL Sedan

See Skyline 1600 Standard Sedan, except for:

PRICE EX WORKS: 747,000 yen.

TRANSMISSION gears: 4, fully synchronized (standard); ratios: I 3.657, II 2.177, III 1.419, IV 1, rev 3.638; lever:

NISSAN Skyline 1600 Standard Sedan

NISSAN Skyline 2000 GT-X Sedan

NISSAN Skyline 2000 GT-X Hardtop

central; axle ratio: 4.111; width of rims: 4.5"; tyres: 6.15 x 14.

PERFORMANCE power-weight ratio: 21.9 lb/hp, 9.9 kg/hp.

BRAKES front disc, rear drum, servo; swept area: front 15.5 sq in, 100 sq cm.

DIMENSIONS AND WEIGHT dry weight: 2,194 lb, 995 kg.

OPTIONAL ACCESSORIES automatic transmission with 3 ratios (I 2.458, II 1.458, III 1, rev 2.182) and steering column lever.

Skyline 1600 GL Hardtop

See Skyline 1600 De Luxe Hardtop, except for:

PRICE EX WORKS: 767,000 yen.

TRANSMISSION width of rims: 4.5"; tyres: 6.15 x 14

PERFORMANCE power-weight ratio: 22.2 lb/hp, 10 kg/hp.

DIMENSIONS AND WEIGHT dry weight: 2,216 lb, 1,005 kg.

Skyline 1800 De Luxe Sedan

See Skyline 1600 Standard Sedan, except for:

PRICE EX WORKS: 737,000 yen.

ENGINE 110.8 cu in, 1,815 cc (3.35 x 3.15 in, 85 x 80 mm); compression ratio: 8.3:1; max power (DIN): 105 hp at 5,600 rpm; max torque (DIN): 111 lb ft, 15.3 kg m at 3,600 rpm; 57.9 hp/l.

TRANSMISSION gears: 4, fully synchronized; ratios: I 3.382, II 2.013, III 1.312, IV 1, rev 3.365; axle ratio: 3.889; width of rims: 4.5"; tyres: 6.15 x 14.

PERFORMANCE max speeds: (I) 27 mph, 44 km/h; (II) 45 mph, 73 km/h; (III) 68 mph, 110 km/h; (IV) 103 mph, 165 km/h; power-weight ratio: 20.9 lb/hp, 9.5 kg/hp.

BRAKES front disc, rear drum, servo; swept area: front 15.5 sq in, 100 sq cm.

DIMENSIONS AND WEIGHT dry weight: 2,194 lb, 995 kg.

OPTIONAL ACCESSORIES automatic transmission with 3 ratios (I 2.458, II 1.458, III 1, rev 2.182) and steering column lever.

Skyline 1800 GL Sedan

See Skyline 1800 De Luxe Sedan, except for:

PRICE EX WORKS: 797,000 yen.

PERFORMANCE power-weight ratio: 21.1 lb/hp, 9.6 kg/hp.

DIMENSIONS AND WEIGHT: dry weight: 2,216 lb, 1,005 kg.

Skyline 1800 GL Hardtop

See Skyline 1800 De Luxe Sedan, except for:

PRICE EX WORKS: 817,000 yen.

PERFORMANCE power-weight ratio: 21.2 lb/hp, 9.7 kg/hp.

DIMENSIONS AND WEIGHT height: 54.92 in, 1,395 mm; dry weight: 2,238 lb, 1,015 kg.

BODY hardtop; 2 doors; separate front seats.

Skyline 1800 GL Station Wagon

See Skyline 1800 De Luxe Sedan, except for:

PRICE EX WORKS: 807,000 yen.

PERFORMANCE power-weight ratio: 21.9 lb/hp, 9.9 kg/hp.

DIMENSIONS AND WEIGHT length: 169.88 in, 4,315 mm; dry weight: 2,304 lb, 1,045 kg.

BODY estate car/station wagon; 4 + 1 doors.

Skyline 2000 GT Sedan

See Skyline 1600 Standard Sedan, except for:

PRICE EX WORKS: 870,000 yen.

ENGINE 6 cylinders, in line; 121.9 cu in, 1,998 cc (4.07 x 2.74 in, 78 x 69.7 mm); compression ratio: 9.5:1; max power

NISSAN Skyline 1600

NISSAN Skyline 2000 GT Sedan

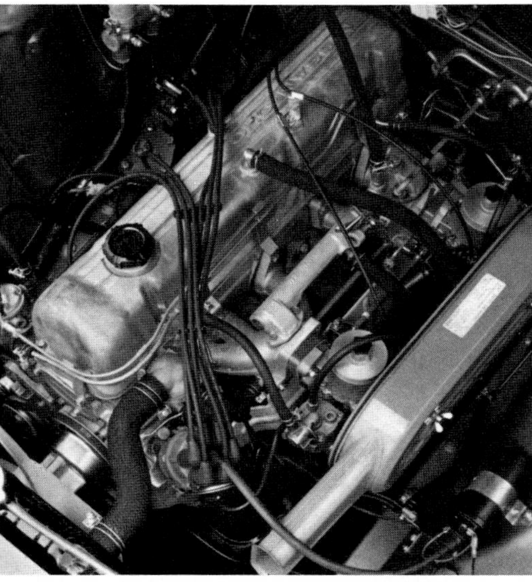

NISSAN Skyline 2000 GT-X

(DIN): 120 hp at 6,000 rpm; max torque (DIN): 123 lb ft, 17 kg m at 4,000 rpm; 60.1 hp/l; 7 crankshaft bearings; lubrication: rotary pump, full flow filter, 10 imp pt, 12 US pt, 5.7 l; 1 Hitachi downdraught twin barrel carburettor; cooling system capacity: 16.7 imp pt, 20.1 US pt, 9.5 l.

TRANSMISSION gears: 4, fully synchronized (standard); ratios: I 3.592, II 2.246, III 1.415, IV 1, rev 3.657; lever: central; axle ratio: 3.900; width of rims: 4.5"; tyres: 6.45S x 14.

PERFORMANCE max speeds: (I) 27 mph, 44 km/h; (II) 45 mph, 73 km/h; (III) 71 mph, 115 km/h; (IV) 109 mph, 175 km/h; power-weight ratio: 20.7 lb/hp, 9.4 kg/hp.

CHASSIS rear suspension: independent, semi-trailing arms, coil springs, telescopic dampers.

STEERING recirculating ball, variable ratio; turns lock to lock: 4.

BRAKES front disc, rear drum, rear compensator, servo; swept area: front 20.5 sq in, 132 sq cm.

DIMENSIONS AND WEIGHT wheel base: 102.7 in, 2,610 mm; rear track: 52.36 in, 1,330 mm; length: 175.59 in, 4,460 mm; height: 54.92 in, 1,395 mm; ground clearance: 6.69 in, 170 mm; dry weight: 2,481 lb, 1,125 kg; turning circle (between walls): 37.4 ft, 11.4 m.

BODY separate front seats.

PRACTICAL INSTRUCTIONS fuel: 98-100 oct petrol; engine sump oil: 10 imp pt, 12 US pt, 5.7 l; gearbox oil: 2.8 imp pt, 3.4 US pt, 1.6 l; tappet clearances: exhaust 0.012 in, 0.30 mm; valve timing: 12° 48° 54° 14°; tyre pressure: front 21 psi, 1.5 atm, rear 24 psi, 1.7 atm.

OPTIONAL ACCESSORIES 5-speed fully synchronized mechanical gearbox (I 3.321, II 2.077, III 1.308, IV 1, V 0.864, rev 3.382), 4.111 axle ratio; automatic transmission with 3 ratios (I 2.458, II 1.458, III 1, rev 2.182).

Skyline 2000 GT Hardtop

See Skyline 2000 GT Sedan, except for:

PRICE EX WORKS: 900,000 yen.

PERFORMANCE power-weight ratio: 20.8 lb/hp, 9.5 kg/hp.

DIMENSIONS AND WEIGHT height: 54.53 in, 1,385 mm; dry weight: 2,503 lb, 1,135 kg.

BODY hardtop; 2 doors.

Skyline 2000 GT-X Sedan

See Skyline 2000 GT Sedan, except for:

PRICE EX WORKS: 975,000 yen.

ENGINE compression ratio: 9.5:1; max power (DIN): 130 hp at 6,000 rpm; max torque (DIN): 127 lb ft, 17.5 kg m at 4,400 rpm; 65.1 hp/l; 2 Hitachi SU type HJG38W-3 horizontal carburettors.

PERFORMANCE power-weight ratio: 19.3 lb/hp, 8.8 kg/hp.

DIMENSIONS AND WEIGHT dry weight: 2,514 lb, 1,140 kg.

Skyline 2000 GT-X Hardtop

See Skyline 2000 GT-X Sedan, except for:

PRICE EX WORKS: 1,005,000 yen.

PERFORMANCE power-weight ratio: 19.5 lb/hp, 8.9 kg/hp.

DIMENSIONS AND WEIGHT height: 54.53 in, 1,385 mm; dry weight: 2,536 lb, 1,150 kg.

BODY hardtop; 2 doors.

Datsun 240K GT Sedan

(only for export)

See Skyline 2000 GT Sedan, except for:

ENGINE 146 cu in, 2,393 cc (3.27 x 2.90 in, 83 x 73.7 mm); compression ratio: 8.6:1; max power (SAE): 130 hp at 5,600 rpm; max torque (SAE): 145 lb ft, 20 kg m at 3,600 rpm; 54.3 hp/l; 1 Nikki downdraught twin barrel carburettor; fuel feed: mechanical pump.

TRANSMISSION axle ratio: 3.545; width of rims: 5"; tyres: 175 SR x 14.

PERFORMANCE max speeds: (I) 31 mph, 50 km/h; (II) 50

DATSUN 240K GT SEDAN

mph, 80 km/h; (III) 78 mph, 125 km/h; (IV) 112 mph, 180 km/h; power-weight ratio: 19.8 lb/hp, 9 kg/hp.

ELECTRICAL EQUIPMENT 60 Ah battery; 60 A alternator.

DIMENSIONS AND WEIGHT tracks: 53.54 in, 1,360 mm front, 52.76 in, 1,340 mm rear; dry weight: 2,580 lb, 1,170 kg.

OPTIONAL ACCESSORIES only automatic transmission with 3 ratios.

Datsun 240K GT Hardtop

(only for export)

See Datsun 240K GT Sedan, except for:

PERFORMANCE power-weight ratio: 20 lb/hp, 9 kg/hp.

DIMENSIONS AND WEIGHT height: 54.53 in, 1,385 mm; dry weight: 2,602 lb, 1,180 kg.

BODY hardtop; 2 doors.

Datsun Z 432 Sports

PRICE EX WORKS: 1,850,000 yen.

ENGINE front, 4 stroke; 6 cylinders, in line; 121.4 cu in, 1,989 cc (3.23 x 2.47 in, 82 x 62.8 mm); compression ratio: 9.5:1; max power (SAE): 160 hp at 7,000 rpm; max torque (SAE): 130 lb ft, 18 kg m at 5,600 rpm; max engine rpm: 7,500; 80.4 hp/l; cast iron cylinder block, light alloy head; 7 crankshaft bearings; valves: 4 per cylinder, overhead, thimble tappets; camshafts: 2, overhead; lubrication: gear pump, full flow filter, 10.6 imp pt, 12.7 US pt, 6 l; 3 Mikuni-Solex horizontal twin barrel carburettors; fuel feed: electric pump; water-cooled, 17.6 imp pt, 21.1 US pt, 10 l.

TRANSMISSION driving wheels: rear; clutch: single dry plate; gearbox: mechanical; gears: 5, fully synchronized; ratios: I 2.957, II 1.858, III 1.311, IV 1, V 0.852, rev 2.922; lever: central; final drive: hypoid bevel; axle ratio: 4.444; width of rims: 5.5"; tyres: 6.95H x 14.

PERFORMANCE max speeds: (I) 37 mph, 60 km/h; (II) 61 mph, 98 km/h; (III) 85 mph, 137 km/h; (IV) 114 mph, 183 km/h; (V) 130 mph, 210 km/h; power-weight ratio: 14.3 lb/hp, 6.5 kg/hp; carrying capacity: 397 lb, 180 kg; acceleration: standing ¼ mile 15.8 sec; speed in top at 1,000 rpm: 15.5 mph, 25 km/h; fuel consumption: 23.5 m/imp gal, 19.6 m/US gal, 12 l x 100 km.

CHASSIS integral, front auxiliary frame; front suspension: independent, by McPherson, coil springs/telescopic damper struts, lower wishbones (trailing links), anti-roll bar; rear suspension: independent, semi-trailing arms, coil springs/telescopic dampers.

STEERING rack-and-pinion; turns lock to lock: 2.50.

BRAKES front disc, rear drum, servo; swept area: front 12.6 sq in, 81 sq cm, rear 54.4 sq in, 351 sq cm, total 67 sq in, 432 sq cm.

ELECTRICAL EQUIPMENT 12 V; 35 Ah battery; 600 W alternator; Mitsubishi distributor; 2 headlamps.

DIMENSIONS AND WEIGHT wheel base: 90.75 in, 2,305 mm; tracks: 53.35 in, 1,355 mm front, 52.95 in, 1,345 mm rear; length: 162.01 in, 4,115 mm; width: 64.17 in, 1,630 mm; height: 50.79 in, 1,290 mm; ground clearance: 6.50 in, 165 mm; dry weight: 2,293 lb, 1,040 kg; distribution of weight: 52.4% front, 47.6% rear; turning circle (between walls): 31.5 ft, 9.6 m; fuel tank: 13.2 imp gal, 15.8 US gal, 60 l.

BODY coupé; 2 doors; 2 seats.

PRACTICAL INSTRUCTIONS fuel: 98-100 oct petrol; engine sump oil: 10.6 imp pt, 12.7 US pt, 6 l, SAE 20W-30, change every 3,100 miles, 5,000 km; gearbox oil: 2.6 imp pt, 3.2 US pt, 1.5 l, SAE 90, change every 31,100 miles, 50,000 km; final drive oil: 2.3 imp pt, 2.7 US pt, 1.3 l, SAE 90, change every 31,100 miles, 50,000 km; greasing: every 31,100 miles, 50,000 km, 5 points; tappet clearances: inlet 0.009 in, 0.23 mm, exhaust 0.015 in, 0.37 mm; valve timing: 30° 50° 50° 30°; tyre pressure: front 33 psi, 2.3 atm, rear 33 psi, 2.3 atm.

VARIATIONS

Competition version.

Fairlady Z Sports

See Datsun Z 432 Sports, except for:

PRICE EX WORKS: 930,000 yen.

ENGINE 121.9 cu in, 1,998 cc (3.07 x 2.74 in, 78 x 69.7 mm); max power (DIN): 130 hp at 6,000 rpm; max torque (DIN): 127 lb ft, 17.5 kg m at 4,400 rpm; 65.1 hp/l; valves: 2 per cylinder, overhead, in line, rockers; camshafts: 1, overhead; lubrication: rotary pump, full flow filter, 7 imp pt, 8.5 US pt, 4 l; 2 Hitachi SU type HJG38W-3 horizontal carburettors; fuel feed: mechanical pump; cooling system capacity: 14.1 imp pt, 16.9 US pt, 8 l.

TRANSMISSION gears: 4, fully synchronized; ratios: I 3.549, II 2.197, III 1.420, IV 1, rev 3.164; axle ratio: 3.700; width of rims: 4.5"; tyres: 6.45 H x 14.

PERFORMANCE max speeds: (I) 33 mph, 53 km/h; (II) 53 mph, 85 km/h; (III) 81 mph, 130 km/h; (IV) 115 mph, 185 km/h; power-weight ratio: 18.3 lb/hp, 8.3 kg/hp.

CHASSIS integral.

ELECTRICAL EQUIPMENT 500 W alternator.

DIMENSIONS AND WEIGHT dry weight: 2,392 lb, 1,085 kg.

PRACTICAL INSTRUCTIONS tappet clearances: inlet 0.010 in, 0.25 mm, exhaust 0.012 in, 0.30 mm; valve timing: 21° 47° 59° 9°.

OPTIONAL ACCESSORIES Nissan automatic transmission with 3 ratios.

NISSAN Datsun 240 Z-G Sports

NISSAN Cedric GX

NISSAN Gloria GX 2-door Hardtop

Datsun 240 Z Sports

See Datsun Z 432 Sports, except for:

PRICE IN GB: £ 1,983.
PRICE IN USA: $ 4,106.

ENGINE 146 cu in, 2,393 cc (3.27 x 2.90 in, 83 x 73.7 mm); compression ratio: 9:1; max power (SAE): 161 hp at 5,600 rpm; max torque (SAE): 146 lb ft, 20.1 kg m at 4,400 rpm; max engine rpm: 6,000; 63.1 hp/l; valves: 2 per cylinder, overhead, rockers; camshafts: 1, overhead; lubrication: rotary pump, 7.2 imp pt, 8.7 US pt, 4.1 l; 2 Hitachi HJG46W horizontal twin barrel carburettors; fuel feed: mechanical pump; cooling system capacity: 10.6 imp pt, 12.7 US pt, 6 l.

TRANSMISSION clutch: single dry plate (diaphragm); axle ratio: 3.900; width of rims: 4.5"; tyres: 6.45H x 14.

PERFORMANCE max speeds: (I) 36 mph, 58 km/h; (II) 57 mph, 92 km/h; (III) 81 mph, 130 km/h; (IV) 106 mph, 170 km/h; (V) 130 mph, 210 km/h; power-weight ratio: 15 lb/hp, 6.8 kg/hp; acceleration: standing ¼ mile 16.2 sec; speed in direct drive at 1,000 rpm: 17.6 mph, 28.4 km/h.

STEERING turns lock to lock: 3.

ELECTRICAL EQUIPMENT 40 Ah battery; 500 W alternator; Hitachi distributor.

DIMENSIONS AND WEIGHT tracks: 53.39 in, 1,356 mm front, 53.03 in, 1,347 mm rear; length: 162.83 in, 4,136 mm; height: 50.63 in, 1,286 mm; dry weight: 2,260 lb, 1,025 kg.

PRACTICAL INSTRUCTIONS engine sump oil: 7.2 imp pt, 8.7 US pt, 4.1 l; final drive oil: 1.8 imp pt, 2.1 US pt, 1 l; tappet clearances: inlet 0.010 in, 0.25 mm, exhaust 0.014 in, 0.35 mm; valve timing: 16° 52° 54° 14°; tyre pressure: front 28 psi, 2 atm, rear 28 psi, 2 atm.

VARIATIONS

(only for export)

TRANSMISSION 4-speed mechanical gearbox (I 3.549, II 2.197, III 1.420, IV 1, rev 3.164), 3.364 axle ratio, 175R x 14 tyres.
PERFORMANCE max speeds (I) 35 mph, 56 km/h, (II) 56 mph, 90 km/h, (III) 86 mph, 139 km/h, (IV) 127 mph, 205 km/h, power-weight ratio 15.2 lb/hp, 6.9 kg/hp.
DIMENSIONS AND WEIGHT dry weight 2,302 lb, 1,044 kg.

OPTIONAL ACCESSORIES Nissan automatic transmission with 3 ratios.

Datsun 240 Z-G Sports

See Datsun 240 Z Sports, except for:

PRICE EX WORKS: 1,500,000 yen.

PERFORMANCE power-weight ratio: 15.4 lb/hp, 7 kg/hp.

DIMENSIONS AND WEIGHT length: 169.49 in, 4,305 mm; width: 66.53 in, 1,690 mm; dry weight: 2,470 lb, 1,120 kg.

Cedric GL Sedan

PRICE EX WORKS: 1,222,000 yen.

ENGINE front, 4 stroke; 6 cylinders, in line; 121.9 cu in, 1,998 cc (3.07 x 2.74 in, 78 x 69.7 mm); compression ratio: 8.6:1; max power (DIN): 115 hp at 5,600 rpm; max torque (DIN): 120 lb ft, 16.5 kg m at 3,600 rpm; 57.6 hp/l; cast iron cylinder block, light alloy head; 7 crankshaft bearings; valves: overhead, in line, rockers; camshafts: 1, overhead;

NISSAN Fairlady Z Sports

NISSAN Cedric GX Sedan

NISSAN Gloria GX 2-door Hardtop

lubrication: rotary pump, full flow filter, 8.3 imp pt, 9.9 US pt, 4.7 l; 1 Hitachi DAH342-3 downdraught twin barrel carburettor; fuel feed: electric pump; water-cooled, 15.8 imp pt, 19 US pt, 9 l.

TRANSMISSION driving wheels: rear; clutch: single dry plate (diaphragm); gearbox: mechanical; gears: 4, fully synchronized; ratios: I 3.549, II 2.197, III 1.420, IV 1, rev 3.164; lever: central; final drive: hypoid bevel; axle ratio: 4.111; width of rims: 5"; tyres: 6.95 x 14.

PERFORMANCE max speeds: (I) 25 mph, 40 km/h; (II) 53 mph, 85 km/h; (III) 87 mph, 140 km/h; (IV) 103 mph, 165 km/h; power-weight ratio: 25.8 lb/hp, 11.7 kg/hp; carrying capacity: 882 lb, 400 kg; fuel consumption: 23.5 m/imp gal, 19.6 m/US gal, 12 l x 100 km.

CHASSIS integral; front suspension: independent, wishbones, coil springs, anti-roll bar, telescopic dampers; rear suspension: rigid axle, semi-elliptic leafsprings, telescopic dampers.

STEERING recirculating ball, servo; turns lock to lock: 4.40.

BRAKES front disc, rear drum, servo; swept area: front 24.8 sq in, 160 sq cm, rear 71.9 sq in, 464 sq cm, total 96.7 sq in, 624 sq cm.

ELECTRICAL EQUIPMENT 12 V; 60 Ah battery; 60 A alternator; 4 headlamps.

DIMENSIONS AND WEIGHT wheel base: 105.91 in, 2,690 mm; tracks: 54.33 in, 1,380 mm front, 54.72 in, 1,390 mm rear; length: 184.65 in, 4,690 mm; width: 66.54 in, 1,690 mm; height: 57.28 in, 1,455 mm; ground clearance: 7.28 in, 185 mm; dry weight: 2,977 lb, 1,350 kg; turning circle (between walls): 39.4 ft, 12 m; fuel tank: 14.3 imp gal, 17.2 US gal, 65 l.

BODY saloon/sedan; 4 doors; 5 seats, separate front seats.

PRACTICAL INSTRUCTIONS fuel: 90 oct petrol; engine sump oil: 8.3 imp pt, 9.9 US pt, 4.7 l, SAE 20W-30, change every 3,100 miles, 5,000 km; gearbox oil: 2.6 imp pt, 3.2 US pt, 1.5 l, SAE 90, change every 31,000 miles, 50,000 km; final drive oil: 1.6 imp pt, 1.9 US pt, 0.9 l, SAE 90, change every 31,000 miles, 50,000 km; tappet clearances: inlet 0.010 in, 0.25 mm, exhaust 0.012 in, 0.30 mm; valve timing: 8° 44° 50° 10°; tyre pressure: front 21 psi, 1.5 atm, rear 21 psi, 1.5 atm.

OPTIONAL ACCESSORIES 4-speed fully synchronized mechanical gearbox (I 3.184, II 1.641, III 1, IV 0.785, rev 2.922), steering column lever, 4.625 axle ratio; Nissan automatic transmission with 3 ratios (I 2.458, II 1.458, III 1, rev 2.182), steering column lever, 4.375 axle ratio.

Gloria GL Sedan

See Cedric GL Sedan.

Cedric GL 2-door Hardtop

See Cedric GL Sedan, except for:

PRICE EX WORKS: 1,280,000 yen.

DIMENSIONS AND WEIGHT height: 55.91 in, 1,420 mm.

BODY hardtop; 2 doors.

Cedric GL 4-door Hardtop

See Cedric GL Sedan, except for:

PRICE EX WORKS: 1,300,000 yen.

BODY hardtop.

Gloria GL 2-door Hardtop

See Cedric GL 2-door Hardtop.

Gloria GL 4-door Hardtop

See Cedric GL 4-door Hardtop.

Cedric GX Sedan

See Cedric GL Sedan, except for:

PRICE EX WORKS: 1,320,000 yen.

ENGINE compression ratio: 9.5:1; max power (DIN): 130 hp at 6,000 rpm; max torque (DIN): 127 lb ft, 17.5 kg m at 4,400 rpm; 65.1 hp/l; 2 Hitachi SU type HJG38W-3 horizontal carburettors.

PERFORMANCE max speed: 106 mph, 170 km/h; power-weight ratio: 22.9 lb/hp, 10.4 kg/hp.

DIMENSIONS AND WEIGHT dry weight: 2,977 lb, 1,350 kg.

Gloria GX Sedan

See Cedric GX Sedan.

Cedric GX Hardtop

See Cedric GX Sedan, except for:

PRICE EX WORKS: 1,380,000 yen.

DIMENSIONS AND WEIGHT height: 55.91 in, 1,420 mm.

BODY hardtop; 2 doors.

Gloria GX Hardtop

See Cedric GX Hardtop.

Datsun 240 C

See Cedric GL Sedan, except for:

PRICE IN GB: £ 1,675.

ENGINE 146 cu in, 2,393 cc (3.27 x 2.90 in, 83 x 73.7 mm); max power (DIN): 130 hp at 5,800 rpm; max torque (DIN): 145 lb ft, 20 kg m at 3,600 rpm; 54.3 hp/l; fuel feed: mechanical pump.

PERFORMANCE power-weight ratio: 22.9 lb/hp, 10.4 kg/hp.

Cedric 2600 GX Sedan

See Cedric GL Sedan, except for:

PRICE EX WORKS: 1,500,000 yen.

ENGINE 156.5 cu in, 2,565 cc (3.27 x 3.11 in, 83 x 79 mm); max power (DIN): 140 hp at 5,200 rpm; max torque (DIN): 159 lb ft, 22 kg m at 4,000 rpm; 54.6 hp/l; 1 Hitachi DAH342-6 downdraught twin barrel carburettor.

PERFORMANCE max speed: 112 mph, 180 km/h; power-weight ratio: 21.2 lb/hp, 9.6 kg/hp.

PRACTICAL INSTRUCTIONS valve timing: 12° 48° 54° 14°.

OPTIONAL ACCESSORIES 4-speed fully synchronized mechanical gearbox with 4.375 axle ratio; bench front seats.

Gloria 2600 GX Sedan

See Cedric 2600 GX Sedan.

Cedric 2600 GX 2-door Hardtop

See Cedric 2600 GX Sedan, except for:

PRICE EX WORKS: 1,600,000 yen.

DIMENSIONS AND WEIGHT height: 55.91 in, 1,420 mm.

BODY hardtop; 2 doors.

Cedric 2600 GX 4-door Hardtop

See Cedric 2600 GX Sedan, except for:

PRICE EX WORKS: 1,630,000 yen.

BODY hardtop.

Gloria 2600 GX 2-door Hardtop

See Cedric 2600 GX 2-door Hardtop.

Gloria 2600 GX 4-door Hardtop

See Cedric 2600 GX 4-door Hardtop.

President A Sedan

ENGINE front, 4 stroke; 6 cylinders, in line; 181.5 cu in, 2,974 cc (3.43 x 3.27 in, 87.2 x 83 mm); compression ratio: 8.7:1; max power (SAE): 130 hp at 4,400 rpm; max torque (SAE): 174 lb ft, 24 kg m at 3,200 rpm; max engine rpm: 4,400; 43.7 hp/l; cast iron cylinder block, light alloy head; 7 crankshaft bearings; valves: overhead, rockers; camshafts: 1, overhead; lubrication: gear pump, 8.3 imp pt, 9.9 US pt, 4.7 l; 1 Hitachi downdraught 4-barrel carburettor; fuel feed: mechanical pump; water-cooled, 28.2 imp pt, 33.8 US pt, 16 l.

NISSAN Cedric 2600 GX 4-door Hardtop

NISSAN President D Sedan

SUBARU Rex GSR Sedan

TRANSMISSION driving wheels: rear; clutch: single dry plate (diaphragm); gearbox: mechanical; gears: 3, fully synchronized; ratios: I 3.184, II 1.641, III 1, rev 2.922; lever: steering column; final drive: hypoid bevel; axle ratio: 3.900; width of rims: 5"; tyres: 7.50 x 14.

PERFORMANCE max speeds: (I) 46 mph, 74 km/h; (II) 76 mph, 122 km/h; (III) 99 mph, 160 km/h; power-weight ratio: 26 lb/hp, 11.8 kg/hp; carrying capacity: 1,058 lb, 480 kg; speed in direct drive at 1,000 rpm: 23 mph, 37 km/h; fuel consumption: 20.2 m/imp gal, 16.8 m/US gal, 14 l x 100 km.

CHASSIS integral; front suspension: independent, wishbones, coil springs, anti-roll bar, telescopic dampers; rear suspension: rigid axle, semi-elliptic leafsprings, anti-roll bar, telescopic dampers.

STEERING recirculating ball.

BRAKES front disc, rear drum, servo; swept area: front 15.8 sq in, 102 sq cm, rear 71.9 sq in, 464 sq cm, total 87.7 sq in, 566 sq cm.

ELECTRICAL EQUIPMENT 12 V; 50 Ah battery; 600 W alternator; Hitachi distributor; 4 headlamps.

DIMENSIONS AND WEIGHT wheel base: 112.20 in, 2,850 mm; tracks: 58.46 in, 1,485 mm front, 58.07 in, 1,475 mm rear; length: 198.62 in, 5,045 mm; width: 70.67 in, 1,795 mm; height: 58.46 in, 1,485 mm; ground clearance: 7.68 in, 195 mm; dry weight: 3,374 lb, 1,530 kg; distribution of weight: 51% front, 49% rear; turning circle (between walls): 38 ft, 11.6 m; fuel tank: 16.5 imp gal, 19.8 US gal, 75 l.

BODY saloon/sedan; 4 doors; 6 seats, bench front seats.

PRACTICAL INSTRUCTIONS fuel: 90 oct petrol; engine sump oil: 7.2 imp pt, 8.7 US pt, 4.1 l, SAE 10W-30, change every 3,100 miles. 5,000 km; gearbox oil: 4.4 imp pt, 5.3 US pt, 2.5 l, SAE 90, change every 24,900 miles, 40,000 km; final drive oil: 2.6 imp pt, 3.2 US pt, 1.5 l, SAE 90, change every 24,900 miles, 40,000 km; greasing: every 12,400 miles, 20,000 km, 19 points; tyre pressure: front 24 psi, 1.7 atm, rear 24 psi, 1.7 atm.

OPTIONAL ACCESSORIES power-assisted steering; separate front seats; electrically-controlled windows; air-conditioning.

President D Sedan

See President A Sedan, except for:

ENGINE 8 cylinders, Vee-slanted at 90°; 243.3 cu in, 3,988 cc (3.62 x 2.95 in, 92 x 75 mm); compression ratio: 9:1; max power (SAE): 195 hp at 5,000 rpm; max torque (SAE): 238 lb ft, 32.8 kg m at 3,200 rpm; max engine rpm: 5,000; 48.9 hp/l; 5 crankshaft bearings; valves: overhead, push-rods and rockers, hydraulic tappets; camshafts: 1, at centre of Vee.

TRANSMISSION gearbox: automatic transmission, hydraulic torque converter and planetary gears with 3 ratios; ratios: I 2.393, II 1.450, III 1, rev 2.094; axle ratio: 3.154.

PERFORMANCE max speeds: (I) 47 mph, 75 km/h; (II) 78 mph, 125 km/h; (III) 115 mph, 185 km/h; power-weight ratio: 18.1 lb/hp, 8.2 kg/hp; acceleration: standing ¼ mile 18.4 sec; speed in direct drive at 1,000 rpm: 24.9 mph, 40 km/h; fuel consumption: 17.7 m/imp gal, 14.7 m/US gal, 16 l x 100 km.

STEERING servo (standard).

DIMENSIONS AND WEIGHT dry weight: 3,539 lb, 1,605 kg.

BODY electrically-controlled windows (standard).

PRACTICAL INSTRUCTIONS gearbox oil: 13.6 imp pt, 16.3 US pt, 7.7 l, automatic transmission fluid; valve timing: 22° 62° 62° 22°.

OPTIONAL ACCESSORIES only separate front seats and air-conditioning.

SUBARU JAPAN

Rex Standard Sedan

PRICE EX WORKS: 327,000 yen.

ENGINE rear, transverse, 2 stroke; 2 cylinders, in line; 21.7 cu in, 356 cc (2.42 x 2.36 in, 61.5 x 60 mm); compression ratio: 6.5:1; max power (DIN): 32 hp at 6,000 rpm; max torque (DIN): 28 lb ft, 3.8 kg m at 5,000 rpm; max engine rpm: 7,000; 89.9 hp/l; cast iron cylinder block, light alloy head; 5 crankshaft bearings; lubrication: gear pump, oil injection to cylinders and bearings, total loss system, 4.4 imp pt, 5.3 US pt, 2.5 l; 1 Hitachi VCM302 downdraught carburettor; fuel feed: mechanical pump; water-cooled, 8.8 imp pt, 10.6 US pt, 5 l.

NISSAN Cedric 2600 GX 4-door Hardtop

NISSAN President D Sedan

SUBARU Rex GSR Sedan

TRANSMISSION driving wheels: rear; clutch: single dry plate (diaphragm); gearbox: mechanical; gears: 4, fully synchronized; ratios: I 3.687, II 2.203, III 1.476, IV 1, rev 3.663; lever: central; final drive: helical spur gears; axle ratio: 3.238; width of rims: 3"; tyres: 4.80 x 10.

PERFORMANCE max speeds: (I) 19 mph, 30 km/h; (II) 34 mph, 54 km/h; (III) 50 mph, 80 km/h; (IV) 68 mph, 110 km/h; power-weight ratio: 33 lb/hp, 15 kg/hp; carrying capacity: 706 lb, 320 kg; acceleration: standing ¼ mile 21.4 sec; fuel consumption: not declared.

CHASSIS integral; front suspension: independent, semi-trailing arms, torsion bars, telescopic dampers; rear suspension: independent, semi-trailing arms, torsion bars, telescopic dampers.

STEERING rack-and-pinion; turns lock to lock: 3.30.

BRAKES drum, single circuit; swept area: front 33.9 sq in, 212 sq cm, rear 33.5 sq in, 216 sq cm, total 67.4 sq in, 428 sq cm.

ELECTRICAL EQUIPMENT 12 V; 26 Ah battery; 35 A alternator; Hitachi distributor; 2 headlamps.

DIMENSIONS AND WEIGHT wheel base: 75.59 in, 1,920 mm; tracks: 44.68 in, 1,135 mm front, 43.90 in, 1,115 mm rear; length: 117.91 in, 2,995 mm; width: 50.98 in, 1,295 mm; height: 50.59 in, 1,285 mm; ground clearance: 6.89 in, 175 mm; dry weight: 1,058 lb, 480 kg; distribution of weight: 38.5% front, 61.5% rear; turning circle (between walls): 26.2 ft, 8 m; fuel tank: 5.5 imp gal, 6.6 US gal, 25 l.

BODY saloon/sedan; 2 doors; 4 seats, separate front seats.

PRACTICAL INSTRUCTIONS fuel: mixture; engine sump oil: 4.4 imp pt, 5.3 US pt, 2.5 l, oil in separate tank; gearbox and final drive oil: 2.3 imp pt, 2.7 US pt, 1.3 l, SAE 80-90, change every 24,800 miles, 40,000 km; greasing: none; tyre pressure: front 16 psi, 1.1 atm, rear 34 psi, 2.4 atm.

Rex Super L Sedan

See Rex Standard Sedan, except for:

PRICE EX WORKS: 413,000 yen.

PERFORMANCE power-weight ratio: 33.7 lb/hp, 15.3 kg/hp.

DIMENSIONS AND WEIGHT dry weight: 1,080 lb, 490 kg.

Rex TS Sedan

See Rex Standard Sedan, except for:

PRICE EX WORKS: 409,000 yen.

ENGINE compression ratio: 7.4:1; max power (DIN): 35 hp at 6,500 rpm; max torque (DIN): 29 lb ft, 4 kg m at 6,000 rpm; 98.3 hp/l.

PERFORMANCE max speeds: (I) 22 mph, 35 km/h; (II) 35 mph, 57 km/h; (III) 52 mph, 83 km/h; (IV) 75 mph, 120 km/h; power-weight ratio: 30.9 lb/hp, 14 kg/hp; acceleration: standing ¼ mile 20.5 sec.

DIMENSIONS AND WEIGHT dry weight: 1,080 lb, 490 kg.

Rex GSR Sedan

See Rex Standard Sedan, except for:

PRICE EX WORKS: 443,000 yen.

ENGINE compression ratio: 7.4:1; max power (DIN): 37 hp at 6,500 rpm; max torque (DIN): 30 lb ft, 4.2 kg m at 6,000 rpm: 103.9 hp/l; 1 Mikuni-Solex 36 PHH horizontal twin barrel carburettor.

TRANSMISSION tyres: 135 JR x 10.

PERFORMANCE max speeds: (I) 22 mph, 35 km/h; (II) 35 mph, 57 km/h; (III) 52 mph, 83 km/h; (IV) 75 mph, 120 km/h; power-weight ratio: 29.8 lb/hp, 13.5 kg/hp; acceleration: standing ¼ mile 19.9 sec.

DIMENSIONS AND WEIGHT: height: 49.41 in, 1,255 mm; ground clearance: 5.71 in, 145 mm; dry weight: 1,103 lb, 500 kg.

Leone 1100 2-door Standard Sedan

PRICE EX WORKS: 459,000 yen.

ENGINE front, 4 stroke; 4 cylinders, horizontally opposed;

LEONE 1100 2-DOOR STANDARD SEDAN

66.4 cu in, 1,088 cc (2.99 x 2.36 in, 76 x 60 mm); compression ratio: 9:1; max power (DIN): 62 hp at 6,000 rpm; max torque (DIN): 63 lb ft, 8.7 kg m at 3,200 rpm; max engine rpm: 6,000; 57 hp/l; light alloy cylinder block with cast iron liners, light alloy head; 3 crankshaft bearings; valves: overhead, push-rods and rockers; camshafts: 1, side lubrication: rotary pump, full flow filter, 5.8 imp pt, 7 US pt, 3.3 l; 1 Hitachi-Stromberg DCG 306 downdraught twin barrel carburettor; fuel feed: electric pump; water-cooled, 10.6 imp pt, 12.7 US pt, 6 l.

TRANSMISSION driving wheels: front; clutch: single dry plate (diaphragm); gearbox: mechanical; gears: 4, fully synchronized; ratios: I 3.666, II 2.176, III 1.480, IV 1.033, rev 4.100; lever: steering column; final drive: hypoid bevel; axle ratio: 4.125; width of rims: 4"; tyres: 6.15 x 13.

PERFORMANCE max speeds: (I) 27 mph, 43 km/h; (II) 45 mph, 72 km/h; (III) 65 mph, 104 km/h; (IV) 90 mph, 145 km/h; power-weight ratio: 26.1 lb/hp, 11.8 kg/hp; acceleration: standing ¼ mile 19.8 sec; fuel consumption: not declared.

CHASSIS integral; front suspension: independent, by McPherson, coil springs/telescopic damper struts, lower wishbones (trailing links), anti-roll bar; rear suspension: independent, semi-trailing arms, torsion bars, telescopic dampers.

STEERING rack-and-pinion; turns lock to lock: 3.80.

BRAKES drum; swept area: front 65.1 sq in, 420 sq cm, rear 26 sq in, 168 sq cm, total 91.1 sq in, 588 sq cm.

ELECTRICAL EQUIPMENT 12 V; 32 Ah battery; 35 Ah alternator; Hitachi distributor; 2 headlamps.

DIMENSIONS AND WEIGHT wheel base: 96.65 in, 2,455 mm; tracks: 49.61 in, 1,260 mm front, 47.44 in, 1,205 mm rear; length: 157,28 in, 3,995 mm; width: 59.06 in, 1,500 mm; height: 54.53 in, 1,385 mm; ground clearance: 6.69 in, 170 mm; dry weight: 1,621 lb, 735 kg; distribution of weight: 64% front, 36% rear; turning circle (between walls): 31.5 ft, 9.6 m; fuel tank: 11 imp gal, 13.2 US gal, 50 l.

BODY saloon/sedan; 2 doors; 5 seats, separate front seats.

PRACTICAL INSTRUCTIONS fuel: 85-90 oct petrol; engine sump oil: 5.8 imp pt, 7 US pt, 3.3 l, SAE 30, change every 3,100 miles, 5,000 km; gearbox and final drive oil: 4.4 imp pt, 5.3 US pt, 2.5 l, SAE 90, change every 24,800 miles, 40,000 km; tappet clearances: inlet 0.012 in, 0.30 mm, exhaust 0.012 in, 0.30 mm; valve timing: 20° 60° 60° 20° tyre pressure: front 24 psi, 1.7 atm, rear 21 psi, 1.5 atm.

Leone 1100 2-door De Luxe Sedan

See Leone 1100 2-door Standard Sedan, except for:

PRICE EX WORKS: 524,000 yen.

TRANSMISSION lever: central.

PERFORMANCE power-weight ratio: 26.5 lb/hp, 12 kg/hp.

DIMENSIONS AND WEIGHT dry weight: 1,643 lb, 745 kg.

Leone 1100 4-door De Luxe Sedan

See Leone 1100 2-door Standard Sedan, except for:

PRICE EX WORKS: 549,000 yen.

TRANSMISSION lever: central.

PERFORMANCE power-weight ratio: 27.6 lb/hp, 12.5 kg/hp.

DIMENSIONS AND WEIGHT dry weight: 1,709 lb, 775 kg.

BODY 4 doors.

Leone 1400 2-door Standard Sedan

See Leone 1100 2-door Standard Sedan, except for:

PRICE EX WORKS: 494,000 yen.

ENGINE 83 cu in, 1,361 cc (3.35 x 2.36 in, 85 x 60 mm); max power (DIN): 80 hp at 6,400 rpm; max torque (DIN): 76 lb ft, 10.5 kg m at 4,000 rpm; 58.8 hp/l.

TRANSMISSION axle ratio: 3.889.

PERFORMANCE power-weight ratio: 20.3 lb/hp, 9.2 kg/hp.

SUBARU Leone 1100

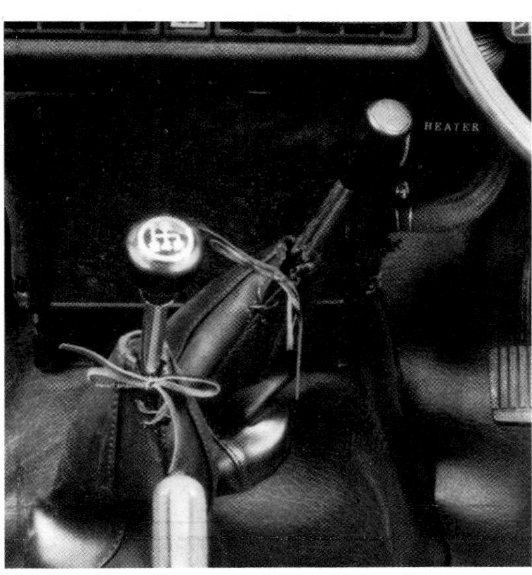

SUBARU Leone 1400 4WD Station Wagon

SUBARU Leone 1400 GL Coupé

Leone 1400 2-door GL Sedan

See Leone 1400 2-door Standard Sedan, except for:

PRICE EX WORKS: 604,000 yen.

TRANSMISSION lever: central.

PERFORMANCE power-weight ratio: 20.8 lb/hp, 9.4 kg/hp.

BRAKES front disc, rear drum.

DIMENSIONS AND WEIGHT dry weight: 1,654 lb, 750 kg.

Leone 1400 4-door Custom Sedan

See Leone 1400 2-door Standard Sedan, except for:

PRICE EX WORKS: 647,000 yen.

PERFORMANCE power weight ratio: 21.5 lb/hp, 9.7 kg/hp.

DIMENSIONS AND WEIGHT dry weight: 1,720 lb, 780 kg.

BODY 4 doors.

Leone 1400 4-door Super Touring Sedan

See Leone 1400 2-door Standard Sedan, except for:

PRICE EX WORKS: 717,000 yen.

ENGINE compression ratio 10:1; max power (DIN): 93 hp at 6,800 rpm; max torque (DIN): 80 lb ft, 11 kg m at 4,800 rpm; 68.3 hp/l; 2 Hitachi DCG 306 downdraught twin barrel carburettor.

TRANSMISSION gearbox ratios: I 3.307, II 2.176, III 1.480, IV 1.033, rev. 4.100; lever: central; tyres 145 SR x 13.

PERFORMANCE max speed: 106 mph, 170 km/h; power-weight ratio: 19 lb/hp, 8.6 kg/hp.

BRAKES front disc, rear drum.

DIMENSIONS AND WEIGHT height: 54.33 in, 1,380 mm; dry weight: 1,764 lb, 800 kg.

BODY 4 doors.

Leone 1400 4WD Station Wagon

See Leone 1400 2-door Standard Sedan, except for:

PRICE EX WORKS: 798,000 yen.

ENGINE max power (DIN): 77 hp at 6,400 rpm; max torque (DIN): 76 lb ft, 10,5 kg m at 3,600; max engine rpm: 6,600; 56.6 hp/l.

TRANSMISSION driving wheels: front and rear with transfer box; ratios: I 4.090, II 2.312, III 1.464, IV 1.029, rev. 4.100; lever: central; tyres: 145 SR x 13.

PERFORMANCE max speeds: (I) 25 mph, 40 km/h; (II) 46 mph, 74 km/h; (III) 73 mph, 117 km/h; (IV) 87 mph, 140 km/h; power-weight ratio: 25.9 lb/hp, 11.7 kg/hp.

STEERING turns lock to lock: 3.20.

BRAKES swept area: front 63.6 sq in, 410 sq cm, rear 26 sq in, 168 sq cm, total 89.6 sq in, 578 sq cm.

ELECTRICAL EQUIPMENT 45 Ah battery.

DIMENSIONS AND WEIGHT wheel base: 96.26 in, 2,445 mm; tracks: 48.43 in, 1,230 mm front, 47.24 in, 1,200 mm rear; length: 159.05 in, 4,040 mm; height: 57.09 in, 1,450 mm; ground clearance: 8.27 in, 210 mm; dry weight: 1,996 lb, 905 kg; distribution of weight: 57.5% front, 42.5% rear; turning circle (between walls): 40 ft, 12.2 m; fuel tank: 7 imp gal, 8.4 US gal, 32 l.

BODY estate car: station wagon: 4 + 1 doors.

PRACTICAL INSTRUCTIONS gearbox and final drive oil: 5.3 imp pt, 6.3 US pt, 3 l; rear final drive oil: 1.4 imp pt, 1.7 US pt, 0.8 l, SAE 90, change every 24,800 miles, 40,000 km; valve timing: 24° 64° 70° 18°; tyre pressure: front 23 psi, 1.6 atm, rear 23 psi, 1.6 atm.

Leone 1400 De Luxe Coupé

PRICE EX WORKS: 597,000 yen.

ENGINE front, 4 stroke; 4 cylinders, horizontally opposed; 83 cu in, 1,361 cc (3.35 x 2.36 in, 85 x 60 mm); compres-

SUBARU Leone 1100 2-door Standard Sedan

SUBARU Leone 1400 4WD Station Wagon

SUBARU Leone 1400 RX Coupé

sion ratio: 9:1; max power (DIN): 80 hp at 6,400 rpm; max torque (DIN): 76 lb ft, 10.5 kg m at 4,000 rpm; max engine rpm: 6,500; 58.8 hp/l; light alloy cylinder block and head; 3 crankshaft bearings; valves: overhead, push-rods and rockers; camshafts: 1, side; lubrication: rotary pump, full flow filter, 5.8 imp pt, 7 US pt, 3.3 l; 1 Hitachi DCG 3066 downdraught twin barrel carburettor; fuel feed: electric pump; water-cooled, 10.6 imp pt, 12.7 US pt, 6 l.

TRANSMISSION driving wheels: front; clutch: single dry plate (diaphragm); gearbox: mechanical; gears: 4, fully synchronized; ratios: I 3.666, II 2.176, III 1.480, IV 1.033, rev 4.100; lever: central; final drive: hypoid bevel; axle ratio: 3.889; width of rims: 4"; tyres: 6.15 x 13.

PERFORMANCE max speeds: (I) 29 mph, 47 km/h; (II) 50 mph, 80 km/h; (III) 73 mph, 117 km/h; (IV) 99 mph, 160 km/h; power-weight ratio: 20.8 lb/hp, 9.4 kg/hp; acceleration: standing ¼ mile 17.8 sec; fuel consumption: not declared.

CHASSIS integral; front suspension: independent, by McPherson, coil springs/telescopic damper struts, lower wishbones (trailing links), anti-roll bar; rear suspension: independent, semi-trailing arms, torsion bars, telescopic dampers.

STEERING rack-and-pinion; turns lock to lock: 3.80.

BRAKES drum; swept area: front 65.1 sq in, 420 sq cm, rear 26 sq in, 168 sq cm, total 91.1 sq in, 588 sq cm.

ELECTRICAL EQUIPMENT 12 V; 35 Ah battery; 30 A alternator; Hitachi distributor; 2 headlamps.

DIMENSIONS AND WEIGHT wheel base: 96.65 in, 2,455 mm; tracks: 49.61 in, 1,260 mm front, 47.44 in, 1,205 mm rear; length: 157.28 in, 3,995 mm; width: 59.06 in, 1,500 mm; height: 52.95 in, 1,345 mm; ground clearance: 6.69 in, 170 mm; dry weight: 1,665 lb, 755 kg; turning circle (between walls): 35.4 ft, 10.8 m; fuel tank: 11 imp gal, 13.2 US gal, 50 l.

BODY coupé; 2 doors; 5 seats, separate front seats.

PRACTICAL INSTRUCTIONS fuel: 85-90 oct petrol; engine sump oil: 5.8 imp pt, 7 US pt, 3.3 l, SAE 10W-30, change every 3,100 miles, 5,000 km; gearbox and final drive oil: 4.4 imp pt, 5.3 US pt, 2.5 l, SAE 90, change every 24,800 miles, 40,000 km; tappet clearances: inlet 0.012 in, 0.30 mm, exhaust 0.012 in, 0.30 mm; valve timing: 24° 64° 70° 18°; tyre pressure: front 24 psi, 1.7 atm, rear 21 psi, 1.5 atm.

Leone 1400 GL Coupé

See Leone 1400 De Luxe Coupé, except for:

PRICE EX WORKS: 649,000 yen.

BRAKES front disc, rear drum; swept area: front 24.2 sq in, 156 sq cm, rear 26 sq in, 168 sq cm, total 50.2 sq in, 324 sq cm.

Leone 1400 GSR Coupé

See Leone 1400 De Luxe Coupé, except for:

PRICE EX WORKS: 719,000 yen.

ENGINE compression ratio: 10:1; max power (DIN): 93 hp at 6,800 rpm; max torque (DIN): 80 lb ft, 11 kg m at 4,800 rpm; max engine rpm: 7,200; 68.3 hp/l; 2 Hitachi DCG 306 carburettors.

TRANSMISSION gearbox ratios: I 3.307, II 2.176, III 1.480, IV 1.033, rev 4.100; tyres: 145 SR x 13.

PERFORMANCE max speed: 106 mph, 170 km/h; power-weight ratio: 18.3 lb/hp, 8.3 kg/hp; acceleration: standing ¼ mile 16.8 sec.

BRAKES front disc, rear drum; swept area: front 24.2 sq in, 156 sq cm, rear 26 sq in, 168 sq cm, total 50.2 sq in, 324 sq cm.

DIMENSIONS AND WEIGHT height: 52.76 in, 1,340 mm; dry weight: 1,709 lb, 775 kg.

PRACTICAL INSTRUCTIONS tappet clearances: inlet 0.010 in, 0.25 mm; valve timing: 40° 76° 76° 40°.

Leone 1400 RX Coupé

See Leone 1400 GSR Coupé, except for:

PRICE EX WORKS: 734,000 yen.

TRANSMISSION gears: 5, fully synchronized; ratios: I 3.307, II 2.157, III 1.518, IV 1.156, V 0.948, rev. 4.100.

LEONE 1400 RX COUPÉ

PERFORMANCE power-weight ratio: 18.7 lb/hp, 8.5 kg/hp; acceleration: standing ¼ mile 16.8 sec.

BRAKES disc, servo.

ELECTRICAL EQUIPMENT 4 headlamps.

DIMENSIONS AND WEIGHT dry weight: 1,742 lb, 790 kg.

SUZUKI JAPAN

Fronte Standard Sedan

PRICE EX WORKS: 329,000 yen.

ENGINE rear, transverse, 2 stroke; 3 cylinders, in line; 21.7 cu in, 356 cc (2.05 x 2.20 in, 52 x 56 mm); compression ratio: 6.8:1; max power (DIN): 31 hp at 6,000 rpm; max torque (DIN): 27 lb ft, 3.7 kg m at 5,000 rpm; max engine rpm: 7,000; 87 hp/l; cast iron cylinder block, light alloy head; 6 crankshaft bearings on ball bearings; lubrication: mechanical pump, injection to cylinders and crankshaft bearings, total loss system, 7 imp pt, 8.5 US pt, 4 l; 3 Mikuni-Villiers VM 22 semi-horizontal carburettors; fuel feed: mechanical pump; air-cooled.

TRANSMISSION driving wheels: rear; clutch: single dry plate (diaphragm); gearbox: mechanical; engine-gearbox ratio: 1.471; gears: 4, fully synchronized; ratios: I 3.182; II 1.875, III 1.238, IV 0.880, rev 2.727; lever: central; final drive: helical spur gears; axle ratio: 4.385; width of rims: 3.5"; tyres: 5.20 x 10.

PERFORMANCE max speeds: (I) 19 mph, 30 km/h; (II) 33 mph, 53 km/h; (III) 50 mph, 80 km/h; (IV) 71 mph, 115 km/h; power-weight ratio: 32.6 lb/hp, 14.8 kg/hp; carrying capacity: 706 lb, 320 kg; acceleration: standing ¼ mile 21.5 sec; fuel consumption: not declared.

CHASSIS integral; front suspension: independent, wishbones, coil springs, anti-roll bar, telescopic dampers; rear suspension: independent, semi-trailing arms, coil springs, telescopic dampers.

STEERING rack-and-pinion; turns lock to lock: 2.75.

BRAKES drum, single circuit; swept area: front 31.6 sq in, 204 sq cm, rear 31.6 sq in, 204 sq cm, total 63.2 sq in, 408 sq cm.

ELECTRICAL EQUIPMENT 12 V; 24 Ah battery; 300 W dynamo; Nihon Denso distributor; 2 headlamps.

DIMENSIONS AND WEIGHT wheel base: 79.13 in, 2,010 mm; tracks: 43.70 in, 1,110 mm front, 42.72 in, 1,085 mm rear; length: 117.91 in, 2,995 mm; width: 50.98 in, 1,295 mm; height: 50.98 in, 1,295 mm; ground clearance: 7.68 in, 195 mm; dry weight: 1,014 lb, 460 kg; turning circle (between walls): 25.6 ft, 7.8 m; fuel tank: 5.9 imp gal, 7.1 US gal, 27 l.

BODY saloon/sedan; 2 doors; 4 seats, separate front seats.

PRACTICAL INSTRUCTIONS fuel: 85-90 oct mixture; engine sump oil: 7 imp pt, 8.5 US pt, 4 l, oil in separate tank; gearbox and final drive oil: 1.8 imp pt, 2.1 US pt, 1 l, SAE 90, change every 6 months; greasing: none; tyre pressure: front 14 psi, 1 atm, rear 24 psi, 1.7 atm.

OPTIONAL ACCESSORIES automatic clutch.

Fronte GU-W Sedan

See Fronte Standard Sedan, except for:

PRICE EX WORKS: 351,000 yen.

ENGINE compression ratio: 7.8:1; max torque (DIN): 29 lb ft, 4 kg m at 4,500 rpm; water-cooled.

PERFORMANCE power-weight ratio: 33.7 lb/hp, 15.3 kg/hp; acceleration: standing ¼ mile 21.6 sec.

DIMENSIONS AND WEIGHT dry weight: 1,047 lb, 475 kg.

OPTIONAL ACCESSORIES automatic clutch not available.

Fronte GAF Coupé

See Fronte Standard Sedan, except for:

PRICE EX WORKS: 399,000 yen.

ENGINE compression ratio: 7.8:1; max torque (DIN): 29 lb ft, 4 kg m at 4,500 rpm; water-cooled.

PERFORMANCE power-weight ratio: 34.1 lb/hp, 15.5 kg/hp.

SUZUKI Fronte GT-W II Sedan

SUZUKI Fronte Station Wagon

SUZUKI Jimny Steel Body

DIMENSIONS AND WEIGHT tracks: 44.09 in, 1,120 mm front, 43.31 in, 1,100 mm rear; height: 47.24 in, 1,200 mm; dry weight: 1,058 lb, 480 kg.

BODY coupé; 2 seats.

Fronte GC-W Sedan

See Fronte Standard Sedan, except for:

PRICE EX WORKS: 431,000 yen.

ENGINE max power (DIN): 34 hp at 6,000 rpm; max torque (DIN): 30 lb ft, 4.2 kg m at 4,500 rpm; 95.5 hp/l; water-cooled.

PERFORMANCE power-weight ratio: 29.8 lb/hp, 13.5 kg/hp; acceleration: standing ¼ mile 20.2 sec.

OPTIONAL ACCESSORIES automatic clutch not available.

Fronte GXPF Coupé

See Fronte GC-W Sedan, except for:

PRICE EX WORKS: 455,000 yen.

PERFORMANCE power-weight ratio: 31.1 lb/hp, 14.1 kg/hp.

DIMENSIONS AND WEIGHT tracks: 44.09 in, 1,120 mm front, 43.31 in, 1,100 mm rear; height: 47.24 in, 1,200 mm; dry weight: 1,058 lb, 480 kg.

BODY coupé; 2 seats.

Fronte GT-W II Sedan

See Fronte Standard Sedan, except for:

PRICE EX WORKS: 446,000 yen.

ENGINE compression ratio: 7.2:1; max power (DIN): 37 hp at 6,500 rpm; max torque (DIN): 30 lb ft, 4.2 kg m at 4,500 rpm; 103.9 hp/l; 3 Mikuni-Villiers VM 24 horizontal carburettors; water-cooled.

PERFORMANCE max speed: 75 mph, 120 km/h; power-weight ratio: 29.5 lb/hp, 13.4 kg/hp; acceleration: standing ¼ mile 19.7 sec.

BRAKES front disc.

DIMENSIONS AND WEIGHT tracks: 44.09 in, 1,120 mm front, 43.31 in, 1,100 mm rear; dry weight: 1,091 lb, 495 kg.

OPTIONAL ACCESSORIES automatic clutch not available.

Fronte GXCF Coupé

See Fronte GT-W II Sedan, except for:

PRICE EX WORKS: 475,000 yen.

PERFORMANCE power-weight ratio: 28.7 lb/hp, 13 kg/hp.

DIMENSIONS AND WEIGHT height: 47.24 in, 1,200 mm; dry weight: 1,058 lb, 480 kg.

BODY coupé; 2 + 2 seats.

Fronte Station Wagon

See Fronte Standard Sedan, except for:

PRICE EX WORKS: 338,000 yen.

ENGINE front, 2 stroke; 2 cylinders, in line; 21.9 cu in, 359 cc (2.40 x 2.42 in, 61 x 61.5 mm); compression ratio: 7:1; max power (DIN): 28 hp at 5,500 rpm; max torque (DIN): 28 lb ft, 3.8 kg m at 5,000 rpm; 78 hp/l; 3 crankshaft bearings; lubricating system capacity: 6.2 imp pt, 7.4 US pt, 3.5 l; 1 Solex downdraught carburettor; water-cooled.

TRANSMISSION gearbox ratios: I 3.683, II 2.218, III 1.418, IV 1, rev 3.683; final drive: hypoid bevel; axle ratio: 5.667; tyres: 4.50 x 10.

PERFORMANCE max speeds: (I) 19 mph, 30 km/h; (II) 30 mph, 48 km/h; (III) 48 mph, 77 km/h; (IV) 68 mph, 110 km/h; power-weight ratio: 39.8 lb/hp, 18 kg/hp; carrying capacity: 662 lb, 300 kg.

CHASSIS front suspension: independent, by McPherson, coil springs/telescopic damper struts, anti-roll bar, lower wishbones; rear suspension: rigid axle, semi-elliptic leafsprings, telescopic dampers.

STEERING recirculating ball.

ELECTRICAL EQUIPMENT 250 W dynamo.

DIMENSIONS AND WEIGHT wheel base: 78.54 in, 1,995 mm; tracks: 44.09 in, 1,120 mm front, 42.52 in, 1,080 mm rear; height: 54.33 in, 1,380 mm; ground clearance: 5.51 in, 140 mm; dry weight: 1,114 lb, 505 kg; fuel tank: 5.5 imp gal, 6.6 US gal, 25 l.

BODY estate car/station wagon; 2 + 1 doors.

PRACTICAL INSTRUCTIONS engine sump oil: 6.2 imp pt, 7.4 US pt, 3.5 l, oil in separate tank; gearbox oil: 1.8 imp pt, 2.1 US pt, 1 l, SAE 90, change every 6 months; final drive oil: 1.4 imp pt, 1.7 US pt, 0.8 l, SAE 90, change every 6 months; tyre pressure: front 20 psi, 1.4 atm, rear 24 psi, 1.7 atm.

OPTIONAL ACCESSORIES automatic clutch not available.

SUZUKI Fronte GXCF Coupé

SUZUKI Fronte Station Wagon

SUZUKI Jimny

Jimny

PRICE EX WORKS: 489,000 yen.

ENGINE front, 2 stroke; 2 cylinders, in line; 21.9 cu in, 359 cc (2.40 x 2.42 in, 61 x 61.5 mm); compression ratio: 7:1; max power (DIN): 28 hp at 5,500 rpm; max torque (DIN): 28 lb ft, 3.8 kg m at 5,000 rpm; 78 hp/l; cast iron cylinder block, light alloy head; 3 crankshaft bearings, on ball bearings; lubrication: mechanical pump, injection to cylinders and crankshaft bearings, total loss system; 4.9 imp pt, 5.9 US pt, 2.8 l; 1 Solex downdraught carburettor; fuel feed: mechanical pump; water-cooled.

TRANSMISSION driving wheels: front and rear; clutch: single dry plate gearbox: mechanical; gears: 4, fully synchronized and 2-ratio transfer box; ratios: I 3.967, II 2.388, III 1.527, IV 1, rev 3.967; transfer box ratios: I 1.714, II 3.012; levers: central; final drive: hypoid bevel; axle ratio: 5.667; width of rims: 4.5"; tyres: 6.00 x 16.

PERFORMANCE max speeds: (I) 16 mph, 25 km/h; (II) 25 mph, 40 km/h; (III) 42 mph, 67 km/h; (IV) 58 mph, 93 km/h; power-weight ratio: 49.2 lb/hp, 22.3 kg/hp; carrying capacity: 551 lb, 250 kg; fuel consumption: not declared.

CHASSIS box-type ladder frame; front suspension: rigid axle, semi-elliptic leafsprings, telescopic dampers; rear suspension: rigid axle, semi-elliptic leafsprings, telescopic dampers.

STEERING recirculating ball; turns lock to lock: 3.20.

BRAKES drum; swept area: front 42.2 sq in, 272 sq cm, rear 42.2 sq in, 272 sq cm, total 84.4 sq in, 544 sq cm.

ELECTRICAL EQUIPMENT 12 V; 24 Ah battery; 175 W dynamo; Nihon Denso distributor; 2 headlamps.

DIMENSIONS AND WEIGHT wheel base: 75.98 in, 1,930 mm; tracks: 42.91 in, 1,090 mm front, 43.31 in, 1,100 mm rear; length: 117.91 in, 2,995 mm; width: 50.98 in, 1,295 mm; height: 65.75 in, 1,670 mm; ground clearance: 9.06 in, 230 mm; dry weight: 1,378 lb, 625 kg; turning circle (between walls): 28.9 ft, 8.8 m; fuel tank: 5.7 imp gal, 6.9 US gal, 26 l.

BODY open; no doors; 3 seats, separate front seats.

PRACTICAL INSTRUCTIONS fuel: 85-90 oct mixture; engine sump oil: 4.9 imp pt, 5.9 US pt, 2.8 l, oil in separate tank; gearbox oil: 1.4 imp pt, 1.7 US pt, 0.8 l, SAE 90, change every 6 months; transfer box oil: 1.2 imp pt, 1.5 US pt, 0.7 l, SAE 90, change every 6 months; final drive oil: 1.4 imp pt, 1.7 US pt, 0.8 l, SAE 90, change every 6 months; tyre pressure: front 16 psi, 1.1 atm, rear 16 psi, 1.1 atm.

Jimny Steel Body

See Jimny, except for:

PRICE EX WORKS: 554,000 yen.

TRANSMISSION transfer box ratios: I 1.562, II 2.571; tyres: 5.60 x 15.

PERFORMANCE power-weight ratio: 52 lb/hp, 23.6 kg/hp; carrying capacity: 441 lb, 200 kg.

DIMENSIONS AND WEIGHT height: 63.58 in, 1,615 mm; ground clearance: 7.48 in, 190 mm; dry weight: 1,455 lb, 660 kg.

BODY estate car/station wagon; 2 + 1 doors.

TOYOTA JAPAN

Publica 1000 Standard Sedan

PRICE EX WORKS: 405,000 yen.

ENGINE front, 4 stroke; 4 cylinders, in line; 60.6 cu in, 993 cc (2.83 x 2.40 in, 72 x 61 mm); compression ratio: 9:1; max power (DIN): 58 hp at 6,000 rpm; max torque (DIN): 57 lb ft, 7.9 kg m tt 4,000 rpm; max engine rpm: 6,200; 58.4 hp/l; cast iron cylinder block, light alloy head; 5 crankshaft bearings; valves: overhead, push-rods and rockers; camshafts: 1, side; lubrication: rotary pump, full flow filter, 5.8 imp pt, 7 US pt, 3.3 l; 1 Aisan downdraught twin barrel carburettor; fuel feed: mechanical pump; water-cooled, 8.3 imp pt, 9.9 US pt, 4.7 l.

TRANSMISSION driving wheels: rear; clutch: single dry plate (diaphragm); gearbox: mechanical; gears: 4, fully synchronized; ratios: I 3.684, II 2.050, III 1.383, IV 1, rev 4.316; lever: central; final drive: hypoid bevel; axle ratio: 4.222; width of rims: 4"; tyres: 6.00 x 12.

PERFORMANCE max speeds: (I) 24 mph, 38 km/h; (II) 42 mph, 68 km/h; (III) 62 mph, 100 km/h; (IV) 87 mph, 140 km/h; power-weight ratio: 25.3 lb/hp, 11.5 kg/hp; carrying capacity: 882 lb, 400 kg; fuel consumption not declared.

CHASSIS integral; front suspension: independent, by McPherson, coil springs/telescopic damper struts, lower wishbones (trailing links), anti-roll bar; rear suspension: rigid axle, semi-elliptic leafsprings, telescopic dampers.

STEERING recirculating ball; turns lock to lock: 3.10.

BRAKES drum, single circuit; swept area: front 35.7 sq in, 230 sq cm, rear 35.7 sq in, 230 sq cm, total 71.4 sq in, 460 sq cm.

ELECTRICAL EQUIPMENT 12 V; 32 Ah battery; 40 A alternator; Denso dstributor; 2 headlamps.

DIMENSIONS AND WEIGHT wheel base: 85.04 in, 2,160 mm; tracks: 48.62 in, 1,235 mm front, 47.24 in, 1,200 mm rear; length: 145.47 in, 3,695 mm; width: 57.09 in, 1,450 mm; height: 54.33 in, 1,380 mm; ground clearance: 6.69 in, 170 mm; dry weight: 1,466 lb, 665 kg; distribution of weight: 56.4% front, 43.6% rear; turning circle (between walls): 31.5 ft, 9.6 m; fuel tank: 8.8 imp gal, 10.6 US gal, 40 l.

BODY saloon/sedan; 2 doors; 5 seats, separate front seats.

PRACTICAL INSTRUCTIONS fuel: 85-90 oct petrol; engine sump oil: 5.8 imp pt, 7 US pt, 3.3 l, SAE 20W-30, change every 3,100 miles, 5,000 km; gearbox oil: 3 imp pt, 3.6 US pt, 1.7 l, SAE 80, change every 18,600 miles, 30,000 km; final drive oil: 1.1 imp pt, 1.3 US pt, 0.6 l, SAE 90, change every 18,600 miles, 30,000 km; greasing: none; valve timing: 16° 50° 50° 16°; tyre pressure: front 17 psi, 1.2 atm, rear 17 psi, 1.2 atm.

OPTIONAL ACCESSORIES automatic transmission with 2 ratios.

Publica 1000 Sedan (Export)

See Publica 1000 Standard Sedan.

Publica 1000 Station Wagon

See Publica 1000 Standard Sedan, except for:

TRANSMISSION tyres: 5.00 x 12.

BODY estate car/station wagon; 2 + 1 doors.

Publica 1000 Hi-De Luxe Sedan

See Publica 1000 Standard Sedan, except for:

PRICE EX WORKS: 455,000 yen.

PERFORMANCE power-weight ratio: 26 lb/hp, 12 kg/hp.

BRAKES front disc, rear drum; swept area: front 16.7 sq in, 108 sq cm, rear 35.7 sq in, 230 sq cm, total 52.4 sq in, 338 sq cm.

DIMENSIONS AND WEIGHT dry weight: 1,510 lb, 685 kg.

TOYOTA Publica 1000 Hi-De Luxe Sedan

TOYOTA Publica 1200 ST Sedan

TOYOTA Corolla 1200 Series

Publica 1200 XL Sedan

See Publica 1000 Hi-De Luxe Sedan, except for:

PRICE EX WORKS: 510,000 yen.

ENGINE 71.1 cu in, 1,166 cc (2.87 x 2.60 in, 75 x 66 mm); max power (DIN): 68 hp at 6,000 rpm; max torque (DIN): 69 lb ft, 9.5 kg m at 3,800 rpm; 58.3 hp/l.

PERFORMANCE max speeds: (I) 25 mph, 40 km/h; (II) 43 mph, 70 km/h; (III) 65 mph, 104 km/h; (IV) 93 mph, 150 km/h; power-weight ratio: 22.4 lb/hp, 10.1 kg/hp; acceleration: standing ¼ mile 18.5 sec; fuel consumption: not declared.

DIMENSIONS AND WEIGHT dry weight: 1,521 lb, 690 kg.

OPTIONAL ACCESSORIES automatic transmission not available.

Publica 1200 ST Sedan

See Publica 1200 XL Sedan, except for:

PRICE EX WORKS: 530,000 yen.

ENGINE compression ratio: 10:1; max power (DIN) 77 hp at 6,600 rpm; max torque (DIN): 70 lb ft, 9.6 kg m at 4,600 rpm; max engine rpm: 6,800; 66 hp/l; 2 Aisan downdraught twin barrel carburettors.

TRANSMISSION tyres: 155 SR x 12.

PERFORMANCE max speed: 99 mph, 160 km/h; power-weight ratio: 20.2 lb/hp, 9.1 kg/hp; acceleration: standing ¼ mile 17.4 sec; fuel consumption: not declared.

BRAKES dual circuit.

DIMENSIONS AND WEIGHT height: 54.13 in, 1,375 mm; dry weight: 1,555 lb, 705 kg.

Corolla 1200 Standard 2-door Sedan

PRICE EX WORKS: 438,500 yen.

ENGINE front, 4 stroke; 4 cylinders, in line; 71.1 cu in, 1,166 cc (2.95 x 2.60 in, 75 x 76 mm); compression ratio: 9:1; max power (DIN): 68 hp at 6,000 rpm; max torque (DIN): 65 lb ft, 9.5 kg m at 3,800 rpm; max engine rpm: 6,300; 58.3 hp/l; cast iron cylinder block, light alloy head; 5 crankshaft bearings; valves: overhead, push-rods and rockers; camshafts: 1, side; lubrication: rotary pump, full flow filter, 6.2 imp pt, 7.4 US pt, 3.5 l; 1 Aisan 3K downdraught twin barrel carburettor; fuel feed: mechanical pump; water-cooled, 8.4 imp pt, 10.1 US pt, 4.8 l.

TRANSMISSION driving wheels: rear; clutch: single dry plate (diaphragm); gearbox: mechanical; gears: 4, fully synchronized; ratios: I 3.684, II 2.050, III 1.383, IV 1, rev 4.316; lever: central; final drive: hypoid bevel; axle ratio: 4.222; width of rims: 4"; tyres: 6.00 x 12.

PERFORMANCE max speeds: (I) 25 mph, 40 km/h; (II) 45 mph, 72 km/h; (III) 66 mph, 107 km/h; (IV) 90 mph, 145 km/h; power-weight ratio: 23.7 lb/hp, 10.7 kg/hp; carrying capacity: 882 lb, 400 kg; acceleration: standing ¼ mile 18.5 sec; fuel consumption: not declared.

CHASSIS integral; front suspension: independent, by McPherson, coil springs/telescopic damper struts, lower wishbones (trailing links), anti-roll bar; rear suspension: rigid axle, semi-elliptic leafsprings, telescopic dampers.

STEERING recirculating ball; turns lock to lock: 3.30.

BRAKES drum; swept area: front 47.1 sq in, 304 sq cm, rear 41.6 sq in, 268 sq cm, total 88.7 sq in, 572 sq cm.

ELECTRICAL EQUIPMENT 12 V; 32 Ah battery; 30 A alternator; Nihon Denso distributor; 2 headlamps.

DIMENSIONS AND WEIGHT wheel base: 91.93 in, 2,335 mm; tracks: 49.41 in, 1,255 mm front, 49.02 in, 1,245 mm rear; length: 155.71 in, 3,955 mm; width: 59.25 in, 1,505 mm; height: 54.13 in, 1,375 mm; ground clearance: 6.69 in, 170 mm; dry weight: 1,610 lb, 730 kg; distribution of weight: 54.5% front, 45.5% rear; turning circle (between walls): 32.1 ft, 9.8 m; fuel tank: 9.5 imp gal, 11.4 US gal, 43 l.

BODY saloon/sedan; 2 doors; 5 seats, separate front seats.

PRACTICAL INSTRUCTIONS fuel: 90 oct petrol; engine sump oil: 6.2 imp pt, 7.4 US pt, 3.5 l, SAE 20W-30, change every 3,100 miles, 5,000 km; gearbox oil: 1.8 imp pt, 2.1 US pt, 1 l, SAE 90, change every 18,600 miles, 30,000 km; final drive oil: 1.4 imp pt, 1.7 US pt, 0.8 l, SAE 90, change every 18,600 miles, 30,000 km; greasing: none; tappet clear-

TOYOTA Publica 1000 Hi-De Luxe Sedan

TOYOTA Publica 1200 ST Sedan

TOYOTA Corolla 1200 De Luxe 2-door Sedan

ances: inlet 0.003 in, 0.08 mm, exhaust 0.007 in, 0.18 mm; valve timing: 16° 50° 50° 16°; tyre pressure: front 20 psi, 1.4 atm, rear 20 psi, 1.4 atm.

Corolla 1200 Standard 4-door Sedan

See Corolla 1200 Standard 2-door Sedan, except for:

PRICE EX WORKS: 463,500 yen.

PERFORMANCE power-weight ratio: 24.3 lb/hp, 11 kg/hp.

DIMENSIONS AND WEIGHT dry weight: 1,654 lb, 750 kg.

BODY 4 doors.

Corolla 1200 De Luxe 2-door Sedan

See Corolla 1200 Standard 2-door Sedan, except for:

PRICE IN GB: £ 935.
PRICE IN USA: $ 2,056.

PERFORMANCE power-weight ratio: 24.3 lb/hp, 11 kg/hp.

DIMENSIONS AND WEIGHT dry weight: 1,654 lb, 750 kg.

OPTIONAL ACCESSORIES Toyoglide automatic transmission with 2 ratios (I 1.820, II 1, rev 1.820), max speed 87 mph, 140 km/h.

Corolla 1200 De Luxe 4-door Sedan

See Corolla 1200 De Luxe 2-door Sedan, except for:

PRICE EX WORKS: 526,500 yen.

PERFORMANCE power-weight ratio 25.4 lb/hp, 11.5 kg/hp.

DIMENSIONS AND WEIGHT dry weight: 1.731 lb, 785 kg.

BODY 4 doors.

Sprinter 1200 De Luxe 4-door Sedan

See Corolla 1200 De Luxe 2-door Sedan, except for:

PRICE EX WORKS: 542,000 yen.

PERFORMANCE power-weight ratio: 25.4 lb/hp, 11.5 kg/hp.

DIMENSIONS AND WEIGHT length: 157.28 in, 3,995 mm; dry weight: 1,720 lb, 780 kg.

BODY 4 doors.

Corolla 1200 De Luxe Coupé

See Corolla 1200 De Luxe 2-door Sedan, except for:

PRICE EX WORKS: 537,000 yen.

PERFORMANCE power-weight ratio: 24.2 lb/hp, 10.9 kg/hp.

DIMENSIONS AND WEIGHT height: 52.95 in, 1,345 mm; dry weight: 1,643 lb, 745 kg.

BODY coupé.

Sprinter 1200 De Luxe Coupé

See Corolla 1200 De Luxe Coupé, except for:

PRICE EX WORKS: 545,000 yen.

PERFORMANCE power-weight ratio: 24.5 lb/hp, 11.1 kg/hp.

DIMENSIONS AND WEIGHT length: 156.30 in, 3,970 mm; dry weight: 1,665 lb, 755 kg.

Corolla 1200 Hi-De Luxe 2-door Sedan

See Corolla 1200 De Luxe 2-door Sedan, except for:

PRICE EX WORKS: 530,000 yen.

PERFORMANCE power-weight ratio: 24.6 lb/hp, 11.2 kg/hp.

BRAKES front disc, rear drum; swept area: front 18.6 sq in,

COROLLA 1200 HI-DE LUXE 2-DOOR SEDAN

120 sq cm, rear 41.6 sq in, 268 sq cm, total 60.2 sq in, 388 sq cm.

DIMENSIONS AND WEIGHT dry weight: 1,676 lb, 760 kg.

Corolla 1200 Hi-De Luxe 4-door Sedan

See Corolla 1200 Hi-De Luxe 2-door Sedan, except for:

PRICE EX WORKS: 555,000 yen.

PERFORMANCE power-weight ratio: 25.8 lb/hp, 11.7 kg/hp.

DIMENSIONS AND WEIGHT dry weight: 1,753 lb, 795 kg.

BODY 4 doors.

Sprinter 1200 Hi-De Luxe 4-door Sedan

See Corolla 1200 Hi-De Luxe 2-door Sedan, except for:

PRICE EX WORKS: 570,000 yen.

PERFORMANCE power-weight ratio: 23.8 lb/hp, 10.8 kg/hp.

DIMENSIONS AND WEIGHT length: 157.28, in, 3,995 mm; dry weight: 1,742 lb, 790 kg.

BODY 4 doors.

Corolla 1200 Hi-De Luxe Coupé

See Corolla 1200 Hi-De Luxe 2-door Sedan, except for:

PRICE EX WORKS: 565,000 yen.

PERFORMANCE power-weight ratio: 24.4 lb/hp, 11.1 kg/hp.

DIMENSIONS AND WEIGHT height: 52.95 in, 1,345 mm; dry weight: 1,665 lb, 755 kg.

BODY coupé.

Sprinter 1200 Hi-De Luxe Coupé

See Corolla 1200 Hi-De Luxe Coupé, except for:

PERFORMANCE power-weight ratio: 24.8 lb/hp, 11.2 kg/hp.

DIMENSIONS AND WEIGHT length: 156.30 in, 3,970 mm; height: 52.95 in, 1,345 mm; dry weight: 1,687 lb, 765 kg.

Corolla 1200 SL 2-door Sedan

See Corolla 1200 Standard 2-door Sedan, except for:

PRICE EX WORKS: 564,000 yen.

ENGINE compression ratio: 10:1; max power (DIN): 77 hp at 6,600 rpm; max torque (DIN): 70 lb ft, 9.6 kg m at 4,600 rpm; 66 hp/l; 2 Aisan downdraught twin barrel carburettors.

PERFORMANCE max speed: 99 mph, 160 km/h; power-weight ratio: 21.9 lb/hp, 9.9 kg/hp.

BRAKES front disc, rear drum; swept area: front 18.6 sq in, 120 sq cm, rear 41.6 sq in, 268 sq cm, total 60.2 sq in, 388 sq cm.

DIMENSIONS AND WEIGHT dry weight: 1,687 lb, 765 kg.

Corolla 1200 SL 4-door Sedan

See Corolla 1200 SL 2-door Sedan, except for:

PRICE EX WORKS: 589,000 yen.

PERFORMANCE power-weight ratio: 22.5 lb/hp, 10.2 kg/hp.

DIMENSIONS AND WEIGHT dry weight: 1,731 lb, 785 kg.

BODY 4 doors.

TOYOTA Corolla 1200 Hi-De Luxe 4-door Sedan

TOYOTA Corolla 1200 SL Coupé

TOYOTA Sprinter 1400 SL Coupé

Sprinter 1200 SL 4-door Sedan

See Corolla 1200 SL 2-door Sedan, except for:

PRICE EX WORKS: 609,000 yen.

PERFORMANCE power-weight ratio: 22.8 lb/hp, 10.3 kg/hp.

DIMENSIONS AND WEIGHT length: 157.28 in, 3,995 mm; dry weight: 1,753 lb, 795 kg.

BODY 4 doors.

Corolla 1200 SL Coupé

See Corolla 1200 SL 2-door Sedan, except for:

PRICE IN GB: £ 1,040.
PRICE EX WORKS: 599,000 yen.

PERFORMANCE power-weight ratio: 29.8 lb/hp, 9.8 kg/hp.

DIMENSIONS AND WEIGHT height: 52.95 in, 1,345 mm; dry weight: 1,676 lb, 760 kg.

BODY coupé.

Sprinter 1200 SL Coupé

See Corolla 1200 SL Coupé, except for:

PRICE IN GB: £ 900.

PERFORMANCE power-weight ratio: 22 lb/hp, 10 kg/hp.

DIMENSIONS AND WEIGHT length: 156.30 in, 3,970 mm; dry weight: 1,698 lb, 770 kg.

Corolla 1400 De Luxe 2-door Sedan

See Corolla 1200 De Luxe 2-door Sedan, except for:

PRICE EX WORKS: 542,000 yen.

ENGINE 85.9 cu in, 1,407 cc (3.15 x 2.76 in, 80 x 70 mm); compression ratio: 8.5:1; max power (DIN): 86 hp at 6,000 rpm; max torque (DIN): 85 lb ft, 11.7 kg m at 3,800 rpm; 61.1 hp/l.

TRANSMISSION gearbox ratios: I 3.587, II 2.022, III 1.384, IV 1, rev 3.484; axle ratio: 4.100; tyres: 6.15 x 13.

PERFORMANCE max speeds: (I) 27 mph, 43 km/h; (II) 47 mph, 76 km/h; (III) 68 mph, 110 km/h; (IV) 99 mph, 160 km/h; power-weight ratio: 21.3 lb/hp, 9.6 kg/hp; fuel consumption: not declared.

BRAKES swept area: front 60.8 sq in, 392 sq cm, rear 54 sq in, 348 sq cm, total 114.8 sq in, 740 sq cm.

ELECTRICAL EQUIPMENT 35 Ah battery; 40 A alternator.

DIMENSIONS AND WEIGHT front track: 49.61 in, 1,260 mm; dry weight: 1,830 lb, 830 kg; distribution of weight: 57.2% front, 42.8% rear.

PRACTICAL INSTRUCTIONS tappet clearances: inlet 0.007 in, 0.18 mm, exhaust 0.013 in, 0.33 mm; valve timing: 16° 54° 58° 12°.

VARIATIONS

ENGINE (export to USA only) 96.9 cu in, 1,588 cc (3.35 x 2.76 in, 85 x 70 mm), max power (DIN) 100 hp at 6,000 rpm, max torque (DIN) 99 lb ft, 13.7 kg m at 3,800 rpm, 63 hp/l.
PERFORMANCE max speed 106 mph, 170 km/h, power-weight ratio 18.3 lb/hp, 8.3 kg/hp.

Corolla 1400 De Luxe 4-door Sedan

See Corolla 1400 De Luxe 2-door Sedan, except for:

PRICE EX WORKS: 567,000 yen.

PERFORMANCE power-weight ratio: 21.8 lb/hp, 9.9 kg/hp.

DIMENSIONS AND WEIGHT dry weight: 1,874 lb, 850 kg.

BODY 4 doors.

Sprinter 1400 De Luxe 4-door Sedan

See Corolla 1400 De Luxe 2-door Sedan, except for:

PRICE EX WORKS: 582,000 yen.

PERFORMANCE power-weight ratio: 22 lb/hp, 10 kg/hp.

TOYOTA Corolla 1200 Hi-De Luxe 4-door Sedan

TOYOTA Corolla 1200 SL Series

TOYOTA Sprinter 1400 SL Coupé

DIMENSIONS AND WEIGHT length: 157.28 in, 3,995 mm; dry weight: 1,896 lb, 860 kg.

BODY 4 doors.

Corolla 1400 De Luxe Coupé

See Corolla 1400 De Luxe 2-door Sedan, except for:

PRICE EX WORKS: 572,000 yen.

PERFORMANCE power-weight ratio: 21.1 lb/hp, 9.6 kg/hp.

DIMENSIONS AND WEIGHT length: 158.07 in, 4,015 mm; height: 52.95 in, 1,345 mm; dry weight: 1,819 lb, 825 kg.

BODY coupé.

Sprinter 1400 De Luxe Coupé

See Corolla 1400 De Luxe Coupé.

Corolla 1400 Hi-De Luxe 2-door Sedan

See Corolla 1400 De Luxe 2-door Sedan, except for:

PRICE EX WORKS: 575,000 yen.

PERFORMANCE power-weight ratio: 21.4 lb/hp, 9.7 kg/hp.

BRAKES front disc, rear drum; swept area: front 24.2 sq in, 156 sq cm, rear 54 sq in, 348 sq cm, total 78.2 sq in, 504 sq cm.

DIMENSIONS AND WEIGHT dry weight: 1,841 lb, 835 kg.

Corolla 1400 Hi-De Luxe 4-door Sedan

See Corolla 1400 Hi-De Luxe 2-door Sedan, except for:

PRICE EX WORKS: 595,000 yen.

PERFORMANCE power-weight ratio: 21.9 lb/hp, 9.9 kg/hp.

DIMENSIONS AND WEIGHT dry weight: 1,885 lb, 855 kg.

BODY 4 doors.

Sprinter 1400 Hi-De Luxe 4-door Sedan

See Corolla 1400 Hi-De Luxe 2-door Sedan, except for:

PRICE EX WORKS: 615,000 yen.

PERFORMANCE power-weight ratio: 22.1 lb/hp, 10 kg/hp.

DIMENSIONS AND WEIGHT length: 157.28 in, 3,995 mm; dry weight: 1,907 lb, 865 kg.

BODY 4 doors.

Corolla 1400 Hi-De Luxe Coupé

See Corolla 1400 Hi-De Luxe 2-door Sedan, except for:

PRICE EX WORKS: 605,000 yen.

PERFORMANCE power-weight ratio: 21.2 lb/hp, 9.6 kg/hp.

DIMENSIONS AND WEIGHT length: 158.07 in, 4,015 mm; height: 52.95 in, 1,345 mm; dry weight: 1,830 lb, 830 kg.

BODY coupé.

Sprinter 1400 Hi-De Luxe Coupé

See Corolla 1400 Hi-De Luxe Coupé.

Corolla 1400 SL 2-door Sedan

See Corolla 1400 De Luxe 2-door Sedan, except for:

PRICE EX WORKS: 619,000 yen.

ENGINE compression ratio: 9.6:1; max power (DIN): 95 hp at 6,000 rpm; max torque (DIN): 89 lb ft, 12.3 kg m at

COROLLA 1400 SL 2-DOOR SEDAN

4,000 rpm; 68.2 hp/l; 2 Aisan downdraught twin barrel carburettors.

PERFORMANCE power-weight ratio: 19.5 lb/hp, 8.8 kg/hp; acceleration: standing ¼ mile 17.3 sec.

BRAKES front disc, rear drum; swept area: front 24.2 sq in, 156 sq cm, rear 54 sq in, 348 sq cm, total 78.2 sq in, 504 sq cm.

DIMENSIONS AND WEIGHT dry weight: 1,852 lb, 840 kg.

OPTIONAL ACCESSORIES 5-speed fully synchronized mechanical gearbox (I 3.587, II 2.022, III 1.384, IV 1, V 0.861, rev 3.484), 4.300 axle ratio, max speed 103 mph, 165 km/h.

Corolla 1400 SL 4-door Sedan

See Corolla 1400 SL 2-door Sedan, except for:

PRICE EX WORKS: 639,000 yen.

PERFORMANCE power-weight ratio: 20 lb/hp, 9 kg/hp.

DIMENSIONS AND WEIGHT dry weight: 1,896 lb, 860 kg.

BODY 4 doors.

Sprinter 1400 SL 4-door Sedan

See Corolla 1400 SL 2-door Sedan, except for:

PRICE EX WORKS: 659,000 yen.

PERFORMANCE power-weight ratio: 20.2 lb/hp, 9.2 kg/hp.

DIMENSIONS AND WEIGHT length: 157.28 in, 3,995 mm; dry weight: 1,918 lb, 870 kg.

BODY 4 doors.

Corolla 1400 SL Coupé

See Corolla 1400 SL 2-door Sedan, except for:

PRICE EX WORKS: 649,000 yen.

PERFORMANCE power-weight ratio: 19.2 lb/hp, 8.8 kg/hp.

DIMENSIONS AND WEIGHT length: 158.07 in, 4,015 mm; height: 52.95 in, 1,345 mm; dry weight: 1,841 lb, 835 kg.

BODY coupé.

OPTIONAL ACCESSORIES with 5-speed mechanical gearbox max speed 106 mph, 170 km/h.

Sprinter 1400 SL Coupé

See Corolla 1400 SL Coupé.

Corolla 1400 SR Coupé

See Corolla 1400 SL Coupé, except for:

PRICE EX WORKS: 661,000 yen.

TRANSMISSION gears: 5, fully synchronized; ratios: I 3.587, II 2.022, III 1.384, IV 1, V 0.861, rev 3.484; axle ratio: 4.300; tyres: 155 SR x 13.

PERFORMANCE max speeds: (I) 25 mph, 40 km/h; (II) 43 mph, 70 km/h; (III) 65 mph, 105 km/h; (IV) 90 mph, 145 km/h; (V) 106 mph, 170 km/h.

DIMENSIONS AND WEIGHT height: 52.76 in, 1,340 mm.

Sprinter 1400 SR Coupé

See Corolla 1400 SR Coupé.

Corolla Levin 1600 Coupé

PRICE EX WORKS: 813,000 yen.

ENGINE front, 4 stroke; 4 cylinders, in line; 96.6 cu in, 1,588 cc (3.35 x 2.76 in, 85 x 70 mm); compression ratio: 9.8:1; max power (DIN): 115 hp at 6,400 rpm; max torque (DIN): 105 lb ft, 14.5 kg m at 5,200 rpm; max engine rpm: 6,800; 72.4 hp/l; cast iron cylinder block, light alloy head; 5 crankshaft bearings; valves: overhead, thimble tappets; camshafts: 2, overhead; lubrication: rotary pump, full flow filter, 6.7 imp pt, 8 US pt, 3.8 l; 2 Mikuni Solex 40 PHH horizontal twin barrel carburettors; fuel feed: mechanical pump; water-cooled, 13 imp pt, 15.6 US pt, 7.4 l.

TOYOTA Corolla Levin 1600 Coupé

TOYOTA Carina 1600 Super De Luxe

TOYOTA Carina 1600 ST Hardtop

TRANSMISSION driving wheels: rear; clutch: single dry plate (diaphragm); gearbox: mechanical; gears: 5, fully synchronized; ratios: I 3.587, II 2.022, III 1.384, IV 1, V 0.861, rev 3.484; lever: central; final drive: hypoid bevel; axle ratio: 4.300; width of rims: 5''; tyres: 175/70 HR x 13.

PERFORMANCE max speeds: (I) 29 mph, 47 km/h; (II) 51 mph, 82 km/h; (III) 73 mph, 118 km/h; (IV) 99 mph, 160 km/h; (V) 118 mph, 190 km/h; power-weight ratio: 16.4 lb/hp, 7.4 kg/hp; carrying capacity: 882 lb, 400 kg; acceleration: standing ¼ mile 16.3 sec; fuel consumption: not declared.

CHASSIS integral; front suspension: independent, by McPherson, coil springs/telescopic damper struts, lower wishbones (trailing links), anti-roll bar; rear suspension: rigid axle, semi-elliptic leafsprings, telescopic dampers.

STEERING recirculating ball; turns lock to lock: 2.80.

BRAKES front disc, rear drum; swept area: front 24.2 sq in, 156 sq cm, rear 54 sq in, 348 sq cm, total 78.2 sq in, 504 sq cm.

ELECTRICAL EQUIPMENT 12 V; 35 Ah battery; 40 A alternator; Nihon Denso distributor; 2 headlamps.

DIMENSIONS AND WEIGHT wheel base: 91.93 in, 2,335 mm; tracks: 50 in, 1,270 mm front, 50.98 in, 1,295 mm rear; length: 155.71 in, 3.955 mm; width: 62.80 in, 1,595 mm; height: 52.56 in, 1,335 mm; ground clearance: 5.91 in, 150 mm; dry weight: 1,885 lb, 855 kg; distribution of weight: 58.5% front, 41.5% rear; turning circle (between walls): 34.1 ft, 10.4 m; fuel tank: 9.9 imp gal, 11.9 US gal, 45 l.

BODY coupé; 2 doors; 5 seats, separate front seats.

PRACTICAL INSTRUCTIONS fuel: 98-100 oct petrol; engine sump oil: 6.7 imp pt, 8 US pt, 3.8 l, SAE 20W-30, change every 3,100 miles, 5,000 km; tappet clearances: inlet 0.011 in, 0.29 mm, exhaust 0.013 in, 0.34 mm; valve timing: 20° 48° 52° 16°; tyre pressure: front 21 psi, 1.5 atm, rear 21 psi, 1.5 atm.

VARIATIONS

ENGINE 8.8:1 compression ratio, max power (DIN) 110 hp at 6,000 rpm, max torque (DIN) 101 lb ft, 14 kg m at 4,800 rpm, 69.3 hp/l.

PERFORMANCE max speed 115 mph, 185 km/h, power-weight ratio 17.1 lb/hp, 7.8 kg/hp.

OPTIONAL ACCESSORIES limited slip differential; final drive oil cooler; 45 Ah battery.

Sprinter Trueno

See Corolla Levin 1600 Coupé, except for:

DIMENSIONS AND WEIGHT length: 156.10 in, 3,965 mm.

Carina 1400 2-door Sedan

PRICE IN USA: $ 2,362.
PRICE EX WORKS: 519,000 yen.

ENGINE front, 4 stroke; 4 cylinders, in line; 85.9 cu in, 1,407 cc (3.15 x 2.76 in, 80 x 70 mm); compression ratio: 8.5:1; max power (DIN): 86 hp at 6,000 rpm; max torque (DIN): 85 lb ft, 11.7 kg m at 3,800 rpm; max engine rpm: 6,400; 61.1 hp/l; cast iron cylinder block, light alloy head; 5 crankshaft bearings; valves: overhead, push-rods and rockers; camshafts: 1, side; lubrication: rotary pump, full flow filter, 6.5 imp pt, 7.8 US pt, 3.7 l; 1 Aisan downdraught twin barrel carburettor; fuel feed: mechanical pump; water-cooled, 11.4 imp pt, 13.7 US pt, 6.5 l.

TRANSMISSION driving wheels: rear; clutch: single dry plate (diaphragm); gearbox: mechanical; gears: 4, fully synchronized; ratios: I 3.587, II 2.022, III 1.384, IV 1, rev 3.484; lever: central; final drive: hypoid bevel; axle ratio: 4.100; width of rims: 4''; tyres: 5.60 x 13.

PERFORMANCE max speeds: (I) 29 mph, 46 km/h; (II) 48 mph, 78 km/h; (III) 75 mph, 120 km/h; (IV) 99 mph, 160 km/h; power-weight ratio: 22.7 lb/hp, 10.3 kg/hp; carrying capacity: 882 lb, 400 kg; fuel consumption: not declared.

CHASSIS integral; front suspension: independent, by McPherson, coil springs/telescopic damper struts, lower wishbones (trailing links), anti-roll bar; rear suspension: rigid axle, twin trailing radius arms, transverse linkage bar, coil springs, telescopic dampers.

TOYOTA Corolla Levin 1600 Coupé

STEERING recirculating ball; turns lock to lock: 3.50.

BRAKES drum; swept area: front 60.8 sq in, 392 sq cm, rear 54 sq in, 348 sq cm, total 114.8 sq in, 740 sq cm.

ELECTRICAL EQUIPMENT 12 V; 35 Ah battery; 30 A alternator; Nihon Denso distributor; 4 headlamps.

DIMENSIONS AND WEIGHT wheel base: 95.47 in, 2,425 mm; tracks: 50.39 in, 1,280 mm front, 50.59 in, 1,285 mm rear; length: 163.58 in, 4,155 mm; width: 61.81 in, 1,570 mm; height: 54.53 in, 1,385 mm; ground clearance: 6.89 in, 175 mm; dry weight: 1,951 lb, 885 kg; distribution of weight: 57.3% front, 42.7% rear; turning circle (between walls): 34.1 ft, 10.4 m; fuel tank: 11 imp gal, 13.2 US gal, 50 l.

BODY saloon/sedan; 2 doors; 5 seats, separate front seats.

PRACTICAL INSTRUCTIONS fuel: 90 oct petrol; engine sump oil: 6.5 imp pt, 7.8 US pt, 3.7 l, SAE 20W-30, change every 3,100 miles, 5,000 km; gearbox oil: 2.6 imp pt, 3.2 US pt, 1.5 l, SAE 80, change every 18,600 miles, 30,000 km; final drive oil: 1.8 imp pt, 2.1 US pt, 1 l, SAE 90, change every 18,600 miles, 30,000 km; tappet clearances: inlet 0.007 in, 0.18 mm, exhaust 0.013 in, 0.33 mm; valve timing: 16° 54° 58° 12°; tyre pressure: front 20 psi, 1.4 atm, rear 20 psi, 1.4 atm.

OPTIONAL ACCESSORIES 5-speed fully synchronized mechanical gearbox (I 3.587, II 2.022, III 1.384, IV 1, V 0.861, rev 3.484), 4.300 axle ratio, max speed 103 mph, 165 km/h; Toyoglide automatic transmission, hydraulic torque converter with 2 ratios (I 1.820, II 1, rev 1.820), 4.300 axle ratio, max speed 93 mph, 150 km/h.

TOYOTA Carina 1600 Super De Luxe 4-door Sedan

Carina 1400 De Luxe 2-door Sedan

See Carina 1400 2-door Sedan, except for:

PRICE EX WORKS: 589,000 yen.

PERFORMANCE power-weight ratio: 23.2 lb/hp, 10.5 kg/hp.

DIMENSIONS AND WEIGHT dry weight: 1,996 lb, 905 kg.

Carina 1400 De Luxe 4-door Sedan

See Carina 1400 2-door Sedan, except for:

PRICE EX WORKS: 609,000 yen.

PERFORMANCE power-weight ratio: 23.7 lb/hp, 10.8 kg/hp.

DIMENSIONS AND WEIGHT dry weight: 2,040 lb, 925 kg.

BODY 4 doors.

Carina 1400 De Luxe Hardtop

See Carina 1400 2-door Sedan, except for:

PRICE EX WORKS: 642,000 yen.

PERFORMANCE max speed: 103 mph, 165 km/h; power-weight ratio: 21.4 lb/hp, 10.8 kg/hp.

DIMENSIONS AND WEIGHT width: 62.20 in, 1,580 mm; height: 52.76 in, 1,340 mm; ground clearance: 6.89 in, 175 mm; dry weight: 2,051 lb, 930 kg.

BODY hardtop.

TOYOTA Carina 1600 ST Hardtop

Carina 1600 De Luxe 2-door Sedan

See Carina 1400 De Luxe 2-door Sedan, except for:

PRICE EX WORKS: 614,000 yen.

ENGINE 96.6 cu in, 1,588 cc (3.35 x 2.76 in, 85 x 70 mm); max power (DIN): 100 hp at 6,000 rpm; max torque (DIN): 99 lb ft, 13.7 kg m at 3,800 rpm; max engine rpm: 6,400; 63 hp/l.

TRANSMISSION axle ratio: 3.900.

PERFORMANCE max speed: 103 mph, 165 km/h; power-weight ratio: 19.9 lb/hp, 9 kg/hp.

OPTIONAL ACCESSORIES 5-speed fully synchronized mechanical gearbox (I 3.587, II 2.022, III 1.384, IV 1, V 0.861, rev 3.484), 4.111 axle ratio, max speed 106 mph, 170 km/h; Toyoglide automatic transmission, hydraulic torque converter with 3 ratios (I 2.400, II 1.479, III 1, rev 1.920), 4.111 axle ratio, max speed 96 mph, 155 km/h.

Carina 1600 De Luxe 4-door Sedan

See Carina 1600 De Luxe 2-door Sedan, except for:

PRICE IN GB: £ 1,130.
PRICE EX WORKS: 634,000 yen.

PERFORMANCE power-weight ratio: 20.4 lb/hp, 9.2 kg/hp.

DIMENSIONS AND WEIGHT dry weight: 2,040 lb, 925 kg.

BODY 4 doors.

Carina 1600 De Luxe Hardtop

See Carina 1600 De Luxe 2-door Sedan, except for:

PRICE EX WORKS: 682,000 yen.

PERFORMANCE max speed: 106 mph, 170 km/h; power-weight ratio: 20.5 lb/hp, 9.3 kg/hp.

DIMENSIONS AND WEIGHT width: 62.20 in, 1,580 mm; height: 52.76 in, 1,340 mm; dry weight: 2,051 lb, 930 kg.

BODY hardtop.

Carina 1600 Super De Luxe 2-door Sedan

See Carina 1600 De Luxe 2-door Sedan, except for:

PRICE EX WORKS: 650,000 yen.

PERFORMANCE power-weight ratio: 20.2 lb/hp, 9.1 kg/hp.

BRAKES front disc, rear drum, servo; swept area: front 24.2 sq in, 156 sq cm, rear 54 sq in, 348 sq cm, total 78.2 sq in, 504 sq cm.

DIMENSIONS AND WEIGHT dry weight: 2,018 lb, 915 kg.

Carina 1600 Super De Luxe 4-door Sedan

See Carina 1600 Super De Luxe 2-door Sedan, except for:

PRICE EX WORKS: 670,000 yen.

PERFORMANCE power-weight ratio: 20.6 lb/hp, 9.3 kg/hp.

DIMENSIONS AND WEIGHT dry weight: 2,062 lb, 935 kg.

BODY 4 doors.

Carina 1600 Super De Luxe Hardtop

See Carina 1600 Super De Luxe 2-door Sedan, except for:

PRICE EX WORKS: 703,000 yen.

PERFORMANCE max speed: 106 mph, 170 km/h; power-weight ratio: 20.7 lb/hp, 9.4 kg/hp.

DIMENSIONS AND WEIGHT width: 62.20 in, 1,580 mm; height: 52.76 in, 1,340 mm; dry weight: 2,073 lb, 940 kg.

BODY hardtop.

Carina 1600 ST 2-door Sedan

See Carina 1600 Super De Luxe 2-door Sedan, except for:

PRICE EX WORKS: 700,000 yen.

ENGINE compression ratio: 9.4:1; max power (DIN): 105 hp at 6,000 rpm, max torque (DIN): 101 lb ft, 14 kg m at 4,200 rpm; 66.1 hp/l; 2 Aisan downdraught twin barrel carburettors.

TRANSMISSION gears: 5, fully synchronized; ratios: I 3.587, II 2.022, III 1.384, IV 1, V 0.861, rev 3.484; axle ratio: 4.111; width of rims: 4.5"; tyres: 6.45 x 13.

PERFORMANCE max speed: 109 mph, 175 km/h; power-weight ratio: 19.4 lb/hp, 8.8 kg/hp.

DIMENSIONS AND WEIGHT dry weight: 2,040 lb, 925 kg.

PRACTICAL INSTRUCTIONS fuel: 98-100 oct petrol.

VARIATIONS

ENGINE 8.8:1 compression ratio, max power (DIN) 100 hp

TOYOTA Carina 1600 GT 2-door Sedan

TOYOTA Celica 1600 GTV Hardtop

TOYOTA Corona 1600 De Luxe Sedan

at 6,000 rpm, max torque (DIN) 100 lb ft, 13.9 kg m at 4,200 rpm, 63 hp/l.
PERFORMANCE power-weight ratio 20.4 lb/hp, 9.2 kg/hp.
PRACTICAL INSTRUCTIONS 85-90 oct petrol.

Carina 1600 ST 4-door Sedan

See Carina 1600 ST 2-door Sedan, except for:

PRICE EX WORKS: 720,000 yen.

PERFORMANCE power-weight ratio: 19.8 lb/hp, 9 kg/hp.

DIMENSIONS AND WEIGHT dry weight: 2,084 lb, 945 kg.

BODY 4 doors.

Carina 1600 ST Hardtop

See Carina 1600 ST 2-door Sedan, except for:

PRICE EX WORKS: 753,000 yen.

PERFORMANCE max speed: 112 mph, 180 km/h; power-weight ratio: 19.9 lb/hp, 9 kg/hp.

DIMENSIONS AND WEIGHT width: 62.20 in, 1,580 mm; height: 52.76 in, 1,340 mm; dry weight: 2,095 lb, 950 kg.

BODY hardtop.

Carina 1600 SR Hardtop

See Carina 1600 ST Hardtop, except for:

TRANSMISSION tyres: 165 SR x 13.

PERFORMANCE power-weight ratio: 19.9 lb/hp, 9 kg/hp.

DIMENSIONS AND WEIGHT height: 52.36 in, 1,330 mm; dry weight: 2,084 lb, 945 kg.

OPTIONAL ACCESSORIES 185/70 HR x 13 tyres.

Carina 1600 GT 2-door Sedan

See Carina 1600 ST 2-door Sedan, except for:

PRICE EX WORKS: 818,000 yen.

ENGINE compression ratio: 9.8:1; max power (DIN): 115 hp at 6,400 rpm; max torque (DIN): 105 lb ft, 14.5 kg m at 5,200 rpm; max engine rpm: 6,800; 72.4 hp/l; valves: overhead, Vee-slanted, thimble tappets; camshafts: 2, overhead; lubricating system capacity: 6.7 imp pt, 8 US pt, 3.8 l; 2 Mikuni-Solex 2GT 40PHH horizontal twin barrel carburettors; cooling system capacity: 13 imp pt, 15.6 US pt, 7.4 l.

TRANSMISSION tyres: 6.45 H x 13.

PERFORMANCE max speeds: (I) 31 mph, 50 km/h; (II) 56 mph, 90 km/h; (III) 81 mph, 130 km/h; (IV) 111 mph, 178 km/h; (V) 115 mph, 185 km/h; power-weight ratio: 18.4 lb/hp, 8.3 kg/hp.

ELECTRICAL EQUIPMENT 40 A alternator.

DIMENSIONS AND WEIGHT ground clearance: 6.69 in, 170 mm; dry weight: 2,117 lb, 960 kg; distribution of weight: 57.5% front, 42.5% rear.

PRACTICAL INSTRUCTIONS fuel: 98-100 oct petrol; engine sump oil: 6.7 imp pt, 8 US pt, 3.8 l, SAE 20W-30; tappet clearances: inlet 0.010 in, 0.29 mm, exhaust 0.013 in, 0.34 mm; valve timing: 20° 48° 52° 16°; tyre pressure: front 21 psi, 1.5 atm, rear 21 psi, 1.5 atm.

VARIATIONS

ENGINE 8.8:1 compression ratio, max power (DIN) **110 hp at 6,000 rpm,** max torque (DIN) 101 lb ft, 14 kg m at 4,800 rpm, 62.3 hp/l.
PERFORMANCE max speed 112 mph, 180 km/h, power-weight ratio 19.2 lb/hp, 8.7 kg/hp.
PRACTICAL INSTRUCTIONS 85-90 oct petrol.

Carina 1600 GT 4-door Sedan

See Carina 1600 GT 2-door Sedan, except for:

PRICE EX WORKS: 838,000 yen.

PERFORMANCE power-weight ratio: 18.8 lb/hp, 8.5 kg/hp.

TOYOTA Carina 1600 GT 2-door Sedan

TOYOTA Celica 1600 GTV Hardtop

TOYOTA Corona 1600 De Luxe Sedan

DIMENSIONS AND WEIGHT dry weight: 2,161 lb, 980 kg.

BODY 4 doors.

Carina 1600 GT Hardtop

See Carina 1600 GT 2-door Sedan, except for:

PRICE EX WORKS: 873,000 yen.

PERFORMANCE max speed: 118 mph, 190 km/h; power-weight ratio: 18.9 lb/hp, 8.6 kg/hp.

DIMENSIONS AND WEIGHT width: 62.20 in, 1,580 mm; height: 52.56 in, 1,335 mm; dry weight: 2,172 lb, 985 kg.

BODY hardtop.

OPTIONAL ACCESSORIES limited slip differential; 185/70 HR x 13 tyres.

Celica 1400 ET Hardtop

PRICE EX WORKS: 572,000 yen.

ENGINE front, 4 stroke; 4 cylinders, in line; 85.9 cu in, 1,407 cc (3.15 x 2.76 in, 80 x 70 mm); compression ratio: 8.5:1; max power (DIN): 86 hp at 6,000 rpm; max torque (DIN): 85 lb ft, 11.7 kg m at 3,800 rpm; max engine rpm: 6,400; 61.1 hp/l; cast iron cylinder block, light alloy head; 5 crankshaft bearings; valves: overhead, Vee-slanted, push-rods and rockers; camshafts: 1, side; lubrication: rotary pump, full flow filter, 6.5 imp pt, 7.8 US pt, 3.7 l; 1 Aisan downdraught twin barrel carburettor; fuel feed: mechanical pump; water-cooled, 11.4 imp pt, 13.7 US pt, 6.5 l.

TRANSMISSION driving wheels: rear; clutch: single dry plate (diaphragm); gearbox: mechanical; gears: 4, fully synchronized; ratios: I 3.587, II 2.022, III 1.384, IV 1, rev 3.484; lever: central; final drive: hypoid bevel; axle ratio: 4.100; width of rims: 4"; tyres: 5.60 x 13.

PERFORMANCE max speeds: (I) 29 mph, 46 km/h; (II) 48 mph, 78 km/h; (III) 75 mph, 120 km/h; (IV) 103 mph, 165 km/h; power-weight ratio: 22.8 lb/hp, 10.3 kg/hp; carrying capacity: 882 lb, 400 kg; acceleration: standing ¼ mile 18.1 sec; fuel consumption: not declared.

CHASSIS integral; front suspension: independent, by McPherson, coil springs/telescopic damper struts, lower wishbones (trailing links), anti-roll bar; rear suspension: rigid axle, twin trailing radius arms, transverse linkage bar, coil springs, telescopic dampers.

STEERING recirculating ball; turns lock to lock: 3.50.

BRAKES drum; swept area: front 60.8 sq in, 392 sq cm, rear 54 sq in, 348 sq cm, total 114.8 sq in, 740 sq cm.

ELECTRICAL EQUIPMENT 12 V; 35 Ah battery; 40 A alternator; Nihon Denso distributor; 4 headlamps.

DIMENSIONS AND WEIGHT wheel base: 95.47 in, 2,425 mm; tracks: 50.39 in, 1,280 mm front, 50.59 in, 1,285 mm rear; length: 163.98 in, 4,165 mm; width: 62.99 in, 1,600 mm; height: 51.57 in, 1,310 mm; ground clearance: 6.89 in, 175 mm; dry weight: 1,962 lb, 890 kg; distribution of weight: 56.7% front, 43.3% rear; turning circle (between walls): 34.1 ft, 10.4 m; fuel tank: 11 imp gal, 13.2 US gal, 50 l.

BODY hardtop; 2 doors; 5 seats, separate front seats.

PRACTICAL INSTRUCTIONS fuel: 85-90 oct petrol; engine sump oil: 6.5 imp pt, 7.8 US pt, 3.7 l, SAE 20W-30, change every 3,100 miles, 5,000 km; gearbox oil: 2.6 imp pt, 3.2 US pt, 1.5 l, SAE 80, change every 18,600 miles, 30,000 km; final drive oil: 1.8 imp pt, 2.1 US pt, 1 l, SAE 90, change every 18,600 miles, 30,000 km; tappet clearances: inlet 0.007 in, 0.18 mm, exhaust 0.013 in, 0.33 mm; valve timing: 16° 54° 58° 12°; tyre pressure: front 20 psi, 1.4 atm, rear 20 psi, 1.4 atm.

OPTIONAL ACCESSORIES 5-speed fully synchronized mechanical gearbox (I 3.587, II 2.022, III 1.384, IV 1, V 0.861, rev 3.484), 4.300 axle ratio, max speed 106 mph, 170 km/h.

Celica 1600 LT Hardtop

See Celica 1400 ET Hardtop, except for:

PRICE EX WORKS: 694,000 yen.

ENGINE 96.9 cu in, 1,588 cc (3.35 x 2.76 in, 85 x 70 mm); max power (DIN): 100 hp at 6,000 rpm; max torque (DIN): 99 lb ft, 13.7 kg m at 3,800 rpm; 63 hp/l.

TRANSMISSION axle ratio: 3.900.

CELICA 1600 LT HARDTOP

PERFORMANCE max speed: 106 mph, 170 km/h; power-weight ratio: 20.2 lb/hp, 9.1 kg/hp.

BRAKES front disc, rear drum, servo; swept area: front 24.2 sq in, 156 sq cm, rear 54 sq in, 348 sq cm, total 78.2 sq in, 504 sq cm.

DIMENSIONS AND WEIGHT dry weight: 2,018 lb, 915 kg.

OPTIONAL ACCESSORIES 5-speed fully synchronized mechanical gearbox (I 3.587, II 2.022, III 1.384, IV 1, V 0.861, rev 3.484), 4.111 axle ratio, max speed 109 mph, 175 km/h; Toyoglide automatic transmission, hydraulic torque converter with 3 ratios (I 2.400, II 1.479, III 1, rev 1.920), 4.111 axle ratio, max speed 99 mph, 160 km/h.

Celica 1600 ST Hardtop

See Celica 1600 LT Hardtop, except for:

PRICE IN GB: £ 1,275.
PRICE EX WORKS: 783,500 yen.

ENGINE compression ratio: 9.4:1; max power (DIN): 105 hp at 6,000 rpm; max torque (DIN): 101 lb ft, 14 kg m at 4,200 rpm; 66.1 hp/l; 2 Aisan downdraught twin barrel carburettors.

TRANSMISSION width of rims: 4.5"; tyres: 6.45 x 13.

PERFORMANCE max speed: 109 mph, 175 km/h; power-weight ratio: 19.5 lb/hp, 8.8 kg/hp; acceleration: standing ¼ mile 17.2 sec.

DIMENSIONS AND WEIGHT dry weight: 2,051 lb, 930 kg.

PRACTICAL INSTRUCTIONS fuel: 98-100 oct petrol.

VARIATIONS

ENGINE 8.5:1 compression ratio, max power (DIN) 100 hp at 6,000 rpm, max torque (DIN) 100 lb ft, 13.9 kg m at 4,200 rpm, 63 hp/l.
PERFORMANCE power-weight ratio 20.5 lb/hp, 9.3 kg/hp.
PRACTICAL INSTRUCTIONS 85-90 oct petrol.

Celica ST Hardtop

(export model for USA only)

See Celica 1600 ST Hardtop, except for:

PRICE IN USA: $ 2,947.

ENGINE 120.1 cu in, 1,968 cc (3.48 x 3.15 in, 88.5 x 80 mm); 53.3 hp/l; cast iron cylinder head; valves: overhead, in line, rockers; camshafts: 1, overhead.

Celica GT Hardtop

See Celica 1600 ST Hardtop, except for:

PRICE EX WORKS: 875,000 yen.

ENGINE compression ratio: 9.8:1; max power (DIN): 115 hp at 6,400 rpm; max torque (DIN): 105 lb ft, 14.5 kg m at 5,200 rpm; max engine rpm: 6,800; 72.4 hp/l; valves: overhead, Vee-slanted, rockers; camshafts: 2, overhead; lubricating system capacity: 6.7 imp pt, 8 US pt, 3.8 l; cooling system capacity: 13 imp pt, 15.6 US pt, 7.4 l.

TRANSMISSION gears: 5, fully synchronized; ratios: I 3.587, II 2.022, III 1.384, IV 1, V 0.861, rev 3.484; axle ratio: 4.111; tyres: 6.45 S x 13.

PERFORMANCE max speeds: (I) 31 mph, 50 km/h; (II) 56 mph, 90 km/h; (III) 81 mph, 130 km/h; (IV) 111 mph, 178 km/h; (V) 118 mph, 190 km/h; power-weight ratio: 18.3 lb/hp, 8.3 kg/hp; acceleration: standing ¼ mile 16.5 sec.

DIMENSIONS AND WEIGHT dry weight: 2,106 lb, 955 kg.

PRACTICAL INSTRUCTIONS engine sump oil: 6.7 imp pt, 8 US pt, 3.8 l; tappet clearances: inlet 0.011 in, 0.29 mm; exhaust 0.013 in, 0.34 mm; valve timing: 20° 48° 52° 16°; tyre pressure: front 21 psi, 1.5 atm, rear 21 psi, 1.5 atm.

VARIATIONS

ENGINE 8.8:1 compression ratio, max power (DIN) 110 hp at 6,000 rpm, max torque (DIN) 101 lb ft, 14 kg m at 4,800 rpm, 69.3 hp/l.
PERFORMANCE max speed 115 mph, 185 km/h, power-weight ratio 19.1 lb/hp, 8.7 kg/hp, acceleration standing ¼ mile 16.6 sec.

TOYOTA Corona 2000

TOYOTA Corona Mark II 1700

TOYOTA Corona Mark II 2000 De Luxe Station Wagon

Celica GTV Hardtop

See Celica GT Hardtop, except for:

PRICE EX WORKS: 863,000 yen.

TRANSMISSION width of rims: 5"; tyres: 185/70 HR x 13.

PERFORMANCE power-weight ratio: 18.5 lb/hp, 8.4 kg/hp.

DIMENSIONS AND WEIGHT tracks: 51.18 in, 1,300 mm front, 51.38 in, 1,305 mm rear; dry weight: 2,128 lb, 965 kg; turning circle (between walls): 35.4 ft, 10.8 m.

Corona 1600 De Luxe Sedan

PRICE EX WORKS: 602,000 yen.

ENGINE front, 4 stroke; 4 cylinders, in line; 96.8 cu in, 1,587 cc (3.17 x 3.07 in, 80.5 x 78 mm); compression ratio: 8.5:1; max power (DIN): 83 hp at 5,400 rpm; max torque (DIN): 91 lb ft, 12.5 kg m at 3,000 rpm; max engine rpm: 5,500; 52.3 hp/l; cast iron cylinder block, light alloy head; 3 crankshaft bearings; valves: overhead, push-rods and rockers; camshafts: 1, side; lubrication: rotary pump, full flow filter, 7.4 imp pt, 8.9 US pt, 4.2 l; 1 Aisan 12R downdraught twin barrel carburettor; fuel feed: mechanical pump; water-cooled, 12.3 imp pt, 14.8 US pt, 7 l.

TRANSMISSION driving wheels: rear; clutch: single dry plate (diaphragm); gearbox: mechanical; gears: 3, fully synchronized; ratios: I 3.337, II 1.653, III 1, rev 4.449; lever: steering column; final drive: hypoid bevel; axle ratio: 4.111; width of rims: 4"; tyres: 5.60 x 13.

PERFORMANCE max speed: 93 mph, 150 km/h; power-weight ratio: 24.7 lb/hp, 11.2 kg/hp; fuel consumption: 31.4 m/imp gal, 26.1 m/US gal, 9 l x 100 km.

CHASSIS integral; front suspension: independent, wishbones, coil springs, anti-roll bar, telescopic dampers; rear suspension: rigid axle, semi-elliptic leafsprings, telescopic dampers.

STEERING recirculating ball; turns lock to lock: 3.50.

BRAKES drum; swept area: front 60.8 sq in, 392 sq cm, rear 54 sq in, 348 sq cm, total 114.8 sq in, 740 sq cm.

ELECTRICAL EQUIPMENT 12 V; 35 Ah battery; 40 A alternator; Denso distributor; 4 headlamps.

DIMENSIONS AND WEIGHT wheel base: 95.67 in, 2,430 mm; tracks: 50.98 in, 1,295 mm front, 50.59 in, 1,285 mm rear; length: 165.16 in, 4,195 mm; width: 61.81 in, 1,570 mm; height: 55.12 in, 1,400 mm; ground clearance: 7.09 in, 180 mm; dry weight: 2,051 lb, 930 kg; distribution of weight: 56% front, 44% rear; turning circle (between walls): 34.8 ft, 10.6 m; fuel tank: 11 imp gal, 13.2 US gal, 50 l.

BODY saloon/sedan; 4 doors; 5 seats, bench front seats.

PRACTICAL INSTRUCTIONS fuel: 91 oct petrol; engine sump oil: 7.4 imp pt, 8.9 US pt, 4.2 l, SAE 20W-30, change every 3,100 miles, 5,000 km; gearbox oil: 3.5 imp pt, 4.2 US pt, 2 l, SAE 80, change every 18,600 miles, 30,000 km; final drive oil: 1.8 imp pt, 2.1 US pt, 1 l, SAE 90, change every 18,600 miles, 30,000 km; tappet clearances: inlet 0.008 in, 0.20 mm, exhaust 0.014 in, 0.36 mm; valve timing: 16° 54° 54° 16°; tyre pressure: front 24 psi, 1.7 atm, rear 24 psi, 1.7 atm.

OPTIONAL ACCESSORIES 4-speed fully synchronized mechanical gearbox (I 3.579, II 2.081, III 1.397, IV 1, rev 4.399), central lever; Toyoglide automatic transmission, hydraulic torque converter with 2 ratios (I 1.820, II 1, rev 1.820), steering column lever.

Corona 1600 Hardtop

See Corona 1600 De Luxe Sedan, except for:

PRICE EX WORKS: 662,000 yen.

TRANSMISSION gears: 4, fully synchronized; ratios: I 3.579, II 2.081, III 1.397, IV 1, rev 4.399; lever: central.

PERFORMANCE power-weight ratio: 24.9 lb/hp, 11.3 kg/hp.

DIMENSIONS AND WEIGHT height: 54.53 in, 1,385 mm; dry weight: 2,073 lb, 940 kg.

BODY hardtop; 2 doors; separate front seats.

Corona 1700 De Luxe Sedan

See Corona 1600 De Luxe Sedan, except for:

PRICE EX WORKS: 652,000 yen.

TOYOTA Corona 2000 SR Hardtop

ENGINE 104.2 cu in, 1,707 cc (3.39 x 2.89 in, 86 x 73.5 mm); max power (DIN): 95 hp at 5,500 rpm; max torque (DIN): 101 lb ft, 14 kg m at 3,800 rpm; max engine rpm: 5,800; 55.6 hp/l; cast iron cylinder head; 5 crankshaft bearings; valves: overhead, rockers; camshafts: 1, overhead; lubricating system capacity: 8.8 imp pt, 10.6 US pt, 5 l; 1 Aisan 6R downdraught twin barrel carburettor; cooling system capacity: 14.1 imp pt, 16.9 US pt, 8 l.

TRANSMISSION gears: 4, fully synchronized; ratios: I 3.579, II 2.081, III 1.397, IV 1, rev 4.399; lever: central.

PERFORMANCE max speeds: (I) 31 mph, 50 km/h; (II) 50 mph, 81 km/h; (III) 83 mph, 133 km/h; (IV) 99 mph, 160 km/h; power-weight ratio: 21.6 lb/hp, 9.8 kg/hp; fuel consumption: 29.7 m/imp gal, 24.8 m/US gal, 9.5 l x 100 km.

BRAKES front disc, rear drum, servo; swept area: front 24.2 sq in, 156 sq cm, rear 54 sq in, 348 sq cm, total 78.2 sq in, 504 sq cm.

DIMENSIONS AND WEIGHT rear track: 50.39 in, 1,280 mm.

BODY separate front seats.

PRACTICAL INSTRUCTIONS engine sump oil: 8.8 imp pt, 10.6 US pt, 5 l; tappet clearances: inlet 0.007 in, 0.18 mm, exhaust 0.013 in, 0.33 mm; valve timing: 15° 45° 50° 10°.

OPTIONAL ACCESSORIES Toyoglide automatic transmission, hydraulic torque converter with 3 ratios (I 2.450, II 1.450, III 1, rev 2.222), max speed 96 mph, 155 km/h; Toyota EAT electronically-controlled automatic transmission with 3 ratios (I 2.400, II 1.479, III 1, rev 1.920).

TOYOTA Corona Mark II 1700 De Luxe Hardtop

Corona 1700 Hardtop

See Corona 1700 De Luxe Sedan, except for:

PRICE EX WORKS: 703,000 yen.

PERFORMANCE power-weight ratio: 22.3 lb/hp, 10.1 kg/hp.

DIMENSIONS AND WEIGHT height: 54.53 in, 1,385 mm; dry weight: 2,117 lb, 960 kg.

BODY hardtop; 2 doors.

Corona 1700 SL Sedan

See Corona 1700 De Luxe Sedan, except for:

PRICE EX WORKS: 768,000 yen.

ENGINE compression ratio: 9.5:1; max power (DIN): 105 hp at 6,000 rpm; max torque (DIN): 105 lb ft, 14.5 kg m at 4,000 rpm; max engine rpm: 6,400; 61.5 hp/l; 2 Aisan SU type horizontal carburettors.

TRANSMISSION axle ratio: 3.900.

PERFORMANCE max speeds: (I) 31 mph, 50 km/h; (II) 52 mph, 84 km/h; (III) 80 mph, 128 km/h; (IV) 106 mph, 170 km/h; power-weight ratio: 19.5 lb/hp, 8.9 kg/hp; speed in direct drive at 1,000 rpm: 16.8 mph, 27 km/h; fuel consumption: 28.8 m/imp gal, 24 m/US gal, 9.8 l x 100 km.

STEERING recirculating ball, variable ratio.

OPTIONAL ACCESSORIES 5-speed fully synchronized mechanical gearbox (I 3.525, II 2.054, III 1.396, IV 1, V 0.858, rev 3.755), max speed 109 mph, 175 km/h.

TOYOTA Corona Mark II 2000 De Luxe Station Wagon

Corona 1700 SL Hardtop

See Corona 1700 SL Sedan, except for:

PERFORMANCE power-weight ratio: 20.3 lb/hp, 9.2 kg/hp.

DIMENSIONS AND WEIGHT height: 54.53 in, 1,385 mm; dry weight: 2,139 lb, 970 kg.

BODY hardtop; 2 doors.

OPTIONAL ACCESSORIES Toyoglide automatic transmission, hydraulic torque converter with 3 ratios (I 2.450, II 1.450, III 1, rev 2.222); 5-speed fully synchronized mechanical gearbox (I 3.525, II 2.054, III 1.396, IV 1, V 0.858, rev 3.755).

Corona 2000 SL Hardtop

PRICE EX WORKS: 827,000 yen.

ENGINE front, 4 stroke; 4 cylinders, in line; 120.1 cu in, 1,968 cc (3.48 x 3.15 in, 88.5 x 80 mm); compression ratio: 9.3:1; max power (DIN): 120 hp at 6,000 rpm; max torque

CORONA 2000 SL HARDTOP

(DIN): 120 lb ft, 16.5 kg m at 4,000 rpm; max engine rpm: 6,400; 60.9 hp/l; cast iron cylinder block and head; 5 crankshaft bearings; valves: overhead, in line, rockers; camshafts: 1, overhead; lubrication: rotary pump, full flow filter, 8.8 imp pt, 10.6 US pt, 5 l; 2 Aisan M-B SU type horizontal carburettors; fuel feed: mechanical pump; water-cooled, 14.1 imp pt, 16.9 US pt, 8 l.

TRANSMISSION driving wheels: rear; clutch: single dry plate (diaphragm); gearbox: mechanical; gears: 4, fully synchronized; ratios: I 3.579, II 2.081, III 1.397, IV 1, rev 4.399; lever: central; final drive: hypoid bevel; axle ratio: 3.700; width of rims: 4.5"; tyres: 165 SR x 13.

PERFORMANCE max speeds: (I) 31 mph, 50 km/h; (II) 55 mph, 88 km/h; (III) 83 mph, 133 km/h; (IV) 115 mph, 185 km/h; power-weight ratio: 18.2 lb/hp, 8.2 kg/hp; carrying capacity: 882 lb, 400 kg; fuel consumption: not declared.

CHASSIS integral; front suspension: independent, double wishbones, coil springs, anti-roll bar, telescopic dampers; rear suspension: rigid axle, semi-elliptic leafsprings, telescopic dampers.

STEERING recirculating ball, variable ratio; turns lock to lock: 3.50.

BRAKES front disc, rear drum, servo; swept area: front 24.2 sq in, 156 sq cm, rear 54 sq in, 348 sq cm, total 78.2 sq in, 504 sq cm.

ELECTRICAL EQUIPMENT 12 V; 35 Ah battery; 40 A alternator; Nihon Denso distributor; 4 headlamps.

DIMENSIONS AND WEIGHT wheel base: 95.67 in, 2,430 mm; tracks: 51.18 in, 1,300 mm front, 50.39 in, 1,280 mm rear; length: 168.11 in, 4,270 mm; width: 61.81 in, 1,570 mm; height: 53.74 in, 1,365 mm; ground clearance: 6.69 in, 170 mm; dry weight: 2,183 lb, 990 kg; distribution of weight: 58% front, 42% rear; turning circle (between walls): 34.8 ft, 10.6 m; fuel tank: 11 imp gal, 13.2 US gal, 50 l.

BODY hardtop; 2 doors; 5 seats, separate front seats.

PRACTICAL INSTRUCTIONS fuel: 98-100 oct petrol; engine sump oil: 8.8 imp pt, 10.6 US pt, 5 l, SAE 20W-30, change every 3,100 miles, 5,000 km; tappet clearances: inlet 0.007 in, 0.18 mm, exhaust 0.013 in, 0.33 mm; valve timing: 16° 60° 56° 20°; tyre pressure: front 21 psi, 1.5 atm, rear 21 psi, 1.5 atm.

VARIATIONS

ENGINE max power (DIN) 125 hp at 5,600 rpm, max torque (DIN) 123 lb ft, 17 kg m at 4,000 rpm, 63.5 hp/l, Toyota EFI electronic fuel injection system.
PERFORMANCE power-weight ratio 17.5 lb/hp, 7.9 kg/hp.

OPTIONAL ACCESSORIES 5-speed fully synchronized mechanical gearbox (I 3.525, II 2.054, III 1.396, IV 1, V 0.858, rev 3.755), max speed 118 mph, 190 km/h; Toyoglide automatic transmission, hydraulic torque converter with 3 ratios (I 2.450, II 1.450, III 1, rev 2.222); Toyota EAT electronically-controlled automatic transmission with 3 ratios (I 2.450, II 1.479, III 1, rev 1.920).

Corona 2000 SR Hardtop

See Corona 2000 SL Hardtop, except for:

PRICE EX WORKS: 827,000 yen.

TRANSMISSION gears: 5, fully synchronized; ratios: I 3.525, II 2.054, III 1.396, IV 1, V 0.858, rev 3.755.

PERFORMANCE max speed: 118 mph, 190 km/h.

CHASSIS rear suspension: anti-roll bar.

Corona Mark II 1700 De Luxe Sedan

PRICE EX WORKS: 707,000 yen.

ENGINE front, 4 stroke; 4 cylinders, in line; 104.2 cu in, 1,707 cc (3.39 x 2.89 in, 86 x 73.5 mm); compression ratio: 8.5:1; max power (DIN): 95 hp at 5,500 rpm; max torque (DIN): 101 lb ft, 14 kg m at 3,800 rpm; 56.2 hp/l; cast iron cylinder block and head; 5 crankshaft bearings; valves: overhead, in line, rockers; camshafts: 1, overhead; lubrication: rotary pump, full flow filter, 8.8 imp pt, 10.6 US pt, 5 l; 1 Aisan downdraught twin barrel carburettors; fuel feed: mechanical pump; water-cooled, 14.1 imp pt, 16.9 US pt, 8 l.

TRANSMISSION driving wheels: rear; clutch: single dry plate (diaphragm); gearbox: mechanical; gears: 3, fully synchronized; ratios: I 3.337, II 1.653, III 1, rev 4.449; lever:

TOYOTA Corona Mark II 2000 GSS Hardtop

TOYOTA Corona Mark II L Sedan

TOYOTA Crown Super Sedan

steering column; final drive: hypoid bevel; axle ratio: 4.111; width of rims: 4.5''; tyres: 6.45 x 13.

PERFORMANCE max speeds: (I) 32 mph, 52 km/h; (II) 65 mph, 105 km/h; (III) 99 mph, 160 km/h; power-weight ratio: 24.7 lb/hp, 11.2 kg/hp; carrying capacity: 882 lb, 400 kg; fuel consumption: not declared.

CHASSIS integral; front suspension: independent, double wishbones, coil springs, anti-roll bar, telescopic dampers; rear suspension: rigid axle, twin trailing radius arms, transverse linkage bar, coil springs, telescopic dampers.

STEERING recirculating ball, variable ratio; turns lock to lock: 4.50.

BRAKES front disc, rear drum, servo; swept area: front 17.4 sq in, 112 sq cm, rear 54 sq in, 348 sq cm, total 71.4 sq in, 460 sq cm.

ELECTRICAL EQUIPMENT 12 V; 35 Ah battery; 45 A alternator; Nihon Denso distributor; 4 headlamps.

DIMENSIONS AND WEIGHT wheel base: 101.77 in, 2,585 mm; tracks: 53.35 in, 1,355 mm front, 52.95 in, 1,345 mm rear; length: 170.28 in, 4,325 mm; width: 63.98 in, 1,625 mm; height: 54.72 in, 1,390 mm; ground clearance: 6.50 in, 165 mm; dry weight: 2,348 lb, 1,065 kg; distribution of weight: 55.9% front, 44.1% rear; turning circle (between walls): 35.4 ft, 10.8 m; fuel tank: 13.2 imp gal, 15.8 US gal, 60 l.

BODY saloon/sedan; 4 doors; 5 seats, bench front seats.

PRACTICAL INSTRUCTIONS fuel: 85-90 oct petrol; engine sump oil: 8.8 imp pt, 10.6 US pt, 5 l, SAE 20W-30, change every 3,100 miles, 5,000 km; tappet clearances: inlet 0.007 in, 0.18 mm, exhaust 0.013 in, 0.33 mm; valve timing: 20° 48° 56° 12°; tyre pressure: front 23 psi, 1.6 atm, rear 23 psi, 1.6 atm.

OPTIONAL ACCESSORIES 4-speed fully synchronized mechanical gearbox (I 3.579, II 2.081, III 1.397, IV 1, rev 4.399), central lever; Toyoglide automatic transmission, hydraulic torque converter with 3 ratios (I 2.400, II 1.479, III 1, rev 1.920), max speed 93 mph, 150 km/h.

Corona Mark II 1700 De Luxe Hardtop

See Corona Mark II 1700 De Luxe Sedan, except for:

PRICE EX WORKS: 757,000 yen.

TRANSMISSION gears: 4, fully synchronized; ratios: I 3.579, II 2.081, III 1.397, IV 1, rev 4.399; lever: central.

PERFORMANCE power-weight ratio: 25 lb/hp, 11.3 kg/hp.

DIMENSIONS AND WEIGHT height: 54.33 in, 1,380 mm; dry weight: 2,370 lb, 1,075 kg.

BODY hardtop; 2 doors; 5 seats, separate front seats.

Corona Mark II 2000 De Luxe Sedan

See Corona Mark II 1700 De Luxe Sedan, except for:

PRICE IN GB: £ 1,290.
PRICE EX WORKS: 737,000 yen.

ENGINE 120.1 cu in, 1,968 cc (3.48 x 3.15 in, 88.5 x 80 mm); max power (DIN): 105 hp at 5,500 rpm; max torque (DIN): 116 lb ft, 16 kg m at 3,600 rpm; 52.8 hp/l.

TRANSMISSION axle ratio: 3.700.

PERFORMANCE max speed: 103 mph, 165 km/h; power-weight ratio: 22.6 lb/hp, 10.2 kg/hp.

DIMENSIONS AND WEIGHT dry weight: 2,370 lb, 1,075 kg.

Corona Mark II 2000 De Luxe Hardtop

See Corona Mark II 2000 De Luxe Sedan, except for:

PRICE EX WORKS: 787,000 yen.

TRANSMISSION gears: 4, fully synchronized; ratios: I 3.579, II 2.081, III 1.397, IV 1, rev 4.399; lever: central.

PERFORMANCE power-weight ratio: 22.8 lb/hp, 10.3 kg/hp.

DIMENSIONS AND WEIGHT height: 54.33 in, 1,380 mm; dry weight: 2,392 lb, 1,085 kg.

BODY hardtop; 2 doors; 5 seats, separate front seats.

TOYOTA Corona Mark II 2000 GSS Hardtop

TOYOTA Corona Mark II L Sedan

TOYOTA Crown Super Sedan

Corona Mark II 2000 De Luxe Station Wagon

See Corona Mark II 2000 De Luxe Sedan, except for:

PRICE EX WORKS: 803,000 yen.

BODY estate car/station wagon; 4 + 1 doors.

Corona Mark II 2000 GSL Sedan

See Corona Mark II 2000 De Luxe Sedan, except for:

PRICE EX WORKS: 820,000 yen.

ENGINE compression ratio: 9.3:1; max power (DIN): 120 hp at 6,000 rpm; max torque (DIN): 120 lb ft, 16.5 kg m at 4,000 rpm; 61 hp/l; 2 Aisan SU type horizontal carburettors.

TRANSMISSION gears: 4, fully synchronized; ratios: I 3.579, II 2.081, III 1.397, IV 1, rev 4.399; lever: central.

PERFORMANCE max speed: 109 mph, 175 km/h; power-weight ratio: 19.8 lb/hp, 9 kg/hp.

DIMENSIONS AND WEIGHT dry weight: 2,381 lb, 1,080 kg.

VARIATIONS

ENGINE 8.5:1 compression ratio, max power (DIN) 115 hp at 6,000 rpm, max torque (DIN) 116 lb ft, 16 kg m at 4,000 rpm, 53.3 hp/l.
PERFORMANCE power-weight ratio 20.7 lb/hp, 9.4 kg/hp.

ENGINE max power (DIN) 125 hp at 5,600 rpm, max torque (DIN) 123 lb ft, 17 kg m at 4,000 rpm, 63.5 hp/l, Toyota EFI electronic fuel injection system.
PERFORMANCE power-weight ratio 19 lb/hp, 8.6 kg/hp.
ELECTRICAL EQUIPMENT 55 A alternator.

Corona Mark II 2000 GSL Hardtop

See Corona Mark II 2000 GSL Sedan, except for:

PRICE EX WORKS: 887,000 yen.

DIMENSIONS AND WEIGHT height: 54.33 in, 1,380 mm.

BODY hardtop; 2 doors; 5 seats, separate front seats.

Corona Mark II 2000 GSS Hardtop

See Corona Mark II 2000 GSL Hardtop, except for:

PRICE EX WORKS: 1,150,000 yen.

ENGINE compression ratio: 9.4:1; max power (DIN): 145 hp 6,400 rpm; max torque (DIN): 130 lb ft, 18 kg m at 5,200 rpm; 73.7 hp/l; valves: overhead, Vee-slanted, thimble tappets; camshafts: 2, overhead; 2 Mikuni-Solex 40 PHH horizontal twin barrel carburettors; cooling system capacity: 15 imp pt, 18 US pt, 8.5 l.

TRANSMISSION gears: 5, fully synchronized; ratios: I 3.055, II 1.899, III 1.296, IV 1, V 0.858, rev 3.755; lever: central; final drive: hypoid bevel, limited slip differential; axle ratio: 4.375; width of rims: 5''; tyres: 165 HR x 14.

PERFORMANCE max speeds: (I) 36 mph, 58 km/h; (II) 57 mph, 92 km/h; (III) 84 mph, 135 km/h; (IV) 109 mph, 176 km/h; (V) 121 mph, 195 km/h; power-weight ratio: 16.8 lb/hp, 7.6 kg/hp.

BRAKES swept area: front 22.3 sq in, 144 sq cm, rear 54 sq in, 348 sq cm, total 76.3 sq in, 492 sq cm.

DIMENSIONS AND WEIGHT height: 53.94 in, 1,370 mm; dry weight: 2,437 lb, 1,105 kg; distribution of weight: 56% front, 44% rear.

PRACTICAL INSTRUCTIONS fuel: 98-100 oct petrol; tappet clearances: inlet 0.011 in, 0.29 mm, exhaust 0.013 in, 0.34 mm; valve timing: 20° 48° 52° 16°.

VARIATIONS

ENGINE 8.5:1 compression ratio, max power (DIN) 140 hp at 6,400 rpm, max torque (DIN) 125 lb ft, 17.2 kg m at 4,800 rpm, 71.1 hp/l.
PERFORMANCE power-weight ratio 17.4 lb/hp, 7.9 kg/hp.
PRACTICAL INSTRUCTIONS 85-90 oct petrol.

Corona Mark II L Sedan

PRICE EX WORKS: 875,000 yen.

ENGINE front, 4 stroke; 6 cylinders, in line; 121.3 cu in, 1,988 cc (2.95 x 2.95 in, 75 x 75 mm); compression ratio:

CORONA MARK II L SEDAN

8.5:1; max power (DIN): 110 hp at 5,600 rpm; max torque (DIN): 116 lb ft, 16 kg m at 3,600 rpm; 55.3 hp/l; cast iron cylinder block, light alloy head; 7 crankshaft bearings; valves: overhead, Vee-slanted, rockers; camshafts: 1, overhead; lubrication: rotary pump, full flow filter, 9.2 imp pt, 11 US pt, 5.2 l; 1 Aisan downdraught twin barrel carburettor; fuel feed: mechanical pump; water-cooled, 19 imp pt, 22.8 US pt, 10.8 l.

TRANSMISSION driving wheels: rear; clutch: single dry plate (diaphragm); gearbox: mechanical; gears: 4, fully synchronized; ratios: I 3.579, II 2.081, III 1.397, IV 1, rev 4.399; lever: central; final drive: hypoid bevel; axle ratio: 4.111; width of rims: 4.5"; tyres: 6.45 x 14.

PERFORMANCE max speeds: (I) 30 mph, 48 km/h; (II) 48 mph, 77 km/h; (III) 71 mph, 115 km/h; (IV) 99 mph, 160 km/h; power-weight ratio: 22.4 lb/hp, 10.1 kg/hp; carrying capacity: 882 lb, 400 kg; acceleration: standing ¼ mile 17.6 sec; fuel consumption: not declared.

CHASSIS integral; front suspension: independent, double wishbones, coil springs, anti-roll bar, telescopic dampers; rear suspension: rigid axle, twin trailing radius arms, transverse linkage bar, coil springs, telescopic dampers.

STEERING recirculating ball; turns lock to lock: 4.50.

BRAKES front disc, rear drum, servo; swept area: front 22.3 sq in, 144 sq cm, rear 54 sq in, 348 sq cm, total 76.3 sq in, 492 sq cm.

ELECTRICAL EQUIPMENT 12 V; 35 Ah battery; 45 A alternator; Nihon Denso distributor; 4 headlamps.

DIMENSIONS AND WEIGHT wheel base: 101.77 in, 2,585 mm; tracks: 53.54 in, 1,360 mm front, 52.95 in, 1,345 mm rear; length: 174.02 in, 4,420 mm; width: 63.98 in, 1,625 mm; height: 55.12 in, 1,400 mm; ground clearance: 6.89 in, 175 mm; dry weight: 2,459 lb, 1,115 kg; distribution of weight: 57.4% front, 42.6% rear; turning circle (between walls): 35.4 ft, 10.8 m; fuel tank: 13.2 imp gal, 15.8 US gal, 60 l.

BODY saloon/sedan; 4 doors; 5 seats, separate front seats.

PRACTICAL INSTRUCTIONS fuel: 85-90 oct petrol; engine sump oil: 9.2 imp pt, 11 US pt, 5.2 l, SAE 20W-50, change every 3,100 miles, 5,000 km; tappet clearances: inlet 0.006 in, 0.14 mm, exhaust 0.008 in, 0.21 mm; valve timing: 20° 36° 48° 8°; tyre pressure: front 23 psi, 1.6 atm, rear 23 psi, 1.6 atm.

VARIATIONS

ENGINE max power (DIN) 120 hp at 5,800 rpm, max torque (DIN) 116 lb ft, 16 kg m at 3,800 rpm, 60.4 hp/l, 2 Aisan SU type horizontal carburettors.
PERFORMANCE power-weight ratio 20.5 lb/hp, 9.3 kg/hp.

ENGINE 9.5:1 compression ratio, max power (DIN) 125 hp at 5,800 rpm, max torque (DIN) 120 lb ft, 16.5 kg m at 3,800 rpm, 62.9 hp/l, 2 Aisan SU type horizontal carburettors.
PERFORMANCE max speed 103 mph, 165 km/h, power-weight ratio 19.7 lb/hp, 8.9 kg/hp.
PRACTICAL INSTRUCTIONS 98-100 oct petrol.

OPTIONAL ACCESSORIES Porsche 5-speed fully synchronized mechanical gearbox (I 3.055, II 1.899, III 1.296, IV 1, V 0.858, rev 3.755), 4.556 axle ratio; Toyoglide automatic transmission, hydraulic torque converter with 3 ratios (I 2.400, II 1.479, III 1, rev 1.920); power-assisted steering.

Corona Mark II L Hardtop

See Corona Mark II L Sedan, except for:

PRICE EX WORKS: 942,000 yen.

DIMENSIONS AND WEIGHT height: 54.72 in, 1,390 mm; dry weight: 2,470 lb, 1,120 kg.

BODY hardtop; 2 doors.

Crown De Luxe Sedan

PRICE EX WORKS: 1,078,000 yen.

ENGINE front, 4 stroke; 6 cylinders, in line; 121.3 cu in, 1,988 cc (2.95 x 2.95 in, 75 x 75 mm); compression ratio: 9:1; max power (DIN): 115 hp at 5,800 rpm; max torque (DIN): 116 lb ft, 16 kg m at 3,600 rpm; max engine rpm: 6,000; 57.8 hp/l; cast iron cylinder block, light alloy head; 7 crankshaft bearings; valves: overhead, Vee-slanted, rockers; camshafts: 1, overhead; lubrication: rotary pump, full flow filter, 9.2 imp pt, 11 US pt, 5.2 l; 2 Aisan MD downdraught twin barrel carburettors; fuel feed: mechanical pump; water-cooled, 19 imp pt, 22.8 US pt, 10.8 l.

TOYOTA Crown Custom Station Wagon

TOYOTA Crown SL Hardtop

TOYOTA Century D Sedan

TRANSMISSION driving wheels: rear; clutch: single dry plate (diaphragm); gearbox: mechanical; gears: 4, fully synchronized; ratios: I 3.579, II 2.081, III 1.397, IV 1, rev 4.399; lever: central; final drive: hypoid bevel; axle ratio: 4.111; width of rims: 5"; tyres: 6.95 x 14.

PERFORMANCE max speeds: (I) 29 mph, 47 km/h; (II) 50 mph, 80 km/h; (III) 71 mph, 115 km/h; (IV) 99 mph, 160 km/h; power-weight ratio: 25.1 lb/hp, 11.4 kg/hp; carrying capacity: 882 lb, 400 kg; speed in direct drive at 1,000 rpm: 17.4 mph, 28 km/h; fuel consumption: 31.4 m/imp gal, 26.1 m/US gal, 9 l x 100 km.

CHASSIS box-type perimeter frame; front suspension: independent, wishbones, coil springs, anti-roll bar, telescopic dampers; rear suspension: rigid axle, lower radius arms, upper torque arm, coil springs, telescopic dampers.

STEERING recirculating ball; turns lock to lock: 4.30.

BRAKES front disc, rear drum, servo; swept area: front 22.9 sq in, 148 sq cm, rear 73.8 sq in, 476 sq cm, total 96.7 sq in, 624 sq cm.

ELECTRICAL EQUIPMENT 12 V; 35 Ah battery; 45 A alternator; Denso distributor; 4 headlamps.

DIMENSIONS AND WEIGHT wheel base: 105.91 in, 2,690 mm; tracks: 54.72 in, 1,390 mm front, 54.33 in, 1,380 mm rear; length: 184.25 in, 4,680 mm; width: 66.54 in, 1,690 mm; height: 55.91 in, 1,420 mm; ground clearance: 6.89 in, 175 mm; dry weight: 2,900 lb, 1,315 kg; distribution of weight: 55.8% front, 44.2% rear; turning circle (between walls): 40 ft, 12.2 m; fuel tank: 15.4 imp gal, 18.5 US gal, 70 l.

BODY saloon/sedan; 4 doors; 5 seats, separate front seats.

PRACTICAL INSTRUCTIONS fuel: 90 oct petrol; engine sump oil: 9.2 imp pt, 11 US pt, 5.2 l, SAE 20W-30, change every 3,100 miles, 5,000 km; gearbox oil: 3.7 imp pt, 4.4 US pt, 2.1 l, SAE 90, change every 18,600 miles, 30,000 km; final drive oil: 2.1 imp pt, 2.5 US pt, 1.2 l, SAE 90, change every 18,600 miles, 30,000 km; greasing: none; tappet clearances: inlet 0.006 in, 0.14 mm, exhaust 0.008 in, 0.21 mm; valve timing: 20° 36° 48° 8°; tyre pressure: front 24 psi, 1.7 atm, rear 24 psi, 1.7 atm.

OPTIONAL ACCESSORIES Toyoglide automatic transmission with 3 ratios; 3-speed mechanical gearbox; steering column lever; bench front seats.

Crown Super Sedan

See Crown De Luxe Sedan, except for:

PRICE EX WORKS: 1,308,000 yen.

PERFORMANCE power-weight ratio: 26.2 lb/hp, 11.9 kg/hp.

STEERING servo.

DIMENSIONS AND WEIGHT dry weight: 3,021 lb, 1,370 kg.

Crown 2300

(Export model).

See Crown De Luxe Sedan, except for:

ENGINE 137.5 cu in, 2,253 cc (2.95 x 3.35 in, 75 x 85 mm); compression ratio: 8.8:1; max power (SAE): 115 hp at 5,200 rpm; max torque (SAE): 123 lb ft, 17 kg m at 3,600 rpm; 51 hp/l; 1 downdraught twin barrel carburettor.

Crown 2600 Super Sedan

See Crown Super Sedan, except for:

PRICE IN GB: £ 1,735 (with automatic transmission).
PRICE EX WORKS: 1,515,000 yen.

ENGINE 156.4 cu in, 2,563 cc (3.15 x 3.35 in, 80 x 85 mm); compression ratio: 8.5:1; max power (DIN): 130 hp at 5,200 rpm; max torque (DIN): 145 lb ft, 20 kg m at 3,600 rpm; 50.7 hp/l; 1 Aisan downdraught twin barrel carburettor.

TRANSMISSION axle ratio: 3.900.

PERFORMANCE max speed: 106 mph, 170 km/h; power-weight ratio: 23.2 lb/hp, 10.5 kg/hp.

OPTIONAL ACCESSORIES Toyoglide automatic transmission with 3 ratios; Toyota EAT electrically-controlled automatic transmission with 3 ratios; air-conditioning.

TOYOTA Crown Custom Station Wagon

TOYOTA Crown SL Hardtop

TOYOTA Century D Sedan

Crown Custom Station Wagon

See Crown De Luxe Sedan, except for:

PRICE IN GB: £ 1,865 (with automatic transmission).
PRICE EX WORKS: 1,105,000 yen.

PERFORMANCE power-weight ratio: 26.2 lb/hp, 11.9 kg/hp.

DIMENSIONS AND WEIGHT length: 184.64 in, 4,690 mm; height: 56.69 in, 1,440 mm; dry weight: 3,010 lb, 1,365 kg.

BODY estate car/station wagon; 4 + 1 doors.

Crown De Luxe Hardtop

See Crown De Luxe Sedan, except for:

PRICE EX WORKS: 1,133,000 yen.

PERFORMANCE power-weight ratio: 24.9 lb/hp, 11.3 kg/hp.

DIMENSIONS AND WEIGHT height: 55.51 in, 1,410 mm; dry weight: 2,878 lb, 1,305 kg.

BODY hardtop; 2 doors.

OPTIONAL ACCESSORIES bench front seats not available.

Crown SL Hardtop

See Crown De Luxe Hardtop, except for:

PRICE EX WORKS: 1,277,000 yen.

ENGINE compression ratio: 9.5:1; max power (DIN): 125 hp at 5,800 rpm; max torque (DIN): 120 lb ft, 16.5 kg m at 3,800 rpm; 62.9 hp/l; 2 Aisan SU type M-B horizontal carburettors.

PERFORMANCE max speed: 103 mph, 165 km/h; power-weight ratio: 23.2 lb/hp, 10.5 kg/hp.

DIMENSIONS AND WEIGHT dry weight: 2,889 lb, 1,310 kg.

OPTIONAL ACCESSORIES Toyoglide automatic transmission with 3 ratios; Toyota EAT electronically-controlled automatic transmission with 3 ratios; electronically-controlled anti-skid brakes; air-conditioning.

Crown 2600 Hardtop

See Crown 2600 Super Sedan, except for:

PRICE IN GB: £ 1,780 (with automatic transmission).
PRICE EX WORKS: 1,580,000 yen.

DIMENSIONS AND WEIGHT height: 55.51 in, 1,410 mm.

BODY hardtop; 2 doors.

Century D Sedan

PRICE EX WORKS: 2,761,000 yen.

ENGINE front, 4 stroke; 8 cylinders, Vee-slanted at 90°; 181.9 cu in, 2,981 cc (3.07 x 3.07 in, 78 x 78 mm); compression ratio: 9.8:1; max power (DIN): 170 hp at 5,600 rpm; max torque (DIN): 181 lb ft, 25 kg m at 3,600 rpm; max engine rpm: 5,600; 57 hp/l; light alloy cylinder block and head; 5 crankshaft bearings; valves: overhead, push-rods and rockers; camshafts: 1, at centre of Vee; lubrication: gear pump, full flow filter, 8.8 imp pt, 10.6 US pt, 5 l; 1 Rochester downdraught 4-barrel carburettor; fuel feed: electric pump; water-cooled, 23.6 imp pt, 28.3 US pt, 13.4 l.

TRANSMISSION driving wheels: rear; gearbox: Toyoglide automatic transmission, hydraulic torque converter and planetary gears with 3 ratios, max ratio of converter at stall 2, possible manual selection; ratios: I 2.400, II 1.479, III 1, rev 1.920; lever: steering column; final drive: hypoid bevel; axle ratio: 3.900; tyres: 7.35 x 14.

PERFORMANCE max speeds: (I) 40 mph, 65 km/h; (II) 62 mph, 100 km/h; (III) 106 mph, 170 km/h; power-weight ratio: 23.4 lb/hp, 10.6 kg/hp; carrying capacity: 1,058 lb, 480 kg; speed in direct drive at 1,000 rpm: 19.1 mph, 30.8 km/h; fuel consumption: 23.5 m/imp gal, 19.6 m/US gal, 12 l x 100 km.

CHASSIS integral; front suspension: independent, by McPherson, air bellows/telescopic damper struts, lower wishbones (trailing links), anti-roll bar; rear suspension: rigid axle, lower radius arms, upper torque arm, transverse linkage bar, coil springs, telescopic dampers.

STEERING recirculating ball, servo.

BRAKES drum, servo; swept area: front 92.7 sq in, 598 sq cm, rear 75 sq in, 484 sq cm, total 167.7 sq in, 1,082 sq cm.

ELECTRICAL EQUIPMENT 12 V; 45 Ah battery; 780 W alternator; Nihon-Denso distributor; 2 iodine headlamps.

DIMENSIONS AND WEIGHT wheel base: 112.60 in, 2,860

CENTURY D SEDAN

mm; tracks: 59.84 in, 1,520 mm front, 60.63 in, 1,540 mm rear; length: 196.06 in, 4,980 mm; width: 74.41 in, 1,890 mm; height: 57.09 in, 1,450 mm; ground clearance: 6.89 in, 175 mm; dry weight: 3,969 lb, 1,800 kg; distribution of weight: 53.9% front, 46.1% rear; turning circle (between walls): 37.4 ft, 11.4 m; fuel tank: 19.8 imp gal, 23.6 US gal, 90 l.

BODY saloon/sedan; 4 doors; 6 seats, bench front seats.

PRACTICAL INSTRUCTIONS fuel: 98-100 oct petrol; engine sump oil: 8.8 imp pt, 10.6 US pt, 5 l, SAE 30, change every 3,100 miles, 5,000 km; gearbox oil: 12.3 imp pt, 14.8 US pt, 7 l, automatic transmission fluid; final drive oil: 3.3 imp pt, 4 US pt, 1.9 l, SAE 90, change every 18,600 miles, 30,000 km; valve timing: 15° 57° 57° 15°; tyre pressure: front 34 psi, 2.4 atm, rear 34 psi, 2.4 atm.

OPTIONAL ACCESSORIES limited slip differential.

Century A Sedan

See Century D Sedan, except for:

PRICE EX WORKS: 2,703,000 yen.

TRANSMISSION gearbox: mechanical; gears: 4, fully synchronized; ratios: I 3.059, II 1.645, III 1, rev 4.079; axle ratio: 3.545.

PERFORMANCE max speeds: (I) 30 mph, 48 km/h; (II) 52 mph, 84 km/h; (III) 78 mph, 126 km/h; (IV) 106 mph, 170 km/h; speed in direct drive at 1,000 rpm: 19.8 mph, 31.8 km/h.

Century B Sedan

See Century D Sedan, except for:

PRICE EX WORKS: 2,356,000 yen.

TRANSMISSION gearbox: mechanical; gears: 3, fully synchronized: ratios: I 3.059, II 1.645, III 1, rev 4.079; axle ratio: 3.545.

PERFORMANCE max speeds: (I) 36 mph, 58 km/h; (II) 67 mph, 108 km/h; (III) 106 mph, 170 km/h; speed in direct drive at 1,000 rpm: 19.8 mph, 31.8 km/h.

Century C Sedan

See Century B Sedan, except for:

PRICE EX WORKS: 2,556,000 yen.

FORD AUSTRALIA

Falcon - Falcon 500 - Futura - Fairmont - Falcon GT Series

1 Falcon	4-door Sedan
2 Falcon	Station Wagon
3 Falcon 500	2-door Hardtop
4 Falcon 500	4-door Sedan
5 Falcon 500	Station Wagon
6 Futura	4-door Sedan
7 Fairmont	2-door Hardtop
8 Fairmont	4-door Sedan
9 Fairmont	Station Wagon
10 Falcon GT	2-door Hardtop
11 Falcon GT	4-door Sedan

Power team:	Standard for:	Optional for:
130 hp	1,2,3,4,5	—
155 hp	6,7,8,9	1,2,3,4,5
170 hp	—	all except 10,11
240 hp	—	all except 10,11
260 hp	—	all except 10,11
300 hp	10,11	—

130 hp power team

ENGINE front, 4 stroke; 6 cylinders, in line; 200 cu in, 3,277 cc (3.68 x 3.13 in, 93.4 x 79.4 mm); compression ratio: 9.1:1; max power (SAE): 130 hp at 4,600 rpm; max torque (SAE): 190 lb ft, 26.2 kg m at 2,000 rpm; max engine rpm: 4,800 39.7 hp/l; cast iron cylinder block and head; 7 crankshaft bearings; valves: overhead, push-rods and rockers, hydraulic tappets; camshafts: 1, side; lubrication: gear pump, full flow filter, 7.6 imp pt, 9.1 US pt, 4.3 l; 1 Autolite downdraught single barrel carburettor; fuel feed: mechanical pump; water-cooled, 15.5 imp pt, 18.6 US pt, 8.8 l.

TRANSMISSION driving wheels: rear; clutch: single dry

FORD Fairmont 2-door Hardtop

FORD Fairmont Station Wagon

FORD Fairlane 500 4-door Sedan

plate (diaphragm), hydraulically controlled; gearbox: mechanical; gears: 3, fully synchronized; ratios: I 2.950, II 1.690, III 1, rev 3.670; lever: steering column; final drive: hypoid bevel; axle ratio: 3.230; width of rims: 5"; tyres: 6.95 L x 14 — station wagon 7.35 x 14.

PERFORMANCE max speed: about 96 mph, 154 km/h; speed in direct drive at 1,000 rpm: 20.5 mph, 33 km/h; fuel consumption: 19.9 m/imp gal, 16.6 m/US gal, 14.2 l x 100 km.

CHASSIS integral; front suspension: independent, wishbones, lower trailing links, coil springs, anti-roll bar, telescopic dampers; rear suspension: rigid axle, semi-elliptic leafsprings, telescopic dampers.

STEERING recirculating ball.

BRAKES drum; swept area: total 154.4 sq in, 996 sq cm.

ELECTRICAL EQUIPMENT 12 V; 45 Ah battery; 38 A alternator; Autolite distributor; 2 headlamps.

DIMENSIONS AND WEIGHT wheel base: 111 in, 2,819 mm; front track: 58.90 in, 1,496 mm - hardtop 60.50 in, 1,537 mm; rear track: 58.50 in, 1,486 mm - hardtop 60 in, 1,524 mm; length: 184.60 in, 4,689 mm - hardtop 186.50 in, 4,737 mm - station wagons 190.30 in, 4,834 mm; width: 76.30 in, 1,938 mm - hardtop 77.50 in, 1,968 mm; height: 55.80 in, 1,417 mm - hardtop 51.90 in, 1,318 mm - station wagons 56.20 in, 1,427 mm; ground clearance: 6.15 in, 156 mm - hardtop 5.40 in, 137 mm - station wagon 6.35 in, 161 mm; turning circle (between walls): 36.6 ft, 11.2 m - hardtop 39.4 ft, 12 m; fuel tank: 14.5 imp gal, 17.4 US gal, 66 l - hardtop 17.5 imp gal, 20.9 US gal, 79 l - station wagons 13.4 imp gal, 16.1 US gal, 61 l.

OPTIONAL ACCESSORIES Select Shift Cruise-o-Matic automatic transmission with 3 ratios (I 2.390, II 1.450, III 1, rev 2.090), max ratio of converter at stall 2, possible manual selection, 3.230 axle ratio; limited slip differential; 185 x 14 or ER70 x 14 tyres with 6" wide rims; power-assisted steering; front disc brakes (diameter 11.25 in, 286 mm), internal radial fins, servo; tinted glass; vinyl roof; GS Rallye equipment only for hardtop; reclining backrests; sunshine roof (not available for station wagons).

155 hp power team

See 130 hp power team, except for:

ENGINE 250 cu in, 4,097 cc (3.68 x 3.91 in, 93.4 x 99.2 mm); compression ratio: 9.3:1; max power (SAE): 155 hp at 4,000 rpm; max torque (SAE): 240 lb ft, 33.1 kg m at 1,600 rpm; max engine rpm: 4,600; 37.8 hp/l.

TRANSMISSION automatic transmission (standard) for Fairmont Series only; axle ratio: Fairmont 2.920.

PERFORMANCE max speed: about 99 mph, 159 km/h; speed in direct drive at 1,000 rpm: 22 mph, 35.4 km/h; fuel consumption: 19.5 m/imp gal, 16.2 m/US gal, 14.5 l x 100 km.

BRAKES (only for Fairmont) front disc (diameter 11.25 in, 286 mm), internal radial fins, servo (standard).

OPTIONAL ACCESSORIES Select Shift Cruise-o-Matic automatic transmission with steering column or central lever and 2.920 axle ratio; 4-speed fully synchronized mechanical gearbox (I 2.780, II 1.930, III 1.360, IV 1, rev 2.780) with central lever and 3.230 axle ratio; air-conditioning; electrically-controlled windows.

170 hp power team

See 130 hp power team, except for:

ENGINE 250 cu in, 4,097 cc (3.68 x 3.91 in, 93.4 x 99.2 mm); compression ratio: 9.3:1; max power (SAE): 170 hp at 4,200 rpm; max torque (SAE): 250 lb ft, 34.5 kg m at 2,200 rpm; 41.5 hp/l; 1 Autolite downdraught twin barrel carburettor.

PERFORMANCE max speed: about 102 mph, 164 km/h; speed in direct drive at 1,000 rpm: 22.4 mph, 36 km/h; fuel consumption: 18.8 m/imp gal, 15.7 m/US gal, 15 l x 100 km.

BRAKES (only for Fairmont) front disc (diameter 11.25 in, 286 mm), internal radial fins, servo (standard).

OPTIONAL ACCESSORIES Select Shift Cruise-O-Matic automatic transmission with 3 ratios (I 2.460, II 1.460, III 1, rev 2.200), max ratio of converter at stall 2, steering column or central lever, 2.920 axle ratio; 4-speed fully synchronized mechanical gearbox (I 2.780, II 1.930, III 1.360, IV 1, rev 2.780) with central lever and 3.230 axle ratio; air-conditioning; electrically-controlled windows.

240 hp power team

See 130 hp power team, except for:

ENGINE 8 cylinders, Vee-slanted at 90°; 302 cu in, 4,950 cc (4 x 3 in, 101.6 x 76.1 mm); compression ratio: 9.5:1; max power (SAE): 240 hp at 5,000 rpm; max torque (SAE): 305 lb ft, 42.1 kg m at 2,600 rpm; max engine rpm: 5,200; 48.5 hp/l; 5 crankshaft bearings; camshafts: 1, at centre of Vee; 1 Autolite downdraught twin barrel carburettor; cooling system capacity: 22.5 imp pt, 27.1 US pt, 12.8 l.

FORD Fairmont 2-door Hardtop

FORD Fairmont 4-door Sedan

FORD Fairlane 500 4-door Sedan

TRANSMISSION gearbox ratios: I 2.710, II 1.690, III 1, rev 3.370; axle ratio: 2.920.

PERFORMANCE max speed: about 112 mph, 180 km/h; speed in direct drive at 1,000 rpm: 25 mph, 40 km/h; fuel consumption: 17.2 m/imp gal, 14.3 m/US gal, 16.4 l x 100 km.

BRAKES (only for Fairmont) front disc (diameter 11.25 in, 286 mm), internal radial fins, servo (standard).

OPTIONAL ACCESSORIES Select Shift Cruise-o-Matic automatic transmission with 3 ratios (I 2.460, II 1.460, III 1, rev 2.200), max ratio of converter at stall 2, steering column or central lever, 2.920 axle ratio; 4-speed fully synchronized mechanical gearbox (I 2.780, II 1.930, III 1.360, IV 1, rev 2.780) with central lever and 2.920 axle ratio; dual exhaust system; air-conditioning; electrically-controlled windows.

260 hp power team

See 130 hp power team, except for:

ENGINE 8 cylinders, Vee-slanted at 90°; 351 cu in, 5,752 cc (4 x 3.50 in, 101.6 x 88.8 mm); compression ratio: 9.7:1; max power (SAE): 260 hp at 4,600 rpm; max torque (SAE): 355 lb ft, 49 kg m at 2,600 rpm; max engine rpm: 4,900; 45.2 hp/l; 5 crankshaft bearings; camshafts: 1, at centre of Vee; 1 Autolite downdraught twin barrel carburettor; cooling system capacity: 24.6 imp pt, 29.6 US pt, 14 l.

TRANSMISSION clutch: 2 dry plates (diaphragm), hydraulically controlled; gears: 4, fully synchronized, ratios: I 2.780, II 1.930, III 1.360, IV 1, rev 2.780; lever: central; axle ratio: 3.000.

PERFORMANCE max speed: about 118 mph, 190 km/h; speed in direct drive at 1,000 rpm: 25 mph, 40 km/h; fuel consumption: 16.6 m/imp gal, 13.8 m/US gal, 17 l x 100 km.

BRAKES (only for Fairmont) front disc (diameter 11.25 in, 286 mm), internal radial fins, servo (standard).

OPTIONAL ACCESSORIES Select Shift Cruise-o-Matic automatic transmission with 3 ratios (I 2.460, II 1.460, III 1, rev 2.200), max ratio of converter at stall 2, steering column or central lever, 2,750 axle ratio; dual exhaust system; 7.35 S x 14 tyres; air-conditioning; electrically-controlled windows.

300 hp power team

See 130 hp power team, except for:

ENGINE 8 cylinders, Vee-slanted at 90°; 351 cu in, 5,752 cc (4 x 3.50 in, 101.6 x 88.8 mm); compression ratio: 11:1; max power (SAE): 300 hp at 5,400 rpm; max torque (SAE): 380 lb ft, 52.4 kg m at 3,400 rpm; max engine rpm: 5,600; 52.2 hp/l; 5 crankshaft bearings; camshafts: 1, at centre of Vee; lubricating system sapacity: 6.7 imp pt, 8 US pt, 3.8 l; 1 Autolite downdraught 4-barrel carburettor; dual exhaust system; cooling system capacity: 24.3 imp pt, 29.2 US pt, 13.8 l.

TRANSMISSION clutch: 2 dry plates (diaphragm), hydraulically controlled; gears: 4, fully synchronized; ratios: I 2.780, II 1.930, III 1.360, IV 1, rev 2.780; lever: central; final drive: limited slip differential (standard); axle ratio: 3.000; width of rims: 6"; tyres: E70 HR x 14.

PERFORMANCE max speed: about 124 mph, 200 km/h; speed in direct drive at 1,000 rpm: 24.5 mph, 39.5 km/h; fuel consumption: 14.9 m/imp gal, 12.4 m/US gal, 19 l x 100 km.

CHASSIS rear suspension: anti-roll bar.

BRAKES front disc (diameter 11.25 in, 286 mm), internal radial fins, servo (standard).

ELECTRICAL EQUIPMENT 4 headlamps, iodine long distance lights.

BODY reclining backrests (standard).

OPTIONAL ACCESSORIES Select Shift Cruise-o-Matic automatic transmission with 3 ratios (I 2.400, II 1.470, III 1, rev 2), max ratio of converter at stall 2.40, 2.750 axle ratio; larger fuel tank; air-conditioning; electrically-controlled windows.

Fairlane Custom - Fairlane 500 Series

1 Fairlane Custom	4-door Sedan
2 Fairlane 500	4-door Sedan

Power team:	Standard for:	Optional for:
155 hp	1	—
220 hp	2	1
250 hp	—	both

155 hp power team

ENGINE front, 4 stroke; 6 cylinders, in line; 250 cu in, 4,097 cc (3.68 x 3.91 in, 93.4 x 99.2 mm); compression ratio: 9.3:1; max power (SAE): 155 hp at 4,000 rpm; max torque (SAE): 240 lb ft, 33.1 kg m at 1,600 rpm; max engine rpm: 4,600; 37.8 hp/l; cast iron cylinder block and head; 7 crankshaft bearings; valves: overhead, push-rods and rockers, hydraulic tappets; camshafts: 1, side; lubrication: gear pump, full flow filter, 7.6 imp pt, 9.1 US pt, 4.3 l; 1 Stromberg downdraught single barrel carburettor; fuel feed: mechanical pump; water-cooled, 15.1 imp pt, 18.2 US pt, 8.6 l.

TRANSMISSION driving wheels: rear; clutch: single dry plate (diaphragm), hydraulically controlled; gearbox: mechanical; gears: 3, fully synchronized; ratios: I 2.950, II 1.690, III 1, rev 3.670; lever: steering column; final drive: hypoid bevel; axle ratio: 3.230; width of rims: 5"; tyres: 6.95 x 14.

PERFORMANCE max speed: about 90 mph, 145 km/h; power-weight ratio: 20.1 lb/hp, 9.1 kg/hp; speed in direct drive at 1,000 rpm: 20.5 mph, 33 km/h; fuel consumption: 19 m/imp gal, 15.8 m/US gal, 14.9 l x 100 km.

CHASSIS integral; front suspension: independent, wishbones, lower trailing links, coil springs, anti-roll bar, telescopic dampers; rear suspension: rigid axle, semi-elliptic leaf-springs, telescopic dampers.

STEERING recirculating ball.

BRAKES drum.

ELECTRICAL EQUIPMENT 12 V; 45 Ah battery; 38 A alternator; Autolite distributor; 4 headlamps.

DIMENSIONS AND WEIGHT wheel base: 116 in, 2,946 mm; tracks: 58.90 in, 1,496 mm front, 58.50 in, 1,486 mm rear; length: 196.30 in, 4,986 mm; width: 73.50 in, 1,867 mm; height: 55.80 in, 1,417 mm; ground clearance: 7 in, 178 mm; dry weight: 3,120 lb, 1,415 kg; turning circle (between walls): 41 ft, 12.5 m; fuel tank: 13.6 imp gal, 16.4 US gal, 62 l.

BODY saloon/sedan; 4 doors; 5-6 seats, separate front seats.

OPTIONAL ACCESSORIES Select Shift Cruise-o-Matic automatic transmission with 3 ratios (I 2.390, II 1.450, III 1, rev 2.090), max ratio of converter at stall 2, possible manual selection, central or steering column lever, 2.920 axle ratio; limited slip differential; power-assisted steering; front disc brakes (diameter 11.25 in, 286 mm), internal radial fins, servo; bench front seats; sunshine roof; air-conditioning.

220 hp power team

See 155 hp power team, except for:

ENGINE 8 cylinders, Vee-slanted at 90°; 302 cu in, 4,950 cc (4 x 3 in, 101.6 x 76.1 mm); compression ratio: 9.5:1; max power (SAE): 220 hp at 4,600 rpm; max torque (SAE): 300 lb ft, 30.3 kg m at 2,600 rpm; max engine rpm: 4,800; 44.4 hp/l; 5 crankshaft bearings; camshafts: 1, at centre of Vee; 1 Stromberg downdraught twin barrel carburettor; cooling system capacity: 22.5 imp pt, 27.1 US pt, 12.8 l.

TRANSMISSION gearbox: Select Shift Cruise-o-Matic automatic transmission (standard for Fairlane 500 only), hydraulic torque converter and planetary gears with 3 ratios, max ratio of converter at stall 2, possible manual selection; ratios: I 2.460, II 1.460, III 1, rev 2.200; axle ratio: 2.920.

PERFORMANCE max speed: about 102 mph, 164 km/h; power-weight ratio: Fairlane Custom 14.1 lb/hp, 6.4 kg/hp — Fairlane 500 15 lb/hp, 6.8 kg/hp; speed in direct drive at 1,000 rpm: 22 mph, 35.4 km/h; fuel consumption: 16.8 m/imp gal, 14 m/US gal, 16.8 l x 100 km.

STEERING (only for Fairlane 500) servo (standard).

BRAKES (only for Fairlane 500) front disc (diameter 11.25 in, 286 mm), internal radial fins, servo (standard).

DIMENSIONS AND WEIGHT dry weight: Fairlane 500 3,305 lb, 1,499 kg.

250 hp power team

See 155 hp power team, except for:

ENGINE 8 cylinders, Vee-slanted at 90°; 351 cu in, 5,752 cc (4 x 3.50 in, 101.6 x 88.8 mm); compression ratio: 9.7:1; max power (SAE): 250 hp at 4,600 rpm; max torque (SAE): 355 lb ft, 49 kg m at 2,600 rpm; max engine rpm: 4,900; 43.5 hp/l; 5 crankshaft bearings; camshafts: 1, at centre of Vee; 1 Stromberg downdraught twin barrel carburettor; cooling system capacity: 24.6 imp pt, 29.6 US pt, 14 l.

TRANSMISSION gearbox: Select Shift Cruise-o-Matic automatic transmission (standard), hydraulic torque converter and planetary gears with 3 ratios, max ratio of converter at stall 2.40, possible manual selection; ratios: I 2.400, II 1.470, III 1, rev 2; lever: central; axle ratio: 2.920.

PERFORMANCE max speed: about 106 mph, 171 km/h; power-weight ratio: Fairlane Custom 12.7 lb/hp, 5.7 kg/hp — Fairlane 500 13.2 lb/hp, 6 kg/hp; speed in direct drive at 1,000 rpm: 22 mph, 35.4 km/h; fuel consumption: 16 m/imp gal, 13.3 m/US gal, 17.7 l x 100 km.

STEERING servo (standard).

BRAKES front disc (diameter 11.25 in, 286 mm), internal radial fins, servo (standard).

DIMENSIONS AND WEIGHT (see 220 hp power team).

HOLDEN Torana 1600 De Luxe 2-door Saloon

HOLDEN Torana GTR XU-1 Saloon

HOLDEN HQ Belmont

HOLDEN AUSTRALIA

Torana 1200 2-door Saloon

ENGINE front, 4 stroke; 4 cylinders, in line; 70.7 cu in, 1,159 cc (3.06 x 2.40 in, 77.7 x 61 mm); compression ratio: 8.5:1; max power (SAE): 56.2 hp at 5,400 rpm; max torque (SAE): 66.5 lb ft, 9.2 kg m at 3,000 rpm; max engine rpm: 6,000; 48.5 hp/l; cast iron cylinder block and head; 3 crankshaft bearings; valves: overhead, in line, push-rods and rockers; camshafts: 1, side; lubrication: gear pump, full flow filter, 5.5 imp pt, 6.6 US pt, 3.1 l; 1 Zenith 30 IZ downdraught single barrel carburettor; fuel feed: mechanical pump; water-cooled, 8.1 imp pt, 9.6 US pt, 4.6 l.

TRANSMISSION driving wheels: rear; clutch: single dry plate (diaphragm); gearbox: mechanical; gears: 4, fully synchronized; ratios: I 3.460, II 2.221, III 1.400, IV 1, rev 3.710; lever: central; final drive: hypoid bevel; axle ratio: 3.899; width of rims: 4"; tyres: 5.50 x 12.

PERFORMANCE max speed: about 83 mph, 133 km/h; power-weight ratio: 33 lb/hp, 15 kg/hp; carrying capacity: 900 lb, 408 kg; speed in direct drive at 1,000 rpm: 15.8 mph, 25.4 km/h; fuel consumption: not declared.

CHASSIS integral; front suspension: independent, wishbones, coil springs, telescopic dampers; rear suspension: rigid axle, trailing lower radius arms, upper oblique radius arms, coil springs, telescopic dampers.

STEERING rack-and-pinion; turns lock to lock: 3.40.

BRAKES drum; swept area: total 126 sq in, 813 sq cm.

ELECTRICAL EQUIPMENT 12 V; 40 Ah battery; 420 W alternator; AC Delco distributor; 2 headlamps.

DIMENSIONS AND WEIGHT wheel base: 95.80 in, 2,433 mm; tracks: 51.30 in, 1,303 mm front, 51 in, 1,295 mm rear; length: 162.20 in, 4,120 mm; width: 63 in, 1,600 mm; height: 53.30 in, 1,354 mm; ground clearance: 5.40 in, 137 mm; dry weight: 1,859 lb, 843 kg; turning circle (between walls): 33.8 ft, 10.3 m; fuel tank: 8 imp gal, 9.5 US gal, 36 l.

BODY saloon/sedan; 2 doors; 4 seats, separate front seats.

PRACTICAL INSTRUCTIONS fuel: 97 oct petrol; engine sump oil: 4.9 imp pt, 5.9 US pt, 2.8 l, SAE 10W-20, change every 6,000 miles, 9,700 km; gearbox oil: 0.9 imp pt, 1.1 US pt, 0.5 l, SAE 90, change every 6,000 miles, 9,700 km; final drive oil: 1.4 imp pt, 1.7 US pt, 0.8 l, SAE 90, change every 6,000 miles, 9,700 km; greasing: every 12,000 miles, 19,300 km, 4 points; tappet clearances: inlet 0.006 in, 0.15 mm, exhaust 0.010 in, 0.25 mm; valve timing: 39° 93° 65° 45°; tyre pressure: front 24 psi, 1.7 atm, rear 24 psi, 1.7 atm.

VARIATIONS

ENGINE 9:1 compression ratio, max power (SAE) 68.9 hp, 59.4 hp/l.
TRANSMISSION 6.20 L x 12 tyres (standard).
BRAKES disc.

OPTIONAL ACCESSORIES Trimatic automatic transmission with 3 ratios (I 2.400, II 1.480, III 1, rev 1.920); 4.125 axle ratio; 6.20 L x 12 tyres; front disc brakes.

Torana 1200 4-door Saloon

See Torana 1200 2-door Saloon, except for:

PERFORMANCE power-weight ratio: 34.5 lb/hp, 15.6 kg/hp.

DIMENSIONS AND WEIGHT dry weight: 1,929 lb, 875 kg.

BODY 4 doors.

Torana 1300 De Luxe 2-door Saloon

See Torana 1200 2-door Saloon, except for:

ENGINE 76.5 cu in, 1,256 cc (3.19 x 2.40 in, 81 x 61 mm); max power (SAE): 62.5 hp at 5,400 rpm; max torque (SAE): 71 lb ft, 9.8 kg m at 3,600 rpm; 49.8 hp/l.

TRANSMISSION tyres: 6.20 L x 12 (standard).

PERFORMANCE power-weight ratio: 29.7 lb/hp, 13.5 kg/hp.

Torana 1300 De Luxe 4-door Saloon

See Torana 1300 De Luxe 2-door Saloon, except for:

PERFORMANCE power-weight ratio: 30.9 lb/hp, 14 kg/hp.

HOLDEN Torana 2250 SL 4-door Saloon

HOLDEN Torana GTR Saloon

HOLDEN HQ Belmont Saloon

DIMENSIONS AND WEIGHT dry weight: 1,929 lb, 875 kg.

BODY 4 doors.

Torana 1300 SL 2-door Saloon

See Torana 1300 De Luxe 2-door Saloon, except for:

PERFORMANCE power-weight ratio: 29.9 lb/hp, 13.6 kg/hp.

DIMENSIONS AND WEIGHT dry weight: 1,869 lb, 847 kg.

Torana 1600 De Luxe 2-door Saloon

See Torana 1200 2-door Saloon, except for:

ENGINE 97.5 cu in, 1,599 cc (3.38 x 2.73 in, 85.7 x 69.2 mm); max power (SAE): 80 hp at 5,500 rpm; max torque (SAE): 96 lb ft, 13.2 kg at 3,200 rpm; 50 hp/l; 5 crankshaft bearings; camshafts: 1, overhead; lubrication: rotary or vane-type pump, full flow filter, 7.9 imp pt, 9.5 US pt, 4.5 l; 1 Zenith 36 IV downdraught single barrel carburettor; cooling system capacity: 14.1 imp pt, 16.9 US pt, 8 l.

TRANSMISSION gearbox ratios: I 2.780, II 1.980, III 1.410, IV 1, rev, 3.060; axle ratio: 4.125; tyres: 6.20 L x 12.

PERFORMANCE max speed: about 90 mph, 145 km/h; power-weight ratio: 25.6 lb/hp, 11.6 kg/hp; speed in direct drive at 1,000 rpm: 14.4 mph, 23.1 km/h; fuel consumption: not declared.

BRAKES front disc, rear drum, servo; swept area: front 14.8 sq in, 95 sq cm, rear 29 sq in, 187 sq cm, total 43.8 sq in, 282 sq cm.

DIMENSIONS AND WEIGHT ground clearance: 5.10 in, 129 mm; dry weight: 2,050 lb, 930 kg; fuel tank: 10.1 imp gal, 12.1 US gal, 46 l.

PRACTICAL INSTRUCTIONS engine sump oil: 7.4 imp pt, 8.9 US pt, 4.2 l, SAE 5W-20 (winter) 10W-40 (summer); gearbox oil: 2.3 imp pt, 2.7 US pt, 1.3 l, SAE 90; tappet clearances (hot): inlet 0.007-0.010 in, 0.17-0.25 mm, exhaust 0.015-0.018 in, 0.37-0.45 mm; valve timing: 24° 56° 56° 24°.

Torana 1600 De Luxe 4-door Saloon

See Torana 1600 De Luxe 2-door Saloon, except for:

BODY 4 doors.

Torana 2250 S 2-door Saloon

ENGINE front, 4 stroke; 6 cylinders, in line; 138 cu in, 2,262 cc (3.12 x 3 in, 79.2 x 76.2 mm); compression ratio: 9.2:1; max power (SAE): 95 hp at 4,600 rpm; max torque (SAE): 120 lb ft, 16.5 kg m at 1,600 rpm; max engine rpm: 5,200; 42 hp/l; cast iron cylinder block and head; 7 crankshaft bearings; valves: overhead, push-rods and rockers, hydraulic tappets; camshafts: 1, side; lubrication: gear pump, full flow filter, 7.5 imp pt, 8.9 US pt, 4.2 l; 1 Bendix-Stromberg downdraught single barrel carburettor; fuel feed: mechanical pump; water-cooled, 15 imp pt, 18 US pt, 8.5 l.

TRANSMISSION driving wheels: rear; clutch: single dry plate; gearbox: mechanical; gears: 3, fully synchronized; ratios: I 3.070, II 1.680, III 1, rev 3.590; lever: steering column; final drive: hypoid bevel; axle ratio: 3.080; width of rims: 4.5"; tyres: A 78 L x 13.

PERFORMANCE max speed: about 99 mph, 160 km/h; power-weight ratio: 24.1 lb/hp, 10.9 kg/hp; carrying capacity: 900 lb, 408 kg; speed in direct drive at 1,000 rpm: 21.9 mph, 35.2 km/h.

CHASSIS integral; front suspension: independent, wishbones, coil springs, telescopic dampers; rear suspension: rigid axle, trailing lower radius arms, upper oblique radius arms, coil springs, telescopic dampers.

STEERING rack-and-pinion; turns lock to lock: 3.30.

BRAKES drum; swept area: front 99 sq in, 638 sq cm, rear 99 sq in, 638 sq cm, total 198 sq in, 1,276 sq cm.

ELECTRICAL EQUIPMENT 12 V; 48 Ah battery; 420 W alternator; Bosch or Lucas distributor; 2 headlamps.

DIMENSIONS AND WEIGHT wheel base: 100 in, 2,540 mm; tracks: 51.80 in, 1,316 mm front, 50.80 in, 1,290 mm rear; length: 172.70 in, 4,386 mm; width: 63 in, 1,600 mm; height: 53.30 in, 1,354 mm; ground clearance: 5.40 in, 137 mm; dry weight: 2,289 lb, 1,038 kg; turning circle (between walls): 38 ft, 11.6 m; fuel tank: 10 imp gal, 11.9 US gal, 46 l.

BODY saloon/sedan; 2 doors; 4 seats, separate front seats.

PRACTICAL INSTRUCTIONS fuel: 97 oct petrol; engine sump oil: 7.5 imp pt, 8.9 US pt, 4.2 l, SAE 5W-20 (winter) 10W-40 (summer), change every 6,000 miles, 9,700 km; gearbox oil: 3.3 imp pt, 4 US pt, 1.9 l, HN-1046, change every 12,000 miles, 19,300 km; final drive oil: 2.5 imp pt, 3 US pt, 1.4 l, SAE 90 EP, change every 6,000 miles, 9,700 km; greasing: every 12,000 miles, 19,300 km or 6 months, 4 points; valve timing: 35° 75° 70° 40°; tyre pressure: front 20 psi, 1.4 atm, rear 20 psi, 1.4 atm.

TORANA 2250 S 2-DOOR SALOON

OPTIONAL ACCESSORIES Trimatic automatic transmission with 3 ratios (I 2.400, II 1.480, III 1, rev 1.920), steering column or central lever; 4-speed mechanical gearbox (I 3.050, II 2.190, III 1.510, IV 1, rev 3.050), central lever; limited slip differential; 2.780 3.360 axle ratios; 5.5" wide rims; front disc brakes; servo brake.

Torana 2250 S 4-door Saloon

See Torana 2250 S 2-door Salon, except for:

PERFORMANCE power-weight ratio: 24.6 lb/hp, 11.1 kg/hp.

DIMENSIONS AND WEIGHT dry weight: 2,338 lb, 1,060 kg.

BODY 4 doors.

Torana 2250 SL 4-door Saloon

See Torana 2250 S 2-door Saloon, except for:

PERFORMANCE power-weight ratio: 24.6 lb/hp, 11.1 kg/hp.

DIMENSIONS AND WEIGHT dry weight: 2,333 lb, 1,058 kg.

BODY 4 doors.

Torana 2850 S 2-door Saloon

See Torana 2250 S 2-door Saloon, except for:

ENGINE 173 cu in, 2,834 cc (3.50 x 3 in, 89 x 76.1 mm); compression ratio: 9.4:1; max power (SAE): 118 hp at 4,400 rpm; max torque (SAE): 168 lb ft, 23.2 kg m at 2,000 rpm; 41.6 hp/l.

PERFORMANCE max speed: about 103 mph, 165 km/h; power-weight ratio: 19.4 lb/hp, 8.8 kg/hp.

Torana 2850 S 4-door Saloon

See Torana 2850 S 2-door Saloon, except for:

PERFORMANCE power-weight ratio: 19 lb/hp, 9 kg/hp.

DIMENSIONS AND WEIGHT dry weight: 2,338 lb, 1,060 kg.

BODY 4 doors.

Torana 2850 SL 4-door Saloon

See Torana 2850 S 2-door Saloon, except for:

PERFORMANCE power-weight ratio: 19.8 lb/hp, 9 kg/hp.

DIMENSIONS AND WEIGHT dry weight: 2,333 lb, 1,058 kg.

BODY 4 doors.

Torana GTR Saloon

See Torana 2850 S 2-door Saloon, except for:

ENGINE max power (SAE): 130 hp; 46 hp/l; 1 downdraught twin barrel carburettor.

TRANSMISSION gears: 4 (standard); lever: central; width of rims: 5.5" (standard).

CHASSIS front suspension: anti-roll bar.

BRAKES front disc (standard).

Torana GTR XU-1 Saloon

See Torana GTR Saloon, except for:

ENGINE 186 cu in, 3,049 cc (3.63 x 3 in, 92.1 x 76.2 mm); compression ratio: 10:1; max power (SAE): 160 hp at 5,200 rpm; max torque (SAE): 190 lb ft, 26.2 kg m at 3,600 rpm; 52.5 hp/l; 3 Stromberg 150 CDS horizontal carburettors; cooling system capacity: 14.1 imp pt, 16.9 US pt, 8 l.

TRANSMISSION gearbox ratios: I 2.540, II 1.830, III 1.250, IV 1, rev 2.540; lever: central; axle ratio: 3.360; tyres: B 70 H x 13.

PERFORMANCE max speed: about 106 mph, 170 km/h; power-weight ratio: 15.1 lb/hp, 6.8 kg/hp.

DIMENSIONS AND WEIGHT tracks: 52.20 in, 1,321 mm front, 51.20 in, 1,296 mm rear; height: 53 in, 1,346 mm; ground clearance: 5 in, 127 mm; dry weight: 2,417 lb, 1,096 kg; fuel tank: 17 imp gal, 20.3 US gal, 77 l.

HQ Belmont Saloon

ENGINE front, 4 stroke; 6 cylinders, in line; 173 cu in, 2,834 cc (3.50 x 3 in, 88.9 x 76.2 mm); compression ratio:

HOLDEN HQ Premier Saloon

HOLDEN HQ Statesman De Ville

HOLDEN Monaro Coupé GTS

Model	Make
RANGE ROVER	ROVER
RAPIER	SUNBEAM
REBEL	RELIANT
REGAL	RELIANT
REKORD	OPEL
REX	SUBARU
RIVIERA	BUICK
ROAD RUNNER	PLYMOUTH
ROTARY	MAZDA
SAFARI	PONTIAC (USA)
SATELLITE	PLYMOUTH
SAVANNA	MAZDA
SCEPTRE	HUMBER
SCIMITAR	RELIANT
SCOUT	INTERNATIONAL
SILVER SHADOW	ROLLS-ROYCE
SIMCA	CHRYSLER FRANCE
SIX	WOLSELEY
SKYLINE	NISSAN
SONETT	SAAB
SOVEREIGN	DAIMLER
SPECIAL	CHEVROLET (RA)
SPEEDSTER	AUBURN SPEEDSTERS
SPIDER JUNIOR	ALFA ROMEO
SPIDER 1600	PUMA
SPITFIRE	TRIUMPH
SPORT	SUNBEAM
SPORT SUBURBAN	PLYMOUTH
SPRINTER	TOYOTA
STAG	TRIUMPH
STATESMAN	HOLDEN
STRATO	CUSTOKA
SUBURBAN	PLYMOUTH
SUNNY	NISSAN
SUSSITA	AUTOCARS
TAUNUS	FORD (D)
THUNDERBIRD	FORD (USA)
TOLEDO	TRIUMPH
TORANA	HOLDEN
TORINO	FORD (USA), IKA-RENAULT
TORONADO	OLDSMOBILE
TOWN AND COUNTRY	CHRYSLER
TRAVELALL	INTERNATIONAL
TYCOON	TRIDENT
URRACO	LAMBORGHINI
VALIANT	PLYMOUTH
VAMOS	HONDA
VANTAGE	ASTON MARTIN
VAREDO	ISO
VARIANT	VOLKSWAGEN
VARZINA	LAWIL
VEGA	CHEVROLET (USA)
VENTORA	VAUXHALL
VENTURA	PONTIAC (USA)
VENTURER	TRIDENT
VERANEIO	CHEVROLET (BR)
VICTOR	VAUXHALL
VISTA CRUISER	OLDSMOBILE
VIVA	VAUXHALL
VOLGA	GAZ
ZASTAVA	ZCZ

Cars called by letters (in alphabetical order)

Model	Make
A 112	AUTOBIANCHI
A 310	ALPINE
DS	CITROËN
E-TYPE	JAGUAR
G15	GINETTA
G21	GINETTA
GS	CITROËN
GT	ANDINO, OPEL
GTJ	OPEL
GT6	TRIUMPH
GT 1.3 JUNIOR	ALFA ROMEO
GT 1300 JUNIOR	ALFA ROMEO
GTA 1300 JUNIOR	ALFA ROMEO
GTE 1600	PUMA
GTO	PONTIAC (USA)
GTX	DODGE (RA)
J 72	PANTHER
JS 2	LIGIER
K 70	VOLKSWAGEN
LTD	FORD (BR, USA)
MARK VI EM	FAIRTHORPE
MGB	MG
N	HONDA
PLUS 8	MORGAN
R130	MAZDA
Ro 80	AUDI NSU
SM	CITROËN
SP	JENSEN
SS	EXCALIBUR, SQUIRE
SSJ	DUESENBERG
SSK	EXCALIBUR
T2-603	TATRA
T SERIES	BENTLEY
TR6 P.I.	TRIUMPH
TX-GT	FAIRTHORPE
TX-S	FAIRTHORPE
TX-SS	FAIRTHORPE
TX TRIPPER	TECHNICAL EXPONENTS
V8	ASTON MARTIN
VX 4/90	VAUXHALL
X 1/9	FIAT (I)
XJ6	JAGUAR
XJ12	JAGUAR
Z	HONDA

Cars called by numbers (in numerical order)

Model	Make
1.3 SUPER 90	G.T.M.
2 CV	CITROËN
2 'S' 130	LOTUS
2.5-LITRE P.I.	TRIUMPH
3.0	BMW
3.5-LITRE	ROVER
4	RENAULT
4/4 1600	MORGAN
5	RENAULT
6	RENAULT
8	RENAULT
12	RENAULT
15	RENAULT
16	RENAULT
17	RENAULT
33	DAF
44	DAF
66	DAF
80	AUDI NSU
95 V4	SAAB
96 V4	SAAB
99	SAAB
100	AUDI NSU, ŠKODA
104	PEUGEOT
105	SYRENA
110	ŠKODA
114	ZIL
117	ISUZU
124	FIAT (I)
125	FIAT (RA)
125 P	POLSKI-FIAT
126	FIAT (I)
127	FIAT (I), GIANNINI
128	FIAT (I), GIANNINI
130	FIAT (I)
132	FIAT (I)
144	VOLVO
145	HONDA, VOLVO
164	VOLVO
181	VOLKSWAGEN
200	MERCEDES-BENZ
204	PEUGEOT
220	MERCEDES-BENZ
223	WARSZAWA
230	MERCEDES-BENZ
250	MERCEDES-BENZ
280	MERCEDES-BENZ
304	PEUGEOT
350	MERCEDES-BENZ
353	WARTBURG
365	FERRARI
404	PEUGEOT
411	BRISTOL
412	VOLKSWAGEN
428	AC
500	FIAT (I), GIANNINI
504	PEUGEOT
520	BMW
530	MATRA SPORTS
590	GIANNINI
600	MERCEDES-BENZ, SEAT
601	TRABANT
650	GIANNINI
802	YLN
850	FIAT (I), MINI (BRITISH LEYLAND), SEAT
911	PORSCHE
914	VOLKSWAGEN-PORSCHE
966	ZAZ
1000	AUDI NSU, MINI (BRITISH LEYLAND)
1100	AUSTIN, MORRIS
1200	AUDI NSU, VOLKSWAGEN
1275 G.T.	MINI (BRITISH LEYLAND)
1300	AUSTIN, CG, MORRIS VOLKSWAGEN, WOLSELEY
1303	VOLKSWAGEN
1430	SEAT
1500	SEAT, TRIUMPH
1600	BMW, FIAT (RA), TVR, VOLKSWAGEN
1602	BMW
1700	RANGER (B)
1800	AUSTIN, BMW, MORRIS
1800 ES	VOLVO
1802	BMW
1900	RANGER (B)
2000	ALFA ROMEO, BMW, LANCIA, TRIUMPH, VAUXHALL
2000 AUTOMATIC	ROVER
2000 SC	ROVER
2000 TC	ROVER
2002	BMW
2150	FNM
2200	AUSTIN, MORRIS
2500	BMW, RANGER (B), TVR
2800	BMW
3000	TVR
3500	ROVER

MAXIMUM SPEED

Up to 65 mph

	mph
LAWIL Varzina	44
LAWIL City	44
STEYR-PUCH Haflinger 700 AP	48
LAWIL Log	50
HONDA Vamos 4	56
SUZUKI Jimny	58
AUTOBIANCHI Bianchina Giardiniera	59
FIAT Campagnola	59
CITROËN Mehari 2+2	62
FIAT (I) 500 Berlina	62
FIAT (I) 850 Familiare	62
HONDA Life Stepvan Super De Luxe	62
TRABANT 601	62
CITROËN 2 CV 4	63
CITROËN Dyane	65
DAIHATSU Fellow Max	65
FIAT (I) 126 Berlina	65

From 66 mph to 80 mph

	mph
ROVER Land Rover	66
CITROËN 2 CV 6	68
FIAT Campagnola A	68
HILLMAN Imp	68
RENAULT 4	68
SEAT 600 E	68
SUBARU Rex	68
SUZUKI Fronte Station Wagon	68
ZCZ Zastava 750	68
DAF 33	70
HONDA Life	71
GIANNINI Fiat Giannini 500 TV	71
MAZDA Chantez	71
MITSUBISHI Minica	71
SUZUKI Fronte	71
VOLKSWAGEN 1200	71
VOLKSWAGEN 181	71
CITROËN Dyane 6	73
MINI (BRITISH LEYLAND) 850 Saloon	73
MINI (BRITISH LEYLAND) Clubman	73
HINDUSTAN Ambassador Mk II	74
AUDI NSU Prinz 4L	75
AUTOCARS Carmel 13/60	75
AUTOCARS Sussita 13/60	75
AZLK Moskvich 412 Diesel	75
AZLK Moskvich 427 Diesel	75
HONDA Life Touring	75
HONDA Z Hardtop	75
HONDA 600	75
MINI (BRITISH LEYLAND) 1000 Saloon	75
RELIANT Bug 700	75
RELIANT Regal	75
RELIANT Rebel 750	75
RENAULT 6 (850)	75
SYRENA 105	75
CITROËN Ami 8	76
DAF 44	76
RENAULT 5 L	76
FORD (D) Escort	78
GIANNINI Fiat Giannini 590	78
LEYLAND INNOCENTI Mini Matic	78
PEUGEOT 204 Break Grand Luxe Diesel	78
SEAT 850	78
VOLKSWAGEN 1300	78
VOLKSWAGEN 1303 Limousine	78
VOLKSWAGEN 1600	78
WARSZAWA 223 K	78
WARTBURG 353 Tourist	78
AUSTIN 1100 Mk III	79

From 81 mph to 100 mph

	mph
AUDI NSU NSU 1000 C	81
HILLMAN Hunter De Luxe Estate Car	81
INTERNATIONAL Scout Station Wagon (113.1 hp power team)	81
JEEP CORPORATION Jeep Commando Series (100 hp power team)	81
MERCEDES-BENZ 200 D	81
OPEL Kadett	81
PEUGEOT 404 Berline Diesel	81
SEAT Diesel 2000	81
VOLKSWAGEN 1300 S	81
VOLKSWAGEN 1303 S	81
WARSZAWA 223	81
WARTBURG 353	81
FORD (BR) Corcel Sedan	82
FORD (GB) Escort 1100	82
INTERNATIONAL Travelall Series (113.1 hp power team)	82
MORRIS Marina 1.3	82
VAUXHALL Viva 1256	82
VAUXHALL Firenza 1256 De Luxe	82
FORD (D) Capri 1300	83
FORD (USA) Pinto 2-dr. Sedan and 3-dr. Runabout (54 hp power team)	83
HILLMAN Hunter De Luxe Saloon	83
HOLDEN Torana	83
AUTOBIANCHI A 112	84
CHRYSLER FRANCE Simca 1100 LS Berline (5 CV)	84
EL NASR Nasr 128	84
FORD (BR) Corcel	84
FORD (D) Taunus	84
GIANNINI Fiat Giannini 650	84
HILLMAN Avenger	84
MERCEDES-BENZ 220 D	84
OPEL Rekord 2100 D	84
PEUGEOT 104 Berline	84
PEUGEOT 504 Berline Diesel	84
RENAULT 6 TL (1100)	84
RENAULT 8	84
SEAT 850 Especial Berlina	84
ZAZ 966	84
ZCZ Zastava 101	84
AUSTIN 1300 Countryman	85
CHEVROLET (ZA) Firenza SL Series (75 hp power team)	85
DAF 66	85
FORD (GB) Cortina 1300	85
TRIUMPH Toledo	85
FIAT 128 Familiare	86
FORD (BR) Aero-Willys	86
FORD (GB) Capri 1300 L	86
RENAULT 5 TL	86
AUSTIN 1300 Super De Luxe	87
AUSTIN Maxi 1500	87
CHRYSLER FRANCE Simca 1000 (5 CV)	87
CHRYSLER FRANCE Simca 1100	87
DAF 66 Super Luxe Coupé	87
DAIHATSU Consorte	87
EL NASR Nasr 125	87
FIAT (I) 127	87
FIAT (I) 128	87
MAZDA Familia	87
MINI (BRITISH LEYLAND) 1275 G.T.	87
MORRIS 1300 Mk III Traveller	87
NISSAN Cherry	87
OTOSAN Anadol	87
PEUGEOT 204 Grand Luxe	87
SAAB 95 V4	87
SEAT 1500	87
SUBARU Leone 1400 4WD	87
TOYOTA Publica 1000	87
TRIUMPH 1500	87
ZCZ Zastava 1300	87
CHECKER Marathon Series (100 hp power team)	88
FORD (BR) Corcel GT Coupé	88
FORD (USA) Torino, Gran Torino, Gran Torino Brougham Series (92 hp power team)	88
VAZ Lada	88
DAF 66 Marathon	89
FORD (USA) Maverick - Maverick Grabber Series (84 hp power team)	89
HILLMAN Hunter Super	89
OPEL Kadett Rallye Coupé	89
OPEL Rekord	89
AMERICAN MOTORS Matador 2-dr. Hardtop and 4-dr. Sedan (100 hp power team)	90
AUDI NSU NSU 1200 C	90
AUDI NSU Audi 80	90
AZLK Moskvich 412	90
AZLK Moskvich 427	90
CHEVROLET (BR) Opala	90
CHEVROLET (BR) Veraneio	90
CHEVROLET (USA) Vega Series (72 hp power team)	90
DODGE (RA) Dodge 1500	90
FORD (D) Capri 1500	90
FORD (D) Consul	90
FORD (GB) Escort 1300	90
FORD (GB) Consul 2000	90
GAZ Volga 24	90
GIANNINI Fiat Giannini 500 Montecarlo	90
HILLMAN Avenger GL	90
HILLMAN Hunter GL	90
HOLDEN Torana 1600	90
HONDA Civic	90
JEEP CORPORATION Jeep Wagoneer Series (100 hp power team)	90
LEYLAND INNOCENTI Mini	90
LEYLAND INNOCENTI Austin J5	90
OPEL Ascona	90
PLYMOUTH Satellite - Satellite Custom (98 hp power team)	90
POLSKI-FIAT 125 P/1300	90
RANGER Ranger Series (86 hp power team)	90
RENAULT 12	90
SAAB 96 V4	90
SEAT 850 Sport Coupé	90
SUNBEAM Sport	90
TOYOTA Corolla 1200	90
TOYOTA Sprinter 1200	90
VANDEN PLAS Princess 1300	90
VOLKSWAGEN Karmann-Ghia	90
VOLVO 145 De Luxe Station Wagon	90
WOLSELEY 1300	90
YLN 802	90
CHRYSLER FRANCE Simca 1000 GLS (6 CV)	91
CHRYSLER FRANCE Simca 1301 Special	91
CITROËN GS	91
FORD (BR) Itamaraty	91
FORD (GB) Cortina 1600	91
JEEP CORPORATION Jeep CJ5 - Jeep CJ6 Series (100 hp power team)	91
PEUGEOT 504 Commerciale	91
VAUXHALL Viva 1256 SL	91
AUSTIN 1300 G.T. Saloon	92
AUSTIN Maxi 1750	92
AUSTIN 1800 De Luxe Saloon	92
FORD (GB) Capri 1600	92
FORD (USA) Pinto Station Wagon (83 hp power team)	92
MORRIS 1800 De Luxe Saloon	92

	mph
PEUGEOT 404 Berline Grand Tourisme	92
VOLKSWAGEN K 70 (75 hp)	92
VOLVO 144 De Luxe Saloon	92
ALFA ROMEO Alfasud Berlina	93
AUTOBIANCHI A 112 Abarth	93
CHEVROLET (RA) Special	93
CHEVROLET (RA) Rally Sport	93
DAIHATSU Consorte GS	93
DODGE (USA) Dart - Dart Custom - Dart Sport - Dart Swinger - Dart Swinger Special Series (95 hp power team)	93
FIAT (I) 128 Rally	93
FIAT (I) 128 S 1100	93
FIAT (I) 124	93
GIANNINI Fiat Giannini 590 Vallelunga	93
GIANNINI Fiat Giannini 127 NP	93
ISUZU Bellett 1600 Special	93
NISSAN Cherry 1200 GL Coupé	93
NISSAN Sunny 1200	93
PLYMOUTH Satellite - Satellite Custom (105 hp power team)	93
RENAULT 15 TL	93
RENAULT 16	93
PEUGEOT 304	93
TOYOTA Publica 1200	93
TOYOTA Corona 1600	93
BUICK Le Sabre - Le Sabre Custom Series (150 hp power team)	94
CHEVROLET (ZA) Kommando Series (142 hp power team)	94
CITROËN GS 1220	94
DODGE (USA) Coronet - Coronet Custom - Charger Series (98 hp power team)	94
LANCIA 2000 Berlina	94
PEUGEOT 304 Coupé	94
PLYMOUTH Valiant - Duster - Valiant Scamp Series (95 hp power team)	94
RENAULT 12 TS Berline	94
AMERICAN MOTORS Hornet - Hornet Sportabout Series (100 hp power team)	95
AMERICAN MOTORS Javelin 2-dr. Hardtop (100 hp power team)	95
MG Midget Mk III	95
MORRIS Marina 1.8	95
PONTIAC Ventura - Ventura Custom Series (100 hp power team)	95
SEAT 850 Sport Spider	95
TRIUMPH Spitfire Mk IV	95
CHEVROLET (USA) Nova - Nova Custom Series (100 hp power team)	96
CUSTOKA Hurrycane	96
CUSTOKA Strato	96
CHRYSLER FRANCE Simca 1000 Special	96
CHRYSLER FRANCE Simca 1100 Special	96
DODGE (RA) Coronado Automatic	96
FIAT (I) 124 Special	96
FORD (D) Capri GT 1700	96
MAZDA Grand Familia	96
NISSAN Sunny Excellent 1400	96
OPEL Manta	96
POLSKI-FIAT 125 P/1500	96
RANGER 1700 2-dr. Saloon	96
ROVER Range Rover	96
SEAT 1430	96
SUNBEAM Alpine	96
VAUXHALL Victor 1800 De Luxe	96
VAUXHALL Victor 3300 SL	96
VAUXHALL Ventora	96
VOLKSWAGEN 412 E	96
ZCZ Zastava 1500	96
AMERICAN MOTORS Ambassador Brougham Series (150 hp power team)	97

	mph
CHEVROLET (USA) Chevelle De Luxe - Chevelle Malibu Series (100 hp power team)	97
FORD (USA) Mustang and Mustang Grandé models (95 hp power team)	97
FORD (USA) Gran Torino Sport Series (137 hp power team)	97
HUMBER Sceptre	97
MERCURY Montego - Montego MX - Montego MX Brougham (92 hp power team)	97
PONTIAC Catalina Series (150 hp power team)	97
RANGER Ranger Series (106 hp power team)	97
AUSTIN Maxi 1750 HL	98
BUICK Century - Century 350 - Century Luxus - Century Regal Series (150 hp power team)	98
CHRYSLER FRANCE Chrysler 160	98
DODGE (USA) Coronet - Coronet Custom - Charger Series (105 hp power team)	98
FORD (BR) Galaxie	98
FORD (BR) LTD Landau	98
FORD (GB) Escort Sport	98
FORD (GB) Escort GT	98
FORD (USA) Station Wagons Series (154 hp power team)	98
MERCURY Comet Series (84 hp power team)	98
OLDSMOBILE Cutlass - Cutlass 'S' Series (160 hp power team)	98
PLYMOUTH Fury I - Fury II - Fury III - Gran Coupé - Gran Sedan Series (150 hp power team)	98
VOLKSWAGEN K 70 (90 hp)	98
AMERICAN MOTORS Matador Station Wagon (110 hp power team)	98
AUDI NSU Audi 80 S	99
BMW 1602 Limousine	99
BMW 1600 Touring	99
CHEVROLET (RA) Rally Sport 250	99
CHEVROLET (RA) Chevy	99
CHRYSLER FRANCE Simca 1000 Rallye	99
DODGE (RA) Polara	99
FIAT (I) 128 S 1300	99
FORD (GB) Capri 1600 GT	99
FORD (USA) Mustang Mach I 2-dr. Fastback (136 hp power team)	99
GIANNINI Fiat Giannini 127 NP-S	99
GIANNINI Fiat Giannini 128 NP 2-dr. Berlina	99
HILLMAN Avenger GLS	99
HOLDEN Torana 2250	99
HONDA 145	99
IKA-RENAULT Torino L	99
ISUZU Florian 1800	99
LANCIA Fulvia Berlina 2ª Serie	99
LEYLAND INNOCENTI Mini Cooper 1300	99
MAZDA Capella 1500	99
MERCEDES-BENZ 200	99
MITSUBISHI Galant	99
NISSAN Cherry X-I Sedan	99
NISSAN Sunny 1200 GX	99
NISSAN Skyline 1600	99
NISSAN President A Sedan	99
OPEL Rekord Coupé	99
PEUGEOT 304 S	99
PEUGEOT 504 Break	99
PLYMOUTH Satellite - Satellite Custom - Satellite Sebring - Satellite Sebring Plus - Satellite Regent Series (150 hp power team)	99
PONTIAC (USA) Le Mans - Le Mans Safari - Le Mans Sport Coupé Series (100 hp power team)	99
RANGER 1700 Coupé	99
SAAB 99 L 2-dr. Saloon	99

	mph
SAAB 99 2.0 EMS 2-dr. Saloon	99
TATRA T2-603	99
TOYOTA Corolla SL	99
TOYOTA Sprinter SL	99
TOYOTA Corolla 1400	99
TOYOTA Sprinter 1400	99
TOYOTA Carina 1400	99
TOYOTA Corona 1700	99
TOYOTA Corona Mk II 1700	99
TOYOTA Corona Mk II L	99
TOYOTA Crown	99
CHRYSLER FRANCE Simca 1501 Special	100
FORD (GB) Escort Mexico	100
HILLMAN Hunter GT	100
MERCURY Montego MX and Montego MX Villager Station Wagon (135 hp power team)	100
MOHS Ostentatienne Opera Sedan	100
MORRIS Marina 1.8 TC	100
PLYMOUTH Suburban - Custom Suburban - Sport Suburban Series (163 hp power team)	100
PONTIAC (USA) Firebird 2-dr. Hartop Coupé (100 hp power team)	100
PONTIAC (USA) Safari - Bonneville Series (170 hp power team)	100
RANGER 1900 2-dr. Saloon	100
ROLLS-ROYCE Phantom VI 7-pass. Limousine	100
ROVER 2000 SC	100
ROVER 2000 Automatic	100
SUNBEAM Rapier	100
TRIUMPH Dolomite	100
TRIUMPH 2000 Mk II	100
VAUXHALL Viva 1800 De Luxe	100
VAUXHALL Firenza 1800 SL	100
VAUXHALL 2300 SL Saloon	100

From 101 mph to 120 mph

	mph
CLAN Crusader	101
FORD (D) Taunus GT	101
FORD (GB) Cortina 1700 GT	101
FORD (USA) Custom 500 - Galaxie 500 - LTD - LTD Brougham Series (158 hp power team)	101
GINETTA G15	101
IKA-RENAULT Rambler	101
MERCURY Montego GT 2-dr. Fastback (137 hp power team)	101
PEUGEOT 504 G.L. Berline	101
PLYMOUTH Suburban - Custom Suburban - Sport Suburban Series (170 hp power team)	101
AMERICAN MOTORS Gremlin Series (100 hp power team)	102
CHEVROLET (USA) Camaro 2-dr. Sport Coupé (100 hp power team)	102
DODGE (USA) Polara - Polara Custom Series (150 hp power team)	102
FORD (D) Granada	102
JEEP CORPORATION Jeep Renegade Roadster	102
OPEL Manta SR	102
PLYMOUTH Road Runner 2-dr. Coupé (170 hp power team)	102
PONTIAC (USA) Catalina Series (175 hp power team)	102
VAUXHALL VX 4/90	102
ALFA ROMEO Giulia Super 1.3	103
AUSTIN 2200 De Luxe Saloon	103
BMW 1802 Limousine	103
BMW 1800 Touring	103

	mph
BMW 2002 Automatic Limousine	**103**
BMW 2000 Automatic Touring	**103**
CITROËN 20	**103**
FIAT (RA) 125 Familiar	**103**
FIAT (I) 132 Berlina 1600	**103**
FNM 2150	**103**
FORD (GB) Cortina 2000	**103**
HILLMAN Hunter GLS	**103**
HOLDEN Torana 2850	**103**
HOLDEN Torana GTR	**103**
HOLDEN HQ	**103**
HOLDEN Monaro	**103**
LANCIA Beta 1400	**103**
MAZDA Capella 1600	**103**
MERCURY Monterey Series (161 hp power team)	**103**
MITSUBISHI Galant L	**103**
MORRIS 2200 De Luxe Saloon	**103**
NISSAN Cherry 1200 X-I Coupé	**103**
NISSAN Datsun Bluebird-U	**103**
NISSAN Laurel 1800	**103**
NISSAN Skyline 1800	**103**
NISSAN Cedric	**103**
NISSAN Gloria	**103**
PONTIAC (USA) Bonneville Series (185 hp power team)	**103**
RANGER 1900 Coupé De Luxe	**103**
RANGER Ranger Series (120 hp power team)	**103**
RENAULT 16 TS	**103**
SAAB 99 2.0	**103**
TOYOTA Carina 1600	**103**
TOYOTA Celica	**103**
TOYOTA Corona Mk II 2000	**103**
WOLSELEY Six	**103**
AMERICAN MOTORS Javelin - Javelin AMX Series (150 hp power team)	**104**
CHEVROLET (USA) Bel Air - Impala Series (145 hp power team)	**104**
CHEVROLET (RA) Chevy Super Sport	**104**
DODGE (USA) Polara - Polara Custom - Monaco Series (163 hp power team)	**104**
FAIRTHORPE Mark VI EM	**104**
FORD (D) Capri GT 2000	**104**
MERCEDES-BENZ 220	**104**
PLYMOUTH Barracuda - 'Cuda Series (150 hp power team)	**104**
VAUXHALL Viva 2300 SL	**104**
VAUXHALL Firenza Sport SL	**104**
BUICK Estate Wagon - Electra 225 - Electra 225 Custom (225 hp power team)	**105**
CHEVROLET (USA) Camaro 2-dr. Sport Coupé (115 hp power team)	**105**
CHRYSLER Newport - Newport Custom (185 hp power team)	**105**
CITROËN DS	**105**
CITROËN DS 20 Berline	**105**
DODGE (USA) Challenger 2-dr. Hardtop (150 hp power team)	**105**
FORD (GB) Consul 2500	**105**
MERCURY Monterey - Marquis and Colony Park Station Wagon (167 hp power team)	**105**
MORGAN 4/4 1600	**105**
OLDSMOBILE Cutlass - Cutlass 'S' - Cutlass Supreme (180 hp power team)	**105**
OLDSMOBILE Vista Cruiser Series (180 hp power team)	**105**
OLDSMOBILE Delta 88 - Delta 88 Royale Series (160 hp power team)	**105**
ALFA ROMEO Junior 1.3	**106**
ALFA ROMEO GT 1300 Junior Z	**106**
ANDINO GT 1100	**106**
AUDI NSU Audi 80 GL	**106**

	mph
AUDI NSU Audi 100 LS	**106**
BMW 2002 Limousine	**106**
BMW 2000 Touring	**106**
BMW 2002 Cabriolet	**106**
BUICK Centurion Series (175 hp power team)	**106**
CHEVROLET (BR) Opala Gran Luxo	**106**
CHEVROLET (BR) Opala Coupé SS	**106**
CHEVROLET (ZA) Constantia 4-dr. Sedan (182 hp power team)	**106**
CHRYSLER FRANCE Chrysler 180	**106**
DODGE (USA) Dart - Dart Custom - Dart Sport - Dart Swinger - Dart Swinger Special Series (150 hp power team)	**106**
FIAT (I) X 1/9	**106**
FIAT (I) 124 Special T	**106**
FIAT (I) 132 Berlina Special 1800	**106**
FIAT (RA) 125 Sport	**106**
FORD (GB) Capri 2000 GT	**106**
FORD (GB) Granada 2500	**106**
GIANNINI Fiat Giannini 128 NP-S 2-dr. Berlina	**106**
GIANNINI Fiat Giannini 128 NP Rally	**106**
IKA-RENAULT Torino S	**106**
HOLDEN Torana GTR XU-I	**106**
HONDA 145 FI Coupé	**106**
ISUZU Bellett 1800 GTN Coupé	**106**
ISUZU 117 1800 N Coupé	**116**
LANCIA Fulvia Coupé 1.3 S 2ª Serie	**106**
LANCIA Beta 1600	**106**
MAZDA Luce Sedan GR AP	**106**
MERCURY Monterey Custom Series (171 hp power team)	**106**
MITSUBISHI Debonair	**106**
NISSAN Laurel 2000	**106**
OLDSMOBILE Toronado Custom Coupé	**106**
PLYMOUTH Valiant - Duster - Valiant Scamp Series (150 hp power team)	**106**
PONTIAC (USA) Luxury Le Mans Series (150 hp power team)	**106**
PONTIAC (USA) Grand Safari Series (200 hp power team)	**106**
RENAULT 15 TS	**106**
RENAULT 17 TL	**106**
SAAB 97 Sonett	**106**
SUBARU Leone 1400 Coupé	**106**
TOYOTA Celica 1600	**106**
TOYOTA Corona 1700 SL	**106**
TOYOTA Crown 2600	**106**
TOYOTA Century	**106**
TRIUMPH 2.5-litre P.I. Mk II Estate Car	**106**
BMW 520	**107**
BUICK Century Grand Sport model (190 hp power team)	**107**
CHEVROLET (USA) Caprice Classic - Caprice Estate Series (175 hp power team)	**107**
CITROËN 23	**107**
DODGE (USA) Polara - Polara Custom - Monaco Series (170 hp power team)	**107**
MG MGB	**107**
PONTIAC (USA) Grand Ville Series (215 hp power team)	**107**
DODGE (USA) Coronet - Coronet Custom - Coronet Crestwood - Charger - Charger SE (150 hp power team)	**108**
OLDSMOBILE Custom Cruiser Series (225 hp power team)	**108**
PONTIAC (USA) Firebird Esprit 2-dr. Hardtop Coupé (150 hp power team)	**108**
TECHNICAL EXPONENTS TX Tripper 1300	**108**
TRIUMPH 2.5-litre P.I. Mk II Saloon	**108**
ALFA ROMEO Giulia Super 1.6	**109**
ALFA ROMEO GTA 1300 Junior	**109**

	mph
CHEVROLET (USA) Chevelle De Luxe - Chevelle Malibu Series (115 hp power team)	**109**
DODGE (BR) Dart	**109**
CG 1300	**109**
CITROËN DSuper 5 Berline	**109**
IKA-RENAULT Torino TS Berlina	**109**
ISUZU Bellett 1800	**109**
ISUZU Florian 1800 TS Sedan	**109**
LANCIA Beta 1800	**109**
MATRA SPORTS 530	**109**
MAZDA Familia Rotary	**109**
MAZDA Savanna	**109**
MAZDA Luce Sedan GR Automatic	**109**
MERCEDES-BENZ 230	**109**
MITSUBISHI Galant Grand Sports	**109**
MITSUBISHI Galant GTO	**109**
NISSAN Datsun Bluebird-U 1800 SSS	**109**
NISSAN Skyline 2000 GT	**109**
OPEL Commodore	**109**
OPEL Admiral	**109**
PONTIAC (USA) Grand Safari Series (230 hp power team)	**109**
TOYOTA Celica ST	**109**
VOLVO 144 Grand Luxe Saloon	**109**
CHEVROLET (USA) Chevelle De Luxe - Chevelle Malibu - Chevelle Malibu Estate - Chevelle Laguna - Chevelle Laguna Estate Series (145 hp power team)	**110**
CHRYSLER New Yorker - New Yorker Brougham - Town and Country Series (208 hp power team)	**110**
MERCURY Marquis - Marquis Brougham Series (202 hp power team, 429 cu in)	**110**
MERCURY Marquis - Marquis Brougham Series (202 hp power team, 460 cu in)	**110**
PONTIAC (USA) Grand Am Series (170 hp power team)	**110**
PONTIAC (USA) Grand Ville Series (250 hp power team)	**110**
PONTIAC (USA) Grand Prix 2-dr. Hardtop Coupé (230 hp power team)	**110**
RANGER 2500 4-dr. Saloon Super De Luxe	**110**
SUNBEAM Rapier H120	**110**
TRIUMPH GT6 Mk III	**110**
TVR 1600 M	**110**
VOLVO 164 Saloon	**110**
AUDI NSU Audi 100 GL	**111**
CHEVROLET (USA) Monte Carlo Series (145 hp power team)	**111**
CITROËN DS 23	**111**
FORD (D) Capri GT 2300	**111**
IMPERIAL Le Baron Series (208 hp power team)	**111**
OLDSMOBILE Ninety-Eight Series (225 hp power team)	**111**
PEUGEOT 504	**111**
PLYMOUTH Duster 340 2-dr. Coupé (240 hp power team)	**111**
VOLKSWAGEN-PORSCHE 914-1.7	**111**
ALFA ROMEO Alfetta	**112**
ALPINE A 110 Berlinette Tour de France 85	**112**
AUDI NSU NSU Ro 80	**112**
BUICK Riviera Hardtop Coupé (250 hp power team)	**112**
CHRYSLER New Yorker - New Yorker Brougham - Town and Country (215 hp power team)	**112**
FAIRTHORPE TX-GT	**112**
FIAT (I) 124 Sport 1600	**112**
GIANNINI Fiat Giannini 128 NP-S Rally	**112**
IKA-RENAULT Torino TS Coupé	**112**
ISUZU 117 1800 Coupé	**112**

	mph
LANCIA Fulvia Sport 1.3 S 2ª Serie	**112**
LANCIA Fulvia Coupé 1600 HF 2ª Serie	**112**
LANCIA 2000 Berlina Iniezione	**112**
MAZDA Rotary Coupé SX	**112**
MAZDA Luce Sedan	**112**
MAZDA Luce Hardtop	**112**
MERCEDES-BENZ 250	**112**
MITSUBISHI Galant GTO XII	**112**
NISSAN Datsun 240K GT	**112**
OPEL Commodore Coupé	**112**
OPEL Commodore GS 4-dr. Limousine	**112**
PONTIAC (USA) Luxury Le Mans Series (175 hp power team)	**112**
RENAULT 17 TS	**112**
ROVER 2000 TC	**112**
THURNER Thurner RS	**112**
FORD (GB) Escort RS 1600	**113**
FORD (GB) Consul 3000 GT Saloon	**113**
FORD (GB) Granada 3000	**113**
OLDSMOBILE Ninety-Eight Series (250 hp power team)	**113**
OPEL Admiral 2800 S	**113**
PONTIAC (USA) Firebird Formula 2-dr. Hardtop Coupé (175 hp power team)	**113**
PUMA 1600	**113**
BMW 520 i	**114**
BMW 2500 Automatic Limousine	**114**
CHEVROLET (USA) Camaro LT 2-dr. Sport Coupé (145 hp power team)	**114**
IMPERIAL Le Baron Series (215 hp power team)	**114**
OPEL Commodore GS Coupé	**114**
PANTHER J 72	**114**
PONTIAC (USA) Grand Am Series (185 hp power team)	**114**
ALFA ROMEO Junior 1.6	**115**
AUDI NSU Audi 100 Coupé S	**115**
DAIMLER Limousine	**115**
FAIRTHORPE TX-S	**115**
FIAT (I) 124 Sport 1800	**115**
FIAT (I) 130 Berlina 3200	**115**
LANCIA 2000 Coupé	**115**
LINCOLN Continental Mk IV 2-dr. Hardtop	**115**
MAZDA Capella	**115**
MAZDA Luce Custom	**115**
MERCURY Cougar - Cougar XR-7 Series (168 hp power team)	**115**
NISSAN Fairlady Z Sports	**115**
NISSAN President D Sedan	**115**
OPEL GT	**115**
RANGER 2500 GTS Coupé	**115**
RENAULT 12 Gordini	**115**
ROVER 3.5-litre	**115**
TOYOTA Carina 1600 GT	**115**
TOYOTA Corona 2000	**115**
LINCOLN Continental Series (219 hp power team)	**116**
PONTIAC (USA) GTO 2-dr. Colonnade Hardtop (230 hp power team)	**116**
SQUIRE S.S. 100 Roadster	**116**
TRIUMPH TR6 P.I.	**116**
TVR 2500 M	**116**
VOLVO 1800 ES Coupé	**116**
DAIMLER Sovereign 2.8-litre	**117**
LOTUS Europa Twin Cam	**117**
VOLVO 164 E Saloon	**117**
ALFA ROMEO GT 1600 Junior Z	**118**
ALFA ROMEO 2000 Berlina	**118**
BMW 2002 Tii	**118**
BMW 2500 Limousine	**118**
CHEVROLET (USA) Corvette Series (190 hp power team)	**118**

	mph
DODGE (BR) Charger	**118**
DODGE (USA) Dart Sport 2-dr. Coupé (240 hp power team)	**118**
FIAT (I) Fiat Abarth 124 Rally	**118**
FIAT (I) 130 Coupé 3200	**118**
FORD (D) Capri GT 2600	**118**
ISUZU Bellett 1600 GTR Coupé	**118**
ISUZU 117	**118**
JAGUAR XJ6 2.8-litre Saloon	**118**
LANCIA Fulvia Sport 1600	**118**
LANCIA 2000 Coupé HF	**118**
MAZDA R130	**118**
MERCEDES-BENZ 280	**118**
MERCEDES-BENZ 280 S Limousine	**118**
OPEL Admiral 2800 E Luxus	**118**
OPEL Diplomat E	**118**
ROVER 3500	**118**
TOYOTA Corolla Levin 1600 Coupé	**118**
TOYOTA Sprinter Trueno	**118**
TOYOTA Celica GT	**118**
VOLKSWAGEN-PORSCHE 914-2.0	**118**
ZIL 114 Limousine	**118**
BENTLEY T Series 4-dr. Saloon	**118**
CADILLAC Calais - De Ville - Fleetwood Series (200 hp power team)	**119**
ROLLS-ROYCE Silver Shadow 4-dr. Saloon	**119**
BENTLEY Corniche	**120**
BMW 2800 Automatic Limousine	**120**
G.T.M. 1-3 Super 90	**120**
ROLLS-ROYCE Silver Shadow Long Wheelbase 4-dr. Saloon	**120**
ROLLS-ROYCE Corniche	**120**
TRIDENT Venturer V6	**120**
TRIUMPH Stag	**120**

Over 120 mph

	mph
ALFA ROMEO 2000 Veloce	**121**
AUDI NSU Audi 100	**121**
CADILLAC Fleetwood Eldorado Series (235 hp power team)	**121**
DODGE (RA) GTX	**121**
LOTUS Elan Sprint	**121**
LOTUS + 2 'S' 130	**121**
OPEL Commodore GS/E 4-dr. Limousine	**121**
TOYOTA Corona Mk II 2000 GSS	**121**
FORD (GB) Capri 3000	**122**
BMW 3.0 S Automatic Limousine	**123**
JENSEN Jensen-Healey	**123**
RELIANT Scimitar GTE	**123**
BMW 2800 Limousine	**124**
DAIMLER Sovereign 4.2-litre	**124**
FORD (USA) Thunderbird 2-dr. Hardtop (208 hp power team, 429 cu in)	**124**
IKA-RENAULT Torino GS Coupé	**124**
JAGUAR XJ6 4.2-litre Saloon	**124**
MERCEDES-BENZ 280 E	**124**
MERCEDES-BENZ 280 E Limousine	**124**
OPEL Commodore GS/E Coupé	**124**
AVANTI Avanti II	**125**
LOTUS Europa Special	**125**
PONTIAC (USA) Firebird Trans Am 2-dr. Hardtop Coupé	**125**
ROVER 3500 S	**125**
TECHNICAL EXPONENTS TX Tripper 2500 P.I.	**125**
TRIDENT Tycoon F.I. 2500	**125**
TVR 3000 M	**125**
BMW 3.0 S Limousine	**127**
BMW 3.0 Si Automatic Limousine	**127**
FORD (D) Capri RS 2600	**127**
MERCEDES-BENZ 350 SE Limousine	**127**
MERCEDES-BENZ 600	**127**
OPEL Diplomat V8	**127**
PORSCHE 911 T	**127**
GINETTA G21	**128**
GILBERN Invader Mk III Saloon	**129**
ALPINE A 310	**130**
FAIRTHORPE TX-SS	**130**
INTERMECCANICA Indra	**130**
MERCEDES-BENZ 350 SL	**130**
NISSAN Datsun Z 432 Sports	**130**
NISSAN Datsun 240 Z	**130**
TECHNICAL EXPONENTS TX Tripper 2500 P.I. De Luxe	**130**
BMW 3.0 Si Limousine	**131**
BMW 3.0 CSi Automatic Coupé	**133**
ALPINE A 110 Berlinette Tour de France 1600 S	**134**
MASERATI Indy America 4200	**134**
JENSEN Interceptor III	**135**
BMW 3.0 CS Automatic Coupé	**136**
ALFA ROMEO Montreal	**137**
BMW 3.0 CS Coupé	**137**
BMW 3.0 CSi Coupé	**137**
MORGAN Plus 8	**137**
PORSCHE 911 E	**137**
BMW 3.0 CSL Coupé	**138**
BRISTOL 411	**140**
DAIMLER Double-Six	**140**
JAGUAR XJ12 Saloon	**140**
TRIDENT Clipper V8 Super 300	**140**
ASTON MARTIN Vantage	**141**
CITROËN SM Injection	**142**
PORSCHE 911 S	**143**
FERRARI Dino 246	**146**
MONTEVERDI High Speed 375/4 Limousine	**146**
EXCALIBUR SSK-SS Series (270 hp power team)	**147**
C.F.P.M. Monica	**149**
ISO Fidia	**149**
DE TOMASO Deauville	**149**
LAMBORGHINI Urraco 250	**149**
MASERATI Merak	**149**
AC 428	**150**
JAGUAR E Type 12V Series III	**150**
JENSEN SP	**150**
LIGIER JS 2	**150**
ISO Grifo G.L.	**151**
MONTEVERDI High Speed 375 L	**152**
PORSCHE Carrera RS	**152**
DE TOMASO Mangusta	**155**
FERRARI 365 GT4 2+2	**155**
ISO Lele	**155**
LAMBORGHINI Espada 400 GT	**155**
MONTEVERDI High Speed 375	**155**
ASTON MARTIN V8	**161**
DE TOMASO Pantera	**162**
LAMBORGHINI Jarama 400 GT S	**162**
MONTEVERDI High Speed Hemi 375 L	**162**
FERRARI 365 GTC 4	**163**
MASERATI Indy America 4700	**165**
DE TOMASO Pantera GTS	**174**
DE TOMASO Longchamp	**174**
FERRARI 365 GTB 4 Berlinetta	**174**
MASERATI Bora 4700	**174**
MASERATI Ghibli Coupé	**174**
MONTEVERDI Hai 450 SS	**174**
MONTEVERDI Berlinetta	**180**
ISO Varedo	**186**
LAMBORGHINI Countach LP 500	**186**
FERRARI B.B. Berlinetta Boxer	**188**

MAKES, MODELS AND PRICES

Page	MAKE AND MODEL	Price in GB £	Price in USA $	Price ex Works
	AC (Great Britain)			
148	428 Convertible	5,800		
148	428 Fastback	—		
	ALFA ROMEO (Italy)			
206	Alfasud 2-door Berlina			—
206	Alfasud 4-door Berlina			1,350,000
206	Giulia Super 1.3			1,665,000
207	Giulia Super 1.6	1,430		1,770,000
207	GT Junior 1.3			1,920,000
207	GTA 1300 Junior			2,465,000
207	GT Junior 1.6	1,760		2,005,000
207	Spider Junior 1.3			1,985,000
208	Spider Junior 1.6			2,070,000
208	GT 1300 Junior Z			2,400,000
208	GT 1600 Junior Z			2,485,000
208	Alfetta			2,180,000
208	2000 Berlina	1,800	4,254	
209	2000 GT Veloce	2,140	5,249	
209	2000 Spider Veloce	2,180	4,948	
	2000 Series:			
	automatic transmission	*207*		*261,000*
	limited slip differential	*35*		*43,000*
	electrically-heated rear window	*17*		*17,000*
	light alloy wheels	*110*		*119,000*
209	Montreal	4,595		5,595,000
	electrically-controlled windows			*59,000*
	air-conditioning			*308,000*
	ALPINE (France)			
86	A 110 Berlinette Tour de France 85			25,900
86	A 110 Berlinette Tour de France 1600 S			36,100
	A 110 Series:			
	engine sump			*420*
	roll bar			*480*
	headrests			*260*
	fog lamps			*280*
	electrically-heated rear window			*660*
87	A 310			46,800
	electrically-heated rear window			*780*
	tinted glass			*720*
	leather upholstery			*2,760*
	AMERICAN MOTORS (USA)			
266	Gremlin 2-door Sedan		2,059	
	V8 engine		*154*	
	automatic transmission		*200*	
	power-assisted steering		*99*	
	servo brake		*44*	
266	Hornet 2-door Sedan		2,249	
266	Hornet 4-door Sedan		2,298	
266	Hornet 2-door Hatchback		2,449	
266	Hornet Sportabout Station Wagon		2,637	
	Hornet and Hornet Sportabout Series:			
	V8 engine		*138*	
	automatic transmission		*200*	
	power-assisted steering		*47*	
	servo brake		*44*	
268	Javelin 2-door Hardtop		2,857	
268	Javelin AMX 2-door Hardtop		3,159	
	Javelin and Javelin AMX Series:			
	V8 engine		*94*	
	automatic transmission		*218*	
	power-assisted steering		*106*	
	servo brake		*44*	
269	Matador 2-door Hardtop		2,848	
269	Matador 4-door Sedan		2,814	
269	Matador Station Wagon		3,140	
	Matador Series:			
	V8 engine		*99*	
	automatic transmission		*226*	
	power-assisted steering		*111*	
	servo brake		*47*	
271	Ambassador Brougham 2-door Hardtop		4,438	
271	Ambassador Brougham 4-door Sedan	2,465	4,422	
271	Ambassador Brougham Station Wagon	2,660	4,822	
	ANDINO (Argentina)			
254	GT 1100			—
	ASTON MARTIN (Great Britain)			
148	Vantage	5,750		
	air-conditioning	*295*		
	headrests	*20*		
148	V8	7,405	21,500	
	AUBURN SPEEDSTERS (USA)			
273	Speedster		—	
	AUDI NSU (Germany, F.R.)			
111	NSU Prinz 4L			5,190
112	NSU 1000 C			5,990
112	NSU 1200 C			6,690
112	NSU 1200 C Automatic			7,190
112	NSU Ro 80	2,439		17,590
113	Audi 80 2-door Limousine			7,990
113	Audi 80 4-door Limousine			8,365
113	Audi 80 L 2-door Limousine	1,070		8,440
114	Audi 80 L 4-door Limousine	1,095		8,815
114	Audi 80 S 2-door Limousine			8,340
114	Audi 80 S 4-door Limousine			8,715
114	Audi 80 LS 2-door Limousine			8,790
114	Audi 80 LS 4-door Limousine	1,175		9,165
114	Audi 80 GL 2-door Limousine	1,239		9,250
115	Audi 80 GL 4-door Limousine	1,305		9,625
115	Audi 100 2-door Limousine		3,695	10,600
115	Audi 100 4-door Limousine		3,805	10,950
115	Audi 100 LS 2-door Limousine	1,487	3,845	
115	Audi 100 LS 4-door Limousine	1,545	3,955	
115	Audi 100 GL 2-door Limousine	1,650	4,345	
115	Audi 100 GL 4-door Limousine	1,650	4,455	
115	Audi 100 Coupé S	2,130		14,700
	AUSTIN (Great Britain)			
148	1100 Mk III 2-door Saloon	716		
149	1100 Mk III 4-door Super De Luxe Saloon	779		

The prices refer to all the models listed in the volume, to the "Optional Accessories" and to the "Variations".
The first column shows the prices of cars produced in or imported into the United Kingdom; the second, the prices of cars produced in or imported into the United States of America; and the third, the prices of cars not imported into the United Kingdom or the United States, expressed in the currency of the country of origin.
The prices expressed in sterling are before adding purchase tax or VAT.
All prices in the USA do not include US transportation fees, state and local taxes; prices of the cars imported into the United States (East Coast) include ocean freight, US excise tax and import duty.
Due to the international monetary situation all prices shown are subject to confirmation.

Page	MAKE AND MODEL	Price in GB £	Price in USA $	Price ex Works
149	1300 Mk III 2-door Super De Luxe Saloon	775		
150	1300 Mk III 4-door Super De Luxe Saloon	803		
150	1300 Mk III Countryman	884		
150	1300 GT Saloon	932		
	1100 and 1300 Series:			
	automatic transmission	*88*		
	reclining backrests	*15*		
	electrically-heated rear window	*9*		
150	Maxi 1500	992		
151	Maxi 1750	1,032		
151	Maxi 1750 HL	1,137		
	Maxi 1750 Series:			
	automatic transmission	*94*		
151	1800 De Luxe Saloon	1,073		
151	2200 De Luxe Saloon	1,197		
	1800 and 2200 models:			
	automatic transmission	*94*		
	power-assisted steering	*60*		
	electrically-heated rear window	*11*		
	AUTOBIANCHI (Italy)			
210	Bianchina Giardiniera			690,000
211	A 112 Berlina			1,038,000
211	A 112 E Berlina			1,096,000
211	A 112 Abarth			1,309,000
	AUTOCARS (Israel)			
338	Carmel 13/60			—
338	Sussita 13/60			—
	AVANTI (USA)			
273	Avanti II Coupé		8,145	
	power-assisted steering		*100*	
	AZLK (USSR)			
247	Moskvich 412	592		
248	Moskvich 412 Diesel			—
248	Moskvich 412 De Luxe	681		
248	Moskvich 412 Diesel De Luxe			—
248	Moskvich 427	660		
248	Moskvich 427 Diesel			—
	BENTLEY (Great Britain)			
152	T Series 4-door Saloon	8,730	25,000	
152	2-door Corniche	11,400	32,800	
152	Corniche Convertible	11,915	35,400	
	BIOTA (Great Britain)			
152	Mini Sports Car	675		
	BMW (Germany, F.R.)			
116	1602 Limousine	1,570		10,645
116	1600 Touring			11,320
116	1802 Limousine			11,195
116	1800 Touring			11,870
116	2002 Limousine	1,773	3,571	
116	2002 Automatic Limousine	1,955		12,995
116	2000 Touring	1,943		12,370
117	2000 Automatic Touring	2,124		13,670
117	2002 Cabriolet			15,490
117	2002 Tii Limousine	2,067	4,286	
117	2002 Tii Touring			14,415
117	520			14,490
118	520 Automatic			15,790

Page	MAKE AND MODEL	Price in GB £	Price in USA $	Price ex Works
118	520 i			15,670
118	520 i Automatic			16,970
119	2500 Limousine	2,729		18,280
119	2500 Automatic Limousine	2,952		19,780
119	2800 Limousine		5,555	19,250
119	2800 Automatic Limousine			20,750
119	3.0 S Limousine	3,334		21,490
119	3.0 S Automatic Limousine	3,556		22,390
119	3.0 CS Coupé	4,093	8,712	
120	3.0 CS Automatic Coupé	5,129		30,450
120	3.0 Si Limousine	3,556		23,590
120	3.0 Si Automatic Limousine			25,090
120	3.0 CSi Coupé	5,129		30,650
120	3.0 CSi Automatic Coupé			32,150
120	3.0 CSL Coupé	5,294		31,950
	BRISTOL (Great Britain)			
152	411	6,450		
	BUICK (USA)			
273	Century Colonnade Hardtop Coupé		3,013	
273	Century Colonnade Hardtop Sedan		3,013	
273	Century 6-passenger Station Wagon		3,423	
273	Century 9-passenger Station Wagon		3,536	
273	Century 350 Colonnade Hardtop Coupé		—	
273	Century 350 Colonnade Hardtop Sedan		—	
273	Century Gran Sport Colonnade Hardtop Coupé		—	
273	Century Luxus Colonnade Hardtop Coupé		3,275	
273	Century Luxus Colonnade Hardtop Sedan		3,248	
273	Century Luxus 6-passenger Station Wagon		3,586	
273	Century Luxus 9-passenger Station Wagon		3,639	
273	Century Regal Colonnade Hardtop Coupé		3,412	
	Century, Century 350, Century Gran Sport, Century Luxus, Century Regal Series:			
	V8 engine		*46*	
	automatic transmission		*236*	
	power-assisted steering		*113*	
	servo brake		*46*	
274	Le Sabre Hardtop Coupé		4,024	
274	Le Sabre Hardtop Sedan		4,079	
274	Le Sabre 4-door Sedan		3,958	
274	Le Sabre Custom Hardtop Coupé		4,107	
274	Le Sabre Custom Hardtop Sedan		4,168	
274	Le Sabre Custom 4-door Sedan		4,047	
274	Centurion Hardtop Coupé		4,286	
274	Centurion Convertible		4,476	
274	Centurion Hardtop Sedan		4,338	
276	Estate Wagon 6-passenger		4,589	
276	Estate Wagon 9-passenger		4,728	
276	Electra 225 Hardtop Coupé		4,781	
276	Electra 225 Hardtop Sedan	3,900	4,889	
276	Electra 225 Custom Hardtop Coupé		4,951	
276	Electra 225 Custom Hardtop Sedan		5,059	
276	Riviera Hardtop Coupé	3,900	5,149	
	CADILLAC (USA)			
277	Calais Sedan		5,938	
277	Calais Coupé		5,771	
277	De Ville Sedan		6,390	
277	De Ville Coupé		6,168	

Page	MAKE AND MODEL	Price in GB £	Price in USA $	Price ex Works
277	Fleetwood Sixty Special Brougham	5,280	7,637	
277	Fleewood Seventy-Five Sedan		11,748	
277	Fleetwood Seventy-Five Limousine		11,880	
	Calais, De Ville, Fleetwood Series:			
	automatic transmission		*77*	
277	Fleetwood Eldorado Coupé	5,280	7,230	
277	Fleetwood Eldorado Convertible	5,400	7,546	
	C.F.P.M. (France)			
87	Monica			—
	CG (France)			
87	1300 Coupé			25,970
88	1300 Spider			27,101
	1300 Series:			
	light alloy wheels			*650*
	iodine fog lamps			*224*
	headrests			*45*
	CHECKER (USA)			
278	Marathon 4-door Sedan		3,954	
278	Marathon Station Wagon		4,211	
278	Marathon De Luxe Limousine		4,612	
	Marathon Series:			
	V8 engine		*109*	
	power-assisted steering		*71*	
	CHEVROLET (Argentina)			
254	Special			—
254	Rally Sport			—
254	Rally Sport 250			—
254	Chevy Standard			—
254	Chevy Super			—
255	Chevy De Luxe			—
255	Chevy Super Sport			—
255	Chevy Super Sport Coupé			—
	CHEVROLET (Brazil)			
258	Opala Especial			—
259	Opala Coupé Especial			—
259	Opala De Luxo			—
259	Opala Coupé De Luxo			—
259	Opala Gran Luxo			—
260	Opala Coupé Gran Luxo			—
260	Opala Coupé SS			—
260	Veraneio			—
	CHEVROLET (South Africa)			
339	Firenza SL 2-door Sedan			—
339	Firenza SL 4-door Sedan			—
339	Firenza SL 2-door Coupé			—
339	Firenza SL Station Wagon			—
340	Kommando 4-door Sedan			—
340	Kommando Station Wagon			—
341	Constantia 4-door Sedan			—
	CHEVROLET (USA)			
278	Vega Notchback Sedan		2,059	
278	Vega Hatchback Coupé		2,159	
278	Vega Kammback Station Wagon		2,284	
	Vega Series:			
	mechanical gearbox		*51*	
	automatic transmission		*163*	
	automatic transmission		*193*	
	power-assisted steering		*92*	

Page	MAKE AND MODEL	Price in GB £	Price in USA $	Price ex Works
279	Nova Hatchback Coupé		2,503	
279	Nova Coupé		2,354	
279	Nova 4-door Sedan		2,382	
279	Nova Custom Hatchback Coupé		2,660	
279	Nova Custom Coupé		2,511	
279	Nova Custom 4-door Sedan		2,539	
	Nova and Nova Custom Series:			
	V8 engine		*86*	
	automatic transmission		*169*	
	power-assisted steering		*100*	
	servo brake		*46*	
281	Camaro 2-door Sport Coupé	2,922	2,732	
281	Camaro LT 2-door Sport Coupé		3,211	
	Camaro and Camaro LT Series:			
	V8 engine		*90*	
	automatic transmission		*210*	
	power-assisted steering		*113*	
	servo brake		*46*	
282	Chevelle De Luxe 2-door Sport Coupé		2,702	
282	Chevelle De Luxe 4-door Sedan		2,669	
282	Chevelle De Luxe Station Wagon		3,033	
282	Chevelle Malibu 2-door Sport Coupé		2,846	
282	Chevelle Malibu 4-door Sedan		2,814	
282	Chevelle Malibu Station Wagon		3,211	
282	Chevelle Malibu Estate Station Wagon		3,404	
282	Chevelle Laguna 2-door Sport Coupé		3,147	
282	Chevelle Laguna 4-door Sedan		3,115	
282	Chevelle Laguna Station Wagon		3,400	
282	Chevelle Laguna Estate Station Wagon		3,587	
	Chevelle De Luxe, Chevelle Malibu, Chevelle Malibu Estate, Chevelle Laguna,			
	Chevelle Laguna Estate Series:			
	V8 engine		*112*	
	automatic transmission		*235*	
	power-assisted steering		*114*	
	servo brake		*46*	
283	Monte Carlo 2-door Sport Coupé		3,364	
283	Monte Carlo S 2-door Sport Coupé		3,509	
283	Monte Carlo Landau 2-door Sport Coupé		3,749	
	Monte Carlo Series:			
	automatic transmission		*210*	
284	Bel Air 4-door Sedan		3,213	
284	Bel Air 6-passenger Station Wagon		3,969	
284	Bel Air 9-passenger Station Wagon		4,078	
284	Impala 4-door Sport Sedan	2,820	3,776	
284	Impala 2-door Custom Coupé		3,792	
284	Impara 2-door Sport Coupé		3,725	
284	Impala 4-door Sedan		3,709	
284	Impala 6-passenger Station Wagon		4,062	
284	Impala 9-passenger Station Wagon		4,171	
284	Caprice Classic 4-door Sport Sedan	2,922	4,075	
284	Caprice Classic 2-door Sport Coupé		4,025	
284	Caprice Classic 2-door Convertible		4,284	
284	Caprice Classic 4-door Sedan		4,008	
284	Caprice Estate 6-passenger Station Wagon		4,314	
284	Caprice Estate 9-passenger Station Wagon		4,423	
	Bel Air, Impala, Caprice Classic and Caprice Estate Series:			
	V8 engine		*334*	
286	Corvette 2-door Sport Coupé		5,561	
286	Corvette 2-door Convertible		5,335	
	Corvette Series:			
	automatic transmission		*97*	
	power-assisted steering		*113*	
	servo brake		*46*	

Page	MAKE AND MODEL	Price in GB £	Price in USA $	Price ex Works
	CHRYSLER (USA)			
286	Newport 2-door Hardtop		4,153	
286	Newport 4-door Sedan		4,080	
286	Newport 4-door Hardtop		4,215	
286	Newport Custom 2-door Hardtop		4,383	
286	Newport Custom 4-door Sedan		4,313	
286	Newport Custom 4-door Hardtop		4,461	
286	New Yorker 4-door Sedan		4,891	
286	New Yorker 4-door Hardtop		5,019	
286	New Yorker Brougham 2-door Hardtop		5,297	
286	New Yorker Brougham 4-door Sedan		5,248	
286	New Yorker Brougham 4-door Hardtop		5,376	
286	Town and Country 6-passenger Station Wagon		5,181	
286	Town and Country 9-passenger Station Wagon		5,265	
	CHRYSLER FRANCE (France)			
88	Simca 1000 LS (5 CV)	670		8,835
88	Simca 1000 GLS Automatic (5 CV)			10,035
88	Simca 1000 GLS (6 CV)	710		9,735
88	Simca 1000 Special	782		10,295
88	Simca 1000 Rallye 1	780		9,995
88	Simca 1000 Rallye 2			12,995
89	Simca 1100 LS Berline (5 CV)	815		11,235
89	Simca 1100 LS (6 CV)	784		11,435
90	Simca 1100 GLS Berline	867		12,635
90	Simca 1100 LS Break			12,135
90	Simca 1100 GLS Break	935		13,335
90	Simca 1100 Special 2-door	955		13,335
90	Simca 1100 Special 4-door	985		13,835
90	Simca 1301 Special Berline	980		13,535
91	Simca 1301 Special Break	1,066		14,035
91	Simca 1501 Special Berline	1,046		
91	Simca 1501 Special Break	1,204		
91	Chrysler 160			15,070
92	Chrysler 180			16,995
	CITROËN (France)			
92	2 CV 4			7,896
92	2 CV 6			8,380
92	Dyane	585		8,580
93	Dyane 6	635		8,980
	Dyane Series:			
	centrifugal clutch	*16*		
	back seat folding down to luggage table	*16*		
93	Mehari 2+2			9,680
93	Ami 8 Berline Confort	701		9,980
94	Ami 8 Berline Club	738		10,440
94	Ami 8 Break Confort	763		10,440
94	Ami 8 Commerciale			10,440
	Ami 8 Series:			
	centrifugal clutch	*16*		
	reclining backrests	*13*		
94	GS Berline	958		12,900
95	GS Break			13,500
95	GS Commerciale			13,500
95	GS 1220 Berline	1,026		13,700
95	GS 1220 Break	1,097		14,300
95	GS 1220 Commerciale			14,300
95	GS 1220 Berline Club	1,087		14,300
95	GS 1220 Break Club	1,153		14,900
95	GS 1220 Commerciale Club			14,900
95	DSpecial Berline	1,404	3,750	
95	DSuper Berline			19,700
96	DS 20 Berline	1,707		22,800
96	DS 20 Pallas			24,800
96	Familiale Confort 20			24,300
96	Break Confort 20			24,300
96	Commerciale 20			21,508
	DS and 20 models:			
	power-assisted steering	*61*		
	electrically-heated rear window	*24*		
96	DSuper 5 Berline	1,545		20,900
96	DS 23 Berline	1,887		25,000
97	DS 23 Pallas	2,107		27,000
97	Familiale Confort 23			26,500
98	Break Confort 23			26,500
98	Commerciale 23			26,500
98	SM Injection	4,420	11,700	
	CLAN (Great Britain)			
153	Crusader	1,125		
	halogen headlamps	*14*		
	sunshine roof	*43*		
	CUSTOKA (Austria)			
82	Hurrycane			26,000
82	Strato			29,800
	DAF (Holland)			
204	33 Saloon	677		
204	33 De Luxe Saloon	715		
204	44 Saloon	809		
204	44 De Luxe Saloon	772		
204	44 C Estate Car	907		
204	66 De Luxe Saloon	876		
204	66 De Luxe Estate Car	1,012		
205	66 Super Luxe Saloon	938		
205	66 Super Luxe Coupé	1,054		
205	66 Super Luxe Estate Car	1,050		
205	66 Marathon Saloon	1,046		
205	66 Marathon Coupé	1,128		
205	66 Marathon Estate Car	1,137		
	DAIHATSU (Japan)			
343	Fellow Max 2-door Standard Sedan			328,000
343	Fellow Max 2-door De Luxe Sedan			373,000
343	Fellow Max 4-door De Luxe Sedan			398,000
343	Fellow Max 2-door Custom Sedan			393,000
343	Fellow Max 4-door Custom Sedan			418,000
344	Fellow Max 2-door Hi Custom Sedan			410,000
344	Fellow Max 4-door Hi Custom Sedan			435,000
344	Fellow Max SS 2-door Sedan			423,000
344	Fellow Max Hardtop TL			423,000
344	Fellow Max Hardtop GXL			476,000
344	Fellow Max Hardtop GHL			458,000
344	Fellow Max Station Wagon			458,000
345	Consorte Standard Sedan			397,000
345	Consorte Super De Luxe Sedan			487,000
345	Consorte PS Sedan			484,000
345	Consorte GS			514,000
	DAIMLER (Great Britain)			
153	Sovereign 2.8-litre	2,443		
154	Sovereign 4.2-litre	2,696		
	Sovereign Series:			
	automatic transmission (2.8-litre)	*46*		
	automatic transmission (4.2-litre)	*82*		
	air-conditioning	*203*		
	electrically-controlled windows	*48*		
154	Double - Six	3,184		
	electrically-controlled windows	*48*		
	air-conditioning	*203*		

Page	MAKE AND MODEL	Price in GB £	Price in USA $	Price ex Works
155	Double - Six Vanden Plas Saloon	4,500		
155	Limousine	4,900		
	electrically-controlled glass partition	*134*		
	electrically-heated rear window	*40*		
	DE TOMASO (Italy)			
211	Mangusta			6,845,000
211	Pantera	5,540	9,995	
211	Pantera GTS	6,198		6,800,000
212	Deauville	7,440		6,500,000
212	Longchamp			6,800,000
	Deauville and Longchamp models:			
	tinted glass	*29*		
	electrically-heated rear window	*169*		
	air-conditioning	*330*		
	DODGE (Argentina)			
255	Dodge 1500			23,510
256	Polara			31,269
256	Polara Coupé			33,355
257	Coronado Automatic			41,491
257	GTX			43,705
	DODGE (Brazil)			
260	Dart 4-door Sedan			—
261	Dart 2-door Coupé De Luxo			—
261	Charger 2-door Coupé			—
261	Charger R/T 2-door Coupé			—
	DODGE (USA)			
288	Dart 4-door Sedan		2,454	
288	Dart Custom 4-door Sedan		2,608	
288	Dart Sport 2-door Coupé		2,369	
288	Dart 340 Sport 2-door Coupé		2,793	
288	Dart Swinger 2-door Hardtop		2,562	
288	Dart Swinger Special 2-door Hardtop		2,407	
	Dart, Dart Custom, Dart Sport, Dart 340 Sport, Dart Swinger, Dart Swinger Special Series:			
	automatic transmission		*178*	
	power-assisted steering		*92*	
289	Challenger 2-door Hardtop		2,902	
	automatic transmission		*223*	
	power-assisted steering		*104*	
290	Coronet 4-door Sedan		2,782	
290	Coronet 6-passenger Station Wagon		3,209	
290	Coronet Custom 4-door Sedan		2,952	
290	Coronet Custom 6-passenger Station Wagon		3,382	
290	Coronet Custom 9-passenger Station Wagon		3,460	
290	Coronet Crestwood 6-passenger Station Wagon		3,632	
290	Coronet Crestwood 9-passenger Station Wagon		3,711	
290	Charger 2-door Coupé		3,725	
290	Charger 2-door Hardtop		2,995	
290	Charger SE 2-door Coupé		3,290	
	Coronet, Coronet Custom, Coronet Crestwood, Charger, Charger SE Series:			
	V8 engine		*92*	
	automatic transmission		*211*	
	power-assisted steering		*114*	
	servo brake		*44*	
292	Polara 2-door Hardtop		3,663	
292	Polara 4-door Sedan		3,640	
292	Polara 6-passenger Station Wagon		4,082	

Page	MAKE AND MODEL	Price in GB £	Price in USA $	Price ex Works
292	Polara Custom 2-door Hardtop		3,849	
292	Polara Custom 4-door Sedan		3,827	
292	Polara Custom 4-door Hardtop		3,917	
292	Polara Custom 6-passenger Station Wagon		4,281	
292	Polara Custom 9-passenger Station Wagon		4,390	
292	Monaco 2-door Hardtop		4,172	
292	Monaco 4-door Sedan		4,114	
292	Monaco 4-door Hardtop		4,235	
292	Monaco 6-passenger Station Wagon		4,646	
292	Monaco 9-passenger Station Wagon		4,775	
	DUESENBERG (USA)			
294	SSJ Roadster		—	
	EL NASR (Egypt)			
338	Nasr 128			—
339	Nasr 125			930
	EXCALIBUR (USA)			
294	SSK Roadster		12,500	
294	SS Roadster		12,500	
294	SS Phaeton		13,500	
	FAIRTHORPE (Great Britain)			
155	Mark VI EM	1,061		
156	TX-S	1,520		
156	TX-SS	1,720		
156	TX-GT	1,720		
	FERRARI (Italy)			
212	Dino 246 GT	4,864	13,885	
212	Dino 246 GTS	5,145	14,485	
212	365 GTC 4	8,662	27,500	
213	365 GT4 2+2			—
213	365 GTB 4 Berlinetta	8,680	25,500	
213	B.B. Berlinetta Boxer			15,500,000
	FIAT (Argentina)			
257	125 Familiar			—
257	125 Sport			—
	FIAT (Italy)			
215	500 Berlina			624,000
	reclining backrests			*11,400*
215	126 Berlina			751,000
	luxury interior			*9,500*
	opening rear windows			*11,400*
215	850 Familiare			1,191,000
215	127 2-door Berlina	759		954,000
216	127 3-door Berlina	808		1,006,000
	127 Series:			
	headrests			*26,000*
	reclining backrests			*11,400*
	luxury interior			*9,500*
	opening rear windows			*11,400*
	electrically-heated rear window	*15*		*14,200*
216	128 2-door Berlina	783	1,992	
216	128 4-door Berlina	819	2,089	
216	128 Familiare	888	2,255	
216	128 Rally	949		1,285,000
	light alloy wheels	*60*		*57,000*
	128 models:			
	reclining backrests			*14,200*
	headrests			*26,000*
	tinted glass with electrically-heated rear window			*26,000*

Page	MAKE AND MODEL	Price in GB £	Price in USA $	Price ex Works
217	128 S 1100 Sport Coupé			1,257,000
217	128 SL 1100 Sport Coupé	1,168		1,342,000
218	128 S 1300 Sport Coupé			1,314,000
218	128 SL 1300 Sport Coupé	1,202	2,650	
	128 models:			
	light alloy wheels			*57,000*
	tinted glass with electrically-heated rear window			*26,000*
218	X 1/9			1,701,000
218	124 Berlina	867		1,266,000
219	124 Familiare	963	2,535	
219	124 Special Berlina	955	2,400	
	automatic transmission	*112*	*200*	
219	124 Special T Berlina	1,030		1,493,000
	5-speed mechanical gearbox			*71,000*
	electronic ignition			*55,000*
	rev counter			*24,000*
	halogen headlamps			*15,000*
	124 models:			
	reclining backrests			*14,000*
	tinted glass with electrically-heated rear window			*26,000*
219	124 Sport Coupé 1600	1,501	3,500	
220	124 Sport Spider 1600		3,644	1,928,000
220	124 Sport Coupé 1800			1,947,000
220	124 Sport Spider 1800			1,994,000
	124 Sport models:			
	5-speed mechanical gearbox			*71,000*
	headrests	*40*		*26,000*
	limited slip differential			*38,000*
	light alloy wheels	*60*		*57,000*
	electronic ignition			*55,000*
	tinted glass with electrically-heated rear window	*30*		*28,000*
	air-conditioning			*246,000*
220	Fiat Abarth 124 Rally			2,930,000
	competition equipment			*57,000*
220	132 Berlina 1600			1,616,000
221	132 Berlina Special 1600			1,701,000
221	132 Berlina Special 1800			1,767,000
	132 Series:			
	5-speed mechanical gearbox			*71,000*
	automatic transmission			*161,000*
	limited slip differential			*38,000*
	light alloy wheels			*57,000*
	electronic ignition			*55,000*
	headrests			*26,000*
	tinted glass with electrically-heated rear window			*28,000*
	rev counter			*24,000*
	air-conditioning			*246,000*
222	130 Berlina 3200			3,969,000
223	130 Coupé 3200			4,914,000
	130 Series:			
	5-speed mechanical gearbox			*—236,000*
	electronic ignition			*70,000*
	limited slip differential			*50,000*
	air-conditioning			*270,000*
	electrically-controlled windows			*100,000*
	tinted glass			*33,000*
	leather upholstery			*180,000*
223	Campagnola A			2,315,000
223	Campagnola C			2,769,000
	Campagnola Series:			
	independent heating			*26,000*
	power take-off			*211,000*
	FIBERFAB (Germany, F.R.)			
120	Bonito			—

Page	MAKE AND MODEL	Price in GB £	Price in USA $	Price ex Works
	FNM (Brazil)			
261	2150			20,000
262	2150 Luxo			22,000
	FORD (Australia)			
396	Falcon 4-door Sedan			—
396	Falcon Station Wagon			—
396	Falcon 500 2-door Hardtop			—
396	Falcon 500 4-door Sedan			—
396	Falcon 500 Station Wagon			—
396	Futura 4-door Sedan	1,805		
396	Fairmont 2-door Hardtop	2,175		
396	Fairmont 4-door Sedan	2,130		
396	Fairmont Station Wagon	2,170		
396	Falcon GT 2-door Hardtop			—
396	Falcon GT 4-door Sedan			—
397	Fairlane Custom 4-door Sedan			—
397	Fairlane 500 4-door Sedan			—
	FORD (Brazil)			
262	4-door Corcel Sedan			—
262	4-door Corcel Sedan Luxo			—
262	Corcel Coupé			—
262	Corcel Coupé Luxo			—
262	Corcel Belina Station Wagon			—
262	Corcel Belina Luxo Station Wagon			—
262	Corcel Belina Luxo Especial Station Wagon			—
262	Corcel GT Coupé			—
262	Aero-Willys			—
263	Itamaraty			—
263	Galaxie			—
264	Galaxie 500			—
264	LTD Landau			—
	FORD (Canada)			
265	Meteor Rideau 4-door Pillared Hardtop			—
265	Meteor Rideau 500 2-door Hardtop			—
265	Meteor Rideau 500 4-door Pillared Hardtop			—
265	Meteor Rideau 500 Station Wagon			—
265	Meteor Montcalm 2-door Hardtop			—
265	Meteor Montcalm 4-door Hardtop			—
265	Meteor Montcalm 4-door Pillared Hardtop			—
265	Meteor Montcalm Station Wagon			—
	FORD (Germany, F.R.)			
120	Escort 2-door Limousine			6,485
120	Escort 4-door Limousine			6,775
121	Escort Turnier			7,035
121	Escort L 2-door Limousine			6,715
121	Escort L 4-door Limousine			7,005
121	Escort L Turnier			7,265
121	Escort XL 2-door Limousine			7,130
121	Escort XL 4-door Limousine			7,420
121	Escort XL Turnier			7,680
121	Escort GT 2-door Limousine			7,920
121	Escort GT 4-door Limousine			8,210
121	Escort 2-door Sport Limousine			7,375
	Escort Series:			
	automatic transmission			*799*
	155 SR x 12 tyres			*64*
121	Taunus 2-door Limousine			7,625
122	Taunus 4-door Limousine			8,000
123	Taunus 5-door Turnier			8,435

Page	MAKE AND MODEL	Price in GB £	Price in USA $	Price ex Works
123	Taunus L 2-door Limousine			7,935
123	Taunus L 4-door Limousine			8,310
123	Taunus L Coupé			8,480
123	Taunus L 5-door Turnier			8,745
123	Taunus XL 2-door Limousine			8,815
123	Taunus XL 4-door Limousine			9,190
123	Taunus XL Coupé			9,325
123	Taunus XL 5-door Turnier			9,625
	Taunus models:			
	97.1 cu in, 1,592 cc engine			*345*
	automatic transmission			*799*
123	Taunus GT 2-door Limousine			9,520
123	Taunus GT 4-door Limousine			9,895
123	Taunus GT Coupé			10,030
123	Taunus GXL 2-door Limousine			10,195
123	Taunus GXL 4-door Limousine			10,570
124	Taunus GXL Coupé			10,705
	Taunus models:			
	6 cylinders engine			*232*
	138.8 cu in, 2,274 cc engine			*572*
	automatic transmission			*799*
	185/70 HR x 13 tyres			*122*
124	Capri 1300			8,365
124	Capri 1500			8,330
124	Capri GT 1700			9,125
	automatic transmission		*183*	
124	Capri GT 2000		2,528	9,670
124	Capri GT 2300			10,230
125	Capri GT 2600		2,821	10,760
125	Capri RS 2600			16,195
125	Consul 2-door Limousine			9,830
126	Consul 4-door Limousine			10,200
127	Consul L Turnier			10,750
126	Consul L 2-door Limousine			10,420
126	Consul L 4-door Limousine			10,790
127	Consul L Turnier			11,340
127	Consul GT 2-door Limousine			11,595
127	Consul GT 4-door Limousine			11,965
	Consul Series:			
	119.3 cu in, 1,955 cc engine			*330*
	138.8 cu in, 2,274 cc engine			*700*
	automatic transmission			*1,060*
	66 Ah battery			*25*
	175 x 14 tyres			*130*
	185 SR x 14 tyres			*360*
	4.400 axle ratio			*67*
127	Granada 2-door Limousine			12,475
127	Granada 4-door Limousine			12,845
127	Granada Turnier			13,395
127	Granada GXL 2-door Limousine			15,185
127	Granada GXL 4-door Limousine			15,555
	Granada Series:			
	153.8 cu in, 2,520 cc engine			*475*
	179.7 cu in, 2,945 cc engine			*670*
	power-assisted steering			*674*
	FORD (Great Britain)			
157	Escort 1100 Standard 2-door Saloon	679		
157	Escort 1100 2-door Saloon	727		
157	Escort 1100 L 2-door Saloon	752		
157	Escort 1100 4-door Saloon	756		
157	Escort 1100 L 4-door Saloon	781		
157	Escort 1100 Estate Car	825		
157	Escort 1100 L Estate Car	850		
	Escort 1100 Series:			
	automatic transmission (except for Standard model)	*100*		
	front disc brakes	*15*		
157	Escort 1300 L 2-door Saloon	780		
158	Escort 1300 XL 2-door Saloon	824		

Page	MAKE AND MODEL	Price in GB £	Price in USA $	Price ex Works
158	Escort 1300 L 4-door Saloon	809		
158	Escort 1300 XL 4-door Saloon	853		
158	Escort 1300 Estate Car	864		
158	Escort 1300 L Estate Car	889		
158	Escort 1300 XL Estate Car	933		
	Escort 1300 Series:			
	automatic transmission	*72*		
158	Escort Sport	835		
159	Escort GT 2-door Saloon	861		
159	Escort GT 4-door Saloon	890		
159	Escort Mexico	1,072		
159	Escort RS 1600	1,480		
159	Cortina 1300 2-door Saloon	803		
160	Cortina 1300 L 2-door Saloon	824		
160	Cortina 1300 4-door Saloon	832		
160	Cortina 1300 L 4-door Saloon	853		
160	Cortina 1300 Estate Car	929		
160	Cortina 1300 L Estate Car	950		
160	Cortina 1600 2-door Saloon	843		
160	Cortina 1600 L 2-door Saloon	864		
160	Cortina 1600 XL 2-door Saloon	936		
160	Cortina 1600 4-door Saloon	872		
160	Cortina 1600 L 4-door Saloon	893		
160	Cortina 1600 XL 4-door Saloon	965		
160	Cortina 1600 Estate Car	969		
160	Cortina 1600 L Estate Car	990		
160	Cortina 1600 XL Estate Car	1,062		
160	Cortina 1600 GT 2-door Saloon	987		
160	Cortina 1600 GT 4-door Saloon	1,016		
160	Cortina 1600 GXL 4-door Saloon	1,123		
161	Cortina 2000 L 4-door Saloon	948		
161	Cortina 2000 XL 2-door Saloon	991		
161	Cortina 2000 XL 4-door Saloon	1,020		
161	Cortina 2000 L Estate Car	1,045		
161	Cortina 2000 XL Estate Car	1,117		
161	Cortina 2000 GT 2-door Saloon	1,028		
161	Cortina 2000 GT 4-door Saloon	1,057		
162	Cortina 2000 GXL 4-door Saloon	1,164		
	Cortina Series:			
	automatic transmission	*72*		
	servo brake	*10*		
162	Capri 1300 L	902		
162	Capri 1600 L	973		
163	Capri 1600 XL	999		
163	Capri 1600 GT	1,101		
163	Capri 2000 GT	1,125		
163	Capri 3000 GT	1,329		
163	Capri 3000 GXL	1,471		
	Capri Series:			
	automatic transmission	*72*		
	165 x 13 tyres	*12*		
	vinyl roof	*17*		
	electrically-heated rear window	*17*		
163	Consul 2000 Saloon	1,070		
164	Consul 2000 L Saloon	1,126		
164	Consul 2500 Saloon	1,157		
164	Consul 2500 L Saloon	1,213		
164	Consul 2500 L Estate Car	1,473		
164	Consul 3000 GT Saloon	1,414		
	Consul Series:			
	automatic transmission	*92*		
	reclining backrests	*18*		
	electrically-heated rear window	*17*		
164	Granada 2500 Saloon	1,400		
165	Granada 2500 GXL Saloon	1,680		
165	Granada 3000 Saloon	1,451		
165	Granada 3000 GXL Saloon	1,731		
165	Granada 3000 Estate Car	1,728		
	Granada Series:			
	automatic transmission	*92*		

Page	MAKE AND MODEL	Price in GB £	Price in USA $	Price ex Works
	FORD (USA)			
294	Pinto 2-door Sedan		1,968	
294	Pinto 3-door Runabout		2,086	
294	Pinto Station Wagon		2,273	
	Pinto Series:			
	V8 engine		*49*	
295	Maverick 2-door Sedan		2,208	
295	Maverick 4-door Sedan		2,263	
295	Maverick Grabber 2-door Sport Sedan		2,389	
	Maverick and Maverick Grabber Series:			
	V8 engine		*39*	
	automatic transmission		*177*	
297	Mustang 2-door Hardtop		2,766	
297	Mustang 2-door Sports Roof		2,823	
297	Mustang 2-door Convertible	3,175	3,105	
297	Mustang Grandé 2-door Hardtop	3,050	2,952	
297	Mustang Mach I 2-door Fastback	3,180	3,003	
	Mustang Series:			
	V8 engine		*41*	
	automatic transmission		*204*	
	power-assisted steering		*103*	
298	Torino 2-door Hardtop		2,762	
298	Torino 4-door Pillared Hardtop		2,731	
298	Torino Station Wagon		3,102	
298	Gran Torino 2-door Hardtop		2,967	
298	Gran Torino 4-door Pillared Hardtop		2,947	
298	Gran Torino Station Wagon		3,243	
298	Gran Torino Brougham 2-door Hardtop		3,130	
298	Gran Torino Brougham 4-door Pillared Hardtop		3,110	
298	Gran Torino Squire Station Wagon		3,486	
298	Gran Torino Sport 2-door Hardtop		3,094	
298	Gran Torino 2-door Sports Roof		3,940	
	Torino, Gran Torino, Gran Torino Brougham, Gran Torino Squire, Gran Torino Sport Series:			
	V8 engine		*44*	
	automatic transmission		*211*	
	power-assisted steering		*112*	
301	Custom 500 4-door Pillared Hardtop		3,540	
301	Galaxie 500 4-door Pillared Hardtop		3,732	
301	Galaxie 500 2-door Hardtop		3,735	
301	Galaxie 500 2-door Hardtop		3,767	
301	LTD 4-door Pillared Hardtop		3,890	
301	LTD 2-door Hardtop		3,882	
301	LTD 4-door Hardtop		3,925	
301	LTD Brougham 4-door Pillared Hardtop		4,031	
301	LTD Brougham 2-door Hardtop		4,034	
301	LTD Brougham 4-door Hardtop	3,615	4,074	
302	Thunderbird 2-door Hardtop	5,305	5,459	
	GAZ (USSR)			
248	Volga 24			—
248	Volga 24 Indenor Diesel			—
	GIANNINI (Italy)			
223	Fiat Giannini 500 TV			685,000
224	Fiat Giannini 500 TVL			755,000
224	Fiat Giannini 500 Montecarlo			845,000
224	Fiat Giannini 590 GT			750,000
224	Fiat Giannini 590 GTL			820,000
224	Fiat Giannini 590 Vallelunga			845,000
224	Fiat Giannini 650 NP			760,000
224	Fiat Giannini 650 NPL			830,000
224	Fiat Giannini 650 NP Modena			845,000

Page	MAKE AND MODEL	Price in GB £	Price in USA $	Price ex Works
224	Fiat Giannini 127 NP			1,130,000
225	Fiat Giannini 127 NP-S			1,250,000
225	Fiat Giannini 128 NP 2-door Berlina			1,350,000
226	Fiat Giannini 128 NP-S 2-door Berlina			1,430,000
226	Fiat Giannini 128 NP Rally			1,480,000
226	Fiat Giannini 128 NP-S Rally			1,800,000
227	Fiat Giannini 132-2000			2,400,000
	GILBERN (Great Britain)			
165	Invader Mk III Saloon	2,063		
	automatic transmission	*120*		
	sunshine roof	*54*		
	GINETTA (Great Britain)			
166	G15	958		
166	G21	2,065		
	GLASSIC (USA)			
303	Glassic Phaeton		6,995	
303	Glassic Roadster		6,995	
	G.T.M. (Great Britain)			
167	1.3 Super 90	1,175		
	HILLMAN (Great Britain)			
167	Imp	546		
168	Imp De Luxe	600		
168	Super Imp	634		
168	Avenger	729		
168	Avenger De Luxe	754		
168	Avenger De Luxe Estate Car	840		
168	Avenger Super	782		
168	Avenger Super Estate Car	880		
168	Avenger GL	882		
169	Avenger GLS	991		
	Avenger Series:			
	91.4 cu in, 1,498 cc engine	*35*		
	automatic transmission	*72*		
169	Hunter De Luxe Saloon	825		
170	Hunter De Luxe Estate Car	936		
	1.7-litre engine	*31*		
	Hunter De Luxe Series:			
	automatic transmission	*108*		
	servo brake	*10*		
170	Hunter Super	884		
	automatic transmission	*77*		
	servo brake	*10*		
	electrically-heated rear window	*12*		
	reclining backrests	*16*		
171	Hunter GL Saloon	963		
	automatic transmission	*77*		
171	Hunter GL Estate Car	1,078		
171	Hunter GT	973		
171	Hunter GLS	1,091		
	HINDUSTAN (India)			
342	Ambassador Mk II			19,064
	HOLDEN (Australia)			
398	Torana 1200 2-door Saloon			—
398	Torana 1200 4-door Saloon			—
398	Torana 1300 De Luxe 2-door Saloon			—
398	Torana 1300 De Luxe 4-door Saloon			—
399	Torana 1300 SL 2-door Saloon			—
399	Torana 1600 De Luxe 2-door Saloon			—
399	Torana 1600 De Luxe 4-door Saloon			—

Page	MAKE AND MODEL	Price in GB £	Price in USA $	Price ex Works
399	Torana 2250 S 2-door Saloon			—
400	Torana 2250 S 4-door Saloon			—
400	Torana 2250 SL 4-door Saloon			—
400	Torana 2850 S 2-door Saloon			—
400	Torana 2850 S 4-door Saloon			—
400	Torana 2850 SL 4-door Saloon			—
400	Torana GTR Saloon			—
400	Torana GTR XU-1 Saloon			—
400	HQ Belmont Saloon			—
401	HQ Belmont Estate Car			—
401	HQ Kingswood Saloon			—
401	HQ Kingswood Estate Car			—
401	HQ Premier Saloon			—
401	HQ Premier Estate Car			—
401	HQ Statesman			—
401	HQ Statesman De Ville			—
401	Monaro Coupé			—
401	Monaro Coupé LS			—
401	Monaro Coupé GTS			—
	HONDA (Japan)			
345	Life De Luxe 2-door Sedan			346,000
345	Life De Luxe 2-door Automatic Sedan			397,000
345	Life De Luxe 4-door Sedan			366,000
345	Life De Luxe 4-door Automatic Sedan			417,000
346	Life De Luxe Station Wagon			394,000
346	Life De Luxe Automatic Station Wagon			417,000
346	Life Custom 2-door Sedan			428,000
346	Life Custom 2-door Automatic Sedan			451,000
346	Life Custom 4-door Sedan			448,000
346	Life Custom 4-door Automatic Sedan			471,000
346	Life Custom Station Wagon			471,000
346	Life Custom Automatic Station Wagon			471,000
346	Life Touring SS 2-door Sedan			389,000
346	Life Touring SL 2-door Sedan			419,000
346	Life Touring GS 2-door Sedan			449,000
346	Life Twin De Luxe 4-door Sedan			404,000
346	Life Twin Custom 4-door Sedan			458,000
346	Vamos 4			345,000
346	Life Stepvan Super De Luxe			403,000
347	Z Hardtop SS			368,000
348	Z Hardtop GT			429,000
348	Z Hardtop GL			449,000
348	Z Hardtop GSS			461,000
348	N 600 Sedan	569	1,473	
348	Z 600 Sedan	644	1,610	
349	Civic Standard 2-door Sedan			425,000
349	Civic De Luxe 2-door Sedan			475,000
349	Civic De Luxe 3-door Sedan			490,000
349	Civic Hi De Luxe 2-door Sedan			495,000
349	Civic Hi De Luxe 3-door Sedan			510,000
349	Civic GL 2-door Sedan			530,000
349	Civic GL 3-door Sedan			545,000
349	Civic			—
349	145 Standard Sedan			511,000
350	145 De Luxe Sedan			591,000
350	145 Custom Sedan			658,000
350	145 SL Coupé			623,000
350	145 GL Coupé			711,000
350	145 FI Coupé			811,000
	HUMBER (Great Britain)			
171	Sceptre	1,175		
	automatic transmission	*41*		
	IKA-RENAULT (Argentina)			
257	Torino L			22,300
258	Torino S			27,700
258	Torino TS Berlina			29,500
258	Torino TS Coupé			30,900
258	Torino GS Coupé			33,500
258	Rambler Ambassador			—
258	Rambler Classic			—
258	Rambler Cross Country			—
	IMPERIAL (USA)			
304	Le Baron 2-door Hardtop		6,669	
304	Le Baron 4-door Hardtop		6,897	
	INTERMECCANICA (Italy)			
227	Indra Coupé			5,450,000
227	Indra Spider			—
	INTERNATIONAL (USA)			
304	Scout Station Wagon		3,422	
	V8 engine		*85*	
305	Travelall 1010 Station Wagon		3,652	
305	Travelall 1110 Station Wagon		3,579	
305	Travelall 1210 Station Wagon		3,706	
	Travelall Series:			
	V8 engine		*77*	
	power-assisted steering		*134*	
	servo brake		*46*	
	ISO (Italy)			
227	Grifo G.L.			8,900,000
228	Lele			9,300,000
228	Fidia			9,900,000
228	Varedo			—
	ISUZU (Japan)			
350	Bellett 1600 Special 2-door Sedan			561,000
350	Bellett 1600 Special 4-door Sedan			591,000
350	Bellett 1600 GTR Coupé			1,110,000
350	Bellett 1800 Sports Sedan			717,000
351	Bellett 1800 GT Coupé			870,000
351	Bellett 1800 GTN Coupé			802,000
351	117 Coupé			1,670,000
352	117 EC Coupé			1,870,000
352	117 1800 Coupé			1,470,000
352	117 1800 N Coupé			1,360,000
352	Florian 1800 De Luxe Sedan			740,000
352	Florian 1800 Automatic Sedan			740,000
352	Florian 1800 TS Sedan			800,000
	JAGUAR (Great Britain)			
172	XJ6 2.8-litre Saloon	2,285	7,683	
172	XJ6 4.2-litre Saloon	2,540		
	XJ6 Series:			
	overdrive	*56*		
	automatic transmission	*93*		
172	XJ12 Saloon	3,082		
173	E Type 12V Series III Convertible	2,785		
174	E Type 12V Series III 2+2 Coupé	3,004	7,732	
	E Type Series:			
	automatic transmission	*144*	*261*	
	JEEP CORPORATION (USA)			
306	Jeep CJ5 Roadster		3,021	
306	Jeep CJ6 Roadster		3,111	
306	Jeep Renegade Roadster		—	
	Jeep CJ5, Jeep CJ6, Jeep Renegade Series:			
	V8 engine		*126*	
	power-assisted steering		*144*	
	servo brake		*45*	

Page	MAKE AND MODEL	Price in GB £	Price in USA $	Price ex Works
306	Jeep Commando Roadster		3,305	
306	Jeep Commando Station Wagon		3,456	
	Jeep Commando Series:			
	V8 engine		*126*	
	power-assisted steering		*144*	
	servo brake		*45*	
307	Jeep Wagoneer Standard Station Wagon		4,451	
307	Jeep Wagoneer Custom Station Wagon		4,689	
	Jeep Wagoneer Series:			
	V8 engine		*212*	
	power-assisted steering		*144*	
	servo brake		*45*	
	JENSEN (Great Britain)			
174	Jensen-Healey	1,620	4,595	
174	Interceptor III	5,580	13,970	
175	SP	5,950		
	LAMBORGHINI (Italy)			
228	Urraco 250	5,400		6,500,000
228	Urraco 250 S	5,700		7,050,000
228	Espada 400 GT	8,390		9,500,000
	power-assisted steering	*250*		*275,000*
229	Jarama 400 GT S	7,580		9,000,000
	power-assisted steering	*250*		*275,000*
230	Countach LP 500			—
	LANCIA (Italy)			
230	Fulvia Berlina 2ª Serie	1,156		1,835,000
231	Fulvia Coupé 1.3 S 2ª Serie	1,542		1,975,000
231	Fulvia 1.3 S 2ª Serie Monte-Carlo			2,050,000
231	Fulvia Sport 1.3 S 2ª Serie	1,880		2,350,000
231	Fulvia Coupé 1600 HF 2ª Serie	1,981		2,575,000
231	Fulvia Sport 1600	2,229		2,700,000
232	Beta 1400			2,050,000
232	Beta 1600			2,300,000
232	Beta 1600 LX			—
232	Beta 1800			2,400,000
232	Beta 1800 LX			—
	Beta Series:			
	tinted glass			*30,000*
	sunshine roof			*80,000*
	electrically-controlled windows			*95,000*
	light alloy wheels			*57,000*
	fog lamps			*22,000*
	electrically-heated rear window			*24,000*
232	2000 Berlina	1,860		2,700,000
333	2000 Berlina Iniezione	2,105		2,900,000
233	2000 Coupé	2,436		3,050,000
233	2000 Coupé HF	2,726		3,300,000
	2000 Series:			
	tinted glass			*30,000*
	electrically-controlled windows			*95,000*
	leather upholstery			*130,000*
	air-conditioning			*300,000*
	LAWIL (Italy)			
233	Varzina			575,000
234	City			585,000
234	Log			700,000
	LEYLAND INNOCENTI (Italy)			
234	Mini 1000			1,083,000
235	Mini 1001			1,185,000
235	Mini T 1000			1,087,000

Page	MAKE AND MODEL	Price in GB £	Price in USA $	Price ex Works
235	Mini Matic			1,172,000
235	Mini Cooper 1300			1,371,000
235	Austin J5			1,215,000
	LIGIER (France)			
98	JS 2			—
	LINCOLN (USA)			
309	Continental 4-door Sedan		7,322	
309	Continental 2-door Hardtop Coupé	5,790	7,088	
309	Continental Mk IV 2-door Hardtop	6,500	8,774	
	LOTUS (Great Britain)			
175	Europa Twin Cam	1,595	5,295	
175	Europa Special	1,960	4,495	
175	Elan Sprint Drophead Coupé	1,940		
176	Elan Sprint Coupé	1,940	5,240	
176	+2 'S' 130	2,250		
	MASERATI (Italy)			
236	Merak			—
236	Indy America 4200	7,750		9,200,000
236	Indy America 4700	8,405	22,500	
236	Bora 4700	8,250	23,900	
237	Ghibli Coupé	8,150		9,800,000
	automatic transmission	*320*		
	MATRA SPORTS (France)			
98	530 LX			22,695
99	530 SX			19,900
	MAZDA (Japan)			
353	Chantez L Sedan			340,000
353	Chantez LX Sedan			375,000
353	Chantez GL Sedan			410,000
353	Chantez GF Sedan			427,000
353	Chantez GF II Sedan			465,000
353	Familia 1000 2-door De Luxe Sedan			493,000
354	Familia 1000 4-door De Luxe Sedan			513,000
354	Familia 1300 2-door De Luxe Sedan			528,000
354	Familia 1300 4-door De Luxe Sedan			548,000
354	Familia 1300 GF Coupé			590,000
354	Grand Familia De Luxe Sedan			560,000
354	Grand Familia De Luxe Coupé			560,000
354	Grand Familia Sedan GL			620,000
354	Grand Familia GF Coupé			640,000
354	Grand Familia Automatic Sedan GL			675,000
354	Grand Familia Automatic Coupé GL			695,000
355	Grand Familia S Sedan GL II			665,000
355	Grand Familia S Coupé GF II			685,000
355	Familia Rotary SS Sedan			618,000
356	Familia Rotary TSS Sedan			618,000
356	Rotary Coupé SX			598,000
356	Rotary Coupé GS			668,000
356	Capella 1500 De Luxe Sedan			618,000
356	Capella 1500 De Luxe Coupé			618,000
357	Capella 1600 De Luxe Sedan			658,000
357	Capella 1600 Super De Luxe Sedan			698,000
357	Capella 1600 Super De Luxe Coupé			738,000
357	Capella 1600 GL Sedan			720,000
357	Capella 1600 GF Coupé			760,000
357	Capella GR Sedan RE-matic			748,000
357	Capella RE GS Coupé			845,000
358	Capella GS Coupé RE-matic			920,000
357	Capella GR Sedan			820,000
357	Capella GR Sedan RE-matic			875,000

Page	MAKE AND MODEL	Price in GB £	Price in USA $	Price ex Works
357	Capella GS Coupé			870,000
358	Capella GS Coupé RE-matic			925,000
358	Savanna RX Sedan			670,000
358	Savanna GR Sedan			700,000
358	Savanna SX Coupé			670,000
358	Savanna GS II Coupé			750,000
358	Savanna GT Coupé			795,000
358	R130 De Luxe Coupé			1,450,000
358	R130 Super De Luxe Coupé			1,750,000
359	Luce Sedan RX			810,000
359	Luce Sedan GR			860,000
359	Luce Sedan GR Automatic			910,000
359	Luce Sedan GR AP			910,000
360	Luce Custom GR			885,000
360	Luce Custom GR Automatic			940,000
360	Luce Custom GR II			975,000
360	Luce Custom GR II AP			1,085,000
360	Luce Hardtop SX			850,000
360	Luce Hardtop GS			905,000
361	Luce Hardtop GS II			1,010,000
361	Luce Hardtop GS II Automatic			1,045,000
361	Luce Hardtop GS II AP			1,045,000
	MERCEDES-BENZ (Germany, F.R.)			
127	200			13,930
128	200 D			14,430
128	220	2,397	6,560	
128	220 D	2,680	6,345	
128	220 D Lang	3,881	6,747	
128	230			16,095
128	230 Lang	3,932		22,477
128	250 Limousine	2,890	7,218	
129	250 C Coupé		8,069	13,369
	250 Series:			
	mechanical gearbox			*616*
	200, 220, 230, 250 Series:			
	automatic transmission	*219*		*1,443*
	air-conditioning			*2,203*
	sunshine roof			*633*
	electrically-heated rear window	*29*		
129	280 Limousine		8,875	18,981
129	280 C Coupé		9,518	21,423
129	280 E Limousine	3,305		20,535
130	280 CE Coupé	3,719		22,977
	280 models:			
	mechanical gearbox			*616*
	automatic transmission	*207*		
	power-assisted steering			*572*
	sunshine roof			*849*
130	280 S Limousine	2,958		23,809
130	280 SE Limousine	3,305	10,283	
131	350 SE Limousine	4,447		28,860
	automatic transmission			*1,443*
	280 S, 280 SE, 350 SE models:			
	mechanical gearbox			*616*
	electrically-controlled sunshine roof			*849*
131	350 SL Roadster	5,121	11,688	
131	350 SLC Coupé	6,785	15,094	
	350 models:			
	automatic transmission	*219*		
	air-conditioning			*2,203*
131	600 Limousine	11,818	32,695	
132	600 Pullman-Limousine	12,902	37,928	
	MERCURY (USA)			
309	Comet 2-door Sedan		2,259	
309	Comet 4-door Sedan		2,314	
	Comet Series:			
	V8 engine		*122*	
	automatic transmission		*178*	
	power-assisted steering		*92*	
310	Montego 2-door Hardtop		2,858	
310	Montego 4-door Pillared Hardtop		2,853	
310	Montego MX 2-door Hardtop		2,981	
310	Montego MX 4-door Pillared Hardtop		2,961	
310	Montego MX Station Wagon		3,340	
310	Montego MX Brougham 2-door Hardtop		3,147	
310	Montego MX Brougham 4-door Pillared Hardtop		3,137	
310	Montego MX Villager Station Wagon		3,514	
310	Montego GT 2-door Fastback		3,356	
	Montego, Montego MX, Montego MX Brougham, Montego MX Villager, Montego GT Series:			
	V8 engine		*112*	
	automatic transmission		*207*	
	power-assisted steering		*112*	
	servo brake		*68*	
313	Cougar 2-door Hardtop		3,295	
313	Cougar 2-door Convertible		3,649	
313	Cougar XR-7 2-door Hardtop		3,602	
313	Cougar XR-7 2-door Convertible		3,826	
	Cougar, Cougar XR-7 Series:			
	power-assisted steering		*103*	
313	Monterey 2-door Hardtop		3,920	
313	Monterey 4-door Pillared Hardtop		3,881	
313	Monterey Station Wagon		4,300	
313	Monterey Custom 2-door Hardtop		4,123	
313	Monterey Custom 4-door Pillared Hardtop		4,044	
313	Marquis 2-door Hardtop		4,660	
313	Marquis 4-door Pillared Hardtop		4,581	
313	Marquis 4-door Hardtop		4,725	
313	Marquis Station Wagon		4,533	
313	Marquis Brougham 2-door Hardtop		5,069	
313	Marquis Brougham 4-door Pillared Hardtop		4,990	
313	Marquis Brougham 4-door Hardtop	4,135	5,134	
313	Colony Park Station Wagon		4,638	
	MG (Great Britain)			
176	Midget Mk III	829	2,520	
176	MGB GT	1,298	3,615	
177	MGB Sports	1,169	3,320	
	MINI (Great Britain)			
177	850 Saloon	574		
178	1000 Saloon	658		
178	Clubman Saloon	702		
178	Clubman Estate Car	755		
179	1275 G.T.	804		
	850, 1000, Clubman and 1275 models:			
	automatic transmission	*88*		
	electrically-heated rear window	*15*		
	MITSUBISHI (Japan)			
361	Minica F4 Standard Sedan			331,000
361	Minica F4 De Luxe Sedan			374,000
361	Minica F4 Custom Sedan			430,000
361	Minica F4 GS			442,000
361	Minica F4 GSL			470,000
361	Minica Skipper FL Coupé			377,000
361	Minica Skipper LL			419,000
361	Minica Skipper GT			452,000
362	Galant FTO GI Coupé			558,000
362	Galant FTO GII			608,000
362	Galant FTO GIII			660,000

Page	MAKE AND MODEL	Price in GB £	Price in USA $	Price ex Works
	VAUXHALL (Great Britain)			
198	Viva 1256 2-door Saloon	741		
198	Viva 1256 De Luxe 2-door Saloon	819		
198	Viva 1256 De Luxe 4-door Saloon	853		
198	Viva 1256 De Luxe Estate Car	920		
198	Viva 1256 SL 2-door Saloon	905		
199	Viva 1256 SL 4-door Saloon	939		
199	Viva 1256 SL Estate Car	1,001		
199	Viva 1800 De Luxe 2-door Saloon	878		
199	Viva 1800 De Luxe 4-door Saloon	912		
200	Viva 1800 De Luxe Estate Car	979		
200	Viva 1800 SL 2-door Saloon	954		
200	Viva 1800 SL 4-door Saloon	988		
200	Viva 1800 SL Estate Car	1,050		
200	Viva 2300 SL 2-door Saloon	1,072		
200	Viva 2300 SL 4-door Saloon	1,106		
200	Viva 2300 SL Estate Car	1,168		
	Viva Series:			
	automatic transmission	*90*		
	front disc brakes with servo	*15*		
201	Firenza 1256 De Luxe	883		
201	Firenza 1800 SL	1,051		
201	Firenza Sport SL	1,140		
	Firenza 1800 and Sport SL:			
	automatic transmission	*90*		
201	Victor 1800 De Luxe Saloon	1,089		
202	Victor 1800 De Luxe Estate Car	1,190		
202	Victor 2300 SL Saloon	1,185		
202	Victor 2300 SL Estate Car	1,278		
202	Victor 3300 SL Estate Car	1,479		
202	VX 4/90	1,336		
	Victor and VX 4/90 models:			
	automatic transmission	*90*		
	reclining backrests	*11*		
202	Ventora	1,535		
	overdrive	*60*		
	automatic transmission	*96*		
	VAZ (USSR)			
249	Lada			—
249	Lada Kombi			—
	VOLKSWAGEN (Germany, F.R.)			
142	1200	715		5,390
143	1300	743		6,330
143	1300 S	808		6,530
	1200 and 1300 models:			
	sunshine roof	*60*		
143	1303 Limousine	847		6,690
144	1303 S Limousine	888		6,890
144	1303 LS Cabriolet		2,599	8,840
44	Karmann-Ghia Coupé		2,750	9,220
[illegible]	Karmann-Ghia Cabriolet		3,099	10,160
[illegible]	181			9,550
[illegible]	1600 A Limousine			7,760
[illegible]	1600 Variant	1,289		8,160
[illegible]	1600 Limousine			8,175
[illegible]	1600 L Limousine			8,560
[illegible]	600 TL			8,560
[illegible]	600 L Variant			8,960
[illegible]	70 (75 hp)	1,571	3,299	
[illegible]	0 L (75 hp)			10,460
[illegible]	(90 hp)			10,190
[illegible]	L (90 hp)			10,670
[illegible]	E 2-door			9,670

Page	MAKE AND MODEL	Price in GB £	Price in USA $	Price ex Works
147	412 E 4-door			10,030
147	412 LE 2-door	1,332		10,110
147	412 LE 4-door	1,381		10,470
147	412 E Variant	1,487		9,670
147	412 LE Variant	1,479		10,510
	412 Series:			
	automatic transmission	*132*		
	sunshine roof	*103*		
	VOLKSWAGEN-PORSCHE (Germany, F.R.)			
147	914 - 1.7			13,360
147	914 - 2.0	2,090		13,760
	VOLVO (Sweden)			
244	144 De Luxe Saloon	1,636		
244	144 Grand Luxe Saloon	2,111		
245	145 De Luxe Station Wagon	1,816		
245	1800 ES Coupé	2,553		
245	164 Saloon	2,284	4,400	
246	164 E Saloon	2,446		
	164 Series:			
	automatic transmission		*180*	
	WARSZAWA (Poland)			
239	223			—
239	223 K			—
	WARTBURG (Germany, D.D.R.)			
110	353	615		
111	353 Tourist	688		
	WOLSELEY (Great Britain)			
202	1300	904		
	automatic transmission	*88*		
	reclining backrests	*15*		
	electrically-heated rear window	*9*		
203	Six	1,328		
	automatic transmission	*94*		
	power-assisted steering	*60*		
	electrically-heated rear window	*11*		
	YLN (China, Taiwan)			
342	802			—
	ZAZ (USSR)			
249	966			—
	ZCZ (Yugoslavia)			
250	Zastava 750 M			—
251	Zastava 750 Luxe			—
251	Zastava 101			—
251	Zastava 1300			—
251	Zastava 1300 Luxe			—
251	Zastava 1500			—
251	Zastava 1500 De Luxe			—
	ZIL (USSR)			
250	114 Limousine			—

14
144
144
144
144
145
145
14
14
1